Y0-BVH-934

TURFGRASS SCIENCE

In Memoriam
Professor Howard Burton Musser
Pioneer Turfgrass Scientist
Pennsylvania State University
September 9, 1893 – August 12, 1968

AGRONOMY

A Series of Monographs Published by the

AMERICAN SOCIETY OF AGRONOMY

General Editor Monographs 1 to 6, A. G. NORMAN

1. C. EDMUND MARSHALL: The Colloid Chemistry of the Silicate Minerals, 1949
2. BYRON T. SHAW, *Editor:* Soil Physical Conditions and Plant Growth, 1952
3. K. D. JACOB, *Editor:* Fertilizer Technology and Resources in the United States, 1953
4. W. H. PIERRE and A. G. NORMAN, *Editors:* Soil and Fertilizer Phosphate in Crop Nutrition, 1953
5. GEORGE F. SPRAGUE, *Editor:* Corn and Corn Improvement, 1955
6. J. LEVITT: The Hardiness of Plants, 1956
7. JAMES N. LUTHIN, *Editor:* Drainage of Agricultural Lands, 1957
   General Editor, D. E. GREGG
8. FRANKLIN A. COFFMAN, *Editor:* Oats and Oat Improvement, 1961
   Managing Editor, H. L. HAMILTON
9. C. A. BLACK, *Editor-in-Chief,* and D. D. EVANS, J. L. WHITE, L. E. ENSMINGER, and F. E. CLARK, *Associate Editors:* Methods of Soil Analysis, 1965. Part 1—Physical and Mineralogical Properties, Including Statistics of Measurement and Sampling; Part 2—Chemical and Microbiological Properties
   Managing Editor, R. C. DINAUER
10. W. V. BARTHOLOMEW and F. E. CLARK, *Editors:* Soil Nitrogen, 1965
    Managing Editor, H. L. HAMILTON
11. R. M. HAGAN, H. R. HAISE, and T. W. EDMINSTER, *Editors:* Irrigation of Agricultural Lands, 1967
    Managing Editor, R. C. DINAUER
12. R. W. PEARSON and FRED ADAMS, *Editors:* Soil Acidity and Liming, 1967
    Managing Editor, R. C. DINAUER
13. K. S. QUISENBERRY and L. P. REITZ, *Editors:* Wheat and Wheat Improvement, 1967
    Managing Editor, H. L. HAMILTON

Monographs 1 through 6, published by Academic Press, Inc., should be ordered from: Academic Press, Inc., 111 Fifth Avenue, New York, New York 10003

Monographs 7—14, published by the American Society of Agronomy, should be ordered from: American Society of Agronomy, 677 South Segoe Road, Madison, Wisconsin, USA 53711

TURFGRASS SCIENCE

Editors

A. A. Hanson

and

F. V. Juska

Forage and Range Research Branch
Agricultural Research Service, USDA
Beltsville, Maryland

Published by the
AMERICAN SOCIETY OF AGRONOMY

Number 14 in the series
AGRONOMY

American Society of Agronomy, Inc.
Madison, Wisconsin, USA
1969

First printing, 1969
Second printing, 1970
Third printing, 1970
Fourth printing, 1971

The American Society of Agronomy, Inc.
677 South Segoe Road, Madison, Wisconsin, USA 53711

Library of Congress Catalog Card Number; 78-100536

Printed in the United States of America

GENERAL FOREWORD

Agronomy—An ASA Monograph Series

"Turfgrass Science" Monograph is made available to the public at a time when turf is both a topic of household importance and a subject of interest to scientists and to consumers. The book represents the fourteenth of a series of monographs prepared by the American Society of Agronomy since 1949 to meet the needs for comprehensive treatment of specific subjects in agronomy, crop science, and soil science. The first six of these monographs were published by the Academic Press, Inc. of New York under the editorship of Dr. A. G. Norman, an eminent member of the society.

As a result of the overall growth of ASA, complete responsibility for the preparation, editing, financing, and publishing of the monograph series was undertaken by the society in 1957 with the seventh volume, *Drainage of Agricultural Lands*. It was followed by *Oats and Oat Improvement* as No. 8 in 1961.

In recent years, the activity relating to publication of monographs has flourished. The colossal task of publishing Monograph No. 9 was completed in 1965. Entitled *Methods of Soil Analysis,* this contribution appeared in two parts: Part I: Physical and Mineralogical Properties, Including Statistics of Measurement and Sampling, and Part II: Chemical and Microbiological Properties. During the same year, *Soil Nitrogen,* Monograph No. 10 also appeared on the market.

The Monograph project remained very much alive in 1966, although no new number was released. In early 1967, *Irrigation of Agricultural Lands,* No. 11, became available. It was soon to be followed by *Soil Acidity and Liming,* No. 12, and *Wheat and Wheat Improvement,* No. 13; and then the present title two years later.

The American Society of Agronomy is closely associated with the Crop Science Society of America and the Soil Science Society of America. The three societies have many objectives and activities in common. They share a large percentage of their memberships and the same national headquarters and staff. This close association makes it possible for the American Society of Agronomy to publish material relating to both crop science and soil science in the "Agronomy" series.

The approximately 7,500 members of the society, organized in 19 professional divisions, including one on Turfgrass Management, provide the society with the supply of scientific knowledge to meet the needs of the public for specific information in many areas. The offering of *Turfgrass Science* is made with the hope that its contents will bring together for users of this commodity the most recent information on the subject and will stimulate investigators to seek answers to the "missing links" in the chain of scientific information related to the genetical development, production, and management of turfgrass irrespective of geographical boundaries or types of uses. Meanwhile, it is hoped that our country may profit from the useful and aesthetic values resulting from the application of turfgrass science.

Matthias Stelly
Executive Secretary
American Society of Agronomy

August 1969

Foreword

Our growing need for turf, whether it be for home lawns, football fields, playgrounds, parks, golf courses, roadsides, or cemeteries, makes this monograph, *Turfgrass Science,* particularly appropriate.

The American Society of Agronomy is happy to publish this material in recognition of the continuous efforts of its members, particularly the members of Division C-5, Turfgrass Management. These men have dedicated themselves to obtaining and utilizing scientific information on turf.

Considerable attention has been given to this subject in the past few years, including research, extension, and applications. This monograph brings together the best thinking in turfgrass science. Since there is much yet to be learned, the book should be of real help in planning future activities and, hence, in speeding progress. Specifically, it should help spur research in vital areas. The concepts of research with a mission and systems analysis might well be considered.

A wide range of subjects is covered, and well qualified people have put much effort into writing the chapters. This monograph is a credit to these men as well as to the American Society of Agronomy. I wish to express appreciation to the authors, editors, and monograph committee members on behalf of the Society.

Lafayette, Indiana
May 1969

Werner L. Nelson, President
American Society of Agronomy

Foreword

Preface

Turf is the most widely grown, most talked about, and least appreciated commodity in the United States. This is the best possible justification that can be advanced for the preparation of a "Turfgrass Science" monograph.

Most homeowners and many employees of public and private enterprises are concerned to a greater or lesser extent with growing turfgrasses. Armed with interest and determination, some of these turf managers gain a sound appreciation of turf production problems, and they learn, through experience, the best combination of practices for the turf that is under their immediate control. The individual may be thwarted, however, in applying his experience over a wider area, either by the limited nature of his experience or by the lack of documented research findings.

Much of the initial work on the development and management of grasses for recreation, beautification, and soil cover was conducted by agronomists who had had some training and experience in growing grasses for pasture and forage. Recognition and definition of research needs led to well organized research by agronomists and horticulturists and to the training of turfgrass specialists. The expansion in turf research, however, often conflicted with public demand for immediate answers to production problems. All too often the prospective turfgrass research specialist became an extension specialist first and a research investigator second. Although times have changed in both public and private agencies, a critical need remains for more and better turfgrass varieties, superior management practices, and improved pest control. A substantial increase in turfgrass research will be needed to develop principles that have broad application and to reduce the hazards and cost of maintaining quality turf.

The possibility of developing a turfgrass monograph has been considered for many years within the American Society of Agronomy. Debate focused on the nature of a monograph that could or should be developed on a production-and-management-oriented commodity—turf. Strong arguments were advanced to confine the presentation to basic aspects of turf production with major emphasis given to soils, physiology, water, genetics, diseases, ecology, etc. It was argued, with considerable justification, that applied turf practices could not be compiled in a manner that would be meaningful on any given site. Conversely, other specialists made an equally strong case for the need to relate available research data to accepted field practice. Many of these individuals stressed the scarcity of research information on turfgrasses which would limit the scope of a technical monograph.

The weights of these opposing arguments are apparent in the organization of the monograph. Introductory chapters on the "History of Turf Usage" and "The Turfgrass Industry" are followed by a series of background chapters that stress the interrelationship of technical information and practice in growing turf. Thus, Chapters 3 through 15 include detailed information on the environment in which turfgrasses are grown, the manner in which they grow and reproduce; and various pests that reduce quality. In this section a chapter on turfgrass ecology (Chapter 8) integrates basic information from many subject matter areas. Subsequent chapters devoted to applied turfgrass production range from regional discussions on lawn care (Chapters 19, 20, and 21) through athletic fields, golf greens and fairways, to roadside turf. Chapters on the principles and practices of seedbed preparation and planting (Chapters 17 and 18) provide an introduction to applied turfgrass management. Authors responsible for applied chapters have had the unenviable task of including essential practices, methods, and techniques, while avoiding excessive duplication with either technically oriented chapters or other applied presentations. They have succeeded to the point where applied chapters stand on their own and provide a starting point for any organized effort to develop a better understanding of plant growth, soils, species, pests, climatic, and other relationships. The title "Turfgrass Science" was selected in preference to either "Turf" or "Turfgrass" to emphasize the relative importance and need for technical information in the interpretation of applied turfgrass production problems.

One finds wide differences of opinion on the merits of various materials and practices. Some of these differences can be attributed to the experience of the protagonists involved, the incorrect interpretation of observations in the absence of factual information, and to obvious deficiencies in turfgrass research. The contributing authors are experienced scientists and turfgrass specialists who have had successful careers in producing quality turf and in assisting others in solving their turfgrass problems. Thus, careful consideration should be given to the concepts included in their various presentations even though the reader may not agree with all of the views expressed. The outlook and horizons of practical turfgrass managers and students will be increased by the diverse approaches that the authors selected for their presentations. In addition, it is hoped that the book will aid in stimulating meaningful research on critical turfgrass production problems.

The editors give special recognition to the many individuals who took time from their busy schedules to contribute to the monograph. Special appreciation is extended to Mrs. Doris Wray, secretary to F. V. Juska, for her valuable assistance in completing this assignment.

Trade names found in this book are used solely to identify materials or equipment and no endorsement of them is implied or intended.

A conversion table for English and metric units may be found on page xviii.

Beltsville, Maryland
April 1969

A. A. Hanson
Felix V. Juska
Editors

Contributors

B. A. App, Agricultural Research Service, USDA, Beltsville, Md.

J. B. Beard, Department of Crop Science, Michigan State University, East Lansing, Mich.

R. E. Blaser, Department of Agronomy, Virginia Polytechnic Institute, Blacksburg, Va.

M. P. Britton, formerly Department of Plant Pathology, University of Illinois, Urbana, Ill.

Glenn W. Burton, Research Geneticist, ARS, USDA, Georgia Coastal Plain Exp. Sta., Tifton, Ga.

J. F. Cornman, Department of Horticulture, Cornell University, Ithaca, N.Y.

J. Ritchie Cowan, Department of Farm Crops, Oregon State University, Corvallis, Oregon

John L. Creech, Agricultural Research Service, USDA, Beltsville, Md.

R. R. Davis, Department of Agronomy, Ohio Agricultural Research and Development Center, Wooster, Ohio

R. E. Engel, Department of Soils and Crops, Rutgers—The State University, New Brunswick, N.J.

Marvin H. Ferguson, President, Agri-Systems of Texas, Inc., Bryan, Texas

Fred V. Grau, President, Grasslyn, Inc., College Park, Md.

A. A. Hanson, Chief, Forage and Range Res. Br., ARS, USDA, Beltsville, Md.

John C. Harper II, Department of Agronomy, The Pennsylvania State University, University Park, Pa.

C. M. Heald, Research Plant Pathologist, Agricultural Research Service, USDA, Weslaco, Texas

Ethan C. Holt, Department of Soil and Crop Sciences, Texas Agricultural Exp. Sta., College Station, Texas

W. L. Hottenstein, Bureau of Public Roads, Washington, D. C.

A. W. Hovin, Forage and Range Res. Br., ARS, USDA, Beltsville, Md.

W. W. Huffine, Department of Agronomy, Oklahoma State University, Stillwater, Okla.

R. D. Ilnicki, Department of Soils and Crops, Rutgers—The State University, New Brunswick, N.J.

F. V. Juska, Forage and Range Res. Br., ARS, USDA, Beltsville, Md.

Ray A. Keen, Department of Horticulture, Kansas State University, Manhattan, Kans.

S. H. Kerr, Department of Entomology, University of Florida, Gainesville, Fla.

J. M. Latham, Jr., Milwaukee Sewerage Commission, Milwaukee, Wis.

Albert W. Marsh, Extension Specialist, Agricultural Extension Service, University of California, Riverside, Calif.

C. Wallace Miller, Department of the Army, Washington, D. C.

H. B. Musser (deceased), Emeritus Professor of Agronomy, The Pennsylvania State University, University Park, Pa.

Gene C. Nutter, Turf-Grass Times and Turf-Grass Publications, Inc., Jacksonville Beach, Fla.

A. T. Perkins, Department of Agronomy, The Pennsylvania State University, University Park, Pa.

V. G. Perry, Department of Entomology, University of Florida, Gainesville, Fla.

Alton E. Rabbitt, National Park Service, Department of the Interior, Washington, D. C.

P. E. Rieke, Department of Soil Science, Michigan State University, East Lansing, Mich.

R. E. Schmidt, Department of Agronomy, Virginia Polytechnic Institute, Blacksburg, Va.

Donald V. Waddington, Department of Agronomy, The Pennsylvania State University, University Park, Pa.

Coleman Y. Ward, Department of Agronomy, Mississippi State University, State College, Miss.

James R. Watson, Jr., Toro Manufacturing Corporation, Minneapolis, Minn.

C. G. Wilson, Milwaukee Sewerage Commission, Milwaukee, Wis.

V. B. Youngner, Department of Agronomy, University of California, Riverside, Calif.

CONTENTS

Conversion Factors for English and Metric Units

To convert column 1 into column 2, multiply by	Column 1	Column 2	To convert column 2 into column 1, multiply by
	Length		
0.621	kilometer, km	mile, mi	1.609
1.094	meter, m	yard, yd	0.914
0.394	centimeter, cm	inch, in	2.540
	Area		
0.386	kilometer^2, km^2	mile^2, mi^2	2.590
247.1	kilometer^2, km^2	acre, acre	0.00405
2.471	hectare, ha	acre, acre	0.405
	Volume		
0.00973	meter^3, m^3	acre-inch	102.8
3.532	hectoliter, hl	cubic foot, ft^3	0.2832
2.838	hectoliter, hl	bushel, bu	0.352
0.0284	liter	bushel, bu	35.24
1.057	liter	quart (liquid), qt	0.946
	Mass		
1.102	ton (metric)	ton (English)	0.9072
220.5	quintal, q	pound, lb	0.00454
2.205	kilogram, kg	pound, lb	0.454
0.0353	gram, g	ounce (avdp), oz	28.35
	Yield or Rate		
0.446	ton (metric)/hectare	ton (English)/acre	2.242
0.892	kg/ha	lb/acre	1.12
0.892	quintal/hectare	hundredweight/acre	1.12
	Pressure		
14.22	kg/cm^2	lb/inch^2, psi	0.0703
0.968	kg/cm^2	atmospheres, atm	1.033
0.9807	kg/cm^2	bar	1.0197
	Temperature		
$\frac{9}{5}$ C + 32	Celsius, C	Fahrenheit, F	$\frac{5}{9}$ (F–32)
	–17.8°	0°	
	0°	32°	
	20°	68°	
	100°	212°	

1 History of Turf Usage

Wayne W. Huffine

Oklahoma State University
Stillwater, Oklahoma

Fred V. Grau

Grasslyn, Inc.
College Park, Maryland

I. Introduction

> Nature! ..... She is the universal artist, creating the greatest contrasts from the simplest material, while achieving, without seeming to strive for it, an ultimate perfection ..... Each of her works has its own peculiar quality; every one of her manifold appearances symbolizes a single concept and yet somehow blending they achieve unity. One must obey nature's laws even while he denies them: he is forced to produce with her aid even when he imagines that he is able to work against her.
>
> "Nature"—A Poetic Fragment
> Johann Wolfgang von Goethe[1]

Turf is one of the blessings of nature. It is both a thing of service and of beauty. The concept of turf as we know it today probably had its origin when man started to domesticate animals. They were herded or tethered to prevent escape and their grazed "islands" conceivably were used by the young of Man for their games and play.

The classic "Dance of the Nymphs" painted by Jean Baptiste Corot in 1851, was romantically inspired by mythology and seemingly performed on an "island" of turf. The mythical field of Mars, "Campus Martius", as described by Zimmerman (1964) where Roman youths performed exercises, rode horses, and drove chariots perhaps evolved into our present stadia with its manicured turf. These and other accomplishments in Agronomy might be attributed entirely to Ceres, the Goddess of Agriculture.

Turf in the modern concept is synonymous with grass which in geological time possibly evolved during the Cretaceous and early Tertiary some 70 million years ago according to Harlan (1956), but the fragments of these fossils are scant. One rich fossil deposit of grassland flora dating from the lower Miocene and later is known from the Great Plains.

---

[1] From *The Arts and Man* by Raymond S. Stites. Copyright 1940, McGraw-Hill. Used by permission of McGraw-Hill Book Company.

II. Biblical References to Grass

In the period of recorded history numerous references to grass are to be found in the Bible. The first chapter of Genesis (1:11-12) reveals the benevolent nature of Creation: "And God said, let the earth bring forth grass, . . . And the earth brought forth grass, . . ." In the fifth book of Moses (Deuteronomy 8:7) is the promise, "And I will send grass in thy fields for thy cattle, that thou mayest eat and be full." Solomon proclaims (Proverbs 19:12), "The king's wrath is as the roaring of a lion; but his favor is as dew upon the grass." Man's brief span is seen by the Psalmist (10:3-15) as the ephemeral life of the flower: "As for man, his days are as grass: as a flower of the field, so he flourisheth. For the wind passeth over it, and it is gone; and the place thereof shall know it no more." Similar expressions were made by Isaiah (40:6-8) and Peter (1 Peter 1:24), both devout naturalists.

While the Scriptures frequently refer to plants and their production, there is distinct scarcity of specific references by name or location to gardens, as pointed out by MacKay (1950). Six gardens are listed in the Old Testament, and two in the New Testament.

The gardens of the Bible would be somewhat like our present day subtropical botanical garden. They were predominantly a garden of trees and a source of water. The earliest gardens according to Rohde (1927) were divided into four parts by four rivers coming from a common source, as depicted in the Hindu Vedas, the accounts of Emperor Babar, and pictured in the design of the famous garden carpets of Persia. The garden design in these carpets shows rectangular beds of flowers and grass, cypress, and fruit trees, with a rectangular pool in the center from which flowed four streams. Gardens of biblical times, with the exception of the Garden of Eden and Ezekiel's paradise, were associated with wealth and stories of them are steeped in mysticism and splendour.

III. Early Use of Turf in Asia

Vast pleasure gardens and magnificent palaces have been the most expensive luxuries of China's emperors, Malone (1934) reports. Emperor Wu Ti (157-87 B.C.) of the Han Dynasty held 30,000 slaves to care for his extensive grounds and buildings. The rarest trees and plants were assembled from throughout his whole empire which extended from Korea to Central Asia.

The simple rectangular Eastern garden design is vividly shown in the Persian garden carpets which date back to the days of the ancient kingdom of Assyria. As mentioned by Rohde (1927) one of the most famous of all garden carpets was made for Chosroes I of Persia, about A.D. 531-579, which represented the plan of a royal pleasure garden.

Firdawsi,[2] the great Iranian poet, who wrote his "Shah nama" or "History of the Kings" about the year A.D. 1000, described the beauties of nature as he wrote of an area along the Caspian Sea:

[2] From *Persian Gardens and Pavilions* by Donald N. Wilber. 1962. Used by permission of Charles E. Tuttle Co., Inc. Tokyo, Japan.

"Mazanderan is the bower of spring . . .
Tulips and hyacinths abound
On every lawn; and all around
Blooms like a garden in its prime
Fostered by that delicious clime."

The Taj Mahal and garden, as Goethe (1955) relates, symbolize the romance that exists among garden-lovers everywhere. The Agra garden, designed by some unknown landscape-artist, dominated the thoughts of Shah Jahan, the Grand Mogul and his love for his wife Mumtaz-i-Mahal.

Sports frequently occupied the day for Akbar, 1556-1605 A.D., the Great Emperor of Hindustan, according to Malleson (1891). Sometimes he would devote the early morning hours to field sports and the late evenings to the game of chaugau, or polo.

IV. Turfgrass Culture in Europe

Rohde (1927) reveals that the rectangular garden plots portrayed in Persian garden-carpets were reflected for centuries in gardens of western Europe. The greatest influence came with the Crusades, when every class of society in Europe was brought into contact with the East.

A part of the classical gardens of Europe was probably devoted to lawns although the first references to that effect only became available in mediaeval times. To this fact Dawson (1949) pays a fitting tribute in his statement, "All lawn lovers should be grateful to Miss Eleanour Sinclair Rohde, who has searched the literature and brought together the early references to lawns in a fascinating article," in Nineteenth Century and After, 1928, CIV,200.

Lawns seem to be sort of a "living fossil" according to some writers. In early times when wild beasts roamed the forests and both were close to the dwellings, the householder grazed his animals close to the house. This was an act of survival for both the man and his animals. The closely-cropped grass became a "symbol" which exists today as a horticultural embellishment and a playground for the young.

A turfgrass sport that has come to us from the crowned heads of Europe is bowls. Monro (1953) found that the association of bowls and war dates back hundreds of years. The game was so popular with the military personnel of England and France in the 1300's that it had to be forbidden as it interfered with their practice of archery. Bowling on the green was the sport in which Sir Francis Drake was engaged (1588) when he was advised of the approach of the Spanish Armada. The original bowling green was the forerunner of our modern golf green.

Golf is a sport played on turf, the finest known to man. It originated in the Low Countries (Holland's Kolf), spread to England and Scotland and thence to the United States about 75 years ago. It originated long before there were mowers to keep the grass clipped closely. "Mowing" was done by sheep which, through a combination of close cropping and "treading", created favorable conditions for the game. As the putting green developed there were times when the game had to stop until the impediments were brushed away.

Cricket, a British game, has persisted for centuries and has been carried to nearly every country, colony, or protectorate occupied by the British ruling class. The demands for perfection in the "pitch," the principal playing surface, place great stress on the grasses. The surface must be firm to the point of hardness and mowed as closely as mowers will cut. Just as cricket has been taken to the far corners of the earth, the British established fine lawns and exquisite botanical gardens wherever they went.

V. Evolution of Turf in the United States

The term turf has been popularized in the United States only within the memory of the living. For many years it carried an unfavorable connotation, especially when it was associated with horse racing and gambling at the track. Little more than 25 years ago the word carried the idea of "golf turf," the playground of the "idle rich."

The Village Green in ancient times has become the "Square," or the "Park" in many old towns. The green was grazed by sheep and goats, and the tight turf was pleasing to the mothers who brought their little ones out for a stroll and sunshine. With houses surrounding the Village Green the turfed area was a natural meeting place for gossip and news, likewise romance.

A hit song and one of the sweetest of the 19th Century, and still a favorite of barber shop quartets as Marcuse (1959) points out, is the one written by John L. Thornton,—"When You Were Sweet Sixteen." The song had its beginning on the village green as told in the chorus:

"I love you as I never loved before,
Since first I met you on the village green;
Come to me, or my dream of love is o'er.
I love you as I loved you when you were sweet,
When you were sweet sixteen."

Turf has been a part of the romantic West of the U.S.A. As early as 1200 A.D. the inhabitants of the midwest, the prehistoric Plains Indians, used sod strips to cover a framework of poles and brush matting to make comfortable dwellings. So far as we can tell the sod was

Figure 1. J. Cramer Sod House Home. Lillian, Custer Co., Nebraska. Nebr. State Historical Society.

stripped from the buffalo-gramagrass prairies. Nothing is known of the methods employed in cutting and lifting the sod.

Typical of the early settlement in the West was the sod house. Figure 1 shows a sod house, about 1886, in Custer County, Nebraska. Charles Grau, a pioneer, father of F. V. Grau, built a sod house such as this in Colorado where he homesteaded. The walls are blocks of sod with joints overlapped. The roof is "shingled" with strips of sod, most certainly buffalograss. These "soddies" were cool in summer and warm in winter but, unfortunately, heavy rains saturated the sod which then continued to drip inside the house for several days after the rain had stopped.

The Plains Indians engaged in several sports, all of which were played on grass sod. One that has been modified to meet modern "civilized" concepts is lacrosse, a popular game in Canada and at a number of American universities. The Indians played it on the grassed plains on foot and on horseback. The game would cover many miles during the course of a day. The excitement of early day sports was captured in the painting of "Indians Playing Ball" by the American artist and traveler George Catlin, in 1832 (Fig. 2).

The first airport built in the U.S. is located in College Park, Md. It has had turf runways since it was started. Turfgrasses were the only covering for most airports until aircraft grew too large and heavy—then it was necessary to install concrete to support the heavy loads and to provide a wearing surface. Today groups of Flying Farmers and others enjoy flying small aircraft and gliders from turfed runways.

With few exceptions burial grounds have been turf covered. The Memorial Gardens of the present day remind one of an extensive turfed park beautifully landscaped. Markers are flush or countersunk to facilitate the operation of maintenance equipment.

VI. Turf Research

Domestic

The first turf research, as revealed by Olcott (1890), appears to have been conducted in the Olcott turf gardens in Connecticut in 1885, and

Figure 2. Indians Playing Ball by George Catlin.

these were continued until the death of J. B. Olcott in 1910. The next step in turf research occurred in 1890 at the Rhode Island Agricultural Experiment Station.

The first mention of turf in the Agricultural Appropriations Act of the Federal Government appears for the year 1901—

> "and the agricultural experiment stations are hereby authorized and directed to cooperate with the Secretary of Agriculture in establishing and maintaining experimental grass stations, for determining .... the best native and foreign species for reclaiming overstocked ranges and pastures, for renovating worn-out lands, for binding drifting sands and washed lands, and *for turfing lawns and pleasure grounds* ..., seventeen thousand dollars: Provided. In addition, the appropriations act for 1901 specified that $6,000 of the amount appropriated be used to purchase and collect seed, roots, specimens, etc. for distribution to experiment stations."

To assure further the distribution of these funds the Act also provided that not more than $6,000 of the amount appropriated shall be expended for salaries in the City of Washington, Distict of Columbia. Although federal allocations of funds for research including turf were made, it was not until the end of World War II that most agricultural experiment stations initiated turf research programs.

The United States Golf Association established its "Green Section" in 1920 to serve both as advisory and research. Their experimental studies in cooperation with the former Bureau of Plant Industry, USDA, at Arlington, Virginia, were directed primarily toward the requirements of golf.

Today, the Agricultural Research Service, U.S. Department of Agriculture, and almost every State Agricultural Experiment Station is involved to some degree in turf research. The initiation of turf research by states is shown in Table 1, which gives dates, locations, early investigators, and persons currently in charge.

The world's first turf research station was established in England on the St. Ives estate at Bingley, Yorkshire, in 1929. Under the able direction of R. B. Dawson this station has achieved a worldwide reputation for its turf research. Turf research was started in New Zealand in 1932, also in Australia in New South Wales. Experimental work was begun in 1935 in Queensland, 1936 in Victoria, and 1948 in Western Australia. Turf research in South Africa was pioneered by C. M. Murray of Capetown. At the end of 1906 Dr. Murray had established grass greens at the Royal Cape Golf Course. A few grass greens had been put down even earlier than this in Durban in 1891 or 1892. The first South African Golf Championship was played on grass greens in 1909 in the Transvaal. The University of Witwatersrand, Frankenwald Turf Research Station, in Johannesburg and the Roodeplaat Experiment Station at Pretoria are actively engaged in turf research.

Table 1. Initiation of turfgrass research in the various states.

State	Turf research initiated	First turf grass conf.	Location	Early investigators	Currently in charge
Alabama	1927	1960	Auburn Univ.	D. G. Sturkie	Ray Dickens
Alaska	1950	None	Univ. of Alaska	H. Hodgson, A. Kallio, A. Wilton, R. Taylor L. J. Klebesadel	R. L. Taylor, L. J. Klebesadel
Arizona	1949	1953	Univ. of Ariz.	S. Fazio, J. Folkner A. Baltensperger	W. R. Kneebone
Arkansas	1959	None	Univ. of Ark.	A. M. Davis	C. L. Murdoch
California	1951	1951	Univ. Cal., Davis	L. Currier, R. Hagan	J. H. Madison
	1948	1949	Univ. Cal., Riverside	V. Stoutemeyer, P. Miller R. E. Endo	V. B. Youngner
Colorado	Early 1940's	1954	Colo. State Univ.	G. Beach, J. Fults	J. Fults, J. D. Butler
Connecticut	1885	None	Univ. of Conn.	J. B. Olcott	W. Washko, R. Peters S. Papanos
Delaware	1965	1968	Univ. of Del.	W. Mitchell, C. Phillips	W. Mitchell
Florida	1945	1953	Univ. of Fla.	R. Bair, G. Nutter	G. Horn, E. Burt A. E. Dudeck
Georgia	1946	1946	Tifton, Georgia	G. W. Burton	G. W. Burton
Hawaii	1963	1965	Univ. of Hawaii	R. Voss, D. Watson, W. McCall	D. P. Watson
Idaho	None	None	Univ. of Idaho	None	None
Illinois	1934	1960	Univ. of Ill.	A. Lang, J. Pieper F. Weinard	T. D. Hughes A. J. Turgeon
Indiana	1942	1937	Purdue Univ.	M. Clevitt, G. Hoffer, G. Mott	W. H. Daniel
Iowa	1931	1932	Iowa State Univ.	V. Stoutemeyer, H. Lantz, S. Edgecomb, E. Roberts	C. F. Hodges A. E. Cott
Kansas	Late 1920's	1950	Kans. State Univ.	J. Zahnley, L. Quinlan	R. Keen, C. Long
Kentucky	1948	None	Univ. of Ky.	E. Fergus, J. Spencer	R. Buckner, L. Stoltz
Louisiana	1960	1963	La. State Univ.	T. E. Pope	W. A. Young
Maine	1958	1962	Univ. of Maine	R. Struchtemeyer	V. H. Holyoke
Maryland	1931	1928	Univ. of Md.	R. Thomas, E. Cory, E. Deal	G. Bean, J. R. Hall
Massachusetts	1927	1931	Univ. of Mass.	L. Dickinson	J. Troll, J. Zak
Michigan	1929	1930	Mich. State Univ.	R. Cook, J. Tyson, M. McCool	J. Beard, P. Rieke
Minnesota	1936	1964	Univ. of Minn.	H. Hayes, H. Schultz	D. White, H. Thomas G. Blake
Mississippi	1956	1960	Miss. State Univ.	C. Johnson, L. Wise	C. Y. Ward
Missouri	1910	1960	Univ. of Mo.	J. Whitten, E. Brown	C. Lobenstein, D. D. Hemphill
Montana	1920's	None	Mont. State Univ.	None	G. Evans, E. Hehn, A. E. Carleton
Nebraska	1927	1963	Univ. of Neb.	F. Keim, F. Grau	E. J. Kinbacher
New Hampshire	1961	1965	Univ. of N. H.	L. J. Higgins	L. J. Higgins
New Mexico	1954	1955	N. M. State Univ.	C. E. Watson	C. E. Watson
Nevada	1965	None	Univ. of Nev.	R. Ruf, R. Post	R. L. Post
New Jersey	1924	1929	Rutgers Univ.	H. Sprague, E. Evaul G. W. Musgrave	R. E. Engel C. Reed Funk
New York	1947	1947	Cornell Univ.	J. F. Cornman	J. F. Cornman
North Carolina	1961	1963	N. C. State Univ.	J. Harris, W. Gilbert	W. Gilbert, W. Lewis
North Dakota	1962	None	N. D. State Univ.	J. Carter*, K. Larson* I. Dietrich*	J. Carter*, K. Larson* D. Hoag*
Ohio	Early 1920's	1938	Ohio State Univ.	F. Welton, G. McClure, R. Davis, K. Bader	R. W. Miller, R. Davis
Oklahoma	1948	1946	Okla. State Univ.	W. Elder, R. Chessmore	W. W. Huffine
Oregon	1930	1948	Ore. State Univ.	H. A. Schoth	N. Goetze, R. Frakes
Pennsylvania	1929	1929	Pa. State Univ.	H. Musser, F. Grau	J. M. Duich
Rhode Island	1890	None	Univ. of R. I.	L. Kinney, H. Wheeler J. A. DeFrance	C. R. Skogley
South Carolina	1959	None	Clemson Univ.	P. M. Alexander	F. B. Ledbetter
South Dakota	1955	None	S. D. State Univ.	William Macksam	D. E. Herman
Tennessee	1938	1947	Univ. of Tenn.	J. K. Underwood	L. M. Callahan
Texas	1940	1946	Tex. A & M Univ.	G. Warner, R. Potts, A. Crain, J. Watson, E. Holt	G. G. McBee, R. L. Duble Wallace Menn
Utah	1958	1964	Utah State Univ.	H. Peterson, K. Allred	W. Campbell, K. Allred
Vermont	1959	1965	Univ. of Vt.	G. M. Wood	G. M. Wood
Virginia	1910-1915	1957	Va. Polytechnic Institute	L. Carrier, A. Smith	R. Schmidt, R. Blaser, J. Shoulders
Washington	1942	1948	Wash. State Univ.	A. G. Law	A. Law, R. Goss
West Virginia	1930	1967	W. Va. Univ.	Collins Veatch	A. Powell, C. Sperow
Wisconsin	1920	1959	Univ. of Wis.	F. Burcalow, E. Nielsen, D. C. Smith, J. Sund	R. Newman, G. Worf, J. Love, P. Drolsom
Wyoming	1962	None	Univ. of Wyo.	Loyd Ayres	Project closed
USDA cooperating	1920	None	Arlington, Va.	John Monteith, Jr.	Project closed
with USGA†	1941	None	Beltsville, Md.	John Monteith, Jr.	F. V. Juska

* Considered resource personnel. † Green Section, U. S. Golf Association.

Literature Cited

Dawson, R. B. 1949. Practical lawn craft. Crosby Lockwood & Son, Ltd. London. 315 p.

Goethe, C. M. 1955. Garden philosopher. The Keystone Press. Sacramento, California. 327 p.

Harlan, J. R. 1956. Theory and dynamics of grassland agriculture. D. Van Nostrand Co., Princeton, New Jersey. 281 p.

MacKay, A. I. 1950. Farming and gardening in the Bible. Rodale Press. Emmaus, Pennsylvania. 280 p.

Malleson, G. B. 1891. Rulers of India. Akbar. Oxford at the Clarendon Press. 204 p.

Malone, Carroll Brown. 1934. History of the Peking summer palaces under the Ch'ing Dynasty. Illinois Studies in the Social Sciences Vol. XIX Nos. 1-2. University of Illinois. 247 p.

Marcuse, M. F. 1959. Tin pan alley in gaslight. Century House. Watkins Glen, New York. 448 p.

Monro, J. P. 1953. Bowls encyclopaedia. Wilke & Co., Ltd. Melbourne, Australia. 295 p.

Olcott, J. B. 1890. Annual report. Connecticut Agr. Exp. Sta. 162-174 p.

Rohde, Eleanour Sinclair. 1927. Garden-craft in the Bible. Herbert Jenkins, Ltd. London. 242 p.

Wilber, D. N. 1962. Persian gardens and garden pavilions. Charles E. Tuttle Co. Tokyo, Japan. 239 p.

Zimmerman, J. E. 1964. Dictionary of classical mythology. Harper & Row Publishers Inc. New York. 300 p.

2 The Turfgrass Industry

GENE C. NUTTER

Turf-Grass Times and Turf-Grass Publications, Inc.
Jacksonville Beach, Florida

JAMES R. WATSON, JR.

Toro Manufacturing Corporation
Minneapolis, Minnesota

I. Development of the Turfgrass Industry

A. Definition and Objectives

Industries may be defined in various ways including geographic influence, scope and size, products, market and trade practices, manpower composition, and public and political policies.

Discussion in this chapter will be confined largely to the North American Continent, which contains a high percentage of the world turf market. The industry is quite young; hence public and political policies have not evolved. Otherwise, the image of the industry will be defined in the ensuing discussion.

By definition, as suggested by Nutter (1965), the turfgrass industry encompasses the production and maintenance of specialized grasses and other ground covers as required in the development and management of facilities for utility, beautification, and recreation. It involves turfgrass science and technology, business management, manpower development, and the manufacturing and marketing of turfgrass products and services.

Beautification refers to those facilities where the prime or partial function is aesthetic (as for example turf usage in commercial or residential landscaping). Recreational facilities include the great and increasing variety of outdoor activities which provide sport and athletic endeavor, exercise and physical conditioning, therapeutic diversion, and healthful outlets for the growing and mythical phenomenon of "Leisure Time". Utility involves those uses of facilities not primarily for aesthetic or recreation purpose, but where turf provides a service function, such as along highways, on airfields, or where erosion control is the prime objective.

Obviously, a given turf area may involve more than one basic function. For example, golf courses and parks serve both recreation and beautification purposes, and a well-landscaped highway serves a utilitarian function while appearing attractive.

1. Facilities for People

While use is the common denominator among the three classes of turfgrass facilities, the underlying theme in the turfgrass industry emphasizes "facilities for people" rather than the earlier agronomic concept which envisioned turf production as the major objective. Today, "use" and "appearance" are given prime consideration. To best serve the particular facility, the turf should be, first, useful and, secondly, attractive. Stress on "use" and "appearance" concepts better relates production and maintenance of turfgrasses to their role in the economy. This approach might be called the "facility concept".

The facility concept not only applies to people using the turfgrass facility—but also to those who are indirectly exposed to the facility. Professional and amateur sports functions may draw thousands of spectators and through the medium of television millions more people observe these events and facilities.

There is also increasing emphasis on the conditioning and grooming of turfgrass facilities for competitive influence, commercial appeal, and public relations. Resorts and commercial apartment complexes are using well-groomed turf as a sales tool. Golf courses compete for player appeal on the basis of turf condition and excellence of grooming. Industrial and institutional grounds become public relations symbols. Even the residential lawn is becoming an ever increasing mark of status in our society.

Thus, we see the turfgrass industry *as a great service industry* revolving around the use of specialized grasses and ground covers which provide facilities for the betterment of our growing population. To some, it is an industry based on luxury and affluence. This is questionable! Who will declare physical conditioning, recreational diversion from mental stress, or the healthy application of leisure time to be a luxury? These are the precepts upon which the turfgrass industry builds and services utility, recreation, and beautification facilities.

B. Evolution of the Industry

The origin of the turfgrass industry would parallel the history of turf usage as related in Chapter 1. There would be a lag, however, because the word "industry" involves the accumulative effect of systematic and distinct endeavor. According to Webster's dictionary, industry refers to a recognized craft or art and a field of business or manufacturing. Obviously, there would not have been such a set up or organization at the outset.

The first equipment and products used in turf were borrowed from the farm. In the choice of mowing equipment, after hand scythes and cradles were abandoned to horse-drawn machines, the sickle-bar mower was brought from the hay field to mow large turf areas (parks and golf courses). The first grasses planted for turf facilities were those common to local farm needs. There were no speciality fertilizers, only barnyard manures, natural compost, guano, fish and bone products, and certain early chemical fertilizers such as ammonium salts and nitrate of soda.

The only weed control in those early days was hand weeding; and there was no irrigation. These early practices seem a long way removed from the complex chemicals used in turf management today, the specialized, hydraulically operated mowing equipment and the sophisticated, automatic irrigation systems.

1. Golf—The Beginning

The turfgrass industry began with the golf course and the maintenance of golf course operations has been the front runner in technical advances and industrial development. Greenskeeping brought the first focus on arts and crafts and later opened the door to profesionalism. Today, the Golf Course Superintendents Association of America represents the most advanced and best organized professional group in the industry. Organized in 1926, it now represents over 2,500 professional golf course superintendents across the North American Continent.

The world-renowned Royal and Ancient Golf Club of St. Andrews (Scotland) originated in 1754 and has been in continous operation ever since (Farley, 1931). Golf "boomed" in the British Isles in the late 19th century and the game gravitated to the U.S. where, in 1888, the first official American golf club became St. Andrew's in Yonkers, N.Y. Gibson (1958) relates that in 1895, 40 additional golf courses were built in the U.S., making the total over 80. The U.S. Golf Association was formed in 1894, the Professional Golf Association in 1916, the Green Section of the USGA in 1920, and the Golf Course Superintendents Association of America in 1926.

By 1920, there were 477 member clubs in the USGA. Then followed the "Golden Age" of the 1920's. By 1931, the number of golf courses in the U.S. had increased to 5,700. The depression of the 1930's closed many golf courses, but growth was rapid after World War II. There are now over 10,000 golf courses in North America and over 11 million golfers. (Anon. 1969c).

In the past, golf has led the industry because of its concentration of activity and commonness of interest. Golf has been the most organized segment of the industry nationally, state-wide, and locally. More recently, other segments have begun to show advanced degrees of unity and organization. These include the sod industry and certain lawn service and pest control groups. Turfgrass trade organizations have now evolved in many states. Turfgrass research and education workers are beginning to coordinate their efforts nationally. Still, these and other segments within the industry have far to go to approach the degree of industry organization existing in golf turf.

II. COMPOSITION OF THE TURFGRASS INDUSTRY

A. Composition of the Industry by Function

An analysis of the turfgrass industry in profile reveals four functional branches. These are (1) The *facilities* branch (that phase dealing with the management and maintenance of turfgrass facilities); (2) The *manufacturing* branch which provides the products; (3) The *servicing* branch which implements the utilization of both products and facilities; and (4) The *institutional* branch which includes schools, colleges, the Extension Service (federal, state, and county) and Experiment Stations (federal, state, and private). Table 1 shows detailed composition by branches. The examples given are not intended to be all-inclusive or restrictive.

Table 1. Functional composition of the turfgrass industry.

BRANCH 1 - Turfgrass Facilities	BRANCH 2 - Manufacturing
Airports	Equipment
Athletic fields	Fertilizers
Bowling and croquet greens	Growth regulator chemicals
Campuses (college and university)	Irrigation system components
Cemeteries and memorial parks	Pesticides, Seed, Sod
Churches and synagogues	Special products (soil components, amendments)
Courthouses and governmental buildings	Supplies, tools, miscellaneous
Exposition and fairgrounds	**BRANCH 3 - Servicing**
Garden apartments	
Golf courses and driving ranges	Distributors and retailers (all products)
Grass tennis courts	Contract services (lawn and landscape maintenance, etc.)
Highway rights-of-way and medians, etc.	Architects and designers, Contractors
Hospitals	Consultants - business and technical
Hotels and motels	Service laboratories (soil testing, chemical, water, etc.)
Housing projects and subdivisions	Research organizations
Industrial parks	Trade and professional organizations
Lawns (residential and commercial)	Information service organizations (USGA Green Section,
Military bases	National Golf Foundation, etc.)
Mobile home villages	Publications
Parks and playgrounds	**BRANCH 4 - Institutional**
Race tracks	
Resorts	Colleges, universities
Retirement villages	Experiment stations
Schools	Vocational-technical schools
Zoos and botanic gardens	Extension service (county, state, federal)
	U.S. Department of Agriculture

To many observers and practitioners in the field, this four-branch profile will be a surprise. In the past, most references to a turfgrass industry usually referred to those activities and functions dealing with the growing of grass or the maintenance of turfgrass areas (facilities branch). Indirectly related was research work at experiment stations and information provided by colleges and extension services (institutional branch).

The inclusion of manufacturing and servicing branches may be particularly unusual to the older concept which primarily considered branches 1 and 4 as comprising the total turfgrass industry. Yet, evidence of the manufacturing and servicing branches are present in all facets of modern turf activities. Today, as the turfgrass industry emerges with a more definite and mature image, all the integral parts become more evident and more important.

B. Manpower Composition of the Turfgrass Industry

The most valuable resource in any industry is its manpower. Likewise, the progress of an industry may be evaluated by the stage of development of its manpower profile. In short, the manpower profile outlines the vertical classification of manpower within the industry. Before turning to a detailed analysis of this profile, it is important to reflect upon the historical development of manpower in the turfgrass industry.

1. Manpower Development

In its early stages, the industry gave little thought to manpower development. Manual labor was more or less plentiful and jobs were filled by convenience without particluar regard for qualifications beyond the need for physical stamina ("a strong back"). In fact, very few turf facilities were managed according to a table of organization; very few had clearly defined job descriptions. Here again, reference is made to golf, since earliest organized turf activities were limited primarily to golf course operations.

Supervisors (primarily greenskeepers) were selected according to experience. Their training was through the apprenticeship system and very few had formal education through the high school level. Some of the early greenskeepers came from Scotland, where they grew up and served apprenticeships in the cradle of golf. Others transferred from the farm. In time, men from these backgrounds blended their knowledge of the soil with the specialized requirements of golf course (and other turf) facilities to develop turf maintenance practices and technologies. While these men had certain management responsibilities, in reality they were technicians. In many cases one man served as labor foreman of the facility (hired and fired the help), as technician (operated sprayers, spreaders, repaired equipment, etc.), and in addition filled out the rest of his 12- to 16-hour day as laborer. Obviously, such working greenskeepers had little time for administrative functions or manpower development. They were involved primarily with the problems of converting forage grasses to the specialized needs of the golf course. Furthermore, some early greenskeepers also served a dual role as golf professionals (pro-greenskeepers).

Gradually, as golf courses increased in number and as maintenance standards were raised, a more definite manpower structure evolved. Working foremen became full-time supervisory greenskeepers and eventually golf course superintendents with broad management responsibilities. Requirements for trained skills increased as mechanization replaced hand methods and as new chemicals were made available. These technological changes resulted in greater job specialization. A mechanic became essential and many golf clubs employed an assistant or a foreman to give closer supervision of labor.

Still the evolution of academic professionalism was slow. Job improvement evolved largely through greenskeeper ingenuity and the need for less laborious methods. There was very little opportunity for educational improvement.

In time, tradesmen (again, mostly greenskeepers) began to visit each other and finally to gather informally for discussion of common problems. At first, trade practices were guarded very jealously. Later, the value of exchanging experiences and ideas became evident. Gradually, some groups began to compile and distribute notes from their meetings. This led to the development of technical (educational) conferences, beginning in the mid-1920's, during the "golden era" of golf. From these meetings and conferences, a higher level of managerial skill evolved in the industry.

Although the growth of golf facilities was retarded by the depression of the 1930's, the financial austerity facing the surviving golf facilities led to more efficient maintenance and to stronger professional growth among greenskeepers and other turfgrass personnel.

The approach of World War II, in the wake of the depression, caused a further reduction in turfgrass operations. Some facilities remained open, but much of the nation's available manpower became involved directly or indirectly in the war effort. Indeed, some turfgrass specialists transferred their activities to such military functions as maintenance of air fields and training bases.

2. *The Postwar Boom*

As the nation recovered from the severe deprivations of the war years, there was an urgent demand to catch up—first on rationed products then on civilian activities. Closed golf courses were renovated and new facilities were planned. Beginning with a 20-year low of 4,800 golf courses (Anon. 1968), the 10-year period from 1946-1955 saw an increase of only 10% in the number of golf courses. This period was followed by a fantastic increase over the next 10 years (1956-1965). This expansion rate continued through the '60's to a projected figure of 10,500 golf course facilities (U.S. only) in 1970.

Manpower requirements for the golf course industry increased at a rate comparable to the growth in golf facilities. Specialization and professionalism increased likewise. For example, in 1951 at its Silver Anniversary Meeting, the National Greenskeeping Superintendents Association changed its name to the Golf Course Superintendents Association of America, and changed the name of their official publication from the *Greenskeepers Reporter* to the *Golf Course Reporter* (Anon. 1951). In 1966, the publication name was changed again to the *Golf Superintendent.* These changes reflect the concern of golf course superintendents in advancing their professional image.

Parallel to the explosion in golf course development was the development in other turfgrass facilities and functions. As manpower development advanced on the golf course, other turfgrass facilities also began to recognize the need for better trained and more specialized manpower. In addition, the manufacturing and servicing branches of the industry moved forward to supply products and services for the expanding facilities.

3. *Schools and College*

Growth at all levels of the industry brought increasing demands to the institutional branch for knowledge and technology. Turfgrass research programs developed at most land grant colleges, and some developed curricula to assist the industry in training manpower.

In addition to university training, some vocational-technical schools and colleges developed training courses specializing in turfgrass management. The first of these was the Stockbridge Winter School at the University of Massachusetts (Anon., 1959). Founded in 1927 under the inspiration of the late Professor Lawrence S. Dickinson, this institution offered an annual 8-week short course beginning in January, which stressed fundamentals of turfgrass production. Many of the nation's leading golf course superintendents are alumni of this pioneering school.

Later the Stockbridge school initiated a 2-year course for turf majors. Other vocational-technical schools have established specialized training courses in turfgrass management. Today, many technical conferences and trade expositions are held across the country on a regional, state, or local basis to provide industry personnel with refresher courses and programs of continuing education and to keep the industry abreast of new products and technologies. The International Turf Conference and Show sponsored annually by the Golf Course Superintendents Association of America features the first and currently the only national exhibit of turfgrass products as well as a national conference on turf (primarily golf) technology. At Miami Beach in 1969, this event reported an attendance of over 3,500 people.

4. Management versus Maintenance

One of the problems confronting manpower development within the facilities branch of the turfgrass industry has been the confusion between the concepts of management versus maintenance. This confusion comes traditionally from the earlier emphasis on agronomic practices and technology as the main pursuit for turf workers, as opposed to managerial functions. It has been further promulgated in books, periodicals, and papers which mislabeled discussions on biological fundamentals as "management" instead of "science or technology."

"Management" deals with people and the manner in which they are organized and directed (Anon., 1961) in order to carry out the objectives and functions of an enterprise. It involves knowledge, skills, and training of people, their habits and attitudes, as well as planning and directing organizational activities.

"Maintenance," on the other hand, refers to things (property and equipment). Turfgrass maintenance, for example, involves preserving a stand of turfgrass in an attractive and healthy condition. Equipment maintenance implies keeping turfgrass machinery in efficient operation or in readiness to function. These maintenance functions involve technology and do not directly involve management.

At the same time, when the technologies of turfgrass maintenance and equipment maintenance are looked upon as *functions of an organization* (a turfgrass facility), then personnel become involved and management takes over. Clarification of the difference between the technologies and management (maintenance versus management) is necessary in order to properly delineate the manpower profile of an industry.

C. The Manpower Profile

Analyses of the manpower resources for the turfgrass industry reveal seven categories of personnel utilization. They are as follows:

1. *Professional*—Occupations requiring specialized knowledge based on academic accomplishment according to prescribed standards
2. *Managerial*—Occupations dealing with the direction of organizations and their resources (in this case turfgrass facilities)
3. *Supervisory*—Occupations involved with overseeing workers in directed pursuits.
4. *Technician*—Occupations requiring specialized (usually practical) knowledge of mechanical or scientific methods.

5. *Trainee or Apprentice*—People in pursuit of occupational training.
6. *Production Manpower*—People who carry out the routine work load of a turfgrass facility.
7. *Sales and Marketing Personnel*—A flexible classification which may utilize personnel from one of the above classifications. People in this category move the products of the manufacturing branch into commerce and may sell specialized services.

Table 2 illustrates in more detail the manpower profile for the turfgrass industry. However, the examples given are not intended to be all inclusive or restrictive.

1. Table of Organization

To further illustrate the degree of manpower specialization that is developing within the turfgrass industry, Table 3 presents a table of organization for an existing progressive turf facility. In the left column, each level of manpower specialization is related to respective categories in the manpower profile given in Table 2.

The organization shown in Table 3 is typical of the trend in manpower development emerging in the industry. Demand for ever-higher grooming standards, advancing technology, and the shortage and cost of labor are the major factors forcing this trend toward more effective utilization of manpower.

III. Value of the Turfgrass Industry

It would be most logical to discuss the value of the turfgrass industry by functional branches as presented in the previous section on com-

Table 2. Turfgrass industry manpower profile.

1. Professional manpower	4. Technician manpower
a. Turf facility architects (golf course, landscape, etc.)	a. Turf equipment mechanics
b. Turf irrigation design engineers	b. Turf irrigation technicians
c. Turf equipment designers and engineers	c. Turf chemical technicians (pest control)
d. Practicing turf agronomists, horticulturists	d. Sod harvesting technicians
e. Turf business and administrative personnel	e. Turf planting technicians
f. Turf trade and professional organization personnel	f. Fertilizer plant technicians
g. Turf education personnel - college teacher, extension service specialists, industry product or development specialists	g. Turf sprayer operator
h. Professional turf consultant - private or industry	h. Turf research field technician
	i. Other related technical personnel
2. Managerial manpower	5. Trainee and apprentice manpower
a. Golf course superintendent	a. College trainees (management or technical)
b. Cemetery superintendent	b. On-the-job training apprentices (operations)
c. Park superintendent	c. Sales trainee
d. Air field manager	6. Production manpower (the work force)
e. College and university grounds superintendent	a. Skilled equipment operators
f. Athletic field manager	b. Semi-skilled maintenance workers
g. Sod production manager	c. Specialized operations worker
h. Seed production manager	d. General (utility) worker
i. Government grounds superintendent	e. Reserve labor
j. Pest control service manager	7. Sales and marketing manpower (may be selected from any of the above classifications)
k. Lawn service manager	a. Market specialists (market analyst, etc.)
l. Lawn and garden supply manager	b. Manufactures representative
m. Irrigation service and supply manager	c. Product demonstrator and exhibit specialist
n. School maintenance superintendent	d. Turf equipment salesman
o. Other turf facility supervisors and specialists	e. Turf fertilizer salesman
3. Supervisory manpower	f. Turf chemical salesman
a. Assistant golf course superintendent (may be managerial in larger operations)	g. Sod salesman
b. Assistant grounds maintenance superintendent	h. Seed salesman
c. Turf maintenance or foreman	i. Irrigation salesman
d. Landscape maintenance foreman	j. Soil product salesman
e. Landscape planting foreman	k. Lawn service salesman
f. Pest control services foreman	l. Turf installation salesman
g. Other supervisory personnel	m. Related sales personnel

Table 3. Table of organization for a 36-hole commercial golf course facility.

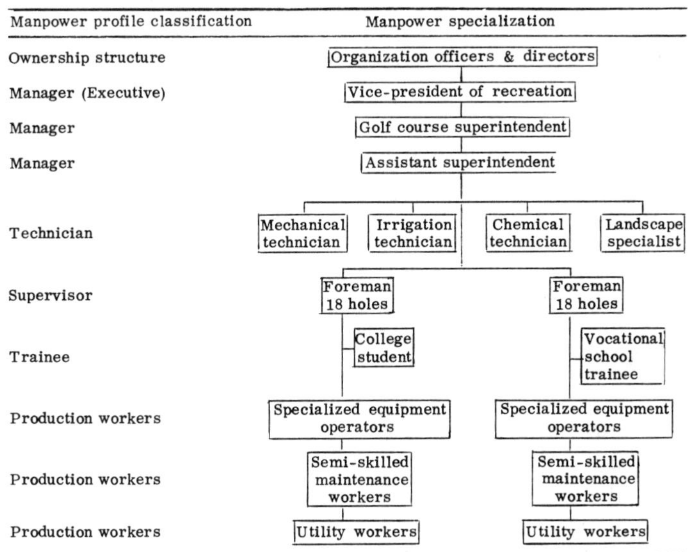

Manpower profile classification	Manpower specialization	
Ownership structure	Organization officers & directors	
Manager (Executive)	Vice-president of recreation	
Manager	Golf course superintendent	
Manager	Assistant superintendent	
Technician	Mechanical technician; Irrigation technician	Chemical technician; Landscape specialist
Supervisor	Foreman 18 holes	Foreman 18 holes
Trainee	College student	Vocational school trainee
Production workers	Specialized equipment operators	Specialized equipment operators
Production workers	Semi-skilled maintenance workers	Semi-skilled maintenance workers
Production workers	Utility workers	Utility workers

position of the industry. Unfortunately, adequate information is not available from all branches to provide such a comprehensive approach. Useful information has been developed for the Facilities Branch—and this will be summarized and presented in this chapter. Only sketchy information is available for a Manufacturing Branch, which is known to be a sizeable and rapidly expanding facet of American commerce.

The probable reason for the delay in emphasis on the Manufacturing and Servicing Branches has been lack of statistics on size, scope, and value of the industry. In fact, according to Nutter (1965) "... this lack of evaluation probably has been the industry's greatest limitation." Such evaluation has been slow for three principal reasons. First, there has been no national, industry-wide medium (such as a trade organization) to gather and communicate such information. Second, it is difficult to evaluate the industry because much of the value involves expenditures for maintenance of facilities rather than the sale of marketable commodities. Thus, market information—hence market value—is not available in terms of production or commodity sales. Third, evaluation has been impeded by classification problems. It relates to agriculture in principle—hence is not considered in the general classification of commerce. Thus, Department of Commerce and Bureau of Census statistics are not available. Conversely, the turfgrass industry has not been recognized generally by many agricultural bodies as a "true phase" of agriculture, primarily because it is not involved with the production of commodities for food, feed, or fiber. Difficulties in classification have left the industry without critically needed information as to its true size and value.

Another reason for the lack of information on the overall value of the industry is its great diversity. The industry represents a broadly horizontal coverage (like an umbrella) of many functions and services.

This horizontal type of industry structure is always more difficult to evaluate comprehensively than a vertical structure wherein interests and activities are more closely aligned and concentrated. Within the turfgrass industry are several vertically oriented sub-industries or segments such as golf and sod. Some information is available from these more advanced segments. Without doubt, as the industry develops maturity and sophistication similar to other major American industries, more detailed statistics will become available.

At the same time, it is realized that the total range of turfgrass activities has emerged as a very large industry that demands recognition, despite lack of definition and internal evaluation. The statistics will bear out this premise.

A. Evaluation of Turfgrass Facility Maintenance

1. Los Angeles County (California)

One of the earliest documented cost surveys of turfgrass facility maintenance was published by the Southern California Golf Association (Beutel and Roewekamp, 1954). This classic survey included both installation and maintenance costs (Table 4).

Considering that these figures were compiled over 15 years ago, it is still staggering that the cost of maintaining principal turfgrass facilities in one county (area approximately 4,083 square miles with over half in mountains and desert; 1954 population, 4,847,043) would exceed $90,000,000 annually.

Detailed information on survey methods and cost data are given in the Los Angeles County Survey. It is interesting to note that in 1954 over 25% of the homes and 50% of the apartment buildings had underground lawn irrigation systems. The breakdown of maintenance costs by type of facility is shown in Table 5.

Table 4. Turfgrass survey of Los Angeles County, Calif., July 1954 (Beutel and Roewekamp, 1954).

Type of turfgrass areas	Number	Acreage	Current installation costs/unit*: Lawn & water system	Equipment & tools	Total†	Annual maintenance costs: Per unit*	Total†
1. Bowling greens	21	7	$5,500	$ 400	$ 123,900	$ 2,900	$ 60,900
2. Cemeteries	62	1,400	11¢	300	7,128,200	1,450	2,030,000
3. Churches	3,218	185	5¢	**	715,100	22§ + 240¶	843,100
4. Parks and athletic fields							
City	44 cities	2,201	9¢	200	9,068,600	1,250	2,751,100
County	91 parks	322	9¢	200	1,324,700	1,250	401,900
5. Factories	575	40	15¢	**	258,700	26§ + 360¶	222,000
6. Government properties (except parks and schools)		442	9¢	200	1,820,000	1,250	552,400
7. Golf courses -- 18 hole	33	2,805	$150,000	20,000	5,610,000	70,100	2,313,300
9 hole	7	280	$75,000	7,000	574,000	30,000	210,000
3-par 9 hole	11	66	$10,000	2,500	137,500	6,000	66,000
Driving ranges	12	12	$2,000	100	25,200	1,000	12,000
8. Residences							
Homes	1,130,400†	50,681	5¢‡	38//	212,656,200	379§ + 180¶	59,907,600
Duplexes	71,000†	2,011	5¢‡	38//	7,988,300	379§ + 180¶	3,318,400
Apartment houses	60,200†	1,824	5¢‡	**	8,396,800	379§ + 240¶	15,139,500
9. Schools - Public	1,066	777	12¢	500	4,593,000	6¢	2,030,000
- Private & parochial	150	108	12¢	500	639,000	6¢	282,000
Colleges	7	193	$4,000	300	829,900	600	115,800
10. Miscellaneous		138	9¢	200	567,800	1,250	172,300
Total		63,490			262,457,700		90,428,300

* Units = green, acre, course, etc. † To nearest hundred. ‡ Plus water sustem. § For water and fertilizer. ¶ For gardener (in only 20% of homes and duplexes). // Each for 80% of units. ** Provided by gardener.

Table 5. Maintenance cost breakdown by facility, Los Angeles County, Calif., 1954.

Maintenance	% of maintenance cost	
	Golf courses	Schools
Labor	76.0	67.0
Equipment repair and replacement	7.8	7.7
Fertilizers and manures	2.5	2.4
Water + power for water supply	9.7	22.1
Miscellaneous	4.0	0.8

Table 6. Estimated annual overall statewide cost for maintenance of turfgrass facilities in five states.

Turf facility	State				
	Michigan Anon., 1969a	Pennsylvania Boster, 1966	Texas Anon., 1964	Florida Anon., 1963	New Jersey Anon., 1956
Lawns	No breakdown	$ 46,300,000	$189,200,000	No breakdown	$46,300,000
Highways	No breakdown	3,800,000	Not available	No breakdown	,900,000
Golf courses	No breakdown	18,500,000	14,900,000	No breakdown	4,000,000
Schools & colleges	No breakdown	3,500,000	3,500,000	No breakdown	700,000
All others	No breakdown	85,100,000	3,900,000	No breakdown	39,000,000
Total	$260,000,000	$157,100,000	$211,600,000	$130,000,000	$56,200,000

2. Evaluation of States

Several states have developed estimates on the overall cost of maintaining turfgrass facilities within their boundaries. Figures from these surveys are compiled and summarized in Table 6.

These data help to illustrate the magnitude of the turfgrass industry. Dates, survey methods, and cost estimates are major variables in Table 6. In fact, only the Texas and Pennsylvania figures are based on systematic survey methods. The other figures are primarily estimates. However, these estimates represent the best available information on an industry that is growing rapidly in every state.

One factor which needs clarification in the surveys listed in Table 6 involves sod and seed production figures. In proper industry alignment, sod and seed production are commodity items which belong in the Manufacturing Branch of the industry—not under the maintenance of turfgrass facilities (Facilities Branch).

3. National Evaluation of Turfgrass Maintenance

The first detailed systematic evaluation of the turfgrass maintenance industry in the U.S. was developed by Nutter (1965). The Texas Survey had just been published (Anon. 1964) and was utilized in development of Nutter's analysis. Population figures from the 1960 U.S. Census Bureau were adjusted to 1965 levels and served as an important basis for developing information on such statistics as the number of residential lawns. Information from many other sources was utilized in developing this national evaluation. Table 7 presents the overall national annual expenditure for the maintenance of 11 basic turfgrass facilities and compares each in percentage of the total annual expenditure. Total maintenance expenditures by region (U.S. Census Bureau Divisions) are shown in Table 8.

Table 7. National annual turfgrass maintenance expenditures by selected facility. (Nutter, 1965).

Facility	Basis of statistics*	Expenditure	% of total
Airports	N.J. survey, 1956	$ 34,606,352	0.8
Cemeteries	N.J. survey, 1965	363,366,704	8.4
Churches	" " "	25,954,764	0.6
Colleges & universities	" " "	17,303,176	0.4
Golf courses	" " "	237,918,674	5.5
Highways	Texas survey	471,511,556	10.9
Lawn-residential		3,002,101,097	69.4
Lawn-commercial	Cal. & N.J. surveys	25,954,764	0.6
Parks-municipal		60,561,117	1.4
Schools-public		38,932,147	0.9
Miscellaneous†		47,583,735	1.1
Total		$4,325,794,086	100.0

* References to state surveys given in Tables 4 and 6. Basis of statistics given where other than projected, adjusted Texas Survey. All statistics adjusted and corrected.
† To include sod and seed production; municipal, state and Federal government building lawns; state and Federal parks, private school, professional athletic facilities and others. Very conservatively estimated. For example Florida alone grows approximately $20,000,000 worth of commercial sod yearly.

Table 8. National annual turfgrass maintenance expenditures by region. (Nutter, 1965).

Region (U.S. Census Bureau Division)	Expenditures*	% of total
New England (Maine, Vt., N.H., Mass., R.I., Conn.)	$183,271,396	4.2
Mid-Atlantic (N.Y., N.J., Pa.,)	496,657,562	11.5
East North-Central (Wis., Mich., Ill., Ind., Ohio)	772,188,186	17.9
West North-Central (N.D., S.D., Minn., Iowa, Nebr., Kan., Mo.)	378,750,526	8.8
South Atlantic (W.Va., Va., Md., Del., D.C., N.C., S.C., Ga., Fla.)	742,864,584	17.2
East South-Central (Ky., Tenn., Miss., Ala.)	374,687,236	8.7
West South-Central (Okla., Ark., La., Texas)	570,179,610	13.2
Mountain (Mont., Idaho., Wyo., Nev., Utah, Colo., Ariz., N.M.)	199,073,182	4.6
Pacific (Alaska, Wash., Ore., Calif., Hawaii)	609,474,712	14.1
Total	$4,326,546,994†	100.2

* Projected from 1960 census figures and the Texas Survey and adjusted, corrected and updated to current evaluations. † While a discrepancy exists between the national evaluation totals appearing in Table 7 and 8, this difference is due to rounding off basic calculations. The difference amounts to only 0.01%.

Table 9. Percentage breakdown of national annual residential lawn maintenance expenditures. (Nutter, 1965).

Maintenance practice	Expenditure*	% of total
Topsoil, compost, topdressing	$ 165,115,560	5.5
Commercial fertilizer	210,147,076	7.0
Chemicals	75,052,527	2.5
Water	1,086,760,596	36.2
Equipment	795,556,790	26.5
Labor	705,493,758	23.5
Total	$3,038,126,307	101.2

* Based on residential lawn total from Table 7 and percentage from Texas Survey.
† Percentages used here are from weighted averages as determined in Texas Survey and corrected and adjusted, updated and projected to current national evaluations for residential lawns.

Since the maintenance of residential lawns represents the largest single turf maintenance expenditure as shown in all of the preceding survey statistics, it was decided that a breakdown of lawn maintenance costs would be of value. Again, the Texas Survey (Anon., 1964) is credited for providing basic statistics for this analysis. Data from Texas were extrapolated, adjusted, and updated to show current national expenditures for residential lawns. Results are shown in Table 9.

Table 10. A comparison of golf course facilities in the U.S. between 1958 and 1968.

Item	Year 1958	1963	1968
Number of golf courses	$ 5,745	$ 7,477	$ 9,615
Total estimated acres	?	740,000	1,031,000
Est. annual maintenance cost	?	175,000,000	360,000,000
Est. capital invested	?	1,900,000,000	2,500,000,000
Number round played	?	?	194,000,000
Number of golfers	3,970,000	7,250,000	11,300,000
Number of golf cars	?	18,000	147,000
Electric		?	117,600
Gas		?	29,400

4. Golf Course Facilities

It would be appropriate to close this section on the value of facilities by presenting a recap on golf courses already stated to require the most sophisticated grooming practices of all turfgrass facilities. Table 10 compares the growth of golf between 1958 and 1968 as taken from information provided by the National Golf Foundation (Anon., 1968).

B. Value of Manufactured Products and Materials

The annual value of manufactured products and materials is a common measure of the scope of an industry. As already indicated, statistics on the comprehensive value of products are not available for the turfgrass industry. However, marketing surveys have been conducted or estimates compiled for certain segments of the industry.

1. Sod

Although sod is produced, rather than manufactured in the traditional sense, it is one of the two basic turfgrass commodities (the other being turfgrass seed). Therefore, it is proper to review statistics on sod and seed marketing under this section on products.

Originally, all sod was cut from pastures. As the value of sodding became evident on athletic fields, housing projects, and other specialized uses, the demand developed for better quality sod. This led to the birth of the cultivated sod industry. Cultivated sod is planted, maintained, and marketed specifically for installation on turfgrass facilities.

Production of cultivated sod has increased at a fantastic pace in recent years. A report from Michigan (Anon., 1969b) indicates that acreage of cultivated sod in that state increased from 2,000 to 20,000 acres from 1955 to 1965. This same report indicates that sod production is the fastest growing agricultural enterprise in Michigan and that the crop is worth "...30 million dollars to growers and another 60 million dollars to those who ship and lay the sod...".

Florida is a major producer of warm-season grass sod. According to an economic study of the Florida sod industry by Brewster (1965), there were over 14,000 acres of sod in production in 1963. Brewster reported that growers received an average price of 3.65c per square foot for sod. Based on these figures, the value of sod in production in 1963 would have been approximately $20 million (based on 40,000 square feet of marketable sod per acre). In addition, growers in Florida showed a capital investment (land, equipment, and buildings) exceeding $15 million.

Table 11. Review of the national (U.S.) cultivated sod industry (March 1969).

Total number of cultivated sod producers	900
Total acreage of cultivated sod in production	160,884 acres
Average acreage in production per farm	179.5 acres
Total acreage marketed annually	74,905 acres
Average acreage marketed annually per farm	86.6 acres
Total wholesale value of sod in production	$100,000,000

Table 12. Estimated production and sale of turfgrass seeds (U.S.) 1968.*

Species (domestic and imported varieties)	Annual production, pounds	Selected selling price/lb	Calculated volume of sales
Bluegrass	50,000,000	$ .40	$20,000,000
Bentgrass	10,000,000	1.50	15,000,000
Fine fescue	30,000,000	.30	9,000,000
Bermudagrass (common)†	10,000,000	.50	5,000,000
Ryegrass	75,000,000	.10	7,500,000
Tall fescue	25,000,000	.20	5,000,000
Totals	200,000,000	----	$61,500,000

* Based on estimated production figures provided by Robert W. Schery, and utilizing assumed selling prices. † Improved bermudagrass varieties are propagated vegetatively.

Further indication of the magnitude of the cultivated sod industry is provided by a recent sod industry survey (Anon., 1969d). A summary of this report is presented in Table 11.

This survey indicated that 41% of the cultivated sod produced was sold to landscapers and 26% directly to homeowners (residential lawns). Over 7% was utilized for commercial lawns, while garden centers accounted for 7% and golf courses 4%. Some 287 salesmen were estimated to be employed throughout the U.S. in marketing cultivated sod.

2. Seed

Statistics on the volume or value of turfgrass seed production have been difficult to acquire from the trade. The nonfarm seed market, as analyzed by the U.S. Census Bureau, includes flower and vegetable (garden) seeds as well as turfgrass seed. The best information on seed production has come through correspondence with individuals in the industry.

In 1968 Robert W. Schery, Director of the Lawn Institute, stated (personal correspondence) "... among the quality (turfgrass) species we are talking about annual disappearance (1968 estimate) in the neighborhood of 100 million pounds, including imports of such specialty items as *Poa trivialis*...". In regard to ryegrass and tall fescue, he advises further that "... total ryegrass production generally runs over 150 million pounds annually and tall fescue generally over 50 million pounds. About half of each species is believed to enter the turf market...".

Due to the great variability in price among varieties and species it is difficult to place an accurate value on the turf seed market. However, utilizing the production figures provided by Schery and assuming an arbitrary but reasonable sale price for each species, an estimated overall value has been calculated for the turfgrass seed market (Table 12).

Several turfgrass species are not included in the above estimates (bahia, centipede, and carpet grasses in the South and redtop, some

Table 13. Nonfarm fertilizer consumption by region, 1965-66 (Mehring, 1967).

Type of usage	Sample: Interviews	Sample: Mean per unit	Region: New England	Middle Atlantic	South Atlantic	East North Central	West North Central	East South Central	West South Central	Mountain	Pacific	Total
	no.	lb	Tons									
Non-farm homes	1,762	58	62,000	255,000	300,000	243,000	85,000	122,000	142,000	48,700	329,000	1,586,700
Industrial plants	27	2,872	5,000	31,500	79,000	84,000	24,000	29,000	28,000	8,000	20,000	308,500
Golf courses	826	51,200	13,100	47,600	56,900	39,200	10,500	20,300	23,200	2,500	13,900	227,200
Highways & Streets	42	9.8 M	3,000	8,000	44,000	25,000	12,000	40,000	28,000	7,000	38,000	205,000
Athletic fields	27	12,454	8,000	13,000	26,000	17,000	8,000	11,000	7,000	2,000	8,000	100,000
College campuses	41	21,376	1,400	15,800	20,000	18,500	5,200	9,300	11,000	1,400	6,500	89,100
Parks	53	177	3,400	13,000	20,000	15,000	7,000	7,400	2,400	2,300	9,000	79,500
Cemeteries	100	15,127	4,300	14,500	25,000	11,700	3,500	5,900	3,900	2,900	5,500	77,200
Government	14	1,328	3,300	7,600	14,400	5,900	3,100	5,500	9,200	7,600	14,500	71,100
Office buildings	61	2,216	3,000	15,000	15,000	5,000	2,000	5,000	5,000	1,000	20,000	71,000
Apartments	22,741	4	2,600	16,400	14,300	3,800	1,800	4,200	5,000	1,800	10,100	60,000
Airports	25	9,212	1,600	5,400	9,300	6,600	5,900	3,400	10,000	6,000	8,000	56,200
Fish ponds	52	50	0	2,000	20,000	6,000	5,000	10,000	8,000	600	3,000	59,600
Secondary schools	18	2,869	2,400	11,300	16,500	8,200	2,100	4,800	4,600	800	2,900	53,600
Hotels	34	917	1,200	6,400	15,800	4,900	2,100	3,500	4,600	800	13,800	53,100
Churches	181	178	1,000	4,900	9,800	6,200	4,300	5,700	3,000	2,100	3,100	40,100
Commercial bldgs.	383	69	1,000	7,000	9,000	4,000	3,000	3,500	3,000	1,000	6,500	38,000
Hospitals	19	3,080	1,300	3,200	3,400	2,800	1,300	2,800	2,800	800	3,000	21,400
Elementary schools	1,432	600	1,400	5,800	5,400	2,800	1,300	900	850	350	1,200	20,000
Motels	25	93	500	1,500	5,200	1,900	1,800	2,600	1,500	800	3,000	18,800
TAA demonstrations	--	--	58	819	3,387	1,531	1,301	7,116	1,695	634	377	16,918
Recreational camps	12	8,850	300	1,200	1,600	2,500	1,100	500	1,200	200	1,300	9,900
Fish hatcheries	--	--	0	1,000	700	2,000	1,000	1,200	500	40	2,060	8,500
Forest seed beds, etc	--	--	100	1,000	2,000	500	50	800	100	50	500	5,100
Capitols & Ct. houses	21	2,388	200	600	1,600	700	400	1,500	600	200	300	6,100
Museums	26	2,895	300	700	400	300	200	600	200	200	300	3,200
Clubs, lodge halls	26	209	100	500	1,000	500	300	300	200	50	150	3,100
Banks	60	212	110	330	590	440	200	420	360	100	400	2,950
Filling stations	31	6	20	75	600	115	50	45	400	100	200	1,605
Funeral homes	27	98	40	410	560	110	80	30	160	20	150	1,560
Miscellaneous	32	11,770	170	310	450	130	60	50	100	20	70	1,360
Libraries	14	116	70	450	300	80	70	30	50	30	200	1,280
Total	--	--	120,968	492,294	722,187	520,406	193,711	309,391	308,615	100,094	525,007	3,292,673

fescues, and the Western grasses). Thus the size of the seed market shown in Table 12 is probably conservative.

3. Fertilizer

According to Mehring (1967), the total nonfarm fertilizer consumption in 1965-66 was estimated to be 3,300,000 tons, or 9.7% of the total production of 33.9 million tons in the 48 mainland states and the District of Columbia. Using U.S. Bureau of Census population estimates of December 1966 and the 1964 U.S. Census of Agriculture Preliminary Reports as a basis, Mehring conducted samples and calculated nonfarm fertilizer consumption by type of usage for each state (Table 13).

Table 13 indicates that the largest single nonfarm use of fertilizer is for lawns and gardens (1,586,700 tons in 1965-66). Quinlan (1967) estimates that approximately 62% of this residential consumption is for lawns, or 983,754 tons annually, which he indicates would have a retail market value of approximately $100,000,000.

Four usage categories (residential and industrial lawns, golf courses, highways and streets, and athletic fields) consume over 73% of the total nonfarm fertilizer production. Table 13 also provides valuable information on the variability in fertilizer consumption, both by region and usage classification.

4. Pesticides

Complete information is not available on the consumption of pesticides for the institutional and consumer turfgrass markets. Data from

Quinlan (1967) indicated that the nonagricultural sales of pesticides (1960 information) totals approximately $120,000,000 annually. Of this amount, 22.7% (or approximately $25 million) is for fungicides; 26.4% (or $31.7 million) for herbicides and 50.9% (or $61 million) for insecticides. Further breakdown by usage classification is not available.

5. *Equipment*

Adequate statistics are not available on the total consumption of equipment and machinery in the turfgrass industry. In most firms, equipment sales are split into two divisions—consumer (sales to amateurs—primarily the high-volume residential outlets) and institutional (turfgrass facilities having professional management).

The Outdoor Power Equipment Institute (OPEI) is the trade organization which services the marketing of power equipment to the consumer division (primarily the lawn trade). This institute has compiled information which compares the growth in sales volume of four major outdoor power equipment items for the years 1946 through 1967 (Table 14).

According to a recent release (Anon., 1968) 1968 sales of power lawn mowers was expected to reach five million units. Riding power mowers showed an 11% increase from 1966 to 1967, reflecting the public's preference for higher priced units.

Assuming an arbitrary average overall retail unit price of $75.00 for power lawn mowers, the sale of five million units in 1968 would total gross sales of $375 million.

A similar breakdown of production or sales is not available for other consumer items or for institutional equipment.

Table 14. Annual shipments by U.S. manufacturers of four power equipment items for the period 1946 through 1967, as compiled by the Outdoor Power Equipment Institute.

	Units shipped			
Year	Power lawn mowers	Motor tillers	Rotary snow throwers	Riding garden tractors
1946	139,018	N/A		
1947	362,000	31,051		
1948	397,000	15,176		
1949	529,000	11,006		
1950	1,080,000	17,211		
1951	1,241,000	26,098		
1952	1,155,000	41,498		
1953	1,275,000	67,922		
1954	1,802,000	75,082		
1955	2,750,000	N/A		
1956	3,200,000	N/A		
1957	3,266,000	129,796	12,000	
1958	3,841,000	173,348	18,000	12,643
1959	4,200,000	251,778	20,000	27,047
1960	3,800,000	315,406	40,000	43,486
1961	3,500,000	277,048	75,000	67,124
1962	4,000,000	317,264	175,000	90,000
1963	3,900,000	306,090	200,000	100,000
1964	4,100,000	291,945	160,000	125,000
1965	4,500,000	340,000	165,000	175,000
1966	4,900,000	325,000	185,000	250,000
1967	4,900,000	350,000	185,000	275,000

IV. Future Outlook for the Turfgrass Industry

Although much information is still needed to comprehensively analyze the turfgrass industry, this start must suffice at this time. Certainly the industry is destined to grow. In fact, it is currently much larger (by almost any standard of measure) than is generally recognized. Undoubtedly its future growth will bring better tools and greater efforts for evaluation.

As the industry looks forward, it becomes evident that population expansion will be accompanied by a commensurate growth in turfgrass facilities. As former agricultural areas become urbanized, residential turf will increase as well as the need for recreational facilities. Spectator sports will continue to gain in popularity. Evidence of this trend is seen in the recent expansion of professional sport facilities (both baseball and football), as well as the increase in golfing events and galleries. The future will call for more parks, more schools and colleges, more super highways, and more cemeteries. Nor can we overlook the role of turfgrass facilities in the world of tomorrow as outlets for leisure time, physical fitness, and mental diversion. The expansion of turfgrass facilities for utility, beautification, and recreation will bring higher demands for turf products, services and manpower.

Optimistically, as standards of living rise in an ever more affluent nation, not only will the demand for products and services increase, but also the means. In turn, distribution and marketing will offer great challenge and opportunity.

A. Technological Horizons

Projections for the turfgrass industry should not be concluded without mention of the technological horizons. Over the past 30 years, the industry has literally "pulled itself up by its bootstraps." Few industries have developed and applied improved methods and practices as rapidly in so short a time. Yet, fantastic as the past has been, it will be dwarfed by future advances in technology.

Trends are toward greater mechanization and mobility in equipment operations and application of computer servicing in administrative functions, electronic implementation of routine operational details, and wider adaptation of chemistry in plant growth control processes. This does not include advances in turfgrass breeding, temperature conditioning, or the application of laser and sonar physics.

Yet, in all the glory of technology, it must not be forgotten that such developments are but *tools* leading to greater efficiency in the management of turfgrass facilities. As the future of the turfgrass industry unfolds, greater stress will be placed on manpower development, for *it is men, not tools* that must motivate and energize the creations and progress of tomorrow. No greater challenge or opportunity has ever faced an industry.

Literature Cited

Anonymous. 1951. Chicago report. Golf Course Rptr. 19(2):20.

__________ . 1956. In New Jersey turf is big business. Golf Course Rptr. 24(8):11.

__________ . 1959. Product: Better superintendents. Golf Course Rptr. 27(7):10.

__________ . 1961. Management for supervisors. Federal Aviation Agency, p.v.

__________ . 1963. Value of Florida agricultural business. Florida Dept. of Agr. Rept., p. 14.

__________ . 1964. Turfgrass maintenance cost in Texas. Texas AES Bull. 1027.

__________ . 1967. Guidelines for assistants and apprentices. Turf-Grass Times 3(2):5.

__________ . 1968. Annual report on golf statistics. National Golf Foundation. Chicago, Ill.

__________ . 1968. Annual report on outdoor power equipment production. Outdoor Power Equip. Inst., Washington, D.C.

__________ . 1969(a). Michigan's $350 million carpet. Mich. AES, Michigan Science in Action, No. 2, p. 5.

__________ . 1969(b). Production of instant turf. Mich. AES, Michigan Science in Action, No. 2, p. 14.

__________ . 1969(c). Over 11 million golfers. Turf-Grass Times 4(3):23.

__________ . 1969(d). Sod industry survey. Weeds Trees and Turf 8(3):36-40.

Beutel, James, and Fred Roewekamp (in cooperation with V.T. Stoutemeyer). 1954. Turfgrass Survey of Los Angeles County. Bull. Southern Cal. Golf Assoc., 12 p.

Boster, Dewey O. 1966. Pennsylvania turfgrass survey. Pa. Dept. Agr. Pub. CRS-42, 36 p.

Brewster, R. H. 1965. An economic study of the Florida cut sod industry. M.S.A. thesis, Univ. of Fla., Gainesville, 33 p.

Colt, H. S., and C. H. Alison. 1920. Some essays on golf course architecture. Charles Schribner's Sons, London.

Farley, G. A. 1931. Golf course commonsense. Farley Libraries, Cleveland Heights, Ohio, p. 1.

Gibson, Niven H. 1958. The encyclopedia of golf. A. S. Barnes and Company, New York, N. Y., p. 15.

Mehring, A. L. 1967. Consumption of fertilizers for purposes other than farming. A report prepared for the National Plant Food Institute.

Nutter, Gene C. 1965. Turf-grass is a 4 billion dollar industry. Turf-Grass Times 1(1):1.

Quinlan, R. J. 1967. Report on sale of chemicals to non-farm market. Commercial Research Department, Toro Mfg., Minneapolis, Minn.

3 Climate and Adaptation

Coleman Y. Ward

Mississippi State University
State College, Mississippi

I. Introduction

Man has long recognized the limitations climate places on species that occur as memoers of indigenous plant communities. Turfgrass species are limited to a given region by a host of environmental variables. Environment has been classified in a number of ways. A recent classification was given by Billings (1952). He states that, "environment includes all external forces and substances affecting growth, structure and reproduction of the plant." The more influential factors of the environment are climatic, edaphic, geographic, and biotic. These factors are interrelated, and each contains subfactors which determine the total effect. Plants respond to all aspects of environment, and to the interrelation or interaction of these various environmental variables. The plant's adaptability is determined by its tolerance to individual and multiple influences of the environment (Wilsie, 1962).

Climate appears to be the most influential factor in determining the region of adaptation of specific turfgrasses. Climate is a dynamic expression of the weather; it is like a fickle woman—ever changing and highly unpredictable (Thornwaite, 1941). In this chapter, climate, as it influences adaptations of turfgrasses will be considered from four aspects—*temperature, moisture, light,* and *wind.* Although physiographic features often influence climate in mountainous regions, broad generalization of climatic conditions are highly predictable over most of the continental U.S.

It is climate that largely determines whether a given turf species is suitable to an area, but soil factors (see Chapter 4) within a given climatic zone determine the extent of adaptation and abundance of a turfgrass species. Biotic factors, especially man's alteration of the natural environment through such practices as irrigation, permit the use of turfgrass species in areas to which they are not naturally adapted.

Turfgrass species, like all living things, respond to the environment, each species having a definite tolerance limit for specific environmental factors. Species growing within a climatic zone or region will persist, and, are said to be adapted as long as the critical tolerance limits of the species are not exceeded. As an example, varieties of bermudagrass, a warm season grass, vary greatly in their tolerance to minimal temperatures. Davis (1967) found the minimal critical temperature for Tifgreen bermudagrass to be 9 F in Raleigh, N.C., whereas R. A. Keen (Personal communication, March 1966) at Manhattan, Kansas, found that certain bermudagrass selections would withstand temperatures as low as minus 30 F.

Much is yet to be learned about the precise effects of individual components of the environment on turfgrasses. Wide and uncontrolled fluctuations in climatic factors under field conditions point out the need for environmental control facilities in management research. Answers to many questions will come from environmental chambers that enable investigators to study several variables simultaneously.

II. Zones of Turfgrass Adaptation

Turfgrass species have been classified into two broad groupings based on their season of most active growth. Those turfgrass species making their grand period of growth each spring and in the cooler months of the fall, with a semidormant period of growth during the hot summer months and cold winter months, have been designated as cool-season species. This group is typified by Kentucky bluegrass. The other broad group of turfgrasses are classed as warm-season, typified by the bermudagrasses. These grasses make their maximum growth during the summer season. They make very little growth at temperatures below 50-55 F and become completely dormant with a browning of all top growth at temperatures below 30 F. Figure 1 shows the broad adaptation zones for warm and cool season species in the U.S. Climate further restricts the species used for turf in certain areas so that some subdivision of the U.S. into major turfgrass regions has been made (Musser, 1962).

A. Turfgrasses for the Cool Humid Regions of the U.S.

This region as seen in Figure 1 comprises an area from Maine, west to the Dakotas, then south along the 98th meridian to Oklahoma. The southern boundary of this zone stretches along the 37th parallel from Oklahoma through central Missouri eastward to central Virginia then

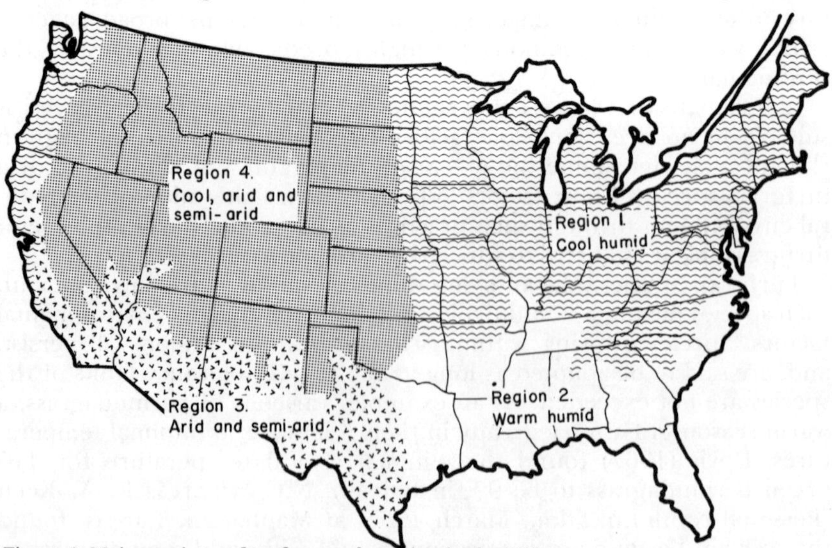

Figure 1. Major regions of turfgrass adaptation in the U.S.

northward to the Washington, D. C., area. The mountainous sections of Tennessee, Georgia, North Carolina, and South Carolina are also included in this region.

1. General Climate of the Region

This region is characterized as a true temperate climate with cold winters and mild to hot summers. The mid-winter mean temperature along the 98th meridian in the Dakotas averages about 5 F, whereas along the regions southern boundary the average is about 35 to 40 F. Thus, it becomes evident that the winters are cold throughout the region, with a temperature gradient of about 2.5 F for each latitude degree of approximately 70 miles (Trewartha, 1941). Mean July temperatures are 75 F to 80 F along the southern part of the region and 65 F along the Canadian border. Total annual precipitation ranges from 45 inches along the Atlantic Coast to about 20 to 30 inches along the western part of the regions, decreasing from south to north.

A somewhat similar cool humid area exists along the Pacific Coast in western Washington, Oregon, and upper California. The turfgrasses adapted to these two areas are similar.

The major turfgrass species of the region are: bentgrasses —creeping, Colonial and velvet; bluegrasses—Kentucky, rough, Canada, and annual; fescues—red, chewings, and tall; ryegrasses— annual and perennial.

Miscellaneous cool season species used for cover and low maintenance turf areas, but more often for forage and pasture are: timothy, orchardgrass, redtop, tall oatgrass, and smooth bromegrass. These species are useful for infrequently mowed areas along roadsides, stream banks, and other outlying areas that need a vegetative cover (Monteith, 1942; Musser, 1962; Daniel and Roberts, 1966).

(For more detailed description of the grasses of this region and their management see Chapters 13 and 19.)

B. Turfgrasses for the Warm Humid Regions of the U.S.

This region, designated as Zone II in Figure 1, extends from peninsular Florida northward to southern Virginia. The northern boundary of this region is approximately the 37th parallel with a more southern boundary where the Appalachian Mountains extend into the region. The western boundary of the region coincides with the 100th meridian, or a line running from Laredo, Texas, to western Oklahoma. The region is traversed by many rivers and has a mean elevation above sea level of about 200 feet.

1. Climate of the Region

The warm humid region is characterized as having a mild temperate climate in the upper part and semitropical climate along the Gulf of Mexico and the peninsula of Florida.

The mean July temperature is about 80 F for the entire area north to south, but winter temperatures are variable and much lower in the upper part of the region. The mean January temperature is about 40 F in the upper South, whereas along the coast and in peninsular Florida it is 65 to 70 F. (Kincer, 1941).

Humidity is high and rainfall abundant, ranging from 40 inches along the Atlantic seaboard in Virginia to 70 inches along the Gulf Coast, then decreasing again to about 20 inches in central Texas and western Oklahoma.

The growing season varies from 200 days in the upper South to 320 plus along the Gulf of Mexico.

The main permanent turfgrasses adapted to this area are: Upper South—bermudagrass (*Cynodon* spp.). Kentucky bluegrass, tall fescue, and zoysiagrass (*Zoysia* spp.); and Lower South—bahiagrass, bermudagrass, carpetgrass, St. Augustinegrass, and zoysiagrass.

The major requirement for good adaptation to the Southeast is tolerance to high summer temperature for prolonged periods. The high temperatures, 90 F and above, are often accompanied by dry periods of 2 to 3 weeks making watering of turf desirable. A limited use is found for Kentucky bluegrass and tall fescue as lawns in the extreme upper South (Schmidt et al., 1965). Tall fescue is much better adapted to the upper South than is Kentucky bluegrass (Wise, 1961)

C. Miscellaneous Grasses of the Southeast

Some turf areas are planted to special purpose grasses for reasons of adaptation and use. Weeping lovegrass, carpetgrass, and dallisgrass are used on roadsides and for golf course roughs. Weeping lovegrass is seeded, the latter two occur naturally (Sturkie and Fisher, 1950; Wise, 1961). All the warm-season grasses lose their color in the fall when temperatures are cooler and days shorter. With the first frost, they turn varying shades of brown and remain dormant until spring. Along the Gulf Coast and in south Florida, turf may be only partially brown in the winter. For a more complete description and discussion of the use of the warm season grasses and their management see Chapters 13 and 20.

D. Turfgrasses for the Arid Southwest

This region encompasses a vast belt from central Texas to California. It is narrowed from north to south by a series of mountain ranges in New Mexico, Arizona, and California. The northern limits of this region are related primarily to low temperatures of the winter season. The 35° N latitude may be used as a guide line for the northern boundary of the region from Texas to California. In California, the region extends as far northward as the 40° latitude in the central valleys and along the coast (Juska and Hanson, 1965; Youngner, 1967).

1. General Climate of the Region

The climate of the region is semi-arid to arid; temperate in the north, with some areas in southwest Arizona and southern California classed as subtropical. The mean summer temperatures of this region are extremely hot, ranging from 82 F in western Texas and New Mexico to 92 in southwest Arizona and southern California. The famed

Death Valley of California averages 100 F for July (Sprague, 1941). It is not uncommon for the temperature in midsummer to exceed 100 F in the shade day after day in the desert sections of these states. The low relative humidity and sparse cloud cover (240 to 280 sunny days annually) of the region lead to cool nights. This fact makes the temperate portion of the region a better environment for cool-season grasses than the hot-humid southeast. For example, with careful management, bentgrasses are used on putting greens in much of this area, but not in the humid-south.

Rainfall for this area is light, ranging from less than 5 inches annually, in parts of Arizona and California to about 20 inches in western Texas. The precipitation in some parts of the region is as low as 1 inch during the warm season (Greening, 1941).

The wind velocity for the interior section of this region is low, averaging about 5 to 6 miles per hour from the southwest.

The growing season ranges from 200 days along the northern limits of the region to 365 days in south California and around Yuma, Arizona.

2. Major Turfgrasses of the Region

All groomed turf in the southwestern states must be irrigated. Since watering of turf is time consuming and expensive, drought tolerance is a key factor in selection of turf species, especially by the home owner. Temperature extremes appear to be the most limiting factor affecting turfgrass adaptation to the southwest. Moisture needs of the grasses are met through irrigation. The dominant grasses of this area are the same warm season species used in the warm-humid Southeast, especially the bermudagrasses and zoysiagrasses. There is little or no carpetgrass and centipede, and the use of St. Augustinegrass is limited to southern California.

Where irrigation is limited, bermudagrass with its deeper root system is the only important fine turf species (Hagan, 1955).

Where no irrigation is practiced, buffalograss and crested wheatgrass are used in areas that receive regular mowing. In restricted mowing areas such as roadsides and areas adjoining flight strips, the native grasses like sideoats grama and black grama (*Bouteloua eriopoda* L.) and introduced grasses such as Lehmann lovegrass (*Eragrostis lehmanniana* Nees.), weeping lovegrass, and crested wheatgrass are seeded (Montieth, 1942). For a more detailed description of the turfgrasses and their management for this region see Chapters 13 and 21.

E. Grasses for the West Central and Intermountain Regions

This region encompasses the vast mid-interior section of the U.S. It is often divided by crop ecologists into two regions, the Northern Great Plains and the Intermountain Region. As may be seen in Fig. 1, this region includes portions of North and South Dakota, Nebraska, Kansas, and the panhandle of Oklahoma on its eastern border. It extends west to the Cascade and Sierra Mountains in Washington, Oregon, and California. This vast area has a highly variable topography except in the Plains States which are characterized by vast level expanses of native grasses (Stoddart and Smith, 1943).

1. Climate of the Region

This region has a subhumid climate along the eastern edge and a semiarid climate throughout most of the western section (Trewartha, 1941). Annual rainfall varies from about 25 inches on the eastern side along the 98th meridian to less than 10 inches in many areas of the drier intermountain plateaus. Fortunately, about 80% of the rainfall comes during the spring and summer season. The region has a climate strikingly continental in character with winters relatively cold and summers relatively warm for the latitude. Midwinter months in North Dakota and Montana have an average temperature of about 0 to 5 F; in Nebraska and Kansas, comparable figures are 25 and 30 F, whereas those in the intermountain regions of Utah and Nevada, and Idaho vary from 10 to 20 F, depending on the elevation. There is much greater diurnal fluctuation in the winter season than in the summer season. On typical midwinter days in North Dakota, the night temperatures drop to about a -10 F while the highest daytime temperatures are below 20 F. In the mountainous states such as Utah, the relatively flat plateau sections with elevations between 3,000 and 5,000 feet have a climate very similar to that of the plains sections of Nebraska and Kansas, whereas in the mountainous sections rising to crests above 10,000 feet, temperatures are colder and more varied. Actual frost seldom forms in Utah owing to the comparatively dry air, though crops may be damaged by temperatures at freezing or lower without frost. Such a condition is known as "black frost."

Summer temperatures over the region are much less varied, ranging from approximately 60 to 65 F as a mean in the northern part of the region to approximately 80 F along the southern regions in Kansas and Oklahoma and in the 60's and 70's in the intermountain regions.

The growing season for this region varies because of wide differences in elevation, which ranges from approximately 1,400 feet for the southern extremities along the 98th meridian to more than 14,000 feet in the western mountain sections. These vast differences in elevation cause a range in length of growing season from 90 days in the northwest to approximately 160 days in the southeast. The greatest diurnal variations in temperature in the U.S. occur in the Plains section of the region, where an advancing polar air mass may bring about a drop in surface temperatures of as much as 60 F in a few hours. Maximum summer temperatures in excess of 100 F have been experienced nearly everywhere in this region and records of 117 F have been reported. Nowhere in the U.S. are turfgrasses subjected to wider fluctuations in temperature. For example, in 1893 at Glendive, Montana, the minimum was -47 F for February and the maximum was 117 F for July, a seasonal range of 164 F (Thornthwaite, 1941).

2. Major Turfgrass Species of the Region

Although the region is large and the climate rigorous, except for native species and a limited use of bermudagrass in the Kansas-Oklahoma region and zoysiagrass along the southern perimeter, the same cool-season turfgrass species used in the Northeast are common to the entire region.

Permanent turfgrasses (c indicates cool-season, w indicates warm-season) adapted to the region are the following:

- (c) Bentgrasses, creeping and colonial
- (c) Bluegrasses, Kentucky
- (w) Buffalograss
- (c) Fescues, red, hard, and sheep

Miscellaneous turfgrasses used include the following:

- (c) Bluegrass, bulbous
- (w) Bluestem, little
- (c) Bromegrass, smooth
- (w) Grama, blue and sideoats
- (c) Ricegrass, Indian
- (c) Wheatgrasses, crested, western, and bluebunch
- (c) Wildrye, Russian

The number 1 turfgrass species for home lawns and utility turf of the region is Kentucky bluegrass (Goss et al., 1962; McCarver, 1966; Martin, 1967). In most of the region, turfgrasses must be irrigated for quality turf. In addition to bluegrass, red fescue, hard fescue, and sheep fescue are used extensively for general-purpose turf (Musser, 1962; Goss, 1962). The bentgrasses represent the chief species for golf putting greens.

Where irrigation is not available or practical, native species are used for turf, especially for golf course fairways, roadside turf, parks, and airfields. Chief among these species is buffalograss which occurs naturally over the areas shown in the map (Fig. 2). Other important native

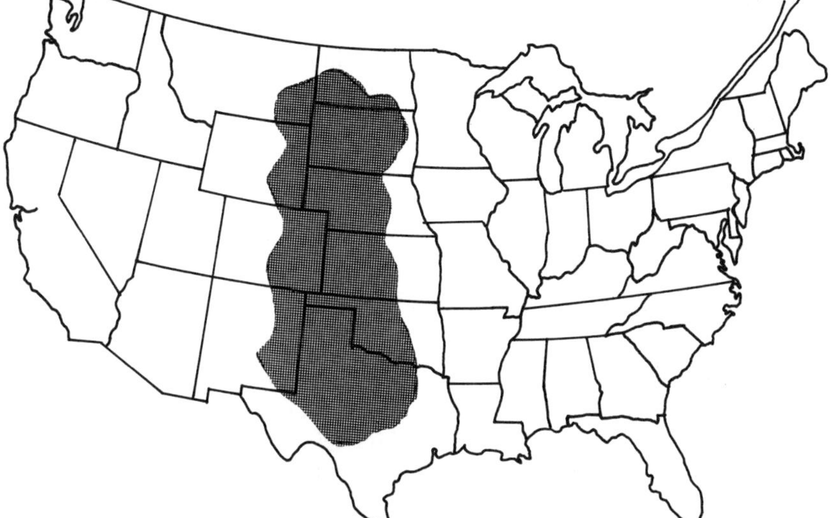

Figure 2. Primary region of adaptation for buffalograss, a native grass used for turf (after Montieth, 1942).

grasses of the area used for low maintenance fairway turf, roadsides, and airfields are blue grama, sideoats grama and a number of native bluegrasses and fine fescues. Other native grasses used for low maintenance turf include western wheatgrass and Indian ricegrass.

Kentucky bluegrass has become naturalized in eastern Kansas, Nebraska, and the Dakotas, and with good management it will make an excellent lawn. Where irrigated, it may be grown throughout the region. It is hardy and survives well in the shade of trees where many other grasses fail. Growth tends to stop during midsummer when soil temperatures exceed 80 F but the species is quite drought tolerant and heat resistant in this dormant period (Keen and Quinlan, 1966).

Fine-leaf fescues are best adapted to cooler sections of the region, particularly intermountain zones at higher elevations. As in the Northeast, it is often planted in mixtures with bluegrass in shaded areas. Very little use is made of red fescue in the southern portion of the region.

Low winter temperatures throughout most of the region prohibit the extensive use of introduced warm-season grasses. Keen (1966) has found common bermudagrass from seed to be adapted only in the extreme southern sections of Kansas. Hybrid bermudagrasses such as Midway and U-3 are better adapted than common bermuda in this region. Some use is made of bermudagrass in Oklahoma and Kansas for putting greens, but W. W. Huffine (personal communication, 1967) estimates that more than 80% of the golf greens in Oklahoma are planted to creeping bentgrass. Zoysiagrasses are used to a limited extent for home lawns in the eastern portion of the region (between the 35th and 40th parallel).

In the foregoing discussion of species adaptation, very broad zones of adaptation were employed; however, it should be emphasized that there are no sharp boundaries in most areas for any given turf species. To illustrate this point, two turfgrasses have been selected to illustrate in more detail the influence of climate on their zone of adaptation.

Creeping bentgrass was chosen from the cool-season grasses and bermudagrass from the subtropical or warm-season grasses.

A modification of an adaptation rating devised by Youngner et al. (1967) is used to indicate the areas where each of the species is used. The zones of adaptation are noted as:

(a) Well adapted. The grass will perform satisfactorily with the maintenance normally required by the grass species.

(b) Adapted with higher maintenance practice. The grass will need more skillful and persistent maintenance to overcome the effects of climate on growth.

(c) Better-adapted grasses available. The grass performs poorly, has weak growth, and is subject to invasion by other grasses and weeds. The turf deteriorates unless expert maintenance is practiced.

(d) Not adapted. The grass will not survive.

The maps in Fig. 3 and 4 cannot take into account all of the variation in microclimate and soil conditions which exist within climatic zones. Hence, boundaries of adaptation depicted should be considered dynamic.

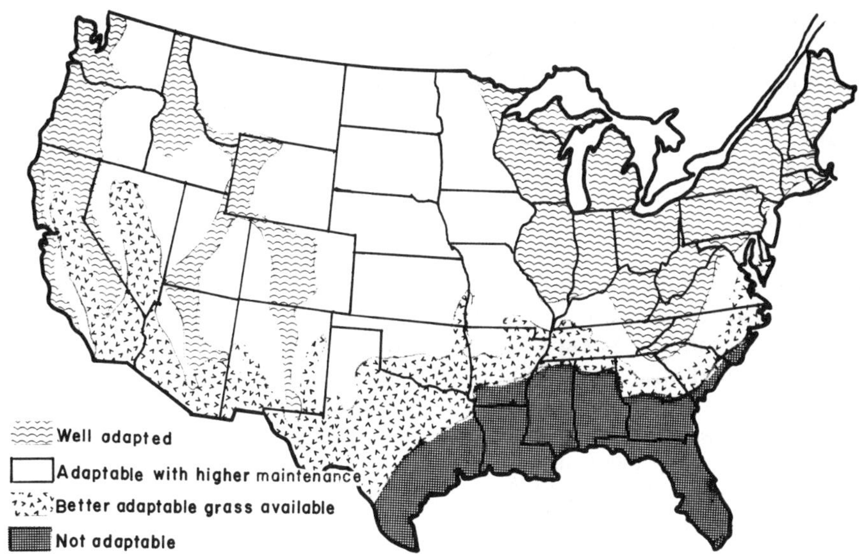

Figure 3. Adaptation of creeping bentgrass to climatic and physiographic regions of the U.S.

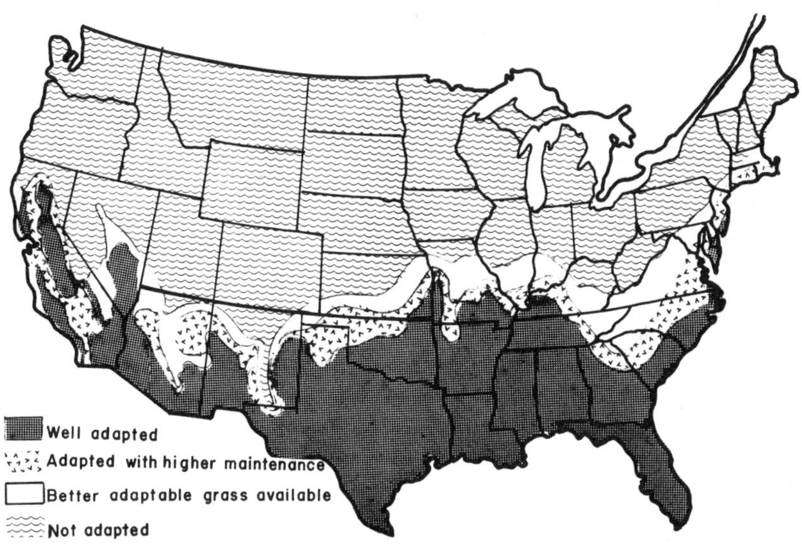

Figure 4. Adaptation of bermudagrass to climatic and physiographic regions of the U.S.

III. Relationships of Climatic Adaptation of Turfgrasses to the Ecology of Their Points of Origin

Most important turfgrasses used in the U.S. were introduced from other continents. A knowledge of the environments in which they originated would be helpful in understanding their adaptation to various regions of the U.S. Investigations have been made to determine the origin of the important cultivated crops (Vavilov, 1951; Harlan, 1951), but turfgrasses have been neglected in these studies. Knowledge of the origin of food crops would obviously receivé first priority.

It is of interest, however, to note the relationships between the latitude and general climate of the "center of origin" of a species and that of the area where it is most widely used in this country. Center of origin refers to the area from which the grass was most likely introduced into this country and not necessarily to its initial point of origin.

The importance of understanding the climatic tolerances of species was illustrated recently in sending wheat and corn varieties to European countries. Wheat varieties from California did well when grown under similar climatic conditions in Greece (Wilsie, 1961).

Nuttonson (1947) has utilized this approach in developing maps on crop geography based on agroclimatic-analogues. He defines climatic-analogues as "areas sufficiently alike with respect to major weather characteristics affecting crop production to offer a fair chance for success of plant material transplanted from one area to its climatic counterpart."

Contrasts in the latitude, mean temperatures and annual precipitation between the point of origin and the center of use of several important turfgrass species are given in Table 1.

Turfgrass species brought to this country from the cool-humid areas around the North Sea in Eurasia are the dominant turf species of the northern U.S. and Canada. These grasses, the bentgrasses, fescues, bluegrasses, and orchardgrass, seem to have adapted to lower latitudes and slightly warmer regions in the U.S. Bentgrasses, for example, introduced from the region of Germany, at 50 to 60° N latitude, are used extensively as far south as 40° N in the U.S. The mean July temperature in northern Europe is about 60 F whereas in the northern

Table 1. Climatic-latitude comparisons of the points of origin and areas of adaptation for some turfgrasses grown in the U.S.

			Ecology of points of origin (or introduction) and centers of use in U.S.*							
			Latitude		Mean Jan. temp, °F		Mean July temp, °F		Annual rainfall, inches	
Species	Point of origin	Use center	Origin	Use	Origin	Use	Origin	Use	Origin	Use
Crested wheatgrass (*Agropyron cristatum*)	Russian Turkestan	Southern Idaho	55 N	43 N	4	22	60	68	18	14
Creeping bentgrass (*Agrostis palustris* Huds.)	Germany & Eurasia	Western New York	52 N	42N	30	24	52	70	25	35
Common bermudagrass (*Cynodon dactylon* L. Pers.)	South Africa	Central Georgia	25 S	33 N	85	48	80	80	30	50
Centipedegrass (*Eremochloa ophiuroides*)	SE Asia near China	South Alabama	23 N	31 N	63	50	85	80	67	55
Tall fescue (*Festuca arundinacea* Screb.)	Northern Europe	Central Kentucky	55 N	38 N	24	36	64	76	24	44
Bahiagrass (*Paspalum notatum* Flugge)	Brazil (Bahia)	Central Florida	13 S	28 N	79	62	74	82	74	50
Kentucky bluegrass (*Poa pratensis* L.)	Eurasia	Northern Illinois	50 N	42 N	25	20	66	74	28	34
St. Augustinegrass (*Stenotaphrum secundatum* (Walt.) Kuntze)	West Indies	Southeast Texas	18 N	30 N	75	54	80	82	61	48

* Points of origin or point from which introduced is often unknown - points of major use in U.S. are based on estimates from available adaptation maps.

U.S. it is about 70 to 75 F. Conversely, the winters in the northern U.S. are colder by some 5 to 10° than those of northern Europe.

Annual rainfall and other forms of precipitation for northern U.S. are somewhat higher than that received by northern Europe (Reed, 1941). Perhaps this compensates for higher summer temperatures in the U.S.

In contrast, subtropical species like bermudagrass, St. Augustinegrass, and bahiagrass seem to have become acclimatized to much cooler regions in the U.S. St. Augustinegrass, a native of the West Indies, about 18° N latitude, is now being grown in the U.S. as far north as the 35th parallel (Wise, 1961). Other examples are illustrated in Table 1.

The adaptation of turfgrass ecotypes from one climatic region to another distant region with similar latitude and climate is illustrated by the work of Klebesadel et al. (1964) in Alaska. They compared the adaptation of Kentucky bluegrass and red fescue established from seed collected in various areas of Alaska with seed from Scandinavian origins. Seed lots of the two species obtained from commercial sources in midlatitude U.S. were included for comparative purposes.

The degree of winterkilling was easily related to point of origin (Table 2). Survival was poorest among seed lots obtained from the U.S. and best for those obtained above 52° N latitude.

It seems certain that a correlation of edaphic and climatic conditions between the point of collection and specific regions in the U.S. might insure greater success in testing turfgrass introductions. When a new species is introduced into an area, it is important that as many ecotypes as possible be collected. If none of the ecotypes are adapted, then hybridization among accessions may produce promising genotypes (Stebbins, 1950).

Population differentiation in *Agrostis tenuis* was studied by Bradshaw (1960). He collected plants of this species from distinctly different habitats and tested them for physiological response in plots varying in altitude, salinity, moisture, lead contamination, and other variables. He found that populations originating from contrasting habitats differed considerably in their ability to tolerate extreme environmental conditions. For instance, the growth of lowland populations in the upland plot was seriously affected by winter conditions, while the growth of upland populations was affected by salt storm spray in the coastal plot. The population from near a lead mine was able to grow in lead-contaminated soil, while the population from normal soil was not. The behavior of each collection could always be related to the environment from which the population originated. Populations from contrasting habitats only a short distance apart showed considerable differences in performance.

Huffine (Personal communication, November 1967) recently made an extensive collection trip for *Cynodon* spp. in parts of Africa, the Middle East, and lower Asia. He returned with more than 700 accessions which are being observed at Oklahoma State University and Plant Introduction Centers in the U.S. A vigorous program to elucidate the cytology and develop inter- and intraspecific hybrids from this material could produce interesting turfgrass types.

Table 2. Latitude of origin, foliar appearance in late fall of seeding year, and winterkilling in rows of red fescue and Kentucky bluegrass (after Klebesadel et al., 1964).

Species and source of accession	No. of lots averaged*	Latitude of seed origin (N. lat.)	Foliar appearance† 10/24/60	Percent winterkill 5/9/62
Festuca rubra				
Alaska:				
'Ruby'	1*	64° 44'	B	10
'Holy Cross'	5*	62° 10'	I-B	8
'Matanuska' (acc. 339)	5*	61° 34'	B	16
" (acc. 342)	1*	61° 34'	I-B	30
" (acc. 343)	5*	61° 34'	I-B	37
" (acc. 344)	5*	61° 34'	B	31
Sweden:				
'Viking'	1	ca. 56°	G	93
Canada:				
'Duraturf'	1	ca. 45° 30'	G	88
'Olds'	1	ca. 52°	G	98
United States:				
'Clatsop'	1	ca. 46°	G	100
'Illahee'	1	ca. 44° 30'	G	98
'Ranier'	1	ca. 44° 30'	G	99
Poa pratensis				
Iceland:				
(acc. 412)	7*	65° ± 1°	G	30
Alaska:				
'Hope' (acc. 282)	2*	60° 56'	G	40
Sweden:				
'Atlas'	1	ca. 56° §	G	83
'Fylking'	1	"	G	83
'Skandia II'	1	"	G	95
Canada:				
'Delta'	1	ca. 45° 30'	G	100
United States:				
'Troy'	1	ca. 48° ‡	G	99
'Park'	1	ca. 48°	G	97
P-4358 (Dwarf)	1	ca. 46° 30'	G	95
'Newport' (C-1)	1	ca. 43°	G	99
'Merion'	1	44° ± 2° ¶	G	100
'Arboretum'	1	44° ± 2° //	G	100
Commercial (Burpee)	1	44° ± 2°	G	100
Commercial (Harris)	1	?	G	100

* Each lot marked (*) represents seed harvested from an individual plant in the spaced plant evaluation nursery established in 1958. Absence of symbol indicates individual commercial accession. † G = green, I = intermediate, B = brown or "cured". Combinations indicate intermediates between main classes. ‡ Original germplasm from 39° ± 3°. § Orignial germplasm from 65°. ¶ Variety selected at ca. 38°. // Variety selected at ca. 38° 30'.

IV. Climatic Factors Affecting Turfgrass Adaptation

Since very early times, it has been recognized that there is a close relationship between the vegetation of a region and its climate. The close identification of climate and vegetation is the consequence of thousands of centuries of plant differentiation and adaptation to climate through natural selection, mutation, hybridization, and changes in chromosome complement. The adaptive power of a turfgrass may hinge on its morphology, such as a thick cuticle, or on its physiology, which may allow it to grow at a low light intensity. Turfgrasses have evolved which are capable of withstanding prolonged drought. For example, crested wheatgrass and buffalograss possess deep root systems and the ability to become semidormant during hot, dry weather. Major climatic factors will be discussed first in general terms and then related to turfgrass adaptation.

A. Temperature

Temperature is often a critical factor in adaptation of turfgrass species. Plants, unlike most animals which maintain a constant body temperature, must assume the temperature of their environment. Their protoplasm is subject to the rigors of large fluctuations in temperature (Clarke, 1954).

Temperature is more predictable than rainfall but is less subject to control by the turf manager than soil moisture and light. The turf manager can rectify drought conditions through irrigation, and light can be controlled to a certain extent by planting or removal of shade trees. Alteration of ambient temperatures over long periods in an outdoor environment is not practical at the present time.

Temperature is an expression of energy. It is easily measured even by an amateur. Solar radiation is the chief source of heat energy received by turfgrasses. The amount of solar energy reaching the earth's surface is measured in gram calories. A gram calorie is the energy required to raise the temperature of 1 gram of water 1 degree centigrade. Solar radiation is expressed in quantitative terms as gram calories per square centimeter per hour (Lemon, 1966).

According to Wilsie (1962), the amount of insolation is dependent primarily on latitude, altitude, season of the year, and relationship to large bodies of land or water. Maps showing average surface temperatures in the U.S. for January and July are given in Fig. 5 and 6.

The July and January isotherms serve as good indicators of the adaptation zones of the major turf species. For example, creeping bentgrass and Kentucky bluegrass, except with special care, are not adapted below the 80 F July isotherm, shown in Fig. 6 (Musser, 1962; Juska and Hanson, 1965; Wise, 1961). On the other hand, bermudagrass requires a temperature above 50 F (Youngner, 1959). Its optimum temperature is apparently near 100 F or above (Brown, 1939). Hence, bermudagrasses are used sparingly above the 80 F July isotherm (Sprague and McCloud, 1962).

Changes in air temperature tend to follow a uniform latitudinal pattern from the equator toward the poles with mean average temperatures decreasing in a northward and southward direction from the equator (Trewartha, 1954). Three general temperature zones have been specified by climatologists: torrid, temperature, and frigid. Most of the U.S. is in the north temperate zone, characterized by warm summers and cool or cold winters. The southernmost extremities of the U.S., which include peninsular Florida, the coastal sections of the Gulf States, the lower Rio Grande Valley of Texas, and portions of southern Arizona and California, have a subtropical climate. In these areas winter temperatures rarely fall to 32 F, which is the "point of killing" for actively growing succulent plant tissue.

The actual low temperature at which turfgrasses are killed or damaged cannot be arbitrarily designated. Sometimes a species is killed at a

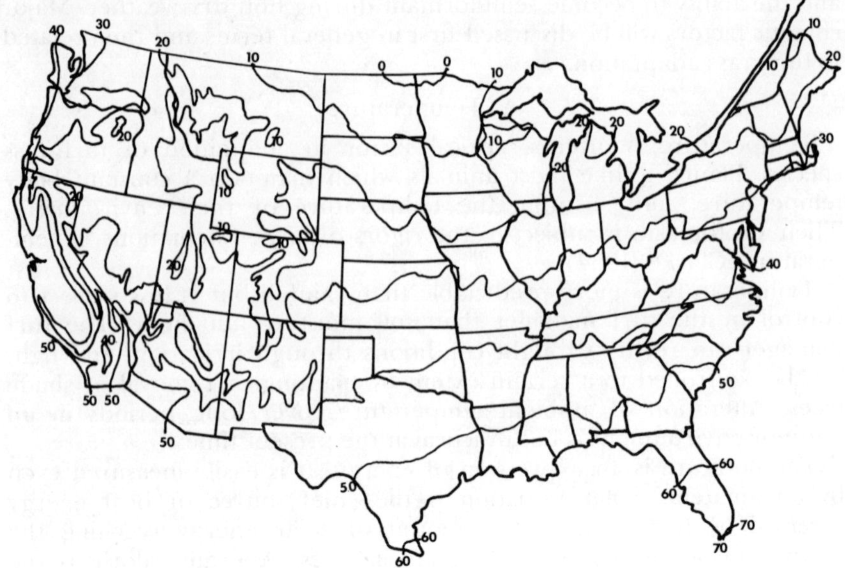

Figure 5. Normal daily average temperature for January (°F 1931-1960) (U.S. Weather Bureau summary, 1966).

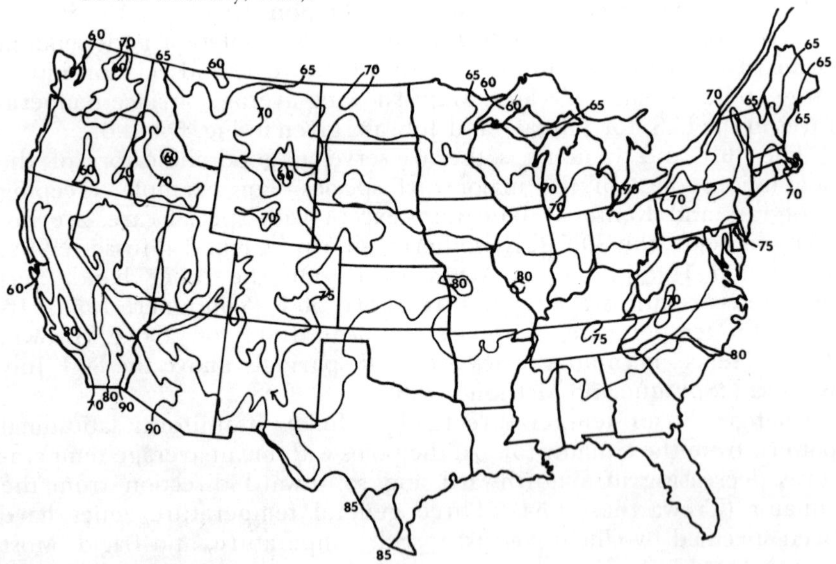

Figure 6. Normal daily average temperature for July. (°F 1931-1960) (U.S. Weather Bureau summary, 1966).

relatively mild temperature during the fall season but is uninjured by the same temperature if the plant is properly hardened and the temperature occurs later in the season. This is illustrated by the work of Davis and Gilbert (1967) in their low temperature injury studies with Tifgreen and Tifdwarf bermudagrasses. As shown in Table 3, these grasses were designated as having winterkilled at 28 F in September,

Table 3. Influence of season on low temperature killing point, in °F., of Tifdwarf bermudagrass.*

	Months, 1965				Months, 1966				
Variety	Sept	Oct	Nov	Dec	Jan	Feb	Mar	Apr	May
Tifdwarf	28	27	23	19	19	18	22	23	28
Tifgreen	28	27	23	21	17	17	20	21	27

* 50% kill as determined by growth of check. After Davis, (1967).

but a temperature of 17 F was required to give the same percentage winterkill in January and February. Plants were again subject to winterkill at about 23 F in very early spring when new growth had just been initiated. These data point toward the importance of proper conditioning of turf for the winter season. Excessive stimulation of turfgrasses with nitrogen fertilization or irrigation may increase succulence and low temperature injury.

Attention should also be given to such generalizations that all varieties of a given species or species within a specific genus tolerate low temperatures. In reality, large differences in low temperature tolerance exist among species and among varieties of a species. For example, Meyer zoysiagrass (*Zoysia japonica*) will tolerate temperatures of -8 to -10 F, manilagrass (*Z. matrella*) will survive 0 to 5 F, while a few hours of frost will kill mascarenegrass (*Z. tenuifolia*) (Youngner and Kimball, 1962).

1. Air Temperature

Air temperatures are controlled by various astronomical and climatic cycles. They are constantly changing due to wind movement, cloud formation, and angle of the sun. Radiation is a primary factor affecting the temperature of plant parts near ground level. According to Sprague and McCloud (1962), the adaptability of a grass species to a given area cannot be determined simply by its ability to withstand a certain minimum temperature, since turf appearance is often the first criteria in measuring suitability for a specific use. Temperatures well above freezing often cause discoloration in leaf tissue of turfgrasses (Madison, 1964).

Soil surface temperatures vary over a wider range than air temperatures (Fig. 7). Because of the great variance in surface temperatures, the standard temperature measurements made by the U.S. Weather Bureau are taken in standard weather shelters at a distance of 5 feet above the soil surface. This height was selected to avoid temperature extremes near the ground. Soil temperatures reach higher maximums than air temperatures do since the transparency of the air allows for little absorption of heat. Air is warmed or cooled by its contact with the earth. By the time air reaches a height of 5 feet, sufficient mixing has taken place to buffer the effect of the radiating soil (Trewartha, 1954; Sprague and McCloud, 1962; Wang, 1963). Raschke (1960) has discussed heat transfer between the plant and environment, pointing out that it takes place in three ways: (*1*) conduction and convection in the form of sensible heat; (*2*) evaporation of water and in the form of latent heat; and (*3*) direct radiation. Since only a small amount of the sun's energy absorbed by green plants is used for photosynthesis, most

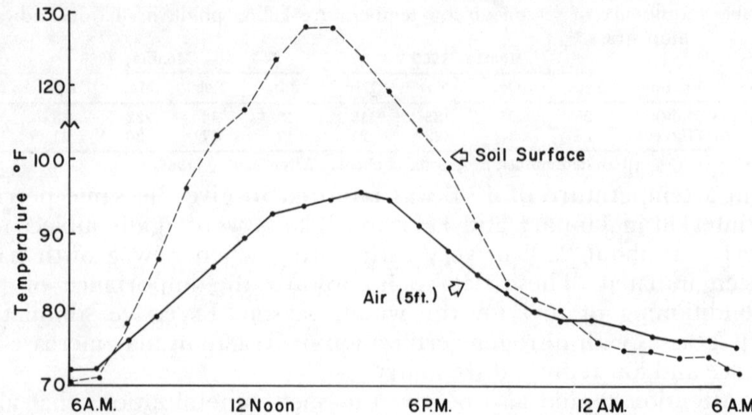

Figure 7. Diurnal fluctuation in air and soil surface temperature on a bright summer day. State College, Miss. (Atwell, S.D., and G.L. Bieber, unpublished data, Miss. Agr. Exp. Sta. 1968).

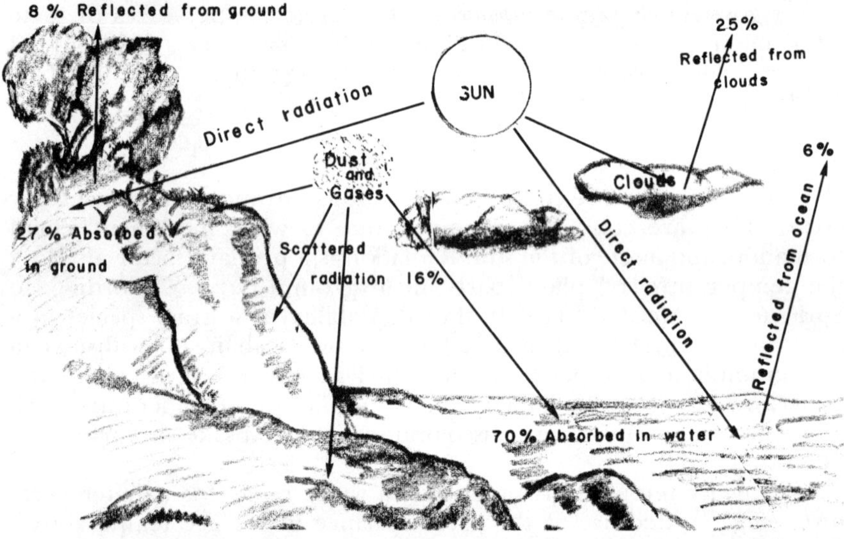

Figure 8. Fate of solar rays through reflection, scattering, and absorption (after Woodsbury. Principles of general ecology. N.Y. Blakistan Co. 1954).

of it goes into heat. The dissipation of solar energy is shown diagramatically in Fig. 8, after Woodsbury (1954).

Diurnal Fluctuations in Temperature

Both air and soil temperatures change constantly and rapidly, but they follow a rather definite diurnal pattern. A typical diurnal change in soil and air temperature is illustrated in Figure 7. At sunrise, air temperature begins to increase and reaches a maximum near midday, declining to a minimum in the early or the late hours of the night. Soil temperature follows the same pattern but has a 2- to 3-hour lag period (Fribourg et al., 1968). This diurnal fluctuation is caused by the earth gaining heat faster than it is re-radiated into the atmosphere. Later in

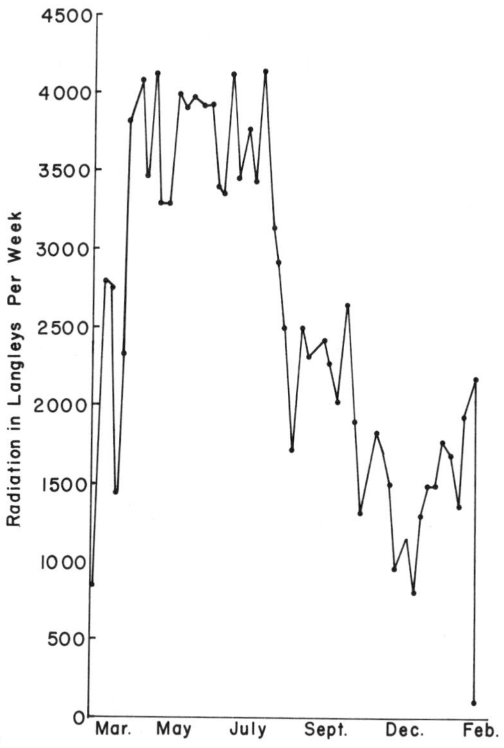

Figure 9. Solar energy received in langleys weekly at Jackson, Tenn. (Fribourg et al. 1967).

the day, a relatively high surface temperature is reached, but re-radiation and conduction begin to exceed insolation, and after sunset radiation from the earth's surface results in a drop in the temperature during the night. This decrease in temperature is hastened by the evaporation of soil moisture from the surface (Chang, 1968).

Seasonal Fluctuations in Temperature

Seasonal fluctuations in temperature are directly related to the incoming solar radiation during the various seasons of the year (Kimball, 1935). Figure 9 shows that the nation receives less radiation during the winter and spring as compared with summer. Growth of turfgrasses within a region and their adaptability to various climatic regions is determined to a large extent by the number of frost-free days occurring during periods of greatest solar radiation. For example, common bermudagrass is best adapted to those areas having a growing season of 200 or more days (Sprague and McCloud, 1962).

Temperature and Turfgrass Adaptation

Turfgrasses, like all plants, have the ability to withstand considerable thermal fluctuation, but they lack the ability to tolerate temperature extremes. All plants have three cardinal temperature points: (a) minimum effective temperature; (b) optimum temperature; and (c) maximum effective critical temperature. These have been defined (Clarke, 1954; Wilsie, 1962; and Chang, 1968) as follows:

a. *Minimum temperature*– lowest temperature at which growth activity occurs
b. *Optimum temperature*– temperature at which growth is most active
c. *Maximum temperature*– highest temperature at which growth occurs.

There are two additional cardinal points, maximum survival temperature and minimum survival temperature. These latter temperatures are linked with time. Thus, a given grass may survive a very high or very low temperature for a few minutes but not for hours. These cardinal temperature points are not easily determined because many variables, such as relative humidity, age of plant, and time of day, influence temperature effects. Agronomists have sought to find temperature limits and the optimum temperatures for many cultivated crop species; turfgrasses have often been neglected.

Sullivan and Sprague (1949) studied the effects of temperature on the root and stubble growth of perennial ryegrass. They clipped ryegrass plants to a height of 1.5 inches above the soil surface and measured regrowth and chemical composition under temperature regimes of 50 to 60, 60 to 70, 70 to 80, and 80 to 90 F. Optimum growth was obtained at 60 to 70 F and minimum growth occurred at 80 to 90 F. Chemical analysis of plant tissue showed that reserve carbohydrates in the stubble and roots were depleted under high temperatures.

Kentucky bluegrass grows over a wide range in temperature. Harrison (1934) found some growth occurring at 100 F, but much more rapid growth occurred at 80 F. A temperature of 60 F appeared to be optimum for sustained growth and development of a Kentucky bluegrass sod.

Most cool-season grasses perform best when daytime temperatures range between 60 and 80 F. Beard and Daniel (1966) obtained rapid root growth of creeping bentgrass at temperatures from 60 to 80 F. Increasing the temperature from 80 to 90 F greatly reduced the number, depth, and thickness of the roots. In addition the roots under the 80 to 90 F condition were not a healthy white color, but were brown and inactive. Schmidt and Blaser (1967) studied the effects of short-term (1 to 2 months) temperature changes on creeping bentgrass growth. High temperature, 36 C, increased the growth and respiration rate of bentgrass but decreased photosynthesis and carbohydrate reserves. They concluded that bentgrasses are weakened by such high temperatures. The best growth of creeping bentgrass is apparently obtained at relatively cool temperatures. The growth parameters shown in Fig. 10 indicate that if temperatures exceed 20 C, creeping bentgrasses decrease in available carbohydrate energy and root growth at the expense of increased leaf growth.

The differential optimum temperature for warm-season and cool-season grasses was demonstrated by Miller (1960). He found the relative rate of photosynthesis for Seaside creeping bentgrass to be 64.6% at 15 C. It increased to a maximum of 100% at 25 C, then decreased to 62.2% at 40 C. Common bermudagrass on the other

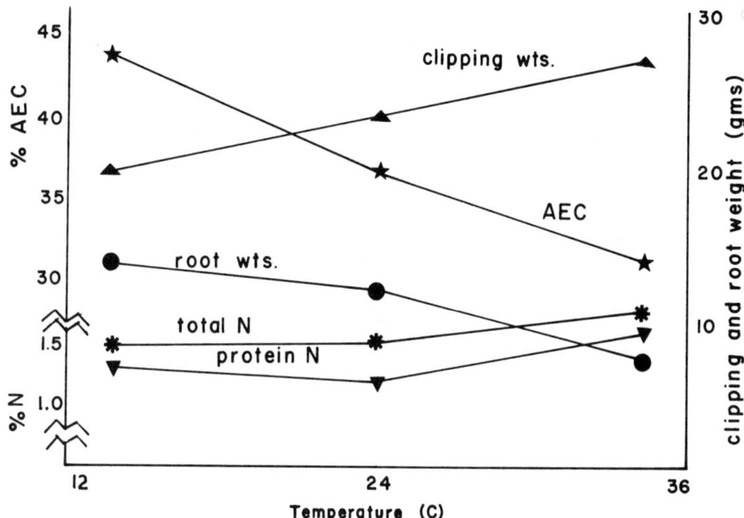

Figure 10. Bentgrass top and root growth and carbohydrate and nitrogen fractions of stolons when grown for 45 days at three temperatures (Schmidt and Blaser, 1967). AEC = acid extractable carbohydrates.

hand, increased from 54.9% at 15 C to a maximum of 100% at 35 C then dropped off to only 97.7% at 40 C.

Tabor (1950) reports that Pensacola bahiagrass initiated growth at 55 F, whereas common bahiagrass required a temperature of 60 F to initiate growth. All strains of bahiagrass tested grew well throughout the summer months with temperatures averaging above 80 F. See later section in this chapter for the influence of temperature on germination of turfgrasses.

2. *Soil Temperature*

As illustrated in Fig. 7, soil temperatures fluctuate in a diurnal pattern but change more slowly than air temperatures. It is not uncommon for soil temperatures near the surface to exceed 130 F during midafternoon of bright, sunny days. In fact, soil temperatures in desert areas have been known to reach 185 F when exposed to the noonday sun (Clarke, 1954). Soil temperatures fluctuate widely in the upper 3 inches, but diurnal fluctuations at lower depths are moderated by the buffering effect of the upper soil layer (Fribourg et al., 1967). Soil temperatures may be modified by applications of water (Duff and Beard, 1966). Temperature changes more slowly in wet soil than in dry soil (Wilsie, 1962). The texture of soils is also important in determining the rate of temperature changes. Sandy soils warm up earlier, loams later, and muck and peat still later in the spring. In the autumn, frost damage to turf may be greatest on coarse-textured soils because re-radiation back into the atmosphere is comparatively rapid after sunset. This relationship is caused by the ability of fine-textured clay soils to hold more water than sandy soils which have large pore sizes. Since water has a higher specific heat than air, it cools and warms at a slower rate than air.

Soil Temperature and Turfgrass Growth

Temperatures at the soil surface may be more important than air temperature in determining turfgrass adaptability. This is because the growing points of turfgrasses, especially those of rhizomes and stolons, are at or near the soil surface. The knowledge of turfgrass response to variation in soil temperature is limited. Beard and Daniel (1966) found root growth of creeping bentgrass correlated with the soil temperature at a 6-inch depth. In their investigation new root growth always followed a sharp drop in soil temperature.

Carroll (1943) found that soil temperature limits survival of turfgrass species more than air temperature does. He exposed turfgrasses to a soil temperature of 5 F and found more injury to annual ryegrass, perennial ryegrass, and velvet bentgrass than to Kentucky bluegrass and colonial bentgrass. Soil temperatures of 120 and 140 F caused severe heat injury directly to the protoplasm. At a soil temperature of 95 F, Darrow (1939) found a reduction in leaf formation and growth in Kentucky bluegrass. Best leaf growth was observed at 59 F. These temperature relationships should be considered carefully when Kentucky bluegrass is to be used for turf.

Julander (1945) showed that bermudagrass and buffalograss were more resistant to injury from high soil temperatures than Kentucky bluegrass, bluestems, and wheatgrasses.

Soil surface temperatures often exceed temperatures at which the enzyme systems of turfgrass tissues function normally. Even during cold weather (low air temperature), soil surface temperature may be high enough to stimulate activity of stolons. Sprague (1955) found the temperature of white clover *(Trifolium repens* L.) stolons to reach 70° in midday even though air temperature was near 32 F. At night temperature of the stolons often dropped lower than the air temperature.

Extremely low or high soil temperatures are probably most detrimental to turfgrasses during the period of establishment. At that time much of the soil is exposed. Direct incoming radiation would heat the soil to very high levels during the day, and rapid cooling would result at night. Young, tender shoots, roots, rhizomes, and especially stolons, would be subjected to this rigorous microclimate and growth could be altered. The failure of turfgrass plantings made in midsummer or late fall is probably related to adverse soil surface temperatures during these seasons. Cool-season turfgrasses should not be planted in the hot summer season (Holyoke and Struchmeyer, 1965; Youngner, 1962). If it is absolutely necessary that plantings be made during midsummer, they should be mulched and carefully watered (Goss et al., 1966).

Soil temperatures are modified by the thatch layer associated with turfgrasses (unpublished data, Thompson and Ward, 1964). Tifgreen bermudagrass with deep layers of thatch (more than 1 inch) went "off color" in the fall about 14 days earlier than plots with less thatch (½-inch or less). Conversely, in the spring the heavily thatched plots were late in developing new leaves because of the insulating effect of the thatch layer.

3. Heat and Cold Tolerance of Turfgrasses

The heat and cold tolerance of any given turfgrass species will depend on many variables such as soil type, moisture content of the soil, relative humidity, season of the year, succulence of the plant tissue, nutritional status of the plants and unknown factors (Laude, 1964; Smith, 1964; and Beard, 1966). Some generalization can be made, however, based on observations and specific research studies.

Beard (1966) found the following ranking of turfgrass species for cold tolerance (resistance to winterkill) in Michigan: *1*) bentgrass; *2*) rough bluegrass; *3*) Kentucky bluegrass; *4*) annual bluegrass; *5*) red fescue; *6*) redtop; 7) tall fescue; *8*) perennial ryegrass; *9*) zoysia; *10*) annual ryegrass; and *11*) bermudagrass. A somewhat different ranking is obtained when turfgrasses are rated for the effect of cold weather on their appearance (winter color). In southern California, Youngner (1962) ranked a number of turfgrasses for winter color. Rated best for winter color was perennial ryegrass, followed by Kentucky bluegrass, bentgrass, red fescue, tall fescue, meadow fescue, St. Augustinegrass, zoysiagrass, improved bermudas, and common bermudagrass. Heat tolerance of these same grasses was as follows in order of decreasing tolerance: zoysiagrass, improved and common bermudagrass, St. Augustinegrass, tall fescue, meadow fescue, Kentucky bluegrass, red fescue, ryegrass, and bentgrass.

It is generally conceded that the creeping bentgrasses are much more cold tolerant than varieties of colonial bentgrass (Beard, 1966).

In overseeding bermudagrass turf in Mississippi, Gill, Thompson and Ward (1962) found ryegrasses more susceptible to low temperature injury than the fine-leaf fescues, which in turn were damaged more than rough and Kentucky bluegrasses.

B. Moisture and Turfgrass Adaptation

Excluding temperature, water is the most important environmental factor influencing turfgrass adaptation. Water is important because: 1) it makes up about 85 to 95% of actively growing turfgrass tissue; 2) it is basic to photosynthetic activity; 3) it maintains turgidity in leaves and serves to transport minerals and other nutrients throughout the plant; and 4) it helps to regulate plant temperature.

1. Precipitation

Most of the water available to turfgrasses comes from condensation of moisture rising as a vapor from oceans, streams, and lakes (Ackermann et al., 1955). The primary form of precipitation is rain. In the U.S. the average annual precipitation is about 30 inches. Some 70%, or the equivalent of 21 inches, goes back into the air as evaporation and transpiration. The remaining 9 inches, or about 30%, enters the streams, lakes, and rivers. The 70% of our total annual water supply lost by evaporation and transpiration, and therefore disregarded in many water studies, is actually the water which is most important to man. It is this portion that sustains plant and animal life (Renne, 1966). While the average annual rainfall for the entire nation is 30 inches, the

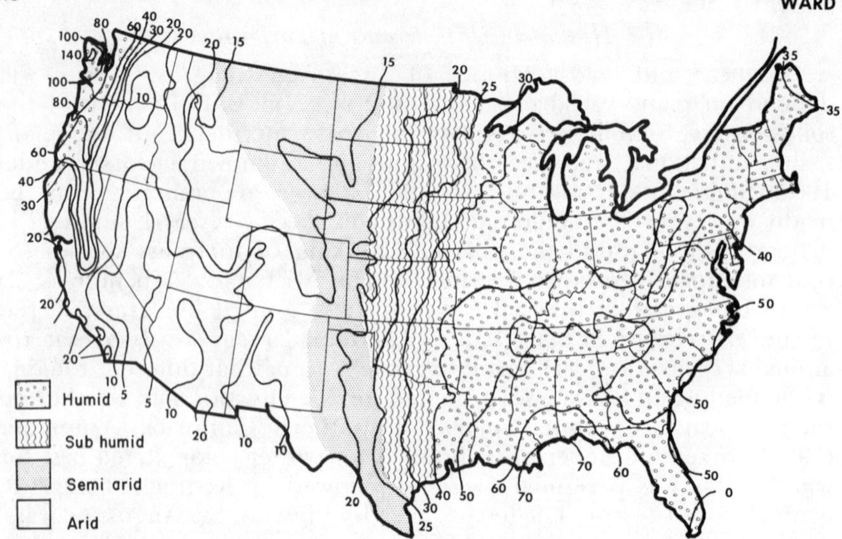

Figure 11. Mean annual total precipitation in inches for period 1898-1941 (after Kincer, 1941).

total rainfall received by some sections is less than 5 inches. A few areas such as the Olympic Forest sections of Washington receive in excess of 140 inches per year. Figure 11 shows the mean annual precipitation for the U.S.

Seasonal distribution is often more important than total precipitation. The eastern half of the nation receives from 30 to 70 inches of rainfall, which is fairly well distributed throughout the year; whereas, rainfall in the Plains region and westward to elevations of about 5,000 feet ranges from 10 to 25 inches annually, 85% of which falls during the growing season. Precipitation along the Pacific Coast varies from less than 10 to more than 100 inches and, except for one small area, it comes almost entirely in the winter season. McDougal (1925) classifies areas in the U.S. according to rainfall patterns as wet, humid, semihumid, semiarid, and arid, as shown in Fig. 11. He emphasizes the fact that temperature is the chief factor determining the effectiveness of rainfall. He equates 55 inches of rainfall at 80 F with 30 inches at 50 F or 15 inches at 20 F. Since the general rainfall patterns within each region have been discussed in an earlier section, further elaboration will not be made here.

In addition to total amount and distribution, a third factor which determines the effectiveness of rainfall is the intensity with which it is received. In the eastern half of the U.S. rainfall tends to be gentle and of a low intensity compared to that received in the Southwest and Plains States. Individual rains in these areas are often received in ineffective amounts, of less than 0.25 inch, and very often the larger rains fall with such intensity that a high percentage is lost in surface runoff. These high intensity rains come as sharp convectional showers caused by the excessive surface heating of unstable air from the Gulf of Mexico. Summer rains of the convectional type are likely to be relatively vigorous, but not of long duration.

Because of the high value of most turf, irrigation is commonly practiced to keep turfgrasses alive during periods of low rainfall; or, where use requires, it is given sufficient water to maintain optimum growth. Without irrigation, most turf would be much less attractive. Many species, presently used for turf in low rainfall areas would be worthless without irrigation. Before the advent of modern irrigation methods golfers putted on "sand greens," rather than on a living carpet of grass. This is done even now in some areas of the Western Plains. Because of the high water costs, home owners in the arid southwest maintain small lawns of well-groomed, drought-tolerant turfgrasses; the remainder of the real estate around their homes is landscaped with nonliving ground covers, such as redwood bark, gravel, and similar materials.

2. *Snow*

Snowfall is an important source of moisture in the upper Midwest, the New England States, and throughout the mountain regions of the West. In these regions, annual snowfall ranges from 30 to 200 inches (Kincer, 1941). Snow not only serves as a source of moisture but forms a blanket of insulation over turf affording excellent protection from the low winter temperatures that characterize northern regions and mountain sections of the U.S. Snowfall increases at higher latitudes and the amounts received south of the 35th parallel are relatively light except in some mountainous areas. Turfgrasses in the colder sections of the U.S. are often covered with snow and ice for long periods of the winter season. Since these turfgrasses are often damaged or "winter killed", it has been theorized that respiratory products such as carbon dioxide were accumulated in toxic amounts under the snow and ice. Beard (1965) at Michigan State, however, found no toxic accumulations of plant respiratory products after 90 days of ice coverage on perennial turfgrasses. He also showed that oxygen diffusion through ice sheets occurs with sufficient rapidity as to cast doubt on the suffocation of turfgrasses under ice sheets.

3. *Dew*

The condensation of moisture in the form of dew often enables turfgrasses to survive in areas of low rainfall. But its presence in humid areas often enhances the buildup of turfgrass diseases. Because dew is closely related to relative humidity, the formation of dew and its importance to turfgrasses are discussed in the section on humidity.

The earth has a fixed supply of water which is used over and over again, appearing in three forms as part of the hydrologic cycle: 1) water in oceans, lakes, streams and underground storage places; 2) water in the soil; and 3) water in the atmosphere.

In the succeeding sections, other parameters of the hydrologic cycle, namely evaporation, transpiration, and humidity, are discussed.

C. Evapotranspiration

Evaporation is usually presented in terms of the inches of water lost through vaporization per day, week, month, or year from a free water surface. Transpiration is that water which is absorbed by the roots, passes through the plants, and is lost to the atmosphere by evaporation through the stomata in the leaves. These two processes combine to give evapotranspiration (ET) (Pruitt, 1964).

Most of the sun's energy which reaches the crop canopy is used in the evaporation of water, if that water is available in the soil moisture reservoir (Wadleigh et al., 1966). During July in the Midwest, up to 2 inches of water a week may be so used. Under such conditions, it makes quite a difference whether this reservoir holds 1 inch or 6 inches of available water. Any factor which limits root penetration influences the capacity of the soil to provide moisture.

Actually the rate of water lost per unit area from the soil due to transpiration by vegetation may be nearly twice as great as that lost from a free water surface due to evaporation. Clarke (1954) lists three atmospheric conditions that greatly modify the rates of evaporation and transpiration. These are *saturation deficit, temperature,* and *wind velocity.* Saturation deficit is the difference between the actual vapor pressure and the maximum possible vapor pressure at the existing temperature. The saturation deficit thus gives more information of ecological significance than the relative humidity alone, since the saturation deficit provides a measure of the capacity of the air to take up additional water. Wilsie (1962) and Shaw and Laing (1966) stress the significance of additional factors, namely: 1) the amount of energy supply and heat demand for water evaporated; 2) the availability of water at the surfaces of the plant where evaporation occurs; and 3) the existence of a transfer mechanism to move the water vapor from the plant surfaces to the atmosphere. Pruitt (1964) adds to these roughness of the crop surface. This factor would obviously affect turbulence caused by wind movement, one of three major factors affecting moisture loss from plants.

Evapotranspiration losses are speeded up with increases in temperature. The converse is equally true, in that evaporation and condensation alter the temperature of the plant environment. The interaction of temperature and moisture is so dynamic that it is difficult, if not impossible, to separate the individual effects of these two factors (Clarke, 1954). Actively growing turfgrasses may use an inch of water every 3 or 4 days during July in the eastern U.S. Spring and fall use rates would be somewhat lower (McCloud, 1959). Hagan (1955) estimates the amount of water used by evapotranspiration from actively growing turfgrasses to range from 1 to 2.5 inches per week depending on geographical location. He found weekly evapotranspiration was only 1 inch in the fog belt of the Californi Coast, but increased to about 3 inches per week in nearby interior valleys and desert areas.

Evapotranspiration from a bermudagrass sod in North Carolina during the growing seasons of 1956-68 averaged about 0.15 inch per day with a maximum daily water use of 0.27 inch in July of 1958 (Van Bavel and Harris, 1962). These data are in close agreement with those of Ekern (1966), who found the water lost through evapotranspiration of bermudagrass sod to approximate that lost from open pan evaporation.

Evapotranspiration from turf is usually low in the winter season and high in the summer. This seasonal variation in water loss is illustrated by data obtained from a perennial ryegrass sod at Davis, Calif. (Table 4). In the winter season, water use by ryegrass was only about 10% of that used in the summer months.

Computed values of evapotranspiration for other areas of the U.S. are given in Table 5. Water use by plants is lower in the New England states and the eastern U.S. than in the central and the western sections of the nation. Evapotranspiration decreases from south to north because of the greater energy received at southern latitudes during the fall, winter, and spring seasons (Brunt, 1944).

1. Transpiration

Transpiration is a process in which water is lost from the plant through leaf stomata. It is rapid during daylight hours and decreases at night to less than 5% of the daytime rate (Briggs and Shantz, 1916). The transpiration rate of crop plants (Slayter, 1967) is influenced by age of the leaf. Since most turfgrasses are mowed frequently, the transpiration rate for turfgrasses should be more constant than for nondefoliated species in which leaves are allowed to mature.

Availability of soil moisture in the root zone probably influences

Table 4. Evapotranspiration from a perennial ryegrass sod at Davis, Calif. (After Pruitt, 1964).

	Inches of water used per month				
Month	1960	1961	1962	Avg	Max. deviation from avg
Jan	1.047	0.628	1.136	0.937	32.7%
Feb	2.153	2.083	1.496	1.911	4.7%
Mar	3.222	2.953	2.856	3.010	7.1%
Apr	4.570	4.859	5.100	4.843	5.6%
May	5.582	6.376	6.269	6.076	8.1%
June	8.709	8.213	8.136	8.353	4.3%
July	8.353	8.555	8.187	8.365	2.3%
Aug	5.643	6.836	6.890	6.457	12.6%
Sept	5.194	4.993	4.929	5.039	3.1%
Oct	3.668	3.543	2.828	3.346	15.0%
Nov	1.568	1.715	1.738	1.674	6.4%
Dec	0.981	0.888	0.855	0.908	8.0%
Total	50.690	51.642	50.420	50.584	---

Table 5. Average evapotranspiration in inches per day for various regions of the U.S.

	Geographical location			
Month	Jackson, Miss.*	Raleigh, N.C.†	Davis, Calif.‡	Durham, N.H.§
Jan	.037	.027	.031	----
Feb	.064	.050	.064	----
March	.085	.074	.100	----
April	.125	.111	.161	.087
May	.143	.137	.202	.123
June	.182	.162	.278	.144
July	.117	.151	.278	.158
Aug	.163	.132	.215	.143
Sept	.132	.106	.167	.111
Oct	.086	.062	.111	----
Nov	.052	.038	.056	----
Dec	.037	.022	.030	----

* Computed (Van Bavel, 1959). † ET/inches/day Calculated. (Van Bavel and Verlinder, 1956). ‡ Actual (Madison, 1964). § Palmer, (1958).

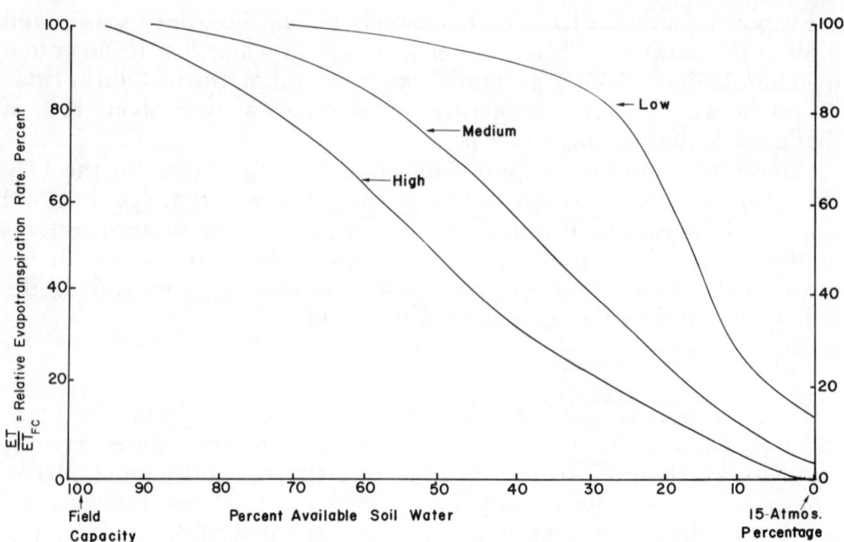

Figure 12. Ratio of actual evapotranspiration to evapotranspiration at field capacity at different levels of soil water for three atmospheric demand conditions (Shaw and Laing, 1966).

transpiration losses more than other factors. As shown in Fig. 12, if more soil moisture is available to plants more is transpired. The high, medium, and low demand curves shown were determined by class A evaporation-pan; rates less than 0.20 inch per day being considered low demand, 0.20 to 0.30 inch average demand, and above 0.30 inch as high demand. Hagan (1955) reported this relationship in a study conducted with Merion Kentucky bluegrass at Davis, Calif., during the hot, rainless summer months. Evapotranspiration losses from the bluegrass turf were approximately 0.19 inch per day during the 14-day period following irrigation; it averaged 0.17 inch per day during the third week; and declined to 0.09 and 0.07 inch for the 4th and 5th weeks, respectively. These data show the possibility of water conservation through the use of grasses which can withstand long periods of drought stress. The desirability of allowing turfgrasses to deplete soil moisture reserves to the point at which the leaves wilt would depend largely on the use being made of the turf.

The rooting depth of the turfgrass can materially affect its adaptability to areas of low rainfall and indirectly its rate of transpiration over a period of time. Turfgrass species vary greatly in their potential rooting depth. This affects their ability to survive during periods of drought or infrequent irrigation. The rooting depth of some common turf species, as measured indirectly by water extraction patterns, was studied on a deep clay soil at Davis, Calif., Table 6 (Hagan, 1953).

Adaptation of turfgrasses to areas where severe drought is a common occurrence should not be based on a single parameter such as rooting depth. The fine-leaf fescues, for example, are known to be more drought tolerant than bentgrasses, yet, in the above study, the fine-leaf fescues did not root as deeply as bentgrasses.

Table 6. Rooting depth at which turfgrasses extracted water from soil.

Species	Depth from which available water extracted, inches
Red fescues	8 to 10
Bentgrasses	12
Kentucky bluegrass	30
Kentucky bluegrass (Merion)	36
Tall fescue	42
Bermudagrasses	48*

* Some roots of bermudagrasses were found at 6 feet and Kentucky bluegrass (Merion) rooted as deep as 5 feet. After Hagan (1955)

Table 7. Adaptation of turfgrasses based on their estimated degrees of drought tolerance.*

Tolerance	Turfgrass	Tolerance	Turfgrass
High	Improved bermuda	Medium	Kentucky bluegrass
	Zoysiagrasses		Perennial ryegrass
	Common bermuda		Meadow fescue
	Tall fescue		St. Augustine
	Red fescue		Colonial bentgrass
Low	Creeping bentgrass		Dichondra

* Data from Youngner (1962).

The adaptation of fine-leaf fescue to droughty situations is related to reduced leaf surface exposure accomplished by rolling of the leaves and the concomitant reduction in water use; whereas bermudagrass is heat and drought tolerant primarily because of its deep root system which extracts water from great depths in the soil.

As we learn more about the moisture needs of turfgrasses, more precise recommendations of species adaptation can be made. Youngner (1962) has ranked the common turfgrasses used in California on the basis of their apparent drought tolerance (Table 7).

The normal rates of evapotranspiration for the area and the type and depth of soil available should be considered in choosing a turfgrass for an area. This knowledge would also be essential to proper watering of established turf (see Chapter 6).

2. *Mechanisms for Reducing Evapotranspiration*

Natural Mechanisms

Turfgrasses possess adaptive characteristics to reduce excessive evapotranspiration, namely: 1) leaf blades wilt or become less turgid; 2) leaf blades roll and curl to expose a minimum surface area to solar radiation; and 3) plants adapt to an adverse environment by increased leaf thickness (Langham, 1941).

Since the number, size, location, and shape of the stomata have a large control on transpiration rate (Waggoner, 1966), turfgrass breeders might well consider selecting plants with fewer and smaller stomata per unit leaf area, to give more drought tolerant varieties. The restrictive action on the number of stomata or closure on CO_2 absorption must be considered, but level of photosynthesis in turfgrasses would seem to be less important than the level in food crops.

Artificial Means for Controlling Transpiration

If turfgrasses could be managed to reduce transpiration and yet maintain their use value their range of adaptation could be enlarged. Mechanical defoliation of forage crops is a chief means of reducing transpiration losses with tall-growing grasses. However, turf plants lose their primary usefulness when severely defoliated. The logical place to attempt botanical control of transpiration is through control of the guard cells in the leaf which open and close the stomates (Bertrand, 1966).

In an attempt to diminish transpiration without detrimental defoliation, workers have experimented with chemicals which reduce stomatal openings when sprayed on the leaves of plants (Gale, 1961). Monomolecular films of long-chain fatty alcohols, chiefly hexadecanol, have been used for this purpose (Gale & Hagan, 1964; Peters and Roberts, 1963). Unfortunately, the decrease in transpiration is more than offset by severe interference with photosynthesis (Slayter and Bierhuizen, 1964).

Waggoner and Hewlitt (1965) sprayed barley plants with a solution of phenyl-mercuric acetate and reduced transpiration. This chemical caused closure of only those guard cells with which it came in contact. Even though the use of this chemical has been found effective in reducing transpiration on various crops, e.g., cotton for 27 days (Slayter, 1964) and corn for 46 days (Waggoner, 1966), it and similar "anti-transpirants" would seem of little value in turf, since frequent mowing would remove the treated leaves.

D. Humidity

Humidity refers to the amount of water vapor in the air. *Absolute humidity,* the total amount of moisture in the air, is of less consequence to turfgrass adaptation than *relative humidity,* which is the amount of moisture in the air as a percentage of the amount which the air could hold at saturation at a given temperature. Therefore, the relative humidity is lowered with an increase in temperature if there is not a simultaneous increase in the total moisture in the air.

The relative humidity of an area greatly influences water loss by evaporation from the soil and transpiration by plants. An area with less than 50% average relative humidity is said to have a dry climate and those with values below 20%are extremely arid (Clarke, 1954).

Relative humidity values for the continental U.S. during midsummer are shown in Fig. 13. Higher values would exist for other seasons of the year. Areas near oceans or other large bodies of water tend to have a constant relative humidity throughout the year. In the interior of the nation, it will fluctuate widely from a high percentage moisture in the air in early morning to a much lower level as the day progresses (Kincer, 1941).

The importance of relative humidity in turfgrass adaptation is associated in part with its effect on the incidence of various turf diseases. Many turfgrass diseases require a moist microenvironment for germination of spores and reproduction. Sprague (1955) found that relative humidity is greater near the ground and within a sod than in the air at some height above the ground. Disease incidence on turfgrasses is much greater in warm humid areas than in the arid Southwest (Couch, 1962).

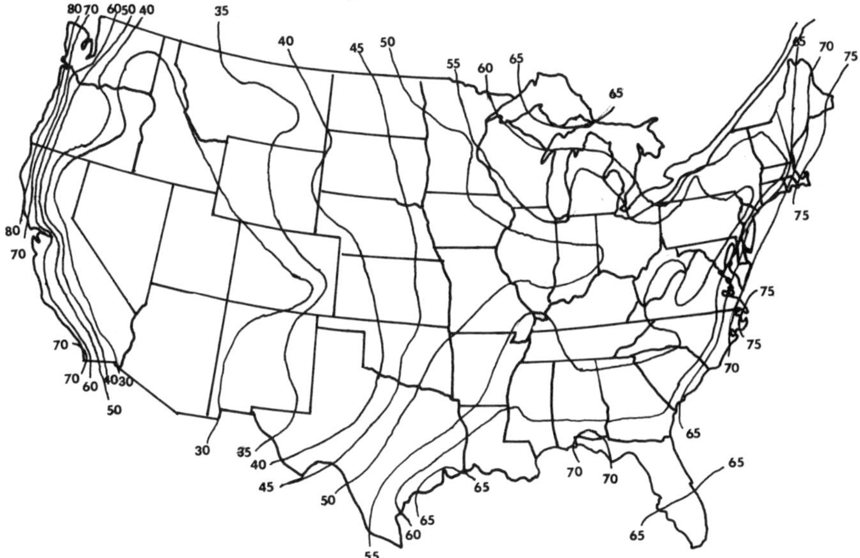

Figure 13. Mean relative humidity, local noon, July for period 1898 to 1940; (Kincer, 1941).

About 540 calories are dissipated in evaporating a gram of water (Lemon, 1966). Hence, increased evapotranspiration from a sod caused by a low relative humidity cools the microenvironment as heat is lost through vaporization of the water. Thus, the low relative humidity of the Southwest enables cool-season turf species to be grown in that region even though temperatures are generally above optimum.

E. Radiant Energy and Adaptation

Difficulties experienced in growing turf in densely shaded areas point up the importance of light to turfgrasses. Grasses are sunloving plants. Even shade-tolerant grasses require, for best growth, more light than may be obtained in many shaded locations. Much higher light intensities are required for the production of a vigorous sod than are necessary merely for growth of the grass.

There are marked differences among turfgrass species in their ability to grow at reduced light intensities (Beard, 1965). The bermudagrasses are notorious for their inability to grow even in moderate shade (Burton and Deal, 1962); whereas, red fescue (Youngner, 1963), among the cool-season species, and St. Augustinegrass (McBee and Holt, 1966), among the warm-season grasses, are well adapted to conditions of reduced light intensity.

In considering the influence of light on the adaptation of turfgrasses, several aspects must be considered; the intensity, duration, and quality of light are important parameters. Light enables turfgrasses to carry on photosynthesis and develop chemical energy needed for growth; it regulates the reproductive processes and excites the enzyme systems within the plants to function in many ways. The adaptation of turfgrasses is influenced greatly by nature's source of light, solar radiation, because its intensity, duration, and quality vary with latitude.

1. Solar Spectrum

Light energy for growing turfgrasses in the field environment has its origin in the sun. The energy of the sun which reaches the earth's surface is equivalent to about 1.6 gcal/cm²/min. This will vary by ±.10 gcal/cm²/min depending on elevation (Clarke, 1954). A more recent reference (Gates, 1965) indicates a more variable range from 2.0 gcal/cm²/min above the atmosphere to 1.34 gcal/cm²/min at the earth's surface.[1] The total energy (about 50,000 kcal per 1,000 sq. ft.) is partitioned into three well known segments of the spectrum, the infrared (greater than 0.7μ), the visible (between 0.4 and 0.7μ), and the ultraviolet (0.4μ). About 52% of the total solar radiation is in the infrared, 44% in the visible range, and 4% in the ultraviolet.

2. Variance in Light Intensity

The amount of light reaching a turfgrass sod at any given latitude and season is influenced by smog, clouds, dust in the atmosphere, and by trees and man-made structures. These not only affect light intensity but alter light quality. Light passing through a canopy of leaves on a tree is lower in blue and higher in red wave lengths than light entering the canopy. A thick stand of trees, such as maples or oaks, may reduce the light intensity by 95 to 99% of the value above the trees (Atkins, 1932).

Trees differ in their seasonal influence on the amount of light that penetrates the canopy. Pine trees reduce light intensity rather uniformly throughout the year, whereas deciduous species, such as the oak, maple, and poplar, reduce the light intensity least in the winter, but more in the late spring and summer when turfgrasses have their greatest need for high light intensity (Shirley, 1945). Light reaching turfgrasses under pine trees may be reduced by 15 to 44% depending on the age of the trees.

Intensities beneath tropical canopies may vary from 0.2 to 1% of full sunlight. Within the range of from 1% to 15% of full sunlight, photosynthesis is almost directly proportional to light intensity provided other factors essential for rapid photosynthesis are available. If all factors are equivalent, photosynthesis continues to increase with light intensity until secondary effects set in, such as high respiration caused by high light intensity and high temperature, excess accumulation of photosynthate in the leaf, water deficit causing closing of stomata or other internal limitations (Shirley, 1945).

The amount of light received by turfgrasses is influenced by the intensity and duration of the light. The normal intensity reaching the earth's surface in the continental U.S. is about 30% lower in March than in June (Kimball, 1928). The angle of incidence or latitude has a definite effect on the intensity and more importantly the duration of

[1] Equivalent to about 9,000 foot-candles or 1.3 langleys.

sunlight. The greatest intensity of sunlight occurs at positions on the earth's surface where the sun is most nearly overhead. A more constant and greater intensity in incident light occurs along the equator in the spring and fall seasons and in the north temperate zones in the summer season. The high intensity (800 gcal/day/cm^2) at the 40 to 60° N latitude in the summer season helps compensate for the short growing season in that region. This fact probably allows grasses like zoysia to be used further north than would otherwise be practical. Figure 9 shows a typical seasonal pattern of solar energy available for plant growth in the eastern states region.

Visible Light

Fortunately for mankind, that portion of the light spectrum most needed by plants for the synthesis of carbohydrates is in the visible wave lengths (Wang, 1963). Chlorophyll pigments, the site of photochemical transformation in the leaves, absorb two distinct regions of the visible spectrum, one at about 0.45 μ and a second at about 0.65 μ. Other pigments have been shown to transfer absorbed photons on to chlorophyll by a resonance process, thus passing along energy needed for photosynthesis from regions of the spectrum where chlorophyll is a poor absorber. According to Lemon (1966), this phenomenon results in an almost constant quantum yield over the visible spectrum. The efficiency of the photosynthetic process is estimated to be in the realm of 1 to 12% with a mean of about 5%.

3. Light Requirement of Turfgrasses

Since turfgrasses are valued for their appearance and not dry matter yield (i.e., excessive clipping weights may be undesirable), and since the two are often not well correlated, determination of light requirements for turfgrasses may be somewhat academic. The light requirements of a turfgrass beyond that needed to keep it alive is largely determined by the use made of the turf area. Turfgrasses in an infrequently mowed lawn which receives no foot traffic would survive on a much lower light intensity than grass on a golf putting green subjected to "heavy play."

A classic example of this relationship was encountered in the now famous Astrodome at Houston, Texas. Engineers unfamiliar with the light requirements of turfgrasses failed in their design to allow sufficient light to enter the dome to insure vigorous growth of the turf. During preliminary trial operations of the Astrodome, the newly laid bermudagrass sod appeared to be adequately supplied with light, but this judgment proved incorrect once the grass was subjected to the rigors of athletic traffic.

Youngner (1962) has ranked the major turf species as to their ability to grow in reduced light (Table 8). Golf course superintendents and home owners who have tried to grow bermudagrass in shade areas would certainly agree with Youngner's rating of this grass. His estimates of the shade tolerance for warm season grasses under California conditions are very similar to the actual response obtained by Burton and Deal (1962) when they subjected several southern turf species to

Table 8. Shade tolerance of turfgrasses.

Degree of tolerance	Estimated tolerance*	Actual shade tolerance of southern grasses†
High	Red fescue	St. Augustinegrass
	Zoysiagrasses	Zoysiagrasses
	St. Augustinegrass	Bahiagrass
	Dichondra	Not tested
	Bentgrass	Not tested
	Tall fescue	Centipedegrass
	Meadow fescue	Not tested
Low	Kentucky bluegrass	Not tested
	Perennial ryegrass	Not tested
	Improved bermudagrass	Improved bermudagrasses
	Common bermudagrass	Common bermudagrass

* Extimated performance in shade. Youngner (1962). † Response when grown under artificial shade. Burton and Deal (1963).

reduced light intensity with plastic shades. As may be seen in Table 8 only the positions of St. Augustinegrass and zoysiagrass are reversed in the estimated and actual tolerance to reduced light.

Because of the importance of trees in landscaping, it is often necessary to compromise with quality in selecting a shade tolerant turf. For example, in the southeast, hybrid bermudagrass is most commonly used on golf tees. But it is not well suited for tees surrounded by a dense planting of trees. In Mississippi, Meyer zoysiagrass is being tested as a replacement for improved bermudagrass on shaded golf tees. However, after two full seasons, it has not healed scars caused by removal of 4 inch divots. Comparable divots made in Tifway bermudagrass healed in 8 weeks or less. Zoysia's slow rate of recovery from injury may limit its use on golf tees (Ward, 1967).

Juska (1963) evaluated the density and disease resistance of 11 varieties of creeping bentgrass when grown under shaded conditions and full sunlight. Black plastic screens which excluded 30% of incident light were used to simulate natural shade of trees. The grasses received uniform cultural treatments and were sprayed at regular intervals with fungicides (PMAS and thiram). Shaded plots were noted to have lower microclimate temperatures, especially near midday. All turf under shade was less dense and lighter green. In general, those varieties which performed best in full sunlight performed best in the shade. Pennlu was a lone exception. It performed better under shade than in full sunlight. Light intensity was found to be a significant factor in determining the growth of C-52 creeping bentgrass at Lafayette, Indiana (Beard and Daniel, 1966).

McBee and Holt (1966) evaluated several selections of bermudagrass and other warm-season turfgrass species for turf quality characteristics under different levels of light intensity (Table 9).

One bermudagrass selection, Floraturf (No-Mow), showed remarkable tolerance to a reduced light environment, an unusual response, since bermudagrasses generally lack shade tolerance. When compared to two other bermudagrasses, Tifway and a Kansas selection under full sunlight the grasses were comparable in turf density; but under artificial shades reducing light to 50% and 35% the No-Mow bermudagrass was vastly superior in density, especially at the lowest light intensity. It was also significantly better in turf density ratings than St.

Table 9. Effect of shade on the percent ground cover of turfgrasses grown at College Station, Texas (After McBee and Holt, 1966).

Grass variety	June % of indident light			July % of incident light			October % of incident light		
	100	35	25	100	35	25	100	35	25
Bermuda									
Tifway	85 a**	16 c	11 bc	100 a	63 c	13 b	100 a	98 a	66 b
T-135	85 a	54 a	12 bc	98 a	94 a	14 b	100 a	99 a	67 b
Floraturf (No-Mow)	59 b	44 ab	29 a	97 a	100 a	63 a	100 a	100 a	99 a
Bahia	47 b	37 b	24 ab	57 c	30 d	12 b	42 c	52 b	28 c
St. Augustine	34 c	18 c	8 c	70 b	87 b	13 b	59 b*	100 a	86 a

* Diseased. ** Those values within a column not followed by the same letter are significantly different at the .05 level by Duncan's test.

Augustinegrass in June and July, and was equal to St. Augustinegrass at the October rating.

Many home owners have established an excellent stand of bermudagrass during early spring, only to have it vanish when trees leafed out to a full canopy. Home owners who insist on a bermudagrass lawn should use it only in sunny areas and rely on zoysiagrass in shaded portions of the lawn. In Zone II, Fig. 1, centipedegrass or St. Augustinegrass may be used in shaded areas for lawn or general turf areas receiving low traffic.

In regions where cool-season grasses are adapted, bluegrasses and bentgrasses are most often supplemented by the fine-leaf fescues in heavily shaded areas (Carleton, 1959; Wise, 1961; Holyoke and Struchtemyer, 1965). The more dense the shade, the higher the percentage of red fescue. Rough bluegrass is often added to turfgrass seed mixtures for lawns with dense shades in cool-humid regions.

The critical light needs of turfgrass species have not been adequately researched. Schmidt and Blaser (1967) grew Cohansey creeping bentgrass sod at 1,500 and 3,000 foot-candles (full sunlight is about 8,000 to 12,000 foot-candles). Top growth was greater and root growth was increased 206% for plants receiving the greater light intensity.

McBee and Holt (1966) found Meyer zoysiagrass to spread more rapidly under 35% and 60% of incident than in full sunlight; Gary and Ward (1967) obtained faster coverage of this species under full sunlight than at 50% and 75% reductions in incident light. Plots mowed at 1 inch covered more rapidly than those mowed at ½ inch regardless of the shade level imposed. After two growing seasons Meyer zoysiagrass had only 30% ground cover where the incident light was reduced by 75%.

Influence of Light on Germination of Turfgrassses

Germination of most viable nondormant seed requires adequate amounts of oxygen and water together with the proper temperature. However, some species require light for germination. Among turfgrass species, Kentucky bluegrass is a notable example (Chippindale, 1949) (See Chapter 7 for more details).

Germination of many common weeds such as crabgrass and annual bluegrass is increased in turf areas as the height of mowing is reduced. While close mowing weakens the permanent turfgrass thus giving less competition to these weeds, it is the greater penetration of light to the weed seeds at the soil surface that brings about the increase in these

Table 10. Effect of mowing height on weed infestation of bluegrass turf in Ohio. 1960. (after Davis et al., 1966)

Variety	Weeds per 10 sq. ft.	
	Mowed 3/4 in.	Mowed 2 in.
Merion	8	0
Penn State K-1	10	1
Delta	102	11
Park	105	8
Common from Ky.	108	5

weeds. Davis and co-workers in Ohio (1966) found Kentucky bluegrass mowed at 3/4 inch to have about 10 times more weeds than when mowed to a height of 2 inches, Table 10.

Invisible Light

About 50% of the light energy reaching the earth is in the invisible infrared and far red region. There is little significant absorption of these waves by vegetation (Gates, 1965). Thus in a turf sod a large percentage of the infrared in solar radiation is transmitted to the soil where its energy is available to heat the soil, evaporate water, and enter thermal radiation exchange in the thatch layer.

Light Interception by Turfgrasses

Plants have been shown to synthesize dry matter at an optimum rate when they intercept 95% or more of incident light (Brougham, 1956). The amount of leaf tissue needed to intercept this percentage of the light varies with plant species. Watson (1947) proposed the term Leaf Area Index (LAI) for describing the ratio of leaf area per unit of soil area. With forage and other food crops the maintenance of a leaf surface area capable of intercepting a high percentage of incoming light is necessary for high production. But, since turfgrasses are important for aesthetic reasons, leaf area as related to dry matter yield may be of little importance.

Grasses for turf have been selected for their ability to produce a dense, close-growing, tightly knit carpet of verdant leaves. Turfgrass sods are deemed most desirable when they are sufficiently dense to prevent exposure of any bare soil. Their ability to do so is primarily dependent on the nature of leaf arrangement and the height of mowing. Grasses like creeping bentgrass and bermudagrass with their more prostrate growth habits would intercept more light per given LAI than upright species such as redtop or tall fescue. Since dry matter production is secondary to aesthetics in turf, the leaf area status of a turfgrass sod is largely a function of use. For example, turf on putting greens is mowed to about 1/4 inch while the same grass species used for a lawn or a fairway would be mowed at 1/2 to 1 inch; the amount of light intercepted would be near maximum in either situation. In this example LAI is incidental to the development of a suitable turf (See Chapter 7 for a more thorough discussion of LAI).

Photoperiod and Turfgrass Adaptation

The response of plants to the relative length of day and night is known as photoperiodism (Borthwick, 1956). The most striking manifestation of photoperiodism is the control of the reproductive cycle of certain plants, although other life processes may be involved. (See Chapter 7 for information on photoperiod effects on turfgrasses.)

F. Wind as a Factor in Turfgrass Adaptation

Wind is important in turfgrass adaptation as with other plants because (1) it mixes the air, thus smoothing out the differentials in carbon dioxide, oxygen, water, and other variables caused by positional boundaries of the soil, crop canopy, and altitude; (2) it often carries sand and other materials which may cover or damage turfgrasses through abrasion; and (3) it buffers temperatures and influences water loss from turf.

1. Wind Patterns

Wind and its pattern of movement, per se, are not as important to turfgrass adaptation as rainfall and temperature but the latter two are greatly influenced by wind movement. Wind brings moisture-laden air from the oceans for rainfall and it mixes the air mass, moderating temperatures in the plant environment. Air moves from an area of high pressure to one of low pressure. Since the rays of the sun fall more directly on tropical than on polar regions the lower latitudes are warmed more than higher ones. Air heated by the equator expands upward and flows poleward aloft (Rossby, 1941). Beginning about 30° N the tropical air mass descends and continues northward as a westerly wind. This flow of tropical air probably increases the northern range of adaptation of some turfgrasses.

In the U.S. the prevailing wind direction is from the southwest. The air movement northward brings warm air from the tropics, which causes precipitation on meeting the returning air mass from the Arctic region. The rotation of the earth causes the winds to flow eastward as they pass from the Gulf of Mexico onto the continent, hence the humid Eastern states receive rain from moisture laden Gulf air. The Midwestern and Plains states receive a much smaller amount of the Gulf air, which explains the lower rainfall pattern of the central states (Trewartha, 1954).

2. Wind Movement and CO_2 and O_2 in the Plant Environment

The air immediately surrounding the earth contains a rather constant composition of nitrogen (78.09%), oxygen (20.93%), carbon dioxide (0.03%) and small amounts of many other gases. Because of CO_2 being released from decaying organic matters and the respiration of roots the CO_2 concentration in the soil is much greater, averaging about 0.2 to 1.0% (Wang, 1963).

The movement of air by convection currents and turbulence is caused by differential heating of the earth surface. This wind or air movement helps bring about a semblance of constancy to the composition of the gas layer as its various components are exchanged by plants and animals.

Since plants utilize CO_2 for photosynthesis and since the normal concentration in the air is low, it is logical to expect that static air surrounding actively photosynthesizing leaves on a bright day would become limiting in CO_2. It has been shown that CO_2 concentration in and around the leaf canopies of corn (Hesketh, 1963), orchardgrass (Hunt et al., 1967), and other plants is sometimes suboptimum for maximum photosynthesis on bright sunny days. In such cases turbulence caused by increased wind speed brings about mixing of CO_2 from areas of higher concentration to areas of lower concentration, increasing CO_2 assimilation. The influence of concentration of CO_2 in the air on assimilation rate was demonstrated by Waggoner et al. (1963). They placed sugarcane (*Saccharum* spp.) leaves in calm and turbulent air at 200 ppm CO_2 and in calm air at 300 ppm CO_2. The cane leaves gave greater response at the 300 ppm CO_2 when grown in still air. But if the air in the chamber containing 200 ppm CO_2 was stirred, the assimilation rate equaled that of leaves exposed to 300 ppm CO_2 in still air.

Since air under field conditions is rarely completely calm, and since the CO_2 concentration is greater near the ground (Daubenmire, 1959), turfgrasses in their natural environment should be adequately supplied with CO_2.

The fact that the grass species vary in their ability to reduce CO_2 at low concentrations (Moss, 1962) implies two important facts: (1) that certain turfgrasses are probably better adapted than others to grow in microenvironments of low CO_2 concentration; and (2) that turfgrass breeders should consider the response of progeny to various CO_2 concentrations.

3. Wind Velocity and Transpiration of Turfgrasses

Wind velocity exerts a major effect on the loss of water from soil and plants through increased evaporation. Thus air turbulence may benefit turfgrasses by increasing the CO_2 concentration around the leaves but concomitantly cause an undesirable increase in transpiration.

As implied in the statement above, wind has a prime effect on the humidity of the atmosphere. The movement of air across the leaf surface moves the moist air surrounding the leaf to layers of dry air above. This reduces the relative humidity and increases transpiration. The rate of evaporation from smooth surfaces increases with the square root of the velocity of the wind. Actual losses of water from plants caused by increased wind velocity vary considerably. Clarke (1954) reports that a wind of only 8 km per hour increases the transpiration by plants 20% over transpiration in still air. A wind velocity of 16 km per hour increased transpiration by 50%. In contrast, Hunt et al. (1967) investigated the influence of wind velocity on evapotranspiration of vegetative stands of orchardgrass under wind tunnel conditions. (These data may be applicable to certain types of turfgrass sods.) Changing wind velocities from 26 cm sec^{-1} to 165 cm sec^{-1} did not influence the rate of evapotranspiration. However, increasing the light intensity from 0.2 to 1.9 cal cm^{-2} min^{-1} significantly increased water loss.

Turfgrasses growing in areas of higher wind velocities must be drought tolerant or have special morphological characteristics to reduce transpiration. Hard fescue growing near the timberline in the Rocky and Sierra Mountains of the West are excellent examples of a turfgrass acclimated to windy environments. This species is low growing and has strongly rolled leaves to reduce the surface exposed to drying winds. Buffalograss and bluegrama are adapted to windy conditions of the Great Plains.

In the colder regions of the U.S. sudden movements of warm dry winds in late winter often cause snow to melt and expose plants to the evaporative power of the air while the soil is still frozen. Consequently, plants may be killed by desiccation through losing water faster than their roots can obtain it. Cool-season turfgrasses are more vulnerable to this type of injury than completely dormant warm-season species.

Winterkilling of turfgrasses often occurs through desiccation (Musser, 1962; Gilbert, 1965; Beard, 1966; Ferguson, 1966). This is especially a problem on bentgrass greens which are usually elevated and more exposed than adjacent turf areas. Loss of turf through desiccation appears to be more serious in the upper Midwest and in Canada than in warmer regions.

4. Mechanical Action of Wind on Turfgrasses

Abrasive action of wind loaded with sand and other particles can be detrimental to turf. The abrasive effect of sand particles as well as physical inundation of turf by sand and other debris laid down by wind are factors in turfgrass adaptation. In mountainous regions the strong winds to which vegetation may be subjected is not always appreciated. For example, on Mt. Washington at 6,300 feet the weather station recorded a wind velocity of more than 75 miles per hour on 85 days between October 1940 and March 1941. The average wind speed for the period was approximately 36 miles per hour. At high elevations low temperatures act with severe winds to produce the familiar dwarfing of grasses and gnarling of woody vegetation (Clarke, 1954).

Dune areas along beaches require tall growing grasses that permeate the soil with a vast network of roots and rhizomes. These grasses stabilize the dunes and because of their height are not easily covered by shifting sands. American beachgrass and seaoats are the more commonly used grasses for such areas. They have leaves which possess a thick, tough cuticle that resists the abrasive action of wind-blown sand. Bermudagrass and other grasses with desirable turf characteristics are easily covered by the shifting sand.

Grasses along roadside shoulders and buffer zones of airport runways are subjected to damage from winds created by high speed vehicles and aircraft. Here, low-growing grasses with wear resistance are best adapted. In such areas the fine-leaf fescues are often used in the north; crested wheatgrass and lovegrasses in the arid west; and bermudagrass and bahiagrass in the south (Montieth, 1942).

G. Microclimate

Microclimate is the climate near the ground as opposed to the gross climate of a region. In turfgrass culture it encompasses the space occupied by the leaves and other aboveground plant parts and to a lesser extent the roots of the sod. Microclimate is important because variance in temperature and other parameters may be greater within a few inches of space near the ground than over a distance of hundreds of miles in the macroclimate (Gieger, 1965).

In recent years, microclimates of sods have been measured in many states in the Northeast (Sprague, 1959) and Southeast (Fribourg et al., 1967). The characteristics of the microclimate have been compared with data taken concomitantly on the macroenvironment using standard U. S. Weather Bureau techniques where applicable. For example, Fribourg et al. (1967) found that air temperatures 3 inches above a tall fescue sod were about 3 F warmer in the summer than air temperatures at the standard 5-foot height in Tennessee, Kentucky, and Virginia. At Blacksburg, Virginia, (1961-1964) the mean minimum January temperature at 5 feet above the ground was 22 F while that 1 inch below the surface of a tall fescue sod was 33 F. During July the mean temperature at 5 feet above the soil was 69 F while that 1 inch below the sod was 77 F. It is not uncommon for the minimum temperature a few millimeters from the soil surface on a clear winter night to be 10 F colder than that obtained from a standard 5-ft. weather station shelter.

Humidity near the soil surface is usually higher than that at 3 to 5 feet above the soil. Sprague (1955) has shown this fact to be important in the incidence of certain diseases of grass plants, since most pathogens require a very humid microenvironment to reproduce in epidemic proportions.

While the microclimate affects a turfgrass sod, the sod also influences the microclimate through transpiration, absorption of heat, and insulation of the soil surface. At Gainesville, Florida, the temperature 1 inch below the soil surface reached 100 F a total of 240 and 590 times during a 6-year period (1959-1964) for sod and bare soil plots, respectively. During this same period the temperature reached 110 F a total of 138 times under bare soil and only 3 times under sod plots. The transpiring sod cooled the microenvironment during the hot summer period (Fribourg et al., 1967).

The general climate of an area largely determines the ability of a turfgrass species to persist but the microclimate determines how well it persists and the ease or difficulty of that persistence.

1. Alteration of Microclimate with Mulches

At no time is the microclimate more important than during the period of germination and seedling development of a newly planted turf area. At this time plants must be adequately supplied with water and oxygen and the temperature must lie within the range necessary for germination and growth. Since bare soils are subject to rapid drying out and change in temperature near the surface, a thin layer of mulch is often used to temper the microclimate of new turfgrass plantings.

Mulches used on new turfgrass plantings help to control wind and water erosion and reduce evaporation of moisture from the thin layer of surface soil in which young germinating seedlings or sprigs are becoming established. Mulches are especially valuable to new seedings made on steep slopes of roadsides, canals, and other "difficult" sites. (See Chapter 18 for description of mulching materials.)

The bulky type mulches, such as grain straw, provide a more desirable temperature moderation of the soil surface than thin layer mulches like wood cellulose (Barkley et al., 1965), woven paper netting, or liquid elastomeric emulsions (Atwell et al., 1968). They also reduce evaporation more effectively, thus maintaining a more desirable microclimate for germination and seedling growth. Atwell et al. (1968) found the temperature at the soil surface to fluctuate 56 F on a sunny day with thin layer mulches as against only 16 F diurnal fluctuation for soil mulched with oat straw at 2 tons per acre. Likewise soil moisture in the upper inch of soil was reduced to the permanent wilting percentage much faster under thin layer type mulches or bare soil treatments as compared to plots mulched with straw (Table 11).

2. Slope and Microclimate

For many years it has been observed that the slope direction of home lawns, terraces, and highway roadsides affects the ease of establishment and stand survival of turfgrasses. South-facing slopes are usually hotter and drier, hence Blaser and Ward (1959) classified them as difficult environments for roadside turfgrasses as compared to north-facing slopes. In developing a site for a home lawn, terraces are to be avoided if possible, because of the difficulty in establishing and maintaining turfgrasses on them (Trew, 1960). Slope exposure also affects the adaptation of turfgrass species. Bermudagrass, a warm-season species, and tall fescue, a cool-season grass, may be found growing on opposite sides of the same highway. The cool-season species will grow on the north-facing slope and the warm-season species is better adapted to the southern exposure (McKee et al., 1965).

According to Chang (1968), the duration and intensity of light striking the soil is greatly modified by slope facing. Thus, the microclimate is altered by orientation of the soil surface in relation to the sun. Cooper (1961) found that microclimate of slopes varied from a cool, moist extreme at the bottom of a north-facing slope to a warm, dry extreme at the top of south-facing slopes. McKee et al. (1965) examined the microenvironment of roadside slopes in Virginia and found that soil temperature at the top of a south-facing slope during May was 5 to 10 F warmer than the base. Air temperature 3 feet above the tops of the slopes showed little relationship to that of the soil surface.

Table 11. How surface mulches affect soil surface temperature and moisture.* (after Atwell et al., 1968)

Mulch material	Temp, °F			Diurnal fluctuation	% H_2O†
	Mean	Max	Min.		
Oat straw	83	92	76	16	16
Liquid latex	89	125	69	56	4
No mulch	88	120	69	51	5
Air temp‡	75.5	88	63	25	

* Conditions sunny and bright. † % water in upper inch of soil 11 days after saturation.
‡ On Sept. 18, 1967.

Sod cover greatly modifies the soil surface temperature (Richards et al., 1952). This is very important because the soil surface represents the region where seeds germinate as well as the site of physiological activity including tiller and leaf development. Soil surface temperatures on bare soil often exceed the critical maximum temperature of many plants. Most nondormant plants are heat killed between 120 and 140 F. However, this temperature must be maintained for several hours to be lethal. Figure 14 shows the close relationship found by McKee et al. (1965) between soil surface temperature and ground cover in stands of tall fescue turf on a roadside in Virginia. They found that sod cover had little effect on soil surface temperatures in early morning and late afternoon, but reduced them 30 to 40° at midday. The high temperature (120 F) obtained on bare soil on south-facing slopes, if maintained for several hours, would probably inhibit germination of many grass species. The north-facing slope was cooler than the south-facing slope except in early morning.

Ward and Holmes (1962, unpublished data) found south-facing slopes of highway roadsides in central Mississippi void of vegetation 3 years after establishment of common bermudagrass. Adjacent north-facing slopes had an 80% cover of bermudagrass. They attributed this difference to the hotter, drier microclimate of the south-facing slopes. A somewhat different situation was found in north Mississippi where the mean temperature is slightly cooler. There bermudagrass persisted well on south-facing slopes and tall fescue dominated the more moist, cooler north-facing slopes. Slope facings should be considered in selecting turfgrasses since they have a marked influence on the establishment and longevity of the sod.

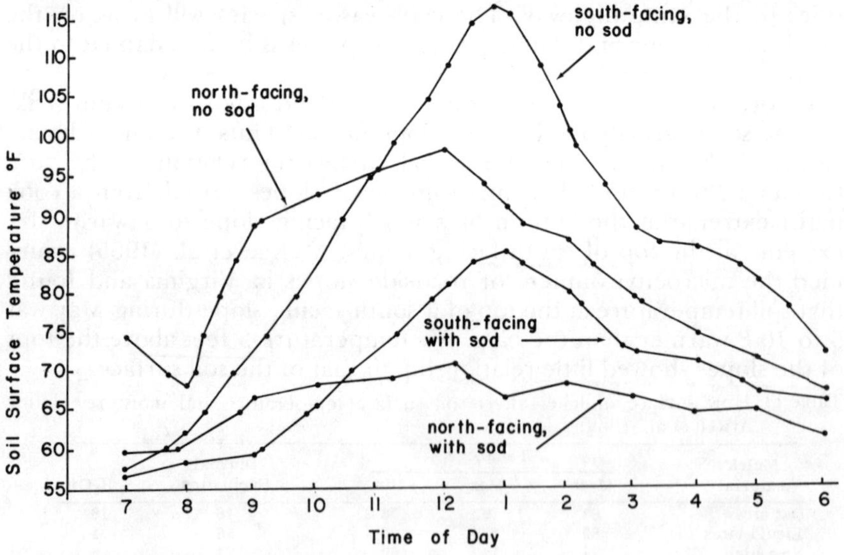

Figure 14. Effect of sod and slope facing on soil surface temperature along a roadside in Virginia, on May 5, 1964 (McKee et al., 1965).

3. Shade and Turf Adaptation

Most adapted turfgrasses can be grown with ease in full sunlight but the same species may perform poorly in shade. It is estimated that 20% of the existing turf areas in the U.S. are maintained under some degree of shade (Beard, 1967). While some shade may at times be beneficial to turfgrasses, their growth and longevity are usually curtailed by the reduced light intensity caused by shade.

Reduced light intensity is but one reason for the poor performance of turfgrasses in shade areas. Trees, the most common cause of shade in turf areas, not only reduce the light intensity up to 99% (Clarke, 1954), but they alter the quality of the light, filtering out a large quantity of the blue and red portions of the spectrum. Thus, the light reaching turf under a canopy of trees may be of sufficient intensity but of such poor quality that the grass cannot carry on photosynthesis at an adequate level. Other factors which reduce turf quality in shaded areas are: (*1*) competition for nutrients and water by tree roots, (*2*), increased relative humidity causing increased activity of turf disease organisms. (*3*) restricted air flow which may lead to slow drying of dew and other precipitation, and (*4*) foot traffic which is often greater in shaded areas that are preferred for entertainment and other outdoor activities.

Shade, then, is not a simple problem but is exhibited most in reduced growth of plants caused directly by reduced light intensities. Light intensities under deciduous hardwood trees approximate 55% in winter when the trees are leafless and decrease progressively as the leaves unfold until a minimum value varying from 1 to 5% is obtained (Shirley, 1945). Beard (1965) found the light intensity under sugar maples (*Acer saccharum* Mersh.) to be approximately 5% of incident sunlight. He selected a uniform woodland area of sugar maples as an experimental site for evaluating the shade tolerance of seven common turfgrasses used in the north central U.S.

The performance of the grasses, under shade conditions, was evaluated over a 3-year period. It was found that rough bluegrass and red fescue performed better than common perennial ryegrass, Kentucky 31 tall fescue, common Kentucky bluegrass, Norlea perennial ryegrass and Merion Kentucky bluegrass. The most significant observation was the effect of disease incidence under shade in reducing turf performance. Powdery mildew was extremely detrimental to Kentucky bluegrass when planted in pure stands. Red fescue was severely injured by *Helminthosporium sativum* during the early phases of the experiment but improved as the experiment progressed. Rough bluegrass showed unusual ability to grow without supplemental irrigation under the shaded conditions of the experiment. Beard believes that the microenvironment of the shade, which included higher relative humidity, extended dew periods, and reduced light intensity, produced a more succulent growth and increased the detrimental effects of disease infestation.

Plants growing in shade not only have reduced top growth but also restricted roots. Blackman and Templeman (1940) showed that nitrogen supply and light intensity markedly affected the leaf-root ratio of

Colonial bentgrass and red fescue. Growth rate of these two species was increased by nitrogen fertilization in full sunlight but in shade the same fertilizer treatments depressed leaf production. The lower light intensity interferred with the elaboration of protein, and nitrates tended to accumulate in the plant tissue. Shaded plants used more organic food substances to produce leaf and stem tissue rather than root tissue. The authors attributed the poor performance of most turfgrasses under shade of trees to the production of leaves tissue at the expense of root development.

The shade tolerance of certain turfgrasses cannot be explained on the basis of any single factor. Considerable research with so-called sun plants and shade plants has been conducted (Blackman and Wilson, 1951). To determine a satisfactory means of classifying plants for their ability to survive under shaded conditions, these workers made measurements on net assimilation rates of plants under varying light intensities. In a study with ten plants, some classified as sun- and others as shade-tolerant species, it was found that reductions in net assimilation caused by shading were similar for all ten species.

4. Syringing of Turf

High-valued turf, such as golf putting greens, justifies special practices too costly for general turf areas. Close mowed, rapidly growing turfgrasses on golf putting greens, especially the bentgrasses, often wilt and may be permanently damaged during periods of prolonged high temperature stress. This is especially true during July and August in the arid Southwest and along the southern edge of the bentgrass belt.

Putting greens and other turfs are often syringed with frequent applications of small amounts of water to protect them from wilting and heat injury during periods of excessively high temperatures (Danner, 1953). Under extreme conditions it may be necessary to irrigate (syringe) greens two or three times daily to prevent injury (Musser, 1962). Newer automatic sprinklers, which have good capacity for quick coverage, have largely replaced hand watering. This management practice mitigates temperature extremes of the microclimate during high temperature stress periods. A light application of water cools the leaf surface through evaporative processes and raises the relative humidity adjacent to the turfgrass plant, alleviating leaf moisture stress that may otherwise develop.

Duff and Beard (1966) stress the need for air movement during syringing operations to reduce surface temperatures. They obtained a significant decrease in temperature of the turf mat immediately after syringing. The reduction in temperature was 6 to 10 F greater when air movement occurred after syringing. This decrease in the microenvironment temperature after syringing persisted for several hours (see Table 12). Ward (1959 unpublished data, Virginia Agricultural Experiment Station) obtained a temporary decrease in soil surface temperatures in stands of Kentucky bluegrass of approximately 30 to 40 F when plots were sprinkler-irrigated between 1:00 and 2:00 p.m. on bright summer days.

Table 12. Effect of syringing on the mat temperature (°F) under 0 and 4 mph air movement regimes and its relationship to the ambient air temperature. (after Duff and Beard. 1966)

Time	Air temp	Turf mat temp under			Mat temp – air temp	
		0 mph	4 mph	Diff.	0 mph	4 mph
8 am	67	60	60	0	-7	- 7
9 am	68	65	63	2	-3	- 5
10 am	70	71	65	6	1	- 5
11 am	73	77	69	8	4	- 4
12 noon	75	80	71	9	5	- 4
12:30 pm	76	76	68	8	0	- 8
1 pm	77	77	69	8	0	- 8
1:30 pm	77	78	69	9	1	- 8
2 pm	78	80	71	9	2	- 7
2:30 pm	76	79	70	9	3	- 6
3 pm	76	77	69	8	1	- 7
3:30 pm	76	75	68	7	-1	- 8
4 pm	76	74	67	7	-2	- 9
4:30 pm	77	73	67	6	-4	-10

The incorporation of syringing as a management practice on bentgrass putting greens will allow the use of this species in warmer regions where it would not otherwise be adapted. This practice should be considered for use on putting greens in all areas where periods of high temperature stress occur. Care should be taken to avoid large applications of water during periods of heavy traffic to reduce the danger of excessive soil compaction.

5. *Air Pollution*

With increased industrialization of the U.S., air pollution in certain areas has reached levels which have deleterious effects on turfgrasses and other plants. The Los Angeles area of California and the Northeast have been most troubled by damage to plants caused by air pollution.

The detrimental effects of smog and other forms of air pollution on plant growth is due to reduced light intensity and the phytotoxicity of smog components such as sulfur dioxide, fluorine (De Ong, 1946), ozone, and certain hydrocarbons (Bobrov, 1952).

Annual bluegrass (*Poa annua* L.) is very sensitive to certain phytotoxic agents in smog and has been proposed as a bioassay indicator plant (Bobrov, 1955).

Smog damage to plants has been reported by a number of workers. In the Los Angeles area smog damage has been reported for spinach, oats, endive lettuce, beets, sugar beets (Middleton et al., 1950), avocado (Taylor et al., 1967), apricot (De Ong, 1946), tomato (Koritz and West, 1953), annual bluegrass (Bobrov, 1955), and bermudagrass (Youngner, 1966).

Typical smog damage of grass leaves, as found in oats and annual ryegrass, depends on two anatomical factors: the number of stomata and the amount of internal air space in the leaf (Bobrov, 1952) per unit area. Plants having more stomata per unit area of leaf are more seriously damaged. In severe smog concentrations a leaf may be completely killed and turn yellow. This damage starts as longitudinal streakings corresponding to the position of the stomatal zones.

In the field, the characteristic response to hydrocarbon oxidation products is seen as tan spotting or transverse banding limited to the region between the tip and midblade of susceptible leaves. The cells which are most seriously damaged are those surrounding stomatal chambers. In plants having a high specific sensitivity to smog, damage is correlated with stomata distribution and activity (Bobrov, 1955).

When plants are affected by smog the youngest and oldest leaves remain virtually undamaged. Newly matured leaves, which have just completed growth by cell expansion, are very susceptible to smog damage (Bobrov, 1952).

Hill and Thomas (1933) reported reduction in yield of alfalfa to be directly proportional to the area of leaf tissue destroyed by lesions of smog damage (sulfur dioxide), indicating that the smog gas does not reduce the yield unless it produces visible effects. However, Bleasdale (1952) showed that air pollution caused a decrease in growth rate of plants particularly ryegrass *(Lolium perenne),* without producing visible injury. He also showed that visible injury was not due to sulfur dioxide. Koritz and Went (1953) obtained similar results on tomato plants. They found that growth of plants fumigated with smog in midday or early afternoon was significantly decreased. Smog appeared to decrease transpiration and water uptake rate.

Smog injury to turfgrasses, especially Tifgreen and Tifway bermudagrass, has been noted by Youngner (1966) and led to the development of a smog-resistant bermudagrass variety, Santa Ana, for use in the Los Angeles area.

It appears that smog injury, since it causes destruction of chlorophyll and spotting, yellowing and browning of leaf tissue, would be more important for its effect on turf appearance than on growth.

Since air pollution is expected to be a more serious problem in the future, turfgrass breeders will be required to add smog resistance to the repertoire of turf quality characteristics now involved in grass breeding programs. Marked differences in response to smog apparently exist among grass species. Antipov (1959) exposed 17 lawn species to conditions of severe air pollution of industrial gases in Russia. He found that quackgrass *(Agropyron repens* L.) showed the highest resistance, 35% survival, followed by red fescue and smooth brome with 21% and 18% survival, respectively. All lawns exposed to industrial gases required more careful maintenance than ordinary city lawns. According to his studies renovation of turf in areas receiving industrial gases was needed every 2 to 3 years.

There is convincing evidence that the nutrient status of turfgrasses is a factor in their adaptation to areas where smog is present. Kendricks et al. (1953) found that plants abundantly supplied with nitrogen were injured five to seven times more than comparable nitrogen-deficient plants. Barley and oats growing with an abundant supply of nitrogen were injured by smog treatments, whereas plants with limited nitrogen were not injured.

Some of the difficulties experienced in growing turfgrasses along airport runways may result from the poor adaptation of certain turfgrasses to exhaust fumes of aircraft.

H. Compensation of Environmental Factors

The use of turfgrass species in areas where they are not best adapted is often feasible because one or more factors of the environment may offset the undesirable effects of another. Many times such compensations are seen in nature.

Shade may compensate for latitude. For example, Kentucky bluegrasses and fine-leaf fescues may be used as turfgrasses much farther south if grown under moderate shade. Shade compensates in part for the higher temperatures found in these regions. Tolerance of the warmer macro-environment is achieved under moderate shade by reduced growth and respiration rates.

Conversely, hybrid bermudagrasses may be grown on putting greens north of the region of their best adaptation if mulched in the winter with straw, polyethelene, or other materials for protection from low temperature injury. In this situation the mulch compensates for latitude or low temperatures (mainly a temperature adjustment).

Management factors often compensate for an undesirable feature of the climate. Tall fescue will survive for many years in the Southeast if mowed at a height of 2 to 3 inches, but may be eliminated in the first hot summer if mowed too closely. This is mainly a temperature adjustment in which the insulating properties of the sod create a more favorable microenvironment and bring about reduced respiration levels in the crown region of the plant. Another example of the compensating effect of mowing height on adaptation is illustrated by data from Davis et al. (1966) in Ohio (Table 10). Mowing bluegrasses at 3/4 inch greatly increased the incidence of weeds. This, no doubt, is related to the amount of light reaching the soil surface and possibly to the weakening of the bluegrass plants through close mowing. It is likely, however, that a home owner might erroneously decide that Kentucky bluegrass is not adapted to Ohio conditions, when in fact the stand was lost due to competition from weeds. In this situation the higher mowing height compensated for the lack of aggressiveness of the bluegrasses.

Since compensations similar to those mentioned above cannot always be implemented, perhaps the best overall approach to growth-limiting environmental factors is an aggressive breeding program. In such a program, the plant breeder must determine the genetic potential for changing the response to day temperature, night temperature, photoperiod, and other environmental factors. In this manner it may be possible to create varieties that closely harmonize with the climate in which they will be grown. An analysis of the genetic basis of climatic response may provide some interesting insight into the problem of evolution, migration, and adaptation of turfgrasses because it will indicate how many genes have to participate to allow invasion of a species into new climatic territory. And it will show the limits of adaptation on the basis of available genetic material in species, for there is no doubt that the genes controlling climatic response are the most important in the survival of the species (Went, 1950).

V. Literature Cited

Ackermann, William C., E. A. Colman, and Harold O. Ogrosky. 1955. Where we get our water—From ocean, to sky, to land, to ocean. Yearbook of Agriculture. Water. pp. 41-51.

Antipov, V. G. 1959. Gas resistance of lawn grasses. Russian (English Summary). Bot. Zurnal. 44: 990-992.

Atkins, W. R. G. 1932. The measurement of daylight in relation to plant growth. Empire For. J. 11:42-52.

Atwell, S. D., G. L. Bieber, and C. Y. Ward. 1968. Effects of mulches on microenvironment temperatures and moisture. Proc. Southern Agr'l. Workers. Vol. 65, pp. 47-48.

Bailey, R. W. 1941. Climate and settlement of the arid region. USDA Yearbook of Agriculture. Climate and Man. pp. 188-196.

Barkley, D. G., R. E. Blaser and R. E. Schmidt. 1965. Effect of mulches on microclimate and turf establishment. Agron. 57:189-192.

Beard, James B. and Charles R. Olien. 1963. Low temperature injury in the lower portion of *Poa annua* L. Crowns. Crop Sc. 3:362-363.

Beard, James B. and William H. Daniel. 1965. Effect of temperature and cutting on the growth of creeping bentgrass (*Agrostis palustris* Huds.) Roots. Agron. J. 57:249-250.

Beard, James B. 1965. Factors in the adaptation of turfgrasses to shade. Agron. J. 57:457-459.

Beard, James B. 1965. Bentgrass (*Agrostis* spp.) varietal tolerance to ice cover injury. Agron. J. 57:513.

Beard, James B. 1966. Winter injury. The Golf Course Superintendent. 34:24-33.

Beard, James B. and W. H. Daniel. 1966. Relationship of creeping bentgrass (*Agrostis palustris* Huds.) root growth to environmental factors in the field. Agron. J. 58:337-339.

Beard, James B. 1967. Shade grasses and maintenance. Proceedings of 38th International Turf Conference, January 5-10, 1967. Washington, D.C. pp. 31-36.

Bertrand, Anson R. 1966. Water conservation through improved practices. Plant Environment and Efficient Water Use, A Monogr. Am. Soc. Agronomy. pp. 207-230.

Billings, W. D. 1952. The environmental complex in relation to plant growth and distribution. Quart. Rev. Biol. 27:251-265.

Blackman, G. E. and W. G. Templeman. 1938. The interaction of light intensity and nitrogen supply in the growth and metabolism of grasses and clover. Annals Bot. 2:765.

Blackman, G. E. and W. G. Templeman. 1940. The interaction of light intensity and nitrogen supply in the growth and metabolism of grasses and clover (*Trifolium repens*). IV. The relationship of light intensity and nitrogen supply in the protein metabolism of the leaves of grasses. Annals Bot. 4:533-587.

Blackman, G. E. and G. L. Wilson. 1951. Physiological and ecological studies in the analysis of plant environment. VI. The constancy for different species of a logarithmic relationship between net assimilation rate and light intensity and its ecological significance. Annals Bot. N.S. 15:63-94.

Blaser, R. E., Timothy Taylor, Walter Griffeth and Willis Skrdla. 1956. Seedling competition in establishing forage plants. A. J. 48:1-6.

Blaser, R. E. and C. Y. Ward. 1959. Seeding highway slopes as influenced by lime fertilizer and adaptation of the species. Proc. of Hwy. Res. Board. 38:21-39.

Bleasdale, J. K. A. 1952. Atmospheric pollution and plant growth. Nature. 169:376-377.

Bobrov, Ruth Ann. 1952. The effect of smog on the anatomy of oat leaves. Phytopath. 42:558-563.

Bobrov, Ruth Ann. 1955. The leaf structure of *Poa annua* with observation on its smog sensitivity in Los Angeles County. Amer. Jour. Bot. 42:467-474.

Boggs, S. W. 1931. Seasonal variation in daylight, twilight, and darkness. Geographical Review. 21:656-659.

Bohning, R. H. and Christel A. Burnside. 1956. The effect of light intensity on rate of apparent photosynthesis in leaves of sun and shade plants. Am. Jour. Bot. 43:557-561.

Borthwick, H. A. 1956. Photoperiodism. Vol. 3, Radiation Biology. McGraw-Hill, New York, New York.

Bradshaw, A. D. 1960. Population differentiation in *Agrostis tenuis* Stibth. III. Populations in varied environments. Phytopath. 59:92-103.

Briggs, L. J. and H. L. Shantz. 1916. Hourly transpiration on clear days as determined by cyclic environmental factors. J. Ag. Res. 5:583-651.

Brown, E. M. 1939. Some effects of temperature on the growth and chemical composition of certain pasture grasses. Mo. Agr'l. Exp. Sta. Res. Bull. 299.

Brougham, R. W. 1956. Effect of intensity of defoliation on regrowth of pasture. Australian Agr'l. Res. 7:377-387.

Brunt, D. 1944. Physical and dynamical meterology. Second Edition. Cambridge University Press, London, 428 pp.

Burton, G. W., J. E. Jackson, and F. E. Knox. 1959. The influence of light reduction upon the production, persistence, and chemical composition of Coastal Bermudagrass *(Cynodon dactylon)*. Agron. 51:537-542.

Burton, G. W. and E. E. Deal. 1962. Shade studies on southern grasses. Golf Course Reporter. 30(8):26-27.

Carleton, Milton R. 1959. Your lawn—how to make it and keep it. D. Van Nostrand, Princeton, New Jersey.

Carroll, J. C. 1943. Effects of drought, temperature, and nitrogen on turfgrasses. Pl. Physiol. 18:19-36.

Chang, J. H. 1968. Climate and agriculture, an ecological survey. A book. Aldine Publishing Co., Chicago, Illinois.

Chippindale, H. G. 1949. Environment and germination in grass seeds. Journal British Grassland Society. 4:57-61.

Clarke, George L. 1954. Elements of ecology. A textbook, John Wiley & Sons, Inc., New York, New York.

Cooper, Arthur W. 1961. Relationships between plant life forms and microclimate in southeastern Michigan. Ecol. Monographs. 31:31-59.

Cott, A. E. and E. C. Roberts. 1964. Lawns. Iowa State University, Pamphlet 312.

Couch, H. B. 1962. Diseases of turfgrass. A textbook. Reinhold Publishing Co., New York, New York.

Daniel, W. H., R. B. Hall, O. C. Lee, G. E. Lehker, and E. G. Sharvelle. 1955. The Lawn—How to establish and maintain. Ind. Agr'l. Exp. Sta. Ext. Bul. 254.

Daniel, W. H. and E. C. Roberts. 1966. Turfgrass management in the United States. Advances in Agronomy. 18:59-326.

Danner, Charles. 1953. Bentgrass greens for the south. USGA Journal and Turf Management. 6:28-31.

Darrow, Robert A. 1939. Effects of soil temperature, pH and nitrogen nutrition on the development of *Poa pratensis*. Botanical Gazette. 101:109-127.

Daubenmire, R. F. 1959. Plants and environment. John Wiley, New York.

Davis, D. L. 1967. Changes in soluble protein fraction during cold acclimation plus the effects of certain nutrients and stress conditions on winter kill of Cynodon spp. A dissertation, North Carolina State University. L. C. 67-11, 274.

Davis, R. R. 1956. Questions and answers on features of meyer zoysiagrass. Ohio Farm Res. 41:44-45.

Davis, R. R., R. W. Miller and M. H. Niehaus. 1966. Kentucky bluegrass for Ohio lawns. Ohio Report, March-April.

De Ong, E. R. 1946. Injury to apricot leaves from fluorine deposit. Phytopath. 36:469-471.

Duff, Thomas D. and James B. Beard. 1966. Effects of air movement and syringing on the microclimate of bentgrass turf. Agron. J. 58:495-497.

Duff, Thomas C. and James B. Beard. 1968. Air movement and syringing-effects on the microenvironment of bentgrass turf. The Golf Course Superintendent. 36:20-23.

Ekern, P. C. 1966. Evapotranspiration by bermudagrass sod *(Cynodon dactylon* L. Pers.) in Hawaii. Agron. J. 58:387-390.

Evans, M. H. 1949. Kentucky Bluegrass. Ohio Agricultural Experiment Station Research Bulletin 681.

Evans, M. W. and John E. Ely. 1933. Usefulness of Kentucky bluegrass and Canada bluegrass in turfs as affected by their habits of growth. Bulletin of the USGA Green Section. 13:140-143.

Escritt, J. R. 1954. Electrical soil warming as an anti-frost measure for sports turf, a further report. Jour. Sports Turf Res. Inst. 8:354-364.

Ferguson, A. C. 1966. Winter injury north of the 49th. The Golf Course Superintendent. 34:38-40.

Fribourg, H. A., R. H. Brown, G. M. Prine and T. H. Taylor. 1967. Aspects of the microclimate at five locations in the southeastern United States. Southern Cooperative Series Bulletin 124. 72 pp.

Gale, J. 1961. Studies on plant anti-transpirants. Pl. Physio. 14:777-786.

Gale, J. and R. M. Hagan. 1965. Contribution of water imbalance on the effect of salinity to plant growth. Annual Rev. of Plant Physiol. 40:36-61.

Gardner, F. P. and W. E. Loomis. 1953. Floral induction and development in orchardgrass. Pl. Physiol. 28:201-217.

Gary, Jack E., Jr. and C. Y. Ward. 1967. The influence of shading on the establishment of meyer zoysiagrass. Proc. Assoc. Sou. Agr'l. Workers. 64:70.

Gaskin, T. 1964. Growing turfgrass in the shade. Park Maintenance. 17(10):90-94.

Gates, D. M. 1965. Radiant energy, its receipt and disposal. Meterol. Monogr. 28:1-26.

Geiger, R. 1958. The modification of microclimate by vegetation and open and hilly country. Proc. Canteberra Symposium. pp. 255-258. UNESCO. Paris.

Geiger, R. 1965. The climate near the ground. Harvard University Press, Cambridge, Massachusetts.

Gilbert, William B. 1965. Winter injury to tifgreen. The Golf Course Reporter. 33:12-19.

Gill, W. J., W. R. Thompson, Jr., and C. Y. Ward. Species and methods for overseeding bermudagrass greens. The Golf Superintendent. Vol. 35:10-18.

Goss, R. L., Kenneth J. Morrison, Alvin G. Law, C. B. Harston, Ben F. Roche, David H. Brannon, M. R. Harris, and Charles J. Gould. 1962. Home Lawns. Washington State University Extension Bulletin 482. 16 pp.

Goss, Roy L. 1966. Turfgrass research in the Pacific northwest. Proceedings of Midwest Regional Turf Conference. March, 1966. pp. 9-13.

Goss, R. L., C. J. Gould, Otis Maloy, A. G. Law, and K. J. Morrison. 1967.

Recommendation for turfgrass management in Washington. Ext. Man. 2783, pp. 1-12.

Graham, J. H. and V. G. Sprague. 1953. The effects of controlled periods on high and low humidities on the development of purple leaf spot of orchardgrass. Phytopath. 43:642-643.

Greening, Gersham K. 1941. Supplemental climatic notes on Arizona. Agricultural Yearbook. Climate and Man. pp. 771-772.

Haagan-Smit, A. M., E. F. Darley, M. Zaitlin, H. Hull, and W. Noble. 1952. Investigation on injury to plants from air pollution in the Los Angeles area. Pl. Physiol. 27:18-34.

Hagan, Robert M. 1953. Know how to water. USGA Journal and Turf Management. Vol. 5:26-30.

Hagan, Robert M. 1955. Watering lawns and turf and otherwise caring for them. Yearbook of Agriculture, Water. 84th Congress, First Session, House Document No. 32, pp. 462-477.

Hagan, Robert M. 1956. Water management. The Golf Course Reporter. Vol. 24:5-17.

Hanson, A. A. and V. G. Sprague. 1953. Heading of perennial grasses under greenhouse conditions. Agron. J. 45:248-251.

Hanson, A. A. and F. V. Juska. 1961. Winter root activity in Kentucky bluegrass *(Poa pratensis* L.). Agron. J. 53:372-374.

Harlan, Jack. 1951. Anatomy of gene centers. Am. Naturalist 85:97-103.

Harrison, C. M. 1934. Responses of Kentucky bluegrass to variations in temperature, light, cutting and fertilizing. Pl. Physiol. Vol. 9:83-106.

Hesketh, J. D. 1963. Limitations to photosynthesis responsible for differences among species. Crop Sc. 3:493-496.

Hiesey, W. M. 1953. Growth and development of species and hybrids of Poa under controlled temperatures. Am. J. Bot. Vol. 40:205-221.

Hill, G. R., Jr. and M. D. Thomas. 1933. Influence of leaf destruction by sulfur dioxide and by clipping on yield of alfalfa. Pl. Physiol. 8:223-245.

Hitchcock, A. S. 1951. Manual of grasses of the United States. USDA Miscellaneous Publication 200.

Holyoke, Vaughn, and Roland A. Struchtemeyer. 1965. Lawns and their care. Univ. of Maine. Ext. Bul. 495. 15 pp.

Hunt, L. A., I. I. Impens, and E. R. Lemon. 1967. Preliminary wind tunnel studies of the photosynthesis and evapotranspiration of forage stands. Crop Sci. 7:575-578.

Juhren, Marcella, Wm. M. Hiesey, and F. W. Went. 1953. Germination and early growth of grasses in controlled conditions. Ecol. 34:288-300.

Julander, O. 1945. Drought resistance in range and pasture grasses. Pl. Physiol. 20:573-599.

Juska, Felix V. 1963. Shade tolerance of bentgrasses. Golf Course Reporter. 3:28-34.

Juska, F. V. and A. A. Hanson. 1965. Lawns. USDA Yearbook of Agriculture, pp. 228-231.

Keen, Ray A. and L. R. Quinlan. 1966. Lawns in Kansas. Agr'l. Exp. Sta. Circ. 32227. Revised. 30 pp.

Kendricks, J. B., Jr., J. T. Middleton, and E. F. Darley. 1953. Predisposing effects of air temperature and nitrogen supply upon injury to some herbaceous plants fumigated with peroxides derived from olefins. Phytopath. 43:588.

Kimball, H. H. 1928. Amount of solar radiation that reaches the surface of the earth, on the land and on the sea, and methods by which it is measured. Monthly Weather Review. 56:393-399.

Kimball, H. H. 1935. Intensity of solar radiation at the surface of the earth and its variation with latitude, altitude, season and time of the day. Monthly Weather Review. 63:1-4.

Kimball, M. H. and F. A. Brooks. 1959. Plant climates of California. Calif. Agriculture 13:7-11.

Kincer, J. B. 1941. Climate and weather data for the United States. Climate and Man. Yearbook of Agriculture. pp. 685-747.

Klebesadel, L. J., A. C. Wilton, R. L. Taylor, and J. J. Koranda. 1964. Fall growth behavior and winter survival of *Festuca rubra* and *Poa pratensis* in Alaska as influenced by latitude-of-adaptation. Crop. Sci. 4:340-341.

Koritz, H. G. and F. W. Went. 1953. The physiological action of smog on plants. I. Initial growth and transpiration studies. Pl. Physiol. 28:50-62.

Langham, D. G. 1941. Effect of light on growth habit of plants. Science 93:576-577.

Laude, H. M., J. E. Shrum and W. E. Biehler. 1952. The effects of high soil temperatures on the seedling emergence of perennial grasses. Agron. J. 44:110-112.

Laude, Horton M. 1964. Plant response to high temperatures. ASA Special Publication No. 5, Forage Plant Physiology & Soil Range Relationships. pp. 15-31.

Lemon, E. R. 1966. Energy conversion and water use efficiency in plants. Plant Environment and Efficient Water Use, ASA Monogr. pp. 28-39.

Lovvorn, R. L. 1945. The effect of defoliation, soil fertility, temperature and length of day on the growth of some perennial grasses. Jour. Am. Soc. of Agonomy 37:570-581.

McBee, G. C. and E. C. Holt. 1966. Shade tolerance studies on bermudagrass and other turfgrasses. Agron. Abstracts, p. 35.

McCalla, T. M. and F. L. Duley. 1946. Effect of crop residues on soil temperature. Agron. J. 38:75-89.

McCarver, Orville W. 1964. Lawns, new and old. Montana State University Extension Folder No. 79. p. 4.

McCloud, Darrell E. 1959. E-T Theory of water loss. Golf Course Reporter. 27:18-20.

McCune, W. E., K. R. Beerwinkle, and G. C. McBee. 1965. The effect of soil heating on winter growth and appearance of warm season turfgrasses. Texas Agr'l. Exp. Sta. Progress Rpt. 2360.

McDougall, Eric. 1925. The moisture belts of North America. Ecology 6:325-332.

McKee, W. H., Jr., A. J. Powell, Jr., R. B. Cooper and R. E. Blaser. 1965. Microclimate conditions found on highway slope facings as related to adaptation species. Hwy. Res. Record No. 93, Roadside Development, Hwy. Res. Board Publication 1309. pp. 38-43.

Madison, John H. 1964. Irrigation-systems and procedures. Calif. Turfgrass Culture, Vol. 14:1-4.

Madison, J. H. 1962. Turfgrass Ecology: Effects of mowing, irrigation, and nitrogen treatment of *Agrostris palustris* Huds., 'Seaside', and *Agrostris tenuis* Stibth., 'Highland' on population, yield, rooting and cover. Agron. J. 54:407-412.

Madison, John H. and Robert M. Hagan. 1952. Extraction of soil moisture by Merion bluegrass (*Poa pratensis* L. Merion) turf, as affected by irrigation frequency, mowing height and other cultural operations. Agron. J. 54:157-160.

Martin, Dean. 1967. Lawns for South Dakota. S. D. State Univ. Ext. Fact Sheet 354. pp. 2.

Middleton, John T., J. B. Kendrick, Jr., and H. W. Schwalm. 1950. Smog in the south coastal area of California. Calif. Agr. 11:7-10.

Miller, D. J. 1960. Temperature effect on the rate of apparent photosynthesis of seaside bent and bermudagrass. Proc. Am. Soc. of Hort. Sc. 75:700-703.

Monteith, John, Jr. 1942. Turf for air fields and other defense projects. Turf Culture. 2:193-239.

Moss, Dale N. 1962. The limiting carbon dioxide concentration for photosynthesis. Nature 193:587.

Moss, Dale N. 1964. Aspects of microclimatology important in forage plant physiology. ASA Special Publication No. 5. Forage Plant Physiology and Soil Range Relationships. pp. 1-14.

Musser, Burton H. 1962. Turf Management. McGraw-Hill Co., New York.

Naylor, Aubrey W. 1939. Effects of temperature, calcium and arsenous acid on seedlings of *Poa pratensis*. Botanical Gazette 101:366-379.

Nuttonson, M. Y. 1947-1950. Ecological crop geography of the ukraine and other areas. Inter. Agro. Clim. Series. Studies 1-13. Am. Inst. Crop. Ecol. Series, Washington, D. C.

Peters, D. B. and W. J. Roberts. 1963. Use of octa-hexadecanol as a transpiration suppressant. Agron. J. 55:79.

Peterson, M. L. and W. E. Loomis. 1949. Effects of photoperiod and temperature on growth and flowering of Kentucky bluegrass. Pl. Physiol. 24:31-43.

Pruitt, W. O. 1964. Evapotranspiration—A guide to irrigation. Calif. Turfgrass Culture. 14:27-32.

Raschke, K. 1960. Heat transfer between the plant and the environment. Annual Rev. Plant Physiol. 11:111-126.

Reed, Wesley W. 1941. The climates of the world. Climate and Man. Yearbook of Agriculture, pp. 672-684.

Reid, M. E. 1933. Effect of shade on the growth of velvet bent and metropolitan creeping bent. Bul. USGA Greens Sect. 13:131-135.

Renne, Roland. 1965-1966. A proper perspective of water in agriculture. ASA Monogr. Plant Environment and Efficient Water Use. Chapter 2:20-26.

Richards, F. J., R. M. Hagan, and T. M. McCalla. 1952. Soil temperature and plant growth. *In* Soil physical conditions and plant growth, pp. 303-480. New York, Academic Press.

Roberts, E. C. and E. J. Bredakis. 1960. Turfgrass root development. Golf Course Reporter. 28:12-24.

Rossby, C. G. 1941. The scientific basis of modern meterology. Yearbook of Agriculture. Climate and Man. pp. 599-655.

Savage, David A. 1933. Buffalograss for fairways in the plains states. The Bulletin of the USGA Greens Section 13:144-149.

Schmidt, R. E. 1962. Overseeding winter greens in Virginia. Golf Course Reporter Vol. 30:1-4.

Schmidt, R. E. and R. E. Blaser. 1967. Effect of temperature, light and nitrogen on the growth and metabolism of Cohansey bentgrass (*Agrostis palustris* Huds.). Crop Sc. 7:447-451.

Shaw, R. H. and D. R. Laing. 1966. Moisture stress and plant response. ASA Monogr. Plant Environment and Efficient Water Use. pp. 73-82.

Shirley, H. L. 1945. Light as an ecological factor and its measurement. Botanical Review, 11:49-7-532.

Slayter, R. O., and J. F. Bierhuizen. 1964. The Effect of seasonal foliar sprays on transpiration and water use efficiency of cotton plants. Agr'l. Meterology. 1:42-53.

Slayter, R. O., and J. F. Bierhuizen. 1965. The influence of several transpiration suppressants on transpiration, photosynthesis, and water use efficiency of cotton leaves. Australian J. Biol. Sci. 17:131-146.

Smith, Dale. 1964. Freezing injury of forage plants. ASA Special Publication No. 5, Forage P. Phys. & Soil Range Relationships. pp. 32-56.

Sprague, Malcolm. 1941. Climate of California. Climate and Man. 1941. Yearbook of Agriculture. pp. 783-797.

Sprague, M. A. and L. F. Graber. 1943. Ice sheet injury to alfalfa. Jour. Amer. Soc. of Agronomy, 35:881-894.

Sprague, M. A. 1955. The influence of rate of cooling and winter cover on the winter survival of ladino clover and alfalfa. Pl. Physiol. 30:447-451.

Sprague, V. G. 1943. The effects of temperature and daylight on seedling emergence and early growth of several pasture species. Soil. Sci. Soc. of Am. Proc. 8:287-294.

Sprague, V. G., H. Neuberger, W. H. Orgell, and A. V. Dodd. 1954. Air temperature distribution in the microclimate layer. Agron. J. 46:105-108.

Sprague, V. G. 1955. Distribution of atmospheric moisture in the microclimate above a grass sod. Agron. J. 47:551-555.

Sprague, V. G. 1959. Forage climates in the northeast. Regional Publication 43, Pa. Agr'l. Exp. Sta. Bul. 653.

Sprague, V. G. and Darrell E. McCloud. 1962. Climatic factors in forage production. Chapter 36. Forages. Iowa State Univ. Press. pp. 359-367.

Stebbins, G. L. 1950. Variation and evolution in plants. Columbia University Press, New York.

Stoddard, L. A. and Arthur D. Smith. 1943. Range Management. Third Edition. McGraw-Hill Book Co., Inc., New York.

Stuckey, I. H. 1941. Seasonal growth of grass roots. Am. Jour. of Botany, 28:486-491.

Stuckey, I. H. 1942. Influence of soil temperature on the development of colonial bentgrass. Pl. Physiol. 17:116-122.

Sturkie, D. G. and H. S. Fisher. 1950. The planting and maintenance of lawns. Ala. Agr'l. Exp. Sta. Cir. # 85, Revised

Sullivan, J. T. and V. G. Sprague. 1949. The effect of temperature on the growth and composition of the stubble and roots of perennial ryegrass. Pl. Physiol. 24:706-719.

Tabor, P. 1950. Some observations of Bahiagrass for soil conservation in the southeastern United States. Agron. J. Vol. 42:362-364.

Taylor, O. C., E. A. Cardiff, J. D. Mersereau, and J. T. Middleton. 1957. Smog reduces seedling growth. Calif. Agric., Vol. 11:9-12.

Thompson, W. R., Jr. 1966. Turfgrass varieties: Part two, South. Turf-Grass Times, Vol. 1, No. 4. pp. 18-21.

Thornthwaite, C. W. 1931. The climates of North America according to a new classification. The Geographical Rev., Vol. 21:633-655.

Thornthwaite, C. W. 1941. Climate and settlement in the great plains. Climate and Man. USDA Yearbook of Agriculture. pp. 177-187.

Thornthwaite, C. W. 1953. Climatology. John Hopkins Univ. Seabrook Laboratory of Climatology.

Thornthwaite, C. W. and J. R. Mather. 1955. The water balance. Publ. in Climate, Vol. 8, No. 1. Drexel Inst. of Technology. Centerton, N. J.

Trew, E. M. 1960. Home Lawns. Texas Agr'l. Extension Bulletin 203. 14 pp.

Trewartha, Glenn T. 1941. Climate and settlement of the sub-humid land. USDA Yearbook of Agriculture. Climate and Man. 167-176.

Trewartha, Glenn T. 1954. An Introduction to Climate. McGraw-Hill, New York.

Van Bavel, C. H. M. 1959. Drought and water surplus in agricultural soils of the lower Mississippi valley area. USDA Technical Bulletin 1209.

Van Bavel, C. H. M. and D. G. Harris. 1962. Evapotranspiration rates from bermudagrass and corn at Raleigh, North Carolina. Agron. J. 54:319-322.

Van Bavel, C. H. M. 1966. Estimating soil moixture conditions and time for irrigation with the evapotranspiration method. USDA—ARS—Publ. 41-11.

Vavilov, N. I. 1951. The origin, variation, immunity and breeding of cultivated plants. Ronald Press, New York.

Wadleigh, C. H., W. A. Raney and D. M. Herschfield. 1966. The moisture problem. Plant Environment and Efficient Water Use, A Monogr. Am. Soc. Agronomy, pp. 1-17.

Waggoner, P. E., D. N. Moss, and J. D. Hesketh. 1963. Radiation in the plant environment and photosynthesis. Agron. J. 55:36-39. U.S. Weather Bureau Climatological Data, National Summary. 1966. Vol. 17:1-133.

Waggoner, P. E. and J. D. Hewlett. 1965. Test of a transpiration inhibitor on a forested water shed. Water Resources Research, Vol. 1:391-396.

Waggoner, Paul E. 1966. Decreasing transpiration in the effect upon growth. In ASA Mongr. Plant Environment and Efficient Water Use. Chapter 4:49-68.

Wallace, R. H. and H. H. Clum. 1938. Leaf Temperatures. Am. Jour. Bot., Vol. 25:83-97.

Wang, J. Y. 1963. Agricultural Meterology, Pacemaker Press, Milwaukee, 693 pp.

Ward, C. Y. 1967. Turf research in Mississippi. Proceedings Southern Turf and maintaining roadside turf in the southeast. Proc. Southeastern Highway Officials. pp. 20-23.

Ward, C. Y. 1967. Tuf research in Mississippi. Proceedings Southern Turf Conference, February 1967.

Watkins, J. M., G. W. Conrey, and M. W. Evans. 1940. The distribution of Canada bluegrass and Kentucky bluegrasses as related to some ecological factors. Jour. Am. Soc. of Agronomy. 32:726-728.

Watson, D. J. 1947. Comparative physiological studies on the growth of field crops. I. Variation in net assimilation rate and leaf area between species and varieties, and within and between years. Ann. Bot. (London) 11:41-76.

Went, F. W. 1950. The response of plants to climate. Science. 112:489-494.

Went, F. W. 1955. Fog mists, dew and other sources of water. Yearbook of Agriculture. Water. pp. 103-109.

Whitton, Gilbert M. 1968. Bahiagrass. Florida Turf, Vol. 1, No. 2: 1-6.

Wilsie, Carroll P. 1962. Crop adaptation and distribution. W. H. Freeman and Co., San Francisco, California.

Wise, L. N. 1961. The Lawn Book. W. R. Thompson Company. State College, Mississippi.

Wolfe, J. N., R. T. Warcham and H. T. Scofield. 1949. Microclimates and macroclimates of Neotoma, a small valley in central Ohio. Bulletin of Ohio Biological Survey. 8:1-267.

Woodsbury, A. M. 1954. Principles of Ecology. Blakiston Co., New York.

Youngner, Victor B. 1959. Growth of U-3 bermudagrass under various day and night temperatures and light intensities. Agron. J. Vol. 51:557-559.

Youngner, Victor B. 1962. Which is the best turfgrass? Calif. Turfgrass Culture, 12:30-31.

Youngner, V. B., J. H. Madison, M. H. Kimball, and W. B. Davis. 1962. Climatic zones for turfgrass in California. Calif. Turfgrass Culture, 12:25-27.

Youngner, Victor B. 1963. Growing turf in shaded areas. Western Landscape News. May, 1963. pp. 4-15.

Youngner, V. B. 1966. Santa Ana, a new turf bermuda for California. Calif. Turfgrass Culture, Vol. 16:23-24.

Youngner, V. B. 1967. Turfgrass adaptation in California. Calif. Turfgrass Culture, 17:13-14.

4 Soil And Soil Related Problems

Donald V. Waddington

The Pennsylvania State University
University Park, Pennsylvania

I. Introduction

"For to all Americans, wherever they live, soil is a basic treasure. Soils produce good yields and keep on doing so if they are well managed. The management of soil is among the oldest of arts, but none is changing more rapidly than it. We know more about taking care of soil than our fathers and grandfathers did. There is much more that we should know." Ezra Taft Benson (1957).

Plant growth is influenced by the following environmental factors: light, mechanical support, heat, air, water, and nutrients (Buckman and Brady, 1960). All of these factors except light are supplied in some degree by the soil. Although it plays an important role in supporting turfgrass growth, soil is often taken for granted in many turfgrass programs. Observations and thoughts may be directed to the grass itself without consideration of the conditions in the soil beneath. The wear and tear of heavy traffic on the grass is easily noticed, but the effects on the soil are not so easily seen. Disease injury and weeds are easily detected; the soil conditions contributing to these problems are not. Fertilizer and water may be applied to turf areas without regard for soil properties which influence the efficiency of these applications. Soils are the result of complex soil forming processes and many complex reactions occur in the soil. The complexity associated with soils should not be a deterrent, but instead an incentive, for more study in order to better understand the importance of soil and soil management in turfgrass production.

There are two branches or concepts associated with soil science. Pedology is the branch which deals with the soil as a natural body and places emphasis on the origin, formation, and distribution of soils. Edaphology considers the soil from the standpoint of higher plants and includes phases of soil science such as soil physics, soil chemistry, soil microbiology, and soil fertility as they relate to soil productivity and plant growth. Joffe (1949), a pedologist, has defined soil as "a natural body of mineral and organic constituents, differentiated into horizons, of variable depth, which differs from the material below in morphology, physical makeup, chemical properties and composition, and biological properties." An edaphological definition by Buckman and Brady (1960) defines soil "as a natural body, synthesized in profile form from a variable mixture of broken and weathered minerals and decaying organic matter, which covers the earth in a thin layer and which supplies, when containing the proper amounts of air and water, mechanical support and, in part, sustenance for plants."

Black (1960) lists the following as the functions of soil in supporting plant life: (1) supplying the necessary mineral nutrients, water, and oxygen and (2) providing an environment for the development of the root system which anchors the plant and absorbs the nutrients and water.

Considerable turfgrass is grown on "made" land, which includes areas filled artificially with earth or trash or both. Made land and other heavily modified areas are not natural bodies and therefore are not true soils according to the definitions given in the preceding paragraph. Artificial soil, modified soil, greenhouse soil, and soil material are terms used to describe these non-soil media which are used for the purpose of supporting plant life. However, the term soil is commonly applied to these other media when one considers their properties, management, or function.

The main components of soils are mineral matter, organic matter, air, and water. The solid materials form the framework of the soil, and air and water occupy the pores within the framework. The balance between these components is important in determining the productivity of a soil. This balance is not only influenced by the kind of soil, but also by soil management practices.

All soils have physical, chemical, and biological properties. Physical properties influence air and water relationships, soil temperature, and the anchorage of plants. Chemical properties affect the amount and availability of plant nutrients in the soil. Biological properties relate to organic matter and to the activities of organisms in the soil. These properties and their relationships to each other determine to a large extent the use and management of soils.

Many reference and text books concerned with soils are available. Some are used as text books in introductory soils courses (Buckman and Brady, 1960; Thompson, 1957; Millar, Turk, and Foth, 1965). Others deal in specific areas such as soil physics (Baver, 1956), soil chemistry (Bear, 1964), soil genesis and classification (Joffe, 1949), soil microbiology (Alexander, 1961), soil survey (Soil Survey Staff, 1951), soil fertility (Tisdale and Nelson, 1966), soil formation (Jenny, 1941), and soil-plant relationships (Russell, 1961; Black, 1957). Current research is published in scientific journals such as the *Soil Science Society of America Proceedings, Agronomy Journal, Soil Science, Journal of Soil Science,* and *Canadian Journal of Soil Science.* Reviews on specific subjects can be found in *Advances in Agronomy* and in *Agronomy, A Monograph Series,* published by the American Society of Agronomy. Reference is made to various publications in the following sections. In some cases, information which is considered "common knowledge" in the soils profession is referenced to give the reader a source of additional information on that particular subject.

II. Soil Formation

Soil formation refers to the development of a soil from an unconsolidated mass of material called parent material. Parent materials are classified according to their geologic origin. They include (1) residual materials such as parent rock, which has been weathered in place, and organic deposits and (2) transported materials which have been moved from their place of origin by the forces of water, wind, ice, or gravity.

A. Factors Influencing Soil Formation

The five major factors influencing soil formation are climate, organisms, topography, parent material, and time. These factors have been discussed thoroughly by Jenny (1941), and some of their effects are listed in the following paragraphs.

Water and temperature are the most important components of the climate factor. Properties of soils formed in arid and humid climates are quite different. Organic matter and nitrogen contents generally increase with increasing rainfall. Products of weathering are leached by percolating water in humid areas, whereas they are leached less from soils in arid regions and these soils contain higher amounts of plant nutrients, with the exception of nitrogen. Clay content, cation exchange capacity, and acidity are soil properties which generally increase with increasing rainfall. Increased temperature favors more rapid and deeper weathering. Clay formation increases and organic matter and nitrogen contents decrease with an increase in temperature. Rainfall and temperature influence soil aggregation by affecting the bases, clay, and organic matter present in the soil.

The organic or biotic factor includes the activities of microbes, vegetation, animals, and man. The properties of organic matter added to the soil vary according to the type of vegetation. Organic matter that is rich in nutrients decays more rapidly and completely than organic matter that is lower in nutrients. Leaf residues of heavy feeders such as grasses return more bases to the soil surface than do the leaves of trees. Man influences soil properties with his irrigation, cultivation, and fertilization practices and by changing the vegetation.

Topography or relief refers to the contours of the land surface. Various conditions caused by topographical features cause differences in soil formation. Slopes may receive less water due to runoff, while depressions receive more. Differences in depth to the water table also cause moisture differences. Relief influences soil depth because soil is removed from slopes by erosion and deposited in depressions. Temperature differences occur due to different exposures to the sun. Weathering proceeds at a faster rate on the warmer southern exposures.

The fineness or coarseness of parent material influences the movement of water during soil formation. Deeper soils are associated with the coarser materials. The resistance of the parent material to weathering influences soil texture. Parent material also has an effect on the nature of the elements released during weathering, the chemical composition of the soil, and soil fertility.

Time is required for the development of soil properties and the formation of horizons, which in turn determine the degree of maturity or age of a soil. A soil is considered mature when the process of soil formation has reached an equilibrium state. The time required for a soil to become mature is dependent on the various soil forming factors. Not all soils develop at the same rate.

B. Profile Development

Layers of soil having distinct properties develop during soil formation. These layers are called horizons. A vertical section through the various horizons is called a soil profile. The characteristics of a profile and its horizons are used as a basis for soil classification. Different profiles typify the different kinds of soils which develop under the influences of the soil forming factors. The soil horizons and their characteristics result from four fundamental processes: (1) accumulation of organic matter, (2) eluviation, (3) illuviation, and (4) differentiation within each horizon (Joffe, 1949). Soils in which these processes act in a similar manner are grouped into one of ten soil orders (Soil Survey Staff, 1960).

Horizons within a profile which have developed due to soil forming processes are designated by the capital letter symbols O, A, and B (Soil Survey Staff, 1962). The O horizons are the organic horizons formed on the surface of mineral soils. Deposition of plant residues gives rise to the formation of O horizons. Organic matter may be found in various stages of decomposition. The characteristics of organic horizons are largely dependent on climate and type of vegetation. Rapid decay is favored by warm, moist conditions. Decay is slower under cooler conditions and under extremely wet, anaerobic conditions.

The A horizon, or eluvial horizon, is formed below the O horizon. The A horizon is characterized by the removal of various constituents by percolating water. Organic acids and elements released during organic matter decomposition move downward into this horizon and react with the rock and mineral matter. Weathering of the parent material releases elements which are leached from this horizon. The finer soil particles are also carried to the underlying horizons.

The eluviated constituents from the A horizon accumulate in the illuvial or B horizon. Clay, iron and aluminum ions, and humus accumulate alone or in combination.

Differentiation also occurs within the O, A, and B horizons, which may be subdivided into layers which are indicated by placing an arabic number after the letter. Thus an organic horizon consisting of essentially unaltered vegetative matter with the original form visible to the eye is called the O1 horizon, whereas an O2 designation is used if the original form of organic matter cannot be recognized with the naked eye. Other examples of subdivisions are shown in Figure 1, which shows a hypothetical soil profile.

III. Soil Survey and Maps

A soil survey involves the following operations: (1) determination of important soil characteristics, (2) classification of soils according to type and other classification units, (3) determination of soil boundaries and

Horizon	Description
01	Organic horizon of undecomposed organic matter.
02	Organic horizon of partially decomposed organic matter. (01 and 02 usually absent on prairie influenced soils and disturbed soils.)
Ap A1	Surface mineral horizon which has an accumulation of well-decomposed organic matter which coats the mineral particles and darkens the soil mass. With plowing or other disturbance A1 and A2 or A3 are mixed. The notation Ap is used in this case.
A2	Subsurface horizon which has lost organic matter, clay, iron or aluminum through eluviation with concentration of resistant sand and silt-sized particles. Platy structure common.
AB A3	Transitional to the B horizon, or C horizon if B is not present, but more like the A than the B or C. If A3 and B1 are present but cannot be separated, AB horizon is designated.
B1	Transitional to the A, but more like the B horizon.
B2	Mineral horizon characterized by one or more of the following: 1. Illuvial concentration of clay, iron, aluminum or organic matter. 2. Residual concentration of iron and aluminum oxides or silicate clay. 3. Coatings of iron and aluminum oxides which give darker, stronger or redder colors. 4. Alteration of parent material through physical and chemical means with formation of silicate clay minerals, liberation of oxides and formation of granular, blocky or prismatic structure.
B3	Transitional to C horizon, but more like the B horizon.
Cg, Cca, Ccs, C	Mineral horizon, other than bedrock, which may or may not be similar to presumed parent material. Has been little affected by soil-forming processes but may be otherwise weathered. Roman numeral prefixes are used to designate C horizons unlike presumed parent material as IIC, IIIC, etc. This designation is also used with other horizons. Cg* = C horizon with intense gleying or reduction of iron compounds. Cca* = C horizon with accumulation of carbonates such as calcium carbonate. Ccs* = C horizon with accumulation of calcium sulfate. * g, ca, cs designations also may be used in other mineral horizons.
R	Underlying consolidated bedrock. If unlike presumed parent material, Roman numeral prefix is used as IIR.

Figure 1. Hypothetical soil profile showing principal horizons (Oschwald et al., 1965).

the plotting of boundaries on maps, and (4) correlation and prediction of the adaptability of soil for various uses (Soil Survey Staff, 1951). Most of the soil surveys conducted in the U. S. are made cooperatively by the Soil Conservation Service of the U. S. Department of Agriculture and the State Agricultural Experiment Stations. Published reports and maps may be obtained from either of these agencies.

A. Soil Series, Type, and Phase

A soil series is a group of soils which have developed from a particular type of parent material and which have horizons of similar arrangement and characteristics, except for the texture of the surface soil (Soil Survey Staff, 1951). A series is usually named after a place in the area where the soil was first described. Examples of soil series are Hagerstown, Houston, and Norfolk.

The texture of the surface soil is used as a basis for subdividing soil series into soil types. The soil type consists of a series name and the name of the textural class of the surface soil. Examples of textural classes are sandy loam, clay, and silt loam. Examples of soil types are Hagerstown clay loam, Houston clay, and Norfolk sandy loam.

The soil phase is used to show variations within soil types. Phase descriptions indicate important features such as slope, erosion, stoniness, and depth. Examples of soil descriptions using phase are Williams stony loam and Cecil clay loam, eroded phase.

The basic unit for soil mapping is the soil type, which is subdivided into phases when necessary to clearly describe the soil. Soil boundaries are placed on aerial photographs by a soil surveyor. The location and plotting of soil boundaries involves considerable field study.

B. Soil Description

A second part of field study in a soil survey is the description of the mapping units. Such a description includes the following information: (1) kind of land form, relief, and drainage; (2) description of parent material; (3) description of the soil profile, including depth, thickness, color, texture, structure, porosity, reaction, presence of organic matter and roots, and chemical and mineralogical composition for each horizon; (4) presence of stones; (5) amount of erosion; (6) principal vegetation; and (7) the land use (Soil Survey Staff, 1951). An example of a soil description follows.

Detailed Description of the Chester Series (Smith, 1967)

The Chester series includes deep, well-drained soils that developed in material weathered from schist and gneiss. These soils are nearly level or undulating. They occur in small areas on upland summits in the southeastern part of the county.

The Chester soils formed in similar material and are adjacent to the less deep, well-drained Manor soils, the moderately deep Glenelg soils, and the deep, moderately well drained or somewhat poorly drained Glenville soils. They are finer textured than the Edgemont and Lansdale soils. The Chester soils are more acid below a depth of 3 feet and contain more mica than the Duffield soils.

Typical profile of Chester silt loam, 3 to 8% slopes, moderately eroded, in cultivated field ½ mile west of Huntingdon Valley in Abington Township:

Ap—0 to 8 inches, dark-brown (10YR 4/3) silt loam containing 2 to 5% fragments of quartz and gneiss; weak, thin, platy structure readily breaking to moderate, fine, granular structure; very friable when moist, nonsticky and nonplastic when wet; strongly acid (pH 5.2); abrupt, wavy boundary. 7 to 10 inches thick.

A3—8 to 10 inches, dark yellowish-brown (10YR 4/4) silt loam containing as much as 4% coarse fragments; weak, very fine, subangular blocky and fine granular structure; friable when moist, slightly sticky and slightly plastic when wet; strongly acid (pH 5.4); clear, wavy boundary. 0 to 3 inches thick.

B1—10 to 16 inches, yellowish-brown (10YR 5/4) to brown (7.5YR 5/4) fine silt loam containing up to 10% small fragments of quartz and gneiss; weak, fine angular and subangular blocky structure but tends toward weak, medium, platy structure; friable when moist, slightly sticky and slightly plastic when wet; medium acid (pH 5.6), clear, wavy boundary. 5 to 8 inches thick.

B21t-16 to 25 inches, dark yellowish-brown (10YR 4/4) fine silt loam or silty clay loam; 2 to 5% small fragments of quartz and gneiss; moderate, medium and fine, angular and subangular blocky structure; has common thin clay films on the surfaces of the peds and in the pores; friable when moist, slightly sticky and slightly plastic when wet; medium acid (pH 5.6); clear, wavy boundary. 8 to 11 inches thick.

B22t-25 to 32 inches, yellowish-brown (10YR 5/6 to 10YR 5/4) silt loam containing 5 to 10% small fragments of quartz and gneiss; moderate, fine, subangular blocky structure; common thin clay films on the surfaces of the peds and in the pores; friable to slightly firm when moist and in place, slightly sticky and slightly plastic when wet; medium acid (pH 5.6); clear, wavy, boundary. 5 to 9 inches thick.

B3—32 to 38 inches, brown (10YR 4/3) gritty silt loam or loam containing 10% coarse fragments; weak, fine subangular blocky structure, slightly firm when moist and in place, slightly sticky and nonplastic when wet; medium acid (pH 5.6); clear, wavy boundary. 5 to 9 inches thick.

C1—38 to 46 inches, brown (10YR 4/3) gritty loam containing 10 to 15% coarse fragments; weak, thick, platy structure breaking to weak, medium, subangular blocky structure; firm when moist and in place, nonsticky and nonplastic when wet; medium acid (pH 5.6); clear, wavy boundary. 6 to 10 inches thick.

C2—46 to 74 inches, dark grayish-brown (10YR 4/2), yellowish-brown (10YR 5/4), and light yellowish-brown (10YR 6/4) sandy loam and gravelly loam; massive, but tends toward weak, thick, platy structure; firm when moist and in place, nonsticky and nonplastic when wet; very strongly acid (pH 5.0); abrupt, broken boundary. 24 to 32 inches.

R—74 to 85 inches; partly weathered gneiss.

The surface layer ranges from dark brown (10YR 3/3 or 7.5YR 4/2) to dark grayish brown (10YR 4/2) in color. The B horizons range from yellowish brown (10YR 5/4) to strong brown (7.5YR 5/6) in color and from silt loam or loam to silty clay loam in texture. The texture of the C horizons ranges from sandy loam or gritty loam to silt loam. In many places the B3 horizon and the C horizons contain mica. In most places coarse fragments of schist, gneiss, or quartzite make up less than 10% of the solum, but the amount increases to as much as 30 to 40% in some places in the C horizons. The thickness of the solum ranges from 34 to 48 inches, and depth to bedrock ranges from 5 to 12 feet.

The notations, such as 10YR 4/3, following soil color are used to quantitatively describe soil color. The suffix t used in the B2 horizons indicates accumulations of translocated silicate clays.

C. Value of Survey Reports and Maps

Interpretation of soil survey information is not directed solely toward agricultural use. This information is also used in urban and suburban planning, highway planning and construction, and recreation area planning. Bauer (1966) has discussed a regional planning program used in southeastern Wisconsin. This program included the use of soil survey data to determine soil capabilities and limitations for wildlife, recreational, and engineering uses as well as for agricultural use. Soil types have been rated according to their suitability for recreational areas such as playgrounds, parks, picnic areas, bridle paths, hiking trails, camp sites, and golf courses.

Montgomery and Edminster (1966) have reported on the use of soil surveys in planning recreation areas. They listed the following factors which may limit the use of soils for intensive-use play areas: wetness, flooding, permeability, slope, surface soil texture, depth to bedrock, stoniness, rockiness, and coarse fragments. Information concerning these factors is available in soil survey reports.

Soils can be divided into three groups according to their limitations for recreational use (Montgomery and Edminster, 1966). Limitations are classified as none to slight in soils having no limitations or ones that are easily overcome. A classification of moderate limitations indicates poorer suitability, but these limitations can be overcome by good planning, design, and management practices. A severe limitation rating indicates that a soil is not suitable for a particular use unless major reclamation work is performed. Soil limitations for intensive use play areas are shown in Table 1.

Soil survey information can be of great value in the planning stages of parks and recreation facilities. Landscape architects, golf course architects, and others having the responsibility of site selection or design should use this information when it is available. Besides indicating the suitability of the soil for growing grass, the report will supply other useful information. Depth of the soil is important when large quantities must be moved to build the desired contours. The suitability of the area for construction of ponds, roadways, and buildings should be considered. The presence of sand, gravel, or peat deposits may influence site selection. Knowledge of the different soil types on a large site should be an aid in selecting a soil which needs a minimum of modification for use on intensively used turf areas. Many important features of a site, which are not obvious as one looks at the surface, are included in the soil survey. Perhaps many of the maintenance problems that are "built in" at the time of construction could be eliminated if survey reports and maps were studied prior to construction.

Soil survey data can also be used in the diagnosis of some soil problems on existing turfgrass areas. However, many of the soil problems have been created by man in his handling of soil. Puddled and compacted conditions caused by heavy equipment operating on wet soil are not described in the soil survey. Neither are shallow soil layers placed over old building foundations, driveways, roadways, and sand

Table 1. Soil limitations for intensive use play areas. (Montgomery & Edminster, 1966)

Soil items affecting use	Degree of soil limitation		
	None to slight	Moderate	Severe
Wetness	Well and moderately well drained soils with no ponding or seepage	Well and moderately well drained soils subject to occasional ponding or seepage of short duration. Somewhat poorly drained soils.	Somewhat poorly drained, subject to ponding. Poorly and very poorly drained soils. Too wet for use for periods of 1 to 5 weeks during season.
Flooding	None during season of use	Subject to occasional flooding. Not more than once in 3 years	Subject to more than occasional flooding during season of use
Permeability*	Rapid, moderately rapid and moderate (.8 - 10 in./hr)	Moderately slow (0.20 to 0.80 in/hr)	Slow and very slow (less than 0.2 in/hr)
Slope	0-2%	2-8%	8% +
Surface soil texture	Sandy loam, fine sandy loam, very fine sandy loam, loam and loamy sand with textural B horizon	Clay loam, sandy clay loam, silty clay, silt loam, loamy sand, and sand.	Sandy clay, silty clay, clay, organic soils, and sand and loamy sand subject to blowing.
Depth to hard bedrock	Over 3 feet	2 to 3 feet†	Less than 2 feet
Stoniness‡	Class 0: No stones or too few to interfer with tillage	Classes 1 and 2: Sufficient stones to interfere with tillage. Intertilled crops may or may not be practicable. Soil can be worked for hay crops and improved pasture.	Classes 3, 4, and 5: Sufficient stones to make use of machinery impracticable
Rockiness‡	Class 0: No bedrock exposures or too few to interfere with tillage	Class 1: Sufficient bedrock exposures to interfere with tillage, but not to make intertilled crops impracticable	Class 2, 3, 4, and 5: Sufficient bedrock exposures to make tillage of intertilled crops impracticable in class 2, and increased bedrock exposure as in classes 3, 4, and 5.
Coarse fragments‡ (2mm-10 in)	Free of coarse fragments	Up to 15% coarse fragments	15% +

* In arid regions soils may be rated one class better. † These soils have severe limitations if slope is greater than 2%. ‡ As per definitions in Soil Survey Manual, pp. 217-221.

traps. These areas which have been largely disturbed by man are usually classified as "made" land.

IV. Soil Physical Properties

Soil physical properties are important in determining the productivity of a soil. They influence water, air, and the temperature relationships as well as soil chemical and microbiological properties.

A. Soil Texture

Soil mineral particles less than 2 mm in diameter are divided according to size into soil separates. Each separate includes particles within certain size limits. Seven separates are recognized in the U.S., whereas only four are recognized by the International Society of Soil Science. The names and size limits for these two systems are shown in Table 2. Soil texture refers to the size of soil particles, and the textural class of a soil is dependent on the proportion of sand, silt, and clay.

The amounts of sand, silt, and clay in a soil are determined by a particle size analysis. The sands are separated by sieving, and smaller particles are determined by methods which are based on the different settling velocities of particles suspended in water (Baver, 1956). Coarse particles settle faster than finer particles, and after a predetermined

Table 2. Soil separate names and size limits.

U.S. Department of Agriculture		Intern. Soc. Soil Science	
Separate	Diameter range, mm	Separate	Diameter range, mm
Very coarse sand*	2.0 - 1.0	Coarse sand	2.0 - 0.2
Coarse sand	1.0 - 0.5	Fine sand	0.2 - 0.02
Medium sand	0.5 - 0.25	Silt	0.02 - 0.002
Fine sand	0.25 - 0.10	Clay	less than 0.002
Very fine sand	0.10 - 0.05		
Silt	0.05 - 0.002		
Clay	less than 0.002		

* Prior to 1947 this separate was called fine gravel. Now fine gravel includes particles between 2.0 and about 12.5 mm in diameter.

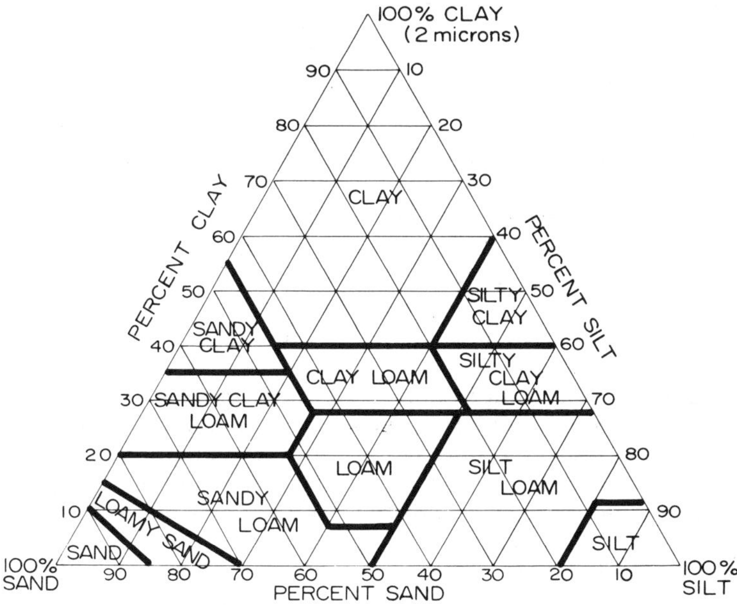

Figure 2. Textural triangle showing the percentages of sand, silt, and clay in the soil classes (Soil Survey Staff, 1951).

settling time the density of the suspension is measured to determine the amount of particles of a given size which are still in suspension. The density of the suspension may be determined by pipetting a sample from the suspension or by using a special hydrometer which is calibrated to give the weight of soil in suspension. Procedures for particle size analyses have been presented by Kilmer and Alexander (1949), Bouyoucos (1962), and Day (1965). After the amounts of sand, silt, and clay are known, the textural class can be determined using the textural triangle shown in Figure 2. Those classes containing the term "sand" in the name can be further divided when one sand separate predominates (Soil Survey Staff, 1951). Examples of such designations are very fine sandy loam and loamy coarse sand.

An important consideration concerning soil texture is the amount of surface area associated with the various soil separates. A given weight of .002-mm clay has 50 times more surface area than the same weight of very fine sand, and 10 times more than silt (Baver, 1956). Many important physical and chemical reactions are influenced by surface area. Clay, having the greatest surface area, is an important binding

Table 3. Average sand, silt, and clay contents and moisture retention values for eleven textural classes. (Peterson et al., 1968)

Textural class	Soil separate			Moisture content at		Available moisture
	Sand	Silt	Clay	1/3 atm	15 atm	
	—— % by weight ——			—— % by volume ——		
Sand	92.5	5.4	2.1	6.8	2.8	4.0
Loamy sand	80.5	15.4	4.1	11.3	3.8	7.5
Sandy loam	61.1	28.0	10.9	22.0	8.9	13.1
Loam	40.0	41.2	18.8	28.0	14.6	13.4
Silt loam	19.6	61.3	19.1	32.3	14.4	17.9
Silt	3.4	89.3	7.3	30.8	9.7	21.1
Sandy clay loam	57.1	19.6	23.3	27.2	16.8	10.4
Clay loam	26.8	41.9	31.3	32.7	21.2	11.5
Silty clay loam	11.3	56.5	32.2	35.2	20.7	14.5
Silty clay	6.5	47.3	46.2	38.9	26.8	12.1
Clay	10.2	31.0	58.8	40.2	29.2	11.0

agent acting in soil aggregation processes. It is also the site of most soil chemical reactions such as those involving absorption and exchange of plant nutrients. Sand promotes good drainage and aeration. Silt is intermediate in size, thus coarse silt particles act similar to sand and the finer silt may contribute somewhat to the chemical activity of the soil. The pore sizes associated with silt are such that they hold much of the available water in the soil. Sand contributes little to the water holding capacity and much of the water associated with clay is not available. The relationship between soil texture and available moisture is shown in Table 3. Note the high amounts of unavailable water held by the finer-textured soils.

The mineralogical composition of the different soil separates is also of importance. Sand and silt particles are derived from various rock fragments and minerals. Quartz is the predominant mineral in the sand and silt fractions of most soils. Clays are primarily composed of secondary minerals which are formed as products of weathering. Examples of these secondary minerals are kaolinite, illite, montmorillonite, and vermiculite.

B. Soil Aggregation and Structure

Soil aggregation refers to the clustering together of soil particles to form secondary particles or aggregates. Aggregation is of particular importance in soils containing appreciable amounts of silt and clay. If these fine particles exist as individual particles, the soil contains many small pores and is tight and compact. When the finer material is aggregated, larger pores are formed, and drainage and aeration conditions become more favorable for plant growth.

Various factors influence the formation of aggregates (Baver, 1956). Forces such as those exerted by roots, freezing and thawing, wetting and drying, and microbial activity bring particles closer together as the first step in aggregate formation. Adsorbed cations influence aggregation by their effects on flocculation of the soil particles. Calcium, aluminum, and hydrogen ions favor flocculation, whereas sodium ions favor dispersion or deflocculation. Poor physical conditions caused by sodium can be improved by replacing the sodium with calcium. Generally the aggregation of acid soils is not improved by additions of calcium, but exceptions do occur. Probably the beneficial effects are indirect. If calcium additions increase root growth and microbial activity, then these factors would favor increased soil aggregation. Clay, organic matter, and colloidal iron hydroxide are important cementing agents which hold aggregates together.

The arrangement of soil particles, including aggregates, determines the soil structure. There are four main types of soil structure: platy, prismlike, blocklike, and spheroidal. Platy structure is characterized by aggregates having horizontal dimensions greater than vertical dimensions. Platy structure is often developed in A horizons of uncultivated soils and may occur in B and C horizons. The clay mineral kaolinite favors platy structure. Prismlike refers to vertically oriented structural units having relatively flat sides which are two to five times as long as the prism is wide. Widths vary in size but may be as much as 6 inches. The term prismatic is used to describe the structure when the tops of the prisms are flat, and columnar is used when the tops are rounded. Prismlike structure develops in the B horizons of heavy soils, especially in arid and semiarid regions. Blocklike structure is well described by its name. Structural units may vary from 1/8 inch to 4 inches. When the sides of the aggregates are distinct the structure is blocky, and if the sides are not distinct and are somewhat rounded at the angles the term subangular blocky is used. Blocky structure is found in subsoils. Spheroidal refers to rounded aggregates and is subdivided into granular and crumb. Crumb structure has aggregates that are more porous than those associated with granular structure. Spheroidal aggregates range in size from 1/25 to 1/2 inch. They are found in surface horizons, especially those high in organic matter. Development of granular structure is great under grass vegetation. Additions of readily decomposable organic matter also favor granulation.

A soil is said to be structureless when there are no observable aggregations or natural lines of weakness which would indicate some orderly arrangement of particles. Divisions within the structureless classification are single grains and massive. Single grain refers to conditions where sandy soils exist with no binding of particles. Massive refers to cases where enough clay or organic matter is present to bind the particles together but there is no definite pattern of structural units.

The stability of aggregates is an important factor which determines the effectiveness of aggregates in maintaining desirable physical conditions. Stable aggregates are not easily broken down and destroyed by wetting or by manipulation during tillage operations. Unstable aggregates break down when wetted due to forces caused by swelling and by escaping air. Raindrops easily disperse weakly cemented aggregates. Soil crusting occurs on bare soils when rainfall has dispersed aggregates and the fine material has been washed into the pores. Close inspection of a crusted soil will show the compacted nature of the crust as compared to the soil beneath it. Excessive tillage and traffic destroy aggregation. These factors will be discussed in the section on compaction.

C. Bulk Density, Particle Density, and Porosity

Bulk density refers to the mass of soil per unit soil volume, including the solids and the pore space. Bulk density is usually expressed in grams per cubic centimeter (g/cc), and may vary from less than 1 in well aggregated soils high in organic matter up to about 2 on highly compacted soils (Russell, 1957). Bulk density values are usually lower for finer textured soils than coarser textured soils. Bulk densities range from 1.0 to 1.3 for clay soils, 1.1 to 1.4 for clay loams and silt loams, and 1.2 to 1.6 for loams, sandy loams, and sands (Thompson, 1957). Organic matter decreases bulk density due to its low particle density and by causing formation of stable soil aggregation. Compaction and excessive tillage cause high bulk densities. Light or moderate tillage, especially on packed soils, can produce lower bulk densities. Thus one soil type can have a wide range of bulk densities depending on the management of the soil.

Particle density refers to the mass per unit volume of the soil particles, excluding pore space. A value of 2.65 g/cc is usually considered typical for most mineral soil particles, but values may be as low as 2.40, or less, if organic matter content in the soil is high (Buckman and Brady, 1960).

The more dense a soil, the higher the bulk density and the closer it approaches the particle density value. The ratio of bulk density to particle density indicates the fraction of the soil which is solid. If it were possible to compress the soil so as to exclude all the pores, the bulk density would be equal to the particle density. At this point the ratio would be 1.0, indicating 100% solid material and no pore space. Of course the solid material in soils is less than 100% and the porosity can be determined by taking the difference between 100% and the solid material. This relationship is shown in the following formula:

$$\%\ \text{porosity} = 100 - \left(\frac{\text{bulk density}}{\text{particle density}} \times 100\right)$$

The porosity of a soil having a bulk density of 1.59 and a particle density of 2.65 would be 40%, viz:

$$\%\ \text{porosity} = 100 - \left(\frac{1.59}{2.65} \mathrm{X}\ 100\right) = 100 - 60 = 40$$

Differences in porosity are usually associated with changes in bulk density rather than particle density. The lower the bulk density, the greater the porosity. Both bulk density and total porosity can be used to characterize the physical condition of a soil. The main value of these properties is in comparing the same soil under different management treatments. Comparing values for different soils may be misleading. Sandy soils having a lower porosity and higher bulk density than fine textured soils may be better drained and aerated because of a greater number of large pores. Fine textured soils having few large pores may be poorly drained and aerated in spite of high porosity values.

The size distribution of pores is of greater importance than total porosity. Large pores are important for air and water movement in the soil, whereas small pores are important for moisture retention. Air porosity (aeration porosity) is the proportion of the soil volume that is filled with air at a given time or at a certain soil moisture content. Usually air porosity is used to designate those pores which drain at a soil moisture tension that approximates the tension at field capacity. In this respect, air porosity is essentially the same as the now obsolete term "non-capillary porosity." Ideally, the air porosity should be about one-half of the total porosity so that the soil will have adequate aeration and drainage as well as moisture holding ability.

D. Soil Water

The soil moisture characteristics for a particular soil are dependent on the pore size distribution within the soil. Thus texture, structure, and organic matter will have a large influence on the movement and storage of water in a particular soil. Soil water relationships are discussed in detail in Chapter 6.

E. Soil Air

Soil air relationships, like those of water, are largely dependent on the nature of the soil pores. Soil aeration refers to the process by which soil air is replaced by atmospheric air, and may be characterized by measuring oxygen and carbon dioxide concentrations, gaseous diffusion rates, and air porosity.

The composition of soil air differs from that of atmospheric air in several respects (Russell, 1952). The carbon dioxide content is higher, oxygen content is slightly lower, and water vapor content is much higher. Respiration of plant roots and microorganisms utilizes oxygen and produces carbon dioxide. Thus the composition of soil air is dependent on the amount of respiration and the exchange of air between the soil and the atmosphere. The composition of air in well aerated soils is similar to that of the atmosphere, whereas higher CO_2 levels and correspondingly lower O_2 levels are associated with poorly aerated soils. Under field conditions the O_2 level will probably become too low before CO_2 becomes too high to limit plant growth.

Exchange of atmospheric air and soil air is brought about by diffusion and the following meterological factors: changes in soil temperature, changes in barometric pressure, wind action, and rain displacing soil air and carrying in dissolved oxygen (Baver, 1956). Diffusion is by far the most important process.

The rate of supply or movement of oxygen in the soil seems to be of greater importance than oxygen concentration in the soil atmosphere.

Platinum microelectrodes can be used to measure oxygen diffusion rates in the soil in order to characterize soil aeration conditions. This method and results obtained using it have been reviewed by Stolzy and Letey (1964). Compaction and high soil moisture content, two conditions commonly found on turfgrass areas, are important factors which limit diffusion. Compaction alters the size, amount, and continuity of pores. Water has a limiting influence because oxygen diffusion through water is about 10,000 times slower than through a gaseous phase such as air.

Considerable variation exists in values of air porosity reported as being critical for the growth of different plants; thus no single value can be given as optimum or minimum for all situations (Grable, 1966).

The subject of soil aeration and plant growth relationships has been reviewed by Clements (1921), Peterson (1950), Russell (1952), and Grable (1966). There is ample evidence showing the need of oxygen in the root zone and the harmful effects to plant growth when supplies are lacking. The uptake of water and nutrients is often decreased by conditions of poor aeration. Hoagland and Broyer (1936) reported that an adequate supply of oxygen is needed for both cation and anion absorption. Harris and van Bavel (1957) found that nutrient uptake by tobacco plants was relatively constant until the O_2 content dropped below 10%. They reported that the sensitivity of several nutrients to decreasing O_2 and increasing CO_2 contents seems to be K > N > P > Mg > Ca. Chang and Loomis (1945) found that potassium uptake was affected the greatest by increasing CO_2 content, and ranked the nutrients in order of reduced uptake as being K > N > P > Ca > Mg. Letey et al. (1961a) reported that increasing O_2 concentration brought about increases in phosphorus and potassium content and a decrease in sodium content of snapdragon plants. Similar results were reported for sunflower (Letey et al., 1961b), barley (Letey et al., 1962), and Kentucky bluegrass (Letey et al., 1964). Calcium and phosphorus accumulation in sunflowers and cotton plants was stimulated by increasing soil oxygen supply (Letey et al., 1961b). Lawton (1945) reported that absorption of potassium by corn is more dependent on aeration than is the uptake of N, Ca, Mg, or P. Hopkins et al. (1950) found that uptake of potassium and phosphorus was affected most by oxygen supply. Cline and Erickson (1959) reported that nitrogen, phosphorus, and potassium contents of pea plants increased with increasing soil oxygen supply, and that calcium and magnesium tended to increase at low oxygen supplies.

Differences in plant tolerance to limiting oxygen supply have been reported by Cannon (1925), who measured root elongation of plants grown with the roots exposed to various oxygen concentrations. He noted that species which naturally occur where the soil may be puddled or water-saturated all or part of the year, exhibit a greater tolerance to oxygen deficiency, and that no species requiring a high percentage of oxygen for root growth has been found to occur in areas where the substratum is saturated part of the year. For instance, *Juncus effusus* and *Nasturtium officinal* (water cress) were found to be tolerant of low oxygen, whereas *Medicago sativa* (alfalfa) was not. Russell (1961) stated that rice, buckwheat, and some willows grow well when the air supply in the root zone is restricted, while tomatoes, and possibly peas and corn, need a very good air supply. Edminster and Reeve (1957) reported that plants normally grown on well drained and aerated soils usually are most sensitive to low oxygen levels, and that those plants which tolerate long periods of little oxygen have special tissues in their stems and roots which conduct oxygen to the roots. In his review, Grable (1966) concluded that diffusion of oxygen from the tops to the roots of plants was the most likely explanation for the ability of some plants to grow in waterlogged soils.

Grasses appear to be more tolerant of poor soil aeration than many other agronomic and horticultural crops. Finn et al. (1961) grew timothy, bromegrass, and reed canarygrass at several soil moisture levels and found them to be quite tolerant of saturated soil conditions. Waddington and Baker (1965) reported that Penncross creeping bentgrass and goosegrass were very tolerant of poor soil aeration and more tolerant than Merion Kentucky bluegrass. All of these grasses were more tolerant than tomato plants. Davis and Martin (1949) reported that various species of *Agrostis* were exceptionally tolerant of flooding. Colonial bentgrass grown in solution culture was found to be tolerant of low oxygen content, and grew satisfactorily at oxygen contents as low as 1 to 2 ppm (Engel, 1951. Studies of turf cultivation and related subjects. Unpublished Ph.D. Thesis. Rutgers University, New Brunswick, N. J.). These results contrast with those of Gilbert and Shive (1941) who observed marked decreases in soybean growth when the oxygen content of the solution culture was 6 ppm. Tomato plants and oats had a higher oxygen requirement than soybeans.

Williamson and Willey (1964) reported that without surface watering tall fescue yields were about the same for water table depths of 9 and 17 inches. When 1 inch of surface water per week was applied, yield with a 16-inch water table was greater than with an 8-inch water table. The difference was attributed to leaching of nitrogen from the root zone. Nitrogen application helped to mask any effects of water table depth on grass yields. Willhite et al. (1965) reported that nitrogen fertilization of timothy may have compensated for unfavorable soil aeration. Waddington and Baker (1965) suggested that liberal fertilization of bluegrass, bentgrass, and goosegrass may have accounted for similar yields and chemical compositions when these grasses were grown under various soil aeration conditions. Grable (1966) concluded that the principle requirement for high yields of grasses grown in poorly aerated soils is adequate fertilization to compensate for fewer roots, less root activity, or both.

When poor aeration is the result of soil compaction, mechanical impedance may also be a factor influencing the root growth and distribution. According to Flocker et al. (1959), the slowing of metabolic processes of plants grown in compacted soil may be attributed to one or a combination of several factors, including poor water utilization, restricted nutrient uptake, lack of oxygen, accumulation of CO_2, and mechanical impedance to root penetration. Mechanical impedance is discussed further in section VII.

Microbial activity is also affected by soil aeration (Alexander, 1961). Good aeration is needed for rapid microbial breakdown of organic materials and also for the conversion of ammonia and organic forms of nitrogen to the nitrate form. Symbiotic fixation of nitrogen by legumes is also favored by good aeration. Low soil oxygen supply suppresses microbial proliferation and enhances denitrification of nitrate nitrogen. Russell (1961) reported that the effects of by-products of anaerobic decomposition such as hydrogen sulfide, methane, and hydrogen have not been studied in any detail, and that the effects of oxygen, carbon dioxide, and by-product gases have rarely been separated in field studies of root growth.

Natural gas leaking from pipe lines can cause anaerobic conditions in the soil by displacing the soil air. Harper (1939) reported the failure of bermudagrass to grow above a natural gas leak. Schollenberger (1930) listed killing of vegetation, darkening of soil, and a peculiar acrid odor as being indicators of natural gas in the soil.

Iron and manganese are more available under anaerobic conditions, and disturbed iron and manganese relationships may be one of the major factors accounting for the detrimental influence of natural gas-saturated soils on vegetative growth (Adams and Ellis, 1960).

F. Soil Temperature

Radiation from the sun is the main source of heat in soils. Heat released from chemical reactions and from within deep strata of the earth are insignificant in influencing soil temperature (Richards et al., 1952).

Factors which influence soil temperature have been discussed by Richards et al. (1952), Baver (1956), and Geiger (1957). The angle at which radiation hits the soil surface influences the intensity of radiation per unit area. Intensity is greatest when the radiation is perpendicular to the soil surface and becomes less as the angle formed with the perpendicular increases. This angle is dependent on the position of the sun in the sky, the latitude, and the slope of the soil surface.

A portion of incoming radiation is scattered in all directions by air molecules and substances suspended in the atmosphere (Geiger, 1957). The heat on a slope caused by this diffuse radiation varies with the angle of the slope, whereas heat from direct radiation varies with both angle and direction of slope. In other words slopes of the same angle, but one facing north and the other south, receive the same diffuse radiation. Differences in temperature due to direction of slope are small in tropical regions. In polar regions the position of the sun gives great differences, but the ratio of direct to diffuse radiation is small. Thus, exposure is not so important in polar regions as in the middle latitudes.

Southern exposures are characterized by higher temperatures and greater variations in temperature than northern exposures. Southern slopes are also drier due to the higher temperatures. Maximum radiation intensity occurs on flatter slopes in summer when the sun is high and on steeper slopes facing the sun in the winter when the sun is low.

Various soil conditions influence soil temperature. Color influences heat absorption; composition and water content influence the specific heat; and compaction and water content influence heat conductivity (Baver, 1956). Dark colored soils absorb more heat than light colored soils. Whether the higher heat absorption will give a warmer soil is dependent on the amount of moisture in the soil. Organic matter is usually the cause of dark soil color, and the temperature in these soils is also influenced by the relatively high specific heat and low heat conductivity of organic materials as well as by the larger amount of water which may be present due to the organic matter. Thus, the darker soil may be warmer when dry, but moisture and other properties will also exert strong influences on the soil temperature.

The specific heat of a substance is the calories of heat needed to raise the temperature of 1g of the substance 1 degree (C).

The specific heat of water is 1.0, and values for dry soils vary from 0.17 to 0.26, with an average of about 0.2. Humus has a value of about 0.45. Heat capacity is the amount of heat needed to produce a given change in the temperature of a substance. It is calculated by multiplying the mass times the specific heat. At a given time and condition the heat capacity of a soil is dependent on the constituents in the soil. When humus or water is added to a soil, the heat capacity increases. Thus the greater the humus content, or the greater the moisture content, the more heat required to bring about a given change in temperature. These relationships account for the coolness of poorly drained or wet soils in the spring.

Heat conductivity varies with the type of soil, moisture content, and compaction. The heat conductivity of various soils has been found to follow the order of sand > loam > clay > peat (Baver, 1956). Air-filled pores are poor conductors, and when air is replaced by water better heat conduction occurs. Heat conduction increases as porosity decreases; therefore, compacted soils conduct heat better than loose soils. A loose, recently tilled soil will be cooler at night and hotter during the day than a more dense untilled soil. At a lower depth the temperature in the dense soil will be warmer during the day, because of deeper penetration of heat, and cooler at night than the less dense soil. Because of poorer conductivity the heat exchange in the loose soil is confined to the tilled layers near the soil surface. Heat conductivity influences melting of snow and the presence of frost. If conductivity is poor there is less heat transfer from lower soil and the surface cools faster. Differences in snow cover after a light snow or in frost cover are often noticeable on areas where the soil has been disturbed in some manner, such as over drainage tile lines or irrigation pipe lines. If excavations have been loosely filled, conduction will be slower than in the surrounding soil. If soil is packed during filling, the conduction will be greater due to denser soil and probably due to more moisture in the packed soil.

Vegetative cover also influences soil temperature. Leaves intercept part of the incoming radiation and shade the soil surface. The soil temperature is lower during periods of warming. Plants also reduce the loss of heat from the soil. A higher maximum temperature and a lower minimum temperature occur on bare soil than on sod-covered areas. A sod-protected soil is also cooler in the summer and warmer in the winter than a bare soil.

Soil temperature influences plant growth and microbial activity. Richards et al. (1952) and Troughton (1957) have reviewed the effects of soil temperature on the growth of grasses. Troughton (1957) compiled a list of optimum temperatures for root growth for various species. Optimum temperatures or ranges, in Fahrenheit degrees, reported for some of the grasses are as follows: Colonial bentgrass, 55 to 70; redtop, 86; carpetgrass, 80 to 90; bermudagrass, 80 to 100; ryegrass, 44 to 63; dallisgrass, 80 to 90; timothy, 55 to 70; and Kentucky bluegrass, 55 to 73. Richards et al. (1952) stated that bermudagrass appears to be favored by temperatures around 95 F, while most cool-season grasses do well in the range of 59 to 72 F. A temperature of 80 F appears to be unfavorable for Kentucky bluegrass root growth. Germination, seedling growth, and heat and cold tolerance of plants are also associated with soil temperatures.

Soil temperature influences various microbial processes in the soil (Alexander, 1961). Organic matter decomposition and various nitrogen transformations are dependent on soil temperature. These relationships are discussed in Section VI.

V. Soil Chemical Properties

Soil chemical properties are closely related to the fertility status of a soil. However, physical and biological processes are also important in influencing the amount and availability of elements. As with physical properties, the soil chemical properties are largely dependent on the amount and nature of clay and humus in the soil.

A. Soil Colloids

Soil colloids consist of very small organic and inorganic particles. Thus, clay and humus are the materials which make up the colloidal fraction of a soil. Not all clay is of colloidal size. Clay is defined as mineral particles having a diameter of less than 2 microns (0.002 mm). Colloidal clay has a diameter of less than 1 micron. The term clay mineral refers to the naturally occurring inorganic crystalline particles. Marshall (1949), Grim (1953), Rich and Thomas (1960), van Olphen (1963), and Jackson (1964) have presented discussions on the nature and properties of clay minerals.

The silicate clays are the predominant clays in temperate regions. These clays have a crystalline structure which is made up of layers of plate-like structural units. Two types of structural units are found in most clay minerals. The alumina unit consists of two sheets of closely packed oxygen and hydroxyl anions between which aluminum cations are positioned such that each cation is surrounded by six anions. Iron and magnesium can occupy equivalent positions. Cations in this configuration are said to have sixfold or octahedral coordination, and the sheets with this coordination are called octahedral layers. The second type of structural unit is the silica unit. Each silicon cation is surrounded by four oxygen anions to give a fourfold or tetrahedral coordination. The arrangement of the tetrahedra in a silica unit is such that three oxygens are in a plane on one side of the silicon and three are in a parallel plane on the opposite side.

The silicate clays can be classified according to their layers of structural units. The two-layer type, or kaolin group, has a structure composed of sheets of one layer of silica tetrahedra and one layer of alumina octahedra. This group is also called the 1:1 crystal lattice group. Kaolinite, a major clay mineral in the Southeastern States, is the most important member of this group.

The three-layer types have a 2:1 crystal lattice consisting of an octahedral layer held between two silica tetrahedral layers. Clays in the montmorillonite group have expandable lattices. The expansion occurs between the 2:1 structural sheets. These clays expand when wetted, and shrink and crack when dried. High internal surface area, high plasticity and cohesion, and high ion absorption are associated with the swelling property. Vermiculite has an expanding lattice, but expansion is not so great as with the montmorillonite group. The presence of potassium ions between the 2:1 sheets of vermiculite causes collapse of the crystal lattice, and potassium fixation occurs. The fixed potassium is only moderately soluble and is less available than water-soluble and exchangeable potassium. The nonexpanding 2:1 clays belong to the illite group. The nonswelling character is attributed to the binding effect of potassium ions between the 2:1 structural sheets. Chlorite is another clay mineral common in some soils. Chlorite is related to the 2:1 clays, but has a magnesium octahedral, or brucite, layer between the 2:1 sheets.

The clay fractions of soils are almost always mixtures of clay minerals. Considerable differences in the kind and amount of clay minerals found within a region may occur, mainly due to parent material influence; however, a general pattern of regional differences does exist (Buckman and Brady, 1960; Jackson, 1964; Toth, 1964). Kaolinite is predominant in many soils in the Southeastern States. In the cool, humid regions kaolinite, illite, and vermiculite have been found as dominating types. In the Midwest, montmorillonite is usually dominant in loessial soils, and illite is dominant in soils formed from glacial till. In the drier desert soils illite and montmorillonite are most abundant. Oxides of silicon, iron, and aluminum are nonsilicate clays which are found in the clay factions of soils.

Humus is the more or less stable fraction of organic matter that remains in the soil after the major portion of organic residues have decomposed. Humus may occur alone or in combination with inorganic colloids (Toth, 1964; Rich and Thomas, 1960).

Soil colloids possess excess negative charges and act as negatively charged ions, or anions, in soil reactions. It is this property which accounts for cation adsorption in soils. Cation exchange is defined as the interchange between a cation in solution and another cation adsorbed on a soil colloid. The principle cations held by soil colloids are Ca^{2+}, Mg^{2+}, K^+, Na^+, NH_4^+, H^+, and Al^{3+}.

B. Cation Exchange Capacity

The cation exchange capacity (CEC) of a soil is the total amount of exchangeable cations that a soil can absorb and is expressed in milliequivalents per 100 g of soil. In chemistry, the term equivalent is applied to elements or compounds which have the same capacity to combine or react. The equivalent weight of a substance is its combining power in grams equivalent to 1 g of hydrogen or 8 g of oxygen. Its milliequivalent weight is the milligrams that will combine with or displace 1 mg of hydrogen. This equivalent or milliequivalent weight of an ion, atom, or molecule is obtained by dividing its atomic or molecular weight (in g or mg, respectively) by its valence. Thus, the milliequivalent weight of Ca^{++} is 20 mg (40/2); that of K^{+} is 39 mg (39/1); of Mg^{++} is 12 mg (24/2); and of Na^{+} is 23 mg (23/1).

If the quantity of an element is expressed as milliequivalents per 100 g of soil, its approximate amount in pounds per acre is easily calculated. Multiplying the milliequivalent value by the milliequivalent weight (mg) would give the milligrams of the element per 100 g or 100,000 mg of soil or the parts per 100,000. Multiplying this product by 20 would give the parts per 2 million or the pounds per acre furrow slice of 6 inches (approximately 2 million pounds of soil). Thus the pounds per acre of Ca^{++} can be obtained by multiplying the milliequivalents of Ca^{++} per 100 g by 400 (20 x 20). To obtain pounds of K^{+}, Mg^{++}, or Na^{+} multiply the meq/100 g by 780, 240, or 460, respectively. Conversely, the milliequivalents per 100 g for the various cations may be obtained by dividing the known amounts of these cations in pounds per acre by the respective factors. The CEC for the soil is then the sum of all the milliequivalents per 100 g.

The cation exchange capacity values for soils are dependent on the amount and kind of soil colloids present in the soil. In general, the greater the clay or organic matter content of a soil, the higher the cation exchange capacity. Coarse-textured soils have low values and fine-textured soils have high capacities.

The CEC values of the individual colloids also have an important effect on the soil cation exchange capacity. The CEC ranges for organic matter and clay minerals are as follows: organic matter, 150 to 500; vermiculite, 100 to 150; montmorillonite, 80 to 150; illite, 10 to 40; chlorite, 10 to 40; and kaolinite, 3 to 15 meq/100 g (Grim, 1953). In soils of a given texture or clay content, the CEC of soils in which illite or kaolinite are the predominant clays will be lower than in soils with clays high in montmorillonite or vermiculite. The high CEC of organic matter points to its importance as a soil colloid. With a CEC of 200 meq/100g, each percent organic matter in the soil would account for 2.0 meq in the soil CEC. Although fine-textured soils usually contain more organic matter the influence of organic matter on soil CEC is of particular importance in coarse-textured soils becuase of their low clay contents.

In general, soils with high cation exchange capacities are more fertile than soils having low exchange capacities. This relationship exists because of the greater amount of exchangeable plant nutrients held in the high CEC soils. Cations added to coarse-textured soils are more easily leached due to less exchange capacity to hold them, as well as due to the more permeable nature of the soil

The base saturation percentage of a soil is the percentage of the total CEC which is occupied by basic cations such as calcium, magnesium, potassium, and sodium (Tisdale and Nelson, 1966). The greater the base saturation of a given soil, the higher the pH and the fertility of the soil. The availability of basic ions increases as base saturation increases but the type of colloid influences this relationship. Organic and 1:1 clay colloids exchange bases more readily at a low base saturation than do the 2:1 clay colloids.

The energy of adsorption of bases by colloids is in the order of Ca > Mg > K > Na, and in humid areas where leaching occurs they tend to accumulate in the same order (Thompson, 1957). Toth (1964) reported that the "ideal soil" is 80% base saturated: 65% Ca, 10% Mg, and 5% K.

The clay fraction of soils also exhibits anion exchange properties (Rich and Thomas, 1960). Anion exchange is greatest in soils in which the dominant clays are kaolinite and oxides of iron and aluminum. Common inorganic anions which may be exchanged are OH^-, Cl^-, NO_3^-, SO_4^{2-}, and $H_2PO_4^-$.

C. Soil Reaction

Soil reaction refers to the acidity or alkalinity of a soil and is expressed as a pH value. pH is an expression used to designate the hydrogen ion activity in a solution and is calculated by taking the negative logarithm of the hydrogen ion activity. The pH scale runs from 0 to 14. A pH of 7 is neutral because the activities of H ions and OH ions are equal. Values below 7 are acid because more H ions are present than OH ions. Above pH 7, OH ions are more abundant and alkalinity exists. The hydrogen ion activity at pH 7 is .0000001 equivalents per liter, and at pH 6 it is .000001 equivalents per liter, or 10 times as much as at pH 7. A soil at pH 5 is 10 times as acid as one at pH 6 and 100 times as acid as one at pH 7. Descriptive terms used to designate pH ranges in soils are as follows: extremely acid, less than 4.5; very strongly acid, 4.5 to 5.0; strongly acid, 5.1 to 5.5; moderately acid, 5.6 to 6.0; slightly acid, 6.1 to 6.5; neutral, 6.6 to 7.3; slightly alkaline, 7.4 to 7.8; moderately alkaline, 7.9 to 8.4; strongly alkaline, 8.5 to 9.0; and very strongly alkaline, greater than 9.0.

The discussion of biological properties (Section VI) includes the relationship between pH and various microbial processes. Important biological processes such as decomposition, nitrogen fixation, and nitrification are favored by pH values in the neutral range. The activity of bacteria and actinomycetes is reduced by low pH, and fungi dominate under these conditions due to less competition from these microorganisms, not because acidic conditions are optimum for fungi.

The effect of low pH in decreasing the release rate of nitrogen from organic materials applies to added fertilizers as well as to plant residues. Bredakis and Steckel (1963) reported that the rate of release of nitrogen from ureaform and natural organic nitrogen fertilizers was greater at pH 6.7 than at pH 5.5. The influence of pH on the natural organics was greatest during the first 3 weeks of incubation and was of little significance over the last 12 weeks when the supply of substrate was considerably lower and probably of a more resistant nature. About 60% of the nitrogen was released from the natural organics and only 30% from the ureaform materials during the first 3 weeks. The pH effect on nitrogen release from ureaform lasted throughout the 15-week experiment. Considering the relatively low plant recovery of nitrogen from these slowly soluble sources, it seems logical that acid soils should be limed to pH levels which will favor maximum nitrogen release and availability.

Soil reaction exerts a strong influence on the availability of certain plant nutrients. The relationship of pH and nutrient availability is shown in Fig. 3. The availability of an element is greatest at the pH values where the respective band is the widest. A pH of about 6.5 is considered most desirable for overall nutrient availability (Truog, 1946). Acid soils have low base saturation, and therefore are less fertile than adequately limed soils. There is less available calcium and magnesium in acid soils. Phosphorus availability is decreased because phosphorus forms insoluble compounds with iron and aluminum. Molybdenum availability decreases with increased acidity. Manganese and aluminum solubility increase, and these elements may reach levels which are toxic to plants. Jackson (1967) has reviewed the aspects of absorption, translocation, distribution, essential functions, and toxicity characteristics of the elements which are of major importance in acid soil infertility.

Overliming and high pH also affect soil fertility (Buckman and Brady, 1960). The availability of copper and zinc becomes less when the pH goes above 7, and deficiencies may occur. Iron, aluminum, and manganese are less soluble in alkaline soils and toxicity is not a problem; however, iron and manganese may be deficient. Boron also becomes less available at pH values over 7.

The effects of pH on toxic substances, nutrient availability, and microbial processes are reflected in plant growth. Jackson (1967) reported that most plants can tolerate pH values as low as 4.0 to 4.5, provided a rather high nutrient supply is maintained and aluminum

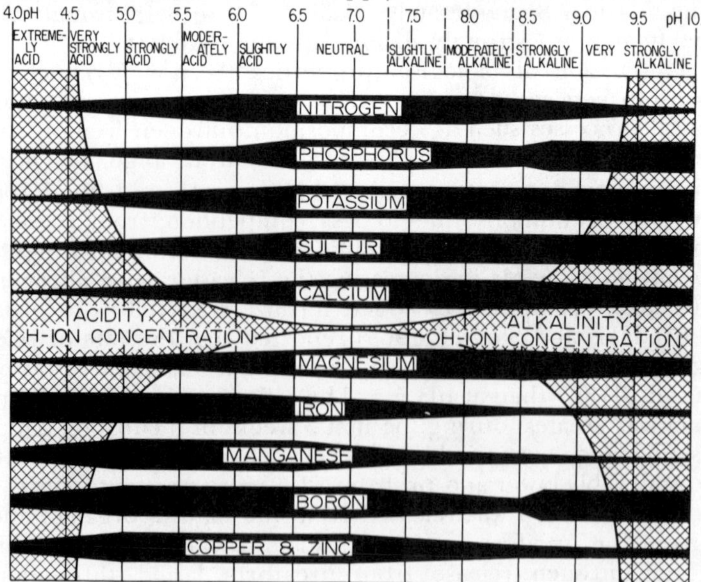

Figure 3. Diagram showing the relationship between soil reaction and nutrient availability (Truog, 1946).

and manganese contents are not excessive. He cited research in which increased calcium and nitrogen supplies were effective in overcoming the toxic influence of high acidity. Research conducted by Hunter (1965) showed that liberal phosphorus fertilization decreased the effects of low pH on the growth of a legume-grass hay mixture. His data clearly indicate a response to phosphorus fertilization; however, the highest level of phosphorus on unlimed soil did not produce so high a yield as the no-phosphorus treatment on limed soil. Phosphorus applications on acid soils are inefficient because considerable quantities may react to form insoluble compounds with iron, aluminum, and manganese. Of course precipitation of aluminum and manganese is desirable if the pH is low enough for them to occur in toxic amounts. Liming decreases soluble iron, manganese, and aluminum, increases phosphorus availability, encourages organic matter decomposition and the release of nutrients from it, favors nitrogen fixation, and increases the availability of molybdenum, calcium, and magnesium. Although phosphorus applications may partially correct for low phosphorus availability on acid soils, liming or a combination of liming plus phosphorus fertilization should be a more economical and beneficial practice.

Plants differ in their response to soil acidity and alkalinity, and are often classified according to the optimum pH range for their growth. Alfalfa is an example of an acid-sensitive plant, whereas azaleas grow best in acid soils. A pH in the range of 6.0 to 7.0 is considered to be best for turfgrass growth due to more favorable nutrient availability and microbial activity (Musser, 1962). Spurway (1941) and Musser (1962) have reported optimum pH ranges shown in Table 4. It would seem likely that grass grown near or below the lower limit of the optimum range would need higher rates of fertilization to keep nutrients at an optimum level. Such a practice could prove to be uneconomical.

Table 4. Soil pH preferences of turfgrasses.

Common name	Optimum pH range	
	Spurway (1941)	Musser (1962)
Annual bluegrass	6.0 - 7.0	5.1 - 7.6
Canada bluegrass	6.0 - 7.5	5.6 - 7.6
Rough bluegrass	6.0 - 7.0	5.8 - 7.6
Kentucky bluegrass	5.5 - 7.5	6.0 - 7.6
Colonial bentgrass	6.0 - 7.0	
Creeping bentgrass	6.0 - 7.0	
Velvet bentgrass	5.5 - 7.0	
Bentgrass		5.4 - 7.6
Redtop	5.0 - 6.0	5.1 - 7.6
Creeping red fescue	5.5 - 6.5	5.4 - 7.6
Chewings fescue	5.5 - 6.5	5.4 - 7.6
Sheeps fescue	4.5 - 6.0	
Tall fescue	6.5 - 8.0	5.4 - 7.6
Ryegrasses	6.0 - 7.0	6.5 - 8.1
Bermudagrass	6.0 - 7.0	5.1 - 7.1
Carpetgrass	6.0 - 7.0	4.7 - 7.1
Centipedegrass		4.0 - 6.1
St. Augustinegrass		6.1 - 8.1
Zoysiagrass		4.6 - 7.6
Buffalograss	6.0 - 7.5	6.1 - 8.7
Crested wheatgrass		6.1 - 8.7
Gramagrass		6.1 - 8.7

Soil pH can be determined by colorimetric and electrometric methods (Peech, 1965a). Colorimetric methods make use of dyes or acid-base indicators which change color with changes in pH. These methods are capable of giving results within 0.3 pH unit of those obtained by the electrometric method. The electrometric method usually involves the use of a glass-electrode pH meter which utilizes a hydrogen ion indicator electrode to determine pH. These methods measure the acidity in the soil solution, which is called the active acidity.

Soils resist change in pH and are said to be buffered. The buffering is due to another component of soil acidity called exchange or potential acidity, which accounts for more of the total soil acidity than does active acidity. Exchange acidity is due to exchangeable hydrogen and aluminum on the soil colloids. The exchange acidity occupies that portion of the soil cation exchange capacity which is not holding exchangeable bases.

Prior to the 1950's, hydrogen was considered to be the main ion involved in soil acidity, but recent research has shown that exchangeable aluminum is largely responsible for soil acidity (Jenny, 1961; Seatz and Peterson, 1964; and Coleman and Thomas, 1967). Aluminum produces hydrogen ions when it undergoes hydrolysis. The reactions involved in hydrolysis can be simply shown as follows:

$$Al^{+++} + H_2O \longrightarrow Al(OH)^{++} + H^+$$
$$Al(OH)^{++} + H_2O \longrightarrow Al(OH)_2^{\ +} + H^+$$
$$Al(OH)_2^{\ +} + H_2O \longrightarrow Al(OH)_3 + H^+$$

An equilibrium exists between active acidity and exchange acidity. If some of the active acidity is neutralized, exchange acidity is released to maintain the equilibrium. If hydrogen is added to the soil solution, the shift is in the other direction. The amount of buffering which occurs in a soil is dependent on the cation exchange capacity of the soil. At a given pH, a soil having a high CEC will have more exchange acidity than one having a low CEC. Clay and humus have already been mentioned as factors which determine the CEC, with the relationship being such that soils high in clay or organic matter are more highly buffered than soils low in these components.

pH measures the active acidity and is a good indicator as to whether a soil needs to be limed. However, pH does not indicate the amount of exchange acidity which must be taken into account and is, therefore, a poor indicator of the amount of lime needed unless more information is available. When only pH data are available, lime recommendations must be adjusted according to the organic matter content and texture of the soil. Various laboratory methods which take exchange acidity into account may be used to chemically determine the lime requirement for a soil (Peech, 1965b).

Barber (1967) has discussed liming materials and their properties. He defined agricultural liming materials as being materials composed of calcium and magnesium compounds which are capable of neutralizing soil acidity. Quicklime (CaO), hydrated lime ($Ca(OH)_2$, limestone, marl, shells, and slags were given as examples. Limestone is the most frequently used material and may be calcite, dolomite, or a mixture of these minerals. Pure calcite is calcium carbonate, $CaCO_3$, and contains 40% Ca. Pure dolomite is calcium carbonate and magnesium carbonate, $CaCO_3$-$MgCO_3$, and contains 26.6% Ca and 13.1% Mg. Mixtures of the two are referred to as dolomitic or calcitic limestones depending on the relative amounts of dolomite and calcite. Dolomite has a greater neutralizing capacity than calcite, but is less soluble than calcite and, therefore, reacts more slowly. Calcium oxide, CaO, is caustic, and both calcium oxide and calcium hydroxide, $Ca(OH)_2$, are powdery, making them difficult and unpleasant to handle.

Two important factors which determine the effectiveness of limestone in reducing soil acidity are chemical purity and particle size (Barber, 1967). The neutralizing capacity of liming materials is expressed as $CaCO_3$ equivalence, with pure $CaCO_3$ being 100. The use of low purity liming materials will decrease the effectiveness of liming unless increased amounts are added. Finely ground limestone particles have more surface area than coarse particles and therefore go into solution more quickly. Agricultural limestone has a range of particle sizes and the particle size distribution can be determined by sieving through various sized sieves. Barber (1967) has summarized research reports on the effects of limestone fineness. He concluded that there is no distinct particle size boundary separating "effective" from "ineffective" limestones. Material coarser than 20-mesh was relatively ineffective while material finer than 60-mesh was highly effective. The percent material passing a 60-mesh sieve characterizes the fineness of most limestones. Limestone with 50% passing a 60-mesh sieve was almost as effective as limestone with 100% passing a 60-mesh sieve.

Economic considerations are important in purchasing limestone. Meyer and Volk (1952) reported that a large portion of limestone should pass a 40-mesh sieve; and when the cost of additional grinding to get it through a 100-mesh sieve is considered, there seems to be little advantage to having it that fine. Tisdale and Nelson (1966) gave an example of a method used in Ohio to determine the efficiency of liming materials. This method assumes 100% efficiency of material passing a 60-mesh sieve, 60% efficiency for material between 20- and 60-mesh, and 20% efficiency for material between 8- and 20-mesh. Consider a limestone in which 100% passes an 8-mesh sieve, 90% passes a 20-mesh sieve, and 60% passes a 60-mesh sieve. The efficiency rating is obtained by multiplying the percent material in each size range by the efficiency rating for that size range as shown below:

less than 60-mesh	60% x 100 = 60%
less than 20, greater than 60	30% x 60 = 18%
less than 8, greater than 20	10% x 20 = 2%
Efficiency rating	80%

Such a method can be used to compare limestones that have the same chemical neutralizing capacity; or if materials have different calcium carbonate equivalents, as well as differences in fineness, multiply the calcium carbonate equivalent by the efficiency rating to obtain the overall effectiveness. Efficiency ratings are useful in calculating equivalent amounts of materials and in determining relative costs of materials. Barber (1967) reported that calculated values of relative effectiveness based on particle sizes were very similar to the values obtained from field experiments.

Liming of acid soils is beneficial to the growth of most plants. Seatz and Peterson (1964) listed benefits obtained from liming soils:

(1) Increased availability of plant nutrients by chemical or biological activity. Availability of N, S, P, Ca, Mg, and Mo is increased.

(2) Decreased solubility of Al and Mn, which may be toxic in acid soils.

(3) Improved soil structure, especially under conditions where organic matter is important in cementation and structure stability.

(4) Increased root activity and better root distribution improves plant efficiency in utilizing available nutrients and water.

The reaction rate of lime in the field is slower than in the laboratory due to poor mixing of soil and lime in the field (Adams and Pearson, 1967; Barber, 1967). Adams and Pearson recommended that limestone should be added at least 2 to 3 months prior to planting, and hydrated lime at least 1 month prior to planting. They stated that reaction rate is affected by the degree of mechanical mixing, and therefore, reaction rates would be expected to be at a minimum when lime is surface-applied to untilled soil.

Lime moves very slowly through the soil, Brown et al. (1956) reported that 2 years after surface applications of limestone on a fine sandy loam, the 1-ton rate had affected the pH only in the upper inch of soil, the 3-, 4-, and 8-ton rates affected the top 2 inches, and the 16-ton rate caused an appreciable change as deep as 4 inches. Longnecker and Sprague (1940) applied 1 ton of hydrated lime and ground limestone to established sod on 12 soil types, and observed a sharp rise in pH in the upper inch of all soils by the end of 6 months. Substantial changes in pH at the 2-, 3-, and 4-inch depths did not occur until after 30 months. These patterns in distribution should be taken into account when sampling for pH determination. Results such as these present a good argument for the recommendation which calls for soil testing and the thorough mixing of limestone into soil prior to turfgrass establishment. Phosphorus, which also moves slowly, should receive the same treatment. The use of mechanical aeration prior to liming provides a means of deeper placement of liming materials on established turfgrass areas.

Materials used to increase the soil acidity include elemental sulfur, sulfuric acid, aluminum sulfate, and iron sulfate. These materials may be used in the improvement of alkali soils in dry regions, and in humid regions they may be used to overcome the effects of overliming or to create a soil reaction more favorable to acid-loving plants (Tisdale and Nelson, 1966). Sulfur is the most effective material. Soil conditions must be favorable for the bacterial conversion of the sulfur to sulfuric acid, and thorough mixing with the soil is important. The acidifying effect from 320 pounds of sulfur will neutralize about 1,000 pounds of limestone ($CaCO_3$). Soil acidity is also increased by the use of acid-forming nitrogen fertilizers such as ammonium nitrate, ammonium sulfate, ammonium phosphate, urea, ureaform, and certain organics (Pierre, 1928, 1934; Wolcott et al., 1965). Nitrate sources of nitrogen, such as KNO_3 and $Ca(NO_3)_2$, decrease soil acidity. The acidity or basicity of a fertilizer is dependent on differences in plant uptake and on biological transformations of the applied cations and anions.

D. Saline and Alkali Soils

Saline and alkali soils occur in arid and semiarid areas, however saline soils may occur near sea water in humid areas. These soils can be defined on the basis of their effect on plants and on the basis of certain soil properties (U.S. Salinity Laboratory Staff, 1954). An alkali soil is a soil which contains sufficient sodium to interfere with the growth of most crop plants. Alkali soils have a pH of 8.5 or higher and the exchangeable sodium is 15% or more of the exchange capacity. Alkali soils may or may not contain excess soluble salts. A saline soil is a nonalkali soil which contains sufficient soluble salts to impair its productivity. The conductivity of the solution extracted from a saturated saline soil is greater than 4 mmhos/cm. Saline soils have an exchangeable sodium percentage less than 15 and a pH usually below 8.5.

A saline-alkali soil contains sufficient exchangeable sodium to interfere with the growth of most crops and also contains appreciable amounts of soluble salts. The exchangeable sodium percentage is greater than 15, the conductivity of the saturation extract is greater than 4 mmhos/cm, and the pH of the saturated soil is usually 8.5 or less.

Saline soils are generally flocculated due to the excess salts, and their permeability is equal to or higher than that of similar nonsaline soils. Saline-alkali soils are also flocculated due to the abundance of soluble salts; however, if the excess salts are leached, the properties of these soils approach those of a nonsaline-alkali soil. The exchangeable sodium in nonsaline-alkali soils causes dispersion, and low permeability is a problem.

Methods of management and improvement of saline and alkali soils have been presented by the United States Salinity Laboratory Staff (1954) and Allison (1964). Consideration must be given to the quality of irrigation water, irrigation practices, and drainage conditions when working with these soils. Soluble salts can be leached, and salinity can be controlled if good quality water is used and if the drainage is such that the dissolved salts can be carried away. Water management is the key to salinity control. In saline soils, irrigation water in excess of crop requirement should be added to maintain a favorable salt balance in the root zone. This excess of water is referred to as the "leaching requirement." Enough water must be used to keep the salts moving downward, and irrigation should be frequent enough to keep the soil from drying between irrigations.

In alkali soils or soils approaching an alkali condition, special amendment, leaching, and management practices are required to improve and maintain soil conditions favorably. The exchangeable sodium must be replaced by other cations. Amendments used for replacement of sodium include soluble calcium salts such as gypsum and calcium chloride; acids and acid formers such as sulfuric acid, sulfur, and iron sulfate; and slowly soluble calcium salts such as ground limestone. The sodium is replaced on the colloids by calcium, hydrogen, or both, and is then removed by leaching. The kind and amount of amendment used is dependent on various soil characteristics (U.S. Salinity Laboratory Staff, 1954).

Plant growth in saline soils is affected mainly by the reduced availability of water due to the high osmotic pressure. The nature of the salts may also be an influencing factor. Plants differ in their tolerance to salt (U.S. Salinity Laboratory Staff, 1954). Bermudagrass and birdsfoot trefoil have high salt tolerances, and perennial ryegrass, tall fescue, and orchardgrass are representative of plants having medium salt tolerances. White clover has a low salt tolerance. Lunt et al. (1961) investigated the tolerance of five turfgrasses to salinity. Seaside creeping bentgrass and Alta tall fescue were found to be more tolerant than Highland Colonial bentgrass and Kentucky bluegrass. *Puccinellia distans* (L.) Parl. (alkaligrass) was more tolerant than these common turfgrass species. The salinity tolerance of seven varieties of creeping bentgrass was determined by Youngner et al. (1967). The topgrowth of all species decreased as salinity was increased. Arlington, Seaside, Pennlu, and Old Orchard were most tolerant. Congressional and Cohansey were intermediate, and Penncross was least tolerant. Seaside showed the best survival under extreme saline conditions, and the best recovery after being removed from salt conditions. Seaside bentgrass has also been shown to be quite tolerant of alkali. Lunt et al. (1964) determined the tolerance of five turfgrasses to soil alkali. Seaside bentgrass and *P. distans* had only moderate growth reduction at exchangeable sodium percentages of 26 to 28% . Alta fescue, Kentucky bluegrass, and common bermudagrass had their growth reduced by 1/3 to 1/2 in this range, but only slight growth reductions occurred with 11 or 12% exchangeable sodium.

VI. Soil Biological Properties

A. Organisms in the Soil

Although soil organisms comprise only a small fraction of the soil mass, they have an essential role in many processes which occur in the soil. The wide variety of organisms found in the soil is shown in Table 5. Several sources of information concerning the nature and activities of soil organisms are as follows: Clark (1957), Buckman and Brady (1960), Russell (1961), Alexander (1961), and Burges and Raw (1967).

The five major groups of soil microorganisms are bacteria, actinomycetes, fungi, algae, and protozoa. Bacteria are the smallest and most numerous, and are important in organic matter breakdown, nitrogen and sulfur transformations, and nitrogen fixation. Heterotrophic bacteria obtain carbon and energy from the breakdown of organic materials. Autotrophic bacteria utilize carbon from carbon dioxide and

Table 5. Chart showing the more important groups of organisms that commonly are present in soils. (Buckman & Brady, 1960)

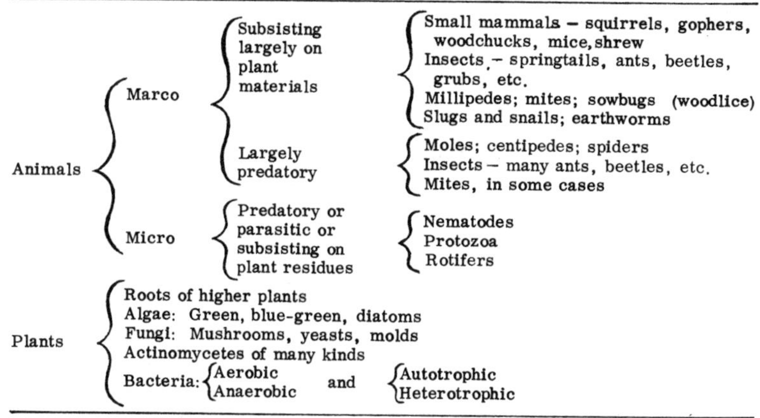

Animals	Marco	Subsisting largely on plant materials	Small mammals – squirrels, gophers, woodchucks, mice, shrew Insects – springtails, ants, beetles, grubs, etc. Millipedes; mites; sowbugs (woodlice) Slugs and snails; earthworms
		Largely predatory	Moles; centipedes; spiders Insects – many ants, beetles, etc. Mites, in some cases
	Micro	Predatory or parasitic or subsisting on plant residues	Nematodes Protozoa Rotifers
Plants	Roots of higher plants Algae: Green, blue-green, diatoms Fungi: Mushrooms, yeasts, molds Actinomycetes of many kinds Bacteria: Aerobic / Anaerobic and Autotrophic / Heterotrophic		

obtain energy from the oxidation of inorganic materials such as sulfur and ammonia.

Actinomycetes are heterotrophic and their main beneficial contribution is in the breakdown of organic matter. The odor of freshly plowed soil is due mainly to actinomycetes.

Fungi occur in fewer numbers than bacteria and actinomycetes, but are highest of the microflora in live weight. The predominant group of fungi found in the soil are the molds. Molds develop over a wide range of soil reactions, and in acid soils they are the main organism responsible for organic matter decomposition. These fungi, as well as bacteria and actinomycetes which act on organic matter, aid in the formation of stable aggregation. Mushroom fungi also occur in soils. Within this group are the types which cause fairy rings in woodlands, pastures, and lawns. Species of *Pythium, Fusarium,* and *Rhizoctonia* are well known as root disease fungi.

Algae are the simplest form of plant life containing chlorophyll. Growth of algae is favored by damp soils and sunlight, however some algae may persist deeper in the soil where light is absent. Algae grow over a wide range of soil reactions, but individual strains do have pH preferences. The blue-green algae can fix atmospheric nitrogen, and are considered to be important in supplying nitrogen for rice in flooded paddies. Algae is one of the first sources of organic matter during soil formation, and accumulated remains of algae are the dominant constituent of some aquatic peats.

Protozoa are single-celled animal life. Most soil protozoa feed on bacteria, and therefore become abundant under conditions which favor the growth of bacteria. Little is known concerning their function in soil. Nematodes, another member of the soil microfauna, are best known for their parasitic members which attack plant roots. The contribution of those that live on decaying organic matter is negligible.

Roots of higher plants are the largest source of organic matter additions to the soil. Roots also contribute to the formation of stable soil aggregation.

Earthworms are perhaps the best known of the macrofauna found in soils. Earthworms mix surface organic residues and underlying soil, and their channels improve water and air movement. Earthworm casts aid in the development of good soil structure. However, earthworm casts on close cut turf are considered objectionable from both the aesthetic and playing viewpoints. Earthworms prefer moist, medium- to fine-textured soils with high amounts of organic matter and adequate amounts of calcium.

Other macrofauna vary in their activities and importance. Some may be beneficial in mixing soil or decomposing organic residues, while others may be injurious to plants. Some spend only part of their lives in the soil.

B. Soil Organic Matter

Soil organic matter refers to the organic fraction of the soil. It includes plant and animal residues at various stages of decomposition, cells and tissues of soil organisms, and substances synthesized by soil organisms. Plant residues, particularly the roots, account for most of the organic matter added to soils.

The organic matter content of cultivated surface horizons of mineral soils ranges from a trace to 15 or 20% of the total soil weight, with values of 3 to 5% being most representative (Buckman and Brady, 1960). Organic soils contain more than 15 to 20% organic matter. The amount of organic matter in a soil is dependent on the amount of organic matter added and the rate at which it decomposes. Conditions which influence organic matter decomposition are discussed in part C.

The effects of organic matter on soil properties have been mentioned in previous sections. Organic matter improves aggregation and influences aeration porosity and moisture retention. Crusting of the soil surface and puddling are decreased by organic matter. Organic matter influences soil temperature through its effects on soil color and moisture content. Increased cation exchange capacity due to organic matter reduces leaching of cations and increases their availability to plants. Organic matter serves as a source of essential plant nutrients and as an energy source for soil organisms.

Organic amendments such as peat and sawdust are often added to soils to alter their properties. Effects of organic amendments on soil properties are discussed in section VIII.

C. Organic Matter Decomposition

Organic matter decomposition concerns the turfgrass grower in several ways. The accumulation of excessive organic residues on the soil surface may be detrimental to satisfactory turf production, thus a rapid breakdown of such organic accumulations is desirable. When organic materials are used to physically modify the soil, the rapidity of their breakdown is also of importance. In this case a long lasting effect is usually desired.

Soil organic matter occurs in various stages of decomposition. The dark, more or less stable, fraction which remains in the soil after decomposition of the major portion of organic residues is called humus. The process of humus formation is called humification.

Mineralization is the process by which elements are converted from organic forms to inorganic forms during microbial decomposition. The main products produced by mineralization are carbon dioxide, water, and minerals.

The major factors controlling humus decomposition are the soil organic matter level, cultivation, temperature, moisture, pH, depth, and aeration (Alexander, 1961). Decomposition of humus is stimulated when readily decomposible organic matter is added to the soil. The effect of cultivation is to decrease soil organic matter to levels below those found under virgin conditions. The temperature and moisture conditions which favor microbial activity will also be favorable for humus decomposition. Humus decomposition is favored by neutral to slightly alkaline soil reaction and is enhanced when acid soils are limed. Decomposition is an oxidation process and is therefore favored by good aeration.

The decomposition of organic materials added to the soil is influenced by the chemical composition of the residue and the following environmental factors: temperature, oxygen, moisture, pH, available minerals, and the carbon-nitrogen ratio of the plant residue (Alexander, 1961). The organic constituents of plant residues vary in their rate of decay. Lignin is slow to decompose. Thus materials having large amounts of lignin are more resistant to microbial breakdown than materials low in lignin. Plant age influences decomposition. Mature plants differ from young, succulent plants by having more of the slowly decomposed components such as hemicellulose, cellulose, and lignin, and less of the more readily decomposed compounds such as proteins and water soluble substances, including sugars, starches, and amino acids.

The optimum temperature range for organic matter breakdown is between 85 and 105 F. Breakdown occurs at temperatures as low as 40 F, but increases as the temperature is increased up to 85 F. Above 105 F decay slows down.

Air and moisture are interrelated in their effects on microbial decomposition. Decomposition becomes slower when oxygen is limited. Water is limiting when an increase in moisture results in more breakdown; but when an increase in moisture slows decay, oxygen is limiting. Soil reaction influences the kind of microorganisms present in a soil and their activity. In acid soils the fungal population is dominant because of decreased competition for the organic materials by the less tolerant bacteria and actinomycetes. Normally decomposition is more rapid in neutral than in acid soils.

A number of mineral nutrients are needed by microorganisms, and a deficiency of any of these would limit microbial activity. The element which has the greatest effect on the decomposition of organic materials is nitrogen. If the material being decomposed is high in nitrogen, the microorganisms are well supplied. However if nitrogen content is low, decomposition will be slow unless supplemental nitrogen is added. The carbon-nitrogen ratio gives an indication of the amount of nitrogen.

Carbon content is usually about 40% of the dry weight. Thus a high nitrogen content would be associated with a narrow carbon-nitrogen ratio. Materials such as blood meal or legume residues have narrow ratios and decompose rapidly. Straw and sawdust have wide ratios and decompose slowly. As materials having wide ratios are broken down, the ratio narrows to a somewhat stable ratio of about 10:1, which is characteristic for humus and which is also the ratio of the soil microbial population. The nitrogen in organic materials having C:N ratios in the range of 20:1 to 30:1 should just meet the needs of the decomposing microorganisms. When materials have C:N ratios wider than this range, decomposition is slow and nitrogen deficiencies may occur because microorganisms utilize inorganic nitrogen from the soil. This conversion of nitrogen from inorganic forms to organic forms in microbial cells is called immobilization. If nitrogen is added to increase the decomposition rate of wide ratio materials, the nitrogen content should be adjusted to about 1.2 to 1.5% on a dry weight basis. Materials such as sawdust (.2% N) and straw (.5% N) would require additions of about 1 pound of nitrogen for each 100 pounds of dry organic material. This amount would satisfy the microorganisms. More would be needed to supply plants growing in the soil. When the C:N ratio is less than 20:1 to 30:1, nitrogen will be released by mineralization, and will be available for plant use. Natural organic nitrogen fertilizers are examples of low C:N ratio materials.

Peats may contain up to 3.5% nitrogen and may have narrow C:N ratios; however decomposition of peats is slow due to the nature of the organic constituents. About half of the nitrogen is of no value as a plant nutrient because it is tied up in very resistant nitrogenous compounds (Anderson et al., 1951). The range of nitrogen in peat humus and hypnum moss peat is 2.0 to 3.5%, but their rates of decomposition differ. Thus release of nitrogen is much slower from the peat humus, which has undergone considerably more decomposition and is higher in lignin content than the hypnum moss peat (Lucas et al., 1965). Spagnum moss peat ranges from 0.6 to 1.4% in nitrogen content, and it decays more rapidly than the hypnum type. If undecomposed or slightly decomposed forms of spagnum are incorporated into the soil, small amounts of nitrogen may be needed (Reuszer, 1957). Reed-sedge peats contain 1.5 to 3.5% nitrogen. They are more resistant to decay than the moss peats and less resistant than peat humus (Lucas et al., 1965). Lipman and Wank (1924) concluded from their investigations that peat is of little value as a source of nitrogen, due to the resistant nature of the organic constituents.

Troughton (1957) reported that "mat" or "thatch," a surface organic accumulation, and "sod bound" conditions, organic accumulation mainly below the ground, are associated with conditions which limit the decomposition of organic matter. Soil acidity and lack of nitrogen have been suggested as conditions which favor this accumulation. The nature of the organic constituents in these residues should also be considered. In a 13-year experiment, liming and topdressing with a 1:1 mixture of a sandy loam soil and coarse sand decreased thatch and sponginess in turf (Rhode Island Agricultural Experiment Station, 1957). In experiments of much shorter duration, about one growing season, Ledeboer and Skogley (1967) applied limestone, fertilizer, and sources of readily available carbon to turfgrasses to determine the effects on decay of thatch. They were unable to detect an influence on thatch decay. They investigated the physical thatch structure and reported that sclerified vascular strands of stems and leaf sheaths were more resistant to decay than clippings or sloughed leaves. Nodes or crown tissues were observed to be most resistant. Less decay occurred when soil was lacking in the organic layer. Where soil topdressing had been practiced, decomposition was more advanced. They concluded that proper soil topdressing of putting green turf is an important factor favoring reduction of thatch accumulation.

D. Nitrogen Transformations

Turfgrasses are very responsive to nitrogen fertilization, and therefore nitrogen is the nutrient element which is used by turf managers to control turfgrass growth. Other essential elements are usually kept at adequate levels and are not limiting. Nitrogen is added in different amounts or withheld in order to regulate the amount of growth. With nitrogen receiving major emphasis in turfgrass fertilization, it is essential to understand how this element behaves in the soil. The nitrogen transformations which take place in the soil will largely determine the efficiency of nitrogen applications.

Nitrogen mineralization is the conversion of organic nitrogen to an inorganic form. The microbiological process in which ammonium (NH_4+) is formed from organic nitrogen is called ammonification. A diverse population, including bacteria, fungi, and actinomycetes, is active in ammonification, and because of this diversity ammonification occurs under a wide range of environmental conditions (Alexander, 1961). Ammonification proceeds slowly when soil moisture content is as low as the permanent wilting percentage, but increases with increasing soil moixture and proceeds under both aerobic and anaerobic conditions. Optimum ammonium release occurs when water or oxygen is not limiting. Ammonification does not occur in frozen soils, but does occur slowly at temperatures just above freezing. The optimum temperature falls within the range of 100 to 140 F. Ammonification occurs to a greater extent in neutral soils than in acid soils.

The ammonium ions in the soil may be fixed in an unavailable form in the lattice of certain expanding type clay minerals, utilized by organisms, taken up by plants, or converted to nitrites and nitrates by the process of nitrification (Tisdale and Nelson, 1966). Nitrification is the biological oxidation of ammonium to nitrate. This conversion occurs in two steps: first, ammonium is converted to nitrite, and second, nitrite is converted to nitrate. A genus of bacteria known as *Nitrosomonas* is important in the nitrite forming step, and another genus, *Nitrobacter,* is responsible for the conversion of nitrite to nitrate. Both of these genera are classified as obligate chemoautotrophs. A chemoautotroph obtains energy for growth from the oxidation of inorganic compounds and uses CO_2 as a source of carbon. The activity of obligate chemoautotrophs is limited exclusively to inorganic oxidations, and only one compound or a small group of related compounds are utilized by an obligate autotroph. Facultative autotrophs may obtain energy from either the oxidation of inorganic materials or organic carbon. Besides the genera responsible for the oxidation of nitrogen compounds, other chemoautotrophic bacteria are also active in oxidation reactions involving sulfur, iron, hydrogen, and carbon (Alexander, 1965).

The *Nitrosomonas* reaction is as follows:

$$2NH_4^+ + 3O_2 \longrightarrow 2NO_2^- + 4H^+ + 2H_2O$$

The NO_2^- is then oxidized in the *Nitrobacter* reaction

$$2NO_2^- + O_2 \longrightarrow 2NO_3^-$$

The energy released in these reactions is the source of energy for the respective nitrifying bacteria. Usually nitrite is oxidized as rapidly as it is formed, but it may accumulate after large quantities of urea, anhydrous ammonia, or ammonium salts have been applied on high-pH soils. Toxicity to *Nitrobacter* is influenced by the amount of ammonium in the soil and the pH. Nitrite does not usually accumulate when the pH is below 7.2, and free ammonia found in alkaline soils appears to be the substance which inhibits *Nitrobacter.*

Environmental factors exert a more strict control on nitrification than on ammonification because a specific population is responsible for nitrification. Nitrification is influenced by various environmental factors (Alexander, 1965). The amount of nitrification varies with the ammonium supply. Generally, ammonification proceeds slower than ammonium oxidation, and nitrite oxidation proceeds faster than these two reactions. Nitrification does not occur at temperatures below freezing, but does occur slowly at temperatures just above freezing. Increases in temperature bring about an increase in nitrification until the optimum range of 85 to 95 F is reached. Nitrification above 105 F is usually insignificant. Nitrification proceeds slowly in acid soils. The optimum pH values for *Nitrosomonas* species fall in the range of pH 7 to 9, and slightly acid conditions limit proliferation of these species.The optimum pH for *Nitrobacter* is neutral to slightly alkaline. Nitrification is an oxidation process and requires oxygen; therefore, nitrification is limited in poorly aerated soil. An oxygen concentration of 20% is considered optimum for nitrification. Moisture conditions are more limiting to nitrification than to ammonification. In very dry soils or extremely wet soils, ammonium levels increase due to decreased nitrification. Nitrification is rapid in soils moistened by rain or irrigation after being dry for a prolonged period.

Nitrate nitrogen may be leached, utilized by plants, immobilized by soil microbes, or lost by denitrification (Tisdale and Nelson, 1966). Denitrification is the biological reduction of nitrate and nitrite to gaseous nitrogen, usually nitrous oxide (N_2O), molecular nitrogen (N_2), or both. Broadbent and Clark (1965) have reviewed the subjects of denitrification, and also chemo-denitrification, which refers to gaseous losses of nitrogen due to chemical reactions involving nitrites. Gaseous losses of nitrogen by the activity of denitrifying bacteria is favored by low oxygen concentrations, alkaline soil reactions, high soil moisture, and high temperatures. Chemo-denitrification occurs under aerobic conditions when the soil pH is 5 or less. Denitrification losses are usually reported to be in the range of 10 to 30% of the applied nitrogen.

Nitrogen may also be lost from the soil by volatilization of ammonia (Alexander, 1961). Under optimum conditions, as much as 25% of the ammonium applied or formed microbiologically may be lost as ammonia. Ammonia volatilization is favored by alkaline soil reactions, warm temperatures, low cation exchange capacity, and low soil moisture. Ammonia is produced when urea breaks down and considerable ammonia losses have been reported from urea applications to grasses. Simpson and Melsted (1962) applied 50, 100, and 150 pounds per acre of urea-nitrogen in solution form to a bluegrass sod. Nitrogen lost as gaseous ammonia 8 to 10 days later was 15.9, 31.1, and 44.5 pounds, respectively. Losses from 50 to 100 pounds applied on bare soil were not measurable, and only 1.4 pounds were lost at the 150 pound rate. Volk (1959) reported that losses of nitrogen as ammonia in a 7-day period following surface application of 100 pounds of dry urea-nitrogen per acre were 20 to 30% for grass sods and 17 to 59% for acid, light sandy soils. Losses from ammonium nitrate and ammonium sulfate were found to be negligible. Losses from urea solutions were similar to those from dry urea on the turf, but were considerably less on soils. Harding et al. (1963) applied 400 pounds of N per acre as urea, ammonium sulfate, ammonium nitrate, and ureaform on the surface of a slightly calcareous Sorrento silt loam, and the percentages of N lost as ammonia were 13.2, 7.8, 1.3, and 1.0, respectively.

Nitrogen fixation is the conversion of elemental nitrogen (N_2) to organic combinations or to forms readily used in biological processes. Certain free-living bacteria and blue-green algae are capable of nitrogen fixation (Jensen, 1965). Fixation also occurs in the free atmosphere due to electrical discharges, and chemical fixation is used in the manufacture of nitrogen fertilizers. The most common free-living bacteria which utilize N_2 are species of *Azotobacter* and *Clostridium*. *Azotobacter* is active under aerobic conditions and *Clostridium* is favored by anaerobic conditions. The activity of both genera is favored by temperatures in the range of 75 to 85 F, a pH near neutral, an adequate supply of minerals and organic substrates, and low levels of available nitrogen compounds. Symbiotic nitrogen fixation is brought about by bacteria which live in association with plants (Alexander, 1961). The most important association in symbiotic fixation involves leguminous plants and *Rhizobium* bacteria. Clover, alfalfa, and crownvetch are examples of leguminous plants. The *Rhizobium* bacteria exist in nodules on the plant roots.

Various environmental factors influence symbiotic fixation of nitrogen (Vincent, 1965). These factors may act on (1) the occurrence and survival of *Rhizobia* outside of the host plant, (2) nodule formation, and (3) nitrogen fixation. In general, the factors which limit symbiotic nitrogen fixation are low pH, high temperatures, droughty soils, ex-

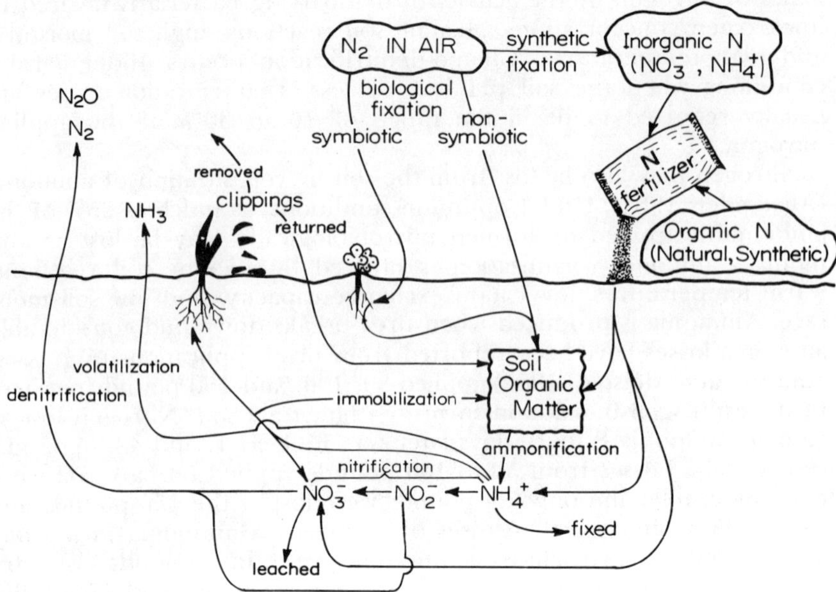

Figure 4. Soil nitrogen cycle.

cessive moisture, presence of available nitrogen compounds, and low levels of calcium, phosphorus, potassium, and other essential elements.

The nitrogen cycle traces the various reactions involved when nitrogen enters a biological environment, including its use by organisms, its release when dead organisms are decomposed, and its conversion to its original form. Figure 4 shows a simplified diagram of the nitrogen cycle as it would apply to turfgrass areas.

VII. Soil Compaction

Soil compactness may occur naturally or it may be brought about by the activity of man. Some subsoils are naturally compact due to a high clay content. Pans are soil layers which are strongly compacted, indurated, or very high in clay content. Genetic pans are natural subsurface layers of low or very low permeability, with a high concentration of small particles, and differing in certain physical and chemical properties from the soil immediately above and below the pan. Clay pans and fragipans are examples of compact genetic pans. A hardpan, also a genetic pan, is a hardened soil layer in which particles have been cemented together with organic matter or with materials such as silica, iron oxides, aluminum oxides, or calcium carbonate. Pressure or induced pans are subsurface layers having a greater bulk density and lower porosity than the soil immediately above or below. They are caused by pressure that has been applied by normal tillage operations or by other artificial means, and are frequently referred to as plow pans, plowsoles, or traffic pans.

On turfgrass areas, compaction from traffic is usually of major concern. This type of surface compaction will be discussed in this section.

Under normal conditions, aggregation and soil permeability are improved where grasses are grown. Traffic on turfgrass areas acts against the natural beneficial effects of grass crops. On intensively used turfgrass areas soil structure may be degraded rather than improved, and compacted conditions may result. In compacted soils the particles are pressed or packed closely together. The pore size distribution is altered, and fewer large pores exist. The air and water relationships may vary drastically depending on the severity of compaction. Ferguson (1950) stated that "surface compaction and poor drainage are the two greatest hindrances that are encountered in the maintenance of proper soil-moisture and soil-air conditions." Some of the conditions which are associated with compaction are hard soil, crusted soil, dry spots, standing water, shallow root systems, and plant indicators such as knotweed and clover. However, the presence of one of these conditions does not always mean that compaction is the cause.

The causes of compaction include traffic from man and machinery, excessive tillage, and raindrop action. Crusts which form on exposed soils following irrigation or rain are an indication of the effect of raindrops. The impact of the raindrops disperses soil aggregates, positions particles into a closer arrangement, and packs them tightly in their new location. Soil pores may be further blocked and reduced in size by the inwashing of fine soil particles carried by the infiltrating water. These crusts may limit movement of air and water and the emergence of seedling plants. Excessive cultivation destroys aggregation, with a more compact soil resulting. It is usually the final tillage operations in preparing seedbeds that are carried to excess. The soil near the surface is very finely pulverized and crusts easily. The effects of foot and machine traffic are usually limited to the upper few inches of soil.

Various soil properties are changed when soils are compacted. The changes in physical properties are most apparent, but chemical and biological properties will be influenced by the changes in the soil physical condition. When soils are compacted, bulk density, heat conductivity, mechanical impedance to roots, and usually moisture retention increase, while aeration porosity, infiltration, percolation, and oxygen diffusion decrease.

Blake and Aldrich (1955) reported that excessive cultivation resulted in lower air space, decreased aggregation, and higher bulk density. Alderfer (1951) reported that the aeration porosity on a heavily trampled bluegrass sod decreased from 33.1% to 6.1% in the 1-inch surface layer. Infiltration decreased from more than 1.50 inches to .35 inch per hour. Table 6 shows the effects of varying degrees of compaction on the bulk density, aeration porosity, and hydraulic conductivity of a loamy sand.

Soil compactibility is dependent on various soil properties. Water acts as a lubricant and allows the particles to slide over each other more easily in moist soils than in dry soils. Compactibility increases with

Table 6. Effect of intensity of compaction on the bulk density, aeration porosity, and hydraulic conductivity of a Freehold loamy sand. (Rosenberg & Willets, 1962)

Compaction intensity	Bulk density, g/cc	Aeration porosity, %	Hydraulic conductivity, in./hr.
Lowest	1.31	21.5	6.5
↓	1.45	20.8	1.4
	1.49	19.9	0.9
	1.60	11.0	0.3
Highest	1.64	10.9	0.2

Table 7. Effect of sand and compaction at three moisture levels on percolátion rate and aeration porosity of Chester soil mixtures. (Swartz & Kardos, 1963)

% available moisture depletion	Sand level, %	Percolation rate, in./hr. Compaction levels			Aeration porosity, % Compaction levels		
		1	2	3	1	2	3
0	30	0.0	0.0	0.0	16.2	14.2	12.4
	50	0.3	0.3	0.0	17.8	15.3	12.9
	70	14.5	10.1	4.3	39.8	34.8	33.3
25	30	0.0	0.0	0.0	14.4	13.9	10.9
	50	1.1	0.6	0.2	21.9	16.9	15.3
	70	15.9	9.8	6.6	40.2	36.1	33.7
50	30	0.3	0.1	0.0	18.3	13.4	10.4
	50	1.2	0.9	0.8	27.7	23.0	22.3
	70	12.7	9.4	5.7	40.2	37.2	31.7

moisture increase until an optimum moisture level for compaction is reached. Above this optimum many of the pores are filled with water and the soil resists compaction. Soil texture also influences compactibility. Meredith and Patrick (1961) determined the compactibility of three subsoils. Each soil exhibited a pronounced optimum moisture content for compaction. An increase in clay content was associated with a lower maximum bulk density and a higher moisture content at which the maximum bulk density was obtained. Data of Swartz and Kardos (1963) show the effects of increased moisture, sand level, and compaction levels on the percolation rate and aeration porosity of different soil mixtures. Percolation and aeration porosity decreased with increased moisture at compaction and with increased intensity of compaction, and increased with increased sand content. Table 7 shows the results obtained from Chester soil mixtures.

Lotspeich (1964) reported that soil compaction and soil strength are influenced by clay content, range of particle sizes, and moisture content. In excess of an optimum content, clay is likely to result in reduced strength and compaction. A multicomponent sand composed of several size fractions favors compaction. Maximum compaction and strength occurs when sizes allow tetrahedral packing with mutual contact of all grains and with films of clay surrounding all particles. A multicomponent sand compacts to greater extent and at lower moisture contents than a one component sand. Interstitial grains provide more contact points for clay to bind thus causing greater strength. A moisture content between 1 and 5 bars tension favors compaction. With lower moisture contents lubrication is insufficient, and with higher contents water interferes due to its volume requirement.

Morgan et al. (1966) reported greater compaction under a set irrigation schedule, which kept the soil relatively wet, than under tensiometer guided irrigation. This work points to the relationship between water management and compaction.

Rosenberg (1964) reviewed the effects of compaction on plant growth. Influencing factors associated with compaction are mechanical impedance, aeration, moisture, and temperature. Air, moisture, and temperature relationships have been discussed elsewhere. Mechanical impedance, or mechanical resistance, refers to the resistance to root and underground shoot penetration in soil. Barley and Greacen (1967) recently reviewed the subject of mechanical resistance. They concluded that mechanical resistance should be regarded as having a widespread influence on the growth of roots and underground shoots, rather than as a factor that operates only in unusually strong soils. Soil moisture influences the ability of roots to penetrate hard layers of soil. As the soil dries, the ability of roots to penetrate decreases. Oxygen and mechanical resistance also interact. Root growth has been shown to be restricted more by mechanical resistance when the soil oxygen level is low (Aubertin and Kardos, 1965; Tackett and Pearson, 1964; Rickman et al., 1966). Taylor et al. (1967) reported that soil which has been slurried is more resistant to penetration than nonslurried soil, and reduction in root elongation was attributed to increases in soil strength. Taylor and Gardner (1963) concluded that soil strength, rather than bulk density, was the critical impedance factor controlling root penetration in the sandy soils of the Southern Great Plains. Soil strength, measured with a penetrometer, increased as bulk density and moisture tension increased.

The degradation of structure cannot be considered a temporary condition (Vomocil and Flocker, 1965). Because the effects of compaction may be long lasting, it is important to manage the soil in a manner which will prevent or minimize compaction. Water management has been mentioned as one factor which influences compaction. Traffic should be held to a minimum on wet soils, and if possible measures should be taken to prevent traffic from being concentrated in one area. Concentrated traffic also causes severe wear and injury to the turfgrasses. Distributing traffic allows these areas to recover. Operating heavy equipment in the same wheel tracks intensifies compaction. Flannagan and Bartlett (1961) observed a striped pattern on turf where a tractor had followed the same course for each mowing. White clover had invaded the compacted soil in the wheel-track areas. The greener color in the compacted strips was attributed to increased nitrogen due to the presence of the clover. A management program which includes the regular use of aerification equipment should minimize the effects of compaction.

Soil modification can also be used to combat compaction. Lunt (1956) reported that placing a 4-inch layer of sandy soil mix on top of a soil susceptible to compaction will protect the soil. Other research has been conducted which shows that increasing the sand content of soils will help to maintain desirable physical conditions when a soil is subjected to compaction. The effects of modification on soil properties are discussed in the next section.

VIII. Soil Modification and Soil Properties

The need for soil modification and the properties and amounts of various amendments used are discussed in detail in Chapter 17. Soils are modified to improve plant-soil relationships, to alter the condition of the playing surface, and to minimize soil management problems. In other words the plant, the player, and the turf manager stand to gain or lose depending on the effectiveness of soil modification. Soil modification of turfgrass soils usually refers to physical modification, and various soil amendments are used to modify or change soil properties. Actually, lime and fertilizers are amendments which modify the chemical properties of soils.

The effectiveness of a physical soil amendment depends on the properties of the amendment, the amount added, the soil to which it is added, and the uniformity of mixing. Although generalities can be made regarding the effects of amendments on soil properties, it may be unwise to base specifications on these generalities.

Peat is commonly used to modify soils. Lucas et al. (1965) have listed the following benefits of peat:

It increases the moisture holding capacity of sandy soils.
It increases infiltration into fine textured soils.
It makes soils more friable and better aerated.
It decreases bulk density and improves root penetration.
It increases the buffer capacity of soils.
It increases microbial activity.
It serves as a slow-release source of plant nutrients.

The effects of soil texture and the kind and amount of organic amendments on soil modification have been shown by Sprague and Marrero (1931). They used well-rotted manure, spent mushroom soil, and cultivated, raw, and moss types of peat to modify clay loam, loam, and sandy soils. The materials were added at rates equivalent to 40 and 80 tons (50% moisture) per acre, and were mixed to a 6.7-inch depth. All of the organic materials increased the moisture holding capacity of each soil. The organic additions slowed water movement in the sandy soil, except with the high application rate of moss peat, and increased water movement in the clay loam. Percolation was decreased by adding the 40-ton rate to the loam, but the 80-ton rate of raw peat and moss peat increased percolation over that obtained with untreated soil. Richer et al. (1949) reported that increased infiltration occurred on golf greens amended with cocoa shells, mushroom soil, and peat. The effects from increasing the amounts of amendments varied with the materials. As the amount added was increased the infiltration rate increased with cocoa shells, mushroom soil, and a Florida peat, but decreased with a New Jersey peat.

Sawdust is another organic material which is used to modify soils (Allison and Anderson, 1951; Anderson, 1957; Bollen and Glennie, 1961; Lunt, 1955, 1961; White et al. 1959). Some beneficial changes in soil properties that have been reported are increases in humus, cation exchange capacity, aggregation, moisture holding capacity, and aeration porosity. Other organic materials which may be used to modify soils have been discussed by Anderson (1950-51).

The persistence of an organic additive is also of importance. Sprague and Marrero (1932) found that cultivated peat persisted in the soil longer than mushroom soil and well-rotted manure. They pointed out that slowly decaying materials give longer lasting physical effects and that rapidly decaying materials are important from the standpoint of nutrient release. Richer et al. (1949) reported that cocoa shells decayed more rapidly than peat, but still maintained good physical conditions with a lower soil organic matter content. This effect was attributed to greater aggregation of silt and clay brought about by the products of decomposition. Lucas et al. (1965) rated peat types according to their value as sources of stable organic matter as follows: peat humus (decomposed) > reed-sedge peat > hypnum moss peat > sphagnum moss peat.

Juncker and Madison (1967) determined the moisture characteristics of sand-peat mixes. As the peat content was increased, the mixtures had a lower bulk density, held more available water, had a lower zone of saturation, and approached wilting conditions more gradually at a high tension. The sand had relatively uniform pore sizes, but the peat had a wider distribution of pore sizes. Larger pores associated with the peat allowed for better drainage at low soil moisture tension, giving a lower zone of saturation. Smaller pores associated with peat accounted for the gradual changes in moisture as the wilting tensions were approached.

The effects of several physical soil amendments were reported in a series of papers by Morgan et al. (1966), Letey et al. (1966), and Valoras et al. (1966). Unamended soil and soil amended with 30% (by volume) peat, lignified redwood, and calcined clay were used in these studies. Water infiltration rates for the soil and amended soils were in the order of soil < peat < lignified redwood = calcined clay, and compactibility was in the order of soil > peat > lignified redwood > calcined clay. Compaction decreased the infiltration into unamended soil and peat amended soil, but had no effect on the other two mixes. Oxygen diffusion rates were lowest in unamended soil, next lowest in the peat mix, and highest in the lignified redwood and calcined clay mixes.

Swartz and Kardos (1963) added medium sand (.5 to .25 mm) to 8 soils to obtain total sand percentages of 30, 50, and 70. The effects of these treatments and a compaction treatment are shown for one of the soils in Table 7. As the sand content was increased, available water decreased and aeration porosity and percolation rate increased. They concluded that the total sand content of a mixture to be subjected to compaction should approach 70%. The size range of 2.0 to 0.25 mm in diameter in the mixes was the dominant fraction in controlling percolation rate. Kunze et al. (1957) reported that 85 to 90% sand (1.0 – 0.5 mm) was needed to produce desirable aeration porosity and permeability levels in modified Houston Black clay soil.

Smalley et al. (1962) used vermiculite, colloidal phosphate, fired clay (calcined clay), and peat to modify a loamy fine sand. All were added at a 10% by volume rate. Also included were 5% colloidal phosphate and 20% vermiculite treatments. All materials except colloidal phosphate increased total porosity. Aeration porosity was increased by fired clay

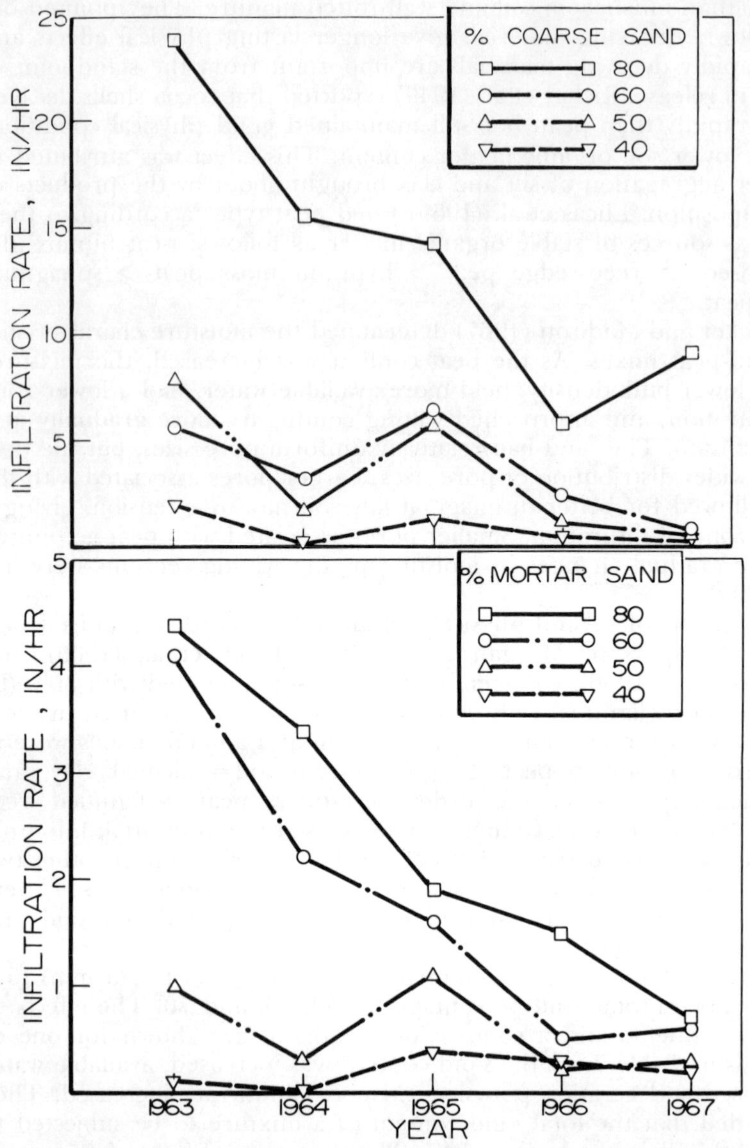

Figure 5. Effects of type of sand (a. coarse sand and b. mortar sand), sand content, and time on infiltration rates of compacted mixtures containing sand, Hagerstown silt loam, and peat (10% by volume).

and peat, but decreased by colloidal phosphate and vermiculite. Hydraulic conductivity increased with fired clay and decreased with the others. With this sandy soil, decreased aeration porosity and hydraulic conductivity from vermiculite additions improved the growth and quality of the turfgrass. Soil modification is not always made with the intent of making a soil more open and permeable. Some soils are too porous and may need moficiation in the opposite direction.

In a Pennsylvania study (G. J. Shoop, 1967. The effects of various coarse textured material and peat on the physical properties of Hagerstown soil for turfgrass production. Unpublished Ph.D. Thesis. Pennsylvania State University, University Park, Pa.) three sands, two slags, calcined clay, and a horticultural perlite were used to modify a silt loam soil. After a sufficient quantity of coarse material was added to reach a threshold value, usually in the order of 50 to 60% on compacted plots, increases in permeability and aeration porosity were obtained. Available moisture decreased as sand, slag, or calcined clay content was increased. Infiltration rates on these plots have been measured each year since these plots were established. The infiltration rates generally show a decrease with time. The greatest changes have occurred with those mixtures which initially had high rates. The effect of sand content and time on infiltration rate is shown in Figure 5.

Results of investigations in Indiana indicated that calcined clay additions increased total porosity, aeration porosity, oxygen diffusion, cation exchange capacity, infiltration, and percolation (R. H. Montgomery, 1961. The evaluation of calcined clay aggregates for putting green rootzones. Unpublished M.S. Thesis. Purdue University, Lafayette, Ind.; M. C. Hansen, 1962. Physical properties of calcined clays and their utilization for rootzones. Unpublished M. S. Thesis. Purdue University, Lafayette, Ind.).

It is obvious that soil physical properties can be altered by additions of organic and inorganic amendments. Modification should be aimed at obtaining suitable moisture retention as well as permeability. To obtain the desired modification, one must have an appreciation of the physical property relationships which occur in soils. To depend upon some magical ratio for soil modification guidance indicates ignorance of these relationships. Thought should also be given to the chemical properties of modified soils and how they might influence soil management. What is the "best" mixture for modified soils? The "best" mixture is any combination of materials which satisfies the objective of obtaining a playable turfgrass area with a minimum of maintenance problems.

Acknowledgments

The author expresses his appreciation to L. T. Kardos, M. R. Heddleson, and G. W. Petersen of The Pennsylvania State University for their suggestions and critical review of this manuscript.

Literature Cited

Adams, F., and R. W. Pearson. 1967. Crop response to lime in the Southern United States and Puerto Rico. *In* R. W. Pearson and F. Adams (ed.). Soil acidity and liming. Agronomy 12:161-206.

Adams, R. S. Jr., and R. Ellis, Jr. 1960. Some physical and chemical changes in the soil brought about by saturation with natural gas. Soil Sci. Soc. Amer. Proc. 24:41-44

Alderfer, R. B. 1951. Compaction of turf soils—some causes and effects. USGA J. and Turf Mgt. 4(2):25-28.

Alexander, M. 1961. Introduction to soil microbiology. John Wiley & Sons, Inc., New York. 472 p.

Alexander, M. 1965. Nitrification. *In* W. V. Bartholemew and F. E. Clark (ed.). Soil nitrogen. Agronomy 10:307-343.

Allison, F. E., and M. S. Anderson. 1951. The use of sawdust for mulches and soil improvement. USDA Circular No. 891. 19 p.

Allison, L. A. 1964. Salinity in relation to irrigation. Advance. Agron. 16:139-180.

Anderson, M. S. 1950-1951. Wastes that improve soil. *In* Crops in peace and war. Yearbook Agr. (US Dep. Agr.) US Government Printing Office, Washington. p. 877-882.

Anderson, M. S. 1957. Sawdust and other natural organics for turf establishment and soil improvement. US Dep. Agr. ARS 41-18.

Anderson, M. S., F. S. Blake, and A. L. Mehring. 1951. Peat and muck in agriculture. USDA Circular No. 808. 31p.

Aubertin, G. M., and L. T. Kardos. 1965. Root growth through porous media under controlled conditions: II. Effect of aeration levels and rigidity. Soil Sci. Soc. Amer. Proc. 29:363-365.

Barber, S. A. 1967. Liming materials and practices. *In* R. W. Pearson and F. Adams (ed.). Soil acidity and liming. Agronomy 12:125-160.

Barley, K. P., and E. L. Greacen. 1967. Mechanical resistance as a soil factor influencing the growth of roots and underground shoots. Advance. Agron. 19:1-44.

Bauer, K. W. 1966. Application of soils studies in comprehensive regional planning. *In* L. J. Bartelli, J. V. Baird, M. R. Heddleson, A. A. Klingebiel, D. O'Harrow (ed.). Soil surveys and land use planning. Soil Sci. Soc. Amer. and Amer. Soc. Agron., Madison, Wisconsin.

Baver, L. D. 1956. Soil physics. 3rd ed. John Wiley & Sons, Inc., New York. 489p.

Bear, F. E. (ed.) 1964. Chemistry of the soil. Reinhold Publ. Corp., New York. 515p.

Benson, E. T. 1957. Foreward. *In* Soil. Yearbook Agr. (US Dep. Agr.) US Government Printing Office, Washington. p v-vi.

Black, C. A. 1960. Soil-plant relationships. John Wiley & Sons, Inc., New York. 332p.

Blake, G. R., and R. J. Aldrich. 1955. Effects of cultivation on some soil physical properties and on potato and corn yields. Soil Sci. Soc. Amer. Proc. 19:400-403.

Bollen, W. B., and D. W. Glennie. 1961. Sawdust, bark and other wood wastes for soil conditioning and mulching. Forest Products J. 11:38-46.

Bouyoucos, G. J. 1962. Hydrometer method improved for making particle size analyses of soils. Agron. J. 54:464-465.

Bredakis, E. J., and J. E. Steckel. 1963. Leachable nitrogen from soils incubated with turfgrass fertilizers. Agron. J. 55:145-147.

Broadbent, F. E., and F. Clark. 1965. Dentrification. *In* W. V. Bartholomew and F. E. Clark (ed.) Soil nitrogen. Agronomy 10:344-359.

Brown, B. A., R. I. Munsell, R. F. Holt, and A. V. King. 1956. Soil reactions at various depths as influenced by time since application and amounts of limestone. Soil Sci. Soc. Amer. Proc. 20:518-522.

Buckman, H. O., and N. C. Brady. 1960. The nature and properties of soils. 6th ed. Macmillan Co., New York. 567 p.

Burges, A., and F. Raw (ed.) 1967. Soil biology. Academic Press, New York. 532p.

Cannon, W. A. 1925. Physiological features of roots, with special reference to the relation of roots to aeration of the soil. Carnegie Inst. of Wash. Publ. No. 368. 168p.

Chang, H. T., and W. E. Loomis. 1945. Effect of carbon dioxide on absorption of water and nutrients by roots. Plant Physiol. 20:220-232.

Clark, F. E. 1957. Living organisms in the soil. *In* Soil. Yearbook Agr. (US Dep. Agr.) US Government Printing Office, Washington. p 157-165.

Clements, F. E. 1921. Aeration and air content. The role of oxygen in root activity. Carnegie Inst. of Wash. Publ. No. 315. 183p.

Cline, R. A., and A. E. Erickson. 1959. The effect of oxygen diffusion rate and applied fertilizer on the growth, yield, and chemical composition of peas. Soil Sci. Soc. Amer. Proc. 23:333-335.

Coleman, N. T., and G. W. Thomas. 1967. The basic chemistry of soil acidity. *In* R. W. Pearson and F. Adams (ed.) Soil acidity and liming. Agronomy 12:1-41.

Davis, A. G., and B. F. Martin. 1949. Observations on the effect of artificial flooding on certain herbage plants. J. Brit. Grassland Soc. 4:63-64.

Day, P. R. 1965. Particle fractionation and particle-size analysis. *In* C. A. Black et al. (ed.) Methods of soil analysis: Part 1. Physical and mineralogical properties, including statistics of measurement and sampling. Agronomy 9:545-567.

Edminster, T. W., and R. C. Reeve. 1957. Drainage problems and methods. *In* Soil. Yearbook Agr. (US Dep. Agr.) US Government Printing Office, Washington. p378-385.

Ferguson, M. H. 1950. Soil water and soil air: their relationship to turf production. USGA J. and Turf Mgt. 3(3)35-36.

Finn, B. J., S. J. Bourget, K. F. Nielsen, and B. K. Dow. 1961. Effects on different soil moisture tensions on grass and legume species. Can. J. Soil Sci. 41:16-23.

Flannagan, T. R., and R. J. Bartlett. 1961. Soil compaction associated with alternating green and brown stripes on turf. Agron. J. 53:404-405.

Flocker, W. J., J. A. Vomocil, and F. D. Howard. 1959. Some growth responses of tomatoes to soil compaction. Soil Sci. Soc. Amer. Proc. 23:188-191.

Geiger, R. 1957. The climate near the ground. Harvard Univ. Press, Cambridge, Mass. 494p.

Gilbert, S. G., and J. W. Shive. 1942. The significance of oxygen in nutrient substrates for plants: I. The oxygen requirement. Soil Sci. 53:143-152.

Grable, A. R. 1966. Soil aeration and plant growth. Advance. Agron. 18:57-106.

Grim, R. E. 1953. Clay mineralogy. McGraw-Hill Book Co., New York. 384p.

Harding, R. B., T. W. Embleton, W. W. Jones, and T. M. Ryan. 1963. Leaching and gaseous losses of nitrogen from some nontilled California soils. Agron. J. 55:515-518.

Harper, Horace J. 1939. The effect of natural gas on the growth of microorganisms and the accumulation of nitrogen and organic matter in the soil. Soil Sci. 48:461-466.

Harris, D. G., and C. H. M. van Bavel. 1957. Root respiration of tobacco, corn, and cotton plants. Agron. J. 49:182-184.

Hoagland, D. R., and T. C. Broyer. 1936. General nature of the process of salt accumulation by roots with description of experimental methods. Plany Physiol. 11:471-507.

Hopkins, H. T., A. W. Specht, and S. B. Hendricks. 1950. Growth and nutrient accumulation as controlled by oxygen supply to plant roots. Plant Physiol. 25:193-209.

Hunter, A. S. 1965. Is phosphorus fertilizer being substituted for lime on acid soil? J. Soil Water Conserv. 20:46-48.

Jackson, M. L. 1964. Chemical composition of soils. p71-141. *In* F. E. Bear (ed.) Chemistry of the soil. 2nd ed. Reinhold Publ. Corp., New York. 515p.

Jackson, W. A. 1967. Physiological effects of soil acidity. *In* R. W. Pearson and F. Adams (ed.) Soil acidity and liming. Agronomy 12:43-124.

Jenny, H. 1941. Factors of soil formation. McGraw-Hill Book Co. New York. 281p.

Jenny, H. 1961. Reflections of the soil acidity merry-go-round. Soil Sci. Soc. Amer. Proc. 25:428-432.

Jensen, H. L. 1965. Nonsymbiotic nitrogen fixation. *In* W. V. Bartholomew and F. E. Clark (ed.) Soil nitrogen. Agronomy 10:436-480.

Joffe, J. S. 1949. Pedology. 2nd ed. Pedology Publ., New Brunswick, N. J. 662p.

Juncker, P. H., and J. J. Madison. 1967. Soil moisture characteristics of sand-peat mixes. Soil Sci. Soc. Amer. Proc. 31:5-8.

Kilmer, V. J., and L. T. Alexander. 1949. Methods of making mechanical analyses of soils. Soil Sci. 68:15-24.

Kunze, R. J., M. H. Ferguson, and J. B. Page. 1957. The effects of compaction on golf green mixtures. USGA J. and Turf Mgt. 10(6): 24-27.

Lawton, K. 1945. The influence of soil aeration on the growth and absorption of nutrients by corn plants. Soil Sci. Soc. Amer. Proc. 10:263-268.

Ledeboer, F. B., and C. R. Skogley. 1967. Investigations into the nature of thatch and methods for its decomposition. Agron. J. 59:320-323.

Letey, J., O. R. Lunt, L. H. Stolzy, and T. E. Szuszkiewicz. 1961a. Plant growth, water use and nutritional response to rhizosphere differentials of oxygen concentration Soil Sci. Soc. Amer. Proc. 25:183-186.

Letey, J., W. C. Morgan, S. J. Richards, and N. Valoras. 1966. Physical soil amendments, soil compaction, irrigation, and wetting agents in turfgrass-management: III. Effects on oxygen diffusion rate and root growth. Agron. J. 58:531-535.

Letey, J., L. H. Stolzy, G. B. Blank, and O. R. Lunt. 1961b. Effect of temperature on oxygen diffusion rates and subsequent shoot growth, root growth, and mineral content of two plant species. Soil Sci. 92:314-321.

Letey, J., L. H. Stolzy, O. R. Lunt, and V. B. Youngner. 1964. Growth and nutrient uptake of Newport bluegrass as affected by soil oxygen. Plant Soil 20:143-148.

Letey, J., L. H. Stolzy, N. Valoras, and T. E. Szuszkiewicz. 1962. Influence of soil oxygen on growth and mineral concentration of barley. Agron. J. 54:538-540.

Lipman, C. B., and M. E. Wank. 1924. The availability of nitrogen in peat. Soil Sci. 18:311-316.

Longnecker, T. C., and H. B. Sprague. 1940. Rate of penetration of lime in soils under permanent grass. Soil Sci. 50:277-288.

Lotspeich, F. B. 1964. Strength and bulk density of compacted mixtures of kaolinite and glass beads. Soil Sci. Soc. Amer. Proc. 28:737-740.

Lucas, R. E., P. E. Rieke, and R. S. Farnham 1965. Peats for soil improvement and soil mixes. Michigan State University Ext. Bull. No. 516. 11p.

Lunt, H. A. 1955. The use of woodchips and other wood fragments as soil amendments. Connecticut Agr. Exp. Sta. Bull. 593. 46p.

Lunt, H. A. 1961. Improving nursery soil by addition of organic matter. Connecticut Agr. Exp. Sta. Circ. 219. 8p.

Lunt, O. R. 1956. Minimizing compaction in putting greens. USGA J. and Turf Mgt. 9(5):25-30.

Lunt, O. R., C. Kaempffe, and V. B. Youngner. 1964. Tolerance of five turfgrass species to soil alkali. Agron. J. 56:481-483.

Lunt, O. R., V. B. Youngner, and J. J. Oertli. 1961. Salinity tolerance of five turfgrass varieties. Agron. J. 53:247-249.

Marshall, C. E. 1949. The colloid chemistry of the silicate minerals. *In* Agronomy 1:1-195.

Meredith, H. L., and W. H. Patrick, Jr. 1961. Effects of soil compaction on subsoil root penetration and physical properties of three soils in Louisiana. Agron. J. 53:163-167.

Meyer, T. A., and G. A. Volk. 1952. Effect of particle size of limestones on soil reaction, exchangeable cations, and plant growth. Soil Sci. 73:37-52.

Millar, C. E., L. M. Turk, and H. D. Foth. 1965. Fundamentals of soil science. 4th ed. John Wiley & Sons, Inc., New York. 491p.

Montgomery, P. H., and F. C. Edminster. 1966. Use of soil surveys in planning for recreation. *In* L. J. Bartelli, J. V. Baird, M. R. Heddleson, A. A. Klingebiel, D. O'Harrow (ed.) Soil surveys and land use planning. Soil Sci. Soc. Amer. and Amer. Soc. Agron. Madison, Wis.

Morgan, W. C., J. Letey, S. J. Richards, and N. Valoras. 1966. Physical soil amendments, soil compaction, irrigation, and wetting agents in turfgrass management: I. Effects on compactibility, water infiltration rates, evapotranspiration, and number of irrigations. Agron. J. 58:525-528.

Musser, H. B. 1962. Turf management. Reveised ed. McGraw-Hill Book Co. New York. 356p.

Oschwald, W. R., F. F. Riecken, R. I. Dideriksen, W. H. Scholtes, and F. W. Schaller. 1965. Principal soils of Iowa. Iowa State University Special Report No. 42.

Peech, M. 1965a. Hydrogen ion activity. *In* C. A. Black et al. (ed.) Methods of soil analysis: Part 2. Chemical and microbiological properties. Agronomy 9:914:926.

Peech, M. 1965b. Lime requirement. *In* C. A. Black et al. (ed.) Methods of soil analysis: Part 2. Chemical and microbiological properties. Agronomy 9:927-932.

Petersen, G. W., R. L. Cunningham, and R. P. Matelski. 1968. Moisture characteristics of Pennsylvania soils: I. Moisture tensions as related to texture. Soil Sci. Soc. Amer. Proc. 32:271-275.

Peterson, J. B. 1950. Relation of soil air to roots as factors in plant growth. Soil Sci. 70:175-185.

Pierre, W. H. 1928. Nitrogenous fertilizers and soil acidity: I. Effects of various nitrogenous fertilizers on soil reaction. J. Amer. Soc. Agron. 20:254-269.

Pierre, W. H. 1934. The equivalent acidity or basicity of fertilizers as determined by a newly proposed method. J. Ass. Offic. Agr. Chem. 17:101-107.

Reuszer, H. W. 1957. Composts, peat, and sewage sludge. *In* Soil. Yearbook Agr. (US Dep. Agr.) US Government Printing Office, Washington, p. 237-245.

Rhode Island Agricultural Experiment Station. 1957. Sponginess in Turf. *In* Rhode Island Agriculture 4(1):5.

Rich, C. I., and G. W. Thomas. 1960. The clay fraction of soils. Advance. Agron. 12:1-39.

Richards, S. J., R. M. Hagan, and T. M. McCalla. 1952. Soil temperature and plant growth. *In* B. T. Shaw (ed.) Soil physical conditions and plant growth. Agronomy 2:303-480.

Richer, A. C., J. W. White, H. B. Musser, and F. J. Holben. 1949. Comparison of various organic materials for use in construction and maintenance of golf greens. Pennsylvania Agr. Exp. Sta. Progress Report No. 16. 6p.

Rickman, R. W., J. Letey, and L. H. Stolzy. 1966. Plant responses to oxygen supply and physical resistance in the root environment. Soil Sci. Soc. Amer. Proc. 30:304-307.

Rosenberg, N. J. 1964. Response of plants to the physical effects of soil compaction. Advance. Agron. 16:181-196.

Rosenberg, N. J., and N. A. Willits. 1962. Yield and physiological response of barley and beans grown in artificially compacted soils. Soil Sci. Soc. Amer. Proc. 26:78-82.

Russell, E. W. 1961. Soil conditions and plant growth. 9th ed. John Wiley & Sons, Inc., New York. 688p.

Russell, M. B. 1952. Soil aeration and plant growth. *In* B. T. Shaw (ed.) Soil physical conditions and plant growth. Agronomy 2: 253-301.

Russell, M. B. 1957. Physical Properties. *In* Soil. Yearbook Agr. (US Dep. Agr.) US Government Printing Office, Washington. p31-38.

Schollenberger, C. J. 1930. Effect of leaking natural gas upon the soil. Soil Sci. 29:261-266.

Seatz, L. F., and H. B. Peterson. 1964. Acid, alkaline, saline, and sodic soils. p. 292-319. *In* F. E. Bear (ed.) Chemistry of the soil. 2nd ed. Reinhold Publ. Corp., New York. 515p.

Simpson, D. M. H., and S. W. Melsted. 1962. Gaseous ammonia losses from urea solutions applied as a foliar spray to various grass sods. Soil Sci. Soc. Amer. Proc. 26:186-189.

Smalley, R. R., W. L. Pritchett, and L. C. Hammond. 1962. Effects of four amendments on soil physical properties and on yield and quality of putting greens. Agron. J. 54:393-395.

Smith, R. V. 1967. Soil survey of Montgomery County, Pennsylvania. U.S. Dep. Agr., SCS. US Government Printing Office, Washington. 187p.

Soil Survey Staff. 1951. Soil survey manual. US Dep. Agr. Handbook No. 18. 503p.

Soil Survey Staff. 1960. Soil classification: a comprehensive system. 7th approximation. US Dep. Agr. US Government Printing Office, Washington. 265p.

Soil Survey Staff. 1962. Supplement to US Dep. Agr. Handbook No. 18. p 173-188.

Sprague, H. B., and J. F. Marrero. 1931. The effect of various sources of organic matter on the properties of soils as determined by physical measurements and plant growth. Soil Sci. 32:35-47.

Sprague, H. B., and J. F. Marrero. 1932. Further studies on the value of various types of organic matter for improving the physical condition of soils for plant growth. Soil Sci. 34:197-208.

Spurway, C. H. 1941. Soil reaction (pH) preferences of plants. Michigan Agr. Exp. Sta. Special Bull. 306. 36p.

Stolzy, L. H., and J. Letey. 1964. Characterizing soil oxygen conditions with a platinum microelectrode. Advance. Agron. 16:249-279.

Swartz, W. E., and L. T. Kardos. 1963. Effects of compaction on physical properties of sand-soil-peat mixtures at various moisture contents. Agron. J. 55:7-10.

Tackett, J. L., and R. W. Pearson. 1964. Oxygen requirements of cotton seedling roots for penetration of compacted soil cores. Soil Sci. Soc. Amer. Proc. 28:600-605.

Taylor, H. M., and H. R. Gardner. 1963. Penetration of cotton seedling taproots as influenced by bulk density, moisture content, and strength of soil. Soil Sci. 96:153-156.

Taylor, H. M., G. M. Roberson, and J. J. Parker, Jr. 1967. Cotton seedling taproot elongation as affected by soil strength changes induced by slurrying and water extraction. Soil Sci. Soc. Amer. Proc. 31:700-704.

Thompson, L. M. 1957. Soils and soil fertility. 2nd ed. McGraw-Hill Book Co., New York. 451p.

Tisdale, S. L., and W. L. Nelson. 1966. Soil fertility and fertilizers. 2nd ed. Macmillan Co. New York. 694p.

Toth, S. J. 1964. The physical chemistry of soils. p 142-162. *In* F. E. Bear (ed.) Chemistry of the soil. 2nd ed. Reinhold Publ. Corp., New York. 515p.

Troughton, A. 1957. The underground organs of herbage grasses. Bull. No. 44. Commonwealth Bur. of Pastures and Field Crops. Com. Agr. Bur., Farnham Royal, Bucks, England. 163p.

Truog, E. 1946. Soil reaction influence on availability of plant nutrients. Soil Sci. Soc. Amer. Proc. 11:305-308.

US Salinity Laboratory Staff. 1954. Diagnosis and improvement of saline and alkali soils. US Dep. Agr. Handbook No. 60. 160p.

Valoras, N., W. C. Morgan, and J. Letey. 1966. Physical soil amendments, soil compaction, irrigation, and wetting agents in turfgrass management: II. Effects on top growth, salinity, and minerals in the tissue. Agron. J. 58:528-531.

van Olphen, H. 1963. An introduction to clay colloid chemistry. John Wiley & Sons, Inc. New York. 301p.

Vincent, J. M. 1965. Environmental factors in the fixation of nitrogen by the legume. *In* W. V. Bartholomew and F. E. Clark (ed.) Soil nitrogen. Agronomy 10:384-435.

Volk, G. M. 1959. Volatile loss of ammonia following surface application of urea to turf and bare soils. Agron. J. 51:746-749.

Vomocil, J. A., and W. J. Flocker. 1965. Degradation of structures of Yolo loam by compaction. Soil Sci. Soc. Amer. Proc. 29:7-12.

Waddington, D. V., and J. H. Baker. 1965. Influence of soil aeration on the growth and chemical composition of three grass species. Agron. J. 57:253-258.

White, A. W. Jr., J. E. Giddens, and H. D. Morris. 1959. The effect of sawdust on crop growth and physical and biological properties of Cecil Soil. Soil Sci. Soc. Am. Proc. 23:365-368.

Willhite, F. M., A. R. Grable, and H. K. Rouse. 1965. Interaction of nitrogen and soil moisture on the production and persistence of timothy in lysimeters. Agron. J. 57:479-481.

Williamson, R. E., and C. R. Willey. 1964. Effect of depth of water table on yield of tall fescue. Agron. J. 56:585-588.

Wolcott, A. R., H. D. Foth, J. F. Davis, and J. C. Shickluna. 1965. Nitrogen carriers: I. Soil effects. Soil Sci. Soc. Amer. Proc. 29:405-410.

Youngner, V. B., O. R. Lunt, and F. Nudge. 1967. Salinity tolerance of seven varieties of creeping bentgrass *Agrostis palustris* Huds. Agron. J. 59:335-336.

5 Nutrition and Fertilizers

R. R. Davis

Ohio Agricultural Research and Development Center
Wooster, Ohio

I. Introduction

Van Helmont's (1648) classical experiment with the willow twig in the early seventeenth century is usually considered the starting point of scientific investigation of the nutrient requirements for plant growth.

Krikorian and Steward (1968) support the hypothesis that Nicholas of Cusa (1401-1464) conducted a similar experiment about one and one-half centuries earlier and should receive the credit usually given to Van Helmont. From this small but very significant start, the science of plant nutrition has developed into a major discipline occupying the time and talents of many researchers. Many questions remain unanswered, however, and the quest for knowledge of specific functions of elements in the metabolic processes of minute plant parts continues at an accelerated rate.

Carbon (C), hydrogen (H), and oxygen (O) are usually considered separately when discussing essential elements, although their essentiality is undisputed. The fact that the plant gets these elements from air, not from native fertility or applied fertilizer, makes this difference of concept valid. Water normally constitutes 70 to 90% of growing turfgrasses and is so important to turfgrass management that it rates a separate chapter (Chapter 6) in this monograph. Carbon, the building block for all life on earth, is usually taken for granted since the plant gets it from the atmosphere. Only recently have attempts been made to increase the small percentage of CO_2 in the atmosphere when growing plants in greenhouses or other confined environment. Thus, CO_2 "fertilization" is now practiced on some high value crops. The use of CO_2 by plants is discussed in Chapter 8.

This leaves 16 elements for consideration in this chapter, namely: nitrogen (N), phosphorus (P), potassium (K), calcium (Ca), magnesium (Mg), sulphur (S), iron (Fe), manganese (Mn), copper (Cu), zinc (Zn), boron (B), and molybdenum (Mo), which have been well established as essential elements; and sodium (Na), chlorine (Cl), silica (Si) and vanadium (V), which have more recently been shown to be either essential or beneficial to some plants under certain conditions. Turfgrasses are not used in pioneering nutrition studies, nor are they as sensitive to minute amounts of a nutrient as are other families of the plant kingdom. Consequently, the necessity of some of the elements for normal growth of turfgrass has never been demonstrated. A few of the other elements in the periodic table are of interest only because they may be toxic to plants.

With knowledge of plant nutrition and chemistry, a modern chemical fertilizer industry has developed in recent years. An "inexhaustible" source of fertilizer nitrogen became available when man learned to combine hydrogen (usually from natural gas) with nitrogen from the air to make synthetic ammonia, an event that occurred at about the time of World War I. Prior to the development of this discovery, most fertilizer nitrogen came from natural organic materials, including animal manures, and a natural deposit of sodium nitrate in Chile. Many natural organics and, more recently, synthetic organics are used to fertilize turfgrasses.

This chapter is not intended to be a complete essay on either plant nutrition or fertilizers. The serious student will find some leads for further study in the bibliography at the end of the chapter. The reviews used as primary references for discussing the functions of fertilizer elements in plants are Hewitt (1963) and Wallace (1961).

II. Major Fertilizer Elements and Their Functions in Plants

A. Nitrogen

If there is any fertilizer element more essential than others for turfgrasses, certainly the vote would have to go to nitrogen. Nitrogenous compounds comprise 40 to 50% of the dry matter of protoplasm, the living and self reproducing substance of plant cells. Thus, nitrogen is an indispensible part of proteins, chlorophyll, amino acids, amides, and alkaloids. Certain nitrogen compounds are mobile in plants and move from older parts to the growing points. This explains why the older leaves first show deficiency symptoms and die prematurely under a nitrogen-deficient condition. Since turfgrasses are maintained in a vegetative condition and prevented from going dormant whenever feasible, their annual nitrogen requirements are higher than for most plants.

B. Phosphorus

Phosphorus, like nitrogen, is directly involved with many vital growth processes in plants. It is a component of nucleic acids and nuclei, essential parts of all living cells. Phosphorus as adenosine triphosphate (ATP) and numerous phosphorylated compounds are involved in practically every synthesizing reaction in the cell. One vital role played by these compounds is that of conservers and suppliers of energy for specific reactions. Other important functions of phosphorus are as phosphate buffers to maintain desirable pH in cells and for special roles in germination of seeds and seedling growth, the ripening of seeds and fruits, and the development of roots.

C. Potassium

Potassium might well be described as the mystery element of plant nutrition. In spite of much study, its specific roles in plants have never been well described. It is not a part of the molecular structure of any of the important plant constituents such as proteins, carbohydrates, fats, and chlorophyll. Upon analysis, potassium is found in all plant parts in relatively large quantities, particularly in leaves and growing points. All of the potassium appears to be in soluble form making it very mobile in plants. Several possible functions of potassium have been suggested by many authors. Among them are processes concerned with the formation of proteins and carbohydrates, water relationships, enzyme action, and photosynthesis. Potassium has been shown to play some role in the winter survival of turfgrasses (Morgan, 1968), in disease resistance (Goss and Gould, 1967, 1968; Couch, 1962), and in increasing the general hardiness of grasses to withstand many adverse conditions (Woodhouse, 1964).

D. Calcium

Turfgrasses as a group are quite tolerant to low levels of calcium nutrition; however, abnormal growth has been observed with very low levels. Of the several functions attributed to calcium, its role in cell walls is most commonly reported. The middle lamella consists largely of calcium pectate which cannot be replaced with compounds of other essential elements. Calcium is throught to have a specific function in the organization of chromatin, or of the mitotic spindle. Hewitt (1963) suggested that calcium is directly involved in chromosome stability and is a constituent of chromosome structure. Calcium has been assigned a role of special importance in root development since defective roots are a common chracteristic of calcium-deficient plants. It probably also has a part in the neutralization of organic acids in cells. Calcium does not appear to move freely from older to younger plant parts although much of it may be soluble. Hence deficiency symptoms first show on young tissue.

E. Magnesium

Magnesium plays a vital role in photosynthesis as a constituent of the chlorophyll molecule. It is involved in many enzyme reactions as an activator. Magnesium is always associated with the enzyme systems concerned with phosphorus metabolism, apparently acting as a carrier for the element. The uptake and transport of phosphorus is strongly influenced by magnesium. It is considered of importance in the formation of seeds which contain phospholipids. Magnesium is quite mobile in plants and deficiency symptoms first show on older leaves as it moves to younger parts.

F. Sulphur

The best known function of sulphur is as a constituent of certain amino acids, such as cystine and methionine, and the proteins that contain them. It is also a part of certain volatile compounds such as mustard oil and organic sulphides. Sulphur plays a role in the conversion of nitrogen fixed by legume root nodules into protein nitrogen. Sulphur does not move readily from the proteins of older leaves to new growth so symptoms of deficiency normally appear first on new growth.

G. Interrelationships Among Major Elements

The interactions among major nutrient elements are numerous and complex. Fortunately for the turfgrass manager, the grasses as a group are quite insensitive to "inbalances" of these elements. The extremely high phosphorus levels observed in the soils of many golf greens in the North Central states causes bentgrass no apparent trouble in obtaining adequate supplies of other major elements. Juska et al. (1965) found that Kentucky bluegrass can tolerate very high levels of P. The fact remains that extreme levels of one nutrient can influence the amount of another nutrient required for an adequacy level. It is a current fad among some soil testing laboratories to put much emphasis on Ca:Mg ratios. Experimental evidence (Key et al., 1962) indicates that much greater extremes than normally found under field condition are necessary before any problem can be expected. A review of many interactions of major elements with some plants (not turfgrasses) is given by Hewitt (1963).

III. Micronutrients and Their Functions in Plants

A. Iron

Iron is essential for normal chlorophyll formation, but it is not a part of the chlorophyll structure. It apparently functions as a catalyst in this regard. Iron is a metal constituent of a number of enzymes concerned with oxidation systems and also of enzymes concerned with the reduction of nitrate to ammonia in plants. The effects of iron deficiency on enzyme activity has been reviewed by Hewitt (1958). Iron is relatively immobile in plants and its mobility is affected by some other elements. Much "iron deficiency" in the plant is in reality "iron immobility." Some relationships between iron and other elements are discussed later in this section.

B. Copper

Copper, like iron, is an essential metal constituent of a number of enzyme systems concerned with oxidation-reduction reactions. Copper deficiency in some plants results in changes in the amino acid pattern and/or higher protein contents, indicating a breakdown of normal nitrogen metabolism. It plays a role in pigment formation in flowers and leaves of some plant species. Copper also has complicated interactions with other essential mineral elements.

C. Manganese

Manganese is also involved as a catalyst of enzyme systems concerned with oxidation-reduction reactions, including a Hill reaction. It plays a role in photosynthesis which remains unexplained. Manganese and iron are closely associated in plant nutrition. An excess of iron may induce manganese deficiency and, conversely, an excess of manganese may induce iron deficiency.

D. Zinc

Zinc is also present in many enzymes concerned with many types of reactions. Tsui (1948) concluded that zinc was required in the tomato for the synthesis of tryptophan, a precursor of auxin. Skoog (1940) concluded that zinc is responsible for keeping auxin in an active state, but not for its synthesis. Zinc deficiency causes large increases in amino nitrogen compounds in tomato, particularly glutamine and asparagine.

E. Boron

Like potassium, no specific function of boron in plants has been identified as a critical role of the element. Among many possible roles suggested are its necessity for the translocation of sugars, its concern with water relations in cells, its role in keeping calcium in a soluble form within the plant and its role in the metabolism of nitrogen compounds to protein. Skok (1958) reviewed possible roles of boron in some detail. Of special interest to turfgrass students is Eaton's (1944) report that Kentucky bluegrass accumulated less boron than any of several other plants studied.

F. Molybdenum

Molybdenum has been shown to be an essential part of the nitrate reductase system of plants (Nicholas and Nason, 1954) and, as would be expected, a deficiency leads to accumulation of high concentrations of nitrate. It is essential for nitrogen fixation by rhizobia so legumes grown on molybdenum-deficient soils often show nitrogen deficiency. Molybdate serves as a catalyst for the chemical hydrolysis of ortho- and pyrophosphate esters (Weil-Malherbe and Green, 1951).

G. Relationships Between Iron and Other Elements

Any nutrient element, if available in excess, may influence the availability of other elements. However, the relationships between iron and other elements are sufficiently unique to rate special treatment. "Lime-induced chlorosis" has been observed on bentgrass golf greens with a high soil pH. The problem can usually be corrected with a spray application of iron sulphate or chelated iron. The induced iron deficiency is further aggravated with a high soil phosphorus level. Excess of either calcium or magnesium carbonate or both can induce the chlorosis.

Iron has been observed to accumulate in the nodes of corn (Hoffer 1930) and sugarcane under potassium deficiency conditions and thus the plant shows iron deficiency. Although this relationship has not been reported in turfgrass, such a possibility could very well exist.

The relationship between iron and manganese was discussed earlier. Excesses of several other metals, including chromium, copper, zinc, cobalt, nickel, and cadmium, may induce symptoms identical with those of iron deficiency.

IV. Mineral Deficiency and Toxicity

The vast majority of nutritional problems on turfgrasses involve only nitrogen, phosphorus, potassium, and lime (calcium and/or magnesium). The usual problem is a limited supply of one or more of these elements. Micronutrient problems on turfgrasses are extremely rare, iron deficiency induced by high pH or by an excess of another mineral(s) being the most likely to cause difficulty. Deficiencies of other micronutrients may develop on very sandy or organic soils.

Berger (1962) reviewed micronutrient deficiencies in the U. S. and reports only iron and copper deficiencies on grasses. Florida, New Jersey, Indiana, Nebraska, Oklahoma, New Mexico, and Texas have reported iron deficiency. Florida, Virginia, and Oklahoma have reported copper deficiency on grasses. The many reports of deficiencies of all the essential micronutrients on other crops emphasize the relative insensitivity of turfgrasses to micronutrient problems.

A. Deficiencies

The appearance of a sod can give the observant turfgrass manager many clues of the nutritional status of the grass. While there are many published reports of deficiency symptoms on important food and fiber

Table 1. Mineral deficiency symptoms on turfgrasses.

Nutrient	Visual deficiency symptoms	Other effects	References
N	Light green or yellow-green color. Leaf dies starting at the tip.	Better root growth in nutrient solutions, more tolerance to some diseases	Juska et al., 1955 Love, 1962 Woodhouse, 1964
P	Dull, blue-green color tending to purple during cool weather. Thin, slow-growing sod.	Seedling more likely to be deficient than mature sod.	Love, 1962 Woodhouse, 1964
K	Yellow streaked leaves followed by browing and dying at tips and margins.	Increased susceptibility to disease and cold injury.	Goss & Gould, 1967 Love, 1962
Ca	Reddish-brown between veins along younger leaf margins. Later tips die and curl.	Symptoms not likely to be observed in field.	Davis, 1949* Love, 1962
Mg	Green or yellow-green strips changing to cherry red. Older leaves affected first.	Increased winter injury.	Embleton, 1966 Love, 1962 Woodhouse, 1964
S	General yellowing of leaves. Gradual firing starting at leaf tip		Love , 1962 Woodhouse, 1964
Cu	Entire plant stunted and yellow. Growing points and tips of younger leaves die.		Woodhouse, 1964
Mo	Pale yellow foliage, bleaching and withering of leaves.		Hewett, 1956 Woodhouse, 1964
Fe	Chlorotic between leaf veins - eventually loss of most chlorophyll.		Wallihan, 1966
Zn	Leaves yellow, smaller, grouped together.		Morgan, 1968
Mn	Chlorosis of younger leaves, yellow-green spots on older leaves, withering at tips.		Walsh, 1945
B	Slow growth, pale green tips of blades, "bronze" tint.		Morgan, 1968

* Davis, R.R 1949. The reaction of four strains of *Agrostis palustris* to various levels of nitrogen, phosphorus, potassium, and calcium. M.S. Thesis. Purdue University.

Table 2. Soil and climatic conditions making deficiencies most likely (Chapman 1966).

Nutrient	Conditions making deficiency likely
N	Sandy soils - high rainfall. Low organic matter soils.
P	Highly leached soils, organic soils, calcareous soils, cold soils.
K	Sandy soils, organic solis, heavily cropped, leached and eroded soils.
Ca	Sandy soils - high rainfall, acid soils - mineral or peat, clay principally montmorillonitic, alkali or sodic soils.
Mg	Acid sandy soils, organic soils
S	Low organic matter soils, small quantity of sulphur brought down in rainfall.
Fe	Calcareous soils, poorly drained soils, high soil levels of P, Mn, Zn, Cu, or Ni.
Cu	Organic soils, alkaline and calcareous soils, leached sandy soils, heavily nitrogen fertilized.
Zn	Acid, leached, sandy soils, alkaline soils, soils derived from granites.
Mn	Thin peaty soils over calcareous subsoil, calcareous silts and clays, poorly drained, high organic matter calcareous soils, very sandy acid mineral soils.
B	Sandy soils, soils derived from acid igneous rock, naturally acid leached soils, acid organic soils, alkaline soils with free lime.
Mo	Highly podosolized soils,well-drained calcareous soils, ironstone soils of Australia, New Zealand, Holland.

Table 3. Methods of correcting mineral deficiencies (Chapman 1966).

Nutrient	Method for correcting deficiency
N	N fertilizer applied to soil or foliar spray of soluble N carrier. Add organic matter to the soil.
P	Apply plant-available source of phosphorus to the soil. Adjust extreme pH.
K	Apply potassium-bearing fertilizer to soil.
Ca	Lime acid soils. Add gypsum or other soluble calcium source where lime is not needed.
Mg	Add dolomitic limestone. Where lime is not needed make a soil or foliar application of epsom salts (magnesium sulfate).
S	Use fertilizer salts containing sulfur (e.g., ammonium sulfate, potassium sulfate, low grade phosphate). Apply gypsum or elemental sulfur.
Fe	Foliar spray of iron sulfate or soil application of chelated iron. Lower pH, improve drainage, reduce phosphorus fertilization.
Cu	Foliar or soil application of copper sulfate. Reduce nitrogen fertilization.
Zn	Foliar spray of zinc sulfate or soil application of zinc chelates.
Mn	Foliar spray of manganese sulfate.
B	Foliar or soil application of borax. Neutralize soils containing free lime.
Mo	Soil or foliar application of sodium or ammonium molybdate. Lime acid soils.

plants, reports of specific symptoms on turfgrass species are rare. Fortunately, symptoms among the many species of the grass family have much in common.

Woodhouse (1964) reported deficiency symptoms in forage grasses, some species of which are also used as turfgrasses. Love (1962) described deficiency symptoms and showed color plate of deficiencies on Seaside creeping bentgrass, Merion Kentucky bluegrass and Pennlawn red fescue. Wallace (1961) and Chapman (1966) describe deficiency symptoms on many plants, including some grasses. Table 1 gives some general deficiency symptoms in brief form and references for further reading. Table 2 contains brief descriptions of soil and climatic factors most likely to result in mineral deficiencies, and Table 3 gives some general methods of correcting them.

B. Excesses or Toxicities

Any mineral element essential for plant growth can be used to excess to the detriment of turfgrasses. All turfgrass managers have observed the lush, soft growth resulting from excessive nitrogen. The report by Cheesman et al. (1965) is one of many showing higher incidence and more severity of attack by some diseases at high nitrogen levels. Carroll and Welton (1938) reported that heavy nitrogen fertilization reduces cold resistance of Kentucky bluegrass. Fortunately, turfgrasses are very tolerant to excessive supplies of many of the essential elements. In a greenhouse study Juska et al. (1965) found no problems on Kentucky bluegrass and red fescue when grown at very high levels of phosphorus. In some field situations, high levels of soil phosphorus have been observed to contribute to iron deficiency.

Most mineral toxicity problems on turfgrasses are man-made, so the long term solution to the problem is to avoid applying excesses. Micronutrients, if applied, should be used with extreme care. Deal and Engel (1965) found a decrease in sod density from iron applied at 1, 10 and 50 pounds per acre. Iron at 50 pounds and zinc at 25 pounds greatly retarded rhizome development. Boron at 7 1/2 pounds per acre was toxic to highly fertilized turf. Oertli et al. (1961) found 10 ppm boron in a nutrient solution toxic to many turfgrass species.

Gregory and Bradshaw (1965) found that colonial bentgrass growing on "mine workings" developed a genetically determined high tolerance for heavy metals. Plants of the same species taken from a pasture were not nearly so tolerant. Tolerances for copper and lead were independent. Plants tolerant to zinc were also tolerant to nickel and vice versa, but this tolerance was independent of copper and lead.

Since minor element deficiencies on turfgrasses are rare and difficult to visually diagnose, a suspected deficiency should be verified before applying something intended for correcting it. Deficiency and toxicity symptoms have much in common. Plant analysis,which is discussed in another section, holds great promise for diagnosing minor element problems.

1. Problems with Salinity

Sodium is considered an essential element for some plants (Brownell and Wood, 1957), and others show positive response to sodium, including some grasses (Gammon, 1953). Also, chlorine has been shown essential on tomatoes (Broyer et al., 1954) and beneficial to some other plants. However, the turfgrass problem with salt is one of excess. Many soils of arid and semi-arid western United States are naturally high in sodium. When water, also high in sodium salts, is added for irrigation, the problem is intensified. Even in humid areas where soils are normally leached, a combination of water high in salts and poor drainage can result in sufficient salt build-up to cause trouble. Turfgrass managers with oceanfront areas have the problem of both foliar burn and salt accumulation in the soil.

Lunt (1966) has reviewed treatments for soils containing an excess of sodium. The goal with such soils is to leach out the sodium or replace it with calcium or magnesium. One way of minimizing the problem is to select a salt-tolerant species and variety. Lunt et al. (1961) found that the salt tolerance rating for general turf quality was Seaside bent > Alta fescue > Kentucky bluegrass = highland bent. Youngner et al. (1967) reported that Arlington, Seaside, Pennlu, and Old Orchard® varieties of creeping bentgrass had the most salinity tolerance, Congressional and Cohansey were intermediate, and Penncross was least tolerant.

2. Arsenic Toxicity

The practice of using compounds containing arsenic as pesticides on turfgrass may result in the build-up of toxic levels. A likely spot for trouble is a golf green on which lead arsenate and/or calcium arsenate has been used for many years to control insects, earthworms, annual bluegrass, and crabgrass. Old orchard sites are also likely to have a high concentration of arsenic in the soil.

Liebig (1966) has reviewed the arsenic problem on many plants. Wilting of new leaves and retardation of root and top growth are common symptoms of arsenic toxicity. With the application of a given amount of arsenic, toxicity problems are more likely on coarse sandy soils and least likely on heavy clay soils (Crafts and Rosenfels 1939). Additions of ferrous sulfate (Vandecaveye et al., 1936), zinc sulfate (Thompson and Batjer, 1950), zinc chelate (Batjer and Benson, 1958), or organic matter (Vincent, 1944) have been reported to reduce arsenic toxicity.

V. Methods of Diagnosing Nutrient Status

When the appearance of a turf and environmental factors indicate a nutritional disorder, steps should be taken to verify the problem. The two most widely used diagnostic techniques are soil tests and analyses of plant part(s).

A. Soil Tests

Soil testing has a history of over 100 years (Anderson, 1960), but only recently has it been used widely to predict plant performance. Viets (1967) sets two criteria for a good soil test:

1. It should extract a portion of the nutrient from the soil that is closely related to or highly correlated with the amount the plant can absorb.
2. The soil test should be cheap, reproducible, and capable of being incorporated into a laboratory routine.

Tisdale (1967) points out that analytical problems in soil testing are minor and can be solved easily. The most important problems to be solved are concerned with correlation of soil tests with plant response.

This is particularly true when trying to relate soil test to turfgrass response. Very little direct correlation work has been done with turfgrasses because no precise measure of turfgrass response is available to relate to soil test results. This lack of a single objective measure for turfgrass response, in contrast with yield for the corn crop, will continue to interfere with progress in developing meaningful correlation data.

Even though most soil test values cannot be precisely related to turfgrass response, a good soil testing service can be very useful to a turfgrass manager. With a test for pH, P, and K, adjustments can be made in the lime and fertilizer program to assure that the soil reaction is favorable and these elements are in adequate supply. Special tests can be arranged if other problems are suspected.

All Land Grant Universities in the U. S. either have a soil testing service or can refer requests to a nearby laboratory. A recent survey of these laboratories in the North Central Region (R. A. Linville, Ohio State University, private communication) shows that 10 of 13 states test turfgrass samples and make lime and fertilizer recommendations. All do not use the same testing procedures so the critical levels for the tested nutrients vary with laboratory and soil type. It is very important that a person interpreting soil test understands the testing procedures used and has some knowledge of turfgrass problems.

Much information other than pH, P, and K levels can be obtained from some laboratories, both university and private. Many university laboratories have options that include calcium, magnesium, nitrates, soluble salts, and a few micro-nutrients. The primary criterion of a good laboratory is its ability to interpret the significance of the results of the test and make appropriate recommendations. Soil testing procedures in common use have been recently reviewed by Black (1965).

Soil tests made and interpreted by the best of laboratories cannot diagnose all turfgrass problems. Many problems such as soil physical condition, chemical damage, excessive shade, diseases, and insects are not explained by a soil test. Neither can a soil test tell much about the nitrogen nutrition of turfgrasses. There is no substitute for a good manager in regulating this most important nutrient element.

Do-it-yourself kits and equipment are available for soil testing. Ohlrogge (1952) has described the Purdue test kit which uses the molybdate test for P and the cobaltinitrate test for K. Bray (1945) developed a nitrate test powder for field testing both soils and plant tissues. Other types of kits are available commercially. Battery powered pH meters and resistance bridges for soluble salt determinations are also available. However, the use of these kits is not recommended unless the operator has a background of experience and training in chemistry. Incorrect soil tests are much worse than no tests at all.

B. Tissue Analyses

Many complicated soil chemical reactions can be bypassed by analyzing plant tissue to determine the quantities of nutrients it has extracted and accumulated from the soil. Hoffer (1926) and Thornton et al. (1939) pioneered the use of tissue tests as a means of making fertilizer recommendations in the U. S. Tissue or whole plant analyses to predict plant nutrient needs have only recently been widely adopted. The development of the direct reading emission spectrograph with computer read-out (Jones and Weaver, 1967) and automated nitrogen analysis has made possible the rapid determinations necessary for a successful plant analysis service.

As with soil testing, the critical problem with plant analyses is correlation with plant response. Again the problem is more difficult with turfgrasses than with many other crops. Hylton et al. (1964) reported the critical nitrate nitrogen level in blade 1 of Italian ryegrass to be 1,000 ppm in a nutrient culture experiment. Chapman (1966) reviews critical levels of essential elements for many crop plants. Jones (1967) shows that it is essential to sample a given plant part at a specific stage of maturity for a plant analysis to be meaningful. Sampling procedures and critical values used by the Ohio Plant Analysis Laboratory are reported. This laboratory analyzed more than 30,000 samples each year in 1966 and 1967, over half of them being research samples to improve interpretation (J. B. Jones, Jr., private communication).

Table 4 illustrates one of the problems of using plant analysis to determine the nutrient status of Kentucky bluegrass, namely, the importance of the time of sampling. The potassium content varies more with time of sampling than with levels of potash fertilization. Soil samples from these plots showed increasing potassium levels with increased fertilization and ranged from an average soil test value of 218 to 511 pounds K per acre. Plots receiving no fertilizer potassium for 8 years showed no evidence of potassium deficiency.

Another problem with spectrographic analysis of turfgrass clippings is the influence of a small quantity of unseen soil on the mineral content of the sample (Table 5). Close mowing and earthworm casts, topdressing, or an uneven surface means a soil contaminated sample. Values for certain elements (Al, Fe, Mn, Si) are dramatically increased while others (K, P) are decreased by the presence of the soil.

The limitations of the present methods of plant analysis do not mean

Table 4. Potassium content of Kentucky bluegrass clippings as influenced by fertilization and date of sampling (unpublished data of R. R. Davis and J. B. Jones, Jr., Ohio Agricultural Research and Development Center).

Treatment	% K in clippings - dry matter basis			
	5/25/64	7/17/64	8/28/64	11/18/64
No K	3.19	2.19	2.75	1.75
10 lb K_2O/A/year	3.21	2.25	2.82	1.84
50 lb K_2O/A/5 years	3.28	2.35	2.89	1.87
60 lb K_2O/A/year	3.47	2.37	2.75	1.89
300 lb K_2O/A/5 years	3.48	2.43	2.91	1.92

Table 5. Influence of cutting height (soil) on the spectrographic analysis of Merion Kentucky bluegrass clippings. (Unpublished data of R.R. Davis and J.B. Jones, Jr., Ohio Agricultural Research and Development Center).

Mowing ht, in.	K	P	Ca	Mg	Na	Si	N*	Mn	Fe	Bo	Cu	Zn	Al	Sr	Mo	Co
	% in dry weight - 10/13/67							ppm in dry weight 10/13/67								
3/4	2.45	0.56	0.43	0.23	<0.01	1.76	5.13	174	2,474	6	11	52	2,878	22	5	4
1 1/2	3.08	0.71	0.34	0.24	<0.01	0.50	5.12	63	431	5	12	50	369	21	2	3

* Kjedahl method

that the technique is useless for turfgrasses. Analyses of appropriate tissue can be very useful in verifying suspected deficiencies or excesses and in trouble-shooting unknown problems. However, the use of routine analysis of turfgrass clippings for making good fertilizer recommendations awaits further research and correlation data.

Quick tests of fresh turfgrass tissue are used by some turfgrass managers as a guide for the fertilizer program. Wickstrom (1967) outlines the steps for using tissue testing in field diagnosis. The Purdue tests (Ohlrogge, 1952), Bray's nitrate test (Bray, 1945), and Melsted's potassium test (Melsted, 1950) are usually used for quick tissue test. As with similar soil tests, their value depends upon the knowledge and experience of the user.

Some land-grant universities now offer a plant analysis service, but the number is likely to increase. A list of laboratories and the service they offer is given by Breth (1968). These universities are the best source of information on the availability and usefulness of plant analysis for turfgrasses.

VI. Fertilizer Sources and Their Characteristics

A. Nitrogen

Natural organic materials were practically the only source of nitrogenous fertilizers in the U. S. until the Chilean nitrate deposits were developed (Taylor, 1953). It was 1870 before the import level reached 1,000 tons of nitrogen. Imports of sodium nitrate reached a peak of 190,000 tons in 1943. By-product ammonium sulfate was an important source of fertilizer nitrogen starting in 1910 and continuing through World War II. Since World War II, synthetic nitrogen taken from the atmosphere has been the principal source of fertilizer nitrogen.

The principal carriers of nitrogen now used in the U.S. are anhydrous ammonia, mixed fertilizers, nitrogen solutions, and ammonium nitrate (Table 6). The natural organics (Table 7) account for less than 1% of the total nitrogen consumption, but they are still quite important in turfgrass specialty fertilizers. No report of ureaform nitrogen use is given in recent statistics (USDA 1967). This form is

Table 6. Nitrogen fertilizer consumption in the United States, year ending June 30, 1967 (USDA 1967).

Carrier	Tons of material	Estimated % N	Estimated tons of N	% of total N
Anhydrous ammonia	2,423,461	82	1,987,238	32
Aqua ammonia	842,231	24	202,135	3
Ammonium nitrate	2,170,015	33½	726,955	12
Ammonium sulfate	845,536	20½	173,335	3
Nitrogen solutions	2,539,253	37	939,524	15
Sodium nitrate	200,685	16	32,110	< 1
Urea	484,100	45	217,845	4
Natural organics	563,682	4	22,547	< 1
Mixtures	21,057,336	--	1,766,321*	29
Other	222,033	--	--	--
Total			6,048,519*	

* Total N and N from mixtures are taken directly from USDA report - other amounts of N are estimates based on tons of material.

Table 7. Approximate N, P, K content of certain natural organic fertilizer materials.

Material	Total N,%	Total P_2O_5,%	Total K_2O,%	Material	Total N,%	Total P_2O_5,%	Total K_2O,%
Animal byproducts				Excreta			
Blood, dried	13.0	2.0	1.0	Manure, cattle, dried	2.0	1.5	2.0
Bone, dissolved	2.0	15.0	-	Manure, horse, dried	2.0	1.5	1.5
Bone meal, raw	4.0	22.5	-	Manure, poultry, dried	5.0	3.0	1.5
Bone meal, steamed	2.5	25.0	-	Manure, sheep, dried	2.0	1.5	3.0
Fish scrap, acidulated	6.0	6.0	-	Sewage sludge, dried	2.0	2.0	-
Fish scrap or meal, dried	9.5	7.0	-	Sewage sludge, activated	6.0	3.0	0.5
Hoof and horn meal	14.0	1.0	†	Plant residues			
Tankage, animal	7.0	10.0	0.5				
Tankage, process	9.0	0.5	-	Castor pomace	5.5	1.5	1.5
Whale guano or tankage	9.5	6.5	†	Cotton seed meal	7.0	3.0	2.0
Wool waste	3.5	0.5	2.0	Garbage tankage	2.5	3.0	1.0
Excreta				Linseed meal	5.5	2.0	1.5
				Rapeseed meal	5.5	2.5	1.5
Guano, bat	8.5	5.0	1.5	Soybean meal	7.0	1.5	2.5
Guano, Peruvian	13.0	12.0	2.5	Tobacco stems	2.0	0.5	6.0
				Tung meal	5.0	1.5	1.5

* Food and Agriculture Organization of the United Nations (1949). These materials vary widely in composition. The figures given are average or typical analyses. † No data.

Table 8. Nitrogen carriers that may be used for turfgrass or seedbed fertilization.

Carrier	Formula	% N	Solubility	Form	How applied
Ammonium chloride	NH_4Cl	26	Soluble	Crystals	Dry or solution
Ammonia liquor	NH_4OH	22-25	----	Low pressure liquid	Soil injection
Ammonium nitrate	NH_4NO_3	33.5	Soluble	Prills	Dry or solution
Ammonium sulfate	$(NH_4)_2SO_4$	21	Soluble	Prills, crystals	Dry or solution
Anhydrous ammonia	NH_3	82	----	High pressure liquid	Soil injection
Calcium cyanamide	$CaCN_2$	20	Decomposes in water	Granular	Dry
Calcium nitrate	$Ca(NO_3)_2 4H_2O$	15.5	Soluble	Prills	Dry or solution
Diammonium phosphate	$(NH_4)_2HPO_4$	18-21	Soluble	Crystals	Dry or solution
Membrane coated prills		-	Slow release	Prills	Dry
Mixed fertilizers			Soluble or slowly soluble	Granular or liquid	Dry or solution
Monoammonium phosphate	$NH_4H_2PO_4$	11-12	Soluble	Crystals	Dry or solution
Natural organics	See table 7		Slowly soluble	Granular or powder	Dry
Potassium nitrate	KNO_3	13	Soluble	Crystals or prills	Dry or solution
Sodium nitrate	$NaNO_3$	16	Soluble	Prills	Dry or solution
Urea	$CO(NH_2)_2$	45	Soluble	Prills	Dry or solution
Ureaform	---	38	Slowly soluble*	Granular or powder	Dry or in suspension

* Ureafrom is 9.5% cold water soluble.

apparently included in the "other" category. Like organics, ureaforms are a small fraction of the total but play an important role in turfgrass specialty fertilizers. A more recent approach to developing slow-release nitrogen sources for specialty fertilizers is the use of membranes to coat soluble nitrogen (Lunt and Oertli, 1962; Lunt, 1963; Beaton et al., 1967). Turfgrass managers in the U. S. now have a wide variety of nitrogen carriers from which to choose (Table 8).

The solubility of nitrogen carriers is considered of major importance by many turfgrass managers. The ideal nitrogenous fertilizer would release nitrogen as the grass needs it over a long period. This ideal is seldom reached since the breakdown of natural organics and ureaform is influenced by temperature, soil moisture, and soil chemical characteristics.

In order to avoid confusion when discussing nitrogen solubility, the following definitions are used in this Monograph:

"Soluble" means quickly soluble in water and includes ammonium nitrate, urea, ammoniated phosphates and other inorganic salts.

"Slowly soluble" nitrogen requires some microbiological and/or soil chemical action before the nitrogen is converted to a plant useable form. This type includes ureaform and the natural organics.

"Slow release" refers to soluble nitrogen coated with plastic or other membranes to restrict contact with moisture.

B. Phosphorus

The primary source of fertilizer phosphorus in the U. S. was waste animal bones until commercial production of phosphate rock began in South Carolina in 1867. South Carolina supplied practically the entire domestic output of mineral phosphate until phosphate mining began in Florida in 1888 (Jacob, 1953). Due to the high grade of the rock and the vast extent of the deposits, Florida soon became the leading source of fertilizer phosphate, a position it still holds today. Mining from deposits in the Western States (Idaho, Montana, and Wyoming) has accounted for an increasing share of the market in recent years (Hill, 1964).

Bones and phosphatic slags are still a major source in some countries, but they supply only a small fraction of the U. S. consumption. The development of phosphate resources has kept pace with the rapidly expanding use of fertilizers. Most fertilizer phosphate is applied as mixed fertilizers or as superphosphate in the U. S. (USDA, 1967). Turfgrass managers have several other sources from which to select (Table 9).

C. Potassium

Wood ashes have been used as fertilizer for centuries. Early settlers in America noted that the Indians applied ashes to their corn fields (Reed, 1953). Hardwood ashes were the source of industrial and fertilizer potash in the U. S. and a thriving export business through the first quarter of the nineteenth century. A rapid decline in the potash industry resulted after the hardwood forests along the Atlantic coast were exhausted. The first factory for processing potassium chloride was erected in Germany in 1861 (MacDonald, 1960), and Germany had a virtual monopoly on world potash supply until World War I. The embargo placed on potash exportation forced development of resources in the U. S. and other countries.

The principal known U. S. potash resources are the Carlsbad District, New Mexico, Searles Lake, California, and Salt Lake Basin, Utah. The U. S. still uses more potash than it produces, although the major

Table 9. Phosphorus carriers that may be used for turfgrass or seedbed fertilization

Carrier	Chemical formula	% P_2O_5	Usual form	How applied
Basic phosphate slag	---	10-12	Fine powder	Dry
Bonemeals	See Table 7	---	Fine meal	Dry
Calcium metaphosphate	$Ca(PO_3)_2$	62-65	Granular	Dry
Diammonium phosphate	$(NH_4)_2HPO_4$	46-54	Crystals	Dry or solution
Mixed fertilizers	---	---	Granular or liquid	Dry or solution
Monammonium phosphate	$NH_4H_2PO_4$	41-52	Crystals	Dry or solution
Phosphoric acid	(H_3PO_4 (in water)	52 (usual form)	Liquid	In solution
Superphosphate	$CaH_4(PO_4)_2H_2O$ + $2CaSO_42H_2O$	18-24	Granular	Dry
Triple superphosphate	$3CaH_4(PO_4)_2$	37-53	Granular	Dry

Table 10. Potassium carriers that may be used for turfgrass fertilization.

Carrier	Formula	$\%K_2O$	Usual form	How applied
Hardwood ashes	-	3-8	Powder	Dry
Mixed fertilizers	-	-	Granular of liquid	Dry or solution
Potassium chloride (Muriate of potash)	KCl	60-62	Crystals	Dry or solution
Potassium nitrate	KNO_3	44	Crystals or prills	Dry or solution
Potassium sulfate	K_2SO_4	50	Crystals	Dry or solution
Tobacco stems	See table 7		Meal	Dry

portion is domestic production (Food and Agriculture Organization of the United Nations, 1966). Canada became a major potash producer with the development of extensive deposits in Saskatchewan. Canadian production has increased rapidly since 1962.

Potash is applied primarily as mixed fertilizers and muriate of potash (potassium chloride) (USDA, 1967). Turfgrass managers have a few other forms of potassium fertilizer to choose from (Table 10).

D. Mixed Fertilizers

Most fertilizers applied to turfgrasses contain at least two of the major fertilizer elements. Thus they are classed as mixed fertilizers. One type of mixed fertilizer is called "granular." In the granulation process, a homogeneous liquid phase is produced using a combination of heat (including heat of chemical reaction) and water. Granulation takes place in the ammoniator, drier, or cooler (Hignett, 1960). With true granulation, each fertilizer particle has the same composition, the particles are sized, and dust is largely eliminated.

Nongranulated mixed fertilizers may contain the same ingredients as the granular type, but the granulation step is omitted. Nitrogen solutions and anhydrous ammonia are the most commonly used nitrogen sources (Smith, 1960). Nongranular fertilizers are more likely to cake and are more difficult to spread uniformily due to wider variation in particle size.

Another way of making dry mixed fertilizers is to mechanically mix the ingredients to give the desired formula. Small "blending" plants are used to custom mix the desired formula and spread it by bulk truck on the customers field. Fertilizer condition becomes relatively unimportant since it does not have time to cake.

Some turfgrass specialty fertilizers are made by absorbing the ingredients on vermiculite, ground corn cobs, or other carrier. Either ureaform or soluble types of nitrogen may be used. The exact process is often the secret of the manufacturer.

Still another type of mixed fertilizer is water-soluble or liquid. The efficient production of ammonium phosphates made available a water-soluble source of phosphorus (Lutz and Pratt 1960). Potassium chloride may be added to provide potash and urea or ammonium nitrate added to supplement the nitrogen supply. The resulting mixture may be marketed as water-soluble concnetrate or as a liquid fertilizer. Liquids have the advantage of easy handling by pumps and pipes.

A newer form of mixed fertilizer is the slurry. With special abrasion-resistant pumps, slurries can be handled like liquids and can be more concentrated than liquids without the "salting out" problem. Special equipment is required for application.

VII. Fertilizer Laws

There is no federal fertilizer law in the U. S. Consequently, there is a wide variety of state laws. Alaska is the only state without a fertilizer law as of January 1, 1968. While all differ in some respect, there is much in common among state laws. Many of the laws are old but have been brought more or less up to date with "Rules and Regulations" issued by the controlling agency. Laws which have been thoroughly revised within the last few years generally follow closely the model law recommended by the Association of American Fertilizer Control Officials (AAFCO). Canada has one Fertilizer Act and Regulations which apply to all the provinces.

A. Guaranteed N-P-K

In 1955 the Soil Science Society of America (SSSA) issued a report on the pros and cons of changing phosphate (P_2O_5) and potash (K_2O) guarantees in fertilizer analysis to the elemental basis as phosphorus (P) and potassium (K). The principal reasons for SSSA supporting the change were: (1) The elemental basis is simpler and easier to understand; (2) Phosphate and potash are misnomers (To be technically correct, P_2O_5 and K_2O should be called phosphorus pentoxide and potassium oxide.); and (3) All other plant nutrients are expressed as the elements.

After the push for a change by SSSA, the AAFCO included a provision in their model fertilizer bill allowing for a gradual change to the elemental basis. Several more recent state fertilizer laws include this provision. However, all state laws still require that a guaranteed minimum analysis of N, P_2O_5, and K_2O appear on the label of each fertilizer container. Due to lack of support by the fertilizer industry for a change to the elemental basis, the AAFCO has apparently given up on such a changeover in the near future. Their latest model fertilizer law (AAFCO, 1967) does not include the provision for reporting P and K content on the elemental basis.

Colorado's law is unique in that it requires all elements listed in the guaranteed analysis to be water soluble. Many states permit and a few require that the source(s) of nitrogen and the percentage of each be listed on the label. Many require that this information be listed on the registration form required before a license is issued for sale.

B. Specialty Fertilizer

Most state laws make a distinction between "commercial fertilizer" and "specialty fertilizer." A common definition states that a "specialty fertilizer" is a commercial fertilizer distributed primarily for nonfarm use, such as home gardens, lawns, shrubbery, flowers, golf courses, municipal parks, cemeteries, greenhouses, and nurseries. Commercial fertilizers used for research or experimental purposes may be included in the definition.

Many states use the label format in AAFCO's uniform State Fertilizer Bill (AAFCO, 1967) for specialty fertilizers. The twenty-second draft of this model bill from AAFCO official publication states: "The following information, if not appearing on the face or display side in a readable and conspicuous form, shall occupy at least the upper third of a side of the container and shall be considered the label."

Net Weight ____________________
(a) Brand Name____________________
(b) Grade____________________
Guaranteed analysis:
Total Nitrogen (N).. ___%
___% Ammoniacal Nitrogen**
___% Nitrate Nitrogen**
___% Water Insoluble Nitrogen*
Available Phosphoric Acid (P_2O_5).............................. ___%
Soluble Potash (K_2O).. ___%
Additional plant nutrients, as prescribed by regulation.
**Potential acidity or basicity ___% or ___lb calcium carbonate equivalent per ton
Name and address of registrant
Notes:
*If claimed or the statement 'organic' or 'slow acting' nitrogen is used on the label.
**If claimed or required."

C. Secondary and Minor Elements

As with specialty fertilizers, many states use the format in the uniform Fertilizer Bill by AAFCO for listing elements other than NPK. The 22nd draft from Official Publication Number 21 states: "Plant nutrients, besides nitrogen, phosphorus and potassium when mentioned in any form or manner shall be registered and shall be guaranteed. Guarantees shall be made on the elemental basis. Sources of the elements guaranteed shall be shown on the application for registration. The minimum percentages which will be accepted for registration are as follows:

Element	%	*Element*	%
Calcium (Ca)	1.00	Chlorine (Cl)	0.10
Magnesium (Mg)	0.50	Cobalt (Co)	0.0005
Copper (Cu)	0.05	Manganese (Mn)	0.05
Iron (Fe)	0.10	Molybdenum (Mo)	0.0005
Sulfur (S)	1.00	Sodium (Na)	0.10
Boron (B)	0.02	Zinc (Zn)	0.05

Guarantees or claims for the above-listed plant nutrients are the only ones which will be accepted. Proposed labels and directions for use of the fertilizer shall be furnished with the application for registration upon request. Warning or caution statements are required on the label for any product which contains 0.03% or more of boron in a water-soluble form or 0.001% or more of molybdenum. Any of the above-listed elements which are guaranteed shall appear in the order listed, immediately following guarantees for the primary nutrients, nitrogen, phosphorus, and potassium."

D. Minimum N-P-K Content

Several states have laws setting a minimum allowable total of N-P-K in fertilizers. Specialty fertilizers and animal manures are usually exempted. A few states have a list of approved ratios and minimum allowable grades which can be sold in the state. Again, specialty fertilizers are usually exempted.

E. Fertilizer-Pesticide Mixtures

The sale of fertilizer-pesticide mixtures in a state may be regulated by the Fertilizer Act or the Pesticide or Economic Poisons Act or both. There is normally the requirement for clear labeling of the pesticide, how much, intended use, and directions for use. Appropriate warning statements concerning the toxicity of the pesticide are usually required. Florida has a detailed law specifying the pesticides that can legally be mixed with fertilizer, the maximum amounts, directions for use, and specification for labeling and handling.

Literature Cited

Anderson, M. S. 1960. History and development of soil testing. Agr. and Food Chem. 8: 84-87.

Association of American Fertilizer Control Officials. 1967. Official Publication No. 21.

Batjer, L. P. and N. R. Benson. 1958. Effect of metal chelates in overcoming arsenic toxicity to peach trees. Proc. Amer. Soc. Hort. Sci. 72: 74-78.

Beaton, J.D., W. A. Hubbard and R. C. Speer. 1967. Coated urea, thiourea, urea-formaldehyde, hexamine, oxamide, glycoluril and oxidized nitrogen-enriched coal as slowly available sources of nitrogen for orchardgrass. Agron. J. 59: 127-133.

Berger, K. C. 1962. Micronutrient deficiencies in the United States. Agricultural and Food Chemistry 10: 178-181.

Black, C.A. Ed. 1965. Methods of soil analysis. Part 2. Chemical and microbiological properties. Agronomy Monograph 9. American Soc. of Agron. Madison, Wisconsin.

Bray, R. H. 1945. Nitrate test for soils and plant tissues. Soil Sci. 60: 219-221.

Breth, S. A. 1968. Plant analysis. What it can do for you. Crops and Soils. April-May, 1968.

Brownell, P. F., and J. G. Wood. 1957. Sodium as an essential element for *Atriplex vesicaria* (Heward) Nature 179. 635-636.

Broyer, T. C., A. B. Carlton, C. M. Johnson, and P. R. Stout. 1954. Chlorine - a micronutrient element for higher plants. Plant Physiol. 29, 526-532.

Carroll, J. C., and F. A. Welton. 1938. Effect of heavy and late applications of nitrogenous fertilizer on the cold resistance of Kentucky bluegrass. Plant Physiol. 14: 297-308.

Chapman, H. D. Ed. 1966. Diagnostic criteria for plants and soils. Univ. of California, Div. of Agri. Sciences. 793 pp.

Cheesman, J. H., E. C. Roberts, and Lois H. Tiffany. 1965. Effects of nitrogen levels and osmotic pressure of the nutrient solutions on incidence of *Puccinia graminis* and *Helminthosporium sativium* infection in Merion Kentucky bluegrass. Agron. J. 57: 599-602.

Couch, H. B. 1962. Diseases of turfgrasses. Reinhold Publishing Corporation. New York, N. Y.

Crafts, A. S., and R. S. Rosenfels. 1939. Toxicity studies with arsenic in eighty California soils. Hilgardia 12: 177-200.

Deal, E. E., and R. E. Engel 1965. Iron, manganese, boron, and zinc: Effects on growth of Merion Kentucky bluegrass. Agron. J. 57: 553-555.

Embleton, T. W. 1966. Magnesium. *In* "Diagnostic criteria for plants and soils". pp. 225-263. (H. D. Chapman, ed.). Univ. of California.

Eton, F. M. 1944. Deficiency, toxicity and accumulation of boron in plants. J. Agr. Research 69: 237-279.

Food and Agriculture Organization of the United Nations. 1949. Efficient use of fertilizers. FAO Agr. Studies 9.

1966. Production Yearbook Vol. 20 pp. 452.

Gammon, N. Jr. 1953. Sodium and potassium requirements of pangola and other pasture grasses. Soil Sci. 76: 81-90

Goss, R. L., and C. J. Gould. 1967. Some interrelationships between fertility levels and Ophiobolus Patch disease in turfgrasses. Agron. J. 59: 149-151.

Goss, R. L. and C. J. Gould. 1968. Turfgrass diseases: The relationship of potassium. USGA. Green Section Record. Vol. 5, No. 5.

Gregory, R. P. G., and A. D. Bradshaw. 1965. Heavy metal tolerance in populations of *Agrostis Tenuis* Sibth. and other grasses. The New Phytologist 64: 131-143.

Helmont, Ioanne Baptista van. 1648. *Ortus Medicinae.* Id est, Initia Physicae Inaudita. Progressus medicinae novus, in Moroborum Ultionem, ad Vitam Longam. Edente Authoris Filio, Franciscus Mercurio van Helmont. Cum ejus Praefatione ex Belgico translata. Amsterodami, Apud Ludivicum Elzevirium.

Hewitt, E. J. 1956. Symptoms of molybdenum deficiency in plants. Soil Sci. 81: 159-172.

Hewitt, E. J. 1958. The role of mineral elements in the acitivity of plant enzyme systems. *In* "Encyclopedia of plant physiology" W. Ruhland, ed. Springer, Berlin.

Hewitt, E. J. 1963. The essential nutrient elements: Requirement and interactions in plant. *In* "Plant physiology III." (F. C. Steward, ed.) Academic Press Inc. New York, N. Y.

Hignett, T. P. 1960. General considerations on operating techniques, equipment and practices in manufacture of granular mixed fertilizers. *In* "Chemistry and technology of fertilizers". (V. Sauchelli ed.) Amer. Chem. Soc. Monograph 148. Reinhold Publishing Corp. New York.

Hill, W. L. 1964. Raw materials. *In* "Superphosphate: Its history, chemistry, and manufacture." U. S. Dept. of Agr. and Tennessee Valley Authority. U. S. Government Printing Office.

Hoffer, G. N. 1930. Testing corn stalks chemically to aid in determining their plant food needs. Purdue Agr. Experiment Sta. Bull. 298.

Hylton, L. O. Jr., D. E. Williams, A. Ulrich and O. R. Cornelius. 1964. Critical nitrate levels for growth of Italian ryegrass. Crop Sci. 4: 16-19.

Jacob, K. D. 1953. Phosphate resources and processing facilities. *In* "Fertilizer technology and resources in the United States," K. D. Jacob, ed. Agron. Monograph 3. Academic Press, Inc. N. Y., N. Y.

Jones, J. B. Jr. 1967. Interpretation of plant analysis for several Agronomic crops. *In* "Soil testing and plant analysis. Plant analysis part 2." SSSA Spec. Pub. #2. Madison, Wisconsin.

Jones, J. B. Jr. and C. R. Weaver. 1967. Determination of mineral composition of plant tissue by direct reading emission spectroscopy. Proc. Pittsburgh Conf. on Analytical Chemistry and Applied Spectroscopy.

Juska, F. V., A. A. Hanson and C. J. Erickson. 1965. Effects of phosphorus and other treatments on the development of red fescue, Merion and common Kentucky bluegrass. Agron. J. 57: 75-78.

Juska, F. V., J. Tyson and C. M. Harrison. 1955. The competitive relationship of Merion bluegrass as influenced by various mixtures, cutting heights and levels of nitrogen. Agron. J. 47: 513-518.

Key, J. L., L. T. Kurtz and B. B. Tucker. 1962. Influence of ratio of exchangeable calcium-magnesium on yield and composition of soybeans and corn. Soil Sci. 93: 265-270.

Krikorian, A. D. and F. C. Steward. 1968. Water solutes in Plant Nutrition: with special reference to van Helmont and Nicholas of Cusa. Bioscience 18: pp. 286-292.

Liebig, G. F. Jr. 1966. Arsenic. *In* "Diagnostic criteria for plants and soils." (H. D. Chapman ed.) Univ. of California Div. of Agr. Sci.

Love, J. R. 1962. Mineral deficiency symptoms in turfgrasses. Golfdom. Vol. 36, No. 9.

Lunt, O. R. 1963. New development in slow-release fertilizers. Golfdom. Vol. 37. No. 5. p. 54.

Lunt, O. R. 1966. Sodium. *In* "Diagnostic criteria for plants and soils." (H. D. Chapman ed.) Univ. of California, Div. of Agri. Sci.

Lunt, O. R. and J. J. Oertli. 1962. Controlled release of fertilizer minerals by incapsulating membrances I. Factors influencing the rate of release. Soil Sci. Soc. of Amer. Proc. 26: 579-583.

Lunt, O. H., V. B. Youngner and J. J. Oertli. 1961. Salinity tolerance of five turfgrass varieties. Agron. J. 53: 247-249

Lutz, W. A. and C. J. Pratt. 1960. Manufacture of concentrated water-soluble fertilizers based on ammonium phosphate. *In* "Chemistry and technology of fertilizers." (V. Sauchelli, ed.) Amer. Chem. Soc. Monograph 148. Reinhold Publishing Corp. New York.

MacDonald, R. A. 1960. Potash: Occurrences, processes, production. *In* "Chemistry and technology of fertilizers." (V. Sauchelli ed.) Amer. Chem. Soc. Monograph 148. Reinhold Publishing Corp. New York.

Melsted, S. W. 1950. A simplified field test for determining potassium in plant tissue. Better Crops with Plant Food 1: 14-17.

Morgan, W. C. 1968. Effects of nutrients on the grass plant. The Golf Supt. Vol. 36, No. 4.

Nicholas, D. J. D. and A. Nason. 1954. A mechanism of action of nitrate reductase from *Neurospora.* J. Biol. Chem. 211: 183-197.

Oertli, J. R., O. R. Lunt and V. B. Youngner. 1961. Boron toxicity in several turfgrass species. Agron. J. 53: 262-265.

Ohlrogge, A. J. 1952. The Purdue soil and plant tissue tests. Purdue Agr. Exp. Sta. Bul. 584.

Reed, J. F. 1953. Potash resources in the United States in relation to world supplies. *In* "Fertilizer technology and resources in the United States." (K. D. Jacob, ed.) Agron. Monograph 3. Academic Press, Inc. N. Y., N. Y.

Skok, J. 1958. The role of boron in the plant cell. *In* "Trace elements." (C. A. Lamb, O. G. Bentley and J. M. Beattie, eds.) pp. 227-243. Academic Press, New York, N. Y.

Skoog, F. 1940. Relationships between zinc and auxin in the growth of higher plants. Am. J. Botany 27: 939-951.

Smith, R. C. 1960. Plant practices in the manufacture of nongranulated mixed fertilizers. *In* "Chemistry and technology of fertilizers." (V. Sauchelli ed.) Amer. Chem. Soc. Monograph 148. Reinhold Publishing Corp. New York.

Taylor, G. V. 1953. Nitrogen production facilities in relation to present and future demand. *In* "Fertilizer technology and resources in the United States." (K. D. Jacob, ed.) Agron. Monograph 3. Academic Press, Inc. New York, N.Y.

Thompson, A. H. and L. P. Batjer. 1950. Effect of various soil treatments for correcting arsentic injury of peach trees. Soil Sci. 69: 281-290.

Thornton, S. F., S. D. Conner and R. R. Fraser. 1939. The use of rapid chemical tests on soils and plants as aids in determining fertilizer needs. Purdue Univ. Agri. Expt. Sta. Circ. 204.

Tisdale, S. L. 1967. Problems and opportunities in soil testing. *In* "Soil testing and plant analysis, Soil testing, part I." SSSA Spec. Pub. 2 Madison, Wisconsin.

Tsui, Chen. 1948. The role of zinc in auxin synthesis in the tomato plant. Am. J. Botany 35: 172-178.

Ulrich, A. and K. Ohki. 1966. Potassium. *In* "Diagnostic criteria for plants and soils" pp. 362-393. (H. D. Chapman ed.) Univ. of California.

USDA. United States Department of Agriculture. 1967. Consumpsion of commercial fertilizers in the United States. Statistical Reporting Service. Crop Reporting Board Sp. Cr. 7.

Vandecaveye, S. C., G. M. Horner and C. M. Keaton. 1936. Unproductiveness of certain orchard soils as related to lead arsenate spray accumulations. Soil Sci. 42: 203-215.

Viets, F. V. Jr. 1967. Soil testing for micronutrient cations. *In* "Soil testing, part I. SSSA Spec. Pub. 2. Madison, Wisconsin.

Vincent, C. L. 1944. Vegetable and small fruit growing in toxic ex-orchard soils of Central Washington. Washington State Coll. Agr. Expt. Sta. Bull. 437.

Wallace, T. 1961. The diagnosis of mineral deficiencies in plants by visual symptoms. Third Edition. Chemical Publishing Co., Inc., New York, N. Y.

Wallihan, E. F. 1966. Iron. *In* "Diagnostic criteria for plants and soils." pp 203-212 (H. D. Chapman, ed.) Univ. of California.

Walsh, T. 1945. Susceptibility of grasses to manganese deficiency. Nature 155: 429-430.

Weil-Malherbe, H. and R. H. Green. 1951. The catalytic effect of molybdate on the hydrolysis of organic phosphates. Biochem. J. 49: 286-292.

Wickstrom, G. A. 1967. Use of tissue testing in field diagnosis. *In* "Soil testing and plant analysis. Plant analysis part II." SSSA Spec. Pub. 2. Madison, Wisconsin.

Woodhouse, W. W., Jr. 1964. Nutrient deficiencies in forage grasses. *In* "Hunger signs in crops." Third Edition. (H. B. Sprague ed.) David McKay Co. New York, N. Y.

Youngner, V. B., O. R. Lunt, and F. Nudge. 1967. Salinity tolerance of seven varieties of creeping bentgrass, *Agrostis palustris* Huds. Agron. J. 59: 335-336.

6 Soil Water—Irrigation and Drainage

Albert W. Marsh

Agricultural Extension Service
University of California
Riverside, California.

I. Introduction

Turfgrass is grown primarily for its appearance, to provide attractive surroundings which will have a pleasing color and texture. It also provides a cover and protective blanket for the stability and retention of soil subject to heavy recreational and athletic use. Like all growing plants, turgrass requires water.

To retain its desirable characteristics, turfgrass must be irrigated in the drier parts of the country, in some places throughout much of the year. Irrigation has proved to be desirable during dry periods which occur unpredictably even in humid areas. Athletic use of turf requires not only a pleasing appearance and stability, but also a relatively standard consistency which will provide for predictable reaction between the ground and the ball used or feet of the players. Irrigation helps maintain this consistency.

II. Soil Water Relations

A. Water Retention

Soil consists of solid particles and the spaces between them which are called pores. Coarse, medium, and fine solid particles are known as sand, silt, and clay, respectively. Soils on which turfgrasses are grown may contain an amount of pores ranging from 40 to 55% of the total soil volume. These pores hold the water and air that are necessary for grass roots.

Water is held in the soil pores by attraction between the water molecules and the surfaces of the solid particles. At a low water content, water is spread as a thin film over the surfaces of all the soil particles. The thickness of the film is dependent upon the amount of water present and the total surface area of the soil particles. Medium textured (loam) soils have a greater particle surface area than coarse textured (sandy) soils so that a given amount of water is spread in thinner films.

When the water films are thin, water molecules are very close to the particle surfaces and are held tightly. The security with which water is held is sometimes expressed in energy units (joules per kilogram) which represent the energy that must be expended to remove a definite amount of water from the soil (Taylor et al., 1961). This energy is more commonly expressed in pressure units of bars or atmospheres (Richards and Richards, 1957), which are about equal numerically, and is called soil suction or soil moisture tension.

When all of the pore spaces are filled with water, a soil is saturated. The energy required to remove a unit of water from saturated soil is zero and the soil suction is zero. Water drains from the soil by gravity initially from the largest pores, where it is held least securely, and air space is created in these pores. The remaining water is somewhat closer to the soil particle surfaces and is held firmly enough to prevent rapid drainage by gravity.

In the process of water use by grass, first the medium and eventually the smaller soil pores lose their water. Water films gradually become thinner, soil suction is greater, and greater energy is required to remove each subsequent increment of water.

B. Soil Water Condition

Soil water condition is a term referring to the relative wetness of soil. Relative wetness is a direct function of the thickness of the water films surrounding the individual soil particles. A fine textured soil might contain twice as much water as a coarse textured soil and still be drier. As will be shown later, the relative wetness or thickness of the water films in soil is closely related to the movement of water in soil and into plant roots. It is, therefore, of some concern to know what this wetness of soil may be at any particular time.

The security with which water is held by a soil is called soil suction as mentioned earlier and can be measured by suitable instruments. Various instruments are available for making such a measurement but the one most adaptable to measuring woil water condition in turfgrass is called a tensiometer. The soil suction measurement is expressed in bars or fractions of a bar. A tensiometer will measure from 0, which is the

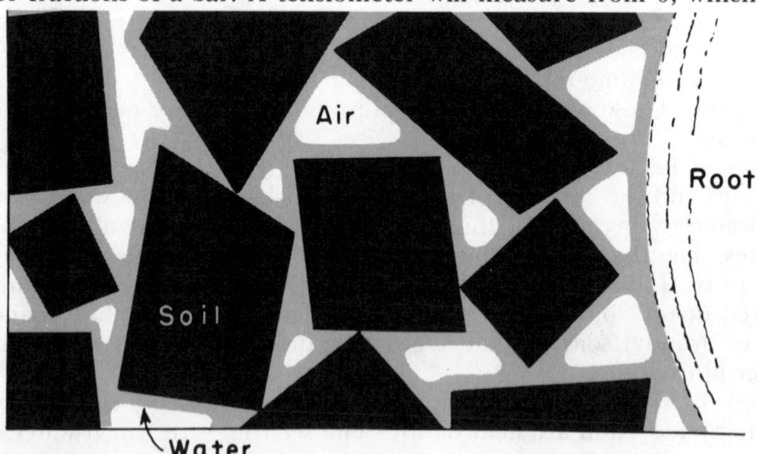

Figure 1. Soil water exists as films surrounding the soil particles.

condition of a saturated soil, to a dryness about equal to 0.8 bar, frequently called 80 centibars (cb.). This measuring device does not cover all of the range of water sometimes called available water but it does cover the range of conditions generally desired for turfgrass culture. The tensiometer gives a reading which is a function of the soil water film thickness. The reading relates directly to the performance of water in the soil water system and to its effect upon plants. For this reason, it does not need calibration for different soil texture (Richards and Richards, 1957).

C. Water Movement in Soil

Water applied by irrigation must first enter the surface of the soil, a process called infiltration. Soil conditions at the surface are often different from those inside the soil and entry rates will differ from transmission rates. Applied irrigation water first encounters the growing turfgrass and its accumulated mat and thatch. Growing grass will usually offer physical protection to the soil granules to help maintain an open structure and the porosity needed for high infiltration rates. Mat and thatch, conversely, tend to form a layer which may impede entry of water because they sometimes become temporarily water repellent when dry. Until they become wet again, irrigation water has difficulty penetrating to reach the soil surface, and runoff occurs.

Traffic on wet soil will compress the soil granules, destroying their structure and seriously reducing the pore space through which water must travel to enter the soil. This process and its result are commonly called compaction, a well known cause of poor water infiltration.

After water has entered the surface of the soil, it is transmitted to other points within the soil in a manner which depends upon existing soil and water conditions. When discussing water movement in soil, there are two types of flow to be considered. They are saturated and unsaturated flow.

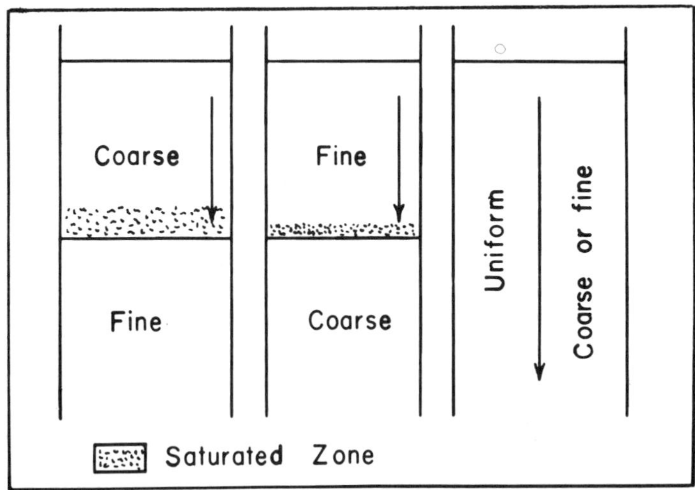

Figure 2. Capillary water movement is impeded by changes in soil texture.

Table 1. Approximate infiltration capacities for various soil textures and slopes.

Soil texture	Infiltration rates, inches/hour		
	Level	Sloping	Steep
Sand	1.0	0.5	0.3
Sandy loam	0.5	0.3	0.2
Loam	0.25	0.18	0.12
Clay loam	0.15	0.1	0.07
Clay	0.10	0.08	0.06

Saturated flow refers to the flow of water through soil when all or most of the pores are filled with water. When saturation exists, the bulk of the flow takes place through the larger pores. Under saturated conditions, gravity is the driving force acting downward and the flow rate is primarily influenced by the size of the larger pores and their proportion in the soil. Saturated flow is, therefore, most rapid in coarse textured soils.

There are restrictions and resistence to the downward saturated flow of water in some soils. If the flow is moving readily through relatively large pores and a change in soil conditions is encountered in which the pore sizes are much smaller, the rate of flow is reduced. Such condition is frequently encountered in turf where a fine textured soil having fine pores is located below the coarser textured surface soil. Water will enter and move through the surface soil rapidly during irrigation but stop when it reaches the fine textured soil. This will produce a perched water table which may persist for several hours or even days.

Much of the time, water movement in soils takes place when the pores are not filled with water and this is known as unsaturated flow. Unsaturated flow is essentially film flow whose rate depends, primarily, on the thickness of the water films existing in the fine and medium pores. If the permeability of soil beneath the soil surface is as great or greater than the infiltration or entry rate of water into the soil surface, the water flow will be unsaturated, even during irrigation.

Water moves by unsaturated flow from one point to another in soil because of a difference in relative wetness between the two points. Water flows from a wetter to a drier soil or from a region where water films are thicker to a region where water films are thinner. The flow of water will take place in the direction of the sharpest gradient or most rapid change between wet and dry soils. It can be up, down, or sideways. The driving force which tends to move water between soils of different wetness is often greater than the force of gravity so that water can move either with or against the force of gravity. Unsaturated flow of water has often been called capillary flow and may be known best to many people by this name.

As with any medium in which flow takes place, whether it is water in a porous medium or electricity or heat in a conductor, there is a resistance to this flow. Resistance to the flow of water in soil arises from two sources. The rate of saturated flow is mainly dependent upon the size of the pores available through which the water can move. Small pores create a greater resistance than large pores to both saturated and unsaturated flow. The other resistance to the flow of water is inversely associated with the thickness and continuity of the water films surrounding the soil particles. The pathway for the flow of water is provided by the water films which become thinner as the soil dries and the resistance to flow increases. For this reason water flows more rapidly in a wet soil than in a drier soil.

Resistance to water flow is related not only to the thickness of the water films through which water can move but also to the continuity of these films. In fine textured soil, the water films surrounding individual soil particles are generally in intimate contact with water films surrounding adjacent soil particles so that flow from one to the other is unrestricted. In coarse textured soils such as sand, there are fewer points of contact between soil particles and thus between adjacent water films. A bottleneck effect is created which limits the rate of water flow in films. Because of this, sandy soils have a rather poor rate of unsaturated water flow compared to finer textured soils. The fact that sandy soils, well known to conduct water rapidly by saturated flow, actually conduct water more slowly by unsaturated flow than fine textured soils is often surprising and confusing. Some of the problems which this peculiar action creates will be described.

When water moving as unsaturated flow through a fine or medium textured soil suddenly encounters a coarse textured soil, its flow is interrupted. The coarse textured soil has large pores through which saturated flow could take place rapidly but when unsaturated, the water films are few and the "bottleneck" points of contact between films seriously restrict the rate of flow. If water is moving laterally, little penetration of the coarse textured soil will occur. If water is moving downward to a soil change and continues to flow to the zone where the flow rate is greatly restricted, an accumulation takes place until a localized condition of saturation is obtained. When the saturated layer exceeds a few millimeters thickness, drops of water (free water as distinct from film or absorbed water) emerge from the finer textured soil downward into the larger pores of the coarser textured soil and move away as saturated flow.

The zone of saturation at the boundary between the two different soil textures does not build up like a perched water table. Nevertheless, a thin zone of saturation continues to persist as long as downward drainage of water occurs and the boundary layer will remain too wet for satisfactory growth of plant roots. This is why soil layers immediately overlying gravel will show evidence, upon inspection, of being too wet much of the time and plant roots will not be healthy. Many people presume that a gravel layer should provide an excellent drainage medium and are surprised when excessive wetness is revealed.

In turfgrass culture the position of a sharp transition in soil texture should preferably not occur in the root zone. While the gravel layer which is intentionally placed in the construction of golf greens (Holmes, 1968) serves to dispose of excess quantities of free water, it will always provide a thin layer of saturated soil at the interface between the two soil textures and this layer should be deeper than the principal root zone of the grass.

The same reason that requires a state of saturation in the soil before water can drip free into an underlying soil containing larger pore spaces (Richards, 1950) applies to the release of water from a soil into a large open space such as a drain tile. Water will not flow into a drain tile unless the soil surrounding the drain tile becomes saturated. At the termination of flow of free water into the drain, a layer of soil immediately adjacent to the drain will remain at a soil water condition equivalent to saturation even though no positive pressure any longer exists. The soil water is now at 0 pressure and 0 suction, in which plant roots will not be healthy. It is for this reason that drain tile should be below the root zone.

D. Soil Aeration

To remain healthy and to be able to absorb water from the soil, plant roots must have oxygen. Like fish, they obtain oxygen from that dissolved in water. The amount of oxygen which soil water can contain is rather limited and would not supply plant roots very long unless it were renewed. It is renewed by the process of diffusion between the oxygen contained in the soil atmosphere and that dissolved in the soil water. The soil atmosphere exists in the soil pores which are not filled with water. The soil atmosphere, in turn, would soon be depleted of oxygen and unable to supply the needs of plant roots unless it were able to be renewed from the oxygen in the atmosphere above the soil surface. This renewal takes place by diffusion through the soil pores. For this diffusion to take place at a rate fast enough to supply plant needs, there must be sufficient pore spaces and open channels through which the diffusion can take place. If the channels are blocked by soil compaction or are filled with soil water, diffusion cannot take place rapidly enough and plant roots will suffer from lack of oxygen.

The most common cause for inadequate oxygen supplies is excessive wetness in the soil that fills pores through which oxygen must diffuse. As stated above, plant roots cannot absorb water unless they have sufficient oxygen. The zealous efforts of an irrigator to provide sufficient water to meet plant needs under conditions of great demand may, in fact, be robbing the plants of their ability to absorb what water is present because the excess water interferes with oxygen renewal. The phenomenon of plants wilting on a hot day while growing in a soil filled with water is generally caused by insufficient oxygen in the root zone.

Equipment has been developed to measure the oxygen availability to plant roots in the soil water system (Lemon and Erickson, 1952 and Letey and Stolzy, 1964). While such equipment is not readily available to turf managers, the measurements that have been made by research scientists have proved that oxygen deficiencies can and do occur under common turfgrass irrigation management conditions (Stolzy and Letey, 1964). They have also shown that indirect measurements and observations can provide considerable insight into the adequacy or insufficiency of soil oxygen. Tensiometers can measure soil water condition and when they indicate a condition close to 0 suction or saturation, it can be reliably assumed that oxygen supplies are insufficient for satisfactory performance of most plants.

The soil chemical and biological systems also respond to a deficiency of soil oxygen. Zones of soil that are frequently or persistently deficient in oxygen become dark colored and develop a characteristic sour odor. When conditions such as these are found while probing in soil beneath turfgrass, it is evident that deficient oxygen conditions are common, generally caused by improper irrigation management and poor drainage. Such evidence suggests that improved drainage conditions should be provided if possible and that a change in irrigation management should be attempted.

III. Effect of Soil Water Condition on Turf

A. Top Growth

It is generally assumed and well supported by observation that in order to maintain a satisfactory top growth and color in turf, there must be adequate soil water in the turfgrass root zone at all times. Any soil water deficiency in the turfgrass root zone will result in visible stress symptoms. If stress symptoms are allowed to persist more than a day or two, the turf will develop brown spots and an unsightly appearance. If the deficiency persists over an extended period of time, some turfgrass may die.

As soil dryness develops in the root zone, the grass will show a darker green color than it did when water was sufficient. If the dryness persists, the green color may acquire a slightly blueish or blue-grey cast. Up to this point, the grass has probably suffered no damage other than that to the pride of its owner or manager. The next stage of drying beyond the blue-grey appearance is that of turning brown. At this point the grass begins to suffer damage that becomes progressively worse as the drought persists.

It is useful to recognize that stress symptoms in turfgrass, as in many other crops, appear whenever the rate of water loss by transpiration from the leaves exceeds the rate of water intake through the roots. Stress may occur at a time when there is a reasonable supply of available water remaining in the root zone. If for any reason the root system of the grass is limited to something less than normal, there may be insufficient root surface available to absorb water at a rate equal to the loss from leaves by transpiration. Stress can be caused by previous management practices which have tended to restrict the root zone and by current management practices which deprive the root zone of the oxygen needed for roots to absorb water.

An excessive water condition in the soil frequently produces top growth which may have a yellowish-green color. This is probably caused by the fact that the excessive irrigation has leached nitrogen from the soil and the growing plant is deficient in nitrogen. The excess water in the root zone may also have reduced the availability of iron and the yellow color is a symptom of iron deficiency.

B. Root Growth

Root growth of turfgrass and the depth of rooting are dependent upon soil condition, grass variety, mowing practice, and irrigation management. Irrigation management which continuously maintains saturation or near saturation in the root zone will restrict rooting depth to the surface few inches of soil. Near the surface, limited aeration is available even in very wet soils because of proximity to the atmosphere.

In such conditions, there is a tendency for new grass roots to develop mainly in the thatch above the soil surface because of the good aeration conditions existing there. When a sizable fraction of the grass roots are in the thatch the turfgrass will require irrigating every day and possibly more than once a day during hot, dry periods. The problem feeds upon itself. The more abundantly or more frequently irrigation is applied, the more frequently it will be necessary to irrigate in order to maintain turf survival. As conditions promote root growth in the thatch, the thatch expands and becomes a distinct problem to over-all turf management.

Roots will penetrate deeper where irrigation management provides water as needed, avoids excessive applications, and permits the soil to dry partially between irrigations. The grass will be healthier and less subject to stress symptoms if severe climatic conditions occur.

C. Development of Pathogens

Turfgrass is subject to various diseases, many of which are caused by fungi and are related to water conditions. Excessive irrigation or too frequent irrigation provides conditions favorable for the growth of fungus diseases. When a system of irrigation management that avoids excessive wetness is followed, fungus diseases are much less prevalent than in turfgrass that is excessively irrigated. Conditions of low soil oxygen created by excessive irrigation favor the development of anaerobic organisms that destroy turfgrass roots.

D. Tolerance of Species to Various Soil Water Conditions

While various soil water conditions affect the performance of most turfgrass species as described above, there are some that differ from most other grasses. They may have greater tolerance to drought or to excessively wet conditions or conversely may have unusual sensitivity to both of these environmental extremes. Performance of such individual species is usually related to the anatomical structure of the grass or to its habit of growth.

It is frequently stated that common bermudagrass is more drought tolerant than most other species and requires less water. The concept of drought tolerance of bermudagrass probably is derived from its inherently deep root system which provides a large reservoir of soil water upon which it can draw. The concept that bermudagrass requires less water than other species does not seem to be supported by fact. When given the amount of water needed for satisfactory maintenance of growth, the amount of water used in transpiration is about equal to that of other grasses (Marsh et al., 1968). This conforms with the theory advanced by Pennman (1948) that all species of ground cover existing in the same atmospheric environment will utilize the same quantity of water if water use is not restricted by drought.

Annual bluegrass is quite intolerant of even moderately dry soil water conditions. This is caused primarily by its extremely shallow root system. Annual bluegrass is unable to absorb water fast enough to meet transpiration needs if the top inch of soil dries moderately even though adequate water still remains at slightly deeper levels in the soil. Likewise, it can also be found that most other grass species which are considered to be drought sensitive act that way primarily because of limited root systems. The distinction between warm-season and cool-season grasses tends to mask actual relative drought tolerance. The observed responses of some grasses to frequent irrigations and wet soil conditions may represent a response to lower temperatures produced by frequent wetting.

Some species of grass appear to do well in excessively wet soil conditions where most other grasses fail. Included are redtop, bentgrasses, and tall fescue. This ability may be related to their resistance to attack by diseases which flourish in excessively wet soil conditions. For some plants this ability has been traced to anatomical differences which provide a mechanism for delivering oxygen to the roots through the stems of the plants rather than through the soil (Valoras and Letey, 1966). Letey (1965) has called this "internal plant aeration" and mentions that some plants develop the ability by anatomical changes after exposure to the adverse environment. Whether turfgrasses perform this way has not been proved but Letey, et al (1966) infer that they may.

E. Soil Compaction

One effect of excessively wet soil water conditions in turf is the susceptiblity of soil to compaction from traffic. Turf used for athletic and recreational purposes is often subject to considerable traffic. Frequently the traffic occurs not long after the turf has been irrigated while the soil is still wet enough to compact easily. Though this effect of soil wetness is not a direct effect upon the grass, it has a very pronounced indirect effect. Compaction reduces the rate of absorption of both water and air into the soil. After soil becomes compacted, careful turf management is required to provide adequate water and oxygen for suitable turf growth. Mechanical aerification can help overcome adverse conditions caused by compaction. Better management practices are needed to prevent or reduce the occurrence of compaction.

IV. Control of Soil Water Condition

With turf responding to various soil water conditions, it becomes important to consider how soil water can be controlled. The means generally available to a turf grower are irrigation, drainage, soil preparation, and soil management.

A. Irrigation

Irrigation is generally the principal means used to control soil water. There are important steps to be followed for an irrigation system to be effective in controlling soil water condition. First, the system must be properly designed for the needs; secondly, it must be installed using good materials and the proper techniques; and thirdly, it must be managed intelligently and skillfully. Subsequent sections consider each of these points.

B. Drainage

Drainage is an important means for controlling soil water condition and one that is sometimes overlooked. Since turfgrass is commonly over-irrigated and occasionally receives heavy rainfall, it is necessary to make provisions for carrying away and disposing of excess surface and soil profile water which is damaging to turf vigor. Natural drainage is adequate in some soils to take care of the excess soil profile water. In other soils conditions within the soil profile impede drainage of water sufficiently that artificial drainage becomes desirable. A subsequent section discusses drainage in more detail.

C. Soil Preparation and Management

Soil physical problems are sometimes responsible for undesirable dryness or excessive wetness in a soil even when suitable irrigation and drainage systems are installed. Advance soil preparation will help to improve the water conductivity of soil (Richards et al., 1964) so that irrigation and drainage management will be less difficult even in shallow profiles. Modified soil is commonly used in the building of new golf greens (Holmes, 1968). Artificial soil preparation is costly but frequently an investment which pays good dividends in terms of reduced water and labor cost, better turf growth, and better playing conditions.

Soil management techniques such as avoidance of soil compaction, use of mechanical aerification, and vertical mowing help to maintain suitable infiltration rates. Good infiltration improves irrigation and reduces runoff. Runoff generally causes wet conditions and ponding in lower places.

V. Irrigation Systems

A good irrigation system is obtained by 1) preliminary planning, 2) suitable design by someone with engineering skills, 3) careful installation, and 4) having the necessary and desirable accessories to contribute to its overall performance. In planning for an irrigation system, the purchaser or intended user should accumulate certain basic information and decide what is needed.

A. Capacity

The first step is to determine the capacity of the system. This will depend upon the water requirement of turf during the hottest and driest period in the growing season. The exact peak use period to be selected for this determination is a matter of choice and judgement. In general, most turfgrass is unable to draw sufficient water supply from soil storage for more than one week. Some turf managers would say that their turf or at least parts of it will be incapable of drawing a water supply from soil storage for as long as a week and that a shorter time should be used in the planning calculation. While this may be true, any stress which might be created in turf if the daily use for 1 to 3 days should exceed the average for the peak period probably would not produce any permanent damage to the turf. Thus, the amount of over-design necessary if planning were based on a maximum 1 or 2-day peak use would be excessive and uneconomical. Planning on the basis of a 1-week peak need does not mean that turf will go without irrigation for 1 week during an extreme climatic period. It merely means that for 1 or 2 or 3 days, which might exceed the average for the peak week, the turf would receive by irrigation 3/4 as much water as it might need and soil storage would have to supply the other 1/4.

Figures for the peak week use are not always readily available, but estimates can usually be obtained from other turf growers in the area who irrigate, a nearby Agricultural Experiment Station, the nearest Agricultural Extension Office, or the Soil Conservation Service Office. Sometimes there are State or Regional Water Agencies who can furnish information of this type.

Some assumed figures can be used to illustrate a solution to this problem. Assume that the peak use per week in midsummer is 1.8 inches. Not many weeks out of the year will require this much water but to meet the need at the critical time, the system must have capacity to apply this much water in 1 week. Assume that this problem is for a golf course which has an irrigable area of 100 acres. Further assume that the water factor of the irrigation system to be installed is 1.4. The water factor of an irrigation system is the number of acre-inches of water which must pass through the system in order to apply beneficially 1 acre-inch per acre to most of the area being irrigated. It takes into account the efficiency of water distribution and application. The difference is lost by runoff, percolation, and evaporation. Many sprinkler irrigation systems in current use for turf have a water factor of 2 or more. Multiply 1.8 inches per week times the water factor of 1.4 times 100 acres to obtain 252 acre-inches per week which the irrigation system must distribute.

Since the flow of water through the various segments of the irrigation system will depend upon the number of hours that the system operates, it is necessary to decide how many hours per week are available for turf irrigation. On golf courses and many other turf areas, it is difficult to irrigate while the turf is in use. Such areas are, therefore, generally irrigated at night. Let us assume that 12 hours per night are available for irrigating 7 nights a week, giving a total of 84 hours during which 252 acre-inches would be applied. This amount divided by 84 gives 3 acre-inches per hour as the flow rate passing through the irrigation system. In other terms, this is 3 cu. ft. per second or 180 cu. ft. per minute, or 1,350 gallons per minute. It is important to have available a water supply equal to this rate of flow or a reservoir supply which can be renewed 168 hours per week while being used only 84 hours per week. With a reservoir, the rate of input would need to be only 1.5 cu. ft. per second or 90 cu. ft. per minute or 675 gallons per minute. The reservoir must have the capacity to hold the input during the hours of non-irrigation. For this example, the capacity needed is about 2 acre-feet (650,000 gallons).

B. Distribution

The ability of a sprinkler irrigation system to distribute water uniformly is one of the important marks of quality. Systems range in quality from good to poor. Very good systems could be installed with techniques and equipment currently available but they seldom are, either for reasons of cost or lack of understanding of the importance of good uniformity. The state of the art or the engineering of irrigation systems has not reached a level where excellent distribution can be obtained within generally acceptable costs.

The need for a high degree of uniformity in distributing water through sprinkler irrigation systems for turf is not sufficiently recognized. Since turf is generally grown for its appearance, there is a desire on the part of most people involved to have turf which looks uniform and healthy without dry brown or yellowish-green spots. A spotted appearance of turf is usually caused by poor water distribution. Turf managers will attempt to eliminate spotted conditions as much as possible even though they have irrigation systems providing poor distribution.

Elimination of spots is usually accomplished by adding more water to green-up the brown spots. To do so increases the amount of water applied to the entire area. Under some circumstances, this may require 1½ to 2 times as much water as would be needed if the irrigation system were providing a uniform distribution. The use of excess water to compensate for poor uniformity of distribution greatly increases water and labor cost. It also produces the problem of disposing of excess water. If soils have restricted infiltration or permeability in any part of the profile, excess water can become a nuisance and lead to degredation of the turf. The attainment of good uniformity in the distribution of irrigation water deserves more attention and concern than it customarily receives.

Lack of uniformity in the distribution of irrigation water from a sprinkler system can often be attributed to budget limitations or the cost cutting procedures. Organizations or individuals intending to install a sprinkler irrigation system frequently estimate how much they will be able to pay for a system and then establish a budget based upon this estimate. When their sprinkler system is designed and submitted for bid, the bid may exceed the budgeted amount. Steps are then taken to reduce costs by eliminating or shortcutting certain phases of the system. This often results in the installation of an unsatisfactory system that does not perform well and eventually costs more, both for current operation and future revision, than the original design. *The buyer eventually pays for a good system whether he gets it or not.*

In addition to cost cutting requests, poor design may be produced by an unqualified designer or highly competitive design-installation combinations that use shortcutting methods. The features usually associated with a poor design consist of excessively wide spacings between sprinklers, use of low cost sprinklers inadequate to perform the job expected of them, or insufficient pipe size to carry the needed volume of water without undue loss of pressure. These are features which the purchaser or ultimate customer is frequently unable to evaluate satisfactorily until the system has been installed and its performance tested. By this time, it is generally too late to make needed changes without great cost.

C. Application Rate

Irrigation systems are designed to apply water to the turf at some preselected rate of application. Because of the large number of sprinkler heads available for use and the different design patterns in which they can be placed, it is possible to install a system which will apply water at rates ranging from 0.10 to 1.0 or more inches per hour.

The desired application rate must be decided. The correct basis for such a decision should be the infiltration capacity of the turf and soil to be irrigated, determined by test wherever possible. Infiltration capacities vary with different types of soil, being higher for coarse textured or sandy soils than they are for fine textured or clay type soils. Infiltration rates are always lower on a slope than they are on level ground. In addition, infiltration rate changes with the wetness of the soil, being higher at the beginning of an irrigation than toward the end.

To be safe, the design application rate of a sprinkler system should be less than the minimum expected infiltration capacity of the soil and turf for approximately 1 hour of irrigation at any time of the year. If the application rate is designed to this level or less, there will not likely be runoff during irrigation. If runoff occurs, it not only wastes sizeable quantities of water but reduces the uniformity of water distribution. The figures in Table 1 represent conservative infiltration capacities that may be used for design purposes when actual data are lacking. Wide variations from these values will be found, but they represent generally safe design rates.

Both high and low application rates have advantages and disadvantages in some respects and are neutral in others. It is often mistakenly believed that a large area of turf, such as a golf course, can be irrigated more quickly with high application rates. For a fixed rate

Table 1. Infiltration capacities for different soil textures and slopes.

	Infiltration rates, inches/hour		
Soil texture	Level	Sloping	Steep
Sand	1.0	0.5	0.3
Sandy loam	0.5	0.3	0.2
Loam	0.25	0.18	0.12
Clay loam	0.15	0.1	0.07
Clay	0.10	0.08	0.06

of water supply a course can be irrigated in the same length of time with either high or low application rates.

For example, a turf area of 100 acres needs a 0.6 inch irrigation, thus requiring 60 acre-inches. There are 12 hours of night time available to irrigate. The water supply rate is 2.5 cu. ft. per second. Flowing for 12 hours, it will supply 30 acre-inches, just half the 60 acre-inches needed. The irrigation will have to be divided into sets either applying 0.3 inches of water to all the area on two successive nights or 0.6 inches to 50 acres the first night and to the other 50 acres the second night. We will choose the latter method for this example though they come out the same.

If a system has a high application rate of 0.6 inches per hour and 0.6 inches is to be applied to 50 acres each night, the available flow will service a set of sprinklers covering 4.17 acres (2.5 acre-inches per hour $\div$ 0.6 inches per hour = 4.17 acres) that need to be operated for just 1 hour. Twelve sets per night can be operated covering $12 \times 4.17 = 50$ acres. If a low application rate such as 0.2 inches per hour were used, the available water flow could service a set covering 12.5 acres (2.5 acre-inches per hour $\div$ 0.2 inches per hour) that would need to be operated for 3 hours. Four sets per night can be operated covering $4 \times 12.5 = 50$ acres.

Higher rates of application are obtained by using larger sprinkler heads which require larger, more costly pipes to convey the greater quantities of water to the sprinkler heads. The larger heads throw water greater distances and can be spaced farther apart, thus reducing the number of heads needed and the number of pipe lines, even though they must be larger. Sprinklers providing high rates of discharge are also affected less by moderate winds.

Low application rates are provided by smaller sprinklers spaced closer together. This requires more sprinklers and a greater number of lateral pipes of smaller diameter and lower cost. Water discharging from smaller sprinklers is more subject to distortions in distribution pattern by moderate wind, though in calm air the distribution is more uniform than from large sprinklers.

D. Types

There are several variations in types of sprinkler irrigation systems used on turf. These can be classified into four general groups. The type of hardware, cost, labor requirement to operate, and application efficiency can also differ widely within groups.

The first group can be called the hose pull system. It consists of buried mainlines usually of steel, located 50 yards or more apart. At strategic points along the mainline there are risers with valves and hose bibs to which a long hose can be connected. The hose is connected to a sprinkler mounted on a stand or skid. The sprinkler is usually the rotary impact type but may be a whirling reaction or wave type. When irrigation is needed, the sprinkler is placed at random in the area which can be reached from the hose bib connection. It will usually be placed on the driest looking spot. At some fixed interval or whenever the operator remembers, the sprinkler will be moved to a new location by pulling on the hose, the procedure from which the name is derived. When all the area reachable by the hose from the hose bib connection has been irrigated, the hose is disconnected and moved to another connection. The labor requirement for such an irrigation system is high, the uniformity of water distribution and the overall efficiency are low. The initial cost is low.

The next group is called the quick coupler system. Buried mains are usually steel but rather than being 50 yards or more apart they are usually between 50 and 100 feet apart. At intervals along the main line, about equal to the distance between mainlines, quick coupling valves are installed. The top of the valve is flush with the turf and is covered with a hinged cap having a spring to keep it closed.

When irrigation is needed, a single rotary impact sprinkler together with a valve operating key is inserted in the quick coupler valve and turned on. As many individual sprinklers are operated simultaneously as the water supply and carrying capacity of the mainlines will permit. It is usually planned so that a balanced number of sprinklers will be operating on each available mainline. Sprinklers are usually moderately large, able to cover a circle of 100-ft. diameter or more. The sprinklers are moved after operating for a fixed interval or whenever the operator can return.

Water application rates with such a system are generally rather high, and runoff or ponding is common. The efficiency of irrigation application and distribution is usually low though it could be considerably higher with proper design and management. Labor costs for operating are high and would be even higher if stringent efforts were made to reach a high efficiency of application.

The third group, which accounts for most of the large turf installations made in recent years, is called solid set system using rotary pop-up sprinklers. They may be impact, cam, or gear driven. Most recent systems are installed with plastic main and lateral lines buried 12 to 18 inches beneath the ground surface, to which are connected permanent sprinklers arranged in a geometric pattern. While rather large sprinklers are sometimes used in these systems, the tendency has been to use medium-sized sprinklers spaced somewhat closer together. This has been made possible by the relatively low cost of plastic pipe.

Proper engineering and hydraulic design are very important for the efficient operation of this type of system. When properly designed, the system is capable of moderate to high application efficiency. The limit of application efficiency to which a system is designed is usually imposed upon the designer by budget considerations. There is a point beyond which an increment of increase in application efficiency may not be justified by the incremental increase in cost.

Most solid set systems of this type are controlled by valves grouped at a central location. In a large operation, such as a golf course, there may be several such centralized locations. Usually the valves are turned on in sequence using a special valve tool. Sequential operation is necessary and desirable. The pipe sizes and thus the cost can be kept lower when not too many sprinklers are operating at one time from a given line. When adjacent lines are operated on a sequential basis, the overlap of water from sprinklers at any one time is reduced and the application rate is less. This helps to prevent runoff. If sprinklers are left running too long, there may be runoff in spite of all other precautions.

Runoff, and the labor of turning valves on and off, can be reduced by using electrically or hydraulically operated valves controlled by clocks in a central control station. This type of central system has become common in most newer installations and is being added to some older installations. With a time clock operation, it is possible to select just when irrigation shall be applied to any one portion of the turf and for how long. If there is a possibility of runoff occurring during extended irrigation, the duration of applications can be reduced with provision made to repeat the operation one or more times during the same night.

The fourth group of sprinkler types involves solid set systems with fixed jet spray type or wave type sprinklers permanently in place. They may or may not be pop-up. This type is usually utilized for small areas such as borders, home yards, odd shaped patterns, and for nonturf areas needing irrigation which lie adjacent to turf. Fixed jet sprinklers can be full-circle or part-circle and thus are able to draw a sharp line between wetted and unwetted areas. They generally have a small radius of coverage ranging from 8 to 25 ft. Because of small area of coverage and lack of rotation, the rate of water application is appreciably higher than from rotary sprinklers, and runoff is a common problem. The wave types have lower application rates than the fixed jets and less runoff.

Operating times for fixed jets generally must be short to avoid runoff. Remote-control valves connected to programmed timers can provide short irrigation intervals and repeated applications to minimize runoff. Efficiency of application is generally much lower than that for the solid set rotary systems because of runoff and because fixed jet sprinklers do not have the mechanical precision of rotary types and are often improperly spaced. The labor requirement is low, particularly where remote-control valves and timers are used.

Previous discussion of types of irrigation systems has referred only to sprinklers because almost all turf is sprinkler irrigated. In arid climates surface flooding is used on a small scale for home yards, schools, and parks where maintenance of a cover at low cost is the prime objective. The land must be level and diked, the water cheap and abundant. The use of surface flooding is declining and will continue to decline.

Subsurface irrigation is relatively new and is the subject of active research. There are advantages in subsurface irrigation but several problems must be surmounted. The outlook is for a gradual but limited expansion of subsurface irrigation for turf. Advantages are: (1) low labor cost to irrigate; (2) little or no evaporation and runoff losses; (3) small pipe sizes because of low flow rates; (4) good fertilizer injection potential; and (5) reduced soil compaction. Problems are: (1) limitation of capillary transport of water by some soils; (2) closeness of pipes needed for uniform distribution; (3) possible clogging of pipe perforations by slimes; and (4) potential salination of surface soil in arid climates.

E. Design

Design of a sprinkler irrigation system for turf consists of selecting appropriate sprinkler heads and designating where they should be placed. The objective is to provide effective irrigation of the area with as high a degree of uniformity, efficiency, and operating flexibility as the skill of the designer can contrive within the price the customer is willing to pay. It also includes selecting the sizes and specifying the location of pipes to deliver water to the sprinklers in the necessary amount and pressure and in logical sequence. It includes selecting and positioning various accessories such as a pump, valves, and controllers. The total design is usually consolidated and presented as a single or multiple working drawing of the system, a descriptive list of all materials needed, and an explanation of the manner and limitations of operation of the system.

A design is needed before a system is purchased or installed because a turfgrass sprinkler irrigation system is a complex assembly of hydraulic and electric components. The system must be designed to fit local needs and conditions from a turfgrass, economic, and engineering standpoint. At present a sprinkler irrigation system design can be made by anyone who thinks he is qualified and is able to convince the system purchaser that he is. He may be an equipment salesman, an equipment manufacturer, an irrigation system installer, a turfgrass superintendent, a landscape architect, or an irrigation engineer specializing in irrigation system design.

A turfgrass sprinkler irrigation system design should start with a meeting between a potential designer and the customer at the site of proposed installation. The customer may be represented by the ultimate user (turf manager) and the buyer, if the two are different. The user should supply information needed by the designer on irrigation requirements (if known), the availability and cost of water to meet these requirements, his proposed system of management including labor supply and cost, and any special problems or considerations peculiar to the site. A map of the area showing all cultural and natural features, elevations, and water supply locations should be provided by the user. If later expansion is anticipated, the designer should be so informed. For a little extra cost he can increase pump and mainline capacities so that the expansion can proceed easily at a later time without expensive

Figure 3. Rotary pop-up sprinklers. Remote control valves. Turf is often associated with odd-shaped shrub borders requiring different sprinkler types.

revisions. The purchaser should indicate the extent to which he is willing to spend money for capital equipment to achieve a uniform turf appearance. He would be prudent to request the designer to make a total cost analysis of two or three alternative designs having different water distribution efficiencies and labor requirements based on local water and labor costs.

If the design is made by anyone except an independent irrigation designer directly employed by the purchaser, the purchaser is advised to ask someone with knowledge of irrigation hydraulics to check the design capability of the system. A person who both designs and bids on a system installation might be tempted to underdesign in subtle ways to permit a low bid. It might be some time after installation before the deficiency was recognized and corrections could prove both difficult and expensive.

When a buyer requests a design from any qualified person or firm, he should state initially the type of performance he wants from the system and then before paying obtain a signed statement that the system will perform as requested. This not only will insure an honest design but induce supervision towards a correct and careful installation.

F. Installation

Installation of a turfgrass sprinkler irrigation system is generally performed by a sprinkler irrigation contractor. In some cases the buyer or ultimate user has a staff possessing the necessary skills, ability, and equipment to make the installation. This procedure is sometimes used to save money by utilizing existing labor and management skills currently on the payroll. Whether the licensed contractor or the do-it-yourself method is cheaper and more satisfactory is a point about which there is considerable disagreement and one which will differ under various circumstances. While lower initial costs favor the do-it-yourself approach, the ability to complete a job by a specified date, the skill and equipment to assemble materials properly, and the responsibility for a soundly assembled system would favor commercial installations.

If the decision has been made to utilize a commercial installer, the design plans are distributed to one or more installers with a request to submit bids for the complete installation. The contract is usually awarded on the basis of the lowest bid submitted, though the purchaser can reserve a freedom of choice if he prefers one bidder over the others. This freedom is sometimes limited for public bodies such as cities and states. It is recommended that a prospective purchaser visit recent installations which have been made by different installers and discuss with turf managers their degree of satisfaction with the installer. Based on this information the private prospective purchaser can avoid awarding the bid to any installer known to have made unsatisfactory installations. Some public agencies prequalify a bidder by a set of standards.

The request for bids should state the guarantees which are expected from the contractor. These guarantees may differ for different situations but generally include a definite time for completion of work and possibly a bond to insure completion, a clause covering damage to existing turf, a clause providing for correction of any material or assembly defects, and the usual personnel and property liability clauses. While the installer should guarantee that the materials specified in the design were installed correctly and skillfully as designated, he will not guarantee water distribution performance of the irrigation system unless he was also the designer.

During installation of the system, some form of supervision should be exercised either by the buyer or the designer. Sometimes problems arise during installation which in the opinion of the installer require adjustments in design specifications. When such an occasion arises, the change should be made only after a meeting and agreement among the buyer, the designer, and the installer. If changes are agreed to, they should be written as amendments into the contract followed by a statement that these changes are made at no cost or at some specified increase or reduction in cost. All parties should attach their signatures to the amendment.

At the conclusion of the installation, the installer should test the entire system to insure that there are no leaks or other workmanship defects and that the various components operate as expected. The installer should also be expected to submit to the buyer a complete "as built" plan of the system which was installed. This latter can be very useful when repairs or replacements of parts are necessary or when the system is to be revised or expanded.

G. Accessories

Accessories for sprinkler irrigation systems, other than pipes and sprinkler heads which are the main components, include pumps, reservoirs, control valves, pressure gauges, fertilizer injectors, and timers. Some are essential on certain types of systems, while others are desirable extras.

A pump is essential in a system which does not receive its water under sufficient pressure to operate the sprinklers. If water is purchased from a city or irrigation district mainline under pressure there is no need for a pump unless water is delivered on a smaller but steady flow for 24 hours a day and is stored in a reservoir for application during a fraction of that day. If water is lifted from a well, a stream, a natural or artificial lake on the premises, or a reservoir, a pump will be needed to lift the water from its ponded condition and inject it into the sprinkler mains at sufficient pressure to operate the sprinklers. Pumps are designed to operate efficiently under a rather limited range of discharge rates, water pressures or heads, and revolutions per minute.

The water head is the sum of the pressure heads at the sprinklers, the lift from water source level to the sprinklers, and the friction loss in the pipes. These are usually expressed in feet. The sprinkler pressure in psi $\times$ 2.31 = pressure head in feet. The lift head is the difference in elevation between the highest sprinkler head and the water source. The friction head in feet is obtained from pipe friction tables which the irrigation design engineer will use. It should not exceed 20% of the pressure head at the sprinklers. Greater friction losses indicate that pipe diameters are too small for the amount of water they carry.

A pump should be purchased that has its greatest operating efficiency within the range of conditions under which it will operate most frequently. Before a pump is selected its performance curves should be examined. A good pump properly chosen will operate at 80% efficiency or better in its range while one operating out of its range may either fail to deliver water as needed or will operate at efficiencies below 80%, possibly as low as 30 or 40%. This will greatly increase the power cost.

For some turf areas, particularly golf courses and public parks, irrigation can be applied only during the "non-use periods" which may not be greater than about 70 hours per week. This may require a flow rate larger than the supply sources can provide. By taking delivery of a lesser amount 24 hours a day or 168 hours per week and storing the water in a reservoir, the larger flows can be furnished for the 70 hours of irrigation. The best reservoir is a natural depression or a ravine which can be dammed. It provides for water storage and makes an ornamental contribution to the area. In areas lacking natural sites, a reservoir of calculated capacity can be excavated using the excavated soil to form dikes and thereby add to storage capacity. The banks of the reservoir can be landscaped to enhance its ornamental appeal. Most reservoirs, natural or artificial, will lose water by seepage. If water is scarce or expensive, this loss should be prevented or minimized. Lining with plastic films eliminates most of the loss and has become a common practice. The plastic sheets are covered with a layer of soil so that they are hidden and protected from mechanical and radiation damage.

Fertilizer injectors can be attached to sprinkler irrigation systems to eliminate the labor of manual or mechanical fertilizer distribution. They enable soluble fertilizers to be distributed through the irrigation water. Available fertilizer injectors are powered either by an external source, such as an electric motor, or by a water-driven pump deriving power from the water pressure in the irrigation system. Fertilizers that are completely soluble in water can be distributed in this manner. However, fertilizers which form highly corrosive aqueous solutions should be used with caution, if at all, to avoid corrosion on the metal parts of the system.

Uniformity of fertilizer applications added through irrigation water will depend on the uniformity of water distribution in the system. Any sprinkler irrigation system is likely to have some areas which recieive two to four times as much water at one irrigation as other areas. This same ratio would hold for the relative amounts of fertilizer received in different areas. The more uniformly the irrigation system applies and distributes water, the more likely it is to do a successful job of applying fertilizers dissolved in the water. Fertilizer injection should not be tried in sprinkler irrigation systems whose distribution has a low uniformity coefficient.

A sprinkler irrigation system needs control valves of one type or another to direct water where needed. Pressure regulating valves can be used where changes in ground elevation make it difficult to maintain equal pressure to all sprinklers in the area. There are also valves which have little effect on pressure but are able to maintain an almost constant volume of flow in a particular section of the irrigation system. Where a system derives its irrigation water from a municipal main, which is also used for potable water, municipal codes in most cities require installation of anti-backflow valves. They prevent any backflow of polluted water from the irrigation system into the city mains if there should be a sudden reduction in pressure in the mains.

Hydraulic and electric remote-control valves are being used with increasing frequency in turfgrass sprinkler irrigation systems to permit remote control of the water flow into any section of the irrigation system. Where such remote-control valves are installed, they are generally associated with a combination timer and controller. The controller allows the turf manager or other operator to open or close any valve which is connected to the controller. It also permits him to set the timer to program a complete irrigation or sequence of irrigations which will proceed without attention. This will be discussed at greater length in the next section.

VI. Irrigation Management

A. Water Use by Turf

A rational basis for the amount and rate of water use by turf was set forth by Pennman (1948). Studies he made with turf formed the basis for his thesis on water use by growing plants. He postulated that any growing plant which covered the surface of the ground as viewed from directly above will use water at a rate directly dependent upon ambient climatic factors. He contended that rate of water loss was dependent only on climatic factors and not on the type of vegetative material growing nor on its density so long as it was dense enough to cover the surface of the ground. Most turf provides such a cover.

While other studies (Van Bavel et al., 1967) have revealed that not all crops use water in direct proportion to climatic factors throughout a year, most growing vegetation follows the hypothesis closely enough so that much use has been made of Pennman's postulate for relating climatic factors to water use rates (Blaney and Criddle, 1950). There are several climatic factors which affect the rate of water use. In diminishing order of influence these include solar radiation, air temperature, air movement, and air humidity.

B. Climatic Measurement

By measuring all of these factors and inserting them in Pennman's or some other formula, it is possible to determine the water use rate for either a short or long period. By solving for a long term period, using average values which have been collected over several years, it is possible to obtain figures which provide a good estimate of the amount of water needed for irrigation in the locality where the measurements are made. Such estimates are useful in designing the correct capacity of an irrigation system. Irrigation designers often lack this information and must extrapolate information obtained from adjacent or other similar localities or make assumptions to the best of their skill from fragmentary data.

Pennman's equation is complicated and requires precise measurements of several weather factors, each involving expensive equipment, attention, and operating skill. The search has continued for alternate ways to accomplish approximately the same end-point. Thornthwaite (1948) has proposed an equation, slightly less complicated than Pennman's, that has reasonable applicability in humid areas. In an effort to further simplify the measurements and calculations for use in areas having less sophisticated climatic measurements, Blaney and Criddle (1950) proposed a relatively simple formula after extensive field studies in the irrigated areas of the western U.S.A. Their procedure requires only local temperature measurements and daylight hours obtainable from published tables relating sunshine hours to day of the year and degree latitude. Because of its simplicity, the Blaney-Criddle formula has been widely adapted both in the U.S. and around the world. Because it uses fewer weather factors, it may not be as correct as the more complex formulas. However, using long term average data, the Blaney-Criddle formula provides an easily calculated, fairly reliable estimate of expected water needs. Its use can be recommended for determining the water requirements necessary to design the capacity for irrigation systems.

The use of water by plants is called transpiration, which basically means the transport of water from the roots to the leaves of the plant and its loss by evaporation from the leaves. Total water use, called evapotranspiration, also includes any loss of water by direct evaporation from the vegetative or soil surface. Since evaporation is the final operation which carries water away from the plant and since it is influenced by all the weather factors which have been mentioned, it has been suggested that direct measurement of evaporation from a free water surface might be a simple, direct, and satisfactory means to assess the water needs of plants.

Considerable work on measuring evaporation from free water sur-

Figure 4. A sunken evaporation pan in the turf area can be used as a guide for irrigation frequency and amount.

faces has been conducted (Rohwer, 1931; Thornthwaite and Holzman, 1942; Bloodgood et al., 1954; Kohler et al, 1955; Pruitt, 1960). Some of this work has been done from large lakes but most of it has been done from containers differing in shape and size. Calibrations have been made to relate the rate of water evaporation from pans to that from growing plants. Unfortunately, none of the containers that have been used produce a rate of evaporation with a constant ratio to transpiration rate from growing plants. Further study is in progress to improve the basis for using measured climatic conditions to evaluate water use. It has the potential for improving irrigation management practices commonly used for commercial and domestic turf.

C. Soil Water Measurement

Soil water measurement has been used by irrigation research scientists in one form or another for more than half a century to guide their irrigation management practices and to define soil water conditions under which the plants were growing in their experiments. Until recently this has been accomplished mainly by soil sampling followed by laboratory weighing and drying. From their research results, scientists recommended that practical irrigation might be improved if it were based upon soil water measurements. However, the sampling method of soil water measurement has not been adopted widely by practical irrigaters because of the time and effort involved.

With a few minor exceptions, the principal effect of irrigation is to increase the relative wetness of the soil and prevent it from becoming too dry. Thus, the most obvious and logical basis for determining the need for irrigation would be information on the dryness or relative wetness of the soil in which plants are growing. Since about 1950 commercial instruments have been available to measure the relative wetness of soil in the root zone of growing plants. Subsequent research as summarized by Stanhill (1957) has served to relate the performance of growing plants to soil water conditions or relative wetness measured by these instruments. As a result, it is possible to base a program for irrigation management on readings of soil wetness obtained from properly installed instruments (Richards and Marsh, 1961).

Instruments for this purpose were used first with various agricultural crops differing in response to soil water conditions. The two types of instruments available for this use are called tensiometers and gypsum electrical resistance blocks. The nature of the instruments and their use have been described by Bouyoucos and Mick (1940), Kelley et al. (1946), L.A. Richards (1949 1954), and S. J. Richards (1957).

Tensiometers measure relatively wet soil conditions while gypsum blocks read better in the moderate to dry conditions. Turf is usually irrigated to maintain a relatively wet soil water condition. Therefore, tensiometers are the only instruments successfully used as a guide to turfgrass irrigation management.

The tensiometer measures a range of soil water condition, expressed in soil suction units of centibars, ranging from 0, a saturated soil, to about 75. The latter value is a degree of dryness at which many plants

Figure 5. Tensiometers are installed almost horizontally just beneath the ground surface for shallow-rooted turf. The tensiometer heads and gauges are contained in a protective box. A lid over the tensiometer box at ground level further protects the instruments and leaves the surface almost normal for most turf uses. Some types of protective boxes have locking lids to minimize vandalism.

Figure 6. Tensiometers can be wired to a controller to allow the irrigation to proceed only when needed.

can live satisfactorily but which most turf managers consider to be too dry for desirable turf conditions. Thus, the tensiometer covers the range of soil water conditions useful for turfgrass irrigation management.

Closely-mowed irrigated turf tends to be shallow rooted. Since it is necessary to place soil water measuring instruments in the active root zone, they generally are placed at depths less than 12 inches and frequently as shallow as 3 inches. Because of this, special installation techniques and modified tensiometers are used for turf. Tensiometers must be installed at carefully selected representative locations and placed so as to avoid changes in the representativeness of the selected location. On turf used for recreational and athletic purposes, tensiometers must be protected from damage and molestation.

Proper location and protection is achieved by installing tensiometers nearly horizontal, completely below the soil surface. The gauge portion of the instrument is contained in an open space below ground level, properly shielded from traffic, unobtrusive, yet accessible to the turf manager for reading and servicing. The sensitive element or porous cup may be located at a very shallow or intermediate depth but should always be slightly lower than the gauge so that air will rise to the filling cap. The reading and servicing of the instruments is done on a periodic basis, preferably in the early morning. It should be done daily during dry or warm weather, less often in cool or wet weather.

D. Frequency and Amount of Irrigation

In general the turfgrass manager decides when to irrigate and how much water to apply. Though he will often be guided by his experience and judgement, there are various guidelines that he may use in reaching a decision.

One guideline which has been widely used is to apply irrigation water when and where the turfgrass shows visible signs of stress, presumably due to shortage of water. With manual systems which require considerable labor and are often short of equipment and water capacity, irrigation is most likely applied when and where turf shows visible drought effects. Even with mechanized and solid-set systems, the turf manager may use the evidence obtained from one or more key spots which, because of nonuniform distribution of irrigation water, show a drought effect slightly sooner than the main turfgrass area. By learning to recognize symptoms in these key spots, the turfgrass manager can irrigate before drought symptoms are obvious to the public.

With totally mechanized or solid-set irrigation systems, it is quite common to irrigate daily. Most turfgrass managers recognize that from an agronomic standpoint, daily irrigation is not desirable. On the other hand, daily irrigation provides some insurance against stress and drought symptoms appearing as a result of unusual hot, dry periods. It helps maintain cordial relations between the turfgrass manager and his employers or patrons. Daily irrigations help to maintain a softer playing surface on golf courses. This is often desired and demanded by players on greens. Daily irrigation can have adverse effects including increased opportunity for soil compaction, excessive use of water and nitrogen because of greater evaporation and leaching, excessive wetness in certain low lying or fine textured soil areas, shallow rooting, and an increase in less desirable grass species.

Daily irrigation is used in warm areas attempting to maintain environmental conditions more conducive to the survival of cool-season grasses. Turfgrass managers have difficulty maintaining certain fine-bladed cool-season grasses on golf greens in warm climates to meet the desires of players. The breeding and development of superior warm-season grass varieties for specialized use may eventually rescue the turfgrass manager from this difficult position.

When a turfgrass manager does not find it necessary or desirable to irrigate daily, he may decide to irrigate on some other calendar basis such as alternate days, twice a week, or once a week. These schedules may prove satisfactory if adjusted to the season of the year and the weather. Although this approach may only approximate the true water needs of the turf, it helps in developing efficient work plans. In irrigation systems where much reliance must be placed on the labor force, it is often more satisfactory to schedule irrigations on a routine and repeatable basis, even though it is not what the turf needs, and generally results in excessive irrigation.

The measurement of evaporation from a free water surface, discussed under climatic measurements, can be used as a guide for scheduling irrigations. Though little used at present, this measurement may gain acceptance as more is learned about its use. The water use rate of turf is less than the evaporation rate from a free water surface by a percentage which varies in different seasons of the year. Irrigation equal to the measured evaporation during summer and 75% of evaporation during other parts of the year would be a liberal basis on which to start. The percentage can be adjusted as local experience is gained. Irrigation could be applied when measured evaporation equals ½ inch, 1 inch, or some other value found to be satisfactory for the local conditions. Measured evaporation must be corrected for rainfall, a difficult problem where rainfall intensity is great enough to produce runoff or the amount absorbed by the soil is sufficient to cause percolation below the root zone.

Some form of soil water measurement is probably the most reliable guide in deciding when and how much to irrigate. However, it is not a very widely used approach in turf irrigation management. Many turf managers who know their ground well have been able to base irrigation decisions on the feel of soil resistance to insertion of a metal probe. Since there are many variations in soil texture, porosity, subsurface drainage, turf rooting characteristics, and degree of compaction it is not possible to describe for any turfgrass manager the particluar feeling or reaction which will tell him when to irrigate. It is a skill which each turfgrass manager must develop for his own location and conditions.

Soil water measuring instruments provide direct measurements to help guide decisions of the turfgrass manager. Use of tensiometers to evaluate soil water conditions in commercial turf has shown that irrigated turf is generally kept wetter than needed. Turf grows well when irrigations are withheld until tensiometer readings reach 15 to 25 cb (Morgan and Marsh, 1965). Irrigation programs which maintain readings between 0 and 5 cb are excessive and contribute to poor root systems. Such conditions are often found on golf greens where readings of 5 to 15 would be better.

Measuring instruments can be wired to clocks and irrigation controllers which then control the irrigation frequency and amount applied. Tensiometers are usually installed at two depths in a selected representative location. The shallow instrument is placed in the dense root zone, the deeper one near the bottom of the active root system. The instruments have adjustable selector switches so that the circuit will close when the tensiometer reading reaches any desired value. The instruments are wired in parallel to the timer so that either one can independently initiate irrigation. The timer is programmed to permit irrigation any day but only at preselected hours. It is desirable to program for several repeat cycles of short duration.

When the clock reaches the selected time for irrigation, it will turn on the water only if the tensiometer has closed the circuit. This is true for each repeated cycle so that irrigation ceases when the soil becomes wet enough to lower the tensiometer reading. If the shallow tensiometer has signalled for irrigation, it may require just a few cycles to complete the irrigation. This serves to avoid excessive water in the deeper part of the root zone. When the lower root zone becomes dry, the deeper tensiometer signals for water. It will take more cycles to satisfy water needs at this depth, but a mild leaching will be accomplished and the infrequent extra wetness is not enough to cause root damage. Irrigations programmed through controllers activated by soil water sensors automatically adjust amounts applied to the actual need. Total amounts of water applied annually will generally be less than with manual control. More research and trial applications are needed before this method can be broadly recommended for all turf but it appears to have substantial possibilities.

E. Irrigating for Special Reasons

There are various special reasons for irrigating other than to replenish the depleted soil water in the turfgrass root zone. For these special reasons, an irrigation may be applied when it would not otherwise be needed.

When grass has just been planted, the seed will lie very close to the soil surface. After initial wetting, the seed starts to absorb water and is then subject to damage from drying. Depending on weather conditions, new seedings may require a light irrigation daily or possibly several times a day. Constant attention will be required until the seed has germinated and established some roots into the soil. New seedlings are often mulched for protection during establishment. Ideal irrigation during this time can be obtained with a clock controller set to irrigate for short intervals several times a day. Soil crusting and washing can be avoided by selecting sprinkler nozzles and a pressure that will produce fine drops and a low application rate.

Turf is fertilized on a regular basis. In general, this is accomplished by applying fertilizer to the turf with mechanical spreaders. An irrigation of 10 to 15 minutes is often applied immediately after fertilizer application to reduce the danger of burning. Irrigation, as such, may not be needed at this time but the fertilizer must be washed off the grass and into the soil. The application time should be sufficiently short so that runoff will not wash the fertilizer away. Fertilizer injection into the sprinkler irrigation system is a practice gaining wider acceptance. Fertilizer injection may take place during a normal irrigation but since much turf irrigation using controllers is done at night, the fertilizer injection may be accomplished as a special application during the daytime hours. The distribution of fertilizers dissolved in irrigation water will be no better than the uniformity of water distribution by the irrigation system. Lack of uniformity could be accentuated further if fertilizer is applied for a rather short period of time. Thus, it would be desirable for fertilizer injections to take place during as many minutes of a normal irrigation as possible. Dilute solutions and a short terminal rinsing period are beneficial.

In some parts of the country, depending on water quality, provision must be made for controlling soil salinity at concentrations that will permit satisfactory turfgrass growth. This may require periodic applications of water in excess of that needed to replenish the supply in the root zone. The additional water will move down through the soil, dissolving salts and carrying them out of the root zone, a process called leaching.

The need for leaching will depend mainly on the quality of the irrigation water. All natural waters except rain contain some dissolved salts, but the concentration is generally too low to be troublesome for turf. Exceptions occur and occasionally water available for irrigation is too salty to use. Somewhat more frequently water supplies have moderate salt concentrations. The water can be used if the salt content is recognized and precautions are taken to minimize adverse effects on plants and soil. Such precautions may be needed when sewage effluents are used for turf irrigation.

A water quality test should be obtained for any water intended for turf irrigation except in high rainfall locations. The results will be reported as electrical conductivity (EC) in micromhos per centimeter or as total dissolved solids in parts per million (ppm). The following table shows a broad classification of water qualities for turf irrigation.

Class	Uses	Total dissolved salts	
		EC	ppm
A	Useful under most conditions	<1000	<650
B	Periodic leaching needed	1000-3000	650-2000
C	Limited usefulness	>3000	>2000

When using waters of class B, the amount of leaching needed will be greater for those of higher concentrations. Some unavoidable but beneficial leaching will occur from rainfall and normal irrigations. The amount of intentional extra leaching needed can be determined best by analyzing soil samples taken periodically. Intentional leaching is needed (Branson, 1966) when the soil analysis shows a concentration of the saturation extract (a standard form of reporting indicated by the symbol ECe) as great as: 4 millimhos for salt-sensitive grasses such as Kentucky bluegrass, Highland Colonial bentgrass, red rescue, meadow fescue; 8 millimhos for medium-salt-tolerant grasses such as Alta tall fescue, perennial ryegrass; 15 millimhos for highly-salt-tolerant grasses such as common and hybrid bermuda grass varieties, seaside creeping bentgrass, and St. Augustinegrass.

If slow soil permeability restricts the intake of excess water needed for leaching, repeated brief applications of water can be used to apply the extra water without runoff. Such a technique or program can be conducted easily with irrigation systems operated by a clock and controller. Where the soil salinity problem is known to arise periodically, leaching irrigations can be scheduled on a periodic basis. Where the periodicity of increasing salt concentrations is less certain, the soil should be sampled two to four times a year and analyzed in a laboratory to determine whether a leaching irrigation is needed.

A swimmer is well aware that on a hot day he feels more comfortable when his body is wet just after emerging from the water than when it is dry and exposed to the sun. Turfgrass, particularly cool-season varieties used on golf greens, may suffer from high temperature on hot summer days. The practice of applying a very light irrigation to the surface of the grass has been widely utilized for no other reason than to cool the grass. This may be done once in the middle of a hot afternoon or several times on extremely hot days. Most turf managers in hot climates follow this practice to preserve turf from deterioration. While the benefits of this practice are real and often observed, the factual basis for the treatment does not appear to have been established by research. It may modify temperatures for a cool-season grass grown under very warm conditions. It may be required because previous irrigation practices and/or natural soil conditions have produced root systems that are incapable of absorbing and transmitting sufficient water to leaves to meet demands on a hot afternoon. The cooling irrigation provides extra water directly at the point of evaporation from the leaf surfaces and lowers the leaf temperature. If improperly performed, the practice may become detrimental in time.

Irrigation is sometimes applied merely to soften the turf to comply with the requests of players, particularly golfers. Golf players appreciate a bounce and roll after their balls hit on a fairway. When shooting to a green, however, they want the ball to stop at or close to the spot where it landed. To provide this, they may request that greens be irrigated just prior to play whether or not the grass needs irrigation for growing purposes. Although this practice is undesirable, it is continued because the course is maintained for the players. Continuing research on soil mixes for greens, as well as on irrigation management techniques, is aimed towards providing the degree of resilience desired by players without creating adverse agronomic effects.

VII. Drainage

Turfgrass areas which are used by people must have drainage to dispose of excess water received either from rainfall or irrigation. The rainfall may be that falling directly on the turf or on higher ground from which it may flow onto turf areas. Drainage is divided into disposal of water which is on the ground surface and that which has percolated into the soil. Surface drainage is needed to prevent excess rainfall from standing in ponds on the turf. Surface drainage may also be needed to carry off excess water caused by runoff from irrigation applications. While irrigation should not yield surface runoff, it is advisable to make provision to handle extra water produced by improper irrigation practices. Internal or subsurface drainage is needed to dispose of excess rainfall or irrigation applications which percolate into the soil faster than they can be disposed of by natural subsoil drainage.

A. Surface Drainage

Provisions for surface drainage from a usable turf area should be made wherever turf is grown. Even in dry climates there are times when rain falls in such unusual quantities that surface drainage becomes essential. Surface drains can usually be constructed at less cost than artificial internal drains and may serve to eliminate or reduce the need for more costly systems. Even where internal subsoil drainage is required, provision for suitable surface drainage will reduce the load on internal drains and increase their overall effectiveness.

Surface drainage should be planned and designed at the time the turf area is established. The design should be based on surface contours of the ground and estimated capacity requirements to carry away surface runoff which may occur during the heavier rainfall periods known for the area. On terrain which has relatively little slope, an initial smoothing of the soil surface will remove small pot holes. These depressions would otherwise hold water and leave soggy spots after the puddles have disappeared.

Grading of the proposed turf area to maintain a continuous downward slope from higher to lower elevations will help carry away water. In this grading process, it is desirable to construct smooth, wide drainways which will be sodded. If it is necessary to make a deep cut in the soil across some saddle in the ground surface, a chanel should be cut to dimensions capable of carrying the estimated maximum flow and lined with erosion-resistant material. There may be places where the slope is too steep to carry drainage water safely in a smooth sodded drainway. Properly cut, shaped, and lined channels should be used in such cases.

Occasionally there are saddles to be breached above which there is a suitable site for a small pond or lake. In addition to an erosion-resistant spillway, the outlet from the lake can proceed through control valves into a culvert to allow water to drain away at a nondamaging rate. In some turf areas a series of multiple-purpose lakes can be developed. They have scenic value, aid in equalizing rate of discharge of surface drainage water, and serve as storage reservoirs for irrigation water. The size of the pond or lake, its planned maximum and minimum surface elevations, and the capacity of the discharge conduits should be based upon the best available information on maximum possible runoff from storms experienced over a 25-year period.

If the anticipated volume of flow for any particular section of a drainway is high or a perennial stream exists, then a channel should be prepared across the turf. Channel dimensions will depend upon expected flow rates. Dimensions should be kept as even as possible and the channel lined with nonerodible material such as gravel, cobble, or masonry. Smooth approaches to the prepared channel will help in turf maintenance and drainage performance. Expensive damage to relatively new drain channels has occurred where hydrologic knowledge and drain design were inadequate.

Outlets are needed for discharge of drainage water from the turf property. The problem is simple if there is a natural stream or drain passing through the property or along one edge. Similarly, if there is a lake on, adjacent to, or near the turf property, the problem of water disposal is simple. Not all turf properties have natural conditions available for such easy discharge of drain waters. Property surrounded by a built-up community may have to arrange for discharge of their drainage into a municipal storm sewer. This will require agreement with local officials and possibly a fee payment for use of the storm sewer.

In some areas, drainage needs are rather common to the entire area and a drainage district may exist or can be formed. This is usually a community enterprise in which all property owners within a given area or natural watershed join forces to dispose of their drainage water. Drainage districts are usually formed according to State enabling legislation. The people involved vote to form a district and confer upon the elected directors of the district the power to levy assessments or taxation needed to construct artificial drainage outlets. These outlets are engineered to meet the needs of each property owner in the district and with sufficient capacity to carry away all the drainage water from the district.

B. Internal Drainage

All natural soils have some natural internal drainage. In some it may be sufficient to take care of all excess water which infiltrates the surface of the soil. In others, natural drainage may be rather slow because of subsurface soil conditions. Where natural drainage is inadequate or too slow to dispose of excess water which infiltrates the surface of the soil, a water table will develop. The water table may be temporary, disappearing within a few days as a result of natural drainage. The water table may persist for an extended period of time and, if so, is quite likely to damage growing ornamentals, particularly shrubs and trees. It may also contribute to salination of the surface soil if the soil water contains more than a small amount of dissolved salts.

An undesirable water table usually can be relieved by artificial internal or subsurface drainage. It should be remembered, however, that drains will discharge water only where there is a water table or when soils are saturated. Wet soils which seem to be wet but are actually unsaturated, will discharge no water into a drain and cannot be improved by such an installation. Other methods for improving such soils should be used. These may include irrigation management to avoid excessive wetness or, where possible, the alteration of subsurface soil conditions. Where rather sharply defined horizontal layers of soil having different textural properties adjoin one another, water moving downward through an unsaturated soil has difficulty passing beyond the boundary between these different soil layers. During initial construction, mechanical mixing of the soil to eliminate the boundary distinction between soil layers will help to promote downward movement of water in unsaturated soils.

Temporary water tables that occur in slowly permeable soils may or may not damage growing plants depending upon how long they exist. If the time required for the temporary water table to disappear seems unreasonably long, it may be helpful to install artificial subsurface drains to remove excess water. If the temporary water table persists for only a few hours to a day or two, it is not likely that artificial drainage can be justified.

Persistent water tables occur where subsoil drainage is poor because of rock or claypan barriers at some point beneath the soil surface. These water tables will vary in depth depending upon the position of the barrier, weather, rainfall, and irrigation management. In general, artificial drainage is not required when the water table is more than 5 or 6 feet below the soil surface. If the water table is less than 4 or 5 feet below the soil surface, steps should be taken to provide artificial drainage. Absence of internal drainage on these sites will create problems in growing deep-rooted plants and in some climates may increase salination of the surface soil and restrict the growth of most turfgrasses.

Because modern irrigation systems for turf have an underground network of plastic pipe, drain tile lines are more easily installed before the irrigation system. Since drain tile are generally installed deeper, they do not interfere with the subsequent installation of the irrigation pipe. It is, therefore, desirable to conduct the investigation for subsoil drainage needs before installing the irrigation system. Such an investigation will not be exact because the act of irrigation may increase the need for drainage. Where there is a doubt, a drainage system should be installed. Most modern golf greens, which are knowingly and consistently over-irrigated, have shallow drain tile installed during construction. They are placed at the interface between the overlying prepared soil and the native soil below, a zone where temporary saturation may easily occur.

When the need for artificial internal drainage is indicated, a survey of all relevant facts should be made in order to decide on the most appropriate method for providing drainage. The first information needed is evidence of water tables, obtained by means of observation wells drilled into the soil. If there is a water table, the ovservation well will fill with water to a level approximately at the water table depth. The observation well is most easily made by boring a 1-inch hole into the soil to a depth of 3 to 6 feet, depending upon existing subsoil conditions. From these measurements, the presence of the water table and its depth beneath the soil surface should be marked on a map of the area. A sequence of measurements should be made to learn how the water table depth varies with time.

When this investigation shows that there is a need for artificial drainage, plans can be initiated for constructing the drain. The first step is to decide what type of drain should be constructed. Open drains as described for surface drainage may serve in part, but generally tile drainage is preferred. However, there are certain conditions which can be satisfactorily drained by construction of vertical wells.

Sometimes a water table is caused by the presence of an impermeable clay layer in the subsoil which in turn is underlaid by more permeable material. Vertical penetration of the impermeable clay layer by a well, tube, or shaft will serve to discharge water into the more permeable layer below. The possibility of using this technique is best learned by drilling a few test holes in the problem area to determine the nature of

Figure 7. Vertical penetration of clay layer may prevent drowning a tree in a turf area if a permeable layer can be reached easily.

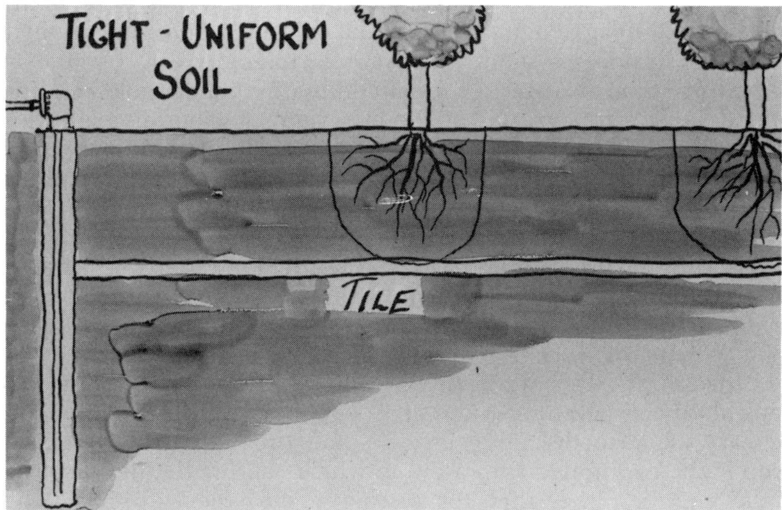

Figure 8. A sump pump elevates tile effluent where collector drain is too high for direct discharge.

various subsoil layers. If the impermeable barrier is a clay layer of great thickness or is a rock layer, there is little opportunity for using the vertical well technique. If the clay layer is not too thick, a few test holes of 4 to 6 inches diameter penetrating the clay should be constructed to learn wheteher they can beneficially dispose of the water table. If they perform satisfactorily, additional vertical wells can be constructed wherever needed. These wells could be constructed either by hand or power augering. While their durability is uncertain, they would probably perform better and longer if backfilled with pea gravel or other stable coarse aggregate material. It would be advisable to check with local water pollution control authorities before installing a large number of wells.

If subsoil conditions do not appear favorable for drainage by vertical wells, the standard horizontal tile line system should be considered. The theory and techniques for drainage and tile line installation have been published in several places (Childs and Collis-George, 1950; Jones, 1952; Luthin, 1957; Edminster and Schwab, 1957; Edminster and Reeve, 1957). In agricultural practice, tile lines are installed at depths of 3 ft. or more in the humid eastern part of the country and at depths of 6 ft. or more in the arid west. The principal reason for utilizing greater depth in the arid west is to avoid the possibility of salination of the surface soil by upward movement of water from the water table. Subsequent evaporation of water at the surface leaves behind a deposit of salt.

Since turf is generally more shallow rooted than many agricultural crops, there may be occasions where tile installations need not be as deep as they would be under similar situations in agriculture. On the other hand, the most deleterious effect of high water tables is often felt by deep rooting ornamental trees and shrubs grown with turf. For such areas, tile should be 4 to 6 feet deep.

Because of the varying possibilities which exist, it is evident that a competent drainage engineer should be consulted before planning and installing a drainage system. The drainage engineer will combine available information relative to subsoil conditions, water table conditions, general surface topography of the area, and possible discharge loads. From this he will plan location of lateral and collector lines with respect to the terrain and potential load factor on the tile, the slope or grade of the tile to provide satisfactory discharge, and suitable outlets for the tile line discharge. As with surface drainage, arrangements must be made for disposal of drain water. Any connection for discharge other than into a lake or perennial stream on the turf property must be made only after proper arrangements with the organization in charge of or controlling the trunk discharge system.

A storm drain discharge may be available but at an elevation higher than the discharge point of the turf tile system. In this situation all tile lines are made to discharge into a sump on the turf property. The sump is then equipped with a pump which can lift the drainage water to the elevation necessary for discharge into the storm drain. The pump motor may be controlled by the water level to cycle on and off, at frequent intervals during periods of large discharge and at infrequent intervals during periods of low discharge. The size of sump needed, the capacity of the pump needed, and the frequency of cycling likely to occur must all be predetermined and designed correctly according to standard engineering calculations. Failure to do so may result in a nonoperative sump pump system.

Literature Cited

Blaney, H. F. and W. D. Criddle. 1950. Determining water requirements in irrigated areas from climatological and irrigation data. USDA Soil Cons. Ser. Tech. Paper 96:1-48. (Processed)

Bloodgood, D. W., R. E. Patterson, and R. L. Smith, Jr. 1954. Water evaporation studies in Texas. Texas Agr. Exp. Sta. Bull. 787. 83 p.

Bouyoucos, G. J. and A. H. Mick. 1940. An electrical resistance method for the continuous measurement of soil moisture under field conditions. Michigan Agr. Exp. Sta. Tech. Bull. 172. 38 p.

Branson, R. L. 1966. Better answers with soil and plant analysis. California Turfgrass Culture 16:1-2.

Childs, E. C. and N. Collis-George. 1950. The control of soil water. Advances in agronomy, II: 234-72.

Edminster, T. W. and R. C. Reeve. 1957. Drainage problems and methods. 1957 USDA Yearbook of Agriculture, Soil. pp 378-85.

Edminster, T. W. and G. O. Schwab. 1957. Drainage in humid areas. Agronomy Monograph No. 7. pp. 371-94.

Holmes, J. L. 1968. Green construction—techniques and materials. USGA Green Section Record 5(6):8-9.

Jones, Lewis A. 1952. Farm drainage. USDA Farmers' Bulletin No. 2046. 37 p.

Kelley, O. J., A. S. Hunter, H. R. Haise, and C. H. Hobbs. 1946. A comparison of methods of measuring soil moisture under field conditions. J. Amer. Soc. Agron. 38:759-84.

Kohler, M. A., T. J. Nordenson, L. R. Denson, and W. E. Fox. 1955. Evaporation from pans and lakes. U. S. Dept. of Commerce Weather Bureau. Res. Paper No. 38. 21 p.

Lemon, E. R., and A. E. Erickson. 1952. The measurement of oxygen diffusion in the soil with a platinum microelectrode. Soil Sci. Soc. Amer. Proc. 16(2):160-63.

Letey, J. 1965. Measuring aeration. Drainage for efficient crop production conference proceedings, Dec., 1965. pp 6-10. (Published by Amer. Soc. Agr. Eng., St. Joseph, Michigan.)

Letey, J., and L. H. Stolzy. 1964. Measurement of oxygen diffusion rates with the platinum microelectrode. I. Theory and equipment. Hilgardia 35(20):545-54.

Letey, J., W. C. Morgan, S. J. Richards, and N. Valoras. 1966. Physical soil amendments, soil compaction, irrigation, and wetting agents in turfgrass management. III. Effects on oxygen diffusion rate and root growth. Agron. J. 58:531-35.

Luthin, J. N. 1957. Drainage of irrigated lands. Agronomy Monograph No. 7. pp 344-71.

Marsh, A. W., F. K. Aljibury, and V. C. Youngner. 1968. Turfgrass irrigation research at the University of California. Proc. 6th Annual Turfgrass Sprinkler Irrigation Conf., Lake Arrowhead. pp 6-9.

Morgan, W. C., and A. W. Marsh. 1965. Turfgrass irrigation by tensiometer controlled system. California Agriculture. 19(11):4-6.

Pennman, H. L. 1948. Natural evaporation from open water, bare soil, and grass. Proceedings Royal Society of London Series A. 193:120-45.

Pruitt, W. O. 1960. Correlation of evapotranspiration with evaporation from pans and atmometers. Correlation of climatological data with water requirement of crops 1959-60 Annual Report. Dept. of Irrigation, University of California, Davis. pp 29-39.

Richards, L. A. 1949. Methods of measuring soil moisture tension. Soil Science 68:95-112.

Richards, L. A. 1950. Laws of soil moisture. American Geophysical Union Transactions. 31:750-56.

Richards, L. A. 1954. The measurement of soil water in relation to plant requirements. Scientific Monthly. 78:307-13.

Richards, L. A., and S. J. Richards. 1957. Soil moisture. Yearbook of Agriculture (USDA), 1957. pp. 49-60.

Richards, S. J. 1957. Time to irrigate. What's New in Crops and Soils. 9(8):9-11.

Richards, S. J., and A. W. Marsh. 1961. Irrigation based on soil suction measurements. Soil Sci. Soc. of Amer. Proc. 25:65-69.

Richards, S. J., J. E. Warneke, A. W. Marsh, and F. K. Aljibury. 1964. Physical properties of soil mixes. Soil Science 98:129-132.

Rohwer, Carl. 1931. Evaporation from free water surfaces. USDA Tech. Bull. 271. 96 p.

Stanhill, G. 1957. The effect of differences in soil moisture status on plant growth: A review and analysis of soil moisture regime experiments. Soil Science 84:205-14.

Stolzy, L. H., and J. Letey. 1964. Measurement of oxygen diffusion rates with the platinum microelectrode. III. Correlation of plant response to soil oxygen diffusion rates. Hilgardia. 35(20): 567-76.

Taylor, S. A., D. D. Evans, and W. D. Kemper. 1961. Evaluating soil water. Utah Agricultural Experiment Station Bul. 426. 67 p.

Thornthwaite, C. W. 1948. An approach toward a rational classification of climate. Geog. Rev. 38:55-94.

Thornwaite, C. W., and Benjamin Holzman. 1942. Measurement of evaporation from land and water surfaces. USDA Tech Bull. No. 817. 143 p.

Valoras, N., and J. Letey. 1966. Soil oxygen and water relationships to rice growth. Soil Science. 101:210-15.

Van Bavel, C. H. M., J. E. Newman, and R. H. Hilgeman. 1967. Climate and estimated water use by an orange orchard. Agr. Meterol. 4:27-37.

7 Physiology of Growth and Development

V. B. Youngner

University of California
Riverside, California

I. Introduction

Scientific literature contains reports of many studies on the growth and development of grasses. Nevertheless, information is meager in many areas, especially concerning growth of grasses in a plant community such as a pasture or turf.

No attempt has been made in this chapter to review all the literature on grass growth and development or even to cover in detail all phases of the subject. Emphasis is placed, instead, on those aspects of particular interest to the turfgrass agronomist. Reference is made only to such research as substantiates statements in the text.

Knowledge of the physiology of growth and development of grasses is important since ultimately all turf management practices must be based upon, or at least modified by, the growth characteristics of the plant.

Growth may be viewed either as increase in length or size or as an increase in dry matter (Black, 1957). Both aspects of growth are inportant to turf culture.

The turfgrasses are herbaceous perennial, rarely annual, species capable of forming a dense sod through the production of numerous shoots that may act as independent units even though attached to others. Roots arise adventitiously from the lower nodes of these shoots to form a dense, fibrous branching root system.

Many turfgrasses have horizontal stems with long internodes above ground (stolons), below the soil surface (rhizomes), or both. These stems initiate roots and new shoots at the nodes or at the tips. Leaves consist of two principal parts; an expanded upper portion, the blade, and a lower portion, the leaf sheath, which clasps around the shoot.

The meristematic regions in grasses are the shoot apex, the root apex, the shoot intercalary meristem located immediately above the nodes and the leaf intercalary meristems at the base of the blade and at the base of the sheath. The shoot intercalary meristem in the turfgrasses is active, increasing internode length thereby, only in stolons, rhizomes, and in the vertical shoots (tillers) at inflorescence development. In the vegetative state, internodes of tillers remain short and leaves arising at the nodes form partially overlapping whorls enclosing the shoot apex, which remains near the ground level. Because of this location of the shoot apex and the leaf intercalary meristems, it is possible to mow turfgrasses frequently without destroying their ability to produce new growth.

II. Seed Germination

The "seed" of turfgrasses is actually a dry fruit, called caryopsis, with the ovary wall (pericarp) attached firmly to the true seed. In most of the turfgrasses the caryopsis is enclosed by the tightly adhering lemma and palea. Scarification or other mechanical treatment may be required to remove these floral parts.

Structure and homologies of tissues of the embryo are discussed by Arber (1934) and Barnard (1964). The grass embryo lies on the lemma side of the endosperm, the mass of stored food in the seed. A typical grass embryo is shown in Fig. 1. In immediate contact with the endosperm is an organ of the embryo called the scutellum or cotyledon which functions in the transport of food from the endosperm to the developing plant during germination. The epiblast is usually regarded as the vestigial remains of the second cotyledon. The part of the embryo that becomes the top of the plant, the plumule or epicotyl, consisting of a first foliage leaf and a growing point, is enclosed in a sheath called the coleoptile, a structure peculiar to the grasses. The

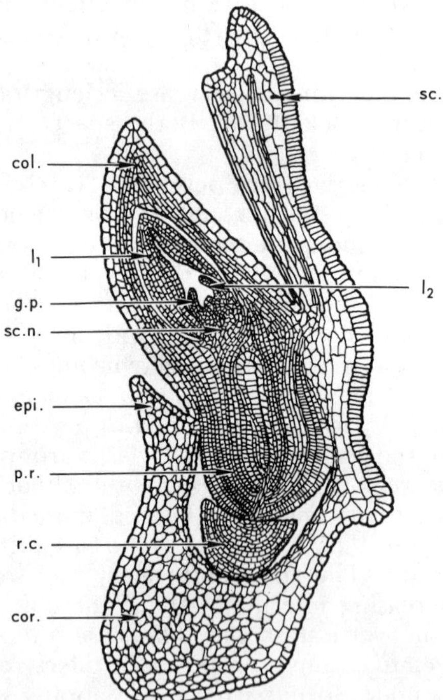

Figure 1. Diagram of grass seed embryo in longitudinal section showing typical structures. Col.—coleoptile; 1_1—first foliage leaf; g.p.—growing point; sc.n.—scutellar node; epi.—epiblast; p.r.—primary root; r.c.—root cap; cor.—coleorhiza; sc.—scutellum; 1_2—second foliage leaf.

Drawing by C. Papp

radicle or primary root is also enclosed in a sheath, the coleorhiza, which emerges from the caryopsis at germination and anchors the seedling with structures similar to root hairs. The primary root subsequently pushes through the side of the coleorhiza.

Many grasses have a distinct segment termed the mesocotyl between the scutellum and the coleoptile (Arber, 1934; Reeder, 1957). The mesocotyl is usually interpreted as the first internode of the stem axis; it may increase in length during germination, the extent of increase depending upon the depth of the seed in the soil.

Mature, freshly harvested seed of many grass species will not germinate readily even under favorable conditions. This lack of germinability has been termed primary dormancy (Crocker and Barton, 1953). Following a period of post-harvest ripening or "after-ripening," during which physiological changes occur in the seed, germinability becomes high. A secondary dormancy may develop when physiologically mature seeds are held in an environment unfavorable for germination. These seeds will not germinate immediately when placed in conditions ordinarily conducive to germination. Secondary dormancy may account in large measure for the persistency of some species in nature (Harris, 1961). Dormancy may be attributed to impermeability of the seed coats to adequate gas exchange, impermeability to water, or existence of inhibitory substances (Vegis, 1964). Some of the ways dormancy may be broken are by leaching to remove inhibitory substances, drying, exposure to low temperature, scarification to break the seed coat, or exposure to light. Treatments with chemicals or growth regulators have broken dormancy in some species. Since the causes of seed dormancy differ among species, no one method of breaking dormancy is universally effective. Dormancy is usually not a practical problem with the turfgrasses, as a period of dry storage provides the time necessary for the after-ripening process. If the seeds are properly handled and planted, there may be no occasion for a secondary dormancy to set in.

Viability is gradually lost in storage, as respiration and other physiological processes occur even under ideal conditions. Moisture and temperature determine the rate at which these processes occur. Viability of grass seeds may be retained at a high level by storing the seeds at a relative humidity below 20% and at temperatures below 30C (Owen, 1956). Optimum moisture levels and temperatures for maintenance of viability of some *Festuca* species is considerably lower.

Gemination may be defined as the various physiological and morphological processes leading to and including the emergence of the first embryo structures from the enveloping seed layers (Ballard, 1964).

Detailed discussions and reviews of seed germination have been given by Crocker and Barton (1953) and Koller et al. (1962). The universal requirements for germination of nondormant seeds are adequate moisture, temperature within a suitable range, and oxygen. Optimum temperatures for germination vary with species from 60 to 90 F. In general, warm-season grasses have a higher optimum than do the cool-season grasses. An alternation of temperature is often beneficial to germination of grass seeds and may be a requirement for germination in some species.

Imbibition of water is the first step in seed germination. If moisture levels are high, saturation of the seed may occur in a few hours. The rate of uptake depends not only upon the moisture level but also on the nature of the seed coats. If floral parts (glumes, lemma, palea) surround the seed, water uptake may be retarded, especially if moisture levels are low (Wellington, 1966). As water is absorbed, cells become turgid but cell elongation may not occur for many hours, depending on the species. In the germination of corn, which has received extensive study, cell elongation is observed first in the coleorhiza approximately 20 hours after water imbibition starts.

Early growth of the embryo during germination is largely by cell elongation as cell divisions are not evident until about the time the radicle tip breaks through the coleorhiza. Extension of the coleorhiza, apparently by cell elongation only, proceeds for only a short distance beyond the point of rupture through the seed coats. The coleoptile, enclosing the first true leaf, breaks through the seed coat at approximately the same time as the radicle emerges from the coleorhiza. At this point germination is complete and subsequent development must be considered seedling establishment.

Energy needed for germination is provided by an increased respiration rate, beginning as soon as the environmental requirements for germination are met. An increased rate of carbon dioxide discharge may be detected almost immediately upon imbibition of water, which is followed shortly thereafter by an accelerated uptake of oxygen.

Enzymes are secreted by the scutellum and certain other embryo tissues that break down the hemicellulose walls of the endosperm and degrade the starch and other reserves of the endosperm. Alpha-amylase, beta-amylase, and maltase are the principal enzymes involved in converting starch to soluble carbohydrates, which are absorbed by the scutellum and transferred to the embryo and developing seedlings. Recent studies have shown that endogenous gibberellins may have an important role in the activation of enzymes and the degradation of proteins during germination (Koller et al., 1962).

Seed germination of some species is inhibited by light while germination of others may be promoted or unaffected. The only turfgrass known to have its seed germination promoted by light is Kentucky bluegrass. Other *Poa* species, such as annual bluegrass, are also thought to be light-sensitive but there is as yet little proof of this. Light control of seed germination is through the same phytochrome system that governs the photoperiodic control of flowering.

III. Seedling Growth and Development

Whalley et al. (1966) recognized three distinct phases in seedling growth of grasses. The first is the heterotrophic stage which begins with the imbibition of water followed by germination and is concluded with the emergence of first leaves above the soil surface and the beginning of photosynthesis. During this stage, the seedling is entirely dependent upon stored food reserves of the seed.

The second phase is the transition stage when the seedling obtains the organic compounds for growth from both photosynthesis and the remainder of the endosperm.

The autotrophic stage begins when the reserves of the endosperm are exhausted and the seedling obtains all its complex organic compounds as products of photosynthesis. The seedling is fully independent at this stage.

Almost immediately after the radicle emerges from the coleorhiza additional seminal or primary roots develop which vary in number depending upon the species. These roots all arise from the embryo itself and generally are well developed by the time the coleoptile appears above the soil surface.

The coleoptile of grasses with a mesocotyl or first internode between the coleoptile and scutellum may be forced up from a considerable depth by elongation of this structure. Thus, the second and later nodes will all be near the soil surface regardless of the depth of the seed. Coleoptile emergence of grasses without this structure is entirely dependent upon growth of the coleoptile itself, and these grasses perhaps require a more shallow planting depth for successful establishment (M. W. Evans, 1927). Growth of the mesocotyl and coleoptile is by both cell elongation and cell division. Growth of the coleoptile is promoted by light while that of the mesocotyl is promoted by dark or inhibited by light (Mer and Causton, 1963; Arber, 1934).

After the coleoptile has extended a short distance above the soil surface the first true leaf breaks through the enclosing coleoptile sheath. As the growing point of the seedling is enclosed by the coleoptile, subsequent foliage leaves also arise through the coleoptile until it withers away. The next seedling structures to develop are the secondary or adventitious roots, which form at the nodes of the new shoot. The time of secondary root formation varies and may be as late as after initiation of the first tiller (Troughton, 1957). Secondary root primordia may be present in the embryo of some species.

The aspects of the mature grass plant are assumed with the appearance of tillers or lateral shoots, which arise from buds in the leaf axils. Each tiller develops its own adventitious root system and is capable of functioning as an independent unit.

The sequence of events in grass seed germination and seedling development is similar for all grasses. However, the time intervals may differ in different species and genotypes within a species and will also be influenced by environmental conditions.

Seedling vigor and rate of seedling establishment of turfgrasses are directly related to the supply of the physical factors necessary for growth—water, air, nutrients, light, oxygen, and carbon dioxide—and to the competition among seedlings for these factors. References frequently are made to competition for space but, as Clements and Shelford (1939) pointed out, space is seldom a limiting factor and competition among plants is actually for the afore-mentioned factors. In turfgrass culture, nutrients and water are usually provided to seedlings in adequate amounts so competition for these factors is greatly reduced.

As seedlings develop, light and, perhaps, soil oxygen are the limiting factors for growth most frequently encountered. Closely planted seedlings will be competing for light as leaves of one shade those of another. This is especially likely if two or more species or strains of genetically different growth rates are planted together. Donald (1963) emphasized that the occurrence of competition must not be assumed just because a factor is in short supply. Seedlings well-spaced will be in their own micro-environment, each seedling independent of those around it. Even though soil oxygen or moisture may be in short supply, there is no competition. Vigor of individual seedlings is also affected by temperature. Grass seedlings must have a well-developed root system before exposure to adverse environmental conditions (Troughton, 1957). Vigor and plant survival will be greatly reduced if seedlings with an undeveloped root system are subjected to temperature extremes, inadequate moisture or low nutrient levels. Therefore, species with slow root development will be more susceptible to unfavorable environmental conditions during the establishment period.

Large seed size generally indicates high seedling vigor in grasses. This relationship is especially close within a seed lot or between seed lots of a single species. A similar relationship was shown among varieties of a single species (Whalley et al., 1966). However, Kneebone and Cremer (1955) demonstrated that among species this relationship is slight. Size of the endosperm rather than size of the embryo causes the effects associated with seed size (Bremner et al., 1963). Thomas (1966) reported that seed weight is one of the main determinants of successful establishment of perennial ryegrass.

Other factors that may affect rate of seedling establishment but have not been clearly demonstrated are the influence of the environmental conditions under which the seed was produced, age of seed, and the conditions of seed storage. The last two factors obviously affect percentage germination but may have little relationship to the subsequent growth of the seedlings from seeds that do germinate.

IV. Growth of Leaves

The stem of the turfgrass plant in the vegetative stage is simply a series of leaf-bearing nodes with unelongated internodes. The stem apex consists of a dome-shaped growing point with crescentric ridges, the leaf primordia, arising alternately on each side (Fig. 2). As the leaves develop from the lower ridges, they form a cowl enclosing the younger leaf primordia and the growing point (Fig. 3).

The number of ridges or leaf primordia of the vegetative apex of grasses may vary among species but is fairly constant for a species within a specific environment. Sharman (1947) classified grass species into three groups according to the length of the vegetative apex:

1. The short apex consisting of not more than three ridges is typical of the cereals. Bermudagrass is a common turfgrass that appears to belong in this group.

Figure 2. Vegetative apex of *Cynosurus cristatus* crested dogtail, consisting of 12 alternating crescentric ridges or leaf primorida. The long type apex according to Sharman's (1947) classification. Vegetative buds, which may develop into tillers, arise in the ridge axils a short time after their formation. Actual length, .75 mm.
Photograph by June Latting

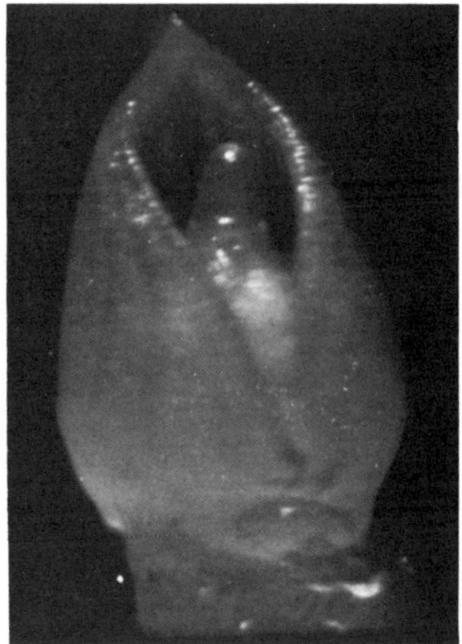

Figure 3. Vegetative apex of *Poa alpina*, alpine bluegrass, consisting of seven ridges or leaf primordia, partially enclosed by an elongating leaf. The intermediate length apex according to Sharman's (1947) classification. Actual length .65 mm.
Photograph by June Latting

2. The intermediate type of 5 to 10 ridges is found among many of the turfgrasses including bluegrass and fescues.

3. The long apex type may bear from 10 to 30 ridges. Annual ryegrass is the only turfgrass known to be in this group.

The exact number for a species will vary slightly with the age of the shoot and the environmental conditions under which it is grown.

A leaf primordium is initiated by periclinal divisions of cells in the two-layered tunica, or outer portion of the stem apex, resulting in the ridge. This is followed by cell divisions along the ridge margin with especially rapid divisions at mid-point to form the leaf tip. Later meristematic activity is restricted to the basal portion of the developing leaf establishing the leaf intercalary meristem. Subsequently this intercalary meristem is divided by a layer of parenchyma cells to form the sheath and blade intercalary meristems which continue the growth of the two leaf parts.

The leaf sheath generally continues to grow after cessation of blade growth; the latter is complete at approximately the time of emergence from the surrounding leaves of the shoot.

Mitchell and Soper (1958) demonstrated that differences in leaf width of perennial ryegrass and dallisgrass are the result of the environmental conditions under which they developed and not those under which the primordium was initiated. Different environments may induce wide variations in the circumference of the subapical meristem but have little affect on the size of the stem apex. Environmental changes affect the carbohydrate nutritional status of the plants and hence the size of the subapical meristem.

Leaf area and rate of leaf emergence were found to vary inversely, leaves being smaller with an increased rate of leaf emergence (Edwards and Cooper, 1963). The rate of leaf emergence per tiller varies greatly according to environmental conditions but is fairly constant under a species for any set of conditions. Climatic factors affecting the rate are temperature, light intensity, and photoperiod. Increased mineral nutrient levels, particularly nitrogen, were shown to have a positive effect on leaf emergence rate (Langer, 1958).

Optimum temperatures for leaf growth of cool-season grasses are usually below 27 C (Mitchell, 1956). Warm-season grasses have an optimum perhaps above 35 C and a minimum of about 10 C (Youngner, 1959, 1961a). Leaf growth increases with increasing daylength, but this effect may be modified by temperature. Youngner (1961a) found that the increase in leaf length with increasing daylength was greater at 27 C than at 21 C for *Zoysia* species.

The photosynthetic rate is maximum in a young, fully expanded leaf; assimilates are translocated and utilized for growth of new tillers, roots, and expanding leaves or stored in roots and crowns. As the leaf ages, photosynthetic activity decreases until the leaf no longer contributes to over-all plant growth and finally dies (Williams, 1964).

Rate of leaf death on a fully developed tiller is fairly constant for a species under a particular environment. As death rate is approximately equal to rate of leaf emergence, the number of living fully expanded leaves on a tiller is also constant (Bean, 1964). Length of leaf life in a turf, then, is dependent upon its particular environmental conditions and may be quite short in a rapidly growing turf. Mowing, as it affects leaf area and light conditions, may be an important factor controlling length of leaf life.

V. Tillering

Tiller buds may be initiated in the axils of young seedlings at an early age and are usually found in the axils of all leaves. Tillers may not necessarily emerge even though primordia are initiated, as tiller development is highly dependent upon environmental conditions. Tiller primordia are initiated by cell divisions in the inner (subhypodermal) layers of the stem apex shortly after appearance of the subtending leaf primordium. Initiation of the primordia appears to be independent of the environment (Soper and Mitchell, 1956). Growth of tillers, as distinct from stolons and rhizomes, is upward (apogeotropic); tillers remain closely oppressed to the parent shoot within the sheaths of the subtending leaf resulting, under favorable conditions, in numerous shoots in a small area. This is called intra-vaginal branching (Arber, 1934).

Development of tillers following bud initiation may be determined by daylength, temperature, light intensity, and nutrients. Rate of tiller development in a turf is the result of the interaction of all these factors as well as clipping height and clipping frequency.

Short days appear to increase the tillering rate of cool-season grasses (Gardner, 1942; Peterson and Loomis, 1949). Therefore, maximum tillering will occur in a turf during early spring and late fall if temperatures and other conditions are favorable. The tillering response of bermuda, zoysia, and other warm-season grasses to photoperiod is not known but may differ from that of cool-season grasses.

Maximum tillering of cool-season grasses occurs at moderate temperatures, optimums varying for different species (Mitchell, 1956). Although Peterson and Loomis (1949) reported only slight strain by temperature interactions for tiller development in Kentucky bluegrass, Youngner and Nudge (1968) showed pronounced differences in tillering at various temperatures among strains of dissimilar climatic origins. Tillering response to temperature of warm-season grasses is not as well-documented. Mitchell (1956) found that the optimum temperature for rate of tillering of dallisgrass is about 80 F. Based on the general temperature responses of warm-season grasses, similar high optimums may be expected for other species in this group.

The low density of turfgrasses grown in shade may result from the reduced tillering rate under low light intensities, as demonstrated by Mitchell (1953) for perennial ryegrass. As tiller buds compete with other parts of the plant for carbohydrates, their development will be increased with increasing light intensity (L. T. Evans et al., 1964). Beard (1965) demonstrated that the numbers of tillers per unit area differ greatly among species and strains of turfgrasses under identical shade conditions.

A young tiller is dependent upon the parent shoot for assimilates until it has developed four or five leaves and its own root system. It may then act as an independent plant although retaining its connection with the parent tiller. The degree to which individual tillers are independent is still a matter of debate (Langer, 1963). Water and nutrients may be translocated from one tiller to another through the vascular connections. Under stress conditions, such as defoliation, assimilates may be translocated from one mature tiller to another (Labanauskas and Dungan, 1956).

Little is known about the length of life of a tiller under turf conditions of frequent clipping and partial prevention of inflorescence formation. A tiller life span of no more than one year as demonstrated by Langer (1956) for timothy is quite probable. Tillers formed in the fall are undoubtedly important to winter survival and spring regrowth. These may not live long into the following summer but may be replaced by spring-formed tillers which, in turn, may be replaced by those formed in the fall. It is probable that any tillers initiating inflorescences die before the end of summer. Under environmental stress newly formed tillers are the first to die (Langer, 1963). Species differ in tiller longevity which, in turn, contributes to the degree of perenniality exhibited in a given environment.

VI. Rhizome and Stolon Growth

Initiation of rhizome and stolon primordia appears to be identical to that of tillers. However, subsequent growth and development differ in several respects. As the growth of a rhizome or stolon is more or less horizontal (diagiotropic), it breaks through the base of the subtending leaf sheath (extra-vaginal branching) instead of remaining within the leaf sheath as do true tillers (Arber, 1934).

Whereas internode elongation of tillers is slight except during inflorescence development, internodes of stolons and rhizomes may increase in length early in their development. During early internode elongation, the entire area between leaf primordia or nodes may be mertistematically active but as the internode grows, cell division activity becomes restricted to the areas directly above each node forming the stem intercalary meristems. Cell elongation, as well as cell division, contributes to stolon and rhizome growth.

Stolons are generally of indeterminate growth, rooting and forming a series of new plants at the nodes as they grow. Some grasses have stolon-like procumbent stems, e.g., crabgrass and dallisgrass, which may root at several nodes before the stem apex turns upward. Rhizomes may be either long and indeterminate, as in bermudagrass, or shorter and determinate with apices turning up and emerging above ground as in Kentucky bluegrass (Oakley and Evans, 1921). Indeterminate stolons and rhizomes may produce branches at some nodes which may in turn branch again. Nodal buds of determinate rhizomes usually remain dormant unless they are severed from the plant or the apical meristem is damaged.

Long days favor rhizome and stolon growth of both cool-season and warm-season turfgrasses (Evans and Watkins, 1939; Youngner, 1961a). Although increase in light energy may be a factor in this long-day response, Youngner (1961a) demonstrated that greater rhizome and stolon growth of *Zoysia* spp. occurs where the additional light period beyond 8 hours is of low intensity artificial light. Optimum temperatures for rhizome and stolon growth may differ and vary with species (Troughton, 1957).

Environmental factors that cause rhizomes to emerge from the soil are poorly understood. Brown (1939) observed that high temperatures or high nitrogen fertility induced rhizome tips of Kentucky bluegrass to emerge. Harrison (1934) found that Kentucky bluegrass rhizomes emerged during the cool, short days of fall. Fisher (1965) suggested that the higher CO_2 content of the soil and the absence of light tend to prevent rhizome bracts or cataphylls of Kentucky bluegrass from becoming leaf-like until the rhizome tip breaks through the soil surface.

Growth characteristics of the cataphylls may influence the downward or upward bending of the rhizome tip.

Growth of Roots

The grass root system consists of two types: the primary or seminal and the secondary, nodal, or adventitious root. The root system of an established turf may consist of roots entirely of adventitious origin, but during the critical period of seedling establishment the young plant is completely dependent on the seminal roots.

The seminal roots have their origin in primordia present in the embryo and may function throughout the life of annual grasses. Seminal roots of perennial turfgrasses seldom live longer than one year, their function gradually being taken over by the secondary root system. The number of seminal roots vary from one to several, depending upon species and variety.

Several attempts have been made to determine the relative importance of the seminal and adventitious root system (Weaver and Zink, 1945; Yates and Jacques, 1953). Results, in general, have been contradictory or inconclusive, in part because the relative importance may differ among species. Seminal roots may be fine and highly branched, this giving them high absorbtive ability, and hence great importance during the first months of a turfs establishment and growth when they are functioning actively.

Adventitious roots form at the lower nodes of the grass stem and may appear as early as the second or coleoptilar node; they will appear as whorls of roots at several successive nodes, thereafter. Many root primordia may form at each node. Adventitious roots also develop at nodes of tillers, rhizomes, and stolons. In dense turf, roots may form at nodes well above the soil surface if moisture is abundant.

The life span of individual nodal roots is not fully known. These roots have been reported to live for a year or more (Stuckey, 1941), a period that may be as long as that of the tiller or shoot they support. The exact length of life may depend on the species, season of development, and on environmental conditions. Roots may continue to function in conducting water and nutrients even after the outer cell layers (cortex) have decayed and only the central stele with its vascular tissue remains (Troughton,1957).

A typical young grass root, diagrammed in longitudinal section in Fig. 4, shows the growth zones recognized by Goodwin and Stepka (1945) in their studies on timothy. The root cap consists of a mass of relatively loose cells, many of which may sluff off as the root grows. It protects the meristematic zone directly behind it. The meristematic region is that portion of the root tip in which transverse cell divisions occur. Growth and cell division is most rapid 200 to 300γ from the tip.

Behind the meristematic region is the zone of elongation in which there is little cell division but a relatively great increase in cell length. Still further back from the root tip lies the zone of cell differentiation in which vascular tissue reaches full development although the initial sieve tubes are formed much nearer the tip. It is in this area that the root

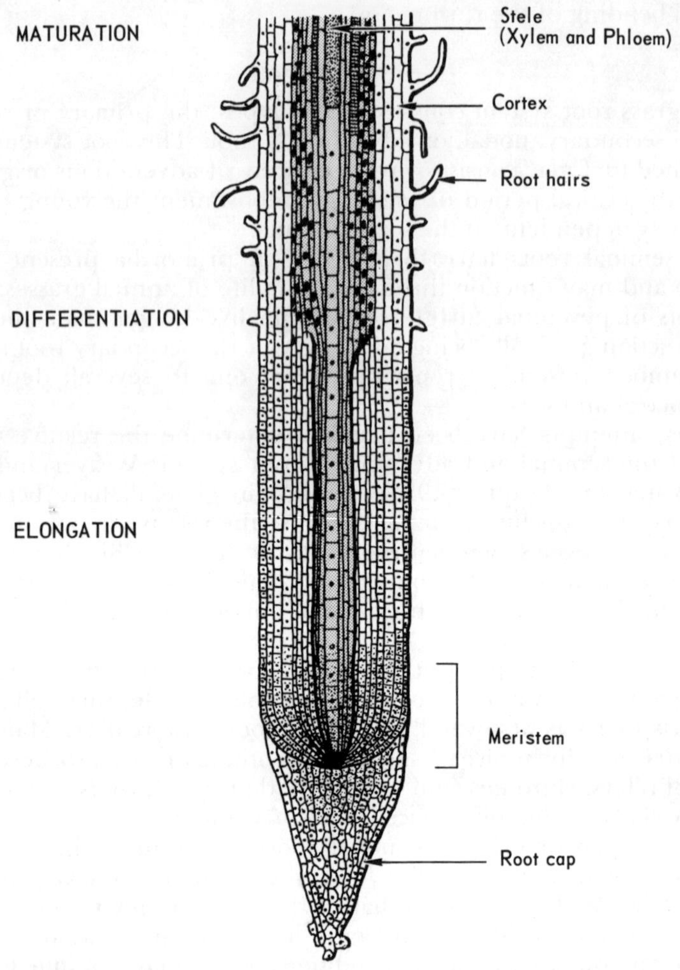

Figure 4. Diagram of tip portion of grass root in longitudinal section showing principal growth zones.

Drawing by C. Papp

begins to serve in full its absorptive function. Xylem vessels are differentiated in the central stele and a dense mass of root hairs develop from the epidermis.

Root hairs form in the zone of cell differentiation of the root tip. Root hairs of grasses persist for a longer time than in many other families and thus may extend for greater distances back from the root tip (Barnard, 1964). In some species, root hairs may develop from any epidermal cell in the zone of differentiation. This is characteristic of the warm-season grasses (panicoid) such as bermuda and zoysia. In the cool-season grasses (festucoid) root hairs develop only from specialized epidermal cells called tricoblasts (Row and Reeder, 1957). Tricoblasts are small cells with dense protoplasm created by unequal cell divisions in the outer (dermatogen) layer of the growing point.

Root growth is influenced by the same environmental factors affecting growth of the shoot. For cool-season grasses, optimum temperatures for root growth are several degrees lower than the optimums for shoot growth. Root temperature, distinct from air temperature, has a pronounced effect on the growth characteristics of grass roots (Brown, 1939; Stuckey, 1942). In general, roots of cool-season grasses held at low soil temperatures (40-50 F) are short, white, and unbranched. At moderate temperatures (60-70 F) roots are longer and profusely branched, while at high soil temperatures they are dark, fewer in number, and fibrous. Tips of roots from high soil temperature may be deformed and discolored, perhaps indicating a general root-tip degeneration.

In California studies at a uniform air temperature of 70 F, roots of Highland colonial bentgrass, Kentucky bluegrass, and bermudagrass were short, thick, and numerous at 50 F root temperature; they were long, thin, and dense at 60 to 70 F; but shorter and fewer in number at 80 F. However, root growth at 50 F was considerably greater for bentgrass and Kentucky bluegrass than for bermuda, and the reduction in root growth at 80 F was least for bermuda. Therefore, maximum root growth of both warm-season and cool-season turfgrasses appeared to take place at moderate root temperatures but with a slightly higher optimum for warm-season than for the cool-season grasses. Shoot growth of the three grasses increased with increasing root temperature (Youngner, unpublished).

Similarly, optimum levels of other environmental factors, such as light and nutrients, for root growth may differ from those for the shoot. However, effects of these factors on root growth can have meaning only if their effects on shoot growth are considered at the same time. This subject is discussed later in this chapter.

VII. Inflorescence Development and Reproduction

To the grower of turfgrasses, development of the grass inflorescence and reproductive organs may hold little interest. However, besides the obvious importance to breeding and seed production, the relationship of inflorescence development to vegetative growth is of significance.

Three stages in the flowering process are generally recognized: (1) induction, (2) initiation, (3) development and differentiation. In induction, certain physiological changes occur in the plant in response to specific environmental conditions. Although no morphological changes are evident, the plant is then ready for the initiation phase wherein stem apices change from the vegetative to the reproductive condition and floral primordia are formed. In the third phase, growth of floral primordia continues and various inflorescence structures and reproductive organs are differentiated.

Many plants, including some cool-season perennial turfgrass, have a period of chilling (a winter condition) as the first requisite for flowering. This chilling, called vernalization, may be effective on seeds of some species following imbibition of water (Chouard, 1960). Winter wheat, rye, and ryegrass are well-known grasses of this type. However, many perennial grasses may not be vernalizable until they have reached a particular stage of seedling development (Ketallapper, 1960; Youngner, 1960; Calder, 1966). This stage of development is often expressed as a minimum leaf number.

The temperature range for the most effective vernalization is from 32 to 50 F, although this chilling also occurs at a reduced rate at both warmer and colder temperatures. The effect of vernalization is quantitative, the longer the chilling period the more prolific the subsequent flowering up to a maximum length of time, beyond which there is no further increase in flowering. Exposure to a period of high temperature during or following chilling will have a devernalizing effect, returning the plant to a state in which it is incapable of flowering (Lang, 1952). The likelihood of devernalization is reduced by a prolonged period of chilling.

Action of the cold is thought to be directly on the shoot apex. The stimulus, resulting from the chilling, may be transmitted to apices of tillers arising from the treated tiller. However, this stimulus is not indefinitely transferable or autocatalytic since late-formed tillers do not flower (Chouard, 1960). Perennial grasses, therefore, require revernalization each year.

Short days may substitute for chilling to produce the vernalization effect in some grasses (Calder, 1966). Perennial ryegrass and several bentgrasses are turfgrasses known to respond to short days. Although short days are generally effective only at warm temperatures Kentucky bluegrass responds only at cool temperatures (Peterson and Loomis, 1949). In this case, neither short days nor low temperatures alone are effective. As L. T. Evans (1964) pointed out, it is doubtful that the same processes are involved as the shoot apex is the receptive organ for vernalization and the leaf for photoperiod.

Flowering of some warm-season grasses is stimulated by exposure to low temperatures for several weeks (Youngner and Spaulding, 1963, unpublished data). Chilling is not obligate for these grasses. This response may be distinct from vernalization and related to an accumulation of carbohydrate reserves under low temperature.

Control of flowering by photoperiod or daylength is common in many families of higher plants including the grasses; a voluminous literature has been compiled on the subject. Where vernalization is also a requirement for flowering, chilling usually must precede photoperiodic induction. Some species require a specific daylength simultaneously with chilling (Lang, 1952).

Plants may be placed in three principal groups according to their photoperiodic response: long-day, short-day, and day-neutral (Lang, 1952; Salisbury, 1961). In addition, plants with long-short-day and short-long-day requirements have been recognized. Long-day plants are those that flower only after exposure to daylengths greater than a critical number of hours. Short-day plants flower only under daylengths shorter than a critical number of hours. Experiments have shown, however, that a plant responds more to the length of the dark period than to the length of the light period. Day-neutral plants flower at any naturally occurring daylength if other flowering requirements are satisfied.

Although a few species will flower after a single day of the proper inductive length, most photoperiodically sensitive plants, including many turfgrasses, require a series of days of inductive length before flowers are initiated. Once induction has occurred, plants continue to flower even if subjected to daylengths that do not promote flowering.

Flowering of most cool-season turfgrasses is promoted by long days (L. T. Evans, 1964). This appears to be an obligate requirement for the ryegrass, red fescue, creeping bentgrass, Kentucky bluegrass, and meadow fescue. Flowering of some other species is accelerated by long days, but under short days these species will flower in time, although less prolifically. Of the warm-season grasses all zoysiagrasses are short-day plants, but certain bermudagrass varieties have a short-day requirement while others may be day-neutral with some acceleration of flowering by long days.

Experimental evidence indicates that a flowering hormone (florigen) is produced in the leaves when a plant is grown at the inductive photoperiod. This hormone is translocated to the shoot apices which then change from the vegetative to the flowering state.

L. T. Evans (1960) proposed from studies on a long-day ryegrass that both promotive and inhibitory substances are produced by leaf blades and that daylength determines the proportion or balance of the two substances; hence, the condition of the shoot apex. In later studies, Evans (1962) showed the presence of promotive and inhibitory substances in short-day grasses, as well.

The existence of ecological races within some species, differing in their photoperiodic or chilling requirements, is of significance to the grass breeder and seed grower (Olmsted, 1944; Hiesey, 1953). Performance of a strain, selected or developed in one area, may be quite different when grown in another latitude or climate. Both flowering and vegetative characteristics may be affected.

Photoperiodic reaction of grasses may be modified by temperature. In general, high temperature, particularly night temperature, has an inhibitory effect on many long-day grasses but a promotive effect on some short-day grasses (Calder, 1966).

High intensity light must precede the dark period for flowering of short-day plants (Salisbury, 1961). For this reason flowering of zoysiagrasses in greenhouses and growth chambers is frequently difficult to induce. However, low intensity light, as at dawn and evening hours, is photoperiodically effective and must be considered in determining the daylength.

Other factors may affect the flowering of grasses although they do not act as major determinants. High nitrogen fertility will increase flowering of some cool-season grasses but will greatly reduce flower production of bermudagrass. Clipping stimulates flower production of kikuyugrass (Youngner, 1961b) but severely restricts flowering of Kentucky bluegrass (Peterson and Loomis, 1949).

Development of the inflorescence has been described for a number of species (Barnard, 1955, 1957; Sharman, 1960; Bonnett, 1961, 1966).

Although they differ in specific developmental details, depending upon the type of inflorescence, the general sequence of events is similar. Following induction, the first visible evidence of change is an elongation of the shoot apex. Soon thereafter the "double ridge stage" can be seen (Fig. 5). Double ridges are formed by lateral bud primordia (spikelet or branch) arising in the axils of leaf primordia. Subsequent development of branches, spikelets, and florets is shown in Fig. 6.

Environmental conditions during this time are determining factors in the course of development and differentiation (Wycherley, 1952; Youngner, 1960). Long days and high temperatures usually increase the rate of development. High temperatures may cause abortion of florets or entire spikelets. In some species a reversal to the vegetative condition (vivipary or vegetative proliferation) may occur under certain day lengths and temperatures. Florets or spikelets are then converted to "plantlets" or "bulbils" which are capable of serving a propagative function. Hovin (1958) showed that temperatures of 85 F day maximum and 68 F night minimum, prior to anthesis of annual bluegrass, lowered greatly the percentage of viable pollen and often caused shriveled anthers. Pistillate organs were not affected. On the other hand, Youngner (1961c) demonstrated a low-temperature-induced male sterility in kikuyugrass.

Both cross- and self-pollination occur in the grass family. Cleistogamy, pollination prior to opening of the florets which assures self-pollination, is found in a number of genera and species. Cleistogamy may be facultative, occurring only under certain environmental conditions, or obligate, occurring at all times regardless of the environment.

Apomixis, production of seed by one of several processes which substitute for the normal sexual method, is common in the grass family. Many bluegrasses produce a high proportion of their seed apomictically, and some grasses such as common dallisgrass are classed as obligate apomictic. It is doubtful if any Kentucky bluegrass selections reproduce entirely by apomixis for even in apomictic selections at least a small percentage of the seed seems to be of sexual origin (Hanson and Carnahan, 1956).

VIII. Top and Root Relationships

Thus far, this discussion has dealt mainly with the independent growth of the several organs and tissues of the grass plant with little consideration of their relationships to each other and of the effects of turf cultural practices. Of particular importance in this respect is the relationship of top to root under various conditions.

In general, environmental conditions favoring top growth of cool-season grasses are unlike those favoring root growth. This may be less true for the warm-season grasses concerning which less research information is available. The frequent clipping practiced on turf, however, may be the single most important factor affecting growth rates and the relative quantities of roots, stems and leaves produced. The

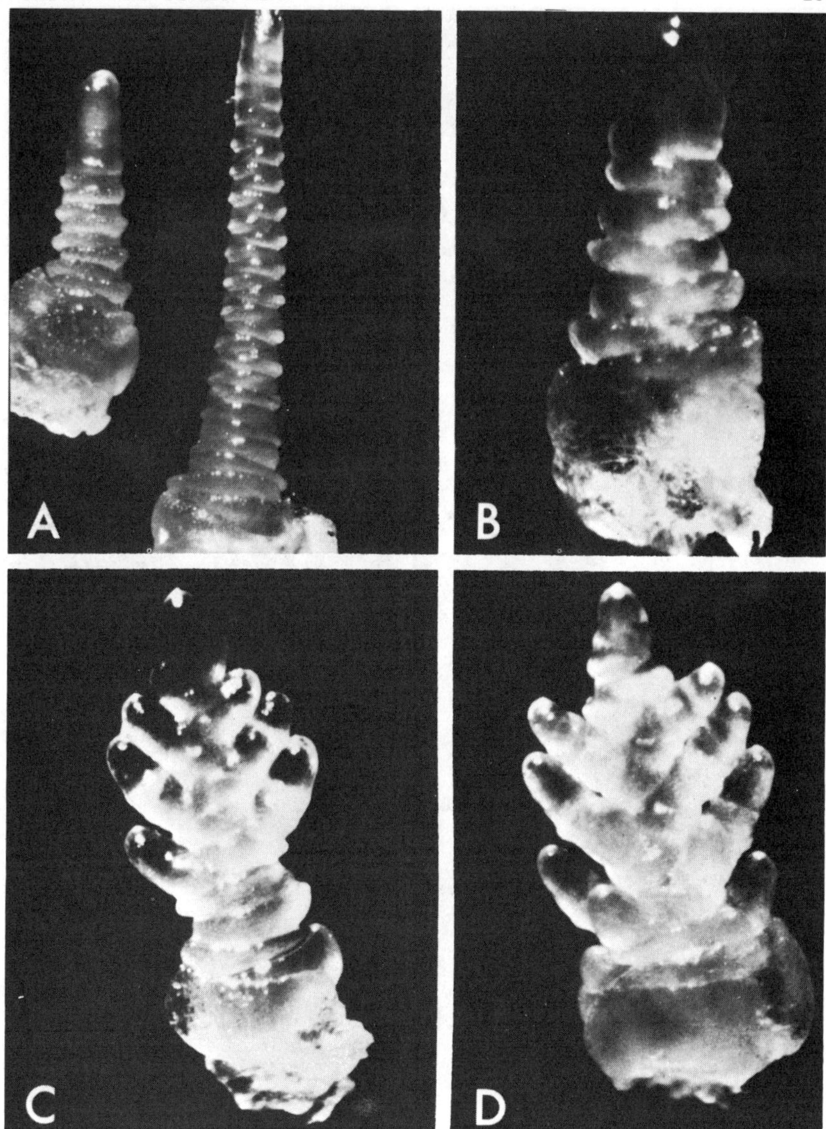

Figure 5. Early stages in the development of the grass inflorescence. A. Transition from vegetative to floral apex in *Cynosurus cristatus*. Left apex is elongating but no double ridge swellings are apparent. Actual length .925 mm. Apex to the right has reached the double ridge stage. Swelling in axils of ridges are spikelet primordia of the developing spike. Actual length 1.57 mm. B,C,D. Early differentiation of the panicle of *Poa artica*. B. Late double ridge stage. Swellings in ridge axils are primary branch primordia. Development is more advanced distally. Actual length .60 mm. C. Late primary branch stage. Secondary branch primordia are beginning to form next to primary branches at the middle of the floral apex. Actual length .85 mm. D. Floral apex with primary and secondary branches differentiated at every node. Apical spikelet differentiated into two glume primordia and the lemma primordium of the basal floret. Actual length .925 mm.

Photographs by June Latting

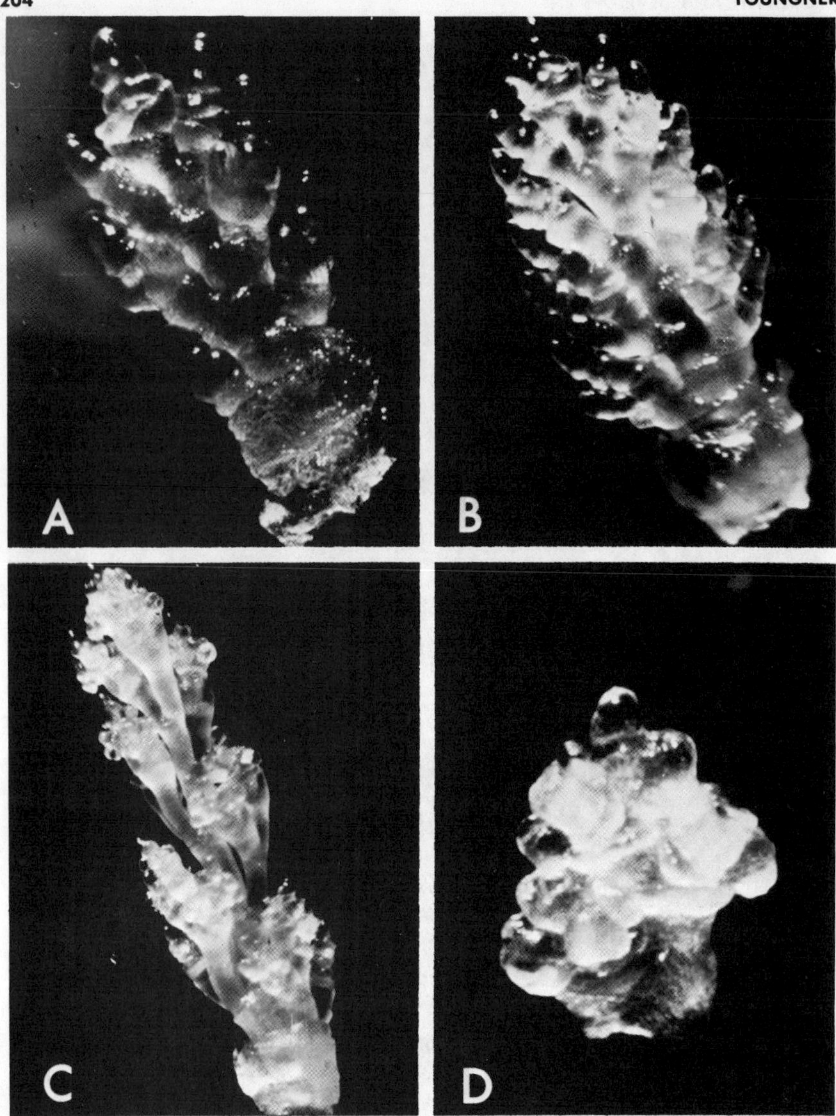

Figure 6. Spikelet and floret differentiation in inflorescence of *Poa artica*. A. Glumes of all spikelets are well differentiated. Lemma primordia are differentiating for basal florets of several spikelets. Apical spikelet shows three well developed lemma primordia above the glumes. Actual length 1.1 mm. B. Beginning of differentiation of structures within florets. Anther is budding on lower left floret of apical spikelet. Shows basipetal panicle differentiation with distal lateral spikelets which have differentiated glumes, lemmas and floret buds further advanced than the proximal spikelets. Actual length 1.7 mm. C. Panicle at pre-boot stage. Panicle and branch axes have begun to elongate. Glumes are elongating around florets of spikelets. Stamens and pistils are differentiated in most florets.. Actual length 3.45 mm. D. Apical spikelet from panicle in C. Lobed anthers on lower three florets and budding on fourth. Ovary infolded on basil floret at left. Lemmas of basal, second and third florets appear as flat ridges below the anthers. Two glumes subtend the spikelet.

Photographs by June Latting

interaction of clipping effects with those of other environmental factors may often prevent proper assessment of their importance.

All turfgrasses have a distinct seasonal cycle of growth, which differs with species and variety and is primarily the result of seasonal changes in temperature, daylength, and light intensity (Etter, 1951; Jacques and Schwass, 1956; Langer, 1959). Maximum root growth of cool-season grasses generally occurs in late fall and early spring when top growth is slow. In regions with mild winters, extensive root growth may also occur during these periods; rate of tillering will also be high. Later in spring, top growth increases while root growth and tillering decline. During summer, growth of all organs of cool-season grasses may decline and there may be a deterioration of the root system. In autumn, top growth increases again followed by increased tillering and root growth. A less specific seasonal pattern is evident for rhizome growth and emergence. Rhizomes are produced in greatest numbers in bluegrass during summer, with emergence in late summer and early fall (Evans and Ely, 1935). However, some rhizome growth seems to occur in all seasons.

An association between onset of flowering and a decline in the root to top ratio has been noted (Troughton, 1956). Although mowing prevents inflorescence production in a turf, initiation and early development of inflorescences occur in many species. The effect of this on root and tiller life of turfgrasses is not known but may be important.

Although the cessation of top growth of warm-season grasses in autumn is obvious, little specific information about the seasonal response of the various structures is available for this group of turfgrasses. Root and top growth of bermudagrass, as evidenced by growth and rooting of stolons, occur simultaneously throughout the warm seasons. Thus, the opposing seasonal responses may not exist to the same degree as noted for cool-season grasses. Root initiation and growth may occur in winter or early spring when no top growth can be observed.

Studies by Troughton (1956, 1960) illustrated the effects of several environmental factors on the relative growth of roots and tops of the turfgrass plant. Increasing the density of stand reduced total growth of several grass species but did not change the relative growth rates of tops and roots. Apparently competition among plants for water, light, and nutrients does not differentially affect growth of roots and tops. Both nitrogen fertilization and more water increased total growth of S-23 perennial ryegrass and increased the relative growth of tops to roots. Higher light intensity also produced more total growth but it increased the growth of roots more than it did the tops.

Three alternative explanations for these responses to changes in environment were suggested by Troughton. One explanation may be that it was an adaptation by the plant to the relative ease with which water, light, and nutrients could be obtained from the environment. For example, if a plant were able to take up more nitrogen per unit weight of roots under high nitrogen levels in the soil than under low, then development of a large root system under low nitrogen fertility would tend to maintain the same balance between nitrogen uptake and photosynthesis. A second explanation may be found in the maintenance of a constant C/N ratio in plant tissues as readily illustrated by the changes in light intensity. At reduced light intensity, photosynthesis would proceed more slowly than nitrogen adsorption, resulting in a low C/N ratio. This would be counterbalanced by increased relative growth of the photosynthetic tissue. Finally, Troughton's observations could be explained on the basis of changes in the relative importance of the functions of the root and shoot systems with changes in environment.

An increased growth of tops relative to roots with higher temperature was also reported for many grass species (Evans et al., 1964). This effect may result from a higher level of assimilates available for the roots at the lower temperatures.

IX. Carbohydrate Reserves

Reserve or available carbohydrates are nonstructural materials that may be stored in various plant tissues and later utilized in respiration and growth. Principal reserves in grasses are sugars, fructosans, starch, and perhaps rarely, if ever, hemicellulose. Cellulose and hemicellulose are principally structural materials and there is little evidence they are ever converted to less complex substances that may act as reserves (Troughton, 1957).

May (1960) pointed out that the term "reserve carbohydrate" has a connotation of purposeful accumulation which cannot be substantiated even though the utilization of these substances is well documented. However, this term is established in the literature and its usage undoubtedly will continue.

On the basis of the principal reserve substance found in the storage tissues, turfgrasses may be placed in the two classes first recognized by DeCugnac (1931). Cool-season turfgrasses store fructosans, sucrose, and reducing sugars but little or no starch. Warm-season turfgrasses store starch, sucrose, and reducing sugars but no fructosans (Okajima and Smith, 1964). These substances are stored primarily in roots, rhizomes, stolons, and crowns (leaf and stem bases) of the grass plant. The relative importance of these parts as storage organs varies with the species.

Carbohydrate reserves are believed to have an important role in providing energy for periods of rapid growth, regrowth following clipping, recovery from injury, and for tillering. Utilization of reserves at these times is well documented but direct evidence supporting their importance relative to current photosynthate in these functions is not extensive. The possible role of carbohydrate reserves in the development of tillers has not been determined, but it is conceivable that reserves may contribute to early tiller growth and favor a high tillering rate.

Seasonal changes in reserve carbohydrate content have been reported for many grasses (Troughton, 1957). Although many variations are evident among species, geographical areas, and the different storage organs, some generalizations may be made. Maximum rate of reserve carbohydrate accumulation in cool-season grasses occurs in late autumn during slow top growth. A gradual decrease in reserves is common during winter. A brief period of accumulation may occur in early spring followed by a rapid decrease associated with the spring flush of top growth. Reserves usually remain low during the summer months although a gradual increase may occur in late summer in some climates.

A similar trend has been shown for bermudagrass turf by Weinmann and Reinhold (1946). As with cool-season grasses, maximum accumulation occurs in autumn and a slow depletion in winter. However, following an initial drop in reserves in early spring there may be gradual increase during summer. These fluctuations are evident for carbohydrates in both roots and rhizomes but storage in rhizomes is several times that in roots. At no time are changes as great as those seen in cool-season grasses.

Seasonal fluctuations in carbohydrate reserves are largely the result of changes in climatic conditions. Temperature is a major factor controlling accumulation and utilization of reserves (Brown, 1939; Sullivan and Sprague, 1949; Miller, 1960). Maximum storage of carbohydrate reserves in unclipped cool-season grasses occurs at temperatures near the minimum for shoot growth. With rising temperature the amount of stored carbohydrates decreases. A depletion of reserves may occur if plants are exposed to very high temperatures for a brief period. Carbohydrate reduction may be especially great if high temperatures are associated with regular clipping. Varieties of a species may differ in their ability to store carbohydrates under identical temperatures (Youngner and Nudge, 1968).

Warm-season grasses may accumulate reserve carbohydrates at higher temperatures than do cool-season grasses. However, McKell and Youngner (1968, unpublished data) showed that maximum carbohydrate storage in bermudagrass also occurs at temperatures near the minimum for shoot growth. A reduction in reserves following short exposure to very high temperature was also noted. The kind of principal reserve carbohydrate, starch in bermudagrass and fructosans in bluegrass, is not altered by changes in temperature. However, the alcohol-soluble sugar content of bluegrass, but not of bermudagrass, increases greatly at cool temperatures. This may be associated with the acquisition of cold hardiness of temperate-climate grasses.

For both warm-season and cool-season grasses, shoot growth increases as temperature rises until an optimum is reached. Thus shoot growth and carbohydrate storage are opposing physiological processes with respect to temperature.

Nitrogen fertilization reduces the level of reserve carbohydrates in grass tissue (Sullivan and Sprague, 1953). This results perhaps from utilization of carbohydrates for the accelerated shoot growth brought about by the additional nitrogen. Depletion of reserves is intensified by clipping following nitrogen application.

The amount of light received by the shoot is a major determinant of carbohydrate reserves as well as all other aspects of growth. The amount of light received is determined by light intensity and photoperiod (Watkins, 1940).

In order for a plant to accumulate reserve carbohydrates the rate of carbohydrate synthesis must exceed the rate of utilization for respiration and growth. Therefore, the quantity of light energy falling on the shoot must exceed the compensation point by a considerable amount if reserves are to be accumulated. Although light saturation of a single grass leaf may be reached at only a fraction of full sunlight, leaves in a turf shade each other, therefore, much higher light intensities may be required for a maximum photosynthetic rate (Alberda, 1957; Wilsie, 1962).

X. Effects of Mowing on Growth

Any discussion of grass growth under conditions of turf culture must consider the many complex effects of frequent and intense leaf removal. Madison (1962) demonstrated that yield of top growth (clippings) is decreased either by reducing the height of mowing or increasing the frequency of mowing. This is consistent with results reported for many forage grasses.

Tillering is stimulated by clipping for the most part, only if the stem apex and its inhibitory effects on lateral buds are removed. Clipping of leaves only will not promote tillering but may actually inhibit lateral bud development (Jameson, 1964).

Of greater significance to turf culture is the effect of mowing on the root system of cool-season grasses. Numerous studies have shown that root growth is retarded by partial defoliation. The lower the height of cut, or the more frequent the clipping, the greater will be the retardation of root growth (Carter and Law, 1948; Jacques and Edmonds, 1952). Root system reduction is usually evident both in weight and length. Clipping may also reduce the number of roots initiated. Thus, the inevitable result of mowing turf is to produce a shallow and thin root system.

Crider (1955) has shown that removal in a single clipping of 40% or more of the top growth of several species stopped root elongation. The larger the percentage removed, the longer the period of root growth stoppage. Many roots on severely defoliated plants did not again grow in length. Severe clipping may be one of the causes of root tip degeneration of turfgrasses frequently observed in the field (Endo, 1967).

Restriction of root growth by clipping is usually interpreted to be the result of decreased carbohydrates for the root system. However, there is little direct evidence supporting this conclusion and it is possible that deficiencies of other leaf-produced growth substances may be involved (Jameson, 1964).

These effects of clipping on the root system may be modified by the growth habit of the species. Weinmann and Goldsmith (1948) found that repeated clipping of bermudagrass did not restrict root growth. They attributed this to the dense prostrate growth habit of bermuda which prevented severe defoliation under these circumstances. This was confirmed by later experiments in which plants were completely defoliated, resulting in severe restriction of root growth.

Clipping also reduces the growth of rhizomes and the number of rhizomes initiated in bluegrass turf (Harrison and Hodgson, 1939). Weight of rhizomes is reduced directly with the frequency of intensity of clipping. As with the root system, rhizomes of bermudagrass are affected little by clipping (Weinmann and Goldsmith, 1948).

The concentration of carbohydrate reserves in roots, rhizomes, and crowns of grasses also is reduced by clipping (Sullivan and Sprague, 1943). The more severe and frequent the clipping the lower will be the levels of carbohydrate reserves. Following a single clipping, reserves in storage organs drop rapidly for several days. If the grass is not again clipped, a gradual increase of the reserve carbohydrates occurs following the period of reduction. However, if the grass is clipped frequently, reserves remain low and may decline further. High temperatures accentuate the loss of reserves from clipping.

These changes in levels of reserve carbohydrates are generally attributed to their translocation to the aboveground plant parts for utilization in the production of new leaf tissue. If sufficient new leaves are allowed to develop, carbohydrates again are accumulated in storage organs.

May (1960) questioned the importance of reserve carbohydrates to regrowth after clipping, suggesting that a carbohydrate level above that needed to initiate new leaf growth is of no benefit. But Ward and Blaser (1961) showed that in orchardgrass regrowth is dependent on reserves; tillers with high carbohydrate reserves produced more total dry matter during the first 25 days following clipping than the tillers with low reserves.

Davidson and Milthorpe (1966a, 1966b) suggested that the concentration of soluble carbohydrates in the bases of expanding leaves is the factor controlling leaf expansion following defoliation. The concentration of carbohydrate in an expanding leaf is dependent upon the photosynthetic contribution of the expanded portion prior to defoliation. Old expanded leaves make little carbohydrate contribution to regrowth. After severe defoliation, regrowth is limited at first by the concentration of soluble carbohydrates in the bases of expanding leaves, next by the rate of photosynthesis, and last by the rate of nutrient uptake by the roots, which had been restricted in growth by the defoliation. Soluble carbohydrates in the leaf bases are important only in the first 2 to 4 days following defoliation. Carbohydrates in bases of old leaves may be free for use in tiller and root development.

High levels of reserves at the beginning of the growing season may be particularly important for turfgrasses. The frequent close clipping of turf, with the consequent regrowth, would seem to create heavy demands on reserves and might lead eventually to exhaustion under certain conditions.

As a result of numerous investigations, the concept that light can become a major limiting or controlling factor in growth of crop and pasture plants has gained wide acceptance. Water, nutrients, or soil air frequently limit crop growth in the field. Carbon dioxide may be a limiting factor under some rather unusual conditions. If these factors are in adequate supply through good production methods, growth will be limited only by the amount of light falling on the crop. As Donald (1951) stated, "When light, and light only, has become the limiting factor governing growth per unit area, the species has achieved the maximum production of which it is genetically capable. Stated differently, the ultimate capacity of a species to produce dry matter depends on the degree to which a community of such plants can exploit the light falling on it." Growth habit, leaf morphology, and leaf arrangements determine what this level of production will be.

In a young stand of pasture or turf the quantity of light is greater than needed by the plants and much of it penetrates through the leaves to the ground. As the plants grow and new leaves are produced, more and more of the incident light is intercepted by the leaf canopy. Eventually, severe competition for light develops among the plants and among the leaves on a plant. As density of the leaf canopy increases, older, lower leaves receive insufficient light and may become parasitic on the younger leaves of the plant. Finally, lower leaves begin to die and, in time, the rate of death of the older leaves equals the rate of appearance of new leaves (Black, 1957). A maximum or ceiling herbage growth has now been reached.

Jewiss and Woledge (1967) demonstrated a progressive decline in apparent photosynthesis with increasing age of leaf on tall fescue. New leaves have the highest photosynthetic efficiency and the best placement for light interception.

Watson (1947) placed these concepts on a quantitative basis, stressing the importance of the ratio of leaf area per unit area of soil surface which he proposed to call the Leaf Area Index (LAI). This is usually expressed as the square feet of leaf area (single surface) per square foot of soil.

Brougham (1955, 1957) showed in clipping studies on pasture plants that 95% interception of incident light and maximum growth rate are reached at a specific LAI for a particular crop regardless of the intensity of clipping. The more severe the prior clipping the longer the time required for this LAI (termed the critical or optimum LAI) to be reached. As the LAI increases above the optimum, lower leaves are shaded causing the growth rate to drop. A maximum LAI and ceiling yield of forage is reached when the rate of death of old leaves from shading equals the rate of new leaf emergence. The critical and maximum LAI varies among species because of differences in growth habit but the principles are broadly applicable.

The significance of these relationships to turf culture have not been determined. Although herbage yield is not a consideration in turf production, a vigorous dense stand of vegetation is usually considered desirable. This might best be achieved by a mowing height and frequency that would maintain a LAI as near the optimum as other requirements of the turf allow. A high net assimilation rate would be maintained thereby permitting good tiller and root development. A LAI above the optimum would have little advantage but might favor thatch accumulation. These considerations would be valid only if nutrition, water, and other requirements for growth are adequate.

Summary

With the foregoing information gathered from many studies and sources, a general but sketchy description of growth of a cool-season grass turf may be offered. Assuming that water and nutrients are adequate and temperature favorable for the species, growth rate of an individual tiller in a young turf will be near maximum, since every leaf will be receiving all the light energy needed. The tillering rate will be high, also, because of the availability of assimilates for translocation to the developing tillers. Despite the rapid growth of the aboveground plant structures, the root system will be expanding as a result of the continuous supply of assimilates and the initiation of roots on the new tillers. Rhizomes will be contributing little to the spread of the turf in the early development stage, but stoloniferous grasses may have a high rate of stolon initiation and growth.

Because tillering of an individual plant is exponential (Patel and Cooper, 1961), growth of the entire turf will be at an accelerating rate during this stage until light or another factor becomes limiting. Little accumulation of reserve carbohydrates in the immature turf will occur.

The effect of mowing an immature turf may be primarily to reduce the total photosynthetic area and consequently to retard the growth rate. Lateral bud development will be retarded by leaf removal unless stem apices (of stolons) are removed; thus, early mowing is not likely to accelerate the spreading of nonstoloniferous turfgrasses as is frequently thought.

As the turf becomes closed, i.e., sufficiently dense for interception of essentially all the incident light by the leaves, growth per tiller and tillering rate decrease but growth rate of the turf will be maximum. Mowing, if close and frequent, may prevent a closed turf conditions from being reached.

Immediately following the first spring mowing of a mature turf, carbohydrate reserves from leaf bases are utilized for the beginning of regrowth. Root growth may cease for several days; the length of time will be greater the more severe the mowing. Cutting of the regrowth will further deplete reserve carbohydrates and again retard root development. Nitrogen fertilization will stimulate top growth and intensify the effects of mowing on carbohydrate reserves and root growth. During the early cool spring season, despite these effects, the total root system will increase in length and weight and many new tillers will be produced.

With the onset of the warm summer season, growth rate of tops will usually decrease, almost all root growth will cease and some dieback of roots will occur. Fewer new tillers will be produced while many of the tillers from the previous season may die resulting in a gradual reduction in turf density. Reserve carbohydrates will be at a very low level.

Cooler late summer and early autumn weather will bring an accelerated rate of top growth, which will gradually decline again as temperatures become lower. With the drop in temperature, root growth will be resumed, tillering will increase and rhizomes will emerge from the soil. Carbohydrates will accumulate in the roots, crown, and rhizomes.

During winter, root growth may continue even if temperatures are too low for any foliage growth. Carbohydrates may be slowly consumed for growth and respiration of roots and other overwintering plant parts.

During the principal growing season, a similar but less pronounced pattern of growth will be evident for the warm-season grasses. Low temperature effects are clearly expressed often with no growth of any plant parts during the coldest part of the winter. A paucity of information still exists, however, on many growth aspects of this important group of plants as compared with the cool-season grasses.

Literature Cited

Alberda, T. H. 1957. The effect of cutting, light intensity, and temperature on growth and carbohydrate content of perennial ryegrass. Plant and Soil 8:190-230.

Arber, A. 1934. The Gramineae. Univ. Press, Cambridge.

Ballard, L. A. T. 1964. Germination. p. 73-88. *In* C. Barnard, (ed.), Grasses and Grasslands, MacMillan & Co. Ltd., London.

Barnard, C. 1955. Histogenesis of the inflorescence and flower of *Triticum aestivum* L. Aust. J. Bot. 3:1-20.

Barnard, C. 1957. Floral histogenesis in the monocotyledons I. The Gramineae. Aust. J. Bot. 5:1-20.

Barnard, C. 1964. Form and structure. p. 47-72. *In* C. Barnard, (ed), Grass and Grasslands, MacMillan & Co. Ltd., London.

Bean, E. W. 1964. The influence of light intensity upon the growth of an S.37 Cocksfoot *(Dactylis glomerata)* sword. Ann. Bot. 28:427-443.

Beard, J. B. 1965. Factors in the adaptation of turfgrasses to shade. Agron. J. 57:457-459.

Black, J. N. 1957. The influence of varying light intensity on the growth of herbage plants. Herb. Abstr. 27:89-98.

Bonnett, O. T. 1961. The oat plant: Its histology and development. Univ. of Illinois, Agr. Exp. Sta., Bull. 672.

Bonnett, O. T. 1966. Inflorescences of maize, wheat, rye, barley and oats: Their initiation and development. Univ. of Illinois, Agr. Exp. Sta., Bull. 721.

Bremner, P. M., R. N. Eckersall, and R. K. Scott. 1963. The relative importance of embryo size and endosperm size in causing the effects associated with seed size in wheat. J. Agr. Sci. 61:139-145.

Brougham, R. W. 1955. A study in rate of pasture growth. Aust. J. Agr. Res. 6:804-812.

Brougham, R. W. 1957. Some factors that influence the rate of growth of pasture. 19th Conf. of the New Zealand Grasslands Assoc. p. 109-116.

Brown, E. M. 1939. Some effects of temperature on the growth and chemical composition of certain pasture grasses. Missouri Agr. Exp. Sta., Res. Bull. 299:1-76.

Calder, D. M. 1966. Inflorescence induction and initiation in the gramineae. p. 59-73. *In* Milthorpe, F. L. and J. D. Ivins, (ed.), The growth of cereals and grasses, Butterworths, London.

Carter, J. F. and A. G. Law. 1948. The effect of clipping on the vegetative development of some perennial grasses. J. Amer. Soc. Agron. 40:1084-1091.

Chouard, P. 1960. Vernalization and its relations to dormancy. Annu. Rev. Plant Physiol. 11:191-238.

Clements, F. E. and V. E. Shelford. 1939. Bio-ecology. Wiley, New York.

Crider, R. J. 1955. Root growth stoppage resulting from defoliation of grass. Tech. Bull. 1102, USDA.

Crocker, W. and L. V. Barton. 1953. Physiology of seeds. Chronica Botanica Co., Waltham, Mass.

Davidson, J. L. and F. L. Milthorpe. 1966a. Leaf growth in *Dactylis glomerata* following defoliation. Ann. Bot. 30:173-184.

Davidson, J. L. and F. L. Milthorpe. 1966b. The effect of defoliation on the carbon balance in *Dactylis glomerata.* Ann. Bot. 30:185-197.

DeCugnac, A. 1931. Recherches sur les glucides des Gramineae. Ann. Sci. Naturelles 13:1-129.

Donald, C. M. 1951. Competition among pasture plants. I. Interspecific competition among annual pasture plants. Aust. J. Agr. Res. 2:355-376.

Donald, C. M. 1963. Competition among crop and pasture plants. p. 1-118. *In* A. G. Norman, (ed.), Advances in Agronomy, Acad. Press, New York.

Edwards, K. J. R. and J. P. Cooper. 1963. The genetic control of leaf development in *Lolium.* Heredity 18:307-317.

Endo, R. M. 1967. Root tip degeneration of turfgrasses, natural and induced. Calif. Turfgrass Cult. 17:17-18.

Etter, A. G. 1951. How Kentucky bluegrass grows. Ann. Mo. Bot. Gardens 38:293-375.

Evans, L. T. 1960. Inflorescence initiation in *Lolium temulentum* L. II. Evidence for inhibitory and promotive photoperiodic processes involving transmissible products. Aust. J. Biol. Sci. 13:429-440.

Evans, L. T. 1962. Day-length control of inflorescence initiatiòn in the grass *Rottboellia exaltato* L. Aust. J. Biol. Sci. 15:291-303.

Evans, L. T. 1964. Reproduction. p. 126-153. *In* C. Barnard, (ed.), Grasses and Grasslands, MacMillan & Co. Ltd., London.

Evans, L. T., I. F. Wardlaw and C. N. Williams. 1964. Environmental control of growth. p. 102-125. *In* C. Barnard, (ed.), Grasses and Grasslands, MacMillan & Co. Ltd., London.

Evans, M. W. 1927. The life history of Timothy. USDA Bull. 1450 p. 1-56.

Evans, M. W. and J. E. Ely. 1935. The rhizomes of certain species of grasses. J. Amer. Soc. Agron. 33:1017-1027.

Evans, M. W. and J. M. Watkins. 1939. The growth of Kentucky bluegrass and Canada bluegrass in late spring and in autumn as affected by length of day. J. Amer. Soc. Agron. 31:764-774.

Fisher, J. E. 1965. The growth of rhizomes in Kentucky bluegrass. Greenhouse, Garden, Grass 5(4):1-6.

Gardner, J. L. 1942. Studies in tillering. Ecol. 23:162-174.

Goodwin, R. H. and W. Stepka. 1945. Growth and differentiation in the root tip of *Phleum pratense.* Amer. J. Bot. 32:36-46.

Hanson, A. A. and H. L. Carnahan. 1956. Breeding perennial forage grasses. USDA Tech. Bull. 1145.

Harris, G. S. 1961. The periodicity of germination in some grass species. New Zealand J. of Agr. Res. 4:253-260.

Harrison, C. M. 1934. Responses of Kentucky bluegrass to variations in temperature, light, cutting and fertilizing. Plant Physiol. 9:83-106.

Harrison, C. M. and C. W. Hodgson. 1939. Response of certain perennial grasses to cutting treatments. Agron. J. 31:418-430.

Hiesey, W. M. 1953. Growth and development of species and hybrids of *Poa* under controlled temperatures. Amer. J. Bot. 40:205-221.

Hovin, A. W. 1958. Reduction of self-pollination by high night temperature in naturally self-fertilized *Poa annua* L. Agron. J. 50:369-371.

Jacques, W. A. and D. B. Edmonds. 1952. Root development in some common New Zealand pasture plants. V. The effects of defoliation and root pruning on cocksfoot *(Dactylis glomerata)* and perennial ryegrass *(Lolium perenne)*. New Zealand J. Sci. and Tech. 34:231-248.

Jacques, W. A. and R. H. Schwass. 1956. Root development in some common New Zealand pasture plants. VII. Seasonal root replacement in perennial ryegrass *(Lolium perenne)*, Italian ryegrass *(L. multiflorum)* and tall fescue *(Festuca arundinacea)*. New Zealand J. Sci. and Tech. 37:569-583.

Jameson, D. A. 1964. Effect of defoliation on forage plant physiology. *In* Forage plant physiology and soil-range relationships Amer. Soc. Agron., Special Pub. #5.

Jewiss, O. R. and J. Woledge. 1967. The effect of age on the rate of apparent photosynthesis in leaves of tall fescue *(F. arundinacea Schreb.)* Ann. Bot. 31:661-671.

Ketallapper, H. J. 1960. Growth and development in *Phalaris* I. Vernalization response in geographic strains of *P. tuberosa*. Ecol. 41:298-305.

Kneebone, W. R. and C. L. Cremer. 1955. The relationship of seed size to seedling vigor in some native grass species. Agron. J. 47:472-477.

Koller, D., A. M. Mayer, A. Poljakoff-Mayber and S. Klein. 1962. Seed germination. Ann. Rev. Plant Physiol. 13:437-464.

Labanauskas, C. K. and G. H. Dungan. 1956. Interrelationships of tillers and main stems in oats. Agron. J. 48:265-268.

Lang, A. 1952. Physiology of flowering. Annu. Rev. Plant Physiol. 3:265-306.

Langer, R. H. M. 1956. Growth and nutrition of timothy *(Phleum pratense)* I. The life history of individual tillers. Ann. Appl. Biol. 44:166-187.

Langer, R. H. M. 1958. A study of growth in sword of timothy and meadow fescue. 1. Uninterrupted growth. J. Agr. Sci. 51:347-352.

Langer, R. H. M. 1959. A study of growth in swords of timothy and meadow fescue. 2. The effects of cutting treatments. J. Agr. Sci. 52:273-281.

Langer, R. H. M. 1963. Tillering in herbage grasses. Herb. Abstr. 33:141-148.

Madison, J. H. 1962. The mowing of turfgrass. II. Responses of three species of grass. Agron. J. 54:250-253.

May, L. H. 1960. The utilization of carbohydrate reserves in pasture plants after defoliation. Herb. Abstr. 30:239-245.

Mer, C. L. and D. R. Causten. 1963. Carbon dioxide: A factor influencing cell division. Nature 199:360-362.

Miller, V. J. 1960. Temperature effects on the rate of apparent photosynthesis of seaside bent and bermudagrass. Proc. Amer. Soc. Hort. Sci. 75:700-703.

Mitchell, K. J. 1953. Influence of light and temperature on the growth of ryegrass *(Lolium* spp.) 2. The control of lateral bud development. Physiol. Plant. 6:425-443.

Mitchell, K. J. 1956. Growth of pasture species under controlled environments. I. Growth at various levels of constant temperature. New Zealand J. Sci. and Tech. 38A:203-215.

Mitchell, K. J. and K. Soper. 1958. Effects of differences in light intensity and temperature on the anatomy and development of leaves of *Lolium perenne* and *Paspalum dilatatum*. New Zealand J. of Agr. Res. 1:1-16.

Oakley, R. A. and M. W. Evans. 1921. Rooting stems in timothy. J. Agr. Res. 21:173-178.

Okajima, Hideo and Dale Smith. 1964. Available carbohydrate fractions in the stem bases and seed of timothy, smooth bromegrass, and several other northern grasses. Crop Sci. 4:317-320.

Olmsted, C. E. 1944. Photoperiodic responses of 12 geographic strains of side-oats grama. Bot Gaz. 106:46-74.

Owen, E. B. 1956. The storage of seeds for the maintenance of viability. Commonwealth Bur. of Pastures and Field Crops, Farnham Royal, Bucks, England. Bull. 43.

Patel, A. L. and J. P. Cooper. 1961. The influence of seasonal changes in light energy on leaf and tiller development in ryegrass, timothy and meadow fescue. J. Brit. Grassland Soc. 16:299-308.

Peterson, M. L. and W. E. Loomis. 1949. Effects of photoperiod and temperature on growth and flowering of Kentucky bluegrass. Plant Physiol. 24:31-43.

Reeder, J. R. 1957. The embryo in grass systematics. Amer J. Bot. 44:756-768.

Row, H. C. and J. R. Reeder. 1957. Root hair development as evidence of relationships among genera of Gramineae. Amer. J. Bot. 44:596-601.

Salisbury, F. B. 1961. Photoperiodism and the flowering process. Annu. Rev. Plant Physiol. 12:293-326.

Sharman, B. C. 1947. The biology and developmental morphology of the shoot apex in the Gramineae. The New Phytol. 46:20-38.

Sharman, B. C. 1960. Developmental anatomy of the stamen and carpel primordia in *Anthoxanthrem odoratum*. Bot. Gaz. 121:192-198.

Soper, K. and K. J. Mitchell. 1956. The developmental anatomy of perennial ryegrass (*Lolium perenne L.)*. New Zealand J. Sci. and Tech. 37A:484-504.

Stuckey, I. H. 1942. Seasonal growth of grass roots. Amer. J. Bot. 28:486-491.

Stuckey, I. H. 1942. Influence of soil temperature on the development of colonial bentgrass. Plant Physiol. 17:116-122.

Sullivan, J. T. and V. G. Sprague. 1943. Composition of the roots and the stubble of perennial ryegrass following partial defoliation. Plant Physiol. 18:556-670.

Sullivan, J. T. and V. G. Sprague. 1949. The effect of temperature on the growth and composition of the stubble and roots of perennial ryegrass. Plant Physiol. 24:706-719.

Sullivan, J. T. and V. G. Sprague. 1953. Reserve carbohydrates in orchardgrass cut for hay. Plant Physiol. 28:304-313.

Thomas, R. L. 1966. The influence of seed weight on seedling vigor in *Lolium perenne*. Ann. Bot. 30:111-121.

Troughton, A. 1956. Studies on the growth of young grass plants with special reference to the relationship between root and shoot systems. J. Brit. Grassland Soc. 11:56-65.

Troughton, A. 1957. The underground organs of herbage grasses. Commonwealth Bur. of Pastures and Field Crops, Harley Berkshire, England. Bull. 44.

Troughton, A. 1960. Further studies on the relationship between shoot and root systems of grasses. J. Brit. Grassland Soc. 15·41-47.

Vegis, A. 1964. Dormancy in higher plants. Annu. Rev. Plant Physiol. 15:185-224.

Ward, C. Y. and R. E. Blaser. 1961. Carbohydrate food reserves and leaf area in regrowth of orchardgrass. Crop Sci. 1:366-370.

Watkins, J. M. 1940. The growth habits and chemical composition of bromegrass as affected by different environmental conditions. J. Amer. Soc. Agron. 32:527-538.

Watson, D. J. 1947. Comparative physiological studies on the growth of field crops. Ann. Bot. 11:41-76.

Weaver, J. E. and E. Zink. 1945. Extent and longevity of the seminal roots of certain grasses. Plant Physiol. 20:359-379.

Weinmann, H. and E. P. Goldsmith. 1948. Underground reserves of *Cynodon dactylon. In* Better Turf Through Research. African Explosives and Chemical Ind., Ltd.

Weinmann, H. and L. Reinhold. 1946. Reserve carbohydrates in South African grasses. J. So. Afr. Bot 12:57-73.

Wellington, P. S. 1966. Germination and seedling emergence. p. 3-19. *In* Milthorpe, F. L. and J. D. Ivins, (ed.), The Growth of Cereals and Grasses, Butterworths, London.

Whalley, R. D. B., C. M. McKell and L. R. Green. 1966. Seedling vigor and early nonphotosynthetic stage of seedling growth in grasses. Crop Sci. 6:147-150.

Williams, R. D. 1964. Assimilation and translocation in perennial grasses. Ann. Bot. 28:419-426.

Wilsie, C. P. 1962. Crop adaptation and distribution. W. H. Freeman, San Francisco.

Wycherley, P. R. 1952. Temperature and photoperiod in relation to flowering in three perennial grass species. Meded. Landbouwh. 52:75-92.

Yates, M. E. and W. A. Jacques. 1953. Root development of some common New Zealand pasture plants. VI. Importance of various roots, particularly the seminal roots of perennial ryegrass *(Lolium perenne.)* New Zealand J. Sci. and Tech. 34:249-257.

Youngner, V. B. 1959. Growth of U-3 bermudagrass under various day and night temperatures and light intensities. Agron. J. 51:557-559.

Youngner, V. B. 1960. Environmental control of initiation of the inflorescence, reproductive structures and proliferations in *Poa bulbosa.* Amer. J. Bot. 47:753-758.

Youngner, V. B. 1961a. Growth and flowering of Zoysia species in response to temperatures, photoperiods and light intensities. Crop Sci. 1:91-93.

Youngner, V. B. 1961b. Observations on the ecology and morphology of *Pennisetum clandestinum.* Phyton. 16:77-84.

Youngner, V. B. 1961c. Low temperature induced male sterility in male-fertile *Pennisetum clandestinum.* Sci. 133:577-578.

Youngner, V. B. and F. J. Nudge. 1968. Growth and carbohydrate storage of three *Poa pratensis* L. strains as influenced by temperature. Crop Sci. 8:455-457.

8 ECOLOGY AND TURF MANAGEMENT

R. E. Schmidt
R. E. Blaser

Virginia Polytechnic Institute
Blacksburg, Virginia

I. Introduction

Over many years communities of plants have developed naturally in response to the complexities of soil, climatic, and biotic interrelationships. Such natural plant communities are evident in all environmental regions in the world—deciduous forests, evergreen forests, short and tall grass prairies, desert shrubs, savanahs, etc. In contrast, cultivated turfgrasses are not natural plant communities; the successful maintenance and use of these species depends on man's influence and knowledge. All ecological factors, climatic, soil, and biotic, and their interplay affect plant survival and must be considered and manipulated to maintain desirable ecological relationships for best turfgrass establishment and maintenance. The response of various turf species to many natural and imposed variables embodies the science of turf management.

Turf management practices such as mowing, fertilization and liming, soil modification, irrigation, dethatching, and control of weeds, insects, and disease influence each other and must be interrelated. For example, fertilizer practice influences thatch accumulation, weed encroachment, and liming requirement and may inhibit or encourage certain disease organisms. In addition, the aforementioned management practices, alone or in combinations, often cause drastic changes in root and canopy microenvironment in turfgrass plantings. Alterations of light, temperature, moisture, and soil aeration can cause adverse or desirable effects.

Turf species and varieties respond differently to the interplay of management and microenvironment. Such differential response among turf plants may be attributed to both morphological and physiological differences that have become stable in genotypes. The area of best adaptation is one where a species survives for long periods under prevailing climatic, soil, and biotic conditions. Grasses are broadly classified as adapted to one of four general climatic regions: cool-moist, warm-moist, cool-arid, and warm-arid regions. However, such classifications are not absolute because differences in elevation within a climatic zone can cause environmental islands; also, environmental conditions and grass adaptation may be altered by management practices. Thus, bermudagrass and Kentucky bluegrass adapted to warm-humid and cool-humid areas, respectively, grow well in some arid environments, if supplied with supplemental irrigation. Bentgrass and other cool season grasses may be used in warm latitudes with special culture. Climatically unadapted grasses often produce good quality turf by manipulating soil, biotic, and management factors.

In this chapter an attempt will be made to explain some micro-environmental-management interrelationships.

II. Turf Usage, An Ecology Factor

The various ways in which grasses are used are as important an influence on their development as the temperature or moisture stresses to which they will be subjected. With modern technology, certain environmental factors can be modified, but use of the grass is often fixed. Thus, turf usage is a primary ecological consideration in selecting adapted grasses.

Grasses used for golf greens, bowling greens, and on other specialized areas must be morphologically and physiologically tolerant of the conditions under which they will be grown and used. Grasses that tolerate extremely close clipping, heavy traffic, and recover quickly from injury are ecologically adapted for such specialized areas as golf greens. Only certain bentgrasses and bermudagrasses provide the firm, smooth, dense, and resilient turf needed for golf putting green use (Musser, 1962; Daniel and Roberts, 1966).

The degree of turf abuse depends on the sport, sequence of sporting activities, amount of traffic, and time of year when it is used. Turf on football fields must have a pleasing appearance during autumn and possess such characteristics as high shear strength, minimum divoting during play, and resistance to abrasion. Modifying the soil properly on a football field before establishing grasses encourages vigorous and deep root systems to improve shear strength. Also, rotating or limiting usage will reduce turf injury from abrasion by traffic. Wear is a serious problem on hard use areas, such as airfields. A wear resistant grass should be used on these areas. Zoysia, bermudagrass, and tall fescue have more resistance to wear than Kentucky bluegrass, ryegrass, fine-leaf fescues, or bentgrass (Youngner, 1961a).

General turf for home lawns, industrial lawns, cemeteries, and institutional grounds usually are subjected to limited and controlled use which simplifies maintenance. Maintenance needed for these types of turf is dictated by the quality of turf desired.

Bermudagrass and Kentucky bluegrass in the warm- and cool-humid regions, respectively, make good lawns, if they are adequately fertilized and irrigated during dry seasons. On the other hand, centipede in the warm-humid regions and fine-leaf fescues in the cool-humid regions will provide better turf than bermudagrass or Kentucky bluegrass under low fertility and if no irrigation is available.

Vegetation along highways must grow under extreme moisture, temperature, and soil environments that are often difficult to alter. Moisture and temperatures on opposite sides of a road in rolling topographies are decidedly different due to slope exposure (McKee et al.,

1965). It is much more difficult to establish and maintain vegetation on sunny than on more shady slopes. The latter have cooler and more moderate temperatures and more available water because of lower evapotranspiration. Exposed subsoils are often droughty because of stoniness or poor water infiltration and possess adverse chemical and physical conditions (Blaser, 1962).

Highway seedings are usually made up of a mixture of several species because of differential responses in germination and survival and growth under variable microclimatic and soil conditions. Soon after establishment sods often degenerate because of low nitrogen levels. Thus, legumes used in seeding mixtures serve to stabilize soils through their growth and added nitrogen for grasses (Blaser, 1963).

Although climax vegetation (undisturbed native vegetation) in humid climates is forest and woody vegetation, it is not practical to establish such vegetation along highways. When native woody vegetation is desired on bare soil areas along newly constructed highways, it is expedient to first establish a grass or grass-legume cover to provide quick soil stabilization and water control. Such sods, if not mowed, serve as ideal environments for the native encroachment of woody vegetation (Blaser and McKee, 1967).

Many thousand miles of coastal and lake beaches are subject to severe wind and water erosion that may create unstabilized dunes. Inland dunes also occur along beachlines and in deltas, deserts, and former lakebeds. These dunes must be stabilized to protect not only recreational areas but also buildings, highways, and agricultural lands.

Vegetation used on sand dunes must thrive in the presence of continuously shifting sand, tolerate sand blasting, and, along coastal shores, persist under continuous salt spray. Plants best adapted to dune stabilization must be perennials, grow rapidly, and persist on substrates low in nutrients.

In the Pacific Northwest, European beachgrass seems to be best adapted for sand stilling (Stoesz and Brown, 1957). Along the Great Lakes and the Atlantic Coast as far south as South Carolina, sand dunes have been successfully stabilized with American beachgrass *(Ammophila breviligulata)*. Tests conducted in Rhode Island and North Carolina show that American beachgrass produces extensive rhizomes that grow rapidly through accumulating sand (Jagschitz and Bell, 1966b; Woodhouse and Hanes, 1966). In Rhode Island, Volga wildrye *(Elymus giganteus* Vahl.) has been used in plantings with American beachgrass because of ease in establishment and its persistence as a shortlived perennial. On dunes from Carolina to Mexico, the adapted plants for dune stabilization are sea-oats *(Uniola paniculata* L.) and sea panicgrass *(Panicum amarum* Ell.) (Stoesz and Brown, 1957).

Although several trees and shrubs, especially Japanese black pine, persisted on Rhode Island beaches, it was projected that grass will have to be the permanent cover for stabilization because of the narrow beaches and severe storms (Jagschitz and Bell, 1966a). North Carolina results indicate that sea-oats, American beachgrass, *Panicum amarum,* and salt meadow cordgrass *(Spartina patens* (Ait.) Muhl.) segregate based on their adaptation (Woodhouse and Hanes, 1966). Sea-oats, high in salt and heat tolerance, usually occupies the "front line" nearest the surf. American beachgrass persists on dunes and back slopes because of its rapid growth through accumulating sand. American beachgrass tolerates hot, dry conditions and does well on high dunes and dry flats behind foredunes. Salt meadow cordgrass is the principal grass on low areas behind the foredune. This grass tolerates salt water and flooding, but it cannot withstand drought or rapid sand build-up (Woodhouse and Hanes, 1966).

On beach areas with heavy traffic, such as parking sites, campgrounds, and walkways, the sand stilling grasses previously mentioned will not persist. Woodhouse and Hanes (1966) suggested bermudagrass or *Paspalum vaginateum* Swartz. for areas south of the Virginia capes. Tall fescue may be used on beaches north of the Virginia capes that are exposed to traffic; it has good salt tolerance (Bernstein, 1958), persists along northern beaches (Jagschitz and Bell, 1966a), and is adapted to hard use (Schmidt and Blaser, 1967b).

III. Turf Establishment

Soil modification, drainage, liming, water control, seeding method, and species components in mixtures have profound effects on initial and subsequent turf composition and quality. Indeed, carefully planned establishment practices to obtain desirable ecological interrelationships between the soil-plant complex will avoid many maintenance problems.

The foundation of good turf culture begins with the soil-root environment. Roots require oxygen, water, mineral nutrients, a preferred pH range, suitable temperature, and carbohydrate energy materials for growth.

Major root functions, mineral nutrient and water intake, depend on physiologically active roots. The roots expend respiratory energy for nutrient absorption, growth, and water absorption from considerable depths. Root development may be inhibited by low oxygen and carbon dioxide accumulation resulting from the respiration of microbes and roots. It has also been reported, however, that increased nutrition may offset the detrimental effects on plants of low oxygen levels in soils (Wooford and Gregory, 1948; Cline and Erickson, 1959).

Although atmospheric air has a desirable oxygen-carbon dioxide ratio, relationships in exchange with soil air may be altered by the size and amount of pore space. This in turn is influenced by surface and internal water control, soil material, and composition.

Installation of adequate drainage in critical areas to remove gravitational water provides for more air exchange to produce better functioning and deeper roots. Roots do not grow or absorb nutrients without oxygen (Letey et al., 1964b). Proper contouring and grading should keep surface water from accumulating and submerging the turf and also eliminate steep slopes where infiltration of water is limited.

It is prudent to stock pile top soil so that it may be replaced after rough grading. Top soil may be used to improve soil physical conditions and nutrient media to obtain good plant-soil relations.

Soil compaction on athletic fields, golf greens, and other specialized turf areas where traffic is heavy interferes with root development and causes unsatisfactory turf (Harper, 1967). Soils of turf areas that will be subjected to heavy traffic should be modified before seeding, to lessen the detrimental effects of compaction in the root zone. Swartz and Kardos (1963) reported that soils modified with less than 50% sand and compacted generally had inadequate aeration, porosity, and percolation rates (less than 1 inch per hour). Soils modified with 70% sand maintained adequate to excessive percolation rates even after compaction but were low in available moisture. Shoop (1967) reported similar results and also showed that the incorporation of 10 to 20% peat had a favorable effect on permeability, aeration, porosity, and available moisture content.

Although turfgrasses appear to survive on less oxygen than many other crops, root development is correlated with soil aeration (Waddington and Baker, 1965; Letey et al., 1964a). Grass species capable of developing large volumes of intercellular air space appear better able to survive environments low in oxygen. Annual bluegrass grown in wet soil has been found to have more air space between the leaf cells than when grown on drier soils (Meusel, 1964). Creeping bentgrass and goosegrass roots have been shown to continue growth at soil oxygen diffusion rates that inhibit Kentucky bluegrass root development (Waddington and Baker, 1965; Letey et al., 1964b).

As seedling plants develop there are dynamic changes in the microenvironment and competition soon develops among species for moisture, nutrients, and light. Such competition shifts botanical composition and the surviving species are responsible for additional changes in the environment. Deficiency of any nutrient will hinder seedling growth, but responses vary with pH and soil nutrient status (Beeson et al., 1947; Blaser et al., 1961). Low nitrogen as compared to high nitrogen in the seedbed has been shown to favor red fescue over Kentucky bluegrass (Roberts and Markland, 1967). Grass species also differ in phosphorus uptake (Juska et al., 1965). Beeson et al. (1947) reported that Kentucky bluegrass was high, redtop was medium, and carpet, bahia, and bermuda grasses were low in phosphorus absorption (content).

The high aluminum solubility in certain low-pH soils is reduced by liming which, in turn, will influence the botanical composition of turfgrass mixtures. On steep slopes along roadsides, tall fescue was persistent and dominant over redtop on limed soils, while the reverse occurred without lime. Fine-leaf fescues, Italian ryegrass, and Sericea lespedeza responded similarly to redtop; but crown vetch, Kentucky bluegrass, white clover, and other species practically failed without the addition of lime (Shoop et al., 1961; Blaser et al., 1961). Other grasses (creeping bentgrass, bermudagrass, western wheatgrass (*A. smithii*), perennial ryegrass, orchardgrass, and smooth brome) showed some response to lime.

During dry weather, seedling emergence may be reduced by soluble salts from liberal fertilization. Damage may result from burning or from concentration that attracts water with subsequent plasmolysis of seedling cells (Kolaian and Ohlrogge, 1959).

Soil amendments, date of seedling, and species in mixtures should be manipulated to insure rapid seedling establishment and suppress weeds. It has been shown that certain annual weeds failed to germinate under dense vegetative canopies (Anonymous, 1968). Dense sods for depressing weeds are encouraged by heavy seeding rates and proper fertilizer use (Kemmerer and Butler, 1964; Roberts and Markland, 1967). On weedy sites, companion grasses for quick establishment may also help to suppress weeds. Many companion grasses cause less severe light reductions than weeds in seedling communities. In addition, competition for light from such erect growing grasses may be easily reduced by early mowing.

The best season for seeding or sprigging depends on the species and the environments where a genotype developed. Soil and microclimatic conditions in early spring and late summer-fall seasons are generally most favorable for establishing cool-season grasses. Conversely, the warm season grassses should be established in late spring or early summer to permit establishment and adequate development before growth is stopped by low temperatures.

The optimum temperatures for seed germination and growth rate of seedlings vary within the cool-season grass group (Blaser et al., 1952, 1956). The percentage of emergence and growth rate of seedlings show differences among species with spring and autumn seasons. With early spring seedings, soil moisture availability is high and temperatures are cool as compared with autumn seedings. Thus, the cool-season species with the lower optimum temperatures for germination become established more quickly in the spring than in the autumn, in the absence of weed competition. On the other hand, the cool-season species that have higher temperature requirements usually become established more readily with the autumn seedings. Earliness of spring or lateness of summer seedings also causes variable emergence and growth rate among species. For example, Kentucky bluegrass-fineleaf fescue mixtures tend to become fescue dominant when seeded in late spring or early fall because fescue has a higher optimum temperature for germination and seedling development than does Kentucky bluegrass.

In the absence of supplemental watering, seedling emergence of slow germinating species is usually better for spring than for late summer seedings because of more favorable moisture (cooler temperatures and more rain). Date of seeding should also be determined by potential weed competition. Certain weeds are competitive in spring; others in fall.

The natural moisture-temperature conditions along with imposed managements have profound effects on the relative emergence and growth rates of seedlings in mixtures and on botanical composition. Thus, seeding rates and ratios should be altered in accordance with expected ecological conditions.

Adequate moisture should be supplied once seed germination has been initiated (Daniel and Roberts, 1966). Corrugated rolling of the seed bed causes miniature depressions that trap water and enhance germination. Also, pressing or drilling seed into the soil helps to protect the seed and seedlings from excessive drying.

Suitable mulching materials applied after seeding improve surface microenvironments for germination and seedling growth (Beard, 1966a; Jacks et al., 1955; Harris and Yoa, 1923; Duley and Kelley, 1939). Barkley et al. (1965) reported turf establishment was enhanced with straw, wood fiber cellulose, and sawdust because soil temperatures were moderated and moisture was improved. Although irrigation improved establishment of Kentucky bluegrass, redtop, and tall fescue, the mulched grasses benefited most from supplemental watering.

Turfgrasses such as bermudagrass, creeping bentgrass, centipedegrass, zoysiagrass, and St. Augustinegrass are normally vegetatively propagated from shredded sprigs. Vegetative material planted in either rows or as plugs is less subject to desiccation and mortality than sprigs broadcast on the soil surface. However, planting in rows or plugging is laborious and causes rough surfaces which are unsatisfactory for special turf areas, such as putting greens.

Broadcast sprigs require favorable moisture at all times for good establishment. Light soil top dressing or applications of mulching materials after sprigging reduces water loss. However, some of these cause weed contamination and have to be removed to lessen competition with newly established grass. Simultaneous hydraulic sprigging and mulching with processed wood fiber cellulose has improved vegetative plantings as this avoids weed contamination, moderates temperatures, and does not need to be removed (Schmidt, 1967b).

IV. TURF MAINTENANCE

Seasonal and year-to-year performance of turfgrasses is strongly dependent upon the manipulation of various management practices that influence the growth and physiology of both warm- and cool-season grasses. Imposing individual or various combinations of cultural management practices should be related to the complex of microenvironmental factors affecting growth. Careful manipulation of management factors may also make species more tolerant to such stress periods as severe temperature deviations, winter dormancy, or disease infestation. Indeed, good management is essential in the development and maintenance of good quality turf.

A. Clipping Interrelationship

Mowing is a major managerial practice for maintaining turf for its designated use and providing the desired degree of fineness and uniformity. Heights and frequencies of mowing affect vigor and determine which species become dominant in mixtures (Juska and Hanson, 1961; Davis, 1958; Madison, 1962a; Roberts and Bredakis, 1960). Mowing may enhance the aesthetic value and playing conditions of turf but, depending on frequency and height, may cause harmful effects on almost all grasses (Davis, 1958; Juska et al., 1955; Harrison, 1934; Gernent, 1936; Harrison and Hodgson, 1939). The removal of active photosynthetic leaves exposes previously shaded and younger leaves (Madison, 1962a).

When considering concurrently plant morphology and turf use, two concepts are exceptionally important in designating the least harmful clipping practices, namely, (1) closeness of clipping or the leaf area left after mowing and (2) height of canopy before it is mowed. Morphologically, small stoloniferous grasses such as bermudagrass and bentgrass tolerate very close mowing with limited harmful effects as many short leaves remain after mowing. After mowing any species, a dense canopy cover that intercepts most of the sunlight should remain. Such a radiant energy intercepting canopy also serves to insulate the soil and moderate the temperature at the soil surface. A shaded soil is more conducive to rapid regrowth of desirable species, which, in turn, will help to suppress the germination and establishment of weedy species.

It is better to base mowing frequencies on canopy height rather than on a date basis. Growth rate after mowing is strongly influenced by combined effects of moisture, fertility, temperatures, and light. Because these factors are only partially controllable, frequencies of mowing may range from 3 to 30 days within a growing season. Allowing top growth to become tall and then cutting closely is very objectionable. Shade from tall grass increases the loss of basal leaves and causes young leaves to grow erect. Thus, mowing will leave an open stubble rather than a dense, leafy turf.

Frequent mowing of turfgrasses will not permit a decrease in mowing height without a reduction in the roots and food reserves (Juska and Hanson, 1961). Madison (1962b) found that a rest from mowing for 2 or 3 days a week, preferably consecutive days, increased Seaside bentgrass vigor. The potential regrowth rate of clipped turf is associated with the combined effects of light intercepted by leaves of the clipped turf and soluble carbohydrates in basal plant tissues. The regrowth rate of turfgrass is associated with leaves remaining in the mowed sod; maximum possible regrowth occurs when there is enough leaf area to intercept about 95% of the light or more. High soluble carbohydrates in basal plant parts (roots, shoots, stolons, and rhizomes) also augment regrowth as well as tillering (Ward and Blaser, 1961; Alberda, 1966; Auda et al., 1966). The best regrowth of mowed sods is attributed to combined influences of residual leaf areas and reserve carbohydrates. Severe leaf defoliation will reduce leaf canopy for light interception and the level of carbohydrate food reserves. Thus, regrowth is progressively slower and lack of light competition allows weed encroachment.

The size and morphology of the grass determines clipping practices. Stoloniferous and rhizomatous grasses will tolerate closer clipping than grasses with a bunchy growth habit (Sprague, 1933; Roberts, 1959; Davis, 1958; Laird, 1930). Similarly, grasses that produce many leaves near the soil surface survive under closer clipping than species that exhibit an upright growth habit (Sprague, 1933; Blaser, et. al., 1952;

Davis, 1967; Madison, 1962a; Juska et al., 1955, 1956; Roberts, 1959; Juska and Hanson, 1961; Goss and Law, 1967; Miller, 1966). In general, an increase in clipping height will enhance turf vigor, reduce weed infestation, and increase wear resistance (Schmidt and Blaser, 1967b; Davis, 1967; Roberts, 1959; Younger, 1962; Madison, 1962a). However, excessively high mowing, especially on stoloniferous grasses, will encourage thatch buildup.

The more severe the defoliation of most grasses the more severe the depression of root, rhizome, and top growth (Gernert, 1936, Harrison, 1934; Harrison and Hodgson, 1939; Roberts and Bredakis, 1960; Goss and Law, 1967). Conditions favoring low carbohydrates in plant tissue have been associated with reduced root and rhizome development (Schmidt and Blaser, 1967a; Hanson and Jüska, 1961).

Mowing management should be associated with seasonal environmental conditions, especially temperature and moisture (Madison, 1962a). Cool-season grasses are often retarded or injured by high temperatures. Thus, clipping height should be kept high during the warmest summer months to provide insulation against temperature increases in the basal canopy and at the soil surface. Also, new shoots do not develop readily during summer from closely clipped cool-season grasses. Cool-season grasses may be mowed closer during early spring and the late summer-autumn season when temperatures are cool.

The removal of clippings is often desirable as this practice may help to reduce thatch accumulation. A heavy thatch layer may interfere with soil aeration and water infiltration which, in turn, reduce root growth. The high moisture retention by surface thatch increases humidity which is conducive to the development and spread of disease. Immediate removal of clippings also promotes quick drying of the canopy and allows full light penetration for regrowth.

Vertical mowing and similar treatments to remove dead vegetation from dense rhizomatous sods will often improve turf by decreasing the detrimental effects of thatch (Thompson and Ward, 1966). However, this practice should be employed only when the grasses are growing vigorously. Late summer or early spring are the best seasons for dethatching cool-season grasses, while late spring and the summer are best for thatch removal from warm-season grasses.

B. Interplay with Fertilization

Fertilizer rates and ratios depend on the nutrient status of soil, species, use, and management of turf. Thus, rapid growth of grass grown for erosion control along highways is not advantageous because of increased costs; conversely, on heavy use areas growth must be reasonably fast to heal damaged areas and to promote covering of bare spots. Clippings are high in nitrogen and potassium; thus, these mineral nutrients must be applied more liberally when clippings are removed rather than returned to the turf. Fertilizer, especially nitrogen, is the key to growth control.

In temperate regions, it is common practice to apply maintenance fertilizer during the late winter-early spring in advance of the spring flush of turf growth. However, release of plant nutrients during winter by weathering of clay fractions and mineralization of organic matter reduce the need for heavy spring applications of nitrogen. Excessive nitrogen use in the spring may overstimulate growth, increase thatch, and disease incidence, and cause adverse physiological effects. Also, excessive fertilizer use adds to operational costs because mowing frequency must be increased.

In warmer temperate regions, where snow cover is limited, the use of maintenance fertilizer on cool-season grasses during the late summer-autumn season has several advantages. *(1)* soil nutrients, especially nitrogen and potassium, are lowest near the end of the growing season. *(2)* New tissue development is stimulated during the transitional autumn-winter season (Stuckey, 1941; Hanson and Juska, 1961; Powell et al., 1967a, b). *(3)* New tissue exhibits greater tolerance to adverse environmental conditions. *(4)* The fall response to fertilizer does not appear to be associated with the adverse physiological effects commonly encountered with overstimulated growth from spring applications of nitrogen. *(5)* There is less competition from aggressive weedy species.

Nitrogen stimulates cell division and expansion (growth and respiration) which has profound physiological and morphological effects on grasses (Alberda, 1966; Schmidt and Blaser, 1967a; Goss and Law, 1967). The effect of nitrogen on growth and physiology differs with species and is interrelated with temperature, moisture, light, and other factors. In a Virginia experiment with tall fescue turf, soluble carbohydrates and top growth varied with nitrogen fertilizer and season of the year (Figures 1 and 2, respectively). The sharp increases in soluble carbohydrates during the autumn-winter season, irrespective of nitrogen rates, are attributed to different temperatures for maximum growth and respiration than for maximum photosynthesis (Brown and Blaser, 1965; Blaser et al., 1966). The cool temperatures restrict top growth, but photosynthesis remains high (Powell et al., 1967a; Schmidt and Blaser, 1967a). Thus, carbohydrates in plant tissues increase. Conversely, during the warm, moist spring, the very rapid top growth with high nitrogen (Figure 2) caused sharp reductions in soluble carbohydrates in the cool season grass stubble (Figure 1). Although photosynthesis is high during spring, the low soluble reserve carbohydrates with high nitrogen are attributed to high energy demands for new tissue (especially tops). With high temperatures, respiration is high as compared with photosynthesis (Schmidt and Blaser, 1967a).

High reserve carbohydrates have been associated with high rates of new tillering, but tillering is slow with low nitrogen (Auda et al., 1966). Tiller growth and root development are stimulated during the autumn-winter period with judicious late season nitrogen applications (Hanson and Juska, 1961; Powell et al., 1967b). Such young tillers would be expected to produce better turf the subsequent year than old tillers. Also, late fall and winter nitrogen fertilization in temperate areas with cool-season grasses has produced and maintained desirable green color during winter with Kentucky bluegrass, creeping bentgrass, and tall fescue at several locations in Virginia. Winter injury to turf has not occurred with these fall and winter nitrogen applications; thus, this tiller and root growth is associated with slow growth and semidormancy, high soluble carbohydrates, and high nitrogen assimilates.

Under summer environments with high temperatures, fertilizer nitrogen applications increase respiration much more than photosynthesis; thus, soluble carbohydrates remain low (Figure 1). During drought that occurred during this study in July, the carbohydrates temporarily increased with both high and low nitrogen. A water shortage apparently restricted carbohydrate utilization for top and root growth (respiration) with a corresponding buildup of carbohydrates. Summer applications of nitrogen can have profound effects on botanical composition and sod maintenance. Encroaching warm-season species, such as crabgrass, respond to liberal N supplies and become very competitive toward cool-season grasses when summer temperatures are high; however, these weedy species are less aggressive when soil nitrogen levels are low.

Nitrogen fertilization during periods of potentially fast top growth generally decreases root: top ratios and root depth; however, Hylton et al. (1965) reported that weights of ryegrass roots increased and later decreased with added increments of N. Such declines in root weights with liberal N appear to be associated with low carbohydrates resulting from high respiration rates and a correspondingly high demand for energy (Schmidt and Blaser, 1967a). Reductions in root growth do not occur with autumn-winter season N applications; carbohydrates are high as cool temperatures restrict top growth.

Bermudagrass roots were slightly restricted by N applications and plant tissues remained high in carbohydrates with high temperatures. Photosynthesis in bermudagrass is apparently higher than that of cool

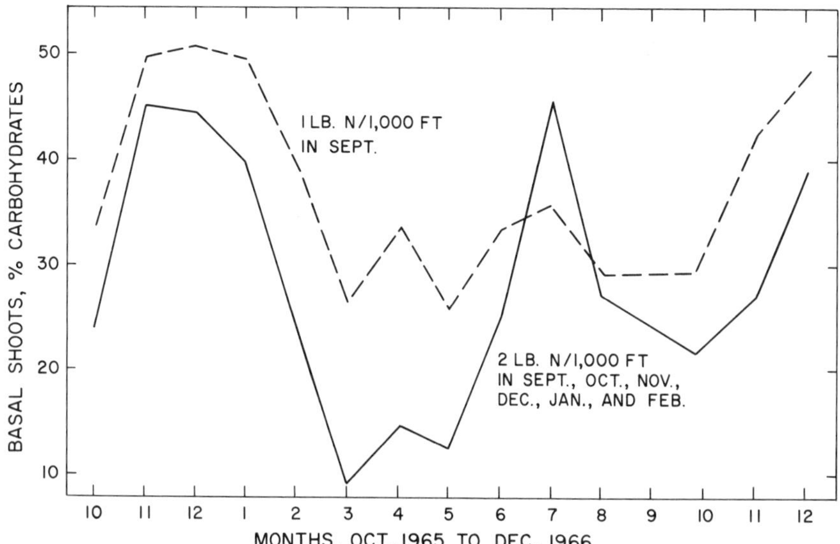

Figure 1. Water-soluble carbohydrates (% dry weight) in basal shoots of Ky. 31 tall fescue during October 1965 to December 1966 with low and high N rates. Grateful acknowledgment is made to F. B. Stewart, Virginia Truck and Ornamental Research Station, for the information in Fig. 1 and 2.

season grasses during warm temperatures (Brown et al., 1966). Bermudagrass and other warm-season grasses should receive N in spring when growth starts and continue during the summer. Late summer N applications sometimes cause winter injury of warm-season species, and later summer or fall N applications encourage the encroachment of cool-season grasses and weeds. However, Gilbert and Davis (1967) reported that bermudagrass winter survival was actually enhanced with N fertilization when phosphorus and potash were concurrently applied at the proper rates.

Nitrogen, the key to growth and quality control of turf, should be used judiciously. Too little is preferable to too much top growth. The requirements vary with species, soils, use of turf, and length of season; recommended annual applications range from 1 to 24 pounds per 1,000 sq. ft.

Although species display differential responses, mineral nutrients should be present in adequate amounts. Metabolism may be disrupted if certain nutrients are low in availability (Wagner, 1967; Kresege and Younts, 1963). Kentucky bluegrasses apparently respond more to phosphorous than red fescue (Juska et al., 1965). Potassium level shifted the botanical composition of grasses because of differences in K requirements (Blaser and Kimbrough, 1968). With high K, tall fescue was aggressive in a fescue-Kentucky bluegrass mixture; the reverse occurred with low K. Many weedy species are aggressive absorbers of K; thus, the botanical composition may become weedy under low soil K. Low soil K and high P may contribute to the aggressiveness of *Poa*

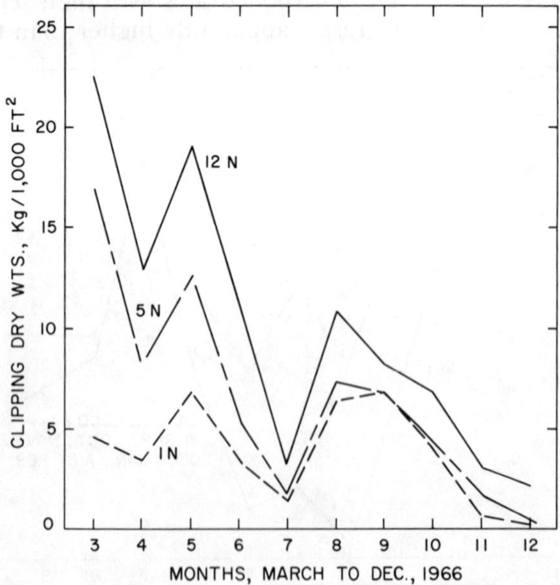

Figure 2. Clipping yields of Ky . 31 tall fescue during 1966 with three rates of N. (1 N - 1 lb/1,000 ft.² in September; 5 N – 1 lb. N in September, October, November, December, and January; 12 N – 2 lb. in September, October, November, December, January, and February.). – 1.0 kg. = 2.2 pounds.

annua in bentgrass greens. This is a common problem as soils data show very low K and very high P availabilities on old golf course greens. Removal of clippings that are three-to tenfold higher in K than P aggravate K shortages in soils. Clipping removal may eventually cause sulphur and trace element deficiencies, especially on sandy soils (Bledsoe and Blaser, 1947). Fertility should be balanced and adequate and the proper management practices selected to control plant succession and botanical composition.

The growth and physiological effects from fertilizer nutrients appear to affect the fungal susceptibility of grasses and disease incidence. The available nitrogen status causes extremes in succulence, nitrogen assimilates, and soluble carbohydrates in plant tissues which, no doubt, hinder some and encourage other diseases. Lukens (1968) associates high soluble carbohydrates in bluegrass tissue with less disease. Jackson and Howard (1967) reported that *Sclerotina* dollar spot and *Corticium* redthread diseases were apparently most serious with low N. Conversely, excessive N apparently increases *Fusarium* patch or *Rhizoctonia* brownpatch. However, Couch (1962) points out that changing soil fertility level to modify or control diseases may interfere with turf use. Further, environmental conditions may shift, increasing susceptibility of the grass to a pathogen other than the organism for which the fertilizer regime was designed to control. As mentioned previously, high humidity found under vigorous canopies may be associated with the harmful effects attributed to fertilizer use.

V. Effects of Soil Environment on the Growth of Turfgrasses

The ratio of solid materials:air:water in soil is changed by factors such as heavy traffic or overwatering (Watson, 1950). With excessive watering or poor drainage, water displaces air from the large pore spaces and compaction aggravates this situation by decreasing these pore spaces (Swartz and Kardos, 1963). This restricts the amount of air in the soil and its movement into soils.

Compaction of soils due to usage occurs at the surface and decreases with soil depth (Vandenber et al., 1957). Removing cores of compacted soils with aerating machines temporarily relieves compaction and helps create a favorable condition for root development (Musser, 1962; Daniel and Roberts, 1966). Filling the aerifying holes with special soil topdressings to resist compaction and yet maintain adequate nutrient and moisture holding capacity will help alleviate conditions caused by heavy traffic.

Soil moisture level is one of the most important factors, yet one of the most complex facets, of turfgrass ecology. Soil moisture induces anatomical and morphological changes of turfgrasses including cuticle thickness and stomotal number and size (Couch et al., 1967). Water availability as it influences growth functions alters the carbohydrate and protein metabolism in plants which influences disease resistance and tolerance to other environmental hazards. Turfgrasses are injured as often by over- as by under-irrigation (Hagan, 1955). Turf frozen under saturated conditions may be subjected to increased hydration and the exertion of hydrostatic pressure on grass tissue increases winter injury (Beard, 1964). Over-irrigation favors weeds (Roberts et al., 1966) and on well-drained soils leaches nutrients and necessitates more frequent fertilization to maintain vigorous turf growth (Hagan, 1955).

Infrequent, heavy watering enhances roots whereas continuous light watering or frequent heavy watering inhibits root development (Schmidt, 1967a). With light, frequent watering, roots are confined to the upper soil layer where moisture was supplied. Frequent, heavy watering changes the soil-air-water ratio and produces poor quality turf (Watson, 1950).

Watson (1950) reported that a cool-season grass mixture lost color during a prolonged drought but serious permanent injury was not observed. Many grasses are able to survive severe drought because axillary buds are below the soil surface and escape xeric conditions or because they assume a dormant condition during dry periods (Blaser et al., 1952). The degree of drought tolerance that species exhibit is not associated with water requirements (Dillman, 1931). It appears that root depth and volume are important in adaptation of grasses to low moisture conditions (Blaser et al., 1952). Turfgrass will grow vigorously only if supplemental water is added to meet the need for adequate nutrient uptake and to prevent disruption of essential physiological processes. Frequency of irrigation will depend upon climate, soil, grass, and turf usage.

VI. Effects of Modifying Temperatures

The capacity to modify environmental conditions has been very important in expanding the area of ecological adaptation for many desirable turfgrass species. Modern irrigation has enabled certain turfgrasses to be grown and used successfully in environments that are naturally unfavorable. Recently, the use of electric soil heating cable systems have maintained frostfree conditions in turf rhizospheres improving winter turf quality of both warm- and cool-season grasses (Barrett and Daniel, 1965).

Plastic covers have been used to protect turfgrasses against desiccation and low winter soil temperatures (Watson and Wicklund, 1962). Ledeboer and Skogley (1967) indicate that plastic screen materials with shade potentials of 30 to more than 50% were beneficial for winter turf growth. This possibly offset the high light intensity that has been reported to destroy chlorophyll at low temperatures (Youngner, 1959).

Syringing and provision for good air circulation can improve the microenvironment on golf greens and other turf areas during hot summers. Duff and Beard (1966) showed that syringing with 0.25 inch of water at noon prevented temperatures from reaching the maximum that would have occurred normally. Air movement at 4 mph reduced the temperature of turf by 13 F in comparison with no air movement.

VII. Competition Among Species

In any turf seeding, using single species or complex mixtures, progressive changes in microenvironment occur as soon as seedlings emerge, shade the soil and each other. Dense, developing seedling populations moderate diurnal temperatures but compete for light, certain nutrients, and moisture. Competition occurs when there is an insufficiency of one or more factors that influences growth (Donald, 1963). Limitation of light is common and severe with the conventional high seeding rates of turfgrass; it is more severe among plants of several species than within seedings confined to one variety or species. Among species in a mixed turf population, severe competition results from differences in speed of germination, seedling emergence, and growth rate (Blaser et al., 1952, 1956; Parks and Henderlong, 1967).

The most aggressive species and varieties produce the best stands and fastest growth. Selected turfgrasses can be ranked for aggressiveness, from most to least, as follows: Italian ryegrass, perennial ryegrass, tall fescue, redtop and fine-leaf fescues, Colonial bentgrass, Kentucky bluegrass (Blaser et al., 1956; Parks and Henderlong, 1967; Erdmon and Harrison, 1947).

The reasons for differential aggressiveness among species is not fully understood. It is strongly influenced by the amount of energy reserves in the seed caropsis, genetic factors, and the physiological response to temperature, moisture, and nutrient status (Blaser et al., 1952). The potential development of competition among species and genotypes differs with the initial microenvironment adjacent to seeds and with season of seeding (Blaser et al., 1956; Erdmann and Harrison, 1947; Juska et al., 1956). For example, fine-leaf fescues and redtop are more aggressive when grown under cool soil temperatures and favorable moisture conditions in early spring than in late spring when temperatures are higher and moisture is less favorable. Tall fescue, redtop, and Colonial bentgrass develop seedling stands quicker than Kentucky bluegrass over much wider ranges of temperature (Blaser et al., 1956).

Aggressive grasses such as annual ryegrass may be disadvantageously used in mixtures. The adverse effects of aggressive short-lived seedlings may persist for many years giving poor cover and uniformity (Juska et al., 1956; Schmidt and Blaser, 1967b; Davis, 1966). Greater uniformity can be achieved by using a single species or several compatible varieties of one species, where the varieties differ in adaptation and disease susceptibility.

There is little relationship between aggressiveness during seedling development and aggressiveness and persistence in later years. Crown vetch and Sericea lespedeza are very nonaggressive during seedling growth (Carson and Blaser, 1962); but in suitable environments, mature plants of these two species are highly competitive to associated grasses. In some areas, stoloniferous grasses, such as the bentgrasses, are very aggressive and dominate cool-season mixtures only to become diseased (Musser, 1948; Davis, 1958; Juska and Hanson, 1959). Zoysiagrass and bermudagrass in warmer regions subdue desirable cool-season grasses, especially under close mowing. Differences of pH and fertility requirements also may influence the aggressiveness of species or varieties (Roberts, 1959; Roberts and Markland, 1967; Skogley and Ledeboer, 1968). Thus, high rates of N fertilizer will generally favor Kentucky bluegrass in seedings planted to mixtures of Kentucky bluegrass and red fescue, (Juska et al., 1955; Roberts, 1959; Roberts, 1965). Aggressiveness of grass associated with legumes for stabilization of soils can be controlled by restricting nitrogen fertilizer (Carson and Blaser, 1962).

Aggressive noncreeping grasses such as tall fescue, can cause unsightly clumpiness when small quantities of seed are incorporated in turfgrass mixtures. Conversely, heavy seeding rates of these species in mixtures will help to produce a desirable uniform turf (Davis, 1958; Youngner, 1961b; Schmidt and Blaser, 1967b; Juska and Hanson, 1959).

The botanical composition of turf mixtures will also be determined to a large extent by the grasses' tolerance to environmental extremes. Beard (1966b) reported that 19 cool-season grasses varied in cold tolerance. Tall fescue has been shown to be an adapted, aggressive turfgrass in Virginia and southern California (Schmidt and Blaser, 1967b; Youngner, 1961b). But when Kentucky 31 tall fescue was used in a mixture with Kentucky bluegrass in central Ohio, the bluegrass became the dominate species because of its low resistance to winter injury (Miller, 1966). Youngner (1961b) suggested that some cool-season grasses may fail in warmer climates because of the lack of cold temperatures required in the initiation of bud development. Redtop and red fescue are highly competitive to Kentucky bluegrass on unirrigated sites (Davis, 1967). Grasses which perform best in full sun were also found best under shade (Juska, 1963; Schmidt and Blaser, 1967b). Beard (1965) concluded that under shade disease resistance influenced competition of grasses more than deficiences in light, moisture, and nutrient supply.

Grasses that become dominant in mixtures are generally characterized by wide adaptation to natural and imposed environmental conditions, excellent persistence during stress periods, and a rhizomatous or stoloniferous growth habit.

VIII. Mutual Beneficial Associations

Although a single species may rank higher than a mixture for uniformity and aesthetic value, mixtures produce an overall higher quality of turf (Juska and Hanson, 1959). No single variety can provide optimum growth under the dynamic microenvironment that occurs in a turfgrass community.

Mixtures are preferred in those situations where environmental factors cannot be manipulated or predicted in terms of species responses. The benefit of a seeding mixture depends on the compatability of grasses, their adaptation to specific environments, and desirable responses to management in terms of appearance, aggressiveness, and disease resistance (Juska and Hanson, 1959; Davis, 1967). Mixtures with small percentages of quickly germinating, short-lived grasses may control erosion and modify the microenvironment until the slower but more permanent species are established (Davis, 1966; Juska et al., 1956). An ideal nurse grass is one that will not offer undue competition to permanent species nor persist to interfere with the aesthetic value and use of turfgrass mixtures.

Species or varieties may also be included in the mixture to offset the disease susceptibility of another grass or to provide an adaptable grass to a site that may be variable in shade or moisture (Juska et al., 1955; Davis, 1966; Juska et al., 1956).

In the transition zone where neither cool- nor warm-season turfgrasses are well adapted, a combination of warm- and a cool-season grass may be advantageous. In southern California, a mixture of bentgrass and bermudagrass produced an outstanding year-round fine turf that was resistant to heavy pedestrian traffic. Combinations of either bermudagrass and Colonial bentgrass or bermudagrass and Kentucky bluegrass proved to be highly satisfactory for general lawn turf (Stoutemyer, 1953).

IX. Ecological Aspects of Winter Turf on Dormant Warm-Season Turf

Cool-season grasses overseeded to provide winter turf on dormant bermudagrass must furnish satisfactory ground cover for up to 7 months under dynamic ecological conditions (Schmidt and Blaser, 1961). Satisfactory winter turf is contingent upon many factors including cool-season species used, rate of overseeding, time of overseeding, seedbed preparation, and winter fertilization. The most critical periods for overseeded turf are the transition from warm- to cool-season grass in the fall and to warm-season grass cover in the spring. The spring transition period is especially critical because the cool-season grass may either delay spring development of the warm-season grass or deteriorate before the warm-season grass initiates satisfactory growth.

Best winter turf has been obtained when the overseeding was correlated with the time that soil temperatures start to decline. The date will vary depending on location. Better winter turf quality in Virginia was obtained from early-October rather than mid-September seedings (Schmidt and Blaser, 1962). Meyers and Horn (1967) obtained satisfactory winter turf in Gainesville, Florida, by overseeding in late November.

It has also been shown that the method of seedbed preparation affects the quality of overseeded winter turf on dormant bermudagrass. The most satisfactory winter turf has been obtained by reducing the competition of bermudagrass by either vertical mowing or close clipping and making certain that seed is placed in contact with soil (Schmidt and Blaser, 1962; Gill et al., 1967).

In Virginia, overseeded annual ryegrass has been abruptly lost with warm spring weather. Pennlawn red fescue maintained good density on fine bermudagrass putting turf during the winter and provided excellent spring transition (Schmidt and Blaser, 1961). In these tests, Seaside creeping bentgrass was slow to establish in the fall, and although inferior during the winter, it was excellent prior to and during the spring transition period. In Florida, there was no difference in the appearance of pure stands of overseeded Penncross creeping bentgrass, Pennlawn red fescue, Kentucky bluegrass, or rough bluegrass (Meyers and Horn, 1967).

Results obtained in Texas showed that rough bluegrass was one of the first overseeded grasses to die with the approach of hot weather (McBee, 1967). Penncross creeping bentgrass and Kentucky bluegrass developed slowly but produced better cover in the latter part of the season.

From Florida data, it was shown that pure stands of winter turf were generally superior to two- and three-grass mixtures. Exceptions were an overseeding combination of creeping bentgrass and red fescue with rough bluegrass and a combination of creeping bentgrass and red fescue. Both of these mixtures provided a more uniform cover than plots with pure species.

In Virginia, mixtures of annual ryegrass and Pennlawn red fescue (2:1, seeded at 45 lb/1,000 sq. ft.) were more desirable than pure stands of either variety on areas infested with annual bluegrass. Pennlawn red fescue overseeded with annual reygrass and/or Seaside creeping bentgrass maintained winter turf quality and provided a satisfactory spring transition period; in addition, annual bluegrass development was inhibited to a large extent by competition from annual ryegrass (and a lesser extent from Seaside bentgrass) (Bingham and Schmidt, unpublished data, V.P.I., 1968).

The rate of overseeding is contingent upon the degree of ground cover that an individual seedling of a particular species will give during the winter months. The amount of seed will be relatively high because of high mortality and the fact that overseeded grasses will not develop much beyond the seedling stage during the winter months. Overseeding rates (lb/1,000 sq. ft.) that have given satisfactory results for putting greens are as follows: fine-leaf fescues, 20-30 lb; annual ryegrass, 60 lb; creeping bentgrass, 4-10 lb; and Kentucky bluegrass, 6-10 lb (Schmidt and Blaser, 1961; Meyers and Horn, 1967). The suggested overseeding rates (lb/1,000 sq. ft.) of the various cool season grasses for lawns are as follows: fine-leaf fescues, 3-5 lb; annual ryegrass, 10 lb; bentgrass, 1 lb; and Kentucky bluegrass, 2-3 lb (Thompson et al., 1963).

It appears that about 1 pound of N per month from a soluble source was necessary to promote satisfactory turf during the winter. Higher rates caused winter injury on common ryegrass. It was also evident that poorer winter turf cover resulted with heavy thatch, than where thatch was controlled on the bermudagrass during the summer (Schmidt and Blaser, unpublished data, V.P.I., 1968).

Literature Cited

Alberda, T. H. 1966. The influence of reserve substance on dry matter production after defoliation. Proc. Xth Inter. Grassl. Cong., pp. 140-147.

Anonymous. 1968. Turn on the light; turn off the weeds. Agric. Res. U.S.D.A. Feb., p. 7.

Auda, H., R. E. Blaser, and R. H. Brown. 1966. Tillering and carbohydrate contents of orchardgrass as influenced by environmental factors. Crop. Sci. 6: 139-143.

Barkley, D. G., and R. E. Blaser, and R. E. Schmidt. 1965. Effects of mulches on microclimate and turf establishment. Agron. J. 57: 189-192.

Barrett, J. R., Jr., and W. H. Daniel. 1965. Electrically warmed soils for sport turfs—Second progress report. Midwest Turf News and Research. Purdue University. No. 33.

Beard, J. B. 1964. The effects of ice, snow, and water covers on Kentucky bluegrass, annual bluegrass, and creeping bentgrass. Crop Sci. 4: 638-640.

Beard, J. B. 1965. Factors in the adaptation of turfgrasses to shade. Agron. J. 57: 457-459.

Beard, J. B. 1966a. A comparison of mulches for erosion control and grass establishment on light soil. Quarterly Bull. Mich. State Agric. Exp. Sta. 48: 369-376.

Beard, J. B. 1966b. Direct low temperature injury of nineteen turfgrasses. Quar. Bull. Michigan State Agric. Exp. Sta. 48: 377-383.

Beeson, K. C., L. Gray, and M. B. Adams. 1947. The adsorption of mineral elements by forage plants: 1. the Phosphorus, cobalt, manganese, and copper content of some grasses. J. Am. Soc. of Agron. 39: 356-362.

Bernstein, L. 1958. Salt tolerance of grasses and forage legumes. Agric. Information Bull. 194, p. 7.

Blaser, R. E. 1962. Soil mulches for grassing. Roadside Development. Highway Res. Board, Washington, D.C. pp. 15-20.

Blaser, R. E. 1963. Principles of making turf mixtures for roadside seedings. Highway Research Record 23, Highway Research Board, Washington, D.C. 23: 79-84.

Blaser, R. E., G. W. Thomas, C. R. Brooks, G. J. Shoop, and J. B. Martin, Jr. 1961. Turf establishment and maintenance along highway cuts. Roadside Development. Highway Research Board, Washington, D.C. pp. 5-19.

Blaser, R. E., and L. Kimbrough. 1968. Potassium nutrition of forage crops with perennials. The role of potassium in agriculture. Am. Soc. Agron., Madison, Wisconsin. pp. 423-445.

Blaser, R. E., R. H. Brown, and H. T. Bryant. 1966. The relationship between carbohydrate accumulation and growth of grasses under different microclimates. Proc. Xth Inter. Grassl. Cong. pp. 147-150.

Blaser, R. E., W. I. Griffith, and T. H. Taylor. 1956. Seedling competition in compounding forage seed mixtures. Agron. J. 48: 118-123.

Blaser, R. E., and W. H. McKee, Jr. 1967. Regeneration of woody vegetation along roadsides. Highway Research Record No. 161. Highway Res. Board, Washington, D.C. pp. 104-115.

Blaser, R. E., W. H. Skrdla, T. H. Taylor. 1952. Ecological and physiological factors in compounding seed mixtures. Adv. in Agron. 4: 179-216. Academic Press, New York, New York.

Bledsoe, R. W., and R. E. Blaser. 1947. The influence of sulphur on the yield and composition of clovers fertilized with different sources of phosphorus. J. Am. Soc. Agron. 39: 146-152.

Brown, R. H., and R. E. Blaser. 1965. Relationships between reserve carbohydrate accumulation and growth rate in orchardgrass and tall fescue. Crop Sci. 5: 577-582.

Brown, R. H., R. E. Blaser, and H. L. Dunton. 1966. Leaf area index and apparent protosynthesis under various microclimates for different pasture species. Proc. Xth Intern. Grassl. Cong. Pp. 108-113.

Carson, E. W., Jr., and R. E. Blaser. 1962. Establishing sericea on highway slopes. Roadside Development, Highway Research Board, Washington, D.C. Pp. 22-43.

Cline, R. A., and A. E. Erickson. 1959. The effect of oxygen diffusion rate and applied fertilizer on the growth, yield, and chemical composition of peas. Soil Sci. Soc. Am. Proc. 23: 333-335.

Couch, H. B. 1962. "Diseases of turfgrasses." Reinhold, New York.

Couch, H. B., L. H. Purdy, and D. H. Henderson. 1967. Application of soil moisture principles to the study of plant disease. Bull. 4, Res. Div. V.P.I.

Daniel, W. H., and E. C. Roberts. 1966. "Turf management in the United States." Adv. in Agron. 18: 259-326.

Davis, R. R. 1958. The effect of other species and mowing height on persistence of lawn grasses. Agron. J. 50: 671-673.

Davis, R. R. 1966. Lawn grasses, mixtures, and blends. Lawn & Ornamental Res. Sum. Ohio Agr. Exp. Sta. 16: 1-2.

Davis, R. R. 1967. Grass mixtures for lawn and golf courses. Res. Sum. Ohio Agric. Res. & Devl. Center 24: 1-8.

Dillman, A. C. 1931. The water requirement of certain crop plants and weeds in the Northern Great Plains. J. Agric. Res. 42: 187-238.

Donald, C. M. 1963. Competition among crop and pasture plants. Adv. in Agron. 15: 1-118.

Duff, D. T., and J. B. Beard. 1966. Effects of air movement and syringing on the microclimate of bentgrass turf. Agron. J. 58: 495-497.

Duley, F. L., and L. L. Kelley. 1939. Effect of soil types, slope, and surface conditions on intake of water. Neb. Agr. Exp. Sta. Res. Bul. 112.

Erdmann, M. H., and C. M. Harrison. 1947. The influence of domestic ryegrass and redtop upon the growth of Kentucky bluegrass and Chewing's fescue in lawn and turf mixtures. J. Am. Soc. Agron. 39: 682-689.

Goss, R. L., and L. G. Law. 1967. Performance of bluegrass varieties at two cutting heights and two nitrogen levels. Agron. J. 59: 516-518.

Gernert, W. B. 1936. Native grass behavior as affected by periodic clipping. Jour. Amer. Soc. Agron. 28: 447-455.

Gilbert, W. B., and D. L. Davis. 1967. Relationship of potassium nutrition and temperature stresses on turfgrasses. Agron. abstr., p. 52.

Gill, W. J., W. R. Thompson, Jr., and C. Y. Ward. 1967. Species and methods for overseeding bermudagrass greens. The Golf Superintendent 35, No. 9.

Hagan, R. M. 1955. Watering lawns and turf and otherwise caring for them. U.S.D.A. Yearbook of Agric. Pp. 462-477.

Hanson, A. A., and F. V. Juska. 1961. Winter root activity in Kentucky bluegrass *(Poa pratensis* L.). Agron. J. 53: 372-374.

Harper, J. C. II. 1967. Athletic fields specification outline, construction, and maintenance. The Penn. State Univ. Ext. Service.

Harris, F. S., and H. H. Yao. 1923. Effectiveness of mulches in preserving soil moisture. J. Agr. Res. 23: 727-742.

Harrison, C. M. 1934. Responses of Kentucky bluegrass to variations in temperature, light, cutting, and fertilizing. Pl. Physiol. 9: 83-106.

Harrison, C. M., and C. W. Hodgson. 1939. Response of certain perennial grasses to cutting treatment. J. Amer. Soc. Agron. 31: 418-430.

Hylton, L. O. Jr., A. Ulrich, and D. R. Correlius. 1965. Comparison of nitrogen constituents as indication of nitrogen status of Italian ryegrass and relation of top to root growth. Crop Sci. 5: 21-22.

Jacks, G. V., W. D. Brind, and R. Smith. 1955. Mulching technology. Communication. No. 49. Commonwealth Bureau of Soil Sci. Farmham Royal, Buchs, England.

Jackson, N., and F. L. Howard. 1967. Disease fungi and turf management. The Golf Superintendent 35 – Feb.

Jagschitz, J. A., and R. S. Bell. 1966a. Restoration and retention of coastal dunes with fences and vegetation. Bull. 382 Agr. Exp. Sta., Univ. of R.I.

Jagschitz, J. A., and R. S. Bell. 1966b. American beachgrass (Establishment-fertilization-seeding). Bull. 383. Agr. Exp. Sta. Univ. of R.I.

Juska, F. V. 1963. Shade tolerance of bentgrass. Golf Course Rept. 2 – Feb.

Juska, F. V., and A. A. Hanson. 1959. Evaluation of cool season turfgrasses alone and in mixtures. Agron. J. 51: 597-600.

Juska, F. V., and A. A. Hanson. 1961. Effects of interval and height of mowing on growth of Merion and common Kentucky bluegrass *(Poa pratensis* L.). Agron. J. 53: 385-388.

Juska, F. V., A. A. Hanson, and C. J. Erickson. 1965. Effects of phosphorus and other treatments on the development of red fescue, Merion, and common Kentucky bluegrass. Agron J. 57: 75-78.

Juska, F. V., J. Tyson, and C. M. Harrison. 1955. The competitive relationship of Merion bluegrass as influenced by various mixtures, cutting heights, and levels of nitrogen. Agron J. 47: 513-518.

Juska, F. V., J. Tyson, and C. M. Harrison. 1956. Field studies on the establishment of Merion bluegrass in various seed mixtures. Mich. Quar. Bull. 38: 678-690.

Kemmerer, H. R., and J. D. Butler. 1964. The effect of seeding rates, fertility, and weed control on the establishment of several lawn grasses. Proc. Amer. Soc. for Hort. Sci. 85: 599-604.

Kolaian, J. H., and A. J. Ohlrogge. 1959. Principles of nutrient uptake from fertilizer bands: I. Accumulation of water around the bands. Agron. J. 51: 106-109.

Kresge, C. B., and S. E. Younts. 1963. Response of orchardgrass to potassium and nitrogen fertilization on Wickham silt loam. Agron. J. 55: 161-164.

Laird, A. S. 1930. A study of the root systems of some important sod-forming grasses. Fla. Univ. Agr. Exp. Sta. Bull. 211.

Ledeboer, F. B., and C. R. Skogley. 1967. Plastic screens for winter protection. The Golf Superintendent. Vol. 35, No. 8 – August.

Letey, J., L. H. Stolzy, O. R. Lunt, and N. Volovas. 1964a. Soil oxygen and clipping height. Golf Course Reporter 32(2) – February.

Letey, J., L. H. Stolzy, O. R. Lunt, and V. B. Younger. 1964b. Growth and nutrient uptake of Newport bluegrass as affected by soil oxygen. Plant and Soil 20: 143-148.

Lukens, R. J. 1968. Low sugar disease "melts-out" bluegrass. Turf-grass Times Vol. 3, No. 5.

Lunt, O. R., R. L. Branson, and S. B. Clark. 1967. Response of five grass species to phosphorus on six soils. Calif. Turfgrass Culture 17: 25-26.

McBee, G. G. 1967. Performance of certain cool-season grasses in overseeding studies on a Tifgreen bermudagrass golf green. Prog. Report 2457. Texas A&M Univ., Texas Agric. Exp. Sta.

McKee, W. H., Jr., A. J. Powell, Jr., R. B. Cooper, and R. E. Blaser. 1965. Microclimate conditions on highway slope facings as related to adaptation of species. Highway Research Board 93: 38-43.

Madison, J. H., Jr. 1962a. Mowing of turfgrass II. Responses of three species of grass. Agron. J. 54: 250-252.

Madison, J. H., Jr. 1962b. Mowing of turfgrass III. The effect of rest on seaside turf mowed daily. Agron. J. 54: 252-253.

Meusel, H. W. 1964. What makes grass wilt? Golf Course Reporter 32(2): 24.

Meyers, H. G., and G. C. Horn. 1967. Selection of grasses for overseeding. Proc. Fla. Turfgrass Mgt. Conf. 15: 47-52.

Miller, R. W. 1966. The effect of certain management practices of the botanical composition and winter injury to turf containing a mixture of Kentucky bluegrass *Poa pratensis* L.) and tall fescue *(Festuca arundinacea,* Schreb.) 7th Turfgrass Conf. Proc. Univ. Ill. Pp. 39-46.

Musser, H. B. 1948. Effects of soil acidity and available phosphorus on population changes in mixed Kentucky bluegrass-bent turf. J. Am. Soc. Agron. 40: 614-620.

Musser, H. B. 1962. "Turf management." McGraw-Hill, New York.

Parks, O. C., Jr., and P. R. Henderlong. 1967. Germination and seedling growth rate of ten common turfgrasses. Proc. W. Va. Acd. of Sci. 39: 132-140.

Powell, A. J., R. E. Blaser, and R. E. Schmidt. 1967a. Physiological and color aspects of turfgrasses with fall and winter nitrogen. Agron. J. 59: 303-307.

Powell, A. J., R. E. Blaser, and R. E. Schmidt. 1967b. Effect of nitrogen on winter root growth of bentgrass. Agron. J. 59: 529-530.

Roberts, E. C. 1959. Changes in turfgrass can be controlled. The Golf Course Reporter. 27(6) – August.

Roberts, E. C. 1965. A new measurement of turfgrass response and vigor. Golf Course Rept. 33 – August.

Roberts, E. C., and F. E. Markland. 1967. Fertilizing helps turf crowd out weeds. Weeds, Trees, and Turf. March.

Roberts, E. C., and E. J. Bredakis. 1960. Turfgrass root development. The Golf Course Reporter. 28: Nov.-Dec.

Roberts, E. C., F. E. Markland, and H. M. Pellett. 1966. Effects of bluegrass stand and watering regime on control of crabgrass with preemergence herbicides. Weeds 14: 157-161.

Schmidt, R. E. 1967a. Growing a vigorous, strong root system on cool season turfgrass. Weeds, Trees, and Turf. July.

Schmidt, R. E. 1967b. Hydraulic vegetative planting of turfgrass. The Golf Superintendent 35 – March.

Schmidt, R. E., and R. E. Blaser. 1961. Cool season grasses for winter turf on Bermuda putting greens. U.S.G.A. Journal and Turf Management. 14(5): 25-29.

Schmidt, R. E., and R. E. Blaser. 1962. Establishing winter Bermuda putting turf. U.S.G.A. Journal and Turf Management 15(5): 30-32.

Schmidt, R. E., and R. E. Blaser. 1967a. Effect of temperature, light, and nitrogen on growth and metabolism of 'Cohansey' bentgrass *(Agrostis palustris* Huds.) Crop Sci. 7: 447-451.

Schmidt, R. E., and R. E. Blaser. 1967b. Evaluation of turfgrasses for Virginia. Bull. 12, Res. Div. V.P.I.

Shoop, G. J. 1967. The effects of various course textured material and peat on the physical properties of Hagerstown soil for turfgrass production. Ph.D. Dissertation. The Penn. State Univ.

Shoop, G. J., C. R. Brooks, R. E. Blaser, and G. W. Thomas. 1961. Differential responses of grasses and legumes to liming and phosphorus fertilization. Agron. J. 53: 111-115.

Skogley, C. R., and F. B. Ledeboer. 1968. Evaluation of several Kentucky bluegrass and red fescue strains maintained as lawn turf under three levels of fertility. Agron. J. 60: 47-49.

Sprague, H. B. 1933. Root development of perennial grasses and its relation to soil conditions. Soil Sci. 36: 189-209.

Stoesz, A. D., and R. L. Brown. 1957. Stabilizing sand dunes. U.S.D.A. Yearbook of Agric. Pp. 321-326.

Stoutemyer, V. T. 1953. Grass combinations for turfs, mixtures of cool season grasses with bermudagrass show promise for year round lawns resistant to weeds. Calif. Agric. — December.

Stuckey, I. H. 1941. Seasonal growth of grass roots. Am. J. Bot. 28: 486-491.

Swartz, W. E., and L. T. Kardos. 1963. Effects of compaction on physical properties of sand-soil-peat mixtures at various moisture contents. Agron. J. 55: 7-10.

Thompson, W. R., Jr., and C. Y. Ward. 1966. Prevent thatch accumulation of tifgreen bermudagrass greens. The Golf Superintendent 34(9) — Sept.-Oct.

Thompson, W. R., Jr., W. J. Gill, and C. Y. Ward. 1963. Overseeding of permanent lawns with cool season turfgrasses for winter color. Miss. Agr. Exp. Sta. Info. Sheet 825.

Vandenber, G. E., A. W. Cooper, A. E. Erickson, and W. M. Corleton. 1957. Soil pressure distribution under tractor and implement traffic. Agric. Engr. 38(12): 854-859.

Waddington, D. V., and J. H. Baker. 1965. Influence of soil aeration on the growth and chemical composition of three grass species. Agron. J. 57: 253-258.

Ward, C. Y., and R. E. Blaser. 1961. Carbohydrate food reserves and leaf area in regrowth of orchardgrass. Crop. Sci. 1: 366-370.

Wagner, R. E. 1967. The role of potassium in the metabolism of turfgrasses. Agron. Abst. p. 55.

Watson, J. R. 1950. Irrigation and compaction on established fairway turf. Ph.D. Dissertation. The Penn. State College.

Watson, J. R., Jr., and L. Wicklund. 1962. Plastic covers protect greens from winter damage. The Golf Course Reporter. Vol. 30 (9).

Woodford, E. K., and F. G. Gregory. 1948. Preliminary results obtained with an apparatus for the study of salt uptake and root respiration of whole plants. Ann. Bot. 12: 335-370.

Woodhouse, W. W., and R. E. Hanes. 1966. Dune stabilization with vegetation on the outer banks of North Carolina. Soils Information Series 8, Dept. of Soil. Sci., N.C. State Univ. at Raleigh.

Youngner, V. B. 1959. Growth of U-3 bermudagrass under various day and night temperatures and light intensities. Agron. J. 51: 57-559.

Youngner, V. B. 1961a. Accelerated wear tests on turfgrasses. Agron. J. 53: 217-218.

Youngner, V. B. 1961b. Population-density studies on cool-season turfgrasses grown in a subtropical climate. J. of the British Grassl. Soc 16: 222-225.

Youngner, V. B. 1962. Wear resistance of cool season turfgrasses. Effects of previous mowing practices. Agron. J. 54: 198-199.

9 Turf Weeds and Their Control

R. E. Engel and R. D. Ilnicki

Rutgers University–The State University of New Jersey
New Brunswick, New Jersey

I. Introduction

The dream of amateur and professional turf growers is a grass area that is absolutely free of weeds. The unpopularity of turf weeds is justified because of their unpleasant contrasts in color and texture. Also, some species such as the crabgrasses *(Digitaria ischaemum* and *Digitaria sanguinalis)* have a less appreciated fault of thinning or destroying stands of cool-season turfgrasses. While turf weeds inflict costly and widespread damage, they are feared less than they were formerly because better methods of control exist. Many weed-free areas have become possible because of improved management practices and better herbicides. Expertise in turf weed control involves fundamental knowledge and precise workmanship.

At one time, weeds were considered plants that had no useful function as cultivated plants. More recently, weeds have been defined as plants growing where they are not wanted. Turf specialists prefer this definition. Thus, this chapter will treat some grasses as weeds which, on other occasions, may be cultivated for turf purposes.

II. Why Do Turf Weeds Occur?

Understanding why weeds occur in turf is important to efficient weed control. Thin turf and bare spots are the most general cause of weeds. The reasons for inadequate turf cover are numerous. Excessive drought kills or thins turf and reduces competition to weed encroachment. Excessive water ultimately destroys turf and often aids establishment or spread of weeds. Severe heat or excessive cold can kill large patches of turf where the first few weeds grow large and reseed before turf is reestablished. Turf diseases, insects, and small animals often destroy modest amounts of turf cover and leave the area vulnerable to weeds. Weeds are encouraged by any use pattern or practice that reduces turf cover, such as heavy traffic, misuse of herbicidal or fertility chemicals, improper fertilization, mowing below optimum cutting height, and removing too much growth at one time. Many of these reflect unfavorably on man's complicity in turf weed problems.

III. Sources and Spread of Turf Weeds

The novice may decide that turf weeds and their seed are everywhere. This is not entirely correct, and those concerned with weeds should realize that guarding against sources and spread of weeds is an important step in most control programs.

Yet, soil is a common source of weeds. Most topsoil has an abundance of weed seed and often contains viable rootstocks of perennial weeds. A study of the quantity of weed seed in Minnesota soil showed 37 of 144 samples had more than 2,000 viable seeds in a cubic foot of topsoil sampled to a depth of 6 inches (Robinson, 1949). Another source reported 1½ tons of weed seed in an acre of farmland (Anonymous, A.C.P. Newsletter, 1954). The number of weed species in topsoil is usually large and commonly contains seed of turf weed species. Only fresh subsoil sites are relatively free of weed seed. Turf weed infestation may trace to soil containing rootstocks and underground structures of quackgrass *(Agropyron repens)*, sedges *(Cyperus* spp.), and bermudagrass *(Cynodon* spp.). Such vegetative sources of contamination deserve attention with the increased use of sod.

Use of stolons and rhizomes in turfgrass establishment is another means of introducing weeds by either seed or vegetative parts. Turfgrass seed lots have often been a source of turf weeds. Examination of 309 lots of Kentucky bluegrass seed showed that 179 lots contained weed seed (Schery, 1965). In this study, 12 different species of turf weeds appeared 9 or more times. While the amount of weed seed by weight is commonly below 2%, this quantity is more than adequate to introduce an unwanted species or give an unattractive lawn.

Many turf soils may have only a trace of troublesome weeds, but this is seldom a long-term deterrent to a serious weed pest as most weeds produce seed abundantly. A study of 101 annuals gave an average seed production of 20,832 seeds per plant (Stevens, 1932). Of course, many of these never develop into mature plants. Yet one stray turf weed of some species is enough to create a major problem within 1 to 3 years. Weed seed is disseminated readily in most cases, and avoiding needless spread is a useful safeguard. Weed seeds may be spread by wind, water, turfgrass materials (propagating materials and topdressing), turfgrass equipment, man, birds, and various other creatures. Two common examples might be the spread of dandelion *(Taraxacum officinale)* seed by wind and the movement of crabgrass and annual bluegrass *(Poa annua)* seed on wet shoes or equipment.

IV. Methods of Attacking or Preventing Turf Weed Problems

Turf weeds are seldom controlled by a single procedure. Most weed control programs stress management for better turf cover and the use of herbicides. A comprehensive look at turf weed control methods would include the use of weed-free seedbeds, weed-free propagation materials, prevention of weed germination or emergence with preemergence herbicides, reducing weed growth and development with management or herbicides, regular mowing to destroy weeds intolerant of mowing, preventing seed set, and destroying the established plants.

A. Weed-Free Seedbeds

Obtaining a weed-free seedbed is feasible for some turf sites. Knowing the weeds that are present helps to determine if this method is useful. On occasions this information can be obtained easily and quickly by observation of the natural site. Some locations may be nearly free of weeds, while others can have excessively large populations of weeds or weed seed in the soil. One to several tillage operations between rains in advance of turf establishment will help reduce weed populations. On weedy sites the reduction in weed competition is often sufficient to permit satisfactory establishment of vigorous turf species. However, tillage alone seldom eliminates all viable weed seed because of seed dormancy and inadequate light or aeration for germination. Also, some underground reproductive parts may be hard to kill with cultivation. When very troublesome species are known to be present even in small quantities, sterilization or fumigation of the soil is a sound approach to control.

Use of temporary sterilants for killing weeds or weed seeds prior to planting turf is theoretically ideal. However, their actual use in turfgrass production has been limited. This type of chemical treatment is most commonly used on sod farms, turf nurseries, putting greens, and show lawns.

Ideally, chemicals used for temporary sterilization should give intense action for a short period of time, then disappear or deteriorate quickly to permit prompt planting of the turf. Calcium cyanamide, methyl bromide, dazomet (tetrahydro-3,5-dimethyl-2*H*-1,3,5-thiadiazine-2-thione), and metham (sodium methyldithiocarbamate) are the types most commonly used. Methyl bromide requires a short delay of 24 to 48 hours between the chemical treatment and seeding, but it requires introduction of the gas under a sealed cover. This adds greatly to cost and limits overall use to comparatively small turf areas. Calcium cyanamide, a dry material, breaks down in a warm, moist soil to form hydrogen cyanamide and various intermediate nitrogen compounds. These are destructive to seeds, plants, and organisms. Areas treated with cyanamide may be seeded in approximately 3 to 6 weeks. The time required for breakdown and safe planting is difficult to predict, but the residues are calcium and nitrogen, which serve as plant nutrients. Metham and dazomet may be introduced into the soil mechanically during tillage or they may be sprayed on the surface of the soil and carried downward with watering. Sealing a loose soil by either rolling or watering reduces escape of the gas. Breakdown and escape of the chemical are rather unpredictable, and this will often require several weeks or more. With both calcium cyanamide and metham, checking the soil with a test seeding of turfgrass or sensitive plant such as tomato before seeding or planting is desirable. Control is better on friable soils than on soils that have large clods, a tight seal, or large air pores.

A variety of additional materials will destroy or reduce weed germination on newly prepared seed beds. Incorporation of ureaformaldehyde solutions, weed-free organic residues such as activated sewerage sludge in large quantity, and various herbicides used preemergence will give such action. The latter are usually unsatisfactory because they do not control a wide enough variety of species, and they may reduce the germination of turfgrasses over a long period following application. While the use of organic residues and the nitrogen materials, activated sewerage sludge, and ureaformaldehyde do not give the most efficient control, this type material is useful on occasion. Incorporation of such materials has the added benefit of supplying nitrogen and improving the soil physically. These applications should be made several weeks in advance of seeding.

B. Preventing Germination and Seedling Establishment

The ugliness and destructiveness of turf weeds is avoided by destroying either weed seeds or weed seedlings beofre they develop into mature plants. This approach is sound and highly effective because control measures are directed at the weakest stage in the life cycle of weedy plants. Two common techniques use either shade (or smother) crops or herbicides. The smother or shade crop can be illustrated by the development of dense, high-cut Kentucky bluegrass to destroy crabgrass seedlings when they germinate. The use of preemergence herbicides has been more important in recent years. Some golf turf growers topdress heavily with weed-free soil on putting greens. Part of their reason is the belief that deep covering of the weed seed discourages germination. While this practice does not destroy weed seeds or seedlings, it may reduce weed emergence.

Control of weeds in turf through preemergence action was suggested by Leach (1927) and was shown to be effective by data reported by Sprague and Evaul (1930). Calcium cyanamide applied to bermudagrass lawns in February was reported to control crabgrass (Sturkie, 1933). On these early occasions, the term preemergence was not used and no attempt was made to elaborate on a mode of action. Welton and Carroll (1938 and 1947) reported the destruction of crabgrass and its embryo with arsenate treatments. Formal recognition of the preemergence method of weed control developed when Slade, Templeman, and Sexton (1945) prevented growth of charlock *(Brassica sinapis visiana)* with α-naphthylacetic acid in 1940. Also, in 1941 they showed that phenoxyacetic acids had preemergence action. Later, this chemical showed some preemergence weed control in turf but it never gave highly effective or consistent results. In 1948 an entomologist in New Jersey observed control of crabgrass in a potato field where chlordane (hexachlorocyclopentadiene) had been used as an insecticide. Shortly afterwards, crabgrass control was observed in turf areas where chlordane had been used for insect control (Grigsby, 1951; Shenefelt, 1952). These observations on chlordane were further substantiated by greenhouse tests by Dybing et al. (1954). Interest in the arsenates was stimulated a short time later by Daniel (1959). In 1959 DCPA (dimethyl tetrachloroterephthalate) and DMPA (O-(2,4-dichlorophenyl) O-methyl isopropylphosphoramidothioate) were released to federal and state experiment stations. These chemicals gave more consistent control and were much safer to the turfgrasses than the previous group. DCPA is currently one of the more popular preemerge herbicides for turf, but DMPA was withdrawn from the market for reasons other than performance. More recently such chemicals as bandane (polychlorodicyclopentadiene isomers), benefin

(*N*-butyl-*N*-ethyl- α,α,α -trifluoro-2,6-dinitro-p-toluidine), bensulide (*O,O*-diisopropyl phosphorodithioate *S*-ester with *N*-(2-mercaptoethyl)benzenesulfonamide), siduron (1-(2-methylcyclohexyl)-3-phenylurea), terbutol (2,6-di-*tert*-butyl-*p*-tolyl-methylcarbamate), and trifluralin (α, α, α-trifluoro-2,6-dinitro-*N,N*-dipropyl-*p*-toluidine) have been tested and sold for preemergence use on turf. D-263 (mixture of 1,1 dimethyl-4,6-diisopropyl-5-inda nylethyl ketone and 1,1 dimethyl-4,6-diisopropyl-7-indanylethyl ketone) and nitralin (4-(methylsulfonyl)-2,6-dinitro-*N,N*-dipropylaniline) have been shown effective for crabgrass control but have not been marketed for such use. Various other chemicals that exhibit a preemergence effect on crabgrass have never received serious consideration for turf because of marketing problems or their lack of safety. Of the current chemicals, DCPA and siduron are most popular with turf growers. Their safety to the established turfgrasses has been good. Siduron is the only herbicide that can be applied with reasonable safety at the time of seeding turfgrasses. Some preemergence herbicides are likely to interfere with turfgrass germination for 1 to 5 months after application (Juska and Hanson, 1964).

The preemergence control of weeds other than crabgrass has met with some success. This group of weeds includes annual bluegrass, goosegrass *(Eleusine indica),* foxtail *(Setaria* spp.), and other annual grasses. The need for annual bluegrass and goosegrass control is great, but the degree of control of these weeds and safety of preemergence herbicides to the turf are often unsatisfactory. Attempts at preemergence control of such weeds seems appropriate only after exploratory trials or when the weed problem is very serious. (See chart for potential herbicides.)

Success with herbicides used before emergence varies greatly with different plants and environmental conditions. Their best use is for control of annual weeds such as crabgrass that exhibit determinate germination. Annual bluegrass germinates any time during the year when the weather is cool and moist; and this may be a partial explanation for the lack of consistently good preemergence control. Variation in the effectiveness of preemergence herbicides may also be related to more complex physical and chemical relationships in comparison with contact-type herbicides. Small changes in the position of preemergence herbicides in the soil with relation to seed germination and emergence are considered critical for other crops (Crafts and Robbins, 1962a). It seems that this could be a critical factor with the use of some current preemergence herbicides on turf. Conclusive information is lacking. Treatments with arsenates and DCPA appear to benefit from an interval between application and germination of the weed, while siduron appears to work as well when applied at or near the time of germination. Siduron is sensitive to light and for this reason results are influenced by rain or irrigation following application. The penetration and behavior of various herbicides may also vary with chemical and thatch residues at the surface of the turf. Very little is known about the significance of these variables in measuring the effectiveness of preemergence herbicides. The inhibiting action of phosphorus on arsenate uptake is one of the best known examples of chemical interference with the action of a turf herbicide (Rumburg, Engel, and Meggitt, 1960a; Juska and Hanson, 1967). Applications of preemergence herbicides on dry carriers have given more consistent control than those made with water spray (Engel, Dunn, and Ilnicki, 1967).While better distribution of dry materials may occur, this does not appear to be the complete explanation. A similar phenomenon is exhibited with field crops (Ilnicki and Everett, 1961). The use of preemergence control of turf weeds will become increasingly important, especially for crabgrass, with the advent of more selective herbicides and improved safety to turf.

C. Avoiding Maintenance Practices that Encourage Growth and Spread of Weeds

Watering beyond the needs of a turfgrass is frequently the cause of serious weed problems. Excessive water can reduce the ability of the turfgrass to grow and survive. In addition, an abundance of water is necessary for weed seeds to germinate and become established when in competition with a mature turf cover. The role of high soil moisture in crabgrass invasion has been shown by research as well as practice (Roberts, Markland, and Pellet, 1966). In warm weather weeds such as crabgrass thrive with an abundance of water, especially if competition from turf species is reduced by summer dormancy. Continuous dampness encourages the spread of crabgrass and chickweed, weeds that creep over the surface by rooting at the nodes.

Most poor management practices contribute to the weed problem. Cutting closer than optimum or thinning of the turf can increase weed populations (Engel, 1966a; Funk, Engel and Halisky, 1966; Youngner and Nudge, 1968). Abrupt lowering of the routine mowing height at a season when the turfgrass lacks vigor may encourage rapid development of a severe weed problem. A good example is the sensational increase in white clover that can occur with drastic lowering of the mower on a Kentucky bluegrass lawn or a bentgrass fairway in the hot, wet weather of late spring or early summer. In 1933, Graber showed that cutting a Kentucky bluegrass turf to ½ inch gave a 7-fold increase in weeds in 1 year. Adequate turf cover for control of weeds does not develop with underfertilization (Sprague and Evaul, 1930). Fertilizer use in excess of grass needs may aggravate turf loss during periods of disease and extreme heat or cold and create voids for weed development (Funk et al., 1966). Fertilization of turfgrasses that are dormant or growing poorly because of unfavorable weather aids spread of hardier weeds. The importance of a dense turf cover for controlling weeds is shown in various ways. An example is provided in a report of turf injury from inorganic mercury fungicides that caused a 100% increase in crabgrass (Sharvelle, 1948). Improper use of herbicides on turf can increase rather than decrease weeds as was illustrated by preemergence crabgrass treatments that controlled crabgrass but not goosegrass (Engel and Dunn, 1967).

D. Preventing Seed Set Without Destroying the Plant

Seed production by annual, biennial, and some perennial weeds is a common necessity for their continuance and spread. This is an especially vulnerable phase in the life cycle of annual weeds because a good seed supply is its only method of spread and survival.

A weed seed crop can be prevented by such elementary means as removing the plant, preventing seedhead development, injuring the flower, killing the seedhead, or encouraging rank foliar growth with abrupt removal of topgrowth before seed matures. The latter method was used formerly by some turf growers to reduce the crabgrass seed crop that otherwise would spread over the turf site.

Flower development is a very critical stage in seed production. Disrupting normal flowering can prevent seed set. Very hot or cold temperatures or chemical treatments may cause serious harm to the flower and prevent seed set. Herbicides have been used to control turf weeds through prevention of seed set. Some growers who have used a light spray of sodium arsenite on annual bluegrass or crabgrass claim injury to the seedheads and reduction in the seed set without killing the weed plant. Inhibition of seedheads on annual bluegrass with maleic hydrazide (1,2-dihydropryidazine-3,6-dione) has been reported (Engel and Aldrich, 1960), but this chemical was impractical for this method of control because it injured seriously the commonly associated bentgrass. Fluorophenoxyacetic acids have been reported as inducing sterility of annual bluegrass (Anderson, Burton, and McLane, 1958). The principle of attacking the weed during critical stages of flower initiation and floral development deserves more consideration. However, this method might be classed as less desirable than preemergence control because it allows the weeds to grow and compete with desirable turfgrasses.

E. Destroying Established Weed Plants Without Killing Turf

Removal of established plants is the oldest and most commonly used method of destroying weeds. It is most effective with annuals where the seed supply in the soil is limited and short-lived. Seedling plants are the easiest to remove. Annual weeds are readily destroyed by cutting roots at the soil surface. This should be done before seeds mature. Biennials and perennials are discouraged by cutting at the soil surface, but many grow back from various underground plant parts. Persistent removal of topgrowth will ultimately destroy these latter two classes of weeds by depletion of reserve carbohydrates. The necessary diligence and amount of work restricts the value of this method. The most useful role of hand weeding is to prevent all seed production by prompt removal of occasional plants found in a nearly weed-free turf. For example, once crabgrass is eliminated from turf, neglect in destroying occasional stray plants contributes to rapid reinfestation.

F. Using Postemergence Herbicides on Established Weeds

Turf growers and research personnel began using such chemicals as ammonium sulfate (Scott, 1924) and arsenicals (Sprague et al., 1930;

Hansen, 1921; Wilson, 1921) long ago. Then sodium chlorate and dinitrophenol were used in the hope of killing weeds without destroying turf. On most turf areas little or no safety margin existed for these chemicals and turf injury was excessive at the rates used for effective herbicidal action. Turf injury prevented their widespread use. In 1945, 2,4-D (2,4-dichlorophenoxy acetic acid) was found effective for destroying established plants of dandelion, plantain (*Plantago major* L.), and buckhorn (*Plantago lanceolata* L.). It was used as a postemergence weed control spray. PMA (phenyl mercury acetate) and potassium cyanate were developed and used for postemergence crabgrass control during the late 1940's. PMA is still used on occasions for control of crabgrass in bentgrass or annual bluegrass turf where the chemical has fungicidal value. When applied at germination, this chemical also gives a preemergence effect. PMA has had limited use because it (a) required 3 to 5 applications at 5- to 10-day intervals for selective effectiveness, (b) was rather ineffective on mature crabgrass plants, and (c) was highly injurious to Merion Kentucky bluegrass. PMA kills grass in an interesting manner. A single heavy application is quite unselective but lighter, more frequent applications cause increasing chlorosis of both the crabgrass and turfgrasses. Death occurs very suddenly and dramatically when the required level of toxicity is developed from the accumulative effects of repeated treatments. The lethal dosage for crabgrass is reached before that of the turfgrasses. No proven explanation for mode of PMA action has been reported, but it has been theorized that a heavy metal such as mercury could cause deterioration of chlorophyll or a sudden precipitation in the protoplasm when critical concentrations are reached.

Figure 1. Crabgrass, a destructive and annoying weed (left), controlled by an application of preemergence herbicide (right). (Courtesy of O. M. Scott & Sons).

Potassium cyanate was developed for crabgrass control shortly after PMA. It has very good and very poor characteristics. It kills quickly and often severely burns the leaves. Thus, it is especially injurious to tender grasses such as bentgrass and annual bluegrass that lack regenerative parts below ground. This chemical is an interesting example of a quickly decomposing chemical that hydrolyzes and leaves a small, harmless residue of potassium and nitrogen. Both research workers and turf growers might use this nearly ideal character of potassium cyanate as a safety standard for future herbicides. The quick breakdown of potassium cyanate was a problem when delay occurred between mixing and application. The contact action and quick breakdown of potassium cyanate makes thorough coverage of the foliage essential, as for other contact herbicides (Crafts et al., 1962b). Wetting agents have improved efficiency of contact herbicides for crabgrass control (Engel and Wolf, 1950). Also, it appears that action of postemergence herbicides is more efficient with the inclusion of 2,4-D (Engel and Aldrich, 1952). Limited data do not show any difference in control with 40, 100, and 360 gal/acre but the increased volume of spray decreased turf injury (Bannerman, 1953). It seems that a reduced concentration of a contact herbicide in the spray solution can reduce localized action. This may offset benefits from better coverage obtained by increasing the volume of spray.

Other useful herbicides that kill established turf weeds include: 2,4-5T (2,4,5-trichlorophenoxy acetic acid); silvex [(2-(2,4,5-trichlorophenoxy) propionic acid], mecoprop (2-[(4-chloro-*o*-tolyl)oxy] propionic acid); dicamba (3,6 dichloro-o-anisic acid); and methanearsonates. All but the latter chemical group are used primarily on the broadleaved weeds in turf. As new herbicides are discovered, choice of turfgrass chemicals will become more specific.

The features of turf herbicides used postemergence are varied. Many injure the plants shortly after contact. Also, slight to moderate turf injury is common except for the most selective types. With an herbicide such as 2,4-D on Kentucky bluegrass or bermudagrass, the margin of selectivity of the weed over the grass is quite large. Some of the earlier materials such as sodium arsenite or potassium cyanate offered a very small margin of safety, and the existing turfgrasses were often forced to grow back from belowground structures for survival. Likewise, sodium arsenite is a hazardous poison.

As for most types of herbicides, knowledge of mode of action of postemergence herbicides and the ultimate reason for death of treated plants is very limited. Dehydration of the plant is often involved. The cause of such water loss varies greatly. Direct withdrawal of moisture occurs when chemicals with a high salt index are applied. An example of this type of herbicide treatment was the intentional fertilizer burn or large applications of other chemicals with a high salt index. The effectiveness of these practices varies greatly with temperature and moisture conditions, the plant's sensitivity to water loss, and the plant's ability to grow back from below ground. Sodium arsenite, applied in a mildly alkaline and buffered solution, softens and hydrolyzes the cuticle, which weakens resistance of the plant to destruction (Crafts and Robbins, 1962c). Plant cells are known to lose ability to regulate loss and retention of water content through a variety of chemical or physical effects on membranes, and this might receive study when considering desiccation phenomenon. While mechanisms of action for most quick-acting postemergence herbicides have not been established, dehydration of the cellular tissues appears to be a frequent cause of death. Also, a death through dehydration can occur when roots are killed or lose their ability to function. 2,4-D and silvex are known to cause abnormal root development in bentgrass (Callahan and Engel, 1965). In addition to reducing capacity for water uptake, this increases the vulnerability of roots to injury from pathogens. Possibly a more important influence of 2,4-D herbicides on desiccation of plants is its rather common disruption of vascular tissues (Callahan et al., 1965). Destruction of or interference with plant enzymes is a second mode of action. Bonner (1950) reports that arsenic poisons the triosephosphate dehydrogenase system and stops production of high energy phosphate bonds needed for respiration. Dalapon (2,2-dichloropropionic acid) is believed to exert part of its action through an enzyme disturbance that interferes with production of pantothenic acid (Hilton et al., 1959). Herbicide action can also be explained by protein precipitation or destruction. The herbicide PMA, containing a heavy metal, may have this type of action. Destruction of the protoplasm contributes to the killing effect of dalapon. Dalapon is used to kill turfgrasses as well as weeds. The chloro-substituted s-triazines such as simazine (2-chloro-4,6-bis(ethylamino)-*s*-triazine) have been shown to kill plants by interfering with the splitting of water into hydrogen and oxygen, an important step in the Hill Reaction of photosynthesis (Klingman, 1961). Numerous investigations on mode of action of 2,4-D emphasize that disruption of an essential activity in the plant, such as maintenance of a food reserve, may cause other harmful effects and death follows from a series of interrelated phenomena.

G. Destroying Both Turf Cover and Weeds

Established turf can deteriorate to a very weedy state that lacks a worthwhile stand of turfgrasses. Without redigging and reducing weed competition, reintroduction of the desired turfgrasses through overseeding is slow and difficult. A complete kill of both weeds and turf vegetation followed by re-establishment of the turfgrasses is a logical step. This can be accomplished by cultivation, but frequently a chemical is used. Soluble fertilizer, sodium arsenite, and potassium cyanate were used in earlier years, and the first two chemicals are still used on some golf courses. More recently, cacodylic acid (hydroxydimethyl=arsine oxide), dalapon, and paraquat (1,1'-dimethyl-4,4'-bipyridinium salts) have been used. This group of chemicals is used prior to the desired cultivation procedure. They hasten destruction of vegetation and aid in preparation of a good seedbed at an early date. In addition, the soil sterilant types, calcium cyanamide, methyl bromide, and metham, which were discussed previously for destruction of weed seed, can destroy both weeds and old turf. However, these are used most commonly after initial tillage to kill weed seed in the surface layers of the tilled soil. Residue problems, cost, availability, and application techniques will influence the choice of chemicals. Moisture, temperature, soil type, and plant species will cause these herbicides to vary in effectiveness. Consideration of the chemical reaction to these conditions is important. Also, growers must recognize time requirements for slow-to-decompose chemicals that will delay seeding schedules.

V. "Non-Turf" Weeds and Secondary Turf Weeds

Weed species that normally do not appear in turf may occur during the establishment of new seedings. Depending on the region, problems may be encountered with such weeds as lambsquarters *(Chenopodium album* L.), pigweed *(Amaranthus retroflexus* L.), wild mustard *(Brassica* spp.), yellow rocket *(Barbarea vulgaris)*, and others. While most of these weeds might be killed with the first freeze or an herbicide treatment, regular mowing is an adequate practice to limit their growth and their temporary suppression of turf. Such annual weeds do not continue to re-establish themselves from year to year because of mowing and the developing turf cover.

Many other plants appearing in poor turf might be classed as secondary turf weeds. Examples are black medic *(Medicago lupulina* L.), common cinquefoil *(Potentilla canadensis* L.), common chickweed *(Stellaria media* L.), ground ivy *(Glechoma hederacea* L.), knawel *(Scleranthus annua* L.), nimblewill *(Muhlenbergia schreberi* J.F.Gmel), quackgrass *(Agropyron repens* L.), red sorrel *(Rumex acetosella* L.), and others. While these may be found in various turf areas from year to year, they are not highly destructive to established turfgrass. They occur because of turf failure or thin cover rather than their ability to overcome a normally healthy turf. If management is changed to assure continuous good turf cover, secondary weeds become insignificant. Herbicides have a limited role for control of these weeds except where such factors as shade or unadapted climate prevent growing of normal, healthy turf of the chosen species.

VI. Control vs. Eradication

Complete elimination of a weed from turf is ideal, but necessarily a practical goal. With the advent of 2,4-D, elimination of dandelion from a turf area seems feasible. Destroying all plants of this species on the site is quite possible, but reinvasion occurs on some sites from airborn seed. Crabgrass can be controlled or eliminated on a practical basis. Where a good turf cover is maintained, continuous prevention of seed set for several years will give extermination. The crabgrass-free condition is easily maintained if there is no convenient source of seed in the general area. Elimination of crabgrass is more difficult where Kentucky bluegrasses perform poorly in warm, moist portions of the temperate zone. However, warm sites in cooler regions with thin turf in the spring and summer offer severe problems. In contrast to complete control is the philosophy guiding the control of annual bluegrass. With current management and materials, few attempts are made to eliminate all annual bluegrass plants. The goal is best described as the reduction of annual bluegrass to minimize large-scale loss of turf in those periods when this species may fail. Even with weed problems that fall in this category, feasible methods of more complete control are desired. Knotweed *(Polygonum aviculare* sp.) is a weed that can be eliminated through the proper use of available herbicides. Eradication of weeds will become more common with the development of better herbicides. Nevertheless, perseverance in preventing weed growth and seed set will continue to be important in controlling and eliminating turf weeds.

VII. The Nature and Action of Herbicides Used on Turf

A. The Phenoxyalkylcarboxylic Acids

The largest family of herbicides used for weed control in turf is the phenoxyalkylcarboxylic acid group, which includes 2,4-D, 2,4,5-T, mecoprop, and silvex. Generally these herbicides are used for controlling dicotyledonous or broadleaf weeds. This chemical family may be further divided into two subfamilies called the phenoxyacetic acids and the α-phenoxypropionic acids.

The phenoxyacetic acid group includes 2,4-D and 2,4,5-T. The α-phenoxypropionic acids include mecoprop (MCPP) and silvex.

Structurally, the phenoxyalkylcarboxylic acids are characterized by the following: (1) an unsaturated 6-carbon ring structure, with several substituents possible on the ring; (2) a side chain consisting of straight chain alkyl groups; (3) an acidic group or a group easily converted to an acidic group at the end of the alkyl group; and (4) an ether linkage or oxygen bridge connecting the unsaturated ring with the alkyl group. It is necessary that the acidic or carboxyl group be at least 2 carbon atoms away from the ring.

Differences in the alkyl group beyond the ether oxygen give rise to the 2 subfamilies indicated above, i.e., an acetic acid group or a propionic acid group. The attachment of the propionic group to the ether oxygen is on the alpha carbon of the group, hence the designation alpha-propionic acids.

Various substitutions are possible on the unsaturated ring, hence the several possibilities within each subfamily. Usually these are chlorine atoms, or methyl (CH_3) groups, or combinations of both. It is possible, therefore, to have identical derivatives of different acids.

The phenoxyalkylcarboxylic acid herbicides are known as growth regulator herbicides because their actions resemble those of naturally occurring plant hormones. While herbicides in various subfamilies differ in specificity, their biological acitvity or weed control activity is similar.

Perhaps the most popular herbicide in this family is 2,4-D. It was first described as a growth regulator by Zimmerman and Hitchcock (1942). A description of its selective action was noted by Marth and Mitchell (1944) who reported the successful removal of dandelion, plantain, and other weeds from Kentucky bluegrass. Later Anderson and Wolf (1947) reported 2,4-D to be effective as a preemergence herbicide in corn. These discoveries ushered in the modern era of chemical weed control and stimulated the investigation of other chemicals for weed control in turf as well as related research.

The phenoxy herbicides, as they are sometimes called, are not highly toxic to humans and other animals. They are noncorrosive, fire resistant, and inexpensive. They are translocated herbicides. Thus in-

Figure 2. Dandelions can be controlled with 2,4-D (right). Seed produced on left will spread into weed-free area. (Courtesy of O.M. Scott & Sons).

complete coverage of the weed during treatment may be effective. Low volume spraying is possible because a few droplets can control susceptible weeds. As little as one gallon of solution per acre is adequate.

Many forms of the phenoxy herbicides are available, including parent acids, salts, and esters. The acid is generally a finely ground powder which can be applied as such or in a liquid carrier. The latter is designated as an emulsifiable concentrate which is diluted with water. The salts include both inorganic and organic forms. Inorganic salts include the sodium and potassium salts. The organic salts, more accurately referred to as amines, are generally the following: dimethylamine, trimethylamine, and some of the oil-soluble amines. Esters are liquid concentrations formulated in diesel oil or some other organic solvents which can be emulsified. Oil formulations are very rarely used for turf weed control.

A further breakdown of the esters shows that there are short chain alkyl esters, which include methyl, ethyl, propyl, isopropyl, and butyl esters, and the heavy esters, or so called low volatility esters, which include butoxyethyl, butoxyethoxypropanol, 2-ethyl hexyl, isooctyl, propyleneglycolbutylether, and other long chain alkyl esters. Ester formulations are named after the alcohol used to react with the parent phenoxy acid to make the ester.

1. Types of Plants Controlled

Phenoxy herbicides are used for control of broadleaf weeds in turf as well as in cereals, pastures, and noncrop areas. Grassy weeds are not effectively controlled by these herbicides; however, young seedlings of grasses may be injured or destroyed when the chemical is applied in close proximity to the seed at time of germination.

2. Physiological Behavior

Phenoxy herbicides are applied to growing plants or to the soil. They are distributed rapidly throughout the whole plant system and susceptible plants soon die. Foliar applications of these herbicides are transported or translocated within the plant, and it is believed that they move with photosynthates. Herbicide droplets that are not intercepted by the foliage reach the ground surface and may enter the plant through the root system. Following uptake by roots, they may move upward in the plant with the transpiration stream. There is considerable research information indicating that translocation both from foliar and root applications is influenced by moisture and the nutritional status of the plant. Annual weeds are very susceptible when they are young. More specifically, these herbicides are absorbed and effect their response in plants that are growing rapidly. Generally, conditions favoring rapid growth such as favorable moisture, favorable nutritional status, and warm temperature are also conducive to a rapid kill from the phenoxy herbicides. Although phenoxy herbicides are not considered to be effective for perennial broadleaf weeds, they are effective in killing these species in the seedling stage, before they assume the perennial habit.

3. Mechanism of Action

This family of herbicides has received more study than any other family of available herbicides. Mechanism of action studies have been conducted on many plants, including crop and weed species. but not much attention has been directed to similar studies on turf species.

Explanation of the mechanism of action and the fate of phenoxy herbicides in plants is complex. Generally, it can be said that there is no agreement on the extent, rate, or pathway of degradation of phenoxy herbicides (Swnson, 1965). These compounds do, however, undergo a variety of reactions in plants.

Respiration of treated plants is generally increased by phenoxy herbicides. However, low dosages tend to stimulate whereas high rates tend to inhibit respiration. Smith (1951) in his review of changes in respiration in relation to toxicity indicated that 2,4-D may exert its influence on the aerobic phase of respiration of both bacteria and higher plants. Recent research has pointed out that the pentose phosphate pathway rather than the glycolytic pathway of glucose metabolism is favored in some plants treated with 2,4-D (Humphreys and Dugger, 1957). Food reserves, as a result, are also affected.

The effect of 2,4-D on photosynthesis is indirect. It is generally accepted that this chemical and related herbicides reduce photosynthetic action.

Cell division and differentiation are also affected by 2,4-D (Gorter and van der Zweep, 1964). Disorganization and disruption occur mostly in the meristematic regions.

The effects of 2,4-D and related herbicides on enzyme activity are not conclusive. The effects appear to differ in various organs of a given plant and with the age of the plant at time of treatment.

Switzer (1957) studied the effect of a number of herbicides, which included 2,4-D and 2,4,5-T, on oxygen and phosphorus uptake using mitochondria isolated from etiolated soybean cotyledons. Both these processes were inhibited at rather low concentrations. Oxygen uptake was changed approximately to the same degree in the presence of pyruvate, *a*-ketoglutarate, and succinate. This indicates that the herbicides had an effect on the whole complex enzyme system rather than on specific enzymes. Phosphate concentrations were increased by 2,4-D, suggesting that this herbicide acted as an uncoupling agent. Excellent reviews on this subject are presented by Wort (1954, 1964) and Woodford et al. (1958).

The fate of phenoxy herbicides in plants and microorganisms has been reviewed by several workers (Swanson, 1965; Audus, 1964; Menzie, 1966; Hilton et al., 1963). Hilton et al. divide the metabolic fate of phenoxy berbicides into: (a) physical and chemical conjugation* with cellular constituents; (b) degradation of the aliphatic acid side chain of the molecule; and (c) ring hydroxylation. These workers mention that the importance of each process seems related to the chemical structure of the herbicide involved. With regard to physical and chemical conjugation, the authors cite several references which indicate that the relative sensitivity of the species to phenoxy herbicides appears to be associated with the amount of unbound herbicide free to move in plants and appears to have some influence on selective action.

Ring hydroxylation seems to be of little importance. However, one investigation was cited (Bach, 1961) in which a number of metabolized components from bean stems incubated with radioactive 2,4-D were found. It was observed that the aromatic nucleus remained intact. Some components contained phenol and alcohol groups but exhibited no aliphatic saturation. In spite of this it was proposed that a partial degradation of the benzene ring occurred without cleavage of the phenol ether linkage.

Decarboxylation of 2,4-D and related herbicides in plants was considered to be of little physiological significance. However, recent investigations show that this process is indeed responsible for resistance in a number of plant species (Luckwill and Lloyd-Jones, 1960). Leaf (1962) noted that the resistance of cleavers *(Galium aparine)* to a 2,4-D related herbicide (MCPA) was attributed to detoxication resulting from loss of both carbon atoms of the side chain.

The most important aspect of side chain degradation is the fact that certain plant species differ in their ability to de-oxidize the side chain of chloro-substituted phenoxyalkylcarboxylic acids. Phenoxy acids with long side chains are nonphytotoxic unless the plant can degrade the side chain to yield an herbicidally active acetic acid derivative (Wain, 1958).

Although the phenoxyalkylcarboxylic acid herbicides as a family are applied directly to plant surfaces in turf, with rates necessary for weed control there is no real danger from long-term herbicide accumulation in soil. Microbial activity helps to dissipate these herbicides from the soil. Under favorable conditions of warm temperature and high ground moisture these herbicides can be completely dissipated before the end of the growing season.

*Adsorption of chemical at physiologically inactive sites. Complexing can occur with proteins, lipoproteins, amino acids, carbohydrates, and some unknowns.

B. Benzoic Acids and Related Herbicides

Another important family of herbicides used on turfgrass weeds are the benzoic acids and related herbicides. The benzoic acids are sometimes considered as growth-regulator-type herbicides similar to the phenoxyalkylcarboxylic acid family because they produce many of the same formative responses. Leopold (1955) pointed out that benzoic acids with three chlorine substituents are auxins, whereas the tetra- and penta- chloro derivatives are not auxins but are effective herbicides. There are several benzoic acid herbicides used in modern weed control technology, but dicamba is the most popular in turfgrass culture. This herbicide, 3,6-dichloro-*o*-anisic acid, almost satisfies the molecular requirements of an auxin; the only difference is the methoxy substituent in the 2 position for chlorine, which would make the latter derivative an auxin by classical definition. Buchholtz (1958) in studies with various chlorinated isomers of benzoic acid for the control of quackgrass observed that isomers having no substituent in the 4 position of the ring structure were able to suppress regrowth of quackgrass. Those isomers with substituents in the 4 or *para* position were herbicidally inactive.

As indicated earlier, the benzoic acid group is similar to the phenoxyalkylcarboxylic family because they produce the same formative effects that the phenoxy acids do. In similar manner, they stimulate respiration, particularly in the actively growing meristematic regions. In contrast to the phenoxy herbicides, benzoic acid herbicides are somewhat more persistent in plants and in the soil. They are not as susceptible to the microbial activities as the phenoxy herbicides.

Zick and Castro (1967) present an excellent review of the dissipation of dicamba in and on living plants. These authors indicated that dissipation of dicamba in plants can occur on the surface of the plant, in leaf tissues, or in root tissues. On the leaf surface dicamba can be dissipated by photodecomposition or volatilization, or both.

The same authors present a review of absorption of dicamba and its ability to translocate within plants. It was found that many plants have the ability to absorb dicamba through the leaves, translocate it basipetally (toward the base) and acropetally (toward the top of the plant), and excrete it through the roots. The amount of root exudation varies from one plant species to another. The chemical is very mobile in plants, moves in both xylem and phloem tissues, and can transfer from one tissue to another.

Broadhurst, Montgomery, and Freed (1966) studied the metabolism of dicamba in wheat and Kentucky bluegrass. A major metabolite formed was identified as 5-hyhroxy-3,6-dichloro-*o*-anisicacid. Two minor metabolites were also identified, the parent compound itself and 3,6-dichlorosalicylic acid. Wheat and bluegrass plants yielded the same metabolites in the same proportions. This study is of special interest because it shows the similarity of metabolic reaction of an agronomic crop and a turfgrass species. Confirmation of this major metabolite was made by Smith, Suzuki, and Malina (1965), also using Kentucky bluegrass as the test species. Zick and Castro indicated that where dicamba is used in agronomic situations, the amounts of metabolites formed are insignificant, and both the hydroxy metabolite and the salicylic acid metabolite are of very low order of toxicity. Hilton (1965) working with several ring-substituted derivatives of benzoic acid, noted that dicamba acted as a direct inhibitor of the conversion of ketopantoate to pantoate in *Escherichia coli.* It was felt that this action was not responsible for herbicidal activity of benzoic acid.

C. The Phthalic Acids

Another family of herbicides used on turfgrass weeds are the phthalic acids. They are dicarboxylic acids and are similar to benzoic acids structurally in that they have 2 carboxyl groups attached directly to the 6-carbon benzene ring. When the carboxyl groups are *para* to each other, the compounds are called terephthalic acids. The two herbicides included in this group are DCPA and OCS-21944. They are actually esters in that the acidic hydrogens of the carboxyl groups have been replaced by other substituents. With DCPA these substituents are methyl groups, and with OCS-21944 they are a methylmercapto and a methyl group. Although DCPA and OCS-21944 are structurally related to the benzoic acids, their physical and biological reactions on turf weeds and grasses are quite different from that of dicamba.

These herbicides must be applied, preemergence, to the soil surface. They are neither absorbed by the foliage nor do they appear to translocate within the plant. Their primary physiological action is that they kill germinating seeds. Once weeds are established, applications of terephthalic acid herbicides are completely ineffective. The exact mechanism of action and the metabolic pathways in both resistant and tolerant weeds as well as in turfgrass species are not known.

D. The Amides

Another family of herbicides used in turf weed control, the amides, include those herbicides that contain the amide moiety. These herbicides can be subdivided into such classes as the substituted ureas or N-phenylureas, amides, and the carbamates. In spite of the diversity of these names, these herbicides are similar in that they contain the peptide linkage or derivations thereof. Because of this structural similarity, their herbicidal activities are quite similar, particularly on some species.

One of the herbicides containing this peptide group used on turf is bensulide. Bensulide actually is a sulfonyl derivative of a primary amine. It is a selective preemergence herbicide that acts on such species as smooth and hairy crabgrasses, annual bluegrass, goosegrass, and certain broadleaf weeds. Because of its physiological action, which kills weeds before germination, it must be applied to the soil before weeds germinate. It should be watered into the soil in order to effect this response. Applications should be made 2 to 3 weeks before annual weeds would be expected to emerge.

The exact physiological or biochemical mechanism or activity in the plant is not known. However, it does interfere with sod rooting and prevents the development of primary roots on germinating seeds. This effect on seedling crabgrass would cause death. Under normal conditions bensulide is not detrimental to established Kentucky bluegrass. However, herbicide injury may occur if turfgrass species are under stress and lack an adequate root system at the time of application. This type injury might be found where turf species have been weakened either by unfavorable weather, poor nutrition, soil compaction, or injury from turfgrass pests.

Bensulide, because of its long residual life, controls weeds over a longer period than other preemergence herbicides. Reseeding of turfgrass into a treated area must be delayed anywhere from 3 months to a year. This could be influenced, however, by such edaphic factors as soil texture, pH, and the amount of water added to the treated area either from natural rainfall or irrigation.

Terbutol is the only carbamate herbicide that has been used in turf weed control. It has good selective preemergence herbicide action on annual bluegrass and crabgrass. Structurally, this herbicide differs from the popular chlorpropham (CIPC) and propham (IPC), which are N-substituted phenylcarbamates, in that the substituted phenyl group is attached to the ester oxygen rather than to the nitrogen atom of the amide moiety. Very little is known about the physiological and biochemical action of terbutol. Apparently absorption occurs through the roots. When application is made to foliage, it remains there without causing any severe injury. It should be applied to turf in the spring before the crabgrass has germinated. It restricts growth of roots and rhizomes at terminal meristems. In grass seedlings it prevents root growth. While terbutol gives good herbicidal action, it can be very harmful to cool-season turfgrass such as bentgrass species. Spring treatment can cause very serious injury to these grasses during the following fall and winter.

Another herbicide included in this amide group is a substituted urea known as siduron. This is a selective herbicide, effective in controlling annual germinating grasses such as the foxtails, barnyardgrass, and the crabgrasses. These grassy weeds may be selectively killed by treatment before they germinate in new seedings or in established plantings of Kentucky bluegrass, bentgrass, fine-leaf fescues, and several forage grasses like smooth brome *(Bromis inermis)*, perennial ryegrass, and orchardgrass *(Dactylis glomerata)*.

A major toxic action of phenylurea herbicides is caused by their interference with photosynthesis (Moreland and Hill, 1962). However, Splittstoesser and Hopen (1967) found that siduron did not inhibit photosynthesis in creeping bentgrass. Work conducted on other species suggests that siduron may disrupt the normal nucleic acid metabolism which is necessary for protein synthesis and cell wall formation (Splittstoesser, 1968). Whether or not this mechanism takes place in turfgrass or weed species has not been established.

E. The Aniline or *p*-Toluidine Herbicides

The aniline family of herbicides is now available for weed control use. At present, some of these new herbicides have label approval for use in turf as well as on several agricultural crops. Because of the presence of a methyl group or modifications of this methyl group, which is in the *para* position to the basic amino group, this family is often designated as the *p*-toluidines. Herbicide representatives in this family are further characterized by 2 nitro substitutions *ortho* to the modified amino group on the 6-carbon aromatic ring and include trifluralin, benefin, and nitralin.

Trifluralin is effective primarily as an herbicide applied preemergence to the soil. Its water solubility is less than 1 ppm and it leaches very slowly. It is strongly adsorbed on clay fractions and soil organic matter and can effect season-long weed control. Turf weeds susceptible to this herbicide include the crabgrasses, foxtails, and barnyardgrass. In some areas use of this herbicide is limited by excessive turf injury.

No information on the mechanism of action of trifluralin in turfgrasses or turf weeds is available. However, its fate and mechanism of action in agronomic and horticultural species may be similar to that found in turfgrasses and turf weeds. Stanifer et al. (1965) reported that swelling of cotton root terminals may be a major morphological effect. Talbert (1965) noted that cell division in soybeans was affected. Further evidence that trifluralin affected some plant tissues was provided by Bayer et al. (1967). These workers studied the effect of trifluralin on primary roots of cotton *(Gossypium hirsutum),* safflower *(Carthamus tinctorius),* and barnyardgrass *(Echinochloa crusgalli* (L.) Beauv.). They found increases in radial expansion near the root tip. The initial radial expansion of treated roots occurred in the region of maximum elongation. With increased duration of treatment there was a gradual decrease in the extent of the meristematic tissue zone. This was the result of progressive vacuolation and subsequent differentiation. The mitotic process was disrupted; however, no one type of mitotic figure prevailed. Some cells underwent normal mitosis. This lack of similar mitotic response in all cells was explained by differences in stage of mitotic division at time of treatment.

Negi et al. (1968) investigated the effects of trifluralin and nitralin, a related aniline herbicide, on mitochondrial activity of sorghum *(Sorghum vulgare),* corn *(Zea mays),* and soybean *(Glycine max),* which included O_2 uptake and oxidative phosphorylation. The activity of trifluralin was more consistent than that of nitralin. It was observed that inhibition of O_2 and P uptake could be involved in the mechanism of action but did not seem to explain selectivity. A greater reduction of uptake occurred in the resistant soybeans than in the susceptible sorghum.

Probst et al. (1968) observed that two metabolic pathways of trifluralin activity take place in soils. Under aerobic conditions, degradation proceeds through dealkylation steps followed by progressive reduction of the ring-substituted nitro groups. Under anaerobic conditions, reduction of the nitro groups preceded the dealkylation process. Most of the trifluralin found in carrot was unchanged, whereas the main metabolite was a dealkylated product. Similar results were obtained by Biswas and Hamilton (1967) who studied the fate of trifluralin in sweet potato and peanut plants. They found that the degradation products included metabolites in which one or both of the propyl groups on the amino N were dealkylated. One or both of the nitro groups substituted on the ring were reduced, and a benzoic or phenolic derivative was formed ultimately.

Benefin differs structurally from trifluralin in that it has an *n*-butyl group and a propyl group attached to the amino N in contrast to trifluralin, which has 2 *n*-propyl groups. It has a water solubility of 70 ppm whereas the solubility of trifluralin is less than 1 ppm. Soil incorporation is necessary to insure activity and this helps to explain why granular preparations are much more effective than liquid sprays. This herbicide has good activity on annual bluegrass, goosegrass, chickweed, knotweed, and crabgrass.

Presumably, the fate of benefin in plants and soil and its mechanism of action is comparable to that of trifluralin. Molecular structural differences between benefin and trifluralin could explain selectivity differences in the various agricultural and horticultural crops.

Nitralin, the third representative in the substituted aniline herbicide family, differs from trifluralin in that a methylsulfonyl substituent occurs on the ring, where the former has a trifluoromethyl group. In addition to the usual weed grasses found in turf that are susceptible to trifluralin and benefin, the foxtails and cheatgrass may be added to the list susceptible to this chemical.

Negi et al. (1968) indicated that nitralin had some effect on mitochondrial activity but their experimental results were not as consistent as those obtained with trifluralin. Its exact mechanism of action and fate in plants and soils have not been ascertained.

F. The *s*- Triazines

Atrazine and simazine, representatives of the family of *s*-triazines, are used extensively on agronomic and ornamental crops. They have found limited use on turf.

s-Triazines are heterocyclic compounds which are ring structures containing nitrogen and carbon in the ring. More specifically, they are triazines because of the 3 nitrogen atoms in the ring. The prefix *s* designates a symmetrical configuration with alternate carbon and nitrogen atoms.

Engel et al. (1968a) in controlling annual weed competition during zoysia establishment found that simazine and atrazine could be safely used on some zoysia varieties and selections, and that simazine was safer than atrazine. Some reductions in stolon development and growth may occur from use of these herbicides. Differences in activity may be explained by the structural differences that distinguish simazine and atrazine. Both are classified as 2-chloro-4,6-bis (alkylamino)-s-triazines. Simazine has two identical amino groups with two-carbon fragments, whereas atrazine has a two-carbon fragment and an isopropylamino group which is a three-carbon fragment. These asymmetric substitutions contribute to a greater water solubility and postemergence contact activity for atrazine and low water solubility and the expression of activity from soil application for simazine (Gysin and Knusli, 1960).

Simazine is absorbed through plant roots with little or no uptake through foliage. It can penetrate the cuticle but moves only in an acropetal direction by diffusion along cell walls and does not enter the living symplast. After being absorbed by the roots it is translocated in the xylem acropetally and accumulates in the apical meristems (Crafts, 1961; Sheets, 1961).

Simazine kills susceptible young seedlings after they have emerged from the soil surface. After emergence they usually turn yellow and die shortly. Moreland et al. (1959) have proposed that simazine exerts its killing action by inhibiting the Hill Reaction, which is a process whereby water is cleaved into hydrogen and oxygen during photosynthesis. The inhibitory action involves bonding of the herbicide through hydrogen bonds with appropriate receptors at or near the active centers in the chloroplasts of the plant. In chloroplasts the proposed site of the photochemical reactions is thought to be the cyclopentanone ring of the chlorophyll molecule (Moreland, 1963).

Metabolic studies with radioactive simazine have indicated that both tolerant and susceptible species degrade simazine, and this occurs primarily in the roots (Montgomery and Freed, 1964). The first step in the degradation process is a dechlorination mechanism to the 2-hydroxy analog (Hamilton and Moreland, 1962) which in turn is further degraded to CO_2 and other products. This nonenzymatic transformation to the hydroxy analog is due to the presence of a "sweet substance" identified as 2,4-hydroxy-7-methoxy-1, 4-benzoxazine-3-one (Castelfranco and Brown, 1962). More recent studies by Shimabukuro (1967) on the metabolism of atrazine revealed that two possible metabolic pathways exist in higher plants. Studies were conducted using two resistant species, corn *(Zea mays* L.) and sorghum *(Sorghum vulgare* Pers.), the intermediate susceptible pea *(Pisum sativum* L.), and two highly susceptible species, wheat *(Triticum vulgare* Vill.) and soybean *(Glycine max* Merr.). Atrazine was metabolized initially by N- dealkylation of either of the two substituted alkylamino groups in all species. Corn and wheat, which contain the "sweet substance" or benzoxazinone, also metabolized this triazine herbicide by hydrolysis or dechlorination in the 2-position of the ring to the 2-hydroxy analog or 2-hydroxyatrazine. Both metabolic pathways detoxify atrazine. The hydroxylation pathway, similar to that observed in simazine, converts atrazine to a completely inactive compound. The dealkylation pathway, also a detoxifying mechanism, produces one or more partially detoxified intermediates. The rate and pathway of metabolism are important in ascertaining tolerance of plants to this herbicide.

Simazine may persist in the soil for some time, but it is broken down by microbial activity. A wide range of soil microorganisms can use simazine as well as atrazine as sources of energy and can utilize the nitrogen from the molecule (Ragab and McCallum, 1961).

Atrazine is similar to simazine in its action but is also toxic when absorbed through the foliage. It has a water solubility of 33 ppm, as contrasted with 5 ppm for simazine. Because of its greater water solubility, its residual characteristics are less pronounced and it is easily moved into the soil. Triazine-susceptible turf plants are more apt to be injured because of this characteristic.

The mode of action of atrazine is similar to that of simazine. As indicated above, another metabolic pathway was observed for atrazine and it is believed that simazine may also undergo detoxication by this dealkylation pathway. Microbial breakdown of both triazines is probably by either one or by both pathways.

G. The Arsenical Herbicides

The arsenicals have been used for weed control in turf longer than any other family of herbicides. The arsenical herbicides may be classified as either inorganic or organic.

The inorganic group includes acid-arsenical spray formulations, sodium arsenite, and calcium arsenate. The organic arsenicals include derivatives of arsonic acid and a derivative of arsinic acid. Common arsonic acid derivatives include methanearsonate (MMA), monosodium methanearsonate (MSMA), monoammonium methanearsonate (MAMA), and disodium methanearsonate (DSMA or DMA). There is only one derivative of arsinic acid, and that is dimethylarsinicacid (cacodylic acid).

The acid-arsenical formulations were used first. They consisted of solutions of arsenic trioxide and sulfuric acid. Before the final spray solutions of the two were prepared, stock solutions were made consisting of arsenic trioxide, sodium hydroxide, and water in specific proportions. Later this stock solution was added to large volumes of water followed by the subsequent addition of sulfuric acid (Robbins, Craft, and Raynor, 1942).

The acid-arsenical formulations, though inexpensive and effective, had several shortcomings. They were corrosive, somewhat hazardous to handle, and ineffective on many deep-rooted perennials. On turf these formulations were used mostly for chemical renovation or total weed control prior to reseeding. Depending on application rate, they could serve as soil sterilants of either short or long duration. The limited use of acid-arsenical spray formulations has given way to more sophisticated herbicides which include other arsenicals.

Sodium arsenite was one of the first herbicides used for selective control of crabgrass in permanent turf. At low concentrations it is effective on crabgrass with slight to severe injury to perennial turfgrasses. Any handbook of chemistry refers to sodium arsenite as metarsenite. It is often a mixture of sodium orthoarsenite and sodium metarsenite. As indicated earlier, effective crabgrass control has been obtained with sodium arsenite when applied to seedlings in the 2-3-leaf stage or later. The permanent turfgrasses may be temporarily discolored but the more durable types such as bermudagrass and Kentucky bluegrass usually recover in a few days under good growing conditions. Spray applications of sodium arsenite were used on occasions to control white clover *(Trifolium repens)*.

As sodium arsenite is mildly alkaline and highly buffered, it softens and penetrates leaf surfaces by hydrolyzing the plant cuticle. After entering the plant, arsenic ions will react with proteins, denature the protoplasm, and cause death. Penetration of sodium arsenite can be enhanced by increasing the alkalinity or by neutralizing and acidifying the solution after dilution to desired strength. The latter acidified solution translocates more readily and under favorable conditions will kill the roots of deep-rooted perennials to a depth of several feet (Robbins, Crafts, and Raynor, 1942).

Sodium arsenite is very poisonous; extreme care must be given to avoid getting dust or spray into the eyes, nose, or mouth or on skin or clothing. It is suggested that goggles be worn and exposure to spray mist should be followed immediately by washing. Care must be taken to avoid breathing the spray mist. Children and pets should be kept away from the chemical and diluted spray. Empty bags and metal containers should be destroyed after emptying. Livestock grazing treated herbage are poisoned. Because of these hazards, use of sodium arsenite is discouraged.

Where used for postemergence crabgrass control, split applications of arsenite were best. Rumberg et al. (1960b), in studies with sodium arsenite and other arsenicals, found split applications superior to single applications for weed control and in reducing injury to desirable turf species.

Calcium arsenate is used for crabgrass control in turf. It is sometimes referred to as calcium orthoarsenate. Depending upon the reaction temperature, commercial calcium arsenates contain $CaHAsO_4$, $Ca_3(AsO_4)_2$, $Ca_5H_2(AsO_4)_4$, $(Ca_3(AsO_4)_3Ca(OH)_2$, $CaCO_3$, and unreacted $Ca(OH)_2$. Tricalcium arsenate ($Ca_3(AsO_4)_2$) is the predominant component. It is applied to established turf either in powder or granular form. It is particularly effective for crabgrass, chickweed, and annual bluegrass. Up to 5 years control of annual bluegrass has been obtained. Its mode of action is expressed through the death of embryos and germinating seeds (Welton et al., 1947). Low-lime calcium arsenate has proven better than the standard formulation. The safety precautions given for sodium arsenite are applicable to calcium arsenate.

At present, organic arsenicals are more widely used for weed control in turf than inorganic arsenicals. Hazards in their use are low. Although used medicinally for some time, it is only recently that they have been registered for killing weeds in turf, particularly crabgrass. Of the organic arsenicals, the derivatives of arsonic acid are by far the more popular. They include MAA, MSMA, MAMA, and DSMA. Generally, these are referred to as the methanearsonates. As indicated, there are different forms available. They are about equal in effectiveness when applied at recommended rates. Killing of crabgrass is easier when the plants are small. However, early season treatment can be unsatisfactory if turf injury is severe or the turf cover is very poor. Usually a second or third application after a 10-day interval is necessary for complete control. Methanearsonates should not be applied to turf when moisture is excessive or the turf is under moisture stress. Chances of turf injury increase with warm, dry conditions and the rate should be reduced if it is necessary to make applications under these conditions. The methanearsonates have been used as selective postemergence treatments on cotton and in noncrop areas, particularly for control of johnsongrass, nutsedge, goosegrass, barnyardgrass, the foxtails, and cocklebur. It should not be used where St. Augustinegrass is the primary turf species. The methanearsonates are used specifically for crabgrass and dallisgrass *(Paspalum dilatatum)* in turf, but some broadleaf weeds may be controlled through a contact-type action. The methanearsonates have been combined with 2,4-D for mixed stands of weeds. The combination is very effective but chances of injury to desirable species increase because of a possible synergistic action. Injury, which is an expression of mode of action, appears first as chlorosis followed by necrosis. The exact mechanism of action is not known. It is suspected that the methanearsonates behave similarly to the inorganic arsenicals.

There is only one popular derivative of arsinic acid, and that is dimethylarsinic acid, also known as cacodylic acid. As contrasted with the arsonates, this herbicide has two methyl groups attached to the arsenic atom and only one acidic hydrogen, whereas the methanearsonates have one methyl group and two acidic hydrogens attached to the arsenic atom. Sodium ions easily replace the hydrogen ions in both of these organic arsenical compounds. When they replace the hydrogen ions of methanearsonic acid the compound then becomes disodium methanearsonate.

Dimethylarsinic acid is a nonselective, postemergence foliar contact type herbicide. Research at Rutgers University has indicated that this herbicide is well adapted for use in pasture renovation as well as in turf renovation (Sprague et al., 1962). It kills crabgrass readily, but severely injures many turfgrasses such as bermudagrass, bentgrasses, fine-leaf fescues, and Kentucky bluegrasses. Because of this, it cannot be used for selective weed control in turf. Studies by Rumburg (1958) have indicated that respiration as measured by oxygen uptake on Kentucky bluegrass is not significantly reduced by cacodylic acid. Phytotoxicity generally is enhanced by the use of anionic surfactants or non-ionic surfactants. Although many early experiments with cacodylic acid involved turf and pasture renovation studies, it is now finding acceptance in other areas of weed control. It has shown some useful defoliating and desiccating properties. Some current experimental uses include cotton defoliation, weed control in fruit and citrus orchards, forestry management, and weed control in new seedling areas. General weed control in and around noncrop areas such as buildings, perennial ornamentals, along fence roads, and spot treatment of noxious weeds also may be included on this use list.

H. Chlordane and Bandane

The last chemical family to be considered for weed control in turf includes chlordane and bandane. Actually these two chemicals are insecticides and are often referred to as the chlorinated hydrocarbon insecticides. Other chlorinated hydrocarbon insecticides include heptachlor, aldrin, dieldrin, and endrin, to mention a few. Oftentimes these insecticides are referred to as the diene insecticides, and sometimes they are referred to as hexachlorocyclopentadienes. All of these insecticides are formed by the 1-4 addition of an olefinic unit to a conjugated diene.

Greenhouse studies by Dybing et al. (1954) showed that insecticide rates of chlordane applied before crabgrass starts to germinate would control crabgrass. However, 10 times this rate was needed for good field control. This is an interesting example of the need to evaluate herbicides under field conditions.

An interesting aspect of chlordane use for preemergence crabgrass control was its original good reputation for safety to turf and the subsequent realization 1 to 2 years later that serious deterioration of the turfgrass was occurring on some areas (Engel and Ilnicki, 1963). This injury appeared most acute during dry, hot growing conditions. Furthermore, chlordane did not prove to be as reliable as other preemergence herbicides.

Bandane, which is similar to chlordane, is a mixture of polychlorodicyclopentadiene isomers containing 60 to 67% chlorine. It has a lower water solubility than chlordane and is leached very slowly from the soil. It will control crabgrass in turf when applied before the crabgrasses germinate. It can also be applied to dichondra lawns to control crabgrass as well as ants, grubs, and Japanese beetles. Recommended application rates are about 35 to 50% of those used for chlordane.

Considerable information is available on the insecticidal mechanism of action of these chemicals. However, the process or processes affected in turf and weed species are not known.

VIII. Weeds of Turf and Their Control

A. Some Turf Weeds of Importance

A limited number of turf weeds deserve special comments because of their widespread occurrence, noxious behaviour, or threat to the future. This does not mean these weeds are considered the worst weeds. Kikuyugrass *(Pennisetum clandestinum),* sometimes planted as a very coarse turfgrass in warmer regions, is little known because of its limited distribution in the U. S. However, where this grass is adapted and encountered, it is recognized as an ugly weed threat. White clover, which is discussed in detail, is a very common weed, but it is scarcely a serious problem because of effective herbicidal control. In contrast, the *Veronica* species, which are listed in the chart, are less common than white clover, but they are often a greater problem because highly effective controls have not been developed. Also, personal opinions vary on which weeds deserve inclusion in one or both listings. Fanciers of bentgrasses, bermudagrasses, or tall fescue might disapprove of including these species on a weed list. Yet, the uninvited and objectionable appearance of these grasses in many turf areas forces recognition of their role as weeds as well as turfgrasses. Many weeds that are of regional significance are unlikely to become a problem in different climatic regions. There is evidence, however, that some warm climate weeds can extend their region of adaptation through the development of winter-hardy races or ecotypes. Similarly, some cool-climate weeds can develop in warmer areas as fall, winter, and spring weeds. It seems likely that additional plant species will be added to turf weed lists with changes in the distribution of both weeds and turfgrass species.

Table 1. Common names, scientific names, growth characters, and controls suggested for troublesome turf weeds.

Common name and scientific name	Life*	Major area of No. America†	Most common habitat	Methods of control‡	
				Cultural§	Chemical¶
Barnyardgrass *Echinochloa crusgalli* (L.) Beauv.	A	Widespr. US & Mex.	Thin seedling turf	-	PE f
Bedstraw *Galium* spp.	A&P	Widespread cooler areas	-	-	Silvex f
Bermudagrass *Cynodon dactylon* (L.) Pers. (primarily)	P	Except colder areas	Warm, humid	-	non-selective
Brome, downy *Bromus tectorum* L.	A	Widespr., esp. west. US	-	-	PE f
Broom sedge, *Andropogon virginicus* L.	P	NE & SE	Infertile soil	Incr. fert.	-
Carpetweed *Mollugo verticillata* L.	A	Warmer & mid lat.	Dry gravelly soils	-	2,4-D g silvex g mecoprop g dicamba
Chamomile, corn *Anthemis arvensis* L.	P	Widespr. So. Can., No. US	-	Dense turf	2,4-D f dicamba fg
Chickweed, common *Stellaria media* (L.) Cyrillo	A, WA	Widespread	Thin turf cool, moist	Incr. turf cover	dicamba g mecoprop g silvex g
Chickweed, field *Cerastium arvense* L.	P	NE-US, SE-Canada	Cool, moist	Incr. turf cover	silvex mecoprop
Chickweed, mouseear *Cerastium vulgatum* L.	P	NE-US, SE-Canada	Cool, moist	Incr. turf cover	silvex mecoprop
Cinquefoil, common *Potentilla canadensis* L.	P	E-N Amer.	Cool, infert.	Incr. fert.	2,4-D dicamba
Clover, white *Trifolium repens* L.	P	Widespread	Moist	N. fert.	dicamba g mecoprop g silvex g
Crabgrass, large *Digitaria sanguinalis* (L.) Scop.	A	Widespread abun. E & So.	Sun, warm moist	Tall dense cover	PE_g, TE_f
Crabgrass, smooth *Digitaria ischaemum* (Schreb.) Muhl.	A	Abund. -NE widespread	Sun, warm moist	Tall dense cover	PE_g, TE_f
Daisy, English *Bellis perennis* L.	P	Pac. NW, Nfd., NE	Cool, moist	Remove	silvex g dicamba g
Dallisgrass - *Paspalum dilatatum* (Poir.)	P	So. US	Warm	-	DSMA f
Dandelion - *Taraxacum officinale* Weber	P	widespread	Humid, fertile	-	2,4-D g
Dichondra - *Dichondra* spp.	P	So. US	Warm, moist	Dense turf	2,4-D
Dock, curly - *Rumex crispus* L.	B	Widespread	-	-	2,4-D + dicamba, fg
Garlic, wild *Allium vineale* L.	A	E-US, So. to Ga. & Ark.	Humid, fertile	Good cover, mow freq.	repeat 2,4-D f dicamba fg
Goosegrass *Eleusine indica* (L.) Gaertn.	A	Warmer sites & regions	Sun, warm, humid	Good turf in spr. & sum.	$PE_{(1,2,3)}^{f}$
Hawkweed, mouseear *Hieracium pilosella* L.	P	Nfd. to No. Car. to Minn.	Cool, moist poor soils	-	2,4-D + dicamba fg
Healall *Prunella vulgaris* L.	P	Widespread	Humid, fertile	Incr. turf cover	2,4-D + dicamba g
Henbit *Lamium amplexicaule* L	WA	E-N. Amer. & Pac. coast	Humid, fertile	Avoid thin fall seedings	2,4-D + dicamba f silvex f
Ivy, ground *Glechoma hederacea* L.	P	So. Can. & No. US	Damp, fertile some shade	Dense turf	silvex f mecoprop f dicamba f
Kikuyugrass *Pennisetum clandestinum* Hochst.	P	SW & So. US	Hot areas	-	non-select. arsonates fp
Knotweed, prostrate *Polygonum aviculare* L.	A	So. Can. & No. US	Compact soil thin sod	Dense turf	dicamba g
Knawel *Scleranthus annus* L.	A	E-US & Can. to Minn. & Fla.	Thin turf, poor soil	Incr. turf cover	dicamba f
Lambsquarters, common *Chenopodium album* L.	A	Widespread	Thin new seedings	Mowing	2,4-D g
Mallow, common *Malva neglecta* Wallr.		Widespread	Thin turf	Incr. turf cover	2,4-D + dicamba g
Mayweed *Anthemis cotula* L.	WA	Widespread	Fertile soil	-	2,4-D + dicamba g
Medic, black *Medicago lupulina* L.	A	Widespread	Thin turf, poor soil	Incr. turf cover	dicamba g silvex g
Moneywort *Lysimachia nummularia* L.	P	E-No. Amer. to Ga. & Kans.	Moist	-	2,4-D
Mosses, *Ceratodon purpureus* Brid. (and other species)	-	Widespread	Moist	Incr. turf cover	-
Nimblewill *Muhlenbergia schreberi* J. F. Gmel.	P	NE coast to Minn. & Tex.	Moist, fertile soil	Incr. turf cover	-
Nutsedge *Cyperus* spp.	P	Widespread	Wet soil	Incr. turf cover	DSMA fp repeated 2,4-D

(continued)

Common name and scientific name	Life*	Major area of No. America†	Most common habitat	Methods of control‡	
				Cultural§	Chemical¶
Onion, wild Allium canadense L.	P	NE coast to Ont.& Tex.	Rich soil	Good turf freq. mow.	2,4-D f dicamba fg
Orchardgrass Dactylis glomerata	P	Cooler N. Am. & SE to Fla. & cent. Calif.	Moist, fertile	Clean seed & soil, dense turf, remove	non-selective
Paspalum, fringeleaf Paspalum ciliatifolium Michx	P	Gulf, So. Atl., & northward	Sandy	Incr. turf cover	arsonates
Pearlwort Sagina procumbens L.	-	Temperate No. Amer.	Cool, moist	Dense turf	-
Pennywort, lawn Hydrocotyle sibthorpioides Lam.	P	Mid Atl. to Ky. & Ind.	Moist, shade	Incr. turf cover	silvex fg
Pineappleweed Matricaria matricarioides (Less.) Porter	A	West. US, sprd. East	Cool	Clean soil & seed	-
Pimpernell, scarlet Anagallis arvensis L.	A	Widespr., mid-Atl. to Pacific	Humid	Incr. turf cover	-
Plantain, broadleaf Plantago major L.	P	Widespread	Mod. to good fertility	Incr. turf cover	2,4-D f
Plantain, buckhorn Plantago lanceolata L.	P	Widespread	Mod. to low fertility	Incr. turf cover	2,4-D g
Puncturevine Tribulus terrestris L.	A	Comm. in SW, occ. MW & E	Thin cover, warm location,	Incr. turf cover	2,4-D g
Purslane, common Portulaca oleracea L.	A	Widespread	Thin turf, rich soil	Incr. turf cover	2,4-D + dicamba g
Quackgrass Agropyron repens L. Beauv.	P	NE, MW, & So. Ca.	Thin turf	Incr. turf cover	-
Sandbur, field Cenchrus pauciflorus Benth	A	Widespread	Sandy	Incr. turf cover	arsonates
Sorrel, red Rumex acetosella L.	P	Widespread	Low fert.	Incr. turf cover	dicamba
Sorrel, yellow wood Oxalis spp.	P	Widespread	Moist, cool	Incr. turf cover	silvex f
Speedwell, creeping Veronica arvensis L.	A	US & So. Can.	Moist, cool	Incr. turf cover	-
Speedwell, purslane Veronica peregrina L.	A	E & Cent. US, Alas. to Can.	Moist, cool	Incr. turf cover	2,4-D + dicamba f
Speedwell, thymeleaf Veronica serpyllifolia L.	P	Widespread	Moist, cool	Incr. turf cover	2,4-D + dicamba f
Spurge, spotted Euphorbia maculata L.	A	Widespread	Thin turf in summer	Incr. turf cover	silvex + dicamba f
Starwort - Stellaria graminea L.	P	E-Can. & US	Moist soils	-	dicamba
Torpedograss - Panicum repens	P	SE US	Sandy soils	-	non-selec.
Thyme, creeping Thymus serpyllum L	P	Comm. to New Eng.-No. Car.	Drier soils	-	dicamba
Timothy Phleum pratense L.	P	Widespr., esp. NE-US	Cool,humid	Clean seed, dense turf	-
Velvetgrass Holcus lanatus L.	P	E. Can., NE MW-Pac. NW	Rich, damp soil	Remove	Non-selec.
Yarrow Achillea millefolium L	P	Widespread	-	Incr. turf cover	2,4-D + dicamba fg
Yellow rocket Barbarea vulgaris R. Br.	B or P	NE, No. Cent. occ. Pac. NW	New seedings fertile soils	Mow & incr. turf cover	2,4-D

* A = annual; B = biennial; P = perennial; WA = winter annual. † U.S. regions: NE = Northeast, MW = Midwest, SE = Southeast, SW = Southwest, Atl. = Atlantic, Pac. = Pacific. ‡ Control = ranging from modest reduction to complete control for various weeds. § Dense turf = high level of fertilization on vigorous turfgrass. Incr. fert. = increased soil fertility. Incr. turf cover = increased turf cover — might be brought about by better nutrition, proper watering, insect control, disease control, traffic control, etc. ¶ PE = preemergence, PE_1 = benefin, PE_2 = bensulide, PE_3 = DCPA, PE_4 = siduron. TE = postemergence, TE_1 = methylarsonates, TE_2 = PMA. Non-selective = a chemical that kills both weeds and grasses and some may require a delay before re-establishing turf — examples are dalapon, paraquat, and cacodylic acid. Chemicals vary in ability to control weeds from excellent to very poor according to designations of g, f and p — g = excellent to good in effectiveness, f = fair to poor in effectiveness, p = poor in effectiveness.

1. Annual Bluegrass (Poa annua L.)

Description.- Unmowed annual bluegrass may be 5 to 20 cm tall and taller. Mature plants may develop in turf cut to putting green height and closer. Rooting at the nodes occurs in some types. Rhizomes are lacking. It has a *Poa* type leaf that is folded and has the double-line through the center of the topside and the boat-shaped blade tip. Its ligule is larger and whiter than most *Poa* spp. and the culms are flattened with blades 1 to 3 mm wide. Most types are distinctly more yellow than *Poa pratensis.* Panicle seedheads are indeterminate and spikelets are compact with 5 to 6 flowers.

Occurrence, Habitat, Life Cycle, Growth Habits, and Nature of the Turf Problem—Annual bluegrass has become widely distributed in North America since its early introduction from Europe. While it is called an annual, many types may persist indefinitely from new tillers that root at the nodes under cool, moist conditions. Seed is produced during most of the growing season and profusely in mid- to late-spring. Seed germination is poor during the first few weeks after harvest and improves over a period of 60 days or more (Cockerham and Whitworth, 1967). Annual gluegrass germination can occur abundantly with the first cool, moist germinating conditions of late summer. Germination may also occur during mild periods in winter and spring. Some local areas experience moderate to abundant germination in spring. Germinating temperatures of 15-25 C are considered optimum. A temperature of 30 C prevented germination of new crop seed (Engel, 1967). Annual bluegrass prefers a moist, fertile soil that has a good supply of nitrogen and phosphorus, but it can persist in areas of comparatively low N fertility and severe soil compaction. It is very susceptible to heat injury, especially when subject to less than optimum moisture. Annual bluegrass is susceptible to most common turf diseases, especially in hot weather. Nearly all annual bluegrass plants are killed in regions where summer temperatures are consistently high, and severe losses are commonplace on warmer sites in the northern U. S. and southern Canada. Heavy winter losses characterize regions that have severe winters and heavy snowfall. Inability of growers and research personnel to find reliable methods to prevent stand losses, especially in hot weather, has made it an unwanted species. Hence in most regions it is classified as a weed. There are a few areas in North America with very mild summers where this grass might be classed as a turfgrass rather than a weed. Annual bluegrass can develop a good root system under favorable conditions (Sprague and Burton, 1937), but a poor root system exists frequently because of high soil temperatures or compact soil. Annual bluegrass has good shade tolerance.

Control—Partial control of annual bluegrass can be achieved by management where the permanent turf species is well adapted. A dense, persistent turf cover, especially in late summer prior to germination of annual bluegrass, will reduce invasion (Sprague et al., 1937; Youngner et al., 1968). Annual bluegrass is seldom a problem in high cut, moderately watered and fertilized Kentucky bluegrass roughs on golf courses of the northern U. S. and southern Canada; yet it may dominate completely in fairways a few feet away. Its takeover of bentgrass turf is less certain if the bentgrass is fertilized lightly and water is less than required for annual bluegrass but adequate for bentgrass. In areas with bermudagrass turf, some growers fertilize to develop a tight turf before the onset of cool weather required for annual bluegrass germination.

Suppression of annual bluegrass with either lead or calcium arsenate has been practiced for a long time. Calcium arsenate has received more attention for this purpose and is considered one of the most effective materials available (Engel, Morrison, and Ilnicki, 1968). Nevertheless, it is difficult to develop a toxic level of this chemical in the soil without encountering loss of turf or a residue in the soil that prevents the germination of turfgrass seed. On areas treated with calcium arsenate greater loss of turf has been observed in periods of hot weather and cold weather stress. Turfgrass species vary greatly in tolerance to arsenates and it is likely that varieties or strains of a species do likewise. Also, as reported previously, the activity of arsenate treatment is influenced by soil phosphorus, pH, and organic matter. To date, trial and error have been relied on in determining treatment rates. Limited research and grower experience suggest that most applications should start with a full treatment. Additional annual treatments would then be reduced to 1/4 or 1/3 the initial rate. The arsenates are poisonous materials that require proper precautions in use.

Among the more recent preemergence herbicides, benefin, bensulide, DCPA, and nitralin can prevent germination of annual bluegrass. However, they have not demonstrated broad effectiveness nor sufficient control. They seem to have little merit in cooler, humid regions where annual bluegrass may survive from year to year. While their damage to established turf may not exceed that of the arsenates, they can be expected to inflict undesirable amounts of injury on sensitive species such as bentgrass.

2. Common Chickweed (Stellaria media (L.) Cyrill)

Other names for this weed are starwort, starweed, winterweed, birdweed, bindweed, satin flower, and tongue-grass.

Description – Stems are low, slender, tufted, much branched, creeping or ascending with a fringe of hairs down one side of the stem. The stems are capable of rooting at the nodes. The leaves are usually not much more than 1.5 cm in length, ovate to oblong, entire, the lower ones on hairy petioles, the upper leaves mostly sessile. These leaves can be so numerous that the plant often covers the ground like a green mat. The flowers are perfect in terminal, leafy cymes or solitary in the axils, and on very slender pedicels. There are five separate sepals. The petals are usually deeply cleft or two-parted, usually shorter than the sepals. The deeply cleft petals form a white star which is set within a larger green one formed by the five oblong and rather pointed hairy sepals. Stamens may range in number from 3 to 7; the usual number is 5. The capsule is ovoid and one-celled and contains many seeds at maturity. The capsule opens at the apex, by what appears to be 6 to 8 teeth, or twice as many as the number of styles. The seeds are 1 mm in diameter and are usually circular to ovate. They are brown, sometimes flattened, roughened, with rows of small tubercles.

Occurrence, Origin, Habitat, Life Cycle, Growth Habits, and Nature of the Turf Problem—Chickweed appears in cultivated fields, gardens, meadows, waste places, and lawns. It was introduced from Europe. It is classified as an annual, and more precisely a winter annual. It reproduces by seed and creeping stems which root at the node. It is often encountered in turf or lawn areas, particularly where open patches occur. Germination usually takes place in the fall; however, it may germinate and become established at other times of the year. It apparently blooms throughout most of the four seasons, and can set seed shortly after flowering.

Control—While chickweed is widespread in turf, it is scarcely a primary weed. Its presence indicates the turf cover lacks density during much of the year. Overcoming this problem is the best single control measure. Improvements in turf cover through adequate soil fertility, proper mowing, and judicious watering should receive high priority. Spraying with an herbicide can give good kill of established plants, and this is very helpful when combined with an improved turf cover. Silvex and mecoprop, two representatives of the α-phenoxypropionic acid family, are effective for the control of this species. Dicamba alone or in mixture with 2,4-D is a very effective herbicidal treatment. 2,4-D has not been too effective for the control of chickweed. However, mixtures of 2,4-D and 2,4,5-T are somewhat more effective.

3. Mouseear Chickweed (Cerastium vulgatum L.)

Description—Stems are tufted, some prostrate, others erect, or ascending, ranging in length from 15 to 30 cm. Stems may root at lower nodes and form dense mats. Leaves are mostly oblong to spatulate. The upper ones are more lance-shaped, 1.3 to 2.5 cm long. Flowers are few to several, in cymose clusters at the tip of the nearly naked stem. The central flower is solitary and always ovoid. There is usually but one flower in a cluster open at a time. The five white petals are cleft at the tip and are longer and somewhat more obtuse than the hairy sepals below them. Sometimes petals are absent. The number of stamens is almost always 10. Styles number 5. The seed capsule is a slender, ovoid structure, faintly-ridged and slightly curved upward. Seeds are very numerous. They are brown in color and quite roughened. This roughened appearance is caused by the tubercles that are present on the seed coat.

Occurrence, Origin, Habitat, Life Cycle, Growth Habits, and Nature of the Turf Problem—Mouseear chickweed is chiefly found in lawns, pastures, and meadows. Occasionally it is found along roadsides and waste places. It is perennial and reproduces both by seeds and creeping stems. It invades lawn areas by becoming established in open patches and where the turf stand is light, but is competitive and spreads in vigorous turf. It makes a dense growth that contrasts with turf and smothers most of the grass in scattered patches where it develops.

Control—Control through management is difficult because this weed competes well with good turf. Hot, dry conditions often destroy it. Where this happens, a dense turf cover at the start of cool growing weather is important to hinder re-establishment of the weed. Control with herbicides is feasible and a number of commercially available herbicides are obtainable. Perhaps the most valuable herbicides are dicamba, silvex and mecoprop. Combinations of 2,4-D with dicamba are used on occasions where dandelion and buckhorn occur. However, 2,4-D by itself is not effective. Applications of effective herbicides should be made in late summer or early fall. Applications may also be made in the early spring.

4. Crabgrass

Smooth crabgrass *(Digitaria ischaemum* Schreb.) is also called small crabgrass and fingergrass. Large crabgrass *(Digitaria sanguinalis* L. Scop.) is also called hairy crabgrass or fingergrass. Other *Digitaria* species occur, but comments on crabgrass will refer to the above two species, which are common weeds in turf.

Description—Both crabgrass species root at the nodes. The stalks of large crabgrass are more robust and the blades and sheaths are hairy, while hairiness of smooth crabgrass is confined to the collar area. Both have a folded leaf bud. Purple color develops in the foliage and seedheads during cool weather of late summer and early fall. This is most pronounced in large crabgrass. Both species have finger-like seedheads with 2 to 6 racemes that range up to 10 and 15 cm, respectively. One-flowered spikelets on short pedicels occur in pairs on one side of the rachis. Spikelets are approximately 2 and 3 mm long, respectively. Both species have a minute first empty glume (possibly lacking in smooth crabgrass) and hyaline margins. Smooth crabgrass has a second empty glume that is nearly as long as the spikelet, while this same structure in large crabgrass is about half the length of the spikelet.

Occurrence, Origin, Habitat, Life Cycle, Growth Habits, and Nature of the Turf Problem—Crabgrass is widespread in warmer and temperate eastern North America, and abundant in local areas of other warm, moist sections. Both species were introduced from Europe. Smooth crabgrass is most common in northeastern U. S., while large crabgrass is most abundant in southeastern U. S., the mid-Atlantic states, and warmer latitudes of the humid, temperate zone. Both species are annuals. They are killed with the first frosts and grow from seed each year. Fresh seed of crabgrass is dormant, but dormancy can be broken by puncturing, scarifying, or soaking in a solution of 500 ppm of ethylene chlorohydrin (Gianfagna and Pridham, 1951). Moist seeds at temperatures of 3 C break dormancy rapidly 25-56 days before germination starts in the spring (Toole and Toole, 1941). The best germination in laboratory tests has occurred at 20-30 C and 20-35 C temperature alternations; 20-40 C gave good germination; and 15-25 C was effective, especially with older seed (Toole et al., 1941). Light aids germination with less than optimum conditions. Seed of both species showed the ability to emerge from a depth of 3.5 cm in some soils (King and Kramer, 1955), but soil compaction gives reduced stands (Watson, 1950). When germination occurs with minimal moisture in a very dry soil, subsequent dry weather will check growth or even destroy the seedlings. With abundant moisture, fertility, light, and warmth, the seedlings grow rapidly. In weak turf, individual plants may spread over a large area by prostrate stems rooting at the nodes. Seedheads usually appear in midsummer and continue to develop until plants are killed by cold weather in the fall. Crabgrass is an unwanted weed in turf because (a) it does not blend in color or texture with most turfgrasses, (b) dense growth may reduce the stand of desirable turfgrasses, and (c) it quickly deteriorates into ugly, grey, bare areas after dying in the fall.

Control—Preventing seed set for several years is required for control. Destroying germination or emerging seedlings can be accomplished with a dense growth of turfgrasses (high cut and fall fertilization on Kentucky bluegrasses) and preemergence herbicides (see Chart). When crabgrass seedlings become established in turf, use a minimal amount of water and fertilizer until the crabgrass is removed or cold weather checks its growth. Destroy with postemergence herbicides where turfgrasses have adequate tolerance. Methylarsonates are appropriate for postemergence crabgrass control. Two to 3 treatments at 7- to 10-day intervals are usually required. PMA is most appropriate for controlling young crabgrass plants in bentgrass turf. PMA causes a minimum of discoloration and keeps certain diseases under control. When only a few crabgrass plants develop in turf, removal by hand may be best.

5. Dallisgrass (Paspalum dilatatum)

Dallisgrass and some related species are also known as paspalumgrass and watergrass.

Description—It is a coarse-textured grass with tufted, glabrous, stout, erect stems 5-17 cm long when unmowed. Rhizomes may be present. Leaf blades are 3-12 mm wide and are long, loose, and glabrous, and the lower ones have a soft pubescence. Seedheads have 2-10 racemes that are 5-10 cm long and spreading. Spikelets are ovoid, acuminate, 2.5-4 mm long, and 2-2.5 mm broad. The glume and sterile lemma are longer than the fruit and silky-villous.

Occurrence, Origian, Habitat, Life Cycle, Growth Habits, and Nature of the Turf Problem—Dallisgrass occurs throught the warmer parts of the U. S. It extends northward locally as far as New Jersey and Oregon in coastal areas. It is a native of South America. Moist, warm areas are the preferred habitat. It is most common in meadows, roadsides, ditches, and high-cut lawn turf, but it can persist and spread under closer cut turf. Its tall seedstalks, contrasting color and coarse texture make its appearance highly objectionable in quality turf. It is classed among the most troublesome turf weeds in the southern U. S.

Control—Where a small number of plants are present, digging them by hand has been a common practice. More recently, methanearsonates of the DSMA or AMA type have become the most common treatment on bermudagrass and zoysia lawns. While proper applications of these treatments are safe to these grasses, they should not be applied where bahiagrass is used for turf. Early spring or summer treatments, when the dallisgrass is starting vigorous growth, are best. Two to four treatments at weekly intervals are usually required. Some growers claim success in killing dallisgrass by covering the turf to shut out light and then removing the cover before bermudagrass is killed.

6. *Dandelion (Taraxacum officinale* Weber)

Dandelion has other but less popular common names. It is sometimes called lion's-tooth, blowball, cankerwort, yellow gowan, witch's gowan, and doon-head-clock.

Description—Dandelion has a large, thick, fleshy tap root that goes deep into the ground as much as 50 cm. Cutting the crown from the tap root will not kill the weed since any part of the root will sprout leaves and make a new plant. The seed achenes are brown, oblong, angled, ridged, and about 3 mm long. They are set around the top with fine spinous tubercles. The tip extending to a slender beak bearing a copious pappus of fine, white hairs.

Leaves are basal, 7 cm to more than 30 cm long, blunt, lance-shaped, varying in outline from oblong to spatulate, coarsely toothed, with the pointed teeth turned toward the base of the leaf, somewhat hairy when young but soon become smooth, spreading on the ground in a flat rosette. Scapes or flower stalks are smooth, hollow, cylindrical, short at first but increasing in length with maturity. Solitary flowers open and close several times before the whole head is fertilized, to the center.

Occurrence, Origin, Habitat, Life Cycle, Growth Habits, and Nature of the Turf Problem—Dandelion is a cosmopolitan weed. It is widespread throughout most of North America. It is found in fields, along roadways, meadows, waste places, and lawns. It is thought to have been introduced from Eurasia, though some authorities believe it is native to North America. It is a perennial that reproduces by seed and sometimes from root fragments. It can bloom almost any time during the year, but particularly in the spring when temperatures are above freezing. Seeds usually are set and dispersed freely within 2 weeks from the onset of flowering. It is objectionable in turf areas because the leaves produce an unfavorable contrast in texture, and the seedheads are unattractive.

Control—Good turf cover reduces dandelions, as can be observed with dense growing species such as bentgrass, bermudagrass, and zoysia. Bare areas encourage invasion. While good turf cover reduces invasion, a dense cover does little to eliminate established plants. 2,4-D is very effective in controlling dandelion. Silvex is effective, 2,4,5-T is less effective, and mecoprop is inadequate. Mixtures of dicamba and 2,4-D are very popular inasmuch as a broad spectrum of weeds, including dandelion, can be controlled. Where an abundance of dandelions has developed, it may be necessary to treat again at 6- to 12-month intervals to control seedling plants. The best treatment time is early to midspring, after the start of good growth and before an abundance of blossoms. Plants killed early allow mature turfgrasses to spread into areas formerly occupied by the weeds. Fall treatments are satisfactory when growing conditions are good.

7. Goosegrass (Eleusine indica (L.) Goertn.)

Goosegrass is also called yardgrass, wiregrass, crowfootgrass, hard crabgrass, silver crabgrass, and Indian eleusine.

Description—Goosegrass is a coarse grass and it has a cluster of tillers that arise from a central part of the plant. The flattened stems or culms are decumbent or prostrate at the base. Leaves are pale green and have loose sheaths which overlap. They are compressed and smooth, but hairy at the throat. The leaf blades vary in length according to vigor of the plant and mowing height. Spikes, 2-10 in number, radiate or digitate at the end of the stalk. Each spike has two rows of spikelets on one side which extend to the tip of the rachis. The spikelets are oppressed, sessile, and are 3-5 flowered, about 5 mm long.

Occurrence, Origin, Habitat, Life Cycle, Growth Habits, and Nature of the Turf Problem—Goosegrass occurs in nearly all parts of North America except the far North. It is widespread in the warm humid areas, and was introduced from the warmer parts of Asia. Goosegrass is common on sunny, warm sites where closely cut turf receives heavy traffic. It is found on lawns, roadsides, farmyards, waste places, and in warm and temperate parts of North America. Golf course greens, tees, and fairways are troubled by this weed. Its coarseness ruins the putting quality of greens. It is a seed-propagated annual. Germination occurs from midspring through summer. High temperatures are required for good germination (Fulwider and Engel, 1959). In temperate climates it blooms any time from June to September and sets seed from July to October.

Control—Perhaps the best method of control is to maintain a dense turf to minimize invasion. Where only a few plants occur, removal of the plants to eliminate the seed supply is an excellent attack.

Chemical weed control from preemergent use of calcium arsenate, bandane, DCPA, and bensulide has been promising in some tests. However, extreme care in selecting herbicides with adequate safety is important. Consideration should be given to the type of turfgrass present in the lawn, rates of application, and proper timing.

8. Yellow Nutsedge

Two common sedges that are problems in turf in the United States are yellow nutsedge *(Cyperus esculentus* L.) and purple nutsedge *(Cyperus rotundus* L.). Sometimes these nutsedges are called nutgrass. Other common names for yellow nutsedge are chufa, northern nutgrass, yellow nutgrass, yellow galingale, coco, cocosedge, rush nut, edible galingale, and earth almond. Purple nutsedge has a number of common names also. These include nutgrass, nutsedge, coco sedge, cocograss, and hydra cyperus. For ease of discussion, each species will be considered separately.

Description—Yellow nutsedge stems are erect, simple, triangular, in cross section (common to all sedges), yellow-green in color, and range anywhere from 3-9 cm tall. These stems arise from perennial tuber-bearing rootstocks. These tubers are 1-2 cm long. Roots are fibrous. Leaves in 3 ranks come from each side of the triangular stem.

They are narrow and grasslike in nature. The midvein is pronounced and the edges of the midvein slightly roughened. The spikes and spikelets are straw-colored or pale yellow-brown, acute, 1-3 cm long, and contain many flattened flowers which are 2-ranked in a somewhat compound terminal umbel.

Occurrence, Origin, Habitat, Life Cycle, Growth Habits, and Nature of the Turf Problem—Yellow nutsedge is widespread in eastern North America, and along the Pacific coast. It is found in other parts of the country as well. Apparently it was introduced from Eurasia; however, some feel that it is native to North America. It is a perennial and propagates by seed and by the tuber-bearing rootstocks. It has become a serious weed problem in turf, particularly where topsoil has come from heavily infested agricultural or crop producing areas. Sedges are very objectionable in turf because of the unsightly contrast in color and texture.

Control—There is no sure method of controlling this species. Many types do not persist over a period of years in closely cut, dense, regularly mowed turf. Turf-tolerant types are expected to become more common. Some success has been obtained with repeated applications of 2,4-D alone or in combination with methanearsenates. Treatments should be applied in early spring when plants are in a tender stage of growth or through the summer when growth is evident. Contaminated soil should be avoided.

9. Purple Nutsedge

Description—Purple nutsedge stems are erect, simple triangular, and similar to yellow nutsedge, but they are generally shorter. Spikelets are chestnut brown in color and seeds are linear to oblong, 3-angled, 1.5 cm long, with the base and apex obtuse. These are covered with a fine network of gray lines. Generally this species resembles yellow nutsedge, but the chestnut brown to purple color of the influorescence sets it apart.

Occurrence, Origin, Habitat, Life Cycle, Growth Habits, and Nature of the Turf Problem—Purple nutsedge is especially prominent in the southeastern U. S. from New Jersey southward and westward to Texas, and in southern portions of the Pacific Coast region. Occasionally isolated plants are found north of this area. It is believed that this species was introduced from Asia. A perennial, it is propagated by seed and by tuber-bearing rootstocks. As with yellow nutsedge, it blooms anytime from July to September and sets seed from August to November. It grows on a wide rage of sites, especially in cultivated crops like cotton. It is a serious problem in turf where topsoil has been obtained from heavily infested agricultural sites.

Control—Same as for yellow nutsedge.

10. White Clover (Trifolium repens)

Description—White clover is a legume with prostrate growth habits. Individual plants can spread rapidly by stoloniferous stems. The plants vary greatly in size, but, most commonly, types occurring in turf are the smaller wild white clover types. The leaves develop from the crown and the nodes of the stolons. They are composed of 3 sessile leaflets and occasionally more. They are broadly elliptical to obovate but vary in size and shape. They may have a crescent-shaped "watermark" on the upper surface. Seedheads are borne on long stalks that arise at the basal nodes, which distinguishes it from alsike clover *(Trifolium hybridum)* that may develop flower stalks at the upper nodes of the stem. The seedheads are ball-like in shape and are composed of 40-100 florets. The individual florets may contain 1-7 rounded bright yellow seeds.

Figure 3. Excellent clover control (left) obtained by use of herbicide to improve appearance of lawn turf. (Courtesy of O. M. Scott & Sons).

Occurrence, Habitat, Life Cycle, Origin, Growth Habits, and Nature of the Turf Problem—White clover is widely distributed in North America. It is classified as an introduced species. It is best adapted to the clay and silt soils of the humid states, but it grows well in most regions if moisture is available and soils have adequate levels of calcium and phosphorus. White clover behaves as a perennial in cool areas and as a biennial in the warmer sections of North America. It appears readily on most turf sites. A few seedlings or scattered plants can spread rapidly through a thin turf. Sudden lowering of the height of cut on cool-season grasses is highly favorable to invasion. White clover is acceptable along roadsides and in meadow-like lawns. However, it is a despised weed on football fields and golf courses. Homeowners often object to clover because it attracts bees and is a source of "grass stains" on clothing. In cool-season turf areas it offers little ground cover during freezing weather, and the flowers are unsightly in late spring.

Control—While white clover can appear readily, frequently, and abundantly in turf, it is not difficult to control. Formerly, many proposed withholding lime (developing a very acid soil) or potassium from turf to discourage this weed. This did not give adequate control and could be deleterious to turfgrasses. Clover can be suppressed, however, when adequate quantities of nitrogen are applied for vigorous growth. Most putting greens are examples of control achieved with adequate nitrogen and a dense turf cover. This is also a good approach to control on home lawns. Where strict control of clover is desired, herbicides can be used with excellent results. Dicamba is best in combining effectiveness and minimum risk to turfgrasses. Mecoprop is safe but somewhat less consistent than dicamba. Silvex gives excellent control of clover but it is too injurious on the more susceptible turfgrasses. Although endothal is effective and leaves no residual effects, it has not been used widely in controlling white clover. Other herbicides may offer some control but they are considered less desirable.

IX. Factors That Influence Results With A Given Herbicide

Consistency of results is an important attribute of turfgrass herbicides. When a chemical lacks this characteristic, it may help to adjust rates either to obtain adequate weed control or to avoid serious turf injury. More research information would improve the consistency of some chemicals. Yet some unpredictability in chemical action on turf is unavoidable because of the many variables that influence biolgical processes. The interaction of variables increases the difficulty. Major variables that influence the action of a herbicide on turf include: (1) temperature, (2) moisture, (3) chemical interrelationships of the herbicide, the plant, and the environment, and (4) genetic or growth stage variability of grass and weed species. Continuing study of the basis for varied behavior of given herbicide treatments has been hindered by rapid changes in the herbicide field.

A. Temperature Effects on Chemical Movement and Reaction

The amount of a chemical absorbed or translocated is affected by temperature. Pallas (1960) found that both high temperature (35 C) and high humidity (70-74%) increased the amount of 2,4-D and benzoic acid absorbed and translocated by bean *(Phaseolus vulgaris)* plants. Chemical activity of most herbicides will vary with temperature and can give qualitative or quantitative changes. Kelly (1949) obtained increased activity of 2,4-D on beans with increased temperature. Callahan, Engel, and Ilnicki (1968) showed that the action of silvex on bentgrass was increased with high temperatures (75-90 F) as compared with low temperatures (50-60 F). Action of sodium arsenite on both weeds and the turf species increases with increasing temperature. On occasions this chemical has produced abnormally large amounts of injury when frost or freezing occurs shortly after application. Yet crabgrass plants treated with sodium arsenite and followed with exposure to temperatures of 60, 75, and 85 F did not show a temperature response (Rumburg, Engel, and Meggitt, 1960b). Calcium arsenate has injured turf severely when applied just prior to periods of cold weather. This has been attributed to either increased action from accumulated soluble arsenicals or chemical interference with plant activities such as seasonal root growth. Temperature may affect herbicidal action directly in many ways other than penetration of the chemical into the plant. Indirect effects may be less conspicuous but very important. Temperature can change the stage of a plant's growth, reduce growth activity, or give changes in soil microorganisms. All of these can be important to herbicidal action. Soil organisms are most active in the range of 75-90 F and their influence on breakdown of chemical residues will be greatest in this temperature range.

B. Moisture Effects on the Chemical

Since most herbicides depend on water as a medium for the chemical reaction, a scarcity of water may slow or prevent herbicidal action. Moisture will also affect herbicidal action through its effect on temperature, chemical deterioration, leaching of the chemical, condition of the plant, and activity of soil organisms. Great differences in water relations in turf occur with both time and site. A canopy of turf growing with a good moisture supply may remain damp on the surface for very short or very long periods of time depending on cloud cover, wind, shade, humidity and temperature. Variations in amount or quantity of moisture in turf caused by rainfall and irrigation practice add to the diversity of moisture influences on herbicide action. The net influence of existing moisture conditions differs greatly with the chemical and its mode of action. Variations in moisture make it especially difficult to anticipate the herbicide's dissipation or movement from the surface and through the soil. Research on water-herbicide relationships has been limited. Both research (Monteith and Bengston, 1939) and experience shows that sodium arsenite treatment of turfgrass foliage loses considerable effectiveness if water is applied soon after treatment. In contrast, 2,4-D sprays need only very short rain- or irrigation-free periods to avoid loss of herbicidal action. Use of 2,4-D as a preemergent treatment has shown that rain may increase the effectiveness of the treatment by providing for the proper positioning of the chemical (Crafts et al., 1962a).

C. Factors Related to the Chemical that Influence Herbicidal Action

Losses of some chemicals after application are often rapid enough to reduce effectiveness. Such losses may arise from volatilization or leaching. The phenoxyacetic acid group include types that were purposely developed with high or low volatility. Leaching is commonly classified as a loss, but movement into the soil may be beneficial for some methods of control. Sodium chlorate is very readily leached. In the past this chemical was leached through the soil to reach the roots of deep-growing plants such as field bindweed *(Convolvulus arvensis).* While many herbicides are not leached easily, movement of the chemical over short distances may cause failure if the chemical moves out of the zone of maximum effectiveness. Light may cause chemical change and loss of some chemicals. In general, N- phenylureas should be washed off turfgrass leaves and into the turf cushion to avoid serious loss through light desensitization (Jordan et al., 1964). Chemicals with long soil life, which includes a number of preemergence types, accumulate in soil and this may require some adjustment in the year to year repetition of treatments. Lack of adjustment in herbicide schedules can result in residues that will impede the establishment of new turfgrass seedings. While dry carriers are preferred for preemergence herbicides, water carriers for herbicides have generally been more efficient for contact and systemic herbicides (Engel et al., 1967c). Formulations can vary greatly and affect the amount of herbicide retained on the plant surface (Ennis, Williamson, and Dorschner, 1952). The importance of concentration of the spray solution has been studied very little. In theory, precise quantities are considered more important for the contact spray treatments.

Time required for herbicide breakdown in soil varies from a few hours to years. The very quick hydrolyzation of potassium cyanate is a good example of quick breakdown. Organic compounds may persist in the soil until their energy material is attacked by the soil organisms (Burger, MacRae, and Alexander, 1962). The lower rates of 2,4-D are decomposed within 4 weeks in good soils that are warm and moist. In dry or frozen soils decomposition is much slower. The pH of the soil was reported earlier to affect the activity of arsenates. Acid soils with good moisture content give more rapid breakdown of 2,4-D. Also, soil texture will affect chemical-physical behavior of herbicides. Sandy soils with low organic matter show more rapid loss of the sodium salt of 2,4-D than other forms. In contrast, 2,4-D moves very slowly in a muck soil. While sandy soils permit greater leaching, they usually are not the safer soils. Their low colloidal content may increase herbicidal activity. Also the low organic matter content may discourage soil organism activity that is required for herbicide decomposition. With refinement in analytical techniques, the role of soil pH, mineral content, and colloidal nature can be investigated more thoroughly for their influence on herbicides.

D. Conditions of the Turfgrass or Weed Plant that Influence Herbicidal Action

Susceptibility to a herbicide will vary with genetic differences within weed and turfgrass species. In addition, various experiments may be distinguished by different varieties, ecotypes, and species of weeds and turfgrasses. Often this source of variation is ignored or test plants are not identified precisely. Such generalized common names as "crabgrass," "chickweed," "bentgrass," and "bermudagrass" are not specific enough to distinguish test plants. Ennis et al. (1952) showed that species influenced such simple responses as herbicide runoff. A great range of variability can occur within a species, as shown by the many varieties and ecotypes within creeping bentgrass (*Agrostis palustris*). Their susceptibility to 2,4-D varies greatly (Albrecht, 1947) and several types appear notably susceptible to the preemergence herbicide, siduron (Juska and Hanson, 1967). Among strains of common zoysia (*Zoysia japonica*). Meyer has good tolerance of triazines, while Midwest has poor tolerance (Engel et al., 1968a). Merion Kentucky bluegrass's intolerance for PMA provides another example of varietal difference within species. Variety and strain differences in maturity rate, waxiness, hairiness, rooting habit, physiology, and biochemical nature must be examined in relation to herbicide response.

Rooting habit of weeds and turfgrasses is important in the use of preemergence herbicides and other long-lasting herbicides that move slowly through the soil. Turfgrass roots may be relatively deep or superficially rooted near the surface, according to either species or growing conditions. Shallow root systems function largely in the surface layer of the soil, where herbicide treatment may be concentrated. Also, turfgrass species have cyclic periods of major root development and their root systems differ in degree of annual development, which increases the difficulty of evaluating a herbicide's safety. Since the relative positions of the roots and herbicide or its residue are difficult to predict, it is equally difficult to establish that a given preemergence treatment will or will not harm the roots. Root systems are most vulnerable to the presence of an herbicide or its residue during periods of maximum regeneration. Partial loss or restriction of the roots may not be manifest in topgrowth. The presence of rhizomes on the grass or weed will greatly reduce the chance for total kill of plants treated with a nonsystemic herbicide.

Stage of growth of weeds and turfgrass plants when treated with herbicides will influence results. Germination and seedling stages are periods of great susceptibility, while susceptibility tends to decrease as plants mature. In general, killing weeds in the seedling stage is not only easier, but also avoids problems associated with their unsightly appearance, their smothering effect on turfgrass plants, and the production of seed. Conversely, herbicide treatment of seedling turfgrasses may be undesirable because of their high sensitivity to damage. Complete loss of stand of turfgrasses is more common at this stage, because young plants have fewer resistant adventitious growth buds at the base of the plant and rhizomes have not developed. Eight- to ten-week-old turf, with the exception of the bentgrasses, has fair tolerance of 2,4-D (Schmidt and Musser, 1958). Dicamba, neburon, and 2,3,6-TBA have been applied without destroying 1-4 leaf stages of Kentucky bluegrass (Canode and Robocker, 1966). Benzonitriles have shown more promise than the phenoxyacetic acid derivatives in controlling broadleaf weeds in young turf with less injury to the young turfgrasses (Legg, 1967). Complete coverage of the foliage is difficult on dense growth of chickweed and other weeds. This can reduce the kill obtained with contact herbicides. In contrast, thin stands of weeds may be difficult to kill for very different reasons. It has been observed that scattered single crabgrass plants or those growing adjacent to a cement curb are more difficult to kill with PMA as compared with those growing closely together in a dense stand. It is suspected that increased vigor may account for the tolerance of scattered weed plants.

Nitrogen availability, moisture, light, temperature, mowing practice, and other environmental variables will determine the physiological condition of treated plants. Depending on the environment, the composition of plants might be described as ranging from high carbohydrate-low nitrogen ("hardened") to low carbohydrate-high nitrogen (soft, lush growth). Low nitrogen, low water, low temperatures, and/or high light intensity are factors that contribute to hardened growth. Some plants develop a degree of dormancy when nitrogen or water supply are very low or limiting. These growth conditions and the physiological status of plants influence results obtained with herbicides. For example, plants under drought stress do not translocate the phenoxy herbicides. In addition, 2,4-D is less effective on dandelions during cold weather or dry, hot periods when plants are dormant.

There are tremendous differences among weed species in periodicity of growth. Knotweed germinates promptly in late winter or early spring, while crabgrass and goosegrass may germinate throughout late spring and summer. The importance of this character was discussed with reference to preemergence weed control; but it, too, may complicate postemergence treatments. Some weeds develop and mature promptly as the season progresses, while others develop throughout the season, and at any one time the population may range from seedlings to mature plants. In general, determinate type plants are easier to control with either preemergence or postemergence herbicides.

X. The Concern and Nature of Turf Injury From Herbicides

Herbicides are becoming increasingly abundant and almost all turf weeds can be destroyed by chemicals. Improvements in herbicide usage have been made possible because new chemicals exhibit selectivity in controlling the weed without harming the turfgrass. Selectivity is the basis for more common use of herbicides. Unfortunately, herbicides with good selectivity are nonexistent for a small percentage, but still sizable numbers of turf weeds. Another major concern in weed control is avoidance of unnecessary injury to the turf. Concern for turfgrass injury involves the relative cover of turfgrasses and weeds. Often the herbicide must permit introduction of more turf into existing turf following treatment.

The decision to use a specific herbicide should be based on the degree of turf injury that is expected and that can be tolerated, as well as the need to destroy the weeds. There are circumstances where growers may elect to tolerate the weed rather than risk serious turfgrass injury. Turf injury may result from improper rate, lack of uniform application, and an inadequate selectivity margin of the herbicide. Temporary injury to turf cover is associated with other problems in addition to its detrimental effect on appearance. Removing a specific weed species can leave turf subject to invasion of other weeds until the cover of desirable grasses is restored. Thus, goosegrass may increase after crabgrass control (Engel et al., 1967b). Restoring a dense cover of desirable turfgrasses may be difficult in some seasons and following the use of certain chemicals that have pronounced residual effects. While long-lasting residues of herbicides are always of great concern in all plant culture, they present a special problem for turf with the absence of tillage. Some of the slow dissipating herbicides or those used repeatedly can result in serious accumulations in the surface of the soil that interfere with or prevent seed germination, root establishment, and the annual rerooting of the turfgrasses.

Recognition of turf injury from herbicides has lacked precision. Those herbicides that injure the turf on contact are the most easily recognized, the most sensational, and receive the most attention. This type of injury kills the foliage quickly and often occurs within the first few days. Such injury causes an unattractive turf and it may temporarily weaken the turfgrasses. Often the turfgrass recovers normal growth in a short time if growing conditions are favorable. However, the dead foliage may be a first stage in the death of the plant. The cause of rapid killing of the turfgrass foliage appears to vary from chemical activity that causes direct desiccation to more complex activity, such as destruction of enzyme systems. Most herbicides require more study of formative or destructive effects on the plant.

Restricted root development of turfgrasses has occurred where preemergence herbicides have been used (Engel and Callahan, 1967; Singh and Campbell, 1965; Bingham, 1967). The ease with which root injury can occur is shown by inhibition in development of bentgrass root tissue when galactose is present (Malca et al., 1965). A reduction in root development of the turfgrass does not mean loss of the grass, but disposes the grass to greater danger during periods of drought stress in either winter or summer. Also, injury to grass roots is thought to serve as a major route of entry for some root pathogens. Often a turf response from an interference with root development may not appear for some months after application of the herbicide. Reduced rhizome development of Kentucky bluegrass (Gaskin 1964) by preemergence herbicides may result from the same factors that interfere with rooting.

While herbicide interference with seed or flower development is a significant factor in controlling weeds, some herbicides can prevent or reduce flower development and seed set in turfgrasses. Maleic hydrazide, which was reported as injurious to bentgrass, is known to inhibit seedheads on annual bluegrass (Engel and Aldrich, 1960). Such chemicals as the phenoxyacetic acid derivatives, CIPC, dicamba, diuron, endothall, paraquat, and 2,3,6-TBA have been used in tests without indication of direct effects on the seed crop (Canode et al., 1967; Lee, 1965; Marth, 1947; Peabody and Austenson, 1965).

Physiological effects of herbicides on turf plants may be as numerous but on a lower order of magnitude as their effects on weeds. A change in cell pH produced by a chemical treatment has drastic effects on either function or plant survival. The role of arsenic in poisoning the sulfhydryl (-SH) enzymes (Bonner, 1950) was discussed previously. Future herbicides will have more sophisticated action on enzyme·systems which will require close concern for their safety to turfgrasses. Many of the physiological effects that herbicides may have when applied to turf are accompanied by indirect effects that influence the total growth of the desired grasses. This was exemplified by herbicidal rates of chlordane that occasionally gave a yellowing of the turf and developed a progressive thinning of turf after several seasons (Engel and Ilnicki, 1963). Part of this appeared to result from the physical condition of the soil, which seemed incapable of supporting normal growth and was undisturbed by earthworms. Depressed vegetative growth is the most subtle damage to turf from herbicide applications. Lower yields of barley and alfalfa caused by arsenic residues in soil were reported by Vandecaveye, Homer, and Keaton (1936). Clipping yields from one test of dicamba, mecoprop, and silvex on bentgrass turf cut to 3/4 inch showed that all three chemicals can cause major reductions in vegetative growth (Engel, 1966b). Small reductions in growth with some of the safer herbicides may go unnoticed in the absence of growth measurements. While this type of herbicide injury may not seem to be serious, it has the potential of contributing to secondary injury. However, physiological disturbances of turfgrass plants that reduce growth will be interrelated with other developments including the accumulation of reserve carbohydrates. These disturbances may be reflected in reduced root development (Juska and Hanson, 1961), increased susceptibility to certain diseases (Lukens, 1968), and poor survival during periods of stress. While most sod-forming grasses can recover rapidly from moderate injury, bare areas, including those caused by a herbicide, increase the opportunities for weed invasion. All degrees of turf injury from herbicide treatments can be self-defeating by encouraging additional weed problems.

XI. Turf Weed Problems of the Future

An evaluation of future problems must consider that several weeds, including goosegrass, sedges, and annual bluegrass, have not reached their maximum distribution. This poses a serious problem, as good herbicides or alternative methods of control do not exist for these and several other weed species.

Weed control in turf will become a more acute problem as turfgrasses are grown on poorer sites and subjected to increased traffic. This will increase the vulnerability of turf to weed invasion and to herbicide injury.

In the future, highly specific and selective herbicide treatments could be developed for each species of troublesome weed. Also, treatments will become more effective in coping with the great variation in conditions of herbicide use and variations in susceptibility of plant varieties and species.

The need for improved specificity in herbicide action will increase with the development of new turfgrass varieties. With pure stands of these more specialized turfgrasses, chemical controls will be desirable for many of the more agressive turf species which will behave as weeds on some sites.

Numerous developments will increase the need for knowledge of the herbicide's mechanism of action. Concern over residues from the long-lasting chemicals will increase. Herbicide use will become more precise, more complicated, and more valuable to turfgrass production.

Literature Cited

Anonymous. Feb. 26, 1954. Weed seeds in soil ACP Newsletter.

Albrecht, H. 1947. Strain differences in tolerance to 2,4-D in creeping bentgrass. J. Amer. Soc. Agron. 39:163-164.

Anderson, Burton R. and Stanley R. McLane. 1958. Control of annual bluegrass and crabgrass in turf with flurorophenoxyacetic acids. Weeds 6:52-58.

Anderson, J. C. and D. E. Wolf. 1947. Preemergence control of weeds in corn with 2,4-D. J. Amer. Soc. Agron. 39:341-342.

Audus, L. J., ed. 1964. The physiology and biochemistry of herbicides. Academic Press, N.Y. 555 pp.

Bach, M. K. 1961. Metabolites of 2,4-dichlorophenoxyacetic acid from bean stems. Pl. Phys. 36:558-565.

Bannerman, Lee W. 1953. A study of the effect of surface active agents on the efficiency of certain herbicides. Master's Thesis, Rutgers University, New Brunswick, N. J.

Bayer, D. E., C. L. Foy, T. E. Mallory and E. G. Cutter. 1967. Morphological and histological effects of trifluralin on root development. Amer. J. Bot. 54(8):945-952.

Bingham, S. W. 1967. Influence of herbicides on root development of bermudagrass. Weeds 15:363-365.

Biswas, P. K. and W. Hamilton. 1967. Degradation of trifluralin in sweet potato and peanut plants. Abst. 6th Int. Congr. Pl. Protect., Vienna. 388-389.

Bonner, J. 1950. Plant biochemistry. Academic Press, Inc. New York. 212.

Broadhurst, N. A., M. L. Montgomery and V. H. Freed. 1966. Metabolism of 2-methoxy-3,6-dichlorobenzoic acid (dicamba) by wheat and bluegrass plants. J. Agr. Food Chem. 14(a):585-588.

Buckholtz, K. P. 1958. The sensitivity of quackgrass to various chlorinated benzoic acids. WSSA Abst. p. 33-34.

Burger, K., I. C. MacRae, and M. Alexander. 1962. Decomposition of phenoxyalkylcarboxylic acids. Soil Sci. Soc. Am. Proc. 26:243-246.

Callahan, L. M. and R. E. Engel. 1965. Tissue abnormalities induced in roots of colonial bentgrass by phenoxyalkylcarboxylic acid herbicides. Weeds 13(4):336-338.

Callahan, L. M., R. E. Engel, and R. D. Ilnicki. 1968. Environmental influence on bentgrass treated with silvex. Weed Sci. 16:193-196.

Canode, C. L. and W. C. Robocker. 1966. Annual weed control in seedling grasses. Weeds 14(4):306-309

Canode, C. L. and W. C. Robocker. 1967. Chemical control of red sorrel in Kentucky bluegrass weed fields. Weeds 15(4):351-353.

Castelfranco, P. and M. S. Brown. 1962. Purification and properties of the simazine-resistance factor of *Zea mays*. Weeds 10:131-136.

Cockerham, S. T. and J. W. Whitworth. 1967. Germination and control of annual bluegrass. The Golf Course Supt. 35:10,14,17,45-46.

Crafts, A. S. 1961. The chemistry and mode of action of herbicides. Interscience Publishers, Inc., New York. 269 pp.

Crafts, A. S. and W. W. Robbins, 1962a. 1962b. 1962c. Weed control. 3rd Ed. McGraw-Hill Book Co., Inc., New York. p. 321, 308, 210.

Daniel, W. H. 1959. Weedy grass control with arsenicals. Midwest Turf 22.

Dybing, C. Dean, Jess L. Fults, and Roger M. Blouch. 1954. Chlordane, chlorobromopropene, and hexachlorocyclopentadiene for preemergence of crabgrass *(Digitaria sanguinalis* L.) and other annual grasses. Weeds 3:377-386.

Engel, R. E. 1966a. A comparison of colonial and creeping bentgrasses for ½—¾ inch turf. New Jersey Agric. Expt. Sta. Bul. 818. 45-48.

Engel, R. E. 1966b. Response of bentgrass turf to dicamba, mecoprop, and silvex herbicides. New Jersey Agric. Expt. Sta. Bul. 816. 85-92.

Engel, R. E. 1967. Temperatures required for germination of annual bluegrass and colonial bentgrass. Golf Course Supt. 20:20,23.

Engel, R. E. and R. J. Aldrich. 1952. Effectiveness of chemical combinations for crabgrass control. Proc. NEWCC 6:265-266.

Engel, R. E. and R. J. Aldrich. 1960. Reduction of annual bluegrass *Poa annua* in bentgrass turf by the use of chemicals. Weeds 8:26-28.

Engel, R. E. and L. M. Callahan. 1967a. Merion Kentucky bluegrass response to soil residue of preemergence herbicides. Weeds 15(2):128-130.

Engel, R. E. and J. H. Dunn. 1967b. Preemergence herbicides for control of goosegrass in cool-season turfgrasses for a series of tests over seven seasons. New Jersey Agric. Expt. Sta. Bul. 818. 93-111.

Engel, R. E., J. H. Dunn, and R. D. Ilnicki. 1967c. Preemergence crabgrass herbicide performance as influenced by dry vs. spray treatments and variation of application date of spring treatments on lawn turf. New Jersey Agric. Expt. Sta. Bul. 818. 112-121.

Engel, R. E., C. R. Funk, and D. A. Kinney. 1968a. Effect of varied rates of atrazine and simazine on the establishment of several zoysia strains. Agron. J. 60:261-262.

Engel, R. E. and R. D. Ilnicki. 1963. Injury to established turfgrasses from preemergence herbicides. Proc. NEWCC 17:493.

Engel, R. E., A. Morrison, and R. D. Ilnicki. 1968b. Preemergence chemical effects on annual bluegrass. The Golf Course Supt. 36:20-21.

Engel, R. E. and Dale E. Wolf. 1950. Wetting agents in chemical control of crabgrass. J. Amer. Soc. Agron. 42:360-361.

Ennis, W. B., R. E. Williamson, and K. P. Dorschner. 1952. Studies on spray retention by leaves of different plants. Weeds 1:274-286.

Fulwider, J. R. and R. E. Engel. 1959. The effect of temperature and light on germination of seed of goosegrass *(Eleusine indica)*. Weeds 7:359-361.

Funk, C. R., R. E. Engel, and P. M. Halisky. 1966. Performance of Kentucky bluegrass varieties as influenced by fertility level and cutting height. New Jersey Agric. Expt. Sta. Bul. 816. 7-21.

Gaskin, T. A. 1964. Effect of crabgrass herbicides on rhizome development in Kentucky bluegrass. Agron. Journ. 56:340-342.

Gorter, C. J. and W. van der Zweep. 1964. Morphogenetic effects of herbicides *in* "The physiology and biochemistry of herbicides" (L. J. Audus, ed.). Academic Press.

Graber, L. F. 1933. Competitive efficiency and productivity of bluegrass with partial defoliation at two levels of cutting. J. Am. Soc. Agron. 25:328-333.

Grigsby, B. H. 1951. The use of chlordane for the control of crabgrass. Michigan State Col. Quart. Bul. 34(2):158-161.

Gysin, H. and E. Knusli. 1960. Chemistry and herbicidal properties of triazine derivatives. *In* "Advances in pest control research" 3:289-358. R. L. Metcalf.

Hamilton, R. H. and D. E. Moreland. 1962. Simazine: degradation by corn seedlings. Science 135:373-374.

Hansen, Albert A. 1921. The use of chemical weed killers on golf courses. USGA Bul. 1:128-131.

Hilton, J. L. 1965. Inhibition of pantothenate biosynthesis by substituted benzoic acid. Weeds 13:267-271.

Hilton, J. L., J. S. Ard, L. L. Jansen, and W. A. Gentner. 1959. The pantothenate synthesizing enzyme, a metabolic site in the herbicidal action of chlorinated aliphatic acids. Weeds 7:381-396.

Hilton, J. L., L. L. Jansen, and H. M. Hull. 1963. Mechanism of herbicide action. Ann. Rev. Plant Phys. 14:353-378.

Humphreys, T. E. and W. M. Dugger. 1957. The effect of 2,4-dichlorophenoxyacetic acid on pathways of glucose catabolism in higher plants. Pl. Phys. 32:136-140.

Ilnicki, R. D. and C. F. Everett. 1961. The effects of several carriers of 2,4-D and its formulations on weed control and on the response of corn (Abst.) Proc. NEWCC 15:242.

Jordan. L. S., C. W. Coggins, Jr., B. E. Day and W. A. Clerx. 1964. Photodecomposition of substituted phenylureas. Weeds 12(1):1-4.

Juska, F. V. and A. A. Hanson. 1961. Effects of interval and height of mowing on growth of Merion and common Kentucky bluegrass. Agron. J. 53:385-388.

Juska, F. V. and A. A. Hanson, 1964. Effect of preemergence crabgrass herbicides on seedling emergence of turfgrass species. Weeds 12:97-101.

Juska, F. V. and A. A. Hanson. 1967. Factors affecting *Poa annua* L. control. Weeds 15:98-101.

Kelly, S. 1949. The effect of temperature on the susceptibility of plants to 2,4-D. Plant Phys. 24:534-536.

King, L. J. and J. A. Kramer. 1955. A review of the crabgrass, *Digitaria ischaemum* and *D. sanguinalis,* with notes on their preemergence control in turf. Proc. NEWC 359-363.

Klingman, G. C. 1961. Weed control as a science. John Wiley and Sons, New York. p. 169.

Leach, B. R. and J. W. Lipp. 1927. Additional experiments in grub-proofing turf. USGA Bul. 7:28.

Leaf, E. L. 1962. Metabolism and selectivity of plant-growth regulator herbicides. Nature 193:485-486.

Lee, William O. 1965. Herbicides in seedbed preparation for the establishment of grass seed fields. Weeds 13:293-297.

Legg, D. C. 1967. Selective weedkiller for use in young turf. J. of Sports Turf Res. Inst. 43:40-48.

Leopold, A. C. 1955. Auxins and plant growth. Univ. of California Press, Berkeley, Calif. p. 354.

Luckwill, L. C. and C. P. Lloyd-Jones. 1960. Metabolism of plant growth regulators I. 2,4-dichlorophenoxyacetic acid in leaves of red and black currant. Ann. Appl. Biol. 48:613-625.

Lukens, R. J. 1968. Low light intensity promotes melting out of bluegrass. Phytopath. 58:1058.

Malca, J. and R. M. Endo. 1965. Identification of galactose in cultures of *Sclerotinia homeocarpa* as the factor toxic to bentgrass roots. Phytopath. 55:775-780.

Marth, P. C. 1947. Yield and viability of Kentucky bluegrass seed produced on sod areas treated with 2,4-D. J. Amer. Soc. Agron. 39:426-429.

Marth, P. C. and J. W. Mitchell. 1944. 2,4-dichlorophenoxyacetic acid as a differential herbicide. Bot. Gaz. 106:224-232.

Menzie, C. M. 1966. Metabolism of pesticides. U.S. Dept. of Interior Special Scientific Report—Wildlife No. 96, Washington, D. C.

Monteith, J. and J. W. Bengston. 1939. Arsenical compounds for the control of turf weeds. Turf Culture 1(1):10-43.

Montgomery, M. L. and V. H. Freed. 1964. Metabolism of triazine herbicides by plants. J. Ag. and Food Chem. 12:11-14.

Moreland, Donald E. 1963. Mechanism of action of herbicides—contributions from studies with the photochemical reaction of isolated chloroplasts. Supp. to Proc. NEWCC 17:105-110.

Moreland, D. E. and K. L. Hill. 1962. Interference of herbicides with the hill reaction of isolated chloroplasts. Weeds 10:229-236.

Negi, N. S., H. H. Funderburk, Jr., D. P. Schultz, and D. E. Davis. 1968. Effects of trifluralin and nitralin on mitochondrial activities. Weed Science 16:83-85.

Pallas, J. E. 1960. Effects of temperature and humidity on foliar absorption and translocation of 2,4-D and benzoic acid. Plant Phys. 35:575-580.

Peabody, D. V. and H. M. Austenson. 1965. Herbicides and their effect on the yield of grass seed. Agron. J. 57:633-634.

Probst, G. W., Tomasz Golab, R. J. Herberg, F. J. Holzer, S. J. Parka, Cornelius Van Der Schans, and J. B. Tepe. 1967. Fate of trifluralin in soils and plants. J. Ag. and Food Chem. 15:592-599.

Ragab, M. T. H. and J. P. McCallum. 1961. Degradation of C^{14} labeled simazine by plants and soil microorganisms. Weeds 9:72-84.

Roberts, E. C., F. E. Markland, H. M. Pellet. 1966. Effects of bluegrass stand and watering regime on control of crabgrass with preemergence herbicides. Weeds 14:157-161.

Robbins, W. W., Crafts, A. S., R. N. Raynor. 1942. Weed control—A textbook and manual. McGraw-Hill Book Company, Inc. New York.

Robinson, R. J. 1949. Annual weeds and their viable seed population in the soil. Agron. J. 41:513-518.

Rumburg, C. B. 1958. The effect of environmental factors on the herbicidal activity and mode of action of selected arsenic compounds. Ph.D. Thesis, Rutgers University, New Brunswick, N. J.

Rumburg, C. B., R. E. Engel, W. F. Meggitt. 1960a. Effect of phosphorus concentration on the absorption of arsenate from nutrient solution. Agron. J. 52:452-453.

Rumburg, C. B., R. E. Engel, and W. F. Meggitt. 1960b. Effect of temperature on the herbicidal activity and translocation of arsenicals. Weeds 8:582-588.

Schery, R. W. 1965. Lawn seed, and what's a weed. Am. Hort. 44:71-83.

Schmidt, R. E. and H. B. Musser. 1958. Some effects of 2,4-D on turfgrass seedlings. USGA Journ. 11:28-32.

Scott, Robert. 1929. Preventing crabgrass seed. USGA Bul. 4:118-119.

Sharvelle, Eric G. 1948. Do turf treatments trouble turf? Midwest Turf Bul. 2(1):1-4.

Sheets, T. J. 1961. Uptake and distribution of simazine by oat and cotton seedlings. Weeds 9:1-13.

Shenefelt, Ray D. 1952. Residual effect of chlordane on crabgrass when applied to lawns for control of sod webworm. J. of Ec. Ent. 45:138.

Shimabukuro, R. H. 1967. Atrazine metabolism and herbicidal selectivity. Pl. Phys. 42:1269-1276.

Singh, R. K. N. and R. W. Campbell. 1965. Herbicides on bluegrass. Weeds 13:170-171.

Slade, R. E., W. G. Templeman, and W. A. Sexton. 1945. Plant growth substances as selective weed killers. Nature 155:497-498.

Smith, F. G. 1951. *In* "Plant growth substances" (F. Skoog, Ed.). Univ. of Wisconsin Press, Madison, Wisc. pp. 111-119.

Smith, M., H. Suzuki, and M. Malina. 1965. Development of analytical procedure for the analysis of dicamba metabolite. J. Asso. of Off. Agric. Chemists 48:1164-1169.

Splittstoesser, W. E. 1968. The effect of siduron upon barley root metabolism. Weed Science 16:344-347.

Splittstoesser, W. E. and H. J. Hopen. 1967. Response of bentgrass to siduron. Weeds 15:82-83.

Sprague, H. B. and G. W. Burton. 1937. Annual bluegrass *Poa annua* L. and its requirements for growth. New Jersey Agric. Expt. Sta. Bul. 630.

Sprague, H. B. and E. E. Evaul. 1930. Experiments with turfgrasses. New Jersey Agric. Expt. Sta. Bul. 497.

Sprague, M. A., R. D. Ilnicki, R. J. Aldrich, A. H. Kates, T. O. Evrard, R. W. Chase. 1962. Pasture improvement and seedbed preparation with herbicides. New Jersey Agric. Expt. Sta. Bul. 803. 72 pp.

Stanifer, L. C. Jr., L. W. Sloane, and M. E. Wright. 1965. The effects of repeated trifluralin applications on growth of cotton plants. Proc. SWC 18:92-93.

Stevens, O. A. 1932. The number and weight of seeds produced by weeds. Am. J. Bot. 19:784-794.

Sturkie, G. 1933. Control of weeds in lawns with calcium cyanamid. J. Am. Soc. Agron. 25:82-84.

Swanson, C. R. 1965. Metabolic fate of herbicides in plants. USDA Bul. ARS-34-36.

Switzer, C. M. 1957. Effects of herbicides and related chemicals on oxidation and phosphorylation by isolated soybean mitochondria. Plant Phys. 32:42-44.

Talbert, R. E. 1965. Effects of trifluralin on soybean root development. Proc. SWC 18:652.

Toole, E. H. and V. K. Toole. 1941. Progress of germination of seed of *Digitaria* as influenced by germination temperature and other factors. J. Agr. Research 63:65-90.

Vandecaveye, S. C., G. M. Homer, and C. M. Keaton. 1936. Unproductiveness of certain orchard soils as related to lead arsenate spray accumulations. Soil Sci. 42:203-213.

Wain, R. B. 1958. Relation of chemical structures to activity for 2,4-D type herbicides and plant growth regulators. Adv. Pest Cont. Res. 2:263-305.

Watson, J. R. 1950. Irrigation and compaction on established fairway turf. Ph.D. Thesis, Pennsylvania State University. pp. 42-48.

Welton, F. A. and J. C. Carroll. 1947. Lead arsenate for the control of crabgrass. J. Am. Soc. Agron. 39:513-521.

Welton, F. A. and J. C. Carroll. 1938. Crabgrass in relation to arsenicals. J. Am. Soc. Agron. 30:816.

Wilson, A. D. 1921. Killing chickweed with arsenite of soda. USGA Bul. 1:126-128.

Woodford, E. K., K. Hally, and C. C. McCready. 1958. Herbicides. Ann. Rev. of Pl. Phys. 9:311-358.

Wort, D. J. 1954. Influence of 2,4-D on enzyme systems. Weeds 3:131-135.

Wort, D. J. 1964. Effect of herbicides on plant composition and metabolism. *In,* "The physiology and biochemistry of herbicides" (Ed. L. J. Audus). Academic Press, N. Y. pp. 291-334.

Youngner, V. B. and E. J. Nudge. 1968. Chemical control of annual bluegrass as related to vertical mowing. Calif. Turfg. Cult. 18:17-18.

Zick, W. H. and T. R. Castro. 1967. Dicamba—dissipation in and on living plants. Bul. Velsicol Chemical Corp., Chicago, Illinois.

Zimmerman, P. W. and A. E. Hitchcock. 1942. Substituted phenoxy and benzoic acid growth substances and the relation of structure to physiological activity. Contrib. Boyce Thompson Inst. 12:321-343.

10 Turfgrass Diseases

M. P. Britton
University of Illinois
Urbana, Illinois

I. Introduction

Two kinds of disease occur in turfgrasses: *infectious diseases,* caused by fungi, bacteria, viruses, and nematodes; and *noninfectious diseases,* caused by nutritional deficiencies, unfavorable environmental conditions, mechanical injury, and genetic defects.

The major infectious diseases of turfgrasses are caused by fungi. There are some virus diseases of the grass species used for turf, but there is no evidence that they occur under turf conditions. Bacterial pathogens of turfgrasses are not an important part in the total disease picture. Bacteria are omnipresent on the surface of the grass leaves, sheaths, and roots. It is probable that future research might reveal bacteria or viruses as pathogens of turf species; our lack of information may be due primarily to lack of investigation. At any rate, the body of knowledge that has accumulated on turfgrass diseases is overwhelmingly concerned with the diseases that are caused by fungi.

Fungi are plants that lack chlorophyll and the ability to utilize the energy of light to manufacture carbohydrates from carbon dioxide and water. They are dependent upon a ready-made source of carbohydrate for their existence. Some of them are adapted to the utilization of the carbohydrates in dead organic matter exclusively, and these are known as saprophytes. Others live only on the living parts of plants, and these are called obligate parasites. Fungi that can adapt to either dead or living tissues are commonly called facultative parasites. The true saprophytes and the facultative forms that are saprophytic most of the time perform a very necessary function in destroying dead plants and animals that otherwise would accumulate on and in soil. When conditions are favorable, obligate and facultative parasites will attack healthy plants and cause diseases. The true saprophytes may enter into the disease picture as secondary invaders. In other words, they may enter the plant later in the stage of decay than the truly parasitic fungi and cause additional damage. Such fungi may be so numerous that the fungus originally responsible for the disease cannot be found or is found only at the advancing margin of the diseased area. The bacteria are important secondary invaders of decomposing plant tissue.

The obligate parasites are usually very well adjusted to living with the plants that are their hosts, at least in the early stages of infection. Often the pathogen does so little damage in the first few days after infection that the invaded cells seemingly function as well as the noninvaded ones. Later, usually when the fungus is producing reproductive spores, damage to the host tissues may be very great.

For the most part, fungi have an over-all structure composed of a much-branched system of thin tubes called a mycelium. The tubes are called hyphae and may or may not be divided into cells by cross walls, depending on the species. On nutrient agar in a petri dish mycelial strands tend to radiate out from a central point and the resulting colony is usually more or less circular in outline. A similar circular colony is formed by the fungi that form fairy rings or large brown patch. A mass of mycelium (colony) is easily seen with the naked eye, individual strands usually are barely visible without magnification. The coarse mycelial strands of the fungi causing dollar spot and brown patch are exceptions.

The mycelium of some fungi may be organized into a tissue of closely packed cells called a sclerotium. A sclerotium is a resting body that remains dormant during unfavorable conditions for growth. When favorable conditions occur the sclerotium may germinate. Germination can occur by the production of structures on which spores are formed or by the production of mycelium. A similar type of structure, the stroma, differs in that the mycelia are loosely arranged; spores are borne in or on it.

Specialized cells or structures are formed on the mycelium that serve to perpetuate the fungus. The most common of these structures are the asexual spores or conidia. Conidia are formed at the tips of specialized mycelial branches called conidiophores. Asexual spores are also produced in specialized fruiting structures. The conidia are usually quite different from the mycelial cells. The walls may be considerably heavier, darker in color and occasionally sculptured. Genetically, they are the same as the mycelium from which they were formed, and upon germination they give rise to another mycelium with the same characteristics as the one on which they were produced. In this way a fungus capable of attacking certain strains of grasses can be perpetuated indefinitely, without genetic changes, and therefore will not lose the ability to attack those strains of grasses.

Sexual spores are another type of reproductive body formed at certain times by most fungi. They differ from asexual spores in that they arise following the fusion of cells or nuclei, usually of different mycelial colonies, in other words, a mating of two fungi. During this process genetic material is recombined and redistributed in the sexual spores, thus the fungus colonies that arise from them are likely to be quite different genetically. Sexual spores may be formed in or on specialized masses of fungus tissue called fruiting bodies. The characteristics of the fruiting bodies are important in the identification of fungi, each species being somewhat different than the others.

The conidia of most fungi are easily detached from the conidiophore by splashing raindrops, wind, mechanical jarring (as in mowing), etc. Splashing raindrops, or droplets from sprinklers, will carry the conidia from the tissue on which they form to healthy tissues up to a foot or more away. Winds will carry some of the conidia for long distances.

Conidia often accumulate on mowers and other equipment and are then spread to healthy plants. This is most likely to happen when wet grass is mowed.

Most conidia are capable of germinating as soon as they are formed, if conditions in the vicinity of the spore are favorable. The temperature must be favorable and the conidium must be in contact with a film of water.

When the spore has become completely hydrated, a slender tube, called the germ-tube, is usually formed and extends out from the spore wall. Germ-tubes often emerge through specific locations on the spore wall called germ pores. The germ-tube grows haphazardly over the surface of the plant. It ceases to elongate when a favorable site for penetration into the plant is encountered. This may be a stomate in a leaf, the surface of an epidermal cell, or a fissue between the cells of some part of the plant. Each species of fungus usually enters through a specific site on the plant. Penetration may occur by the tip of the germ-tube growing into the plant through an open stomate or a wound. More commonly, when the tip of the germ-tube has encountered a suitable site for penetration, the tip enlarges into a structure called an appressorium. The appressorium serves to fasten the fungus to the host surface during the penetration process. Penetration is accomplished by the growth of a peg-like hypha from the bottom of the appressorium through the cell wall or stomatal opening.

The protoplasm of the spore migrates through the germ-tube as it grows and when the appressorium has formed, the entire protoplast of the spore moves into it. It is essential that moisture be present during the growth of the germ-tube and appressorium. If these structures dry out, the fungus will be killed. Following penetration, the mycelium of the fungus grows inside the host plant, spreading between the cells or penetrating into the cells. If the fungus penetrates into the cells of the host, the cells of the mycelium are in direct contact with the host protoplasm which is utilized for food.

Special absorbing organs called haustoria are formed by some fungi. Haustoria occur inside the cells of the host plant and are outgrowths of the mycelium that grows between the cells, or in some cases on the outside of the host plant. If the mycelium is entirely between the cells of the host, nutrients are absorbed through the host cell wall or membrane. In many cases, the host cells will have been killed, or the membranes destroyed, by toxins or other substances produced by the fungus. The toxins diffuse through the plant tissue in the vicinity of the mycelium, and the advance of the fungus mycelium is through the dead or dying cells. In such situations the zone of dead plant tissue is usually surrounded by a zone of chlorotic (yellowed) tissue.

II. Effect of Environmental Factors on Turfgrass Diseases

A. Climatic Factors

Temperature influences nearly every function of fungi. For each fungus there is a temperature above which it will not grow, the maximum temperature, and a temperature below which growth is prevented, the minimum temperature. A few fungi are capable of growth below 32 F, but most are restricted by temperatures between 32 and 40 F. The maximum temperature tolerated varies widely from about 75 to 122 F.

Most fungi reach an optimum growth rate quite near the maximum temperature and grow more and more slowly as the minimum temperature is approached. There is an optimum temperature for the production of spores as well as for growth of mycelium. The two optima may be different. The ability of most fungi to cause disease in grasses is temperature related. Studies by Endo (1963a) and Freeman (1960) show that the minimum temperature for the growth of *Pythium aphanidermatum* (Edson) Fitzpatrick, the cause of *Pythium* blight, is 50 F, the maximum slightly more than 95 F, and the optimum temperature for growth is near 90 F. Freeman (1960) showed that the fungus grew in the soil at 50 F, but did not infect the grass plants. At 67 F, grasses were infected and death of 50% of the plants occurred in 8 to 24 hours. As the temperature was increased, the time required for the fungus to kill 50% of the plants was reduced. Thus at 86 F, 4 to 8 hours were required and at 95 F only 2 to 4 hours. It is not known whether this is due solely to the effect of temperature or the growth rate and pathogenicity of the fungus. It is possible that high temperature might alter the metabolism of the host grasses so that they would be more susceptible to attack.

Strains of the same fungus species vary in their response to temperature. In California, Endo (1961a) reported low temperature and high temperature strains of *Rhizoctonia solani,* the cause of brown patch. The cardinal temperatures for the low temperature strain were a minimum below 40 F, optimum between 60 and 70 F, and a maximum near 90 F. This strain was pathogenic over a wide range of temperatures, 40 to 80 F, but killed the plants slowly and the optimum temperature for disease development was 60 to 70 F. The high temperature strain had a minimum of 40 F, an optimum near 80 F, and a maximum above 90 F. Plants were infected over a range from 60 to 90 F, but the damage was greatest at 80 to 90 F.

Moisture in the form of films or droplets on plant surfaces is necessary for the germination of most fungus spores. Spores are partially dehydrated during their maturation and they must absorb water before they can complete the germination process. Germination tubes of most fungi are thin-walled and in the absence of free moisture become rapidly dehydrated, and the protoplast of the germinating spore is killed. If germination results in the formation of motile zoospores, as in *Pythium* spp., free water is necessary as a medium in which the zoospores swim to suitable infection sites on the host plant.

The mycelia of fungi like *Sclerotinia homeoecarpa* (dollar spot) and *Rhizoctonia solani* (brown patch) can easily be seen in the early morning on wet leaf surfaces and in the guttation droplets on leaf tips. With the onset of drying conditions, they rapidly wither and disappear. Free moisture is necessary for their continued growth over the leaf surfaces.

Normally the moisture in the live tissues of an invaded host plant is sufficient to support the growth of the fungus pathogen. When the host plant tissues are killed, they tend to dry out, and further growth and sporulation of fungi in these dead tissues will be curtailed as long as the tissues remain dry, In many cases, the mycelium will survive in dry dead plant tissue in a dormant condition, and sporulation of the fungus will occur if the tissue is moistened.

Perhaps a less obvious role of water is that of an agent of dissemination of the fungus pathogen. Spores are splashed from their place of formation to growing plants by raindrops and droplets from sprinklers. Run-off water from rainfall or irrigation will carry spores, sclerotia, and perhaps mycelial fragments from one location to another. The streaking of *Pythium* blight toward low areas on putting greens is an example of such spread.

Too much water in the soil for prolonged periods of time is detrimental to growth and survival of grass roots. Plants that are damaged in this fashion may be less able to survive attacks of leaf and crown diseases.

Too little water may also increase disease damage. During drought periods diseased turfgrass plants often die. This is illustrated in the case of stripe smut in Kentucky bluegrass (Kreitlow and Myers, 1955; Hodges, 1967).

Couch et al. (1960) reported that significantly greater dollar spot development occurred on Kentucky bluegrass maintained with irrigation practices that allowed the plants to extract the soil moisture to 3/4 field capacity or below than when soil moisture was maintained near field capacity.

The humidity of the air exerts an influence on turfgrass disease occurrence in that free water cannot exist for long on plant surfaces unless the air is nearly saturated with water. High humidity usually exists at night and in the early morning hours. On cloudy days, the humidity remains high until late morning, and the wet leaf surface period is extended, thus prolonging conditions favorable for growth and penetration of fungus pathogens.

Light intensity is a factor in the occurrence of powdery mildew on Kentucky bluegrass. This disease is most abundant on grass in shaded areas. The reason for the increase in disease severity in shade is not known. However, healthy Kentucky bluegrass plants grown in shade do not grow as vigorously as plants in full sunlight (Gaskin and Britton 1962). In addition, temperatures tend to be lower in shaded areas and cooler temperatures tend to be accompanied by higher humidities.

Wind is a factor of great importance in disease occurrence. Spores of many fungi are disseminated widely by wind, especially the spores of fungi that cause rusts, smuts, and mildews. Air movement also facilitates evaporation of water from leaf surfaces and withering of mycelium of fungus pathogens on the plant surfaces. In locations where air movement is impeded by surrounding trees, shrubs, or topography, there will be a rapid rise in air temperature above that experienced in an exposed area. In addition, the air in these pockets tends to be more humid. Turfgrasses in such locations may be damaged more frequently by high temperature diseases than turfgrasses in exposed areas. In areas exposed to wind, the heated, moist air close to the turf is rapidly dissipated by mixing with the cooler, drier air above it.

The alkalinity or acidity of the soil influences the incidence of turfgrass disease primarily because of the effect pH has on the pathogen. The pH of the soil affects the growth and reproduction of some fungus pathogens directly. It may also act indirectly by affecting certain biological and chemical processes in the soil. For instance, the saprophytic soil organisms are affected differently by soil pH, and as the relative prevalence of various kinds of saprophytes may affect the prevalence and activity of pathogens, pH may influence disease development through its effect on the makeup of the soil microflora. The effects of pH on the occurrence of specific turf diseases have not been intensively studied in the field. However, the fungus *Ophiobolus graminis* Sacc. occurs primarily on grasses and cereals in coarse-textured alkaline soils (Dickson, 1956). Smith (1956, 1959a) in Great Britain, found that development of the *Ophiobolus* patch disease on turfgrasses was favored by the application of limestone. However, Gould et al. (1961) reported the occurrence of this disease in western Washington on turfgrass grown on soils with a pH of 6.0 to which lime had not been applied. Another indirect effect of soil pH on disease occurrence is that of determining the availability of nutrient elements to plants. In alkaline soils, phosphate, calcium, iron, and manganese may be present in insoluble forms and, therefore, unavailable to plants. Couch et al. (1963) found that the availability of calcium, particularly a deficiency of calcium, had a pronounced influence on increasing the proneness of Highland bentgrass to *Pythium* blight.

B. Management Factors

The management practices necessary to the maintenance of turf have a decided effect on disease incidence and development. Most cultural practices exert an indirect effect on disease development by modifying certain factors of the micro-environment that in turn affect disease incidence. Others are directly involved with disease development or with the severity of damage caused by disease. These effects are abundantly illustrated by the basic turf management practice—mowing.

Within limits, as the height of cut is lowered greater numbers of smaller plants occur in an area. The individual plants are crowded closely together causing *1*) a greater degree of shading of the soil surface and *2*) a greater restriction of air movement in the plant zone than would be found in unmowed situations. These conditions would tend to extend the wet period necessary for disease initiation.

On putting greens, the individual plants are very small, and attack by a fungus pathogen may involve an entire leaf and sheath in a very short time. The same infection on an unmowed plant of the same species might result in only a spot on a leaf blade.

The wounds caused by mowing constitute the primary avenue of entry for some of the most important turf pathogens (Couch et al. 1966; Rowell, 1951). On putting greens, cut leaf tips are close together, and mycelial bridging from one leaf tip to another by fungi is an important means of spread from infected plants to adjacent healthy ones. At a higher cut there are fewer cut leaf tips in close proximity, and bridging from one to another is more limited. A commonly observed illustration of this is provided by the occurrence of half circles of brown patch at the edge of bentgrass putting greens. The disease occurs on the closely clipped bentgrass and does not spread into the same variety of bentgrass mowed at a higher cut on the collar of the green.

The spores of some fungi are readily dislodged by the mower. Spores, mycelia, and infected leaf fragments adhere to mowing equipment and are then spread to healthy plants. This is more likely to happen if the grass is mowed when it is wet. Under dry conditions the dislodged spores are caught by air currents and are carried by winds to other plants.

Mowing can be beneficial. In the case of fungi that attack plants primarily through the cut leaf tips such as *Rhizoctonia solani, Fusarium* spp. and *Curvularia* spp., infections usually do not progress very rapidly down to the meristematic tissue at the base of the leaf. Therefore, once the disease is controlled, the diseased portion of the leaf is pushed upward by basal growth of the leaf and is removed by mowing. Thus in 2 to 3 weeks, or less in light attacks, the damaged leaf tissue is removed and the affected areas are healed.

The application of fertilizer to turfgrass if properly done is beneficial in that it stimulates the desired level of growth needed for a particular use. The application of fertilizer elements to turfgrass will not change the inherent susceptibility or resistance of the grasses to diseases. However, the severity of the disease attack on a susceptible host may be greater under certain levels of fertility than others. Couch and Bloom (1960), Bloom and Couch (1960), and Moore et al. (1963) reported that the changed disease proneness of susceptible turfgrasses is probably not due to a single nutritional factor but rather to a combination of environmental factors including fertility.

The application of fertilizer may increase disease severity by making growth conditions more favorable for the pathogen. Glutamine is an abundant constituent of turfgrass guttation fluids formed after fertilization with readily soluble nitrogen fertilizers (Curtis, 1944; Healy, 1967). The glutamine in the guttation droplets is used by *Helminthosporium sorokinianum* to develop multiple infection structures, the result being increased leaf spot infection on creeping bentgrass (Healy, 1967). Other workers have suggested that other organic constituents of guttation fluids also may enhance disease development on close-cut turf by providing nutrients for the saprophytic growth of the pathogens on the host surface (Endo, 1963; Rowell, 1951).

Recovery from disease damage is dependent upon regrowth of the plants to replace the killed tissues. The beneficial effect of high nitrogen fertility in avoiding severe dollar spot damage is probably the result of rapid growth of the grass during periods of reduced activity of the pathogen (Couch and Bloom, 1960). Early recommendations for treatment of brown patch damage stress the need for nitrogen and light topdressing immediately after damage to promote regrowth of the grass in affected areas (Oakly, 1924, 1925; Monteith, 1925). Such recommendations would not be generally applicable today as nitrogen fertility is maintained at a considerably higher level.

Maintenance practices that prevent or limit the development of thick layers of thatch on the soil surface are largely beneficial to disease prevention. Some turf pathogens like *R. solani* and *Fusarium* spp. grow saprophytically in the thatch. Other pathogens, including *Helminthosporium* species, produce spores on the dead material in the thatch layer (Healy and Britton, 1968). Mechanical removal of the thatch layer is beneficial in eliminating much of the material that could be used by fungi.

The benefits derived from the addition of nonsterilized soil and composted topdressing materials are perhaps not as obvious, but they may be equally important in limiting disease occurrence. Such topdressings contain a wide range of beneficial bacteria and fungi that hasten thatch decomposition. Also, organisms that are antagonistic to pathogenic fungi are replenished. The physical action of burying some of the leaves with soil would mechanically prevent spores from being dispersed; and most spores do not survive for long in moist soil.

Syringing, the application of a small quantity of water to turfgrass, if properly done, can result in lowered disease incidence on putting greens. Syringing in the early morning will wash the guttation droplets from leaf tips. Two things that tend to reduce disease development are accomplished since 1) the grass dries more quickly once the droplets are dispersed and 2) the guttation fluids and the glutamine and other organic materials in it are washed from the grass plant into the soil and thatch. Mechanical methods of guttation drop removal promote drying but distribute the fluids over the surfaces of the leaves where the constituents can be used for the growth of pathogens.

Syringing putting greens during midday, where restricted air movement allows high temperatures to develop in the turf, can lower the maximum temperature reached in the turf (Duff and Beard, 1966). It should be practiced with considerable discretion. Great benefit in disease prevention by the limited temperature lowering is not likely, and indiscriminate syringing can produce moisture saturation of the turf and increased disease development.

III. Control of Turfgrass Diseases

The professional turfgrass manager and those persons who give advice to the general public should know how to recognize the turf diseases that occur in their locality. Recognition should be based on knowledge of the symptoms exhibited by grasses and signs of the pathogen. However, the kind of grass, the time of year that the disease occurs, and the prevailing weather conditions are helpful in diagnosis.

Many turf diseases are endemic to a region and occur year after year when conditions favor the pathogen. The occurrence of these diseases can be anticipated, and some of them can be avoided by the selection of turfgrass species that are immune or varieties that are resistant to the disease. The damage from most diseases can be kept to a minimum by adherence to correct cultural practices and the judicious use of fungicides.

A. Resistant Varieties

There are a great many degrees of disease resistance in plants. An immune plant is one that is not attacked by a particular pathogen. A susceptible plant is one that is severely damaged by disease. Resistant plants are intermediate in reaction. A highly resistant plant may exhibit slight development of the disease under ideal conditions for development; a slightly resistant plant may be almost as severely damaged as the fully susceptible ones. Varieties of plants that are considered highly resistant or immune in certain areas because no disease attacks have been observed may prove to be more susceptible in other areas. This may be because of more favorable environmental conditions for disease development or the presence of genetically different races of the pathogen. The determination of the degree of resistance of a new variety should be accomplished with greenhouse inoculations under ideal conditions for the pathogen, and should be supplemented by field testing at many locations throughout the country. Claims of resistance for new turfgrass varieties that have not been so tested should be viewed with a certain degree of skepticism.

B. Cultural Practices

The primary cultural practices that affect disease incidence on turf are those that involve mowing, watering, and, to a lesser extent, soil fertility or fertilizer use. In general, the chances for disease damage are increased as the height of mowing is decreased and as the use of water and fertilizer is increased. The cultural operations followed in the maintenance of turf are dictated by the intended use of the area, and the degree to which they can be modified to minimize disease incidence is limited but important.

C. Fungicides

Fungicides are chemicals that are used to destroy fungus pathogens or to render them incapable of further growth. Most fungicides are designed to prevent the pathogen from infecting the host plant. This may be accomplished in several ways such as (1) the destruction of spores, mycelia, and sclerotia in the soil or thatch, reducing the likelihood of disease initiation; (2) the application of protective sprays and dusts on the plant surfaces that destroy the pathogens present and, through residual action, prevent infection by pathogens subsequently deposited on them; and (3) the application of systemic fungicides that prevent infection. The latter type may also eradicate fungi that have become established in the host plant. Some of the newer systemic fungicides show considerable promise in controlling some of the turfgrass pathogens.

Turfgrass fungicides are formulated primarily as wettable powders. In these, the active ingredient is carried on finely ground clay materials so treated with adjuvants that they are easily suspended in water. Excellent coverage of exposed plant surfaces is obtained with such formulations. Special materials that stick the particles to leaves are used in these formulations. During subsequent re-wetting of the leaves by dew or light showers, some redistribution of the active ingredient occurs; however, this movement is usually not sufficient to protect the new growth of leaves. Some of the fungicide is removed by mowing; some is washed from the leaves. There is also a loss in effectiveness by degradation of the active ingredient. Therefore, fungicides must be applied periodically to keep leaf surfaces adequately protected. Part of the fungicide is deposited in the thatch and upper soil layer, especially if it is applied with a lot of water. Benefit can be expected from this because of the destruction of inoculum. However, since many beneficial organisms may also be destroyed, some thought should be given to replenishing them through topdressing with nonsterilized soil or compost. Emulsifiable concentrates are formulated with various liquid organic solvents that contain special adjuvants that make them miscible in water. Such formulations perform essentially in the same manner as the wettable powders and provide excellent coverage of plant surfaces.

Fungicides incorporated on granules do not provide much protection to plant surfaces. Most of the granules are deposited on or in the thatch layer. Granular materials are effective in the control of organisms that make some saprophytic growth in the thatch as in the case of snow mold caused by *Typhula itoana* and *Fusarium nivale*. In addition, they may reduce the production of spores of leaf-infecting pathogens in the thatch.

In general, dust formulations are not used on turfgrass. They are disagreeable to apply and usually do not provide as complete coverage as wettable powders and emulsifiable concentrate formulations.

There are a number of excellent fungicides for use against diseases of turfgrasses. In selecting fungicides, one should keep in mind that a product may give effective control of a disease in an area where conditions for disease development are mild and fail to control the same disease in another area where conditions favor severe disease development. The decision to use a particular material should be based on tests that have been conducted locally. Instructions for the use of fungicides are placed on the label by the manufacturer. These should be read carefully and followed. A list of diseases for which control can be expected when the fungicide is properly used is also included on the label.

IV. Important Turfgrass Diseases

A. Various Diseases

BROWN PATCH

PATHOGEN: *Rhizoctonia solani Kuhn (Pellicularia filamentosa* (Pat.) D. P. Rogers

HOSTS: Annual bluegrass, bahiagrass, bermudagrass, centipedegrass, colonial bentgrass, creeping bentgrass, Italian ryegrass, zoysiagrass, Kentucky bluegrass, perennial ryegrass, red fescue, redtop, rough bluegrass, St. Augustinegrass, tall fescue, velvet bentgrass and others.

Occurrence:

Brown patch is important at times in nearly all of the U.S. and Canada. It is most prevalent in midsummer in the southern part of the cool-season grass region and in the southern states. The disease rarely occurs in regions with cool summers such as the coastal region of the Pacific Northwest (Gould, 1963). In the northern states it is particularly destructive to bentgrasses (Monteith and Dahl, 1932). Kentucky bluegrass is seldom damaged severely, and for some time was thought to be immune (Oakley, 1924; Monteith, 1926; Piper and Oakley, 1921). Annual bluegrass, rough bluegrass, the various fescues, and the ryegrasses are moderately susceptible. Brown patch is a serious disease of all the major grasses used for turf in the South (Freeman, 1967). St. Augustinegrass and Japanese lawngrass are somewhat more susceptible than bermudagrass, centipedegrass, and bahiagrass. In the South the disease is particularly active in the spring and fall months (Zummo and Plakidas, 1958).

Symptoms:

Brown patch occurs in more or less circular areas varying from a few inches to several feet in diameter (Fig. 1). The infected portions of the plants are first water-soaked and dark-colored, they then wilt and become light-brown as the tissue dies. Generally, not all of the plants in an area are infected. In closely mowed grass, the color of the area is determined by the proportion of healthy to diseased leaves. In early stages of development, when only a small number of leaf blades have been killed, a patch may be largely green with only a slight discoloration marking the outline of the diseased area. If the disease is allowed to progress, the number of killed leaves in the affected area will increase and impart a distinctly brown appearance. Eventually, all leaves in the area may be killed. In the early morning when the grass is wet, an affected area that is rapidly enlarging laterally is often ringed

Figure 1. Brown patch *(Rhizoctonia solani)* caused this injury to St. Augustinegrass turf.

by a narrow zone of dark-colored, recently-infected grass. Hyphae of the pathogen are often abundant on the darkened leaves. The hyphae and the dark ring disappear rapidly with the onset of drying conditions; i.e., wind and sunlight; but on cloudy, humid days they may be seen at midday.

Close examination of individual plants of creeping bentgrass reveals that infections vary from partial destruction of leaf blades to complete killing of the plant. Usually the infection is confined to the leaves and sheaths, and diseased areas recover their green color rapidly by regrowth of leaves once the disease has been stopped (Monteith, 1926).

On some of the coarse grasses, limited infections may appear on the sheaths as elliptical light-colored eye spot lesions with brown borders (Sprague, 1950). On St. Augustinegrass the rotting of leaf sheaths may progress inward, and in such cases entire leaf fasicles can be pulled from the plant with little effort (Zummo and Plakidas, 1958). Where the grass is thinned, a root and stem rot is usually evident. Freeman (1967) points out that centipedegrass is subject to attacks that involve only the leaf blades. The light tan lesions may traverse the leaf blade, killing the distal portion.

Disease Development:

Rhizoctonia solani survives periods of conditions unfavorable for growth as sclerotia in the thatch or the upper layers of soil. The sclerotia can germinate over a range of temperature from 46 to 104 F. The optimum temperature for germination is about 80 to 85 F (Dahl, 1933b). The fungus is present in most soils, especially acid ones. It is capable of saprophytic growth in the soil (Kerr, 1956) and also invades the roots of a great many grasses causing a mild root necrosis (Sprague, 1950; Endo, 1961; Britton and Rogers, 1963; Lukens and Stoddard, 1961). Practically nothing is known of the importance of such infections.

When a sclerotium germinates, hyphae grow out from its surface (Dickinson, 1930). These proliferate and grow radially to form a roughly circular colony in the upper portion of the soil or thatch. During warm, humid conditions, when grass plants are wet, the fungus hyphae grow up onto the leaves and sheaths of the grass plants. In closely clipped bentgrass turf, hyphae gain entrance into the leaves mainly through the cut ends of the leaves (Rowell, 1951). Entry through stomates also occurs, in which case penetration is preceded by the formation of appressoria (Monteith, 1926; Dodman et al., 1968). Stomatal penetration is common on coarse grasses where discrete spots result. After entry into the leaf, the hyphae grow between the leaf cells, rapidly ramifying throughout the tissue until the leaf is filled with mycelium (Monteith, 1926). The contents of the cells oozes out into the intercellular spaces; the leaf becomes watersoaked, and dark in color. Leaves in this condition are killed rapidly when exposed to sunlight or drying wind, and they shrivel and turn brown as cells collapse.

Leaf infection of susceptible grasses occurs in the range of 73-90 F; however, disease development is more severe at 80 to 85 F. Hot weather is brown patch weather; minimum temperatures are usually high (near 70 F), as are the maximum temperatures (near 90 F). Thus, average daily temperatures fall within the range at which infection occurs (Dahl, 1933a).

Saprophytic growth of *R. solani* on plant surfaces occurs only with free moisture and high humidity, and moisture must be present before the fungus can parasitize the grass. Rowell (1951) reported that guttated water was much more effective in stimulating the occurrence of brown patch than water from rain or sprinkler irrigation. Hyphae of the pathogen commonly grow from one guttation droplet to another on the tips of leaf blades, and masses of mycelium can often be found in the droplets. The nutrients in guttated water contribute to the rapid saprophytic growth of the pathogen near the site of penetration. It has long been known that removal of guttation droplets in the early morning by watering or mechanical means has been effective in reducing the occurrence and severity of brown patch.

The humidity of the air exerts an influence on brown patch in that free water cannot exist for long on the leaf surfaces unless the air is nearly saturated with water. These conditions usually occur at night and in the early morning hours. This is when brown patch areas are actively enlarging laterally. On cloudy days, the humidity remains high later in the morning, extending the wet period, and thus prolonging the conditions necessary for further infection. Once the humidity of the air has been lowered sufficiently to allow the moisture to evaporate, further spread of the fungus from plant to plant is checked.

Control:

The frequency and severity of brown patch can be materially lessened by providing surface and subsurface drainage that rapidly removes the excess water from irrigation or heavy rainfall (Dickenson, 1930; Dahl, 1933c, 1933d). Bloom and Couch (1960) showed that the moisture content of the soil within the range readily available to plants did not alter susceptibility to brown patch.

An abundance of readily available nitrogen in the soil often results in greater frequency and severity of brown patch if other conditions are favorable for the disease. Data presented by Bloom and Couch (1960) indicate that this is not because of an increase in plant vigor or succulence. They proposed that particular combinations of nitrogen with other elements and pH, in some manner, change the proneness of plants to infection. It is possible that the increase in brown patch severity following applications of soluble nitrogen may be caused by a higher concentration of nitrogenous materials in the guttated water which would promote greater saprophytic and parasitic activity of *R. solani.* A number of fungicides give excellent control of this disease.

DOLLAR SPOT

PATHOGEN: *Sclerotinia homeoecarpa* F. T. Bennett

HOSTS: Annual bluegrass, bahiagrass, bermudagrass, centipedegrass, colonial bentgrass, creeping bentgrass, Italian ryegrass, Kentucky bluegrass, red fescue, redtop, sheep fescue, St. Augustinegrass, velvet bentgrass, and zoysiagrass.

Occurrence:

Dollar spot on turfgrasses has been reported from Canada, most of the U.S. and the British Isles. It apparently does not occur in the coastal region of the Pacific Northwest (Gould, 1963). It is a common disease of bentgrass putting greens and Kentucky bluegrass and fine-leaf fescue lawns in the northern regions of North America (Couch and Bloom, 1960; Couch and Moore, 1960). In the South, bermudagrass, zoysia, and bahiagrass are severely affected by dollar spot (Freeman, 1967).

Symptoms:

The name, dollar spot, was derived from the usual occurrence of dead, bleached spots in bentgrass putting green turf about the size of a silver dollar (Fig. 2). The spots rarely enlarge beyond that size; however, if not controlled with fungicides, they may become so numerous that the individual spots overlap to produce large, irregular areas of dead turf. In the early morning, while the grass is wet, wisps of the white mycelium of the causal fungus may be observed on diseased turf. The mycelium dries and disappears as the sun and wind dry the grass blades. The mycelium may persist for some time beneath the sheaths (Endo, 1961).

On turf maintained at a higher cut, the diseased areas of turf tend to be significantly larger with occasional spots being 10 or 12 inches in diameter. Damage caused by *S. homeoecarpa* is readily distinguished from most other turfgrass disorders by the presence of characteristic lesions on the leaf blades of plants at the margin of the affected areas. The lesions are light tan and have a reddish brown border. Some extend downward from the leaf tip, and may be an inch or so in length. Isolated lesions on leaves are shorter. They usually extend completely across the blades of Kentucky bluegrass. The lesions tend to occur along the margin of blades of coarser grasses (Freeman, 1967). Infection of culms and leaves of unmowed bermudagrass and bahiagrass has been reported (Bain, 1962; Gudauskas and McGlohon, 1964). Roots and rhizomes were not attacked.

Figure 2. Injury to bermudagrass turf from dollar spot *(Sclerotinia homoecarpa)*.

Disease Development:

Sclerotinia homeoecarpa survives periods of unfavorable conditions as sclerotia. The sclerotia are black and occur as paper-thin flakes. They usually germinate by resuming mycelial growth. Occasionally conidia and cupulate spore-bearing structures (apothecia) are formed, but they are not thought to be of much importance in disease development.

According to Monteith and Dahl (1932) the pathogen gains entry into the plant via the cut leaf tips and through stomates when the plant surfaces are wet. Endo (1966) has observed appressorium formation, and it is probable that stomatal invasion is accomplished after the formation of appressoria. The invaded tissues are first water-soaked and dark-colored, becoming bleached-tan when dry. If the disease is checked shortly after infection occurs, only the leaf blades are affected, and the turf quickly recovers if it is growing rapidly. If the disease is not controlled the fungus will kill the infected plants, and healing of the diseased turf areas is much slower.

Primary roots of creeping bentgrass in quartz sand culture are damaged by a toxin produced by *S. homeoecarpa* (Endo, 1963a; Endo et al, 1964; Endo and Malca, 1965). The roots are not invaded by the fungus. The toxin destroys the apical meristem and cortical tissues of the root. A similar deterioration of roots of creeping bentgrass is caused by D-galactose, but it is not known if D-galactose is the toxic principle (Malca and Endo, 1965). Endo and Malca (1965) report that similar root damage has been observed following advanced foliar infection in the field. They suggest that the marked reduction in length and number of roots of cool season turfgrasses may be caused, in part, by toxic compounds from decomposing plant debris and microorganisms.

The fungus is capable of mycelial growth over a wide range of temperatures (50 to 90 F), and is pathogenic to grasses between 60 and 80 F. Disease development is usually most rapid between 70 and 80 F; however, strains of the fungus vary in their response to temperature (Bennett, 1937; Freeman, 1967).

A high incidence of dollar spot has been noted in seasons with low rainfall (Howard et al., 1951; Smith, 1955). Couch and Bloom (1960) demonstrated experimentally that low soil moisture levels increased the disease proneness of Kentucky bluegrass to *S. homeoecarpa*.

The incidence of dollar spot is lower on turfgrasses maintained with adequate nitrogen than on turf grown with a deficiency of nitrogen (Monteith, 1929, Endo, 1966). Monteith and Dahl (1932) suggested that an adequate supply of readily available nitrogen enabled the grass to recover quickly from attacks of dollar spot. Couch and Bloom (1960) reached a similar conclusion when their investigation revealed that Kentucky bluegrass was less susceptible to *S. homeoecarpa* at low nitrogen levels than at normal levels. Endo (1966) noted that washed mycelia of *S. homeocarpa* made little growth in sterile water on green leaves and did not infect them unless guttation fluid or 0.5% sucrose was added with the mycelia. Growth of the fungus was vigorous on yellow senescent leaves, and infection occurred on them readily in sterile water. The data indicate that *S. homeoecarpa* requires a food base for saprophytic growth and infection. Endo (1966) suggests that plants lacking nitrogen are more likely to supply the required food base in the form of senescent or dead foliage than plants receiving adequate nitrogen.

Control:

Dollar spot is not a disease that destroys grass quickly, especially if adequate nitrogen fertility is provided and if the soils are maintained near field capacity by irrigation. Under these conditions, attacks are usually mild and damaged leaves are mowed off and replaced quickly once the disease has been controlled with fungicides. Several fungicides give adequate control, and the cadmium compounds have generally given excellent control with a fairly long residual effect.

RED THREAD

PATHOGEN: *Corticium fuciforme* (Berk.) Wakef.
HOSTS: Annual bluegrass, bermudagrass, colonial bentgrass, creeping bentgrass, Kentucky bluegrass, perennial ryegrass, red fescue, velvet bentgrass, and others.

Occurrence:

Red thread is an important disease of turf in northern Europe, England, and North America. In the U.S. it is important on red fescue, bentgrasses, and Kentucky bluegrass in the northeastern states and in the Pacific coastal states (Muse and Couch, 1965; Gould et al., 1967; Sprague, 1950; Endo, 1963a). In these regions it occurs primarily in the early spring and fall during cool, wet weather. It has also been reported on bermudagrass lawns in Mississippi during December (Filer, 1966).

Symptoms:

The fungus forms coral-pink, thinly gelatinous masses on leaves and sheaths of grass plants. The gelatinous stromata are joined together by a pink web of mycelium. The fungus growth is very conspicuous when the grass is wet. The gelatinous masses are formed of strands of branched hyphae that are bound together by the fusing of branches and by the gelatinous walls. They often extend from the tips of leaves as coral-pink appendages. These are usually pointed but may be branched. The stromata harden when they dry. Basidia and basidiospores are borne on the surface of the mycelial masses. The affected areas are usually more or less circular and vary in diameter from a few inches to a foot or more. The leaves and often the sheaths are killed. The infected leaf tissue is first watersoaked, but rapidly dies and becomes light-tan when dry.

Disease Development:

The pathogen survives unfavorable conditions as fragments of dried stroma and as dormant mycelium in the residues of diseased plants. The stroma resume growth and mycelia penetrate the leaves through stomata. Basidiospores are produced on the stroma in abundance, but they are probably not too important in the spread of the pathogen (Couch, 1962).

The pathogen spreads from plant to plant by mycelial growth from the gelatinous masses on infected leaves. Fragments of dried stroma may be carried by wind or mechanically on mowers, etc.

Corticium fuciforme is capable of growing over a wide range of temperature (Erwin, 1941; Endo, 1963a). Growth occurs from slightly above 32 F to about 86 F. Optimum temperature for growth in culture was between 60 and 70 F. Filer (1966) reported that the disease developed when soil temperatures were between 40 and 54 F, but ceased when the temperature dropped to 32 F. Sprague (1950) indicated that the disease occurred with *Fusarium nivale;* and Gould et al. (1967) reported that the disease was serious only when the grass was growing slowly because of cool temperature or because it was under-fertilized with nitrogen.

Control:

A number of fungicides give adequate control of red thread when the turf is properly fertilized.

PYTHIUM BLIGHTS

PATHOGENS: *Pythium aphanidermatum* (Edson) Fitzpatrick and *Pythium ultimum* Trow.

HOSTS: Annual bluegrass, bermudagrass, colonial bentgrass, creeping bentgrass, Italian ryegrass, Kentucky bluegrass, perennial ryegrass, tall fescue, red fescue, redtop, rough bluegrass, velvet bentgrass, and many others.

Occurrence:

Pythium blight is primarily a disease of cool season grasses (Moore and Couch, 1961). Freeman and Horn (1963) found that only bermudagrass, of 28 varieties of the various warm-season grasses tested, was susceptible to attack by *P. aphanidermatum.* Injury to bermudagrass was slight when compared to damage on cool-season grasses. During winter months in the southern states, the disease is a serious problem on putting greens overseeded with ryegrasses. In the northern states, the disease occurs during the hottest periods of summer. Under favorable environmental conditions for the development of *Pythium* blight, entire stands of both seedling and mature grass can be destroyed in a few hours.

Symptoms:

On closely-mowed creeping bentgrass turf, *Pythium* blight appears as a circular spot varying in diameter from less than an inch to several inches; most are less than 2 inches in diameter. In the early morning, the infected plants are water-soaked and dark-colored, and a cottony growth of mycelium is usually abundant on matted leaves in diseased areas. With the onset of drying conditions the mycelium disappears and the grass blades dry and become reddish brown. The diseased spots often are clustered so that their margins coalesce and large irregular areas of turf are killed. Often the killed areas occur as long streaks a foot or so wide, apparently the result of the spread of spores from an initial point of infection by either running water or mowing equipment.

The over-all damage to Kentucky bluegrass and other turfgrasses mowed at lawn height is similar to that on putting greens. However, the individual spots of infected grass tend to be somewhat larger. At the margins of the affected areas, plants can usually be found with leaves that are only partially blighted. The individual lesions on leaves are straw-colored and resemble dollar spot lesions, but unlike the latter they do not have reddish brown margins. Oospores form in dead tissue and can be seen by microscopic examination.

Disease Development:

Both species of *Pythium* are capable of surviving as soil saprophytes and as root parasites of turfgrasses (Endo, 1961; Kraft et al., 1967; Sprague, 1950). Conidia and oospores of *P. ultimum* germinate by the formation of a germination tube. They rarely germinate indirectly to form motile zoospores. Sporangia and oospores of *P. aphanidermatum* germinate by the production of motile zoospores. Kraft et al. (1967), using time-lapse photography, showed that the zoospores of *P. aphanidermatum* infected primary roots of creeping bentgrass directly through the cell wall of root hairs. The zoospore became encysted on a root hair, formed an appressorium, and the cell wall was penetrated by a peg-like growth from the appressorium. The process of penetration and death of the root hair cell occurred in less than an hour. In 24 hours, infections by one or a few zoospores at a single site was followed by limited colonization of adjacent host cells; infection by many zoospores resulted in extensive colonization and root necrosis. No information is available on the mode of entry of these fungi into leaves and sheaths of grasses.

Local spread of the pathogen from leaf to leaf is accomplished by mycelial growth from infected plants to healthy ones. Running water may carry conidia and sporangia several feet from their place of formation. Zoospores are motile and can move short distances in water films. The pathogens can be transported over great distances in soil and infected plant parts.

Pythium blight is generally regarded as a hot weather disease, since rapid killing of plants occurs at temperatures of 85 to 95 F. Freeman (1960) points out that infection can occur at temperatures as low as 68 F; and if short periods of high temperatures occur on successive days, the grass can be severly damaged even though average daily temperatures are relatively cool. Regardless of temperature, the disease does not become active unless there is an abundance of moisture and plants are wet. In the northern states, serious outbreaks occur during periods of extremely hot weather with heavy rainfall or high humidity and heavy dews. A sudden drop in temperature or a dry atmosphere will check further spread of the disease.

Control:

Since abundant moisture is an important requisite for the development of *Pythium* blight, overwatering in periods of high temperature should be avoided. Putting greens and other fine turf areas should be constructed so that the surface drainage will remove heavy rainfall rapidly and subsurface drainage will bring the soil to field capacity quickly.

Pythium blight is difficult to control with fungicides. However some benefit is derived from preventive applications of the commonly used turf fungicides if the putting green has good drainage. In the Midwest, the disease is frequently seen on fairways and approaches where drainage is poor and fungicides are not applied, but not on the putting surface or collar.

Mercury fungicides and Dexon (p-dimethylaminobenzenediazo sodium sulfonate) applied as a preventive program during periods of weather favorable for disease development are recommended on bermudagrass greens overseeded with ryegrass (Freeman, 1967).

FUSARIUM BLIGHT

PATHOGENS: *Fusarium roseum* (Lk.) Snyd. & Hans. f. sp. *cerealis* (Lk.) Synd. & Hans. *Fusarium tricinctum* (Cda.) Snyd. & Hans. f. sp. *poae* (Pk.) Snyd. & Hans.

HOSTS: Annual bluegrass, colonial bentgrass, creeping bentgrass, Kentucky bluegrass, red fescue, and many other grasses.

Couch and Bedford (1966) reported that the bentgrasses are the most susceptible species, followed by Kentucky bluegrass and red fescue. The disease occurred frequently in stands of Merion Kentucky bluegrass; Newport was fairly resistant. Other varieties varied in susceptibility at different temperatures and with different isolates of the causal fungi.

Occurrence:

The pathogens are widespread and the occurrence of these species on blighted turf has been reported from the mid-Atlantic states, the midwestern states, and California (Couch and Bedford, 1966; Bean, 1966; Endo, 1961; Healy, 1967).

Symptoms:

The damage done to turf by this disease is quite characteristic. At first, diseased areas of grass are light-green, but they fade to tan and then to light straw-color in 36 to 48 hours (Couch and Bedford, 1966). They vary in size from a few inches to two or more feet in diameter. The dead areas may be circular, crescent shaped, streaked, or in circles with a patch of live grass in the central portion. Plants are killed when crown tissues are destroyed. Extensive damage occurs when diseased areas are numerous and coalesce.

Leaf lesions are irregularly shaped and often extend full width of the leaf blade. As they develop, the color of the leaf fades from a light green to tan. Many lesions extend from the cut leaf tip toward the base (Couch and Bedford, 1966; Healy, 1967). Endo (1961) isolated *F. roseum* from reddish brown to light -brown areas on stem bases and crowns of creeping bentgrass, annual bluegrass, and Kentucky bluegrass. Bean (1966) isolated species of *Fusarium* from rotted crowns of Merion Kentucky bluegrass as well as from leaf lesions.

Disease Development:

Couch and Bedford (1966) reported that macro-conidia of the causal fungi germinated within 12 hours after being placed on plants, but penetration of leaves was not evident during the first 36 hours. Penetration occurred most frequently through cut leaf tips, and subsequent development of the mycelium in the leaf was greatest following this type of penetration. Direct penetration occurred at the junctions of epidermal cells without the formation of appressoria. Mycelial growth within the leaf was both intercellular and intracellular.

The causal fungi are closely associated with dead residues of grass. Saprophytic mycelium develops profusely on thatch material that has not been disintegrated, and conidial production is profuse under favorable conditions. Couch and Bedford (1966) suggested that high soil nitrogen encouraged the development of *Fusarium* blight in the field because there was greater accumulation of thatch under high nitrogen. The number of leaves and cut leaf tips is increased under high nitrogen regimes, and this would increase the number of potential infection sites. Crown tissues and roots of grasses are invaded by mycelia of *Fusarium* spp. growing saprophytically in grass residues (Dickson, 1956). In rotted crowns, *Fusarium* spp. are commonly associated with species of *Curvularia, Helminthosporium,* and *Rhizoctonia* (Endo, 1961).

The causal fungi exhibit considerable variability in regard to pathogenicity. Couch and Bedford (1966) reported that three isolates of *F. roseum* were equally pathogenic on Highland colonial bentgrass and Pennlawn red fescue at 77, 86, and 95 F. Isolates of *F. tricinctum* and *F. roseum* from seaside creeping bentgrass were most pathogenic to Merion Kentucky bluegrass at 86 and 95 F, respectively. An isolate of *F. roseum* from Merion was most virulent on Merion at 86 F. Healy (1967) found that pathogenic isolates of *F. tricinctum* and *F. roseum* could be obtained from creeping bentgrass and annual bluegrass on golf greens throughout the growing season. Approximately 50% of the *Fusarium* isolates were pathogenic. In general, these isolates were more pathogenic to annual bluegrass than to creeping bentgrass, and pathogenicity was increased by the presence of bentgrass leaf extracts on the leaf surface. These extracts were similar to juices that exude from cut leaf tips and other wounds on leaves. The occurrence of wound extracts on cut leaf tips might explain the great amount of penetration through the cut leaf tips.

Control:

The disease has not been a serious problem on bentgrass putting greens where preventive fungicide schedules are followed with regularity, although the pathogens are present during most of the growing season. The disease is serious on Kentucky bluegrass lawns maintained at high nitrogen levels. No satisfactory control has been obtained with fungicides on lawns. It seems probable that effective control of the disease in lawns will be dependent on the use of effective methods of limiting the build-up of excessively thick layers of thatch.

OPHIOBOLUS PATCH

PATHOGEN: *Ophiobolus graminis* Sacc.

HOSTS: Annual bluegrass, colonial bentgrass, Kentucky bluegrass, perennial ryegrass, red fescue, redtop, rough bluegrass, tall fescue, velvet bentgrass, and others.

Occurrence:

This disease of turfgrasses is not widespread. It occurs in England and in northern Europe and in the coastal region of the Pacific Northwest in North America (Gould et al., 1961a). Monteith and Dahl (1932) theorized that *O. graminis* might be an important cause of turf disease under certain conditions. However, it has not been found on turf over most of North America even though the pathogen is widely distributed on wheat and barley in the U.S. and Canada (Sprague, 1950).

Symptoms:

Gould et al. (1961a) described the appearance of the disease on Astoria colonial bentgrass. The disease at first was seen as light-brown areas of grass a few inches in diameter. These increased in size rapidly, some attaining a diameter of more than 2 feet. The bentgrass was killed and did not become re-established for several months. The central portions of the dead spots were readily invaded by annual bluegrass and weeds. The plants killed by *O. graminis* had a dry rot of the main roots, crowns, and basal shoot tissues. In western Washington, fruiting bodies of the pathogen occurred on the dead plants in November, 5 months after the diseased areas appeared.

Disease Development and Control:

Ophiobolus graminis is capable of saprophytic existence on undecomposed grass debris. Infection of healthy grass plants is accomplished by the mycelium in the thatch layer penetrating the roots, crowns, and basal shoot tissues during moist conditions. As a result of such infections, the leaves and sheaths wither and die.

In England, Smith (1956) reported that *Ophiobolus* patch development was enhanced by the application of limestone and checked by addition of ammonium sulfate and monoammonium phosphate. Organic mercury fungicides suppress disease development (Smith, 1956; Jackson, 1959; Gould et al., 1961a).

POWDERY MILDEW

PATHOGEN: *Erysiphe graminis* DC.

HOSTS: Bermudagrass, Kentucky bluegrass, red fescue, sheep fescue, redtop, and other grasses.

Occurrence:

Powdery mildew is a minor disease on all of the above hosts except Kentucky bluegrass. It has become an increasingly important disease in recent years on the Merion variety. The problem has been intensified by the use of high rates of nitrogen fertilizer that produce a dense growth of grass and an ideal environment for the mildew fungus.

The disease is generally more damaging to the grass in shaded and protected areas, although it does occur in severe form in fields of Merion sod during late fall and early spring. It is an important cause of the deterioration of bluegrass lawns in shaded areas as the fungus significantly reduces the growth of leaves, roots, and rhizomes (Gaskin and Britton, 1962). Many plants are killed outright, and many others are so weakened that they winter-kill or die from drought.

Symptoms:

Powdery mildew appears first as small, superficial patches of white to light-gray fungus growth on leaves and sheaths (Figure 3). The patches enlarge rapidly and become powdery as conidia are produced. The leaf tissues under the patches of mildew become yellowed and then turn tan or brown as tissue is killed. The older, lower leaves are often completely covered by mildew. Severely infected leaves gradually dry up and die. In severe outbreaks, the turf is a dull white, as if dusted with flour.

The fungus survives the winter as mycelial mats on live leaves of Kentucky bluegrass and as cleistothecia on dead plant tissue (Sprague, 1950). Tremendous numbers of conidia are produced on the mycelial mats in the spring. These spores are carried by wind and cause new infections during cool (optimum 65 F), humid, cloudy weather. The

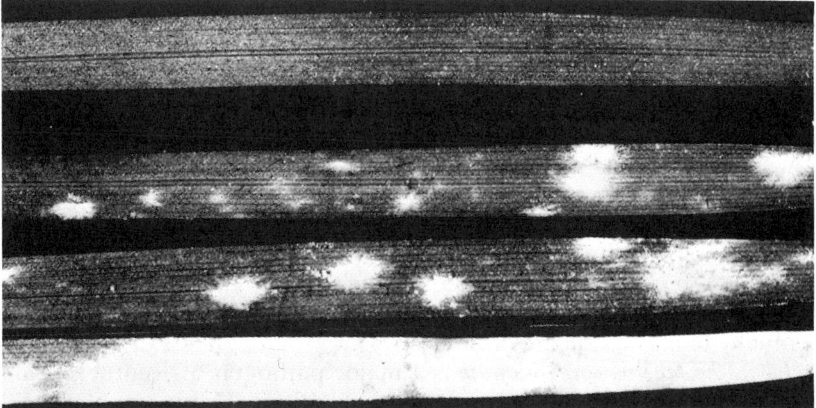

Figure 3. Powdery mildew *(Erysiphe graminis)* infected Kentucky bluegrass. Note bottom leaf almost completed faded; healthy leaf at top of photo.

conidia germinate in the absence of free water (Cherewick, 1944; Yarwood, 1936). Infection is accomplished by germination tubes penetrating through host cell walls. Specialized feeding branches called haustoria develop inside the epidermal cells of the host. The mycelium of the fungus grows on the surface of the host. Conidiophores are formed, and conidia are formed in chains on their tips. During late fall, cleistothecia may form on mycleial mats on dying leaves. Cleistothecia appear as barely visible dark-brown to black, round bodies, Ascopores are produced in them in the early spring and can initiate new infections.

Control:

Kentucky bluegrass varieties differ in their susceptibility to powdery mildew. The variety Merion is very susceptible, and Anheuzer Dwarf is highly resistant; other varieties exhibit varying degrees of resistance intermediate to these. The fungicides Karanthane (2,4-dinitro-6-(2-octyl) phenyl crontonate) and Parnon (alpha, alpha-Bis (p-chlorophenyl)-3 oyridinemethanol) give excellent control.

B. Diseases Caused by Species of Helminthosporium

HELMINTHOSPORIUM LEAF SPOT AND FOOT ROT OF KENTUCKY BLUEGRASS

PATHOGENS: The major pathogens are *Helminthosporium vagans* Drechsl. and *H. sorokinianum* Sacc. ex Sorokin. *H. dictyoides* Drechsl. and a number of other species of *Helminthosporium* also parasitize Kentucky bluegrass (Bean and Wilcoxson, 1964; Sprague, 1950). Most of them are not generally destructive.

Occurrence:

Helminthosporium vagans is the major pathogen causing "melting-out" in the northeastern U.S. (Halisky and Funk, 1966; Halisky et al., 1966; Couch and Cole, 1957; Couch and Moore, 1960). Halisky and Funk (1966) found that *H. vagans* was active during the entire year in New Jersey. Couch and Cole (1957) reported that in Pennsylvania leaf spotting was most prevalent in the cool months of spring and late fall, with the crown and root rotting phase occurring during the warm, dry summer months. Similar observations were made by Mower (1961) in New York and by Endo (1961) in California. Sprague (1950) reports that *H. vagans* is most active during late winter and early spring in the Pacific Northwest and during the summer and fall in the northern Great Plains. Bean and Wilcoxson (1964) did not isolate *H. vagans* in Minnesota, but reported the frequent occurence of *H. dictyoides*. Bean (1964) also reported that *H. dictyoides* was commonly isolated from Kentucky bluegrass near Washington, D. C.

Helminthosporium sorokinianum is a major pathogen of Kentucky bluegrass in the Midwest (Bean and Wilcoxson, 1964; Weihing et al., 1957), in New York (Mower, 1961), and in California (Endo, 1961), especially during the summer months. In New Jersey, Halisky and Funk (1966) isolated *H. sorokinianum* from Kentucky bluegrass throughout the year.

Symptoms:

The leaf spots produced by the major pathogens are essentially identical. Occasionally both *H. vagans* and *H. sorokinianum* are isolated from the same plant (Endo, 1961). Identification of the causal fungi can be accomplished only by microscopic examination of the spores produced on leaf lesions or on fungus colonies grown on artificial media.

Lesions on leaves are first seen as small water-soaked areas. These soon become uniformly dark-colored. The color varies from a dark reddish browh through purplish black. As the spots enlarge the centers become necrotic, changing from brown at first to a straw-color (Figure 4 and 5). The larger spots may be 3/8 inch long and 1/8 inch wide. Lesions in all stages of development may be present on leaves at one time.

On sheaths, lesions tend to be somewhat larger and the margins are less distinct. The color of the necrotic tissues is usually brownish.

If lesions extend completely across the base of a leaf blade or sheath, the entire leaf distal to the lesion is killed and the dead leaf soon drops from the plant. In severe cases, nearly every leaf on the plants will be killed. As a rule, the youngest leaf is the last to be injured.

Weihing et al. (1957) reported that leaf killing caused by *H. sorokinianum* was temperature related. Only leaf spotting occurred at 68 F; leaf spots and some necrosis occurred at 77 F; and a few leaf spots and extensive necrosis occurred at temperatures above 86 F. Some of the plants were killed at 95 F.

Infection originating in the outer leaf sheath may extend inward to the progressively younger sheaths and eventually into the apical meristem (Drechsler, 1930). The resulting crown rot is characterized by a reddish brown rot at first; later the rotted tissues are dark-colored. The rot may also involve roots and rhizomes.

Disease Development:

The fungi survive periods of weather unfavorable for infection as

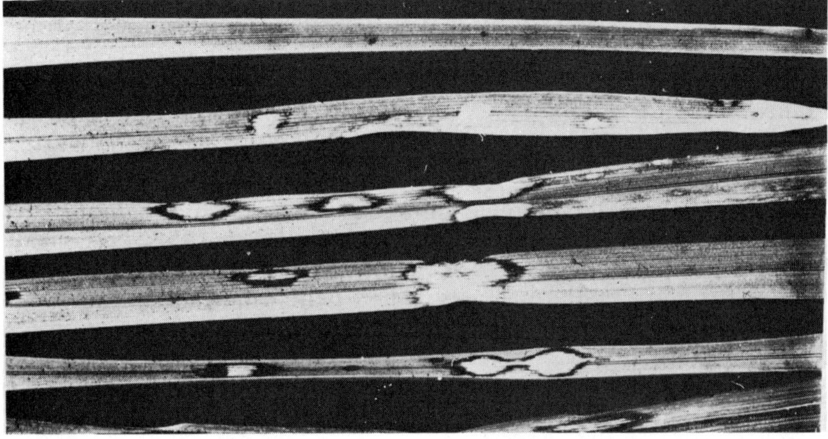

Figure 4. *(Helminthosporium* spp.) leaf spot lesions on five Kentucky bluegrass leaves below; healthy leaf is at the top.

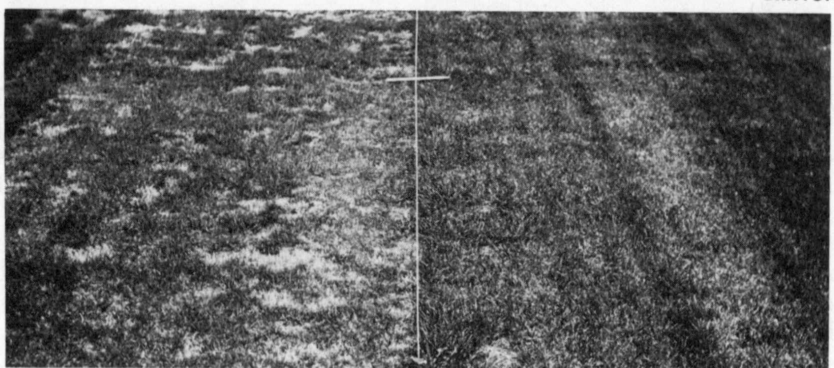

Figure 5. Typical *Helminthosporium,* leaf spot, injury to common Kentucky bluegrass. On the left mowed at 1 inch; on the right mowed at 2 inches.

spores and dormant mycelium in lesions on the debris of plants killed by the disease. The spores are splashed onto healthy leaves and sheaths by water droplets during rains or sprinkler irrigation and are also carried by winds.

The spores germinate in water by the production of one or more germ tubes. Germ tubes arise from the end cells of the spores of *H. sorokinianum* and *H. dictyoides,* and from all cells of the spores of *H. vagans.* Penetration into the host plant may occur through stomates or between the cells of the host epidermis and is usually preceded by the formation of an appressorium (Weihing et al., 1957; Bean and Wilcoxson, 1964a; Mower, 1961). Inside the host, hyphae grow between cells. Host cells adjacent to the hyphae, and at a considerable distance from hyphae are disrupted and killed (Mower, 1961; Mower and Millar, 1963). The fungi grow aggressively as saprophytes in dead tissue, eventually producing spores. Spores can be produced on the necrotic portions of large lesions (Drechsler, 1930), and are produced in abundance on dead leaves that have fallen from the plant.

Bean and Wilcoxson (1964b) demonstrated that *H. vagans, H. sorokinianum,* and *H. dictyoides* were capable of infecting the roots of seedling bluegrass plants. *H. vagans* was slightly more pathogenic than the other species. Infection occurred equally well at temperatures between 47 and 90 F.

Control:

The best control of *Helminthosporium* leaf spot and foot rot is obtained through the use of resistant varieties. Merion Kentucky bluegrass exhibits nearly complete immunity to these fungi under field conditions. Mower and Millar (1963) have shown that the resistance of Merion is related to the failure of the pathogen to penetrate the cuticle at the junction of epidermal cells. When penetration did occur, symptoms developed as in the susceptible varieties. Halisky and co-workers (1966a) reported that the varieties Pennstar, Anheuser Dwarf, and Merion exhibited a high degree of resistance. Moderate resistance was shown by Cougar and Newport. Delta, Arboretum, Park, and common were highly susceptible.

Leaf spot and foot rot of Kentucky bluegrass are most damaging when close mowing is practiced (Drechsler, 1929, 1930; Halisky et al, 1966a; Williams and Schmidt, 1964). Consequently, susceptible varieties of Kentucky bluegrass should be mowed as high as practical, consistent with the use of the turf.

Susceptible varieties are more severely damaged by leaf spot and foot rot under high fertility, especially high nitrogen (Halisky et al., 1966a). The use of excessive amounts of nitrogen fertilizer should be avoided on lawns composed of susceptible varieties.

A number of fungicides can be used to reduce the severity of the leaf spot phase of the disease. To be most effective, applications must be started in the early spring about the time Kentucky bluegrass begins to grow. They must be reapplied periodically as long as conditions are favorable for leaf spot development.

HELMINTHOSPORIUM DISEASES OF BENTGRASS

MAJOR PATHOGENS: *Helminthosporium erythrospilum* Drechsl. *Helminthosporium giganteum* Heald & Wolf. *Helminthosporium sorokinianum* Sacc. ex Sorok.

Occurrence and Hosts:

Helminthosporium erythrospilum is common on redtop and creeping bentgrass in the midwestern states and the central Atlantic states. Colonial bentgrass and velvet bentgrass are somewhat resistant. *Helminthosporium giganteum* is primarily a pathogen of bermudagrass and is most abundant in the southern states. Drechsler (1928, 1929) reported this pathogen on creeping bentgrass in Michigan, Indiana, Illinois, Ohio, Minnesota, and Virginia, and on velvet bentgrass in Virginia. He suggested that the northward extension of the fungus on creeping bentgrass might because of the commerical distribution of infected bentgrass stolons from sources within the natural range of the pathogen. *Helminthosporium sorokinianum* has been reported on creeping bentgrass in the midwestern states (Klomparens, 1953; Healy and Britton, 1968) and in California (Endo, 1961, 1963). In Illinois and California, *H. sorokinianum* is the species found most commonly on creeping bentgrass.

Symptoms:

Each pathogen forms characteristic leaf spots on the leaves of unmowed host plants or plants mowed at lawn height. Those formed by *H. erythrospilum* during periods of wet weather have tan centers and are bordered by a zone of reddish brown. Under sonewhat drier conditions the central portion tends to remain brownish or reddish brown and infected leaves tend to wither and die even though soil moisture is plentiful (Drechsler, 1935). An eyespot lesion is also typically formed by *H. giganteum;* however, the central portion is whitish and the margins dark-brown. If several lesions occur on the same blade, withering of the leaf portion distal to the lesions results (Drechsler, 1928). The lesions formed by *H. sorokinianum* are usually entirely dark-colored, but a few may have light-colored centers and dark margins when fully developed (Drechsler, 1929). Therefore, positive identification can be made only by microscopic examination of the spores of the fungi isolated from lesions.

Identification is even more difficult on putting greens. The leaves of creeping bentgrass on putting greens are much smaller than on unmowed plants. Consequently, lesion size is restricted, and leaves are killed by girdling more quickly. In particular, the eyespot lesions form less frequently.

Healy and Britton (1968) reported that leaf spots on creeping bentgrass resulting from infection by *H. sorokinianum* first appeared as water-soaked spots 0.1 mm in diameter between the veins of the leaf; these enlarged to 0.5 to 1.5 mm and became dark-brown. Chlorotic zones often were observed at the outer margins of dark-colored lesions Occasional spots with small straw-colored centers were formed. The over-all appearance of leafspotted creeping bentgrass putting greens was a reddish brown. Leaf spotting was the only symptom observed in May, September, and October in Illinois. A similar appearance is imparted by leaf spotting caused by *H. erythrospilum*.

Leaf blighting caused by girdling of the leaves by lesions of *H. sorokinianum* occurred in June, July, and August (Healy and Britton, 1968). In addition, during hot, humid weather, infected leaves turned dark-gray, as though wilted, withered and died. In over-all view, the disease at this time imparts a smoky-blue cast to infected areas. Ordinarily, a high percentage of the plants in the areas are killed.

According to Endo (1961), under California conditions the infection of leaves of creeping bentgrass and annual bluegrass by *H. sorokinianum* usually resulted in a general yellowing followed by necrosis and browning. Leaf spotting was uncommon, but a typical root and crown rot was noted.

On bentgrass putting greens, *H. giganteum* lesions occur as small, dead, bleached areas; the zonate margins are usually not evident (Drechsler, 1929). In over-all view, severely infected turf has a gray appearance because of the numerous light-colored lesions.

Disease Development:

All of the *Helminthosporium* species overwinter as dormant mycelium in plant parts killed by the fungus pathogens. Under favorable conditions of moisture and temperature the dormant mycelium resumes growth, and spores are produced that comprise the initial inoculum. Conidia of *H. giganteum* are short-lived and probably are not important in overwintering (Drechsler, 1928). Conidia of *H. sorokinianum* and probably *H. erythrospilum* may persist in a viable condition for several months and thus are important in surviving periods unfavorable for growth.

Conidia of *H. sorokinianum* germinate by the production of thin-walled germ tubes from the end cells. In water a single appressorium usually develops on the germ tubes at infection sites on the leaf epidermis. Approximately 10% of the infections occur through stomata

(Healy and Britton, 1968). Endo and Amacher (1964) showed that the percent germination was increased by suspending conidia in guttation fluids from barley. Endo and Oertli (1964) also reported that greater numbers of appressoria were formed on branched germ tubes when guttation fluid was present. A corresponding increase in infection and severity of the disease on creeping bentgrass also occurred with the spores in guttation fluids. Healy and Britton (1968) reported similar results with guttation fluids, glutamine, which is a common constituent of guttation fluids, and sterilized extracts from bentgrass leaves. Glutamine is most abundant in guttation fluids of grasses immediately following fertilization with soluble nitrogen fertilizers (Curtis, 1944; Healy, 1967). The leaf extracts are similar to the wound exudates produced during mowing. Apparently glutamine and nutrients in the leaf saps are utilized by *H. sorokinianum* in saprophytic growth on the surface of bentgrass leaves. This results in an increase in the total amount of protoplasm in the germ tubes, and thus multiple appressoria are formed on branched germ tubes. Large lesions are formed as a result of multiple penetrations (Healy and Britton, 1968). Hyphal growth from each penetration is sparse and affects only a few of the host cells. A lesion developing from a single penetration is minute in comparison to those from multiple penetration. The large lesions tend to girdle the leaves, killing the tissues distal to them; single small lesions do not girdle the leaves. Sporulation was never observed on lesions on live leaves by Healy and Britton (1968), but it was abundant on dead leaves in the thatch.

Control:

The increased severity of the disease caused by *H. sorokinianum* on bentgrass putting greens during the summer months is undoubtedly due in part to the increased prevalence of guttation fluid on the leaves. It may also be affected by the more rapid release of nitrogen from organic sources during hot weather, or by the application of soluble nitrogen. Either of these could result in increased glutamine content of the guttation fluids. Consequently, the guttation droplets should be removed early in the morning, preferably by syringing. Mechanical removal tends to spread guttation fluids over the leaf surfaces.

Since glutamine is found in guttation fluids only when too much soluble nitrogen is present in the soil, fertilization practices should be followed that would avoid excessive nitrogen and yet provide good growth of the grass.

The organic fungicides like Dyrene (2,4-dichloro-6-o-chloroaniline -s-triazine), Daconil 2787 (tetra chloroisophthalonitrile), Fore (a co-ordination product of zinc ion and manganese ethylene bisdithiocarbamate), and Actidione (cyclohexamide) give control.

HELMINTHOSPORIUM DISEASES ON BERMUDAGRASS

PATHOGENS: *Helminthosporium cynodontis* Margi. *Helminthosporium triseptatum* Drechsl. *Helminthosporium stenospilum* Drechsl. *Helminthosporium rostratum* Drechsl. *Helminthosporium giganteum* Drechsl.

Occurrence:

Freeman (1964) noted simultaneous infection of bermudagrass by two or more species in over 50% of the samples studied. Not all species are equally damaging to the grass. The diseases caused by these species are common throughout the range of bermudagrass and are of considerable importance during periods of mild weather, especially in the spring and fall when the grass is semidormant.

Symptoms:

The leaf spots produced by *H. giganteum* are distinctive. The leaf spots produced by the other species are not readily distinguishable (Freeman, 1964). All are small (1 to 4 mm long), brown to purple lesions. The lesions tend to be congregated on the leaf blades near the collar. Heavily spotted leaves become reddish brown, wither, and die. The over-all color of severely infected turf may be reddish or purplish. Death of the leaves causes a thinning of the turf, and infection of sheaths and crowns results in death of plants, often in patches.

Control:

Most of the recently released bermudagrass varieties have some resistance to the commonly occurring species of *Helminthosporium.* Freeman (1967) reported that Dyrene, thiram, Acti-dione, or organic mercury fungicides give effective control.

OTHER HELMINTHOSPORIUM DISEASES

Helminthosporium dictyoides, in addition to causing a leaf spot in Kentucky bluegrass, causes a severe disease of red fescue (Couch and Cole, 1957). The disease commonly occurs throughout the region where red fescue is adapted and may be severe during midsummer. At first the grass is chlorotic and then turns light-brown. The diseased plants soon fall to the ground to form patches of "sunken" grass. The patches range in size from a few inches to several feet in diameter.

The symptoms on individual leaves are small, reddish brown spots that extend across the width of the leaf. Yellowing and necrosis of the blade outward from the infected area are caused by rapid girdling of the leaves.

On tall fescue, in the early development of leaf spot symptoms, a fine network of light and dark-brown lines may be formed in the infected area. This pattern has given rise to the name netblotch for this disease. The netblotch symptom usually disappears as the lesions age and become solid-colored.

Italian ryegrass and perennial ryegrass are also susceptible to *H. dictyoides.* The leafspots are somewhat similar to those on tall fescue. Another fungus, *Helminthosporium siccans* Drechsl. (*Pyrenophora lolii* Dovaston), is commonly isolated from leafspots on both species of ryegrass. A crown and root rot is common during the summer months. The disease cycle is apparently similar to that of *H. vagans* on Kenthcky bluegrass.

Control:

In Illinois, red fescue lawns can be grown satisfactorily only with low levels of fertility and little supplemental water. With maintenance considered normal for Kentucky bluegrass, red fescue is killed out, apparently by *H. dictyoides*. Fungicides were not effective against this disease in Pennsylvania (Couch and Cole, 1957).

C. Rust Diseases of Turfgrasses

There are a number of rust fungi that are capable of parasitizing the grass species used for turf. Only a few of them occur frequently enough, and with sufficient intensity, to be damaging to turfgrasses, although they may do considerable damage to unmowed grasses grown for seed production, hay, or pasture (Hardison, 1963).

All rust fungi that damage turfgrasses are species of *Puccinia,* and their life cycles are similar, although the hosts they attack may be quite dissimilar. In addition, all of the species are able to survive from year to year in the absence of an alternate (aecial) host, although such hosts may occur and be important locally. Therefore, the following discussion will be concerned only with the spore stages that occur on the grass hosts.

PATHOGENS: On bluegrasses: *Puccinia graminis* Pers., causing stem rust; *Puccinia striiformis* West., causing stripe rust; *Puccinia brachypodii* Otth var. poae-nemoralis (Otth) Cummins & H. C. Green, causing leaf rust. On ryegrasses and tall fescue: *Puccinia coronata* Cda., causing crown rust. On bermudagrass: *Puccinia cynodontis* Desm. On St. Augustinegrass: *Puccinia stenotaphri* Cumm. On zoysiagrasses: *Puccinia zoysiae* Diet.

RUSTS ON KENTUCKY BLUEGRASS

Leaf Rust

Leaf rust caused by *Puccinia brachypodii* var. *poae-nemoralis* is a minor disease of widespread occurrence. It can be distinguished from the other rusts on Kentucky bluegrass by the presence of colorless, capitate paraphyses in the uredial pustules and by urediospores with colorless walls and scattered germ pores. The author has observed this rust on Kentucky bluegrass in March and April in Kentucky and southern Illinois in such abundance that the leaf blades of the grass were distinctly yellowed. At other times of the year, uredial pustules are sparse on leaves of Kentucky bluegrass in lawns and cause no appreciable discoloration or apparent damage.

Stem Rust

Stem rust caused by *Puccinia graminis* is the commonly occurring rust on Merion Kentucky bluegrass. Many grass species are susceptible to this fungus, including creeping bentgrass (Britton and Cummins, 1959). However, the disease is not as important on bentgrass turf or the other susceptible turfgrass species as it is on Kentucky bluegrass. Stem rust occurs throughout the U.S. and Canada wherever Kentucky bluegrass is grown.

Symptoms:

A severely rusted bluegrass lawn has a yellowish to reddish brown cast due to chlorosis of the leaf blades and the presence of brick-red uredial pustules and necrotic tissues. On hot, dry days infected leaves may fold as though suffering from drought.

Symptoms on individual leaves consist of brick-red pustules of spores emerging through a lengthwise rupture of the host epidermis. The individual pustules are mostly longer than wide and may be surrounded by green, yellow, or dead leaf tissue depending upon the age of the pustules and the susceptibility of the host plant. Pustules are usually separate from one another and definitely do not occur in seriate arrangements. Urediospores tend to be oblong; walls are brown and echinulate, usually with three germ spores (Britton and Cummins, 1959). Paraphyses do not occur in the uredia. Telial sori are rarely formed in mowed bluegrass. The few that have been observed were on leaf sheaths near the soil line. Teliospores are not important in the disease cycle of the rust on this host and are of little value in identification because of their infrequent occurrence.

Urediospores germinate in a film of water by the production of a germ tube. An appressorium is formed over a stomate and a penetration peg develops between the guard cells. This peg terminates inside the substomatal air space in a swelling called a vesicle; hyphal branches originating from the vesicle grow between the cells of the leaf mesophyll. The host cells are penetrated by special branches of the hyphae called haustoria. In a susceptible host plant, the cells show little evidence of damage during the first few days after infection, but are killed during urediospore formation. Urediospores are formed 10 to 15 days after infection; the shorter interval occurs when air temperatures are between 70 and 80 F. Teliospores usually form in tissue that is maturing or drying out slowly, like stems; in turf this type of tissue is rarely formed.

Disease Development:

In California, rust has been observed on Merion Kentucky bluegrass during every month of the year (Endo, 1961). In more northern areas, stem rust urediospores are killed by low temperatures, and the first infections to occur in these regions each year are probably caused by urediospores blown in from the south where the fungus has overwintered as dormant mycelium or as actively growing uredia. The mycelium of *P. graminis* is capable of surviving winter conditions in live leaves of Kentucky bluegrass as far north as Lafayette, Indiana (Britton, 1958). Survival of the mycelium is dependent upon the survival of the infected leaf, as *P. graminis* is an obligate parasite and, therefore, cannot grow or survive in dead tissue. The dormant mycelia result from late fall infections. Low temperatures arrest the development of mycelium during the cold months. With the advent of warm weather in early spring, the mycelia resume growth and form urediospores. Sporulation from overwintered mycelia was observed on March 29, 1957, at Lafayette (Britton, 1958). Secondary spread and infection from the initial infections was slight during late spring and early summer when the bluegrass was growing rapidly and was mowed frequently. A rapid build-up to severe levels does not occur until growth of the lawn is slowed by high temperature, dry soils; or depleted nitrogen fertility.

Britton and Butler (1965) found that in rapidly growing Kentucky bluegrass lawns the three youngest leaves were usually free of rust. The reason for this is that these leaves are oriented in an upright position that allows the older portion of the leaf to be removed by regular mowing. If mowing is done at weekly intervals stem rust infections on the tips of the leaves are removed before spores are formed. If the grass is not mowed regularly these infections will produce spores. Also, if the growth rate of the grass is reduced to the extent that infected tissue is not removed by mowing, the leaves will become rusted. As the leaves become older they become oriented below the height of mowing and are severely rusted and killed prematurely.

Stem rust infections often are severe in late summer and early fall. Late in the fall a fungus parasite *(Darluca filum* [Biv. ex Fr.] Cast.) kills many of the urediospores. The presence of *D. filum* in a uredium causes the surrounding host tissue to turn purplish, forming spots that can be mistaken for *Helminthosporium* leaf spots. They are easily distinguished from *Helminthosporium* by the presence of a rust pustule in the center of each spot.

Stripe Rust

Stripe rust, caused by *Puccinia striiformis,* occurs in the Pacific Coast States and in the Intermountain Region. It is more important than stem rust over much of this area and has become especially serious in bluegrass seed fields (Hardison, 1963).

Britton and Cummins (1956) reported that the varieties Merion, Newport, Delta, and Park and a number of numbered Kentucky bluegrass selections were susceptible to this rust. In the field, the Merion variety is particularly susceptible. The varieties Windsor, Prato, and Fylking are also attacked.

Symptoms:

A severely rusted lawn appears orange to brown in color. Growth of the grass is less vigorous. The uredial pustules are characteristically bright yellow and become arranged seriately in long, narrow, chlorotic streaks running lengthwise of the leaf and sheath between the veins. Urediospores resemble those of *P. brachypodii* in that they have colorless cell walls and scattered germ pores and are irregularly circular to ovoid in shape. They differ in not having capitate paraphyses in the uredia. Paraphyses occasionally occur but these are spatulate in shape.

Disease Development:

Stripe rust is active in the winter months in California and Oregon (Endo, 1961; Hardison, 1963). It is most severe during the cool, moist periods of early spring and late autumn. The mycelium is dormant in the perennial grasses during the winter in northern regions, and urediospores may remain viable over the winter and cause infections the following spring. Spore germination, penetration, and development of infections are similar to those of *P. graminis;* however, the mycelium, once inside the leaf, grows more extensively, giving rise to the long rows of uredia.

RUST ON BERMUDAGRASS

Bermudagrass rust is caused by *P. cyanodontis.* Rust is widespread and damaging on bermudagrass throughout the area where this grass is grown. The general appearance of severely rusted lawns is similar to the damage caused by the rust diseases of Kentucky bluegrass. The uredial pustules on leaves are orange and longer than wide. Teliospores form in the older pustules, causing them to become brown or black.

RUST ON ZOYSIAGRASS

Rust on zoysiagrass is caused by *P. zoysiae.* This rust disease is new to the U.S., having been found for the first time in 1964 (Kreitlow et al., 1965). It is presently distributed throughout the southeastern U.S. from Washington, D. C., to Kansas (Freeman, 1965; Kazelnicky and Garrett, 1966; Gudauskas and McCarter, 1966; Kreitlow et al., 1965; Bain, 1966). The disease is favored by cool temperatures and is retarded by hot weather. Freeman (1965) reported a severe attack in Florida during January. The rust was prevalent until April when it subsided with the beginning of warm, dry weather. In Georgia, the rust appeared around the first of May and subsided in June when the maximum daytime temperatures exceeded 70 to 75 F (Kazelnicky and Garrett, 1966). Rust development is greatest in the shaded portions of lawns (Kreitlow et al., 1965; Kozelnicky and Garrett, 1966), with severity increasing as shading is intensified.

The rust occurs on the Meyer variety of *Zoysia japonica,* the variety Emerald *(Z. japonica* x *Z. tenuifolia), Z. matrella,* and *Z. tenuifolia.*

An orange discoloration is imparted to severely rusted lawns and the lawn is thinned and unthrifty in appearance. The uredia are bright orange and occur on both leaf surfaces.

CROWN RUST

Crown rust caused by *Puccinia coronata* is a common disease of Italian ryegrass, perennial ryegrass, and tall fescue. The fungus is widely distributed wherever these hosts are grown. The uredia are bright yellow, and the symptoms are similar to those produced by the other rusts.

Control of Rusts

The Newport Kentucky bluegrass variety is essentially immune from infection by *P. graminis.* The resistance is the result of a hypersensitive reaction to infection (Britton, 1958; Britton and Butler, 1965). Park exhibits a high degree of resistance, as do Delta, Common, and similar types. This field resistance is expressed by the development of low numbers of uredia and is not due to a hypersensitive reaction of the host plant. Merion, Prato, Delft, and Windsor are highly susceptible.

Maintaining vigorous growth by watering and fertilizing as needed and removal of infected leaf tissue by regular mowing will keep the youngest three leaves essentially free of stem rust and leaf rust on Kentucky bluegrass. The over-all appearance of the turf is that of a nonrusted lawn, even though the older leaves may be badly rusted. In addition, the density of the stand is maintained.

A number of fungicides are effective in the control of the rust diseases.

D. Smut Diseases

There are several smut fungi that attack turfgrasses. Some of these destroy the inflorescences of the grasses and are of major importance in seed production. Occasionally they are found in lawns; however, the damage done to turf is usually negligible. The leaf smuts, as the name implies, occur primarily in the leaves and sheaths of grasses, and these are important pathogens of turfgrasses. The leaf spot smuts caused by species of *Entyloma* are found infrequently, although they occasionally are damaging (Fischer, 1951). The smuts that produce long linear sori on leaves and sheaths, stripe smut and flag smut, are destructive and widespread on several cool-season turfgrasses.

STRIPE AND FLAG SMUTS

PATHOGENS: *Ustilago striiformis* (West.) Niessl—stripe smut. *Urocystis agropyri* (Preuss) Schröt.—flag smut

Occurrence:

On unmowed grasses, flag smut tends to sporulate in the upper leaves, especially the flag leaf, whereas stripe smut sporulates in nearly all leaves. Under close mowing, both smuts sporulate in all leaves and sheaths, and symptoms on grass plants are identical. Identification is accomplished only by microscopic examination of the teliospores. The teliospores of *U. striiformis* are single cells; the teliospores of *U. agropyri* consist of a spore ball of one or two fertile cells surrounded by several empty cells.

Thirumalachar and Dickson (1953) found that flag smut is most prevalent in the early spring and that stripe smut predominated in late May and June.

Symptoms:

Diseased plants in unmowed stands of grass exhibit various degrees of stunting. In addition, the leaves of infected plants of Kentucky bluegrass and bentgrasses tend to remain erect and stiff rather than lax and spreading. The most conspicuous symptom is the occurrence of narrow, linear telial sori on the leaves and leaf sheaths. When the sori are first visible they are covered by the host epidermis, and their color is a dull gray. When the host epidermis is ruptured, the black, dusty spore mass is revealed. Sori are small when they first appear, but, as spore production continues, the sori coalesce and form the typical linear stripes that sometimes extend the entire length of the leaf and into the sheath. As the sori develop and the epidermis is ruptured, the leaves die from the tip, becoming curled, brown, and shredded.

Infection centers in new seedings can often be detected from a considerable distance by the brown appearance of patches of grass caused by the death of infected leaves. Nearly all plants in such areas will be diseased. In lawns with high numbers of infected plants, a distinct browning is often noted during hot, dry weather.

Infected plants are readily killed by drought and high temperatures (Davis, 1924; Kreitlow, 1943; Kreitlow and Meyers, 1944; Leach et al., 1946; Fischer, 1940; Hodges, 1967). Dead areas of grass often appear during midsummer in heavily infected lawns. Sometimes the damage is so extensive that the lawn must be reestablished. Infected plants may also be predisposed to invasion by other pathogens that kill them (Kreitlow and Meyer, 1944).

Disease Development:

The pathogen survives as perennial mycelium in the crowns of infected plants and as spores in the soil and thatch. New infections can arise from soil borne spores penetrating through the coleoptile of seedling plants (Davis, 1926; Thirumalachar and Dickson, 1953; Hodges, 1967). Hodges (1967) showed that penetration from soil borne teliospores could also occur in the lateral buds on crowns and rhizome nodes of mature plants, and the tillers and rhizomes from these would be diseased. Earlier workers had suggested that tillers and rhizomes could be penetrated by soil-borne teliospores (Leach et al., 1946). The mycelium in perennially infected crowns will invade the new plants arising from rhizomes and tillers from that crown.

Thirumalachar and Dickson (1953) reported that infection hyphae from germinated spores enter the host epidermal cells or between them by direct penetration. The infection hyphae form after conjugation of compatible cells of the promycelia of teliospores. In the coleoptile, growth of the mycelium is mostly inside the host cells. Advance of the mycelium toward the crown primordium is mainly in parenchyma tissue and along the walls of the xylem and phloem cells in the subcrown internode. In the crown primordium the hyphae become established in the differentiating tissue of the culm apex. Leaves, tillers, and rhizomes arising from such crowns are infected as they develop. The mycelium grows with the developing infected organs and eventually produces spores.

Hodges (1967) found that the fungus did not grow into the crown when infection occurred through lateral buds. Only the tissues produced from the bud were invaded, i.e., the tillers and new plants from rhizomes were smutted but the parent plant remained healthy.

The low incidence of smut in new lawns would indicate that only limited infection of seedling plants occurs. The large number of infected plants observed in lawns 4 or more years old is apparently the result of the penetration of lateral buds and the spread of the fungus from perennially infected crowns (Hodges, 1967). Watering contributes to such a build-up, as it prevents the death of perennially infected plants during drought periods. The disease would be expected to be more prevalent in varieties that tiller profusely, since such varieties would produce more lateral buds; and the Merion variety does tiller profusely.

The Merion variety of Kentucky bluegrass is very susceptible (Kreitlow and Juska, 1959; Gaskin, 1966; Halisky et al., 1966a). Most other varieties exhibit somewhat better resistance to the disease than Merion. However, Gaskin (1966) presented evidence that races of the pathogens exist and pointed out that it would be difficult to predict the resistance or susceptibility of a variety from a field plot tests conducted in one locality.

Control:

Methods for controlling this disease have not been developed. However, some promising results have been obtained with systemic fungicides (Hardison, 1966, 1967).

E. Cold Weather Diseases

FUSARIUM PATCH AND PINK SNOW MOLD

PATHOGEN: *Fusarium nivale* (Fr.) Ces. [*Calonectria graminicola* (Berk. & Br.) Wr.]

When the pathogen causes disease in the absence of snow, the disease is called *Fusarium* patch; the damage produced under snow or at the margins of melting snowbanks is quite different and is referred to as pink snow mold.

HOSTS: Annual bluegrass, Colonial bentgrass, creeping bentgrass, Italian ryegrass, Kentucky bluegrass, perennial ryegrass, redtop, red fescue, rough bluegrass, sheep fescue, tall fescue, velvet bentgrass, and many other grasses.

Occurrence:

Fusarium patch is the most common disease of turf in western Washington (Gould, 1957; Gould et al., 1961) and in the British Isles (Smith, 1953). In these areas the disease is most active in the wet, cool months of autumn and spring with reduced activity during winter and summer. In the northern tier of states of the U.S. disease activity begins in cool, wet periods of late fall, continues under melting snow during winter and spring and with diminished intensity in cold wet weather in the early spring.

Symptoms:

In the absence of snow, *Fusarium* patch on putting greens and other closely-mowed turf occurs in distinct, nearly circular spots varying from less than an inch to several inches in diameter. The majority are about the size of dollar spot patches. The diseased areas are yellowish at first, then turn tan or white as the leaves die. Mycelium of the causal fungus is not readily apparent on these leaves except at low temperatures (32 to 45 F) and with abundant moisture.

Under snow, the disease develops when temperatures are high enough to melt the snow. A snow cover over unfrozen soil commonly melts from the bottom upward, forming ideal conditions for disease development. Infected areas under these conditions are irregularly circular, from a few inches to a foot or more in diameter, and during development the grass is covered with a profuse growth of white aerial mycelium. The infected leaves tend to be matted together with the mycelium. The areas so damaged feel slimy when wet, and the surface drys to form a crust. The grass beneath the crust is often wet, and the fungus may continue to grow beneath it. Plants in such areas are often killed. Under less ideal conditions for disease development, the patches have less aerial mycelium on them, and the leaves of infected plants tend to remain erect and do not mat extensively. In such areas the damage is largely confined to the leaves, and plants are not killed, but recovery may be slow. Occasionally, spots will show a tinge of pink when observed in sunlight.

Disease Development:

The optimum temperature range for development of the disease is 32 to 40 F (Dahl, 1934). Disease development becomes slower at higher temperatures and ceases at about 60 F. In culture, the growth of the fungus is greatest between 60 and 77 F; growth ceases at about 32 and 88 F. The reason that the fungus is pathogenic at lower than optimum temperatures for its growth is not known, but it may be caused by physiological changes in host plants at the lower temperature.

The mycelium, conidia, and perithecia develop on the dead grass residues in the thatch. Dahl (1934) reported that when the fungus became actively parasitic, the mycelium grew up onto the leaves of the grass and penetrated through stomata after forming appressoria. The hyphal growth inside the leaf is intercellular at first, becoming intracellular as the cells of the leaf die. The rate of disease spread is directly dependent upon the rapidity of mycelial growth over the leaf surface as new infections occur along the entire length of the leaves through stomata; therefore, with rapid growth, many penetrations occur along more of the leaf. Once the leaf is killed, the fungus also penetrates into the leaf directly through the cell walls of the epidermis. Lateral spread of the fungus is largely by mycelial growth from diseased leaves to adjacent healthy ones and is rapid in wet, cold weather when aerial mycelial growth is profuse. When temperatures or moisture conditions are less favorable, the external mycelial growth is limited, and infection along the leaf and spread from leaf to leaf is slowed.

Conidia are produced on masses of mycelium (sporodochia) that grow out of the stomata of dead leaves. At first these occur in rows, but may enlarge so that they cover much of the leaf surface. The importance of conidia and ascospores in initiating infections is unknown. It is probable that they are carried by wind or splashing water to leaves and that new infections may arise from them in a manner similar to mycelial penetration (Couch, 1961).

Attacks by *F. nivale* are influenced by certain cultural practices. High nitrogen levels on putting greens tend to increase the development of *Fusarium* patch (Gould et al., 1961). Smith (1959) reported that attacks of *Fusarium* patch disease were frequently observed to follow the application of ground limestone and suggested that a high pH in the upper soil regions increased disease incidence. A late fall application of a nitrogenous fertilizer that promotes growth of the grass tends to favor the development of pink snow mold (Dahl, 1934), especially if the grass is not mowed and the long leaves mat together. Wet, cold conditions are prolonged under matted leaves, deep thatch layers, and straw mulches; and this tends to favor disease development.

TYPHULA BLIGHT (SNOW SCALD, GRAY SNOW MOLD, SPECKLED SNOW MOLD)

PATHOGEN: *Typhula itoana* Imai

HOSTS: Annual bluegrass, Colonial bentgrass, creeping bentgrass, Italian ryegrass, Kentucky bluegrass, perennial ryegrass, red fescue, rough bluegrass, tall fescue, velvet bentgrass, and others.

Occurrence:

Typhula blight occurs in the northern U.S. and Canada. It does not occur as far south as pink snow mold; however, both often occur on the same turf areas. The disease caused by *T. itoana* is strictly associated with cold weather and snow and is most frequently found where the snow is deep or drifted and slow to melt in the spring.

Symptoms:

Damaged areas as large as 2 feet in diameter are exposed by the melting of the snow cover in the spring. These are covered with a white or light-gray growth of mycelium, and the mycelium and dead leaves are matted together. A ring of fluffy, aerial mycelium is often massed at the margin of these areas. They may be distinguished from damage caused by *F. nivale* by the presence of small sclerotia embedded in the leaves, sheaths, and other plant parts (Remsberg, 1940). The sclerotia in moist leaves are pinkish-orange when they are developing, amber to reddish brown when mature, and dark brown or nearly black in dry leaves. The surface of developing sclerotia is smooth but becomes roughened as maturity is reached. The shape of the sclerotia is variable, but they tend to be irregularly spherical. Plants overrun by mycelium lost their green color, wither, and turn brown and then bleached-white.

Disease Development:

The pathogen persists through warm periods as sclerotia. They germinate in late fall when temperatures are low and moisture is plentiful. Germination is accomplished by the production of small club-shaped fruiting bodies. These are less than an inch long; the upper portion is pink, the basal portion white. Basidiospores are produced on them and these are distributed by air currents. Following fusion of compatible basidiospores, mycelial colonies form in the thatch, and these develop into primary infection centers. At temperatures slightly above freezing, (32 to 40 F) the hyphae from these colonies grow up from the thatch and over-run the plants. Damage to plants ranges from killing leaves to invasion and rotting of the crown and root tissues. The disease is checked as the temperature rises, moisture decreases, and sunlight increases.

OTHER SNOW MOLDS

In canada an unidentified low-temperature basidiomycete causes a snow mold type of damage to turfgrasses and other plants (Broadfoot, 1936; Broadfoot and Cormack, 1941; Lebeau, 1964; Ward and Thorne, 1965). On turf, the damaged patches are distinctly smaller than those caused by *F. nivale.* A light-gray mycelium is often formed on plants in these areas. The fungus appears to be active at lower temperatures than *F. nivale* with an optimum temperature for disease development near 32 F (Lebeau, 1964). Another cold weather pathogen, *Sclerotinia borealis* Bub. and Vleug, is found in even colder regions (Lebeau, 1964).

Control:

Snow mold damage can be minimized by selecting turfgrasses that are somewhat resistant to damage. In general, Kentucky bluegrass is fairly resistant; red fescue, annual bluegrass, Colonial bentgrass and creeping bentgrass are very susceptible (Beard, 1966, Dahl, 1934; Lebeau, 1964). Beard (1966) reported that varieties of creeping bentgrass varied widely in susceptibility to *T. itoana.* The varieties Seaside and Cohansey were very susceptible; Pencross, Washington, and Toronto were moderately susceptible. Congressional was quite resistant, as was the Astoria variety of Colonial bentgrass. Dahl (1934) reported that Metropolitan creeping bentgrass is highly resistant to *F. nivale.* The Washington variety has moderate resistance to crown invasion, although leaves are readily killed. Kallio (1966) reported that common Kentucky bluegrass was the most resistant to snow mold followed by Park, Newport, and Merion, in that order.

Gould et al. (1961) recommended that fungicides be applied on a biweekly schedule for the control of Fusarium patch. Their data indicate that an alternating schedule of phenyl mercury and cadmium chloride fungicides would generally provide good control and the least damage to turf. Excellent control and long residual action have been obtained with a finely-ground mixture of mercurous and mercuric chlorides (Gould et al., 1965).

To prevent the development of the diseases caused by *F. nivale* and *T. itoana* under snow, fungicides must be applied during the cold, rainy weather in the fall and prior to the first snowfall. Fungicides should be applied again in spring or late winter if the disease is active. Since *F. nivale* can continue to cause damage after the snow has melted, regular fungicide treatments may be required to prevent damage during the cold, wet, early spring weather.

Under severe disease conditions, the organic and inorganic mercury fungicides and the cadmium compounds have given good control when properly applied. Other fungicides that give inadequate control under severe conditions are used successfully in areas where disease development is slight.

FAIRY RINGS

A great many soil-inhabiting fungi are capable of causing fairy rings in lawns, pastures, and native grasslands (Shantz and Piemeisel, 1917). Some commonly occurring ones are *Agaricus campestris* Fr., *Marasmius oreades* Fr., and *Lepiota morgani* Pk.; the latter one is deadly poisonous if eaten!

Recognition:

Fairy rings usually appear as circles or areas of dark green grass in lawns that are well provided with soil moisture (Figure 6). A ring of dormant or dead grass may develop on the inside or outside of the greener circle. During dry weather, expecially in the fall, the dead area is normally outside the green ring. The following spring while the soil is moist the fungus occupies the soil outward from the dead ring and the growth of the grass outside the ring is stimulated and dark green in color. In addition, a second ring of green is sometimes observed inside the dead ring. After rains or heavy irrigation, mushrooms (fruiting bodies of the causal fungi) may appear in the circle of green grass.

Fairy rings are first seen as a tuft of stimulated green grass or a cluster of mushrooms. The fungus mycelium grows only outward from this central cluster in the surface foot or so of soil. The advancing margin of the fungus is actively growing; the receding margin is dying. The stimulation that shows up as greener grass is due to the increased

Figure 6. Fairy ring *(Agaricus campestris)* with stimulated grass and fruiting bodies (mushrooms) of the fungus on the outer edge.

amount of nitrogen made available to the grass by the fungus as it breaks down organic matter. The ring of dormant or dead grass is associated with depletion of soil water.

Filer (1965b) reported that *Marsamius oreades* parasitizes Kentucky bluegrass, red fescue, and Colonial bentgrass. The fungus hyphae penetrate the cortical cells of roots, causing their death. Filer (1965a) also reported that some isolates of *M. oreades* produce hydrogen cyanide in culture, and he suggested that turfgrass roots might be damaged by cyanogenic compounds in nature.

Control:

The eradication of fairy rings is nearly impossible, short of excavating the infested soil and replacing it with uncontaminated soil, and even this may fail to work. Suppressing the disease symptoms is more practical for the majority of cases. Eventually the organic matter in the soil that can be used by the fungus for growth is depleted and the fairy rings disappear.

The development of the ring of dormant or dead grass can be prevented by forcing large quantities of water into the soil to a depth of 1 or 2 feet with a tree-root feeder attachment on a garden hose. The rings must be treated at the first signs of wilting and treatments must be repeated whenever the grass shows signs of wilting. This does not kill the fungus, but it prevents the formation of rings of dormant or dead grass.

The dark green rings can be made less conspicuous by applying nitrogen fertilizer to the lawn so that the color difference is not as great.

Organic mercury fungicides have been recommended for control of fairy rings. By and large, their use involves rather detailed application techniques of drilling holes in the infected soil at intervals and repeatedly filling them with fungicide solutions. The results are usually not very spectacular. Stripping the sod from the infected area and fumigating with soil fumigants is usually effective, but costly and laborious.

SLIME MOLDS

The slime mold generally found on lawns is *Physarium cinereum* (Batsch) Pers. Occasionally other species may occur. The slime molds

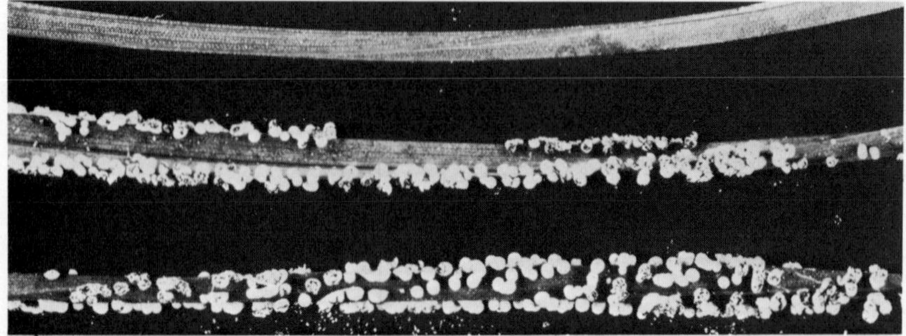

Figure 7. Slime mold fungus *(Physarium cinereum)* clings to the two Kentucky bluegrass leaves below; clean leaf at top.

are primitive fungi that lack cell walls during the vegatative phase of growth. They are capable of amoeba-like movement and creep over the soil surface and plant debris ingesting particles of organic matter, fungi, and bacteria. This stage, called a plasmodium, is rarely seen. Plasmodia of *P. cinereum* are watery-white; other species have plasmodia that are gray, cream, yellow to orange, red, violet, blue, green, or brown. The plasmodia occur in irregular shapes from less than an inch to a foot or more in diameter.

The reproductive stage of *P. cinereum* consists of purplish spores encased in grayish white calcareous fruiting structures on the leaves and stems of low-growing plants in the lawn, i.e., grasses, clover, and weeds. The fruiting bodies resemble cigarette ashes in over-all appearance and are easily rubbed off the plants (Figure 7).

The slime molds are not parasitic and technically do not cause disease. They merely use the plant leaves and stems as a support for their reproductive structures. However, slight damage may occur when leaves are smothered or shaded for several days by the fruiting bodies.

No control is usually recommended other than breaking up the spore masses by raking, brushing, or hosing with a stream of water. Mowing the grass usually destroys them.

V. Glossary of Mycological Terms

Apothecium (apothecia)—An open, saucer-shaped, disc-like sexual fruiting body bearing asci, characteristic of the discomycetes. (See perithecium.)

Ascocarp—A fruiting body producing asci.

Ascospores—Spores borne in an ascus.

Ascus (asci)—A sack-like structure characteristic of the Ascomycetes, in which sexual spores occur (usually 8 in number); these are the ascospores.

Asexual—Without sex.

Basidiospore or Sporidium (sporidia)—Small spores borne on a basidium.

Basidium (basidia)—A club-shaped structure or stalk bearing the basidiospores (often called promycelium in the smuts and rusts).

Blight—Rapid discoloration and death of the tissues over certain portions of plants.

Cleistothecium (cleistothecia)—A completely closed ascocarp.

Conidiophore—Mycelium stalk bearing conidia.

Conidium (conidia)—An asexual spore usually produced at the tip or side of a hypha or conidiphore.

Damping-off—The rapid rotting of seedlings, usually at the soil surface.

Facultative parasites—Organisms that usually live as saprophytes but under certain conditions may become parasitic.

Facultative saprophytes—Organisms that usually live as parasites but under certain conditions are capable of saprophytic growth.

Flagellum (flagella) or Cilium (cilia)—A whip-like structure that projects from free cells, such as bacteria and zoospores, and that functions as an organ of locomotion.

Fruiting body—A structure bearing spores.

Fungicide—An agent that inhibits or kills fungi.

Fungus (fungi)—A cryptogamic plant, not differentiated into root, stem, and leaf, devoid of chlorophyll.

Germ-tube—The hypha developed by a spore upon germination. By growth and branching, a germ-tube usually develops into the mycelium.

Haustorium (haustoria)—A special mycelial organ that usually develops within the host cell and absorbs nutrients.

Host or Suscept—The plant or animal upon which a parasite lives.

Hypha (hyphae)—The mycelial-like threads or vegetative growth of a fungus.

Immunity—Exemption from infection.

Infection—The process of gaining entrance and becoming established as a parasite.

Inoculum—That portion of a pathogen which is transferred to a host. It usually consists of spores, bacteria, mycelial fragments, nematode cysts, or virus particles.

Lesion—A localized diseased area.

Mycelium—The vegetative structure of a fungus, made up of the filamentous hyphae.

Necrosis—The death or disintegration of cells and tissues.

Obligate parasite—Organisms that can live only as parasites.

Obligate saprophyte—Organisms that can live only as saprophytes.

Oospore—A sexual spore produced in an oogonium, formed by the union of male and female gametes.

Paraphysis (paraphyses)—A sterile, hair-like structure in a hymenium.

Parasite—An organism that lives in or upon some living plant or animal from which it receives part or all of its food materials.

Pathogen—A disease-producing organism.

Pathogenicity—Ability of an organism to cause disease.

Primary infection—Infection instituted by a pathogen after a period of rest, usually in the spring.

Pustule—A local elevation of the epidermis that may rupture to expose the causal agent.

Race (physiologic race)—A name given to a subdivision of fungi within a species. Races within a species differ qualitatively in their ability to infect certain hosts, but show little, if any, difference morphologically.

Resistance—The sum of the qualities of the host and causal agent that retard the activities of the causal agent.

Saprophyte—An organism growing on dead organic matter.

Sclerotium (sclerotia)—A hard, dense, compact mass of mycelium with a specialized outer coat or rind.

Secondary infections—Infections initiated by a pathogen from primary or other secondary infections, without an interposed resting or dormant period.

Septate—With cross-walls.

Sign—The manifestation of disease by the presence of structures of the causal agent. (See symptoms.)

Sorus (sori)—A cluster of sporangia or spores usually covered first by the epidermis of the host.

Sporangium (sporangia)—A cell that contains one or more asexual spores.

Sporodochium—A densely packed group of short conidiophores.

Strain—A subdivision within a species or variety that differs quantitatively from other forms of the same organism.

Stripe—An elongated, narrow lesion with parallel sides.

Stroma (stromata)—A cushion-like, mycelial mass of tissue on or in which fructification usually occurs.

Susceptibility—The sum of the qualities of a plant and causal agent that allows the development of the causal agent.

Symptoms—Disease responses presented by the plant itself.

Systemic infection—A type of infection involving the entire plant.

Teliospore—A thick-walled resting or overwintering spore, produced by rust and smut fungi.

Urediospore—Binucleate repeating spore produced by certain rust fungi.
Uredium (uredia)—A cluster of urediospores.
Virus—A minute, infectious nucleo-protein that causes disease.
Zoospores—Motile spores provided with one or more flagella.

Literature Cited

Bain, D. C. 1962. *Sclerotinia* blight of bahia and Coastal bermudagrasses. Plant Dis. Reptr. 46:55-56.

Bain, D. C. 1966. *Puccinia zoysiae* in Mississippi. Plant Dis. Reptr. 50:770.

Bean, G. A. 1964. The pathogenicity of *Helminthosporium* spp. and *Curvularia* spp. on bluegrass in the Washington, D. C., area. Plant Dis. Reptr. 48:978-979.

Bean G. A. 1966. Observations on *Fusarium* blight of turfgrasses. Plant. Dis. Reptr. 50:942-945.

Bean, G. A., and R. D. Wilcoxson. 1964a. *Helminthosporium* leaf spot of bluegrass. Phytopathology 54:1065-1070.

Bean G. A. and R. D. Wilcoxson. 1964b. Pathogenicity of three species of *Helminthosporium* on roots of bluegrass. Phytopathology 54:1084-1085.

Beard, J. B. 1966. Fungicide and fertilizer applications as they affect *Typhula* snowmold control on turf. Quart. Bull. Michigan Agr. Exp. Sta. 49:221-228.

Bennett, F. T. 1937. Dollarspot disease of turf and its causal organism, *Sclerotinia homoeocarpa* N. sp. Ann. Appl. Biol. 24:236-257.

Bloom, J. R., and H. B. Couch. 1960. Influence of environment on diseases of turfgrasses. I. Effect of nutrition, pH, and soil moisture on *Rhizoctonia* brown patch. Phytopathology 50:532-535.

Britton, M. P. 1958. The identity, epiphytology and control of stem rust of Merion bluegrass. Ph.D. Thesis, Purdue University.

Britton, M. P., and J. D. Butler. 1965. Resistance of seven Kentucky bluegrass varieties to stem rust. Plant Dis. Reptr. 49:708-710.

Britton, M. P., and G. B. Cummins. 1956. The reaction of species of *Poa* and other grasses to *Puccinia striiformis*. Plant Dis. Reptr. 40:643-645.

Britton, M. P., and G. B. Cummins. 1959. Subspecific identity of the stem rust fungus of Merion bluegrass. Phytopathology 49:287-289.

Britton, M. P., and D. P. Rogers. 1963. *Olpidium brassicae* and *Polymyxa graminis* in roots of creeping bent in golf putting greens. Mycologia 55:758-763.

Broadfoot, W. C. 1936. Experiments on the chemical control of snowmold of turf in Alberta. Scientific Agr. 16:615-618.

Broadfoot, W. C., and M. W. Cormack. 1941. A low-temperature basidiomycete causing early spring killing of grasses and legumes in Alberta. Phytopathology 31:1058-1059.

Cherewick, W. J. 1944. Studies on the biology of *Erysiphe graminis* D. C. Can. J. Res. 22:52-86.

Clinton, G. P. 1905. The *Ustilagineae,* or smuts of Connecticut. Connecticut State Geol. and Nat. Hist. Surv. Bul. 5. 43 p.

Couch, H. B. 1962. Diseases of turfgrasses, Reinhold Publishing Corporation, New York. 289 p.

Couch, H. B., and E. R. Bedford. 1966. *Fusarium* blight of turfgrasses. Phytopathology 56:781-786.

Couch, H. B., and J. R. Bloom. 1960. Influence of environment on diseases of turfgrasses. II. Effect of nutrition, pH, and soil moisture on *Sclerotinia* dollar spot. Phytopathology 50:761-763.

Couch, H. B., and H. Cole, Jr. 1957. Chemical control of melting-out of Kentucky bluegrass. Plant Dis. Reptr. 41:205-208.

Couch, H. B., and L. D. Moore. 1960. Broad spectrum fungicides tested for control of melting-out of Kentucky bluegrass and *Sclerotinia* dollar spot of seaside bentgrass. Plant Dis. Reptr. 44:506-509.

Curtis, L. C. 1944. The exudation of glutamine from lawn grass. Plant Physiol. 19:1-5.

Dahl, A. S. 1933a. Effect of temperature on brown patch of turf. Phytopathology 23:8.

Dahl, A. S. 1933b. Effect of temperature and moisture on occurrence of brownpatch. U.S.G.A. Green Section Bul. 13:53-61.

Dahl, A. S. 1933c. Effect of watering putting greens on occurrence of brownpatch U.S.G.A. Green Section Bul. 13:62-66.

Dahl, A. S. 1933d. Relationship between fertilizing and drainage in the occurrence of brownpatch. U.S.G.A. Green Section Bul. 13:136-139.

Dahl, A. S. 1934. Snowmold of turf grasses as caused by *Fusarium nivale.* Phytopathology 24:197-214.

Davis, W. H. 1924. Spore germination of *Ustilago striaeformis.* Phytopathology 14:251-267.

Davis, W. H. 1926. Life history of *Ustilago striaeformis* (Westd.) Niessl which causes a leaf smut in timothy. J. Agr. Res. 32:69-76.

Dickson, J. G. 1956. Diseases of field crops. McGraw-Hill Book Company, New York. 517 p.

Dickinson, L. S. 1930. The effect of air temperature on the pathogenicity of *Rhizoctonia solani* parasitizing grasses on putting-green turf. Phytopathology 20:597-608.

Dodman, R. L., K. R. Barker, and J. C. Walker. 1968. Modes of penetration by different isolates of *Rhizoctonia solani.* Phytopathology 58:31-32.

Drechsler, C. 1928. Zonate eyespot of grasses caused by *Helminthosporium giganteum.* Agr. Res. 37:473-492.

Drechsler, C. 1929. Occurrence of the zonate-eyespot fungus *Helminthosporium giganteum* on some additional grasses. Agr. Res. 39:129-136.

Drechsler, C. 1931. Leaf spot and foot rot of Kentucky bluegrass caused by *Helminthosporium vagans.* Agr. Res. 40:447-456.

Drechsler, C. 1935. A leaf spot of bentgrasses caused by *Helminthosporium erythrospilum,* N. Sp. Phytopathology 25:344-361.

Duff, T. D., and J. B. Beard. 1966. Effects of air movement and syringing on the microclimate of bentgrass turf. Agron. J. 58:495-497.

Endo, R. M. 1961. Turfgrass diseases in southern California. Plant Dis. Reptr. 45:869-873.

Endo, R. M. 1963a. Influence of temperature on rate of growth of five fungus pathogens of turfgrass and on rate of disease spread. Phytopathology 53:857-861.

Endo, R. M. 1963b. Turf-grass disease situation in California in 1963. Golf Course Reptr. 31:27-30.

Endo, R. M. 1966. Control of dollar spot of turfgrass by nitrogen and its probable bases. Abs. Phytopathology 56:877.

Endo, R. M., and R. H. Amacher. 1964. Influence of guttation fluid on infection structures of *Helminthosporium sorokinianum.* Phytopathology 54:1327-1334.

Endo, R. M., and I. Malca. 1965. Morphological and cytohistological responses of primary roots of bentgrass to *Sclerotinia homeocarpa* and D-galactose. Phytopathology 55:781-789.

Endo, R. M., I. Malca, and Emmylou M. Krausman. 1964. Degeneration of the apical meristem and apex of bentgrass roots by a fungal toxin. Phytopathology 54:1175-1176.

Endo, R. M., and J. J. Oertli. 1964. Stimulation of fungal infection of bentgrass. Nature 201:313.

Erwin, L. E. 1941. Pathogenicity and control of *Corticium fuciforme* (Berk.). Wakef. Rhode Island Agr. Exp. Sta. Bul. 278. 34 p.

Filer, T. H. 1965a. Damage to turfgrasses caused by cyanogenic compounds produced by *Marasmius oreades,* a fairy ring fungus. Plant Dis. Reptr. 49:571-574.

Filer, T. H. 1965b. Parasitic aspects of a fairy ring fungus, *Marasmius oreades.* Phytopathology 55:1132-1134.

Filer, T. H. 1966. Red thread found on Bermuda grass. Plant Dis. Reptr. 50:525-526.

Fischer, G. W. 1940. Fundamental studies of the stripe smut of grasses *(Ustilago striaeformis)* in the Pacific Northwest. Phytopathology 30:93-118.

Fischer G. W. 1951. A local, winter-time epidemic of blister smut, *Entyloma crastophilum* on Kentucky bluegrass at Pullman, Washington, Plant Dis. Reptr. 35:88.

Freeman, T. E. 1960. Effects of temperature on cottony blight of ryegrass. Abs. Phytopathology 50:575.

Freeman, T. E. 1964. *Helminthosporium* diseases of Bermudagrass. Golf Course Reptr. 32:24-26.

Freeman, T. E. 1965. Rust of *Zoysia* spp. in Florida. Plant Dis. Reptr. 49:382.

Freeman, T. E. 1967. Diseases of southern turfgrasses. Florida Agr. Exp. Sta. Tech. Bul. 713. 31 p.

Freeman, T. E., and G. C. Horn. 1963. Reaction of turfgrasses to attack by *Pythium aphanidermatum* (Edson) Fitzpatrick. Plant Dis. Reptr. 47:425-427.

Gaskin, T. A. 1965. Varietal reaction of creeping bentgrass to stripe smut. Plant Dis. Reptr. 49:268.

Gaskin, T. A. 1966. Evidence for physiologic races of stripe smut *(Ustilago striiformis)* attacking Kentucky bluegrass. Plant Dis. Reptr. 50:430-431.

Gaskin, T. A., and M. P. Britton. 1962. The effect of powdery mildew on the growth of Kentucky bluegrass. Plant Dis. Reptr. 46:724-725.

Gould, C. J. 1957. Turf diseases in western Washington in 1955 and 1956. Plant Dis. Reptr. 41:344-347.

Gould, C. J. 1963. Some practical aspects of disease control. Golf Course Reptr. 31:1-5.

Gould, C. J., R. L. Goss, and M. Eglitis. 1961a. *Ophiobolus* patch disease of turf in Western Washington. Plant Dis. Reptr. 45:296-297.

Gould, C. J., R. L. Goss, and V. L. Miller. 1961b. Fungicidal tests for control of *Fusarium* patch disease of turf. Plant Dis. Reptr. 45:112-118.

Gould, C. J., V. L. Miller, and R. L. Goss. 1965. New experimental and commercial fungicides for control of *Fusarium* patch disease of bentgrass turf. Plant Dis. Reptr. 49:923-927.

Gould, C. J., V. L. Miller, and R. L. Goss. 1967. Fungicidal control of red thread disease of turfgrass in western Washington. Plant Dis. Reptr. 51:215-219.

Gudauskas, R. T., and S. M. McCarter. 1966. Occurrence of rust on *Zoysia* species in Alabama. Plant Dis. Reptr. 50:885.

Gudauskas, R. T., and N. E. McGlohon. 1964. *Sclerotinia* blight of bahiagrass in Alabama. Plant Dis. Reptr. 48:418.

Halisky, P. M., and C. R. Funk. 1966. Environmental factors affecting growth and sporulation of *Helminthosporium vagans* and its pathogenicity to *Poa pratensis.* Phytopathology 56:1294-1296.

Halisky, P. M., C. R. Funk, and S. Bachelder. 1966a. Stripe smut of turf and forage grasses—its prevalence, pathogenicity, and response to management practices. Plant Dis. Reptr. 50:294-298.

Halisky, P. M., C. R. Funk, and R. E. Engle. 1966b. Melting-out of Kentucky bluegrass varieties by *Helminthosporium vagans* as influenced by turf management practices. Plant Dis. Reptr. 50:703-706.

Hardison, J. R. 1963. Commercial control of *Puccinia striiformis* and other rusts in seed crops of *Poa pratensis* by nickel fungicides. Phytopathology 53:209-216.

Hardison, J. R. 1966. Systemic activity of two derivatives of 1, 4-oxathiin against smut and rust diseases of grasses. Plant Dis. Reptr. 50:624.

Hardison, J. R. 1967. Chemotherapeutic control of stripe smut *(Ustilago striiformis)* in grasses by two derivatives of 1,4-oxathiin. Phytopathology 57:242-245.

Healy, M. J. 1967. Factors affecting the pathogenicity of selected fungi isolated from putting green turf. Ph.D. Thesis, University of Illinois.

Healy, M. J., and M. P. Britton. 1968. Infection and development of *Helminthosporium sorokinianum* in *Agrostis palustris.* Phytopathology 58:273-276.

Healy, M. J., M. P. Britton, and J. D. Butler. 1965. Stripe smut damage on 'Pennlu' creeping bentgrass. Plant Dis. Reptr. 49:710.

Hodges, C. F. 1967. Etiology of stripe smut, *Ustilago striiformis* (West.) Niessl, on Merion bluegrass, *Poa pratensis.* Ph.D. Thesis, University of Illinois.

Howard, F. L., J. B. Rowell, and H. L. Keil. 1951. Fungus diseases of turf grasses. Rhode Island Exp. Sta. Bul. 308.

Jackson, N. 1959. *Ophiobolus* patch disease fungicide trials, 1958. J. Sports Turf Res. Inst. 9:459-461.

Kallio, A. 1966. Chemical control of snow mold (Sclerotinia borealis) on four varieties of bluegrass *(Poa pratensis)* in Alaska. Plant Dis. Reptr. 50:69-72.

Kozelnicky, G. M., and W. N. Garrett. 1966. The occurrence of *zoysia* rust in Georgia. Plant Dis. Reptr. 50:839.

Kerr, A. 1956. Factors influencing the development of brown patch in lawns of *Sagina procumbens* L. Aust. J. Biol. Sci. 9:322-338.

Klomparens, W. 1953. A study of *Helminthosporium sativum* P. K. & B. as an unreported parasite of *Agrostis palustris* Huds. Ph.D. Thesis, Michigan State University.

Kraft, J. M., R. M. Endo, and D. C. Erwin. 1967. Infection of primary roots of bentgrass by zoospores of *Pythium aphanidermatum.* Phytopahtology 57:86-90.

Kreitlow, K. W. 1943. *Ustilago striaeformis* II. Temperature as a factor influencing development of smutted plants of *Poa pratensis* L. and germination of fresh chlamydospores. Phytopathology 33:1055-1063.

Kreitlow, K. W., and F. V. Juska. 1959. Susceptibility of Merion and other Kentucky bluegrass varieties to stripe smut *(Ustilago striiformis).* Agron. J. 51:596-597.

Kreitlow, K. W., F. V. Juska, and R. T. Haard. 1965. A rust on *Zoysia japonica* new to North America. Plant Dis. Reptr. 49:185-186.

Kreitlow, K. W., and W. M. Meyers. 1944. Prevalence and distribution of stripe smut of *Poa pratensis* in some pastures of Pennsylvania. Phytopathology 34:411-415.

Leach, J. G., C. V. Lowther, and Mary A. Ryan. 1946. Stripe smut *(Ustilago striaeformis),* in relation to bluegrass improvement. Phytopathology 36:57-72.

Lebeau, J. B. 1964. Control of snow mold by regulating winter soil temperature. Phytopathology 54:693-696.

Lukens, R. J., and E. M. Stoddard. 1961. Wilt diesase of golf greens and its control with nabam. Abs. Phytopathology 51:577.

Malca, I., and R. M. Endo. 1965. Identification of galactose in cultures of *Sclerotinia homeocarpa* as the factor toxic to bentgrass roots. Phytopathology 55:775-780.

Moore, L. D., and H. B. Couch. 1961. *Pythium ultimum* and *Helminthosporium vagans* as foliar pathogens of gramineae. Plant Dis. Reptr. 45:616-619.

Moore, L. D., H. B. Couch, and J. R. Bloom. 1963. Influence of environment on diseases of turfgrasses. III. Effect of nutrition, pH, soil temperature, air temperature, and soil moisture on *Pythium* blight of Highland bentgrass. Phytopathology 53:53-57.

Monteith, J., Jr. 1925. July experiments for control of brown-patch on Arlington experimental turf garden. U.S.G.A. Green Section Bul. 5:173-176.

Monteith, J. Jr. 1926. The brown patch disease of turf, its nature and control. U.S.G.A. Green Section Bul, 6:127-142.

Monteith, J. Jr. 1929. Some effects of lime and fertilizer on turf diseases. U.S.G.A. Green Section Bul. 9:82-99.

Monteith, J., Jr., and A. S. Dahl. 1932. Turf diseases and their control U.S.G.A Greens Section Bul. 12:85-186.

Mower, R. G. 1961. Histological studies of suscept-pathogen relationships of *Helminthosporium sativum* P. K. & B., *Helminthosporium vagans* Drechsl., and *Curvularia lunata* (Wakk.) Boed. on leaves of Merion and common Kentucky bluegrass *(Poa pratensis* L.) Ph.D. Thesis, Cornell University.

Mower, R. G., and R. L. Millar. 1963. Histological relationships of *Helminthosporium vagans, H. sativum,* and *Curvularia lunata* in leaves of Merion and common Kentucky bluegrass. Abs. Phytopathology 53:351.

Muse, R. R., and H. B. Couch. 1965. Influence of environment on diseases of turfgrasses. IV. Effect of nutrition and soil moisture on *Corticium* red thread of creeping red fescue. Phytopathology 55:507-510.

Oakley, R. A. 1924. Brown-patch investigations. U.S.G.A Green Section Bul. 4:87-92.

Oakley, R. A. 1925. Some things we have learned about brown-patch. U.S.G.A Green Section Bul. 5:75-77.

Osner, G. A. 1916. Leaf smut of timothy. Cornell Univ. Agr. Exp. Sta. Bul. 381.

Piper, C. V., and R. A. Oakley. 1921. The brown-patch disease of turf. U.S.G.A Green Section Bul. 1:112-115.

Remsberg, Ruth E. 1940. Studies in the genus *Typhula.* Mycologia 32:52-96.

Rowell, J. B. 1951. Observations on the pathogenicity of *Rhizoctonia solani* on bentgrasses. Plant Dis. Reptr. 35:240-242.

Shantz, H. L., and R. I. Piemeisel. 1917. Fungus fairy rings in eastern Colorado and their effect on vegetation. J. Agr. Res. 11:191-245.

Smith, J. D. 1955. Fungi and turf diseases. Jour. Sports Turf Res. Inst. 9:35-59.

Smith J. D. 1956. Fungi and turf diseases 6. *Ophiobolus patch* disease. J. Sports Turf Res. Inst. 9:180-202.

Smith, J. D. 1959a. Fungal diseases of turfgrasses. Bul. Sports Turf Res. Inst. p. 57-61.

Smith, J. D. 1959b. The effect of lime application on the occurrence of *Fusarium* patch disease on a forced *Poa annua* turf. J. Sports Turf Res. Inst. 9:476-470.

Sprague, R. 1950. Diseases of cereals and grasses in North America. The Ronald Press Co., New York. 538 p.

Thirumalachar, M. J., and J. G. Dickson. 1953. Spore germination, cultural characters, and cytology of *Ustilago striiformis* and the reaction of hosts. Phytopathology 43:527-535.

Ward, E. W. B., and G. D. Thorne. 1965. Evidence for the formation of HCN from glycine by a snow mold fungus. Abs. Phytopathology 55:1081.

Weihing, J. L., S. G. Jensen, and R. I. Hamilton. 1957. *Helminthosporium sativum,* a destructive pathogen of bluegrass. Phytopathology 47:744-746.

Williams, A. S., and R. E. Schmidt. 1964. Studies on dollar spot and melting out. Golf Course Reporter 32:36-40.

Yarwood, C. E. 1936. Tolerance of *Erysiphe polygoni* and certain other powdery mildews to low humidity. Phytopathology 26:845-859.

Zummo, Natale, and A. G. Plakidas. 1958. Brown patch of St. Augustine grass. Plant Dis. Reptr. 42:1141-1147.

11 Harmful Insects

B. A. App

Agricultural Research Service, U.S.D.A.
Beltsville, Maryland

S. H. Kerr

University of Florida
Gainesville, Florida

I. Introduction

The control of injurious insects is one of the constant problems of turf establishment and maintenance. It has been conservatively estimated (USDA, 1965) that the damage to turf due to insects is around 5% of its value and amounts to several hundred million dollars annually. All the common kinds and varieties of turfgrasses are attacked by insects, more than 60 species of which are recorded as pests. However, the insect species are not universally distributed and vary in abundance from year to year and location to location because of such factors as climate, presence or absence of natural enemies, and the abundance of food plants. As a result, only a few species are sufficiently abundant at any one time to justify control measures.

The insect pests of turf can be roughly divided into three groups—those that feed below the surface of the soil, those that eat the leaves and stems, and those that suck plant juices. The damage shows up in several ways: insect feeding may weaken the plants and cause a general unthrifty condition; patches of grass may be consumed, which gives the turf an uneven appearance; or areas of the turf may turn yellow or brown and die. Also, many other insects are found in or on turf areas, some that may indirectly damage turf by their burrowing or nest building habits, and others that cause little or no damage but are annoying and may bite or sting.

The presence of insects in turf often goes unnoticed until considerable damage has occurred. All the yellowish, brownish, or dead spots and the unthrifty areas of turf are not caused by insects. Nematodes, diseases, drought, and lack of proper soil nutrients are often responsible instead. It is important to be certain what is causing the injury. The home owner and turf specialist should learn to recognize the major turf pests and become familiar with the types of damage they cause. Also, frequent examinations of the turf should be made so that insect infestations can be detected early and the proper treatment applied at the right time. It is the purpose of this chapter to briefly describe the major insect pests of turf, the damage they cause, and ways in which they can be controlled.

II. Soil Inhabiting Insects

A. Grubs

Grubs are the larvae of many species of beetles belonging to the family Scarabaeidae. Although the adult beetles differ considerably in color, structural markings, and habits, the grubs themselves and the injury they cause to turf are quite similar. Full-grown larvae are from 1 to 1½ inches long, soft bodied, and white to grayish white; they have brown heads, six prominent legs, and are generally found in a curled position. The hind part of the body is smooth and shiny, and the dark contents of the stomach shows through the skin. These pests feed on the roots of grass 1 to 2 inches below the surface, which causes the grass to turn brown and die. In severe infestations, the grubs cut off the roots, and the sod can be easily lifted or rolled up (Fig. 1). Moles, birds, and skunks feed on these grubs and often tear up the turf as they search for them.

White grubs. The white grubs (Fig. 2), principally *Phyllophaga* spp., are the most widely distributed group that infests turf. There are over 150 species in the U. S., one or more that are found in all areas though they

Figure 1. White grub injury to turf.

Figure 2. White grubs.

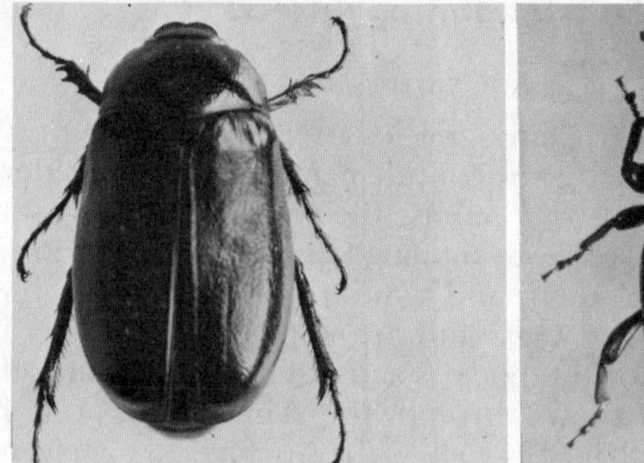

Figure 3. Adult May beetle (left) and adult billbug (right).

are more abundant in the eastern half of the country. The adults are the familiar May beetles or June bugs (Fig. 3) that often fly to lights on warm nights in the spring. The beetles are hard-shelled, and most of them vary from yellow-brown to blackish though some are bright blue-green or yellow with metallic lustre (Ritcher 1966); they feed at night on the foliage of trees and shrubs and sometimes completely strip them.

The length of the life cycle of the *Phyllophaga* varies from 2 to 4 years depending on latitude (Luginbill 1953). Most have a 3-year cycle north of the Ohio river, but some that have a 3-year cycle in the north complete their cycle in 2 years farther south. In a typical 3-year cycle, the adults emerge in May and June and mate and lay their pearly white eggs in the soil. A single female deposits an average of 50 eggs (Ritcher 1940). Hatching requires 15 to 21 days. The young grubs feed on decaying and living vegetable matter during the first summer.

Late in the fall they go deeper into the soil to spend the winter. During the second summer they feed on grass roots and cause most of their damage. Then, as cold weather approaches, they again go deeper into the soil. The next spring they feed for a short time; but in June they move downward in the soil and change to the pupal stage. They transform to adults in about a month but remain in the pupal cell until the following May or June.

The masked chafers. The grubs of the northern masked chafer, *Cyclocephala borealis* Arrow, and a closely related species, the southern masked chafer, *C. immaculata* (Olivier), are sometimes called annual white grubs because they complete their life cycle in one year. The adults are about ½ inch long and brown. The males are somewhat darker than the females. These beetles are strong fliers and are strongly attracted to lights. No food is taken by the adults since their mouth parts are nonfunctional. The grubs, however, do extensive damage to lawns and turf areas.

The northern masked chafer is found from Connecticut south to Alabama and west to California, and the southern masked chafer is common in the southeastern states and as far north as Kentucky. Ritcher (1940) indicated that in the inner bluegrass region of Kentucky the population of southern masked chafers often equaled that of all other species of May beetle grubs combined. Polivka (1965) said that in Ohio the northern masked chafer varied in abundance from year to year but was sometimes the predominant species.

The oriental beetle. So far as is known, the oriental beetle, *Anomala orientalis* Waterhouse, was accidentally introduced into Connecticut around 1920 and has since spread into Massachusetts, New York, and New Jersey. The grubs sometimes cause severe damage to turf. The adults are about 1/2 inch long and straw colored with darker markings. There is a single generation each year.

The Asiatic garden beetle. Another accidentally introduced pest is the Asiatic garden beetle, *Maladera castanea* (Arrow). These grubs, too, sometimes damage turf. The species was first found in New Jersey in 1921, and it is now found in scattered locations from Massachusetts to South Carolina and west to Ohio. The adult is about 1/4 inch long and velvety brown; the underside of the body is covered with short yellow hairs. There is only one generation per year. Adults are most abundant from mid-July to mid-August.

The European chafer. As its name implies, the European chafer, *Amphimallon majalis* (Razoumowsky), was introduced from Europe. In 1940 it was found damaging turf in Wayne County, New York. Isolated infestations have since been found in Connecticut, Massachusetts, New Jersey, West Virginia, Pennsylvania, and Ohio. The grubs damage winter grain, legumes, and other plants (Gambrell, 1954) in addition to turf.

The insect has a one-year life cycle. The adults are about 1/2 inch long and light tan to chocolate brown. They are most numerous in June and July, and when numbers of them are in flight their buzzing noise and appearance are such that they are easily mistaken for a swarm of bees. The adult beetles feed little and do little damage.

The Japanese beetle. The Japanese beetle, *Popillia japonica* Newman, is another of our pests of foreign origin. It was first found in New Jersey in 1916, and it now occurs from southern Maine to North Carolina and Georgia and west to Kentucky, Illinois, Michigan, and Missouri.

The grubs of the Japanese beetle spend about 10 months of the year in the soil feeding on the roots of plants, particularly grasses. They are about 1 inch long when full grown. Large populations severely damage turf areas.

The adults are slightly less than 1/2 inch long. They are shiny metallic green with coppery-brown wing covers and six small patches of white hairs along the sides and back of the body. The beetles make their appearance in early summer and are abundant for 4 to 6 weeks. They fly during the day and are most active on warm, sunny days. The females burrow about 3 inches into the ground, usually in turf areas, and deposit their eggs. There is a single generation per year.

Green June beetle. Injury to turf by the green June beetle, *Cotinis nitida* (L.) is largely caused by the little mounds of earth thrown up on the surface by the grubs as they burrow through the soil. These mounds disfigure the turf and may smother the grass. Also their burrowing may uproot seedlings or cause the soil to dry out so the grass may suffer from lack of moisture. These grubs normally feed on organic matter in the soil.

The adult beetles are somewhat flattened, nearly 1 inch long, and velvety green with bronze or yellowish edges. They are quite common in the Eastern states as far north as Long Island, New York, and west to southern Illinois. They are present from June to August and are most active during the day. The eggs are laid in soil rich in organic matter. The grubs are about 2/3 grown by fall and complete their development the following spring. When full grown, they are plump and yellowish white, have brown heads, and are about 2 inches long and 1/2 inch wide. The grubs come to the surface at night and move about on their backs assisted by stiff ambulatory bristles. There is one generation per year.

B. Ants

Ants are social insects that live in colonies made up of a queen and workers similar to honey bees, *Apis mellifera* L. Several species nest in turf, and, when they are numerous, the mounds of soil they excavate are unsightly and may smother the grass and cause much damage. In addition their tunnels may allow the soil to dry out around the roots of plants, which often causes the death of the plants. Also, ants may prevent grass seeds from germinating by feeding on them or by storing them in their nests. Schread (1964) lists four species, three of which commonly nest in lawns—the cornfield ant, *Lasius alienus* (Foerster), a red ant, *Formica palliedefulva* Latreille, and the pavement ant, *Tetramorium caespitum* (L.). A fourth species, the Allegheny mound ant, *Formica exsectoides* Forel, is capable of nesting in lawns, but the large mounds it builds are usually disturbed before injury becomes severe. A few ants sometimes found in turf, such as fire ants, *Solenopsis* spp., and harvester ants, *Pogonomyrmex* spp., can inflict a painful bite and sting.

C. Bees and Wasps

A few species of bees and wasps (Hymenoptera) may damage lawns by their nest building habits. Kelsheimer and Kerr (1957) mentioned the unsightly mounds of a mound-building bee, *Nomia heteropoda* (Say). These bees are annoying because they continually fly around the yard, but there are no records of people being stung by them. During July and August in the eastern U. S., the cicada killer, *Sphecius speciosus* (Drury), may be seen buzzing and darting around the yard. These wasps are about 1 1/2 inches long and have a yellow and black body. They are very energetic and dig holes about 3/4 inch in diameter and mound up the dirt around the entrances. The hole extends about 6 inches into the soil. Several branches then extend 6 to 8 inches and terminate in roughly globular cells. The female wasp captures a cicada, stings it, places it in one of the cells, and lays an egg on it. The egg hatches in a few days, and the larva feeds on the cicada. These wasps are not vicious but, when molested, they can inflict a painful sting.

D. Periodical Cicada

When nymphs of the periodical cicada, *Magicicada septendecim* (L.), emerge to become adults, they leave small holes in the soil that may be particularly numerous under trees. These nymphs do not damage lawns. The adults are about 1⅝ inches long and have a mostly black body and reddish legs and eyes; the veins in the wings are orange. The females lay their eggs in pockets cut in the twigs of trees. The young nymphs drop to the ground and burrow into the soil where they suck juices from the roots of trees. Development to the adult stage requires 17 years in the northern states and 13 years in the southern states.

E. Billbugs

Several species of billbugs damage turf. The adults (Fig. 3) are hard-shelled beetles from ⅕ to ¾ inch long with a long snout or bill that carries a pair of strong jaws at the tip. The larvae are legless, white, as much as ⅝ inch long, and have a hard yellowish brown or reddish brown head. The adults burrow in the grass stems near the soil surface, and the larvae feed on the roots, often cutting them off so the grass is easily pulled out.

In general, billbugs pass the winter as adults, but in the warmer parts of the country other stages may survive the winter. The eggs are laid in cells cut in the grass stems and hatch in a few days to 2 weeks. The larva feeds for several weeks and then changes into a pupa, usually in a cell in the soil. The pupa changes to an adult in a few days and may remain in the pupal cell for the winter or may emerge and be active until the advent of cold weather.

Sphenophorus phoeniciensis Chittenden, the so-called Phoenix billbug, attacks bermudagrass lawns in the southwest. Klostermeyer (1964) reported that *S. cicatristriatus* Fahraeus caused considerable damage to turf in the state of Washington. A hunting billbug, *S. venatus vestitus* Chittenden, causes severe damage to zoysiagrass (Kelsheimer, 1956; Juska, 1965). This billbug occurs from Maryland to Florida, west as far as Missouri and Kansas, and in Hawaii. It feeds on several grasses, but with the increased planting of zoysiagrass in the eastern U. S., it has become very destructive to this grass. The larvae feeding on the roots cause the grass to turn yellow or brown in circular or irregular patches; then the grass can be pulled up with little or no resistance. The damage is sometimes confused with fertilizer burn.

F. Wireworms

Turf areas are sometimes damaged by wireworms (Elateridae). They are cylindrical, hard, wirelike larvae 1 to 1½ inches long and usually yellowish or brown that feed on the roots and bore into the underground parts of the plant. The adults are ½ to ¾ inch long, brownish, grayish, or nearly black, and tapered at both ends. They are called click beetles because, when they fall on their backs, they right themselves by flipping into the air and making a clicking sound.

G. Mole Crickets

Mole crickets feed on the roots of grasses. In addition, their burrowing through the soil allows the soil to dry out and uproots some plants. Newly seeded turf may be severely damaged by only a few crickets. These insects are most active at night when they may come to the surface to feed. The adult crickets are about 1½ inches long, light brown or grayish brown, and covered with fine hairs that give them a velvety appearance. They have beady eyes and stout front legs with shovellike feet that are well equipped for digging. Kelsheimer (1950) listed four species found in the southeast—the short-winged mole cricket, *Scapteriscus abbreviatus* Scudder, the northern mole cricket, *Gryllotalpa hexadactyla* Perty, the southern mole cricket, *S. acletus* Rhen and Hebard, and the changa, *S. vicinus* Scudder. Kelsheimer (1950) indicated that the southern mole cricket and the changa were important species in Florida.

Mole crickets overwinter as partly grown nymphs that mature in late spring. The females deposit their eggs in cells in the soil. The eggs hatch in 20 to 35 days, and the young resemble the adults except that they are wingless. There is only one generation per year.

III. Insects That Eat Leaves and Stems

A. Lawn Caterpillars

Sod webworms. Several kinds of caterpillars, such as sod webworms, armyworms, and cutworms, damage turf grasses. The sod webworms are the most important. They are the larvae of small, whitish or grayish moths often called lawn moths that are frequently seen flying over the lawn in the early evening. They can be recognized by their habit of folding their wings close around their bodies when at rest (Fig. 4). The females drop their eggs at random as they fly over the turf, and they hatch in a week to 10 days. The larvae feed on the grass leaves and then, as they grow older, they build themselves burrows or tunnels close under the soil surface that are lined with silk. The larvae are most active at night when they chew off grass blades near the ground. The injury is first noticed as irregular brown spots and later as ragged uneven patches of growth. Large populations may severely damage large areas of grass. Full-grown larvae are about ¾ inch long, brownish or greyish, and usually spotted (Fig. 4). They pass the pupal stage in cells in the soil. There are several generations per year, and the winter is usually passed in the larval stage.

There are many species of sod webworms, and one or more occur in all areas of the U. S. Most of those found in lawns belong to the genus *Crambus.* Bohart (1947) listed *C. bonifatellus* (Hulst) and *C. sperryellus* Klots as important species in California. The bluegrass webworm, *C. teterrellus* (Zincken), is widely distributed in the eastern U. S. (Ainslie, 1930). *C. laqueatellus* Clemens and *C. trisectus* (Walker) (damage turf

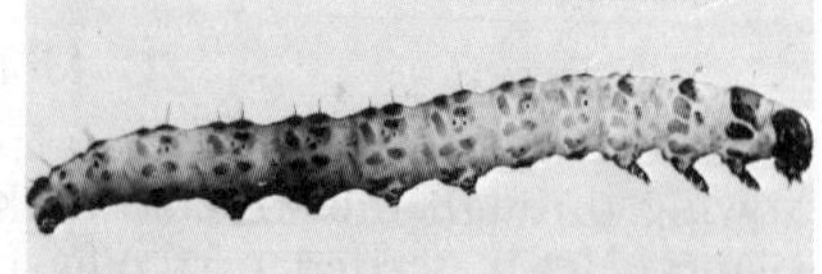

Figure 4. Sod webworm and larva.

areas in Connecticut (Johnson 1944). Crawford and Harwood (1964) listed several species that are troublesome in Washington grass seed fields but reported *C. topiarius* Zeller, the cranberry girdler, as most destructive. A tropical sod webworm, *Herpetogramma=(Pachyzancla) phaeopteralis* (Guenee), is the most important species in Florida (Brogden and Kerr, 1964). A burrowing sod webworm, *Acrolophus popeanellus* (Clemens), infests lawn grasses in Maryland and Virginia west to Kansas and in Louisiana; the dirty-white larvae of this species live in silk-lined tubes about 3/8 inch in diameter extending 2 to 3 inches into the soil.

The fall armyworm. The fall armyworm, *Spodoptera frugiperda* (J. E. Smith), is the most common armyworm found in turf. The full-grown larvae are about 1½ inches long, vary from light green to almost black, and have several stripes along the sides. Also there is a yellowish white inverted Y on the head. These larvae feed on a wide range of plants but prefer grasses. They feed mostly at night and consume grass leaves. In turf areas, they cause the grass to look ragged and bare. When heavy outbreaks occur, the larvae may devour the grass down to the ground.

The adults are ash-gray moths with mottled forewings with irregular white or light gray spots near the extreme tips. When the wings are expanded, they measure about 1½ inches across. The moths are most active at night, and the females lay their egg masses on grass leaves or other foliage. These masses may contain a hundred or more eggs and are covered with a light grayish fuzz from the female's body. The larvae feed 2 to 3 weeks and then burrow 2 to 3 inches into the soil to pupate. In the South, there may be as many as six generations per year, but there is only one in the northernmost part of the insect's range. The fall armyworm does not overwinter except in the warmer parts of the southern U. S. Infestations that cover much of the eastern half of the country and sometimes extend as far north as Massachusetts and as far west as Montana are the result of northward migrations of the moths each year.

The armyworm. Another caterpillar found less commonly in lawns is the armyworm, *Pseudaletia unipuncta* (Haworth). The larvae are similar in size and appearance to larvae of the fall armyworm. The moth has a wing spread of 1½ inches and is brownish with a small white spot near the center of each front wing. This insect is present in much of the U. S. east of the Rocky Mountains and occasionally occurs in New Mexico, Arizona, and California. It usually overwinters as a larva but sometimes as a pupa. There are usually three generations per year.

Cutworms. Cutworms are the larvae of night flying moths of the family Noctuidae. Several species are occasionally found in turf. They are usually minor pests that feed on the leaves and cut off the grass near the soil surface. Turf areas may also serve as a reservoir for cutworms that migrate into flower beds and cut the plants (Schread 1964). Cutworms are plump, nearly smooth caterpillars 1½ to 2 inches long that vary from grey to brown to nearly black. Some species are spotted; others are striped. When they are found in the soil, they are usually in a coiled position. The moths are brownish or grayish. They lay their eggs on plants in grassy areas. There may be one to four generations per year depending on locality and species.

Nomophilia noctuella (Denis and Schiffermüller). This insect has no approved common name but is sometimes called the lucern moth (Jefferson and Swift, 1956), the celery stalk worm, the soil webworm (Smith, 1942), or the clover nomophila (Treece, 1960). The larvae prefer clover and other legumes but will feed on grasses and are occasionally found in lawns. They are slender grayish or greenish spotted caterpillars that reach a length of about 1 inch. Like the sod webworms which they resemble, they make small horizontal silken tubes near the base of the plants. The adult is a small brownish moth with mottled darker front wings. This insect is widely distributed over the U. S. and produces two to four generations per year.

Skippers. Skippers are so called because the adults have an erratic flight habit of suddenly darting from place to place. The larvae have large heads and strongly constricted necks. Larvae of the fiery skipper, *Hylephila phyleus* (Drury), and the field skipper, *Atalopedes campestris* (Boisduval), feed on grasses and are common throughout the U. S. They are minor pests of turf grasses. The larvae of the fiery skipper are about 1 inch long and brownish yellow. The male butterflies are orange-yellow spotted with black, the wings of the female are dark brown with orange-yellow spots. The species was reported to sometimes injure bentgrass lawns in California (Jefferson and Swift, 1956). The field skipper is common and is most important as a pasture pest, but the larvae sometimes damage bermudagrass lawns (Warren and Roberts, 1956).

Grass loopers. Several species of striped grass loopers, *Mocis* spp., feed on grasses. When these larvae become abundant, they may invade lawns and turf areas. The larvae feed on the blades of the grass. When full grown, they are about 2½ inches long and vary from cream to blue-gray, brown, black, or orange. They have large black-and-white spots, and stripes extend the full length of the body.

B. Other Foliage and Stem Feeders

Grasshoppers. There are many species of grasshoppers that differ widely in their food preferences and feeding habits. They are not normally pests of well-kept turf, but when they are abundant and other food is scarce they may invade turf areas.

Frit fly. The frit fly, *Oscinella frit* (L.), is of European origin where it has long been a pest of grains. It is present in several states and has been found in well-kept turf in Connecticut (Schread, 1964). The adult flies are black and about 1/16 inch long. They lay their eggs on the grass, and the young maggots bore into the stems. There are several generations per year.

IV. Insects That Suck Juices From Roots, Stems, or Leaves

A. Lawn Chinch Bugs

Chinch bugs, *Blissus* spp., feed on grasses, and some species of these insects are serious pests of lawn grasses. The hairy chinch bug, *Blissus hirtus* Montandon, is frequently injurious to bentgrasses in the northeastern U. S.; the southern chinch bug, *B. insularis* Barber, is a major pest of St. Augustinegrass in the southeastern part of the country. The species *B. leucopterus* (Say) is the common chinch bug that damages grains and corn but is sometimes a pest of bermudagrass in the lower area of the Midwest.

The life histories of chinch bugs that have been studied are generally similar (Eden and Self, 1960; Kerr, 1966a; Komblas, 1962; Leonard, 1966; Luginbill, 1922; Shelford, 1932; Webster, 1907). The females lay a few eggs a day over a period that may last several weeks, and 100 to 500 eggs per female is the range commonly observed.

The time for the eggs to hatch and for the nymphs to develop to adults varies widely, depending largely on temperature. In warm weather the eggs hatch in about 1½ weeks, but it may take as much as a month in cooler weather. Typically, there are five nymphal instars, though some individuals may have only four and others may have six or seven. The total length of the nymphal stage has ranged from 26 to 70 days, and the time from egg to adult from 35 to 95 days. Pre-oviposition periods range from 5 to 14 days.

In the northeastern U. S., the hairy chinch bug has two generations per year with possibly a partial third in part of its range. The southern chinch bug has three generations and a partial fourth where it has been studied in Louisiana and northern Florida, but it probably has at least five generations in southern Florida and the subtropical parts of its range.

The hairy chinch bug overwinters as an adult, usually in tufts of meadow grasses or under plant debris in meadows, along woods borders, and around foundations of houses. It leaves its hibernating quarters in the spring (early in May in Connecticut). The southern chinch bug continues to breed the year around where it has been studied in northern Florida and Louisiana, but the rate of development is greatly slowed in the winter. Where they continue to be active during the winter, the greater part of these populations will be adults.

The adults hibernate or enter a dormant condition during the coldest weather in the northern part of the range.

Adult lawn chinch bugs are 1/6 to 1/5 inch long and black with white wings folded over the back. On the outer margin of each wing is a small, triangular black spot. The wings of some individuals reach to the tip of the abdomen, but in others they may extend only half the length of the abdomen (Fig. 5). Nymphs range from 1/20 inch long (newly hatched) to nearly adult size. The smallest ones are bright red. As they grow larger, the color darkens, first to orange, then to gray, and then to black. They have a transverse white band just behind the wing pads.

Chinch bugs insert a slender piercing beak into the grass and suck the plant juices. Studies with the chinch bug, *B. leucopterus,* on sorghum showed that the salivary juices of the insect and the plant materials reacted to form a substance that blocked some food transport passages in the plant; this interaction was probably an important type of plant injury (Painter, 1928).

Chinch bugs occur in aggregations in scattered patches rather than being evenly distributed over the lawn, but they are usually found in

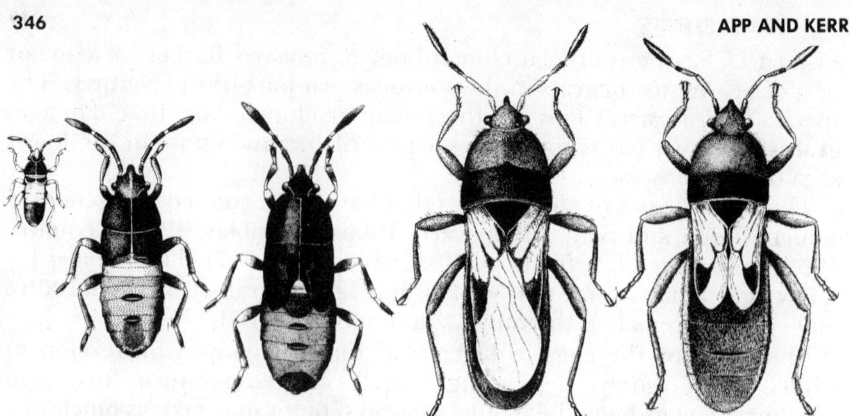

Figure 5. Three chinch bug nymphs (left) and long- and short-winged adult forms.

the open, sunny areas of the lawn and may be as numerous as several hundred per square foot. The grass turns yellowish in irregular patches that are at first only 2 or 3 feet in diameter. If the bugs are allowed to continue feeding, the grass dies and turns brown. The injured areas enlarge and fuse, and eventually all but the heavily shaded areas may be killed.

There are many reasons for declining patches of grass in lawns. To determine whether chinch bugs are the cause, examine the grass in the yellowing marginal areas of injured patches—not in the brown, dead grass. Simply spread the grass back with your fingers, and look down near the soil surface. Chinch bugs are active, especially in warm weather, and if they are present you can see them scurrying about. It is a rule of thumb that if this type of inspection reveals chinch bugs easily, then control is needed. A way to determine the presence of chinch bugs positively, even when few are present, is to use water in a metal cylinder (Fig. 6). Home gardeners could use a large shortening can or coffee can with both ends removed. One end of this cylinder is sharpened and set firmly into the turf. Heavy grass runners could be cut with a knife before the cylinder is pushed in if necessary. The cylinder is then filled with water. Chinch bugs, if they are present, will float to the top in 5 to 10 minutes.

B. Scale Insects

Scale insects are small, inconspicuous, and easily overlooked. Several species infest turf and suck the juices from the plant. Some attack the aboveground parts, and others attack the roots. Infested turf becomes unthrifty, may be lighter in color, and appears to lack fertilizer. In severe infestations, the grass turns yellow and then brown and finally dies. Damage may be more noticeable during dry periods.

The life histories of most scale insects infesting grasses are quite similar. The newly born scales, called crawlers, are active and run about over the plant. In a few days, they settle down, insert their mouthparts into the plant, lose their legs and antennae, and begin a sessile existence.

Figure 6. Metal cylinder used to diagnose chinch bug infestations.

Rhodesgrass scale. The rhodesgrass scale, *Antonina graminis* (Maskell), is found in the Gulf States and westward to southern California. It is most important as a pest of rhodesgrass, *Chloris gayana* Kunth, and other pasture grasses, but in many areas it severely damages turf grasses. The adults are globular 1/8 inch in diameter, dark purplish brown, and covered with a cottony secretion. Most of them are attached to the plant near the crown, but some may be found on stem nodes. In south Texas, some development takes place throughout the year, and five generations have been reported (Chada and Wood, 1960).

Odonaspis ruthae Kotinsky. This scale has no approved common name though it is usually referred to as the bermudagrass scale and sometimes as Ruth's scale. The adults are about 1/16 inch long, tapered toward the rear, and encased in a hard, white scale. They are found attached to the plant nodes.

Ground pearls. Probably several species of ground pearl, *Margarodes* spp., attack the roots of grasses. One species, *M. meridionalis* Morrison, attacks bermudagrass, St. Augustinegrass, and centipedegrass in the southern part of the U. S. but damage is most noticeable on centipedegrass. The females deposit masses of eggs and cover them with a cottony secretion. The emerging young cover themselves with hard, globular shells that are whitish, somewhat irridescent, and resemble small pearls. They vary in size but may reach about 1/8 inch in diameter.

C. Leafhoppers

Many species of leafhoppers (family Cicadellidae) infest lawns. They are tiny wedge-shaped insects about 1/5 inch long ranging in color from yellow to green and grey and are often mottled or speckled. The young resemble the adults except for size and lack of wings. As the name implies, they move short distances by hopping. In addition, the adults can fly, and the nymphs of some species can run rapidly over the plants. Both nymphs and adults can retard grass growth by sucking the sap from the stems and leaves. Damage appears as whitened areas often mistaken for drouth or disease damage. New turf seedings may be so severely damaged that they must be replanted.

D. Spittlebugs

Spittlebugs are more a curiosity than a pest in well-managed turf. The young or nymphs live within a mass of spittle and suck plant juices. The adults resemble and act somewhat like leafhoppers but are more robust. Two species are sometimes found in lawns. The meadow spittlebug, *Philaenus spumarius* (L.), is found in the northeastern and midwestern states. When these yellowish green nymphs are present in lawns, they are usually feeding on clover or weeds rather than on grass. The adults are about 1/4 inch long, gray or brown, and variously marked with darker brown. The two-lined spittlebug, *Prosapia bicincta* (Say), is a grass feeder that is occasionally found in turf areas in the southeastern states. These nymphs may feed on bermudagrass, St. Augustinegrass, and centipedegrass. They are ivory-colored with brownish heads and thoraces. The adults are about 3/8 inch long, dark brown to black, and have two orange lines across the wings. This species has two generations per year in the south (Byers, 1965).

E. Mites

Mites are close relatives of insects, and several species suck the sap of grasses and cause a blotching or stippling of the leaves. Continued feeding may cause severe chlorosis and death of the leaf. In severe infestations, brown and dead stolons are common, and entire plants may be killed. *Oligonychus stickneyi* (McGregor) was reported to infest grasses in Florida (Wolfenbarger, 1953) and in Arizona (Bibby and Tuttle, 1959). Banks grass mite (formerly called the timothy mite), *Oligonychus pratensis* (Banks), is widely distributed and feeds on many plants. Malcolm (1955) reported that it was a serious pest in grass seed fields in Washington but that it was not an important pest of well-managed lawns in that area. Bibby and Tuttle (1959) recorded this species from bermudagrass. In 1959, an eriophyid mite, now called the bermudagrass mite, *Aceria neocynodonis* Keifer, was found seriously damaging bermudagrass turf in Arizona (Butler and Tuttle, 1961). These creamy white mites are extremely small, only 1/100 of an inch. They cause the plant to grow abnormally with shortened internodes and rosetted or tufted growth, and heavily infested plants turn brown and die. This mite has since been recorded in most southern states from Florida to southern California. Another mite commonly found in turf is the clover mite, *Bryobia praetiosa* Koch. These reddish mites are about 1/30 inch long and are more of a household pest than a turf pest. They feed mainly on clover and other plants but sometimes build up large populations that migrate into houses, particularly in the spring and fall. They are entirely plant feeders, but their presence in the home may be a serious nuisance.

V. Pests That Cause Little Damage But Are a Nuisance

A. Sowbugs and Pillbugs

Sowbugs and pillbugs are not insects. They belong to the class Crustacea which also includes the crabs, crayfish, and lobsters. They reach a length of about 1/2 inch, are slate gray, and have seven pairs of legs. The name pillbugs is given to some species that roll themselves into a tight ball when disturbed. Pillbugs and sowbugs are usually found in dark damp places, under boards, stones, and decaying leaves, and in damp basements where they may be a nuisance. They feed mainly on decaying vegetable matter, but they sometimes attack living plants including grasses.

B. Millipedes and Centipedes

Millipedes, thousand-legged worms, belong to the class Diplopoda, and centipedes, hundred-legged worms, to the class Chilopoda. They are usually brownish, many-segmented, and coil up when disturbed. Centipedes are rather flattened and move rapidly, millipedes are rather cylindrical and move more slowly. They usually feed on decaying vegetable matter but occasionally attack living plants. Also, they sometimes become numerous in lawns and are troublesome when they crawl into homes, swimming pools, and other places. Some centipedes can inflict a painful bite, but most species are not dangerous.

C. Spiders and Scorpions

Spiders and scorpions belong to the class Arachnida. Spiders are sometimes abundant in turf areas, and scorpions are occasionally found in such areas in the warm parts of the U. S. Neither damages lawns, and both may be considered beneficial since they feed on and destroy other insects. All spiders have a pair of venomous jaws used to poison their prey. In spite of a nearly universal dislike for spiders, few are dangerous. The black widow spider, *Latrodectus mactans* (F.), is the most venomous spider in North America. This shiny black spider with a red hourglass mark on the underside is sometimes found in lawns. Scorpions are most common in the Southwest. They have a stinger at the tip of the abdomen and can inflict a painful sting that is probably never fatal.

D. Ticks

Ticks also belong to the class Arachnida. They do not injure lawns but sometimes drop to the grass from infested dogs or rodents. Most of them will attack man, and pain may result from their bite. Some species transmit diseases such as tick fever.

E. Chiggers

Chiggers, *Trombicula* spp., often called red bugs, are the six-legged "larvae" or immature stages of certain mites. They are rounded, orange-yellow, less than $^1/_{150}$ inch long, and nearly invisible without magnification. They are most common east of the Rocky Mountains but have been recorded in Arizona and California. There are several species, but *Trombicula alfreddugesi* (Oudemans) is most widely distributed. Chiggers do not damage lawns but invade them from surrounding grassy or wooded areas where vegetation is abundant. They annoy people by attaching themselves to the skin, and as they feed they inject a fluid that causes intense itching and red blotches. They also attack other animals.

Chiggers winter as adults slightly below the soil surface. Eggs laid in the spring hatch into the six-legged form that is troublesome to man. After feeding, these forms drop off and transform to eight-legged nymphs and finally to adults. The two latter forms do not attack man but are probably predaceous on eggs of certain insects. There may be several generations per year depending on location.

F. Fleas

Fleas (Siphonaptera) are small wingless insects that feed on warm-blooded animals. The adults jump or crawl from one host to another. The females lay eggs that drop to the ground and hatch into larvae. These larvae do not bite animals but feed on organic matter. Fleas occasionally spread to lawn areas from infested dogs and cats or nearby animal quarters. When numerous, they bite and annoy people.

G. Earwigs

Earwigs are beetlelike insects occasionally found in lawns. When full grown, they are reddish brown, about $^3/_4$ inch long, and bear a pair of forceps at the rear of the body. The widespread belief that these insects crawl into peoples' ears is not true. They feed on all sorts of food and are sometimes abundant in lawn clippings. Earwigs damage many flowers and other plants and often are a nuisance in the home where they are much disliked because of their appearance and foul odor. The European earwig, *Forficula auricularia* L. is a common species found in the northeast and some western states. The striped earwig, *Labidura riparia* (Pallas), and the ring-legged earwig, *Euborellia annulipes* (Lucas), are common species around residences in the southeast.

VI. Control With Insecticides

Most insects attacking turf can be controlled with insecticides. However, one of the first lines of defense against insects is to follow the recommended cultural and maintenance practices for turf. A well-managed, vigorous turf, though it is a continual attraction for insects, can support a greater population of insects without serious harm than one in poor condition. Poor, unthrifty turf may be caused by insects or by a combination of factors; thus one should determine that insects are the cause before applying an insecticide.

There are three general types of insecticides used to control turf insects. One group known as chlorinated hydrocarbons includes aldrin, chlordane, dieldrin, heptachlor, and toxaphene. These insecticides are widely used to control turf pests, give good control of many pests, and have a long period of effectiveness. However, some of these insecticides leave undesirable residues so they cannot be used where there is any chance that the land will be grazed. A second group called the organophosphates include tetrapropyl thiopyrophosphate (Aspon(^{R}), = NPD(^{R})), carbophenothion, diazinon, Dursban(^{R}), ethion, malathion, and Nemacide(^{R}). These are highly effective against some turf insects, but they do not have as long a period of effectiveness as the hydrocarbons and their residues dissipate more rapidly. A third group, the carbamates, includes carbaryl (Sevin(^{R})), and Bay 39007 (Baygon(^{R})) which have about the same residual life as the organophosphates. The chemical names of the above insecticides are given in Table 1.

Insecticides are marketed in several formulations: dusts, wettable powders, emulsifiable concentrates, granules, and oil solutions. Oil solutions are not recommended for use on turf since they may burn the grass. Use of the other formulations depends on the equipment available. In general, sprays are preferred over dusts. Granular insecticides are easily applied if the right equipment is used.

Insecticides are sold under different trade names and in different-sized packages. It is important to know the ingredients in a brand-name item to be certain that the right insecticide is obtained. Also size of the package should be determined by the need; it is not good practice, especially for safety, to store insecticides from year to year.

No one insecticide is effective against all turf pests. Table 2 lists the

Table 1. Chemical names of pesticides suggested for controlling turf insects.

Aspon$^{(R)}$, NPD$^{(R)}$	Tetrapropyl thiopyrosphosphate
Aldrin	At least 95% 1, 2, 3, 4, 10, 10-hexachloro-1, 4, 4a, 5, 8, 8a-hexahydro-1, 4-endo-exo-5, 8-dimethanonaphthalene
Bay 39007 (Baygon$^{(R)}$)	o-isopropoxyphenyl methylcarbamate
Chlordane	At least 60% 1, 2, 4, 5, 6, 7, 8, 8-octachloro-2, 3, 3a, 4, 7, 7a-hexahydro-4, 7-methanoindene and not over 40% related compounds
Carbaryl (Sevin$^{(R)}$)	1-naphthyl methylcarbamate
Carbophenothion (Trithion$^{(R)}$)	S-[(p-chlorophenylthio) methyl] O,O-diethyl phosphorodithioate
Diazinon	O, O-diethyl O-(2-isopropyl-4-methyl-6-pyrimidinyl) phosphorodithioate
Dieldrin	Not less, than 85% of 1, 2, 3, 4, 10, 10-hexachloro-6, 7-epoxy-1, 4, 4a, 5, 6, 7, 8, 8a-octahydro-1, 4-endo-exo-5, 8-dimethanonaphthalene
Dursban$^{(R)}$	O, O-diethyl O-3, 5, 6-trichloro-2-pyridyl phosphorothioate
Ethion	O,O,O, O'-tetraethyl S, S'-methylenebisphosphorodithioate
Heptachlor	1, 4, 5, 6, 7, 8, 8-heptachloro-3a, 4, 7, 7a-tetrahydro-4, 7-methanoindene
Malathion	S-[1, 2-bis(ethoxycarbonyl) ethyl] O, O-dimethyl phosphorodithioate
Nemacide$^{(R)}$ (VC-13)	O-2, 4-dichlorophenyl O, O-diethyl phosphorothioate
Toxaphene	Chlorinated camphene containing 67-69% chlorine

Table 2. Insecticides suggested for controlling lawn insects.

Pest	Insecticide	Amount*
Ants	Aldrin	1
	Chlordane	4
	Dieldrin	1
	Heptachlor	1
Armyworms and cutworms	Chlordane	2
	Dieldrin	0.35
	Heptachlor	1
Bermudagrass mite	Diazinon	2
Billbugs	Diazinon	3
Chinch bugs	Tetrapropyl thiopyrophosphate (Aspon(R), NPD(R))	3.5
	Bay 39007 (Baygon(R))†	3.5
	Carbaryl (Sevin(R))	4
	Carbophenothion (Trithion(R))‡	2.5
	Diazinon	3
	Dursban(R) §	0.37
	Ethion	3.5
	Nemacide(R) (VC-13)	9
White grubs	Aldrin	1
	Chlordane	4
	Dieldrin	1
	Heptachlor	1
Japanese beetle grubs	Aldrin	1
	Chlordane	4
	Dieldrin	1
	Heptachlor	1
	Toxaphene	9
Milky disease spores	2 g dust per spot at 3-, 5-, or 10-foot intervals or 8 ounces dust broadcast/1,000 ft²	
Leafhoppers	Malathion	0.75
Mole crickets	Chlordane	2
	Dieldrin	1
	Heptachlor	1
Scale insects	Malathion	4
Sod webworms	Aldrin¶	1
	Carbaryl	4
	Chlordane¶	2
	Diazinon	4
	Heptachlor¶	1
	Dieldrin¶	1
	Toxaphene¶	2

* Ounces active ingredient to apply per 1,000 ft². † Currently approved for use only in Florida. ‡ See precautions. § Currently approved for use only by Pest Control operators. ¶ Use of these materials in some locations has sometimes given less than satisfactory control of webworms.

insecticides commonly suggested for the control of the more important ones. Most other insects discussed will need control only occasionally. The table does not attempt to include all insecticides that are approved for use against turf insects. Trade names are used for some insecticides solely to provide specific information. Mention of a trade name does not constitute a warranty of the product by the U. S. Department of Agriculture. Recommendations of insecticides are constantly being improved and changed, and it is a good practice to check with county agents and state experiment stations for the latest information on turf insect control.

A. Equipment

Many kinds of equipment can be used to apply insecticides to turf, but the type used must be designed to handle the material being applied. However, the formulation and equipment are not as important as being certain that the correct amount of material is applied. Any equipment must therefore be properly calibrated to dispense the correct amounts. Applying more is wasteful since it does not increase effectiveness, and applying less is also wasteful because it will not give satisfactory control.

Dusts. Dusts are less frequently used than other formulations. They can be applied by power equipment or hand-operated dusters.

Sprays. Wettable powders and emulsifiable concentrates can be applied with power sprayers and hand-operated compressed air sprayers. Jar attachments for a garden hose give satisfactory results, the type that requires 10 to 15 gallons of water to empty the jar is preferred. One such jarfull is used to cover 500 square feet.

Granules. Most fertilizer distributors, either power or hand-operated, can be calibrated to apply granular insecticides.

B. Application Suggestions

Ants. If only a few nests are present, apply insecticide around the openings of individual nests. If an area is generally infested, a broadcast treatment should be applied.

Armyworms and cutworms. It is best to treat the grass in late afternoon or evening and delay watering until the next day. For armyworms, best results will be obtained by applying the insecticide when the caterpillars are small.

Bermudagrass mite. Treatment should be applied in the spring as soon as the grass turns green. Application at 1- to 2-month intervals may be needed throughout the season. Good management practices help improve the appearance of infested bermudagrass.

Billbugs. More than one treatment may be needed for billbugs. On zoysiagrass, application of a treatment in mid-May soon after the grass turns green and then one in mid-August and one in mid-September have given effective control.

Chinch bugs. Many insecticides among the organophosphate and carbamate insecticides are effective in controlling lawn chinch bugs (Kerr, 1966b). Most hydrocarbon insecticides are no longer effective because the insects have developed resistance to them. Materials effective against the southern chinch bug are also effective against the hairy chinch bug (Polivka, 1963; Schread, 1963). Several other materials would probably perform well against the hairy chinch bug in areas where one does not have to contend with the extremes of conditions frequently encountered in the Gulf States.

The recommended formulations for control of lawn chinch bugs are emulsifiable concentrates, wettable powder sprays, and granulated insecticides. Proper application is the key to successful control and is especially important with the difficult conditions in the south. It is desirable to have the turf moist at the time of application. Therefore, since it is not always possible to arrange for irrigation shortly before treatment, emphasis is given to the use of high gallonage in spraying. In power spraying, the typical method for commercial operations, the insecticides should be diluted so that 15 to 20 gallons of spray are applied per 1,000 square feet. In the very thick turf thatches encountered in some places, 30 gallons per 1,000 square feet are routinely applied by commercial operators. In Florida, spray operators use nozzles with orifices that deliver a fan-shaped spray with relatively coarse droplet size that is ideal for applying such drenching treatments. However, even when nozzles with huge orifices are used, pressure at the nozzle should not exceed 100 psi. to avoid the shattering of droplets and the formation of an undesirable mist.

The home gardener can use jar attachments to a garden hose as discussed. However, granular insecticides perform just as well against chinch bugs and are much easier for the home gardener to handle. After application, the granules should be washed off the grass blades into the turf thatch, and for this a light irrigation is sufficient. One cannot emphasize too strongly the need for thorough coverage with the recommended amount of material. The careful use of a well-calibrated fertilizer spreader is recommended for application of granules.

A single application of recommended insecticide provides about six weeks of control under subtropical conditions, and in some areas of the Gulf States, four or more applications are sometimes used between April and November. Two applications should be sufficient to keep lawn chinch bugs under control through the spring and summer in northern states.

Grubs (white, chafer, Japanese beetle). The grub population can be determined by carefully digging and removing a square foot of soil 2 to 3 inches deep in several places in the lawn in the fall or spring and carefully examining the soil. If grubs average three or more per square foot, an insecticide should be used. Applications can be made any time that the ground is not frozen. The formulation is not as important as the correct amount. The turf should be watered immediately after application to wash the insecticide down to the soil surface. Insecticides are not completely effective against those grubs that are present at the time of treatment, but they will control subsequent populations. A properly applied treatment will control grubs for 2 to 5 years (Polivka 1965).

Japanese beetle grubs can also be controlled by applying milky disease spores. Use a preparation containing 100 million spores per gram. For greater effectiveness, the spore dust should be applied on a community-wide basis. Generally, it may require several years for the disease to spread and become fully effective. Spore dust should not be applied to soil that has been treated with an insecticide. Although the insecticide does not harm the spores, it reduces the grub population and thereby greatly lowers the chance of establishment and spread of the disease.

Leafhoppers. Leafhoppers are active insects and readily migrate back into turf from untreated areas. If populations are high, treatments may have to be applied at 4- to 5-week intervals during the season.

Mole crickets. Areas infested with mole crickets should be treated as soon as the damage is noted. After treatment, 15 to 20 gallons of water should be applied per 1,000 square feet to wash the insecticide to the soil.

Scale insects. Grass scales are difficult to control, but insecticides are of some help. Heavy infestations will require 2 or 3 treatments 3 to 4 weeks apart. Insecticides have not been effective against ground pearls.

Sod webworms. Sod webworms feed mainly at night, so the insecticide should be applied in the late afternoon or evening and watering delayed until the next day. It is advisable to mow the grass before the insecticide is applied. Since most sod webworms produce more than one generation, more than one application of insecticide may be needed. Turf areas should be carefully watched for the appearance of small irregular brown patches, and when they are found they should be carefully examined for webworms. Granular formulations have not given as good webworm control as other formulations.

C. Precautions

Insecticides used improperly can cause injury to man and animals. Use them only when needed, and handle them with care. Follow the directions, and heed all precautions on the container label. Insecticides should be kept in closed, well-labeled containers in a dry place where they will not contaminate food or feed and where children and animals cannot reach them.

In handling any insecticide, avoid repeated or prolonged contact of it with skin and the inhalation of dusts, mists, and vapors. Wear clean, dry clothing, and wash hands and face before eating or smoking. Wash clothing daily.

When handling or mixing concentrates, avoid spilling them on the skin and keep them out of the eyes, nose, and mouth. If any is spilled, wash it off the skin immediately with soap and water. If you spill it on your clothing, remove the clothing immediately and wash the contaminated skin thoroughly. Launder clothing before wearing it again. If it gets in the eyes, flush with plenty of water for 15 minutes and get medical attention.

To protect honey bees and other pollinating insects, make applications during hours when the insects are not visiting the plants. Avoid drift into bee yards and adjacent crops in bloom.

To protect fish and wildlife, do not contaminate streams, lakes, or ponds with insecticides. Do not clean spraying equipment or dump excess spray material near such water.

Do not apply insecticides to turf areas when people or animals are on them, and do not allow insecticides to drift to areas where they might injure people or animals or contaminate food or feed. Thoroughly water-in any insecticides that are used to control soil insects.

Keep children and pets off treated lawns and turf areas until the insecticide has been washed off by sprinkling and the grass has completely dried.

Carbophenothion is highly toxic and may be fatal if swallowed, inhaled, or absorbed through the skin. It should be applied only by a person who is thoroughly familiar with its hazards and who will assume full responsibility for proper use and comply with all the precautions on the label.

Literature Cited

Ainslie, G. G. 1930. The bluegrass webworm. USDA Tech. Bull. 173

Bibby, F. F., and D. M. Tuttle. 1959. Notes on phytophagous and predatory mites of Arizona. J. Econ. Entomol. 52(2):186-190.

Bohart, R. M. 1947. Sod webworms and other lawn pests in California. Hilgardia 17(8):267-308.

Brogden, J. E., and S. H. Kerr. 1964. Home gardeners lawn insect control guide. Florida Agri. Exp. Sta. Circ. 213A.

Butler, G. D., and D. M. Tuttle. 1961. New mite is damaging to bermudagrass. Prog. Agr. Ariz. 13(1):11.

Byers, R. A. 1965. Biology and control of a spittlebug, *Prosapia bicincta* (Say) on Coastal bermudagrass. Georgia Agr. Exp. Sta. Tech. Bull. N.S. 42.

Chada, H. L., and E. A. Wood, Jr. 1960. Biology and control of the rhodesgrass scale. USDA Tech. Bull. 1221.

Crawford, C. S., and R. F. Harwood. 1964. Bionomics and control of insects affecting Washington grass seed fields. Washington Agri. Exp. Sta. Tech. Bull. 44.

Eden, W. G., and R. L. Self. 1960. Controlling chinch bugs on St. Augustinegrass lawns. Auburn Univ. Agr. Exp. Sta. Prog. Rept. Ser. 79.

Gambrell, F. L. 1954. A soil-inhabiting pest of grasses and nursery plantings. N.Y. State Agr. Exp. Sta., Geneva, N.Y. Farm Res. 20(4):2-3.

Gambrell, F. L., S. C. Mendall, and E. H. Smith. 1942. A destructive European insect new to the United States. J. Econ. Entomol. 35(2):289.

Jefferson, R. N., and E. J. Swift. 1956. Control of turfgrass pests. South. Calif. Turfgrass Culture 6(2). April.

Johnson, J. P. 1944. Miscellaneous insect notes. Conn. Agr. Exp. Sta. Bull. 488:420.

Juska, F. V. 1965. Billbug injury in zoysiagrass turf. Park Maintenance 18(5):38.

Kelsheimer, E. C. 1950. Control of mole crickets. Florida Agr. Exp. Sta. Circ. S-15.

Kelsheimer, E. C. 1956. The hunting billbug, a serious pest of zoysia. Proc. Fla. State Hort. Soc. 69:415-18.

Kelsheimer, E. G., and S. H. Kerr. 1957. Insects and other pests of lawns and turf. Florida Agr. Exp. Sta. Cir. S-96.

Kerr, S. H. 1966a. Biology of the lawn chinch bug, *Blissus insularis*. Florida Entomol. 49:9-18.

Kerr, S. H. 1966b. Recommendations for commercial lawn spraymen. Florida Agr. Exp. Sta. Circ. S-121C.

Klostermeyer, E. C. 1964. Lawn billbugs—a new pest of lawns in eastern Washington. Irrigation Exp. Sta. (Prosser) E. M. 2349.

Komblas, K. N. 1962. Biology and control of the lawn chinch bug, *Blissus insularis*. Ph.D. thesis. Louisiana State Univ. Baton Rouge.

Leonard, D. E. 1966. Biosystematics of the "Leucopterus complex" of the genus *Blissus* (Heteroptera: Lygaeidae). Connecticut Agr. Exp. Sta. Bull. 677.

Luginbill, P. 1922. Bionomics of the chinch bug. USDA Bull. 1016.

Luginbill, P., and H. R. Painter. 1953. May beetles of the United States and Canada. USDA Tech. Bull. 1060.

Malcolm, D. R. 1955. Biology and control of the timothy mite, *Paratetranychus pratensis* (Banks). Washington Agr. Exp. Sta. Tech. Bull. 17.

Painter, R. H. 1928. Notes on the injury to plant cells by chinch bug feedings. Ann. Entomol. Soc. Amer. 21:232-242.

Polivka, J. B. 1963. Control of the hairy chinch bug *Blissus leucopterus hirtus.* Mont. in Ohio. Ohio Agr. Exp. Sta. Res. Circ. 122.

Polivka, J. B. 1965. Effectiveness of insecticides for the control of white grubs in turf. Ohio Agr. Res. Dev. Center Res. Circ. 140.

Ritcher, P. O. 1940. Kentucky white grubs. Kentucky Agr. Exp. Sta. Bull.

Ritcher, Paul O. 1966. White grubs and their allies. Oregon State Univ. Mono. Studies Entomol. 4.

Schread, J. C. 1963. The chinch bug and its control. Connecticut Agr. Exp. Sta. Circ. 223.

Schread, J. C. 1964. Insect pests of Connecticut lawns. Connecticut Agr. Exp. Sta. Circ. 212 (Rev.)

Shelford, V. E. 1932. An experimental and observational study of the chinch bug in relation to climate and weather. Illinois Nat. Hist. Survey Bull. 19:487-547.

Smith, R. C. 1942. *Nomophila noctuella* as a grass and alfalfa pest in Kansas (Lepidoptera, Pyralididae). J. Kansas Entomol. Soc. 15(1)25-34.

Treece, R. E. 1960. Pest is attacking alfalfa. Ohio Farm Home Res. May-June, 42-43.

U. S. Department of Agriculture. 1965. Losses in agriculture. Agr. Handbook 291.

Warren, L. O., and J. E. Roberts. 1956. A hesperid, *Atalopedes campestris* (BDV), as a pest of bermudagrass pastures. J. Kansas Entomol. Soc. 29(4):139-141.

Webster, F. M. 1907. The chinch bug. USDA Bur. Entomol. Bull. 69.

Wolfenbarger, D. O. 1953. Insects and mite control problems on lawn and golf. grasses. Florida Entomol. 36(1):9-12.

12 Nematodes and Other Pests

C. M. Heald

Agricultural Research Service, USDA
Weslaco, Texas

V. G. Perry

University of Florida
Gainesville, Florida.

I. Introduction

Nematodes of many types are found abundantly in turf, apparently in all areas of the world. Many of the early nematologists, such as DeMan of Holland, reported prior to 1900 on the occurrence of nematodes, parasitic or otherwise, from meadow lands. Such species as *Pratylenchus pratensis* (De Man) Filipjev, and *Rotylenchus uniformis* (De Man) Filipjev, were described from meadow habitats. However, the early work was taxonomic, and only recently has attention been directed toward nematodes as pathogens of turfgrasses.

Research into the pathogenic capabilities of the so-called ectoparasitic nematodes by Christie et al. (1952, 1954), Christie and Perry (1951), and Perry (1953a) made possible an understanding of nematode damage to turfgrasses in Florida. Subsequently, the introduction of the relatively nonphytotoxic nematicides containing 1,2-dibromo-3-chloropropane (DBCP) and O-(2,4-dichlorophenyl)O,O-diethylphosphorothioate (V-C 13) provided nematologists with chemical tools for demonstrating the effects of nematodes through control. Numerous trial applications of these nematicides and others were made in Florida during the period 1952-55, and in most cases significant growth response was noted. Gradually the use of nematicides on golf greens and home lawns has become a standard practice in certain parts of Florida where high quality turf is desired.

For the most part, experimental tests to determine the type and extent of nematode damage to most grasses have not been conducted. However, the pathogenicity of a few parasites has been established on several major turfgrasses. Perry et al. (1959) proved that a spiral nematode, *Helicotylenchus digonicus* Perry, causes severe injury to Kentucky bluegrass in Wisconsin. Sledge (1962) and several subsequent workers have shown that the pseudo root-knot nematode, *Hypsoperine graminis,* of turfgrasses is highly injurious to several grasses. DiEdwardo and Perry (1964) proved that the cyst nematode, *Heterodera lenceilyma* DiEdwardo and Perry, is an important pathogen of St. Augustinegrass (Fig. 1). Similarity of symptoms produced on row crops with those on turfgrasses by such pests as the sting nematodes, *Belonolaimus longicaud-*

Figure 1. Roots of St. Augustinegrass infected with females of the cyst nematode *H. leuceilyma.*

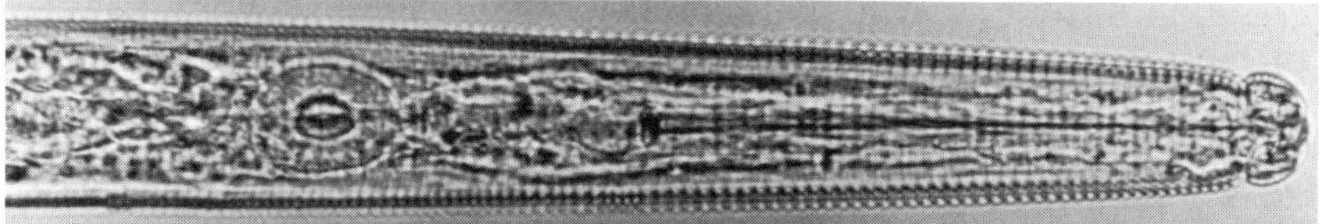

Figure 2. Esophageal region of *B. longicaudatus* showing stylet and esophageal glands.

atus Rau, has led to recognition of them as pests of turf. Grass growth following applications of nematicides has also increased our knowledge of the extent of injury by nematodes. Thus, available evidence shows that nematode parasites are significant factors in the production of quality turf, at least in certain areas of the U.S.

Plant parasitic nematodes are microscopic animals. All inhabit the soil as eggs and in early larval stages. They are round in cross-section and usually are eel-shaped, but later stages of some, such as root-knot nematodes, become swollen to a kidney or pear shape. Nematodes range from 1/10 to about 1/75 inch in length and are transparent. These tiny animals are surprisingly well developed in that they have efficient and complex internal organs. Reproduction is similar to that of other animals which produce and deposit eggs from which the early larval stage emerges. Most species have males and females, but some reproduce by parthenogenesis. The larvae usually develop to the second life cycle stage within the egg shell, and they may either hatch immediately or remain inactive for several months or even years as with cyst nematodes. Overwintering may occur at any stage of the life cycle but more commonly as larvae within the egg shell.

Plant parasitic nematodes are equipped with an oral spear for feeding (Fig. 2). This spear is a hollow needle-like structure which is used to puncture and enter individual plant cells. Near the base of the esophagus are located at least three glands which produce enzymes and possibly other materials for purposes of food digestion. One of these glands is in a dorsal position, and the materials produced by it are secreted through the stylet during feeding. These secretions act to partially digest and, thus, liquefy the contents (protoplasm) of cells being fed upon. The liquefied material is then sucked into the nematode esophagus and passed to the intestine for further digestion and storage until energy is needed by the animal. Most food energy is used for reproduction since nematodes move very little in the soil.

Some mechanical injury to plants results when nematodes penetrate roots and individual cells, but most plant effects are due to the esophageal secretions. These secretions act in a variety of ways and affect the morphology and physiology of plant hosts. In some cases (root-knot and cyst) the hosts respond to the feeding of nematodes by producing a group of peculiar, enlarged cells called giant or nectarial cells upon which the nematodes feed. With root-knot nematodes the plant host also produces an increased number of cells near the giant cell; this results in a galled or enlarged root. In contrast the ectoparasitic nematodes, such as sting and stubby-root nematodes, usually feed at or near root tips by inserting their spears into the developing cells. The esophageal secretions act to curtail further cell division by the host and cause a cessation of root growth. This results in a stubby, shallow root system of most grasses. Other nematodes feed along the sides of older roots while wholly or partially embedded within the roots.

The exact mechanism of injury to hosts by nematodes thus varies among parasites and among hosts. The nature of the esophageal secretions varies with the nematode species which accounts for much of the variation in pathogenicity among nematode species. Symptoms of unthriftiness expressed by hosts have been attributed to abbreviated or dead roots, blockage of vascular elements, and physiological disturbances due to actions by the esophageal secretions. At times secondary pathogens, usually fungi or bacteria, may enter roots already invaded by nematodes. This causes a disease-complex involving nematodes and other micro-organisms.

II. Nematodes Which Damage Turf

The sting nematode (*Belonolaimus* spp), morphologically, is one of the largest nematodes that feed on turf, ranging in length up to 3 mm. The nematode is noted for its long stylet which it uses vigorously in feeding. Generally, the nematode is found in sandy soils and is most prevalent on turf in Florida and Georgia. However, it can become established on golf greens and in nurseries in many areas of the U. S. if it is introduced. In Florida, Christie et al. (1954) examined 60 turf samples and found the sting nematode present in 36. They described the nematode injury as a "stubby-root" symptom. The turf had abnormally few rootlets and root tips were "knob-like" in appearance. These symptoms were noticed on St. Augustine, centipede, bermuda, and zoysia grass turf. In a greenhouse experiment, Rhoades (1962) found that the sting nematode, *B. longicaudatus,* caused a severe chlorosis of common St. Augustinegrass and that root weights were reduced up to 69% during an 8-month period. In other greenhouse studies, Winchester and Burt (1964) found that the same species of sting nematode caused severe turf yellowing and stunting of tops and of roots of Ormond bermudagrass. DiEdwardo (1963) reported in greenhouse trials that the sting nematode is capable of causing severe injury to Tifgreen bermudagrass and found a 50% reduction in plant weight of nematode-inoculated plants. Numerous other reports (Brodie and Burton, 1967; Good et al., 1956, 1959; Heald and Burton, 1968; Jackson et al., 1961; Lautz, 1959; Nutter and Christie, 1958; Winchester and Burt, 1964) implicate the sting nematode as causing severe injury to several turf grasses. A sting nematode *(B. longicaudatus)* is presently known to be widespread in Florida; it is considered the most important pest of turfgrasses in Florida.

The awl nematode *(Dolichodorus* spp) is mentioned here because it ranks with the sting nematode in its effect on turf and because it is very similar in morphological features. The pest is not found commonly but occurs frequently on lake front property. Christie et al. (1954) reported finding high populations of the awl nematode in 2 of 10 turf samples taken in Florida. Perry (1953b) has found this nematode a serious pest of turfgrass where it occurs.

The stubby-root nematode *(Trichodorus* spp) is a relatively small animal. Its stylet is curved in a unique manner and it feeds exclusively at root tips. In a turf survey in Georgia, Good et al. (1959) revealed that of 387 grass samples examined, 205 contained populations of the stubby-root nematode. Greenhouse studies of two species of the stubby-root nematode in Florida by Rhoades (1965) showed that *T. proximus* caused reduced growth of St. Augustinegrass by destroying the root tips as a result of its feeding action. Damage to the grass was much greater than that caused by *T. christiei,* a more common species of stubby-root found on turf. In other studies in Florida, Rhoades (1962) reports *T. christiei* as a major parasite of St. Augustinegrass causing 25% reduction in top weight and 49% reduction of root weight. The major effect on the grass was reduction in root size with fewer and shorter rootlets and stubby tips on the rootlets.

The name spiral nematode usually refers to several genera: *Helicotylenchus, Rotylenchus, Peltanigratus,* and *Scutellonema.* They are called "spirals" because of the C- shape they assume when relaxed or at rest. They usually range from about .6 to 1 mm in length. Careful microscopic examination is required to note morphological differences among the genera.

Perry et al. (1959) made a detailed study of *H. digonicus* on Kentucky bluegrass turf in Wisconsin and described a disease known as "summer dormancy" which is caused by this nematode. They found that the nematode could withstand the freezing winter temperatures and commence feeding in the spring as new root growth began. By the advent of the summer season, the nematode had limited the turf roots to the top 1 or 2 inches of soil. With the onset of high summer temperatures and moisture stress the disease symptoms appeared. Unpublished research by C. M. Heald showed that a species of the spiral nematode *H. nanus* caused significant reduction of roots and vegetative parts of common bermudagrass under greenhouse conditions. Other researchers (Good et al., 1956, 1959; Sommerville et al., 1957) have implicated the genera of spiral nematodes as causing significant injury to turf grasses.

The lance nematode (*Hoplolaimus* spp), named for its strongly developed stylet, is one of the most commonly found genera in turf surveys. The nematode is similar, morphologically, to the spiral nematode and is found in a variety of soil types. DiEdwardo (1963) has shown that lance nematodes cause severe stunting to Tifgreen bermudagrass, decreasing growth by 50% in greenhouse comparisons between inoculated and non-inoculated plants. A turf survey by Somerville et al. (1957) reported lance nematodes in 12 of 20 states. There are many other reports (Christie, 1956; Christie et al., 1954; Good et al., 1959; Nutter, 1955; Nutter and Christie, 1958; Parris, 1957) of the association of this nematode with damaged turfgrasses.

Stylet nematodes (*Tylenchorhynchus* spp) are often referred to as pests of turf although there are varying reports as to damage it causes. In Georgia, Powell (1964) found that turf infected with *T. maximus* showed a marked improvement when treated with a nematicide. However, in a Massachusetts greenhouse trial, Troll and Rohde (1965) reported that no reduction in top growth of nematode infected turf compared to controls was noted on Kentucky bluegrass, annual ryegrass, and creeping red fescue. They concluded that the stylet nematode (*T. claytoni*) did not cause discernible injury. Several other researchers (Good et al., 1959; Parris, 1957; Somerville, 1957; Taylor et al., 1963) have reported the presence of stylet nematodes in turfgrasses.

Ring nematodes (*Criconemoides* spp) are so named because of the heavy annulation of the cuticle. Specimens are very short and usually equipped with a long stout stylet. The exact role of these parasites is questionable, but in some areas injury to turf has been attributed to certain species. Tarjan (1964) collected turf samples showing chlorotic symptoms of nematode injury and containing a nematode population of 93% ring nematodes. After chemical treatment of the turf in a greenhouse experiment, he found significant increases in grass weight when compared with nontreated turf. Other reports (Christie et al., 1954; Good et al., 1959; Kelsheimer and Overman, 1953; Somerville, 1957) implicate ring nematodes as parasites of turfgrasses.

Lesion nematodes (*Pratylenchus* spp), so named because of the small lesions they cause on the roots of host plants, have been found in several surveys of turf, but there is only one report of them causing significant injury to turf. In greenhouse tests, Troll and Rohde (1965) found *P. penetrans* to significantly reduce root growth of annual ryegrass, but not Kentucky bluegrass and creeping red fescue.

The last three genera to be discussed in detail are all very similar in appearance in that the adult females swell and assume a lemon or pear shape. At this stage of development, the specimens are no longer mobile, and remain in a stationary position for the remainder of their life cycle.

Root-knot nematodes (*Meloidogyne* spp) are commonly recognized by the galls or knots formed on roots. Host ranges include most economic plants. These nematodes enter the root systems and stimulate irregular cell growth which, in turn, forms a gall. The nematode is usually embedded in the root tissue with only a small portion of the posterior end exposed. There are several reports (Gaskin, 1965; Hodges et al.,

1963; McBeth, 1945; Riffle, 1964) of the root-knot nematode attacking turfgrasses. Generally speaking, root-knot nematodes have not created problems in turf equal to certain other genera, and their importance as turf pests appears limited to certain areas.

The pseudo-root-knot nematode (*Hypsoperine* spp) was described by Sledge and Golden (1964) and since that time has attracted much attention as a parasite of turfgrasses. Although the nematode morphologically appears very similar to the root-knot nematode, it causes only slight swellings at infection sites on grass roots. Adult females are usually embedded completely in the root tissues although some variations have been noted. Sledge (1962) has observed that under natural conditions St. Augustinegrass infected with the pseudo-root-knot nematode became chlorotic and died. Histopathological studies by Mirza and Perry (1967) showed that the nematode caused extensive damage to the roots of St. Augustinegrass. In a greenhouse test, Dickerson (1966) found that zoysiagrass was stunted and became slightly chlorotic when heavily infected. The pseudo-root-knot nematode was also found to prevent normal development of roots and suppress vegetative growth of Tifdwarf bermudagrass (Heald 1969). These greenhouse studies also confirmed field observations that the nematode is a parasite to Tifdwarf bermudagrass. Other reports (Bell and Krusberg, 1964; Orr and Golden, 1966; Van Weerdt, 1959) have shown that the nematode is widespread and probably causes extensive turf damage in many areas. Some difficulty has been encountered in control of this pest and higher rates of nematicides than those normally used are suggested.

Cyst nematodes (*Heterodera* spp) are very similar in size to root-knot and pseudo-root-knot nematodes, but unlike these two, cyst nematodes are found with only the head and neck inserted in roots with the oval portion of the body outside. DiEdwardo and Perry (1964) published the first report of a cyst nematode infecting a turfgrass. They found that a new species, *H. leuceilyma,* is pathogenic to St. Augustinegrass. It causes a distinct interveinal chlorosis of the foliage and produces symptoms similar to iron deficiency. Top and root growth were reduced, and disease symptoms in the greenhouse tests were similar to those seen in lawns.

There are several other genera which probably cause injury to turf, but because research on pathogenicity is lacking they have not been implicated as serious parasites of turf. The following is a list of other nematodes which have been found in turf samples in the U. S.: dagger nematodes (*Xiphinema* spp); sheath nematodes(*Hemicycliophora* spp); pin nematodes (*Paratylenchus* spp); stem and bulb nematodes (*Ditylenchus* spp); and species of *Panagrolaimus, Eucephalobus, Aphelenchoides,* and *Aphelenchus* which have no specific common names.

The general symptoms of nematode injury to turfgrasses may appear on the foliage as slight to severe chlorosis and declining growth usually in circular to irregular patches. These symptoms are generally more evident in periods of hot weather, moisture stress, and under poor fertility management. However, under the most ideal conditions, such as turf on golf greens, nematode injury will become evident once populations have increased to damaging numbers. Damage to roots may appear as sparseness of roots, discoloration, a stubby root condition, galled or slightly swollen rootlets, or a combination of these symptoms depending on the species of nematodes attacking the grass.

III. Control of Nematodes

There is one important consideration which precedes nematode control, and this is to be certain the turf problem is caused by plant parasitic nematodes. In order to detect nematode populations, soil and root samples should be taken from several areas where nematode damage is suspected, placed in plastic bags and forwarded to a nematologist for identification. Soil samples are washed and screened by various procedures to separate the nematodes from the soil, and the parasites are examined microscopically. Roots are usually placed in a mist chamber for a sufficient time to allow the nematode to exit and be collected for identification.

Control of nematodes in turf is a difficult task because these tiny parasites are in the soil feeding on or within roots. Chemicals used for control must be such that they will kill the nematodes in or around the roots without causing significant damage to the turf. To date, eradication has not been obtained in turf because nematodes are found at all depths in the soil where roots grow. Two types of nematode control are possible: chemical and nonchemical. Much more emphasis has been placed on chemical control because other means have not proved effective. We will not discuss specific treatments in this section, but will attempt to classify the chemicals as to whether they are fumigants or nonfumigants.

Numerous investigators (Bell and Krusberg, 1964; Brodie and Burton, 1967; Lautz, 1958; Nutter and Christie, 1958; Nutter and Whit-

Figure 3. Roots of bermudagrass turf treated and not treated with Dasanit showing response due to control of the sting nematode.

ton, 1957; Perry, 1953a; Perry et al., 1959; Powell, 1964; Tarjan, 1964; Troll and Rohde, 1966; Winchester and Burt, 1964) have experimented with a large range of nematicides with varying results. This variation is probably due to conditions such as method of application, soil temperature, soil type, soil moisture, and other variables.

Chemicals which act as fumigants are not satisfactory on established turf because of their phytotoxic effects on grasses. A fumigant for turf use should, when placed in the soil, convert to a gas, penetrate the soil, and kill the nematodes without causing significant injury to the grass roots. Such materials are usually applied to the turf in liquid form and immediately washed into the soil with 1/2 to 1 inch of water. The materials may also be injected at 6- to 8-inch depth on approximately 12-inch centers with a hand fumagun, but this procedure is very slow and time consuming.

Fumigants are especially useful if they are applied prior to planting turf. The material may then be injected into the soil at 8 to 10 inches with a chisel applicator at rates sufficient to reduce the population by 70 to 95%. Chemicals are also available that will give additional weed and fungus control when covered with polyethylene or similar cover at time of application.

Recently a number of nonvolatile nematicides have been investigated. These materials are also applied to the turf surface and washed in with irrigation water. However, there is no fumigant action from the materials, and the nematode must come in contact with the chemical. Among the nonvolatile nematicides are a group known as organophosphates. Some of these materials when applied to the turf are picked up by roots and become systemic in plants. Insecticidal benefits are also obtained from some of these materials. Excellent control and turf response have been obtained from many of the nonvolatile nematicides, and several states have approved them for use on turf.

The merits of nonchemical control have hardly been investigated because none of the standard nematode control measures such as fallowing, flooding, or crop rotation will apply to turf management. However, we will cite a few examples where attempts have been made. Workers (Heald and Burton, 1968; Nutter and Christie, 1958) have shown that fertilizers containing organic nitrogen in the form of processed sewage sludge will suppress nematode populations. This brings about an increase in root and turf growth when compared with inorganic sources of nitrogen. Nutter and Christie (1958) have speculated that the sewage sludge may create soil conditions which favor the development of nematode predators, thereby keeping the nematodes in check. At present it is not known to what extent this method of control is practiced. Heald and Wells (1967) recently reported a method of control by soaking cores of turf in hot water at temperatures lethal to the nematode but not to the turf. This method of control will be useful in obtaining propagation material free of nematodes. Resistance of grasses to nematodes has been reported by several workers (Gaskin, 1965; McBeth, 1945; Riggs et al., 1962). Sledge (1962) reported that *Hypsoperine graminis,* the pseudo-root-knot nematode, attacks several species of turfgrass. In these studies the nematode did not complete its life cycle on Ormond bermuda, Emerald zoysia, and Florantine St. Augustinegrass. Recent work by the authors has shown that different strains of St. Augustinegrass vary in their susceptibility to the pseudo-root-knot nematode.

Although a few turfgrasses show resistance to certain nematode species, there is no single grass that is resistant to all species of nematodes. Little attention has been given to the possibility of breeding nematode-resistant turfgrass varieties.

To date, nematode control in turf is not adequate, and research must continue in this field to produce, hopefully, a means or a chemical that will give long-term control of most nematodes that attack turf.

A. Suggestions for Nematode Control

The nematicides suggested for control of the nematode problems of turfgrasses are listed in Table 1. These have proved effective at the rates given in the southeastern U. S., especially so in Florida. Others may prove effective in different areas.

These materials are applied to the surface and then drenched into the soil with water. Emulsifiable liquids should be applied with low pressure sprayers, and then additional water should be applied by sprinkler irrigation. Granular formulations may be applied dry and the treated areas then irrigated. Apply a minimum of 100 gallons of water per 1,000 sq ft of turf area. Better results are obtained with irrigation of up to 1 inch of water. The irrigation must immediately follow application in order to minimize the chances of foliage burn by the chemicals.

Organophosphate nematicides affect nematodes differently than do fumigants such as DBCP. Populations are reduced much more gradually by the organophosphates, but the turf response often is visible sooner. In any case, application should be made when the grass is beginning to grow (early spring). Any response by the grass should be visible within 4 weeks. The degree of the response is determined by the type and quantity of nematode parasites present.

Table 1. Chemicals suggested for nematode control on established turf.

Nematicides*		Active ingredient/acre	Cautions for use	Use
1, 2 dibromo 3-chloropropane liquid or granular	Nemagon(R) Fumazone(R) (DBCP)	5 gal or 86 lb	May cause skin burn	Home and professional
O, O-diethyl O-(2-isopropyl)	Sarolex (R) (Diazinon)	30-40 lb	Avoid contact. Do not breathe fumes	Home and professional
O, O-diethyl O-(P-methylsulfinyl) phenyl phosphorathioate	Dasanit(R) (Bayer 25141)	10-20 lb	Highly toxic but granular formulation can be handled with caution	Professional use only
O-ethyl S, S-dipropyl phosphorodithioate	Mocap(R) (UC 9-104)	15-20 lb	" " "	Professional use only

* These chemicals are not registered for turf use in all states. Care must be taken to check with state authorities before using.

IV. Other Pests of Turf and the Extent of Their Injury

Moles are furry little animals with sharp-pointed teeth, concealed eyes and ears, with front paws turned outward and supporting stout claws used to make unsightly tunnels in turf areas. Contrary to the thoughts of many people, these creatures do not feed on the roots of plants, but rather on earthworms, grubs, and other similar creatures harbored in the turf. Several methods of control are suggested, such as trapping, poison bait, and control of food supply with insecticides.

Rodents such as mice, ground squirrels, gophers, etc. can cause extensive injury to turf by burrowing numerous holes and runways. Mice may work under snow cover and the damage not detected until spring. Gophers, especially the pocket gopher, cause extensive damage to turf by tunneling through an area and throwing up large piles of soil at tunnel exits. These pests can be controlled by traps and various poison baits. In some cases, lethal gases can be introduced in tunnels and runways with favorable results.

Earthworms are generally known to aerate the soil and some turf authorities believe they are beneficial to turf soil. However, others consider the earthworm to be a nuisance because of castings left on the surface of the turf. Earthworms are also known to be a source of food for some burrowing animals and from this standpoint are also undesirable. Many of the nematicides and insecticides normally used in turf maintenance will also control earthworms, so it is felt that an active pest control program should take care of earthworm problems.

Household pets, mainly dogs, can be a problem in turf management. Many seem to follow the same route daily causing trails and other unsightly problems in the turf. Chemical repellants have been suggested for very small areas, but are not practical otherwise. The sting from the pellet of a boy's BB-gun has proven to be an effective repellant when all else fails.

Literature Cited

Bell, A. A., and L. R. Krusberg. 1964. Occurrence and control of the genus *Hypsoperine* on zoysia and bermuda grasses in Maryland. Plant Dis. Reptr. 48: 721-722.

Brodie, Bill B., and G. W. Burton. 1967. Nematode population reduction and growth response of bermuda turf as influenced by organic pesticide applications. Plant Dis. Reptr. 51: 562-566.

Christie, J. R. 1956. Identity and distribution of soil nematodes. Florida Agr. Exp. Sta. Ann. Rept.: 86-87.

Christie, J. R., A. N. Brooks, and V. G. Perry. 1952. The sting nematode, *Belonolaimus gracilis,* a parasite of major importance on strawberries, celery, and sweet corn in Florida. Phytopathology 42 (4): 173-176.

Christie, J. R., J. M. Good, Jr., and G. C. Nutter. 1954. Nematodes associated with injury to turf. Proc. Soil Sci. Soc. Fla. 14: 167-169.

Christie, J. R., and V. G. Perry. 1951. A root disease of plants caused by a nematode of the genus *Trichodorus*. Sci. 113:491-493.

Dickerson, O. J. 1966. Some observations on *Hypsoperine graminis* in Kansas. Plant Dis. Reptr. 50: 36-38.

DiEdwardo, A. A. 1963. Pathogenicity and host-parasite relationships of nematodes on turf in Florida. Florida Agr. Exp. Sta. Ann. Rept.: 109.

DiEdwardo, A. A., and V. G. Perry. 1964. *Heterodera Leuceilyma* n. sp. *(Nemata: Heteroderidae),* a severe pathogen of St. Augustine grass in Florida. Florida Agr. Exp. Sta. Bull. 687. 35 pp.

Gaskin, T. A. 1965. Susceptibility of bluegrass to root-knot nematodes. Plant Dis. Reptr. 49: 89-90.

Good, J. M., J. R. Christie, and J. Nutter. 1956. Identification and distribution of plant parasitic nematodes in Florida and Georgia. (Abst.) Phytopathology. 46: 13.

Good, J. M., A. E. Steele, and T. J. Ratcliffe. 1959. Occurrence of plant parasitic nematodes in Georgia turf nurseries. Plant Dis. Reptr. 43: 236-238.

Heald, C. M. 1969. Pathogenicity and histopathology of *Meloidogyne graminis* infecting Tifdwarf bermudagrass roots. J. Nematology 1(1):9-10.

Heald, C. M., and G. W. Burton. 1968. Effect of organic and inorganic nitrogen on nematode populations on turf. Plant Dis. Reptr. 52: 46-48.

Heald, C. M., and H. D. Wells. 1967. Control of endo- and ecto-parasitic nematodes in turf by hot-water treatments. Plant Dis. Reptr. 51:905-907.

Hodges, Clinton F., Donald P. Taylor, and Michael P. Britton. 1963. Root-knot nematode on creeping bentgrass. Plant Dis. Reptr. 47: 1102-1103.

Jackson, James E., J. M. Good, and Glenn W. Burton. 1961. Five-year study of nitrogen sources for 328 Bermuda. Golfdom, Sept.

Kelsheimer, E. G., and Amegda J. Overman. 1953. Notes on some ecto-parasitic nematodes found attacking lawns in the Tampa Bay area. Proc. Fla. State Hort. Soc. 66: 301-303.

Lautz, William. 1958. Chemical control of nematodes parasitic on turf and sweet corn. Proc. Fla. State Hort. Soc.: 38-40.

Lautz, W. H. 1959. Increase of *Belonolaimus longicaudatus* on various plant species in artifically inoculated soil. Plant Dis. Reptr. 43: 48-50.

McBeth, C. W. 1945. Tests on the susceptibility and resistance of several southern grasses to the root-knot nematode, *Heterodera marioni.* Proc. Helminth. Soc. of Washington 12(2): 41-44.

Mirza, Kishwar, and V. G. Perry. 1967. Histopathology of St. Augustinegrass roots infected by *Hypsoperine graminis* Sledge and Golden. Nematologica 13: 146-147 (Abst.).

Nutter, G. C. 1955. Nematode investigations in turf. Florida Agr. Exp. Sta. Ann. Rept.: 58.

Nutter, Gene C., and J. R. Christie. 1958. Nematode investigations on putting green turf. Proc. Fla. State Hort. Soc.: 445-449.

Nutter, G. C., and G. M. Whitton. 1957. Nematode investigations on turf grasses. Florida Agr. Exp. Sta. Ann. Rept.: 120-121.

Orr, Calvin C., and A. Morgan Golden. 1966. The pseudo-root-knot nematode of turf in Texas. Plant Dis. Reptr. 50: 645.

Parris, G. K. 1957. Screening Mississippi soils for plant parasitic nematodes. Plant Dis. Reptr. 41: 705.

Perry, V. G. 1953a. Return of nematodes following fumigation of Florida soils. Proc. Fla. State Hort. Soc.: 112-113.

Perry, V. G. 1953b. The awl nematode *Dolichodorus heterocephalus,* a devastating plant parasite. Proc. Helmin. Soc. Wash., 20(1): 21-27.

Perry, V. G., H. M. Darling, and G. Thorne. 1959. Anatomy, taxonomy and control of certain spiral nematodes attacking bluegrass in Wisconsin. Univ. Wis. Res. Bull. 207. 24 pp.

Powell, W. M. 1964. The occurrence of *Tylenchorhynchus maximus* in Georgia. Plant Dis. Reptr. 48: 70-71.

Rhoades, H. L. 1965. Parasitism and pathogenicity of *Trichodorus proximus* to St. Augustine grass. Plant Dis. Reptr. 49: 259-262.

Rhoades, H. L. 1962. Effects of sting and stubby-root nematodes on St. Augustine grass. Plant Dis. Reptr. 46: 424-427.

Riffle, Jerry W. 1964 Root-knot nematode on African Bermuda grass in New Mexico. Plant Dis. Reptr. 48: 964.

Riggs, R. D., J. L. Dale, and M. L. Hamblen. 1962. Reaction of Bermuda grass varieties and lines to root-knot nematodes. Phytopathology 52: 587-588.

Sledge, E. B. 1962. Preliminary report on a *Meloidogyne* sp. parasite of grass in Florida. Plant Dis. Reptr. 46: 52-54.

Sledge, E. B., and A. Morgan Golden. 1964. *Hypsoperine graminis (Nematoda: Heteroderidae),* a new genus of species of plant-parasitic nematode. Proc. Helminth. Soc.: 83-88.

Somerville, A. M., Jr., V. G. Young, Jr., and J. L. Carnes. 1957. Occurrence of plant parasitic nematodes in soil and root samples from declining plants in several states. Plant Dis. Reptr. 41: 187-191.

Tarjan, A. C. 1964. Rejuvenation of nematized centipedegrass turf with chemical drenches. Proc. Fla. State Hort. Soc. 77: 456-461.

Taylor, D. P., M. P. Britton, and H. Carol Hechler, 1963. Occurrence of plant parasitic nematodes in Illinois golf greens. Plant Dis. Reptr. 47: 134-135.

Troll, J., and R. A. Rohde. 1965. Pathogenicity of the nematodes *Pratylenchus penetrans* and *Tylenchorynchus claytoni* on turfgrasses. (Abst.). Phytopathology 56: 1285.

Troll, J., and R. A. Rohde. 1966. The effects of nematicides on turfgrass growth. Plant Dis. Reptr. 50: 489-492.

Van Weerdt, L. G., W. Birchfield, and R. P. Esser. 1959. Observations on some subtropical plant parasitic nematodes in Florida. Soil and Crop Sci. Soc. Fla. Proc. 19: 443-451.

Winchester, J. A., and E. O. Burt. 1964. The effect and control of sting nematodes on Ormond Bermuda grass. Plant Dis. Reptr. 48: 625-628.

13 Species and Varieties

A. A. Hanson

F. V. Juska

Agricultural Research Service, USDA
Beltsville, Maryland

Glenn W. Burton

Agricultural Research Service, USDA
Tifton, Georgia

I. Introduction

Turf production begins with grass, not just any grass, but rather a grass species, and more often a variety of that species, and sometimes mixtures containing several grass species and varieties. Thus, gaining knowledge of the grasses adapted for turf use is an essential preparation, either for conducting intensive studies or for strengthening a casual interest in growing and managing turf.

The grass family (or Gramineae) contains over 5,000 species of which 1,400 or more are found within the borders of the continental U. S. It is the most valuable family of flowering plants known to man. It includes all major cereal grains (wheat, oats, barley, rye, rice, millet, sorghum, and corn), sugarcane, bamboo, and numerous forage grasses utilized in livestock production for grazing and conserved feed. The grasses also provide sources of many other products ranging from paper to perfume. They are extremely important in stabilizing the soil and for reducing the harmful effects of water and wind erosion. The relatively few species adapted for turf use (less than 25 according to accepted classification systems) have one characteristic in common, namely, the ability to tolerate mowing at regular intervals. Similarly, many undesirable weedy grasses have a high tolerance to close, frequent mowing.

The grasses in Table 1 appear in alphabetical order under their technical or botanical names and are cross-referenced to the accepted common names. Common names are often uncertain in their application, with different plants bearing the same name or the same plant having different names in different locations. Language differences among countries add further confusion to the correct use of common plant names. It is for these reasons that systematic botanists rely on Latin in naming and identifying plants. The Latin name is followed by the authority (or authorities) credited with naming the species, e.g., *Poa pratensis* L. (The L. refers to Linnaeus, who published Species Plantarum in 1753.)

In the U. S. a fair degree of uniformity prevails in the common names applied to cultivated grasses. Credit for this uniformity can be

Table 1. Common and botanical names of some turf, forage, and weed grasses.

Name	Description no.
bahiagrass-Paspalum notatum	37
beachgrass, American-Ammophila breviligulata	10
European-Ammophila arenaria	9
bentgrass, Colonial-Agrostis tenuis	8
creeping-Agrostis palustris	7
velvet-Agrostis canina	6
bermudagrass-Cynodon dactylon	19
bermudagrasses-Cynodon spp.	18
bluegrass, annual-Poa annua	41
Canada-Poa compressa	42
Kentucky-Poa pratensis	44
rough-Poa trivialis	45
upland-Poa glaucantha	43
bromegrass, smooth-Bromus inermis	16
bromesedge-Andropogon virginicus	11
buffalograss-Buchloë dactyloides	17
canarygrass, reed-Phalaris arundinacea	39
carpetgrass-Axonopus affinis	12
carpetgrass, tropical-Axonopus compressus	13
centipedegrass-Eremochloa ophiuroides	25
crabgrass, large-Digitaria sanguinalis	22
smooth-Digitaria ischaemum	21
dallisgrass-Paspalum dilatatum	35
fescue, Chewings-Festuca rubra var. commutata	31
hard-Festuca ovina var. duriuscula	29
fescue, meadow-Festuca elatior	27
red-Festuca rubra	30
sheep-Festuca ovina	28
tall-Festuca arundinacea	26
goosegrass-Eleusine indica	23
grama, blue-Bouteloua gracilis	15
sideoats-Bouteloua curtipendula	14
Japanese lawngrass-Zoysia japonica	48
kikuyugrass-Pennisetum clandestinum	38
lovegrass, weeping-Eragrostis curvula	24
manilagrass-Zoysia matrella	50
orchardgrass-Dactylis glomerata	20
paspalum, field-Paspalum laeve	36
quackgrass-Agropyron repens	3
redtop-Agrostis alba	5
ryegrass, annual-Lolium multiflorum	33
perennial-Lolium perenne	34
St. Augustinegrass-Stenotaphrum secundatum	46
timothy-Phleum pratense	40
velvetgrass-Holcus lanatus	32
wheatgrass, crested-Agropyron desertorum	2
fairway-Agropyron cristatum	1
streambank-Agropyron riparium	4
zoysiagrass-Zoysia spp.	47

given to the activities of various professional societies, public agencies, and to the published listing of common names included in the Federal Seed Act.[1] Names recognized in the Federal Seed Act are very important, as this act governs the correct labeling of seed moving in interstate commerce.

Descriptions of important turfgrasses are given in this chapter together with selected forage species (that may be used for soil stabilization and often appear as weeds in turfgrass areas), species for special purposes (sand dune stabilization), and some significant annual and perennial weedy grasses. Emphasis is given to growth habit, vegetative characteristics useful in identifying grasses in the nonflowering state, general region of adaptation and use, and varieties available for specialized and general-purpose turf.

Grasses are often confused with grass-like plants belonging to either the Rush family (Juncaceae) or the Sedge family (Cyperaceae). Grasses can be distinguished from members of these two families by the two-ranked arrangement of the leaves (leaves in two vertical rows) and by culms (stems) that are usually hollow, cylindrical or flattened, with conspicuous nodes. Members of the Cyperaceae possess three-ranked leaves (leaves in three vertical rows) and culms filled with pith, rarely hollow, generally three-sided, with inconspicuous nodes. The Juncaceae have three-ranked leaves born on cylindrical culms filled with chambered or open sponge-like pith. Nodes on the culms are not conspicuous as in the Cyperaceae.

Plant parts of value in identifying nonflowering grasses include the bud shoot, ligule, auricles, collar, sheath, and blade. Points of separation among these characters are as follows:

[1] Rules and Regulations under the Federal Seed Act. Agricultural Marketing Service, USDA. Service and Regulatory Announcements No. 156. Issued March 1940. Reprinted with amendments, August 1963.

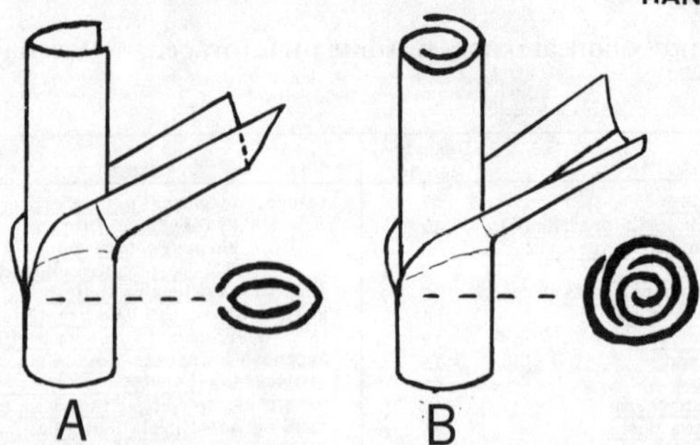

Figure 1. Vernation: A—leaf folded in bud-shoot. B—Leaf rolled in bud-shoot.

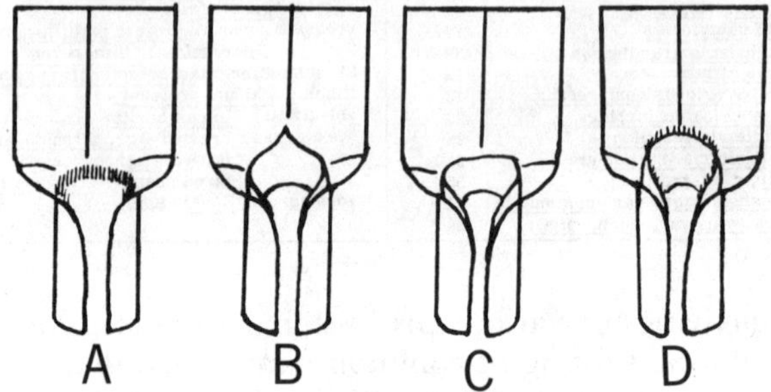

Figure 2. Ligule shapes and margins: A—Fringe of hairs. B—Acute. C—Truncate. D—Ciliate margin.

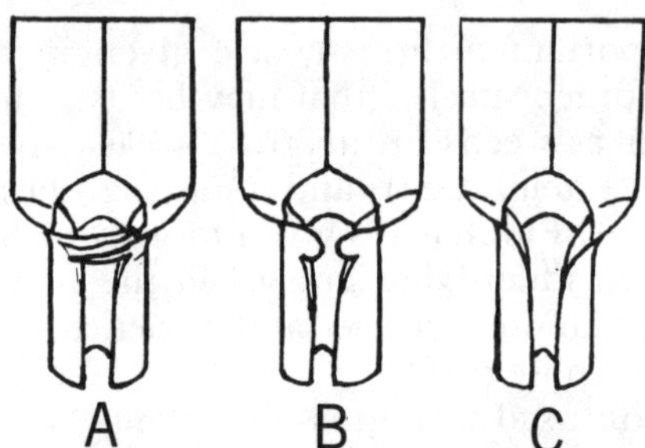

Figure 3. Auricles: A—Clawlike. B—Rounded. C—Absent.

Leaves: Arrangement of leaves in bud shoot (vernation) is an important feature in identification. Leaves may be either folded with margins meeting but not overlapping (Fig. 1A) or rolled lengthwise with margins overlapping (Fig. 1B).

Ligule: A tongue-like outgrowth at the junction of the blade and sheath, clasping the culm or bud shoot. It may be a fringe of hairs (Fig. 2A), membranous with various conformations (Fig. 2B-acute, Fig. 2C-truncate, and Fig. 2D-ciliate) or absent (rarely).

Auricles: Appendages projecting from each side of the collar. May vary in length and shape from clawlike (Fig. 3A) to blunt rounded appendages (Fig. 3B). Auricles are often absent (Fig. 3C).

Collar: A meristematic band or growth zone marking the division point between the blade and the sheath. The band may be broad (Fig. 4A), or narrow (Fig. 4B), or divided by the midrib (Fig. 4C).

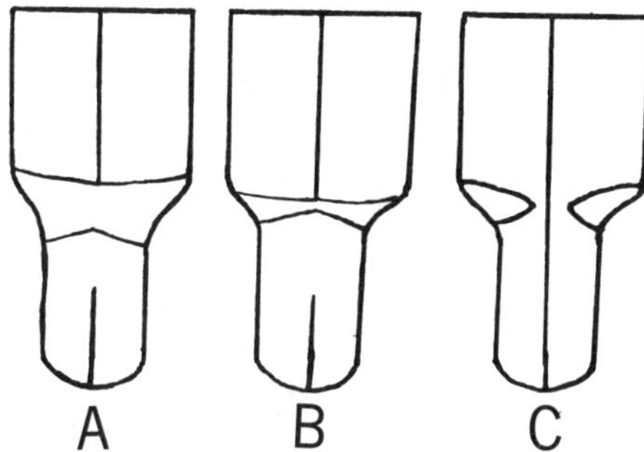

Figure 4. Collar: A—Broad band. B—Narrow band. C—Divided by midrib.

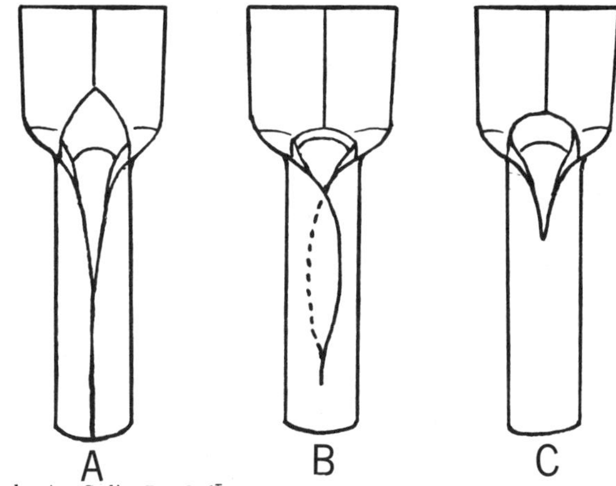

Figure 5. Sheath: A—Split. B—Split to near base with margins overlapping. C—Closed (Note ligule shapes: A—Acute. B—Truncate. C—Rounded.)

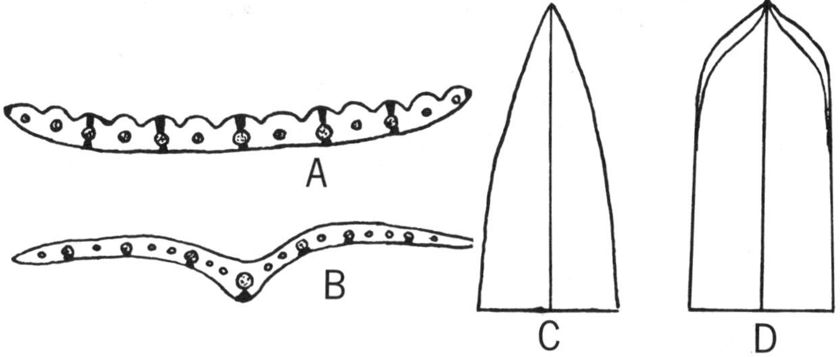

Figure 6. Blade surface and tips: A—Blade ridged and not keeled. B—Blade not ridged and keeled. C—Taper-pointed open. D—Boat-shaped open.

Usually glabrous, but may be pubescent, and generally a lighter green than blade or sheath.

Sheath: The tubular basal portion of the leaf enveloping the culm or young growing leaves. In cross section it may be compressed or rounded and occasionally keeled by the midrib. It may be split with or without overlapping margins (Fig. 5A), split to near base (Fig. 5B), or closed (Fig. 5C).

Blade: The free, nonclasping part of the leaf above the collar and ligule. Width and length of the blade vary with variety, management, plant density, and age, so that general statements on texture are about as meaningful as specific measurements. There are several other blade characteristics, however, that are helpful in identification. The upper blade surface may be deeply ridged or smooth (Fig. 6A and 6B), while the midrib may be prominent on the under surface forming a distinct keel (Fig. 6B). The blade tip in *Poa pratensis* has a characteristic boat shape (Fig. 6D).

II. Identification of Grasses by Vegetative Characters[2]

Group I. Leaf blade rolled in bud shoot.

A. Auricles present.

B. Blade glossy on under surface; margin of ligule not ciliate; auricles blunt to clawlike.

C. Auricles with short hairs. *Festuca arundinacea* (26)[3]

CC. Auricles glabrous

D. Blade scabrous on margins, ligule generally 0.5 mm long or less. *Festuca elatior* (27)

DD. Blade smooth on margins near base, ligule generally 1.0 mm long or more. *Lolium multiflorum* (33)

BB. Blade not glossy on under surface; margin of ligule ciliate or lacerate; auricles stiff, clawlike.

C. Collar minutely pubescent; midrib not pronounced on under surface of blade; upper surface not prominently ridged. *Agropyron repens* (3)

CC. Collar glabrous; midrib conspicuous on under surface of blade; upper surface of blade prominently ridged. *Agropyron cristatum* (1)

AA. Auricles absent or rudimentary.

B. Ligule a fringe of hairs. *Zoysia japonica* (48) (If *Cynodon dactylon* is placed here because of very slight rolling of leaves in bud shoot, then it can be distinguished by well-expanded leaves up to stolon tip vs. restricted leaf development near ends of most *Z. japonica* stolons.)

BB. Ligule membranous

C. Sheath closed

D. Sheath and blade glabrous *Bromus inermis* (16)

DD. Sheath and blade pubescent (several weedy bromegrass species)

CC. Sheath split (margins generally overlapping)

D. Hairs present (on sheath or on blade or on collar).

E. Sheath compressed

F. Sheath glabrous *Digitaria ischaemum* (21)

FF. Sheath pubescent

[2] This vegetative key was adapted from Nowosad, Swales, and Dore (1936).
[3] Numbers in parentheses refer to species descriptions which follow this listing of characters.

G. Stolons or creeping stems present *Digitaria sanguinalis* (22)

GG. Stolons absent

H. Blades flat, soft, dense, velvety, short, hairy above. *Holcus lanatus* (32)

HH. Blades not dense, velvety, short, hairy above.

I. Ligule with dense row of whitish hairs at back. *Paspalum notatum* (37)

II. Ligule without whitish hairs at back.

J. Ligule rounded to acute; sheaths densely hairy below, sparsely so above. *Paspalum dilatatum* (35)

JJ. Ligule truncate; sheaths sparsely hairy on margins and midnerve *Paspalum laeve* (36)

EE. Sheath not compressed (ligule membranous, ciliate, sometimes appearing as dense fringe of hairs). *Bouteloua curtipendula* (14)

DD. Glabrous throughout.

E. Ligule long (more than 1.5 mm long).

F. Margin of collar sparsely ciliate; ligule with prominent notch on either side; culms with bulbous base. *Phleum pratense* (40)

FF. Margin of collar glabrous; ligule without a notch on either side; culms lack bulbous base.

G. Ligule white, papery, 2 to 8 mm long, acute or obtuse; blade 6 to 15 mm wide. *Phalaris arundinacea* (39)

GG. Ligule thin-membranous, 1.5 to 4 mm long, rounded or acute; blade 1.5 to 7 mm wide.

H. Stolons absent; rhizomes present *Agrostis alba* (5)

HH. Stolons long, leafy, prostrate. *Agrostis palustris* (7)

EE. Ligule short (less than 1.5 mm long), truncate

F. Blade about 1 mm wide, smooth above and below. *Agrostis canina* (6)

FF. Blade about 2 to 3 mm wide, smooth to rough above and below. *Agrostis tenuis* (8)

Group II. Leaf blade folded in bud shoot.

A. Auricles present; lower sheaths reddish at base; glabrous throughout. *Lolium perenne* (34)

AA. Auricles absent.

B. Ligule a fringe of hairs.

C. Sheaths greatly overlapping between each apparent node (gives multiple leaf effect), rhizomes and stolons. *Cynodon dactylon* (19)

CC. Sheaths not greatly overlapping between nodes (or basal only), no rhizomes, stolons present.

D. Blade petioled above ligule. *Stenotaphrum secundatum* (46)

DD. Blade not petioled above ligule.

E. Blade with few long hairs scattered on both surfaces. *Buchloe dactyloides* (17)

EE. Blade without long hairs scattered on both surfaces.

F. Blade 1 to 2.5 mm wide, sharp point, scabrous or pubescent on upper surface especially near base. *Bouteloua gracilis* (15)

FF. Blade 4 to 8 mm wide, obtuse, glabrous or ciliate at base. *Axonopus affinis* (12)

BB. Ligule short-membranous; short ciliate.

C. Collar continuous, broad (constricted by fused keel), pubescent, ciliate, tufted at lower edge. *Eremochloa ophiuroides* (25)

CC. Collar divided, narrow, mostly hairy on margins. *Andropogon virginicus* (11)

BBB. Ligule membranous.

C. Hairs on margin of collar, sheath hairy at top. *Eleusine indica* (23)

CC. No hairs at margins of collar, sheath glabrous or densely puberulent.

D. Blade prominently ridged on upper (inner) surface, narrow to bristle-like.

E. Ligule less than 0.5 mm long or obsolete; sheath split; leaves glaucous, blue-green; plant tufted. *Festuca ovina* (28)

EE. Ligule about 0.5 mm long; sheath closed nearly to top; leaves generally dark green; plant not tufted. *Festuca rubra* (30)

DD. Blade not prominently ridged on upper (inner) surface, flat, not bristle-like.

E. Median lines present; tip of blade boat shaped, abruptly pointed.

F. Ligule truncate, short (less than 1.0 mm long).

G. Sheath keeled; blade broadest at base gradually tapering to apex; foliage blue-green, often glaucous; minute hairs on margin of collar absent. *Poa compressa* (42)

GG. Sheath not keeled (ligule usually 0.5 mm long); blade parallel-sided; foliage deep green, not glaucous; minute hairs often present on margin of collar. *Poa pratensis* (44)

FF. Ligule obtuse or acute, long (more than 1.0 mm long).

G. Blade truncate at base and tapering to a narrow boat-shaped tip; sheath usually scabrous; perennial. *Poa trivialis* (45)

GG. Blade not tapering (parallel-sided), often puckered; tip abruptly pointed and boat-shaped; sheath smooth; annual. *Poa annua* (41)

EE. Median lines absent; tip of blade taper-pointed; blade broad, plant tufted. *Dactylis glomerata* (20)

III. Description of Species

1. *Agropyron cristatum* (L.) Gaertn, fairway wheatgrass (other names– fairway crested wheatgrass and crested wheatgrass)

Origin: Introduced from Russian Turkestan in 1906. Indigenous to eastern Russia, western Siberia, and central Asia.

Description: A coarse-textured, cool-season, perennial bunchgrass. Plant type variable; foliage light, bluish green. *Leaves*– rolled in the bud shoot. *Ligule*– membranous, truncate, lacerate (up to 1.5 mm long). *Auricles*– clawlike. *Collar*– divided, light or yellowish green, smooth to ciliate. *Sheath*– round, split, smooth, slightly scabrous, sometimes with soft pubescence. *Blade*– flat or slightly involute, tapers to sharp point, prominent veins, often soft pubescence on upper surface, margins scabrous. *Inflorescence*– erect, flattened spike. In general, glumes have pronounced awns.

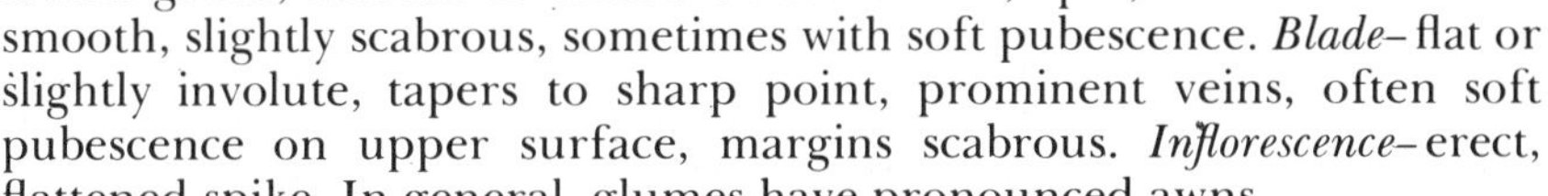

Adaptation and use: A very drought-tolerant, cold-resistant grass, adapted throughout much of the Canadian prairies and the Northern Great Plains and Intermountain Regions in the U. S. It grows well on most productive soils from light sandy loams to heavy clays. Rated as low in tolerance to alkali soils and prolonged flooding. Fairway is used extensively for pasture and hay in western Canada and to a lesser extent in the U. S. It is shorter, denser, finer stemmed and less productive than crested wheatgrass (*Agropyron desertorum*), but better suited for dryland lawns and general-purpose turf.

Varieties: Although some selection has been practiced, no improved varieties are available for turf use.

2. *Agropyron desertorum* (Fisch.) Schult., crested wheatgrass (other names– standard crested wheatgrass, desert wheatgrass)

Origin: Introduced from Russian Turkestan in 1906. Indigenous to eastern Russia, western Siberia, and central Asia.

Description: A coarse-textured, cool-season, perennial bunchgrass. A tetraploid species (28 chromosomes) that is generally coarser in appearance than diploid (14 chromosomes) fairway wheatgrass (*A. cristatum*). However, types vary from leafy, fine-stemmed plants to those that are very coarse, with few leaves and stiff stems. Vegetative characteristics similar to fairway wheatgrass. Glumes may have pronounced awns, short awns, or no awns.

Adaptation and use: Used for pasture, hay, and erosion control in Northern Great Plains; important for range seeding westward to the Cascade and Sierra Nevada mountains and south to northern Arizona and New Mexico. Most successful in areas with 9 to 15 inches of rainfall, except in southern portion of range where 12 to 15 inches are required. It has performed best at elevations of 5,000 feet or more in southern areas. The elevational limit is usually given as 8,500 to 9,000 feet. Not as acceptable as fairway wheatgrass for dryland turf plantings but of value in conservation plantings and for soil stabilization.

Varieties: Improved varieties have been developed for forage use.

3. *Agropyron repens* (L.) Beauv., quackgrass.

Origin: Indigenous to Eurasia, probably introduced into U. S. from Europe during Colonial Period.

Description: A coarse-textured, cool-season, sod-forming perennial. *Leaves*–rolled in bud shoot. *Ligule*–membranous (0.2 to 1 mm long), truncate to rounded, may be finely toothed or ciliate. *Auricles*–claw-like, slender. *Collar*–medium, occasionally divided, sometimes minutely hairy. *Sheath*–round, mostly short, hairy, split. *Blade*–tapering to sharp point, sometimes glaucous, harsh–scabrous on margins, usually sparsely pilose, smooth below. *Inflorescence*–long, narrow spike with spikelets placed side to rachis.

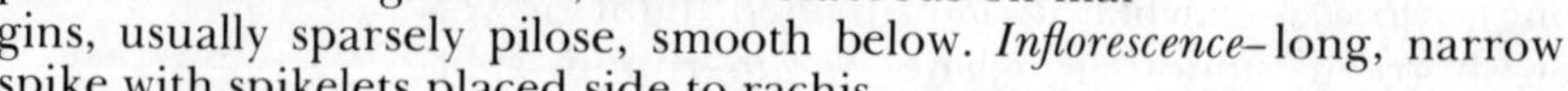

Adaptation and use: Widely distributed in northern states and south and west to North Carolina, Arkansas, Utah, and California. Existing stands may be used for pasture and forage. Troublesome, persistent weed in cultivated and abandoned fields and in turf.

4. *Agropyron riparium* Scribn. and Smith, streambank wheatgrass.

Origin: Indigenous to western North America.

Description: A coarse-textured, cool-season, sod-forming perennial. Resembles thickspike wheatgrass *(A. dasystachyum* (Hook.) Scribn.). It is drought tolerant and possesses vigorous rhizomes. Top growth relatively short.

Adaptation and use: Found from Montana to Washington and south into Nevada, Utah, and Colorado. Valuable for ground cover because sod is resistant to erosion. Well adapted for use on roadsides, airports, and irrigation canal banks.

Varieties: Sodar. Released by the Idaho and Washington AES[4] and Plant Materials Centers, SCS, USDA,[5] Aberdeen, Idaho, and Pullman, Wash. Produces open sod highly competitive to weeds and other plants under dryland conditions.

5. *Agrostis alba* L., redtop.

Origin: Introduced from Europe during Colonial Period.

Description: A cool-season, rhizomatous perennial. *Leaves*–rolled in bud shoot. *Ligule*–membranous, rounded to acute (1.5 to 5 mm long). *Auricles*–absent. *Collar*–prominent, glabrous, divided, may be oblique. *Sheath*–round, smooth, split. *Blade*–flat, tapering to sharp point, up to 10 mm wide, prominently ridged on upper surface, rough above and below, margins rough. *Inflorescence*–a reddish, spreading panicle. (Distinguished from creep-

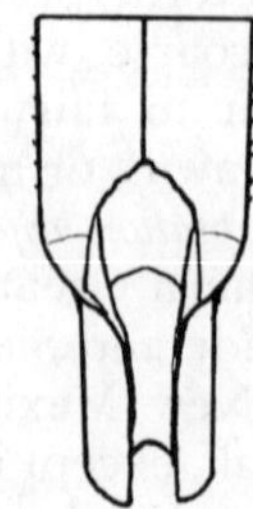

[4]AES–State Agricultural Experiment Station or Stations.

[5]The Agricultural Research Service and Soil Conservation Service of the U. S. Department of Agriculture (USDA) appear as ARS and SCS, respectively.

ing bentgrass *(A. palustris)* by absence of long surface stolons and from Colonial bentgrass *(A. tenuis)* by longer ligule and broader blades.)

Adaptation and use: Widely distributed throughout cooler sections of the U. S., especially in Northeastern and North Central States. Under humid conditions it tolerates a wide range of soil and moisture conditions. Grows on acid soils and poor clay soils of low fertility. Used as temporary grass in lawn seed mixtures, for pastures, erosion control, and occasionally for hay. Competes with other grasses included in mixtures, becomes stemmy, coarse textured, and soon dies under close, frequent mowing.

Varieties: None available.

6. *Agrostis canina* L., velvet bentgrass.

Origin: Introduced from Europe during Colonial Period.

Description: A fine-textured, cool-season, stoloniferous perennial. *Leaves*–rolled in bud shoot. *Ligule*–membranous, rounded to acute (0.4 to 0.8 mm long). *Auricles*–absent. *Collar*–medium broad. *Sheath*–round, smooth, split. *Blade*–flat, smooth above and below, margins scabrous. *Inflorescence*–loose, spreading panicle.

Adaptation and use: Well adapted to cool, humid regions, especially coastal portions of the Northeastern States, much of New England, and milder sections of the Pacific Northwest. Comparatively tolerant to infertile soils but does not thrive on poorly aerated and poorly drained sites. In contrast to other bentgrasses, it will make satisfactory growth in partial shade as well as in full sunlight. Where adapted, velvet bentgrass is very aggressive under close, frequent mowing. It is used primarily for turf purposes, including bowling greens, putting greens, and in mixtures for home lawns and parks. Turf quality is good.

Varieties: Common sources have been used in most seedings and vegetative plantings. Earlier varieties, such as Piper, Raritan and Kernwood, have not gained any degree of prominence.

Kingstown. Released by the Rhode Island AES, Kingston, in 1963. Selected for color, vigor, density, texture, and resistance to several diseases. Semibrilliant dark green color, excellent vigor, and high dollar spot resistance. Promising in tests.

7. *Agrostis palustris* Huds., creeping bentgrass (other names—carpet bentgrass)

Origin: Introduced from Europe during Colonial Period.

Description: A fine-textured, cool-season, stoloniferous perennial. *Leaves*–rolled in bud shoot. *Ligule*–membranous, rounded or obtuse, finely lacerate-toothed or entire, minutely hairy on back (0.6 to 3 mm long). *Auricles*–absent. *Collar*–distinct, usually oblique. *Sheath*–round, smooth, split. *Blade*–flat, distinctly ridged on upper surface, slightly keeled on lower surface, scabrous on surfaces and margins. *Inflorescence* – narrow, dense, pale or purple panicle.

Adaptation and use: Well adapted to cool, humid regions, especially coastal marshes from Newfoundland to Maryland and from British Columbia to northern California, and occasionally along ditch banks in Texas and New Mexico. Range of use on putting greens has been extended through application of good management practices. Tolerates low temperatures and thrives on relatively poor, wet soils. Used extensively on putting greens and bowling greens and occasionally for lawns. High maintenance requirements restrict its value for lawn use.

Varieties: Propagated either vegetatively or by seed. Seed sources include Seaside and Penncross varieties. A number of vegetatively reproduced varieties have been selected from established greens of South German mixed bentgrass. South German mixed bentgrass probably included up to 75% Colonial bentgrass and varying amounts of velvet and creeping bentgrass.

Major Seeded Types:

Penncross. Released by the Pennsylvania AES University Park, in 1954. Name applied to first-generation seed produced by random crossing of three vegetatively propagated clones. Selected for improved turf quality, density, disease tolerance, and rate of recovery from damage. Somewhat variable especially in years immediately after establishment. Performance rated as satisfactory to good over a wide range of environmental conditions.

Seaside. A recognized source of creeping bentgrass characterized by extreme variability. Turf quality lower than that of most selected varieties. Generally rated as below average in disease resistance. Develops patches of individual strains, exhibiting marked differences in texture, color, graininess, and disease susceptibility.

Major Vegetative Varieties:

Arlington (C-1).[6] Selected at Arlington, Va., by U.S. Golf Association Green Section and Crops Research Division, ARS, USDA. Tough, rather slow growing, bluish-green in appearance. Requires high level of soil fertility, careful attention to irrigation practices, and close mowing to reduce swirl. Some tolerance to dollarspot and melting-out (*Helminthosporium* – *Curvularia* complex) but susceptible to brown patch. Grows well in warm weather. Combines well with Congressional (C-19) if not subjected to overwatering.

C-52. (Also sold under trademark "Old Orchard") Selected at Old Orchard Grass Nursery, Madison, Wis., in 1934. Good color and texture, and some tolerance to dollarspot. Tendency to thin out during

[6]C numbers used to identify strains in cooperative studies conducted by U. S. Golf Association Green Section and Crops Research Division, ARS, USDA, Arlington, Va.

hot weather. Well adapted and used rather widely in parts of the Midwest.

Cohansey (C-7). Selected at Pine Valley Golf Club, Clementon, N. J. Vigorous, aggressive, yellowish-green. Tolerates frequent watering and possesses wide adaptation to climatic conditions. Exhibits some tolerance to brown patch and melting out, but susceptible to dollar spot. Performs satisfactorily in warm areas.

Collins (C-27). Selected at Arlington, Va., by U.S. Golf Association Green Section and Crops Research Division, ARS, USDA. Dark green, rather nonaggressive, somewhat comparable to Seaside in disease susceptibility.

Congressional (C-19). Selected at Congressional Country Club, Rockville, Md. Attractive dark green, good texture, hardy, starts growth early in spring and retains color well into fall and winter. Susceptible to brown patch. Good variety either alone or in combination with Arlington (C-1) and/or Collins (C-27).

Evansville. Released by the Indiana AES, Lafayette, in 1963. Dark-green collection from Evansville Country Club, Evansville, Ind. Described as a dense-growing variety possessing resistance to dollar spot and some tolerance to brown patch.

Metropolitan (C-51). Selected at Arlington, Va., by U. S. Golf Association Green Section and Crops Research Division, ARS, USDA, Difficult to manage as turf tends to become fluffy and grainy. Very susceptible to melting-out.

Pennlu. Released by the Pennsylvania AES, University Park, in 1954. One of three parental clones, 10(37)4, in Penncross variety. Selected for disease tolerance, good vigor, density, and texture. Appears to have acceptable tolerance to a wide temperature range.

Pennpar. Released by the Pennsylvania AES, University Park, in 1966. Medium texture, medium dark green color, and produces good putting surface without severe graining or mottling. Selected for resistance and tolerance to snow mold, brown patch, red leaf spot, and dollar spot. Some tolerance to turfgrass herbicides, not exceedingly vigorous, and easier to manage than Penncross.

Toronto (C-15). Selected at Toronto Golf Club, Long Branch, Ontario, Canada. Vigorous, aggressive, dark green, fine-textured variety that requires careful management. Susceptible to brown patch and dollar spot. Well adapted in eastern Canada and midwestern U.S.

Washington (C-50). Selected at Arlington, Va., by U.S. Golf Association Green Section and Crops Research Division, ARS, USDA. Washington and Metropolitan were the first named varieties of creeping bentgrass in the U.S. Light green, excellent texture, some disease tolerance and resistance to heat. It has a comparatively short growing season; growth starts slowly in spring and ceases in early fall. Assumes purple tinge with cool weather.

8. *Agrostis tenuis* Sibth., Colonial bentgrass (other names—Rhode Island, browntop, New Zealand, Prince Edward Island)

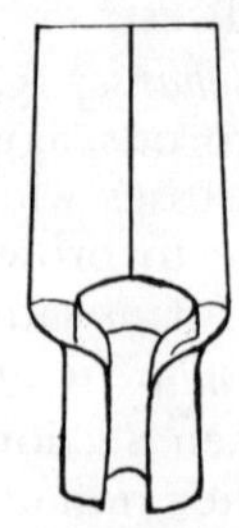

Origin: Introduced from Europe during Colonial Period.

Description: A fine-textured, cool-season, sod-forming perennial. Tufted appearance spreading by short rhizomes and sometimes stolons to form close turf. *Leaves*–rolled in bud shoot. *Ligule*–membranous, truncate, entire or finely toothed, short (0.3 to 1.2 mm long), sparsely, and minutely hairy on back. *Auricles*–absent. *Collar*–distinct, narrow, oblique. *Sheath*–round, smooth, split. *Blade*–sharp pointed, distinctly ridged on upper surface, slightly keeled on under surface, margins and upper surface scabrous. *Inflorescence*–open delicate panicle.

Adaptation and use: Adapted to cool, humid regions. Naturalized in areas of well-drained, sandy-loam soils of low fertility in northern U. S. and Canada. Grows well on heavy, fertile soils. Persists on acid soils that will not support Kentucky bluegrass. Inferior to velvet and creeping bentgrass for putting greens. Used as a lawn grass west of the Cascade Mountains in Washington and Oregon, and in New England, and as a component in general-purpose lawn mixtures in many northern states. Very competitive and may dominate other desirable grasses included in new seedings. Replacement of other species is objectionable in regions where Colonial bentgrass is subject to severe disease damage.

Varieties: Astoria. Released by the Oregon AES, Corvallis, in 1936. Traces to a collection made in northwestern Oregon. It cannot be readily distinguished on the basis of growth habit or color from common Colonial. Somewhat more robust but not under all conditions.

Common. Common Colonial seed is certified in Washington State. Most of the production traces to seed collected originally from native stands in southwestern Washington, north of Columbia River to Olympia.

Exeter. Released by the Rhode Island AES, Kingston, in 1963. Selected from collections made in Rhode Island, Connecticut, and Massachusetts. Similar to Astoria but becomes green earlier in the spring and holds color better in summer. Bright green, some leaf spot resistance, and leafier than other varieties.

Highland. Released by Oregon AES, Corvallis, in 1934. A distinctive type selected from collections made in southern Willamette Valley, Oregon. Characterized by bluish-green color; erect, robust culms; and large pyramidal panicles semiclosed after blooming. In some tests it has been rated as a slightly stronger creeper than Astoria and Common.

Holfior. Developed by D. J. van der Have, Netherlands, in 1940. Described as darker green than Astoria, with moderate rate of spread, upright growth habit, and less tendency to mat as severely as other varieties.

9. *Ammophila arenaria* (L.) Link, European beachgrass.

Origin: Introduced from Europe. Native to coastal sands of northern Europe.

Description: A tough, coarse, erect perennial with scaly, creeping rhizomes and dense, spikelike panicles. Produces heavy growth on unstable beach sand of low fertility. Young plants resist scouring, withstanding the cutting effect of wind-driven sand particles. Plants grow rapidly to a height of about 5 feet and can emerge through heavy sand deposits. The root system is deep, and the spread from rhizomes rapid. Individual plants form large clumps and spread to unvegetated areas.

Adaptation and use: Well adapted to erosion control on sandy soils. Plants produce large amounts of vegetative material and provide initial stabilization on shifting dune areas. Growth stops when sand is stabilized. Areas stabilized with beachgrass should be planted to permanent grasses or to woody species. Planting stock is collected when plants are nearly dormant—from late fall through early spring. Old plants are dug and stems cut back to about 20 inches. About five culms are planted to a depth of 8 inches (12 inches above surface) in hills spaced from 18 inches to 3 feet apart. Closer planting and nitrogen fertilizer is recommended for rapid dune stabilization. New plants develop from buds at the base of the stems.

Varieties: No varieties are available, but selections range from tall, coarse, bunch types to short, fine, creeping types.

10. *Ammophila breviligulata* Fernald, American beachgrass.

Origin: Indigenous to North America.

Description: Resembles European beachgrass except for smaller size of its ligule.

Adaptation and use: Found on shores of Great Lakes, along the Atlantic Coast from Newfoundland to North Carolina, and along Pacific Coast. Adapted for the same purposes as European beachgrass. It does not appear to be as sensitive to high temperatures following planting. Often preferred to European beachgrass because of its longer planting season and greater persistence. Permanent vegetation must be planted as for European beachgrass but not as soon.

Varieties: None available. Aggressive types have been identified and are maintained at certain Plant Material Centers, SCS, USDA.

11. *Andropogon virginicus* L., broomsedge.

Origin: Indigenous to North America.

Description: A coarse-textured, warm-season, perennial bunchgrass. *Leaves*–folded in bud shoot. *Ligule*–membranous, acute to truncate, ciliate (0.4 to 2 mm long). *Auricles*–absent. *Collar*–small, divided, mostly hairy on margins. *Sheath*–much compressed, keeled, long hirsute on margins. *Blade*–flat, hirsute near base above, smooth to rough below, margins rough-scabrous and ciliate. *Inflorescence*–narrow panicle with feathery branches.

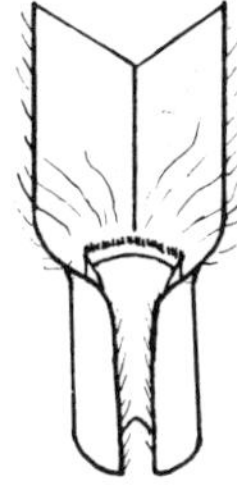

Adaptation and use: Found throughout much of the eastern U. S., from Massachusetts and New York westward to Michigan and Iowa and south to Texas and Florida. A common weedy species in old fields and open woods. It grows on sterile hills and light soils, and is often associated with low soil fertility. Not adapted for turf purposes, and of little agricultural value except to provide cover on depleted sites.

12. *Axonopus affinis* Chase, carpetgrass.

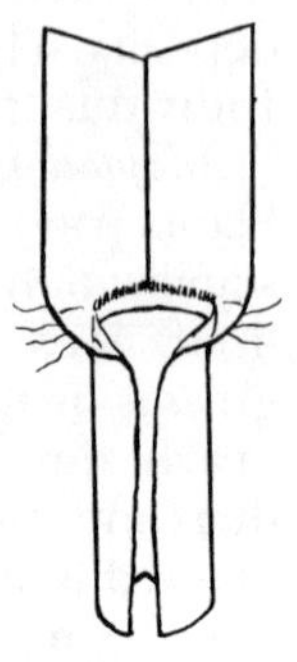

Origin: Indigenous to Central America and West Indies. Presumably introduced into U. S. early in Colonial Period.

Description: A warm-season, low-growing, sod-forming perennial that spreads both by stolons and seed. Light green color. *Leaves*–folded in bud shoot. *Ligule*–short, pubescent fringe, fused at base (about 1.0 mm long). *Auricles*–absent. *Collar*–continuous, narrow, glabrous or occasionally with few hairs. *Sheath*–glabrous and compressed. *Blade*–glabrous or ciliate at base, obtuse, margins scabrous near apex (about 4 to 8 mm wide). *Inflorescence*–three racemes on filiform stem.

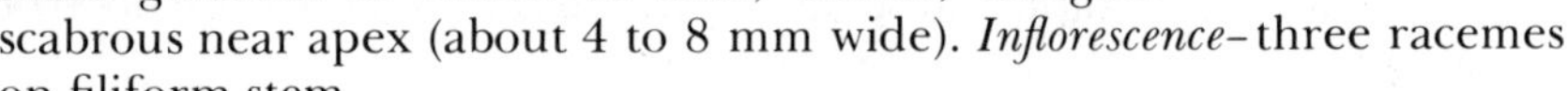

Adaptation and use: Well adapted to virgin soils of the Coastal Plain in southeastern U. S., from southern Virginia to Mexico and inland to Arkansas and north central Mississippi and Alabama. Most abundant on lowland areas from coastal North Carolina to Florida and westward to Texas. Invades infertile upland sites within its region of adaptation. Grows well on sandy or sandy loam soils where moisture is near surface most of the year. Does not thrive either in swamps or where seepage is continuous. Carpetgrass is not drought resistant and becomes chlorotic at pH of 7 or above. Regarded as a good lawn grass in lower Coastal Plain. It is established from seed and makes a dense turf that tolerates moderate shade, and requires little care other than mowing. Rate of spread and density can be improved with application of fertilizer. Carpetgrass is common in permanent pastures and is very useful in erosion control and for planting road banks and firebreaks.

Varieties: None available.

13. *Axonopus compressus* (Swartz) Beauv., tropical carpetgrass.

Origin: Indigenous to Central America and the West Indies. Presumably introduced into U. S. early in Colonial Period.

Description: A warm-season, low-growing, sod-forming perennial. Vegetative characteristics similar to *Axonopus affinis.*

Adaptation and use: Less winter-hardy than common carpetgrass. Found only in Florida and southern Louisiana. Grows best on moist sandy or loamy soils, especially those rich in organic matter, and withstands temporary flooding. Grows well in partial shade. Used in permanent pastures under subtropical and humid tropical conditions and for lawns and erosion control. Propagated vegetatively.

Varieties: None available.

14. *Bouteloua curtipendula* (Michx.) Torr., sideoats grama.

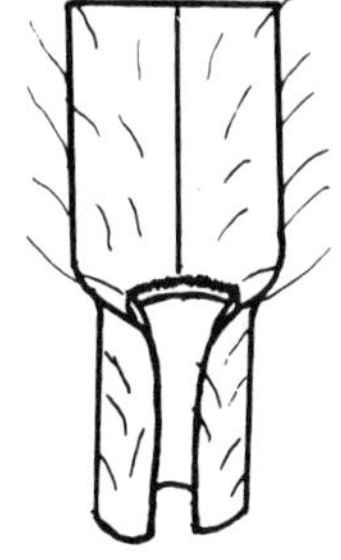

Origin: Indigenous to North America.

Description: A warm-season, slightly spreading, perennial bunchgrass. Has short, scaly rhizomes but assumes bunch form. *Leaves*– rolled in bud shoot. *Ligule*– membranous, truncate, lacerate, ciliate, sometimes appears as dense fringe of hairs (up to 1 mm long). *Auricles*– absent. *Collar*– medium broad, continuous, with few hairs at mouth. *Sheath*– round, split. *Blade*– scabrous above, smooth below, with scattered long hairs mainly on upper surface, margins scabrous to ciliate, tapering to sharp point. *Inflorescence*– spikes mostly twisted to one side of slender axis, often purplish, spreading or pendulous.

Adaptation and use: Major range grass throughout much of the Great Plains but widely distributed in North America. Generally found on favorable sites in Great Plains in association with bluestems *(Andropogon* spp.) Replaced in drier areas by blue grama. Used primarily for grazing and conservation purposes but occasionally for non-irrigated general-purpose turf in semi-arid regions.

Varieties: Several varieties have been released for forage use: namely, Butte, Coronado, El Reno, Pierre, Premier, Trailway, Tucson, Uvalde, and Vaughn.

15. *Bouteloua gracilis* (H.B.K.) Lag. ex Steud., blue grama.

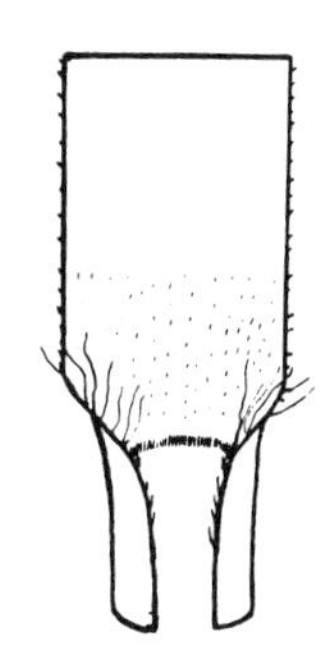

Origin: Indigenous to North America.

Description: A warm-season, densely tufted perennial. Under favorable conditions, culms in contact with soil will root at nodes to form new plants which, together with occasional very short rhizomes, lead to development of a comparatively dense sod. Fine, curling, basal leaves have grayish-green color. *Leaves*– folded in bud shoot. *Ligule*– dense fringe of hairs (up to 0.5 mm long). *Auricles*– absent. *Collar* – continuous, medium broad, with long hairs on inside of margins. *Sheath*– round, split. *Blade*– scabrous or pubescent on upper surface especially near base, glabrous below. Narrow leaves, prominently veined above and below, tapering to sharp point. *Inflorescence*– usually 2 spikes, sometimes 1 or 3 spreading at maturity, rachis not projecting beyond spikelets.

Adaptation and use: Widely distributed in North America but of primary importance as range grass in Great Plains. Tolerates more drought and alkali than sideoats grama. Used in range seeding, conservation plantings and as turfgrass on some unirrigated sites in parts of the Great Plains.

Varieties: Little use has been made of improved types selected to date.

16. *Bromus inermis* Leyss., smooth bromegrass.

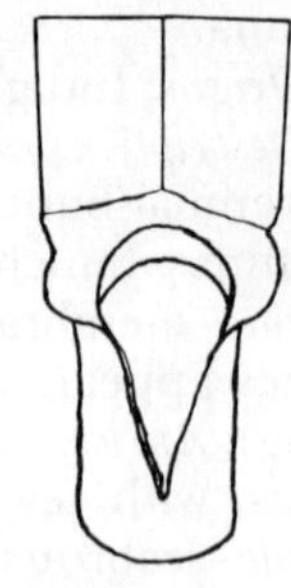

Origin: Introduced from Hungary in 1884. Indigenous to eastern Europe and the USSR.

Description: A coarse-textured, cool-season, sod-forming, rhizomatous perennial. *Leaves*– rolled in bud shoot. *Ligule*– membranous, truncate to rounded (about 1 mm long). *Auricles*– absent. *Collar*– medium broad and divided. *Sheath*– round, smooth, occasionally short, hairy on lower sheath, closed to near top. *Blade*– smooth above and below, margins smooth to rough. *Inflorescence*– open, nodding panicle.

Adaptation and use: Well adapted to cool temperate regions in the northern U. S., with major region of adaptation and use corresponding to the Corn Belt. Resistant to drought and temperature extremes, grows on variety of soil types but makes best growth on deep, fertile, well-drained silt loams and clay loams. Used primarily for hay and pasture. Valuable grass for controlling soil erosion and has been used for stabilizing roadbanks. Not recommended for turf.

Varieties: Two distinct types are recognized; namely, "Northern"—adapted to western Canada and Northern Great Plains; and "Southern"—adapted to Corn Belt States and Central Great Plains. A number of improved varieties have been developed for forage use.

17. *Buchloe dactyloides* (Nutt.) Engelm., buffalograss.

Origin: Indigenous to North America.

Description: A fine-leaved, warm-season, sod-forming perennial that spreads by stolons. Foliage is grayish-green. *Leaves*– rolled in bud shoot. *Ligule*– short fringe of hairs. *Auricles*– absent. *Collar*– narrow, indistinct, with long hairs at mouth. *Sheath*– round, split, and smooth. *Blade*– distinctly veined, with few long hairs scattered on both surfaces, generally less than 3 mm wide. *Inflorescence*– dioecious, pistillate heads 3 to 4 mm thick, staminate culms slender with 2 or 3 spikes.

Adaptation and use: Found on dry plains from western Minnesota to central Montana, south to northwestern Iowa, Texas, Arizona, and northern Mexico. Major species in Central and Southern Great Plains. Adapted to soils with high clay content and does not succeed on sandy soils. It is drought resistant, tolerant to alkali and to intensive grazing. Buffalograss is an important range grass and is used occasionally for turf on non-irrigated sites.

Varieties: No varieties developed specifically for turf.

18. *Cynodon* L. C. Rich, bermudagrasses. *Cynodon dactylon* (L.) Pers., is the most important *Cynodon* species adapted for turf and forage use. However, a number of other species have been introduced into the U. S. Although these species are identified by both botanical and com-

mon names, they are most often recognized as bermudagrasses from the standpoint of use. Improvement efforts are characterized by extensive hybridization among species, and for that reason all improved varieties are listed under *C. dactylon.* Recognized species, which have been used on occasion for either turf or forage, are as follows:

a) *Cynodon bradleyi* Stent, Bradley bermudagrass. A fine-textured grass with hairy leaf blades. Distinguished from *C. transvaalensis* and *C. magennisii* by absence of rhizomes. Spreads by creeping stolons.

b) *Cynodon magennisii* Hurcombe, Magennis bermudagrass. A hybrid between *C. dactylon* and *C. transvaalensis.* A fine-textured grass resembling *C. transvaalensis.* Does not produce viable seed.

c) *Cynodon plectostachyus* (K. Schum.) Pilg., stargrass. A coarse-textured forage grass, characterized by stoloniferous growth habit, hairy leaves, and absence of rhizomes. Used for forage in tropical and some subtropical areas. Not winter-hardy in Georgia.

d) *Cynodon transvaalensis* Burtt-Davy, African bermudagrass. A fine-textured grass with narrow, soft, hairy leaves. Uganda is a very fine-textured, low-growing, nonaggressive variety.

e) *Cynodon* sp., giant bermudagrass. A robust bermudagrass type identified in irrigated areas of the southwestern U. S. Appears to be a diploid form of *C. dactylon.* Distinguished from common bermudagrass by greater vigor and lack of pubescence. May be found as objectionable contaminant in some seed lots of common bermudagrass.

19. *Cynodon dactylon* (L.) Pers., bermudagrass (other names include couchgrass, wiregrass, and devilgrass)

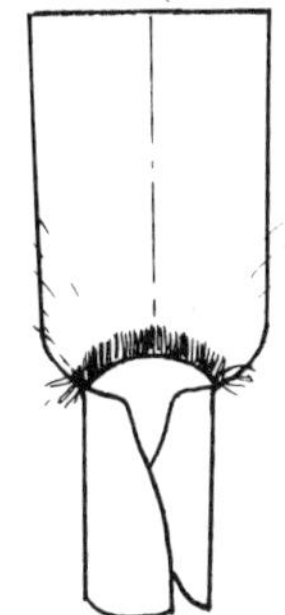

Origin: Introduced in 1751 or earlier. Primary center of origin placed in Africa.

Description: A warm-season, sod-forming perennial that spreads by stolons and rhizomes. Turns off-color in cool weather and brown after frost. In common with other Cynodon species, the leaves are borne on stems which produce long internodes alternating with one or more very short internodes. This characteristic gives the impression that the species has multiple-leaved nodes. *Leaves*– folded in bud shoot. (Arrangement of leaf blade in bud shoot has been described as rolled in some keys and folded in others. This may be attributed to variation among samples or to difficulties in establishing this characteristic. In general, blades in *Cynodon dactylon* do not overlap in bud shoot, although there is some indication of slight overlap in some specimens. They are never tightly rolled as in *Zoysia* spp.). *Ligule*– a fringe of hairs (2 to 5 mm long). *Auricles*– absent. *Collar*– continuous, narrow, glabrous, hairy on margins. *Sheaths*– compressed to round, loose, split, smooth to sparsely hairy, tuft of hairs at throat. *Blade*– soft, sharp-pointed, smooth to sparsely pubescent, margins scabrous. *Inflorescence*– four or five digitate spikes.

Adaptation and use: Adapted to tropical and subtropical parts of the world, it grows throughout the warmer regions of the U. S.—from

Maryland to Florida, west to Kansas, Oklahoma, and Texas, and at lower elevations in southwestern states. Although of lesser importance in cooler regions, the northern range has been extended through natural selection and the development of winter-hardy varieties. Now found on favored sites in southern New England and in southern portions of Ohio, Indiana, and Illinois. Grows on a wide range of soils, from heavy clays to deep sands provided fertility is not limiting. Makes satisfactory growth on both acid and calcareous soils and has high tolerance to saline conditions. May persist on relatively infertile soils but has high nitrogen requirement for good-quality turf and high forage yield. Tolerates some flooding but does not thrive on water-logged soils. Although rated as drought tolerant in humid regions, cannot be grown in arid regions without supplementary water. Not shade tolerant. Slight differences in shade tolerance exist among varieties. Common bermudagrass is used for general-purpose turf, hay, pasture, and erosion control. A number of improved varieties have been developed for turf and forage use.

Varieties: Most improved varieties are sterile or nearly so and must be propagated vegetatively. Those that do produce seed, such as U-3, do not breed true for type. Sources of bermudagrass seed are restricted at present to common and Giant. Improved forage varieties include Coastcross 1, Coastal, and Suwannee developed by the Georgia AES, Tifton, and the Crops Research Division, ARS, USDA. These two agencies cooperated with the Oklahoma AES, Stillwater, in releasing the winter-hardy variety, Midland. Greenfield, a vigorous selection from common, was released by the Oklahoma AES.

Bayshore. Released by the Florida AES, Gainesville. Considered to be a natural hybrid between *C. dactylon* and *C. transvaalensis.* Sometimes identified as Gene Tift. Light green, fine texture, some resistance to leaf spot diseases. Adapted for use on putting greens in South Florida.

Everglades. Released by the Florida AES, Gainesville, in 1962. Considered to be a natural hybrid between *C. dactylon* and *C. transvaalensis.* Dark green, fine texture, close growing, vigorous putting-green type. Much superior to common in turf quality and resistance to foliar diseases. Adapted throughout Florida.

Floraturf (No Mow). Proposed for release by the Florida AES in 1969. Tested under the name, "No Mow". Collected on the Mobile Country Club and assumed to be the product of a natural cross. Very dark-green, short-leaf, medium-coarse texture, low-growing, prostrate type. Unmowed grass 4 to 6 inches tall in full sun. Relatively shade-tolerant, susceptible to *Helminthosporium* leaf spot, very susceptible to mites, and average in susceptibility to parasitic nematodes. Suitable for home lawns, golf tees and fairways, and industrial turf plantings.

Midway. Released by the Kansas AES, Manhattan, in 1965. A sterile triploid between Uganda *(C. transvaalensis)* and winter-hardy *C. dactylon.* A medium-textured lawn grass that produces relatively few seedheads. More winter-hardy in Kansas than U-3 and rated as tolerant to mites and leaf spot in Arizona test. Adapted for lawn use in southwestern Kansas.

Ormond. Released by the Florida AES, Gainesville, in 1962. Attractive, blue-green color, vigorous, relatively prostrate growth habit, medium texture, some tolerance to leaf diseases, susceptible to dollar spot, lacks cold tolerance. Well adapted in Florida for lawns, golf tees, fairways, and recreational areas.

Pee Dee. Released by the South Carolina AES, Clemson, in 1968. A mutation selected from an early South Carolina planting of Tifgreen (Tifton 328). Dark green, disease resistant, and less upright growth habit than Tifgreen. (See also Tifdwarf).

Royal Cape. Released by the University of California, Los Angeles, and the Crops Research Division, ARS, USDA, in 1960. Selected in about 1930 on Royal Cape Golf Course near Mowbray, South Africa. Released on basis of late-fall and early-spring growth, good color, texture, vigor, and spread; tolerance to saline soils; and limited production of seedheads. Adapted for use in hot desert areas of Lower Colorado River Basin.

Santa Ana. Released by the California AES, Los Angeles, in 1966. Dark-green seedling selected from progeny of South African introduction. Characterized by medium texture, good vigor, high wear resistance, resistance to *Eryosphyid* mite, and a high level of smog tolerance. Well adapted in Southern California where it exhibits short winter dormant period. May be subject to winter killing and disease damage in colder areas. Recommended for golf tees, playgrounds, athletic fields, and other heavy-use turf.

Sunturf. Released in 1956 by the Alabama, Arkansas, Oklahoma, and South Carolina AES at Auburn, Fayetteville, Stillwater, and Clemson, respectively. Fine leaves, dark green, rapid spread, few seedheads, sometimes damaged by rust.

Texturf IF: Released by the Texas AES, College Station, in 1957. Fine texture, light green, recovers rapidly in spring, produces relatively few seedheads, susceptible to leaf diseases. Because of disease susceptibility not recommended for Gulf Coast and eastern Texas.

Texturf 10. Released by the Texas AES, College Station, in 1957. Medium texture, dark green, recovers rapidly in spring, produces relatively few seedheads. Fair resistance to leaf diseases improves autumn color. Sensitive to chlorinated hydrocarbon insecticides, turning straw colored following application of these materials. Recovers in 5 to 7 days with no permanent damage. Dense turf but slower in producing cover than common.

Tifdwarf. Released by the Georgia AES, Tifton, and Crops Research Division, ARS, USDA, in 1965. Evidence suggests that Tifdwarf is a vegetative mutant that occurred in Tifgreen (Tifton 328) at Tifton before the first planting stock was sent out for early testing. A dwarf type with small, short leaves, stems, internodes, and seedheads; tolerates 3/16″ cutting height better than Tifgreen. In other comparisons with Tifgreen, it is darker green, requires less fertilizer for comparable degree of greenness, and comparable in disease resistance. A highly regarded variety for golf greens in southeastern U. S.

Tiffine. Released by the Georgia AES, Tifton, and Crops Research Division, ARS, USDA, in 1953. An F_1 hybrid between *C.dactylon* and *C. transvaalensis.* Tested as Tifton 127. Lighter green, more disease resistant, much finer texture than common. Used for fine lawns and putting greens.

Tifgreen. Released by the Georgia AES, Tifton, and Crops Research Division, ARS, USDA, in 1956. Best of several F_1 hybrids between *C. dactylon* and diploid *C. transvaalensis* from Africa. Tested as Tifton 328. Disease resistant, dark green, and widely adapted throughout much of southeastern region for use on golf greens. Better putting surface than Tiffine and outstanding variety for fine lawns.

Tiflawn. Released by the Georgia AES, Tifton, and Crops Research Division, ARS, USDA, in 1952. Tested as Tifton 57. An F_1 hybrid selected for rate of spread, dense turf, and superior disease and frost tolerance. Requires less fertilizer and is more wear resistant than common bermudagrass. Particularly well suited as heavy-duty turf.

Tifway. Released by the Georgia AES, Tifton, and Crops Research Division, ARS, USDA, in 1960. An F_1 hybrid between *C. transvaalensis* and *C. dactylon.* Selected for dark color and stiff leaves. Rated as equal or superior to Tiffine and Tifgreen in disease resistance, density, weed resistance, seedhead production, and rate of spread. Well suited for use on fairways, tees, and home lawns.

Tufcote. Released by the Maryland AES, College Park, Plant Materials Center, SCS, Beltsville, and Crops Research Division, ARS, USDA, in 1962. Stiff leaves, comparatively rapid spread; released on basis of winter hardiness and wear resistance, for use in conservation plantings and on athletic fields.

U-3. Released by the U.S. Golf Association Green Section and Crops Research Division, ARS, USDA, in 1947. Selected for moderately fine leaves, cold hardiness, rapid spread, and wide adaptation. Adapted for use on lawns, parks, and golf course tees and fairways.

20. *Dactylis glomerata* L., orchardgrass (other name—cocksfoot).

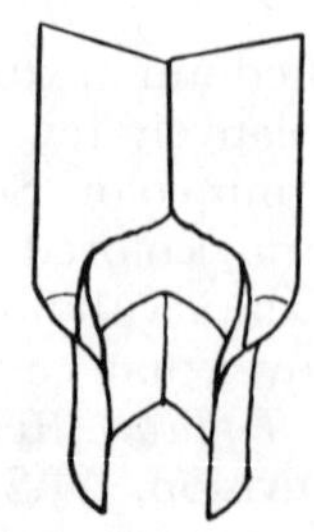

Origin: Introduced during colonial times from Europe. Indigenous to western and central Europe.

Description: A coarse-textured, cool-season, perennial bunchgrass. *Leaves*- folded in bud shoot. *Ligule* -membranous, truncate, often with awn-like point at apex (2 to 10 mm long). *Auricles*- absent. *Collar*- broad, distinct, glabrous, and divided. *Blade*- V-shaped in cross-section at base, sharply keeled below, gradually tapering to acute point, deep furrow over midrib, margins almost smooth to scabrous.

Adaptation and use: Found in eastern Canada southward to northern portions of Gulf Coast States, and from Atlantic Coast to edge of Great

Plains. Also adapted to high rainfall and irrigated areas in the Intermountain Region and Pacific Coast. Less winter-hardy than smooth brome, timothy, and Kentucky bluegrass; more drought tolerant than timothy and less than smooth brome; and not exacting in soil requirements. Orchardgrass responds well to high levels of soil fertility and is used primarily for hay and pasture purposes. It is a troublesome weed in turf.

Varieties: Several improved varieties have been released for forage use.

21. *Digitaria ischaemum* (Schreb.) Schreb. ex Muhl., smooth crabgrass.

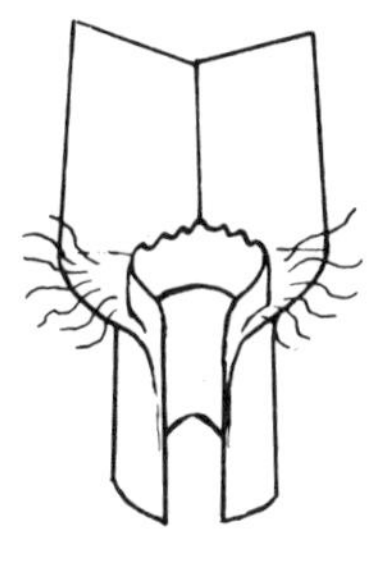

Origin: Introduced from Eurasia.

Description: A coarse-textured, warm-season annual that spreads by decumbent, branching stems, rooting at the nodes. *Leaves*–rolled in bud shoot. *Ligule*–membranous (1.5 to 3 mm long), obtuse to truncate, slightly undulate. *Auricles*–absent. *Collar*–narrow to broad, distinct, often divided, few flexuous hairs at margin. *Sheath*–compressed, glabrous, split, basal ones sometimes sparsely hairy. *Blade*–smooth above but mostly with few hairs near base, margins glabrous or sparsely ciliate, smooth or scabrous, dull green or tinged with purple (about 5 to 10 mm wide). *Inflorescence*–2 to 6 digitate racemes at or near summit of culm. Distinguished from *D. sanguinalis* (large crabgrass) by smaller size and glabrous, usually purplish sheaths.

Adaptation and use: Widely distributed from Quebec to Georgia and west to Washington and California. Troublesome weed in turf areas.

22. *Digitaria sanguinalis* (L.) Scop., large crabgrass (other names—common crabgrass, crabgrass, and fingergrass).

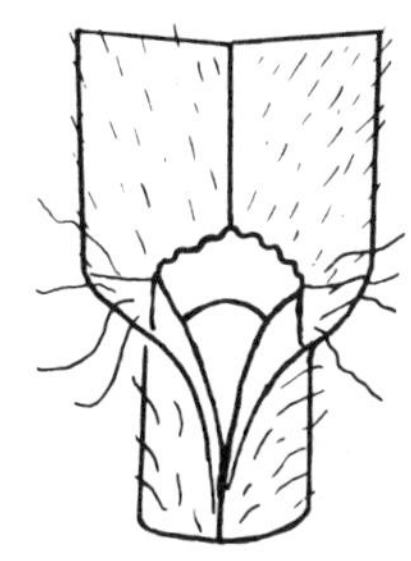

Origin: Introduced from Europe.

Description: A coarse-textured, warm-season annual that spreads by decumbent, branching stems, rooting at the nodes. *Leaves*–rolled in bud shoot. *Ligule*–membranous (0.5 to 3 mm long), rounded to acute, sometimes undulate or toothed, often reddish. *Auricles*–absent. *Collar*–broad, mostly divided by midrib, hairy at least on margins. *Sheath*–compressed, split, long hairy, green but sometimes purplish-veined. *Blade*–pilose on both surfaces with a few longer hairs at base on upper surface, keeled below, margins scabrous and occasionally hairy (about 4 to 18 mm wide). *Inflorescence*–several digitate racemes at or near summit of culm.

Adaptation and use: Found throughout the U. S. at low and medium altitudes, but more common in eastern and southern states. A serious weed in lawns and cultivated areas.

23. *Eleusine indica* (L.) Gaertn., goosegrass.

Origin: Introduced from tropical regions.

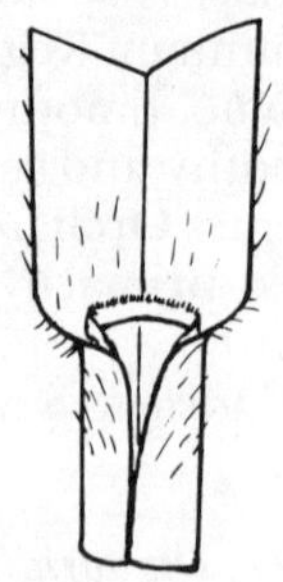

Description: A coarse-textured, warm-season, annual bunchgrass. Flat stemmed with prostrate growth habit. *Leaves*–folded in bud shoot. *Ligule*–membranous (0.6 to 1 mm long), truncate, pubescent on back, margin sometimes short ciliate. *Auricles*–absent. *Collar*–broad, crooked cilia on margins. *Sheath*–flattened, hairy at top, split overlapping margins sometimes hairy. *Blade*–sparsely long, hairy near base above, smooth and keeled below, margins smooth to rough or sometimes long hairy. *Inflorescence* –two to several spikes at or near summit.

Adaptation and Use: Widely adapted from Massachusetts to South Dakota, south to Florida and Texas. Found in Intermountain Region, Oregon and California. A common weed, especially troublesome in turf.

24. *Eragrostis curvula* (Schrad.) Nees, weeping lovegrass.

Origin: Introduced from Africa in 1927.

Description: A warm-season, perennial bunchgrass. Develops dense tufts; leaf blades narrow and may be glabrous or hairy; grows rapidly; drought resistant; includes many different "forms."

Adaptation and use: Well adapted to the Southern Great Plains and in parts of the Southwest, it can also be grown successfully in the southeastern states. In the Great Plains winter killing is common north of the Oklahoma-Kansas line. Regarded as a useful forage grass, especially in Oklahoma, and as a valuable species for soil conservation purposes. Its rapid establishment and adaptation to poor soils are important characteristics in conservation plantings. Not suitable for use as a turfgrass.

25. *Eremochloa ophiuroides* (Munro) Hack., centipedegrass.

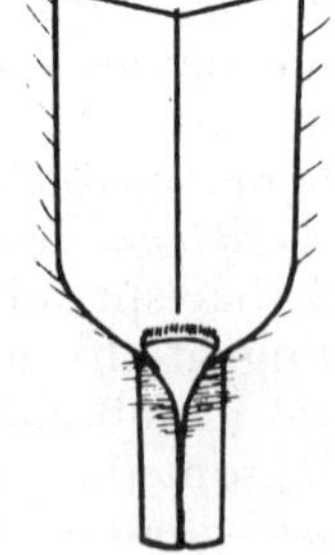

Origin: Indigenous to southeastern Asia. Introduced from seed found in baggage of Frank N. Meyer, USDA plant explorer who disappeared on his fourth trip to China in 1916.

Description: A warm-season, sod-forming perennial, creeping by thick, short-noded, leafy stolons. *Leaves*–folded in bud shoot. *Ligule*–short, membranous with cilia, cilia longer than purplish membrane (total length about 0.5 mm). *Auricles*–absent. *Collar*–broad, continuous, constricted by fused keel, pubescent, ciliate, tufted at lower edge. *Sheath*–glabrous with grayish tufts at throat, very compressed, margins overlapping. *Blade* –compressed or flattened (about 3 to 5 mm wide), short, keeled, ciliate with margins papillose toward base, otherwise smooth. *Inflorescence* –solitary spikelike racemes.

Adaptation and use: Well adapted to soils and climatic conditions in southern U. S. It has survived as far north as northern Alabama and Raleigh, N. C. Grows successfully on comparatively poor soils. It is well regarded as a low maintenance, general-purpose turf and lawn grass. Frequently sprigged in new lawns but may be seeded.

Varieties: Common type used most extensively.

Oklawn. Released by Oklahoma AES, Stillwater, in 1965. Selected for tolerance to drought and extreme temperatures, grows in shade as well as in full sun, resistant to insects and diseases, does not require high management practices.

26. *Festuca arundinacea* Schreb., tall fescue.

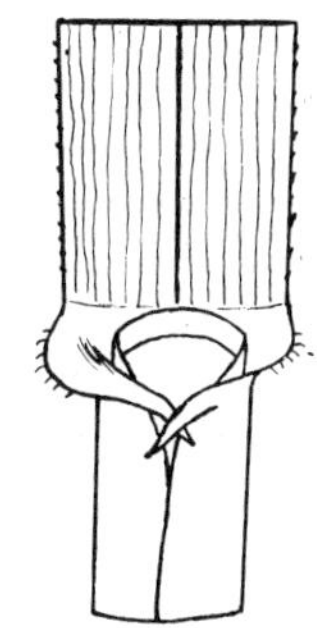

Origin: Indigenous to Europe. Thought to have been introduced to North America in mid-1800's or earlier. Recognized as having value as forage plant in late 1930's.

Description: A coarse-textured, cool-season, perennial bunchgrass. Individual plants may develop broad crowns especially in thin stands. Plants increase in size through tillering although occasional plants develop a few short, thick rhizomes. *Leaves*-rolled in bud shoot. *Ligule*-membranous, truncate (generally 0.4 mm but up to 1.2 mm long). *Auricles*-small, short, pubescent. (Note absence of hairs on auricles of annual and perennial ryegrass). *Collar*-broad, divided, somewhat hairy on margins. *Sheath*-round, generally smooth, split. *Blade*-mostly 5 to 10 mm wide, smooth to rough above, glossy below, prominent midrib, margins scabrous. *Inflorescence*-erect or nodding panicle.

Adaptation and use: Has been grown successfully throughout much of the continental U. S. Not adapted in arid regions except under irrigation. Winter survival poor at some locations in northern tier of states, with short life in Southern Coastal Plain attributed to disease. Not specific as to soil type but does best on heavy soils, tolerates wide range in pH level, wet to comparatively dry sites, and poor drainage. A major pasture and forage grass in the southern states, from North Carolina to central Georgia westward to Arkansas and Missouri, in the western portions of Washington and Oregon, and in some irrigated areas in the Intermountain Region. Useful general-purpose turfgrass for home lawns, athletic fields, institutional areas, and roadsides in certain eastern and southern states. Bunchgrass growth habit objectionable when included in complex seed mixtures or when found as a contaminant in seed of major cool-season turfgrasses. Poor quality tall fescue seed may be contaminated with seed of other hay and pasture species, such as orchard, timothy, and ryegrasses.

Varieties: Available varieties have been developed and promoted primarily for pasture purposes. The value of these varieties for turf will depend on differences in growth habit and disease resistance. Attempts have been made to improve turf quality by selecting for prostrate, rhizomatous types. Available evidence indicates that disease resistance must be stressed in attempts to improve turf quality.

Alta. Released by the Oregon AES, Corvallis, and Crops Research Division, ARS, USDA, in 1940. This variety, which was selected from a series of plant introductions on the basis of winter survival, became the major source of Oregon-grown tall fescue seed. In the eastern and southern U. S. Alta is generally rated slightly below Kentucky 31 in turf quality when evaluated for density and persistence.

Fawn. Released by the Oregon AES, Corvallis, in 1964. Developed for improved forage and seed yields from named varieties and foreign introductions. No evidence to suggest that it possesses characteristics that merit consideration in turf production.

Goar. Certified by the California Crop Improvement Association in 1946. Selected at the Imperial Valley Field Station, El Centro, Calif., for better growth during periods of high summer temperature.

Kenmont. Released by the Montana AES, Bozeman, in 1963. A direct increase of a naturalized variety collected in Kentucky and identified as Kentucky 59 G1-32. Reported to form a denser sod than Kentucky 31 in Montana. Although not widely evaluated for turf, it may warrant testing where winter survival is a potential threat.

Kentucky 31. Released by the Kentucky AES, Lexington, in 1940. Represents an ecotype collected from William Suiter's farm in Menifee County, Ky., in 1931. Accepted as somewhat superior for turf purposes to other named varieties. Superiority generally credited to higher percentage of prostrate plants and to better persistence.

Kenwell. Released by the Kentucky AES, Lexington, and Crops Research Division, ARS, USDA, in 1965. Developed from naturalized strains for forage use. It possesses resistance to several foliar diseases and looks promising in preliminary turfgrass trials. Further testing for turf purposes would be justified.

Traveler. Selected by Fred V. Grau, College Park, Md., as a turfgrass type. In comparative tests its performance has been somewhat comparable to Kentucky 31.

27. *Festuca elatior* L., meadow fescue.

Origin: Introduced from Europe during Colonial Period.

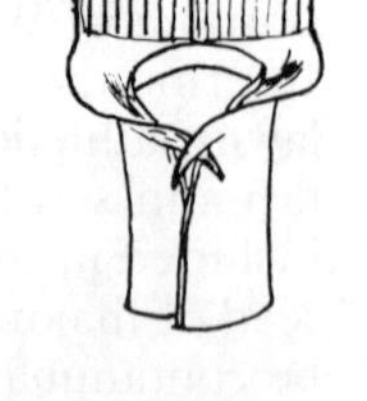

Description: A cool-season, short-lived, perennial bunchgrass. *Leaves*-rolled in bud shoot. *Ligule*-membranous short (0.2 to 0.5 mm long), truncate to obtuse. *Auricles*-clawlike or blunt. *Collar*-broad, distinct, glabrous. *Sheath*-not compressed, not keeled, glabrous, reddish to purple at base, split. *Blade*-bright green (about 3 to 8 mm wide), upper surface dull, scabrous, prominently ridged, lower surface glossy smooth, margins scabrous. (Note: annual ryegrass—smooth leaf margins; perennial ryegrass—folded in bud shoot.) *Inflorescence*-erect or nodding panicle.

Adaptation and use: Well adapted throughout humid parts of the northern U. S. Grows well on heavy, moist, fertile soils, and withstands poor drainage. It is susceptible to rust and less persistent than tall fescue. Used to some extent for pasture and erosion control. Seldom planted for turf except as a component in poor quality lawn seed mixtures.

Varieties: Several named varieties are available but have little value as turfgrasses.

28. *Festuca ovina* L., sheep fescue.

Origin: Indigenous in Northern Hemisphere.

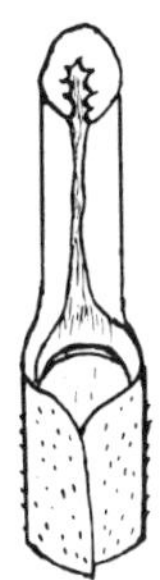

Description: A fine-textured, cool-season, perennial bunchgrass. *Leaves*- folded in bud shoot. *Ligule*- membranous (about 0.3 mm long), rounded. *Auricles*- absent. *Collar*- medium broad, divided, indistinct. *Sheath*- flattened, smooth or short hairy, split *Blade*- bristle-like (about 1 to 2 mm wide), smooth to rough above, deeply ridged on upper (inner) surface, pale bluish-green, glaucous. *Inflorescence* - narrow panicle.

Adaptation and use: Adapted to northern half of continental U. S., where it makes satisfactory growth on dry, sandy, gravelly, or rocky soils. Used to limited extent as durable turfgrass on sandy soils, and for erosion control.

Varieties: None in commercial production.

29. *Festuca ovina* var. *duriuscula* (L.) Koch, hard fescue.

Origin: Introduced from Europe.

Description: A fine-textured, cool-season, perennial bunchgrass. Similar to sheep fescue except that leaf blades are wider and tougher.

Adaptation and use: Similar to sheep fescue but rated as less drought tolerant. Useful in erosion control and soil improvement in parts of Pacific Northwest. Seldom used for turf.

Varieties: Durar. Released by Washington, Idaho, and Oregon AES's and Plant Materials Center, SCS, USDA, Pullman, in 1949. Plants selected from old planting and evaluated for conservation use. Resembles large form of sheep fescue.

30. *Festuca rubra* L., red fescue (other name—creeping red fescue).

Origin: Introduced from Europe during Colonial Period.

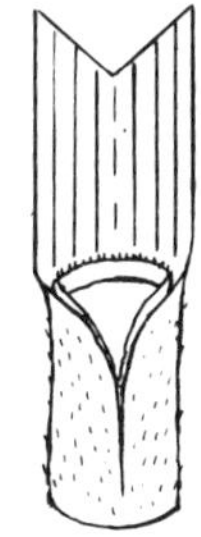

Description: A fine-textured, cool-season, sod-forming perennial. Most plants possess short rhizomes, but includes plants with strong rhizome development to those with tufted growth habit. *Leaves*- folded in bud shoot. *Ligule*- membranous (about 0.5 mm long), truncate. *Auricles*- absent. *Collar*- indistinct, narrow, continuous, glabrous. *Sheath*- not compressed, not keeled, split part way, sometimes finely pubescent. *Blade*- thick, V-shaped to closely folded (often about 1.5 to 3 mm wide), deeply ridged on upper surface, smooth below, margins smooth. *Inflorescence*- narrow, contracted panicle.

Adaptation and use: Well adapted to cool, humid regions of the U. S. Requires moderate to good drainage but grows on poor, droughty sites and on highly acid soils. A major turfgrass species for open sun and moderate shade. Forms dense wear-resistant turf when seeded heavily. Subject to severe disease damage in southern portion of its range.

Varieties: Large quantities of common red fescue seed are used in lawn grass mixtures. Seed imported from Canada and Europe is comparable in most respects to common but inferior to improved varieties that are adapted in specific areas.

Arctared. Released by the Alaska AES, and Crops Research Division, ARS, USDA, in 1965. Developed from single plant collection on basis of winter survival. Has good color and would be of interest where winter injury is a serious problem. Not widely tested in major red fescue region.

Golfrood. Developed by D. J. van der Have, Kapelle-Biezelinge, Netherlands, from plants collected in saline coastal areas. Selected for rust resistance, narrow leaves, color, and turf quality. Limited testing in the U. S.

Illahee. Released by the Oregon AES, Corvallis, and Crops Research Division, ARS, USDA, in 1950. Selected on the basis of turf quality from imported seed lot. It possesses a fair level of disease tolerance, and is recommended and grown in many parts of the eastern U. S.

Jamestown. Released by Rhode Island AES, Kingston, in 1967. Selected from local collection on basis of uniformity, color, tolerance to mowing and disease resistance. Has looked promising in comparative tests.

Pennlawn. Released by the Pennsylvania AES, University Park, in 1954. Selected from local collections for density, disease tolerance, spread, and tolerance to close mowing. Good performance and fair level of disease tolerance in many comparative tests.

Rainier. Released by the Oregon AES, Corvallis, and Crops Research Division, ARS, USDA, in 1944. Selected from introduced seed lot for uniform dark green color, good turf development, and seed yield. Generally rated as inferior to Illahee and Pennlawn in disease resistance.

Ruby. Developed by D. J. van der Have, Kapelle-Biezelinge, Netherlands. Selected for rust resistance, creeping habit, summer color, and turf quality. Growth habit and appearance under mowing similar to Rainier but with better overall performance at Minneapolis, Minn.

Wintergreen. Released by the Michigan AES, East Lansing, in 1968. Selected from introductions for turf quality. In Michigan tests rated superior to Pennlawn in color, density, uniformity, and management requirements. Comparable to Pennlawn in disease resistance, but possesses superior quality with minimum water and nitrogen. Range of adaptation not established.

31. *Festuca rubra* var. *commutata* Gaud., Chewings fescue.

Origin: Probably introduced from Europe during Colonial Period. First cultivated extensively in New Zealand.

Description: A fine-textured, cool-season, perennial bunchgrass similar to red fescue in appearance, except for more erect growth habit and absence of rhizomes.

Adaptation and use: Similar to red fescue but preferred by some for use in shade.

Varieties: Cascade. Released by the Oregon AES, Corvallis, in 1966. An authentic source of stock seed developed by bulking 12 seed lots of Oregon-grown Chewings fescue from as many commercial fields. No selection practiced within seed collections. In turf plots stock seed source appeared identical to commercially grown Chewings fescue.

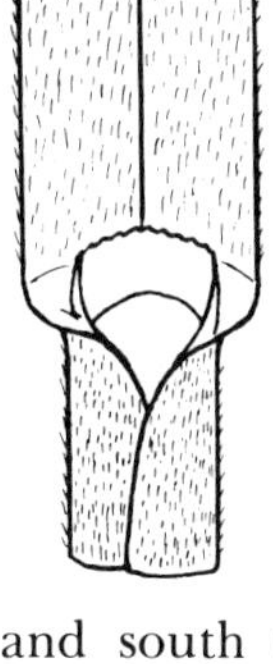

32. *Holcus lanatus* L., velvetgrass.

Origin: Introduced from Europe during Colonial Period.

Description: A coarse-textured, cool-season, perennial bunchgrass. *Leaves* -rolled in bud shoot. *Ligule*-membranous, rounded (up to 3 mm long). *Auricles*-absent. *Collar*-divided, hairy. *Sheath*-flattened, dense, velvety, short, hairy, split. *Blade*-dense, velvety, short, hairy above and below, margins short, hairy. *Inflorescence*-long contracted panicle.

Adaptation and use: Found in open ground and meadows and on moist sites from Maine to Colorado and south to Georgia and Louisiana. Common along Pacific Coast. Classed as weedy grass but where abundant may be utilized to limited extent for grazing and hay. Not suited for turf. An objectionable weed in some turfgrass seed lots.

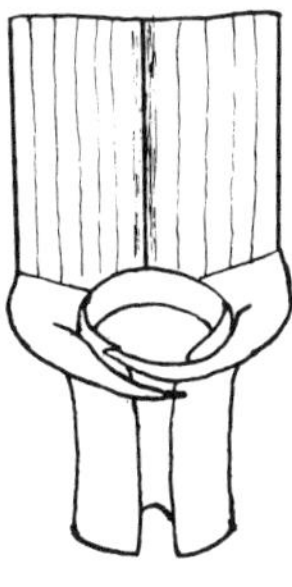

33. *Lolium multiflorum* Lam., annual ryegrass (other names—Italian and common ryegrass).

Origin: Introduced from Europe during Colonial Period.

Description: A cool-season, annual or short-lived perennial bunchgrass. Coarse-textured in thin stands but fine-textured at heavy seeding rates. *Leaves*-rolled in bud shoot. *Ligule*-membranous (0.5 to 2.0 mm long), obtuse. *Auricles*-pointed, sometimes blunt or clawlike. *Collar*-broad, distinct, continuous, glabrous, pale to yellowish-green. *Sheath*-not compressed, not keeled, glabrous, split, green, pinkish at base. *Blade* -soft, bright green, upper surface dull, prominently, ridged, lower surface smooth, glossy and slightly keeled, margins smooth. *Inflorescence* -long, narrow, flat spikes with awned spikelets.

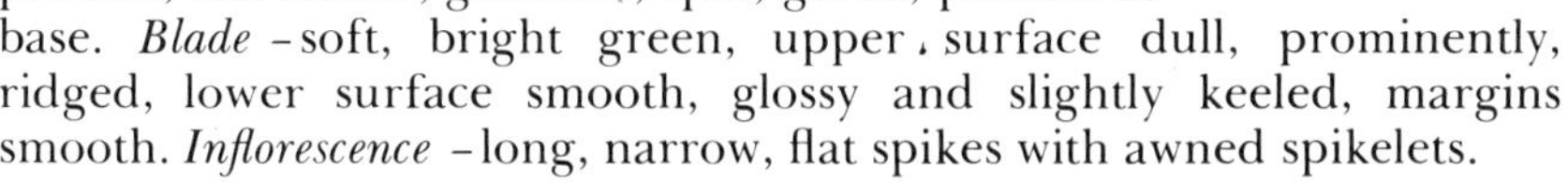

Adaptation and use: Adapted to cool, moist conditions and fertile soils. It dies during the summer in the southern states and does not persist where winter conditions are severe, especially in the northern tier of states. Widely used for pasture and forage purposes, for temporary lawns, as a component in inexpensive turfgrass seed mixtures, and for overseeding warm-season turfgrasses in the southern states.

Varieties: Common seed sources are used extensively in lawn seed mixtures, in overseeding warm-season perennial turfgrasses and for temporary cover. These seed lots are predominantly annual ryegrass, but may include varying amounts of genetic mixture with perennial ryegrass.

Astor. Released by the Oregon AES, Corvallis, in 1964. Selected for persistence and forage yield from Danish seed source. Considered well adapted to coastal areas of Oregon and southwestern Washington. Little information on merits for turf.

Gulf. Released by the Texas AES, College Station, and Crops Research Division, ARS, USDA, in 1958. An increase of the rust-resistant variety La Estanzuela 284. Valuable pasture variety but little used for turf purposes.

Magnolia. Released by the Mississippi AES, State College, and Crops Research Division, ARS, USDA, in 1965. Selection practiced for improved rust resistance within a series of plant introductions. Little information as to value for turf purposes.

Wimmera 62. Released by the California AES, Davis, and Plant Materials Center, SCS, USDA, Pleasanton, in 1962. Obtained through natural selection from Australian source. Awnless; thought to represent a hybrid between *Lolium rigidum* and *L. multiflorum.* Recommended for brush-burn seedings in certain dry areas. Little information on usefulness in turf plantings.

34. *Lolium perenne* L., perennial ryegrass.

Origin: Introduced from Europe during Colonial Period.

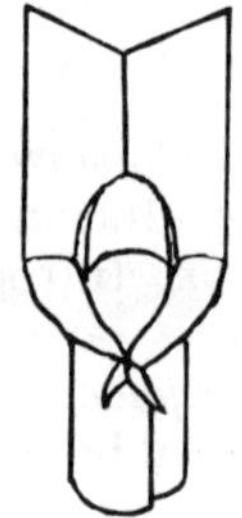

Description: A cool-season bunchgrass that behaves as an annual, short-lived perennial or perennial depending on environmental conditions. *Leaves*- folded in bud shoot. *Ligule*- membranous (0.5 to 2.0 mm long), truncate to obtuse, may be toothed near apex. *Auricles*- small, soft, clawlike. *Sheath*- usually compressed but sometimes almost cylindrical, glabrous, pale green, reddish at base, closed or split. *Blade*- bright green, keeled, prominently ridged on upper surface, smooth and glossy on lower surface, margins slight scabrous. *Inflorescence*- long narrow, flat spikes with unawned spikelets placed edge to rachis.

Adaptation and use: Adapted to moist, cool environments that have either mild winters or a uniform snow cover during winter months. Not specific as to soil type but grows well on heavy soils. Requires medium to high soil fertility for satisfactory growth. A good-quality pasture and forage grass. Appreciable quantities of seed used to provide temporary turf. It is often included as a component in inexpensive lawn seed mixtures. Seldom recommended for turf seedings because of competition with the establishment of other species, and the coarse appearance of surviving plants.

Varieties: Seed certified as to species, but not variety, has been available for many years.

Linn. Released by the Oregon AES, Corvallis, in 1961. Represents a direct increase of an authentic source of perennial ryegrass seed as determined by field inspections and comparative tests. No selection practiced.

Manhattan. Released by New Jersey AES, New Brunswick, in 1967. Leafy, fine-textured variety selected for persistence and turf quality.

NK100. Developed by Northrup, King & Company, Minneapolis, Minn., and released in 1962. Selected for persistence, leafy growth habit, and seed production. Reported to produce good turf in areas where perennial ryegrass is adapted.

Norlea. Released by the Canada Department of Agriculture, Ottawa, Ontario, in 1958. Selection practiced for winter survival within a world-wide collection of seed lots. It exhibits good winter hardiness and persistence but is damaged by rust in some areas.

Pelo. Developed by D. J. van der Have, Netherlands, and released in the U. S. by Northrup, King & Company in 1964. Improved with respect to winter hardiness and rust tolerance. Reported to develop good turf in area of adaptation.

35. *Paspalum dilatatum* Poir., dallisgrass.

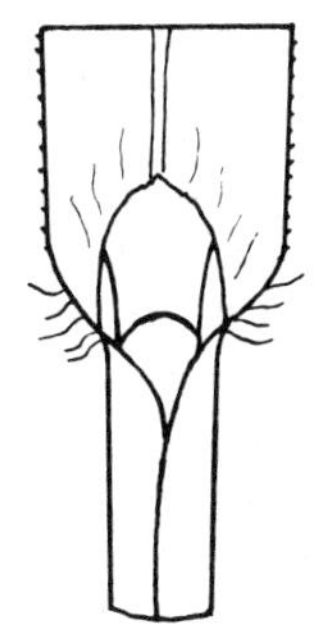

Origin: Introduced from South America, possibly from Uruguay or Argentina, during middle of 19th century.

Description: A coarse-textured, warm-season, slightly spreading, perennial bunchgrass. *Leaves*-rolled in bud shoot. *Ligule*-membranous, acute to obtuse (2 to 5 mm long). *Auricles*-absent. *Collar*-glabrous, narrow to broad, continuous, often hairy on margins. *Sheath*-compressed,slightly keeled, split, often pilose near base of plant, otherwise glabrous. *Blade*-flat, keeled, tapering to rounded narrow base, glabrous or with few hairs near base, margins smooth to scabrous. *Inflorescence*-3 to 5 one-sided racemes (spikelike branches) with flat, round to oval seed.

Adaptation and use: Found from New Jersey to Florida westward to Tennessee and eastern Texas. Adapted throughout the Cotton Belt where annual rainfall is 30 inches or more. Makes best growth on moist, fertile, bottom land but grows well on heavy soils in the Piedmont and where high fertility levels are maintained in lowland areas of the Coastal Plain. Better adapted than bermudagrass on wet sites. More tolerant to extremes of drought and moisture when grown on heavy clay soils. A palatable, nutritious pasture grass that performs well in association with lespedeza and white clover. It is an objectionable weed in turfgrass areas.

Varieties: Selected forage types include a prostrate form developed by the Georgia AES, Tifton, and Crops Research Division, ARS, USDA. Available material not promising for turf.

36. *Paspalum laeve* Michx., field paspalum.

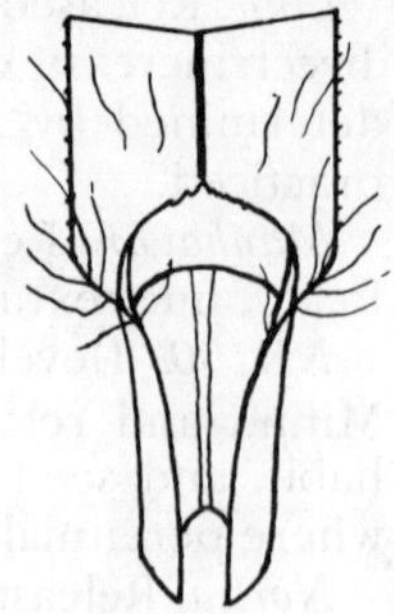

Origin: Uncertain.

Description: A coarse-textured, warm-season, perennial bunchgrass. *Leaves*-rolled in bud shoot. *Ligule*-membranous (1 to 2.5 mm long), generally acute to truncate. *Auricles*-absent. *Collar*-continuous, narrow, glabrous; margins may be hairy. *Sheath*-compressed, split, glabrous, may be hairy at top. *Blade* -smooth above, mostly long, hairy near base, smooth and keeled below, margins scabrous. *Inflorescence* -2 to 5 spreading or ascending racemes.

Adaptation and use: Found from New Jersey to Ohio south and west to Florida, Arkansas, and eastern Texas. Some value as forage but objectionable weed in lawns and other turf areas.

37. *Paspalum notatum* Flugge, bahiagrass.

Origin: Introduced from Brazil in 1913. Thought to have been introduced earlier in ship ballast by presence near several southern seaports.

Description: A coarse-textured, warm-season perennial that spreads slowly by short, stout rhizomes. Includes at least six major types that differ appreciably in their morphological characteristics. Generalized vegetative characteristics are as follows: *Leaves* -rolled in bud shoot. *Ligule* -membranous, with dense row of whitish hairs at back (about 1 mm long). *Auricles* -absent. *Sheath* -compressed, keeled, rather glossy, glabrous or ciliate toward summit or rarely pubescent throughout. *Blade* -flat or folded at base, usually sparsely ciliate toward base, sometimes almost to summit, otherwise glabrous. *Inflorescence* -2, rarely 3, one-sided racemes (spikelike branches).

Adaptation and use: Some varieties adapted to sandy soils of coastal areas from central North Carolina to eastern Texas. Well adapted on sandy soils that are comparatively infertile. Extensive root system provides some measure of drought tolerance, but it grows best in areas with high or well distributed rainfall. Bahiagrass is very aggressive. Competitive ability attributed to decumbent growth habit, good seed production, fair shade tolerance, and development of tough, coarse sod. Used primarily for pasture and soil conservation purposes in the southeastern U. S. A serious weed in fine turf. The Paraguay variety is used occasionally for general-purpose turf.

Varieties: Argentine. Released by the Florida AES, Gainesville, and Crops Research Division, ARS, USDA, in 1949. Leaves wider than those of Pensacola but narrower than common. Medium cold tolerance.

Common. Small with broad leaves, lacking in cold tolerance.

Paraguay. Origin obscure. Coarse, tough, with shorter and hairier leaves than Pensacola. Used sparingly for general-purpose turf.

Paraguay 22. Introduced from Paraguay in 1947. Released informally for pasture purposes. Not adapted for turf.

Pensacola. Approved as superior forage variety by the Florida AES, Gainesville, in 1944. Differs from common in possessing higher tolerance to low temperatures, narrower leaves, smaller seed, and in exhibiting a greater response to soil nutrients.

Tifhi-2. Released by the Georgia AES, Tifton, and Crops Research Division, ARS, USDA, in 1961. A hybrid variety developed for improved forage yield.

Wilmington. Seed distributed by the Soil Conservation Service, USDA, in 1943. A narrow-leaf variety with good cold tolerance.

38. *Pennisetum clandestinum* Hochst. ex Chiov., kikuyugrass.

Origin: Introduced from Africa in middle 1920's.

Description: A relatively coarse-textured, warm-season, sod-forming perennial that possesses stout rhizomes and stolons. Stems are horizontal to weakly upright and produce numerous leaves. Leaves are folded in the bud shoot, covered with soft, short hairs, and somewhat flattened near tips. Sheaths are hairier than the leaves and the ligule is a fringe of hairs. Flowering stems are topped with 2 to 4 flowers which bloom on short side shoots. Fertile and male-sterile strains are recognized. Anthers and stigmas are exserted on the fertile strains but only stigmas on the male-sterile. Planted vegetatively using sprigs or chopped stems.

Adaptation and use: Adapted to higher elevations (6,000 to 10,000 feet) in moist tropics. Not well suited to warm, damp conditions that prevail at low elevations. Introduced to southern California, Arizona, Texas, and Florida, Damaged by leaf spot in Florida. Where adapted it is useful for pasture, erosion control and general-purpose turf. Introduced for erosion control in southern California, it has invaded turf areas and cropland. Not recommended as turfgrass in continental U. S.

39. *Phalaris arundinacea* L., reed canarygrass.

Origin: Indigenous to North America, also Europe and Asia.

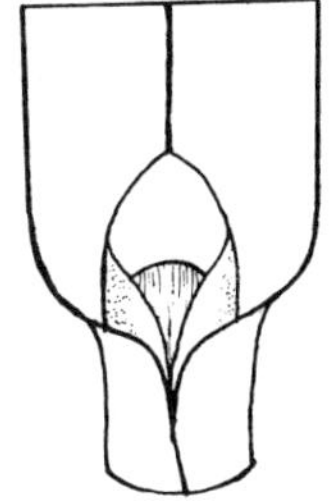

Description: A coarse-textured, cool-season, sod-forming perennial with long, scaly rhizomes. In thin stands, often grows in clumps from a few to several feet in diameter. *Leaves*- rolled in bud shoot. *Ligule*- membranous, white, papery, acute to obtuse, minutely hairy on back (2 to 5 mm long). *Auricles*- absent. *Collar*- distinct, glabrous, continuous, oblique. *Sheath*- not compressed, split, glabrous, smooth. *Blade*- flat, sharp-pointed, glabrous or rarely very sparsely hairy at base, indistinctly ridged on upper surface; midrib prominent below; margins scabrous, slightly ciliate at base. *Inflorescence*- densely flowered, narrow to spreading panicle.

Adaptation and use: Widely distributed throughout the northern half of the U. S. Abundant in Michigan, Wisconsin, Minnesota, and Iowa, and along the Pacific Coast from Washington to northern California. Well adapted to poorly drained soils subject to flooding but can be grown on drier upland soils. Does not grow well in salt marshes or on alkali soils. Used primarily for soil conservation purposes and in some areas for pasture and forage. Useful for gully control, grassed waterways, along streambanks, and around farm ponds. Not suitable as a turfgrass.

Varieties: Improved varieties have been developed for forage and conservation purposes.

40. *Phleum pratense* L., timothy.

Origin: Introduced from Europe during Colonial Period.

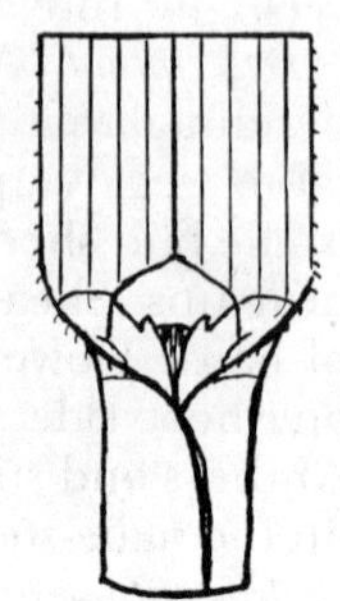

Description: A coarse-textured, cool-season, perennial bunchgrass. Lower internodes on stems enlarge to form haplocorm. *Leaves*– rolled in bud shoot. *Ligule*– membranous, obtuse to acute, distinct notch on either side (1.0 to 4.5 mm long). *Auricles*– absent. *Collar*– broad, distinct, continuous, margins sparsely ciliate. *Blade*– flat, sharp-pointed, glabrous, ridges on upper surface low and rounded, margins scabrous. *Inflorescence*– densely flowered, cylindrical, spikelike.

Adaptation and use: Adapted throughout cool, humid regions of the Northern United States. Prefers clay, loams, or heavy soils, long-lived in cool, humid regions, winter-hardy, fairly shade tolerant, but not resistant to close, continuous grazing. Poor recovery with limited moisture; does not tolerate drought, high temperatures, or alkaline soils. An important hay grass that is also used in pasture mixtures, for silage, and for conservation purposes. It is not adapted for turf use. An objectionable weed in lawns and other turf areas.

Varieties: Several improved forage varieties have been developed.

41. *Poa annua* L., annual bluegrass.

Origin: Introduced from Europe during Colonial Period.

Description: A cool-season, annual bunchgrass, with low-growing tufted growth habit. *Leaves* – folded in bud shoot. *Ligule* – membranous (0.8 to 3 mm long), acute, entire. *Auricles* – absent. *Collar* – distinct, glabrous, V-shaped. *Sheath* – compressed, slightly keeled, glabrous, split part way only. *Blade* – flat or V-shaped, smooth above and below, light green, not glossy, margins glabrous but slightly scabrous toward tip, tip boat-shaped, two distinct light lines may be seen along midrib by transmitted light. *Inflorescence* – small, open, few-branched panicle.

Adaptation and use: Found throughout the U. S. Grows during the winter in warm regions. A very troublesome weed in turf areas.

42. *Poa compressa* L., Canada bluegrass.

Origin: Introduced from Europe during Colonial Period.

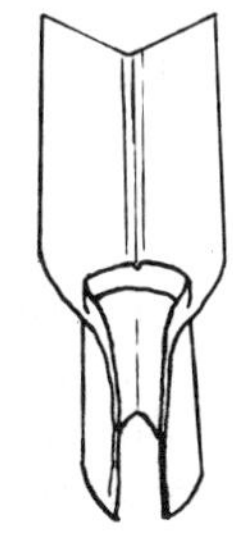

Description: A fine-textured, cool-season, sod-forming perennial that spreads by rhizomes. Plants have characteristic bluish-green color. *Leaves*– folded in bud shoot. *Ligule*– membranous (0.2 to 1.2 mm long), truncate. *Auricles*– absent. Collar – narrow, glabrous, divided by midrib. *Sheath*– strongly compressed, sharply keeled, glabrous, split. *Blade*– flat or slightly V-shaped, keeled below, tapering throughout length to boat-shaped tip, glabrous, bluish-green, somewhat glaucous; margins slightly scabrous; two distinct light lines may be seen along midrib by transmitted light. *Inflorescence*– a narrow, short-branched panicle. In contrast to *Poa pratensis* leaves are pale bluish or glaucous green, rather than deep green, and never shiny and always glabrous. *Ligule* is more conspicuous.

Adaptation and use: Widely distributed from Newfoundland to Alaska, south to Georgia, Oklahoma, New Mexico, and California. Most common in northern states. Found in association with Kentucky bluegrass but only dominant on soils that are too acid, droughty, or deficient in phosphate, nitrogen, or other nutrients for good growth of Kentucky bluegrass. Used primarily for pasture and soil conservation purposes on less productive soils. May be useful in turfgrass plantings on soils that are too dry for Kentucky bluegrass, but value limited by disease susceptibility in warmer regions and by poor recovery after mowing.

Varieties: None available.

43. *Poa glaucantha* Gaudin, upland bluegrass.

Origin: Thought to be indigenous to North America and Europe.

Description: A cool-season, perennial bunchgrass. Plants mostly glaucous with culms compressed in tufts. Resembles both *Poa nemoralis* and *Poa interior* and to some extent Canada bluegrass *(Poa compressa)*.

Adaptation and use: Found in the northern U. S., especially in Minnesota, Montana, and Wyoming. Limited use in Pacific Northwest for erosion control and general-purpose turf.

Varieties: Draylar. Released by Washington AES and Plant Materials Center, SCS, USDA, Pullman, in 1951. Received as plant introduction from Turkey. Adapted for use as ground cover on low-fertility soils.

44. *Poa pratensis* L., Kentucky bluegrass.

Origin: Introduced from Europe during Colonial Period.

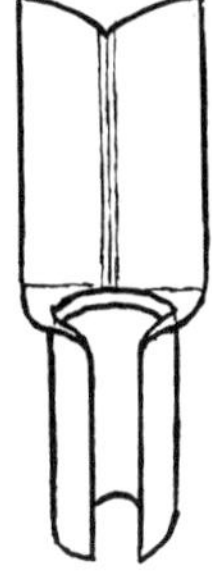

Description: A fine-textured, cool-season, rhizomatous perennial that produces a dense sod under favorable conditions. *Leaves* – folded in bud shoot. *Ligule*– membranous, very short (0.2 to 0.6 mm long), truncate. *Auricles*– absent. *Collar*– medium broad, slightly divided by midrib, may have fine hairs on margins. *Sheath*– compressed but not sharply keeled, glabrous, closed when young but later split. *Blade*–usually V-shaped, keeled below, parallel-sided, and abruptly narrowed to boat-shaped tip, sometimes minutely pubescent, margins smooth to slightly scabrous; two distinct light lines may be seen along midrib by transmitted light. *Inflorescence*–open, pyramidal panicle.

Adaptation and use: Widely distributed throughout the U. S. at all altitudes below alpine regions except in arid regions. Found in all states; it is a major grass in the northeastern and midwestern regions but comparatively uncommon in the Gulf States. Kentucky bluegrass grows on heavy soils of moderate fertility but is best adapted to productive soils of limestone origin. Often the dominant species in pastures and turf areas where soils have a pH of 5 or higher and comparatively high levels of available phosphorus. Never abundant on infertile soils. Not drought resistant but can survive long, dry periods in dormant state. Within major region of adaptation annual precipitation varies from 20 to 50 inches, and temperatures range from -30 F to about 105 F. A valuable grass for lawns, pastures, and soil conservation purposes; it ranks as the major turfgrass in the northern U. S.

Varieties: Common Kentucky bluegrass seed, stripped from fields in Kentucky and in the region stretching from western Missouri and eastern Kansas northward to Canada, is used very extensively for turf purposes. Substantial quantities of Kentucky bluegrass seed is imported from northern Europe (especially The Netherlands and Denmark), and on some occasions seed of named varieties may be marketed without any designation as to variety. Imported seed lots may be seriously contaminated with *Poa annua* and *P. trivialis,* and in some tests persistence has been inferior to domestic seed lots. Likewise, an unadapted named variety is less satisfactory than domestic sources of common Kentucky bluegrass. Efforts to preserve reliable sources of domestic Kentucky bluegrass seed are apparent in the development of certified Kenblue and certified South Dakota common. The named varieties described below vary in performance and availability. Where information is available, the major region of adaptation is identified.

Arboretum. Selected at the Missouri Botanical Garden, St. Louis, from collections made in old pastures and lawns. Generally rated as comparable to good common seed lots.

Campus. Developed by Gebr. van Engelen, Netherlands. Moderately susceptible to leaf spot and rust and not rated as tolerant to extreme temperatures. Fair turf-forming properties and exhibits characteristic shade of dark green.

Cougar. Released by the Washington AES and Plant Materials Center, SCS, USDA, Pullman, in 1964. Selected for low growth habit and adaptation to irrigated areas in Pacific Northwest. Rated as moderately susceptible to susceptible for leaf spot, stripe smut, and mildew in midwestern and eastern U. S.

Delft. Developed by Cebesco, Netherlands. Tests in some areas indicate intermediate levels for color, vigor, and disease tolerance. Although moderately susceptible to leaf spot and rust, it appears to possess stripe smut tolerance.

Delta. Released by the Canada Department of Agriculture, Ottawa, in 1938. Selected for vigor and mildew resistance. Well adapted to northern, cooler sections of the country where disease problems are less severe.

Fylking. (U. S. Patent pending) Developed at the Swedish Plant Breeding Station, Svalof. A low-growing variety adapted to close mowing, it is described as having moderate to good resistance to leaf spot, rust, *Fusarium roseum,* and stripe smut. Recommended for use in some areas on basis of available data.

Kenblue. Developed by the Kentucky AES, Lexington, and Crops Research Division, ARS, USDA, in 1966. Represents seed collected from fields in central Kentucky, and selected on basis of age of stand and performance in comparison with imported seed lots, named varieties, and other sources. Represents certified source of domestic seed.

Merion. Released by the U.S. Golf Association Green Section and Crops Research Division, ARS, USDA, in 1947. Tested as B-27. Selected for low growth habit, good color, and high level of resistance to *Helminthosporium* leaf spot. Subject to damage from stem rust, stripe smut, and *Fusarium roseum,* especially in warmer areas. Maintains important place in cooler sections where diseases are less important.

Newport. Developed by the Carnegie Institution of Washington, Stanford University, and released by the Plant Materials Center, SCS, USDA, Pullman, in cooperation with the Washington and Oregon AES at Pullman and Corvallis, respectively. Selected on the basis of vigor and color. An excellent seed producer, it generally looks promising in new seedings. In much of the midwestern and eastern U. S. quality declines rather rapidly in older plantings. Loss of stands generally attributed to damage from one or several diseases and/or damage from low temperatures. Generally rated as inferior to good sources of common. Newport, Newport C-1, C-1, and Altra C-1 are synonymous.

*Nu Dwarf**. Developed by R. H. Rasmussen, Hooper, Nebraska. Selected for dwarf character and aggressive growth in area of adaptation. Not typical dwarf type. Poor performance in eastern U. S. attributable to disease susceptibility.

Nugget. Released by the Alaska AES and Crops Research Division, ARS, USDA, in 1965. A dark green variety selected for winter hardiness and disease tolerance. Very promising in areas where Kentucky bluegrass is subject to severe winter damage.

Park. Released by the Minnesota AES, St. Paul, in 1957. A mixture of 15 selected, apomictic lines. In Minnesota described as superior to Merion in seedling and plant vigor, rust resistance, and sod formation. In many comparative tests, performance has been about comparable to

* These varieties are patented. Provisions of the U.S. Patent Law protect the original clone and all vegetative increases from it. Protection does not extend to seed produced from patented clones.

good common sources. The good quality of Minnesota-grown Park seed is a significant factor in establishment.

Pennstar. Released by the Pennsylvania AES, University Park, in 1967. Tested as K5(47). Selected for disease resistance. A dark green variety that is similar to Merion in general appearance. A promising variety that has performed well in a number of comparative tests. Susceptible to sod webworm damage, but this should not constitute a serious hazard.

Prato. Released by D. J. van der Have, Kapelle-Biezelinge, The Netherlands. Vigorous growth habit and some tolerance to disease. Susceptible to stripe smut, but has shown promise in portions of the upper Midwestern U. S.

South Dakota Certified. A certified source of domestic common Kentucky bluegrass. Eligible seed fields must be at least 10 years old, and some fields are nearly 50 years old.

Troy. Released by the Montana AES, Bozeman, and Crops Research Division, ARS, USDA, in 1955. A vigorous pasture type adapted to cooler parts of the Kentucky bluegrass region. Not outstanding in disease resistance.

Warren's A10.* Released by Warren's Nursery, Chicago, Ill. Dense, leaf spot resistant, with somewhat finer texture than Merion. A sexual variety that must be propagated vegetatively.

Windsor.* Developed by O. M. Scott and Sons Company, Marysville, Ohio, and released as component in proprietary lawn-seed mixtures in 1962. Selected for dense cover, low growth habit, and disease tolerance. Satisfactory performance in some areas but only average in others.

45. *Poa trivialis* L., rough bluegrass (other names—roughstalked bluegrass).

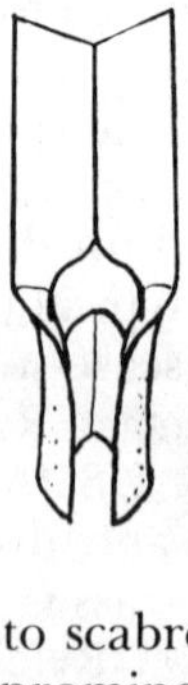

Origin: Introduced from Europe during Colonial Period.

Description: A fine-textured, cool-season, sod-forming perennial that spreads by stolons. *Leaves*–folded in bud shoot. *Ligule*–membranous (2 to 6 mm long), acute, entire, sometimes ciliate. *Auricles*–absent. *Collar*–broad, distinct, glabrous, divided by midrib. *Sheath*–compressed, sharply keeled, generally scabrous, split part way only, green or purple tinted. *Blade*–flat, slightly tapering from base to tip which is narrowly boat-shaped, keeled, glossy, smooth to scabrous below; slightly scabrous on upper surface; median lines not prominent; margins scabrous at least near tip; bright green color. *Inflorescence*–oblong, open panicle. Distinguished by scabrous sheath and glossy under-surface of the blade.

Adaptation and use: Found from Newfoundland and Ontario south to North Carolina and west to South Dakota and Colorado, and along Pacific Coast. Best adapted to rich soils and moist locations. Grows well in wet meadows and along ditch banks. Shade tolerant but not drought resistant. Tolerates comparatively heavy shade when soil moisture and fertility are not limiting. Short-lived on dry sites. Included in many lawn and turf seed mixtures developed for shady areas.

Varieties: None available.

46. *Stenotaphrum secundatum* (Walt.) Kuntze, St. Augustinegrass.

Origin: Probably introduced during Colonial Period or earlier. Indigenous to West Indies and common in tropical Africa, Mexico, and Australia.

Description: A rather coarse-textured, warm-season, sod-forming perennial, that spreads by aboveground stolons and rhizomes. *Leaves*–folded in bud shoot. *Ligule*–inconspicuous fringe of hairs (about 0.3 mm long). *Auricles*–absent. *Collar*–continuous, glabrous, broad, narrowed to form short stalk or petiole for blade. *Sheath*–compressed, keeled, loose, slightly ciliate toward summit and along margins. *Blades*–commonly smooth, glabrous, bluntly obtuse. *Inflorescence*–short, flowering culms bear terminal and axillary, fleshy racemes, with spikelets imbedded.

Adaptation and use: Restricted by winter killing to Gulf Coast states and to milder parts of California. Very subject to winter damage north of line from Augusta, Ga., to Birmingham, Ala. Grows best on fertile, well-drained soils with a pH of 6 to 7. Requires abundant moisture. Does not tolerate either low soil fertility or poor drainage. Well adapted under heavy shade when provided with adequate water and soil nutrients. Very subject to damage from chinch bugs and brown patch. Used primarily for lawns. Also important for pastures on muck soils of southern Florida. Propagated vegetatively by planting sprigs.

Varieties: Bitter Blue. Selected by tradesmen on lower east coast of Florida. Origin obscure. Name has been misused on occasion for unimproved sources. In comparison with common it has closer internodes, shorter, narrower leaves, improved leaf density, and more prostrate growth habit. It has an attractive blue-green color. The variety does not tolerate continuous wear and is best adapted for ornamental turf.

Floratine. Released by the Florida AES, Gainesville, in 1959. A low-growing, finer-textured variety that has an attractive blue-green color. Produces dense turf of short (about 1½ inches) narrow (10/32 inch) leaves. Average internode length about 1.8 inches as compared with 2.0 inches for Bitter Blue and 3.0 inches for common. Tolerates close mowing and has survived at ½ inch. Rate of coverage and other characteristics similar to Bitter Blue.

Roselawn. Released by the Florida Everglades Experiment Station, Belle Glade, in 1943, for pasture use on organic soils of south Florida.

47. *Zoysia* Willd., zoysiagrass. Three species are recognized as having value for turf purposes in the U. S. These species *(Zoysia japonica, Z. matrella,* and *Z. tenuifolia* Willd. ex Trin.) are distinguished primarily on the basis of size, vigor, coarseness, and winter hardiness. Although there is some question as to their status as legitimate species, the species

concept can be followed in describing turf characteristics. *Zoysia japonica* is variable but on the average coarser, more vigorous, and more winter-hardy than the other two species. *Zoysia matrella* is intermediate in texture and winter hardiness, while *Z. tenuifolia* is the finest, least winter-hardy, and least aggressive. Although some seed of *Z. japonica* (Japanese lawngrass) has been imported from Korea, most plantings are established vegetatively. All improved varieties are propagated vegetatively.

48. *Zoysia japonica* Steud., Japanese lawngrass.

Origin: Introduced from Asia prior to 1895.

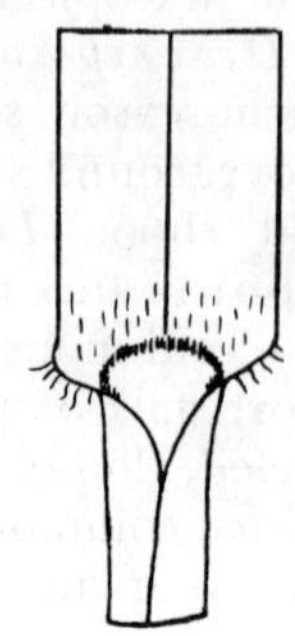

Description: A warm-season, sod-forming perennial that possesses both stolons and rhizomes and includes both coarse and comparatively fine-textured types. Turns off-color in cool weather and brown after frost. *Leaves*–rolled in bud shoot. *Ligule*–a fringe of hairs (up to 0.2 mm long). *Auricles*–absent. *Sheath*–round to slightly flattened, split, glabrous but may have tuft of hair at throat. *Blade*–smooth or occasionally short, hairy above with at least few long hairs near base, smooth below, margins smooth to scabrous and occasionally long, hairy near base. *Inflorescence*–short, terminal, spikelike. Vegetative characteristics resemble those of bermudagrass *(Cynodon dactylon)* but leaves more distinctly rolled in bud shoot.

Adaptation and use: Grown from mild, coastal areas of New England south to Florida, and westward to eastern portions of the Great Plains, and under irrigation in the southwestern states. Best adapted to areas that have long, warm-growing season. Persists on infertile sites, but prefers heavy soils and requires fertilizer for good growth and color. Responds to lime on very acid soils. Not highly drought resistant but survives long, dry periods in humid regions. Less salt tolerant than bermudagrass. Used primarily for lawns and general-purpose turf and to some extent for erosion control.

Varieties: Meyer. Released by Crops Research Division, ARS, USDA, and U.S. Golf Association Green Section in 1951. Tested as Z-52. Selected for leaf width intermediate between typical *Zoysia japonica* and *Z. matrella*, and for winter hardiness. A relatively vigorous vegetatively propagated variety, that is used to some extent throughout the species' range of adaptation. It is well adapted to the Mid-Atlantic region.

49. *Zoysia japonica* x *Z. tenuifolia*.

Varieties: Emerald. Released by the Georgia AES, Tifton, and Crops Research Division, ARS, USDA, in 1955. A vegetatively propagated F_1 hybrid between *Zoysia japonica* x *Z. tenuifolia*. Combines in varying degrees greater winter hardiness, non-fluffy growth habit, and faster rate of spread of *japonica* parent with finer leaves, denser turf, and dark green color of *tenuifolia*. Better shade and frost tolerance than bermudagrass. Best adapted in southeastern U. S. north to Maryland.

50. *Zoysia matrella* (L.) Merr., manilagrass.

Varieties: FC 13521. Released by Alabama AES, Auburn. A vegetatively propagated introduction of *Z. matrella* characterized by fine, dark green leaves, and dense growth habit. Tolerates considerable shade, susceptible to drought but recovers rapidly when moisture becomes available. A good lawn grass in warmer portions of the southeastern U. S.

References

Bennett, Hugh W., R. O. Hammons, and W. R. Weissinger, 1952. The identification of 76 species of Mississippi grasses by vegetative morphology. Mississippi AES, Tech. Bull. 31.

Burton, Glenn W. 1951. The adaptability and breeding of suitable grasses for the southeastern states. Advances in Agron. 3:197-241.

Carrier, Lyman. 1917. The identification of grasses by their vegetative characters. USDA Bull. 461.

Chippindall, Lucy K. A. 1955. The grasses and pastures of South Africa. Part 1. A guide to the identification of grasses in South Africa. Central News Agency, Cape Town, South Africa.

Clarke, S. E., J. A. Campbell, and W. Shevkenek. 1944. The identification of certain native and naturalized grasses by their vegetative characteristics. Dominion of Canada Dep. Agr., Pub. 762, Tech. Bull. 50.

Fults, Jess L. 1956. Colorado turfgrasses. Colo. A&M Coll., Fort Collins, Ext. Ser. Circ. 2663.

Hanson, A. A. 1965. Grass varieties in the United States. ARS, USDA, Agr. Handbook 170.

Hitchcock, A. S. 1950. Manual of the grasses of the United States. USDA, Misc. Pub. 300.

Hughes, H. D., Maurice E. Heath, and Darrel S. Metcalfe. 1962. Forages. Iowa State Univ. Press, Ames.

Juska, F. V., and A. A. Hanson. 1964. Evaluation of bermudagrass varieties for general-purpose turf. USDA, Agr. Handbook 270.

Madison, John H., and William B. Davis. 1966. Know your turfgrasses. Univ. of Calif. Agr. Ext. Ser., Turfgrass Series, Sept.

Nowosad, F. S., D. E. Newton Swales, and W. G. Dore. 1936. The identification of certain native and naturalized hay and pasture grasses by their vegetative characters. Macdonald Coll., McGill Univ., Tech. Bull. 16.

Phillips, C. E. 1962. Some grasses of the northeast. Univ. of Del., Field Manual No. 2.

Weintraub, F. C. 1953. Grasses introduced into the United States, USDA, Agr. Handbook 58.

14 Improving Turfgrasses

Glenn W. Burton
Agricultural Research Service, USDA
Tifton, Georgia

I. Importance and Need for Better Varieties

The living green carpet called "turf" is the product of one or more genotypes interacting with an environment generally altered by management. Thus, genotype, environment, and management all influence and limit turf quality. Frequently to grow better turf, the environment must be improved by introducing drain tile, removing huge shade trees, watering, liming, fertilizing, etc. Much of turf management is, in effect, an alteration of the environment to favor the genotype desired. Cutting heights and frequencies and disease and insect control measures are dictated by the genotypes selected and the use to which they will be put. Obviously, the best turf is realized when genotype, environment, and management are balanced.

Frequently, the balance required for good turf can be most easily and economically achieved by changing the genotype to more nearly fit the existing environment. Substituting carpetgrass for bermudagrass in low, wet areas will eliminate the need for drain tile. Planting a shade-tolerant grass like St. Augustine can save many a tree that would have to go if bermudagrass were to be used. By choosing centipedegrass, a homeowner can avoid the expense of insecticide treatments required to control the chinchbug on a St. Augustinegrass lawn. These genotypes differ so greatly that taxonomists classify them into different genera.

Generally, much variability between genotypes can be found or created within a species. Manipulating this variability to develop improved varieties within a species is the responsibility of the geneticist and plant breeder. Given adequate support, he can develop improved varieties that will more nearly balance the existing environment and will materially reduce management costs. Breeding the weed-resistant Tifway bermudagrass has solved many of the weed problems associated with common bermudagrass turf and has saved millions of dollars that might have been required to control the weeds in common bermudagrass turf (Burton, 1960). Developing Tifdwarf bermudagrass, with a putting green quality comparable to bentgrass, has helped to satisfy the insatiable demand for better putting greens in areas unsuited to bentgrass culture (Burton and Elsner, 1965). A chinchbug-resistant St. Augustinegrass could save Florida homeowners the $20 million spent annually for insecticides to control this pest.

The monetary support for turfgrass breeding has been extremely limited. Some of today's improved turfgrass varieties were developed as byproducts of pasture and forage grass breeding. Many were picked out of nature's breeding basket by keen observers whose main job was not plant breeding. Very few originated in well-supported plant breeding programs. Yet, the ever-expanding turfgrass industry ranks among the top agricultural enterprises in the U.S. Strong, strategically located turfgrass breeding programs, organized with adequate interdisciplinary assistance, would pay tremendous dividends in terms of better turf. Surely those who determine the direction of agricultural research cannot long continue to overlook this need.

II. General Requirements

To be classed as a turfgrass, a species must be able to make a green, reasonably dense, wear-resistant carpet when mowed frequently. More specifically, the ideal turfgrass should be tolerant of drought and frost injury in order to remain green for long periods of time. To extend its area of usefulness, it should be able to withstand both high and low temperatures.

To reduce mowing requirements and give a better appearance when neglected, the perfect turfgrass should have a low growth habit. If man's dream of a lawn grass that requires no mowing is ever realized, it will most certainly be with a low-growing species that produces few, if any, seedheads.

The turfgrass breeder will always endeavor to make his improved varieties pest resistant. Among the many pests he must consider will be the diseases, insects, and nematodes parasitic on the grass. He will achieve improved weed resistance by increasing the density of the new variety, but as he does so he will add to the problems of thatch and insect control. Herbicide tolerance will be highly important, particularly if chemicals will be needed to control weeds.

In most instances, low forage yields will be sought. Notable exceptions will be varieties planted along roadsides, where they must compete with weeds under an infrequent mowing regime. Here, vigorous varieties, more like pasture and hay types, will be more successful.

Although turfed areas are frequently planted only "once in lifetime," ease of propagation cannot be overlooked. Damaged turf must be repaired. Establishment costs, directly related to ease of propagation, will influence the extent to which a new turfgrass variety will be used to plant new areas or replace less satisfactory types. Improving ease of establishment without sacrificing other desired traits will always improve the species and increase its use.

Seedheads detract from the appearance of turf. Grasses, like bahiagrass that produce tall, rapidly growing seed stalks throughout the summer, may have to be mowed twice a week to maintain a smooth turf. If mowing is delayed, seeds are frequently scattered into adjacent lawns, where they may develop into serious weeds. If the grass must be propagated by seed, good seed yields will be required. If vegetative propagation is practicable, however, complete elimination of seedheads will improve the appearance of the turf and will help to prevent its spread into areas where it is not wanted.

III. Germ Plasm Sources

Good germ plasm is essential for successful turfgrass breeding. Like gold, it is "where you find it" and it is not easy to find.

Turfed areas that have been in turf for many years frequently yield varieties that prove to be rare gems. This is particularly true where the turf was originally established from seed of a heterozygous variety. Most of the superior vegetatively propagated bentgrass varieties, such as Arlington, Cohansey, and Congressional, were discovered on golf greens where their superiority under golf green management had allowed them to reach noticeable proportions (Hanson, 1959). Tiflawn bermudagrass, for football fields and heavy-duty turf, was first selected for turf plot evaluation because it had survived in an old, neglected, space-plant nursery, where hundreds of sister hybrids had disappeared (Burton and Robinson, 1951). Differences in disease reaction and mode of reproduction have been observed among regional collections of Kentucky bluegrass (Hanson and Juska, 1965).

Introductions from foreign countries offer an excellent source of turfgrass germ plasm. Most of the species used for turf in the U. S. are not native to this country. Their greatest diversity is most likely to occur near their centers of origin or in secondary centers, where they have hybridized with indigenous material. Likewise, plants resistant to disease and insect pests are most likely to be found close to their original home. Bermudagrass, for example, originated in Africa and genes for resistance to the disease, insect, and nematode pests of common bermudagrass have likewise come from that continent.

Frequently, related species or even genera can supply characteristics not available in the natural variants of a turfgrass. Brought together by hybridization, the desirable traits of the parent species may complement each other and give rise to hybrid varieties superior to either parent. Most of the improved bermudagrass varieties, such as Tifgreen and Tifway, are F_1 hybrids between tetraploid *Cynodon dactylon* and diploid *Cynodon transvaalensis*. The latter species imparts fineness, softness, and increased density to the triploid hybrids (Burton, 1960, 1964). The sterility that usually occurs in species hybrids poses no serious problem if vegetative propagation is practicable.

IV. Breeding Methods Determined by Mode of Commercial Propagation

A. Vegetative Propagation

A vegetatively propagated turfgrass greatly facilitates its genetic improvement. Breeding such species requires only that a superior plant be developed. Progeny testing to ascertain the performance of succeeding generations can be omitted, and the time required to produce a superior variety can be reduced proportionally.

Interspecific and intergeneric hybridization, usually beset with sterility problems, may be freely used because seed for propagation is not needed. The sterility of such hybrids prevents pollen shed and helps to keep them restricted to the areas where planted. Non-pollen-shedding bermudagrass triploids, such as Tifway, have been particularly attractive to people allergic to bermudagrass pollen.

The reduction or elimination of seedheads can become a major objective in breeding vegetatively propagated turfgrasses, and few genetic changes could do more to lower maintenance costs and improve turfgrass appearance.

Vegetative propagation simplifies the description and identification of the new variety. At present, only vegetatively propagated grass varieties may be patented. Purity of the new grass can be maintained with less effort. Only a wall or a few feet of space are required to isolate one vegetatively propagated grass from another.

B. Seed Propagation

Seed propagation usually reduces turfgrass establishment costs. It is essential for the development of turf from bunchgrasses and is highly desirable for the establishment of turf from slow-spreading, rhizomatous species, such as Kentucky bluegrass.

Breeding superior seed-producing turfgrass varieties is much more difficult and time-consuming than the genetic improvement of vegetatively propagated species. In both instances, plants with the desired turf characteristics must be selected and tested. If the new variety is to be seed-propagated, however, it must produce good seed yields in the seed-producing area. Since the environment in the seed-growing area is usually very different from that in the breeding or use area, seeding habits of new varieties must be studied where the seed will be grown.

If the seed-propagated selections reproduce sexually, they must be progeny tested in spaced-plant nurseries and close-seeded plots. Possible genetic shifts, resulting from growing seed in a different environment, must be ascertained and finally must be provided for.

Seedhead elimination or reduction cannot be a breeding objective in seed-propagated varieties. It may be achieved, in some instances, by developing photoperiod-sensitive varieties that flower and produce seed in the seed-producing area, but remain vegetative where grown for turf. Near the equator in South America, where a uniform 12-hour day is experienced, certain varieties of bahiagrass, *Paspalum notatum,* rarely produce seedheads and are considered excellent turfgrasses. Given a 13- to 14-hour day, these grasses seed profusely throughout the long-day season. Although generally propagated vegetatively at the equator, these bahiagrass varieties could be planted with seed harvested in regions that have a longer day.

V. Breeding Methods Determined by Mode of Reproduction

Efficient plant breeding requires a knowledge of the mode of reproduction of the material to be improved. An understanding of the cytogenetic relationships between the members of the one or more species involved will also greatly facilitate the genetic improvement program.

The first step in any well-organized plant breeding program is the collection of germ plasm. This involves bringing together members and closely related species of the turfgrass to be improved.

A systematic survey and classification of the germ plasm collection might well be the next step. An examination of a small, spaced-plant progeny of each accession can throw much light on its mode of reproduction. A spaced planting of a selfed progeny will also suggest how important characters in a selected plant are inherited.

Chromosome numbers should be counted as soon as possible. Genome relationships, particularly between species to be hybridized, should be established. Self- and cross-fertility relationships should be determined. In order to get the breeding work underway, however, such studies should first be confined to the best plants, the ones to be involved in the first breeding effort.

A. Asexual Reproduction

Vegetative propagation of turfgrasses by sprigs may be considered one type of asexual reproduction. The genetic improvement of vegetatively propagated grasses merely requires the collection or creation of variable plants and the selection and evaluation of superior individuals.

Apomixis is another form of asexual reproduction that occurs in a number of grasses. *Poa bulbosa,* an example of vegetative apomixis, develops small, seed-like bulbils in its flowering panicles instead of seeds. These bulbils may be used to propagate the grass. Apospory, a form of agamospermy, in which maternal tissue differentiates to form seed embryos, is the type of apomixis generally encountered in grasses. Since the word "apomixis" has usually been used instead of "apospory" to describe this phenomenon in grasses, apomixis will be used in that context for the remainder of this chapter.

Since apomixis allows for vegetative reproduction of a genotype through its seed, it combines the advantages of vegetative and seed propagation. Although apomixis is heritable, the genetic mechanisms whereby it is transmitted from parent to offspring are not well understood. Burton and Forbes (1960) found evidence that apomixis in tetraploid bahiagrass was controlled by a single recessive gene in the homozygous (nulliplex) condition. Taliaferro and Bashaw (1966) reported that apomixis in buffelgrass, *Pennisetum ciliare,* occurs in plants with the genetic constitution, A-bb. They postulated the genetic constitution of a naturally occurring sexual plant to be AaBb, where gene B conditions sexuality and is epistatic to gene A, which controls apomixis. Even when the mode of inheritance is not understood, apomixis may be used to facilitate turfgrass improvement as exemplified in Merion bluegrass (Hanson, 1959).

A uniform spaced progeny from open-pollinated seed suggests that the parent plant is either highly self-pollinated or reproduces by apomixis. The existence of apomictic reproduction may be confirmed by examining embryo sacs of the accession. If the origin of asexual embryo sacs can be established cytologically or if multiple embryo sacs are produced, the uniform progeny can be attributed to apomixis.

If apomixis is facultative, as in Kentucky bluegrass, most apomictic plants will produce some sexual offspring that will differ from the parent plant. Improvement by selection within progeny of such plants may be possible (Brittingham, 1943).

If apomixis is of the obligate type that occurs in many warm-season grasses, such as the tetraploid bahiagrasses, sexual offspring will not be produced (Bashaw, 1962; Burton and Forbes, 1960). Seedlings from obligate apomictic plants are exactly like their female parent regardless of the male parent used to produce the seed. Somatic mutation, natural or induced, will create a low frequency of changes but attempts to select superior plants in the seedling progeny of a grass that reproduces by obligate apomixis have not been fruitful (Bashaw, 1962; Burton, 1962; Burton and Forbes, 1960).

Grasses that reproduce by apomixis (particularly the obligate type) may best be improved by hybridizing apomictic males with sexual female plants (Bashaw, 1962; Burton and Forbes, 1960). This technique allows the male parent to contribute half of the hybrid's germ plasm, just as if it were sexual. Some of the hybrids from such matings will be apomictic in the F_1 or F_2 generation, depending on the genetic constitution of the sexual female parent. If propagation by apomixis is intended, the mode of reproduction of hybrid offspring must be tested. If a plant is apomictic, it will produce embryo sacs with multiple embryos and will give rise to a uniform progeny. Five spaced plants from open-pollinated seed will usually classify the mode of reproduction of a single plant where obligate apomixis is involved. Only those selections that reproduce by apomixis need be evaluated for turf qualities.

B. Sexual Reproduction

Grasses that reproduce sexually, such as red fescue, tall fescue and bermudagrass, are usually further classified with reference to the amount of cross-pollination that occurs in nature. Grasses that are naturally self-pollinated generally give rise to uniform offspring that are like their parents. Although a few chance hybrids between such plants may occur, selection within seedling offspring is not likely to be very fruitful. Thus, self-pollinated grasses are usually improved by mating plants that carry different desired traits. Selection in advanced generations for the combination of traits sought will, after five or six generations, give rise to reasonably homozygous plants that will breed true.

Naturally cross-pollinated grasses are usually heterozygous. If they are self-fertile, variable progeny can be produced by selfing selected plants. The loss in vigor, generally associated with inbreeding and frowned upon in forage crop improvement, may be desirable in turfgrasses (Dudeck and Duich, 1967).

Naturally cross-pollinated grasses are well suited to population breeding methods, such as mass selection. Actual procedures may vary from roguing out a few undesirable plants in a spaced planting before flowering to removing a few superior plants to an isolated area for seed production.

Frequently, such grasses carry a self-incompatibility mechanism that causes individual plants to be self-sterile but cross-fertile (Burton and Hart, 1967). Superior seed-propagated F_1 hybrids can be produced in such grasses by interplanting vegetatively two or more self-sterile, cross-fertile clones in isolated seed-production fields (Burton and Hart, 1967). Penncross bent seed, as purchased on the market, comes from seed fields planted to three vegetatively propagated clones of creeping bentgrass (Hanson, 1959). The clones are heterozygous and the commercial Penncross seed, a mixture of the three possible crosses between three clones, gives rise to a variable population. The frequency of vigorous hybrid plants carrying the traits of the selected parent clones is great enough, however, that golf greens planted with Penncross seed have usually been better than those seeded to other bentgrasses. Harvesting seed only from fields planted to the three selected clones insures against population drift and guarantees that Penncross seed will always contain essentially the same genotype frequencies. However, not all golf greens planted to Penncross bent can be expected to look the same when 10 years old. Genotypes surviving on one green may be quite different from those surviving on another green in a different environment.

VI. Techniques for Creating Variation

A search for naturally occurring variants offers one of the most fruitful methods of acquiring the variable germ plasm essential for a successful breeding program. Plants that have been able to survive and increase enough to be noticeable must possess many of the traits required of superior turfgrasses. Most of today's turfgrass varieties originated in this way. If not worthy of increase themselves, they may be most valuable as parents in a breeding program. Thus, a very good clone of common bermudagrass, selected by Greenskeeper W. G. Thomas from the fourth green of the Charlotte Country Club, Charlotte, N. C., became one of the parents of the highly successful Tifgreen bermudagrass (Tifton 328) (Burton, 1964).

Inbreeding heterozygous, sexually reproducing plants offers a particularly promising method of developing desirable variation in turfgrasses. Genes for dwarfness, short seed stalks, and seedlessness are usually recessives that rarely appear (or survive if they do appear) in cross-pollinated populations. Genes for pest resistance may also be recessive. Thus, a search of large, spaced-plant nurseries, planted to selfed progeny of selected heterozygous plants, provide a good opportunity for finding superior turfgrass types. If too much vigor is lost from inbreeding, some of it may be recovered by intermating unrelated plants with similar turf characteristics.

Hybridization is one of the commonest methods used to create variation in plants. When hybrids are made, the F_1 is usually more vigorous but otherwise intermediate to the parents in most characteristics, except for those controlled by dominant genes. The F_2 generation will generally include plants ranging from the extremes of one parent to the other for most of the traits considered, and will provide new combinations of characteristics not seen in the parent and F_1 plants. If the parents are heterozygous, as they will generally be, a large F_2 generation from a number of F_1 plants of the cross may be expected to contain dwarfs and other recessive characters not seen in either parent. Intraspecific hybrids will be the easiest to make and can usually be advanced to the F_2 generation without difficulty.

Interspecific and intergeneric hybrids are more difficult to make and will generally give rise to sterile F_1 hybrids. If the hybrids have superior turf characteristics and can be propagated vegetatively, their sterility may be an asset, as in the case of the triploid bermudagrass hybrids. If the hybrids are not superior as turfgrasses and/or cannot be commercially propagated by vegetative means, an effort to advance them another generation should be made. Where the parents contribute different genomes, doubling the chromosome number of the F_1 hybrid may lead to the development of a fertile amphidiploid. If the chromosomes in the F_1 hybrid pair with a high frequency, doubling of the chromosome number to increase fertility is much less likely to succeed. Backcrossing the F_1 hybrid to one or both parents may yield a few seeds and produce useful variants. The possibility of developing vegetatively propagable hybrids by crossing sterile interspecific or intergeneric hybrids with another stoloniferous or rhizomatous species should not be overlooked.

Mutagenic agents will create variation as they increase mutation frequencies. At optimum dosages, chemical and radiation mutagenic agents are about equally effective in increasing mutation frequency. Generally, however, treatment with radiation, such as X rays or thermal neutrons, results in chromosome breakage and rearrangement and reduces seed set. Mutagenic agents, such as ethyl methane sulfonate, do not cause noticeable chromosome aberrations and, consequently, affect seed set very little (Burton and Powell, 1966). Thus, chemical mutagenic agents may be preferred if seed production of the treated material is desired. If, however, sterility to eliminate pollen and facilitate control is a desirable characteristic in vegetatively propagable material, heavy radiation would be the recommended treatment.

Since most induced mutants behave as recessives and since paired loci are rarely affected by a single treatment, M_1 plants from treated seed may show comparatively few mutations, particularly if the treated seeds were homozygous. Such material must be advanced to the M_2 generation to permit full expression of the mutagenic-agent effects. Mutagen-treated heterozygous seeds will give rise to much greater variation in the M_1 generation because treatment of the dominant gene at any heterozygous locus allows the associated recessive to be expressed.

Creating variation in apomictic material is most difficult, particularly if obligate apomixis is involved. Where sexual female plants are lacking, treatment with mutagenic agents is about the only known method for increasing variability. Hanson and Juska (1962) treated seed of the facultative apomictic Merion bluegrass with thermal neutrons to increase the number of aberrant plants up to 11-fold. Although most of the mutants were inferior to the parents, a few had turf potential. Most of their mutants tested in the M_3 generation were apomictic.

Most plants that reproduce by apomixis are highly heterozygous. Treatment of such germ plasm with mutagenic agents will give rise to many mutant or offtype plants in the M_1 generation (Burton and Jackson, 1962). Carrying these mutants to the M_2 generation, generally gives uniform progeny like the mutant parent—proof that the mutant is also apomictic. Sometimes M_2 progenies are variable but if so, there will usually be more than one plant of each variant. When these variants are advanced to the M_3 generation, they give uniform progeny to prove that they are also apomictic. Thus, variations that sometimes appear in certain M_2 progeny are due to sectoring in the M_1 generation, where several mutant sectors in one plant contribute seed for the M_2 test.

There is no evidence to prove that apomictic plants can be made sexual by treatment with mutagenic agents. Thus, induced mutants of apomictic plants may be expected to continue to breed true by apomixis. Since most induced mutants are likely to be inferior to their apomictic parents, literally thousands of spaced plants from treated seed should be examined in a breeding program designed to improve the turf qualities of an apomictic grass by mutagen treatment.

Many of man's superior fruits, such as the Delicious apple, arose as bud mutations in vegetative material. There is good reason to believe that Tifdwarf bermudagrass originated as a natural mutant in the vegetative stolons of Tifgreen, a sterile triploid (Burton and Elsner, 1965).

Since mutagenic agents merely step up the frequencies of natural mutations, it should be possible to create variation in sterile or non-seed-producing grasses by subjecting stoloniferous material to treatment with mutagenic agents. To facilitate the discovery of mutants, vegetative material should be subdivided into single sprigs before treatment and should be handled as space-planted seedlings after treatment.

VII. Techniques for Selfing and Crossing

Genetic improvement, except for vegetative mutation, must be preceded by floral induction and seed production. Hybridization is greatly facilitated when the parents can be made to flower at the same time. Floral induction is subject to both genetic and environmental control. Frequently, grasses native to the tropics fail to flower when moved to areas with summer days longer than 12 hours. Reducing the daily photoperiod to 12 hours will usually bring such grasses into flower. Every species and genotype has an optimum photoperiod that must be known and simulated if genotypes are to be made to flower at will.

Hill or row plantings produce more heads and flower for a longer period than dense plantings. Removing dead winter growth with a spring fire will increase seedhead formation in bahiagrass several fold. Adequate fertilization, particularly with nitrogen, can induce heavy, prolonged flowering in a starved, nonflowering grass sod. Temperature has a significant effect on floral induction in most species.

Age affects floral induction in some grasses. The female parent for Tiflawn bermudagrass was a dwarf *Cynodon dactylon* seedling that failed to produce any seedheads until the sod was 3 years old. The variety, No Mow bermudagrass, planted at Tifton, Georgia, in the spring of 1965, failed to flower until 1967, when it produced a great profusion of seed stalks. Thus, the turfgrass breeder will do well to study the floral behavior of his breeding stocks in order to learn how to bring them into flower at will.

Selfing requires that grass flowers be isolated from all foreign pollen. Enclosing heads in bags before anthesis begins has been the method generally used to self most grasses. Selfing bags must be porous enough to allow for moisture and gaseous interchange but tight enough to prevent pollen penetration. Bags made from glassine or kraft paper, sealed with waterproof glue, have usually met these requirements. In addition, individual bags must be small enough and light enough to keep from breaking the stalks bearing the bagged heads. The seed stalks of many turfgrasses are so fragile that supports for the bags must also be provided. Where many heads flower over a short period, it may be desirable to enclose the entire plant in a large glassine or parchment bag.

If only a few plants are to be selfed, isolation may be found in the windows of offices and laboratories. This requires that heads to be selfed must be moved to these rooms, which can be easily accomplished with potted plants. Seed stalks of many grasses will flower and mature seed if they are cut close to the soil surface just prior to anthesis, placed immediately in tap water, and kept in the water until mature. Many heads can be placed in a bottle of water, which, in turn, is located in a window where the heads will receive some light. Although seed set is frequently two to three times less and seed size is smaller than in normal field plantings, the procedure has been very effective with bermuda and bahiagrass.

Hand emasculation of grass florets is a tedious, time-consuming procedure that may be necessary to produce hybrids but should be avoided wherever possible. Basically, hand emasculation involves the removal of the three anthers in each grass floret without allowing them to shed any pollen. It may be most easily accomplished at the time the florets open and begin to exsert their anthers during normal anthesis. At this stage, the anthers will dehisce naturally and shed pollen very easily unless great care is exercised. Creating a dense, artificial fog will delay anther dehiscence and make the anther walls less likely to fracture when removed with tweezers (Burton, 1948).

Anthesis in many species is light-stimulated and temperature-influenced. Flowering may be delayed in grasses that flower soon after sunrise by keeping them in a dark chamber. If it is necessary to delay flowering several hours beyond the normal time, lowering the temperature in the dark chamber to 40 to 50 F will be desirable. Reduced temperature may be used to slow down the normal rate of anthesis to facilitate emasculation and increase the time during which florets can be emasculated.

Male-sterility, as it makes emasculation unnecessary, greatly facilitates crossing procedures. Genetic male-sterility, usually controlled by a recessive gene, is very useful in developing hybrids that are to be advanced to the F_2 generation for selection because the F_1 is usually fertile. Cytoplasmic male-sterility, of value in a commercial F_1 hybrid breeding program, poses problems in the production of hybrids to be carried to the F_2 generation for the selection of new recombinants. If the male parents, crossed with cytoplasmic male-sterile plants, fail to carry fertility-restorer genes, the F_1 hybrids will be sterile and cannot be advanced to the F_2 generation. Both mechanisms will give rise to either F_1 or F_2 plants that cannot be selfed.

Male-sterility may be temporarily created in a number of grasses by altering the environment of the flowering culm. Immersing heads several days before anthesis in hot water at 116 to 119 F for 1 to 5 minutes has generally rendered grasses male-sterile. Low temperatures, around 32 F, have also caused male-sterility. Coastal bermudagrass has on occasion produced only sterile anthers shortly before the first killing frost in the fall.

Generally, the greatest seed set results if emasculated or male-sterile grasses are pollinated at the time that pollination normally occurs. A group of male heads ready to flower, placed in a bottle of water, will supply an excellent source of pollen. This may be collected in a bag and dusted on the male-sterile florets. It is frequently simpler and more effective, however, to place the bouquet of male heads in close proximity to the female heads. These may be enclosed with the female heads in a bag or may be isolated with the female heads in the windows of offices, as suggested for inbreeding.

Self-incompatibility allows for the production of hybrids without emasculation simply by bringing together two self-sterile, cross-fertile genotypes in the flowering stage. Bundles of culms ready to flower, placed in bottles of water, can be paired in isolation to create hybrids. Shaking the heads each morning will favor pollen movement and increase the number of hybrids produced. This is an excellent technique for producing polycrosses.

Mutual pollination consists of bringing together heads of two self-fertile, cross-fertile plants in isolation during anthesis. Pairing in isolation equal numbers of flowering culms in bottles of water offers one of the best ways of making hybrids by this technique. Obviously, the method depends largely on chance to create hybrids. If there are no incompatibilities and if the number of pollen grains and florets are similar for both parents, half of the seeds should be hybrids and the other half should be selfs. This method is very easy and will allow for the production of many more hybrids than could be produced by hand emasculation. If the parent plants possess noticeably different characteristics, if the hybrid seeds are kept separate by female parent, and if selfed progeny of each parent are space planted along with the hybrid progeny, it should be quite easy to identify the hybrid plants. If the plants hybridized are heterozygous, the selfed plants will generally be less vigorous than the hybrids. Incorporating a recessive marker gene, such as white stigma color in bahiagrass where normal stigma color is red, will verify chance hybrids produced by the mutual-pollination technique.

VIII. Selection and Evaluation

Success of a plant breeder is determined in no small measure by his ability to identify and isolate the superior plants in a large, variable population. To facilitate the first operation, individual seedlings started in the greenhouse are usually space planted far enough apart to allow each to express its characteristics with a minimum of competition. Weeds must be controlled, and fumigating with methyl bromide before planting or spraying with herbicides immediately after planting (and as frequently thereafter as needed) will save much labor in this phase of the operation. The amine salt of 2,4-D, applied at a rate of 1 to 2 pounds of acid equivalent per acre immediately after planting and at monthly intervals thereafter, usually gives excellent control of most weeds. Using 2,4-D to control weeds also permits an evaluation of the tolerance of the seedlings to this commonly used herbicide.

Locating the space planting on a coarse, deep sand will help to screen the population for root-system development. Only those plants with deep, extensive root systems will be able to make good growth on such soils.

Where resistance to a specific disease is sought, it may be possible to inoculate and screen the seedlings for disease resistance in flats while they are still in the greenhouse. Generally, a grass resistant to a disease in the seedling stage will retain the resistance throughout its life cycle. This technique may also be used in breeding for insect and nematode resistance.

Generally, the most promising plants can be removed from a spaced planting at the end of one or two seasons of observation. It will be well, if possible, however, to leave the space planting without care for several years thereafter to observe persistence when plants are neglected. Occasional mowing may be required to reduce excess top growth and weeds and facilitate observations. It is not uncommon for one or more superior plants to appear after such treatment.

Space plantings will not supply all the information needed to prove the worth of a new turfgrass. Small plots, managed as the turf will be treated by the ultimate user, are needed to appraise the turf properties of promising spaced plants. If the new variety will ultimately be propagated vegetatively, the test plots can be established in this way. Since rate of spread is an important characteristic in a new grass, this information can be obtained as the plots are established. It will be important to establish each plot with comparable sprigs located in the same way if relative ratings are to have significance.

If the new turf variety is to be established from seed, it may still be desirable to evaluate each selection in a vegetatively established plot test in order to better appraise its turf properties. A spaced-plant progeny test will also be required to establish the breeding behavior of each superior selection. A selfed progeny test will reveal the presence of any undesirable recessive traits that need to be removed. An open-pollinated progeny test will suggest the contribution that the selection may make to a new seed-propagated, synthetic variety. If it appears practicable to plant commercial seed fields vegetatively to two or more superior clones (as in the production of Penncross bentgrass seed), a spaced-plant progeny test of each singlecross from a diallel mating of superior clones will be desirable. Finally, test plots of each new hybrid or synthetic must be established from seed produced under conditions to simulate ultimate commercial seed production.

Plot tests should be located on uniform soil and receive uniform management throughout the test period. Seeding rates comparable to commercial rates should be used. Square plots, ranging from 1 to 3 square yards in size, will usually be adequate. New selections should be replicated at least twice, and if there are many entries it will be desirable to replicate the checks a number of times. Since the best varieties currently available must be surpassed by any new entry, the best varieties should be included in the test as checks. This will permit at all times a direct comparison between currently available varieties and any new selection.

Management should simulate that generally given grasses that the new varieties may replace. Grasses bred for golf greens must be mowed daily at heights of 3/16 to 4/16 inch. They must be top-dressed with soil as golf greens are. Their tolerance of the chemicals (fertilizers, insecticides, herbicides, and nematocides) used in golf green maintenance must be established. If they must be overseeded with winter grass in regular practice, test plots must also be overseeded. Grasses that show promise for more than one use need to be managed as for each potential use. Making a management variable, such as mowing height or fertilizer rate, a part of the selection-evaluation test by splitting each plot with the management treatments may be a desirable practice.

The criteria used for the evaluation of spaced plants and plots of selected plants will include those characteristics listed under General Requirements at the beginning of this chapter. Practically all criteria used to evaluate turfgrass selections require or permit visual appraisal. Color, one of the more important turf characteristics, is difficult to measure with machines but is easy to classify visually. Injury due to drought, frost, chemicals, disease, or insects will change turf color. Thus, a comparative color rating of a group of turfgrass genotypes, from 1 to 5 or 1 to 10, made at monthly intervals with additional ratings after frosts, etc., will indicate which genotypes were most pleasing to the eye and least affected by adversity. Rate of establishment, ground cover, and sod density can likewise be easily described with a relative rating system that gives the densest plots a rating of 1 and the least-dense plots a rating of 10. Weed resistance may be easily described by a visual rating that gives weed-free plots a rating of 1 and the weediest plots a score of 10. Forage yield, an important measurement in forage breeding, is generally unimportant in turfgrasses except that it be low and this can be estimated visually. Even stolon length, plant height, and seedhead abundance, characters that can be measured, can be more rapidly classified with a visual rating system.

Giving the most desirable plants a rating of 1 for each trait described greatly simplifies obtaining an overall summary of the observations that will apply to a group of plants. Thus, the clones with the lowest average rating over a testing period will generally be the best. Ratings for color and sod density should be taken at least once a month. In addition, ratings should be taken at any other time that differences due to treatment or environment occur. Artificial shades, placed over different grasses, furnish the best method for appraising their shade tolerance (Burton and Deal, 1962). Wear resistance, important for fairways, playgrounds, etc., can be appraised by rating plots subjected to uniform golf-cart traffic (Burton and Lance, 1966). Precision and accuracy in rating may be improved by training, by rating the plots or plants two or three times whenever ratings are made, or by averaging ratings made by two or more people. Where plots are replicated, ratings may be analyzed statistically.

Regional tests add replication to local tests and indicate the area in which each grass is adapted. Rainfall, one of the major regional differences, is frequently compensated for by artificial watering. Thus, grasses adapted at Tifton, with 50 inches of rain, also do very well in Arizona, with less than 5 inches of natural rainfall. As a matter of fact, superior humid-region grasses frequently do even better in arid sections when watered because of more sunshine and less of the high humidity that favors the development of plant diseases. Thus, there is a much greater need for regional tests to set latitudinal limits for new varieties than to establish their longitudinal adaptation. Cool-season grasses have a southern limit due to summer heat and plant diseases, and winter cold determines how far north a tropical grass may be dependably grown. Thus, regional tests, located north and south of the breeding center, will usually be worth much more than east and west tests. Drainage, irrigation, and fertilization can usually overcome soil differences experienced in different regions. Since turf can usually bear the costs of these soil amendments, regional tests to appraise soil type adaptation are not too important.

There is no substitute for ultimate user evaluation. He must be pleased if the new grass is to succeed. Tifgreen (Tifton 328) was given this kind of test by a number of golf course superintendents before it was released. Unfortunately, such tests frequently lead to premature release. Generally, new grass varieties that are consistently superior for at least 3 years in well-replicated tests at one location, where they are exposed to major diseases and insects, will have wide adaptation in the same longitudinal regions and will please the ultimate user.

Literature Cited

Bashaw, E. C. 1962. Apomixis and sexuality in buffelgrass. Crop Sci. 2: 412-415.

Brittingham, W. H. 1943. Type of seed formation as indicated by the nature and extent of variation in Kentucky bluegrass and its practical implications. J. of Agr. Res. 67: 225-264.

Burton, Glenn W. 1948. Artificial fog facilitates *Paspalum* emasculation. J. Amer. Soc. Agron. 40: 281-282.

Burton, Glenn W. 1951. The adaptability and breeding of suitable grasses for the Southeastern states. Adv. in Agron., Vol. III: 197-241.

Burton, Glenn W. 1960. Tifway bermudagrass. U.S.G.A. J. and Turf Managemt., pp. 28-30, July issue.

Burton, Glenn W. 1962. Conventional breeding of dallisgrass, *Paspalum dilatatum* Poir. Crop Sci. 2: 491-494.

Burton, Glenn W. 1964. Tifgreen (Tifton 328) bermudagrass for golf greens. U.S.G.A. Green Sect. Rec., pp. 11-13, May issue.

Burton, Glenn W., and Elwyn E. Deal. 1962. Shade studies on Southern grasses. Golf Course Reptr., pp. 26-27, Aug. issue.

Burton, Glenn W., and J. Earl Elsner. 1965. Tifdwarf—a new bermudagrass for golf greens. U.S.G.A. Green Sect. Rec. 2(5):8-9.

Burton, Glenn W., and Ian Forbes, Jr. 1960. The genetics and manipulation of obligate apomixis in common bahiagrass *(Paspalum notatum)*. Proc., 8th Intl. Grassl. Cong., Reading, Berkshire, England, pp. 66-71.

Burton, Glenn W., and R. H. Hart. 1967. Use of self-incompatibility to produce commercial seed-propagated F_1 bermudagrass hybrids. Crop Sci. 7: 524-527.

Burton, Glenn W., and J. E. Jackson. 1962. Radiation breeding of apomictic prostrate dallisgrass, *Paspalum dilatatum* var. *pauciciliatum*. Crop Sci. 2: 495-497.

Burton, Glenn W., and Clarence Lance. 1966. Golf car versus grass. The Golf Supt. 34 (1): 66-70.

Burton, Glenn W., and Jerrel B. Powell. 1966. Morphological and cytological response of pearl millet, *Pennisetum typhoides,* to thermal neutron and ethyl methane sulfonate seed treatments. Crop Sci. 6: 180-182.

Burton, Glenn W., and B. P. Robinson. 1951. The story behind Tifton 57 bermuda. Sou. Turf Fdn. Bull., pp. 3-4, Spring issue.

Dudeck, A. E., and J. M. Duich. 1967. Preliminary investigations on the reproduction and morphological behavior of several selections of Colonial bentgrass, *Agrostis tenuis* Sibth. Crop Sci. 7: 605-610.

Hanson, A. A. 1959. Grass varieties in the United States. Agr. Handbook No. 170, A.R.S., USDA.

Hanson, A. A., and F. V. Juska. 1962. Induced mutations in Kentucky bluegrass. Crop Sci. 2: 369-371.

Hanson, A. A., and F. V. Juska. 1965. The characteristics of *Poa pratensis* L. clones collected from favorable and unfavorable environments. Proc., 9th Intl. Grassl. Cong., Sao Paulo, Brazil, pp. 159-161.

Taliaferro, C. M., and E. C. Bashaw. 1966. Inheritance and control of obligate apomixis in breeding buffelgrass, *Pennisetum ciliare*. Crop Sci. 6: 473-476.

15 Producing High Quality Seed

J. Ritchie Cowan

Oregon State University
Corrallis, Oregon

I. Introduction

In the production and management of high quality turf, the most important investment is the purchase of high quality seed. This means that care must be exercised in selecting the appropriate kind or kinds and the appropriate variety or varieties. Too frequently, little attention is given to the seed purchase and every effort made to procure seed at the lowest possible price. A good stand of the appropriate grass or grass mixtures is basic to the adoption of improved management practices.

There are three cardinal rules which should be observed in purchasing seed: (a) purchase the right kind and variety adapted to the particular use of the turf; (b) insist on certified seed where varietal purity is important; (c) make certain the best quality of seed has been procured. Caution in purchasing seed is extremely important for it may take 2 or 3 years to identify poor seed lots on the basis of field performance. The purchase of certified seed, however, provides the purchaser a guarantee of seed kind, variety, and quality. All certified seed containers are labeled as to kind and variety and have a purity analysis on them (Fig. 1). These labels are extremely important to the purchaser and should be filed for future reference. If problems arise in a year or two which were the result of poor quality seed, then by referring to these labels it should be possible to determine their origin. Frequently, these labels are discarded at the time of purchase. They could become some of the most important records which the turf manager has in his files.

Not too many years ago, the production of seed for turf was a byproduct of pasture or hay production. If conditions warranted, the farmer would harvest the crop for seed. Seed production today has become a major enterprise in many parts of the country and the world. A farmer may devote his entire operation to the production of seed. Growers who are predominantely seed producers obtain seed crops having higher quality than seed produced as a sideline. The professional grower will have a greater investment in equipment and facilities to produce his seed crop than the nonspecialist. The price of the seed may reflect this increase in capital investment, but such seed will quite likely be less expensive than "sideline" seed when judged in terms of turf quality.

The production and use of seeds for lawns and turf have increased in the past few decades to match almost any agriculture enterprise (see Chapter 2). More than 100 million pounds of grass seed are used annually. With greater emphasis placed on recreation needs, beau-

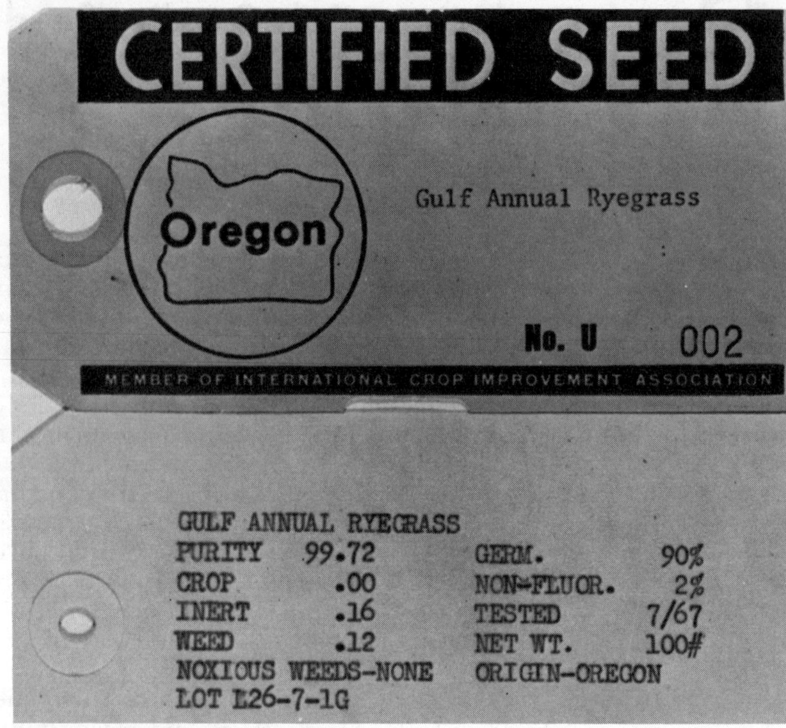

Figure 1. Seed certification label at the top reflecting state of origin, variety, kind and lot number. Seed analysis label below reflecting mechanical quality and germination potential.

tification, and erosion control, further expansion can be anticipated in the production of turfgrass seed.

The production of high quality turf is very expensive. Since the proper seed is a prerequisite in growing high quality turf, it is most important that every effort by expended to use good quality seed. There are many factors in the production process that influence, rather markedly, seed quality. Thus, the purchaser may be at a loss to know if he is securing the best possible seed. This problem can be met, especially for large quantities, by requesting bids in accordance with specified requirements. The purchaser must then accept the fact that seed produced to meet these requirements may demand a higher price. On the other hand, the premium paid for high quality seed is a comparatively small investment when measured against the cost of seeding failures or controlling objectionable weeds. Such specifications could require certain standards for purity, such as freedom from other crops and weed seeds, minimum germination, certification as to variety and kind, moisture condition of the seed when shipped, and kind of containers in which it is to be shipped. These and other factors could have a very significant bearing on seed quality, as will be shown later in this chapter. Tall fescue and orchardgrass seed in fine-seeded grasses, or bentgrass in Kentucky bluegrass seed, or vice versa, can be as serious as any weed in the production of high quality turf. A few seeds of these coarse-seeded grasses or of other fine-seeded kinds can become a very serious deterrent to the production of high quality turf of fine grasses, particularly in the production of sod. Thus, it is conceivable that the purchaser could insist on seed lots free of coarse grasses and, possibly, of seed of other turfgrass species. These are some of the items that can be considered in making direct purchases or in developing specifications for competitive bidding. They provide the purchaser with an opportunity to describe in some detail the type of product needed for a specific turf seeding.

Seed certification officials are trained and knowledgeable in the technical phases of seed production. By inspecting fields prior to their establishment or during the production cycle they are able to recognize potential difficulties that might reduce seed quality. Their knowledge of various requirements and their ability to recognize proper labels indicating the kind and quality of planting stocks are highly important. They can also help to identify problems or potential problems in the processing and handling of seed. Seed laboratories are staffed with analysts who have the equipment to provide quick, accurate seed analyses. These analyses are only as accurate as the sample used. Sampling must be done by trained personnel who understand the importance of drawing representative samples. The value of seed certification and seed analyses is maintained through proper labelling and sealing of seed containers. The services are rendered by officials who are unbiased and work under the same rules and regulations regardless of the part of the country in which they are located. The regulations under which they operate are designed for the protection of the consumer and to reflect the reputation of the producer and handler (Parsons, Garrison, and Beeson, 1961).

Of primary importance in purchasing seed is the kind or kinds needed. The term "kind" is used to identify the species, e.g., Kentucky bluegrass *(Poa pratensis)* bentgrass *(Agrostis sp.),* or fine fescue *(Festuca rubra).* Within most kinds, there are a number of varieties available. These varieties have been developed for various reasons, including resistance to specific diseases, improved texture, superior persistence, and others (see Chapter 13). Thus, it is extremely important that the purchaser know the nature and characteristics and adaptation of the variety or varieties selected for use. Quite frequently, the user will desire a combination of kinds and/or varieties. Where possible, it is wise to purchase seed lots that are pure as to kind and variety and subsequently mix them prior to planting. If mixtures are purchased, then the label must be examined carefully to see if the various kinds and varieties conform with local recommendations. Otherwise, the purchaser may find to his sorrow that the "bargain" mixture contained a small percentage of fine-leaved perennial turfgrasses and substantial quantities of coarse-textured grasses.

The ability of a variety to produce seed is influenced by genetic factors and the environment under which the seed crop is produced. Seed yields are also influenced by management practices. Some varieties that produce indifferent quality turf may produce excellent seed yields and, conversely, certain good turfgrasses may produce comparatively low seed yields. In general, seed of high yielding varieties will appear on the market at lower prices. This emphasizes again the importance of knowing the potential performance of the variety being purchased under the conditions where it is to be used. The average commercial seed yield for Merion Kentucky bluegrass is approximately 400 pounds per acre. Under similar conditions Newport Kentucky bluegrass will yield 1,500 pounds per acre.

The several important steps in producing quality seed are provided here in summary form. The primary factor is planting pure seed on clean land. This can be done by using only high quality seed stocks and by knowing the history of the land. There are cultural techniques available to keep contaminants, in the form of volunteers, to a minimum. These volunteers can cause two problems. If the volunteers are of the same kind as the species being grown, contamination can result from cross-pollination. If the volunteers are of a different kind, they can be the source of undesirable and incompatible mixtures. Contaminants which are readily visible can be eradicated by spot spraying or hand roguing. Care must be exercised as harvesting equipment moves from one variety to another to make certain that it has been properly cleaned, in order to avoid mechanical mixing. The same precautions must be exercised when processing seed to make certain that all pieces of equipment involved in processing are properly cleaned before starting the processing of another seed lot.

Once the seed has been processed, then a final check is made on the quality. The procedure is standard for all official laboratories. An official test is important. Representative seed samples are evaluated for purity, germination potential, and any undesirable quality factor such as the presence of disease, etc. Traditionally, seed analytical work has been based on hand separations. All components within the seed sample must be accounted for when it is analyzed.

It is rather difficult to devise equipment which will do this in the manner required by seed analytical rules and regulations. These rules have been developed and co-ordinated by the A.O.S.A. (Association of Official Seed Analysts, 1965) and the I.S.T.A. (International Seed Testing Association, 1966). They provide uniformity of interpretation both nationally and internationally. In recent years mechanical devices such as the vibratory separator (Hardin, 1967), the continuous seed blower, and the microscopic inspection station have been developed. These devices permit more accurate analyses of seed to be accomplished more efficiently. Larger samples can be examined in less time than required for the standard hand analyses. This advancement in seed technology expedites the merchandising of the seed and gives the customer greater assurance of high quality.

II. Production of Seed

A. Field Selection and Isolation

The grower must give primary consideration to the location of the area or field for seed production in relation to surrounding crops in order to provide adequate isolation from pollen which might contaminate the seed crop. Most turfgrasses are cross-pollinated. The one exception is Kentucky bluegrass which reproduces apomictically. There can be some crossing which will result in "off types" or aberrants. The ICIA (International Crop Improvement Association, 1963) has set up minimum standards for isolation so the possibility of contamination from cross-pollination from another variety of the same species will be reduced to the minimum. Studies by Knowles (1966) and Copeland (1968) have been very helpful in establishing practical limits for isolation. The farmer must either provide the required distance from other varieties of the same kind or discard border areas sufficient to meet the isolation requirements. Isolation distances for three turf species are shown in Table 1.

In addition to contamination from neighboring fields, contamination from volunteer plants along ditch banks and roadsides can be very serious. Therefore, the seed grower must make certain that all such plants near the production field are removed or suppressed from producing pollen at the time the seed field is pollinating.

The seed field may be located on the leeward side of natural barriers such as canyons, wooded areas, major drainage ditches, or canals and derive some isolation in this manner. However, these natural barriers can also harbor natural vegetation which might contaminate the crop. Therefore, the grower and the seed certification inspector will take special note of the vegetation in the immediate vicinity of the seed field so that it will not be a source of contamination. In general, most plants growing in undisturbed areas tend to flower later than the same kind growing under cultivated conditions. This provides some measure of natural protection. The good seed grower is alert to this problem and puts forth every effort to see that contaminants are either clipped or sprayed well in advance of heading and to avoid contamination by pollen which might otherwise blow into the production field.

Table 1. Isolation distance for fields of 5 acres or larger.

Class of seed produced	Kentucky bluegrass	Red fescue	Colonial bentgrass
		Isolation distance, feet	
Foundation	165	900	900
Registered	165	300	300
Certified	16	150	150

B. Seedbed Preparation

A good seedbed is an important prerequisite to obtaining a good stand. There are also other factors which influence the land preparation for the production of high quality seed. If the field has been previously used for production of the same kind of seed there is always the chance that some old clumps may have persisted or there may be seed in the ground which is brought to the surface during land preparation. This source of contamination could prove to be a major obstacle in the production of high quality seed. Studies by Rampton (1966), Toole and Brown (1946), and Lewis (1961) have shown that seed of various species vary in the time during which they will remain viable

Table 2. Percentage of whole seed recovered of 400 seed samples buried in 1961. (H. H. Rampton, Oregon State Univ. Personal Communication.)

Year	Annual ryegrass	Perennial ryegrass	Orchard-grass	Kentucky bluegrass	Chewings fescue	Colonial bentgrass
1962	30	0.1	8	30	7	41
1963	4	0.1	0.3	4	2	20
1964	4	0	0	1	0	13
1965	0	0	0	0	0	17
1966	0	0	0	0	0	13
1967	0	0	0	0	0	12

* Rampton, H.H. Farm Crops Dept., Oregon State Univ. Personal Communications.

when buried in the soil. Some will produce viable plants after several years if brought close enough to the surface. Others deteriorate very rapidly, as shown in Table 2. Thus, the cropping history of the field is of extreme importance to the seed certification inspector. In fact, it is the opinion of many in seed certification that an accurate documenting of land history is a much more useful criterion in judging fields for potential contaminants than inspecting the field at heading time. It is better to identify potential problems prior to the establishment of fields for seed production. Contamination from volunteer plants could disqualify fields for certification with serious loss to the grower.

It has been traditional in the production of seed to require an interval between the production of any variety of a specific kind or species and the production of another variety of the same species. It was, of course, the hope that during this time any seeds in this soil would decompose and not provide a source of contaminating pollen and/or seed to the variety being grown. Unfortunately, when seed is the major if not the only farm enterprise, it is uneconomical to have large tracts of land held idle for long periods because of this restriction. In addition to contamination from previous crops, weed populations in new seedings may be very heavy. In the past, weed contamination was so severe that it was almost impossible to process the first seed harvest from perennial crops in such a way that they could meet certificaiton standards. To meet these very practical problems facing seed growers cooperative research between the Oregon State University and the Agricultural Research Service (Lee, 1965) took a new approach to the preparation of fields for seed production. The philosophy was simple. Some way had to be found to establish seed fields without disturbing the soil immediately before planting.

Normally in seedbed preparation, the soil is rather thoroughly cultivated and seed brought close to the surface will germinate. If the land is reworked to destroy these plants more seed will be brought to the surface. It was theorized that if the land was thoroughly worked and adequate moisture was available a crop of vegetation would appear. If this vegetation could be destroyed and without reworking the soil, a system could be developed that would reduce, and perhaps eliminate, possible sources of contamination. Extensive research by Lee (1965) has shown that it is possible to devise a system to meet this objective. (See Fig. 2).

The use of herbicides can be very helpful in establishing grass stands for seed production. For maximum effectiveness in controlling germi-

Figure 2. Pure stands of a variety and a kind can be achieved as shown in this field for certified production of Manhattan perennial ryegrass on the Carey Strome Seed Farm, Oregon. The stand is 6 weeks old and established on a chemically prepared seedbed. (Photo by R. W. Henderson, Oregon Agricultural Experiment Station.)

nating weeds without injury to the crop it is absolutely essential that recommendations be followed accurately. Successful use of herbicides in establishing new plantings requires careful, well-timed land preparation. In Oregon best results are obtained by summer fallowing to destroy established perennial plants prior to seeding. The fields should be worked immediately after the previous crop harvest. Late fall cultivation of the field to be seeded is advised to control many early germinating weeds that might later be too large for control by herbicides. The key to this practice is spraying fall-tilled fields in late November or December, after maximum germination of weed seeds, with IPC plus 2,4-D or paraquat. The fields must not be tilled following the spraying. Seeding can then be done between February 15 and March 15. Drilling is preferable to broadcast seeding. At the time of seeding, an additional spraying of paraquat is usually recommended. Broadleaf weeds may appear in the seed field but can be controlled with various chemicals, such as 2,4-D, dicamba, or diuron. With this cultural approach, no cultivation or disturbance of the soil is required. All weeds or undesirable crop plants are controlled by spraying. This method has provided pure stands of a given variety and kind for the production of high quality seed during the first year of production. There are some seeds in the soil which could ultimately be a source of contamination, but they are not brought close enough to the surface for germination. This procedure has enabled growers to shift more readily from one variety to another, if they follow accepted cultural practices in establishing subsequent crops. Knowledge that this can be done is of extreme importance to the seed buyer. It provides assurance that genetically pure seed can be obtained from areas that are given over to continuous seed production, where changing from one variety to another on relatively short notice is a necessity. Nonspecialists may not be in a position to adopt practices that provide maximum protection to the consumer.

C. Planting Method and Rates

A uniform, thin stand is desired for good seed production. All seeding should be done by precision drills which space the rows and uniformly distribute the seed within the row. The rows will be spaced from 6 to 30 inches apart. Some seed crops do not lend themselves to the row type cultural practice because of their spreading growth habits. They soon develop a solid stand. The seed grower will follow cultural practices which will keep the stand uniform and not too thick by appropriate burning of residue and spraying to remove volunteers.

Only high quality seed is used for planting stock. Seeding rates are kept low. They vary depending on the kind; and sometimes variety will influence the rate of seeding. Recommended rates of seeding per acre are 1 pound for bluegrass, 3 pounds for red fescue, and 2 pounds for bentgrass.

Seed can be harvested from a stand over several years if the grower follows appropriate cultural procedures to eliminate the possibility of volunteers. Usually the plant breeder will designate the number of years that a stand may be eligible for producing a specific class of certified seed.

D. Weed Control

It is extremely difficult to remove some undesirable crop and weed seeds from the desired seed after it has been harvested. Therefore, it is essential that every effort be made to keep seed fields free of undesirable plants, both weeds and other crops. One technique, which has been employed for many years by seed growers is to produce the crop in rows. This provides an opportunity to quickly identify undesirable plants and to remove them by hoeing or by spot spraying with chemicals such as atrazine and monuron. A machine for spot spraying has been built by a seed grower. It has a pressure tank, spray container, and hose with a boom. The movement through the field is controlled by a pneumatic button on the end of a long handle. Other machines which are not so flexible are mounted on tractors. Workers walk in front of the tractor carrying a spray boom and spot spray undesirable contaminants.

This method of management allows a seed grower to harvest several crops from the same stand of a perennial species. This is to the advantage of the ultimate consumer. The investment in crop establishment is substantial and the price per unit of seed can be reduced when growers harvest several crops from the same field. Wholesale seedmen know the farmers who use good cultural and weed control practices and select these growers for contract seed production.

E. Harvesting

Time of harvesting is extremely important to both producer and consumer. If the producer harvests too late, then a great deal of shattering loss of seed will result, and production per acre will be reduced substantially. If the crop is harvested at an immature stage, there is an increase in poor-quality, shrunken seed with low germination. Both of these extremes have a direct bearing on seed quality and price to the consumer.

Klein (Klein, Leonard M. 1965. Personal communication. Farm Crops Department, Oregon State University.) has established that moisture content of seed hand stripped from a standing crop can serve as an excellent criterion for the grower to use to initiate harvest. He found the content at optimum mowing time to be 27% for Chewings fescue, 24% for creeping red fescue, and 28% for Kentucky bluegrass. These determinations were based on windrowing the crop before harvesting.

Thus, it is possible to cut at an immature stage and obtain high quality seed by letting seeds mature on the stems while they are in the windrow. Most grass seeds will shatter rather easily when they become overripe. Therefore, it is much more satisfactory to windrow than to combine directly. Crops must be quite mature and the moisture content of the seed low for direct combining; otherwise, there is danger of spoilage due to heating of freshly harvested seed. Direct combining of grass seed crops has been replaced by windrowing primarily because of added flexibility and improved seed quality.

The self-propelled windrower has increased the flexibility of grass seed harvesting (Fig. 3). With this machine it is possible to cut grass seed on the immature side and have the crop complete its development in the windrow. Substantial acreages of seed can be windrowed at any given time. Once it is in the windrow, it is possible to combine it on a more orderly time table without the pressure that is typical of direct combining operations.

In order to produce seed efficiently and economically, it is necessary to operate on a reasonably large scale. The grower who has as his main enterprise the production of seed may grow several kinds and/or several varieties of the same kind. In the harvest operation it is essential that the equipment be cleaned very thoroughly after the harvest of one variety and before equipment is moved to harvest a second variety. Good seed growers exercise extreme care in cleaning their harvesting machinery.

Figure 3. Self-propelled windrowers in a field of Smith Brothers Newport bluegrass near Peoria, Oregon in July, 1968. (Photo by R. W. Henderson, Oregon Agricultural Experiment Station.)

Figure 4. Double threshing unit combine harvesting Merion Kentucky bluegrass, Buckner Brothers Farm, Albany, Oregon. (Photo by Lenard Klein, ARS, USDA, Corvallis, Oregon.)

Precise adjustments in the threshing and cleaning mechanisms of the combine are very important. The ground speed at which the combine moves can influence quality and quantity of seed harvested. Harmond, Smith, and Park (1961) discuss the operation of threshing equipment. It requires considerable experience to adjust a combine to satisfactorily harvest velvet bentgrass, with about 12 million seeds per pound and then shift to a red fescue crop, with approximately 200,000 seeds per pound.

Frequent handling of any commodity will increase production costs. Therefore, seed growers must use techniques which will minimize the number of times that material must be handled. At one time, it was standard practice to put all seed into sacks for removal from the field to the processing plant. This is slow, time consuming, and expensive. Most seed now produced in a major seed production enterprise is handled in bulk. As the seed is threshed, it is carried temporarily in the bulk bin of the combine (Fig. 4). At regular intervals it is unloaded into tote boxes. In the production of certified seed, it is extremely important that these boxes be carefully constructed. Mechanical contamination can occur just as readily from poorly constructed tote boxes as from a contaminated combine. The corners must be properly finished to facilitate cleaning with compressed air. Once the tote box is full it must be fitted with tight cover. Usually some kind of plastic material is used. All containers, whether tote boxes or sacks, must be accurately labelled to maintain identity during transit and temporary warehouse storage. Bulk handling can be done without contamination, but it demands expert care and attention.

III. Maintenance of Seed Fields

Once the seed crop is harvested, certain post-harvest maintenance operations are needed on a perennial grass field if subsequent crops of high quality seed are to be produced. The field will be covered with refuse resulting from the threshing operation. There can be seeds which have been light or blown over during the threshing operation which could constitute a source of volunteers. Weed seeds can be scattered about the field in the threshing operation. There could be volunteers which might increase the need for spot spraying.

Rampton (H. H. Rampton, Oregon State University, Personal communication) has shown that burning the refuse from grass seed fields after harvest has a beneficial effect on subsequent seed crops. The burning performs an important sanitation job, for straw can be a potential carrier of disease (Hardison, 1964). In addition, it is not economical to remove the straw, and residues reduce or nulify the effectiveness of spraying for weed control. Therefore, it has become standard practice to burn the residue on grass seed fields.

Chilcote (1967) has shown that an early burn shortly after harvest is most desirable. It will remove the residue with little damage to the crowns of the plants and increase yields of seed the subsequent year. In areas where this practice is common, summer rainfall is minimal. Chilcote also found that when surface temperatures during the burning are high, which is characteristic under dry conditions, there seems to be a stimulating effect to the plants, causing a greater production of seed head primordia for the subsequent seed harvest. Burning tends to reduce the "sod-binding" problem in older stands which is positively correlated with low yields. There is, however, an air pollution problem associated with this management practice; although less pollution results from early, rapid burns than from burning at a later stage (Chilcote). At later stages the moisture content is higher due to humidity and green aftermath growth, and the slower burn produces greater air pollution.

As soon as the fall rains have commenced the grower must give attention to a well planned spray program to control volunteer seedlings and weeds. Attention must also be given to fertilization. In general, fertilizer should be applied in the fall to promote the development of new tillers. Nitrogen is an important nutrient. In the western Oregon grass seed growing area it is advantageous to apply nitrogen at a light rate in the fall (15 to 20 pounds per acre) and at a heavier rate in late winter and early spring in one or two applications (80 to 100 pounds per acre). Nitrogen applications will not increase yields unless the supply of phosphorus is adequate. The good seed grower carefully programs fertilizer applications in accordance with soil test recommendations. There are management and cultural practices which demand continuous attention of the professional seed grower throughout the entire year. Good agronomic practices in seed fields provide the consumer with good quality seed at reasonable prices.

IV. Seed Processing

The objectives of seed processing are twofold: (1) to remove all undesirable crop and weed seeds and (2) to provide a uniform product. Seeds that are well developed and plump will perform much better than those which are poorly developed. Seed from the combine will contain varying quantities of light, poorly developed seed, chaff, and other inert material which must be removed. It is extremely important that this phase of seed production be carefully and expertly handled. If too much seed is lost in the cleaning operation, the grower's profit will be reduced. On the other hand, if a great deal of undesirable material and potential contaminants are left in the seed then the ultimate consumer will not be able to produce a desirable turf. Therefore, it is extremely important for the seed grower who does not have his own processing plant to contract with a reliable and knowledgeable firm to process his seed. In general, the separation of undesirable material and the grading for size are accomplished by some method of vibrating and passing the seeds through various sizes of screens. A machine with vibrating screens and air passing through them will provide for major separation. For finishing or final separation, generally only one contaminant can be removed per machine. There are indent disk and cylinder separators, velvet rolls, spirals, inclined drapers, vibrators, electronic separators, color separators, and other devices which can be used for difficult separations (Klein, Henderson and Stoesz, 1961). Brandenburg and Harmond (1966) have shown that cleaning specifications based on the physical dimensions of the seed will yield a high-quality product.

In order to have an efficient operation where large quantities of seed may be processed it is necessary to have elaborate and extensive elevator systems. These systems increase the possibility of contamination when changing from one variety to another since seed can lodge in the bottoms of legs or in conveyor cups. In processing the seed it is quite possible to seriously reduce the germination potential if the seed is not carefully handled. Brandenburg and Harmond (1964) have devised a technique for fluidizing the conveyance of seed, from one area of the processing plant to another, in which seed flows through a tube in a stream of air. This technique is extremely valuable in producing high-quality seed. First, it eliminates damage to the seed. Second, and equally important, it provides an excellent method for cleaning the transport system. The method should be of extreme interest to the consumer since it provides a means whereby the quality of seed can be maintained and mechanical mixing can be prevented.

Analysis of the seed may be made one or many times (Fig. 5). It is not uncommon to have a preliminary evaluation made after the first cleaning to determine what progress is being made in removing undesirable materials. This analysis can provide the operator with guidelines for adjusting equipment to remove specific contaminants. After seed has been processed to where the operator considers it satisfactory in purity, then an official sample is drawn by a representative of the Seed Certification Agency. This official sample will be used to provide the information for the analysis tag. All seed that moves in interstate transport must have an analysis tag to reflect the kind, variety, purity, and germination. In some states this is also a requirement for within-state movement. For certification, it is necessary that the seed meet certain minimum standards of purity and germination. As far as small seeds are concerned, automatic samplers are not currently being used officially, However, work by Grisez (1967) has established that an auto-

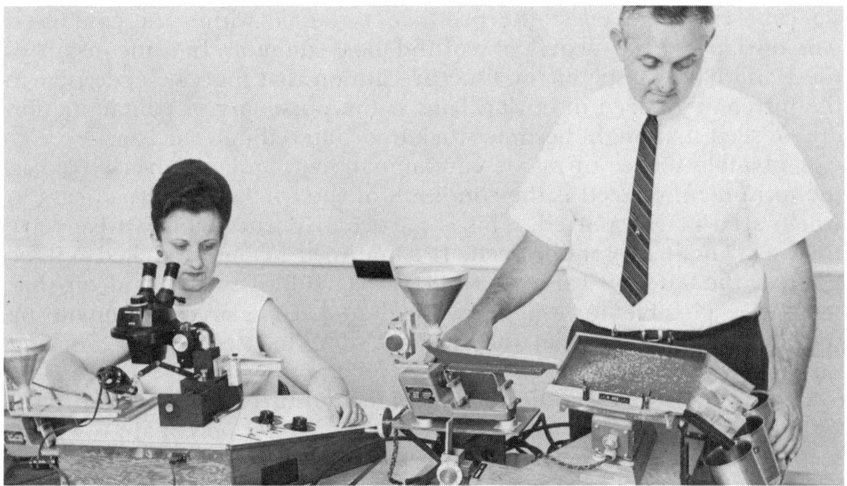

Figure 5. On the left a seed analyst uses the Microscopic Inspection Station while a Seed Technologist operates a vibrator separator which expedites seed purity analyses Oregon State University Seed Laboratory, Corvallis. (Photo by R. W. Henderson, Oregon Agricultural Experiment Station.)

matic sampler can be used satisfactorily for obtaining a representative sample directly from the leg of the cleaner. This has many advantages because it would permit continuous, comprehensive sampling of all seed in a given lot. At the same time it provides some economies for the seed processor in warehousing different varieties. If the seed sample must be drawn after the seed has been processed and placed in bags, then these must be stored in such a manner that all bags can be sampled with ease. If a sample has been taken from the leg of the cleaner in the final stages of processing before the seed is put into sacks, then it is possible to save warehouse space through compact storage. The processor and the owner must also record the quantity of seed in each lot which is represented by a given sample. This record is extremely important in order to determine the amount of seed produced from a given area. Production figures are examined by the certification agency prior to issuing tags to make certain that they are in agreement with expected production from a given acreage and variety.

V. Seed Shipments

A great deal of effort can be expended to keep seed lots separate, pure as to variety, and free from mechanical mixtures during production, and then purity can be contaminated or identity lost in shipment. Thus care must be exercised in selecting appropriate containers to preserve identity and quality. Seed is most commonly merchandised in sacks. These may be burlap, cotton, or paper. The larger the unit that can be used the less costly it will be to the producer. Still, it must be packaged in a unit that is convenient and suitable for the purchaser. The home owner prefers to have the seed in small units. For this use, paper is most satisfactory. It provides a means whereby the merchandiser can readily advertise the product contained within the container. The burlap bag is probably one of the most common. In some instances these will have plastic liners. One precaution that must be exercised in the purchase of seed in burlap bags is the possibility of contamination due to seed that might become stuck to or filtered into the bag.

A possible source of major contamination frequently overlooked in the movement of seed is the condition of the trucks or railroad cars in which seed is transported. This is particularly true if burlap bags are used as containers for the seed. If some seed has been spilled on the floor of the truck or car and a burlap bag full of seed is laid on this, then it is possible for this stray seed to become a contaminant by sticking to the bag or, in the case of very fine seed, even working through the burlap.

Ching et al. (1964) indicate that high moisture is one of the most serious factors causing deterioration in vitality and potential growth of seed. Chewings fescue is very susceptible to fluctuations in moisture content and high moisture. Therefore, once the seed has been processed and dried to 9% moisture level or lower, it is important that this level be maintained or substantial drops in germination can be expected over relatively short periods of time. Chewings fescue can drop in germination as much as 50% within 3 or 4 months if the moisture content goes up 10%. Therefore, the type of container can be extremely important in maintaining a uniform low level of moisture. Sacks with special plastic liners are one way in which this can be accomplished. Both multiwall paper and burlap bags are available with these liners. These types of containers reduce, if not eliminate, the possible uptake of moisture from surrounding air in warehouses.

In the future, large containers may be used in bulk seed shipments. These containers made from cardboard or large laminated paper sacks might have a capacity of several hundred pounds and necessitate mechanical handling. In the event that seed is moved in this manner, it is extremely important that it be properly identified as it may be bulked from smaller containers and repackaged for retailing. Thus, the supervision of a certification official is needed to avoid the loss of variety identity. It can be to the advantage of the purchaser to specify the type of container in which the seed must be put, as well as the nature and condition of carrier that will be used for transport.

VI. Maintenance of Varieties

The development of a variety is an expensive process. The cost will be directly related to the time needed to isolate superior selections, develop stable lines and varieties, and evaluate their turf characteristics. A good variety can be expected to more than pay for the investment in development because of superior characteristics—pest resistance, persistence, texture, etc. As new varieties possess desirable characteristics it is most important that every effort be made to maintain their identity. If the consumer, as a result of information obtained through publicity desires to buy a specific variety or varieties, then assurance must be given that the seed provided will perform in accordance with the original variety. It is almost impossible to identify varieties on the basis of the physical appearance of their seed. In some instances, it is possible to develop certain tests which can identify one variety from another within a certain kind, but this is the exception rather than the rule.

Plant breeders in Sweden were among the first to recognize that some labelling procedure must be evolved to provide variety identification and protect the consumer. The philosophy developed by the Swedish workers was brought to Canada in the early 1900's. A similar system was being developed in the U. S. about the same time. Recognizing the significance of the movement of seed from one state to another and also from one country to another, the U. S. and Canada created a voluntary organization known as the International Crop Improvement Association (ICIA) which developed a set of minimum standards for certification. Certification of seeds has as its primary goal the protection of the genetic identity. The early workers engaged in developing seed certification placed much emphasis on mechanical quality and purity. Thus, minimum standards for germination and purity were incorporated in certification procedures. Thus, the purchaser of certified seed not only had the assurance of variety purity but also minimum standards for germination and purity. Wholesalers and/or retailers may wish to have standards of mechanical quality higher than those set as minimum standards for seed certification. Thus, there can be contracts issued requiring that standards above the minimum for germination and purity be met.

Frequently, in merchandising seed, it becomes important to have certified seed relabeled because of the need for repackaging. It may be a case of where the seed moves from a major producing area on a wholesale basis in large containers and it is more expedient for merchandising to have it repackaged into smaller containers in another state where it will be retailed. In this event a provision is made between state certifying agencies so that there can be a recertification of the new containers. This must be done under the supervision of the certifying agency in the state in which this repackaging is done. The recertifying agency recognizes the labels affixed by the original certifying agency but will affix its own state labels and keep a record in its files of the amount of seed recertified. This is an important service in that seed may move freely from one region of the country to another and yet be repackaged for convenience in merchandising without loss of identity.

When a new variety has been developed the plant breeder has a small quantity of seed which is identified as breeder seed. Under normal circumstances the originating plant breeder accepts the responsibility for the maintenance of this initial stock seed. Further multiplication usually is done by a commercial seed production agency.

The Breeder seed may be released directly to elite seed growers for the production of Foundation seed. Registered seed is harvested from a Foundation planting. In the multiplication of some varieties, the plant breeder may choose to recommend that the registered class not be used in the increase program. This restriction is based on the premise that an adequately rapid multiplication can be made on a commercial basis without this generation, and thus there will be less likelihood of either genetic change or contamination during seed multi-

Table 3. Minimum seed quality standards for red fescue.

	Foundation	Registered	Certified
Pure seed - minimum %	98.0	98.0	98.0
Other crops - maximum %	0.10	0.10	0.25
Inert matter - maximum %	2.0	2.0	2.0
Smut balls	None	None	Trace
Weed seed - maximum %	0.10	0.30	0.30
Germination - minimum %	90.0	90.0	90.0

plication. The certified seed class is produced from planting either Foundation or Registered seed. Therefore, in the certification system as used in the U.S., there are four classes of seed, Breeder, Foundation, Registered, and Certified. This system is frequently referred to as the limited generation method of handling certified seed. Certified seed cannot be used for the production of certified seed. The commercial seed producer must always purchase Foundation or Registered for the production of Certified seed. There are more rigid requirements for the production of Foundation and Registered seed than there are for Certified seed, as illustrated in Table 3 for red fescue. Thus, the Certified seed is the commercial class of seed for use by the ultimate consumer whereas Foundation or Registered are for the most part used for the production and maintenance of seed stocks of a given variety. This limited generation system provides for adequate steps in an orderly increase of a variety without causing it to be unduly expensive to produce. At the same time, the product which is made available to the ultimate consumer is not far removed from the original stock released by the plant breeder. This is extremely important in cross-pollinated crops which are heterogenous in nature.

Regardless of how superior a new variety of grass may be for turf production, it is of no value until seed of it is available and planted. Obviously limited seed supplies of new varieties will restrict their use. Until seed production became a primary enterprise of farmers, it was not possible to have large volumes of any given variety available in the channels of commerce at any given time. With the advent of extensive seed production in the western U. S., western developed varieties were grown almost exclusively. When a surplus supply existed, outside markets were sought. In many instances, these varieties were not necessarily well adapted to other areas.

Eventually, varieties developed by plant breeders in non-seed growing areas were taken to the western seed growing areas for multiplication. It is possible that a variety grown under entirely different climatic conditions for seed production might not be maintained in exactly the same composition as originally synthesized by the plant breeder. Therefore, it was extremely important that research be conducted to establish whether or not genetic changes occur when varieties are grown for seed outside the region where they are adapted for turf purposes. Research by Garrison and Bula (1961) has established that it is possible to multiply varieties outside of their area of adaptation without the danger of genetic shift. However, their researches show the importance of examining varieties for stability when seed is produced outside of their region of adaptation. One of the protections that should be utilized when multiplying seeds of varieties outside their region of adaptation is provision for limitation of generations. Management and cultural practices that may have abnormal effects on growth, flowering, and seed setting habits must not be used. The control of volunteer plants is necessary. Adequate isolation from other fields of the same crop is required. Seed certification standards include the essential requirements to safeguard against serious genetic shifts. Thus, production of seed in different regions has had no major effect on the performance of crop varieties. Seed of European and Japanese varieties are regularly increased in western U. S. and returned for use in the originating country. These seed lots have given very satisfactory performance.

Literature Cited

Association of official seed analysts. 1965. rules for testing seeds. Proc. Assoc. Off. Seed Anal. Vol. 54:2.

Brandenburg, N. R., and Harmond, J. E. 1966. Separating seeds by length with special indent cylinders. Oregon Agr. Exp. Sta. Tech. Bull. 88.

Brandenburg, N. R., and Harmond, J. E. 1964. Fluidized conveying of seed. Agr. Res. Ser. U.S.D.A. Tech. Bull. No. 1315.

Chilcote, D. O. 1967. The benefits of burning early. Oregon's Agricultural Progress, Spring-Summer, 1967.

Ching, T. M., Schoolcraft, I., Rowll, P., Taylor, H., and Davidson, B. 1963. Change of forage seed quality in commercial warehouses in western Oregon. Agron. J. 55:379-382.

Copeland, L. O. 1968. Measurement of outcrossing in *Lolium* Spp. as determined by fluorescence tests. Ph.D. thesis. Oregon State University.

Garrison, C. S., and Bula, R. J. 1961. Growing seeds of forages outside their regions of use. Seeds, Yearbook of Agr. p. 401-406.

Grisez, J. P. 1967. A comparison of four methods of sampling small seeds. M.S. thesis. Oregon State University.

Hardin, E. E., and Grisez, J. P. 1967. Vibratory separator—a new research tool. Agron. J. 59:384.

Hardison, John R. 1964. Justification for burning grass fields. Proc. 24th annual meeting of the Oregon Seed Growers League. p. 93-96.

Harmond, Jesse E., Smith, James E., Jr., and Park, Joseph K. 1961. Harvesting the seeds of grasses and legumes. Seeds, Yearbook of Agr. 394-401.

International Crop Improvement Assoc. 1963. Minimum seed certification standards. Pub. No. 20.

International Seed Testing Assoc. 1966. International rules for seed testing. Proc. Int. Seed Testing Assoc. 31:1.

Klein, L. M., Henderson, James, and Stoesz, A. D. 1961. Equipment for cleaning seeds. Seeds, Yearbook of Agr. 307-321.

Knowles, R. P. 1966. Annual report of the International Crop Improvement Assoc. 48:93-95.

Lee, W. O. 1965. Herbicides in seedbed preparation for establishment of grass seed fields. Weeds 13 (4): 293-297.

Lewis, J. 1961. The influence of water level, soil depth and type on survival of crop and weed seeds. Proc. Int. Seed Test. Assoc. 26 (1):68-85.

Parsons, Frank G., Garrison, C. S., and Beeson, Keller. 1961. Seed certification in the United States. Seeds, Yearbook of Agriculture. 394-401.

Rampton, H. H. 1966. Longevity and dormancy in seeds of several cool-season grasses and legumes buried in soil. Agron. J. 58:220-223.

Toole, E. H., and Brown, E. 1946. Final results of the Duvel buried seed experiment. J. Agr. Res. 72 (No. 6):201-210.

16 Producing Quality Sod

J. B. Beard
P. E. Rieke

Michigan State University
East Lansing, Michigan

I. Introduction

Sod is a term used to describe plugs, blocks, squares, or strips of turfgrass plus the adhering soil which are used for vegetative planting. It is also used to describe the process whereby an area is planted with turf. During the 1960's the term sod became closely associated with the commercial sod production industry. Sodding is a term used to describe the operation of establishing a turfgrass area with sod.

The practice of sodding was described as early as the 17th century in Great Britain. Meadows and pastures containing low-growing, perennial grass species were utilized as the source of sod.

Recommendations concerning sodding at that time involved cutting the sod at a considerable depth with as much as 4 inches of soil moved with the sod. Tamping the sod following laying was stressed. It was not until the 1920's that turfmen utilized sodding to any significant extent, however. During this period, most of the sod was obtained from sod strippers. Sod stripping is the practice of harvesting sod from pastures and similar areas which were originally established for another purpose. Also, in the 1920's several commercial sod production operations were initiated in Michigan and New England. In contrast to sod striping, commercial sod production, or what is sometimes referred to as nursery or cultivated sod production, encompasses the establishment, maintenance, and harvesting phases involved in producing quality sod. Much of the commercial sod production of the 1920's and 1930's involved bentgrass species. During this period a majority of the sod laid was obtained from sod stripping operations and was a comparatively low-quality product of high cost.

It was not until approximately 1950 that any significant expansion in the commercial sod production industry occurred. Factors which contributed to this expansion were (a) the development of a mechanical sod cutter, (b) release of improved sod forming turfgrass varieties, and (c) the availability of 2,4-D for broadleaf weed control (Johanningsmeier, 1965). Since neither the Federal nor State Crop Reporting Services included sod in their surveys, there are no accurate figures available on the sod acreage or value of the sod industry through 1968. During the 1960's commercial sod production was one of the most rapidly expanding agricultural industries. Michigan led in the expansion of cool-season turfgrass production while Florida ranked as the leader in warm-season turfgrass production. Estimates have been

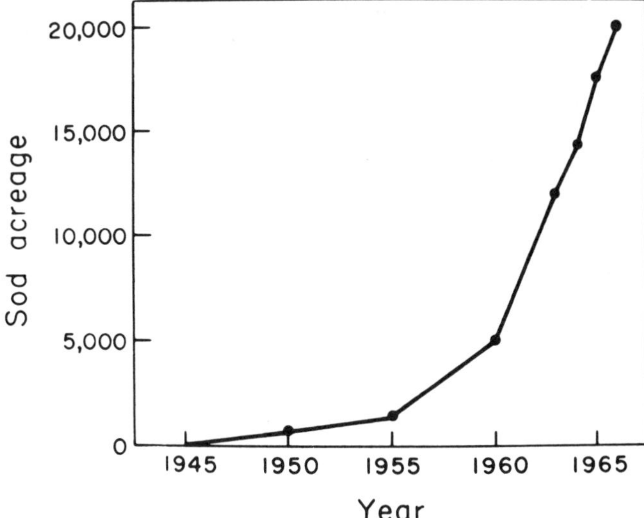

Figure 1. Growth rate in acreage of the commercial sod production industry in Michigan from 1945 to 1966. (Rieke, Beard, and Lucas, 1968).

developed on the growth rate of the sod production industry in Michigan (Fig. 1). It can be noted that the rapid expansion in Michigan started in 1960. The expansion rate of commercial sod production in other states parallels that for Michigan although somewhat delayed. Since 1960, sod stripping operations have been almost nonexistent in Michigan except as a source of sod for roadside slope stabilization.

Sod production operations are now limited primarily to the North American continent. Since 1965, sod production operations have been established within shipping distance of most major population centers in the United States. In 1965, it was estimated that 100,000 acres of sod were being grown on the North American continent (Anonymous, 1965). It should be emphasized that this is only an estimate. Michigan, Florida, Illinois, Wisconsin, New York, Maryland, and New Jersey have sizable acreages.

The rapid expansion of the sod production industry during the 1960's was the result of several key factors. (Beard and Rieke, 1964). One is an acceptance by the public of sodding as a quick and relatively easy means of obtaining a quality lawn. The ability to achieve an "instant" quality turf is quite attractive to the consumer. He has immediate use of the area. A second factor has been a favorable economic climate with the resultant high rates of new home and commercial business construction and the availability of funds for purchasing sod. A third factor is that sodding can be done anytime during the growing season, assuming irrigation is available, while effective seeding is usually restricted to certain periods (Miller, 1962). Two types of sod enterprises have evolved. One type includes all phases of production, harvesting, shipping, and laying. Enterprises of this type are common throughout the East Coast area. The second type is based on the establishment, production, and harvesting of sod, with separate organizations responsible for shipping and laying. This latter type of enterprise predominates in the midwest production area.

Where adequate deposits of organic soil are available, the trend has been toward an increasing percentage of sod being produced on these soils. For example, in 1963 50% of the sod grown in Michigan was produced on organic soil. In 1968, 5 years later, 75% was produced on organic soil. A similar trend is developing in other states where adequate organic soil deposits are available.

The sod production industry in the U. S. is quite young in comparison with most agricultural industries. Much of the early production technology associated with the sod production industry has been developed through the practical experiences and trial and error methods employed by individual growers. Scientific literature concerning sod production is practically nonexistent. Therefore, the authors of this chapter are forced to base the following discussion primarily on general observations and experiences rather than on the results of detailed scientific studies.

II. Factors in the Development of the Commercial Sod Production Industry

The problems involved in producing and marketing sod must be studied carefully before entering into a sod production operation. The key considerations in the development of a successful commercial sod farming operation include: (a) markets, (b) soil, (c) climate, (d) water availability, (e) capital investment, (f) equipment, (g) labor supply, and (h) technology.

Markets. No structured marketing and distribution system has been developed in the sod production industry. Therefore, it is important to make surveys and establish market outlets prior to entering or expanding a sod production operation. The primary market for sod is allied with new home, business, and institutional construction (Woodhouse, 1965). A favorable economic climate with resultant high rates of new construction will insure continued stability and growth of sod markets. A second market for sod is in the renovation of existing turfs, especially athletic fields, park grounds, and playfields. Damaged or worn areas can be quickly replaced with a quality turf by sodding.

The relative supply of sod now available to a market area and the potential growth rate of the market in the area should be considered. When contemplating marketing sod in an entirely new area, one must keep in mind that the acceptance of sodding by the public has been relatively slow in the past. An active, vigorous educational program will help in the development of new markets.

Another consideration is the accessibility to the market area and the current price level in that area. Michigan growers are exporting sod to markets at distances up to 400 miles. Factors which enable marketing at such distant points include (a) a good road system between production and market areas and (b) an adequate differential between the market price and the production cost to cover shipping expenses.

Soil. It is important that the soil on which the sod is grown is of a texture which is conducive to seeding, growing, and harvesting as well as being compatible with the ultimate site on which the sod is laid. Briefly, the land selected should have a topography which is level to no more than gently rolling. Consideration should be given to soil texture, depth, drainage, presence of stones, roots, and other debris which would interfere with harvesting operations. In addition, the land should be free of weedy, perennial grasses. Factors in soil selection are discussed in detail in the section on site selection and development in this chapter.

Climate. The longest possible effective growing season for the particular turfgrass variety being produced is desired. For example, Kentucky bluegrass, which is the predominant species produced in the cool-season region, will establish most rapidly when soil temperatures are in the range of 55 to 65 F. The warm-season turfgrasses have an optimum establishment rate when soil temperatures are in the range of 80 to 90 F. The effective growing season for a particular turfgrass is that period when soil temperatures are within this optimum range. The effective growing period of a region can be obtained through a detailed study of the climatic data.

A second aspect of climate is precipitation. Both the quantity and distribution of precipitation during the growing season must be considered. About 1 to 1½ inches of precipitation per week is desirable for commercial sod production. The poorer the distribution and the lower the quantity of precipitation received the greater the amount of water that must be supplied through irrigation. This, of course, will increase production costs.

The third aspect is a climate which is most favorable for turfgrass growth and least favorable for disease activity. A favorable climate for disease activity will lengthen the time required to produce a sod crop and will lower production efficiency.

Water Availability. Some supplemental irrigation is required for most commercial sod production operations. An adequate water source is necessary for irrigation and may be provided by a deep well, stream, or impounded water. Irrigation is particularly important during the initial 4 weeks of germination and seedling establishment. It may be necessary for a period of 3 to 4 weeks prior to harvest, particularly during summer dormancy periods when satisfactory color and growth can only be achieved through irrigation.

Water quality is also important. In some regions salt content of the water restricts regular water use. This applies to either surface or ground water sources. Water quality is based on: (a) total concentration of soluble salts; (b) relative proportion of sodium to other cations; (c) concentration of boron and other elements that may be toxic; and (d), under some conditions, the bicarbonate concentration as related to the concentration of calcium plus magnesium (Richards, 1954).

Capital Investment and Equipment. The development of a sod production operation requires the purchase of many pieces of specialized equipment. Included are such items as harrow, plow, landleveler, sod roller, cultipacker-seeder, land roller, sod cutter, disc, fork lift, sweeper, and mowing equipment. Also required are tractors and other power units for pulling loaded trucks and trailers from the production field. Wheeled machinery used on organic soils are frequently equipped with flotation devices in the form of over-sized balloon tires or metal extension rims. This specialized equipment requires substantial capital investment. In addition, a sizable investment is also needed for an irrigation system. No detailed studies have been made concerning the minimum investment required to develop an efficient sod operation.

Labor and Technology. The labor requirement for sod production is substantial, particularly for sod harvesting operations. Securing an adequate, reliable labor supply is certainly a concern in developing a sod production operation. With labor costs continually increasing, a number of new developments in mechanical harvesting equipment have been introduced since 1965. It is anticipated that this trend in mechanization of the sod production industry will continue.

Finally, sod production requires specialized technology, much of which must be developed through experience and research by private and public organizations. High quality sod will have greater consumer acceptance, a wider range in market potential, and a higher market price. Lower grades of sod are frequently sold at a lower price for use in steep slope stabilization on newly constructed roadsides..

III. Site Selection and Development

An efficient sod production enterprise must be based on selection of a site and its development. Consideration should be given to soil type, land clearing, drainage and water control, leveling, access roads, and development of an efficient irrigation system.

Considering market requirements and availability of land, perhaps the most basic decision to be made is whether to grow sod on organic or mineral soil. Michigan, Florida, Illinois, Indiana, Wisconsin, and Minnesota have appreciable acreages of sod grown on organic soils. In other regions of the country sod is grown predominantly or exclusively on mineral soils.

The topography of the land should be level to no more than gently undulating. On sloping soils, seed or even seedlings may be eroded, especially on soil types which have a low infiltration rate. This results in expensive reseeding operations, lack of uniformity in stand, and time lost in production. In addition, low areas may tend to dry more slowly, which interferes with seeding, mowing, and harvesting.

Consideration should be given to; (a) depth of the soil, (b) uniformity of the soil with depth and within a field, (c) need for tile drainage and drainage ditches, and (d) feasibility of lowering the entire drainage system. The land should be free of stones, gravel, hardpan layers, stumps, logs, or other materials which would interfere with tillage and harvesting operations. If new land is being opened for sod production where trees have been growing, expensive clearing operations will be necessary.

The field should be free from weedy perennial grasses such as quackgrass, bentgrass, reed canarygrass, johnsongrass, and bermudagrass, as well as nutsedge. These grasses must be eradicated prior to seeding in order to produce quality sod. With the exception of nutsedge the above weedy grasses can be effectively controlled with amitrol-T or dalapon followed by a period of fallow cultivation. Fumigation is practiced in some regions for weed, insect, and nematode control, but this results in increased production costs.

Organic Soils. Organic soils, by the nature of their formation, are free of stones and provide smooth, flat areas which facilitate establishment, maintenance, and harvesting of high quality sod. However, trees, stumps, and roots which have grown on these soils in the later stages of their development must be removed. Clearing operations can be very expensive, requiring special equipment for lifting roots out of the soil and removing them from the field. It is best to remove roots to at least the plowing depth. The smaller pieces of wood cannot be economically removed and may interfere with seeding and harvesting operations.

The organic soils range from essentially undecomposed sphagnum peat, which is not common in existing sod growing areas, to finely-divided, well-decomposed muck high in mineral soil content. The composition of the deposit may vary considerably with depth.

On most sites artificial drainage will be required since organic soils were formed under poorly-drained conditions. The drainage water from organic soils may have to be lifted by pumping into the drainage outlet which increases production costs (Fig. 2). A drainage reservoir allows pumping to be gauged by a float valve which maintains the water table at a constant level. If the land is quite level, the water table can be changed during the growing season through the use of adjustable sluice gates between lateral and main tile lines. This allows variation of water table level at different points in the field and at different times of the growing season. It is particularly desirable to lower the water table during establishment and harvest periods. Controlling the water table can contribute to more efficient water use and should reduce the rate of subsidence of organic soils.

Figure 2. Pumping station for drainage of water from an organic soil deposit.

Figure 3. Metal flotation wheels used on sod production equipment.

During periods of high rainfall, especially in the spring, the lack of soil stability on organic soils may restrict maintenance and harvesting operations. Special flotation wheels such as metal extension rims or balloon tires (Fig. 3) are necessary at such times. These wheels are often used throughout the year to prevent formation of ruts which would interfere with sod harvesting.

On many organic soil sites drainage ditches must be dug to allow removal of large quantities of water during periods of excess moisture. The spoil from these ditches can be used for building access roads if the material is mineral in nature. If the organic deposit is deep, it may be necessary to excavate the organic material and replace it with a mineral base to provide stable access roads. The access road is particularly essential for support of heavy trucks used during harvesting.

Highly weathered organic soil (muck) is particularly susceptible to wind erosion. In the past, trees have been used as windbreaks, but they take large areas out of production. As a result the trend has been to control erosion during turfgrass establishment by maintaining a moist surface seedbed through frequent irrigations.

Mineral Soil. In selecting a mineral soil as a site for sod production, consideration must be given to soil texture. Management requirements will vary depending upon texture. Sandy loams and loams provide a reasonable balance of soil properties. The water and nutrient holding capacities are much greater than for sand, while the problems with compaction and drainage are less than for soils higher in clay. For example, more care must be exercised in controlling traffic following precipitation or irrigation on soils high in clay in order to avoid serious compaction.

From the consumer's viewpoint it is preferable that sod used on heavy traffic areas, such as putting greens, should be grown on soils of loamy sand or coarse sandy loam texture. These soils will be less subject to compaction, although they are more difficult to handle during harvesting and laying operations. It is desirable to use sod grown on soil of similar texture to that of the use area when heavy traffic conditions prevail. When sod grown on clay loam soil is laid on a sandy site, water movement and drainage are impaired.

The profile of mineral soils must be examined for the presence of hardpan layers, zones of appreciable clay accumulation, changes in soil texture, and depth to the water table.

These factors influence water movement and drainage, and on a long-term basis may restrict the number of crops that can be removed.

Soil maps, available from the Soil Conservation Service, can aid in assessing factors such as drainage, susceptibility to wind and water erosion, texture, depth of soil, and presence of stones.

In general, production of marketable sod can be accomplished more rapidly on organic soil than on mineral soil. Twelve to 18 months are normally required for production of high quality sod on organic soils. Under similar climatic and management conditions approximately 6 months more are needed on mineral soils. In Michigan, a harvestable sod crop has been produced on an organic soil in only 3 months after a spring seeding of Merion Kentucky bluegrass. However, this short production time is atypical and has been achieved only under ideal conditions.

Sod grown on organic soil weighs less per square yard than that grown on mineral soil. An acre of mineral soil to a depth of 6⅔ inches weighs about 2,000,000 pounds. In contrast, a similar depth of organic soil weighs about 600,000 pounds per acre, depending on the degree of decomposition of organic matter and the percentage of mineral materials in the soil. Satari (1967) reported a bulk density of 0.24 to 0.37 g/ml for Houghton muck on which he was studying sod production factors. One square yard of sod grown on organic soil and cut at ¾ inch weighs 25 to 30 pounds depending on the moisture content. For mineral soils, the weight of 1 square yard is approximately twice that amount. The lighter weight of sod grown on organic soil facilitates harvesting and laying operations. In addition, the lighter weight results in larger payloads and lower shipping costs in transporting sod to distant markets.

Irrigation System. Development of an irrigation system is an important facet of a progressive sod operation. If permanent water lines are necessary, they are most easily installed when drainage ditches, tile lines, and access roads are being installed. Allow for settling of the soil over tile and irrigation lines so that these areas will not be lost to production.

In planning an irrigation system, consideration must be given to the effect of local climatic and soil conditions in determining the volume of water needed. The effects of prevailing winds on water distribution from sprinkler systems must be kept in mind as well as the water-holding capacity and infiltration rate of the soil. For detailed discussion of factors affecting irrigation see Chapter 6.

IV. Turfgrasses Utilized in Sod Production

The selection of turfgrass species and varieties to be grown for commercial sod production is dictated primarily by the sod forming characteristics of the particular species or variety, the market demand, and adaptation to the environment where the sod is to be marketed. The characteristics desired in a turfgrass to be utilized in sod production include; (a) rapid, vigorous establishment from seed or vegetative plant parts; (b) rapid, vigorous rhizome and/or stolon formation which results in a tight sod; (c) tolerance to diseases, insects, heat, cold, and moisture stress; (d) good density, color, and uniformity; and (e) a wide range of adaptation to various soils and environments. The following discussion of turfgrass species and varieties will cover only the aspects of specific concern in sod production. A detailed description of the adaptation, characteristics, and utilization of the individual species and varieties is presented in Chapter 13.

A. Cool-season Turfgrasses

Kentucky bluegrass is the predominant turfgrass species utilized for commercial sod production in the cool-season region of North America. The vigorous rhizome development of Kentucky bluegrass plus its broad adaptation to cool, humid environmental conditions are the principle reasons for its wide use.

Merion is the predominant variety of Kentucky bluegrass utilized for commercial sod production. This is due primarily to the vigorous sod forming characteristics and leafspot resistance of Merion. There are a number of situations in which Merion is not the preferred variety from the standpoint of ultimate adaptation and use by the consumer. For example, the powdery mildew susceptibility of Merion causes it to thin out completely under dense shade. Also, Merion requires high maintenance and there are many situations such as large, general-purpose turfs where it would be better to utilize a low maintenance variety, particularly when funds are not adequate to maintain the proper level of quality. Other Kentucky bluegrass varieties being grown for sod include A-20, Cougar, Delta, Fylking, Kenblue, Newport, Park, Prato, Windsor, and others.

The blending of two, three, or four Kentucky bluegrass varieties is a very desirable practice in commercial sod production. The sod will be distributed for use on a wide range of soil, environmental, and cultural conditions. Utilizing a blend of several turfgrass varieties, one of which is adapted to low maintenance, one to high maintenance, one to sandy soils, one to heavy soils, or one to shaded areas and one to full sunlight, will provide a wider genetic base and broader adaptability to any cultural or environmental situation. The component of the blend which is best adapted to the particular environmental and cultural regime under which it is grown will become the dominant variety.

Red fescue has not been widely used in commercial sod production. This is due to the comparatively weak rhizome development of the currently available red fescue varieties and to the lack of leafspot resistance which reduces marketability and rooting capability during the mid- to late summer period. There is a definite need for red fescue sod for use in shaded environments and on droughty soils. A red fescue variety is needed which can be utilized by the commercial sod production industry for the above-mentioned purposes. If such a red fescue variety is developed, Kentucky bluegrass-red fescue mixtures will become more widely utilized in sod production. Mixtures of Kentucky bluegrass and red fescue are now grown for sod production but the acreage is not extensive. This type of mixture is more widely adapted to both full sunlight and shaded environments.

A minor percentage of the sod production acreage is devoted to the production of creeping bentgrasses, primarily Penncross. Bentgrass sod is utilized for rapid establishment of closely mowed sports turfs such as putting greens and on certain high-maintenance lawns. High-maintenance costs, especially for mowing and disease control, reduce the market potential for bentgrass sod. Production of bentgrass sod should be isolated to avoid contamination of other fields such as Kentucky bluegrass.

In the transition belt between the warm-season and cool-season turfgrasses, a portion of the sod production acreage is devoted to tall fescue or mixtures of tall fescue and Kentucky bluegrass. Tall fescue has comparatively weak sod forming characteristics due to the lack of adequate rhizome development. Therefore, the production period is somewhat longer and the depth of soil cut during harvesting is thicker in order to facilitate moving and handling. The development of an improved tall fescue variety with a reasonable degree of rhizome formation would be an important contribution in terms of desirability for use in commercial sod production.

B. Warm-Season Turfgrasses

St. Augustinegrass, bermudagrass, centipedegrass, zoysiagrass, and bahiagrass are the primary warm season turfgrasses which are utilized for sod production. St. Augustinegrass is the major species used in Florida. Almost all of the production is on organic soil. Bitterblue, Common, and Floratine rank as the preferred varieties of St. Augustinegrass for sod production. Bermudagrass is grown for sod throughout the warm humid region. Tifgreen and Ormond are two of the most commonly grown varieties. Emerald and Meyer are the main zoysiagrass varieties. Centipedegrass sod is grown primarily on sandy peat soils. Bahiagrass sod is grown on sands and established from seed. Varieties normally grown include Pensacola, Argentine, and Paraguay.

V. Establishment

The establishment of a uniform population of grass is essential to efficient sod production. Open areas must be reseeded or harvesting delayed until the sod fills in naturally. Competition from weeds is more serious under these conditions.

Tillage and soil preparation are important factors in good establishment and in the capacity of the land to produce succeeding crops. Any of a number of tillage operations may be used, but in most cases plowing is an initial step. The soil should normally be tilled to a depth of 8 inches or more. Rototilling is sometimes utilized for uniform soil preparation.

For new sod fields or those infested with weedy perennial grasses, special control programs may be necessary. An application of amitrole-T or dalapon followed by summer fallowing with tillage about every 14 days has been used successfully. Fumigation is required on some soils for the control of nematodes where warm season species are to be planted.

Proper nutritional levels can be critical in establishment. Lime and seedbed fertilizer should be applied at rates indicated by soil test and worked into the soil. Careful records should be kept of soil tests for each field or for major areas within fields. Lime should be applied to raise soil pH to 5.5 to 6.0 on organic soils and to 6.0 to 6.5 on mineral soils. The Kentucky bluegrasses prefer the higher pH ranges. Thirty to 60 pounds of nitrogen per acre can be worked into the seedbed. The higher rates of nitrogen are commonly used on mineral soils.

Fertilizer should be worked into the soil and followed by a flotation operation. The latter operation is important in eliminating wheel tracks and other small depressions which might interfere with seeding and harvesting.

Most warm-season turfgrasses, with the exception of bahiagrass, are planted by sprigs or plugs throughout the growing season. Bermudagrass and zoysiagrass are often completely reestablished from plugs or sprigs after each harvest. In general, St. Augustinegrass and centipedegrass are harvested from the same field annually without reestablishment. This is achieved by cutting a 12-inch width of sod and leaving a 2-inch ribbon of sod between each harvested strip. This 2-inch ribbon is then depressed into the organic soil by rolling. Approximately 30,000 square feet of sod may be harvested per acre using this technique.

The original establishment of St. Augustinegrass, bermudagrass, zoysiagrass, and centipedegrass is vegetative. Bermudagrass and zoysiagrass can be established from sprigs or plugs using a special planter. The planting rate is 300 to 400 bushels per acre for bermudagrass and 350 to 450 bushels per acre for zoysiagrass. The other two species are established primarily from 3-inch plugs spaced on 3-foot centers. Approximately 1,000 to 1,500 square feet of sod are required to plant 1 acre by plugging.

Seedings of cool-season turfgrasses should be made when temperature and moisture conditions are adequate for germination. Late-summer seedings are most successful, especially in the northern climates, because of the more favorable soil temperature and moisture conditions. This allows sufficient time for the development of a root system strong enough to withstand the effects of winter desiccation and heaving.

A spring seeding is the second choice, but the young seedlings will be subjected to greater competition from annual weeds and grasses as well as moisture and temperature stresses. Uniform stands are more difficult to achieve during the spring.

Dormant seedings may be used in regions where temperatures stay below freezing for extended periods during the winter. However, the chance of achieving a successful stand is substantially reduced. The seed will germinate in early spring, and some of the disadvantages of spring seedings are overcome. Dormant seedings are more likely to be successful in areas where the land is not subject to spring flooding or serious water and wind erosion.

Solid set irrigation allows successful seeding at almost any time during the growing season except late fall in northern regions. Irrigation is also helpful in preventing blowing of seed or loss of seedlings by wind erosion.

Seeding rates vary with germination and purity of the seed, condition of the seedbed, environmental conditions, and the availability of irrigation. Excessive rates of seeding have been found to give a more rapid initial cover but the rate of sod formation is decreased. Emphasis must be placed on the use of high quality seed free of weed seeds. The seed lot used should be free from annual bluegrass, rough bluegrass, and bentgrass. The preferred per acre seeding rates for Michigan are: (a) 25 to 40 pounds for Kentucky bluegrasses, (b) 60 to 100 pounds for red fescue, and (c) 35 to 60 pounds for a mixture of bluegrass and red fescue.

A uniform seeding is essential. Planting operations will vary with the equipment available. Cultipacker type seeders are the most widely used means of seeding since the seed is placed at a shallow depth and firmed by rolling in a single operation. Adequate contact of the seed with the soil cannot be over emphasized. The seed can also be broadcast, mixed lightly into the soil, and rolled. This requires additional labor and is not practical for large acreages.

It is possible for Kentucky bluegrass sod to re-establish from rhizomes left in the field following harvest. As many as five crops have been removed from a field without tillage and reseeding. However, the rate of establishment of successive crops is sometimes reduced. This procedure has been combined with attempts to seed directly into the soil left in the field.

Irrigation used to supplement natural precipitation can greatly enhance uniform germination and establishment, especially during midsummer. Frequent light rates of water application maintain more favorable surface soil moisture for germination and seedling growth. As much as 0.2 inch of water per day has been used in two applications on spring seedings and 0.4 inch in 4 applications for establishment during the summer in Colorado (Wilkins, 1966).

VI. Maintenance

Following establishment, the primary objective is to encourage sod development, by enhancing root and rhizome or stolon growth. These organs hold the sod intact and permit harvesting and handling (Fig. 4). Management practices which encourage root and rhizome growth of sod do not necessarily coincide with those employed on other turfgrass areas where the quality of the aboveground portion of the plant is of primary concern.

Mowing frequency is influenced by the height of cut and the rate of growth. A mowing frequency of every 2 to 3 days is desirable for Kentucky bluegrass. A 5- to 10-day mowing interval is more common for warm-season turfgrass species. A general rule of thumb is to remove no more than one-third of the leaf area at any time. Sharp,

Figure 4. Good sod handling characteristics are a function of proper root and rhizome development.

properly adjusted equipment should always be used. Seven- to nine-unit, reel-type gang mowers are used almost exclusively. Mowing height will depend on the turfgrass species and stage of growth. A height of 1.2 to 1.7 inches is preferred for the Kentucky bluegrasses and red fescues; 0.5 inch or less for the bentgrasses; 0.7 to 1.2 inches for bermudagrass and zoysiagrass; 1.2 to 2 inches for centipedegrass, and 1.3 to 2.5 for St. Augustinegrass and bahiagrass.

If mowing is delayed during rainy periods, it may be necessary to remove excess clippings. Before harvesting older sods it is sometimes desirable to vertical mow and remove dead plants and clippings.

Assuming that adequate phosphorus and potassium were incorporated into the seedbed, maintenance fertilization usually involves only nitrogen, except for isolated cases where other nutrients are found to be limiting. It is important to have sufficient nitrogen available to the young seedling for vigorous growth and rapid sod formation.

Evaluation of management variables in sod production research must include some measure of the root and rhizome development. A device (Fig. 5) has been developed to determine the weight required to tear a sod piece (Rieke, Beard, and Hansen, 1968).

Satari (1967) used this technique to evaluate the effect of nitrogen applied to Merion Kentucky bluegrass grown on an organic soil, Houghton muck (Table 1). The higher rates of nitrogen, applied monthly, decreased sod strength of 5-month-old sod. Weights of roots and rhizomes in soil plugs taken from these plots were also decreased

Figure 5. Apparatus to measure sod strength by determining weight required to tear a sod piece (Rieke, Beard, and Hansen, 1968).

Table 1. Effect of monthly nitrogen application rates on Merion Kentucky bluegrass grown for sod on Houghton muck (Satari, 1967).

Monthly N application lb/acre)	Root and rhizome wt. g*	Sod strength, October (pounds)	% total available carbohydrates in rhizomes	
			Aug 3	Sep 21
0	110	38	11.5	19.4
15	122	31	10.0	18.0
30	88	19	9.3	16.4
60	85	18	9.0	17.0

* Contained in 13.6 sq. in. plug, September 15.

by increasing nitrogen. A positive correlation was found between sod strength measurements and the weights of roots and rhizomes.

Increasing nitrogen increased the growth rate of the turfgrass and resulted in decreased levels of soluble carbohydrates in the rhizomes on both August 3 and September 21, as illustrated in Table 1.

The influence of soil nitrogen level as affected by climatic factors must be considered, especially on organic soils which contain appreciable nitrogen. Sod strength data for 1967 on the same soil show an increase from 32 pounds to 60 pounds when nitrogen was increased from 0 to 15 pounds per acre per month. Additional monthly increments of nitrogen up to a total of 60 pounds per acre did not significantly change sod strength from the 15-pound treatment. Greater leaching and cooler temperatures resulted in lower available nitrogen in the organic soil in 1967 than in 1965.

The timing of nitrogen application is important in promoting sod development. Kurtz (1967) seeded Merion Kentucky bluegrass on Fox sandy clay loam in May. Nitrogen was applied in July, August, and September. As total applied nitrogen was increased from 0 to 4 pounds per 1,000 square feet, the number of rhizomes and the average length of rhizomes increased significantly. Doubling the rate of nitrogen application in September significantly increased average rhizome length over the regular monthly nitrogen rate. Sod strength was also increased by the higher nitrogen rates applied in September.

Most nitrogen is applied in the spring and fall depending on the time of seeding. Light rates of nitrogen are applied in the summer as needed for maintenance of color or to green-up the grass before harvest. Nitrogen is normally applied at intervals of 4 to 6 weeks, depending on the maintenance program.

Nitrogen use should be based on (a) rate of nitrogen release from the soil, especially in organic soils, (b) requirements of the turfgrass species or variety, (c) soil texture, (d) moisture regime, including irrigation, (e) season of year, and (f) growth rate of the grass, especially as affected by temperature. There is no simple means of measuring nitrogen release from the soil for use in nitrogen recommendations. Consideration must be given to the organic matter content of the soil, soil temperature, and moisture relations that influence the release of nitrogen from soil organic matter by microorganism activity.

Specific fertilizer recommendations for sod production are difficult to make because of variations in soil, climate, and management factors. Grasses having a higher nitrogen requirement for long term turfgrass maintenance also need a higher nitrogen level for sod production.

Nitrogen usage by growers varies considerably but is generally consistent in the Midwest and on the East Coast. Annual rates as high as 250 pounds nitrogen per acre are common for Merion Kentucky bluegrass and bentgrass. Frequently, lesser amounts are applied, depending on growth of the grass and moisture conditions. The higher rates are more common on mineral soils. Common Kentucky bluegrass and red fescue normally receive lower nitrogen rates.

In the South and on the West Coast where the growing season is longer, greater amounts of nitrogen are typical. For example, in Florida, as high as 100 to 200 pounds per acre of nitrogen are used annually on centipedegrass, 200 to 250 pounds on St. Augustinegrass, and 200 to 300 pounds on bermudagrass.

Soluble nitrogen carriers are widely used for sod production because of lower cost and rapid response. The trend is toward light and more frequent applications. Distribution equipment used includes aerial, drill-type, and broadcast-type applicators. Nitrogen may also be applied through the irrigation system if properly designed.

Deficiencies of secondary nutrients and micronutrients in sod are problems only on certain soils. Exceptions are copper and iron on some organic soils in Florida. Iron and manganese may be needed on highly alkaline mineral soils for bentgrass sod. Knowledge of the grass and soil tests should be helpful in predicting possible deficiencies of these nutrients.

Irrigation is essential for sod production in warmer climates and is being more widely utilized in cooler regions. Irrigation supplements natural precipitation, insures more uniform establishment, and enhances the rate of sod formation. Rates and amounts of water applied depend upon soil texture, natural precipitation, potential evapotranspiration, and rate of grass growth. Consideration may be given to water table influences especially on organic soils. Subsurface irrigation is used on some organic soils in Michigan and Florida. Frequent irrigations at low rates are common during the establishment period, but as the sod crop matures less frequent applications are made at heavier rates.

Tensiometers have been used as sensing elements to determine irrigation needs. However, the problem of soil variability and the temporary nature of the turf have limited utilization of these instruments.

Surface leveling by rolling is a common practice and is particularly effective on organic soils. Effects of winter heaving, ruts, and other small depressions can frequently be corrected. It is important to roll in early spring and just after establishment. A sod crop may be rolled three to four times per year. This operation greatly facilitates harvesting operations.

Most broadleaf weeds can be controlled with 2,4-D, silvex, mecoprop, or dicamba. The more difficult to control broadleaf weeds may require repeat applications. Postemergence control of certain annual weedy grasses such as crabgrass, bermudagrass, foxtail, and goosegrass is accomplished with DSMA and MSMA in two applications, 7 to 10 days apart.

Weedy perennial grasses should be eradicated prior to seeding the crop. Quackgrass, bentgrass, nutsedge, and annual bluegrass are the most important perennial weedy grasses in the cool, humid production regions. Torpedograss, vaseygrass, bermudagrass, nutsedge, and pangolagrass are the most serious grassy weeds in warm-season sod production (Burt, 1963). The weed infestation should decline after the first few years of production unless a new source of weeds is introduced. Perennial weedy grasses along drainage ditches must not be permitted to seed.

Root and leaf feeding insects should be controlled. Chinch bugs, sod webworms, and army worms can cause serious injury in the South.

In the past, diseases have not been a problem in sod production of Kentucky bluegrass. *Fusarium* blight, powdery mildew, and *Helminthosporium* leafspot have restricted sod formation of certain varieties. Brown patch is a serious problem on St. Augustinegrass and centipedegrass. Dollar spot and leafspot can be problems on bermudagrass. Specific control measures for the above pests are discusssed in Chapters 10 and 11.

VII. Sod Quality

Sod is ready to harvest as soon as the rhizomes and roots have knitted sufficiently to permit handling the sod pieces without tearing. The time required to produce a marketable crop of Kentucky bluegrass sod varies from 3 months in more favorable climates, particularly in the northern cool, humid region, up to 2 years under less favorable conditions. The time required to produce a red fescue sod is substantially longer than for Kentucky bluegrass. The production time for most warm-season turfgrasses is usually a minimum of 12 months and may require as long as 2 years, particularly for zoysiagrass. In general, bermudagrass and St. Augustinegrass require a shorter production time than zoysiagrass or bahiagrass, with centipedegrass ranking intermediate between these two groups. A bermudagrass sod crop can be produced in 6 to 9 months.

A high quality turf possesses the following characteristics: (a) uniformity; (b) good density; (c) acceptable color; (d) freedom from serious weeds, weed seeds, insects, diseases and nematodes; (e) adequate sod strength for handling; (f) sufficient maturity, in terms of carbohydrate reserves, to root effectively; and (g) a minimum amount of thatch.

In an effort to protect the ultimate consumer, sod certification programs have been initiated in many states (Ousley, 1965). The primary function of certification is to specify the genetic purity and genetic identity of the sod. In addition, assurance of freedom from noxious weeds and insects is sometimes given. Published standards for grades of sod quality have also been developed by some grower associations (Woodhouse, 1965).

VIII. Sod Harvesting and Shipping

The time to harvest sod in northern climates extends from as early in the spring as the equipment can get on the fields until late fall or early winter when the soil freezes. It is desirable for the sod to be moist when cut but excessive moisture should be avoided to reduce shipping costs and facilitate handling. Mechanical cutters which cut the sod into thin layers with widths of 12, 18, or 24 inches are used (Fig. 6). Kentucky bluegrass sod is generally harvested in lengths which give a total area of either a square yard or a yard and one-half per piece. Warm-season grasses are cut in units of 1 x 2 feet.

The thickness of the sod removed is an important factor in the productive life of the sod field as well as in handling and laying. The thickness of cut will vary depending on the turfgrass species, uniform-

Figure 6. Typical sod cutter utilized in sod harvesting.

ity of soil surface, type of soil, density of sod, and degree of rhizome and root development. Rhizome or stolon development is the most critical factor in both sod strength and in the sod rooting capability. It is significant to both grower and consumer that thin-cut sod is easier to handle and roots faster than thick-cut sod (Anonymous, 1925; Hodges, 1958). Sod cut too thick is initially more drought resistant but is slower to root. Sod cut too thin is prone to injury from atmospheric drought.

The poorer the sod strength and density, the thicker the sod must be cut in order to facilitate handling. Bluegrass, bermudagrass, and zoysiagrass sods are usually cut at a depth of 0.5 to 0.8 inch, red fescue at 0.7 to 1 inch, and bentgrass as shallow as 0.3 inch. St. Augustinegrass, bahiagrass, and centipedegrass are cut at 0.8 to 1.3 inches. For best operation the sod cutting knife should be sharp at all times. The frequency of knife replacement will vary with the cutting conditions and type of soil.

The sod strips of bluegrass and fescue are usually folded or rolled for convenience in handling and laying. St. Augustine, centipedegrass, and bahiagrass are usually cut in 1 x 2-foot pieces, and stacked flat on pallets with 500 square feet per pallet. For many years the sod was rolled and loaded manually. Since 1966, a number of different types of mechanical sod rollers have been developed to facilitate the harvesting operation and reduce labor costs (Nutter, 1966). There are three basic types of mechanical sod harvesting operations (Fig.7). One involves the use of a sod cutter followed by an independent unit which mechanically rolls the sod. The second involves a sod cutter followed by a mechanical sod roller which also has a conveyer for loading trucks or pallets. The third involves a unit which cuts, mechanically rolls, and conveys the sod to the truck or to pallets (Anonymous, 1967). After loading the truck, a canvas is frequently placed over the top of the load to reduce drying during shipment.

The amount of soil removed with the sod is a function of the depth of cutting and the frequency of harvest. Rieke, Beard and Lucas (1968) reported that on Houghton muck slightly more soil is removed by sodding than is lost by natural subsidence under a row crop such as onions.

A. Post-Harvest Physiology

Sod is a perishable commodity which can be stored for only a limited time. Heating damage to sod during shipment is a problem to the sod industry, particularly when shipping to distant markets. The time before lethal effects from heating are observed will vary from 12 to 60 hours. Preliminary investigations indicate that the lethal effects occur when temperatures in the Kentucky bluegrass sod stack reach approximately 105 F (J. W. King and J. B. Beard, 1966, unpublished data). A certain amount of injury will sometimes be evident at temperatures as low as 100 F. The killing temperature for warm-season species is probably higher. Bermudagrass heats up the most rapidly of the warm-season turfgrasses.

Factors which contribute to rapid heating of sod include high soil

Figure 7. Two procedures utilized in sod harvesting: conveyer (above) and pallet handling (below).

temperature at the time of harvest, high nitrogen fertility level, excessive irrigation, and the presence of clippings. Another factor involved is disease activity. For example, *Helminthosporium* leafspot disease activity on certain turfgrasses appears to increase sod heating. Observations indicate that sod is most prone to heating during the period when the grass is initiating seed heads.

The higher the soil temperature at the time of harvest the more rapidly lethal temperatures are reached. When the soil temperature factor is of concern, harvesting in early morning would be preferred since the minimum soil temperatures generally occur between 6 and 8 a.m. When sod loads are to be shipped long distances, the use of a ventilation system through the load will assist in alleviating the heating problem. Artificial cooling of a sod load has also been utilized to avoid excessive heating. This practice involves the use of a vacuum cooling process and has proven quite effective (Anonymous, 1964). However, cooling costs result in a substantial increase in the market price of the sod. For this reason, vacuum cooling has not been widely used in the commercial sod production industry.

Acknowledgment

Most of the material included in this chapter is based on work done at Michigan State University. It is published as a contribution from the Michigan Agricultural Experiment Station, East Lansing, as Paper No. 4670.

References

Anonymous. 1925. How thick to cut sod for putting greens. U.S.G.A Green Section Bul. 5(8):172-173.

Anonymous. 1964. Vacuum cooling of sod aids shipping problems. American Nurseryman. 120(6):52-54.

Anonymous. 1965. WTT survey shows sod industry headed for vast expansion, increased sales. Weeds, Trees, and Turf. 4(8):22-25.

Anonymous. 1967. Richlawn's "Turfmaster" eases sod harvesting. Weeds, Trees, and Turf. 6(2):26-28.

Beard, J. B. and P. E. Rieke. 1964. Sod production in Michigan. Michigan State University Extension Mimeo p. 1-7.

Burt, E. O. 1963. Weed control in turf nurseries. Proc. University of Florida Turf-grass Management Conf. 11:141-143.

Hodges, T. K. 1958. Cutting sod for rhizome value. Proc. 1958 Midwest Regional Turf Conf. p. 40-42.

Johanningsmeier, E. D. 1965. Sod production. 6th Illinois Turfgrass Conf. p. 1-4.

Kurtz, K. W. 1967. Effect of nitrogen fertilization on the establishment, density, and strength of Merion Kentucky bluegrass sod grown on a mineral soil. M.S. Thesis. Western Michigan University.

Miller, R. A. 1962. Seed sod study. Illinois Turfgrass Con. Proc. p. 39-45.

Nutter, G. C. 1966. Sod production expands and mechanizes. Turf-Grass Times 1(3):12-19.

Ousley, J. E. 1965. The effects of turfgrass certification in Florida. Golf Course Reporter. 33(2):42-46.

Richards, L. A., editor. 1954. Diagnosis and improvement of saline and alkali soils. USDA Agr. Handbook 60.

Rieke, P. E., J. B. Beard, and R. E. Lucas. 1968. Grass sod production on organic soils in Michigan. Proc. Third Int. Peat Congress. Quebec City, Canada.

Rieke, P. E., J. B. Beard, and C. M. Hansen. 1968. A technique to measure sod strength for us in sod production studies. Agron. Abst. p. 60.

Satari, A. M. 1967. Effects of various rates and combinations of nitrogen, phosphorus, potassium and cutting heights on the development of rhizome, root, total available carbohydrate and foliage composition of *Poa pratensis* L. Merion grown on Houghton muck. Ph.D. Thesis, Michigan State University.

Wilkins, J. Russell. 1966. Sod production. 12th Annual Rocky Mountain Regional Turfgrass Conf. p. 15-17.

Woodhouse, J. 1965. How sod is grown in Canada. Golf Course Reptr. 33(2):48-50.

17 Guide to Seedbed Preparation

H. B. Musser
A. T. Perkins

The Pennsylvania State University
University Park, Pennsylvania

I. Introduction

The production of a good quality permanent turf that can be maintained successfully depends upon sound establishment practices. These include the preparation of complete plans and specifications for the job, and all of the preliminary operations of land clearing, trash removal, provision for drainage and irrigation, and soil modification. Establishment also involves all grading and tillage operations, the correction of soil acidity, fertilizer use, and final seedbed preparation.

"Built in" mistakes at the time an area is being prepared often are directly responsible for failure to maintain a satisfactory turf and may necessitate major expenditures when it is found later that they must be corrected. Good quality turfgrass cannot be maintained on areas where poor drainage, either surface or internal, is a chronic problem, and poor soil conditioning and preparation invariably result in inadequate stands of grasses. These and many other construction errors are the direct causes for much of the poor quality turf that is characteristic of so many turfgrass areas. Many serious mistakes can be avoided if the entire operation is adequately planned before actual construction begins.

II. Initial Planning

Advance planning is essential to provide assurance that there will be timely completion of all operations incidental to seedbed preparation. Optimum seeding times vary in different climatic regions. If best results are to be obtained, construction operations must be so adjusted that their completion will coincide with the best time for seeding in any locality (See Chapter 3). Also it is desirable in order to avoid confusion and unnecessary "backtracking" after actual construction begins, and to ensure that the various operations will progress in a systematic manner. Finally, it can prevent many irritating and often costly delays due to failure to have materials, equipment, and labor available when needed.

A. Drawings and Specifications.

The preparation of a complete set of working drawings is an essential part of the initial planning of any construction operation. These will show the design, dimensions, contours and elevations, grade levels, and location of special structures such as drainage and irrigation systems. Complete drawings are particularly desirable for sports areas such as athletic fields and golf courses, where contours and grades must meet specific requirements. They should be to scale, with contours, elevations, and fixed grade levels plainly marked. Where complete or partial modification of the construction profile above the subgrade is required, a cross section drawing is necessary, showing all features of the profile, including location of drainage and irrigation lines and thickness of all layers of superimposed materials.

The drawings should be accompanied by a complete set of specifications which outline the work to be done, the methods to be followed, and the quality and quantities of all materials to be used (See Chapter 27). A good set of plans and specifications is particularly desirable for turfgrass areas where the construction work is to be contracted. Under all circumstances they provide a useful reference that will help to avoid errors during construction operations. In order to accomplish this objective, however, they must be prepared in sufficient detail to provide complete directives for all phases of the work.

B. Construction Planning.

All phases of actual construction operations should be planned in advance. This will include clearing and the disposal of trash and waste materials. On rolling terrain where cuts and fills will be required to bring the area to fixed grade levels, estimates should be made of the quantity of fill material needed. Where quantities are in excess of estimated amounts available from cutting operations, sources of additional soil should be located. Provision also must be made for preservation of topsoil and for sources of additional material if determination of the on-site quantities that are available show that it will be needed. If modification of the existing soil is required, either because of low quality or because good quality topsoil cannot be obtained, it will be necessary to determine the kind and quantity of modifying materials to be used and to make advance plans to obtain them (See Soil Modification section of this chapter).

The need for drainage and irrigation should be determined and specifications prepared for the design and type of systems to be installed (See Chapter 6).

Most natural soils do not contain sufficient quantities of plant nutrients to ensure normal development of new grass seedlings. Also, soils may require applications of lime to correct acidity. Good initial planning will include determination of the kinds and amounts of lime and fertilizer needed and provision for their timely delivery to the construction site (See Chapter 4).

The choice of a grass or mixture of grasses is an important item of initial planning. Grasses vary in their climatic adaptations and in other important characteristics which may or may not adapt them for use under the conditions to which they will be subjected. Only those types should be considered that have a satisfactory history of performance in the region where the turf is to be grown. The ability to withstand wear and tear and the type of maintenance required for best performance are among the more important characteristics that must be considered (See Chapters 8 & 13).

If the turf is to be established by seeding, the kind and quantity of seed needed should be determined. Sources should be investigated and arrangements made for procurement. This also applies to vegetative planting stock and sod. Both seed and planting stock may vary materially in quality. Advance planning will permit price and quality comparisons and avoid failures because products are not true to type or are received in poor condition.

The amount and type of labor and equipment needed for construction will depend on the size of the job, the degree of finish demanded, and the time limits for completion. A fine lawn will require more intensive treatment than the rough on a golf course. Similarly, areas designed for specialized use, such as athletic fields and golf course greens, must be prepared more carefully than those that will be subjected to less concentrated traffic. Labor is one of the most expensive items. Each construction operation should be carefully studied to determine when and where it may be possible to use mechanical equipment most economically. Thus, it may be possible to use equipment such as the Meeker harrow or a steel mat for final grading and smoothing, rather than hand raking. Costs often can be reduced materially if advance planning includes estimates of labor and equipment requirements.

III. Construction

A. Sequence of Operations.

The most economical and systematic construction results when an orderly sequence of operations is followed. This often eliminates expensive and time consuming "backtracking" and assures completion of each stage of construction operations in logical order. It will avoid unnecessary conflict between one operation and another and may prevent the partial or entire destruction of a completed job to do one that should have been completed earlier. Thus, it is easier and less expensive to install tile drains and water lines before final grading and seedbed preparation. Similarly, if lime and fertilizer are applied prior to final tillage and grading, they can be worked into the soil to the required depth during these operations.

The following outline gives the logical sequence of operations:

1. Clearing and trash removal
2. Location of borrow pits
3. Stockpiling topsoil and rough grading
4. Installation of drainage and irrigation systems
5. Subgrade fitting
6. Placing topsoil

7. Application of lime, basic fertilizer, and soil modifying materials
8. Deep tillage and preliminary smoothing
9. Application of starter fertilizer
10. Final grading and smoothing
11. Seedbed firming, if necessary

On large areas, such as golf courses, cemeteries, and parks, where the work will be done in sections, many construction operations will be carried on concurrently to provide efficient use of labor and equipment. On small areas, such as home lawns, where the work is to be done as a single unit, the above sequence will apply *in toto*.

B. Clearing.

Clearing is the first essential construction operation. It includes the removal of stones (minimum size specified in specifications), trash, and any other material that might interfere with subsequent construction operations or create poor conditions for turfgrass production. It is of particular importance in wooded areas. Clearing woodlands should include the complete removal of all brush, logs, and stumps. If such materials are buried in grading they eventually will decay and leave undesirable depressions that destroy grade uniformity and permit water to pond during rains or irrigation. A common method for disposal of such material is to bulldoze it into piles for burning on the site.

Removal of rock outcrops also is an essential part of clearing operations. When these occur, they should be cut to at least 12 to 15 inches below fixed grade levels. Sufficient soil then can be added to provide for satisfactory grass establishment and maintenance.

B. Borrow Pits.

On rolling terrain or steep slopes it may be necessary to make cuts and fills to bring the area to the desired grade levels. Where sufficient fill material cannot be obtained by cutting down high points above fixed grade levels, the required amounts must be obtained by purchase or by taking it from some other location on the property. Such locations are known as borrow pit areas. Care should be used in their selection to ensure that they do not interfere with the construction or use of the turfgrass area and are not left in an unsightly or hazardous condition after construction has been completed. This also applies to the approaches to them, created in the process of transporting soil to other locations. Provision should be made for grading out and seeding the pit slopes, or for screening them with ornamental plantings.

C. Stockpiling Topsoil.

Topsoil is an extremely variable material. It ranges in quality all the way from practically sterile sand with very low moisture holding capacity and fertility, to tight clays that are poorly drained and highly subject to compaction. It may vary in depth from an inch, or less, to several feet, or more. Where the quality is good enough (See Chapter 4) and a sufficient quantity is present to justify its preservation it should be removed from all areas requiring cuts and fills, from borrow pit sites, building sites, and all areas requiring installation of complete internal drainage structures and soil modification. Stockpiling should be done at locations that will not interfere with other construction operations and will permit its replacement with a minimum of handling.

Topsoil can be handled in various ways. On areas of limited size it can be picked up and stockpiled with a high lift or front end loader. If the soil is so hard that the scoop will not cut it, several passes with a rotovator will loosen it sufficiently to be worked. On larger areas the usual method is to bulldoze it into piles or lift and move it with a soil pan. Extreme care should be used in handling soil with a high silt or clay content. If worked when wet, it will develop lumps and clods. When these dry out they are very difficult to break up and spread uniformly.

D. Rough Grading.

After clearing and stockpiling topsoil, the entire area should be rough graded. This will include cutting down high points and filling depressions to conform to the grade levels specified on the plans. To obtain a grading job free from undesirable pockets and other irregularities, grade stakes should be set at intermediate points between fixed grade levels. Strings are stretched between the stakes and "sighted in" to give the desired slopes. After the height has been marked on the stakes the strings are removed and the soil graded to the marked points on the stakes.

In marking grade levels on stakes in fill sections, the marks should be made at a height above the desired permanent grade to compensate for settling. Allowances will vary with the depth of the fill and character of the soil. An allowance of 1½ to 2 inches per foot of depth should be made for silty or clayey soils in good physical condition. If the fill material is loose and cloddy, the allowance must be increased. Settling will be less for soil with a high sand content. Extreme allowances for settling may be avoided by placing fills in layers of about a foot in depth and rolling after placement of each layer. If this practice is followed, rolling soil with a high silt or clay content must be avoided. This will cause serious compaction that will prevent normal movement of air and water and result in severe drainage problems.

On areas from which the topsoil has been removed, a subgrade should be established at a level below the finished grade that will allow for the depth of topsoil that is to be replaced. All subgrades should conform to specified finished grades and contours. If a coarse drainage layer is to be used under a layer of topsoil, the grade stakes should be marked to show the thickness of both drainage and topsoil layers.

The most desirable grade on any type of turfgrass area is a gentle, uniform slope from the highest point. The slope should be gradual without sharp breaks or pockets. A desirable grade is a fall of ¼ inch per foot, except on athletic fields and other specialized areas where grades must conform to standard requirements (See Chapter 22). In grading lawns around homes and other buildings grade levels should be adjusted to ensure drainage of surface water away from foundations. Terraces and steep slopes should be avoided. They are difficult to maintain and are prone to soil moisture deficiencies due to rapid runoff of water. Fertilizer losses by washing also are excessive. Where it is necessary to drop a slope more than a maximum of 3/4 to 1 inch per foot, terrace construction with retaining walls is recommended wherever possible.

E. Drainage and Irrigation.

The next step in construction operations is the installation of all permanent drainage and irrigation lines. Where internal drainage is required and a permanent irrigation system is to be installed, opening the necessary ditches will interfere less at this time than at any other with subsequent construction operations. See Chapter 6 for complete directions for the design and installation of drainage and irrigation systems.

F. Conditioning the Subgrade.

Operation of equipment during construction and rough grading, especially if the soil is wet, often will create a layer of heavily compacted soil of varying thickness at the surface of the subgrade. Unless broken up, this compacted layer may persist for a long period of time, causing sogginess and poor aeration in the root zone of the grass. The construction program should provide for correction of this condition before the topsoil is put in place. On large areas a disk or springtooth harrow will do an effective job, if compaction is only moderate. Where it is severe, it will be necessary to use rotovating or heavy scarifying equipment (See Chapter 28). For small areas, such as moderate-size lawns, a sturdy garden cultivator or small rotovator can be used effectively.

A second condition which may require correction occurs when an impervious subsoil underlies a relatively shallow layer of topsoil. This may create an even more serious problem than mechanical compaction of the subgrade. It will prevent normal movement of surplus water out of the topsoil, resulting in chronic problems of saturation and poor aeration. In some instances it can be corrected by the use of deep chiseling or mole drain equipment which will open channels for movement of water. In extreme cases it will be necessary to install a complete internal drainage system to provide for adequate movement of water out of the topsoil.

G. Placing Topsoil.

Placement of topsoil can be done in various ways. On small- to medium-size areas it can be placed in uniformly distributed piles and spread with a mechanical scraper or blade, followed by hand finishing to bring it to uniform depth and required grade levels. The use of large soil moving equipment is more efficient on large areas.

The settled depth of a topsoil layer should be at least 6 inches, provided normal slope and subgrade conditions exist. This will require an application of 7 to 8 inches of material. On steep grades and terraces, and where there are underlying rock outcrops, the depth should be increased to 12 to 14 inches to ensure maintenance of adequate moisture and nutrients.

If the topsoil contains stones that will interfere with later soil preparation and seeding operations, they should be removed. On areas of less than 8,000 to 10,000 sq. ft. they can be hand picked. On larger areas the use of a mechanical stone picker after the soil has been spread will do a more complete and efficient job than hand picking. A third method that will remove the stones more completely than either hand or mechanical picking consists of processing soil through a soil shredder prior to spreading. This has the added advantage of breaking up lumps and clods which might interfere with later tillage and seeding operations. Soil shredders are available in a range of sizes that will meet the requirements of any operation. The best equipment of this kind is designed to deliver the processed soil directly onto trucks or distributing machines for placement and spreading. Shredders are equipped with receiving hoppers which permit feeding soil into them with high lifts or front end loaders. Where trucks are used to transport the soil to receiving areas, the common practice is to place it in uniformly spaced piles and spread it by blading. Equipment also is available that transports and spreads in one operation. The success and acceptability of any topsoil operation, both as to uniformity in depth and proper grade levels, depends primarily upon the efficiency of the equipment operator.

H. Soil Modification.

If the topsoil on a construction site is not of satisfactory quality for turfgrass production, and good soil cannot be obtained at a reasonable price, the existing soil material often can be modified to improve its physical condition and adapt it to turfgrass requirements (See Chapter 4). This is standard practice in the construction of golf course putting greens and other installations where optimum physical condition is essential to meet maintenance and use demands (See Chapter 23). Although soil modification is less common on general turfgrass areas, it frequently is a more economical and sounder practice than to purchase poor or mediocre topsoil at a high price.

Modifying materials used on general lawn areas should be spread on the surface following installation of drainage and irrigation lines and preliminary tillage to loosen the soil and prepare it for mixing the materials. The kind and quantity to be used will depend upon the character of the soil to be modified. Domestic peats have been used more extensively than any other material for conditioning sandy soils. They will increase both moisture holding capacity and fertilizer retention. From 1 to 2 cu. yds. should be applied per 1,000 sq. ft. of area under average conditions. Specialized structures, such as golf course greens and tees, normally require larger quantities (See Chapter 23). Other natural organic materials, rotted manures or well rotted sawdust, can be used at the same rates, but both decompose much more rapidly than peat. Several classes of synthetic materials also are available. The calcined clays and processed micas are among the most important of these. Their rate of application will depend on the type of material

Table 1. Volume of soil amendments to add for various treatment depths. (After McNeely and Morgan. Courtesy *Turf-Grass Times.)*

Amendments as % of amended soil	Depth in inches								
	4	5	6	7	8	9	10	11	12
	Cubic yards								
5	0.61	0.77	0.93	1.08	1.23	1.39	1.55	1.71	1.86
10	1.23	1.54	1.85	2.16	2.47	2.78	3.09	3.40	3.71
15	1.85	2.32	2.78	3.24	3.70	4.17	4.63	5.09	5.55
20	2.47	3.09	3.71	4.32	4.94	5.55	6.17	6.79	7.40
25	3.08	3.86	4.63	5.40	6.17	6.95	7.72	8.49	9.27
30	3.70	4.64	5.56	6.48	7.41	8.33	9.26	11.18	12.10
35	4.32	5.40	6.48	7.57	8.64	9.72	10.80	11.87	12.95
40	4.94	6.18	7.41	8.64	9.88	11.13	12.34	13.61	14.81
45	5.55	6.95	8.33	9.72	11.10	12.52	13.88	15.17	16.67
50	6.17	7.72	9.26	10.80	12.34	13.88	15.42	16.96	18.50
55	6.78	8.49	10.19	11.88	13.58	15.28	16.98	18.67	20.37
60	7.41	9.26	11.11	12.86	14.81	16.67	18.52	20.37	22.22
70	8.64	10.80	12.96	15.11	17.28	19.44	21.60	23.77	25.92
80	9.88	12.35	14.81	17.28	19.76	22.22	24.69	27.16	29.63

used and the degree of modification required. Table 1 gives the volumes of amendments needed for various treatment depths to provide different modification percentages.

The inability of most native soils, under certain turfgrass situations, to withstand the use demands placed on them often necessitates modification of these soils. Most commonly, these are heavy, fine-textured soils that are subject to compaction and require the addition of sand, organic matter, or other modifying materials, to minimize this effect. The principle involved in such additions is to substitute sand or other coarse aggregates for part of the fine-textured particles of the soil. The use of sand for this purpose is a sound practice, but the user should be familiar with the variable nature of sand and the different effects this variability can cause. Also, the quantity needed to achieve the desired result varies, but a minimum value does exist. Soil modification research has shown that sand with a narrow range in particle size is best suited for providing long term relief from compaction (See Chapters 4 & 23). Research also has established guidelines for determination of the proper quantity of sand to use. In general, as the silt and clay content of a soil increases, the amount of sand required increases. In studies of Houston black clay, Kunze (1956, "The effects of compaction of different golf green soil mixtures on plant growth"—Unpublished M.S. Thesis, Texas A & M Univ.) found that a sand of uniform size, 0.5 to 1.0 mm. in diameter, was most desirable for plant growth and that 80% sand of this character was needed. In contrast, the Hagerstown silt loam used by Shoop (1967) required only 50% sand to produce desirable physical conditions. Shoop also found that as the fineness increased the amount of sand increased. A mixture containing 40% of the well graded coarse sand gave the same results as one containing 60% mortar sand which is finer in texture. Conversely, a very sandy soil, such as the Arredondo loamy fine sand used by Smalley (1962) did not benefit by adding more sand, but required additions of materials to increase the water holding capacity.

Due to the great variability in soil conditions and types, blanket recommendations for the proper ratio of sand, soil, and organic materials for soil modification are of doubtful value. If modification is to be done, care should be exercised to avoid complications resulting from the use of insufficient quantities of coarse-textured materials. The evidence indicates that soils containing high proportions of silt and clay should be amended with a minimum of 1½ to 2 cu. yds. of peat and 10 tons (cu. yds.) of sand per 1,000 sq. ft. Larger quantities of sand will be required as the silt-clay content of a soil passes into the clay sector of the textural classification. Also, synthetic materials, such as calcined clays, expanded shales, and blast furnace slag, can be substituted for sand on a 1:1 basis.

I. Mixing Operations.

Mixing modifying materials with the soil can be done either on- or off-site. When mixed on-site they should be worked into the soil to a minimum depth of 5 to 6 inches. The best procedure is to spread them uniformly on the surface of the loosened soil and work them in by repeated harrowing, disking, or rotovating. If both sand and peat are used, the peat should be applied first and the sand spread on top of it. The heavier sand will help to work in the lighter peat more uniformly. A convenient formula for determining the quantities to be used is: Volume of finished mix (area × depth) × required percent of modifying materials = required quantity (volume).

If the topsoil is to be modified before spreading, the mixing can be done by processing it through a soil shredder with the modifying materials. The operation consists in first determining the required number of shovel or scoop loads of each material that will be needed to provide the desired ratio of topsoil, sand, and peat. The calculation of quantities needed is based on the desired proportions of each material in the finished product. Thus, if a 6-inch layer of modified soil, containing 1 part peat (10%), 4 parts sand (40%), and 5 parts topsoil (50%)- is to be used, one shovel or scoop of peat would be put into the shredder for every 4 of sand and 5 of topsoil. The 6 inch layer would require 500 cu. ft. of the mix per 1,000 sq. ft. of area (1,000 sq. ft. × ½ ft.), or 50 cu. ft. of peat, 200 cu. ft. of sand, and 250 cu. ft. of topsoil. Quantities for any other ratio of materials may be calculated in the same way. If the topsoil that is to be used contains any appreciable quantity of stones, it should be processed through the shredder to remove them before the mixing operation. Otherwise, the ratio of modifying materials to topsoil will be narrowed because of the volume of stones removed in the mixing operation.

Actual off-site mixing operations may vary widely depending on the need of the individual construction job. Where only limited quantities of modified soil are needed, the usual practice is to hand feed the required proportions of each ingredient into the mixing machine and follow with several turnings of the processed pile with a front end loader or power scoop. Various mixing methods have been devised where large total quantities are needed. One of the most efficient of these is a continuous process operation in which the various ingredients are delivered into a three-compartment hopper blender. The desired proportions of each are fed onto a conveyor belt through adjustable gates at the bottom of each compartment of the hopper and delivered into the mixing machine. No further turning or handling is required and the mixture can either be stockpiled for later use or discharged directly into trucks for transport to the site.[1]

Off-site mixing ensures a more complete and uniform mixture to the full depth of the modified layer of soil than normally can be obtained by on-site mixing. In the latter operation lighter materials tend to float and it becomes very difficult to work them in uniformly to the desired depth. Pockets of high or low concentration often develop that may create serious maintenance problems.

J. Application of Lime and Basic Fertilizer.

The basic principles which govern the use of lime and fertilizer for turfgrass production, and determination of the kind, quantity, and quality that should be applied are presented in Chapters 4 and 5. Lime and basic fertilizer materials (phosphates, potash, and trace elements) are most effective when worked deeply into the soil. The most practical and efficient method of doing this is to spread required quantities of each on the surface, along with any modifying materials that are to be used, and work in everything in a single tillage operation. Effective incorporation can be obtained by thorough disking, harrowing, or rotovating.

In making lime applications, the full amount needed for acidity correction, as shown by soil tests, should be used. A cyclone type spreader is more satisfactory for distribution than a hopper type (See Chapter 28). The finely pulverized lime packs in the hopper of the latter and often will not feed through the bottom openings uniformly. Practically all lime suppliers are equipped to do custom spreading. Where applications are to be made on large areas, it often is very convenient and economical to include them in the contract price.

The term basic fertilizer applies to those plant nutrients that should be worked deeply into the soil, as distinguished from fertilizers that are used more efficiently and economically as surface dressings and worked in very lightly. Basic fertilizers usually do not include nitrogenous materials. There is a relatively rapid release of all or a part of the nitrogen and substantial quantities may be lost by leaching before deeply placed nitrogen can be utilized by young seedlings.

In making lime and fertilizer applications, it is essential that distributing equipment be properly set (calibrated) to deliver the correct quantity per unit of area. Different brands and mixtures flow through spreaders at different rates. For accurate application, the spreader should be reset every time a different brand or grade is used.

K. Starter Fertilizer.

The starter fertilizer is applied as part of final seedbed preparation just prior to seeding. It should be material carrying a liberal quantity of nitrogen to ensure an adequate supply of this nutrient in the shallow root zone of developing seedlings. It can be a complete fertilizer with a

[1] A detailed description of this method is given in Turf-Grass Times, Vol. 1 No. 6, July-Aug. 1966. "Soil Mixing operations" H. B. Musser.

high nitrogen content or a material furnishing nitrogen only. The former is preferred when any appreciable time intervenes between preliminary seedbed fitting and final preparation and seeding. This helps to ensure that there will be an adequate supply of available nutrients in the shallow root zone of new seedlings.

If nitrogen in the starter fertilizer is in a soluble form, the quantity applied should be adjusted to supply a maximum of 1 to 1½ pounds of actual nitrogen per 1,000 sq. ft. This would require 10 to 15 pounds of a 10-5-5 complete fertilizer or 5 to 7½ pounds of ammonium sulfate (20% nitrogen). A total of 4 to 5 pounds of actual nitrogen can be used when only slowly soluble nitrogen sources are applied. One advantage in using the latter form is that slowly soluble and delayed release sources lengthen the interval between nitrogen applications. When only a soluble nitrogen source is used as a starter on a fall seeding, a second application usually will be required within a 2- to 3-week period. This may create problems because of the difficulty of operating distributing equipment on soft seedbeds and the danger of burning the new seedlings. Repeated applications at such a short interval are not necessary when slowly soluble forms are used at recommended rates. Fall seedings will not require further treatment until the following spring. Similar guidelines apply to spring seedings and vegetative plantings. Repeated applications of soluble nitrogen will be required in approximately 2 weeks after seedling emergence. They will not be necessary for 6 to 8 weeks after seedling emergence when slowly soluble forms are used.

L. Final Grading.

Final grading serves to work the starter fertilizer into the surface soil to the required depth and to smooth and condition it for seeding. Before final grading begins, all grade stakes that have been removed or misalined should be reset and the grade levels marked on them. As for rough grading, it may be necessary to again stretch strings between the fixed grade levels and set stakes at intermediate points to ensure smooth, uniform slopes. Hand raking is the usual practice in grading small areas of 10,000 sq. ft. or less. Grading and fitting tools, such as soil blades, the Meeker harrow, wire mats, and plank drags can be used on larger areas.

Applications of starter fertilizer and final grading should be delayed until just prior to seeding. If these are completed too long in advance of seeding and rains occur in the interim, the surface of the fitted soil may crust and extra tillage will be required to recondition it. Also, the longer the interval between final seedbed preparation and seeding, the greater will be the chances of nutrient losses by leaching.

It is essential that final grading include provision for adequate firming of the seedbed if it is in a loose, open condition following grading operations. On large areas the use of heavy seeding equipment, such as the cultipacker seeder, often will provide sufficient firming unless the soil is extremely light and open. Under the latter conditions, rolling prior to seeding is good practice. On small areas, where light seeding equipment is used, firming may be inadequate, especially where the seedbed has been prepared with a rototiller or similar tool that leaves the soil loose and open, and there has been little rain to settle it prior to seeding. In such instances, rolling is essential to prevent excessive drying out during the period of seed germination.

Literature Cited

Harper, J. C. II. 1968. Athletic fields: specification outline, construction, and maintenance. Pennsylvania State University, Bul. U. Ed. 7-750.

Musser, H. B. 1962. Turf management, Chapter 6. McGraw-Hill Co., Inc. New York.

Shoop, G. J. 1967. The effects of various coarse textured materials and peat on the physical properties of Hagerstown soil for turfgrass production. Ph.D. Thesis, The Pennsylvania State University.

Smalley, R. R., W. L. Pritchett, and L. C. Hammond. 1962. Effects of four amendments on soil physical properties and on yield and quality. Agron. J. 54: 393-395.

Supplemental Readings

Cornman, J. F. 1965. Home lawns. Cornell Univ. Ext. Bul. 922.

Ferguson, M. H. 1953. Be sure your new seeding produces turf. U.S.G.A. J. Vol. VI, No. 5: 30-31.

Ferguson, M. H. 1965. After five years: the Green Section specifications for a putting green. U.S.G.A. Green Section Record 3, No. 4.

Holmes, J. L. 1967. Putting green construction. U.S.G.A. Green Section Record. 4, No. 6. p. 13.

Keen, R. A., and L. R. Quinlan. 1966. Lawns in Kansas. Kansas Agr. Exp. Sta. Cir. 327.

McNeeley, W. H., and W. C. Morgan. 1968. Review of soil amendments. Classification and development. Turf-Grass Times 3: No. 23, p 2.

Musser, H. B. 1966. Soil mixing operations. Turf-Grass Times 1, No. 6. p 6.

Musser, H. B., J. M. Duich, and J. C. Harper II. 1965. Guide for preparation of specifications for golf course construction. Special Bul. Agr. Ext. Serv. The Pennsylvania State Univ.

Musser, H. B., J. M. Duich, and J. C. Harper II. 1967. Turfgrass guide. Pennsylvania State Univ., Bul. U. Ed. 6-330.

Ohio State University. 1966. Your lawn. Coop. Ext. Serv. Bul. 271.

Pennsylvania Highway Dept. 1968. Specifications, roadside development. Sect. 800.0-804.3.

Pope, T. E., and P. Gray. 1966. Establishing and maintaining turf on Kentucky athletic fields, school grounds, and other recreational areas. University of Kentucky, Coop. Extn. Serv. Bul. 609.

Schmidt, R. D., J. F. Shoulders, R. E. Blaser, and A. S. Beecher. 1965. Turfgrass guide for lawns and other turf areas. Virginia Polytechnic Inst. Agr. Ext. Serv. Cir. 818.

Skogley, C. R. 1962. Building a new lawn. Univ. of Rhode Island Ext. Serv. Bul. 183.

Tate, H. F., and S. Fazio. 1965. Lawns for Arizona. University of Arizona., Coop. Ext. Serv. Bul. A-6.

Underwood, J. K. 1964. Tennessee lawns. Univ. of Tennessee, Agr. Ext. Serv. Publ. 326.

Univ. of Minnesota. The home lawn. 1967. Agri. Ext. Serv. Ext. Folder. 165.

U.S. Golf Assoc., Gr. Sect. 1960. Specifications for a method of putting green construction. U.S.G.A. J. and Turf Mgt. 13: No. 5, p 27.

18 Guide to Planting

H. B. Musser
A. T. Perkins

The Pennsylvania State University
University Park, Pennsylvania

I. Introduction

There are three methods of planting that can be used for the establishment of turfgrasses. These are seeding, vegetative planting, and sodding. The success of any planting operation not only depends upon the thoroughness of seedbed preparation, as outlined in Chapter 17, it also will be affected by the many factors relating to the quality, characteristics, and accepted planting methods for individual species and varieties. Perfect seedbed preparation is of little consequence if seed placement is too deep or if vegetative planting stock is in such poor condition that it cannot recover from the shock of handling. A thorough understanding of these and many other related items is essential to the production of good initial stands of grass.

II. Seeding

A. Seed Quality.

Purity, viability (germination), and trueness to type are the principal factors affecting seed quality. Purity refers to the actual percentage of pure seed of a species, variety, or specific mixture that is present in any particular lot of seed. It will be reduced by the amount of foreign material (chaff, stems, etc.), weed seed, and seed of other crops that are present. Viability is the percent of the seed that is alive and will germinate when subjected to standard laboratory tests. Trueness to type refers to the total amount of seed that is true seed of the species, variety, or mixture designated. Federal and most state seed laws require the labeling of each package to show the percentages of each species or variety present, the germination with the date of testing, and the percentages of foreign material, weed seed, and other crop seed. The label also may be required to show any noxious weeds present. The requirements for container labeling are designed to protect the consumer. Labels should be examined carefully before purchase to determine whether the seed conforms to standards of purity, viability, and other quality factors, as outlined in the following discussion.

B. Purity.

Standards of purity have been established for seed of most species and varieties of grasses. Table 1 gives acceptable purity percentages for a number of these. It will be noted that purity of the various grasses varies within wide limits; ranging from a minimum of 40% to a maximum of 98%. Individual seed characteristics are partially responsible for the wide differences. It is much easier to clean and process some kinds of seed than others. Also, the purity of any lot may be related to the method of production. Usually, the cleanest seed is produced when fields are row planted (See Chapter 15).

Table 1. Quality characteristics of good seed of turfgrasses.

Grass	Minimum purity, %	Minimum germination, %	Approx. no. seeds/lb
Bahiagrass	75	80	160,000
Bermudagrass	98	85	1,750,000
Buffalograss	85	50	(Burs) 36,500
Canada bluegrass	95	85	2,250,000
Carpetgrass	90	90	1,125,000
Chewings fescue	95	85	600,000
Colonial bentgrass (all varieties)	98	85	7-8,000,000
Creeping bentgrass (all varieties)	98	85	6-7,000,000
Crested wheatgrass	90	85	325,000
Dallisgrass	75	60	160,000
Gramagrasses	40	75	5-800,000
Indian ricegrass	90	85	140,000
Kentucky bluegrass	85	75	2,250,000
Kentucky bluegrass (Merion)	90	75	2,250,000
Kentucky bluegrass (other varieties)	95	75	2,250,000
Little bluestem	40	60	260,000
Orchardgrass	95	85	750,000
Red fescue (U.S. grown) (all varieties)	98	85	600,000
Red fescue (Canadian grown)	97	85	600,000
Red fescue (Denmark grown)	95	85	600,000
Redtop	92	85	5,750,000
Rhodesgrass	90	75	2,000,000
Rough bluegrass	90	80	2,500,000
Tall fescue (all varieties)	98	85	500,000
Velvet bentgrass	90	90	8,000,000
Weeping lovegrass	95	85	1,500,000
Western wheatgrass	85	80	125,000

Compilation from Turf Management (Musser, 1962) and Standard Seed Specifications (Atlantic Seedsmen's Association, 1966).

Weed seed content is an important item affecting seed quality. At first glance, 1 or 2% of weed seed per pound may not appear to be too objectionable. Actually, this may mean the seeding of 10 to 50 or more weed seeds per square foot, depending upon the rate of seeding. It is particularly serious if most of the weeds are of noxious species. Noxious weeds are defined as those species that are most difficult to eradicate and are most likely to compete seriously with the grass. Federal and most state seed laws list noxious weeds by name and specify the permissible maximum content in any lot of seed offered for sale.

The quality of any lot of seed is reduced by the percentage of foreign or inert material it contains. This includes hulls, pieces of stems, soil particles, or any other material not removed in the cleaning process. Foreign material content will vary widely depending upon the kind of seed and the degree of cleaning. When it is present in excessive quantities it should be considered in conjunction with other quality factors in determining the comparative value of competing seed lots. Also, high quantities are an indication of the degree of care exercised in cleaning the seed and preparing it for marketing.

Seed laws require that the container label show the percentages of other crop seed present. This refers to cereal grains and any species of grasses other than those specifically listed on the label. The presence of any appreciable quantity of crop seed is undesirable because it often germinates and seriously competes with the young grass of the species or variety seeded. High quantities in a seed lot indicate poor production and seed processing methods, or they may be the result of deliberate mixing. They will materially reduce stands of desired grass and may cause serious maintenance and eradication problems in established turf.

C. Viability.

The quality of any given lot of seed will depend upon the percentages of live seed of the particular species or varieties it contains. Viability is determined by standard laboratory tests approved by the Association of Official Seed Analysts.

Different species and varieties of grasses will vary materially in the normal percentages of viable seed which they may be expected to contain. This variation is due to such variables as unfavorable growing conditions, time of harvesting, improper processing, unsatisfactory seed storage, and to the blending of seed lots differing in average percent germination. Substantial quantities of light, poorly developed seed may or may not be removed in the cleaning process. Table 1 shows the germination percentages that should be expected for good quality seed of the various grasses.

D. Trueness to Type.

Varietal purity becomes a very important quality factor when specifying seed of a given variety. The best assurance of protection against the possibility of getting a high proportion of off-types in an improved variety is to purchase only certified seed. The value of certification rests on the difficulty or impossibility of distinguishing many improved varieties on the basis of seed characteristics. Seed certification programs regulate the methods under which seed of improved varieties may be produced and provide for inspection of producing fields and harvested seed (See Chapter 15 for a discussion of seed certification). Purchasers of certified seed should retain the certification tags until the character of the turf produced provides assurance that the seed conformed to certification standards.

E. Seeding Operations.

Successful turfgrass establishment by seeding depends upon seeding at the correct time, using the correct quantity of seed per unit of area, and proper distribution, covering, and soil firming. Unsatisfactory stands often are the direct result of failure to meet all of these essential requirements in the seeding operation.

1. Time of Seeding.

Grasses are classed as warm-season or cool-season, based upon their temperature tolerance (See Chapters 8 & 13). The optimum time for seeding warm-season grasses is late spring or early summer. This provides the longest possible period for establishment before temperatures drop to critical levels. Conversely, cool-season grasses, most of which are highly tolerant to low temperatures, should be seeded in early fall or early spring. Best establishment with these species is obtained under cool growing conditions.

Late summer or fall seedings of warm-season grasses are seldom successful, except in the Deep South where temperatures normally do not fall below freezing for any appreciable time. Under average conditions seedings should not be made later than early July for most warm-season grasses. The closer the seeding time of cool-season grasses approaches hot weather, the greater the chances of poor establishment or complete failure. Late spring seedings are subject to damage from high temperatures and drought and may suffer from excessive weed competition. Under average conditions, fall seedings should not be made later than mid-October and spring seedings not later than the third week in May in cooler sections of the northern U. S. It should be recognized that the above date limitations are not absolute. Temperatures vary in different regions from season to season, for different elevations, or other causes. The dates serve to indicate the most desirable times under average conditions and provide a basis for determining the chances for successful establishment if it is necessary to make seedings at other than optimum times.

"Dormant seedings" of cool-season grasses sometimes are used where construction and seedbed preparation have not been completed until late fall. They are most successful when winter temperatures remain low enough to inhibit germination. Germinating seed is very susceptible to injury by freezing. Poor establishment from dormant seedings may result when temperatures rise to the germinating range of the species planted and these higher temperatures persist for any appreciable period. In making dormant seedings, the safest method is to seed on frozen ground and apply a straw or other protective mulch cover to reduce thawing. This not only eliminates or at least minimizes the chances for germination during mild periods, but also provides protection against losses of seed by washing or blowing (See section on Mulching).

2. Seeding Rate.

Seed quality will affect the seeding rate of grasses. Obviously, low percentages of purity and germination will reduce the number of viable seeds in any lot and require heavier rates to compensate for the reduction. Seeding rates also will vary among species because of differences in the size and weight of seeds. Table 1 gives the approximate number of seeds per pound for several turfgrass species.

Recommended rates for standard quality seed of the different species are given in Table 2. These rates are based first on the determination of the actual number of plants required per unit of area to ensure establishment of a good cover that will permit seedling grass to compete successfully with weeds. One to two thousand plants per square foot will be needed to meet these requirements (Unpublished data, Pa. Agr. Exp. Station).

Table 2. Standard seeding rates for good quality seed of turfgrasses.

Grass	Seeding rate, lb/1,000 sq. ft.	Grass	Seeding rate, lb/1,000 sq. ft.
Bahiagrass	4 - 8	Ryegrasses	5 - 6†
Bermudagrass (hulled)	2	Ky. bluegrass(all varieties)	2 - 3
Bermudagrass (unhulled)	4 - 8	Little bluestem	$\frac{1}{4}$ - $\frac{1}{2}$
Buffalograss (burs)	1 - $1\frac{1}{2}$	Orchardgrass	2 - 3
Canada bluegrass	2 - 4*	Redtop	1 - 2‡
Carpetgrass	2	Rough bluegrass	[illegible] - 4
Red & chewings fescue	3 - 5	Sheep fescue (hard fescue)	2 - 3
Colonial bentgrass	1 - 2	Smooth brome	1 - 2
Creeping bentgrass	1 - $1\frac{1}{2}$	Tall fescue	4 - 8
Crested wheatgrass	$\frac{1}{2}$ - 1	Timothy	$\frac{1}{2}$ - 1
Dallisgrass	2 - 4	Velvet bentgrass	$1\frac{1}{2}$
Gramagrasses	3/4 - $1\frac{1}{2}$†	Weeping lovegrass	$\frac{1}{4}$ - $\frac{1}{2}$

* Seldom seeded alone, 10 to 25% in mixtures seeded at 2 to 4 lb. † Seldom seeded alone, except improved varieties, 25% in mixture seeded at 4 to 5 lb. ‡ Seldom seeded alone, 5 to 10% in mixtures seeded at 1 to 4 lb.

The second step in determining seeding rate for any given lot of seed is to calculate the actual reduction in the number of pure live seed per unit of weight due to less than 100% purity and germination. Thus, if 1 pound of pure red fescue seed contains 600,000 seeds (See Table 1) and the package label shows 98% purity and 85% germination, the actual number of good seed per pound would be approximately 500,000 seeds. If 1,000 plants per square foot are required to ensure a good stand, 1 pound of this seed should be sufficient to plant 500 sq. ft. of area. From a practical standpoint, a further reduction must be made to compensate for expected mortality in viable seed after it is planted. Mortality rates vary with seed size, condition of the seedbed, and the initial quality of the seed. Small seeds may be buried so deeply in the seeding operation that seed reserves are exhausted and the seedlings die before emergence. Seedling losses can be very heavy on loose seedbeds because of uneven planting depth and rapid drying in the surface zone. Finally, seed lots that show low germination in laboratory tests often show abnormally high mortality in the field. Low germination indicates that the seed has been weakened. Although sprouting may occur under the ideal conditions of a laboratory test, many seeds will be of such low vitality that they cannot grow and develop under more rigorous field conditions (See Chapter 7). Mortality rates will often vary between 25 and 50%, depending upon environmental conditions.

Seeding rates of mixtures are based, primarily, upon the percentages of the various ingredients they contain. The actual number of seeds of each species in the mixture will depend upon the percent of seed of each grass present, as shown on the label, and should be adjusted as previously outlined, to the percentages of purity and germination. Further deductions are made to reflect the estimated mortality in each species, to show the number of seeds per pound in the mixture which can be expected to produce plants. Seeding rate is based on the number of plants required per unit of area (See calculation steps in Table 3).

Table 3. Seeding rate calculation for a seed mixture that will produce a 50-50 stand of Kentucky bluegrass and red fescue at the ideal seedling population of 1,200,000/1,000 sq. ft.*

	Known values		Seed label		Calculations				
	Mortality rate, %*	Seeds /lb	% purity	% germ.	% live seed†	% field survival‡	Seedlings expected§	Lb seed needed¶	% in mix
Bluegrass	50	2,250,000	90	80	72	36	810,000	0.75	30
Red fescue	30	600,000	95	90	85.5	60	360,000	1.75	70
Total							1,170,000	2.50	100

* Unpublished data, The Pennsylvania Agr. Exp. Sta. † % purity × germination. ‡ % live seed × (100 - mortality). § Per pound of seed = seeds per pound × % field survival. ¶ 0.50 × total population ÷ seedlings expected per lb.

Adjustment in seeding rates to the various proportions of ingredients in a mixture will not in itself provide assurance of a satisfactory turf. An almost endless variety of mixtures are commercially available. These vary widely in the percentages of desirable grasses. Some mixtures are prepared for definite purposes, as for shade or use on specialized areas such as athletic fields. However, others are put together purely on a price basis, usually for competitive purposes. Most state seed laws require that the percentages of ingredients in a mixture be stated on the label. It is essential that labels be examined carefully, particularly for low-priced products. If a mixture that contains less than 60 to 70% of desirable permanent species is selected, results may be very disappointing. Mixtures should be avoided that contain over 25% of temporary species, such as common ryegrass. In addition, relatively small quantities of coarse grasses like timothy and orchardgrass are very objectionable. These coarse species develop more rapidly than most good permanent grasses. All of them have a dense bunch type habit of growth. When present in any appreciable quantity, they not only compete seriously with desirable turfgrasses, but also produce a coarse, bunchy turf that is uneven in appearance and difficult to maintain.

3. Seeding Methods and Equipment.

Any seeding method which distributes the seed uniformly and provides for adequate covering and firming the soil is satisfactory. A standard practice that will ensure the greatest possible uniformity is to divide the total quantity of seed to be used on an area into two equal parts. Seedings are then made in two directions, at right angles to each other. This necessitates adjustment of equipment to deliver half of the total quantity that is to be used.

There are three general classes of mechanical seeding equipment—the grass seed drill, the hopper type distributor, and the broadcast seeder. Both hopper and broadcast types are built in small sizes adapted for use on small areas.

Grass seed drills are designed to distribute the seed, cover it, and firm the soil in a single operation. They are the least desirable type of seeder for turfgrasses since they deposit the seed in drill rows that are from 6 to 8 inches apart. Under stress of unfavorable weather conditions the grass in the rows may not close in and produce a solid cover for several months. Also, it is difficult to adjust them so that the seed will not be planted too deeply in light soil. They may be equipped with fertilizer attachments so that the seed and starter fertilizer can be applied in one operation.

Hopper distributors are of two types. The simple and less expensive type broadcasts the seed onto the seedbed. These seeders usually are equipped with an agitator inside the hopper which forces seed through adjustable size openings in the bottom. All of the small hopper type seeders designed for use on small areas are in this class. The second type of hopper seeder is designed to broadcast the seed, cover, and firm the soil in a single operation. Most of them also are equipped with fertilizer attachments that apply the fertilizer along with the seed. They are similar to grass seed drills except that they can be set for shallow seeding more easily, and they broadcast the seed instead of planting it in rows. The larger sizes are from 6 to 10 feet wide and are excellent for seeding large areas. These seeders are relatively heavy and so constructed that they will firm the soil both before and after the seed is deposited. Some are equipped with special attachments that help to assure uniform covering and smoothing of the soil surface. Most of them also have attachments that apply the fertilizer with the seed.

Broadcast seeders distribute the seed by throwing it out onto the surface of the seedbed in a circular pattern by means of a gravity impeller that rotates parallel to the surface. They are the fastest type of seed distributing equipment in that they will cover a swath 6 to 20 or more feet in width, depending upon their size. Since they deposit the seed on the surface they must be followed by some method of covering and soil firming. An added disadvantage is the difficulty in obtaining uniform seed distribution when mixtures contain seed that differs materially in size and weight. The larger, heavier seeds will be thrown farther than the light, chaffy types, and the turf may show alternate strips of the grasses used in the mixture.

4. Calibration.

Regardless of the type of seeder used, it is essential that the equipment be properly set (calibrated) to deliver the desired seeding rate for the specific species or mixture used. A simple method of calibrating a hopper type seeder is to spread a strip of building paper on the ground, fill the hopper, set for the desired rate, and operate the machine for a measured distance. The weight of the seed discharged on the paper will be the amount actually applied to the calculated area (distance traveled times width of the spreader). The quantity that would be applied per 1,000 sq. ft. can be calculated from this figure, and proper adjustment in setting made for a higher or lower delivery rate. Some hopper distributors come equipped with shallow trays that can be suspended below the hopper to catch the seed as it is discharged. A variation of this method of calibration is to place a measured quantity of seed in the hopper and operate the seeder until all of it is discharged. The linear distance covered times width of the hopper will be the area covered by the measured quantity of seed. The rate of seeding is calculated from this, and necessary adjustments are made in settings to obtain the desired rate.

Calibration of broadcast seeders is somewhat more difficult. The simplest method is to place a measured quantity of seed in the spreader and measure the area covered when operated at a constant speed. When this has been determined, repeated adjustments are made until the desired rate is reached. Calibration of broadcast seeders is less accurate than for hopper types because of the greater difficulty in determining accurately the exact size of the area covered by the former.

5. Covering and Firming.

Seed must be covered to ensure maximum germination and emergence. The most important consideration is that they are not buried so deeply that their reserve nutrients will be exhausted before the seedling plant can emerge and form a root system. Proper covering will also prevent injury to the germinating seed due to drying. Depth of planting will vary with seed size. Small seeded species should not be covered to a depth exceeding 1/4 inch. Acceptable depths for large seed types are within the range from 1/2 to 3/4 inch. Mechanical seeders equipped with covering attachments have adjustments that can be set for varying planting depths.

Seed deposited on the surface by hand seeding or by simple broadcast seeders which do not have covering and firming devices can be covered with various kinds of equipment. Very light hand raking is used on areas of limited size. On larger areas covering can be done satisfactorily with shallow-set spike tooth harrows, chain and Meeker harrows, weeders, steel mats, or plank and brush drags. The best germination is obtained when the soil is firmed following covering so that the soil particles will make close contact with the seed. Moisture is absorbed more readily by the seed, and large soil pores that are responsible for rapid drying out are reduced. Firming by rolling is the standard practice where equipment is used that does not cover and firm. There is no necessity for using heavy rolling equipment to obtain satisfactory firming. A 250-lb. water ballast roller, either empty or partially filled depending upon soil conditions, or a standard farm type cultipacker should be sufficient to provide the necessary firming. A single roller normally is satisfactory for small areas. They can be used in gangs of three or more to speed up operations on large areas.

Any method of firming, whether by rolling or the use of multipurpose equipment, must be adjusted to the character and condition of the seedbed soil. Soils with a high silt-clay content cannot be rolled when they are wet, or even noticeably moist, without danger of developing serious surface compaction. Compaction danger is reduced materially where soils have a high organic matter content or high percentages of coarse sand.

6. Seeding in Regions of Limited Rainfall.

Special seeding methods must be used in regions of limited rainfall where supplemental irrigation is not available. Under these conditions dryland grasses, such as crested and western wheatgrasses, buffalograss, and the gramagrasses are used. Where trashy seedbed preparation has been practiced (the working in of liberal quantities of organic residues from previous crops), seedings can be made directly into the seedbed with a seed drill. If this is not practicable, seedings of annual crops, cereal grains or sudangrass, should be made in the season prior to planting the permanent grass. The annual crop should be planted on a prepared seedbed in the spring and permitted to grow to as near maturity as weather conditions during the season will permit. The crop is cut in the fall, leaving a 6- to 8-inch stubble. The permanent grass is seeded into this stubble the following spring, using a seed drill with a heavy disk-type furrow opener. If there is any appreciable precipitation during the winter before seeding the permanent grass, the dead roots and stubble of the temporary crop usually will retain sufficient moisture to establish the grass.

III. Mulching

The use of a mulch on newly seeded turfgrass areas is one of the oldest and soundest practices employed in the establishment operation. As the final step in the procedure, it acts as a short term insurance policy to provide for the successful development of the turfgrass stand. Not all successfully established seedings have required the protection afforded by a mulch, but many seeding failures can be attributed to its absence.

The advantages of mulching go beyond the protection it provides against soil erosion. When properly applied it reduces the rate at which the soil dries out. It prevents surface crusting, dissipates the energy of falling raindrops, and has a modifying effect on temperature.

A. Materials.

Many materials have been tried as mulches, but the extensive literature on the subject indicates that when properly applied, straw gives best results. The favorable moisture relationships created in the seedbed by use of straw is one of the chief advantages. Adams (1966) found that a 2-inch thick application of straw eliminated runoff and reduced evaporation while decreasing the impact of raindrops thereby increasing infiltration. This same increase in infiltration was observed by Mannering and Meyer (1963) using wheat straw as the mulching material. The importance of such moisture conserving characteristics is well illustrated by the work of McGinnies (1960). He found that as moisture stress increased, the germination of six range grasses was delayed and that total germination after 28 days decreased. The most favorable moisture relationships created by straw are achieved by increased infiltration and moderation of temperatures which reduce evaporation losses.

Other natural materials used for mulching include hay, sawdust, and wood cellulose fiber. Hay can be placed in the same category as straw as to its effectiveness. One important consideration in selecting a suitable hay material is to use only immature, first cut to avoid weed contamination often found in mature hay and later season cuttings. Sawdust falls short of either straw or hay as a mulching material. The most serious objection to its use is its lightness and tendency to float. A second consideration has been examined by Waddington et. al. (1967). He found that fresh sawdust from several wood species inhibited germination and stand of several turfgrass varieties. Wood cellulose fiber products which can be mixed with seed and fertilizer to produce a slurry are being used by many state highway departments (See Chapter 25).

A number of synthetic materials have been used as mulches. Several of these have value and have been employed successfully in specialized establishment situations. Where quick cover on limited areas is desired, clear polyethylene covers can be used. Army and Hudspeth (1960) found that such material provided favorable conditions for seed germination and early turfgrass development. They recommended their use on areas such as earth dams, waterways, terrace channels, and ridges. For mulching slope areas where inaccessibility is a problem, sprayable mulches offer definite advantages. In addition to wood celulose fiber slurries, elastrometric polymer emulsions, diluted 9:1 by volume with water, are available for spray applications. In comparing a black elastic emulsion with wood cellulose fiber, straw, and sawdust, Barkley et. al. (1965) found the straw and wood fiber to be the best materials and that the black emulsion was not beneficial in their experiment. It should be noted that this experiment was made on July 5 and that the black color of the emulsion resulted in soil temperatures in excess of 100 F. This may have been responsible for the unfavorable effects of the emulsion on germination. This material may offer definite advantages for seeding during periods of below optimum temperatures. In addition, the elastic emulsion is available as a green concentrate which does not present this same temperature problem. Other specialized mulching materials include mesh netting and jute mats (See Chapter 25).

B. Rates of Application.

Rate of application for straw and hay mulches are well agreed upon. Most studies indicate that 1½ to 2 tons per acre are very satisfactory (Cheph et. al., 1963; Barnett et. al., 1967; Musser, 1962; and Richardson and Disecker, 1965). Rates for synthetic sprayable products vary with individual materials and label recommendations should be followed. Polyethylene covers vary in thickness and selection of the most suitable grade must be determined by the amount of handling anticipated, roughness of the terrain, and whether re-use is contemplated. Four- and six-mil covers are most commonly used for mulching.

C. Methods of Application.

Application techniques for hay and straw depend primarily on the size of the area to be covered. On the average home lawn and on relatively level areas up to an acre in size, hand application is satisfactory. Where steep slopes require mulching or where large areas are involved, such as cemeteries, industrial lawns, or golf courses, a mechanical mulch blower is more efficient. This machine chops the straw and blows it over the seedbed. Some models are available which feed an asphalt material into the straw and serve to bind the mulch on the treated area. This same technique can be used for hand-applied mulches if the necessary spraying equipment is available. However, hand-applied straw mulch is generally held in place by crisscrossing the mulched area with binder twine anchored at the edges of the area with stakes.

Placing a polyethylene cover involves nothing more than pulling it over the seeded area and anchoring the four sides to eliminate the possibility of wind damage. Narrow gauge, wire "J" pins can be used for this purpose when re-use is anticipated. The edges of the cover can be bound with heavy-duty polyethylene tape to reduce the liklihood of pin holes developing into large tears. Application of other types of covering materials involves similar techniques (See Chapter 25).

More sophisticated equipment is required for applying sprayable mulches. The elastic emulsion is applied by a proportioning device which is equipped with an agitator to keep the concentrate from settling. The proportioned material is removed from the drum by the siphoning action provided by pressure from an external water source. The material is then discharged through a regular 1-inch hose equipped with a fan-shaped nozzle to break up the spray. Uniform application is important to avoid sealing the soil surface by overlapping. The color of these materials helps to reduce the danger of serious overlapping.

Hydro-mulching is the term applied to the application technique developed for wood cellulose fiber mulches. The machine consists of a tank truck equipped with a permanently mounted adjustable spray gun and large-volume pumping equipment. As the tank is being filled with water, the fertilizer, seed, and wood fiber mulch are added. The tank is equipped with agitation devices to ensure a homogenous slurry. When thoroughly mixed the material is sprayed on the prepared area. Distances up to 150 feet can be reached with large hydro-mulcher guns (See Chapter 25).

Removal of the various mulches following plant emergence may or may not be necessary. When hay or straw has been applied heavily, with no soil visible, it should be removed when the grass has grown to a height of about ½ to 1 inch. A bamboo or wire leaf rake is a good tool for this purpose. Light applications of hay or straw, 50% soil visible, can be left to decompose. Polyethylene covers must be removed as soon as uniform seedling emergence has occurred. The best approach is to lift the cover from the area and move it off of the seedbed before rolling or folding for storage.

In summer, mulches are optional on level seedbed areas when adequate supplies of water are available for irrigation. Nevertheless, it is recommended that all substantial turfgrass seedings be mulched, and it is an absolute necessity that every sloping area receive the protection that a properly applied mulch affords.

IV. Vegetative Planting

Turf propagation by vegetative planting is confined, from a practical standpoint, to those species and varieties of grasses that produce numerous creeping stems (stolons) and for which seed is not available. Species most commonly propagated in this way include most varieties of creeping and velvet bentgrass, bermudagrass, the zoysiagrasses, and St. Augustine grass. Vegetative planting frequently is used for the production of turf from improved varieties developed by systematic breeding and selection programs. It has several advantages. If planting stock is produced properly, it assures uniform turf identical to the parent plant. An exception to this is where stock is taken from fields that originally were produced from seed or from unselected material.

When properly managed, vegetative plantings will produce mature turf more quickly than by seedings of the same species. It also makes possible commercial production of improved varieties more quickly than where new types are seed propagated. A disadvantage, particularly when planting stock comes from a single parent, is that adaptation to a wide range of conditions may be limited. An individual parent may be susceptible to attacks by certain disease-producing organisms or it may not be able to adjust to specific environmental conditions. When these occur, turf damage will be more severe than with plantings that include many types with varying degrees of resistance to fungus attacks and unfavorable growing conditions. An added disadvantage is higher establishment costs. Costs of planting stock normally will be from 5 to 10 times higher than seed costs per unit of area. Also, the labor involved in planting is much greater.

A second method of vegetative planting is with sod plugs or small pieces of sod. Plugs have been used most frequently for the establishment of turf of the zoysiagrasses, although this method can be used for the production of turf of any sod-forming species.

Vegetative planting has been used to a limited extent to propagate noncreeping grasses. Here, groups of tillers obtained by dividing individual plants are used to establish clonal plantings. This method applies primarily to increasing grasses that tolerate low moisture or other unfavorable environmental conditions. It has been used most frequently on areas such as sand dunes and steep cut and fill sections to check wind and water erosion.

A. Quality of Materials.

The availability of true-to-type planting stock is of prime importance in the establishment of good quality turf by vegetative planting.

Off-types may occur in nurseries where the stock is grown unless there is constant supervision to ensure prompt removal when they appear. To assure the production of true-to-type planting stock most states growing commercial stock have adopted certification regulations that apply to the production of improved varieties. Because of the very serious danger of getting off-types in uncertified material, the use of certified stock is recommended.

Planting stock must be fresh. Good turf establishment depends upon the ability of the stolons or sprigs to produce new shoots and roots at the stem nodes. Anything that reduces the vitality of the stock will affect new growth. Stock that has been permitted to dry out to any appreciable extent will lose some of its vigor. Heating also will destroy viability. Material that is held in tightly packed containers may be injured seriously in 1 to 2 days, due to the respiration of the green material (See Chapter 16 for accepted methods of handling and shipping planting stock). If nursery stock is to be held for any appreciable time between receipt and planting, it should be spread out in a thin layer on a reasonably flat area and covered with burlap or some other moisture-absorbing material. The cover should be kept damp at all times. This will prevent excessive drying or heating, provided the layer is not more than 6 to 8 inches in thickness. Good planting stock also should be free from soil and other foreign matter which may carry injurious insects and weed seeds.

B. Soil Preparation.

Construction and tillage operations for vegetative planting should be the same as for seeding (See Chapter 17). Where planting stock is to be broadcast on a prepared surface and covered by topdressing, firming the surface with a light roller before the stock is spread is a good practice. This will reduce moisture loss from the soil and assist in leveling depressions caused by trampling and equipment.

C. Preparation of Planting Stock.

Planting stock should be chopped or shredded to facilitate separation and distribution. The cut pieces of stolons or sprigs should average not less than 6 inches in length and carry at least two nodes. This is particularly desirable where mechanical planters are used. Unless planting material is well separated, operations will be slowed down materially. Commercial nurseries supplying the stock are equipped to prepare it properly for planting.

D. Planting Methods.

Two general methods are commonly used for vegetative planting. The first of these is row sprigging. It is preferable in regions where high temperatures may cause rapid drying of the soil during the planting operations. The method permits planting to a depth where soil moisture is more constant. Rows can be planted by hand or with mechanical equipment which has been developed for this purpose.

Hand planting is common on areas of limited size. It consists of first opening furrows to a depth of 3 to 4 inches and from 8 to 12 inches apart. The planting material is dropped into the furrows and firmed down with the feet. It is covered and the soil above firmed by rolling. Mechanical planters have furrow opening, covering, and firming attachments. Row planting rates will vary from 2 to 4 bushels of planting stock per 1,000 sq. ft., depending upon the condition of the stock and width of rows. Where water is available the planted area should be kept damp by frequent light watering until the new growth is well established.

Broadcast planting usually is preferred in regions of moderate temperatures. It consists in spreading the planting stock in a thin layer on the prepared surface and covering it with prepared topdressing or tucking it into the soil with a blunt disk or sheepsfoot roller. Distribution can be by hand on small areas or with spreading equipment such as manure spreaders on large areas. Mechanical planters also can be used. Rates of planting will vary from 5 to 10 bushels of planting stock per 1,000 sq. ft. The topdressing material can be screened soil that has been modified to conform with the physical character of the soil in the planting bed.

In planting specialized areas, as golf course greens, it is desirable to broadcast the stock in 3- to 4-foot strips acrosss the area and topdress and roll each strip before planting the next one. Boards often are used to define the outer edge of the strip. Workmen doing the planting can work from these, thus preventing excessive trampling during planting operations. The surface of the bed should be dampened with a fine spray prior to spreading the planting stock and the entire area should be well watered as soon as planting has been completed.

E. Sod Plugs and Plant Clones.

Propagation of turf with sod plugs consists of setting the plugs into a prepared seedbed on 12- to 16-inch centers. Plugs are cut from an established sod and vary from 2 to 4 inches in diameter. This type of establishment is expensive due to high initial cost of the plugs, amount of labor involved in setting them, and high mortality, particularly when planting small-diameter plugs. It can be justified only where the grass will produce a solid turf within a reasonable period of time. Otherwise, serious weed infestations may develop between the plugs, which not only compete with the grass and check its spread but also present a very unsightly appearance.

The use of plant clones (divisions) is confined to specialized plantings. The beachgrasses *(Ammophila spp.)* and broomsedge *(Andropogon virginicus)* are planted in this manner for wind and water erosion control on sand dunes and other rough areas where other species will not survive. The most successful establishment has been obtained when the plants are collected when dormant. They are divided into small clusters of stems attached to sections of the basal crown of the plant and set on 2- to 3-foot centers on the area to be protected. Because of their habit of growth and the severe conditions to which they are subjected, they seldom produce a solid turf. However, when well established they will provide good protection against excessive soil movement.

V. Sodding

Sodding is the most expensive method of turfgrass propagation. Comparisons show that costs will be from 5 to 7 times greater than for seeding, and 3 to 4 times higher than for vegetative planting. This is due to the high initial cost of the sod and to the extra labor required for handling and laying. It is the quickest method of producing a mature turf. It can be done at any time during the growing season with proper handling and watering. Under favorable conditions, well laid sod will produce a usable turf within 10 days to 2 weeks. This compares with an establishment period of 2 to 4 months for seedings, and 8 to 10 weeks for vegetative plantings. The rapid establishment of turf by sodding justifies its use, in spite of high costs, wherever a quick mature turf cover is needed. Sodding is particularly useful for the repair of turfgrass on sportsfields where injury has been severe and replacement is necessary within the shortest possible time. It may be the only satisfactory method for producing a good cover on terraces and steep slopes where establishment by seeding or other methods is always a problem.

A. Sod Quality.

Sodding is highly questionable unless good quality sod of desirable grasses is used. Sod taken from old pasture fields usually is thin, often is infested with weeds, and may contain mixtures of grasses that will not produce a desirable turf. Commercial nurseries that grow cultivated sod under approved management practices are the most satisfactory sources.

An essential quality requirement of good sod is that it be true to type. This applies not only to sod of individual species and varieties, but also to mixtures of grasses. Because of the difficulty of accurate identification of the various grasses in a close clipped turf, some of the larger producing states have set up certification standards for commercial sod production (See Chapter 16). These include limitations on the content of off-types and other quality factors. The use of certified sod is the best available guarantee of a good quality product.

Where certified sod is not available, the sod should be examined prior to purchase to determine the quantity of troublesome weeds, its freedom from injury by diseases and insects, its physical condition, and its handling qualities. Any appreciable weed content is always undesirable. However, some species are more competitive with the grass than others. These should not be tolerated and sod containing them should be avoided (See Chapter 9 for weed descriptions and identification). Sod that has been injured by disease and insects is undesirable. While such turf may not be dead, it could be injured so severely that it will not recover or recover very slowly from cutting and handling (See Chapters 10 and 11).

Sod that has dried out or heated materially in the stack or roll should not be used. It may grow eventually, depending upon the degree of deterioration, but the development of an acceptable cover will be greatly delayed. Loss of color (distinct yellowing) of the foliage usually is good evidence of reduced vigor. Sod pieces can be cut in any convenient size for handling. When sod is in good condition and well knit, it can be handled easily in strips 4 to 6 feet in length and 12 to 16 inches in width. The thickness of the pieces will affect their ease of handling. A mature Kentucky bluegrass turf should be cut so that not more than 1/2 inch of soil is carried by the roots below the crowns of the plants. Good quality sod of bentgrass, bermudagrass, zoysiagrass, and other stoloniferous species can be cut even thinner.

Commercial nurseries may follow different methods of cutting and handling. The sod may be cut into flat pieces of convenient size and stacked onto platforms that are handled by dollies. Or it may be cut into strips and rolled (See Chapter 16).

B. Soil Preparation, Handling, and Laying.

The soil bed on which the sod is to be laid should receive the same type of preparation as for seeding and vegetative planting. It should be firmed by rolling and any depressions dressed out with extra soil to provide a smooth, uniform surface. Just prior to laying the sod the bed should be dampened if necessary with a fine spray to avoid placing the roots in contact with excessively dry soil.

If the sod is to be held more than 24 to 48 hours before being laid, it should be spread on a flat surface, grass side up, and kept moderately watered. This entails extra handling and emphasizes the desirability of scheduling deliveries so that sod will not have to be held too long before being used. Care should be exercised in handling so that individual pieces will not be torn or stretched out of shape. Irregular pieces interfere with a uniform job of fitting and are difficult to seal properly.

The accepted procedure in laying sod is to match the first course against a straight line running across the area. This can be defined by a series of boards from which the operators can work, or with a tightly stretched string. Laying successive courses is adjusted so that the joints of adjacent courses do not coincide. Pieces should be fitted against each other as tightly as possible and firmed by light tamping as they are laid, to provide uniform contact with the soil. When laid on terraces or steep slopes, where slippage is likely to occur, each piece should be held in place with a wooden stake or metal pin driven through the sod into the soil base.

Following laying, prepared soil should be worked thoroughly into the joints and seams between the pieces to prevent excessive drying at these points. The sod should be watered regularly until there has been sufficient rooting to hold it in place. At this point water should be withheld until the surface becomes reasonably dry. This will permit broadcasting topdressing over the area, if necessary, and light rolling to smooth out minor surface irregularities.

During the establishment period newly laid sod should be checked frequently and watered whenever there is the slightest evidence of wilting or loss of color. Under droughty conditions daily watering may be required until it is well rooted and growth has started. The rate of development of new growth will determine when mowing and other maintenance practices should begin (See Chapter 16).

Literature Cited

Adams, J. E. 1966. Influence of mulches on runoff, erosion, and soil moisture depletion. Soil Sci. Soc. Am. Proc. 30:110-114.

Army, T.J., and E. B. Hudspeth, Jr. 1960. Alteration of the microclimate of the seed zone. Agron. J. 52:17-22.

Barkley, D. G., R. E. Blaser, and R. E. Schmidt. 1965. Effect of mulches on microclimate and turf establishment. Agron. J. 57:189-192.

Barnett, A. P., E. G. Diseker, and E. C. Richardson. 1967. Evaluation of mulching methods for erosion control on newly prepared and seeded highway backslopes. Agron. J. 59:83-85.

Cheph, W. S., N. P. Woodruff, F. H. Siddoway, D. W. Fryrear, and D. V. Grmbust. 1963. Vegetative and nonvegetative materials to control wind and water erosion. Soil Sci. Soc. Am. Proc. 27:86-89.

McGinnies, W. J. 1960. Effects of moisture stress and temperature on germination of six range grasses. Agron. J. 52:159-162.

Mannering, J. V., and L. D. Meyer. 1963. The effects of various rates of surface mulch on infiltration and erosion. Soil Sci. Soc. Am. Proc. 27:84-86.

Musser, H. B. 1962. Chapter 6 in turfgrass management. Pages 118-153. McGraw-Hill Co., Inc., New York.

Richardson, E. C., and E. G. Diseker. 1965. Establishing and maintaining roadside cover in the Piedmont Plateau of Georgia. Agron. J. 57:561-564.

Waddington, D. V., W. C. Lincoln, Jr., and J. Troll. 1967. Effect of sawdust on the germination and seedling growth of several turfgrasses. Agron. J. 59:137-139.

Supplemental Reading

Juska, F. V., and A. A. Hanson. 1959. Evaluation of cool-season turfgrasses alone and in mixtures. Agron. J. 51:597-600.

Madison, J. H. 1966. Optimum rates of seeding turfgrasses. Agron. J. 58:441-443.

Musser, H. B. 1962. Chapter 6 in turfgrass management. Pages 118-153. McGraw-Hill Co., Inc., New York.

Musser, H. B., J. M. Duich, and J. C. Harper. 1967. Turfgrass guide. Pennsylvania State University, Public. U. Ed. 6-330.

Ohio State University. 1966. Your lawn. Coop. Ext., Ser. Bul. 271.

Pope, T. E., and P. Gray. 1966. Establishing and managing turf on Kentucky athletic fields, school grounds, and other recreational areas. University of Kentucky. Coop. Ext. Serv. Cir. 609.

Schmidt, R. E., J. F. Shoulders, R. E. Blaser, and A. S. Beecher. 1965. Turfgrass guide for lawns and other turf areas. Virginia Polytechnic Inst., Agr. Ext. Serv. Cir. 818.

Tate, H. F. and S. Fazio. 1965. Lawns for Arizona. University of Arizona Coop. Ext. Serv. Bul. A-6.

USDA. Better lawns. 1966. Home and Garden Bul. 51.

19

Turfgrasses Under Cool, Humid Conditions

F. V. Juska

Agricultural Research Service, USDA
Beltsville, Maryland

J. F. Cornman

Cornell University
Ithaca, New York

A. W. Hovin

University of Minnesota,
St. Paul, Minnesota

I. Introduction

The cool, humid region of the United States includes the states in the Northeast, North Central, Appalachia, and the Pacific Coastal Northwest (Fig. 1). Temperature and moisture limit the adaptation of specific turfgrasses to this region. With adequate irrigation, grasses adapted to the cool, humid region can be extended into the northern plains and mountainous areas of the west.

The best permanent grasses for lawns, golf courses, parks, cemeteries, airfields, athletic fields, highway roadsides, institutional and industrial sites in the cool, humid region are Kentucky bluegrass, red fescue and Chewings fescue, creeping bentgrass, Colonial bentgrass, and rough bluegrass. Tall fescue, bermuda, and zoysiagrasses are important in the transition zone which is shown as the cross-hatched area extending westward from New Jersey to Missouri and northeastern Kansas. The ryegrasses and redtop are used throughout much of the region but are of limited value for permanent turf. Botanical names, characteristics, habit of growth, varieties, and identification of these and other grasses appear in Chapter 13.

The development and maintenance of acceptable turf depends on the use of adapted grasses and varieties, soil conditions, and management. Common problems associated with the site or with management include improper watering, improper use of fertilizer and pesticides, improper mowing, excessive traffic, too much shade, and poor drainage.

Turf management problems in the region differ with latitude. In the northern portion, snowmold is more severe than in the transition zone where snow cover is of short duration. Leaf spot and *Fusarium* blight that destroy turf of Kentucky bluegrass or mixtures of Kentucky blue-

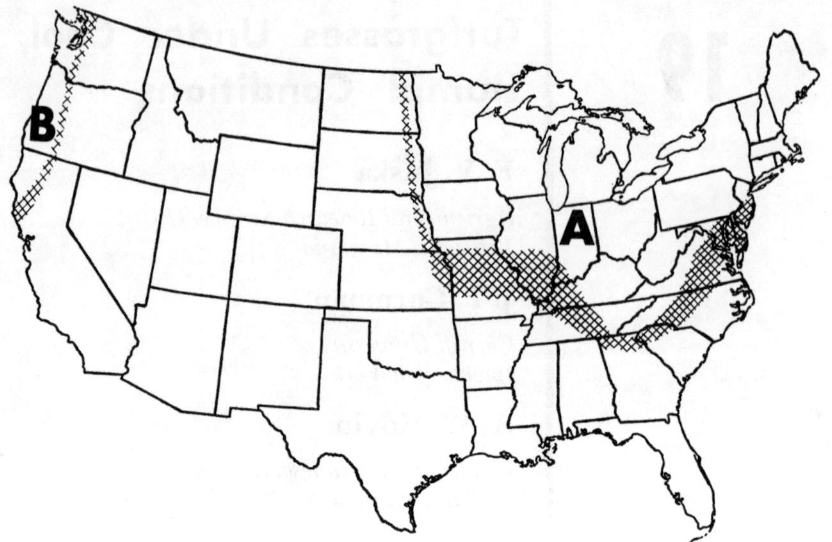

Figure 1. Cool, humid regions of turfgrass adaptation. A. Kentucky bluegrass, fineleaf fescues, and Colonial bentgrass; in addition, tall fescue, bermuda, and zoysiagrasses in the transition zone from New Jersey and Maryland westward to Missouri and northeastern Kansas. B. Colonial bent, Kentucky bluegrass, and fineleaf fescues.

grass and fine-leaf fescues are more severe in the transition zone because of higher temperature and humidity. Differences in latitude influence the choice of rates and timing of fertilizer application. Kinds of weeds in turf also vary with latitude; crabgrass, in particular, is a more serious problem further south. In the transition zone neither cool- nor warm-season grasses are well adapted. Because they have fewer disease problems, bermuda, tall fescue, and zoysiagrasses find reasonable acceptance in the transition zone. Bermuda and zoysia perform well as summer turf but are disliked by many because of their long period of winter dormancy. Insect problems also differ: zoysia turf is damaged by billbug infestations in the south while the cool-season grasses are injured more severely by chinch bugs along the Eastern Seaboard, and frit fly injury has been found on well-kept turf in New England.

Additional problems peculiar to the cool, humid region are discussed in more detail in appropriate portions of the chapter. Adherence to the major management principles outlined in this chapter should aid materially in the establishment and maintenance of good turf.

II. Factors Affecting the Choice of Grass Species

A. Climate

Climatic variation within the region is of prime importance in the selection of grasses or varieties. The predominant turfgrasses in the transition zone are Kentucky bluegrass varieties or mixtures of Kentucky bluegrass and red and Chewings fescue. Bermudagrass is accepted for use on tees, fairways, and athletic fields while zoysia is used mostly for home lawns. In this zone, tall fescue is also planted for athletic fields, play areas, and to some extent for home lawns. Further north in the region Kentucky bluegrass is the most widely accepted species, especially in sunny locations. Merion Kentucky bluegrass has remained a favored variety throughout much of the region, particularly in the northern portion, because of its deep green color, density, resistance to leaf spot, and its ability to withstand closer mowing. Stripe smut, powdery mildew in shady areas, rust in the more southern region, and *Fusarium* blight are diseases detrimental to Merion.

With the exception of very limited areas of the U. S. bentgrass is not generally recommended for lawn use unless considerable time and money are to be spent in maintaining the lawn. Throughout New England and the Pacific Coastal Northwest, where climatic conditions are ideal for bentgrass, lawns of this type may be maintained successfully with average maintenance.

B. Light Intensity

Reduced light intensity in shady areas affects grass development. In deep shade grasses have longer internodes, smaller leaves, and are more yellow in color because less chlorophyl is formed. Grasses under low light intensity become succulent and more susceptible to diseases, thus making it more difficult to maintain turf.

At best, it is difficult to maintain good turf cover under trees, particularly if they are shallow rooted. The following maintenance practices may considerably improve turf grown under shade. (a) Use shade-tolerant grasses (red fescue, Chewings fescue, rough bluegrass, and tall fescue). (b) Remove all unnecessary trees. This may enhance the landscape design. (c) Head up and prune the lower limbs and unnecessary limbs to allow more light to enter the grass area. (d) Prune shallow roots. Many shallow roots may be removed without harm to the tree. (e) Apply lime if indicated by a soil test. (f) Do not overstimulate the grass with nitrogen. Apply fertilizer lightly three or four times a year to provide nutrients for both the grass and trees. (g) Fertilize the grass early in the spring, before tree leaf growth begins, to promote early vigorous grass growth. (h) Remove fallen branches and leaves. Leaves allowed to accumulate on the turf may smother the grass. (i) Water deeply. Wet the soil to a depth of 6 inches or more; then do not water again until the grass begins to turn blue or wilts slightly.

The amount of shade in a lawn area will determine the species of grass that is to be selected. Red and Chewings fescues are the most important shade-tolerant grasses. Rough bluegrass is a shade-tolerant perennial that is useful in the northern portions of the region under normally moist conditions. Rough bluegrass will not tolerate the hot temperature of the transition zone. Tall fescue alone or in mixture with red fescue finds some use in the transition zone.

C. Use or Function

Use or function is very important in selecting adapted grasses and appropriate management programs. Although Kentucky bluegrass predominates in the cool, humid region, other permanent turf species may be preferred for special purposes, such as cemeteries, airfields, industrial areas, institution rough areas, lawns, and other turf.

Kentucky bluegrass and fine-leaf fescues are widely used in the cool, humid region for cemeteries, particularly in cemeteries with many trees. Colonial bentgrass finds some use for this purpose in the Pacific Coastal Northwest and portions of New England. Coarse-leaved, bunch-type grasses are particularly undesirable in cemeteries. Bermudagrass should be avoided for cemetery turf because of its length of dormancy and the labor required to clip stolons around markers.

Permanent grasses between airport runways should be sod-forming grasses. Kentucky bluegrass and fine-leaf fescues produce a dense, durable turf over much of the cool, humid region of the U. S. and should be the main component of most airport turf mixtures. The major requirements for effective ground cover on airfields are controlling dust and soil erosion (Rabbitt, 1949). The elimination of airborne dust is most essential for the protection of aircraft engines and sensitive instruments. Coarse, bunch-type grasses such as timothy, orchardgrass, and smooth bromegrasses should not be used. Mixtures should be compounded according to the climatic and soil adaptations of the component grasses. In general, Kentucky bluegrass will grow better on heavier, more fertile soils, while the fine- leaf fescues would be recommended for less fertile and sandy soils.

Institutional and industrial rough area turf may consist of species not especially adapted to the production of a dense turf. Hay-type grasses—orchard, timothy, tall fescue, and brome—may be planted either alone or in mixtures with Kentucky bluegrass and fine-leaf fescues. Rough areas located in back of institutional and particularly industrial sites are maintained to provide cover largely to control dust and soil erosion. Use of the turf and degree of maintenance available will determine the choice of species.

D. Site, Soil Type, and Traffic

The site will have an effect on species selection, fertilizer requirements, irrigation, and other maintenance needs. The fine-leaf fescues are considered to be more drought tolerant and are frequently included in mixtures with Kentucky bluegrass for sandy sites. Kentucky bluegrass is best adapted to loam soils but with proper management will do well on heavy soils. Turf on southern exposures must be watered more frequently and may be more susceptible to some fungus diseases. Bentgrasses will grow at a lower soil pH level than Kentucky bluegrass. Tall fescue, in its area of adaptation, will tolerate wet sites better than Kentucky bluegrass. Soil type—sand, loam, or clay—will influence soil compaction and maintenance requirements. Heavy clays and loam are subject to compaction under heavy traffic. Sandy soils will need more frequent irrigation, fertilization, and lime applications.

For control of erosion on slopes, mixtures of grass species are frequently planted. A seed mixture suitable for slopes should include rapidly germinating species. Ryegrass, fine-leaf fescues, and redtop germinate more rapidly than Kentucky bluegrass. Mixtures that include these grasses and Kentucky bluegrass are suitable for planting on most slopes. Redtop and ryegrass do not form permanent turf, but after they have served their purpose, Kentucky bluegrass and fine-leaf fescues will predominate. In the area of its adaptation tall fescue, either alone or in mixtures, is useful for stabilizing slopes. Tall fescue germinates fairly rapidly, forms a permanent turf, and may be used on slopes that are mowed frequently or infrequently.

Temporary cover with nonpermanent species is used on sites that cannot be seeded at proper seasons of the year. Rapidly germinating annual or perennial ryegrasses are frequently planted for this purpose. After the ryegrass cover has served its purpose, the seedbed is prepared and seeded to permanent species. Temporary cover is also used to stabilize and prevent soil erosion on construction and other sites that are to be regraded and later planted to permanent-type grass species. Seedbed preparation and planting are covered in Chapters 17 and 18.

Traffic will have a serious effect on the turf quality and its management. Areas such as playgrounds, athletic fields, and some parks receive tremendous punishment. If traffic is a problem, periodic aerification will help to obtain better seed establishment, better water infiltration, and entry of fertilizer nutrients. Due to constant traffic and insufficient time for seedling establishment, it is frequently necessary to replace deteriorated areas with sod. Natural pathways may develop on golf courses, school grounds, and parks. The problem is often best solved with the construction of concrete or blacktop walks or roads. Soil compaction and its correction are covered in Chapter 4.

E. Adaptive Limitations of Grasses

Lawns range widely in quality from those that are excellent to those that lack density and contain many weeds. The use of unadapted species, varieties, or mixtures is one of the more important causes of poor lawns. Kentucky bluegrasses and red fescues and mixtures of these two species are best adapted for most of the cool, humid region. In the transition zone of the cool, humid region tall fescue is adapted over a wide range of soils. It provides an acceptable coarse-leaved lawn when seeded at the rate of 6 to 8 lb/1,000 ft^2, in areas where Kentucky bluegrass is very difficult to maintain (Underwood, 1964). Tall fescue is also better adapted than Kentucky bluegrass for lawns with hard use, on steep slopes, sunny exposures, and shady areas in the transition zone.

In the transition zone very few lawns of bermudagrass have been planted because of its aggressive growth and long dormancy. Bermuda is utilized primarily for fairways and tees on golf courses. Varieties most commonly available are U-3, Tifgreen, and Tufcote. Common bermuda is also seeded or sprigged in new fairways in mixtures with cool-season grasses. Meyer and Emerald zoysia are utilized to a limited extent for lawns in the transition zone. Because of its slow recovery from injury, very little zoysia is used on golf courses. The Meyer variety is more winter-hardy than Emerald, has a broader leaf, and is more popular.

The availability of water should be considered in the selection of a grass species for turf. Where water is limited, fine-leaf fescue or mixtures of fine-leaf fescue and Kentucky bluegrass are preferable. Bentgrasses are shallow rooted, require more water, and should not be selected for turf where the water supply is uncertain.

Personal preferences must also be taken into consideration. Some homeowners take great pride in maintaining their lawns. They select species on the basis of quality, learn how to manage them properly, and are not satisfied with less than an excellent, dense, weed-free turf.

F. Mixtures

Mixtures of two or more cool-season species are used very widely for lawns and turf areas throughout the cool, humid region of the U. S. Seed mixtures may provide suitable turf under variable conditions where a single species will not give satisfactory turf. Turfgrasses in mixtures must be evaluated in terms of their specific environmental requirements and their response to management practices. Environmental factors to be considered in the selection of a species for a seed mixture are usage, shade or sun, soil type, drainage, fertility, fungus diseases, slopes, cutting height, rate of growth, and climate. Suggested seed mixtures and adapted species for turf from several state experiment stations are listed in Table 1.

In the transition zone Juska and Hanson (1959) found that a mixture of 75% Merion and 25% red fescue or mixtures of common Kentucky bluegrass with red fescue produced a higher quality turf after 5 years than either of the bluegrasses seeded alone. The plots were located on a silt loam soil having a pH of 6.0. After two seasons of growth, lime was added at the rate of 2,000 lb/A. Each year two applications of 3 lb of nitrogen/1,000 ft^2 were made using activated sewage (6-3-0) in the spring and a complete fertilizer (10-10-10) in the fall. The grasses were mowed at 1¾ inches weekly, except during periods of flush growth when it was necessary to mow more often. Clippings were removed only during periods of flush growth. Weed control measures were not employed. Supplemental irrigation was used during periods of extensive drought. Merion seeded alone was superior to mixtures of Merion plus common and Merion plus red fescue for the first 4 years after which Merion was severely injured by stripe smut. Colonial bentgrass was the most aggressive species planted. In mixtures containing other species, bentgrass soon dominated the mixture and invaded adjacent plots and reduced turf quality under the management conditions of this experiment. Mixtures containing ryegrass and redtop with a substantial amount of Kentucky bluegrass, but no bentgrass, eventually produced an acceptable turf. The poorest results were with mixtures that did not contain any Kentucky bluegrass. Findings from this study suggest that mixtures of long-lived, adapted perennials, excluding

Table 1. Grass species and seed mixtures suggested by several state experiment stations for use in the cool, humid region of the U.S.

State	Sunny locations	Shaded or partially shaded	Hard use and utility areas
Illinois	Ky. bluegrass varieties alone or in combination	Red fescue 75% Ky. bluegrass 25%	Ky. 31 tall fescue 60% Ky. bluegrass 20% Red fescue 20%
Indiana	Blends of Ky. bluegrass varieties 100%	Dry - red fescue, 50%; Ky. bluegrass, 30%; redtop, 5%; ryegrass, perennial 15%. Moist - red fescue, 50%; rough bluegrass,40%; bentgrasses, 5%; redtop, 5%.	Ky. 31 tall fescue 80% Ky. bluegrass 20%
Maryland	Common Ky. bluegrass 50% Merion Ky. bluegrass 50% (Droughty soils) Common Ky. bluegrass 40% Merion Ky. bluegrass 40% Red fescue 20%	(Dense shade) Common Ky. bluegrass 25% Red fescue 75% (Wet and shady) Red fescue 35% Rough bluegrass 45% Common Ky. bluegrass 20%	Ky. 31 tall fescue 80% Common Ky. bluegrass 20% Merion Ky. bluegrass 40% Common Ky. bluegrass 40% Red fescue 20%
Maine	Merion or common Ky. bluegrass alone Merion or common Ky. bluegrass 65% and red fescue 35% Dry, sandy soils - red fescue 80% and ryegrass 20%	Dry - red fescue 50%, common Ky. bluegrass 30%, and ryegrass 20% Moist - rough bluegrass 40%, red fescue 50%, and redtop 10%	Ky. 31 tall fescue 80% and Ky. bluegrass 20% Common Ky. bluegrass 20%, red fescue 30%, and Ky. 31 tall fescue 40%
Michigan	Blends of Ky. bluegrass with a minimum of 20% Merion on areas of high maintenance 70-40% Red fescue 30-60%	Moist - Ky. bluegrass 20-30% Red fescue 70-40% Rough bluegrass 10-30% Dry - Ky. bluegrass 20-50% Red fescue 80-50%	Ky. bluegrass 70-50% Red fescue 30-50%
New Jersey	Ky. bluegrass 40-100% Red fescue 0-35% Improved perennial ryegrass 0-20%	Ky. bluegrass (ex. Merion) 10-40% Red fescue 60-90% Improved perennial ryegrass 0-20% (for wet soils include 20-30% rough bluegrass in lieu of red fescues.)	Ky. 31 tall fescue 50-75% Ky. bluegrass 25% Improved perennial ryegrass 0-25% or Ky. bluegrass 50-75% Red fescue 0-25% Improved perennial ryegrass 25-50%
New York	Ky. bluegrass-red fescue mixtures. 55% or more Ky. bluegrass, red fescue 65% or more in dry sites	Dry - Red fescue, 65% or more, remainder Ky. bluegrass Moist - Red fescue 65% Rough bluegrass 20% Ky. bluegrass 15%	Ky. bluegrass 55-35% Red fescue 45-65%
Ohio	Common Ky. bluegrass or blends 100%	Common Ky. bluegrass 40-50% Red fescue 50-60% Dense shade, red fescue 100%	Southern Ohio - Ky. 31, 100% or the main component in mixture with Ky. bluegrass or red fescue
Pennsylvania (Southeastern)	Blends of three or more varieties of Ky. bluegrass 100% A mixture 40-65% Merion and 35-60% blends of Ky. bluegrasses	Heavy shade - red fescue 60-70% and rough bluegrass 30-40%. Moderate - red fescue 50-60%, Ky. bluegrass 15-25%, and rough bluegrass 15-25%	Ky. 31 tall fescue 100% Blends of three or more varieties of Ky. bluegrass 100%
(Other locations)	Mixture of 35-65% blends of Ky. bluegrasses and 35-65% red fescue		Ky. 31 tall fescue 100% Ky. bluegrass 35-65% & red fescue 35-65%
Rhode Island	Merion, common Ky. bluegrass, or Exeter bentgrass 100%	Mixtures for lawns, athletic fields, other tough turf areas: No. 1 - red or Chewings fescue, 50%; common Ky. bluegrass, 25%; Merion Ky. bluegrass, 25%: No. 2 - red fescue, 40%; common Ky. bluegrass, 30%; Merion Ky. bluegrass, 10%; Italian ryegrass. 20%.	
Virginia (No. Piedmont and west of Blue Ridge)	Merion Ky, bluegrass 30-65% Common Ky. bluegrass 30-65% Redtop 0-5% Ky. bluegrass 95-100% Redtop 0-5%	Ky. bluegrass 30-50% Red fescue 45-65% Redtop 0-5% Ky. 31 tall fescue 100%	Ky. 31 tall fescue 100% Ky. 31 tall fescue 70% Ky. bluegrass 30-65% Redtop 0-5%
Washington (West of Cascades)	Red fescue 60% Astoria or Highland bentgrass 40%	Red fescue 60% Astoria or Highland bentgrass 40%	Merion Ky. bluegrass 100% Alta tall fescue 80% Merion Ky. bluegrass 20%

bentgrasses, will produce a desirable turf under home lawn care. In many cases suitable prepackaged mixtures are available; if not, the grass species may be bought separately and mixed.

The fine-leaf fescues in mixtures with Kentucky bluegrass will form a turf suitable for shady and droughty sites. Eventually the species best adapted will be the main component in the turf. Under conditions of shade and poor drainage a mixture of Kentucky bluegrass and rough bluegrass will provide satisfactory cover. Mixtures may also provide some insurance against the loss of the entire lawn because the components in a seed mixture vary in their resistance to different fungus diseases (Juska and Hanson, 1959). Bentgrasses should not be used in mixtures unless one wants a bentgrass lawn (Davis et al., 1966; Juska and Hanson, 1959). The aggressive bentgrasses will soon crowd out other grasses. However, bentgrass will make an excellent lawn if it is given the high degree of maintenance that is required south of its area of adaptation.

Turf of a single grass species is uniform in texture, color, and more attractive than mixtures. Properly managed where growth is not limited by shade, soil drainage, or other variables, a single species can provide a superior turf. In the transition zone of the cool, humid region Kentucky bluegrass seeded alone is very susceptible to leaf spot disease unless properly maintained. Even though pure stands of Merion will develop into a most attractive lawn, it is generally desirable to include red fescue or other Kentucky bluegrass varieties in mixture with Merion because of its susceptibility to several fungus diseases. For play areas, lawns, and general turf in the transition zone, Kentucky 31 tall fescue seeded alone at recommended rates makes a more attractive turf than its mixture with fine-leaf fescue, ryegrass, or bluegrass. For fine uniform turf, in areas where adapted, Colonial bentgrass should be seeded alone and not in mixtures; however, a mixture of fine-leaf fescue and Colonial bentgrass is recommended for turf west of the Cascades in Washington and Oregon.

Available funds will determine the level of maintenance that can be applied on any given turf area. Funds must be provided for labor, equipment, fertilizer, lime, irrigation, fungicides, and for managerial staff. Variations in turf quality in parks, lawns, airfields, cemeteries, etc., frequently are due to the availability of funds for maintenance. Money is not the entire answer, for management is an essential ingredient in determining the success or failure of a maintenance program.

III. Irrigation

No uniform answer can be given with respect to quantity and frequency of water application (Hagan, 1955). Several variables must be considered when watering turf—height of cutting, traffic, isolated dry spots, rate of fertilization, compaction, soil type, rainfall, organic matter, etc. With the number of variables no given amount of water can be recommended per week. A bentgrass turf must be cut short and frequently. This turf, because of shallow roots, will require more watering than turf cut at a height of 2 inches.

Judgment, based on observation and experience, is generally required to determine when and how much water. This can be readily determined by looking over the turf, particularly against the sun, for signs of the grass turning bluish in color and showing a slight indication of wilting. When these signs are obvious, sufficient water should be applied to wet the soil to a depth of 6 or more inches. Do not water again until the grass begins to show slight signs of turning off-color or wilting. If the sprinkling pattern is not uniform and isolated dry spots appear, it may be necessary to water these by hand. Use of a soil probe is most helpful; if the soil at a depth of 6 inches or more is friable, no further watering is needed. Slight moisture stress between waterings will tend to develop deep rooting while overwatering tends to increase soil compaction and shallow rooting.

Turf may be watered at any time of the day or night. The incidence of disease may be somewhat greater with night watering, but night watering may be dictated by watering restrictions or traffic. If disease is a problem it is generally advisable to water early enough in the day to allow the grass leaves time to dry out before night. Overwatering is more harmful to grass growth than underwatering. A statement that 1 or 2 inches of water should be applied a week would be erroneous since rainfall and the other factors must be considered. Sandy soils, because of larger pore space, require less water at one time than heavy soils but must be watered more frequently. For further information see Chapter 6.

IV. Mowing

Frequency of mowing is governed by many factors including habit of growth, choice of species, fertilization, irrigation, soil type, climatic conditions, and function or use. Height of mowing must be adjusted to the grass and its habit of growth because turfgrasses vary considerably in their tolerance to height of cut. Function or use of the turf will also influence height of mowing. Bentgrasses for fairways or lawns are not mowed as closely as those for golf course putting greens. Turf composed of upright-growing, cool-season grasses like Kentucky bluegrass, fine-leaf fescues, tall fescue, and ryegrass should be mowed at a height of 1½ to 2 inches. Most grasses in rough or utility areas should be mowed to a height of 2 to 3 inches. Close mowing of upright-growing, cool-season grasses, especially during hot weather, may weaken or destroy turf (Juska and Hanson, 1961). Mowing too closely weakens the plants, causes shallow rooting, lowers resistance to drought, increases susceptibility to fungus diseases, and encourages thinning of turf. In addition, close mowing brings more light to the ground surface and encourages the germination and growth of weedy grasses and broadleaf plants.

Colonial bentgrass, a fine-textured, leafy grass, that spreads by short stems or stolons, should be mowed comparatively short. The neatest-appearing bentgrass turf is mowed at 1/2- to 3/4-inch height for home lawns. In general, seeded or vegetative varieties of creeping bentgrass should be avoided for general turf because they produce more thatch and after a few years present a serious thatch removal problem.

Because of their stoloniferous habit of growth and numerous basal leaves, the warm-season bermuda and zoysiagrasses should be mowed closer than upright-growing grasses. Vigorous bermudagrass turf should be mowed two to three times a week at 3/4 inch height. For best appearance, mow zoysia weekly at 3/4- to 1-inch height during the summer and less frequently during cooler weather of the spring and fall.

Mow as soon as there is sufficient top growth to remove. Adjust the mower to the proper height for the principal species of turf. Do not permit the grass to grow unusually tall and then cut it back to the normal height. If the grass is excessively tall, increase the height of cut and gradually return to the normal cutting height over a period of several weeks. Cutting excessively tall grass back to normal mowing height is very damaging, especially during warm weather. Turf recovers slowly if most of the leaf area has been removed. The stemmy, remaining turf is less dense and more susceptible to weed invasion. For better appearing turf, mow frequently enough so as not to remove over one-third of the leaf. There may be periods during the spring and fall when it may be necessary to mow every 3 or 4 days. The closer cut lawns require more frequent mowing to maintain a good appearance. Less frequent mowing will be required during the summer months when grass grows more slowly. Continue mowing until growth stops in the fall. Do not allow excessive growth to remain over winter because of danger of smothering grass and encouraging disease infestation.

A. Level of Maintenance

Turfed areas may be arbitrarily classified into two major maintenance categories: a) High maintenance (golf courses, grass tennis courts, lawns, parks, and athletic fields); and b) medium to low maintenance (play areas, airfields, highway rights-of-way, streambanks, shore areas of ponds, roughs on golf courses, industrial and some institutional turf). The degree of turf maintenance within each category will also differ according to personal taste, funds and labor available, and aesthetics.

Roughs on golf courses are mowed less frequently than fairways. On the other extreme, bentgrass putting greens require a very high intensive maintenance program. In general, parks, lawns, institutional and cemetery turf should have average or above average maintenance depending on the quality of turf desired. On the other extreme, turf grown on steep highway roadsides, some industrial sites, and airfields may be mowed once a year with little or no other maintenance. Inaccessible areas as found on steep banks of highways may never be mowed. Most turf falls in the intermediate class requiring an average maintenance program depending on individual needs and requirements.

Unless growth is excessive, clippings need not be removed on most turfed areas (Cornman, 1965). Clippings left on lawns mowed at proper intervals will filter into the turf, decay, and provide nutrients for future growth. Clippings left on turf that is fertilized regularly add very little to thatch formation. Grass which is produced under higher nutritive levels generally contains less lignified material than that grown under lower levels of fertility. Zoysia clippings decay slowly and hence should be removed after each mowing to help prevent thatch formation.

B. Thatch

Thatch or mat, a common term in turf management, denotes an undecomposed layer of stems, stolons, roots, and rhizomes. Thatch formation is not generally increased to any appreciable extent by clippings left on regularly mowed turf. Clippings decompose readily if water and fertility conditions are favorable. With demands for the production of excellent turf, thatch has become a serious problem in the maintenance program. Several factors that contribute to thatch formation are newer turf varieties with more vigor and density than older varieties and increased production of stems, roots, and rhizomes. Turf areas irrigated during the summer months have prolonged the season of active grass growth. Cool temperatures may contribute to thatch formation because of reduced bacterial activity. Low pH in the thatch layer, high levels of nitrogen, and use of fungicides produce environmental conditions conducive to thatch formation. The type of grass species utilized for turf will also determine the quantity of thatch accumulation. Grasses with a creeping habit of growth like zoysia, bermuda, and creeping bentgrasses form more thatch than upright growing grasses.

According to Butler (1965) there are some possible benefits from a limited amount of thatch formation in turf. Thatch provides shade and lowers soil temperatures. With some thatch soil temperatures are lower during the day and higher at night. It also provides some protection from frost and low temperatures. Thatch may reduce water loss, protect soil from drying winds, aid in the reduction of weed populations, recycle nutrients, and provide a cushion for play.

Some adverse effects of thatch formation listed by Butler (1965) are: Retention of water in the thatch otherwise available to the soil, reduced air infiltration into the soil, abundance of roots in the thatch layer, increased disease problems, and perhaps increased insect infestation.

There are no quick remedies once the accumulation of thatch on general-purpose turf has become excessive. Topdressing with soil on large areas to hasten thatch decay is not practicable. It is generally necessary to remove thatch mechanically. The most practical equipment to use in dethatching turf are vertical mowers and machines with flexible tines. The vertical mower has revolving blades which cut into the thatch and remove it to the surface, where it may be taken off by raking or other means. The machines with flexible tines lift the debris to the surface. On small turf areas raking, spring and fall, is of some benefit. The soil aerifier, which removes small cores of soil to a depth of 4 inches, is also helpful in thatch reduction. The cores of soil, when broken, lightly cover the thatch and hasten decomposition through increased bacterial action. The holes remaining in the soil also provide aeration, increase water infiltration, and aid fertilizer entry into the soil. Yearly applications of 10 to 15 pounds of lime/1,000 ft^2 may reduce thatch formation by holding the pH in thatch at a higher level to increase bacterial action and thereby increasing decomposition.

The best time to dethatch is in the early spring and/or early fall when turf is growing actively. Dethatching during the hot summer months is not recommended because of turf injury and slow recovery after the thatch removal process.

V. Annual Fertilizer Requirements

The quality, kind of fertilizers, and other amendments required for the establishment of a new lawn or turf are discussed in Chapter 18. Annual fertilizer requirements for established turfgrasses are dependent on several variables. The selected grass species will influence fertilizer needs. Soil, rainfall, mowing frequency, and climate are other variables. Fertilizer requirements for turf are calculated on the percentage of nitrogen in a complete analysis fertilizer containing N-P-K or one which contains nitrogen alone. Nitrogen is the element most often lacking in turf because grasses use large amounts of nitrogen, and this element is readily leached from the soil by excessive rainfall and irrigation. The approximate annual requirements of nitrogen for turfgrasses grown under average conditions in the cool, humid region of the U. S. are given in Table 2. Lesser amounts of fertilizer will be needed on turf maintained under minimum care.

Table 2. Approximate annual nitrogen requirements for several turfgrasses.*

Grass	Lb/1,000 ft^2	Grass	Lb/1,000 ft^2
Bentgrass, Colonial	4 - 6	Fineleaf fesuces	2 - 3
Bermudagrass	5 - 10	Tall fescue	3 - 5
Merion Kentucky bluegrass	5 - 6	Zoysiagrass	4 - 6
Kentucky bluegrass	2 - 4	Ryegrass	3 - 4
Rough bluegrass	2 - 4		

* Range in application rates summarized from State Experiment Station publications for turf grown under cool, humid conditions.

Soil type affects the quantity of fertilizer required for turf. Nutrients are more readily leached from sandy than from heavy soils. The quantity of organic matter in the soil will affect fertilizer needs. As organic matter breaks down, nitrogen and other nutrients are released for plant growth. Organic matter also helps materially to prevent nutrients from leaching. Other factors which affect the quantity of fertilizer needed for adequate turf growth are: length of growing season, summer dormancy, temperatures, function or use, quantity of rainfall or irrigation, excellence of turf desired, and whether or not clippings are removed. A soil test should be taken to determine specific fertilizer needs.

Removal of clippings from turf will increase the need for a higher level of fertilization, especially for nitrogen. Schery (1961) states that dry clippings from an acre of Kentucky bluegrass contains approximately 120 pounds of N, 40 pounds of P_20_5, and 100 pounds of K_20. Davis et al. (1966) mentions that bentgrass clippings contain about 3 parts nitrogen to 1 part P_20_5 and 2 parts K_20. The variations in the ratios obtained for nutrients removed by turfgrasses may be due, in part, to luxury feeding of some of the plant elements. Juska et al. (1965) have shown that the percentage uptake of P from grass clippings was greatest with the first increment of 218 pounds of P/A. A slight but gradual increase in percent uptake of P was found with the addition of each 218-pound increment through 873 pounds of P. This may suggest that luxury feeding of nitrogen, phosphorus, and potash may change the ratios for N-P-K recovered in grass clippings.

If soil tests indicate adequate quantities of P and K, nitrogen alone in the form of urea, ammonium nitrate, ureaform, ammonium sulfate, etc., may be used. For all practical purposes, fertilizer analyses of 20-10-5, 10-10-10, 12-6-6, 20-10-10, or similar ratios, appear to be entirely adequate for turf even when applied year after year. Potash leaches quite readily from the soil, and it is doubtful that this element would accumulate in excessive quantities to be toxic to turf. Phosphorus does not leach readily from the soil, and may accumulate to very high levels; however, Kentucky bluegrass and red fescue can tolerate high rates of phosphorus (Juska et al., 1965).

Fertilizer should be applied according to the requirements of the species or predominant component of the turf mixture. Apply sufficient fertilizer to keep the grass growing vigorously, but avoid overstimulation with nitrogen. Halisky et al. (1966) and Juska and Hanson (1963) found that soft, succulent grass stimulated in the spring with high levels of nitrogen was more severely damaged by *Helminthosporium vagans* (melting-out) than Kentucky bluegrasses growing at lower fertility levels. No more than 1 to 2 lb/1,000 ft^2 of soluble nitrogen should be applied at any one time on most Kentucky bluegrass turf or mixtures of Kentucky bluegrass and fineleaf fescues. Higher rates of urea formaldehyde or slowly soluble nitrogen may be applied at one time because of slower nitrogen release and because of less danger of fertilizer burn and overstimulation of turf. Annual fertilizer applications may differ from those listed in Table 2 depending on the manager's objective. For minimal maintenance of a common Kentucky bluegrass turf without supplemental irrigation in the transition zone, Juska and Hanson (1967) reported that reasonable turf density can be obtained with one annual fall application of nitrogen. The amount of nitrogen will vary with environmental conditions, but in all probability need not exceed 2 lb/1,000 ft^2 where there is no supplemental irrigation.

Kentucky bluegrass, fine-leaf fescues, tall fescue, rough bluegrass, and bentgrasses should generally be fertilized in the spring and fall. Recommendations from most state experiment station bulletins are generally in agreement with fall and spring fertilizer applications for cool-season grasses; however, there are exceptions as to exact timing in spring and fall months. This may be accounted for, in part, by the length of the growing season, quality of turf desired, and whether slowly soluble, soluble, or a mixture of these fertilizers is used. There is merit in waiting until after the flush spring growth of grass has occurred before making the spring application of a nitrogen fertilizer. This practice will help to prevent excessive succulent growth. In the spring apply enough fertilizer to keep the grass growing vigorously, but avoid overstimulation. Allow the grass to "harden off" with the approach of hot weather. Reducing the amount of spring-applied nitrogen will lessen the frequency of mowing.

Favorable or unfavorable results may be obtained with split fall or late fall applications of nitrogen fertilizers. In the northern portion of the cool, humid region where snowmold can be a serious problem in turf under prolonged snow cover, Lukens and Stoddard (1959) report that heavy fertilization prevents turf from "hardening off" before winter and thus favors the development of snowmold. In the transition zone, Hanson and Juska (1961) obtained a fourfold increase of root growth from December to April harvest with a split application of fertilizer made in September and again in late October. That there is an increase in root growth during the winter months when the soil is not frozen is supported by Stuckey (1941). She found Kentucky bluegrass root tip cells dividing at temperatures approaching 32 F. Snowmold disease is seldom a serious problem in the transition zone; thus a split fall (September, late October) and a light late spring application of soluble nitrogen appears advantageous for good turf density and for reducing the probability of heavy leaf spot infestations.

Summer applications of nitrogen-containing fertilizers for cool-season grasses are not generally recommended. However, with the availability of excellent preemergence crabgrass herbicides, light applications of nitrogen fertilizer in early summer is becoming a more common practice. An application of not over ½ pound of soluble nitrogen will not overstimulate turf and will improve color. The response of turf receiving an early summer application of nitrogen will depend on the rainfall pattern or irrigation.

Fertilize warm-season grasses, bermuda and zoysia, in late spring and during the summer months when they are growing most actively. Warm-season grasses are more variable in their nitrogen requirements than cool-season grasses (see Table 2). The first application should be made after bermuda and zoysiagrasses have started to break dormancy in the spring. The first and subsequent applications made during the growing season should not exceed 2 pounds of soluble nitrogen/1,000 ft^2. The last application of nitrogen in the transition zone is generally made by mid-September. Frequency of fertilizer application is also dependent on the source of nitrogen. Fertilizer with soluble sources of nitrogen must be applied more frequently and in smaller amounts than fertilizer in which the source of nitrogen is slowly soluble.

Precautions must be taken to prevent fertilizer injury to turf. Careless use of soluble nitrogen either applied alone or in combination with P and K is perhaps the most frequent cause of severe injury to turf. Pulverized sources containing soluble nitrogen are the most hazardous. The pulverized form of fertilizer clings to the leaves and if not washed off will burn the grass after dew has dissolved the fertilizer. In the spring before grass growth begins there is less danger of burning turf with soluble sources of nitrogen. Most state experiment station bulletins recommend watering turf after an application of soluble fertilizer. In the interests of safety it is recommended that not over 1 pound of soluble nitrogen in the pulverized form be applied at one time. Complete analysis fertilizer such as a 10-10-10 and similar types may be obtained in granular or pelleted forms. Granular and pelleted forms of fertilizer sift through the grass thus greatly reducing the danger of injury to turf. Greater quantities of slowly soluble or a mixture of at least 50% slowly soluble and soluble fertilizer may be applied at one time. Slowly soluble fertilizers release nitrogen at a slower rate so that the danger of burning turf is greatly decreased.

Method of fertilizer application must also be considered in discussing turf injury. Overlapping with the fertilizer spreader doubles the application rate which may show up as burnt strips at a later date. The rotary or broadcast spreader is preferred for pelleted and granular fertilizer material. A swath 10 to 15 ft wide may be covered at one time with little danger of under or overlapping.

Davis et al. (1966) list several precautions to avoid fertilizer burn: a) Do not apply more than 2 pounds of soluble nitrogen/1,000 ft^2 at one time. b) Spread evenly. c) Do not overlap or spill fertilizer. d) Apply fertilizer when foliage is dry. e) Pulverized materials are more likely to stick to the leaves than granulated or pelleted materials. f) Water immediately after application. g) Slowly soluble forms of nitrogen or complete fertilizer with slowly soluble nitrogen is less likely to scorch turf.

VI. Major Pests

A. Weeds

Correct cultural practices are a prerequisite for weed control in turf. A dense, properly maintained turf will seldom present a severe weed problem. Avoid those practices that lead to thin weed-infested turf, such as mowing too closely, planting unadapted species, and improper use of water and fertilizer. After the causes of a poor turf are corrected, herbicides may be used in any good turf maintenance program.

Weeds infesting turf may be divided into two general classes—broadleaf plants and undesirable grass weeds. Among the more common broadleaf weeds found in turf in the cool, humid region are dandelion, plantains, ground ivy, chickweed (common and mouseear), speedwells, henbit, knotweed, wild garlic or onion, red sorrel, and woodsorrel. The grass weeds include crab (hairy and smooth), nimblewill, tall fescue, foxtail, bent, timothy, orchard, brome, and bermuda grasses.

Most broadleaf weeds may be eradicated with one of the phenoxy herbicides such as 2,4-D, 2,4,5-T, silvex, and mecoprop, or with a mixture of two or three of them. When using these materials, care must be taken to prevent injury to trees, shrubs, and flowers. Dicamba with 2,4-D will also eradicate most of the broadleaf plants mentioned, but precautions must be taken to prevent injury to desirable plants because dicamba is readily absorbed by roots.

Crabgrass and foxtail are easily controlled with an application of one of the preemergence herbicides. Applied properly about the time *Forsythia suspensa* is in bloom, either benefin, bensulide, DCPA, siduron, or terbutol will provide good preemergence control of crabgrass and foxtail. For postemergence control of crabgrass, DSMA or MSMA are effective. Spot nonselective control of tall fescue, timothy, orchard, and bromegrasses may be obtained with dalapon, paraquat, or petroleum distillate. If a few isolated clumps of these perennial grasses are in the turf, it may be more desirable to remove them with a spade. Nimblewill and bentgrasses are difficult to remove with herbicides without injury to desirable grasses. An application of a petroleum distillate or paraquat will kill the portion of the plant above ground. Then the grass may be removed with a garden rake and reseeded in the fall. Bermudagrass is a serious weed in lawns in the transition zone. Fumigation with methyl bromide will give 100% control, but it is relatively expensive, tedious, hazardous, and seldom practical for home use because of extensive landscaping on many lawns. For detailed information about herbicide rates, method of application, chemical and botanical names, refer to Chapter 9.

B. Insects

The larvae of several beetles (May, Japanese, Chafer, Asiatic, and Oriental) feed on the roots of turf in the region. Grubs of these beetles may be readily controlled with an application of chlordane, dieldrin, or heptachlor. The hairy chinch bug, which may be very destructive to turf, can be controlled with either diazinon, carbaryl, ethion, or Nemacide.® Sod webworms feed on the stems and leaves of grasses. The insecticide effective for chinch bugs will also control sod webworm. The hunting billbug destroys zoysia turf. Control may be obtained with one or more applications of diazinon.

Moles and skunks, which feed on grubs and insects, may be destructive in turf. Eliminating grubs and insects from turf will discourage the presence of these troublesome animals. For detailed control of these and other insects, see Chapter 11.

VII. Turf Renovation

Renovation is the restoration or renewal of a deteriorated turf. Turf of cool-season grasses should be renovated during cool, moist conditions that prevail in spring and again in the fall. In the northern portion of the region turf may be renovated either in early spring or fall. Fall is the preferred time to seed in much of the region. Renovation should begin in late summer or early fall to permit sufficient time for germination and establishment of new grass seedlings before the onset of cold weather. The extent of a renovation program is dependent on the degree of turf deterioration. Renovation may involve either handraking and seeding a few dead spots or reworking the entire turf area with power equipment (vertical mowers, aerators, spikers), with or without the application of contact herbicides. Turf consisting of at least 50% adapted perennial grasses is considered worth renovating instead of complete rebuilding and the preparation of a new seedbed.

Before renovation the cause of turf deterioration should be corrected or renovation may become an annual requirement. The most common causes for turf deterioration are: a) poor maintenance practices; b) injury due to insects, diseases, and winter killing; c) poor physical properties of soil; d) use of unadapted grasses; and e) low fertility and unfavorable soil reaction. It is advisable to obtain a soil test before renovation so that adequate quantities of fertilizer and lime may be supplied to correct any deficiencies.

If broadleaf weeds are a problem, one of the first steps to be taken is to spray for weed control. Use the appropriate herbicide— 2,4-D, 2,4,5-T, or silvex or other herbicides—at recommended rates at least 2 weeks before renovation. Summer annual grasses like crabgrass and foxtail may be eradicated with two applications of DSMA or MSMA spaced at 7-day intervals. Postemergence herbicides for annual weed control should be applied 3 to 4 weeks before renovation. For specific information on weed control, refer to Chapter 9.

Preparation of a suitable seedbed without destruction of desirable grasses is the second step in renovation. Motorized vertical mowers or slicers are available for renovation of turf areas. These machines cut through weedy grasses without undue injury to existing permanent grasses. The blades of the machines are set to cut through the thatch layer, remove excess debris, and provide a rough seedbed suitable for seeding. It may be necessary to go over the area several times with a vertical mower before sufficient thatch is removed and a proper seedbed prepared for seeding. After each use of the vertical mower, thatch and debris brought to the surface should be removed.

Some aerifiers remove small cores of soil and add soil to the surface to provide a better seedbed. Aerifiers and spikers are frequently used in conjunction with vertical mowing in the preparation of the seed bed. On large areas a disk with the blades set straight may be employed. Whichever implement is used, care must be taken not to uproot or destroy desirable grasses. On small lawns renovation and seedbed preparation may be done with a garden rake. Alternate mowing and raking will remove thatch, crabgrass, bentgrass, nimblewill, and other material to provide a seedbed without the destruction of desirable grasses. Regardless of the equipment or method used to renovate, it is necessary to prepare the turf area so that seed will come in contact with the soil. Seed planted on thatch will not become established because of lack of moisture.

In some cases, even though less than 50% of desirable grasses are present in a turf area, it may be advisable to renovate rather than work the soil because of inconvenience and erosion problems. A combination of a contact grass-killing herbicide and mechanical renovation is becoming popular. It is easier to establish a new seeding after killing old vegetation and renovating the area to provide a rough seedbed. Davis et al. (1966) reports that experience has shown that a chemical plus renovation will give better kill of undesirable plants than either used alone.

Unfortunately an ideal herbicide to eradicate all undesirable vegetation is not available. Methyl bromide, a soil fumigant, will kill all vegetation including most seeds but requires special applicators and must be applied under a gas-proof cover. Methyl bromide cannot be used under trees or close to shrubs. Paraquat[1], a contact herbicide, will give quick kill of most vegetation and complete browning within 48 hours. More than one application will be necessary for bentgrass and tall fescue. Paraquat will not kill bermudagrass, and eradication of quackgrass is questionable. Paraquat will not effectively control some types of broadleaf weeds. Cacodylic acid is also a contact herbicide. Its effect on grasses and weeds is similar to paraquat. Burt (1966) reports that paraquat is inactivated shortly after contact with the soil, thus there is no-waiting period before the treated area is planted. Cacodylic acid leaves little or no residue in the soil and seeding may be done immediately after renovation (Davis et al., 1966).

After a rough seedbed has been prepared, apply fertilizer at the rate of 1 to 1½ pounds of soluble nitrogen/1,000 ft^2 as 10-10-10, 20-10-10, 20-10-5, or similar analysis. If a soil test indicates sufficient quantities of P and K in the soil, then a fertilizer containing only nitrogen may be used. If the soil pH is below 6.5, add ground or pulverized agricultural limestone in accordance with directions given in soil test recommendations. If contact herbicides have not been used to kill all vegetation, fertilizer should be applied over the turf area when grass is dry to prevent injury to existing desirable grasses.

Seed adapted grass species or grass seed mixtures at recommended rates listed in Chapter 18. After seeding, rake the area lightly to cover the seed and then firm the seedbed with a roller. For large renovated turf areas, the seed may be covered with a flexible tine harrow, steel mat, or a section of chain-link fence. The renovated turf should be watered as needed to hasten germination. When the existing grasses have attained mowing height, begin mowing and continue until grass growth has stopped in the fall.

VIII. Summary of Management Practices

Except for climate, factors affecting growth and quality of turf may be modified extensively in the turf management program. While not much can be done about the weather, the response of turf to tempera-

[1]Extremely hazardous. Must be used in accordance with instructions.

ture and moisture depends on a variety of soil conditions and management practices. Adoption of a few basic principles in turf management will aid in maintaining an excellent turf and will materially improve a poor one. It does not require an expert to have good or at least acceptable turf. By providing the basic requirements for good grass growth, most problems associated with poor turf can be resolved. The four most common reasons for inferior turf are: use of unadapted species, improper mowing, improper fertilizing, and indiscriminate watering. However, fungus diseases and insects are often responsible for serious damage. The careful operator looks for signs of injury and resorts immediately to accepted remedial measures. Many new grass species, fertilizers, equipment items, and pesticides are now available to make maintenance of a good turf less burdensome.

The basic requirements for maintenance of good turf under cool, humid conditions are as follows:

1. Select a grass species or grass mixture that is adapted to your locality, soil conditions, and the maintenance program that is to be followed. If you plan to follow a low maintenance program, do not select Colonial bentgrass or Merion Kentucky bluegrass for your turf. Several Kentucky bluegrass varieties or mixtures of Kentucky bluegrasses and fineleaf fescues are adapted throughout most of the cool, humid region. The trend toward the use of blends of Kentucky bluegrass varieties rather than a single variety is becoming more widely accepted because of disease problems. In the region west of the Cascades in the States of Washington and Oregon a mixture of bentgrass and red fescue is recommended.

Do not plant mixtures containing tall fescue, perennial ryegrass, or other undesirable forage grasses because of their unsightly appearance and clumping habit. Tall fescue, which is adapted for some turf areas in the transition zone, should be planted alone at 6 to 8 lb/1,000 ft^2. In dry sites and shady areas use a mixture of 50% or more fine-leaf fescues in a mixture with Kentucky bluegrass. Under naturally moist, shady conditions above the transition zone rough bluegrass should be included in the mixture. Bentgrass should be avoided in mixtures with bluegrass and fine-leaf fescues in the transition zone. Under most conditions, bentgrass forms unsightly patches in the turf, may eventually become the predominant grass species, and requires high maintenance for a desirable turf.

2. Mow grasses in accordance with the species that predominate in the turf. Mow at proper frequencies so as not to remove over 1/3 of the leaf area at one time. Frequent mowing at 3- to 4-day intervals may be necessary for upright growing species during flush seasons of growth in early spring and fall. Except for the summer months when mowing may be less frequent, weekly mowing may be adequate except for zoysia, bermuda, and bentgrasses. Clippings need to be removed only on heavily fertilized turf or when the grass is rapidly growing. Occasions may arise when the grass has not been mowed for 2 or more weeks. It is then advisable to raise the mowing height and, over a period of time, gradually lower the mower to the proper cutting height.

3. Thatch may become a problem with most grass species, particularly on turf that is well supplied with nitrogen-containing fertilizer and irrigated to prolong its season of growth. Thatch may be removed with a steel rake or with one of several types of mechanical equipment, after which the debris is raked and removed from the turf.

4. Turf should be fertilized to provide the basic requirements for best grass growth. Apply enough fertilizer to keep the grass growing vigorously, but avoid overstimulating with nitrogen. Select a fertilizer in which the percent of nitrogen is equal to or larger than that of phosphorus and potash. Under most conditions with soluble sources of nitrogen, it is best to apply not over 1 lb of N/1,000 ft^2 at one time. At this rate, more frequent applications will be required, but more even growth of grass will be attained and danger of fertilizer burn will be greatly reduced.

Granular or pelleted fertilizers are often preferred because of easier distribution and less danger of burning turf. Fertilizer should be applied on turf when the grass is dry to prevent fertilizer burn. Fertilizer seldom needs to be watered into the soil when properly applied in correct quantities and when the grass leaves are dry. Avoid applications of soluble sources of nitrogen during peak seasons of grass growth in the spring or fall. Slowly soluble sources of nitrogen may be applied at higher rates. They will not stimulate turf growth as rapidly, will last longer, and will not be as likely to burn the turf.

5. Use visual observations to decide when to water turf. Look over the turf toward the sun for signs of the grass turning bluish in color and showing slight indications of wilting. Grass needing water will show footprints more readily and longer than turf that does not require water. After one or more of these signs become apparent sufficient water should be applied to wet the soil to a depth of 6 or more inches. Do not water again until the grass begins to show signs of needing more water.

6. Fall renovation of cool-season turf should be undertaken in late summer to permit sufficient time for the grass seed to germinate and become established before winter. On small lawns with only a few bare spots, hand rake to remove thatch, fertilize, broadcast seed, rake lightly, and water as needed.

The following steps should be used for the renovation of larger turf areas:

a) Apply 2,4-D or other appropriate phenoxy materials to eradicate broadleaf weeds. Allow an interval of at least 2 weeks before seeding.

b) Renovate with mechanical equipment (slice or tine) to remove thatch. Several passes with a renovator may be necessary. Remove debris from the turf.

c) After preparation of a rough seedbed, apply 1 to 2 lb N/1,000 ft^2 in the form of 10-10-10, 20-10-5, 20-10-10, or similar analysis.

d) Apply lime if needed.

e) Seed adapted grasses, Kentucky bluegrass or blends of Kentucky bluegrass at the rate of 2 to 3 lb/1,000 ft^2; if in mixture with fine-leaf fescues, seed 3 to 4 lb/1,000 ft^2; and bentgrass, 1 to 2 lb/1,000 ft^2.

f) Rake or drag a steel mat over the area to lightly cover the seed.

g) Water lightly until seedlings are established.

h) Continue mowing at the proper height for the predominant grass species.

7. Major pests. Most broadleaf weeds may be eradicated with herbicides. Early fall is the best time to control broadleaf weeds. Preemergence crabgrass herbicides give good to excellent control of crabgrass as it germinates in the spring. Apply according to label instructions about the time forsythia is in bloom.

Grubs and insects may be controlled with insecticides. The prevalence of moles, skunks, and other insect- and grub-feeding animals will decline when their food supply is eliminated.

Follow the instructions and precautions on the label with the use of all pesticides to avoid injury to man, animals, turf, and shrubbery.

Literature Cited

Burt, E. O. 1966. Paraquat an exciting new herbicide for all turf. Turf-Grass Times 2:1, 4.

Butler, J. D. 1965. Thatch—a problem in turf management. Turfgrass Conf. Proc., Univ. of Ill., p. 1-3.

Cornman, J. F. 1965. Home lawns. Cornell Univ. Ext. Bull. 922, 31 p.

Davis, R. R., et al. 1966. Your lawn. Ohio State Univ. Ext. Bull. 271, 31 p.

Hagan, R. M. 1955. Watering lawns and turf and otherwise caring for them. Yearbook Agr., US Dep. Agr., p. 462-477.

Halisky, P. M., C. R. Funk, and R. E. Engel. 1966. Melting out of Kentucky bluegrass varieties by *Helminthosporium vagans* as influenced by turf management practices. Plant Dis. Reptr. 50:703-706.

Hanson, A. A., and F. V. Juska. 1961. Winter root activity in Kentucky bluegrass *(Poa pratensis* L.). Agron. J. 53:372-374.

Juska, F. V., and A. A. Hanson. 1959. Evaluation of cool-season turfgrasses alone and in mixtures. Agron. J. 51:597-600.

Juska, F. V., and A. A. Hanson. 1961. Effects of interval and height of mowing on growth of Merion and common Kentucky bluegrass *(Poa pratensis* L.). Agron. J. 53:385-388.

Juska, J. V., and A. A. Hanson. 1963. The management of Kentucky bluegrass on extensive turfgrass areas. Park Maintenance 16:22-27.

Juska, F. V., A. A. Hanson, and C. J. Erickson. 1965. Effects of phosphorus and other treatments on the development of red fescue, Merion, and common Kentucky bluegrass. Agron. J. 57:75-78.

Juska, F. V., and A. A. Hanson. 1967. Effect of nitrogen sources, rates, and time of application on the performance of Kentucky bluegrass turf. Amer. Soc. Hort. Sci. 90:413-419.

Lukens, R. J., and E. M. Stoddard. 1959. Diseases and other disorders of turf. Circ. 208, Conn. Exp. Sta., p. 1-11.

Rabbitt, A. E. 1949. Vegetation on airfields. Soil Conservation, Bur. of Yards and Docks, Dep. Navy, p. 43-47.

Schery, R. W. 1961. The lawn book. Macmillan Co., New York, N. Y.

Stuckey, I. H. 1941. Seasonal growth of grass roots. Amer. J. Bot. 28:486-491.

Underwood, J. K. 1964. Tennessee lawns. Univ. of Tenn. Ext. Bull. 326, 45 p.

Supplementary Reading

Better lawn seed mixtures. 1966. Ext. Bull. 357, Coop. Ext. Ser., Rutgers—The State Univ., New Brunswick, N. J.

Building a new lawn. 1964. Bull. 183, Ext. Ser., Univ. of Rhode Island, Kingston, R. I.

Chemical weed killers 1967 guide. 1967. Bull. 533, Coop. Ext. Ser., Univ. of Maine, Orono, Me.

Common lawn weeds. 1966. Circ. 577-A, Coop. Ext. Ser., Univ. of Kentucky, Lexington, Ky.

Diseases of turfgrasses. 1962. Huston B. Couch. Reinhold Publ. Corp., New York, N. Y.

Establishing a lawn in Kentucky. 1965. Misc. 326, Coop. Ext. Ser., Univ. of Kentucky, Lexington, Ky.

Establishing and managing turf on Kentucky athletic fields, school grounds, and other recreational areas. 1966. Circ. 609, Coop. Ext. Ser., Univ. of Kentucky, Lexington, Ky.

Evaluation of bermudagrass varieties for general-purpose turf. 1964. Agri. Handbook No. 270, A.R.S., U.S.D.A.

Grasses and seed mixtures for lawn turf. 1965. Ext. Bull. 178, Ext. Ser., Univ. of Rhode Island, Kingston, R. I.

Handbook on lawns. 1956. Brooklyn Botanic Garden, Brooklyn, N. Y.

Home lawns. 1962. Ext. Bull. 482, Ext. Ser., Washington State Univ., Pullman, Wash.

Home lawns. 1958. Circ. 445, Ext. Ser., Univ. of Wisconsin, Madison, Wis.

Home lawns for Oregon. Station Bull. 516, Oregon State Coll., Corvallis, Ore.

How to have an attractive lawn. 1965. Circ. 729, Coop. Ext. Ser., Univ. of Illinois, Urbana, Ill.

Lawns. 1967. 67-14, Coop. Ext. Ser., The Univ. of Connecticut, Storrs, Conn.

Lawns. 1965. Yearbook of Agri., Consumers All, pp228-231.

Lawn care in Maryland. 1965. Ext. Bull. 171, Coop. Ext. Ser., Univ. of Maryland, College Park, Md.

Lawn diseases—How to control them. 1967. Home and Garden Bull. No. 61, U.S. Dept. of Agri.

Lawn weeds: Identification and control. 1967. Circ. 873. Coop. Ext. Ser., Univ. of Illinois, Urbana, Ill.

Lawn weed control with herbicides. 1967. Home and Garden Bull. No. 123, U.S. Dept. of Agri.

Lawns and their care. 1965. Bull. 495, Coop. Ext. Ser., Univ. of Maine, Orono, Me.

Lawns for better living. 1964. Pampl. 312. Coop. Ext. Ser., Iowa State Univ., Ames, Iowa.

Making a new lawn. 1966. Leaf. 308-A, Coop. Ext. Ser., Rutgers—The State Univ., New Brunswick, N. J.

Response of Kentucky bluegrass, creeping red fescue, and bentgrass to nitrogen fertilizers. 1960. Prog. Rpt. 214, The Pennsylvania State Univ., University Park, Pa.

Starting a lawn. 1967. Circ. 963, Coop. Ext. Ser., Univ. of Illinois, Urbana, Ill.

The Lawn Book. 1961. Robert W. Schery, The Macmillan Co., New York, N.Y.

The lawn—how to establish and maintain. 1966. Ext. Circ. 438, Coop. Ext. Ser., Purdue Univ. Lafayette, Ind.

Turfgrass guide for lawns and other turf areas. Mixtures, fertilization, management. 1966. Circ. 818, Coop. Ext. Ser., V.P.I., Blacksburg, Va.

Turfgrass guide for lawns, recreation areas, and roadsides. 1966. The Pennsylvania State Univ., University Park, Pa.

Turf management. 1962. H. Burton Musser, McGraw-Hill Book, Co., New York, N. Y.

Your lawn and its care. 1966. Ext. Bull. 362, Coop. Ext. Ser., Rutgers—The State Univ., New Brunswick, N. J.

20 Turfgrasses Under Warm, Humid Conditions

Ethan C. Holt

Texas Agricultural Experiment Station
College Station, Texas.

I. Introduction

Temperature and moisture are the major climatic factors determining species adaptation within the warm, humid region. Temperature is by far the more important of these two because irrigation can be used to supplement natural rainfall. Within the warm, humid region climatic conditions vary considerably. From north to south there is a range in frost free days from less than 200 to more than 320. Average January temperatures vary from 33 F in South Missouri to 67 F in South Florida. Summer rainfall (June-August) ranges from an excess of 20 inches on the East coast to less than 6 inches in Central Texas. Thus, a variety of grasses and management practices are necessary to meet turf needs and demands in the warm, humid region.

The Piedmont and other areas of Virginia, North Carolina, and South Carolina have climatic conditions suitable for growing the cool-season grasses such as Kentucky bluegrass at higher altitudes. Similarly, sections of Tennessee, Kentucky, Arkansas, and Missouri are in the transition zone between warm, humid and cool, humid conditions. These areas present problems with cool-season grasses because of relatively high temperatures, high humidity, and drought. On the other hand, warm-season grasses have a long dormant season in the areas and may be subject to winter-kill.

The warm, humid region is generally characterized by high rainfall and shallow, infertile soils. Because of the nature of the soils, a relatively short period without rainfall results in moisture stress. Many lawns and general turf areas are developed on old cultivated field sites; thus, weeds are frequently a problem. Furthermore, even a short lapse in maintenance can result in turf becoming thin and depleted and subject to weed invasion. Likely, the two most serious problems confronting turf growers are weed control and fertility level. In addition, in the coastal region, disease and insect control on St. Augustinegrass are absolutely necessary if a grass cover is to be maintained.

II. Factors Affecting Choice of Grass

Very few of the hundreds of grasses in the warm, humid region of the U. S. are suitable for turf usage. Turfgrasses are not permitted to grow normally. Food materials essential for growth and development of roots and stems are produced in the leaves; yet, the leaves are removed at frequent intervals through the growing season. Only a few grasses are able to withstand such treatment and still produce desirable turf.

Choice of a turfgrass depends on geographic location, season of use, degree of shade, kind of usage, turf quality desired, availability of irrigation water, and amount of time and money the turf grower is willing to spend on establishment and maintenance.

A. Climatic Factors

Turfgrasses are classified as warm-season (growing in the spring, summer, and early fall) and cool-season (growing in late fall, winter and spring). The southern 2/3 of the warm, humid region has a long warm growing season and mild winters. The permanent turf grasses are predominantly perennial, warm-season types. Cool-season annuals or perennials which behave as annuals are used in combination with the warm-season perennials. The upper 1/3 of the area has a longer winter and a shorter warm growing season. As a result both warm-season and cool-season perennial grasses may be used.

The primary perennial warm-season grasses are bermuda, St. Augustine, zoysia, centipede, bahia, and carpet grasses. The important cool-season perennial grasses are Kentucky bluegrass, tall fescue, and red fescue. Improved varieties are available in several of these species. The characteristics and limitations of species and varieties are discussed in Chapter 13. A number of cool-season grasses which are either annuals or serve as annuals are used for temporary cover or for overseeding the warm-season grasses. These include annual and perennial ryegrass, redtop, and rough bluegrass. In the deep South, the perennial cool-season grasses also may be used as annuals for winter color and cover. These include Kentucky bluegrass, red fescue, and Colonial bentgrass.

B. Light and Shade

The amount of sunlight determines to a large extent selection of the turfgrass to be used. Many grasses will tolerate little shade while others may do equally well in shade or sun. The general behavior of a shade-susceptible grass when exposed to shade is internode and leaf elongation which results in an open turf. As light becomes more limited a gradual loss of stand occurs. One of the problems encountered under field conditions is the establishment of trees and turf at the same time or the establishment of trees after turf establishment. Young trees produce little shade and no area is permanently shaded. As the tree grows not only is the shade larger but some areas adjacent to the tree may never receive direct sunlight. This is particularly true of low-canopy trees such as live oak, water oak, and cedars. If a shade-susceptible grass was established initially, extensive bare areas may develop as the trees grow. Even shade-tolerant grasses may do poorly in dense shade when direct sunlight is never received.

Under conditions of continuous dense shade some alternative would have to be introduced. There are ground cover plants which thrive at very low light intensities. If continuous shading is due to a low canopy or drooping branches such as with live oaks, water oaks, and willow, some of the lower tree branches might be removed. If continuous shade is due to a dense stand of trees, the stand might be thinned to provide some direct sunlight.

Warm-season grasses may be grouped generally in three categories for shade tolerance, as follows:

Tolerate little shade – bermuda and carpet grasses
Tolerate partial shade – zoysia, centipede and bahia grasses
Tolerate heavy shade – St. Augustinegrass

Among the cool-season perennial grasses, red fescue and tall fescue are the most shade tolerant, while the Kentucky bluegrasses will tolerate some shade.

Some exceptions to the above groupings have been reported recently. McBee and Holt (1966) observed that Floraturf (NoMow) bermudagrass produced a satisfactory turf under 65% continuous (artificial) light reduction (Table 1). The grass survived and produced reasonably acceptable turf under 75% shade but showed some of the usual symptoms of excessive shading: attenuated growth, reduced density, poorer color. Actually, Floraturf quality was better under 35% of incident light than in full sunlight. Both this study and a more recent study (McBee, G. G. Unpublished data, Texas Agricultural Experiment Station, College Station, Texas) indicate that Floraturf bermudagrass is almost as shade tolerant as St. Augustinegrass. It has been suggested (McBee and Holt, 1966) that internode length might be an indicator of shade tolerance in the bermudagrasses. The internode elongates under reduced light resulting in the short internode types under shade having the general appearance of longer internode types in full sunlight.

Most of the grasses which will grow under shade conditions will also tolerate full sunlight if they have adequate moisture. Thus, the fact that a grass is shade tolerant does not limit its usefulness to shaded areas. In fact, bentgrasses showing the most shade tolerance also have been found to grow best in full sun.

Table 1. Density ratings and percent ground cover for grasses grown. under three levels of light intensity, July.

	Density ratings*			% ground cover		
	% of incident light			% of incident light		
Grass variety	100	35	25	100	35	25
Tifway bermudagrass	1.0	4.0	5.0	100	63	73
St. Augustinegrass	3.3	2.8	5.0	70	87	13
Floraturf bermudagrass	1.0	2.2	4.3	97	100	63

* 1 = best, 5 = poorest. (McBee and Holt, Agron. J. 58:523-525. 1966).

C. High vs Low Maintenance Turf

Anticipated maintenance practices may influence the choice of turfgrass and variety. St. Augustinegrass requires more water and control of diseases and insects than bermudagrass does to be grown successfully. Thus, if shade is not a factor, the individual may reduce maintenance costs some by choosing common bermudagrass rather than St. Augustinegrass. An extreme example of low maintenance requirements is buffalograss which is sometimes used on farm and ranch lawns in the extreme western fringe of the region. Buffalograss requires no supplemental water and little fertilization and mowing for survival. Centipedegrass in the Southeast is another example of a low-maintenance grass. Centipede will not tolerate heavy fertilization and requires little mowing. In fact, care should be taken to avoid over-fertilization and in using it on sites where it may escape and become a problem in pastures because of its density and competetiveness under low fertility conditions.

The fine-leafed bermudagrass varieties produce a superior turf compared with common bermudagrass, but they require closer and more frequent mowing, more thatch control, and more frequent fertilizer applications. Common bermudagrass, which might be considered a low-maintenance grass, will respond to intensive management and produce a superior turf. The fine-leafed bermudagrasses are high-maintenance grasses and will not perform satisfactorily under limited maintenance. Bahiagrass, used primarily for rough turf such as road shoulders and airfields, will perform satisfactorily under moderate to low maintenance conditions. Thus, the warm-season grasses can be classified by maintenance requirements as: low—centipede and bahia grasses; moderate—zoysia, St. Augustine, and common bermuda grasses; and high—the fine-leaf bermudagrasses.

D. Traffic

St. Augustinegrass and centipedegrass are sensitive to traffic and should not be used where heavy traffic is anticipated. If shade or other factors dictate the use of these grasses, then adequate walks, barriers or other methods of controlling and directing traffic should be employed. St. Augustinegrass grows rapidly and will recover quickly from injury, but centipedegrass, because of its slow growth, recovers slowly from any kind of injury. The bermudagrasses and zoysiagrasses will withstand heavy traffic. If the traffic is such that the surface cover is worn out, bermudagrass recovers more rapidly than zoysia.

E. Site

The specific site may dictate the choice of species or variety. Steep slopes and cuts that require quick cover for erosion control should not be established to slow growing species and varieties except in the form of solid sod. Poor soil conditions which cannot be improved immediately may dictate the use of a species with a wide range of adaptation to soil conditions.

F. Funds for Establishment

The availability of funds for establishment also influences the selection of a particular turfgrass. All of the improved bermudagrasses, zoysiagrasses, and St. Augustinegrass must be established vegetatively. Cost of planting material and labor requirements for planting are both greater for vegetative propagation than for seeding. Vegetative planting stock of some zoysiagrass and fine-leaf bermudagrass varieties may be expensive.

G. Fine Turf

Numerous grasses provide an excellent cover and satisfactory appearance for home lawns, for public and commercial buildings, institutional buildings and cemeteries. However, texture, density and color, which influence appearance, differ widely among adapted grasses. The fine-leaf bermudagrass varieties provide an unusually good quality turf when properly managed. Examples of fine-leaf varieties are Sunturf, Tifgreen, Tifway, and Tifdwarf. More intensive management including the use of specialized mowing equipment is required in the maintenance of fine turf, but the reward is a distinctive lawn or turf area.

H. General Turf

Grasses suitable for air fields, industrial areas and low maintenance (rough) turf generally are quite different from those used for home lawns, cemeteries, public buildings, and other such sites. On the latter sites the turf cover has both an aesthetic value and a utilitarian purpose. A turf cover is required on airfields, industrial areas, and other rough turf sites primarily for utility purposes—to control wind and water erosion, to reduce fire hazard, and to provide some protection of surface for traffic.

Mowing and fertilization are much less frequent on rough turf sites and irrigation may be non-existent, at least after establishment. If grasses are to reduce fire hazard rather than present a fire hazard under drought conditions, they must be drought tolerant. Thus, grasses which require high maintenance are not suitable for such sites.

In the southern part of the region, grasses adapted for rough turf purposes include common bermudagrass and bahiagrass while in the transition zone tall fescue, Kentucky bluegrass, and common bermudagrass generally meet the requirements. In the westerly part of the region, common bermudagrass, bahiagrass, buffalograss, King Ranch bluestem, and weeping lovegrass are used successfully.

I. Grass Mixtures

In some situations a combination of two or more grasses has an advantage over either species or variety alone. This is especially true in areas that are variable because of soils, moisture, shade, traffic, etc. Individual varieties or types in the mixture tend to predominate under the conditions to which they are best adapted. As an example, mixtures of Kentucky bluegrass and red fescue are used in the transition zone for seeding partially shaded lawns. Kentucky bluegrass becomes the dominant species in open areas and red fescue in shaded areas. Similarly, climatic conditions vary both within the growing season and from year to year. A mixture of grasses such as common and Merion Kentucky bluegrass may provide a more uniform and continuously good turf in their area of adaptation than either variety alone.

The creeping grasses do not perform well in mixtures because the more aggressive member of the association tends to crowd out the other variety and because most of them have to be established vegetatively. Bermuda, St. Augustine, centipede, and zoysia grasses are grown almost exclusively in pure stands for the above reasons. Some of the rhizomatous, sod-forming grasses grown in the lower half of the warm-humid region form such a dense, highly competitive turf that other grasses do not grow well in association with them. These grasses include bahia, carpet, and zoysia. Common bermudagrass and, under special conditions, fine-leaf bermudagrass may be overseeded with winter-annual grasses. Such a mixture or combination has the characteristic of extending the season of turf utility and beauty with a minimum of competition between components of the mixture. Dense-growing types such as St. Augustine, zoysia and centipede grasses are not compatible even with winter-annual overseedings.

Use of grass mixtures, other than overseeding of winter annuals, is limited largely to the northern Piedmont and shaded or partially shaded areas in the transition zone between warm-season and cool-season grasses. The seed mixtures shown in Table 2 are suggested in these areas and where cool-season grasses are to be used.

Table 2. Seed mixtures suggested for sunny and shady areas.

Species or variety	% by weight	Species or variety	% by weight
Sunny areas		Shady areas	
Merion Kentucky bluegrass	30- 65	Kentucky bluegrass (Merion or Common)	30-50
Common Kentucky bluegrass	30- 65	Red fescue	45-65
Redtop	0- 5	Redtop	0- 5
or		or	
Kentucky bluegrass (Merion or Common)	95-100	Kentucky 31 fescue	70
Redtop	0- 5	Merion Kentucky bluegrass	15
		Common Kentucky bluegrass	15
		or	
		Kentucky 31 fescue	100

III. Maintenance Practices

A. Mowing

Proper mowing is important in maintaining a healthy, vigorous turf. Factors in proper mowing include both height and frequency of mowing as well as the use of a sharp, well-adjusted mower. If the mower does not cut properly, the leaf portions remaining on the plant are damaged, thereby creating an off-color appearance, delaying recovery, and increasing the probability of disease damage.

B. Habit of Growth

Since turf grasses differ in both growth habit and rate of growth, mowing practices must be adjusted for species and varieties within species and for season of the year. Mowing should begin as soon as the new grass is tall enough to mow. The frequency of mowing depends on the rate of growth and will vary with species and growing conditions. More frequent mowings are required under favorable growing conditions and with rapidly growing varieties. As a general rule, mowing should be often enough so that no more than 1/3 of the leaf area is removed at any one mowing.

C. Mowing Heights

Height of mowing depends largely on the species or variety and to some extent on preference of the turf user. Creeping types of grasses can withstand closer mowing than bunch-type grasses. Optimum heights vary from 1/2 to 1 inch for fine-leaf bermudagrass to 2 to 3 inches for tall fescue.

Grasses which are clipped closely must be mowed frequently to avoid excessive leaf removal at one time. Infrequent mowing results in shading and death of lower leaves. Mowing then results in almost complete defoliation, slower recovery, and partial loss of stands under extreme conditions. When mowing height must be reduced, it should be done gradually. Mowing height is sometimes increased under hot, dry conditions, especially with cool-season grasses to provide more soil surface shading and a larger reserve system for the plant.

D. Effects of Improper Mowing

Improper mowing can result in deterioration of the turf. Mowing too close, which does not allow adequate leaf area for photosynthesis, depletes and weakens the plant, reduces the root system, encourages thinning of the turf, and may result in weed invasion. Results (McBee, 1967) of a study at College Station (Table 3) indicate a significant change in density of bermudagrass turf with 1 year of close mowing at a weekly interval. More frequent mowing would have been desirable for the 1/2-inch height. In Mississippi where Meyer zoysia and Tifway bermuda were cut weekly at 1/2 inch for several years, weed invasion was 3 to 4 times as great as where the grasses were cut to 1 inch (Personal correspondence with Coleman Y. Ward, Mississippi State University, January 16, 1968). Mowing too close also allows excessive

Table 3. Color, density and thatch ratings for Texturf 1F bermudagrass turf mowed at four heights (mowed weekly).

Mowing ht. (inches)	Relative ratings		
	Color*	Density†	Thatch†
0.5	1.0	3.5	1.0
1.0	3.0	2.0	2.0
1.5	4.0	1.0	3.0
2.0	4.0	1.0	4.0

* 1 = best, 5 = poorest. † 1 = least, 5 = most.

Table 4. Mean maximum soil temperatures under bermudagrass sod.

Month	Air temp., F	Soil temperature, F		
		Stubble height, inches (N added, lb/A)		
		2(0)	2(120)	5(120)
June	89	90	88	87
July	95	97	93	91
August	95	96	93	90
September	84	87	85	80
Density (stems/sq. ft.)		163	198	236

soil drying and baking, increased soil moisture loss through evaporation, and heat damage to grass during the summer. The data in Table 4, taken from a bermudagrass study in East Texas (1968), show that surface soil temperatures in a thin turf exceed soil temperatures in a dense turf by 2 to 4 degrees. Similarly, soil temperatures under a short turf may be as much as 5 degrees higher than under a tall turf. Clipping too high results in excessive accumulation of vegetative matter on the soil surface, which encourages insects and diseases and these weaken and thin or destroy the turf. The deleterious effects of close mowing can be reduced within limits by increasing the frequency of mowing.

E. Removing Clippings

Grass clippings represent the succulent actively growing protion of the plant and as such are high in plant nutrients. The clippings may contain 3 to 5% nitrogen, 0.5% phosphorus, and 2.0% potassium. Thus, it can be seen that large amounts of plant nutrients are removed in the clippings. This raises the question as to whether clippings should be removed or if they should be allowed to return to the soil. There is no specific answer to the question. Several factors must be considered and ultimately the individual must decide for himself. Heavy clippings that tend to mulch the grass rather than the soil should be removed if at all possible. Heavy clippings are unsightly, help to spread disease, encourage thatch accumulation, and may kill areas of grass by smothering. If a dense turf is present or the stubble is tall, clippings do not easily settle to the soil since the growth holds them and pushes them upward.

If the turf is cut frequently so that the amount of clippings is small, there is less need to catch or remove them. If the turf is thin or relatively open, a reasonable amount of clippings serves as a soil mulch, conserving moisture, reducing soil temperatures, and returning plant nutrients to the soil as they decompose.

The nature of clippings also may influence the decision regarding their disposition. Tender, succulent clippings, upon drying, form only a small amount of residue which decomposes rapidly. More mature fibrous clippings, such as from zoysiagrasses, are more resistant to decomposition and may accumulate to such an extent as to create a problem.

If thatch accumulation is beginning, is already formed, or is a potential problem, clippings will hasten the accumulation and aggravate the problem. Under such conditions the clippings definitely should be removed. Thus, the amount of clippings, density of the sod, nature of the clippings and presence or potential of thatch build-up are more important factors in determining clipping removal than nutrient removal as such.

F. Thatch Prevention and Control

Thatch is described or defined as a layer of undecomposed stems, stolon, roots, leaves, and clippings which collect between the soil surface and the green vegetation. It produces a mat or cushion effect. For this reason many home owners consider it desirable. However, it is known to interfere with desirable air and water movement and to encourage diseases. Thick thatch may prevent water from entering the soil during rain or watering, and may even cause areas in the turf to die from lack of moisture. It also creates excellent environmental conditions for disease organisms.

The development of thatch can be delayed and sometimes reduced through proper mowing and removal of clippings as described previously. Tall mowing especially encourages thatch build-up in such grasses as St. Augustinegrass. Mowing practices alone probably will not prevent the accumulation of undecomposed stems and stolons in creeping grasses such as St. Augustinegrass and the fine-leaf bermudagrasses. In fact, the fine bermudagrass varieties produce thatch on golf greens maintained at 3/16-inch mowing height. Tifway bermudagrass has been noted particularly for thatch accumulation problems.

Before thatch accumulates to the point of becoming a serious problem, it should be removed. A vertical cutting mower is the most effective implement for doing this. It moves the thatch to the surface where it can be picked up with a reel mower and collection pan or a rake. The turf may have to be cut several times in different directions if a heavy thatch has accumulated. Vertical mowing every 4 to 6 weeks reduced thatch accumulation and weed invasion and improved the mowing quality of Sunturf bermudagrass and Emerald zoysia in Mississippi (Mississippi Agricultural Experiment Station 80th Annual Report, 1967.). Drought tolerance also appeared to be increased by vertical mowing. A gradual increasing of the mowing height during the growing season improved the appearance and mowing ease of the turf. If a vertical mower is not available, the warm-season grasses may be cut as closely as possible with a regular mower run in several directions and with the clippings removed. Hand raking or combing the cool-season grasses to remove thatch is preferred to close mowing. Thatch removal should be done when the grass is growing well. This would be spring and early summer for warm-season grasses and spring or early fall for cool-season grasses. Thatch removal may result in severe to complete defoliation of the turfgrass. Such severe mechanical treatments should be used well in advance of the time when the turf will become dormant, so that the grass will recover fully before the onset of low or high temperatures.

G. Thatch—Relationship With Other Problems

Thatch, as already indicated, interferes with water and oxygen movement into the soil. Rooting, which normally occurs at the nodes of creeping grasses, is prevented and existing root systems are reduced in depth. Thatched conditions may require more nitrogen than normal to insure decomposition of the organic material. Thatch makes proper mowing difficult if not impossible. Thatch in the dense growing grasses such as fine-leaf bermudagrasses frequently results in scalping during mowing. In heavily thatched turf, only a shallow area of green leaves is found at the surface below which are brown stems and leaves. Removal of the green leaves by mowing results in brown spots and areas.

Disease organisms such as brown patch *(Rhizoctonia solani)* seem to thrive under thatch conditions and also are more difficult to control. The applied fungicide should move to the soil surface for best results and this is difficult if not impossible in a dense thatch. The same is true for insecticides which require movement into the sod for effectiveness.

IV. Fertilization

Proper turfgrass fertilization is often neglected, especially by the homeowner. Grass needs adequate nutrients just as do other plants and crops. Costs of fertilizer for the maintenance of healthy, vigorous turf are small in comparison with the quality of turf obtained. When clippings are caught and removed from the turf area, increased fertilizer rates will be necessary, since the clippings would return some plant food to the soil when they decompose.

Plant food for turf should carry a high percentage of nitrogen with enough phosphorus and potassium to assure good vigor and health. Nitrogen is the key element in turf production. It produces vegetative growth and gives the plant a deep green color. Other elements are necessary also, especially phosphorus, potassium, and calcium. A nutritional balance must be maintained among the major elements. This is done by feeding with a complete fertilizer at least once and sometimes twice each year and the addition of lime as necessary to maintain the proper soil pH. Many other elements play important roles in the nutrition of plants and these are discussed in Chapter 5.

The root system develops during the fall and early spring. Deep and extensive root growth may be promoted by making plenty of plant food elements available during these seasons. Nitrogen applied separately during the growing season is used in producing top growth. Choice of type and grade of fertilizer material to use depends on price, availability, and ease of handling.

Complete fertilizers containing phosphorus, potassium, and slow-release or slowly soluble nitrogen are available. Such fertilizers usually contain both water-soluble (soluble) and water-insoluble (slowly soluble) nitrogen, to be referred to as a slow-release type more than 50% of the nitrogen must be slowly soluble. These usually cost more per pound of plant nutrients than fertilizers containing no slowly soluble nitrogen. However, they do have the advantage of slower and more uniform nitrogen release.

The additional nitrogen to be applied between spring and fall applications of complete fertilizer may be from one or a combination of several sources including: (1) slowly soluble organic sources such as processed sewage sludge, (2) slowly soluble synthetic sources such as urea-formaldehyde formulations that have a high percentage of insoluble nitrogen, or (3) soluble sources including ammonium nitrate, ammonium sulfate, and sodium nitrate.

Nitrogen from organic-type sources usually costs more, but becomes available more slowly, is available over a longer period of time, and helps to avoid overstimulation. Soluble types should be applied in smaller amounts and more frequently than the slowly soluble types. The soluble types are more likely to burn grass. Fertilizer should not be applied to wet grass because of the danger of burning. Generally, the fertilizer should be washed off the grass and into the soil immediately after application. Application of nitrogen fertilizer to perennial cool-season grasses should be reduced or eliminated in the summer since these grasses are often semidormant. Normally only one-half or less of the amount applied in the spring and fall should be used during the summer period on cool-season perennial turf. Warm-season grasses in the upper ⅓ of the area have a shorter growing season and produce less growth than in the more southerly areas; thus, somewhat smaller amounts of nitrogen may be required. Over stimulation of warm-season grasses in late fall should be avoided. Succulent growth may be more susceptible to frost damage and winter kill.

Table 5 gives a general guide to fertilizer use on warm-season grasses adapted to various parts of the warm, humid region.

Table 5. Fertilizer program for maintaining warm-season grasses.

Varieties	Time of application	Plant food needed per 1,000 square feet					
		If more than 50% of N is slowly soluble			Soluble inorganic fertilizer		
		N	P_2O_5	K_2O	N	P_2O_5	K_2O
		Upper warm humid region					
Bermudagrass, Zoysiagrass	Mar 15 to Apr 1	4	2	2	1½	1½	1½
	May 10 to 20				1½	0	0
	July 1 to 15	1½	0	0	1½	0	0
	Sept 1				1	0	0
	Oct 1 to 15*	2	1	2	1½	1	2
Totals		7½	3	4	7	2½	3½
		Lower warm humid region					
Bermudagrass, Zoysiagrass	Mar 1 to Apr 1	4	1½	1½	2	1½	1½
	May 1 to 15				1½	0	0
	June 15 to 30	2	0	0	1	0	0
	Aug 1 to 15				1	0	0
	Sep 15 to Oct 1	2	1	1½	2	1	1½
Totals		8	2½	3	7½	2½	3
St. Augustinegrass, Bahiagrass	Mar 1 to Apr 1	4	1	1	2	1	1
	June 15 to 30	2	0	0	1½	0	0
	Sep 1 to 15	1	1	1	1½	1	1
Totals		7	2	2	5	2	2
Centipedegrass	Mar 1 to Apr 1				1	½	1
	Sep 1 to 15				½	0	0
Totals					1½	½	1

* Or after overseeding with ryegrass. If soil is low in P and K, 1½ lb each of P_2O_5 and K_2O should be added.

V. Major Pests

A. Weeds

Proper turfgrass management is the best means of controlling or minimizing weeds. When the right grass is used and properly established, fertilized, mowed, and watered, weed problems are likely to be at a minimum. If the turfgrass thins out and weeds invade the turf, the management program should be reviewed for possible weaknesses. However, some weed problems are likely to occur even with optimum management and chemical control practices are necessary.

The most critical grassy weed problems are produced by crabgrass, dallisgrass, bahiagrass, goosegrass, sandbur, and nutsedge. These grasses and sedges can be controlled or significantly reduced in bermudagrass, zoysiagrass and Kentucky bluegrass turf by post-emergence use of any one of the organic arsenical herbicides. These materials cannot be used safely on St. Augustine, centipede, and bahia grasses. More than one application of the materials may be necessary for some weedy plants such as dallisgrass and nutsedge. Pre-emergence and early post-emergence control of crabgrass, goosegrass, and sandbur are possible with pre-emergence herbicides such as DCPA, bensulide, and benefin. Winter-annual grassses such as *Poa annua,* rescuegrass, and other annual bromes are sometimes problems and require control. Dormant season applications of endothal, paraquat, and naphtha are effective on these weedy grasses. However, great care must be exercised to make certain the permanent grass is completely dormant.

It is more difficult to pin point the broadleaf weed problems. These represent a broad spectrum of plants in terms of season of growth, plant characteristics, and responses to herbicides. These are likely to include dock, plantain, clovers, knotweed, chickweed, henbit, cranesbill, evening primrose, and cudweed. Generally, herbicides such as 2,4-D and dicamba will control these weeds. Some temporary damage may occur on some grasses.

Some weeds which present major problems do not fall in either of the above categories and include wild onion or wild garlic.

B. Diseases

Properly managed turf is less likely to be attacked by disease and, if attacked, likely to recover more rapidly than is poorly managed turf. Several practices and conditions can favor turf diseases. Thatch and heavy clippings are probably the worst of the controllable factors that contribute to turf diseases. They create a moist chamber effect which favors disease organisms. Small, frequent applications of water have somewhat the same effect. Frequent, heavy watering leads to excessive tenderness and shallow roots, especially in poorly drained soils. Such growth is often more susceptible to disease damage and certainly less capable of recovering than healthy turf.

The identification of many disease organisms is difficult because the primary causal organism is often masked by a secondary invader. Because a fungicide which controls one organism may be ineffective on another, proper identification of the organism is important. Recommended chemicals should be applied as directed by the manufacturer. Even though the proper fungicide is used, results may be unsatisfactory unless it is applied thoroughly and properly. Many fungicides are poisonous and should be handled according to directions.

Disease prevention is an important step in maintaining a uniform green living carpet. The ability to recognize disease symptoms before a serious problem develops is a prerequisite to efficient and effective disease control. Most disease-control chemicals act as protectants and serve to prevent infection from microorganisms that enter the plant tissue and cause diseases.

There are numerous turf diseases of varying degrees of intensity—from those which completely kill the plant to others which are not much more than a nuisance. The most serious and prevalent diseases are brown patch, dollar spot, Pythium blight, gray leaf spot of St. Augustinegrass, *Helminthosporium* leaf spots, and rusts. Broad-spectrum and specific fungicides are available for the control of most major turf diseases.

Nematodes sometimes damage turf and require treatment. Symptoms are nonspecific but include loss of vigor and general thinning of the stand. Positive identification is possible only through soil analysis in a plant disease diagnostic laboratory. Nematicides should not be applied to newly seeded areas. Annual nematicide application is usually necessary where nematodes are a serious problem.

C. Insects

Insect invasions of turf are almost impossible to prevent. Many insects live in turf, but fortunately only a few cause enough damage to require control measures. Damage from insect attacks can be reduced by prompt control of the insect and by having the grass in a vigorous and healthy condition. If a sound management program of fertilization, mowing, and watering is followed, the grass will be able to recover from insect attacks much more rapidly.

Control practices are determined to a large extent by the type of damage inflicted and the location of the insect in the turf or soil.

1. Insects which infest the soil and attack below-surface stems and roots include grubs, mole crickets, and billbugs. These insects generally can be controlled with aldrin, dieldrin, heptachlor, or chlordane.

2. Insects that feed on leaves and stems or suck juices include sod webworms, chinch bugs, armyworms and cutworms, scale insects such as ground pearl and rhodesgrass scale, mites, leafhoppers, and spittlebugs. Many of these insects can be controlled with diazinon, carbaryl, chlordane, heptachlor, and toxaphene. However, some require specialized treatment.

The chinch bug is probably the most serious lawn insect pest in the warm, humid region. St. Augustinegrass is very susceptible to attack and centipedegrass turf may be damaged. Recommended insecticides include ethion, carbophenothion, and diazinon. Repeated use of these may be necessary for season-long protection.

The sod webworm is another serious pest of turfgrasses in the south. The sod webworm is the larvae of a small, brown moth. The sod webworm lives in the soil and comes out at night to feed on leaves of the grass. During the day it hides in a silken web just below the surface of the ground. Control is generally obtained with carbaryl, diazinon, chlordane, or heptachlor.

Scale insects are difficult to control and in some cases no effective controls have been developed. Generally, malathion and other insecticides have been recommended.

3. Pests that inhabit turf but do not necessarily feed on the plants include slugs and snails, millipedes and centipedes, sowbugs and pillbugs, chiggers and ticks, ants, wasps, and bees. Some of these pests build nests in the soil, thereby, damaging grass roots and possibly covering grass leaves. Generally, a wide range of insecticides will control these pests.

Specific insecticides and rates of application for control of various insects may be found in Chapter 11.

VI. Turf Renovation

A turf area should be renovated when the stand of a desirable grass is too poor to recover against weed competition and when fertilization by itself will not bring back a good, weed-free stand in a reasonable time. Major factors likely to contribute to loss of stand are soil compaction, lack of fertilization, and traffic. In the renovation process the problem which caused the loss of stand should be corrected as far as possible. Other factors might include a change in soil pH, mowing practice, shade, and soil-water relationships. If the causative problem is not corrected, the results of renovation will be short lived.

Cool-season grasses are generally more difficult to renovate than warm-season grasses because they are more sensitive to environment and lack the strong creeping growth habit of most warm-season turf grasses.

Renovation may be partial or complete depending on the situation and the desire of the individual concerned. Partial renovation is particularly appropriate when only spots or small areas require attention. Partial renovation might involve degree of intensity instead of area: such as correction of the causative factor and re-establishment of the desired turf grass.

Other than for limited spots or areas, complete renovation is likely to be more successful than partial renovation. Complete renovation may take one of two forms: (1) Complete destruction of existing vegetation, usually chemically, followed by seeding or sprigging directly in the dead residue. (2) Complete destruction of existing vegetation, tillage, seedbed preparation including fertilization and re-establishment of the desired turfgrass. The former is cheaper and more quickly executed, but less likely to be successful. It does not involve correction of problems which may have led to deterioration of the initial turf. Also, successful establishment of new seedings or sprigs on a poorly prepared seedbed is unlikely.

Complete renovation to correct existing problems and re-establish turf should involve the following steps.

1. Prepare a good seedbed by complete tillage. This will serve also to correct soil compaction problems which may have contributed to loss of turf cover. This may turn up a new crop of weed seed which will emerge and compete with the new grass and make weed control measures necessary.

2. Add top soil, sand, and organic matter as needed to correct soil surface and physical condition problems. Top soil may be needed to fill depressions or raise the turf area generally. Sand may be added on heavy clay soils or organic matter on light soils to improve aeration and soil structure.

3. Add a complete fertilizer consisting of nitrogen, phosphorous, and potassium in accordance with a soil test.

4. Add lime to correct pH and supply calcium.

5. Work the fertilizer, top dressing, and lime into the soil. Smooth (fine grade) and firm the surface.

6. Re-establish to desired turfgrass. This may involve changing species or varieties if failure of the turf was due to a poorly adapted type or to a change in conditions such as increased shading. The choice of species and variety should be based on factors outlined earlier in this chapter.

7. Newly planted or sprigged turf should not be allowed to become dry. Irrigation may not be needed throughout the region or after establishment in parts of the region. However, irrigation during establishment is highly important to prevent loss of seedlings or new growth. The waterings should be light and frequent enough to prevent the surface from drying. As the young seedlings develop, or as the sprigs or seed begin to take root and grow, the frequency of watering should be reduced and the amount applied at any time increased.

8. Newly established areas should be mowed as soon as the grass is 1½ to 2 inches high. Mowing should be frequent enough so that only the tips of leaves are removed, never the entire leaf or stem.

9. Newly established turf on renovated areas is likely to become weedy before the area is completely covered with grass. The grass should be encouraged by proper mowing, adequate fertilization, and judicious amounts of water. Herbicides for the control of weeds may be applied before seeding some grasses, following sprigging of some vegetative varieties, and after emergence of the grass. More detailed information on specific weed control practices is given in Chapter 9.

10. One or two light applications of nitrogen approximately 1 month apart after emergence may be desired to keep the grass growing actively during the establishment phase. After establishment, the appropriate fertilizer schedule presented earlier in this chapter should be followed.

VII. Turf Management Program

A good turf does not just happen. It is the result of a well planned and continuing management program. The following is suggested as a brief guideline to the development and maintenance of a pleasing and useful turfgrass cover.

1. Select an adapted grass, taking into consideration both the geographic location and specific site including, especially, shade.

2. Apply fertilizer according to needs and recommendations.

3. Prepare a good seedbed and establish the turf according to recommended procedures.

4. Mow at appropriate height and intervals using a sharp, well-adjusted mower.

5. Follow a regular fertilizer schedule to maintain active, continuous growth during the growing season.

6. Irrigate as needed during both the growing season and the dormant season.

7. Control turf diseases, insects, and weeds using appropriate chemicals and application practices.

8. Remove or control thatch accumulation during the growing season.

9. Use grass mixtures or overseeding where appropriate to extend the season of turf use.

10. Renovate thin areas which may develop and correct or adjust the management program to maintain healthy turf.

Acknowledgment

The author is grateful to co-workers throughout the warm-humid region who have supplied information which has been used freely without specific reference and who reviewed the material and made helpful suggestions.

Literature Cited

Holt, Ethan C. and J. A. Lancaster. 1968. Yield and stand survival of 'Coastal' bermudagrass as influenced by management practices. Agron. J. 60: 7-11.

McBee, George G. 1967. Effects of mowing heights on Texturf IF bermudagrass turf. Soil and Crop Sciences Dept. Tech. Report No. 10, Texas A & M University.

McBee, George G., and E. C. Holt. 1966. Shade tolerance studies on bermudagrass and other turfgrasses. Agron. J. 58: 523-525.

Mississippi Agricultural Experiment Station, 80th Annual Report. 1967. p. 15-16.

Supplementary Reading

Carolina Lawns. 1963. North Carolina Agr. Ext. Serv. Circ. 292.

Guide for chemical control of turfgrass diseases and turfgrass weeds. 1967. Va. Agr. Ext. Serv. Circ. 1034.

Robertson, R. L. Insects of lawns and turf and their control. Unnumbered memo, North Carolina Ext. Serv.

Schmidt, T. E., J. F. Shoulders, R. E. Blaser, and A. S. Beecher. 1965. Turfgrass guide for lawns and other turf areas. Va. Agr. Ext. Serv. Circ. 818.

Thompson, W. R., Jr. and C. Y. Ward. 1966. Prevent thatch accumulation of Tifgreen bermudagrass greens. The Golf Superintendent, Nov. - Dec.

Thompson, W. R., Jr. 1964. Mowing and fertilization. Miss. Agr. Expt. Sta. Turfgrass Mimeo Series No. 8.

Thompson, W. R., Jr. 1964. Insect control in turf. Miss. Agr. Expt. Sta. Turfgrass Mimeo Series No. 12.

Trew, E. M. 1962. Home lawns. Tex. Agr. Ext. Serv. Bul. 203.

Underwood, J. K. Tennessee lawns. 1964. Univ. of Tenn. Agri. Ext. Serv. Bul 326.

Wise, Louis N. The lawn book. W. R. Thompson. State College, Mississippi. 250 pp.

21 Turfgrasses Under Semi-Arid and Arid Conditions

Ray A. Keen

Kansas State University
Manhattan, Kansas

I. Introduction

The arid and semi-aird region, west of 98° W. longitude in the U. S. (See Fig. 1 in Chapter 26), is a region of extremes which must be recognized in the planning and construction stages of turf production, or failure is almost certain. While general aridity is a problem, heavy rains of "cloudburst" proportions must be provided for in surface drainage. Northern latitudes and high altitudes result in short, cool growing seasons, comparable with those in the New England States, where irrigation is available.

Southern subtropical and desert regions are being used increasingly for recreation and residence. Turf production under such conditions is further complicated by alkaline or saline soils and irrigation waters. The "winter resort" or "summer resort" period of residence of many sites is a complicating factor in that permanent turf may have to survive long periods of neglect during the more disagreeable seasons of the year. In driving from a downtown site in a valley to a home in a high-altitude surburb of many western cities the change in climate and the change in recommended turfgrasses may be equivalent to driving from Memphis to Chicago.

II. Choice of Grass

The grasses listed in Chapter 13 are all usable, but not generally available in the arid region. In choosing from the relatively few adapted in an area, one must consider these limiting factors:

1. Duration of use. A perennial turf receiving year-round care versus a quick green cover during the mild season of the year. If perennial, what extremes of temperature and traffic will be encountered? If snow cover is present at high altitudes the grass is not subject to extreme air temperatures. On recreation areas, at what season must turf recover from traffic and injury and at what height must it be maintained to make play enjoyable?

Where summer temperatures exceed 100 F, will water always be available for irrigation and cooling or will there be periods of severe stress while prior water rights are met.

2. Light intensities are generally high in the semi-arid and arid region with more ultraviolet at higher altitudes. Disease problems may

be less because of intense light and dry air but the line between sun and shade may be more drastic. Shade from trees and structures is a factor if present more than 50% of the daylight hours. Kentucky bluegrass may survive only where shaded. Tree canopies may be less dense in this region but traffic may be concentrated under trees increasing the stress on both trees and turf.

3. Function or use of turf. Few grasses perform well under both high- and low-maintenance. Low-maintenance turfs are found along roadsides, airport landing strips, golf course roughs, and ski slopes. They prevent water and wind erosion and trap snow and dust. They should tolerate infrequent high mowing, low fertility, and drought and be fire resistant with as long a green period as possible. Bromegrass, tall fescue, wheatgrasses, and native bunch grasses are commonly used in rough turf. In warmer areas, buffalograss, grama grasses and bermudagrass in the coarser common and giant forms are persistent in rough areas.

High-maintenance grasses form turf when mowed relatively often at heights of 1½ inch or less. Irrigation, fertilization, cultivation, and other cultural practices are on a regular schedule. Such turf is demanded for the finest athletic fields, golf tees, and greens and "show" lawns around commercial establishments. A few home owners will devote the time and money required for high-maintenance turf.

4. Site factors that affect choice of grass are the soil factors of texture, drainage, fertility, pH or alkaline reaction, salinity and other local complications of vegetation and air drainage, aspect (direction of slope), wind movements, or waste from oil or mining operations that support the local economy. Too often the production of turf on a site is the last consideration; grading operations having long since removed or buried the top soil essential to success. Subsoil problems of outwash gravels, claypans, or caliche may require special drainage, flushing or capillary barriers to prevent upward movement of salts. Choosing a salt-tolerant grass may not be a long-term answer. Alkaligrasses, saltgrass, buffalograss, bermudagrass, and Seaside creeping bentgrass are salt tolerant, at least to seawater.

5. Choice of grass for use under stress of traffic will be influenced by the season of traffic. The grass must have ability to recover from injury and to grow during the stress period. Where warm season turf is subjected to winter traffic while dormant, the practice of overseeding with cool-season grasses as practiced in the South (Chapt. 20) is recommended. Not all bermudagrasses are equally hardy under winter traffic, even when overseeded with cool-season grasses. U-3, Tufcote, and K1-51 bermudagrasses are tolerant of winter traffic in this increasing order.

6. The funds and/or time available for maintenance will influence the choice of grass. In general, fine-textured, closely mowed turf is more expensive than taller, coarser textured grass. Some native grasses may survive with little care other than occasional mowing or grazing, plus weed and brush control. Maintaining a grass outside its region of optimum use is more expensive; e.g., zoysia may require twice as much acidifying material as fertilizer on soils above 7.6 pH. Taller grasses, in

addition to needing less frequent mowing, have deeper root systems adapted to less frequent and deeper irrigation. The ability to survive drought by dormancy is a desirable factor where prolonged drought restricts water use to household purposes in the arid region. Any special equipment required for mowing, cultivating, removing thatch, or controlling pests may be an important economic factor to consider in choosing a turfgrass.

7. Grasses for temporary cover or erosion control are usually large seeded and quick germinating. They may be perennial grasses where permanent erosion control is the goal in waterways, along roadsides, or on ski slopes. Crop grasses are often used for temporary cover. They include oats, wheat, barley, sudangrass, millet, and others adapted to the season and soil. In the northern arid region bermudagrass from seed may provide temporary summer cover and acceptable playing turf. Conversely annual and domestic ryegrasses, annual, rough and Canada bluegrasses, fine-leaf fescues and bentgrasses are used for winter cover in southern arid regions. Temporary or permanent control of wind erosion in the arid region, without available irrigation, is almost impossible if attempted with grass alone. Existing vegetation should not be disturbed without irrigation water available. Where the annual planting season is short, a lagging construction schedule may delay establishment of turf cover a full year. Then severe erosion often increases costs. Wind erosion can contribute to substantial dust deposits on established turf (Fig. 1).

Figure 1. Dust is a problem in semi-arid and arid regions. Profiles show dust accumulation on a newly constructed golf course in Kansas.

Permanent turf without irrigation in the arid and semi-arid areas will rely heavily on native species. Buffalograss is almost the only sod-forming grass that will grow with less than 15 inches of precipitation a year.

A few bermudagrasses will compete in the southern range on deep soils. Wheatgrasses, the bunchy blue and black gramas, and alkaligrasses *(Puccinellia* sp.) will grow under increasingly arid conditions but cannot be said to form sod, since it takes increasing amounts of soil and surface to provide water for the bunches of grass. Mowing must be as high as practical, under arid conditions, to get maximum root development. All management practices are directed toward maximizing the retention and utilization of precipitation.

Many outwash plains are naturally stabilized by surface gravel layers as a result of wind and water actions. Where disturbed by construction, such layers may be replaced with sized gravel to trap water and retain seed until vegetative cover is again established. Gravel is impractical near operational areas at airports that accommodate jet aircraft or near launching sites of missiles where exhaust blasts will drive loose gravel at bullet velocities.

Selecting irrigated grasses to blend with native grasses in season may greatly simplify camouflage operations when required on industrial and military sites in the arid region.

8. Mixtures are not desirable for the finest turf, where a single species, cultivar, or clone will give more uniform results and make for uniform maintenance schedules. Mixtures of grasses may be indicated where less than perfect turf is acceptable. "Shotgun" mixtures, containing several different grasses, are widely used to cover large areas on which soils, drainage, exposure, and other factors are varied or disturbed. Except where grown as improved grasses under cultivation, the indigenous species are often available in quantity only as "Mixed Native Grasses." As a general rule they should not be used much more than 200 miles north or south of their source; closer is better.

The role of the grasses included in the mixture should be verified. A "nursegrass" becoming a weed that robs the permanent grass of vigor and stand is well documented. However, the western and crested wheatgrasses and untreated buffalograss seed are slow to establish so that companion or temporary grasses are desirable if moisture is available for both. Otherwise, mulching with straw, hay, or stubble, after one or more years of fallow, may be preferred. Buffalograss seeds are clustered in an impervious burr that permits germination over a period of years. Uniform germination, without overwintering, is obtained by soaking the seed in weak potassium nitrate solutions and chilling it for 1 or 2 months after which it is dried and sold as "treated" seed. Untreated seed is often fall planted but germination may occur over two or more springs.

Mixing cool-season and warm-season grass seeds is not recommended because the time of seeding is improper for one of the two. Where cool-season and warm-season grasses are desired for year-round color the best results have been obtained by overseeding the cool-season grass into a cultivated or renovated warm-season grass at the end of the warm season. Merion or similar Kentucky bluegrass cultivars or varieties seeded into Meyer zoysia in late August or early September is an example. To retain such a mixture for any reasonable period, management practices should favor the weaker grass.

III. Mowing

With the possible exception of buffalograss, which may benefit from removal of shade competition, most grasses are not benefitted by mowing. Dense, uniform, smooth turf never develops without mowing, so the paradox of mowing results in a compromise between minimum removal of green leaf and maximum height that use of the turf will allow. Excessive removal of blades results in an imbalance between top and roots, which retards growth while food reserves are used in new growth. When the grass plant is under drought or high temperature stress, severe defoliation may result in dormancy or death of the plant. Frequent mowing at a uniform height results in minimum "shock" to the plant and maximum density of foliage. As height of cut is lowered, importance of frequent mowing increases.

Temperature is an important determinant of the height at which mowing is tolerated. In the north, and at high altitudes, where soil and night temperatures are cool the fine-leaf fescues and some bluegrasses will tolerate ½-inch mowing. At higher temperatures they require 1- to 3-inch mowing to survive, even in the shade of trees or buildings. Bentgrasses, fine-leaf zoysias and bermudagrasses will tolerate ¼-inch, daily mowing under putting green conditions. Infrequent mowing of these species, even at 1 inch, can result in loss of turf on a hot day.

Buffalograss and coarse, tall-growing bermudagrass, though stoloniferous, will not tolerate mowing below 1 inch; higher is better if mowing is less often than weekly.

The tall fescues, ryegrasses, plains bluegrasses, wheatgrasses, and native bunchgrasses are least tolerant of mowing. Under rough turf cover conditions they may be mowed about 3 inches high each time they reach 4 inches; this removes about ⅓ of the leaf area and supports deep roots. Better stand is realized than when the rough areas are mowed after seed formation and at the end of the season only.

Mixtures of warm- and cool-season grasses can be regulated by height and frequency of mowing. Close frequent mowing in hot weather will favor the warm-season grass while higher, less frequent mowing favors the cool-season grass, especially in cool weather when the warm-season grass is dormant.

Infrequent mowing allows the tall grass to shade the lower blades. The sudden removal of tall grass exposes otherwise protected grass to the elements and checks root growth. Light reaching the soil level will enhance the germination and survival of crabgrass and many other weeds that are photosensitive. Even a well-kept sward can be lost in a single mowing at the usual height if it is allowed to become tall during a vacation period or a protracted wet spell without mowing, especially if the days are hot and clear following the severe mowing. Recovery is hastened by careful irrigation, mowing, light fertilizing, or other practices that minimize stress on the grass. Applying weed control chemicals may well be delayed until the grass has recovered.

Clipping removal does not differ among regions. Clippings always are removed from the finest turf. Removal is not necessary on other areas if the clippings are so short they disappear into the cut grass. If they lie on the mowed surface, and especially if they have bunched because the grass was wet or the mower windrowed the clippings, they should be removed, or scattered by a second mowing. Piles of clippings may smother the grass or serve as incubators for disease spores to be spread at the next mowing.

Where clippings are removed, extra fertilizer will be required to replace the nutrients removed in the clippings. The accumulation of clippings adds little to the organic fraction of the soil and to the cushion of thatch, mat, and fibre as the increasingly decomposed residue is called. This layer is largely the woody residue of stems, rhizomes and stolons that becomes a problem when it is so thick that roots and rhizomes fail to enter the soil below. That happens in a season or two in the semi-arid region when grass is grown with maximum fertility and irrigation on poor or impervious soil. Corrective measures, in addition to physically removing the thatch and mat, should improve the physical character of the soil as a growing medium.

Thatch is primarily a crop residue problem. A healthy lawn is an efficient producer of vegetation. By cultivating, or topdressing with soil or compost, thatch can be beneficially incorporated into the soil profile. This must be a continuing process so it may raise the level of the turf above sidewalks, drives and other structures. If the thatch layer is more than 1 inch thick it may be too much to decompose without burying an undecomposed layer that will interfere with growth and may aggravate disease problems. If the layer of thatch is loose and dry, above moist soil protecting deep rhizomes, it can be burned. That usually is prohibited, because of the fire hazard, by local laws against burning. A wide assortment of hand and power tools are available to rake, slice, puncture, cut, and remove thatch residue. If the only living grass is in and above the thatch and mat, machines must be used carefully and repeatedly to avoid thinning the stand and inviting weed invasion.

Surface thatch is best removed at the beginning of the growing season, to expose live rhizomes and stolons for earlier growth. Water may be required in dry seasons to prevent exposed stolons and rhizomes from drying before the root system is functioning. Deep layers of thatch and mat are further reduced during the period of maximum growth when the scars of removal are quickly healed by new shoots that develop where rhizomes are severed.

IV. Fertilizing

Fertilizer requirements vary so widely, even in short distances, in the semi-arid and arid regions that no specific recommendations can be made. A successful fertilizer program should begin with a soil test that is interpreted in terms of turf rather than for an orchard or field crops. Grasses are reasonably uniform in requirement for the major nutrients, (nitrogen, phosphorus, and potassium), but soils vary greatly in their supply of these materials. Some, in the arid region, may even be excessively high in potassium or nitrate. Many well-fertilized lawns have excess phosphorus and potassium.

In the arid region the minor nutrient elements may be a greater problem by being present in toxic amounts or, oftener, by being deficient or unavailable because of the pH of the soil is too high from excess calcium, sodium, or other salts. Iron deficiency chlorosis is common, with many local byproducts of mining, smelting, or refining on the market to correct the deficiency. County agents, extension turf specialists, or soil scientists should be consulted on local problems. Where water is the limiting factor for growth, a small amount of nitrogen, and/or phosphorus may considerably improve utilization of the limited water available.

As a general rule fertilizers more acid in reaction, such as ammonium sulfate, are preferred to less acid ones such as sodium nitrate (Table 1). Where the water supply is from wells or surface runoff, it may be desirable to acidify the water before applying it to fine turfgrass. Acidifying equipment should be professionally installed to avoid damaging irrigation equipment or turf, or injuring personnel. Some landscape contractors acidify soil with commercial sulfuric acid at the beginning of construction if no vegetation is growing on the site.

Table 1. Salt index and lime equivalents of selected fertilizers.

Fertilizer	Analysis*	Salt index†	Acidity‡	Basicity§
Ammonia, anhydrous	82-0-0	47.1	148	--
Ammonium nitrate	35-0-0	104.7	60	--
Ammophos	21-53-0	34.2	74	--
Ammonium sulfate	21-0-0	69.0	110	--
Calcium cyanamid	21-0-0	31.0	--	63
Calcium nitrate	11-0-0	52.5	--	21
Potassium chloride	0-0-60	116.3	0	0
Potassium nitrate	13-0-46	73.6	--	23
Potassium sulfate	0-0-54	46.1	0	0
Sodium nitrate	16.5-0-0	100.0	--	29
Superphosphate	0-20-0	7.8	0	0
Superphosphate	0-48-0	10.1	0	0
Urea	46-0-0	75.4	80	--

* $N-P_2O_5-K_2O$. † Ratio of change in osmotic pressure of soil solution based on equal weight of $NaNO_3$ as 100. After Rader et al. (1943). ‡ Expressed as lb $CaCO_3$ to neutralize 100 lb fertilizer. § Neutralizing power of 100 lb fertilizer expressed as lb $CaCO_3$.

In the northern semi-arid regions, and at high altitudes farther south, returning clippings to the turf will return some nutrients as they decompose. Organic matter from decomposed clippings may be more important in retaining applied fertilizers than it is as a source of nutrients, except on "mountain loams" and other organic soils brought down from high-elevation peat beds and cultivated silty mucks.

A single application of 1 to 2 pounds of nitrogen per 1,000 square feet is sufficient for cool-season grasses where the growing season is short and soil temperatures are low. At the other extreme bermudagrass or bentgrass golf greens in the southern desert, under heavy irrigation with clippings removed daily, may require 8 to 16 pounds of nitrogen per 1,000 square feet during the 12-month growing season. Where Kentucky bluegrasses and fine-leaf fescues are grown under high summer temperatures, disease losses will be less if nitrogen rates are kept low during the warm period.

A. Timing Fertilizer Applications

As a general rule, fertilizers are first applied shortly before or at the beginning of the growing season of the grass involved. On cool-season grasses, for summer turf with a short season, a single application in late winter or early spring may be sufficient. Where cool-season grasses are used for winter color and cover, applications are made in late fall or early winter and again at the beginning of the growing period.

Where cool-season grasses are grown with a split growing season (winter wheat climate, Zones 5-7, Fig. 1, Chap. 27), the major fertilizer application will be made in late summer at the beginning of the "fall" growing season. A second fertilization in late winter or early spring will hasten "green up" and growth in the spring. Rate of growth and color will be guidelines for further applications, always remembering that soft lush grass may be more susceptible to disease in very hot weather where cool-season grasses are to be grown through the summer with irrigation.

The first application of nitrogen fertilizer to warm-season grasses will be made in spring, after thatch removal, on established turf. Local phenological criteria may be established for homeowner guidance, e.g., the blooming of forsythia, lilac, spiraea, redbud, dogwood, or other showy plants that indicate that the growing season of bermudagrass and zoysia turf has arrived. Succeeding applications are based on growth, color, and recovery from traffic wear, remembering that excess nitrogen may result in extra mowing and faster thatch accumulation.

Fertilization of buffalograss is based on a different concept of management from that for more aggressive grasses. Buffalograss is a poor competitor and intolerant of shade. While it may benefit from fertilizer applications, they should be made when competing weeds will not benefit more than the buffalograss. Grassy, annual weeds are the more serious competitors because they grow rapidly if excess moisture becomes available, but broadleaf winter annuals are also serious competitors if autumn rains are abundant. Tolerance of buffalograss to herbicides is not well documented. It is easily damaged, especially by herbicides that reduce root depth since its tolerance to drought is based on the ability of 1 to 2 inches of top growth to support 4 or 5 feet of root depth.

In addition to the side effects of disease and weeds encouraged by excess or improperly timed fertilizer applications, damage can also occur from fertilizer applications through salt effect. Most fertilizers can burn the blades and shoots of the grass plant if applied to damp plants and not watered in promptly. Where the soils have a high salt content, as they often do in arid regions, fertilizers with a high salt index (Table 1) may damage turf by raising the salt content of the soil. This effect is related to the osmotic value of the dissolved fertilizer.

Those fertilizers with a high index readily wilt and damage the plant, especially when they are added to a naturally high saline soil. Organic fertilizers of limited solubility and low osmotic value cause little salt damage but are more slowly available because the organic nitrogen compounds must be oxidized before they can enter the plant. Withholding water can cause loss of stand, especially on newly seeded areas under arid conditions where the plant uses much water for cooling. Heavy irrigation to leach excess salts downward should preceed fertilizer applications under such conditions. Organic or low-salt-index fertilizers should be considered.

V. Major Pests

Under the widely variable conditions in this region, including sparsely populated areas with unusual, indigenous species, pests may be as surprising as they are serious. The presence of irrigated turf in the arid region may attract mammals from moose to mice, with most of the damage done by rodents or animals that prey on them. Jackrabbits may be serious in some years. Burrowing rodents, including prairie dogs and smaller species that burrow below the snow, can destroy turf over large areas, often along the borders of adjacent fields or rough areas. Poison baits or fumigants are usually recommended. Legal aspects should be cleared with the county game protector, state game warden, or other civic authority.

Grasshoppers are probably the commonest insect pest of turf in the semi-arid region. Control is easy with chemicals, except when they are migrating or concentrated into turf areas from harvested fields or attracted to the city lights. Prompt action is required to save turf and ornamental plants. Control measures considered safe in the field may not be suited to protecting turf where contact with humans and pets is expected.

Many local species of grubs, including the wheat white grub, are readily controlled by chlordane or dieldrin used as recommended on the container. Annual applications may be necessary if the chemical is trapped in the thatch layer and removed.

The many species of sod webworms may require careful timing of pesticide applications for control. Early spring applications may be effective for those that overwinter as grubs. In the southern part of its range, buffalograss is attacked by a nocturnal, subterranean webworm that harvests buffalograss blades and pulls them through a silken tube into its hole and devours them. Damage is severest on raised, well drained, or compacted areas. Chlordane at 10 pounds per acre has given control. Other lepidopterous species include cutworms and army worms that may build to surprising populations when they move in from surrounding areas.

Arid conditions favor the development of sucking insects, including chinch bugs, which may require unusual control measures if resistant to common insecticides. Greenbugs or aphids are pests locally in some years. Malathion is a safe control if necessary.

Bermudagrass throughout its range is damaged by several scale insects that are found below the leaf sheaths or underground. Malathion sprays applied during the crawler stage are recommended. Several species of billbugs that attack native grasses may move to cultivated grasses. They may prove difficult to eradicate because they feed below the thatch at the soil line where they are hard to reach with control chemicals. Dieldrin has been recommended.

Also moving from wild to cultivated grasses are the "frit flies," a small, shiny gnat that will alight on golf balls or other white objects. Their damage is commonly mistaken for disease that doesn't respond to fungicides. Resistant populations build up where the same insecticide is used for some time. A change to a different type of insecticide will often give effective control.

Eriophyid mites are nearly invisible pests that cause stunting, tufting, or rosetting of bermudagrass and buffalograss and sometimes trapping of the tips of terminal leaves. Diazinon has given control, also sulfur dust when air temperatures are below 85 F. Clones of bermudagrass with good resistance are, therefore, preferred over susceptible clones that require control measures.

Weed pests in this region likewise run from algae through ferns, cacti, sedges, and tumbleweeds to zygadenus (deathcamas). Of first importance is correct identification of the weed. Common field and range weeds can be identified by county agricultural agents. Unusual weeds should be sent to the state Agricultural Experiment Station or the curator of the Botanical Herbarium. Pressed dried plants with flowers and/or fruits attached are preferred. Where seed is present the state seed testing laboratory may give a quicker reply.

After identifying the weed, recommended control measures may be attempted; however, it should be recognized that control of one weed may release a suppressed weed that requires different control measures. A thick, dense turf is one of the best weed control measures. Weed problems usually follow some failure in management that opens the turf to weed invasion. In the arid region many weeds are well adapted for wind dispersal, from seeds alone in flight or the entire aboveground portion of a plant tumbling for miles and scattering seed with each revloution. Such dispersal may nullify attempts to control weeds by sterilizing the soil before seeding or planting in it.

VI. Turf Renovation

When a sward has deteriorated to the point where normal maintenance practices can no longer restore it, renovation is attempted through a program somewhat short of rebuilding the lawn. Before renovating, the cause of failure should be determined so that any management practices that contributed to the loss of turf may be corrected. In addition to the common disease, insect, and climatic factors that cause loss of turf, any one or more of the management factors of mowing, irrigation, fertilizing, and cultivating, or controlling pests or weeds can be misapplied or improperly timed and this leads to dead grass. Reseeding alone will not greatly improve a lawn, for the new plants will do no better than the old ones. Conditions that will give vigor to both old and new plants must be created.

VII. Summary

A. How to Grow a Good Lawn

1. Improve the fertility of the soil with fertilizers. Increase organic content of the soil by adding peat, compost, or manure. Have at least 6 inches of good topsoil. Do not overfertilize. Test soil.
2. Before planting a lawn, cultivate, rake and roll the topsoil to produce a fine, firm seedbed.
3. Choose the grass best adapted to the region, kind of use, and care to be provided. Kentucky bluegrass is best for Zones 3-5 and shady areas elsewhere. Bermudagrass and zoysia are best for Zones 6-9. Buffalograss and crested wheatgrass are best for unirrigated areas.
4. Plant grasses at the beginning of their growing seasons, cool-season grasses in September, warm-season in April-May.
5. Mow lawns as often as there is anything to cut. They cannot be mowed too often. The shorter a lawn is cut, the oftener it must be mowed. Cut cool-season grasses 2 to 3 inches high; warm-season grasses, 1 inch or less.
6. Fertilize cool-season grasses in September and March. Fertilize warm-season grasses in May and as often thereafter as they lose their dark green color.
7. Water lawns before the grass wilts. Soak the soil at least 12 inches deep. If water runs off, apply it more slowly or aerate the turf to relieve compaction and to admit water, air, and fertilizers to the roots.
8. Control white grubs, chinch bugs, and sod insects with a recommended insecticide, used according to directions.
9. Control weeds before they go to seed. Small seedling weeds are easiest to kill.
10. Remove clippings that are so long they lie on top of the grass. Accumulated clippings, stems, roots and leaves should be removed in the spring to prevent thatch and localized dry spots.

B. Warm-Season Grass Calendar, Zones 6-8

April: Remove thatch from established lawns. For new lawns, prepare seedbed and finish grading. Control weeds on area to be planted. Determine best grass for area, based on use and budget.

May: Plant warm-season grasses as early as possible in warm soil. Fertilize well and keep moist until established. Begin mowing as soon as grass is high enough to mow. Fertilize and apply needed weed control sprays to establish lawns.

June: If lawn loses color, apply 1 pound of nitrogen per 1,000 square feet. Mow weekly at 1 inch or 2 or 3 times a week at ½ inch. Apply crabgrass post-emergent sprays if needed.

July: Continue mowing and fertilizing as in June and spray with insecticide if birds start flocking to lawn for webworms and/or grubs. Water when needed.

August: Continue mowing one or more times a week and water as needed. Apply last fertilizer this month; later applications benefit chickweed and henbit.

September: Raise mower ½ inch to add to winter mulch. Continue mowing until frost. Aerify and overseed with ryegrass or bluegrass before the 15th if green winter color is desired.

October: Apply chickweed and henbit sprays at 2-leaf stage. Water thoroughly before ground freezes if soil is dry. Keep leaves raked and added to compost pile.

November: After grass is dormant and tops are dry a winter lawn paint can be applied.

C. Cool-Season Grass Calendar, Zones 4-6

August: Prepare seedbed and finish grade. Control weeds on area to be seeded. Determine best grass for area, based on use and budget. Do not permit established lawn to wilt. Keep growing with irrigation.

September: Seed as early as possiblle, fertilize well, keep moist until established. Renovate and fertilize well, keep moist until established. Renovate and fertilize established lawns. Spray weeds on established lawns.

October: Mow new lawns as soon as grass is 2 inches high. Mow weekly or oftener at 2 inches. Keep leaves removed as they fall from trees. Compost the leaves.

November: If the ground is dry, irrigate before the ground freezes. Keep fallen tree leaves raked.

Dec. to Feb.: Prepare seedbed for spring lawn when ground can be worked.

March: Seed spring lawns as early as possible. Fertilize well with fertilizer that carries insecticide like aldrin or chlordane to control grubs in both new and old lawns. Apply crabgrass pre-emergent materials now to established lawns.

April: Apply weed control sprays and insecticides before gardens are planted. Apply low-volatile 2,4-D during warm, calm days.

May: Make second application of fertilizer plus the insecticide needed. Cultivate, perforate, or aerify any hard spots in the lawn that won't take water.

June: Raise mower to cut 3 inches high. Watch for disease if season is wet. Spray for sod webworms, if present. Apply post-emergent crabgrass sprays as needed.

July: Water lawn before wilting occurs. Fertilize lightly, if needed. Mow lawn each week. Remove slime mold spores with a broom, burlap, or stream of water if their mass threatens to smother grass.

Supplementary Reading

Dittmer, H. J. 1950. Lawn problems of the Southwest. Univ. of N. M. Press, Alburquerque.

Folkner, Joseph S. 1959. Construction, renovation and management of athletic fields. Report 158, Arizona Agr. Expt. Sta.

Keen, Ray A. and L. R. Quinlan. 1966. Lawns in Kansas. Circ. 327. Kansas Agr. Expt. Sta.

Love, J. R. 1967. Salinity and its related problems in turfgrass. The Golf Supt. 35(6):20-21.

Lunt, O. R., C. Kaempffe, and V. B. Younger. 1964. Tolerance of five turfgrass species to soil alkali. Agron. J. 56:481-483.

Lunt, O. R., V. B. Younger, and J. J. Dertli. 1961. Salinity tolerance of five turfgrass varieties. Agron. J. 53:247-249.

Rader, L. F., Jr. L. M. White, and C. W. Whitaker. 1943. The salt index—a measure of the effect of fertilizers on the concentration of the soil solution. Soil. Sci. 55:201-218.

Tate, H. F. and S. Fazio. 1965. Lawns for Arizona. Bull. A-6. Arizona Agr. Expt. Sta.

Tate, H. F. and J. S. Folkner. 1966. Turf on large recreation and play areas. Bull. A-48. Arizona Agr. Expt. Sta.

Younger, V. B., J. H. Madison, M. H. Kimball, and W. B. Davis. 1962. Climatic zones for turfgrass in California. California Agr. 16(7):2-4.

22 Athletic Fields

John C. Harper II

The Pennsylvania State University
University Park, Pennsylvania

I. Introduction

Playing safety and pleasing appearance dictate that athletic fields be adequately turfed. In the true sense, functional value of athletic field turf is far more important than its aesthetic properties. Accurate records are available to show marked injury reduction on dense, wear resistant turf in comparison to sparsely turfed, often dusty, athletic areas. A direct correlation has been reported between dusty athletic fields and the frequency of respiratory ailments. To the spectator, the school or college administrators, the professional team owners, and the TV cameras pleasing appearance is a necessity.

Production and maintenance of quality athletic field turf depends on the grass species or varieties used, proper design and construction, adequate drainage, soil fertility, and a comprehensive maintenance program which recognizes the problems involved. Any area lacking in any of these considerations will be virtually impossible to keep in acceptable playing condition.

II. Specification Guide

No athletic field turf can be any better than the construction and planning specifications for that field. Specifications should be clear and complete, covering in detail all methods and materials used in the operation in order to provide a definite basis on which bids can be made and to assure the use of proper techniques and quality materials. Good specifications operate to the mutual benefit of the contractor and the owner.

Specifications will vary between individual jobs due to differences in soil and climatic conditions and the proposed use of the area. Certain things, however, should be common to all specifications. Chapter 27, Specifications for Turfgrass Establishment, should be consulted for information on the preparation of specifications.

III. Construction, Grading, and Drainage

Subsurface, as well as surface, drainage is of utmost importance on any athletic area. Water-logged soils are not conducive to optimum root development so necessary in providing vigorous turf growth. In addition, soggy conditions at the soil surface restrict footing, slows down play, and may lead to serious injury. Naturally well-drained subsoils normally will provide adequate internal drainage.

On heavy soils some type of underdrainage blanket generally is required, especially on fields that must be used under all types of weather conditions. Crushed limestone or washed gravel normally are the most effective materials for this purpose, although cinders and similar materials have been used. Sharp angular material of 1- to 2-inch diameter is preferred over rounded material such as river gravel. The subsurface beneath the drainage blanket should be contoured in the same manner as will be the finished grade. This permits the stone or gravel to be laid down in a layer of uniform thickness, retains the desired contour, and will assure uniform thickness of the topsoil layer.

Soil compaction is a major problem on athletic fields. Its primary cause is foot trampling and the use of heavy equipment either in construction or maintenance, especially if the soil is wet. Compaction seals the surface and prevents normal movement of air and water into and through the soil. For this reason, tiling of the entire playing area, with the exception of seepage spots or high water tables, may be of little value because of surface compaction which impedes water movement into the tile lines. Good contouring of the surface will aid substantially in reducing compaction by providing for rapid removal of excess surface water. Tile systems should be placed in the most advantageous design to pick up this excess surface water. Contouring and tiling will vary considerably with the type of playing area involved.

Football gridirons may be crowned to provide excellent surface drainage without interfering with play. The design should provide for a 12- to 18-inch crown (1.25 to 1.87%) sloping uniformly from the center of the field to the side lines without pockets. The side lines should be level. Tile lines are placed in slight swales along the side lines with catch basins to remove water more rapidly than it will be absorbed through the soil.

Fields designed for football are not acceptable for use as soccer fields. The high crown on the former makes side shots in soccer very difficult. The crown on soccer fields should not exceed 1%. The actual height of the crown from midfield to side lines will vary considerably as the rules of soccer permit fields to be a minimum of 150 feet and a maximum of 300 feet in width. Tile systems with catch basins along the side lines should be constructed in the same manner as for football fields.

Baseball diamonds will vary considerably with the type of baseball being played. Official rule books of the Little League, State Interscholastic Athletic Associations, the National Collegiate Athletic Association, and the Professional Leagues should be consulted when laying out diamonds. Normally, baseball diamonds should have the pitcher's mound elevated approximately 10 inches above home plate and the base paths. The fall from the mound should be turtle-backed and not abrupt to the edge of the mound area. The infield area from the edge of the mound to the base paths should have not more than a 1% grade. Removal of surface water from the infield can be accomplished by placing tile lines on the outer edge of the infield skinned area. These lines should be drained away from the playing area in any manner conforming to local conditions. The outfield should be graded to a 1% slope from the center in all directions with the water carried off at the edge of the field by a catch basin tile system.

IV. Soil Modification

Soil compaction is the most common cause of poor turf on athletic fields. Constant traffic and the use of heavy maintenance equipment can squeeze soil particles into a highly impervious mass especially in the surface ½ to 1 inch. Heavy soils with high proportions of silt and clay compact more readily than lighter sandy soils containing large quantities of coarse particles.

Compaction reduces the rate of movement of air and water through the soil. This results in stagnant conditions that prevent grass roots from functioning normally. They first become shallow and may eventually die. As a result, the turf weakens, loses its vigor, and density, and is more susceptible to mechanical injury.

The effects of compaction on heavy soils can be minimized by adding physical conditioning materials when the field is built. Materials most commonly used for this purpose are sand and some form of organic matter. Calcined clays are also being used in some areas of the country. The quantity and quality of sand used will depend upon the character of the soil to be treated. Heavy clays and silts may require as much as 50 to 60% sand by volume mixed to a 5-inch depth to improve their resistance to compaction while retaining the firmness necessary for good playing conditions. Soils with higher contents of natural sand do not require as much additional sand for conditioning.

Graded sands with the fines removed are best adapted for use as physical conditioners. The specifications should designate the type as washed ground rock, etc., and the sieve analysis as indication of particle size range. It is currently believed that a minimum range of particle sizes with less than 10% passing a No. 60 sieve is most desirable. A majority of particles should be approximately of the ½- to 1-mm size range (passing a No. 18 sieve, being retained on a No. 35 sieve).

Recent research has indicated that calcined clays which have been calcined at 1,600 C or higher may be used successfully in place of sand as a physical conditioner. It may be necessary to use a greater amount of the calcined clay to achieve the same effect. In addition to the effect on physical condition, calcined clays will increase the total water-holding capacity of the soil but do not materially increase the available water-holding capacity.

Various types of organic materials also are effective in reducing soil compaction. Raw or cultivated reed sedge peat and moss peats are well adapted for this purpose. Both types, but especially the moss peats, should be run through a hammer mill or some type of grinder to facilitate later incorporation of the materials into the soil. They have a high moisture absorptive capacity and improve aeration of the soil.

Where peats are used, it is seldom necessary to apply them at rates of over 10 to 15% by volume. Depending upon the depth to which they are mixed, this would require 1 to 2 cubic yards of peat per 1,000 square feet of area.

Other types of organic materials may be used to make soils more resistant to compaction. These include raw sewage sludge, tannery wastes, seed hulls, and well-rotted sawdust. Most of these materials, because of their faster rate of decomposition, are effective for a much shorter time than peats. The quantity applied must be estimated on the basis of their moisture content, physical character, and the relative persistence in the soil. Raw sewage sludge may contain 70% or more water so that relatively high rates of application will be necessary to obtain the required quantity of dry matter. Seed hulls usually are light and fluffy and are difficult to mix into the soil uniformly when applied at heavy rates. Rotted sawdust decomposes relatively slowly and can be used in volumes approximating the rate of application for peats.

Where soils are extremely sandy, colloidal phosphate may be added to improve the physical and chemical properties of the soil. Colloidal phosphate, which is a phosphatic clay, will reduce the percolation rate and increase the water-holding capacity and cation exchange capacity of the soil.

The maximum value of any soil-conditioning material is obtained only when it is uniformly mixed into the soil to a specified depth. Best results are obtained by mixing the physical amendments and the soil off-site with a Royer®, Lindig®, or similar type shredder. When mixing physical amendments into the soil on-site, various tools such as rotary hoes, rotovators, or disks can be used. If both sand and organic matter are to be mixed into the soil, the organic matter should be laid down first with the sand on top. Tillage tends to float the light organic material upward while the heavy sand moves downward. The operation should be checked repeatedly to assure that a thorough job is done. Layers of any given material must be avoided. Disruption of the soil continuity may cause serious drainage problems. Tillage depth should be a minimum of 6 inches. If no drainage blanket is used under the topsoil, tillage should be sufficiently deep to mix a minimum of 3 inches of the subsoil with the topsoil. This will provide a transition zone between the subsoil and the topsoil without a sharp line of demarcation between the two.

V. Establishment

A. Soil Test.

A complete soil test to determine lime and fertilizer requirements provides the best guide for proper establishment. The test should provide the pH and lime requirement of the soil, the amounts of phosphorus, potassium, calcium, and magnesium in the soil, the cation exchange capacity of the soil, and the percent saturation of potassium, calcium, and magnesium. Soil tests may be obtained through land-grant universities or through commercial laboratories. Soil tests should be interpreted and recommendations made by trained agronomists familiar with the particular soil testing procedure used. Attempts should not be made to compare soil tests run by different laboratories.

B. Seedbed Preparation.

Seedbed preparation is one of the most critical operations in constructing an athletic area. Improper seedbed preparation or preparation under adverse weather or soil moisture conditions may result in complete seeding failure. Working soils containing excessive moisture, especially with heavy equipment, will destroy the physical condition of the soil. Destruction of the soil physical condition increases soil compaction with resultant reduction in aeration and drainage of the soil. Compaction impedes the movement of fertilizer nutrients, water, and air into the soil. The basic premise in modifying soils with sand and/or organic matter is to reduce the compactability of the soil.

Physical condition of the soil can also be destroyed by over tillage. This is especially true if a rapidly revolving tine-type rotary tiller is used. This machine tends to beat the soil so much that soil structure is destroyed. Rotovators, on the other hand, are quite satisfactory for seedbed preparation. Rotovators, in contrast to rotary tillers, are equipped with shovel-like cultivators which revolve relatively slowly. Plowing provides an acceptable method of tillage, provided care is taken to work out, by disking and floating, the unevenness caused by the furrows. Depending on the soil involved, tillage by disking alone, may be satisfactory. The final seedbed should be a homogeneous mixture of the original soil, physical amendments, lime, and fertilizer and completely free of hollows, other depressions, and soft spots.

C. Lime.

The soil reaction affects the activity of soil microorganisms, the availability of plant nutrients, and the activity of disease-causing fungi. Soil microbial activity is essential to the decomposition of clippings and other organic matter and to the breakdown of certain types of fertilizer materials and their subsequent conversion to nutrient forms that can be utilized by the plants. At pH values over 7.5 or under 5.5, certain plant nutrients can become limiting through the formation of insoluble compounds. Fungi which cause 99% or more of turf diseases are favored by high acidity. Grasses grow best within certain pH ranges. It is fortunate that grasses make their optimum growth, nutrients are most available, soil microorganism activity is greatest, and fungi activity is reduced at a pH range of 6.0 to 7.5.

Lime is the most economical and readily obtainable material for correcting soil acidity. Many county agricultural extension offices, land-grant universities, and commercial soil testing laboratories have equipment to make lime requirement tests. Properly taken soil samples that are representative of the area should be submitted and lime applications based on the results of the test. Test recommendations are based on standard ground limestone. Its value is based on chemical composition (oxide equivalent) and degree of fineness. Ground limestone exists as calcium carbonate (calcite) or as a mixture of calcium and magnesium carbonates (dolomite). Standard ground limestone contains a minimum of 50% lime oxides (calcium oxide plus magnesium oxide), 98% passing a 20-mesh sieve and at least 40% passing a 100-mesh sieve. Application rates should be enough to meet the full lime requirement. Lime should be applied prior to preliminary tillage operations and worked into the soil to a minimum depth of 5 or 6 inches.

D. Basic Fertilizer.

Soils vary widely in the quantities of available plant nutrient materials which they contain. Nutrients most likely to be deficient are nitrogen, phosphorous, and potassium. Soil tests will provide adequate information on the need for phosphate and potash, and should be the basis for the basic fertilizer application. When soil tests show medium to low levels of these materials, liberal applications should be made in preparing the seedbed for turf. Normally, adequate quantities of phosphate and potash can be supplied by an application of 75 pounds per thousand square feet of an 0-20-20 fertilizer or the equivalent. The material should be applied prior to tillage operations and worked into the soil to a depth of 5 or 6 inches.

E. Starter Fertilizer.

Soil tests are not a reliable measure for determining the quantity of nitrogen that should be used. They show only the quantity of soluble nitrate nitrogen present at the time of testing. This type of nitrogen is utilized or lost very rapidly so a soil test may not show the true situation. Three basic facts control the use of nitrogen for turfgrass establishment. These are the needs of the grass itself, the kind of nitrogen applied, and the depth to which it is mixed into the soil. It is seldom necessary to apply a total of more than 1 to 1½ pounds of quickly available nitrogen per thousand square feet to meet the normal requirements of the young seedling grass. If larger quantities are applied, losses from leaching may be greater and there is danger of over-stimulation that may make the young grass more susceptible to damping-off and other diseases. This immediately available nitrogen may be exhausted quickly requiring reapplication within 4 or 5 weeks after emergence of the seedlings. The necessity for a second application in such a short time may be avoided by supplementing the initial application with additional nitrogen (3 to 5 lb. per 1,000 $ft.^2$) derived from materials such as natural organics or ureaform compounds which release nitrogen slowly. Such materials can be mixed into the soil with much less danger of loss before the grass roots can utilize the nitrogen which they supply.

It is best to apply fertilizers containing nitrogen just prior to seeding. These should also carry phosphate and potash even though previous applications of these materials have been made. This will insure that liberal quantities of the nutrient materials will be available to developing seedlings. The starter fertilizer should be worked into the soil to a depth of not more than 1 inch. If a material containing nitrogen in a soluble form is used, the nutrient ratio of N-P_2O_5-K_2O should be approximately 1-1-1. A grade such as 10-10-10 would conform to this. The fertilizer should be applied at a rate to supply about 1 to 1½ pounds of each nutrient per 1,000 square feet. If a fertilizer containing 35% or more of the total nitrogen as water-insoluble nitrogen is used, the ratio of nitrogen to the other nutrients can be increased to 2-1-1 or 3-1-1 and the material applied at a rate to supply 3 to 5 pounds of nitrogen per 1,000 square feet.

Prior to the application of the starter fertilizer, the seedbed should be firmed to indicate the presence of pockets or soft spots in the seedbed. Such areas must be eliminated by regrading. The starter fertilizer may be worked into the top 1 inch of soil with a York® rake or similar tool.

F. Pesticides.

It is sometimes desirable to treat the seedbed with some type of pesticide if a serious weed or insect problem is present. In areas where nematodes are a problem, a nematicide may be used prior to seeding to alleviate this condition. A combination problem such as nematodes and an undesirable grass or weed can best be controlled with a temporary soil fumigant such as methyl bromide. This material is a gas under pressure that must be applied to the soil under a gas-proof cover. In contrast to many other temporary soil sterilants, there is no soil residual and the area may be safely seeded within 48 to 72 hours after removal of the cover (a longer period may be required for vegetative material). Following the use of a temporary soil sterilant the soil surface should be disturbed as little as possible.

In the crabgrass region of the U. S., siduron, a preemergence crabgrass control herbicide may be applied to give crabgrass control without injuring the desirable turfgrass seedlings. The material should be applied following the seeding and firming operation in order to insure an unbroken chemical barrier at the soil surface.

G. Seeding.

(Refer to Table 1 for recommended grass species and varieties)

The most important items in seeding turfgrass areas are uniform distribution, proper covering, and firming the soil around the seed. Various types of mechanical seeders will distribute seed uniformly when they are correctly calibrated and operated. These can be divided into two general classes: (1) the hopper and cyclone types which drop the seed on the surface of the seedbed, and (2) the cultipacker type which distributes and covers the seed and firms the soil in one operation. If the hopper or cyclone type is used, seed must be covered by light raking or harrowing followed by light rolling to firm the soil. In either case, the seeder should be calibrated to determine the proper setting for the kind of seed and desired seeding rate.

Calibrating can be done in various ways. A simple method is to hang a shallow pan under the seed hopper and operate the equipment at a

Table 1. Turfgrasses for athletic fields.

Region*	General area	Northern portions & High elevations	Southern portions & Seacoast
1	Tall fescue; Ky. bluegrass blends; Ky. bluegrass - red fescue; Pelo, Manhattan, Pennfine ryegrass†		Bermudagrass: U-3 Tufcote
2	Bermudagrass: Common Tiflawn Texturf 10 Tifway Santa Ana	Tall fescue; Ky. bluegrass blends; Pelo, Manhattan, Pennfine ryegrass†	Zoysia, Centipede, Bahia
3	Bermudagrass: Common Tiflawn Tifway Tifgreen Ormond Centipede; Bahia		
4	Ky. bluegrass blends; Tall fescue; Ky. bluegrass - red fescue	Pelo, Manhattan, Pennfine ryegrass†	Bermudagrass: U-3, Common Tifgreen Tiffine Tifway
5	Ky. bluegrass blends; Tall fescue: Pelo, Manhattan, Pennfine ryegrass† (Irrigation required)		Bermudagrass: U-3, Common Tifgreen Tiffine Tifway
6	Ky. bluegrass blends; Tall fescue; Pelo, Manhattan, Pennfine ryegrass†		

* See figure 1, regions of grass adaptations. † To be used in combination with Ky. bluegrass blends and Ky. bluegrass-red fescue mixtures.

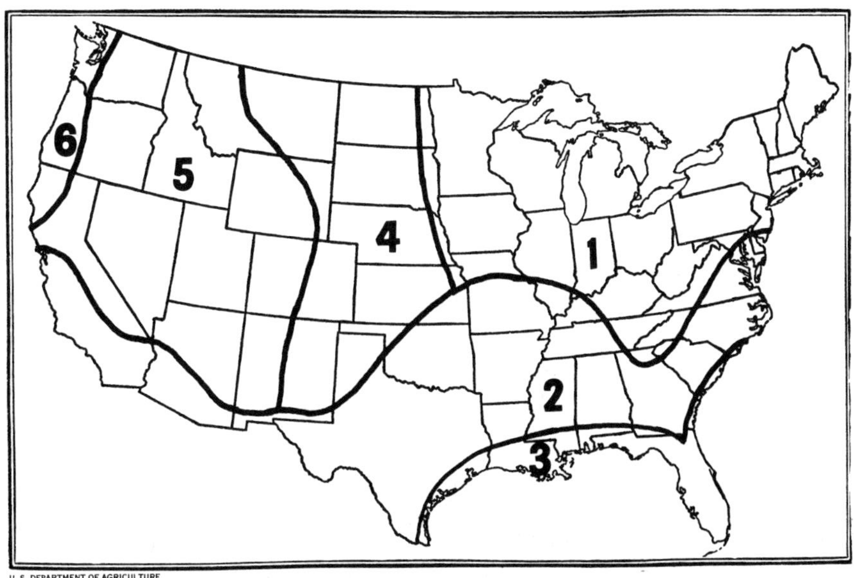

Figure 1. Regions of grass adaptations in the U.S.

standard speed for a given distance at a trial setting. The distance traveled multiplied by the width of the hopper will give the area covered. Seed discharged into the pan can be weighed to show the quantity used on the area covered. Settings can then be adjusted to deliver more or less as desired. Cyclone seeders normally are calibrated by a trial and error method. If a known amount of seed is placed in the seeder and completely run out, the amount of seed applied to a specific area can be calculated. By adjusting the seeder opening and repeating this process, reasonably accurate calibration can be obtained. To secure maximum uniformity in distribution, it is desirable to set the machine to deliver half of the total rate desired. This will permit making two passes over the area. Best results are obtained when the second pass is made at right angles to the first.

Dormant seeding may be used to advantage when construction schedules prevent seeding at optimum times. The object is to gain several weeks growing conditions in early spring. The principle of dormant seeding is to sow seed during winter when weather conditions normally prevent germination and seedling establishment of all species. It should be emphasized that dormant seedings seldom are as successful as conventional seedings.

Hydro-seeding offers a fast method of applying starter fertilizer, seed, and mulch in one operation and is becoming increasingly popular. A slurry of seed, fertilizer, and a mulching material such as wood fiber or other cellulose material is prepared in a large agitation tank and pumped through a spray gun onto the area to be planted. Commercial hydro-seeders or hydro-mulchers currently available vary in their capacity but models are available that are capable of fertilizing, seeding and mulching 7 acres per hour or fertilizing and seeding 12 acres per hour.

H. Mulching.

Mulches are used primarily to protect against washing prior to germination and establishment of the new turf and to prevent rapid drying out of the seedbed which might delay or injure germination. They are effective, also, in protecting late fall seedings from winter injury.

Materials most commonly used are straw or some form of hay or coarse grass clippings. Mulching rates with these materials vary from 1½ to 2 tons per acre, depending upon how uniformly they are spread. Machines have been developed that spread mulch mechanically. These do an excellent job and should be used if available. However, hand spreading is not difficult and can be done rapidly.

Various methods of holding the mulch in place can be used. It can be weighed down by placing boards or brush at intervals over the area. These can be removed as soon as the mulch has been thoroughly wetted down and flattened into place and before the seed has germinated. A system of stakes and tie-down strings also is effective. For best results, the stakes should be placed on about 40-foot centers and the strings stretched between them in a systematic design.

Where equipment is available, the mulch cover can be sprayed with emulsified asphalt at a rate of 1/10 gallon per square yard. The asphalt serves as a binding material that holds the mulch in place. This method requires special spraying equipment. It is expensive and there is little evidence that it is effective enough to justify the additional cost and trouble involved.

If the mulch has not been spread uniformly and it is so heavy on certain areas that the young seedlings have difficulty in growing through it, part of it should be removed. Where the grass shows green above the mulch, it can be left on without danger of injury to the turf.

Wood fiber or other cellulose mulches may be applied with a hydro-mulcher. Properly applied mulch of this type does not need to be removed.

I. Vegetative Planting.

(Refer to Table 1 for recommended grass species and varieties).

Establishment of turf by vegetative planting is limited to those grasses that spread by creeping stems or runners. The process consists of shredding sod grown in nurseries for this purpose and planting the material on a prepared seedbed. The shredded sod can be broadcast over the entire area or planted in spaced rows. If broadcast, it must be covered to a depth of 1/4 to 1/2 inch with prepared topdressing soil. If planted in rows, the runners are set in open furrows 2 to 3 inches deep and covered by backing soil over them. In either case, seedbed preparation should be the same as for seeding and the entire area firmed by light rolling after planting.

From 5 to 10 bushels of shredded planting stock will be required per 1,000 square feet of area to be planted if the broadcast method is used. When planted in rows 1 bushel of planting stock will plant about 600 feet of row. Rows can be spaced from 12 inches or less, to 2 feet, depending on the kind of grass and how quickly complete cover is required. Zoysia rows require closer spacing than bermudagrass because of its slower growth rate..

J. Sodding.

Sodding is the most expensive method of initial turf establishment. It involves cost of the sod, whether bought commercially or grown in a sod nursery. Its use on an athletic field is limited to those situations where it is necessary to provide a mature, wear-resistant turf cover in a short time. A properly laid sod on a well-prepared sodbed will knit and be ready for use within 2 to 8 weeks depending on the grass species, the sod quality, and the weather conditions. In contrast, comparable turf cannot be produced by seeding in less than 3 months to a full growing season.

A successful sodding operation depends on the quality of the sod, its condition, and the care used in preparing the sodbed and laying the sod. Unless quality sod is used, results will not justify the high cost involved in establishing turf by this method. It should be dense and well knit, so that it can be cut as thin as possible, and in long strips that can be rolled to facilitate handling. Thin-cut sod weighs less, lies better, and roots quickly. Quality sod of the grasses adapted for use on athletic fields should have a maximum root and soil thickness of 1/2 to 3/4 inch. It should be cut in strips 12 to 16 inches wide and 5 to 6 feet long. This makes a convenient size roll for handling. If cut sod is to be held for several days before laying, it should be spread out flat, grass side up, in a cool place and kept moist. Rolled or stacked sod will weaken and yellow rapidly and will not be in good condition to start growth promptly when laid.

Preparation of the sodbed, including liming, fertilization, and soil conditioning, should be the same as for seedbeds. The surface should be firmed by rolling, and, if dry, it should be wet down with a fine spray just prior to laying sod.

The first course of sod should be laid to a line that has been squared to the longitudinal axis of the field. Sods of the next course are matched against the first so that the joints between pieces in the adjacent courses do not coincide. The sod is tamped lightly as it is set to insure good contact with the soil surface at all points. Any openings that occur in the seams between the pieces should be filled with prepared topdressing to prevent excessive drying out at these spots. In periods of dry weather, a regular watering program should be followed until the sod has rooted.

Freshly laid sod should not be rolled. Rolling at this time often causes the sod to creep ahead of the roller and usually does more harm than good. After rooting has occurred, a light roller can be used to smooth out minor irregularities.

K. Establishment Maintenance.

Newly seeded areas or vegetatively planted areas should be provided with sufficient irrigation to insure germination and rooting of the seedlings or rooting of the vegetative material. Moisture is especially critical when the seed coat begins to swell and the seedling emerges and during the first few days following vegetative planting.

As soon as the new seeding or vegetative planting exceeds its normal cutting height by 1/4 to 1/3, it should be clipped to the height at which it will be maintained. A frequency of clipping should be maintained that will result in removal of no more than 1/4 of the total leaf surface at any given mowing.

L. Repair.

Little or no repair work is required on newly established athletic areas if all establishment operations have been properly carried out. Washes or depressions should be brought to grade using the same soil or soil mixture used on the overall field. Liming, fertilizing, seeding and mulching should be done as previously described for the initial seeding.

VI. Maintenance

A good maintenance program is just as necessary to insure athletic field turf of satisfactory quality as sound establishment methods. The essentials of such a program are that it should:

a. Produce tough grass with maximum wear resistance
b. Maintain high density to resist weed invasion and encroachment of undesirable grasses
c. Encourage deep rooting to provide good anchorage and firm footing
d. Adjust mowing height to grass requirements and playing demands
e. Fertilize and water at such times and in such manner as to provide steady growth with maximum quality
f. Consider the endurance limits of the turf in scheduling use of the field
g. Repair injuries due to wear or other causes promptly.

The following outline of maintenance operations and methods is designed to meet these requirements.

A. Mowing.

Grass should be cut often and at a height adjusted to the predominating grass in the mixture. Merion Kentucky bluegrass, common Kentucky bluegrass, and the red fescues or mixtures of these grasses should not be cut to a height of less than 1½ to 2 inches. Kentucky 31 tall fescue should not be cut to a height of less than 2 to 2½ inches. Frequency of mowing is governed by the growth rate of the grass. Cutting should not remove more than ¼ to ⅓ of the total leaf surface at a given clipping. If this practice is followed, it is not necessary or desirable to change the mowing height at any time. Bermudagrass should be kept ½ inch high by frequent mowing. When cut higher it becomes spongy and loose and does not provide a good footing or a dense turf. Other warm-season grasses should be cut at approximately ¾ inch.

B. Watering.

Irrigate only when the grass shows signs of wilting and discoloration because of lack of water. Equipment should be adjusted to apply water only as fast as the soil will absorb it. A soil-sampling probe can be used to determine the rate and depth of moisture penetration. Sprinklers should be operated until water has penetrated to a depth of at least 6 inches. Traveling types of sprinklers will provide more uniform water distribution than stationary kinds, unless the latter are checked often. Periodic aeration will speed up water penetration and usually results in more efficient water use.

C. Aeration.

Constant trampling often causes the development of a compact impermeable surface layer of soil. This condition can be aggravated by mowing, rolling, or the use of other heavy equipment when soils are wet. Compaction cannot be avoided under such conditions and, when it develops, grass roots are injured because of lack of sufficient moisture and air to assure normal functioning. In addition, it becomes more difficult for water and fertilizer to penetrate into the soil.

Various types of aerating tools have been devised to break through the compacted soil layer mechanically and remove a soil core. Size of openings made by these machines varies with the diameter of the hollow tines or spoons used. For athletic field use such openings should be about 3/4 to 1 inch in diameter. Equipment having solid tines or spikes should not be mistaken for aerating equipment. Aerators always remove a soil core whereas solid tine spikers do not. Spikers actually increase soil compaction as the movement of the soil to all sides by the penetration of the solid tine forces the soil into a denser mass.

Fields should be systematically aerated a minimum of three times per year. Heavy aeration (6 to 8 times over the area) in the spring prior to fertilization and/or overseeding is recommended followed by light aeration (1 to 3 times over) in late summer or early fall prior to fertilization. Aeration at these times should be followed by dragging with a chain drag or a section of chain link fence. At the close of the fall playing season again aerate at the heavy rate but do not drag the area following aeration. By allowing the aeration holes to remain open, freezing and thawing of moisture in the holes will improve the effectiveness of aeration. Where a field is in constant use it is sometimes necessary to give it additional aerations during the season. A good rule to follow is to aerate whenever the turf begins to show the effects of soil compaction.

D. Lime Applications.

Soils should be tested every 2 or 3 years for lime requirement. This service is available at no cost at most county agricultural extension service offices. Lime should be applied whenever the soil shows a pH test of less than 6.2 or a lime requirement of more than 1,000 pounds of limestone per acre. Applications can be made at any time. Usually it is most effective and convenient to apply limestone in late fall following thorough aeration or during the winter on frozen turf. Ground agricultural limestone is the recommended form of lime to use. Where soil tests show a deficiency of magnesium, ground dolomitic limestone should be used.

E. Fertilization.

The maintenance fertilizer program should be based on complete soil test results. Required amounts of phosphate and/or potash vary greatly with the natural soil fertility, establishment fertilization, and previous maintenance fertilization. Most athletic areas will require two complete fertilizer applications per year although some fields may require only one complete fertilizer application supplemented with nitrogen applications. Occasionally fields having high phosphate and potash levels will require only nitrogen applications. When a single application of a complete fertilizer is made, cool-season grasses such as Kentucky bluegrass and fescue are benefited most by fall applications.

Bermudagrass and zoysia should receive the application in the spring. Where soil tests show low levels of phosphate and/or potash, it may be necessary to make additional supplemental applications of superphosphate, potash, or phosphate-potash fertilizers one or more years in the fall until these soil levels are satisfactory.

Rate of application of the complete fertilizer will vary with the species or variety of grass, the soil fertility level, the fertilizer grade and the type of nitrogen contained in the fertilizer. Cool-season grasses require the major plant nutrients (nitrogen, phosphate, potash) in an approximate 2-1-1 or 3-1-2 ratio. Warm-season grasses require a fertilizer ratio of approximately 4-1-2.

Red fescue, common Kentucky bluegrass, and named varieties of Kentucky bluegrass other than Merion require approximately 4 pounds of nitrogen, 2 pounds of phosphate, and 2 pounds of potash per 1,000 square feet per season. Merion Kentucky bluegrass and Kentucky 31 tall fescue require approximately 5 to 7 pounds of nitrogen per 1,000 square feet with corresponding increases in phosphate and potash. Warm-season grasses may require as little as 4 and as much as 20 pounds of nitrogen per 1,000 square feet per season. This is due to the variance in requirements between species, between varieties of bermudagrass, and the length of the growing season.

The ideal fertilizer program provides uniform growth over the entire growing season. The type of nitrogen-carrying materials in a fertilizer is very important in determining how such a program can be obtained. Basically, nitrogen materials are divided into two broad groups—quickly available and slowly available.*

The quickly available materials are water-soluble and the nitrogen is immediately available to the plants. The results are a sudden flush of growth and a rapid depletion (2 to 6 weeks) of the available nitrogen. Thus, it will be necessary to make frequent light applications of these materials in order to obtain uniform growth over a long time and to prevent possible burning. Quickly available nitrogen materials include ammonium sulfate, ammonium nitrate, nitrate of soda, ammonium phosphate, calcium nitrate, urea, and others.

Slowly available nitrogen materials relase most of their nitrogen over relatively long periods. These materials depend on soil bacteria for decomposition and to transform the resultant compounds into nitrogen forms available to the plant. The activity of these bacteria, in turn, depends on moisture and temperature conditions. Under high temperatures and adequate moisture supply the breakdown of these materials is accelerated. Under conditions of low moisture or cool temperatures, the breakdown will be much slower. Within slowly available materials there are three groups—natural organic materials, ureaform, and IBDU.

Natural organic materials include activated or processed sewage sludge, animal and vegetable tankage, manures, soybean meal, cottonseed meal, etc. Because these natural organic materials vary greatly in

* The terms quickly available and slowly available are synonymous with soluble and slowly soluble.

their chemical composition there will be a wide variation in the rate of decomposition, although all of them will release their nitrogen at a slower rate than the quickly available nitrogen sources.

Ureaform compounds are synthetic materials made by the chemical union of urea and formaldehyde. Within a given ureaform material there is actually a series of chemical compounds with varying degrees of solubility. As the soil microorganisms decompose these materials, the more soluble materials break down first, followed by each successive compound. Thus, a small amount of nitrogen is constantly being released over a relatively long time. This permits the user to apply heavy applications of these materials at infrequent intervals. Care must be taken not to confuse urea (quickly available nitrogen) with ureaform (slowly available nitrogen).

It has been generally accepted by definition that a turfgrade fertilizer should be a complete fertilizer containing a minimum of 10 units of nitrogen, an approximate 2-1-1 to 4-1-1 ratio, and 35% or more of the total nitrogen as water-insoluble nitrogen (slowly available). Many fertilizer companies manufacture fertilizers meeting these requirements specifically for the turfgrass industry.

It must be pointed out that quality athletic field turf can be produced with any nitrogen source provided the nitrogen is used properly. When quickly available (soluble) sources of nitrogen are used it is suggested that single application rates do not exceed 1 pound of nitrogen per 1,000 square feet. When slowly available nitrogen sources are used, single application rates may be as high as 4 or 5 pounds of nitrogen per 1,000 square feet. The danger of "burning" with quickly available sources of nitrogen also dictates that application rates be low and applications frequent.

As a result of excessive rainfall or other unusual growing conditions, nitrogen supply may be depleted prior to making scheduled fertilizer applications. Under these conditions, supplemental nitrogen applications at light rates may be beneficial to the turf. This may be most easily accomplished by applying pelleted urea at a rate of 85 to 100 pounds per acre as indicated by the needs of the grass.

F. Weed Control.

It is impossible to prevent damage to athletic field turf. Weeds, clover, and other undesirable plants come into the injured areas. Unless these are removed promptly, they will prevent desirable grasses from healing the scars. Chemical treatments usually are the most effective means of control.

Broadleaf weeds such as dandelion, broadleaf plantain, and narrow leaf plantain (buckhorn) can be controlled with 2,4-D. Clover, knotweed, chickweed, and sorrell are susceptible to dicamba. Crabgrass can be controlled with any of several pre-emergence or post-emergence herbicides. For the latest recommendations on weed control in turfgrass areas, obtain the latest Agricultural Extension Service publication on turfgrass weed control from your county Agricultural Extension office.

In using herbicides, the directions on the manufacturers labels for rates of application and care in handling must be followed.

G. Disease and Insects.

A number of diseases and insects may cause serious injury to turfgrasses. The first step in a control program is to determine the cause of the trouble. Identification, particularly of diseases, often is difficult. Since many diseases and some insects require specific treatment, diagnosis of the cause of injuries should be checked with a competent authority, such as the county agricultural extension agent or university turf specialists, before expensive control measures are undertaken. Effective control measures have been developed for many diseases and insects. For the latest recommendations, contact the Agricultural Extension Service through your county office.

H. Use-Discipline.

There is a limit to the amount of traffic that even the best-managed turf can withstand without excessive injury. This must be recognized if frequent costly repairs are to be avoided. Some of the things that often can be done to reduce injury are the following.

a. Schedule a minimum of use when fields are wet;

b. Where size of area permits, rotate play areas to permit a recovery period for turf showing the effects of wear;

c. Avoid concentrated trampling, such as practicing band formations, whenever possible;

d. Limit or withhold use of new seedings or vegetative plantings until a mature turf has developed;

e. Do not use area in spring until the turf has recovered from winter dormancy;

f. Keep off when there has been surface thawing of frozen turf.

VII. General Repair and Renovation

A well-designed repair and renovation program should be a standard part of athletic field turfgrass management. The method must be adjusted to the way in which the field is used.

A. Repair by Reseeding.

Where a field is in frequent use, repair by reseeding usually will not produce enough improvement to justify the time and expense involved. This method is practicable only when the field is out of play long enough to permit new seedings to become fully established. This will require 2 to 3 months for bermudagrass and 3 to 6 months for cool-season grasses.

1. Reseeding with permanent grasses

a. Apply proper weed killer to eliminate weed species present. Some herbicides require a waiting period before proceeding to the next step.

b. Mow area closely (3/4 to 1 inch) and remove all clippings, leaves, and other debris.

c. Aerate thoroughly (6 to 8 times over).

d. Apply ground limestone according to lime requirement test.

e. Apply fertilizer according to soil test.

f. Aerate 6 to 8 times over to work some of the limestone and fertilizer into the soil and to improve the seedbed.

g. Seed with one of the seed mixtures suggested for establishment. Choose seed mixture most similar to the existing turf. Seeding rate should be adjusted to the amount of existing grass on the field. If turf loss has been 50% or less, use half of the normal establishment seeding rate. On completely bare areas, use full establishment seeding rate.

h. Drag area with a piece of chain link fence or steel mat to break up aeration cores and to work lime, fertilizer, and seed through the existing turf into aeration holes.

i. Roll lightly to firm loose surface soil.

2. Reseeding with ryegrass

There is sometimes need for quick temporary cover on areas that connot be otherwise treated. Ryegrass can be used to advantage under such circumstances. Preparation should be the same as outlined above for permanent seedings. Use annual or perennial ryegrass at a rate of 6 to 8 pounds per 1,000 square feet. Temporary seedings of ryegrass normally will not persist beyond the season of planting. Permanent seedings should be made at the first opportunity.

Improved varieties of perennial ryegrass, such as Pelo, Manhattan, and Pennfine, may be used in place of annual or common perennial ryegrass and normally will provide greater persistence.

B. Repair by Plugging and Sodding.

This is the only satisfactory method of maintaining an adequate turfgrass cover on heavily and continuously used fields. Its essential features consist of setting sod plugs into small damaged areas of not over 5 to 6 inches in diameter and patching larger areas with sod from a nursery maintained for this purpose.

A hole cutter, similar to one used for setting cups on a golf course, is the best tool for plugging. A 3-inch-deep plug is cut out of the area to be repaired and replaced with a sod plug from the nursery.

Sodding can be done at any time during the growing season if the turf is handled carefully and watered properly. The first step in resodding is to remove the old turf from the damaged area. Small sections can be lifted with a hand tool. Some type of power sod cutter should be used for larger areas. Soil preparation prior to sodding should be the same as outlined for new seedings. The prepared surface should be firmed by rolling. If the soil is dry, apply water in a fine spray to dampen it to a depth of 1 to 2 inches just prior to laying the sod. Sod pieces of any convenient size can be used. Where large areas are involved, strips 5 feet long by 1 foot wide are very satisfactory. Sod should be cut as thin as possible. A well-knit Kentucky bluegrass or fescue sod can be cut so that not more than a half inch of soil is present below the crowns of the grass plants. Bermudagrass sod can be cut even thinner. Sod should be laid as soon as possible after cutting. If it must be held for more than 1 to 2 days, particularly when temperatures are above 70 to 75 F, it should be unrolled and kept watered until used.

Sod can be purchased from commercial growers or, when land is available, can be grown in your own sod nursery. The sod nursery is by far the more economical and satisfactory source of material. It not only assures turf composed of the desired grasses but also provides for the prompt use of cut sod. A nursery of 10,000 square feet will supply enough sod to meet average renovation requirements.

VIII. Heating Cables

The use of electric heating cables under athletic field turf is in its infancy in the U. S. Only a few major stadiums have installed heating cables. These include Falcon Stadium at the U. S. Air Force Academy in Colorado Springs, Colorado, and Lambeau Field at Green Bay, Wisconsin.

Current information would indicate that there may be some practibility in using underground heating cables for athletic fields if normal temperatures are not extreme. Heating cables proved to be of no value in the 1967 National Football League championship game at Green Bay, because air temperatures dropped well below zero. Additional research and practical experience is required to determine the true value of soil warming from an agronomic standpoint as well as the economic feasibility of such systems.

IX. Grass Colorants

The use of grass colorants or dyes may be justified in special instances but are not considered as a normal maintenance practice. Athletic fields planted to warm-season grasses, especially bermudagrass, tend to go off-color near the close of the playing season. In those parts of the U. S. where these grasses are adapted, grass colorants can be used to give the playing field spectator appeal. Likewise, they may be used as a temporary measure where disease, insect, or mechanical damage has occurred to the turf. They have been used extensively when football games are televised in color. In correspondence with turfgrass workers at 38 land-grant universities and colleges, approximately 50% felt that grass colorants were only temporary expedients for the situations indicated above and would recommend them for these purposes only.

X. Artificial Turf

Considerable interest has been generated in recent years through the introduction of artificial turf. The development of artificial turf has stimulated further consideration of the construction of closed or domed stadiums where light limitations and other factors make it virtually impossible to grow acceptable turf.

A number of colleges and universities have recently installed artificial turf on their outdoor stadiums or practice fields. These installations will be watched with interest in the next few years. Player acceptance, wearability, maintenance costs, etc. are still to be determined.

It would appear that artificial turf at present has a very limited application and may be considered as an inferior substitute for good turfgrass in situations where it is impossible to grow grass.

Supplemental Reading

Anderson, S. R., K. L. Bader, R. Guarasci, A. E. Hoffman, and R. W. Miller. Sept. 1964. Turf renovation and management of the Ohio State University Football Stadium. Progress Report, Agronomy Dept., Ohio State University, Columbus, Ohio.

Bader, K. L., R. R. Davis, and O. L. Musgrave. 1964. Turf for heavy use areas. Leaflet 115. Ohio Cooperative Extension Service, Columbus, Ohio.

Barrett, J. R., and W. H. Daniel. 1965. Electrically warmed soils for sports turf. Midwest Turf News and Research, 2nd Progress Report, No. 33.

Barrett, J. R. and W. H. Daniel. 1966. Turf heating with electric cable. Journal of the American Society of Agronomy, Vol. 47, No. 10.

Burton, Glenn W. Tiflawn (Tipton 57) Bermudagrass. Leaflet, Georgia Coastal Plain Experiment Station, Tifton, Georgia.

Burton, Glenn W. Football field construction and maintenance for the South. Leaflet, Georgia Coastal Plain Experiment Station, Tifton, Georgia.

Cornman, J. F. 1967. 1967 Cornell recommendations for turfgrass. New York Agricultural Extension Service, Ithaca, New York.

Davis, F. F., and G. E. Harrington. 1948. Sod is ideal for playing fields. Grass, 1948 Yearbook of Agriculture. United States Department of Agriculture.

Deal, E. E. 1965. Turf on athletic fields and play areas. Fact Sheet 168, University of Maryland Agricultural Extension Service, College Park, Maryland.

Drage, C. M. Selecting turfgrasses for lawns, parks, athletic fields, play areas and cemeteries in Colorado. Leaflet, Colorado State University Department of Horticulture, Fort Collins, Colorado.

Engel, R. E., and G. H. Ahlgren. 1954. Turf management on athletic fields. Leaflet 119, New Jersey Agricultural Extension Service, New Brunswick, New Jersey.

Folkner, J. S. August 1957. Construction renovation and management of athletic fields. Report No. 158, University of Arizona Agricultural Experiment Station, Tucson, Arizona.

Folkner, J. S. August 1960. Athletic fields—the southern approach. The Golf Course Reporter, Vol. 28, No. 6.

Goss, R. L. August 1960. Athletic fields—covering the western viewpoint. The Golf Course Reporter, Vol. 25, No. 6.

Harper, J. C. August 1960. Athletic fields—on eastern problems. The Golf Course Reporter, Vol. 28, No. 6.

Harper, J. C. January 1965. Athletic field maintenance. Leaflet, Pennsylvania Agricultural Extension Service, University Park, Pennsylvania.

Harper, J. C. 1968. Athletic fields—specification outline, construction and maintenance. Pennsylvania Agricultural Extension Service, U. Ed. 7-750, University Park, Pennsylvania.

Juska, F. V., and A. A. Hanson. 1965. Consumers all, 1965 yearbook of agriculture. United States Department of Agriculture, pp. 228-231.

Lantz, H. L., and B. Taylor. March 1954. Maintenance of athletic turf. Leaflet, Iowa State University, Ames, Iowa.

Mascaro, T. Improving athletic field turfgrass. Bulletin No. 2, West Point Products Corporation, West Point, Pennsylvania.

Mascaro, T. August 1960. Athletic fields—why, when, and how renovation. The Golf Course Reporter, Vol. 25, No. 6.

Meyers, H. G., and G. C. Horn. May 1967. Construction and maintenance of football fields. Florida Turf Grower, Florida Agricultural Extension Service, Gainesville, Florida.

Miller, R. W. September 1967. The effects of certain management practices on the botanical composition and winter injury to turf containing a mixture of Kentucky bluegrass and tall fescue. Research Summary, Ohio Agricultural Research and Development Center, Wooster, Ohio.

Musser, H. B., J. C. Harper, and J. M. Duich. 1962. Athletic fields, specification outline, construction and maintenance. U. Ed. 2-411, Pennsylvania Agricultural Extension Service, University Park, Pennsylvania.

Parks, W. L., L. M. Callahan, and C. E. Coffey. Turf establishment and maintenance of football fields in Tennessee. University of Tennessee Athletic Department, Knoxville, Tennessee.

Tate, H. F., and J. S. Folkner. 1966. Turf on large recreation and play areas. Bulletin A-48, Arizona Agricultural Extension Service, Tucson, Arizona.

Taylor, B. S., and E. Roberts. August 1960. Athletic fields—speaking from the Midwest. The Golf Course Reporter, Vol. 28, No. 6.

Wilcox, H. 1964. Safe athletic fields, American School Board Journal.

Wilcox, H. June 1965. Safer athletic fields. Athletic Journal.

Watson, J. R., Jr. 1956. Renovation and management of athletic field turfgrass. Leaflet, Toro Manufacturing Corporation, Minneapolis, Minnesota.

Youngner, V. B. April 1963. Turfgrasses on heavy traffic areas. Western Landscaping News.

Youngner, V. B. September 1964. A report on playground turf. Western Landscaping News, Vol. 4, No. 9.

Youngner, V. B. April 1967. Turfgrass adaptation in California. California Turfgrass Culture, Vol. 17, No. 2.

23 Putting Greens

Marvin H. Ferguson

Agri-Systems of Texas, Inc.
Bryan, Texas

I. Introduction

In a model round of golf, the player who does what is expected of him on every shot will play 36 of his 72 strokes *on* the putting green and he will play 18 more *to* the putting green. Thus 3/4 of the golf strokes in a model round will be made on or onto the putting green. It is no wonder that golfers demand excellent turf on this relatively small but tremendously important area.

Because the putting green is so important in the game, a group concerned with building a golf course and the architect who serves them can justify great effort toward making the putting surface as nearly perfect as possible. Many factors are involved and all should be considered.

II. Location

A person familiar with golf course maintenance can visit a golf course under construction and predict with amazing accuracy which greens on the new course will be easily kept and which will cause difficulty. This prediction is based on the need for good air circulation over the surface of the green, the importance of surface drainage, the detrimental effects of shade, and knowledge of traffic patterns attributable to design features.

Location of the green is as important to the maintenance of that green as it is to the integrity of the golf hole. When the location is unsuitable on either count, the architect has failed.

Air circulation if one of the prime requirements of good putting turf. Close mowing of greens and the compaction imposed by traffic are invariably associated with relatively shallow root systems. Shallow roots require frequent applications of water; this in turn causes high humidity unless air movement disperses the moisture vapor. High humidity, a favorable temperature, and a susceptible host plant provide ideal conditions for serious disease infestation in the presence of a pathogenic organism. Thus a cardinal rule in locating a green is to avoid barriers that will intercept the prevailing breeze during hot months. The rule has been violated countless times because a particular location has strategic value or because the natural setting provides an attractive location. Strategic values and beauty are important, but if the putting surface is poor, these attributes quickly lose their charm.

Drainage is always a consideration. Surface water draining from higher ground should not flow over the green. Seeps arising from slopes should be intercepted upslope from the green or else the green should be relocated. Finally, the green and the bunkers and mounds surrounding it should be so located and shaped that surface water resulting from heavy rains will move quickly away.

Shade is a detriment to good turf. Trees in the vicinity of the green are tolerable and in some cases desirable, but they should not shade the green for more than a few hours each day. Neither should trees be so near that their roots become troublesome in the green.

Another matter affecting the location of a green is its relationship to the tee of the next hole. Players can be guided without their being aware of being guided if a green is so shaped and oriented in relation to the following tee that the placement of the flagstick and the tee markers for the next hole enables the use of alternating traffic patterns. Conversely, the thoughtless arrangement of flagstick placement areas, tee orientation, and bunkering can prescribe paths where no relief from traffic is possible.

III. Design Features

Slopes and contours are a major concern in putting green maintenance. Slopes surrounding the putting green should be gentle enough to permit the use of gang mower units, but steep enough to support good surface drainage. On the putting surface, slopes should generally be arranged to carry surface water off the green in more than one direction. Slopes should never drain all surface water off the front of the green in the approach area.

Contours on the putting surface can add much to the character of the green and may affect the difficulty of play very greatly. They are desirable so long as they are gentle. Maintenance suffers when they become severe. The area available for flagstick placement is diminished by sharp contours, and relatively large greens are required for adequate traffic distribution. If greens are both small and heavily contoured, then flagstick areas become worn and compacted.

IV. Size

It is almost axiomatic—according to books and articles on golf architecture—that the size of the green must be related to the length of the approach shot. There is one difficulty associated with this philosophy. Frequently on the short three-par holes, golf shots are played with a high trajectory and ball pitting of the turf becomes quite serious. If the size of the green restricts the availability of flagstick placement area such a surface may suffer badly. It would appear that imaginative bunkering and contouring will permit the use of a small target area on a relatively large green. Thus flexibility in the play of the hole and satisfactory flagstick space may both be provided while retaining the difficulty associated with the small target.

The absolute size of putting surfaces is a matter of debate among partisans of various architectural styles. The range in actual putting surface is from about 4,000 square feet to about 12,000 square feet. There are a few extremes, of course, on either side of this range. From the maintenance viewpoint, about 6,500 to 7,500 square feet is preferable. A green of this size, if not severely contoured, will provide adequate room for frequent flagstick movement. Smaller greens suffer from traffic concentration while larger ones increase the area to be maintained intensively.

V. Construction

Golf course design and golf course construction have been considered an art rather than a science. The individuality and the character of golf courses in this country have resulted from the artistic talents of many qualified architects.

Likewise, construction methods have been developed as a result of individual experiences and individual preferences. It is a tribute to those whose efforts have gone into golf course building as well as to those who maintain them that so many courses have stood up well over the years.

The pace of golf activity and the traffic on golf courses is presently at a peak which has never been equaled in our country. Many construction methods that were satisfactory in an earlier day, will no longer produce greens that will withstand the wear now imposed upon them.

Because of these considerations, the United States Golf Association Green Section has since 1948 interested itself in construction methods and in a study of the physical problems of soils used in putting greens. Research in these matters has been sponsored by the Green Section at Beltsville, Md.; at Oklahoma State University, Stillwater; at the University of California, Los Angeles; and, since 1954, at Texas A&M University, College Station.

In these studies it has been found that problems of construction procedures and the physical behavior of soils cannot be separated. The two matters are related and must be considered together if the desired result is to be produced. The procedures outlined here may be used as the basis for construction specifications which a club may submit to prospective golf course builders.

Such specifications will place no limitations upon the individuality and artistry of the architect. They will, however, provide a guide for the builder and for the club which wants to be assured that their greens will provide good playing conditions for many years.

The basic considerations underlying all specifications involve provision for good drainage and resistance to compaction. These ends cannot be achieved without some compromise. A highly permeable soil which drains readily offers some problems in the establishment of turf. It is loose and may create difficulty in changing cups. These are minor problems, however, when weighed against the advantages of rapid drainage, good aeration, deep rooting, indirect protection against diseases, protection against over-watering, protection against salt problems, resistance from pitting by golf balls, and providing a putting surface which without being overly wet will hold a shot.

The methods and specifications outlined in the following pages represent the best thoughts of the USGA Green Section staff and of numerous soil scientists who have given serious attention to the problem. It is hoped that they will result in more satisfactory putting greens throughout the nation.

A. Subgrade

The contours of the subgrade should conform to those of the proposed finished grade, with a tolerance of plus or minus 1 inch. The subgrade should be constructed at an elevation 14 inches below the proposed finished grade. The subgrade should be compacted sufficiently to prevent future settling which might create water-holding depressions in the subgrade surface and corresponding depressions in the putting surface.

Where terrain permits, it is possible to build the subgrade into the existing grade or to cut it into the subsoil. It is not necessary to elevate or "build up" the green unless design considerations dictate the desirability of doing so.

It will be noted that courses of materials above the subgrade consist of 4 inches of gravel, 1½ to 2 inches of coarse sand, and 12 inches of topsoil. Thus the total depth will be 17½ to 18 inches. However, this fill material will settle appreciably, and experience indicates that 14 inches will be the approximate depth of these combined materials after settling.

B. Drainage

Tile lines of at least 4-inch diameter should be so spaced that water will not have to travel more than 10 feet to reach a tile drain. Any suitable pattern or tile line arrangement may be used, but herringbone or gridiron arrangements will fit most situations.

Cut ditches or trenches into the subgrade so tile slopes uniformly. Do not place tile deeper than is necessary to obtain the desired amount of slope. Tile lines should have a minimum fall of .5%. Steeper grades can be used but there will seldom be need for tile line grades steeper than 3% to 4% on a putting green.

Tile may be agricultural clay tile, concrete, plastic, or perforated asphalt-paper composition. Agricultural tile joints should be butted together with no more than ¼ inch of space between joints. The tops of tile should be covered with asphalt paper, fiberglass composition, or with plastic spacers and covers designed for this purpose. The covering prevents gravel from falling into the tile.

Tile should be laid on a firm bed of ½ to 1 inch of gravel to reduce possible wash of subgrade soil up into tile line by fast water flow. If the subgrade consists of undisturbed soil, so that washing is unlikely, it is permissible to lay tile directly on the bottom of the trench.

After the tile is laid, the trenches should be backfilled with gravel, being careful not to displace the covering over the joints.

C. Gravel and Sand Base

a. The entire subgrade should be covered with a course of clean washed gravel or crushed stone placed to a minimum thickness of 4 inches.

The preferred material for this purpose is washed pea gravel of about 1/4 inch diameter particle size. Larger gravel or stone may be used, but it is important that changes in size between this course of material and the succeeding one overlying it not be too great. Otherwise, smaller particles from overlying material will wash into the gravel, clog the pores or drainage ways and thereby reduce the effectiveness of the gravel.

The maximum allowable discrepancy appears to be 5 to 7 diameters. In other words, if 1/4 inch pea gravel (about 6 mm) is used, then the particles of the overlying course of sand should not be less than 1 mm in diameter. If stone of 1-inch diameter were used, it would be necessary to include a course of pea gravel to prevent the movement of smaller soil aggregates into the stone.

b. When the gravel is in place, assuming that pea gravel has been used, a 1½ inch layer of coarse washed sand (commercial concrete sand is satisfactory) should be placed to a uniform thickness over the gravel.

The tolerance for error in the thickness of gravel and sand courses should be limited to plus or minus .5 inch.

A profile of a properly constructed putting green is illustrated in Figure 1.

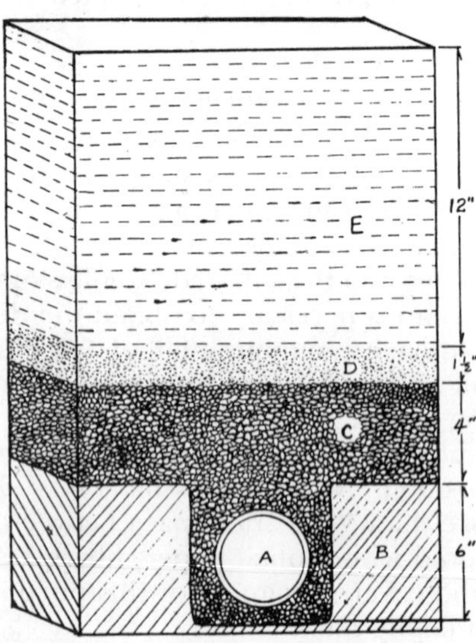

Figure 1. Profile of putting green with trench and tile line, in cross-section. A. 4-inch diameter tile. B. Subgrade of native soil or field material. C. Gravel. D. Coarse sand. E. Topsoil mixture.

D. "Ringing" the Green

When the courses of gravel and sand are in place and outlets have been established for subsurface water (through tile lines), the green should be "ringed" with the soil which is to be used for aprons and collars. This soil should be placed around the green and any contours established in such a way that they will blend into the putting surface.

The next step is to fill the depression, which represents the putting surface, with the prepared topsoil mixture described in the following paragraphs.

E. Soil Mixture

A covering of topsoil mixture at least 12 inches in thickness should be placed over the sand and gravel layers.

The soil mixture should meet certain physical requirements including permeability and porosity—*after compaction.*

Permeability: After compaction, with soil water at approximately field capacity, a core of the soil mixture should permit the passage of not less than 1/2 inch of water per hour nor more than 1 1/2 inches per hour when subjected to a hydraulic head of .25 inches. This technique is described by Ferguson, Howard, and Bloodworth (1960).

Porosity: After compaction, a sample of the soil mixture should have a minimum total pore space of 33%. Of this pore space, the large (non-capillary) pores should comprise from 12 to 18% and capillary pore space from 18 to 27%.

Information with respect to bulk density, moisture retention capacity, mechanical analysis, and degree of aggregation as provided by a soil physicist may be helpful in further evaluating the potential behavior of a putting green soil.

Few natural soils meet the requirements stated above. It will be necessary to use mixtures of sand, soil, and organic matter. Because of differences in behavior induced by such factors as sand particle size and gradation, the mineral derivation and degree of aggregation of the clay component, the degree of decomposition of the organic matter, and the silt content of the soil, it is impossible to make satisfactory recommendations for soil mixtures without appropriate laboratory analyses.

The success of the method of construction herein described is dependent upon the proper physical characteristics of the soil and the relationship of that soil to the drainage bed underlying the green. Therefore a physical analysis of soil should be made before the soil components are procured. When the proper proportions of the soil components have been determined, it becomes extremely important that they be mixed in the proportions indicated. A small error in percentages in the case of a plastic clay soil can create serious problems. To insure thorough mixing and the accurate measurement of the soil components, "off site" mixing is advocated.

Any public or private physics laboratory which is equipped with the facilities to carry out the measurement described by Ferguson et al (1960) can prescribe a soil mixture for putting green use.

F. Soil Covering, Placement, Smoothing and Firming

When soil has been thoroughly mixed off site it should be transported to the green site and dumped at the edge of the green. Padding the edge of the green with boards may be necessary to prevent disturbance by wheeled vehicles of the soil previously placed around the outside of the putting surface. A small crawler-type tractor suitably equipped with a blade is useful for pushing the soil mixture out onto the prepared base. If the tractor is always operated with its weight on the soil mixture that has been hauled onto the site, the base will not be disturbed.

Grade stakes spaced at frequent intervals on the putting surface will be helpful in indicating the depth of the soil mixture. Finishing the grade will likely require the use of a level or transit.

When the soil has been spread uniformly over the surface of the putting green it should be compacted or firmed uniformly. A roller usually is not satisfactory because it "bridges" the soft spots.

"Footing" or trampling the surface will tend to eliminate the soft spots. Raking the surface and repeating the footing operation will result in having the seed or stolon bed uniformly firm. It should be emphasized that the raking and footing should be repeated until uniform firmness is obtained.

Whenever possible after construction, saturation of the soil by extensive irrigation is suggested. Water is useful in settling and firming the surface. This practice will also reveal any water-holding depressions which might interfere with surface drainage.

G. Fumigation of Soil and Establishment of Turf

These steps may be accomplished by following well-known conventional procedures (see Chapter 18).

H. Irrigation Systems

A part of greens construction is provision for irrigation facilities. Ability to control the irrigation of putting greens is the key factor. Ideally, the job should be done by hand watering, but, because of labor costs this is impossible.

Any method based upon the use of set sprinklers must have flexibility. Changes in wind direction may call for the use of sprinklers placed in several different positions. In general, it will be necessary to provide at least five locations at intervals around the green. Locations will be dictated by shape of the green and wind patterns. In addition to permanent sprinkler positions it is desirable to have at least one outlet where a hose may be attached. This is useful in hand showering, spot watering, and in filling in a blank in an irrigation pattern that may result from unusual wind conditions.

Low precipitation rates for greens are desirable. Some automatic systems may use higher precipitation rates, but apply water for very short intervals and depend upon recycling to accomplish the wetting of the soil without runoff.

I. Choice of Grass

In most parts of the U. S. putting green grasses are a variety of either creeping bentgrass or fine-leaf (hybrid) bermudagrass. Seaside and Penncross are the only two creeping bentgrasses planted from seed.

Seaside is a heterogeneous population of creeping bentgrass occurring naturally in coastal areas of the Pacific Northwest. Because of tremendous genetic variability, some of the seedlings in a planting of Seaside bentgrass will be suited to a given environment. At the same time many seedlings fail to survive and the eventual turf is composed of several dozen of the surviving clones. Thus, ultimately greens take on a mottled appearance as the surviving clones enlarge with age.

Pencross bentgrass is a synthetic variety created by the cross pollination of three vegetative selections of creeping bentgrass. There is some genetic variability but not nearly so much as with Seaside.

Numerous vegetatively planted creeping bentgrasses are available. Among them are Arlington (C-1), Cohansey (C-7), Toronto (C-15), Congressional (C-19), Washington (C-50), and Old Orchard (C-52). These grasses provide very uniform turf. Where they are well-adapted, they are often preferred. Their range of adaptation is not so great, however, as that of the seeded types. In choosing a grass for a new golf course, it is well to check with superintendents of nearby golf courses to learn their experience with the vegetatively planted selections.

Where bermudagrass is used for putting greens, Tifgreen is the most widely planted single variety. Recently Tifdwarf, apparently a vegetative mutation arising from Tifgreen, has begun to find favor.

Several other bermudagrass selections are available but their use is limited.

J. Collars and Aprons

The areas around putting surfaces should be prepared carefully. This part of the golf course is maintained less intensively than the putting surface but more intensively than fairways.

Areas adjacent to greens are abused by the turning of mowers, and sometimes they are subject to additional traffic from hand pulled carts and from caddies dropping golf bags. The grass should be of a type that will tolerate mowing to about ½ inch. In the cool season grass region, this implies the use of bentgrass. In the bermudagrass region, the area surrounding the green is usually planted to the same grass that is used on the putting surface.

K. Preparation and Planting

After soil is prepared and placed on greens in accordance with the preceding discussion, it is firmed, raked repeatedly and watered several times to effect thorough settling. Fertilizer materials are incorporated into the surface portion of the soil in the final grading stages.

Sterilization is normally accomplished by fumigation with methyl bromide. Fumigation requires about 48 hours. The gas is injected beneath polyethylene sheets. After the film is removed an aeration period of at least 48 hours is required to allow all the gas to escape from the soil prior to seeding. If stolons are to be planted, an aeration period of 7 to 10 days is desirable. Greens are then ready to plant.

If greens are seeded, rates varying from 2 to 5 pounds of seed per 1,000 square feet are used. Seed is divided into two lots and sown in two operations. The second lot is sown while moving in a direction at right angles to the direction used in sowing the first lot. Seed may be raked in lightly or covered with a light topdressing. Watering must be very frequent, using a fine spray mist, until seeds have germinated and seedlings have become established.

In planting a green with stolons, rates of 2 to 10 bushels of loosely packed stolons per 1,000 square feet are used. The rate of planting will affect the rapidity of establishment. Stolons are broadcast by hand over the areas to be planted. Usually a light topdressing is used to cover the stolons, but some contractors use a machine consisting of a series of closely spaced straight disks to push the stolons into the loose soil.

In either operation, it is imperative that a moist environment be maintained until the stolons have established roots and begun to grow.

VI. Reasons for Construction Steps

The first seven steps in the construction procedures above tell *how* the work should be done. It is advisable to re-examine each step in order to explain *why* it should be done that way.

The Subgrade—When a new green is built and the subgrade is contoured, it frequently happens that there is a rather large amount of fill. It is very difficult to compact filled areas sufficiently to preclude further settling. However, the builder must strive to prevent further settling if at all possible. If uniform layers of gravel, sand, and soil overlay the subgrade, it is obvious that any settling of the subgrade will result in corresponding settling at the top. Therefore, the thorough compaction of filled areas is necessary if the green is to maintain the contours built into it.

Tile Drainage—It is commonly believed that the use of a gravel layer provides adequate drainage and that the installation of tile is a needless expense. No doubt there is good reason for this belief on specific sites. However, when large amounts of water are moving through soil following a heavy rain or rapid irrigation, and where the water must move a considerable distance to reach an outlet, tile lines aid in the removal of excess water. It is also true that despite the best efforts to compact the subgrade, it sometimes settles after construction and "pockets" appear. Tile lines help to remove such trapped water. A putting green is expensive to build and the relatively small additional cost of adding tile drainage appears modest for the insurance provided.

Gravel and Sand Base—A few examples can be found where builders have used tile and then assumed that the gravel base could be omitted. This assumption results from the lack of understanding on water movement in soils. Lateral movement of water is relatively small unless there is a barrier which impedes its downward movement (see Fig. 2). Therefore, when tile is placed near the surface it must be very closely spaced if it is to remove much excess water. Conversely, if it is spaced at intervals of more than 4 or 5 feet it must be placed very deeply.

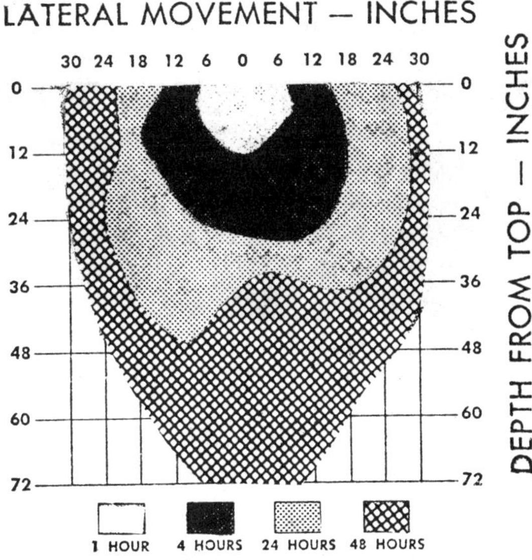

Figure 2. Infiltration of water into Yolo loam from an irrigation furrow kept filled for various lengths of time. Note that vertical movement exceeds lateral movement. (Adapted from Hendrickson and Veihmeyer, 1933).

When a gravel layer is placed over the tile, it provides a medium whereby water can move laterally very easily. Thus tile can be placed just at the bottom of the gravel layer and spaced at intervals of 10 to 20 feet, depending upon the degree and direction of slope.

The layer of coarse sand used over the gravel base is for the sole purpose of preventing soil particles from moving downward into the gravel and thereby impeding drainage. It is necessary to build up with successively finer layers of material in order to keep fine soil on top of coarse materials.

Ringing the Green—Some builders place topsoil around the edges of the green after the sand and gravel are in place. They will then proceed to place the putting green soil mixture on top of the gravel and bring it to the finished grade.

There is one disadvantage to placing a heavier topsoil contiguous to the porous putting green soil mixture. Moisture is sometimes drawn out of the putting green edge because of the greater tension exerted by fine-textured soil. This disadvantage can be overcome by using something like polyethylene plastic sheeting as a vertically placed moisture barrier between the "ring" of topsoil and the soil mixture on the putting surface. In the absence of such a moisture barrier, the edge of the putting green may dry out faster than the remainder of the green.

The Interface—When soils of different textures are placed in layers, the zone where they meet affects the movement of water. The interface between the two soils produces a sort of textural barrier. Figure 3 is a photograph showing that water does not move from a layer of fine soil into a lower layer of a coarser-textured soil until the fine-textured soil becomes saturated. The reason for this failure of water to readily cross the "textural barrier" is a matter of surface tension. When sufficient gravitational force (weight) accumulates, the tension force is overcome and water then drains out through the sand and gravel.

Figure 3. Principle of the perched water table. (From W. H. Gardner, Washington State University, 1953).

The "textural barrier" then can be used to increase the water holding capacity of an open-textured soil. If irrigation is stopped just before the soil reaches the saturation point, no drainage occurs. On the other hand, in the case of a heavy rain, the soil will not hold too much water. It is paradoxical that the soil overlying such a "textural barrier" can be made to hold more water than it would without the gravel layer, but it cannot be made to hold enough water to be harmful to plants.

The Soil Mixture—The compounding of a soil mixture based on laboratory tests is one of the essential elements of the Green Section Specifications. Putting green construction is costly and the costs rise sharply when soil materials must be purchased elsewhere and brought to the site. Therefore, it is important to use soil and sand that are available within reasonable hauling distance of the building site. It is expected that organic matter will normally be imported but its relatively light weight allows freight costs to be kept to acceptable levels.

Because of cost considerations, the amendments used in putting green soils must be relatively inexpensive. Materials such as vermiculite, perlite, and calcined clays may be useful as soil amendments but the builder must consider whether the costs are justifiable.

In a relatively sandy soil, where water holding capacity is low and percolation rates are high, porous soil amendments offer some appeal. They serve to increase the total water holding capacity of the soil. Because of added surface, however, more of the water is held at tensions too great to be available for plant use. Thus the increase in available moisture in the soil is not as great as the increase in total water.

Vermiculite increases water holding capacity, and it provides greater resiliency to the soil when it is included in the mixture. It has been reported, however, that vermiculite tends to lose its structure under the effects of traffic. The expanded "accordion-like" structure breaks down to individual platelets and the beneficial effects are lost.

Perlite has performed well in some experimental mixtures. It may find a place in soil mixtures. At the present time, there is not sufficient experience upon which to base a recommendation.

Calcined clay products have been used in putting green soil modification and in some cases these materials have been incorporated into new greens. There is considerable variability in the products offered as soil amendments. Some are harder and more stable under repeated freezing and thawing cycles. These are materials that have been fired at higher temperatures or for a longer period.

The harder materials provide more promise of stability for a putting green soil. Such a material may substitute in part for sand because it provides a substantial noncapillary porosity, if used in sufficient quantity. The chief consideration with respect to the use of calcined clay in new construction is cost. The quantities required to produce desirable effects in soil mixtures usually result in rather expensive mixtures.

In some cases greens have been built and called "Green Section Specification" greens where the builder has borrowed a formula based on his neighbor's laboratory tests. This is a dangerous practice because soils, sands, and organic matter are likely to vary widely within a community. In some experimental plots where the same sand and the same organic matter were used but where two different high clay content soils were used, a suitable mixture required 40% of one soil and less than 10% of the other.

Some critics of laboratory methods argue that one cannot substitute laboratory measurements for good judgment. True! *But how much better is a judgment based on physical facts rather than on "feel" or visual estimates!*

Soil Covering, Placement, Smoothing, and Firming—It may be well to reiterate that soil should be mixed "off site." It is virtually impossible to do a satisfactory job of mixing soil materials in place on the green site.

Establishment of Turf—Because recommended soil mixtures are porous, some greens have been rather slow to become established. Frequent, light fertilization of newly seeded or vegetatively planted greens provides one method of speeding establishment.

On occasion, sodding may be used in establishing or repairing greens. This is a satisfactory procedure *provided the sod is grown on the same soil mixture as is used in the green.* Growing sod on a heavier soil and then moving it to a porous putting green soil can lead to serious problems. The textural change between soil in the sod and that in the putting green will cause the sod layer to hold too much water. Roots tend to be very short.

USGA Green Specifications—The steps outlined for constructing putting greens will provide excellent results if they are followed exactly and completely. This fact has been amply demonstrated in numerous construction programs.

Equally demonstrable is the fact that going just part of the way with these procedures is an invitation to failure. A great many years of research have gone into the study of each phase of these methods.

The relationship between soil texture and soil depth is important. Because the topsoil mixture is placed over a bed of gravel and because a textural barrier is created at the juncture of soil and gravel a sort of false water table is formed. A zone of saturated soil will lie just above the interfacial area. The depth of this zone of saturation will depend upon soil texture. If a fine-textured soil is used the zone of saturation will be deeper than if a porous soil is used. If one uses a heavy soil, he must either use a much deeper seedbed or he must leave out the gravel layer. If one mixes a soil that is sandy and too deep, it will be droughty.

These are negative ways of saying that if you undertake to construct a putting green by this method, follow the instructions completely.

How Expensive?—Some clubs have been deterred from building putting greens by this method because they have thought that construction costs would be excessive. It is obviously impossible to provide costs for a given area because of variations in the cost of soil materials, gravel, and labor. However, information on quantities of materials needed should help in projecting cost estimations. The following quantities of materials are required per 1,000 square feet of putting surface:

Gravel	4-inch depth—12.3 cubic yards
Sand	1½-inch depth—4.6 cubic yards
Soil mixture	12-inch depth—37.0 cubic yards
Tile	approximately 100 lineal feet

VII. Management of Greens

A. Mowing

Of all management practices, mowing is most regular, most frequent, and it is among the most important in producing the kind of turf needed for putting. Mowing provides an even surface, with grass blades all cut at the same height, a surface where a golf ball will be supported on the tips of the blades.

Putting greens are normally mowed at heights ranging from 3/16 to 5/16 inch. The "fastness" or "slowness" of a putting green is determined in part by the kind of grass but primarily by the mowing practices employed. For championship play, a very closely mowed, fast green is desirable. A skillful putting touch is rewarded on such a green. High handicap golfers prefer a green that is slower, and these conditions call for a mowing height of about ¼ inch or slightly above.

On courses where the standards of maintenance are high, daily mowing is practiced. Sometimes Monday is devoted to other work and greens mowing may be skipped for the one day.

Frequency of mowing is related to the rate of growth and the height of cut. As a rule, the closer the cut the more frequently mowing is required. When grass is growing rapidly, frequent mowing is essential.

"Grain" is one of the problems encountered on closely mowed greens. "Grain" results from the tendency of grass to lie down and grow in one direction. It is important therefore, to change the direction of mowing each day. Most superintendents make frequent use of brushes during those seasons when grass is growing rapidly. Brushing helps to keep the grass upright.

Sharp, well-adjusted mowers are a necessity. Any tendency for the blades of the reel to pinch leaves against the bed knife will result in bruised, torn leaf tips. This will produce a grayish appearance on the green.

Vertical mowing is a relatively new practice but a very useful one. Knives rotating in a vertical plane at very high speeds will cut surface runners and prostrate leaves. Thus when the machine is adjusted so that blades cut at the turf surface, the machine tends to combat grain and creeping tendencies in the grass.

If the machine is set to cut down to the soil surface, it may be useful in removing thatch that has accumulated beneath the live turf at the surface. Used in this way, the verti-cut produces a drastic effect. It should be used in this way only in seasons when turf is growing actively and will make a rapid recovery.

Thatch may be diminished by several other practices. These are sometimes used singly, but more often the superintendent will use a combination of several practices such as cultivation, topdressing, raking, double cutting, and vertical mowing.

Inasmuch as thatch is defined as the accumulation of material between the soil surface and the live upper portion of the turf, it is very difficult to remove it without seriously damaging the putting surface. Therefore, practices such as deep vertical mowing and raking must be used with restraint.

Some thatch-forming materials are decomposed and become incorporated into the soil. These materials decompose more rapidly if they can be mixed with soil. It is in this way that topdressing and cultivating contribute to thatch control. Cultivation by punching holes or slitting the turf allows some soil to be brought to the surface where it sifts back down through the turf. If new soil is applied at this time as a topdressing, this material also works down into intimate contact with the thatch and forms vegetation. When thatch is perforated and mixed with soil, it no longer sheds water. Also, when it is mixed with soil, it is less susceptible to the footprinting so characteristic of a heavily thatched, "cushiony" green.

B. Wear Control

One of the enemies of putting green turf is traffic. We have indicated that a heavy accumulation of thatch is undesirable. At the other end of the scale is a turf that is too thin and that is seriously damaged by the footprints of golfers.

Good management from the standpoint of irrigation, fertilizer use and mowing are the first line of defense against traffic. At times, this is not enough. The superintendent must try to distribute traffic sufficiently so that turf is not damaged so severely that recovery will be slow.

Multiple flagstick locations and frequent movement of the flagstick position will serve to distribute traffic. Traffic flow over a green may sometimes be controlled to some degree by the location of the flagstick in relation to the tee markers on the next hole.

Much of the controllability of traffic on putting greens is either built in at the time of construction or it is left out. The position of bunkers, mounds, swales, trees, and the orientation of the green with respect to the next tee are all factors which influence the way golfers will approach and leave the putting green. If these factors are brought together in such a way as to permit changes in traffic flow, the superintendent may have some opportunity to rest some areas of the green when necessary. Without ample foresight, traffic control may be precluded by the design of the green.

C. Operations in Management

The mowing of the putting surface itself has been discussed. The mowing of areas surrounding the putting surface is another important operation. Usually the fringe or collar of the green is mowed at a height intermediate between the putting surface and the fairway height. This fringe is normally about 30 inches wide, though there is no standard width.

The fringe may be subject to some additional wear caused by the turning of putting green mowers. Where possible, putting green mowers should be turned in wide sweeping turns. This is difficult to teach because most mower operators appear to take pride in an ability to make a sharp, quick turn.

Topdressing has been mentioned as a step in the control of thatch. It has other uses. Soil added to the surface helps to smooth greens that may have become pitted. Following cultivation, topdressing falls into the holes or slits. It is new loose soil with good structure that tends to relieve the compaction of soils which have been subjected to traffic and loss of structure.

In areas where overseeding is practiced, topdressing is used to provide a medium for seed germination in the fall. It is also used as an agency for facilitating transition from wintergrass to bermudagrass in spring.

In general, material used for topdressing should be similar to the soil materials in the putting green. The exception to this is the case where soil in the green is unsuitable and overly susceptible to the effects of compaction. Under these circumstances a more desirable material should be used. Some greens which were hard and compacted have been improved remarkably by the use of a topdressing soil that was resistant to compaction.

Techniques for applying topdressing have been revolutionized by the advent of engine-powered spreaders. These machines permit the even spreading of topdressing material with far less labor than required by manual techniques.

Amounts of topdressing cannot be specified because of great variations in conditions where topdressing may be used. An average treatment would call for about 1/4 cubic yard per 1,000 square feet.

Cultivation may be used as an individual practice or in conjunction with topdressing. In some cases, it is believed that cultivation may be a partial replacement for topdressing. Soil that is brought to the surface in cultivation is spread over the turf and worked back into the surface.

Cultivating machinery is generally of three types. The hollow curved spoon was used on some of the first powered machines. Such a spoon enters the soil, creates subsurface soil movement and then exits. The surface hole is relatively small compared to the disturbed area beneath the soil. Such a tool does a great deal to fracture and loosen the soil. It leaves the surface roughened for a few days and is the source of some player complaints.

One of the widely used principles at the present time is that of a straight hollow tine which is pushed straight into the soil and is pulled straight out. These hollow tines range from 1/4 to 1/2 inch in size and are usually spaced on about 2-inch centers. Even though the cores are relatively small, the close spacing results in removal of a rather large amount of soil. The small size of cores and the straight-in, straight-out principle of operation combine to leave the putting surface in fairly good condition. There is not a serious amount of interference with play and the small holes "heal" rapidly.

More recently, machines have been offered which cultivate through a slitting effect. Slits are made by rapidly revolving thin steel blades. Soil is brought to the surface and deposited along either side of the slit. The surface is left in fairly good condition. At the present time, this principle of cultivation seems to be growing in favor but it has not yet achieved the popularity of the hollow tined cultivator.

Spiking may be considered a form of cultivation, though it does little to stir the soil. Spiking is used to penetrate thatch and any crust that may tend to form at the surface of a putting green. This crusting effect is difficult to describe or to explain. Apparently, it results from water lying almost constantly at the soil surface, the effect of players' footprints, the passage of maintenance equipment over the area, the growth of algae, the accumulation of dust, leaf fragments, and other detritus. During summer months, as a result of these and perhaps other factors, greens often reach a state where water penetrates slowly. Spiking is a practice that does little damage to turf but which opens the surface of the soil and increases the rate of water infiltration.

D. Irrigation

Irrigation of putting greens is one of the most critical of all management practices. It is the practice which, if done improperly, can lead to the loss of turf in a few hours.

Even under the best management and the best environmental conditions, bentgrass roots tend to become short in hot weather. It is not uncommon to find that most roots under a putting green turf are less than 1 inch long. To keep enough moisture in this 1 inch of soil to support the plant, and at the same time to avoid too much water which would exclude air, is a kind of tightrope act that the superintendent must perform.

The troubles are compounded by the necessity for close mowing, the constant threat of disease, the incessant foot traffic of golfers, the frequent summer showers, and the complaints of the golfer "off his game" that the greens "are too hard, they won't hold a shot, why don't you water them." This last factor is very real and very troublesome.

Unfortunately, most golfers have only a limited knowledge of plant growth principles and soil-water relationships. They equate hard surfaces with dry greens and soft surfaces with wet greens. When their approach shot to the green—often poorly played and with a low trajectory—fails to stop on the putting surface, they conclude that the green is dry. Thus, many putting greens are irrigated to please one of the superintendent's employers, a club member, rather than to provide for the needs of the grass. This kind of irrigation increases the problem of shallow roots.

Most successful golf course superintendents apply most of the necessary irrigation to putting greens at night or in early morning. Then during the hot part of the afternoon, greens are showered as necessary to prevent wilt. Over-irrigation or excessive rainfall may result in "wet wilt" or "scald" on greens. This phenomenon occurs when soil is saturated and when roots are taking up water at a slower rate than it is being lost from leaf surfaces. Wet wilt can be overcome by showering lightly to reduce transpiration. The objective of the irrigator is to wet leaf surfaces but to add no more water than necessary to the soil.

The principles governing the irrigation of putting greens can be set forth rather simply, but the practice whereby the superintendent must deal with all the modifying factors is a very difficult task indeed. One cannot outline a definite irrigation program for any group of putting greens. Their proper management requires accurate observation and competent performance of irrigation procedures.

E. Fertilization

Putting green fertilization is a more critical operation than is the fertilization of most turf areas. There is a rather wide spread between amounts of fertilizer used in different parts of the country.

Bentgrasses are normally fertilized in spring and fall with very little being applied in hot weather. During winter months there is practically no fertilizer used in northern areas but in the south moderate amounts may be applied.

Research which has dealt with the removal of nutrient elements in clippings indicates that a ratio of 3-1-2 (N-P_2O_5-K_2O) is the proportion found in well-fertilized greens. This has led to the adoption of such a nutrient ratio as a goal for optimum fertilization. It may be argued that this ratio is subject to change by any number of modifying factors. However, from the standpoint of practice it appears to be a satisfactory standard.

Most superintendents try to provide an adequate quantity of phosphorus and potash and then they adjust nitrogen in relation to color and the production of clippings.

In the eastern section of the U. S., some clubs may use as little as 5 to 7 pounds of nitrogen per 1,000 square feet per year on bentgrass greens. By contrast, as much as 15 to 18 pounds of nitrogen per 1,000 square feet is used on the bentgrasses in parts of the West. Generally, the low rates are the result of a belief that disease incidence is lessened by a slower, sturdier growth. In less humid regions, where disease is less troublesome, additional fertilizer is used to produce upright growth and a more pleasing color.

Bermudagrasses generally are fertilized somewhat more heavily than bentgrasses. The use of as much as 18 pounds of nitrogen per 1,000 square feet per year on bermudagrass greens is quite common. Fertilization at rather frequent intervals throughout the summer is the normal procedure. Growth is allowed to slow before overseeding in the fall. After overseeding, moderate rates of a slowly soluble form of nitrogen are used during the winter.

During spring transition, fertilizer can be used as a tool in effecting the transition from wintergrass to bermuda. Heavy fertilization of the cool-season grasses at the time weather becomes very warm will result in their rapid growth and ready susceptibility to wilting. At the same time, additional fertilizer for the bermudagrass causes it to make faster growth.

Deficiencies of the trace elements are not thought to be common in putting greens. One exception is iron. The causes of chlorosis on putting greens may be manifold but an application of about 2 ounces per 1,000 square feet of iron sulfate as a spray will usually correct chlorotic conditions.

F. Pest Control

At the present time, fungus diseases must be considered the most serious pests of putting green turf. The preceding discussion about the peculiar needs of putting greens with respect to irrigation practices will provide a basis for understanding the persistence of diseases. The soil must be kept almost constantly moist, and frequently water lies at the surface of compacted soils for a considerable length of time. Turf is bruised daily by the operation of mowers and by foot traffic.

Most of the fungi which produce turf diseases can be controlled by fungicides that are available. However, there is a problem of identification. The golf course superintendent usually relies on grass symptoms for identification. Such symptoms, together with an awareness of temperature and humidity as well as other environmental factors gives an observant person a reasonably good basis for identification. If an application of fungicide clears up the trouble, the superintendent assumes that the fungicide he used is good for control of the disease he suspected.

Because of the difficulties of positive identification of disease-causing organisms in the field and the overlapping of gross symptoms, those fungicides which are commonly called "broad spectrum" formulations have found a great deal of use. The mercury-containing compounds are especially useful, but they are also phytotoxic at higher dosage levels. Combinations of organic mercury compounds with thiram provide fairly good control of most diseases and may be used at safe dosage levels. Cadmium compounds, in combination with thiram, have demonstrated excellent fungicidal effectiveness.

Organic compounds with demonstrated fungicidal value are becoming available at a very rapid rate and any listing of these materials is out-of-date very quickly. Those materials which are widely used often reflect the aggressiveness of the sales campaign rather than the effectiveness of the product.

There is no question about the need for turf fungicides in putting green management. However, they should be relegated to a position second to management practices in disease control.

On bentgrasses the most serious diseases during the playing season occur when temperatures are quite high. This period coincides with the need for very careful watering and it is the time when turf is weakest and least able to recover from injury. It is therefore necessary to avoid any management practice that would render the turf more susceptible to disease. Fertilizer should be used sparingly or not at all in hot weather. Irrigation should provide for the needs of the turf, but no excess water which would tend to diminish soil oxygen should be applied. Flagstick locations must be changed frequently to prevent excessive wear in any one area. Phytotoxic herbicides and fungicides are to be avoided. Cultivation, vertical mowing, and topdressing are practices which should be delayed until conditions for recovery are more favorable. Any practice which will weaken or bruise turf will cause it to be damaged more severely by any diseases which may occur. Sometimes the best management consists of performing only those operations which are absolutely necessary.

There are numerous publications which describe the various turf diseases and their control. They are also discussed in a separate chapter of this publication.

Weeds on putting greens have ceased to be a serious problem with few notable exceptions such as *Poa annua.* Golf course superintendents have learned to sterilize topdressing and new seedbeds. They have come to use preemergence materials quite effectively in controlling crabgrass and goosegrass.

Poa annua in bentgrass greens is the one problem weed that has defied general control. In bermudagrass greens there are several weed problems that attend the practice of overseeding. In this case pre-emergence herbicides would preclude the establishment of winter grasses. When the winter grass is established, it is so young that the use of post-emergence herbicides for control of weeds is usually not advisable.

The answer to this problem appears to lie in the area of seed sources. Many of the weed species found in overseeded greens appear to be almost certainly introduced with the cool-season grass seed. Some efforts at recleaning imported seed have resulted in a diminution of weeds in winter turf.

Insects on putting greens need not be a problem. There are presently no insect pests that cannot be controlled effectively with available insecticides coupled with appropriate management practices. When insect damage does occur, it is the result of faulty observation, so that damage occurs before the presence of the insect is detected.

Nematodes are recognized as a problem on putting greens. However, injury appears to be difficult to identify and to measure. Symptoms of nematode-infested putting greens are primarily associated with a decline in vigor of the turf. The amount of decline in vigor may sometimes be demonstrated by treating part of a putting green with a nematicide. Broad scale treatment of turf for nematodes is not practiced, but it appears likely to increase.

Algae make a rather serious problem on poorly turfed putting greens, usually where a compacted surface opposes water infiltration and free water lies at the surface of the green. Therefore the key to control is good drainage and good water infiltration. Topdressing and cultivation will help to create conditions where algae will not thrive. However, these practices must be carried out in seasons when the grass is growing well and algae are seldom a serious problem until midsummer. Therefore, temporary control treatments must be employed.

Hydrated lime, dusted on the surface of an algae-infested green, will usually provide some degree of control. Lime should be used at very light rates, no more than 2 to 3 pounds per 1,000 square feet. Control may be obtained with zineb or a combination of zineb and maneb.

G. Renovation

Renovation is a term with varied meanings. It can mean complete rebuilding or simply a slight modification. For our purposes, it is considered to be treatment exceeding the more drastic maintenance operations but less than complete rebuilding.

Renovation is indicated when playing qualities have declined below acceptable standards and when maintenance practices will not correct the condition. It is also indicated when some feature is requiring an excessive expenditure for maintenance.

Greens with seriously compacted soil but fairly good provisions for subsurface drainage can have the turf removed, soil amendments worked into the soil, and new turf planted. When the turfgrass strain is unsatisfactory, the sod can be removed or killed out and a different grass planted in its place.

Renovation usually implies limited work and leaving the golf course in play while the work is being accomplished. Therefore, timing becomes important. The object is to perform the work as quickly as possible and with as little interference to play as possible. The time must be chosen with an eye to weather factors which would influence the re-establishment of grass; a time when labor is available; a time when play is not too heavy; and at a time when funds are available.

The many remifications and variabilities attending renovation projects precludes a comprehensive discussion of "how" to go about the job.

The greatest onus on the superintendent faced with a need for improvement is the decision of whether to renovate or to rebuild. Rebuilding usually is more costly, but unless the superintendent can be sure that renovation will completely correct the deficiencies that dictate the undertaking, he may be wise to rebuild rather than go half way.

VIII. Winter Greens

Bermudagrass greens are often overseeded for winter play. For years ryegrass has been the favorite for overseeding. With the advent of the finer bermudagrass varieties—Tiffine, Tifgreen, and Tifdwarf—

fine-leaf grasses have become important in overseeding bermuda greens. These include Seaside creeping bentgrass, red fescue, rough bluegrass, redtop, and Kentucky bluegrass. Despite its shortcomings, ryegrass alone or in mixtures continues to be used in the northern portion of the bermudagrass belt, where temperatures drop suddenly and play is often heavy in early fall.

More thought should be given to seedbed preparation for mixtures of small-seeded species than for ryegrass seeded alone. Heavy topdressing with topsoil and matting is apparently sufficient for ryegrass seeded alone. With fine-seeded grasses, aeration should take place about 1 month before overseeding. Topdressing with soil is important but smaller amounts should be used. One method that has proven successful is to topdress before seeding, mat the soil into the green, power spike several times, and seed. The new seeding is topdressed again and dragged with a mat to cover the seed lightly. It is important that the green be kept watered for optimum germination.

Because of seed-size differences among the finer-textured species, they are frequently seeded individually to obtain better distribution of each species. After several years of testing in the bermudagrass belt, the Milwaukee Sewerage Commission found that a mixture of 4 lb rough bluegrass, 3 lb Kentucky bluegrass, 10 lb red fescue, and 1 lb Seaside creeping bentgrass per 1,000 sq ft provided the most suitable mixture for overseeding the finer varieties of bermudagrass. This mixture may be varied according to the geographical location. For example, red fescue is more suitable in northern areas and at higher elevations. Rough bluegrass ranks superior under most playing conditions where early play is desirable. Red fescue, rough bluegrass, and ryegrass can be relied on for early mid-season play. Kentucky bluegrass and creeping bentgrass do not develop rapidly. Kentucky bluegrass is a desirable component in the Gulf Coast region.

Supplementary Reading

Alderfer, R. B. Compaction of turf soils-some causes and effects. USGA Journal, Vol. IV, No. 2, June, 1951.

Brooks, Cecil R. Growth of roots and tops of bermudagrass as related to aeration and drainage in stratified golf green soils. Unpublished Doctoral Dissertation. Texas A&M University, 1966.

Cornish, Geoffrey. Course construction. The Golf Course Reporter, August, 1958.

Davis, R. R. The physical condition of putting green soils and other environmental factors affecting the quality of greens. Ph.D. Thesis, Purdue University, 1950.

DeFrance, J. A., Simmons, J. A., and Allen, C. H. Jr. Preparation, planting, and developing a putting green with stolons. Rhode Island Agricultural Experiment Station, March, 1950.

Dunning, Bob, et al. Green construction. Golfdom, September, 1956.

Dunning, Bob. Full package deal for improved maintenance. Golfdom, January, 1961.

Ferguson, M. H. Compaction, drainage and aeration. United States Golf Association Journal and Turf Management. 3 (2): 32-33, 1950.

Ferguson, M. H. Soil water and soil air: their relationship to turf production. USGA Journal, Vol. III, No. 3, July, 1950.

Ferguson, M. H. When you build a putting green make sure the soil mixture is a good one. USGA Journal, Vol. III, No. 6, November, 1955.

Ferguson, M. H. Soil modification—practices with putting green soils. Proceedings 1957 Turf Conference of Midwest Regional Turf Foundation.

Ferguson, M. H. Soils. USGA Journal, Vol. XII.

Ferguson, M. H., Howard, H. L., and Bloodworth, M. E. Laboratory methods for evaluation of putting green soil mixtures. USGA Journal, Vol. XIII, No. 5, September, 1960.

Garman, W. L. Permeability of various grades of sand and peat and mixtures of these with soil and vermiculite. United States Golf Association Journal, and Turf Management 5: Number 1, 27-28: 1952.

Gordon, William F. Design with respect to maintenance practices. USGA Journal, Vol. XII. No. 2, June, 1959.

Hendrickson, A. H. and F. J. Veihmeyer 1933. The maintenance of predeterminal soil-moisture conditions in irrigation experiments. Proc. Am. Soc. Hort. Sci. 30: 421-425.

Holmes, James L. Factors in building a green. Golf Course Reporter, March-April, 1959.

Howard, H. L. The response of some putting green soil mixtures to compaction. Unpublished M. S. Thesis. Texas A&M University, 1959.

Humbert, R. P. and Grau, F. V. Soil and turf relationships. Part 1—USGA Journal, Vol. 11, No. 2, June 1949; Part 11—USGA Journal, Vol. 11, No. 3, July, 1949.

Kunze, J. R. The effect of compaction of different golf green mixtures on plant growth. Unpublished M. S. Thesis. Texas A&M University, 1956.

Kunze, J. R., Ferguson, M. H., and Page, J. B. The effects of compaction on golf green mixtures. USGA Journal, Vol. X, No. 6, November, 1957.

Lambert, L. E. GCSA guide for golf course construction. Golfdom, April, 1961.

Lunt, O. R., Miller, P. A., and Wyckoff, C. G. Seedbed preparation for turfgrass. Golf Course Reporter, August, 1955.

Lunt, O. R. Minimizing compaction in putting greens. USGA Journal, Vol. IX, No. 5, September, 1956.

Lunt, O. R. Soil types for putting greens. Southern California Turfgrass Culture, Vol. 8, No. 2, April, 1958.

Moote, Robert F. Golf course reporter. September-October, 1961.

Musser, H. B. Turf management. 356 pp. McGraw Hill, 1950. Revised, 1962.

Pair, John and Keen, Ray A. Comparing percentages of green mixtures. USGA Journal and Turf Management. July, 1962.

Radko, A. M. Renovation vs rebuilding, USGA Journal, Vol. XII, No. 1, April, 1959.

Wolfrom, Clarence. Building and rebuilding greens. Golf Course Reporter, July, 1958.

The National Golf Foundation. Planning and building the golf course. 804 Merchandise Mart, Chicago, Illinois. 60654.

Sprinkler Irrigation Association. Minimum installation Specifications for turf sprinkler irrigation systems. 1966. Washington, D. C.

USGA Green Section. Irrigation of golf courses (Symposium). USGA Green Section Record, March, May, and September, 1966.

USGA Green Section. The putting green. USGA Green Section Record, March 1968.

24 Golf Fairways, Tees and Roughs

C. G. Wilson
J. M. Latham, Jr.
Milwaukee Sewerage Commission
Milwaukee, Wisconsin

I. Fairways

A. Playing Requirements

The low scoring, scratch, or tournament golfer sets the standards for fairway turf acceptance. This is the way it should be. Golf is a sport. As such, it never will and never should accede to the often heard clamor for mediocrity.

It will be of interest to review some of the golf courses selected over the years by the United States Golf Association for their major tournaments as shown in Table 1. Many factors are considered, but first and foremost is that it must be a great test of the game. To be a great test it must have the turf to match player requirements, i.e., a close, tight, and frequently cut turf so that the player's club will not catch the grass before it makes contact with the ball in playing the fairway shot.

With but one exception the reader will note among the grasses listed in Table 1 the absence of lawn grasses like Kentucky bluegrass and red fescue. The reason is simple. Other than at high altitude with irrigation under generally arid conditions, these cool-season species have not lent themselves to close cutting and proper play of the game. This may change with the advent of preemergence herbicides that keep out the weedy grasses like annual bluegrass, thus allowing a closer height-of-cut.

Table 1. Locations of some U.S. Golf Association tournaments.

Club	Tournament	Year	Fairway grass
Baltusrol, New Jersey	Open	1967	Bentgrass
Merion, Pennsylvania	Amateur	1966	Bentgrass
Bellerive, Missouri	Open	1965	Bermudagrass
Canterbury, Ohio	Amateur	1964	Bentgrass
Cherry Hills, Colorado	Open	1960	Ky. bluegrass
Winged Foot, New York	Open	1959	Bentgrass
Southern Hills, Oklahoma	Open	1958	Bermudagrass

* United States Golf Association, 40 East 38th Street, New York, New York.

Merion Kentucky bluegrass was heralded by many as the answer to a bluegrass that would deliver what the golfer wanted. Unfortunately, it has met with as many failures as successes. While resistant to leaf spot diseases that sooner or later take their toll of common and other widely acclaimed selections, Merion is plagued by other diseases. A *Fusarium* blight has wiped out large plantings in Pennsylvania and New York, and the grass is quite susceptible to powdery mildew and stripe smut. New systemic fungicides may halt the decline of Merion and reestablish it as a desirable fairway grass, although at the same time making it more costly to maintain.

USGA Green Section Director Al Radko has said that if the golf ball were square instead of round, so it would sit on top of sparse vegetation, golfers would not insist on close cutting. As there is no likelihood of this happening, player requirements for the 18 fairway strokes in a perfect round will continue to demand the highest standards of maintenance. These include close cutting, irrigation, weed, disease and insect control, excellent drainage and mechanical cultivation, to alleviate compaction from men and machines.

There are, of course, many exceptions to the high standards set for championship play. Several courses with sand putting "greens" exist in the plains states and parts of the West. There are good buffalograss fairways in southern Kansas near Wichita where rainfall is light and irrigation is unavailable. Crested, western, or fairway wheatgrass, or gramagrass, or, for that matter, anything that will grow is tolerated on low-budget courses in the northern plains where there is little competition for the golfer's dollar. In the South, low-budget courses have mixed fairways of almost every southern grass imaginable, including St. Augustine, centipede, bahia, crabgrass, carpetgrass, and many others.

Saline soils pose a definite problem for fairway development and maintenance. The area involved is so vast that the cost of major soil improvement would be prohibitive. Fortunately, some native grasses are adaptable to these conditions. *Puccinellia distans* shows promise on fairways at Utah Copper Country Club, Magna, Utah, provided adequate nitrogen is supplied. *Paspalum vaginatum* is performing well at Sea Island, Georgia, Gulfstream, Florida, and at other locations in the subtropical area. Some creeping bentgrasses exhibit salt tolerance along the northeast Atlantic coast. Seaview Country Club near Atlantic City, New Jersey, has low fairways that are often covered by tidal overflows where creeping bents are the only grasses to persist.

In northern humid regions there are many nonirrigated Kentucky bluegrass and red fescue fairways cut high (1½") that, over most of the year, provide excellent turf but low golfer acceptance. Because they do not please the critical golfer, more and more of these fairways are being irrigated, which necessitates a change in the grass.

When golfers have a choice of where to play, the superb test of golf and high quality grass at a good course will be picked. Fairway irrigation, as an example, does more than grow grass. It keeps the golfer's handicap strokes realistic throughout the playing season.

B. Fairway Grasses

Through the elimination process of what's best for the game, it is easy to see that few possibilities exist as this is written. In the South, Southwest, and West at lower elevations bermudagrass is preferred. Excellent fairways can be developed and maintained from seed, although the trend in the South is toward the use of improved selections planted vegetatively. Ormond is still favored in Florida and has withstood the test of time. Tifway is being widely used in recent plantings, and some clubs are trying such putting green varieties as Tifgreen and Tifdwarf. In general, the finer the strain and more vigorous the hybrid, the greater the thatch problem in the absence of intensive management.

The bermudagrass varieties developed by several experiment stations have many favorable attributes. In lawn and athletic field areas these grasses represent great advances in the production of high quality turf. Golf course fairway systems, amounting to some 30 to 100 acres, pose a gigantic problem as to mowing requirements and thatch removal. When fertility is high enough to fulfill the promise of optimum color, density, and reduced seedhead formation, thatch production is tremendous. When a good golfer cannot hit a controlled iron shot on these fairways, complaints begin to mount up. (Fig. 1)

Figure 1. These well-managed common bermudagrass fairways at Southern Hills Country Club, Tulsa, Oklahoma, rival improved bermudagrasses. (Courtesy O. J. Noer Research Foundation.)

About this time the walking golfers begin to complain about tiring because of deeper turf. Then the superintendent begins to notice the appearance of spring dead spot which the authors feel is related to thatch on plantings 3 or 4 years old. McCoy (1967) reported the same thing.

In the transition zone, sometimes referred to as the crabgrass belt, U-3 bermudagrass has been widely used with varying degrees of success. Most of the original plantings in the Philadelphia area have winterkilled. St. Louis, Louisville, Washington, D. C., and Kansas City have extensive fairway plantings of the U-3 variety. Next to outright winterkill, spring dead spot is the most serious malady on bermudagrasses in the northern range of their use in the South and Plains States. This has prompted some to consider zoysiagrass. At the Alvamar Hills Golf Course, Lawrence, Kansas, 18 fairways were planted to Meyer and common zoysia in 1967. This is the most widescale planting to come under play. Time will tell whether or not zoysia will become an important fairway grass in the crabgrass belt. New, cold-tolerant varieties of zoysia and bermudagrass have been released, namely, Midwest zoysia and Midway bermudagrass.

Recurrent problems with U-3 in the St. Louis and Kansas City areas have prompted some golf course superintendents to select winter-hardy "native" bermudagrass strains growing on their courses. Although coarser textured, they appear to be more winter-hardy and have less tendency toward thatch accumulation. In St. Louis and Springfield, Mo., these selections green up earlier and overrun U-3 bermudagrass.

Ray Keen at Kansas State University, Manhattan, has developed good winter-hardy bermudagrass strains. He cautions that winter hardiness will be reduced by nitrogen applications made from August 1 until the grass becomes dormant in the fall.

There is a serious lack of grass breeding activity in the northern U. S. In the South, G. W. Burton and co-workers have been responsible for many improved bermudagrasses widely used in golf (see Chapter 13). The most recent improvement for fairways is Tifway. Burton has devoted much time and effort to developing efficient methods for vegetatively planting sterile or largely sterile hybrid bermudagrass varieties. There should be an equal opportunity to select superior stoloniferous bentgrasses for vegetative planting on northern fairways. Bentgrasses are valued on northern fairways because of their adaptation to close mowing (1/2 to 3/4 inch).

Several commercially developed varieties of Kentucky bluegrass are being evaluated in the field. They may prove capable of withstanding the closely mowed treatment given fairway turf.

In the northern humid areas, west of the Cascade mountains in the Northwest, at high elevations with irrigation and where winter temperatures are severe, the bentgrasses deserve first consideration. Beard (1964) found Toronto creeping bentgrass to be the most cold tolerant of the cool-season species used in his trails at Michigan State. Grasses tested were Kentucky, rough, and annual bluegrass, red fescue, Toronto creeping bentgrass, and Penncross and Colonial bentgrass from seed.

The bentgrasses are among the most heat tolerant of our cool-season fairway grasses. They are widely used in desert areas where summer temperatures often reach 120 F or higher. Use there naturally relates to putting greens, but the point should not go unnoticed. Because of their density and ability to withstand close cutting they are undoubtedly the most weed free of all cool-season grasses. Properly managed, creeping bentgrasses have a reasonable level of drought resistance and good tolerance to high concentrations of soluble salts.

Possibly the most frequent condemnation one hears pertains to the annual bluegrass problem on bentgrass fairways. Nothing could be farther from the truth. It is Kentucky bluegrass and red fescue that are most subject to annual bluegrass invasion under close mowing. Bentgrasses, in fact, will persist at mowing heights and management levels that will eliminate Kentucky bluegrass and red fescue. The second, and probably the most severe condemnation, is that bentgrasses are so very expensive to maintain. As an example, fairway recommendations with respect to nutrients are often related to putting green requirements which, if nothing else, are wasteful and expensive. Here again, the talk is not from fact, but from supposition. People relate to experience in fields other than the one in question. Perhaps bentgrasses are condemned for fairway use because they are costly to maintain on putting greens.

Other than the need for more frequent mowing under low height-of-cut, which applies to any grass, bentgrasses perform well under the same or lower maintenance standards that are recommended for Kentucky bluegrass. Thus, we must stop equating putting green requirements with fairway needs if bentgrasses are to find their proper place in fairway use.

On new plantings the authors favor a mixture of grasses despite the fact that the turf will be maintained for bentgrass (Wilson, 1969). The inclusion of Kentucky bluegrass at seeding will give more body to the fairway turf in the early stages of development. The authors like to use red fescue even though they realize that it will not persist. Red fescues have the ability to germinate quickly, but even more important, they continue to grow well immediately following germination. This helps reduce erosion and weeds. Some of the new improved perennial ryegrasses such as Pelo, Manhattan, Norlea, NK-100, and others, may serve a similar worthwhile purpose, but have not been adequately tested as this is written.

A seed mixture that has done well, provided fertilization is adequate, consists of 50% Kentucky bluegrass, 30 to 35% red fescue, and 15 to 20% bentgrass seeded at 100 pounds per acre. Certified seed free from annual bluegrass should be specified. Oats or additional ryegrass is often specified where erosion will be a problem and has merit under such conditions. In these seed mixtures there is little reason to specify selections of Kentucky bluegrass or red fescue; and annual ryegrass will do just as well as perennial ryegrass. Seed used in mixtures should be free of annual bluegrass.

The bentgrasses deserve more careful thought than has been given in the past. Highland Colonial bentgrass is the cheapest. It has given the poorest results for fairway purposes. Penncross creeping bentgrass, while vigorous, has a bad tendency towards puffiness under fairway height of cut and, thus, in our opinion, should not be considered. Colonial bentgrass seed, identified as such, should not be considered because it is often Highland. This leaves Astoria Colonial bentgrass and Seaside creeping bentgrass; and the authors favor the use of both. Astoria is preferred for its broad gene base, pleasing apple green color, and the fact that it contains a high percentage of true creeping types. Exeter Colonial surpasses Astoria in performance at the University of Rhode Island, so is worthy of consideration in New England. It also looks promising in the Midwest. Seaside offers the greatest tolerance to saline conditions and contains a wide variety of true creeping types. A 50-50 mixture of Astoria and/or Exeter and Seaside is therefore advocated in the original seeding mixture. This same mixture at 20 pounds per acre is suggested for overseeding to upgrade Kentucky bluegrass or annual bluegrass fairways.

Annual bluegrass is a major grass component in most irrigated close cut fairways in the North. As long as it can be maintained as a perennial it provides an excellent playing surface. Unfortunately, it is weak in both hot and cold weather. Losing it once during the calendar year is

Figure 2. The excellent bentgrass fairways and Kentucky bluegrass roughs at the Milwaukee Country Club, Milwaukee, Wis., are typical of the best golfing conditions in the northern United States. (Courtesy O. J. Noer Research Foundation.)

serious enough, but many courses have had it "go out" in the winter and again in the summer of the same year. As this cannot be tolerated, golf course superintendents are experimenting with preemergence herbicides to control annual bluegrass.

A small percentage of annual bluegrass often comes with the grass seeds we purchase. Concern on this point in New York and Maryland has resulted in laws specifying that the number of annual bluegrass seeds present must be stated on the seed tag. Other states are following or are expected to follow this practice, which should result in cleaner seed in the future.

Annual bluegrass started to take over fairway turf when the height-of-cut was dropped following World War II. Prior to that time, high-cut Kentucky bluegrass-red fescue mixtures probably offered sufficient shade to reduce annual bluegrass germination and invasion. Furthermore, the bluegrass-fescue mixture was more competitive at the higher cut. Frequent irrigation had not yet become prevalent. Other factors concerning annual bluegrass "take over" are listed elsewhere in this monograph.

From the practical standpoint, those course managers who have yet to lower the height-of-cut, but who may well be forced into doing so, would be well advised to overseed with bentgrass when the mowing height is lowered. It is far easier to establish bentgrasses before annual bluegrass takes over.

Rough bluegrass is another *Poa* species often present in irrigated, close-cut fairways in northern regions. Beard (1966) rated it as highly cold tolerant. It seems especially well adapted to wet areas where drainage is poor. Rough bluegrass also does well under wet, shaded conditions and is sometimes suggested for use on tees where such conditions prevail. However, as with annual bluegrass, it is not a strong summertime or hot-weather performer.

The improvement of fairway grasses rests with the turfgrass breeders. The golf industry badly needs superior creeping bentgrass varieties for fairway use. One word of caution is important. While bentgrasses are ideal for fairways they should never be used in the rough.

C. Design

Design concepts are not within the province of agronomy. Neither should they be left in the hands of well-meaning club officials or the golf course superintendent. By the same token a golf architect, regardless of his reputation, should not be expected to have the last word on things relating to agronomy. Ideally, one field of endeavor should complement the other. The wise club will employ the services of both, and this is where the big breakthrough for the future lies.

Golf architects' fees vary depending on the work involved and the reputation of the man. Some have agronomic training, and a few employ agronomists or utilize their services on their jobs. A forward looking guess will see more clubs utilizing golf turfgrass agronomists. This must be done before and not after the fact. It is too late to alter building specifications once the contracts have been signed.

D. Fertilization

Not enough fertilizer is being used during construction, and too much is often recommended for established fairways. The best hint as to nitrogen needs for establishment comes from sod growers. It is not uncommon for them to apply 10 pounds or more of actual nitrogen per 1,000 square feet over a 7-month growing season. This is to grow a marketable sod in 12 to 18 months. Yet, many specifications for new fairway establishment call for only 1 pound of elemental nitrogen per 1,000 square feet. It is small wonder that such fairways are plagued with erosion, weeds, thin turf, and slow development.

The intricacies of financing are such that a new course demands rapid establishment. There are building lots to be sold, new members to recruit, and strong pressures for instant turf. Those who advise on new plantings do the customer a disservice in telling him to economize on fertilizer during the important establishment period.

Soil tests should be the guide for phosphorus, potash, and lime, provided they are based on actual fairway requirements. The only choice remaining is the source of plant food nutrients. One should not use much more than 1 pound of soluble nitrogen per 1,000 square feet as a surface application, in order to avoid seed injury and waste. Worked into the seedbed, these sources can be used at somewhat higher rates.

One successful practice for rapid establishment of both cool- and warm-season grasses is to apply 10-10-10 or similar analysis fertilizer along with activated sewage sludge, 6-3-0, a natural organic source of slowly soluble nitrogen. The rates of these at the start are ½ ton and 1 ton per acre, respectively. This is followed approximately 3 weeks after germination with supplemental applications of nitrogen from ammonium sulfate and natural organic alternated every 3 to 4 weeks until the desired stand is achieved. The rate on subsequent treatments is 1-pound actual nitrogen per 1,000 square feet for ammonium sulfate and 2-pounds for the natural organic. On fall plantings in the North the initial treatment is followed with a "dormant application" of natural organic provided ground conditions are favorable for the transport of equipment. A dormant application of chemical fertilizer has proven to be dangerous under dry, open winter conditions because it enhances desiccation.

New courses can also be established using only inorganic sources of nitrogen, phosphorus, and potassium. Sometimes ureaform and/or natural organics are used in the mixture to provide safer and more slowly soluble sources of nitrogen. It is generally unwise to exceed the 1-pound rate of elemental nitrogen in soluble form on young or established turf. Furthermore, it has been demonstrated in many trials that more frequent applications of soluble nitrogen are needed to maintain growth levels comparable to those obtained with slowly soluble nitrogen.

Ammonium sulfate has consistently ranked best among the quickly soluble nitrogen sources in Florida Experiment Station trials. Unfortunately, it is seldom the choice of those in the fertilizer mixing business because other nitrogen sources—urea, ammonium phosphate, or ammonium nitrate—are either more convenient or cheaper for use in mixed goods. Volk (1964), in investigating the gaseous loss of nitrogen from various compounds, states, "We can no longer say that a pound of nitrogen is a pound of nitrogen (irrespective of source)."

Once the fairway is established the rate of fertilizer application should change drastically. True, one can always add extra nitrogen and get more color but, one might add, at the expense of excessive growth. Fairway turf differs from other agricultural crops because the object is to produce a good sward rather than a heavy crop of clippings. Edenic values aside, one should strive for a playable turf, and color is not a good measure of playing value. Enough fertilizer must be used to maintain density, to heal the ravages of traffic, and to keep down weeds. Nature furnishes about 3 pounds of nitrogen per acre from rainfall and lightning. In addition, the biological breakdown of grass clippings and other organic matter constitute an important source of nitrogen. The remaining nitrogen needs must be supplied by man. Little thought has to be given to phosphorus and potash provided the initial levels are satisfactory, because as clippings decay these elements are returned to the turf. Clippings, incidentally, are good sources of plant food nutrients. They analyze roughly at a 5-2-4 to 6-2-3 analysis for N-P_2O_5-K_2O and when they remain in place return considerable nitrogen, phosphorus, and potash to the soil, as shown in Table 2.

Table 2. Percent nutrients in putting green clippings.*

Grass	N	P_2O_5	K_2O	SO_3	Soil reaction
Wash. creeping bentgrass	4.83	1.80	3.24	Not run	pH 7.2
Common bermudagrass	4.62	1.35	2.86	1.18	pH 6.8
Tifgreen bermudagrass	5.37	1.31	2.12	1.72	pH 6.3

* Turf Service Bureau, Milwaukee Sewerage Commission, Milwaukee, Wis. Bulletins 2 and 6.

The figures in the table are composite averages for the growing season. Soil reaction was slightly acid to slightly alkaline with high levels of phosphorus and potash. The clipping yields were taken from greens in play—Brynwood Country Club, Milwaukee, Wis., for the bentgrass test and the Memphis Country Club, Memphis, Tenn., for the common and Tifgreen bermudagrass samples.

Additional testing showed that the same ratios exist in healthy fairway clippings and that grass roots contain approximately 1% more phosphoric acid than leaves.

As to actual fertilizer levels used in fairway maintenance, the authors point to a few successful case histories. At Southern Hills Country Club, Tulsa, Okla., excellent common bermudagrass fairways have been maintained for years with three 800- to 1,000-pound applications of activated sewage sludge per acre per year. The turf has also remained free from "spring deadspot" that has plagued many other courses, in the same area, on which common bermudagrass is maintained with ammonium nitrate. Under subtropical conditions and a 12-month growing season at Miami Shores Golf Club, Miami Beach, Fla., a fourth application at the same rate has been required every 3 or 4 years.

In terms of actual nitrogen per 1,000 square feet the 4 to 6 pounds applied yearly is considerably lower than the 10 to 12 pounds of soluble nitrogen suggested for bermudagrass by some experiment stations. At these levels 2 to 3 pounds of phosphate and only 1/4 to 1/2 pound of potash are used. Yet this has been enough to maintain soil levels of both. At the same time, as much sulphur and iron have been applied yearly as fringe benefits.

Excellent irrigated bentgrass fairways on the Flossmoor Country Club, Chicago, Ill., are grown with only one 1,000-pound-per-acre August application of activated sewage sludge. Slightly more than double this amount is used at the Milwaukee Country Club, Milwaukee, Wis. At this club three 800-pound-per-acre applications have been applied in mid-June, late August, and late November since 1932 in growing high-quality bentgrass on irrigated fairways. The late George Hoffer (1949, unpublished data) was surprised to find that tissue tests of fairway clippings showed the same 5-2-4, N-P_2O_5-K_2O analysis as did the greens despite the low level of potash furnished by activated sewage sludge. The late O. J. Noer (1949, unpublished data) drew attention to the return of potash to the soil as clippings decayed, and to the approximate 0.75% potash contained in activated sludge.

Incidentally, the late November application on the Milwaukee Country Club is made on frozen ground, when the turf is dormant, in lieu of spring feeding. The fairways at the club have never needed fungicide treatments. The turf has been tight and free from thatch without resorting to mechanical raking. Some spot treatment is done to control the occasional broadleaf weeds. After Labor Day in some years the superintendent applies 1 to 3 weekly applications of sodium arsenite at 1-pound-per-acre to check clover and annual bluegrass. Experience at the Milwaukee Country Club has convinced the authors that irrigated bentgrass fairways are not costly to maintain in comparison with other irrigated cool-season grasses.

The amount of fertilizer required depends on many factors. Sandy soils need more than clays, while peat seldom, if ever, requires nitrogen. The depth of the soil is important. Where roots are restricted by hardpans or false water tables more in total but less per application should be used. The length of growing season, height of cut, use of irrigation, annual rainfall, amount of traffic, and condition of the turf have a bearing on total requirement and frequency of application. Soil tests taken at the proper depth of 2 inches are the best guide for phosphate, potash, and lime needs. They are not reliable for nitrogen. Color, density, and presence of weeds, especially clover, are the best indicators for nitrogen needs. Not only is each course an individual problem but with 30 to 100 acres of fairways stretched out over 6,000 to 7,000 yards, each course has special areas that require individual attention. Thus, no hard and fast rules on actual fertility needs can be given. It is further realized that soluble nitrogen alone or in combination with ureaform or other organic sources can be used, although more total nitrogen may have to be applied.

Individual golf course conditions and supervision determine the fertilization applied. Many grades and quantities are used depending upon the region, experiment station recommendations, and local sales organizations. It is, however, unfortunate to see a soil testing laboratory recommend 10-10-10 analysis even though phosphorus and potash levels in the soil are high and clippings remain. It is expensive to apply a complete fertilizer when either phosphorus or potash is not needed.

E. Irrigation and Drainage

Fairways should be irrigated if for no other reason than to keep play uniform. Traps that come into play during a wet season become obsolete after a prolonged dry spell. A difficult par four hole becomes an easy birdie when fairways are hard packed from drought, and the poor golfer who lowers his handicap on dried-out fairways has difficulty in winning when he plays a tournament on an irrigated course.

With irrigation, good drainage becomes of paramount importance, especially where rainfall is a factor. In keeping the soil near field capacity with sprinklers, stringent provisions must be made to handle excess rainfall. Surface drainage is by far the most important. Tile drains will not work unless they are placed below the water table. It is not necessary nor desirable to make every level fairway a "hogback" to shed water. They can be tilted from right to left and left to right on the same fairway. Where this is done in the landing area, a further premium can be placed on the tee shot.

In hilly country, provision has to be made sooner or later to stop seepage. The intercepting tile is placed in the rough and, if it is to be effective, a backfill of pea gravel or other coarse aggregate must come all the way to the surface of the ground. The least expensive location of the line is determined by digging a series of post holes on approximately 30-foot spacings directly up the slope from the wet area. The tile is then placed between the dry hole and the one partially filled with water. The auger holes are used to determine the shallowest placement depth that will be effective in draining the seepage area.

Similar slit trench drains are used successfully to remove excess water from pocketed and relatively level fairway areas. A 3-inch wide, self-powered ditch digger is used to cut trenches 2 feet deep leading from the area where water tends to pond to the adjacent rough. No tile is used. The trenches are backfilled to the surface with pea gravel or aggregate of similar size. Grass spreads rapidly to cover over the narrow trench with few, if any, objections from golfers.

Another area where intercepting tile lines can be used to good advantage is in front of pitched greens that seep to cause a wet, soggy approach. This has been a common problem in recent years where architects have used a gravel blanket over the subgrade, before adding sandy topsoil, but have failed to specify tile drains. This water is picked up by placing an oarlock or horseshoe type interceptor in front of the green collar deep enough to include the depth of the gravel blanket as well as that of the topsoil. Here again it should be backfilled to the surface with pea gravel, provided the intention is to control surface runoff as well. The butt or drainage end of the tile should be carried off into the rough or a non-play area.

Shallow soils, especially with a clay or silt texture, are virtually impossible to drain internally. It is only with depth that they can draw down or drain properly. J. R. Love (1967, unpublished data) at the University of Wisconsin estimates that 2 feet of loam soil is needed above a gravel blanket in order to achieve proper drainage. It is a mistake to place a thin layer of topsoil over the subgrade before planting where such soil differs appreciably in texture from the underlying strata. Where sandy soil is placed in a shallow layer over clay, it will take water more rapidly than the clay can disperse it. Conversely, a shallow layer of loam over sand or gravel will be constantly and continuously wet, because of the perched water table where the loam meets the sand.

An automatic irrigation system is preferred when labor is scarce and expensive. It can be designed to meet the customer's needs provided water is available. Probably its greatest single advantage rests in the direct control that it provides the superintendent. Automation doesn't guarantee proper watering. This can only be accomplished by excellent design, the right components properly installed, and programming in the hands of a knowledgable superintendent.

Deep and infrequent watering is ideal for most agricultural crops, including turfgrasses. Unfortunately, there is no way to replenish a serious water deficiency in the profile of a loam soil with one night of irrigation. Also, as mentioned before, if the soil is permitted to dry out to this extent, there will be a serious decline in the uniformity of playing conditions on fairways. Thus, most courses find themselves committed to watering every night or every second or third night. In order to water deeply and infrequently, the members would have to resign themselves to a course shutdown, so that fairways could be irrigated night and day in order to replace water losses.

Heavier soils, in terms of "draw bar pull," will not accept water at a rate much in excess of 1/3 inch per hour. Where the water evapotranspiration rate is 1 to 1 1/2 inches per week, as in the East and upper Midwest, the system must be designed to replenish this amount. In the desert areas of the Southwest, water use rates can reach 3 to 3 1/2 inches per week, and design must take these differences into consideration.

One other point on water should not be overlooked. Although peat fairways seldom need irrigation from the standpoint of color or inducing growth, watering will help to keep them smooth. Watering will also prevent a conflagration during dry weather from a carelessly tossed cigarette.

F. Weed Control

Annual bluegrass is the worst weed problem on irrigated northern fairways, while the sedges and nutgrasses are the most difficult to control in bermudagrass. Annual bluegrass is also becoming more of a problem on bermudagrass fairways. Excessive nitrogen levels, low cutting, and too much water and traffic are credited by many with the increase in annual bluegrass since World War II. Not to be overlooked is the indiscriminate use of 2,4-D and related products that appear to have had a deleterious effect on the vigor of bentgrasses. The same products have affected the growth of some bermudagrass varieties.

When 2,4-D first came on the market it was considered by some people as a panacea for weed problems, and, as a consequence, it was applied to excess on fairway areas. It was reputed to kill dandelion and plantain even when applied on dormant turf when the weeds were not growing. These late fall applications at excessive rates probably helped to open the turf for annual bluegrass invasion, especially during dry seasons. Currently, rates have been reduced and 2,4-D is now combined with mecoprop or dicamba to control clover, chickweed, and knotweed. The important point, still, is to be circumspect with fall treatments as this is the time when most of the damage from their use occurs and, one might add, the injury is seldom seen until the following year.

Insofar as possible, fairways should be managed to discourage annual bluegrass. It is important to determine the nature and extent of invasion. If it has replaced a large percentage of the perennial turfgrasses, a complete renovation may be necessary. Under these circumstances the turf must be destroyed prior to reseeding. One favorite method is to use sodium arsenite at very heavy rates (20 to 30 pounds actual per acre) followed by thorough seedbed preparation with aeration and renovation tools, and reseeding with more desirable bentgrass species. This should be done as early in August as possible to give the bentgrass a fair chance to become established before annual bluegrass germinates in the fall. Complete renovation will succeed when done properly, although follow-up preemergent control is usually necessary.

Where annual bluegrass is present in reasonable amounts along with desirable grasses, preemergence chemical control is practical. Newer materials like bensulide, DCPA, and turbutol are worthy of trial in limited areas. The arsenicals as preemergent chemicals have been used successfully for many years. Further, when used properly they are not injurious to overseedings and they control crabgrass and chickweed as well as annual bluegrass. Lead arsenate is an old standard that is quite effective. Now that tricalcium arsenate (calcium arsenate) is available in granular form, it is replacing lead arsenate to a large degree. The proper approach in using arsenicals requires the gradual buildup of toxic levels and their maintenance with light annual applications.

Arsenicals, as with most fungicides and insecticides, can kill people as well as turf pests. Thus, handling precautions printed on the label must be followed.

Effective postemergence weed control on bermudagrass fairways in the South depends on an early start and repeated herbicide applications throughout each growing season. DSMA with or without 2,4-D is well accepted in controlling weedy grasses and sedges in bermudagrass. Treatments with DSMA or the closely related MSMA products will do a good job provided they are used with persistence and care.

Dormant bermudagrass is subject to invasion by cool-season weeds and grasses. Sodium arsenite as a postemergent treatment will eliminate these cool-season species. As soils are cooler in the spring the rate is normally 5 to 8 pounds per acre. The heavier rate is more effective in controlling chickweed and henbit. Wild onion and garlic can also be a problem when bermudagrass is dormant. These weeds can be controlled with 2,4-D and related compounds but more than one application is required.

In the past it was not uncommon to "burn off" winter weeds by applying soluble nitrogen shortly before the bermudagrass initiated growth. This practice is questionable because the fertilizer burn can damage the new growth of bermudagrass. Any delay in bermudagrass growth can increase the severity of crabgrass invasion.

Preemergence controls on bermudagrass fairways have not been widely used as this is written. Much remains to be learned concerning the persistence of preemergence chemicals in soils, especially where fairway turf will be overseeded to improve winter color and playing conditions.

G. Insect Control

Mole crickets and scale insects have been the worst problems on bermudagrass fairways, although there is some evidence that cutworm and sod webworm damage may be of increasing importance in improved fine-leaf selections. Poison baits are excellent for controlling mole crickets. Scale insects are difficult to control unless timing is perfect, with the application made during the crawler stage. Diazinon and carbaryl insecticides are of value in controlling scale insects, especially in those areas where resistance to the hydrocarbon insecticides is suspected. Diazinon also has been used at heavy rates for nematode control. The billbug has been difficult to control on zoysia. For billbugs, Florida entomologists suggest disulfoton, applied only by commercial operators at 7 to 10 pounds per acre and thoroughly watered.

Chinch bugs are serious on St. Augustinegrass and in the North sometimes cause injury to cool-season fairways, especially during dry weather. A *Hyperodes* weevil has been responsible for the loss of annual bluegrass in the metropolitan New York area. Other than for this weevil, available insecticides can be relied on to control insects on cool-season grass fairways. Again, if resistance to chlorinated hydrocarbons is suspected, they should be replaced with either organic phosphates or carbamates.

Soil insecticides will control grubs and will discourage earthworm activity when applied at about double the rate suggested for grub control. Lessening the number of grubs is also effective in discouraging moles.

Gopher damage is widespread in the South and West. Trapping, shooting, and gassing are widely accepted practices and effective, provided vigilance is followed by the workmen. Gopher injury has been observed to be more troublesome on new courses and on those surrounded by tracts of wilderness.

Nematode injury is often observed on sandy soils in Florida and on the coastal islands of the southeastern coast. The cost of nematicides is such that most clubs wait until grass decline is apparent and then spot-treat localized areas.

H. Disease Control

Fairways in the South are seldom, if ever, treated for diseases. Leaf spot is widespread on most southern grasses, and brown patch and dollar spot have been reported on bermudagrass. Inducing better growth is an accepted and less costly method of masking the condition even though it falls short of actual control. Where fairways are overseeded for winter color the use of fungicide-treated seed will reduce the possibility of cottony blight damage to germinating seedlings.

A few irrigated northern courses practice some degree of disease control on fairways. Both pink and gray snowmold damage can be severe on annual bluegrass and bentgrasses. Leaf spot, rust, powdery mildew, and stripe smut can create problems on Kentucky bluegrass. The bentgrasses, Kentucky bluegrass, and the fine-leaf fescues are attacked by both dollar spot and brown patch. The point worth noting here is that bentgrasses are not unique in being plagued by disease problems.

As mentioned in these case histories, much can be done by proper management to lessen the inroads of disease. As nitrogen levels are increased, dollar spot disease is lessened. When comparing similar rates of applied nitrogen from different sources, Roberts (1963) and Roberts and Markland (1966) report less dollar spot where activated sewage sludge was used. Cook et al. (1964) say the same, plus a reduction in brown patch where sludge had been compared with inorganic 10-6-4. At the Coastal Plain Experiment Station, Wells (1957) found less cottony blight disease where activated sewage was used in comparison with ammonium nitrate, urea, and ureaform. Possibly the most unfortunate point of all is that protective fungicides on northern fairways may have done more to perpetuate annual bluegrass than the more desirable bentgrasses. This is not to say fungicides will never be needed. They will be, and increasingly so, as more one-crop grass areas on large acreages are planted and nurtured to perfection. Many turfgrass pathologists agree that a good fungicide will only do the job it is capable of doing when other essential maintenance practices are correct.

I. Special Problems

The increase in play coupled with irrigation has caused a substantial increase in compaction problems. As a result several companies now manufacture specialized equipment capable of cultivating the soil underneath established turf without unduly disturbing the sod. There is no doubt that these aerating and spiking machines will be used with increasing frequency in the years ahead. (Fig. 3)

Figure 3. This group of golfers and caddies on a starting tee illustrate the wear and compaction from foot traffic that grasses and soils must withstand. (Courtesy O. J. Noer Research Foundation.)

Several problems associated with their use have been observed. The first relates to the tendency to use them at the least effective time of the year in an effort to avoid golfer complaints. As an example, it is not unusual to observe superintendents aerating both before and after the growing season has ended. When done late in the season these cultivations open the soil for winter weed invasion. Conversely, in the North they are often used early in the spring when frost action should have taken care of compaction problems. Their use has also been observed following an application of a preemergence herbicide, thus destroying its effectiveness.

The authors believe in the value of aeration and spiking equipment, but there is need for common sense in fitting these machines into the overall management program. One cannot be quite as certain as to where mechanical rakers, sweepers, and vertical mowers fit in fairway management programs. Obviously, where management has permitted excessive thatch and mat accumulation, dethatchers have a place and some type of sweeping or windrowing equipment must be used to remove the duff. Their use to keep thatch from developing is questionable and, as mentioned before, clipping removal means additional fertilizer usage.

Mowing equipment must be kept sharp and properly adjusted. Cutting should be done as growth dictates and not on arbitrary schedules. Care should also be taken to mow in different directions with cross cutting as needed to reduce grain and "washboarding" caused by mowing at high speeds.

Where play is heavy, one can expect increasing attention to divot repair in major landing areas, using soil, seed, and fertilizer to promote rapid healing. Cart paths of macadam or other nonturf materials will increase in length and width to handle the increased mechanization of maintenance equipment, as well as the golfers who prefer to ride instead of walk. Even now, there are a few courses who have a complete highway system throughout the entire course for the use of power carts.

II. Tees

Standards for tees are established by the requirements for good playing conditions. Tees should be almost level, furnish a relatively dry surface, provide for a firm stance in making tee shots, and be of sufficient size to allow tee markers to be moved and thereby permit injured turf to recover.

Methods of seedbed preparation for tee soils are similar to those used on greens, except that on most courses modification with sand and organic materials is not as extensive. It is essential, however, to insure good moisture holding capacity and a comparatively high level of soil fertility.

The same grasses recommended for fairway use are adapted for planting tees. Bermudagrass, including improved varieties, is standard in much of the southern U. S. except in shade where zoysia is preferred. In the transition zone, a portion of the bermudagrass tee area may be set aside for winter play and seeded to annual ryegrass or to a mixture of cool-season grasses. The remaining portion is often mulched heavily to prevent winter kill. Kentucky bluegrass and red fescue mixtures have been used extensively on tees in cool, humid regions, but under high cut they are not well accepted. Where irrigation is available, many of these tees have been replaced by Colonial and creeping bentgrasses. Astoria Colonial and Seaside creeping bentgrass are common components in seed mixtures used on new tees in the northeastern, midwestern, and northwestern regions. The bentgrasses are preferred because they maintain dense turf under close cutting and heal divot scars more rapidly than Kentucky bluegrass and fine-leaf fescues. Rough and annual bluegrasses are encouraged under heavily shaded conditions. (Fig. 4).

Figure 4. Close-cut bentgrass or bermudagrass tees give the golfers optimum shot-making potential. (Courtesy O. J. Noer Research Foundation.)

Turf on tees should be cut at a height that will permit the ball to stand clear of the grass without being teed too high. This is the same as putting green height to critical golfers. Daily cutting of well fertilized bentgrass and bermudagrass will often be necessary. Close clipping is essential on both to reduce the development of a spongy turf. Periodic topdressing is required for the same reason and to maintain a level surface. Clipping may be less frequent with slower growing grasses such as Kentucky bluegrass, fine-leaf fescue, zoysia, buffalo, blue grama, and centipede grasses. New seedings of Kentucky bluegrass and the fine-leaf fescues should reach a height of 1½ to 2 inches before the first cutting. These grasses will generally be maintained at 1¼ inches in the Midwestern and Eastern States. Merion and comparable dwarf varieties of Kentucky bluegrass have been maintained at a ¾-inch cutting height when grown under irrigation in cool regions and this will satisfy some golfers. New plantings of bentgrass, bermudagrass, and other strongly creeping grasses can be cut at ¾ or ½ inch as soon as the initial growth reaches a height of 1 to 1¼ inches.

Fertilizer schedules for bentgrass and bermudagrass tees where clippings are removed are similar to those developed for greens (see Chapter 23). Kentucky bluegrass, fine-leaf fescues, and most other species, where clippings remain, are fertilized in keeping with fairway practice. In watering tees, every attempt should be made to permit the maximum amount of time between watering and heavy play. This practice improves playing conditions and helps to reduce compaction. Aeration and spiking are standard practices to improve water intake and to provide a dry surface. Disease, insect, and weed control practices are the same for tees and greens.

Tee markers should be moved before the turf shows evidence of severe injury. Divot scars should be filled with good-quality topdressing material. Vigorously growing creeping bentgrass and bermudagrass, supplied with adequate nitrogen, may heal scars rapidly without seeding. On the other hand, seeding is recommended for large scars on Kentucky bluegrass, fine-leaf fescues, and Colonial bentgrass. Constant play on restricted areas may damage turf beyond repair. The alternative to play from bare ground or a synthetic grass substitute involves increasing tee size and restoring the damaged area by either complete renovation and reseeding or sodding.

III. Roughs

Roughs are usually the most neglected areas of the golf course. In the past, it was a common practice to permit roughs to be occupied by naturally occurring vegetation that was mowed only occasionally. The rank growth of grass obtained under these conditions slowed play. The common trend now is to plant roughs with the same species used on fairways. The one exception is bentgrass which is not satisfactory for roughs because of its spongy growth habit at the higher mowing height required on roughs. Acceptable cover and playing conditions for roughs are obtained by adjusting height and frequency of cut and by applications of fertilizer as needed.

The toughest roughs are bermudagrass and dense Kentucky bluegrass, cut high. Among the species utilized for roughs in the northern region are Kentucky bluegrass, fine-leaf fescues, and sometimes tall fescue. Crested and western wheatgrass, smooth brome, grama, and weeping love grasses have proven satisfactory in the Great Plains. In the humid section of the southeastern region bermudagrass is preferred, or centipedegrass where it is adapted.

In the construction of new golf courses, it has become a common practice to use the same establishment practices on roughs and fairways. The roughs will vary in width depending on the design and area available. Differences in turf quality to meet demands of play are obtained by the adjustment of clipping height and other maintenance practices. Fertilizer applications, adjustment of soil pH, and other soil treatments will depend on local conditions and the grasses planted. Refer to Chapter 18 for seeding rates.

On existing thin turf, it may be necessary to make a light overseeding to obtain greater turf density. Usually extra nitrogen will accomplish the same purpose, provided soil tests are satisfactory for phosphate, potash, and lime.

Height and frequency of mowing will depend on the grass species and policy with regard to playing conditions. The trend today is to mow an intermediate or "step down" height adjacent to the fairway. Otherwise the ball slightly off line is penalized more severely than the shot falling way off line in the direction of play. In general, roughs composed of sod-forming species are cut with reel mowers at a height below that used for bunch grasses. Rotary or hammer knife mowers adapted to cut high are used for roughs consisting of coarse grasses and weeds. Non-use areas should be planted with grass species that will require a minimum of care, tolerate existing soil conditions, provide cover, and prevent erosion.

Literature Cited

Beard, J. B. 1964. The effects of ice, snow and water covers on Kentucky bluegrass, annual bluegrass, and creeping bentgrass. Crop Sci. 4:638-640.

Beard, J. B. 1966. Winter injury. The Golf Supt., pp. 24-27, 30, January

Cook, R. N., R. E. Engel, and S. Bachelder. 1964. A study of the effect of nitrogen carriers on turfgrass disease. Pl. Dis. Rptr. 48:254-255, April.

McCoy, R. E. 1967. A study of the etiology of spring dead spot. M. S. Thesis. Oklahoma State University, Stillwater, Okla.

Roberts, Eliot C. 1963. Relationships between mineral nutrition of turfgrass and disease susceptibility. The Golf Course Rptr., pp. 52-54, 57, May.

Roberts, Eliot C. and Flave E. Markland. 1966. Dollar spot tests yield tips. Golfdom, February.

Volk, G. M. 1964. Florida research report 9(1), January.

Wells, H. 1957. Number of cottony blight spots with different nitrogen sources. Proc. Southeastern Turfgrass Conf.

Wilson, C. G. 1969. Overseeding bermuda greens. Paper presented at Golf Course Superintendents Assoc. Meeting, Miami Beach, Fla. Jan. 23, 1969.

Supplemental Reading

Anonymous. Better bent greens, Fertilization and Management 1959. Bulletin No. 2 published by Milwaukee Sewerage Commission, Milwaukee, Wis.

Anonymous. Better bermudagrass greens and tees. Bulletin No. 6 published by Milwaukee Sewerage Commission, Milwaukee, Wis.

Anonymous. Better fairways, northern golf courses, theory and practice. 1960. Bulletin No. 3 published by Milwaukee Sewerage Commission, Milwaukee, Wis.

Ferguson, Marvin H. 1968. Building golf holes for good turf management by the green section staff of the United States Golf Association, edited by M. H. Ferguson.

Hagan, Robert M. 1955. Watering lawns and turf and otherwise caring for them. Yearbook Agr., U.S. Dept. Agr., pp. 462-477.

Juska, Felix V. and A. A. Hanson. 1961. Effects of interval and height of mowing on growth of Merion and common Kentucky bluegrass *(Poa pratensis* L.) Agron. J. 53:385-388.

Juska, Felix V. and A. A. Hanson. 1967. Factors affecting *Poa annua* L. control. Weeds 15:98-101.

McCloud, Darrel E. 1959. Theory of water loss. The Golf Course Rptr., pp. 18-20, July.

Youngner, V. B., O. R. Lunt, and F. Nudge. 1967. Salinity tolerance of seven varieties of creeping bentgrass, *Agrostis palustris* Huds. Agron. J. 59:335-336.

25 Highway Roadsides

W. L. Hottenstein

Bureau of Public Roads
Washington, D. C.

I. Introduction

Completion of the Interstate System of Defense Highways will add more than 1,000,000 acres of roadside area to an existing total of 2,500,000 acres. The right-of-way of a modern highway contains areas of earth that comprise 60 to 75% of the total area. If left bare, the construction-scarred portion of this vast acreage probably would erode and be unsightly. Erosion on an extensive scale can destroy an appreciable part of the highway investment and create serious hazards for the motorist. Turf-forming grasses which cover the majority of roadside areas are the most effective and rapidly developing ground cover and are a prime factor in the economic, aesthetic and safety requirements of a complete highway.

The need to control erosion along highways provided the initial impetus for so-called roadside development work. It was during the first tremendous drive to construct a network of all-weather surface roads for automobiles in the 1920's that highway engineers began to note with alarm the results of erosion on newly constructed cross sections. Structures were undermined, drainage installations were vitiated, and severe damage was inflicted by deposition of subsoil in water supply facilities and on agricultural lands beyond right-of-way boundaries. Damage caused by erosion necessitated additional expenditures for maintenance. Economics became the prime factor which motivated highway administrators to employ professionally trained men to develop methods and techniques for establishing vegetation on those roadside areas disturbed by construction.

It is interesting to reflect that during the early decades of highway construction the indifference of engineers to erosion probably evolved from the land-use concept which guided our forefathers in the nineteenth century. Natural resources were then considered to be practically inexhaustible. Little thought was given to the possible consequences of pollutants poured into clean streams and clear, sparkling lakes. Only passing notice was given to destructive logging, mining and farming practices which contributed to irreparable damage from fires, erosion, and siltation. These evils all too frequently were accepted as the inevitable associates of progress.

Agronomists, landscape architects, and foresters employed by state highway departments during the 1920's and 30's to implement erosion control operations emphasized the use of vines and shrubs. It was soon evident, however, that labor and material costs for the extensive plantings required had a limiting effect. This, plus the fact that woody species needed two or more years to develop an erosion resistant ground cover, made the shift to other forms of vegetation a matter of practical necessity. During the late 1930's a significant effort was directed toward the development of techniques and materials for establishing and maintaining turf species on roadside areas.

The grasses are an extremely adaptable family of plants. By varying species and manipulating management techniques a wide range of environmental effects can be achieved on a highway right-of-way. The milieu of an urban setting is expressed with neatly mowed areas of uniformly textured turf, while the ecological associations of a natural swamp or marsh situation may be made an integral part of the rural highway landscape with appropriate grasses and maintenance methods. Subsequent portions of this chapter will describe the most important facets of turf establishment and management along highways in the several climatic regions of the U. S.

Erosion control, maintenance, and the need to evolve new land-use concepts in a nation where land and water resources were harshly exploited have been mentioned. There is another important area of consideration in which grass plays a major role. Highways today are much more than a facility to hasten the movement of traffic and to make transportation more convenient. Highways today are for people. They are an integral part of urban and rural America. It is, therefore, essential that highways be so designed, located and developed that they form a visually acceptable element in the motorist's environment, as well as that of residents adjacent to the right-of-way.

A major reason for the current emphasis on highway beautification is the increase in pleasure driving as a form of recreation. More leisure time and a developing awareness of environmental quality and safety are other factors which make more important the need to create and maintain a highway environment that is visually attractive. Grass is the single most useful form of vegetation to accomplish such a goal.

II. Turf Uses

A. Erosion Control

Measures to effectively control erosion on highway roadsides have been the subject of intensive study by the Roadside Development Committees of the Highway Research Board and American Association of State Highway Officials for over three decades. Today the importance of erosion control is second only to the need for adequate design and location considerations. To achieve an effective and harmonious control between the highway right-of-way and the adjoining countryside, it is still imperative that vegetation—normally turf—be used to control erosion on construction scars with a minimum of delay, thereby making possible their restoration as an integral part of an aesthetically pleasing, unobtrusive, and natural roadside environment. The "complete highway" is not a reality until all soil areas are protected with appropriate vegetation.

Knowledge of basic soil erosion factors influencing soil erosion is of major importance in recognizing problems and arriving at solutions. These principle factors which influence soil erosion have been summarized by A. W. Johnson (1957).

1. Slopes

Good cross-section design is a basic factor in attaining successful erosion control. It is axiomatic that cut and fill slopes be constructed as flat as economically possible. As slopes become steeper, there is a rapid increase in erosion control cost and a corresponding decrease in effectiveness and performance of control measures. Slopes designed as flat as economically practical, with adequate rounding at both top and bottom and with appropriate transitional grading between cuts and fills, will improve appearance and highway safety, facilitate establishment of a vegetative cover, and reduce maintenance costs. Other considerations relating specifically to erosion control include climate, geologic formations, soil types, and drainage design that considers adjacent land elements as well as the roadway itself.

Unfortunately, flat slopes are uneconomical of attainment in many sections of the U. S. Erosion control problems increase in difficulty, but not importance, with increased gradient and height of cut and fills. Special methods, materials, and equipment have been developed to cope with these problems. Industry is constantly adding new ones. Solutions frequently involve additional measures to control surface water and runoff, such as *(1)* drainage channels designed for need; *(2)* culverts located with regard to erosion dangers, drop structures to prevent ditch erosion, aprons at outlets to minimize scour; *(3)* intercepting ditches for minor drainage from above the highway, flume and special ditch design for handling farm terrace water, and diversion channels from culvert outlets to natural drainage; *(4)* gutter paving; and *(5)* berms and spillways on large fills and inside of elevated curves.

2. Drainage Channels

Drainageways present special problems involving safety, appearance, and adjoining lands. Vegetative cover as a control has limitations with respect to channel capacity and premissible velocity. In addition to mechanical erosion control methods such as temporary check dams or permanent-type construction, there have been many experiments designed to stabilize and protect intercepting dikes and channels pending establishment of suitable vegetation. Many materials in addition to concrete and asphalt linings have been used, including jute netting, glass fibers (alone or with asphalt), paper netting, and glass fiber matting. Although the results have not been uniformly conclusive, the variety of materials suggests that industry is aware of the problem and is cooperating in the development of suitable materials for special erosion control problems.

3. Special Areas

Erosion control methods have evolved from special problem areas. For instance, seeding and fertilization by helicopter or other aircraft have been used successfully to establish vegetation on high cut and fill slopes that could not be worked with conventional equipment. Costs were comparable with other mechanical means. Sandy soils require specialized treatment, particularly where high winds are the erosive problem. To be successful in such cases, each top grain of sand must be stabilized. Crushed rock or gravel materials have proven effective and their application can be followed by seeding and fertilization where vegetation is practical. Seeding, fertilization, and straw mulch tied down with wire netting have been used successfully.

Sand dune control is a difficult and costly stabilization problem. Culms of European and American beachgrass are normally employed as the first step in stabilization, followed by the seeding of various grasses and legumes. Shrubs and trees are planted for the final cover.

Under any condition, speed in establishing vegetation is a prime factor in obtaining effective erosion control at low cost. Often extensive seedbed preparation is avoided by employing proper erosion control procedures immediately after construction.

Special attention is called to the two bibliographies published by the Highway Research Board (1960, 1965). The references listed in these bibliographies offer more pertinent and detailed information on the many facets of soil erosion control than is possible here.

B. Safety—Stabilization, Sight Distance and Emergency Areas.

Modern high-speed transportation arteries must have clear, obstruction-free recovery areas adjacent to the travel lanes. Drivers who swerve or are forced from the pavement to a roadside area must have safe zones for such emergencies.

On recently completed expressways, motorists are provided several important features: *(1)* a streamlined cross section with flattened slopes and swale-type drainage ditches, *(2)* stabilized areas devoid of fixed traffic hazards, and *(3)* roadside areas with a vegetative cover of turf made up of grasses adapted to the existing environmental conditions.

Experience has clearly demonstrated that turfgrass is one of the most adaptable and useful ground covers and contributes to the safe use of roadside areas. Turf is the most rapidly established vegetative cover that controls erosion, stabilizes slopes, and provides safe off-highway emergency parking and stopping areas. It can be economically maintained, and it contributes a pleasing appearance for both the highway user and adjacent residents.

Equally important are safe, adequate, and unobstructed sight lines along and from all highways. Safe stopping distances are essential on high-speed traffic lanes. Unimpaired sight distances must be maintained at all intersections, railroad grade crossings, intersecting roads and relatively unimportant driveways and local streets. Visibility can be maintained by low-growing, functional turfgrasses that can be kept in such a manner that sight distances are devoid of visual limitations.

C. Appearance.

Travel lanes framed with a turf cover provide a transition for the natural environment of the rural countryside, as well as for the suburban and urban situation. Residential streets and boulevards in towns and cities also include areas of grass. The reasons for developing these areas in this manner are numerous; grass properly established and cared for improves the appearance of the landscape, makes the areas more desirable for a variety of uses, and prevents the erosive action of wind and water.

A turf cover adds pleasure and comfort to the highway user and permits an unobstructed view of distant scenes of the rural countryside, as well as providing desirable visual values in the urban environment.

1. Texture–Rural, suburban and urban.

High speed travel along modern expressway systems makes detail of the turf relatively unimportant. Of particular importance are ecologically adapted species with desirable functional and aesthetic values. It is generally conceded that turf with a coarse texture is best suited to rural areas and that turf of a finer texture is better in areas of lawns, parks, cemeteries, etc., and in suburban and urban areas.

It should be remembered, however, that the controlling criteria for the use of this element in the highway picture are ease and economy of establishment and maintenance, functional value, and appearance for the motorist and for the owner of abutting property.

2. Recreation.

Recreational driving is the predominant use of highways. Highway travel for pleasure or business should be a pleasant and safe experience for the motorist.

Unending ribbons of concrete with unimproved roadside areas are monotonous and unsafe. It is, therefore, essential that highway facilities include locations for the motorist to stop, rest, relax, and perhaps enjoy a picnic lunch. Small parks along the roadside with interesting paths to explore should be provided for the highway user. Scenic overlooks, historic sites, and other recreational facilities are valuable roadside assets.

3. Restoration of sites.

Immediately after construction operations, slope stabilization, erosion control, and roadside rehabilitation should be undertaken. The most efficient and economical method for accomplishing these objectives is through the establishment of a grass cover. Seeding, fertilizing, and mulching should be done immediately after the grading operations. Obviously, it is important to establish a vegetative cover on the raw soil to eliminate erosion and the equal evils of stream sedimentation and pollution. An aesthetically pleasing roadside area is a dividend which grass contributes in addition to the functional purposes it serves.

4. Conservation.

The importance of exercising good conservation practices during construction cannot be overemphasized. Existing plant materials should not be disturbed beyond the limits of construction. Preservation of native species reduces the necessity for extensive replanting.

It is, however, necessary to distrub many areas which must be covered with grass initially. In order to reduce maintenance operations, and to provide a more aesthetic appearance, the regeneration of native species of woody plants should be encouraged. Planned and well-developed highway roadsides will become more interesting and will be more economical and less hazardous to maintain. Native growth usually abounds beyond the construction limits and through sensible management practices this vegetation can be encouraged to extend over the slopes and other roadside areas. In this way roadsides become an integral part of the adjacent environment.

III. Design Elements

A. Cross Section and Grade (3-dimensional)

The proper design of the highway cross section contributes to the attractive appearance of the highway, successful establishment of turf, and reduced maintenance costs. Roadside slopes with appropriately designed grades fitted into the terrain are basic elements in the appearance of the highway and should be given priority over other roadside design features.

With a flat gradient a slope will look better and be safer, turf will be established more readily, and mowing will be easier if it should be required. The assets inherent in flatter slopes are recognized by many state highway departments. In actual practice, such slopes may be difficut to justify because of the additional construction costs and because standard cross sections are frequently used regardless of slope height. To achieve proper grading, a contour grading plan should be used and different gradients employed for varying slope heights.

Rounding the top of a slope permits easier mowing and eliminates a starting point for erosion where the planes of the slope and the original ground form an angular section. The angular section invites erosion and the sod may be scalped in mowing. Rounding (blending a slope with the original surface) the toe of a slope is also important for the same reasons noted above. The fact that the rounded slope looks much better can be considered a bonus. On any highway project where attention is given to appearance and ease of maintenance, a rounded slope is an essential requirement. Where snow drifting is a problem, the design and construction of flat and well-rounded slopes will minimize this winter hazard.

It is difficult to categorically state what is the best slope ratio. It may be appropriate, unless the elevation is great, to use a slope that is 3:1 or less. Depending on elevation, slope ratios may vary from 3:1 to 10:1. The guiding principal for the design of a cross section should be that of blending the grading into the terrain so that it appears to be an integral part of the landscape.

The grading of bridge embankments presents special problems because of embankment heights and the usually steep slope section directly beneath the bridge. In some instances sodding the "nose" of the embankment would be better than attempting to seed turfgrasses. However, a more desirable practice from the standpoint of safety and maintenance would be to flatten the embankment even though this could mean an increase in cost. It is not possible to grow turf in areas directly underneath bridges except in those special cases where the structures are very high and the areas beneath receive sufficient sunlight and moisture to support a turf cover. In situations where turf cannot be grown, suitable surfacing should be used.

The cross-section design of parking and public use areas in roadside safety rest areas should be planned for ease of pedestrian movement and graded for rapid drainage to insure dry areas for the convenience of the motorist.

B. Earth stabilization

The soil upon which turf is to be grown must be at its natural angle of repose and the area must be stable from the viewpoint of soil mechanics before the establishment of turf can be expected. An adequate turf cover will prevent surface erosion but will not control a heavy seepage or flow of water from beneath the surface. Often the areas of slippage or heavy seepage are not discovered until the actual construction of the highway slope. In such situations they may be controlled by adequately designed "french" drains and, in some serious cases, by placing a stone blanket on the area of seepage in order to prevent sloughing. Where sloughing occurs, the problem should be resolved in cooperation with a soil mechanics engineer.

Assuming a reasonable slope-grade and suitable soil, it is generally easier to establish turf on a fill than on a cut slope. The requirements for a specific area must be considered when designing the treatment to establish a turf cover.

The maximum degree of slope ratio upon which grass should be attempted to be grown is commonly agreed to be 1.5 horizontal to 1 vertical. However, there can be some variation because of soil types. A ratio of 2 horizontal to 1 vertical is usually considered maximum for the successful establishment of turf on a large scale.

Occasionally a fill slope constructed of rock is covered with soil, and grass is planted. In such situations, the angle of repose of the rock fill may be less than 2 horizontal to 1 vertical, but the placement of soil behind and in the crevices between the rocks makes for a stability not possible without the rock.

Topsoil may be removed from the area of the road prism, depending upon the depth of fill. In some states the height of the fill beyond which stripping is not required is 6 feet. In any event, all topsoil to be removed should be stockpiled and used on median areas, slopes requiring flattening beyond the normal highway prism, and other locations. Any excess of topsoil should be stockpiled for use on nearby projects where topsoil may not be available.

Although turf can be grown on subsoil containing at least 10% fines (particles of soil passing through a sieve with 200 openings per square inch), a higher percentage is desirable. Approximately 50% fines is the optimum. In most situations, the percentage of fines should not exceed 80%. It is not considered economically feasible to salvage topsoil with less than 20% fines. The seeming contradiction between the ability to grow turf on soil containing a minimum of 10% fines and the salvage of topsoil with a minimum of 20% fines is understandable after a study of the economics involved.

Numerous studies have shown that the organic component of topsoil is not essential for turf establishment. With proper fertilization, soil completely lacking in organic material, but containing sufficient fines, can be successfully used for turf establishment.

The depth of topsoil required for turf growth depends on the kind of turf, nature of the underlying soil, degree of slope, type of maintenance the turf will receive and, to a lesser extent, the availability and cost of topsoil. It is not practical to spread topsoil less than 2 inches in depth unless the area is relatively level and the underlying material has enough fines in it to aid in the establishment of turf. There is little value in placing topsoil over 6 inches in depth unless very special considerations are involved.

On some slopes a smoothly bladed subgrade and a thick layer of topsoil will contribute to serious slippage after the upper layer becomes saturated with water. Bonding the topsoil and subsoil is very important and may be accomplished by loosening the surface of the subsoil prior to placing the topsoil. In some situations slope exposure will contribute to slippage of the upper layer because of freeze-thaw cycles in late winter or early spring. This is particularly noticeable where the slope exposure is to the south and the soil is heavy.

C. Environmental and Management Considerations.

The type of turf desired is an important factor. Environmental considerations should take into account whether or not an area is to be mowed and, if so, how often. In many sections of the country nonmowed areas will be invaded by woody plants and this will start a return to the natural vegetation. To the extent consistent with safety and appearance, woody plants, particularly low shrubs, should be encouraged to invade roadside slope areas. Such regeneration can be encouraged by not mowing existing desirable woody species found near adjacent fence lines.

In areas where mowing is not contemplated, plants other than grasses may be desirable substitutes or additions to the initial seed mixture. Plants such as crown vetch and birdsfoot trefoil are excellent in the regions and soils where they will thrive.

It is essential that the vegetation maintenance plan for an area be determined in advance of actual establishment so that the turf produced will lend itself to the type of management considered proper. Major management considerations for the different areas are discussed below.

1. Rural

There are many kinds of rural highways. They range from Interstate highways on completely new locations with little or no adjacent development to older roads with a relatively large number of dwellings adjacent to the right-of-way. Hence no hard and fast rules can be made to cover the wide variation of conditions prevailing along various classes of rural highways. Some may pass through long stretches of heavily wooded sections where management will differ from that in open farm land. In some locations, particularly in areas principally devoted to agriculture, it is required that all roadside areas between right-of-way lines be mowed to prevent the growth of noxious weeds.

On the Interstate system there will be many locations where mowing is neither required nor desirable. These will include high, steep cuts and fills which might be impossible to mow and where the objective should be to encourage the establishment of the natural woody growth. In some areas where a wide median area was stripped of all vegetation and grass established, it may be desirable to leave major portions of the area unmowed in order to achieve a more natural environment, encourage the regeneration of woody species, and decrease mowing costs (Fig. 1).

Figure 1. Economical, functional, and aesthetic benefits are derived by not mowing slopes and other roadside areas not immediately adjacent to the traffic lanes in rural areas. Here sumac and other desirable shrubby species interspersed with wild flowers provide a permanent erosion-proof ground cover of volunteer native plants.

A maintenance fertilizer program, following the initial contract application, may be required on rural highways where topsoil has not been used.

2. Suburban.

Suburban highways, which often become urban, generally require a higher degree of maintenance than is called for on rural highways. Higher design criteria may include flatter grades, the use of topsoil to produce a high quality turf, the careful selection of a seed mixture, and a maintenance fertilizer program. Generally, the turf will be mowed to a height of 3 to 4 inches several times a year and herbicides used to eliminate weed growth and produce a more attractive appearance.

Areas of turf along suburban routes should be mowed and not allowed to return to native woody material, except in those locations where the roadsides include existing woodland, stream beds, edges of marshes, or other natural sites.

3. Urban.

Roadside turf in urban areas is often the only grass that the motorist or the urban pedestrian sees in the course of a day, and designs for roadside areas should be made with this in mind. In urban areas, requirements for topsoil, seed, and fertilizer should be carefully studied. (Refer to Seeding Charts, Tables 1 to 6, Areas of Frequent Mowing)

Table 1. Chart for highway seeding in Northeast Region, including Maine, New Hampshire, Vermont, Massachusetts, Rhode Island, Connecticut, New York, New Jersey, Pennsylvania, Delaware, Maryland, and West Virginia.

		Seeding rate - pounds per acre (mixture)						
		Slopes		Medians & areas adjacent to shoulder*	Interior areas of interchanges			
Grasses or legumes	Best seeding time	Mowed	Un-mowed		Mowed	Un-mowed	Non-mow areas†	Special purpose areas
Red fescue	Apr - Jun	30-40					30-60	
Tall fescue	and	25-30				40-50		
Ryegrass, annual	Aug - Oct	8				8	8	45‡
Birdsfoot trefoil		0-10					0-15	
Ryegrass, perennial	Apr - Jun		45					
or Red fescue	and		35-40			35-40	45	
and Crown vetch	Aug - Oct		25-35			25-30		
Ky. bluegrass	Apr - Jun			20-25	20-25§	or		20¶
Red fescue	and			45-50	45-50	65-70		35-45¶
Redtop	Aug - Oct			4	4	4		8-16¶
or								
Ryegrass, annual				8	8	8		
Reed canarygrass	May - June							50//
Redtop	Aug - Oct							16-20//

* Areas of frequent mowing. † Areas planned for natural regeneration. ‡ Temporary. § Little or no Ky. bluegrass in sandy areas. ¶ Drainageways. // Wet areas.

4. Safety Rest Areas.

A growing number of roadside safety parking areas makes it mandatory that thought be given to the design of turf areas at such locations. The turf here should be grown on topsoil and should be of such a character that it will withstand a moderately large amount of pedestrian traffic and wear, particularly at picnic sites. Where picnic tables are provided, a pad of cement or bituminous asphalt should be placed at the table location rather than to attempt to maintain grass under and immediately around the table. Often the picnic areas are located under mature trees and heavy shade may reduce turf density.

D. Conservation.

The establishment of turf on highway roadsides is necessary for the important purposes of protection of the roadside slopes and for visual appearance.

In some woodland areas, especially on new locations along the Interstate highways, turf provides a means of preventing soil erosion until woody species become reestablished. There is some evidence that grassed areas tend to suppress certain woody plants but after initial invasion by blackberry, sumac, trembling aspen, and fire cherry the

Table 2. Chart for highway seeding in Southeast Region, including Virginia, North Carolina, South Carolina, Georgia, Florida, Alabama, Mississippi, Louisiana, Arkansas, and Tennessee.

		Seeding rate - pounds per acre (mixtures)				
Grasses or legumes	Best seeding time	Slopes	Medians & areas adjacent to shoulders*	Interior areas of interchanges	Non-mow areas†	Special purpose areas
Va., Tenn, Western N. C., Northwestern S. C., Northeastern Ga., Northern Ark.						
Ky. bluegrass	Mar - May		40	40		
White clover	Aug - Oct		3	3		
or						
Ky. bluegrass		30	20	20		
Redtop	Aug - Oct	5	5	5		5‡
White clover		2	2	2		
or						
Ky. bluegrass	Aug - Oct		40	40		40
Red fescue			20	40		40
or						
Tall fescue		40	40	40	40	40
With one of the following:						
White clover	Aug - Oct	2	2	2		2
Annual lespedeza		20	20	20	20	20
Sericea lespedeza		30			30	
Crown vetch		5			5	
Southeastern Va., Eastern N. C., Southeastern S. C., Miss., Ala., Ga., Northern La.						
Bahiagrass	Feb - June	25	25	25	25	
Annual lespedeza		20	20	20	20	
or						
Bahiagrass	Feb - June			25	25	25
Sericea lespedeza				20	20	
Bermudagrass	Feb - June	15	15	15	15	15
With one of the following:						
Crimson clover	Aug - Nov	25	25	25	25	25
Annual lespedeza		20	20	20	20	
Sericea lespedeza				30	30	
or						
Weeping lovegrass	Mar - Aug	5		5	5	
With one of the following:						
Annual lespedeza		20				
Sericea lespedeza		30		30	30	
Crown vetch		5		5	5	
Southern Louisiana, Mississippi, Alabama, Florida						
Bahiagrass		25		25	25	
Sericea lespedeza	Feb - June	20		20	20	
Centipedegrass			10-15			
Annual ryegrass	Aug - Sept	5-25	5-25	5-25	5-25	5-25§
Browntop millet	Apr - Sept	30	30	30	30	
Sudangrass		40	40	40	40	

* Areas of frequent mowing. † Areas planned for natural regeneration. ‡ Drainageways. § Temporary.

more tolerant and longer-lived species such as the oaks and maples move in.

A major benefit to conservation is the natural appearance gained by the establishment of turf which contributes to the harmony of the highway with its environment.

IV. Establishment Practices

A. Properties of Roadside Soils

In preparing a good seedbed for establishing new plantings of small seeded grasses and legumes the soil should be finely divided and firm to allow rapid movement of water from the soil to the seed. Normal highway construction usually removes friable topsoil and leaves a difficut environment for plants.

1. Physical Properties.

Soil is said to be a mixture of highly weathered minerals together

Table 3. Chart for highway seeding in Central Region, including Kentucky, Ohio, Indiana, Michigan, and Illinois.

		Seeding rate - pounds per acre (mixtures)					
						Special purpose areas	
Grasses or legumes	Best seeding time	Slopes	Medians & areas adjacent to shoulder*	Interior areas of interchange	Non-mow areas†	Urban	Drainage-ways
Tall fescue, Ky. 31		40	40	40	40	40	40
Kentucky bluegrass	Feb - Apr	20	20	20	20	20	20
Perennial ryegrass or red fescue	and Aug - Sept	10	10	10	10	10	10
Clover‡		3	3	3	3	3	3
Kentucky bluegrass			25-30			25-30	
Red fescue	Feb - Apr		18-20			18-20	
Perennial ryegrass or redtop	and Aug - Sept		8-10			8-10	
Clover‡			4- 5			4- 5	
Tall fescue, Ky. 31	Feb - Apr	35-40	35-40	35-40	35-40		35-40
Red fescue	and	10-12	10-12	10-12	10-12		10-12
Redtop or perennial ryegrass	Aug - Sept		8-10	8-10	8-10		8-10
Clover‡		4- 5	4- 5	4- 5	4- 5		4- 5
Tall fescue, Ky. 31		35-40		35-40	35-40		
Bermudagrass	Apr - May	10-15		10-15	10-15		
Red fescue or red top		4- 6		4- 6	4- 6		
Clover‡		3- 4		4- 4	3- 4		
Tall fescue, Ky. 31		40-45			40-45		
Kentucky bluegrass	Feb - Apr	18-20			18-20		
Crown vetch		10-12			10-12		
Crown vetch	Feb - Apr	18-20			18-20		
Perennial ryegrass		6- 8			6- 8		

* Areas of frequent mowing. † Areas planned for natural regeneration. ‡ White Dutch, Ladino, or Alsike clover.

with an organic fraction capable of supporting plant growth. However, roadsides rarely present an opportunity to seed on good agricultural soils, but rather a seedbed must be prepared from subsoil or geologic materials which are extremely low in plant food, void of organic matter, and possess a structure which is not conducive to the preparation of a fine seedbed. Soil material along roadsides will range in texture and physical composition from very rocky in the mountainous sections to very dense marine clay in swampy areas. A seedbed must be prepared for all situations whether wet or dry, sand or clay.

Because the subsoil is exposed in construction operations, the physical nature of the roadside seedbed is often more difficult to amend than its chemical properties. This is especially true where highly compacted or dense clays and raw parent material are a part of the roadside.

a. Topsoil.

If a good seedbed can be prepared from soils in a given region it can usually best be prepared from the topsoil. "Topsoil" designates the highly weathered surface horizon of a soil. It is usually the most friable and fertile layer of a soil horizon and contains larger amounts of organic matter than the sublayers. Except where highways are built in very level terrain such as the Great Plains, most of this desirable topsoil is removed during grading operations. Ideally it should be stockpiled and spread about 4 to 6 inches deep over selected subsoil areas exposed in the construction process. This practice, though ideal from an agronomic standpoint for level median and other areas where a fine quality of turf is required, is not practical for use on extensive slope areas,

Table 4. Chart for highway seeding in North Central Region, including Iowa, Kansas, Minnesota, Missouri, Nebraska, North Dakota, South Dakota, and Wisconsin.

		Seeding rate - pounds per acre (mixture)				
Grasses or legumes	Best seeding time	Slopes	Medians & areas adjacent to shoulders*	Interior areas of interchanges	Non-mow areas‡	Special purpose areas
Northern Plains areas - Low precipitation (N.D., S.D., Western Nebr., Northwestern Minn.)						
Oats§	Mar - Jun	16		16	16	9-73(Tempo-
Rye¶	and	24		24	24	9-73 rary)
Buffalograss	Aug - Oct	2	5-25	2	2	
Intermediate wheatgrass		3-17		3-17	3-17	
Slender wheatgrass		1- 4	1	1- 4	1- 4	
Crested wheatgrass		3-16	3	3-16	3-16	
Alfalfa//		3- 6	2- 7	3- 6	3- 6	
Smooth brome		4-16**		4-16	4-16	15 Drains
or						
Switchgrass		2- 4		2	2	
Indiangrass	Mar - Jun	3		3	3	4
Little bluestem	or	1- 3		1- 3	1- 3	
Big bluestem	Aug - Oct	1		1	1	4
Intermdeiate wheatgrass		3-17		3-17	3-17	
Crested wheatgrass		3-16		3-16	3-16	15
Sideoats grama		2- 4		2- 4	2- 4	15
Hairy vetch//		3		3	3	3
Perennial ryegrass			3			
Kentucky bluegrass			2- 6			
Blue grama			2			
Buffalograss			5-25			
Sudangrass						11-13(Temp.)
Central Plains areas - Low precipitation (Western Kansas, Nebraska)						
Annual ryegrass		6	6			
Tall fescue		15	15			
Kentucky bluegrass		6	2- 6			
Western wheatgrass	Mar - June	3- 4				
Switchgrass	and			2- 4	2- 4	
Smooth brome	Aug - Oct		6	6	6	
Alfalfa		3- 6	2- 7	4-13	4-13	
White clover				3-15	3-15	
Blue grama			2	3	3	
Sand lovegrass				2- 5	2- 5	
Sand dropseed				2- 4	2- 4	
Buffalograss				18	18	
Cool humid lake states - Eastern Minn., Wis., Iowa, Missouri						
Crown vetch		5		3	3	
Tall fescue		10		10	10	10
Smooth brome	Mar - Jun	6		6	6	6
Birdsfoot trefoil	and	4		4	4	
Switchgrass	Aug - Oct	3		3	3	3
Alfalfa		5		5	5	
Perennial ryegrass		4		4	4	4
Reed canarygrass						10-30 Wet areas
		Rural	Urban			
Tall fescue		25				
Kentucky bluegrass		8	40			
Birdsfoot trefoil	Mar - Jun	3				
White clover	and	3				
Perennial ryegrass	Aug - Oct	8	8			
Red fescue			18			
Redtop			8			

* Areas of frequent mowing. ‡ Areas planned for natural regeneration. § Spring. ¶ Fall. // Not to be used in areas where herbicides applied. ** High rate with mulch.

particularly in rugged topography. (Refer to Seeding Charts for species appropriate for various raodside areas.)

b. Subsoil.

Most soils have a higher percentage of clay in the subsoil (B-horizon) than is found in the topsoil (A-horizon). This is especially true of soils in humid sections.

Subsoils high in clay content allow very slow percolation of water. Aeration is slight or lacking. Root penetration is limited. For these

Table 5. Chart for highway seeding in Northwest Region, including Washington, Oregon, Idaho, Montana, Wyoming, Alaska, and Northern California.

		Seeding rate - pounds per acre (mixtures)				
Grasses or Legumes	Best seeding time	Slopes	Medians & areas adjacent to shoulder*	Interior areas of interchanges	Non-mow areas†	Special purpose areas
Western Oregon and western Washington						
Red fescue	Mar - Apr	10-25	10-25	10-25	10-25	30-40
Chewings fescue		8-20	8-20	8-20	8-20	20-30
Perennial ryegrass	and	3-12	2-12	3-12	3-12	15-20
White Dutch clover		3- 6	3- 6	3- 6	3- 6	4- 5
Highland bentgrass	Sept - Oct	3	3	3	3	4- 5
Ky. bluegrass, Newport		5	5	5	5	5
Eastern Oregon and eastern Washington						
Hard fescue	Mar - Apr	10-20	10-20	10-20	10-20	20-30
Crested wheatgrass		10-30	10-30	10-30	10-30	30-40
Big bluegrass, Sherman		10	10	10	10	20-30
Perennial ryegrass	October	5	5	5	5	5-10
Irrigated Lawn areas						
Ky. bluegrass, Merion	Mar - Apr			50-80		
Chewings fescue	and			80		
Red fescue	October			80		
Under 12" precipitation						
Crested wheatgrass	Spring	5-10	5-10	5-10	5-10	5-10
12" to 20"+ precipitation						
Pubescent, crested or streambank wheatgrass	Spring	10-20	10-20	10-20	10-20	10-20
Hard fescue	and	20	20	20	20	20
Winter clover	Fall	4	4	4	4	4
Alaska						
Crown vetch	Jun - Jul	25			25	25
Red fescue		40			40	40
Smooth brome		95			95	
Chewings fescue		25			25	
Ky. bluegrass		40	40			
Red fescue		60	60			
Smooth brome, Manchar		15			15	
Oats		15			15	
Northern California						
Annual ryegrass	Late summer	100-200				
Barley		100				

* Areas of frequent mowing. † Areas planned for natural regeneration.

reasons heavy clay soils are droughty and are very susceptible to erosion.

In general, roadside slopes composed of clay subsoils are plastic when wet, very firm when moist, and hard when dry. Subsoil has not been exposed to surface weathering and the soil-building action of plant roots; therefore, it usually "breaks up" into large clods rather than fine particles when tilled.

2. *Chemical Properties*

Subsoil materials used as a seedbed for most roadside plants are inherently low in plant nutrients. The chemical composition of these soil materials is strongly related to the geologic parent material. The fertility and pH of the subsoils will be similar to the parent material from which it was derived.

a. pH.

In the humid sections of the eastern U. S. the roadside seedbed is

Table 6. Chart for highway seeding in Southwest Region, including Arizona, Southern California, Colorado, Nevada, New Mexico, Oklahoma, Texas, and Utah.

Grasses or legumes	Best seeding time	Seeding rate - pounds per acre (mixtures)				
		Slopes	Medians & areas adj. to shoulder*	Interior areas of interchanges	Non-mow areas†	Special purpose areas
Arizona						
6 - 10" precipitation						
Lehman lovegrass	June	2	2	2		
10 - 16" precipitation						
Lehman lovegrass	June	2	2	2		
Boer lovegrass	June	2	2	2		
Blue grama	June	3	3	3		
10 - 20" precipitation‡						
Western wheatgrass	June	8	8	8		
Crested wheatgrass	or	5	5	5		
Pubescent wheatgrass, Luna	October	4	4	4		
Alkali sacaton		5	5	5		
Sand dropseed	June	1	1	1		
Spike dropseed	June	2	2	2		
Blue grama	June	2	2	2		
Indian ricegrass	October	4	4	4		
Smooth brome	Jun or Oct	5	5	5		
California						
Annual ryegrass alone or with barley	Late summer or early fall	200				
Colorado						
Under 15" precipitation‡						
Blue grama	Late fall	1	1	1	1	1
Sideoats grama	or early	3	3	3	3	3
Western wheatgrass	spring	5	5	5	5	5
Buffalograss (treated)		6	6	6	6	6
Yellow sweetclover		3	3	3	3	3
Sand lovegrass		1	1	1	1	1
Madison vetch		4	4	4	4	4
Crested wheatgrass		3 - ½	3 - ½	3 - ½	3 - ½	3 - ½
15" - 30" precipitation‡						
Blue grama		1	1	1	1	1
Sideoats grama	Late fall	3	3	3	3	3
Little bluestem	or early	2	2	2	2	2
Big bluestem	spring	3	3	3	3	3
Sand dropseed		½	½	½	½	½
Madison vetch		4	4	4	4	4
Western wheatgrass		5	5	5	5	5
Smooth brome		6	6	6	6	6
Orchardgrass		2	2	2	2	2
Intermediate wheatgrass		5	5	5	5	5
Pubescent wheatgrass		5	5	5	5	5
Hard fescue		2	2	2	2	2
Slender wheatgrass		4	4	4	4	4
Meadow foxtail		2	2	2	2	2
Over 30" precipitation‡						
Intermediate wheatgrass		5	5	5	5	5
Orchardgrass	Early	2	2	2	2	2
Smooth brome	summer	6	6	6	6	6
Mountain brome	and	4	4	4	4	4
Pubescent wheatgrass	early	5	5	5	5	5
Kentucky bluegrass	fall	1 - ½	1 - ½	1 - ½	1 - ½	1 - ½
Timothy		2	2	2	2	2
Nevada						
Irrigated lawn areas						
Kentucky bluegrass	Late spring	3	3	3	3	3
Red fescue, Rainier		1	1	1	1	1
Chewings fescue		1	1	1	1	1
White Dutch clover		½	½	½	½	½
Oklahoma						
Coarse-textured soils, 15 - 30" precipitation‡						
Weeping lovegrass		6½	6½	6½	6½	
Sand lovegrass	Feb 20 -	½ - 1		1	½ - 1	
Sand bluestem	May 20 in	1½ - 2		2	1½ - 2	
Switchgrass	west portion	1½			1½	
Sideoats grama	Apr 1 - May 31	2 - 2½	3 - 4	2½ - 3½	2 - 2½	5
Blue grama	in east por-	1 - 2½	2 - 5	1½ - 2	1 - 1½	3
Bermudagrass, common	tion	3	3	3	3	3

(continued)

Grasses or legumes	Best seeding time	Seeding rate - pounds per acre (mixtures)				
		Slopes	Medians & areas adj. to shoulder*	Interior areas of interchanges	Non-mow areas†	Special purpose areas
Oklahoma (cont)						
Fine-textured soils						
Weeping lovegrass	Feb 20 -	6½	6½	6½	6½	
Sideoats grama	May 20 in	2½ - 3½	2½ - 3½	2½ - 3½	2½ - 3½	3½
Blue grama	west portion;	1½ - 2	1½ - 2	1½ - 2	1½ - 3½	2 - 3½
Buffalograss	Apr 1 - May 31	2½ - 4	3 - 4	3 - 4	3 - 4	4
Bermudagrass, common	in east portion	3	3	3	3	3
Miscellaneous soils;‡						
Weeping lovegrass	Feb 20 - May	6½	6½	6½	6½	
Yellow bluestem	20 in west;	2 - 2½	2½ - 3½	2½ - 3½	2 - 2½	3½ - 5
Blue grama	Apr 1 - May 31	1 - 1½	1½ - 2	1½ - 2	1 - 1½	2 - 3
Bermudagrass, common	in east portion	3 - 6	3 - 6	3 - 6	3 - 6	6 - 12
Over 30" precipitation‡						
Weeping lovegrass	Apr 1 - May 31	6½	6½	6½	6½	
Switchgrass	in west portion;	1 - 2	1½ - 3		2½ - 3	
Little bluestem		1 - 2	1½ - 3	1 - 3	1 - 2	2 - 3
Sideoats grama	Apr 7 - June 10	2 - 2½	2½ - 3½	2½ - 3½	2 - 2½	3½
Bermudagrass, common	east portion	3 - 6	3 - 12	3 - 12	3 - 6	3 - 12
Buffalograss						4
Yellow bluestem		½			½	
Tall fescue						16
Smooth brome						9
Texas						
15 - 25" precipitation						
Northwestern Texas						
Sandy soils:						
Sideoats grama	Feb 1 -	½	½	½		½
Green sprangletop	Jun 1	2	2	2		2
Switchgrass		2½	2½	2½		2½
Plainsbristlegrass		4	4	4		4
Bermudagrass			7			
Weeping lovegrass					1½	
Heavier soils:						
Sideoats grama	Feb 1 -	½	½	½		½
Green sprangletop	June 1	2	2	2		2
Western wheatgrass		3½	3½	3½		3½
Blue grama		½	½	½		½
Southwestern Texas						
Buffalograss	Feb 1 -	1	1	1		1
Rhodesgrass	June 1	1½	1½	1½		1½
Yellow beardgrass		2	2	2		2
Sideoats grama		½	½	½		½
Over 30" precipitation						
Bermudagrass (hulled)	Feb 1 -	7	7	7		7
Green spangletop	May 15	2	2	2		2
Weeping lovegrass (Deep sands)		1½			1½	
Bermudagrass (unhulled)	Sep 1 -	7	7	7		7
Annual ryegrass	Dec 15	12	12	12		12
Weeping lovegrass (Deep sands)		1½			1½	
Irrigated lawn area						
Bermudagrass	Feb 1 - June 1§	7	7	7		
St. Augustinegrass¶	Mar - June	Sodding	Sodding	Sodding		
Utah						
Under 15" precipitation						
Clay and loam soils:						
Crested wheatgrass	Sep - Feb	15	7 - ½	7 - ½	7 - ½	43
Streambank wheatgrass		15	7 - ½	7 - ½	7 - ½	43
Sandy soils:						
Crested wheatgrass	Sep - Feb	14	7	7	7	
Streambank wheatgrass		10	5	5	5	
Sand dropseed		6	3	3	3	
15" - 30" precipitation						
Crested wheatgrass	Sep - Feb	10	5	5	5	
Streambank wheatgrass		10	5	5	5	
Smooth brome		10	5	5	5	

* Areas of frequent mowing. † Areas planned for natural regeneration. ‡ Mixtures vary, use components given below to total 15-20 lb pure live seed/acre. § Depending on latitude. ¶ Spot sodding, 8 to 10" centers, in southern 1/2 and eastern 2/3 of state.

usually acid in reaction. Whereas in the western U. S. the alkaline parent material and low rainfall combine to produce subsoils in which the pH ranges from 7 to 9. Sometimes strong alkali deposits exposed in construction must be buffered with gypsum, organic matter, or topsoil before seedings can be established.

In the southeastern states extremely acid backslopes have been exposed in road construction through "lignite" soils. These soils require as much as 20 tons of lime per acre to neutralize acids in the surface layer (Ward et al., 1963).

b. Fertility.

Most soils along roadsides in the humid section of the U. S. need additions of plant food to support a ground cover. Nitrogen is universally lacking in amounts adequate to sustain healthy grass sods. This is related to the very low organic matter content of exposed subsoil along roadsides. With few exceptions, U. S. soils are low in phosphorus. Many subsoil areas contain less than 10 pounds of available phosphorus per acre. The same is often true for potassium, although soils, in general, are more abundantly supplied with potassium than nitrogen or phosphorus.

3. Organic Matter.

Organic matter in soils is influenced by climate, topography, kind of vegetation, nature of the parent material, and time.

More plant growth, hence more organic matter, is produced in humid areas than in dry climates, but it is also decomposed more rapidly in warm and humid climates. In the U. S. the percentage of organic matter in the soil decreases from north to south because rate of decomposition overrides production. Organic matter is important to the rooting zone of roadside turf because it supplies nitrogen (soil organic matter is about 5% N), helps develop a more stable soil structure, and holds water and nutrients.

Unfortunately, most soils are inadequately supplied with organic matter. The average subsoil contains less than 1% organic matter, a fact which makes for poor stability of structure. High intensity rains tend to "puddle" soils low in organic matter. This causes rapid surface sealing during rains, so that a high percentage of the rainfall is lost as runoff.

Amending soils with organic matter is not practical on roadsides except where high intensity management is to be practiced after establishment. Small areas, like lawns around rest stops or roadside parks, are situations which might justify the use of organic soil amendments such as peat or sawdust.

B. Seeding and Fertilization.

1. Seedbed Preparation.

Regardless of species, seeding method, fertilizer, and mulching practice, a well prepared seedbed is advantageous for the establishment of roadside seedings.

Ideally, the soil should be tilled 6 to 8 inches deep with the top 4 inches pulverized into small aggregates. However, due to soil texture and structure and topography, the seedbed rarely can be broken below 4 to 6 inches, thus leaving the surface cloddy. On flattened slopes and median areas the best method of seedbed preparation involves the use of a tractor-mounted disk-harrow. If this leaves the seedbed cloddy, a tractor-mounted rotary tiller or cultipacker should be used to pulverize clods into smaller aggregates. Where a hard soil condition exists it may be necessary to chisel plow the soil before disking, following which the surface may need further smoothing and conditioning. A spike tooth harrow worked parallel with the roadway is an excellent tool for this purpose since it not only helps pulverize and firm the seedbed but also leaves horizontal grooves. These grooves act as miniature checks for seed and rain water, thus creating a more favorable environment for germination.

A word of caution should be added here about safety in seedbed preparation on steep slopes. To avoid accidents, only tractors with a low center of gravity should be used on such areas. Where regular farm tractors are used, dual wheels and the widest wheel spacing possible should be used. Slopes too steep for a tractor to operate safely must be worked with specialized equipment. Two approaches are possible: *(1)* till the seedbed with an attachment on a crane from the roadbed, or *(2)* till the seedbed with equipment which hangs from a tractor at the top of the slope. Where adequate space for operating a tractor is available at the top of slopes, a heavy spike-toothed chain (clodbuster) is an excellent tool for soil preparation. Chains made for this purpose have a ball or swiveled weight at the end which rolls along the base of the slope and as the tractor moves the chain turns rapidly, the spikes digging into the seedbed. Several passes may be needed to pulverize the seedbed to the desired texture (Fig. 2).

Figure 2. The "clodbuster" is an effective tool to prepare a seedbed on slope areas which are too hazardous for conventional equipment.

2. Fertilization.

To support an erosion-resistant sod most roadside soils must be fertilized at high rates. The initial application of phosphorous and potassium should be sufficient to meet the needs of plants for 1 to 2 years (Blaser and Ward, 1959). Sufficient nitrogen should be applied to supply the new turf for 6 to 12 months. Adequate lime should be applied to adjust the pH to 6.0 to 6.5.

Within a given geographic region the initial fertilizer treatment given a new roadside planting would be similar. However, routine soil analyses for pH and phosphorous and potash should be made. These can be made on the soil obtained from test borings made for the grade and drain phase of the highway project. Abnormal soil situations which require special amendments or a change in the average rate of fertilizer and lime should be noted.

Regardless of the amount and kind of fertilizer and lime applied, it is desirable to incorporate it to a depth of 4 to 6 inches during seedbed preparation. Fertilizer may, however, be applied on the surface if steep terrain makes it hazardous to operate equipment safely.

The amount of fertilizer applied in establishing a sod on roadsides is usually greater than amounts used in seeding farm pastures but not as great as the amounts used in establishing fine turf. Except in the western U. S. where soils are well supplied with potassium, a complete fertilizer with a 1-2-1 ratio of N, P_2O_5, and K_2O should be incorporated into the seedbed. The rate varies from region to region, but in the humid east about 1,000 pounds per acre of a 10-20-10, or a similar fertilizer, is used. Higher rates may be applied on very infertile soils. Somewhat lower rates are used in the drier western states where a 1-2-0 ratio of N, P_2O_5, and K_2O is normally used.

3. Seeding

Conventional farm equipment such as grain drills and cultipacker seeders may be used for roadside seeding where the terrain is reasonably level and the soil is not too rocky. However, on roadsides there are slopes which are too steep for conventional equipment. On these areas seedings are made by several methods: *(1)* manually with cyclone seeders, *(2)* with tractor or truck-mounted centrifugal seeders or *(3)* most often a "hydroseeder" with which the seed and fertilizer are sprayed onto the seedbed (Fig. 3).

The development of a sod in a short time is an essential consideration in compounding mixtures for roadside seedings. The seeding rate and species used on roadsides for the various regions of the U. S. are given in the accompanying tables. In general, seeding rates on roadsides are several times higher than those used for planting pastures. For example, tall fescue is seeded at 10 to 15 pounds per acre in pasture but on roadsides it is planted at 40 to 60 pounds per acre. The need for the higher seeding rates are attributable to high seed losses caused by the poor quality seedbed.

It is often necessary in seeding on highly erosive soils or when seeding "out of season" to use a rapidly growing companion species such as ryegrass, millet, or a small grain. Care should be taken to keep the seeding rate of these species low (5 pounds of ryegrass, 15 pounds of millet, or ½ bushel of small grain); otherwise, they shade out desirable permanent grasses.

Figure 3. Slurries of seed, fertilizer, ground limestone, and sometimes cellulose fiber-type mulch, are pumped through a "hydroseeder" to provide basic ingredients for a turf cover on steep and difficult slopes.

4. Equipment.

One reason for many of the past seeding failures on roadsides has been inadequate equipment. In some sections lime and fertilizer are still applied to the seedbed by hand from a bag, or with a shovel from a truck bed. Fortunately, this method is rapidly fading from the scene. In recent years several innovations in equipment for planting, mulching, and fertilizing roadsides have been developed. Chief among these is the "hydroseeder" which permits the planting of slopes from distances up to 200 feet. This equipment consists of a large slurry tank and centrifugal pump powered by a gasoline engine. Along with water, the seed and other desired ingredients (i.e., fertilizer, lime, fungicides, and even certain types of mulch) are placed in the tank under constant agitation. The resulting slurry is then sprayed onto the slope or other areas at a prescribed rate. The size of the slurry tank varies from 250 to 1,500 gallons, the latter containing sufficient seed, water, and fertilizer to cover from 1 to 2 acres. If wood cellulose fiber mulch is added to the slurry, the area covered by a "single fill" is reduced by 50%. Some slurry machines are capable of pumping sprigs with the mulch and fertilizer. They are often used to relime or refertilize steep slopes which are inaccessible to conventional equipment.

In addition to the slurry applicators, specially designed "air guns" for blasting pelleted fertilizers onto slope areas have been developed. These "guns" operate by compressed air, and consist of a suction pipe and controlled orifice nozzle which blasts a fan pattern of pelleted fertilizer up to 80 feet. In rural areas, airplanes are sometimes used to apply fertilizers to roadsides.

C. Mulching.

1. Purposes.

A good mulch is the most important single material, next to properly selected seed, required for the successful development of a highway turf. Indeed, erosion of an unprotected soil surface may create greater maintenance expenses than the initial cost of shaping, seeding, fertilizing and mulching. Many people concerned with roadside development are of the opinion that a good mulch is more important on slopes than a topsoil cover.

The success of hydroseeding in spraying seed on slopes depends on the use of a suitable mulch. This technique, followed by mulching with hay, was developed over 25 years ago, and provides a successful method for establishing turf on highway slopes. The method can be used, with or without topsoil, at about 1/3 the cost of other practices. Today, turf is established on highway slopes in humid regions at a price per unit area that is much lower than that of 30 years sgo.

Mulch is required for temporary stabilization of a disturbed soil surface until a cover of vegetation can be established. An effective mulch serves a many-fold function, i.e., it protects the soil surface against wind and water erosion, holds the seed in place, protects the seed from rapid temperature fluctuations, reduces surface evaporation, protects the seed from direct sunlight, permits the penetration of rainwater into the soil, and helps prevent the formation of a crust on the soil surface.

2. Materials.

Hay and straw have long been the universal mulching materials used on highway areas. Indeed, some states still depend upon the use of these materials over a seeding of cereal rye for the initial establishment of growth on highway slopes, and depend upon the gradual development of native grasses and weeds to stabilize the area. This practice is being supplanted by the judicious use of grass and legume species adapted to local soil and climatic conditions. In the past few years the scarcity of good mulch hay, presence of undesirable weed seed, costly labor and equipment requirements for placing hay mulch, the improved quality requirements for turf, and the magnitude of current highway construction programs have shown the need for other and more suitable mulching materials and faster means of application.

In the past decade materials such as sodium silicate, liquid dispersed polyethylene, various synthetic plastic emulsions, latex formulations, and petroleum resins have been tried as soil binders and mulches with varying degrees of success. Latex formulations are on the market today, but have not proved either as versatile or as efficient as hay. A thin film of these materials on the slope is easily ruptured and does not readily permit the gentle entry of water through the soil surface.

Petroleum, resin-based stabilizer emulsions, although still in the experimental stage, have shown some promise for stabilizing very sandy areas against wind erosion until seedlings emerge.

Materials such as bran, crushed corncobs, bagasse, sugar-beet pulp, cocoa, and peanut hulls have been tried with varying degrees of success, but the importance of these will probably be limited to those areas where these by-products are available locally. In most cases these materials will require a heavy application of asphaltic emulsions to hold them in place. Some states have had success with light applications of wood chips over seeded areas.

A significant development has been the wood fiber mulches manufactured by chemically or mechanically reducing pulpwood to discrete fibers that will readily take up water and which can be mixed, with proper agitation, in water slurries of seed and fertilizer for application to the soil surface as a heavy spray.

Wood fiber mulch applied uniformly at rates of about 1 ton per acre will hold seed in place and provide a fairly effective erosion cover that approaches that afforded by hay. Wood fiber mulch is free of weed seed, more fire retardant than hay or straw, permits the gentle entry of water through the soil, prevents the formation of a surface crust, and requires less equipment and labor for application. However, wood fiber mulch will not usually last as long as properly applied hay or straw mulch, is more expensive, and does not provide the same degree of insulation. The user must evaluate these two materials carefully in making a choice as to which should be used for a particular area.

Fiberglass, as continuous filaments, applied with a compressed air gun has been tried in many areas and probably has a place under certain limited conditions; however, it lacks some of the requirements of a good general purpose mulch. Since it defies decomposition, the long, tough filaments can pose a hazard to mowing operations, and it is difficult to anchor on slopes unless it is tied in place with a heavy application of binder such as an asphaltic emulsion.

Nettings of various types made of paper or jute serve well to hold hay or straw on steep slopes; however, the labor requirements for installation make the use of asphaltic emulsions more economical.

Heavy jute netting has been used with some degree of success as a mulch material; however, since the wide mesh does not effectively reduce surface evaporation or buffer the soil surface against temperature fluctuations, its use is usually limited to ditch lining.

Excelsior matting is perhaps one of the better manufactured mulch materials for slope surfaces. The loose mat of tough, coarse fibers protects the soil surface from evaporation and direct sunlight, and permits the entry of water into the soil. The greatest disadvantage of the material for slope protection is the high labor requirement for installation. The time required for installation and high initial material cost tend to cancel its attractive features.

3. Application and Anchoring.

Hay or straw is efficiently applied to highway slopes with modern mulch blowers. Most of these machines are so constructed that bales of mulch can be fed directly into the machine, which separates the stems and blows them through a nozzle that can be directed vertically and horizontally by the operator, thus permitting placement on almost any portion of a slope surface. The better machines can blow the mulch as much as 200 feet under calm weather conditions, and by adding flexible plastic tubes can blow mulch to even greater distances. Recent models are equipped to inject asphaltic emulsion at the outlet of the nozzle, thus permitting a uniform application which causes the hay or straw to stick together as it falls on the soil surface. Hay or straw mulch is applied at rates of 1 to 2 tons per acre, with the latter rate generally being more satisfactory. Application rates for asphaltic emulsion range from 200 to 800 gallons per acre. The emulsion can be applied as a separate spray after placing the mulch, but the injection method is more desirable (Fig. 4).

Figure 4. Applying hay or straw mulch to slope areas is effectively and economically accomplished with a mulch-blower.

Hay or straw mulch can also be held in place on relatively level, sandy areas by cutting it into the soil surface with a heavy cutaway disk harrow, brush harrows, or a tractor-drawn mulch-packer.

Recently developed petroleum resin-based stabilizer emulsions are designed primarily for the protection of sandy areas from wind erosion. These materials are mixed with water in a tank truck and are applied as a coarse spray under low pressure to the soil surface at rates as low as 1/4 gallon per square yard. Limited use for a short time does not permit a complete evaluation of these materials.

Wood fiber mulches can be applied with a hay mulch blower but application in this manner leaves much to be desired. These materials preferably should be applied as a slurry spray. Approximately 1 ton per acre should be applied uniformly for mulching slopes, 1/2 ton per acre is sufficient for level areas. Slurry mixes containing wood fiber mulch can be delivered to distances in excess of 100 feet, depending upon the efficiency of the hydroseeder and wind conditions. The slurry can also be pumped through several hundred feet of hose to more distant and difficult to reach areas.

D. Sprigging and Sodding.

The development of efficient seeding and mulching techniques during the past 25 years has almost eliminated the need for other methods to propagate grasses and legumes on highway areas. In the East, for example, very little sprigging of grass species is used except on golf courses. Of interest, however, is a recent development in which bermudagrass or bentgrass sprigs are mixed in a slurry with wood fiber mulch and sprayed on the soil surface. The operation requires a hydroseeder equipped with a gear-type pump; fiber is applied at rates near 3,000 pounds per acre.

Most sprigging in the Northeast will be confined to the sprigging of American beachgrass for sand-dune stabilization in those areas where encroaching sand poses a problem to highway safety and maintenance. This operation consists of digging beachgrass culms from an adjacent area and transplanting them by hand or with modified tractor drawn tree or tomato transplanters. Best results have been obtained by planting the culms 18 inches apart in rows 18 inches to 3 feet apart. It would appear that the application of petroleum resin-based stabilizer emulsions over the area immediately after sprigging the beachgrass might promote establishment of new plants by reducing the abrasive action of blowing sand.

The most expensive method of turf establishment is sodding. However, its use may be justified on certain steep, short slopes. Good quality bentgrass and bermudagrass sod should be cut to a thickness of 1/2 to 3/4 inches, Kentucky bluegrass and the fine-leaved fescues should be cut to a thickness of 1 to 1 1/4 inches.

Sod should be laid on a well prepared, friable, but firm soil surface as soon after cutting as possible. The sod should be tamped lightly as it is set to ensure complete contact with the soil surface. Water must be applied regularly to prevent drying of the edges. On steep slopes sod should be secured with wooden pegs to prevent slippage during heavy rains.

E. Special Liners for Drainageways.

Drainageways that carry water most of the year and those with grades in excess of 4% should be permanently paved with bituminous or concrete materials.

Drainageways that carry water for only short periods and those with grades less than 4% can be stabilized with vegetative cover. It is important to select those species of grasses and legumes which will thrive under local drainageways conditions. Lists of such species for a given location can usually be obtained from the local offices of the Agricultural Experimental Station or the Soil Conservation District (See tables).

Since it is difficult to determine when drainageways may be carrying peak water loads, it is essential to protect the seeding or new seedlings until a resistant sod is developed. Several materials for such ditch linings have been developed in recent years.

Hay and straw mulch does not serve well for protecting waterways since it tends to be floated away under high water conditions and can cause damage by plugging catch-basins and blocking drainageways.

The time-tested material for protecting drainageways has been Dutch-type burlap. This burlap has a loose weave, weighs 4 to 6 ounces per square yard, and is made in strips 5 feet wide. Fifty-foot rolls are economical and can be handled with ease. Successful installations require a clean and uniform surface grade completely stripped of all vegetation. The soil should be friable, but firm. The burlap is laid from the extreme downstream end; the centerline of the burlap strip should coincide longitudinally with the centerline of the drainageway bottom. Special staples are used to pin the burlap to the soil by inserting them along the centerline of the ditch bottom and along both edges. Upstream ends of the burlap must overlap the downstream end by at least 12 inches, with staples placed 6 inches apart across the overlap. Soil should be carefully raked over the edges of the burlap on both sides of the drainageway to a depth of at least 2 inches and to a width of at least 1 foot. Prior to placing the burlap the soil surface of the drainageway should be fertilized and seeded.

Jute netting with a weave consisting of 1.6 to 1.1 yarn count has been used extensively for lining drainageways while sod is being established. This material is placed in the same manner as burlap, and has gained acceptance in many states.

Excelsior matting may serve well as a ditch liner and can be installed, including stapling, in a manner similar to that employed in placing burlap. The matting is relatively easy to place and its thickness and loose weave provides an insulating effect which promotes rapid germination and emergence of grass seedlings.

Some states have had success with the continuous filament fiberglass material applied carefully over freshly seeded drainageways. A light application of asphalt emulsion is used to anchor the fiberglass.

Fiberglass mats stapled to drainageways and coated with asphalt emulsions or bituminous materials have been used in many states. The success of establishing turf under these mats is dependent upon the porosity and thickness of the mat and the thickness and type of bituminous coating.

Fiberglass mats coated heavily with bituminous materials are not a durable or economical substitute for ditch paving.

Wood fiber mulch mixed with asphalt emulsion, or wood fiber mulch followed by an application of asphalt emulsion at about 800 gallons per acre, has also been used to provide drainageway protection; however, it appears that the better materials for drainageway protection until the sod develops are burlap, jute netting, and excelsior matting.

V. Management Practices

A. Maintaining Fertility and pH Levels—Soil Amendments.

Quality turf along the roadside is achieved and maintained only so long as an adequate and continuing program of fertilization is in effect. An erosion-resistant cover of grass does not happen because the seed was sown and an indulgent mother nature provided the elements necessary for growth. Steel bridges need repainting, concrete pavements must be patched and resurfaced, and grass, for functional reasons, must be fertilized and given the benefit of other cultural practices to maintain a dense erosion resistant cover.

Because of the harsh environment for growth, good management is even more critical on most highway right-of-ways than on golf courses and home lawns. Proper fertilizer use is very important on these difficult sites. Rule-of-thumb guidelines for roadside fertilization include: *(1)* Use maximum amounts of fertilizer to produce a dense turf quickly; *(2)* Provide nutrients which are adequate for the least fertile soil in the area where turf is to be maintained; *(3)* Expect all soils to be deficient in nitrogen. Following these guidlines on average roadside areas disturbed by construction should help to maintain a thick turf and dense root system that will protect soils from erosion.

Fertilizer must be used in sufficient amounts to supply adequate nutrients for the range of soils and soil materials in the area. Grading operations often create more extensive soil differences than would be expected for normal variation between soil series over a wide area. Subsoils and many topsoils do not contain sufficient nitrogen for normal grass growth. Available quantities of other plant nutrients, especially phosphorus, may be lacking. Thus, it is important that information regarding subsoil properties be utilized with data on topsoils in planning roadside fertilizer and liming programs. A mixed fertilizer containing nitrogen, phosphorus, and potassium applied in accordance with soil test information insures against deficiencies in nutrient supplies or imbalance among the several essential elements.

It is generally recognized that a soil which has been disturbed requires twice as much fertilizer to produce a given plant stand as the same soil prior to the grading operation. Costs for hauling and spreading topsoil are excessive. Annual fertilizer applications can be made over a 20-year period on poor soils at 1/5 to 1/10 the initial cost of topsoil. In addition, there are few topsoils of sufficiently high fertility to maintain a turf cover without added fertilizer.

Poor establishment and inadequate response to maintenance fertilizer result when nitrogen is withheld or restricted. Response to varying amounts of phosphorus and potassium is much less marked. Some nitrogen may be lost through leaching, but phosphorus and potassium contained in plants are returned to the soil for reuse from season to season. Every ton of grass (air dry) contains about 30 pounds of nitrogen, 10 pounds of phosphorus, and 30 pounds of potassium.

Maintenance fertilizer should be applied when the turf shows evidence of poor growth and vigor. Heavy single applications should be avoided. Grasses maintained at higher than minimum fertility levels are costly because of excessive mowing expenses. Roadside turf requires nitrogen refertilization to prevent degeneration. Readily soluble nitrogen sources or mixtures of ureaformaldehyde (1/2 to 1/4) and readily soluble sources (1/2 to 3/4) are being used with good results. For normal grass maintenance 30 to 50 pounds of nitrogen per acre should be adequate per application. Symptoms of trace element deficiency on roadside areas are rare. If adequate fertilization practices are maintained throughout the first 2 years following establishment, and perhaps during the third on certain types of soil, the need for annual applications will decrease.

Well-fertilized grass makes more efficient use of water. A thick turf and dense root system helps slow water movement and keeps it in the rootzone. Grass which is adequately fertilized develops a deep root system which is very important under roadside conditions.

Fertilized turf protects soil from the sun and keeps temperatures lower than the air. Thin turf does not cover the soil and soil temperatures increase to the detriment of grass plants.

It has also been demonstrated that a vigorous turf offers more competition with undesirable weeds. Thus, proper fertilizer use can reduce populations of certain unattractive weeds.

Although soil materials used in construction may vary greatly in relatively short distances, experience has shown that soil tests provide excellent guidelines to follow, particularly in determining the status of pH levels and phosphorus and potassium content of the soil. The importance of adjusting soil pH for the proper utilization of plant nutrients cannot be overemphasized.

Soil pH values may vary from 5.5 to 7.5 under roadside conditions. Values below 4.5 usually have a detrimental effect on the establishment of vegetative cover. Some acid soils are high in aluminum and other metallic ions which retard establishment and thin turf stands. Lime should be used when soil tests and experience with the soils involved indicate it is necessary. As a general rule, apply lime to soils which have pH levels below 6.0. Agricultural ground limestone, at least 50% of which passes a 100-mesh sieve, is recommended.

Successful management of a turf cover is attained on soils with a wide range in percentages of organic matter. High levels of organic matter, although desirable, are not essential and need not be added if in low supply. Turf tends to increase the organic matter content of soils through normal growth processes. Microbiological populations normally associated with organic matter, and usually rich in nitrogen, phosphorus, and other readily available plant nutrients, increase following sod establishment.

B. Weed Control.

The primary objective of any highway erosion control program is to establish a dense and permanent vegetative cover on areas disturbed during construction. When this objective has been achieved, roadsides will be safer for vehicles out of control and soil erosion will be minimal. Weed growth can be a serious deterrent to the establishment of a desirable turf.

There are several reasons why weeds are undesirable. Many annual weeds because of restricted root development and sod formation do not have the same soil-holding ability as the permanent grasses. Furthermore, annuals that develop in late spring and die with the first fall frost offer little protection from erosion during most of the spring, fall and winter seasons. Perennial weeds have deep root systems and are difficult to eliminate. Most of them do not develop a dense, erosion-resistant cover.

While most weeds do not provide effective erosion control, they compete detrimentally with permanent grasses for moisture, nutrients, and light. Weeds produce a fast, lush growth and in the process utilize large quantities of moisture and soil nutrients. Broadleaf weeds shade lower-growing grasses and reduce the amount of carbohydrates that they produce. Lower carbohydrate production reduces growth rate and the vigor of permanent grasses. Good weed control practices can reduce or eliminate competition from weedy plants.

Control practices are dictated by the reproductive and physiological characteristics of the species. Perennial weeds, which reproduce by seed and vegetative means, present an entirely different control problem than those which reproduce only by seed. Each species of plant is physiologically different. This means that chemicals toxic to one species may not eradicate another. To some extent, the type of control is governed by the topography. That is, chemical weed control may be necessary in areas that are inaccessible to mowing.

There are two basic methods of weed control—cultural and chemical. Cultural methods should first be employed, and only when they fail should chemical methods be considered. Use of weed-free seed and mulch is an important step in weed control. Seed should be obtained from an established seed dealer or a certified grower and should be from the latest available crop meeting requirements of the State's Department of Agriculture or other regulatory agency. Purity requirements should be as high as practical. Seed containing high weed seed levels and noxious weeds should be rejected. Mulch, too, should be free of weeds.

Grass species that will develop best and give the greatest competition to weed species should be selected for each area. Because grasses generally have a more pronounced response to fertilizer, a program providing optimum nutrient levels will greatly aid the survival and competitive ability of the seeded grasses. Purity and germination levels, set as high as practical, will aid in assuring a strong, healthy, weed-free turf.

Mowing is the most widely used cultural method for control of both annual and biennial weeds. If the seed heads of the annuals are removed prior to maturity, these plants will not be able to reseed or become reestablished the following year. Biennial weeds may be treated in the same manner, but two seasons of mowing will be required in order to control or reduce plant populations. To a lesser degree, perennial weed populations may be controlled by mowing, thus enabling desirable species of grass to achieve dominance. Seed production can be reduced but vegetative reproduction cannot be controlled by mowing. Food reserves in perennial weeds are at comparatively low levels when flower buds appear. Repeated mowing at this stage of growth will gradually reduce food reserves, weaken regrowth, and reduce competition. Control of this type requires timely mowing and thus it is sometimes impracticable for highway use.

The second method of weed control is the use of selective phytotoxic chemicals. Caution in the application of these chemicals must be emphasized. Chemicals should be selected which have little effect on seeded grasses but are toxic to broadleaf plants. Unfortunately, many desirable species for highway use are legumes and usually these are broadleaf in character. When selecting a herbicide, first consideration should be the selectivity of the chemical. The chemical should affect only weedy plants and not harm desirable species. In general, spot spraying with a selective chemical of low volatility is the most efficient method for the control of perennial weeds along highways.

C. Mowing Requirements—Height, Needs and Equipment.

Highway mowing is an important and useful maintenance operation when correctly performed. It enhances the natural beauty of the roadside and, more important, it improves highway safety by providing definition to roadside areas beyond the travelway. Also, in snowbelt states, it removes the tall grasses which may increase snow accumulation on shoulders and pavements. Mowing may also aid in controlling the invasion of right-of-way areas by undesirable species.

There are several factors which, in general, should influence the time of mowing. Very early spring mowing, although it may be desirable, is not recommended because the taller grasses will shade out the germinating weeds. At this time of the year the areas are usually wet, and mowing equipment may become stuck, cause rutting, and damage large areas of turf with potential erosion problems as a result. Another factor is the packing of the soil by the wheels of equipment, causing damage to the root structure of the grass. Unless the mower blades are very sharp, grass plants may be actually pulled from the soil rather than being cut.

Areas established with the shorter growing grasses may require routine mowing depending on their growth rate. In general, mowing for these areas (medians, adjacent to shoulders, some interchange islands, etc.) should take place when the height is 50% above the desired mowing height.

Areas established in the taller grasses should not require mowing other than for spot weed control. Such weed control mowing should be delayed until the time of year when seed heads of the weeds are present but have not yet reached maturity.

Fall mowing is not recommended. The grass plants should have the opportunity to mature and harden off before winter. Mowing may stimulate lush growth which makes the plants more susceptible to winter kill.

On many portions of the right-of-way, legumes are useful as a long-lived nurse crop, aiding the establishment of the permanent grass cover. Mowing height need not be based on legumes in the area. The lower growing legumes such as white clover and birdsfoot trefoil, are sometimes used as more permanent species with the lower growing grasses in medians, rest areas, etc. Legumes easily withstand the same mowing regime used for grasses. When used for slope protection, legumes such as crown vetch usually should not be mowed more than two times during the establishment period and then should be cut high for control of undesirable species.

Another consideration is the root-shoot balance maintained by the grass plant. Normally the part of the plant above ground balances with the part below ground. A reduction in one may cause a reduction in the other. Close mowing will not only reduce the leaf surface of the plant but force a corresponding reduction in the root system. Thus, the plant's effectiveness in erosion control is reduced, as is its resistance to extended periods of hot, dry weather.

Seed production of grass species is generally eliminated by mowing. Seed production is not essential for those grasses that reproduce by rhizomes or stolons. Bunch grasses, however, must produce seed for perpetuation and to increase the extent of turf areas. On newly seeded roadsides, the production of seed is an important factor in the establishment of a dense, functional turf.

While seed production is hindered by mowing, the vegetative reproduction of some species, such as Kentucky bluegrass, is stimulated by mowing. When the seed head, or top of the plant, is removed the plant's food reserve is used to increase normal vegetative reproduction rather than for seed production. If too much of the leaf area is removed at this stage recovery may be slow.

Mowing needs differ on various parts of the right-of-way. In general, areas that require mowing are the medians, parts of interchange islands, and along the foreslopes to frame and define the roadway. Areas that require more intensive mowing should be established in grass species that will tolerate such cutting. Backslopes, fill areas and, generally, the remaining parts of the right-of-way do not require mowing except where necessary for weed control.

As complex as it may seem, the selection of the right mowing height is not difficult. Grass plants will withstand a great deal of abuse. Even under the worst possible mowing regime, it may take several years to kill out a species of vigorously established turf.

For highway purposes, grasses and legumes may be divided into two general groups—those which will tolerate low mowing (4- to 5-inch minimum mowing height) and those which may only occasionally be mowed at such a height. The following is a listing of some of the more commonly used species showing tolerance to close mowing.

Tolerant	Less Tolerant
Grasses	*Grasses*
Bentgrass	Bluestem, big and little
Bermudagrass	Brome, smooth
Bluegrass, Canada	Canarygrass, reed
Buffalograss	Mixed native grasses
Fescue, red and tall	Orchardgrass
Redtop	Switchgrass
Ryegrass	Wheatgrass, crested
St. Augustinegrass	
	Legumes
Legumes	Crownvetch
Birdsfoot trefoil	Hairy vetch
Clover, white	

Safety should be the prime consideration in selecting highway mowing equipment. Mowers should have a low center of gravity and wide-set wheels with flotation tires to provide optimum safety, reduce turf damage, and prevent rutting. They should be designed so that their operation does not throw debris or foreign objects into the path of vehicles passing by.

Most highway mowing equipment is tractor-drawn or tractor-mounted. Small lawn-type rotary mowers may be used for trimming in rest areas or other special-use locations. Small, self-propelled, sickle-bar type mowers are useful for maintaining comparatively inaccessible and rough areas that are mowed infrequently. The use of scythes for hand control of weeds cannot be justified except in special areas not accessible to field equipment.

The four types of mowers generally used are: reel, sickle-bar, rotary, and flail.

Reel mowers are used extensively in some sections of the country, but are limited to those portions of the right-of-way which are comparatively level and smooth. They are especially designed for use on fine-textured turf. Reel mowers usually have the highest maintenance requirements of all mowing equipment.

The sickle-bar mower has been used for highway mowing longer than other types. It is still especially valuable for use in tall grass or weeds. However, this type of equipment does not produce as uniform or as level a cut as some of the others. Speed is also a limiting factor.

Rotary mowers are the most widely used type of mowing equipment on highway rights-of-way. They produce a fairly uniform, level cut but many throw foreign objects into travel lanes. Because of this hazard there has been a reduction in the widespread use of this type of equipment, particularly in urban areas.

Flail mowers are the most recent type of equipment to be developed. Turf cut with these units has a rougher, more ragged appearance, but not as uneven as that cut with sickle-bar mowers. Objects are not thrown with this type of mower, which is an extremely important safety feature.

Cutting units should be kept sharp, regardless of the type of mower used. Dull cutting knives will tear leaves, cause premature browning of leaf blades, and may increase disease incidence.

A carefully planned roadside mowing and maintenance program is becoming more and more essential as the acreage of turf expands and traffic volume and vehicle speeds are increased. Since many maintenance budgets are inadequate to carry out all required operational functions, careful evaluation of mowing requirements is essential.

Several steps are important in analyzing mowing practices including *(1)* classification of roadside areas, based on existing right-of-way conditions and desired mowing standards; *(2)* determination of performance characteristics of mowers of different widths, types, and sizes; *(3)* establishment of a periodic mowing cycle to attain desired standards; *(4)* rating of mowers for a particular type of right-of-way by field performance tests; *(5)* appraisal of operating costs including depreciation, repair, maintenance, and fuel cost; and *(6)* consideration of factors in the assignment of mowers which would identify the character of the area to be mowed, duration of the mowing cycle, available machine time for each cycle, average production rate for each type in accordance with the classification of the right-of-way, special requirements, and the cost and time involved.

The classification factors that are considered of prime importance are *(1)* size and shape of the roadside areas; *(2)* topographical conditions such as steepness of slopes, relatively flat areas, drainage channels, and surface configuration; *(3)* geological conditions such as bogs and soil types; *(4)* obstructions such as utility poles, culverts, signs, etc.; and *(5)* turf density and height of cut desirable.

With such management techniques in effect, greater operating efficiency and better supervisory control are possible, thus reducing or preventing an increase in the cost of this necessary maintenance operation.

D. Growth Retardants.

In recent years a limited number of growth retardant chemicals have been developed for use on turf areas. As a management tool, these materials make it possible to decrease the exposure of maintenance workers and their equipment to the highway user, thus providing safer travel arteries and reducing mowing costs.

Thus far, maleic hydrazide has been the most effective growth retardant for roadside use. It has not been widely accepted, however, because of critical requirements with respect to time of application. Research is continuing and, hopefully, new materials or improved formulations and application techniques may be developed that will improve the effectiveness of growth retardants. In some areas proper use of presently available control chemicals has reduced the number of mowings by 50% or more, while at the same time improving appearance. Under such circumstances mowing equipment can be more efficiently utilized, maintenance costs reduced, and traffic safety enhanced.

E. Insect and Disease Control.

It is just as important to apply good management practices on roadside turf as on lawns, parks, and golf courses. Various insect pests and diseases have been known to destroy extensive areas of turf with the ultimate threat of complete loss of vegetative cover, the creation of large unsightly areas, and an increase in costly erosion.

Crowded turf plants compete for air and soil space, light, water, and nutrients. Humidity is an important factor in the spread of disease organisms from plant to plant. Spores of fungi are carried from infected areas by wind, water, and mowing. Some of the major diseases found in roadside areas are leaf spots and blights, anthracnose, red thread, copper spot, Ophiobolus patch, spring dead spot, and Fusarium blight. Successful disease control requires sound cultural practices beginning with clean seed and soil. A fungicide should only be used when the cultural and other management practices are not completely effective.

As with diseases, insect pests can be a devastating problem in many areas. Vigilance on the part of knowledgeable, trained personnel is important so that sod webworm, beetle grubs (Japanese and Asiatic), chinch bugs, and the like are kept under control. It is essential that potential invasions be averted by the application of appropriate insecticides in order to avoid future loss of large areas of turf. By the eradication of grubs, the problem of moles may also be overcome, the latter often being the indirect cause of erosion problems and other adverse effects. Caution must be exercised in the choice of insecticides and the quantity applied in order to prevent any harmful effect on desirable wildlife; there must also be an awareness of the possibility of movement of insecticide residue into drainage systems and adjacent streams with the consequent effects on aquatic biota.

Proper turf management can provide favorable conditions for growing healthy roadside grass and aid in reducing the damaging effects of diseases and insects. A vigorously growing turf is also more resistant to traffic damage and weed invasion. It is important to provide good surface and subsurface drainage as well as to sow high-quality, adapted, disease-resistant grasses and seed mixtures. A sound fertilization program, with lime and other soil amendments as required, is essential in any roadside turf management program. It is extremely important not to mow too closely because higher cuts improve root depth and tolerance to drought and high summer temperatures. If the soil becomes compacted, an aerifier should be used so that proper amounts of air, water, and nutrients may reach the root systems of desirable species.

F. Reseeding—Renovation, Aeration.

Roadside turf areas are probably subjected to more physical damage than any other location where turf is used. Accidents, vehicles forced or driven off the paved areas, improper mowing practices, and numerous other incidents cause rutting and breaks in the turf cover. Failures in interception drainage ditches, excessive periods of adverse weather (too wet, too hot, or too dry) and the use of de-icing compounds are some of the principal causes of damage.

It is, therefore, extremely important to repair turf as soon as possible after damage occurs. The placement of topsoil, fertilizer, seed, and mulch should be performed as necessary. In some locations, it will only be necessary to renovate turf in so-called spot areas. In extensively damaged areas, where there is an almost complete loss of turf, restoration will involve methods similar to initial seeding operations. It is imperative that there be constant surveillance so as to detect damaged turf areas promptly, thus hastening repair and the renovation process. This will help to avoid damage which may result from delayed maintenance.

Perhaps one of the most neglected maintenance items of roadside turf is soil aeration. The generally poor soil conditions and severe soil compaction caused by vehicular traffic and mowing equipment are factors that should be given more consideration. Inasmuch as modern, efficient equipment has been developed, aeration can be easily accomplished. The quality as well as the functional value of roadside turf will be enhanced by including this operation in many maintenance programs.

It must be emphasized that proper management practices for roadside turf areas are essential. The knowledge of and need for sound cultural practices must be recognized and implemented in order to achieve highway roadsides that are safe, functional, and aesthetic.

VI. Conclusion

Turf on roadside areas has been portrayed in the preceding portions of this chapter as a basic element in the complete highway. Species, establishment practices, and management techniques have been described and design considerations have been indicated.

Except in arid sections of the U. S., grass is indeed the indispensable plant on the highway roadside. Grass contributes substantially to highway economy by controlling erosion. An effective cover of turf eliminates the deposition of eroded soil in ditches and drainage facilities. Grass covered roadsides afford protection to agricultural lands and streams and water supplies contiguous to the highway.

By preventing erosion grass also makes highways safer. Originally designed surface contours with swaled ditches, smooth shoulders, and flat slopes can be maintained with grass to insure safer operation of motor vehicles when they leave roadway pavements in emergency situations (Fig. 5).

Figure 5. Mowed turf is necessary in some areas to achieve a desirable environmental relationship between highway right-of-way and abutting properties.

Improved appearance is perhaps the most obvious value which grass contributes to the motorists pleasure. It is a basic component in the highway environment and provides an appropriate setting for trees and shrubs. Well maintained grass provides the frame for the highway picture and tends to assure the driver and his passengers that the highway is safe, aesthetic and utilitarian—a "complete highway."

Acknowledgements

The principal author of this chapter was assisted in its preparation by members of the Roadside Development Committee, Highway Research

Board, university personnel engaged in research relating to the establishment and management of vegetation on highway rights-of-way, and professionals in state highway departments. Particular recognition is due W. C. Greene, Landscape Architect, Bureau of Public Roads, for his dedicated assistance. Others who made possible the national scope of this chapter are: John Ryan, New York; Edward Button, Connecticut; Charles Anderson, Maryland; Mark Astrup, Oregon; Roy Rodman, Texas; Harold Dolling, Iowa; Kenneth Arnold, Kentucky; Lawrence Foote, Minnesota; R. E. Holmes, Mississippi; Robert Wakefield, University of Rhode Island; Coleman Ward, University of Mississippi; Wayne McCully, Texas A & M University; Norman Goetze, Oregon State University; D. B. White, University of Minnesota; and Eliot Roberts, University of Florida.

Literature Cited

Bellingham, Francis J. 1964. Hydraulic seeding on motorway, verges and other marginal areas as practiced in England, Twenty-Third Ohio Shortcourse on Roadside Development. pp. 44-48.

Blaser, R. E. and C. Y. Ward. 1959. Seeding highway slopes as influenced by lime, fertilizer, and adaptation of species, Virginia Council of Highway Investigation and Research, Reprint No. 21.

Bredakis, Evangel J. and John M. Zak. 1965. Timing of seeding throughout the growing season. Twenty-Fourth Ohio Shortcourse on Roadside Development. pp. 65-69.

Buckman, Harry O. and Nyle C. Brady. 1960. The nature and properties of soils, Chapter 3, pp. 55-68.

Highway Research Board. 1960. A selected bibliography No. 26, pp. 11-17.

Highway Research Board. 1965. Bibliography on roadside development, pp. 10-14.

Johnson, A. W. 1957. Erosion control along American highways. American Society of Agricultural Engineers, East Lansing, Michigan.

Mannering, J. V. 1966. Infiltration and soil surface, Twenty-Fifth Ohio Shortcourse on Roadside Development, pp. 103-106.

Soil Survey manual, 1952, United States Department of Agriculture Handbook, No. 18, pp. 231-235.

Stamm, R. H. 1966. Fast seeding and mulching, Mid-west Regional Turf Conference Proceedings, pp. 72-74.

Ward, C. Y., S. L. Simpson, W. J. Gill and H. D. Palmertree, 1963. Seeding highway roadside in the southeastern United States as influenced by species adaptation, fertilization, and mulching. Southeastern Association of State Highway Officials Proceedings, 22nd Annual Meeting, pp. 149-155.

26 Ground Cover Plants

John L. Creech
Agricultural Research Service, USDA
Beltsville, Maryland

I. Introduction

Ground covers include a wide range of low-growing plants which can substitute for grass, cover bare ground where grass will not grow, or prevent erosion where rough terrain makes grass maintenance difficult. In addition, ground covers provide a pleasing landscape effect through color, form, and other horticultural qualities for which plants are generally enjoyed. Annuals, herbaceous perennials, and woody plants may serve as ground covers. While we regard broadleaved evergreens as the most desirable, conifers and deciduous plants are entirely suitable.

Ground covers range in size from plants that are as low in habit as grass to shrubby species that attain 3 feet or more in height. Some ground covers function because of their grass-like habit *(Liriope* and *Ophiopogon)* while others depend on the matting of stems and leaves *(Pachysandra)* or interlocking of branches *(Juniperus* and *Cotoneaster)* to cover the ground. Unlike grass, which requires continual mowing, ground covers are expected to maintain themselves to a great extent when once established.

As with grasses, a single ground cover species will not fit all situations even if the over-riding factor of climatic hardiness is excluded. Consequently, long lists of recommended plants have been developed for regional or local purposes. Wyman (1961) describes nearly 250 plants which make acceptable ground covers, yet his list is restricted to the central and northern parts of North America. Many additional ground covers are recommended in bulletins of State Experiment Stations and botanic gardens because of local preference.

In the final analysis, the choice of ground cover species will be governed largely by the availability of plants from reliable nurserymen. Thus, while many plants are recommended for use as ground covers, a relatively limited number of species is in general use. Since the factors that determine a good ground cover are not common in most plants, we may not expect any marked change in the selection of ground covers now available. Horticulturists, however, continue to evaluate newly introduced species in order to expand the range of useful ground covers.

II. Hardiness

Most plant descriptions include a hardiness rating, numerically keyed to a plant hardiness zone map. Such maps are essential guides to predicting the adaptability of plants to broad climatic regions. They are isotherm maps based upon average minimum temperatures derived from long-term weather records. There are two major hardiness zone maps for the U. S., the USDA Plant Hardiness Zone Map (1960) and the Arnold Arboretum Hardiness Map (1967). In addition to these, Canada has its own hardiness map (1967). Since there are interpretive inconsistencies among them, we must be careful to use published zone references with the correct map. Many states have used these major maps to draw local hardiness maps giving temperature information on a more precise basis. The USDA hardiness map divides the country into 10 zones and lists plants that are hardy in each (Fig. 1). These plants, in turn, serve as indicators for additional species adapted climatically to a given region. Weston and Harshbarger (1962), in cooperation with horticulturists throughout the country, used the USDA map to rate many garden plants for hardiness.

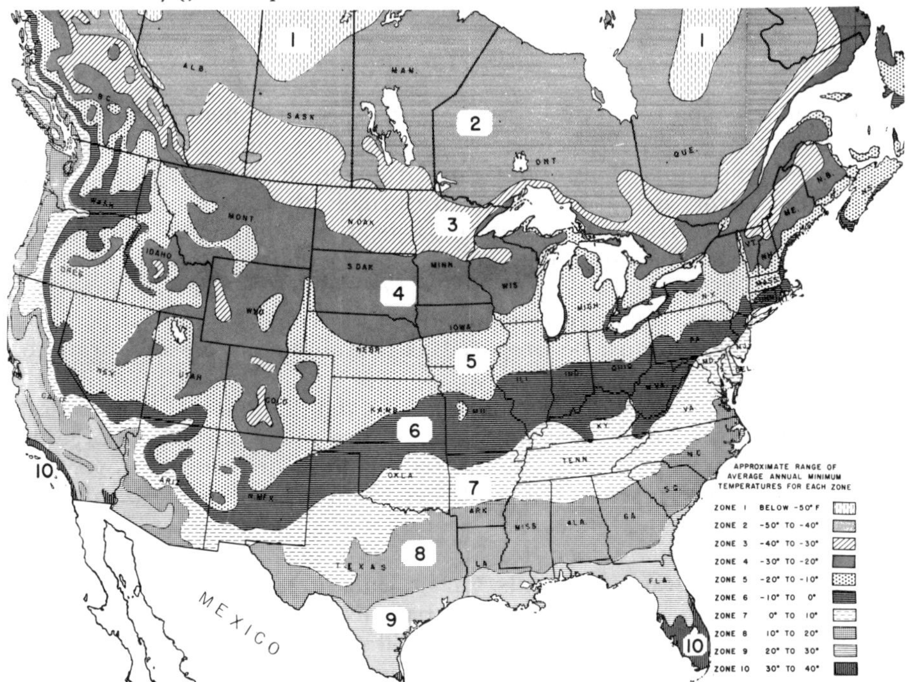

Figure 1. Plant-hardiness zone map. ARS, USDA. Miscell. Pub. 814.

Others factors are as important as minimum temperatures in determining plant adaptation. Soil type, rainfall, summer temperatures, and daylength are significant. Certain additional conditions govern whether a plant can thrive without unusual attention. Light intensity, frost occurrence, snow cover, wind, humidity, length of sustained low or high temperature periods, drainage, and competition from other plants become especially significant when plants are left to "shift for themselves" as are most ground covers. Since these factors are not depicted easily, plant hardiness maps remain the most useful single guide to plant adaptability.

Because of their habit, ground covers may perform better in cold climates than related upright plants. This applies to areas where a snow cover is present or when some other type of protection can be provided, such as covering the planting with pine needles, straw, and branches. In climates where few exotic species are satisfactory ground covers, native plants are often used. Smithberg and Johnson (1965) recommend various native heaths for sandy, acid soils in the severe climate of Minnesota. These include bearberry *(Arctostaphylos uva-ursi)*, blueberry *(Vaccinium angustifolium)*, and wintergreen *(Gaultheria procumbens)*. Perhaps the least use of ground covers occurs in areas with low rainfall and low humidity. For example, they are rarely used in Arizona except where sprinkler irrigation can be used effectively. But, H. F. Tate (personal communication, 1967) says that by controlling this single factor trailing lantana, English ivy, junipers, honeysuckle, dichondra and lippia can be used in small areas.

III. Planting

The selection of ground covers and the planting methods vary from region to region. Therefore, we are making only general cultural recommendations. The underlying principle in preparing a site for ground covers is that conditions are usually the poorest for the best plant growth. Dense shade, dryness, heat, poor drainage, exposure, and other similar conditions are usually involved, singly or in combination in most sites. Furthermore, because of this service function ground covers usually receive a minimum of care once they are established. The site must be prepared as thoroughly as possible prior to planting.

Soil preparation—Work the soil to a good depth, no less than 6 inches, with the objective of increasing the moisture retention. Spread organic matter, such as peat moss, well-rotted manure, or leaf mold over the surface of the area to a depth of several inches and spade it into the soil. Poorly drained soils may require tiling. Johnson et al. (1966) recommend prepared beds for highway plantings. This eliminates competition from grass and weeds. On difficult sites where the entire area cannot be worked, individual holes have to be prepared. These should be dug deep enough to partially back-fill with mixed soil before setting the plants. Use top soil for the rest of the refill.

Slopes can be effectively planted with ground covers if not too steep. A low bank from 2 to 4 feet high can be protected from erosion without any additional preparation beyond that described above. When the slope is very steep, retaining walls have to be constructed. Sloping areas are usually dry and sunny so plants must be selected for tolerance to periodic drought. The practice is to use vigorous or rather large plants, such as junipers or cotoneasters under these circumstances.

Fertilizer—A complete fertilizer is essential at the time the site is prepared. Apply 5-10-5 at the rate of 3 to 6 pounds to 100 square feet, with the heavier rate suggested for areas that have not been fertilized previously.

It is usually inadvisable to alter the soil pH to meet requirements for specific plants. Rather, species adapted to existing pH conditions should be chosen; i.e., ericaceous plants for acid soils, and legumes or species tolerant of alkaline soils for other areas. Extremely acid soils, however, can be improved by the application of from 10 to 25 pounds of dolomitic limestone to 100 square feet.

Time of planting—Although ground covers can be established throughout the growing season, early spring is the appropriate time for most localities. This allows a maximum growing period before winter arrives.

Planting distance—The objective of establishing a ground cover is to close in the site as rapidly as possible. Small ground covering species such as pachysandra *(Pachysandra terminalis)* or bugle-weed *(Ajuga reptans)* may be put as close as 4 to 6 inches apart. Large specimens, such as creeping juniper *(Juniperus horizontalis)* or rock spray cotoneaster *(Cotoneaster horizontalis)* can be planted as much as 4 feet apart. Obviously, closer planting will accomplish the objective more rapidly but requires more plants.

For general guidelines, the Utah Association of Nurserymen estimates that 100 plants will cover an area in relation to planting distance as follows:

Planting distance—inches	Area covered—sq. feet
4	11
6	25
8	44
10	70
12	100
18	225
24	400

IV. Maintenance

A well-established ground cover planting requires (or more frequently receives) relatively minor maintenance. Watering, weeding, mulching, and application of fertilizer in early spring are the main requirements. To avoid burning the foliage, scatter a pelleted form of commercial fertilizer such as 5-10-5 over the planting when the foliage is dry, at the rate of 2 to 3 pounds per 100 square feet.

In cold climates with no permanent snow cover, plantings in bright sun may require protection and conifer branches laid loosely over the beds are useful for this purpose (Fig. 2). These recommendations apply to plantings of limited expanse, such as around dwellings and public areas where well-groomed plants are essential.

Ground covers as a rule require only pruning to remove dead wood and keep the planting in bounds. Some species that are used on level ground can be mowed. For example, the dwarf bamboos, *Sasa pumila* and *Sasa veitchi,* and the lily turfs, *Liriope spicata* and *Ophiopogon japonicum,* can be cut with either a rotary or reel mower right along with adjacent grass areas.

Figure 2. Winter protection is afforded ground covers by covering loosely with pine branches.

Ground covers will show winter injury just as do other plants. Evergreen species present a particular problem when the foliage has been "burned" following an extremely dry winter. It is sometimes possible to shear such plantings or individually prune out damaged branches. Plantings of juniper are sometimes so badly winter damaged that bare soil areas develop. The only solution is to replant with healthy specimens rather than to wait until the old planting fills in the gap.

A. Weed Control

Ground covers are relatively slow to close over bare ground as compared to grass. Consequently, there will be a weed problem, especially during the first year. A mulch of wood chips, straw, or other organic refuse will control most weeds, as well as retain moisture. In small plantings, weeds can be controlled by hand when they break through the mulch. Clean cultivation is not desirable on slopes since it encourages erosion.

B. Propagation

The propagation of most ground covers is simple. The plants are easily divided and this is the most common method of propagation. Woody species are also rooted from cuttings and the legumes are propagated from root pieces or seeded. Annuals and some perennials are seeded either in place or transplanted from seed flats. Most of the larger plants such as junipers, cotoneasters, and roses are set out as nursery plants.

V. Ground Covers for Highway Plantings

We have gained most of our information on ground covers from their use in residential and urban landscaping. Recent programs of highway and suburb beautification have created a demand for ground covers to stabilize banks and to improve the scenic beauty around bridge abutments and open drainage channels.

Because these programs are very recent, they must rely on ground covers already in vogue for home planting purposes. However, several interesting ground covers have evolved from such programs and seem to be equally promising in more formal settings. Crownvetch *(Coronilla varia)*, the milkvetches *(Astragalus)*, birdsfoot trefoil *(Lotus corniculatus)*, and *Lespedeza* species are among the plants selected by the University of Tennessee (1967) for roadside revegetation.

The use of ground covers under highway circumstances is the most demanding. Only a limited number of species will meet the requirements of low cost maintenance and adaptability to an extremely unfavorable environment.

A. Some Recommended Ground Covers

As pointed out initially, the best sources of information for selection of ground covers are the local horticultural institutions and nurserymen. The plants shown in Table 1, arranged by scientific name, have been selected from national and local listings. The descriptions are brief, including scientific name, common name, hardiness range according to the USDA Plant Hardiness Zone Map, plant description, and recommended method of propagation. No attempt has been made to cover all species and in some instances groups of related species are

Table 1. An alphabetical listing of ground covers.

Common name	Scientific name	Common name	Scientific name
Aaronsbeard St. Johnswort	Hypericum calycinum	Heartleaf Bergenia	Bergenia cordifolia
Andora Juniper	Juniperus horizontalis fma.	Iceplant	Mesembryanthemum sp.
	plumosa	Japanese Garden Juniper	Juniperus procumbens
Barrenwort	Epimedium app.	Japanese Holly	Ilex crenata 'Helleri'
Bearberry	Arctostaphylos uva-ursi	Japanese Spurge	Pachysandra terminalis
Bearberry Cotoneaster	Cotoneaster dammeri	Kumazasa Bamboo	Shibataea kumasaca
Bugle-Weed	Ajuga reptans	Memorial Rose	Rose wichuraiana
Capeweed	Lippia nodiflora	Moss Sandwort	Arenaria verna
Chenault Coralberry	Symphoricarpos chenaultii	Periwinkle	Vinca minor
	'Hancock'	Purple Heart	Setcreasea purpurea
Coralberry	Symphoricarpos orbiculatus		(see Zebrina)
Cowberry	Vaccinium vitis-idaea	Rock Spray Cotoneaster	Cotoneaster horizontalis
Cranberry Cotoneaster	Cotoneaster apiculata	Sand Strawberry	Fragaria chiloensis
Creeping	Liriope spicata	Sarcococca	Sarcococca hookeriana
Creeping Thyme	Thymus serpyllum		var. humilis
Crownvetch	Coronilla varia	Sargent Juniper	Juniperus chinensis var.
Daylily	Hemerocallis spp.		sargentii
Dichondra	Dichondra repens	Savin Juniper	Juniperus sabina
Dwarf Hollygrape	Mahonia repens	Sericea	Lespedeza cuneata
Dwarf Lilyturf	Ophiopogon japonicus	Shore Juniper	Juniperus conferta
Dwarf Polygonum	Polygonum reynoutria	South African Daisy	Gazania X splendens
English Ivy	Hedera helix	Small-leaved Cotoneaster	Cotoneaster microphylla
Germander	Teucrium chamaedrys	Strawberry Geranium	Saxifraga sarmentosa
Goldmoss Stonecrop	Sedum acre	Veitch Bamboo	Sasa veitchii
Groundivy	Nepeta hederacea	Wandering Jew	Zebrina pendula
Ground Bamboo	Sasa pumila	Waukegan Juniper	Juniperus horizontalis
Hall's Honeysuckle	Lonicera japonica var.		fma. douglasii
	halliana	Weeping Lantana	Lantana sellowiana
		Wintergreen	Gaultheria procumbens

discussed in a composite fashion. Disease and insect control is not considered here and the reader should consult local authorities since problems are most likely to relate to several kinds of trees and shrubs in a mixed planting. Not all states publish separate bulletins on ground covers. Some include the subject in publications on turf and lawn grasses. The references at the end of this plant list are by no means complete but serve to indicate that ground covers are becoming increasingly important in community, roadside, and home beautification.

Ajuga reptans L.—Zones 5-9
Bugle Weed
A creeping perennial, 4 to 8 inches tall, with practically evergreen foliage, blue or purple flowers in terminal spikes. This ground cover is recommended by most states including some beyond the recommended hardiness Zone 5. It thrives in either sun or shade, is a rapid grower, and tolerates most soil conditions. Bugle can be used alone or in combination with other small plants. Propagate by seed or division.

Arctostaphylos uva-ursi (L.) Sprengel—Zones 2b-9a
Bearberry
A fine-textured, broadleaved evergreen, grows to 12 inches tall with trailing stems, dark lustrous foliage, and bright red fruits in late summer. It is excellent for stoney, sandy, and acid soils, particularly for sandy banks. It is also excellent for dune control on the seashore. Because of its hardiness, bearberry is recommended along the northern tier of states where soils are acid. Unfortunately, it is difficult to transplant and best obtained as sods or pot-grown plants.

Arenaria verna L.—Zones 2-9
Moss Sandwort
A low growing moss-like perennial particularly suited to planting in small areas, and between flagstones. It has a broad range of adaptation but requires good soil, moist partial shade, and some winter protection in cold, exposed sites. Propagate by division or seed.

Bergenia cordifolia Sternb.—Zones 5a-10
Heartleaf Bergenia
A creeping, clumpy perennial growing to 12 inches tall, foliage thick and heavy, flowers pink in May. Requires ordinary soil and stands sun or partial shade; suited for residential purposes. Propagate by division.

Coronilla varia L.—Zones 3-7
Crownvetch
This perennial legume from northern Europe is used frequently to cover dry, steep slopes and highway cuts. It forms a dense cover about 2 feet tall and bears numerous small pink flowers in midsummer. Crownvetch spreads by creeping rootstalks, a single plant covering up to 6 sq. ft. of ground. It performs best on neutral soil but tolerates slightly acid conditions. Once established it provides an attractive cover and reduces erosion with low maintenance costs. Some recent selections are Chemung (N.Y.), Emerald (Iowa), and Penngift (Pa.). Crownvetch is seeded at the rate of 20 pounds of scarified seed per acre. Seed should be inoculated with crownvetch inoculum immediately before seeding.

Cotoneaster apiculata Rehd. & Wils.—Zones 5-9
Cranberry Cotoneaster
C. dammeri C. Schneid.—Zones 6-10
Bearberry Cotoneaster
C. horizontalis Decne.—Zones 6-10
Rockspray Cotoneaster
C. microphylla Wall. ex Lindl.—Zones 7-10
Small-leaved Cotoneaster

The cotoneasters with their flat horizontal habit and abundant bright red fruits make excellent ground covers. They are especially useful on banks and rough areas. Because of their presistant foliage and striking habit, *C. dammeri* and *C. microphylla* are especially recommended. The cotoneasters are subject to fire blight, red spider, and lace bug. *Cotoneaster apiculata* appears to be the hardiest of the group. All do best in full sun and are often used as accent plants in combination with other ground covers. Propagate by cuttings in early summer.

Dichondra repens Forst.—Zones 9-10
Dichondra

A native herb of the southern states with runner-like stems. Dichondra with its small kidney-shaped leaves is popular in California. It seldom exceeds 1 to 2 inches in height and rarely requires clipping. Because it spreads rapidly, a good covering develops in 2 or 3 months. Dichondra cannot be surpassed for either sunny or shady locations. Although Dichondra will survive along with grasses, it will not remain weed-free. Responds to regular irrigation and occasional fertilizer applications. Poor drainage and winter cold may lead to *Alternaria* root rot. It is also susceptible to damage from insects and other diseases. In the warmer portions of southern California it provides a cover which can be kept green the year round. There is no advantage in substituting Dichondra for Kentucky bluegrass or red fescue in areas where these grasses are adapted. On a less extensive scale, Dichondra is used as a ground cover in Florida, and in other parts of the southeastern region. Efforts are being made to determine its merits as far north as South Carolina.

Planting Dichondra seed is better than transplanting because plugs or cuttings may introduce diseases and nematodes. If plugs or clumps are used, they should be an inch or more in size. Plugs should be planted either on 6-inch or 1-foot centers.

Epimedium alpinum L.—Zones 4-8
E. grandiflorum Morr.—Zones 4-8
E. pinnatum Fisch.—Zones 4-8
Barrenwort

All of the epimediums are good ground covers. These compact perennials grow to 12 inches and maintain a uniform height throughout the season. The leaves are compound and the foliage dense, often persisting well into the winter. The flowers are white, yellow, or lavender according to variety. Epimediums grow well in semishade and tolerate almost any soil. They are particularly useful as underplantings for evergreens and shrubs and have been rated highly in all localities where they succeed. Propagate by division.

Euonymus fortunei (Turcz.) Hand.-Mazz.—Zones 5-10
Wintercreeper

A clinging evergreen vine, native to Japan, with several good varieties. It is commonly used as a wall plant as well as a ground cover. The variety, *radicans* (Miq.) Rehd., is perhaps the most useful because of its uniform leaves and rapid growth. It is good on banks and slopes since it holds its leaves through the winter. Colorata is a vigorous form with purplish foliage in winter. The USDA recently released a variety, Longwood, that has fine foliage, makes rapid growth and is extremely hardy. Scale insects may become a serious problem with all varieties. Propagate by division or summer cuttings.

Fragaria chiloensis (L.) Duchesne—Zones 6-10
Sand Strawberry

An excellent ground cover because of its rampant, running habit. It grows in most soils and particularly sandy types. Its appearance is not unlike that of the cultivated strawberry both in flower and fruit. *Duchesnea indica* is quite similar but the flowers are yellow and the fruit is not palatable. Both *Fragaria* and *Duchesnea* are propagated by division.

Gaultheria procumbens L.—Zones 5-7
Wintergreen

An extremely useful evergreen ground cover for acid soils and moist shady areas. It grows to 4 inches tall, spreads by creeping rootstocks and is perhaps best used in naturalized plantings. It falls into the same category of useful but minor ground covers as partridgeberry *(Mitchella repens)* and trailing arbutus *(Epigaea repens)*. Propagate by division.

Gazania X *splendens* Henderson—Zones 9-10
South African Daisy

In California, the perennial South African Daisy is used in parking strips and similar sites. The plants are 6 to 12 inches tall, with daisy-like flowers, from white to orange, that appear continually throughout the year. Once established, this plant will thrive for the entire season with little water. There are no serious pests or diseases in dry climates. Propagate by seed; several named varieties.

Hedera helix L.—Zones 5-9
English Ivy

This evergreen vine is a shade loving plant (Fig. 3). It grows 6 to 12 inches tall, has coarse foliage, forms a dense cover and is often employed under conditions where it can spread on the ground and then climb adjacent walls. One of our best evergreen ground covers with many varieties.

It is cultivated as far north as Massachusetts and south to Florida although in the latter state, the Algerian Ivy *(Hedera canariensis)* is more widely used. The leaves are lobed in juvenile plants and entire in the adult form. In the Los Angeles, Calif. area, thousands of acres are covered by ground covers and ivy is the one most in use. Ivy can be propagated by merely pulling branches free and rooting the pieces in a new site.

Hemerocallis hybrids—Zones 3-10
Daylily

The daylily, although variable in height, makes an excellent ground

Figure 3. English Ivy *(Hedera helix)* is a ground cover with wide adaptability. It grows well under most trees and shrubs.

cover, or more properly, naturalizing plant. It thrives in road cuts and banks under both dry and boggy conditions. With its long flowering period and almost complete freedom from insects and diseases, the daylily is becoming a popular plant in large-scale highway planting operations. Propagate by division.

Hypericum calycinum L.—Zones 6-10

Aaronsbeard St. Johnswort

This semi-evergreen shrub makes an ideal ground cover for semi-shade and sandy soil. It grows to 1 foot tall and is of special value because the bright yellow flowers appear in mid-summer and continue until frost. The foliage turns reddish in autumn. Some of the hypericums are aggressive, noxious weeds and should be considered with caution. Propagate by seed, division, or summer cuttings.

Ilex crenata Thunb.—Zones 6-10

Helleri Japanese Holly

This variety of Japanese holly has a low habit, fine evergreen foliage and can be kept down to 2 feet tall (Fig. 4). When planted in mass, it makes a good medium height ground cover for small banks and semi-shade areas. Because it is slow growing, Helleri is best established as large nursery plants.

Juniperus chinensis var. *sargentii* Henry—Zones 4-10

Sargent Juniper (Fig. 5)

J. conferta Parlatore—Zones 4-10

Shore Juniper (Fig. 5)

J. horizontalis fma. *douglasii* Rehd.—Zones 3-9

Waukegan Juniper

J. horizontalis fma. *plumosa* Rehd.—Zones 3-9

Andorra Juniper

Figure 4. Individual plants of *Ilex crenata* will ultimately fill in to a solid mass, completely covering this island.

Figure 5. Mass Juniper ground covers provide variation in texture and color. This massive use of ground cover at Longwood Gardens, Kennett Square, Pennsylvania, consists of *Juniperus conferta* (left) and *Juniperus chinensis* var. *sargentii* (right).

J. procumbens (Endl.) Miq.—Zones 4-9
Japanese Garden Juniper
J. sabina L.—Zones 3-9
Savin Juniper

The several species of juniper are highly recommended as evergreen ground covers wherever they can be grown. The plants are highly variable and by use of cultivars different color forms can be had, ranging from light green to steel blue and often turning purple in the winter. Plant habit is likewise variable ranging from prostrate to upright but rarely exceeding 3 feet tall. They are recommended for sunny dry areas and once established require little attention (Fig. 6). Junipers do well from seashore into the coldest parts of the country. Among the largest of the plants used for ground covers, spacing is often up to 4 feet apart. The junipers are among the best plants for highway use. The varieties of *J. sabina,* Skandia and Arcadia, hardy selections from Canada, especially are recommended for this purpose. Propagate by cuttings in late summer.

Figure 6. A newly planted bank with *Juniperus horizontalis* 'Wilton' shows both wide spacing and use of wood chips for weed and erosion control.

Lantana sellowiana Link & Otto – Zones 8-10
Weeping Lantana

A trailing shrub with hairy branches up to 3 feet long. The flowers are rose-lilac in compact heads and appear almost all year in warmer parts of Florida. Lantana is best adapted to sunny sites and does well regardless of soil quality. It is highly salt tolerant but is killed by temperatures below 25 F. It is frequently mixed with junipers or used as a hanging cover for walls. Propagate by cuttings or seed.

Lespedeza cuneata (Dumont) G. Don – Zones 6-9
Sericea

Several of the lespedezas are now in use as stabilization plants. Sericea has proven particularly valuable from Maryland southward as a perennial ground cover on highway banks. Sericea grows to 3 feet tall and bears small white flowers in short spikes. It thrives in heavy soil and appears disease-free. Propagate by seed or division.

Lippia nodiflora Michx. – Zones 9-10
Capeweed

A creeping, perennial herb often found on sanddunes, along roadsides, and waste areas of the southern states. The leaves are spatulate, greenish to purple in color. The flowers are light pink, in spikes appearing almost continually. With its extremely low habit, rapid rate of spread, and tolerance to sun and shade, Lippia is a highly recommended grass substitute. It withstands trampling, can be mowed like grass, responds to fertilizing, and is more drought resistant than common warm-season lawn grasses. Propagate by sod pieces or stem cuttings.

Liriope spicata Lour. – Zones 5-10
Creeping Lilyturf

This grass-like, evergreen perennial, to 12 inches tall, is second to none in tolerance to heat, dryness, intense sun, or deep shade. In addition to its linear, dark green leaves, Liriope produces attractive purple flowers on spikes above the leaves. It can be mowed or left alone, grows in almost any kind of soil, and can stand direct exposure to salt spray without injury. Once established, Liriope forms a dense mat from which small divisions can be removed for propagation.

Lonicera japonica var. *halliana* (Dippel) Nichols.—Zones 5-9
Hall's Honeysuckle

A climbing, twisting vine with evergreen to semi-evergreen foliage and white flowers turning to yellow, highly fragrant. An extremely vigorous plant for sun or partial shade where it will not get out of bounds. In some areas it has become a serious pest, shrouding trees and shrubs. It is essential that it be pruned yearly for control and may only be useful where the winter is severe enough to keep it under control. South of Maryland it is a most serious weed species. Propagate by division or cuttings.

Mahonia repens (Lindl.) G. Don—Zones 6-9
Dwarf Hollygrape

An evergreen shrub to 10 inches tall native to the Pacific Northwest. Hollygrape makes a good ground cover for sun or shade. It grows well in any kind of soil and covers rapidly. In colder climates, the holly-like, compound leaves are likely to be injured. The flowers are yellow in short terminal spikes. Propagate by division.

Mesembryanthemum spp.—Zones 8-10
Iceplant

The several species of succulents classed as iceplants are among the most widely used ground covers in Southern California. With brilliant flowers that open only in full sunlight, these plants are useful for banks, roadsides, and for bedding purposes. The most commonly grown genera are: *Carpobrotus, Cephalophyllum, Delosperma, Drosanthemum, Lampranthus,* and *Malephora,* although they were previously lumped under *Mesembryanthemum.*

Although the dazzling flowers are the main show, the gray foliage is excellent all year long. In cold climates, iceplants are choice temporary summer ground covers for newly prepared gentle banks until such time that grass is planted. Propagate by seed or cuttings.

Nepeta hederacea (L.) Trev.—Zones 3-9
Groundivy

A creeping perennial to 3 inches tall with rounded leaves and forming a low mat. It does well in average soil in either sun or shade. Since it is also a weed in lawns it may become a pest if not confined. A form with white or pink leaf margins is sometimes mixed with the species. Propagate by division.

Ophiopogon japonicus (L. f.) Ker—Zones 7-10
Dwarf Lilyturf

The dwarf lily turf is a low growing perennial to 10 inches tall, similar in most characteristics to *Liriope*. However, the flowers are not as showy and the plant is somewhat less hardy in the north. The plants are lower in habit and *Ophiopogon* seems the preferred in the South. Propagate by division.

Pachysandra terminalis Sieb. & Zucc.—Zones 5-8
Japanese Spurge

This Japanese plant, growing to 6 inches tall, with its spreading habit and evergreen foliage is considered one of our best ground covers for semishade (Fig. 7). It grows well under trees, spreads by underground stems, and covers quickly. There are few faults to find with Pach-

Figure 7. *Pachysandra terminalis* is one of the best ground covers for neat, compact growth.

ysandra and it is particularly suited to formal landscape design. A variegated variety is often used but it is slower growing than the green form. Pachysandra has no serious pests but may occasionally be subject to scale. Propagate by division or cuttings.

Polygonum reynoutria Makino—Zones 4-10

Dwarf Polygonum

A dwarf deciduous plant with oval leaves, 3 to 6 inches long, and pink flowers in summer. It grows in full sun, is extremely hardy and covers rapidly. In its native Japan, it is found on rocky or gravelly hillsides. The foliage turns red in the autumn. Recently, *Polygonum affine* has attracted attention as a compact, dwarf ground cover. Propagation is by division.

Rosa wichuraiana Crep.—Zones 5-9

Memorial Rose

This rose is a prostrate, trailing plant with semi-evergreen lustrous foliage. It serves well as a bank cover and for dune erosion control. The flowers are white and very effective in summer. The stems will root where they contact the soil. In Japan it grows along the beaches just above the tidal area and is highly tolerant to salt spray. Other roses that are showy roadside ground covers are *R. virginiana, R. rugosa,* and *R.* X Max Graf. Propagate by seed or cuttings.

Sarcoccoca hookeriana var. *humilis* (Stapf) Rehd. & Wils.—Zones 6-10

Sarcoccoca

A shrubby evergreen from China with glossy leathery leaves 1 to 2 inches long, small white, fragrant flowers. This ground cover is for more formal use such as edging for larger plants and around the base of trees. It tolerates shade and can be sheared if it gets too tall. Propagate by division or cuttings.

Sasa pumila (Mitf.) E. G. Camus—Zones 6-10

Ground Bamboo

S. veitchii (Carr.) Rehd.—Zones 6-10

Veitch Bamboo

Shibataea kumasaca (Zoll.) Nakai—Zones 6-10

Kumazasa Bamboo

The dwarf bamboos are excellent grass substitutes and can be grown as an adjunct to grass since they spread rapidly. The bamboos are excellent soil binders for use along irrigation ditches and hard-to-control banks. Dwarf bamboos can be mowed and treated like warm-season grasses. In many respects, culture is similar to that for zoysia. The foliage gets brown in winter and new growth does not develop until late in the spring. Propagation is by rhizome pieces or transplanting small clumps.

Saxifraga sarmentosa L.—Zones 7-9

Strawberry Geranium

A tufted herbaceous perennial, growing to 15 inches, spreading by runners. The leaves are basal, clustered, and round, reddish below. The flowers are white, borne well above the foliage in summer. It does best in partial shade around the base of other plants, in rock gardens, and areas with heavy clay or loam. Propagate by runners.

Sedum acre L.—Zones 4-10

Goldmoss Stonecrop

The sedums are useful ground covers for dry areas and grow only inches tall. *S. acre* scarcely reaches 4 inches. It is creeping and forms mats of tiny foliage so that it is particularly useful between stepping stones and in rocky places. Propagate by division or cuttings.

Symphoricarpos chenaultii Rehd. Hancock—Zones 5-9

S. orbiculatus Moench—Zones 3-9

Coralberry

A native deciduous shrub up to 3 feet tall but shorter in *S. chenaultii* Hancock. Spreading rapidly by underground stems. These species are especially useful for soil erosion and thrive in poor soil either in full sun or partial shade. The foliage is fine textured and the plants form neat mats where a tall cover is acceptable. Propagate by division or cuttings.

Teucrium chamaedrys L.—Zones 6-10

Germander

This is a small, woody perennial with upright habit to 10 inches tall, especially useful as a border for walks. The foliage is glossy green and persistent and responds to pruning. The flowers are purple or rose in terminal spikes appearing in midsummer. Suitable for sun or partial shade but in some areas, such as Missouri, a winter protecting mulch may be needed. Propagate by division or summer cuttings.

Thymus serpyllum L.—Zones 5-10

Creeping Thyme

A creeping evergreen with grayish foliage used for edging and between stepping stones. It is also excellent for small areas in place of grass as it rarely exceeds 3 inches in height. There are several varieties in California where they are widely used because of their fine texture and tolerance to trampling. Propagate by division.

Vaccinium vitis-idaea L.—Zones 5-9

Cowberry

This small evergreen shrub to 1 foot tall makes an excellent ground cover for acid soils. It is among the species suited to colder parts of the country. It bears small pink flowers and dark red berries. Cowberry will not tolerate summer heat and is limited to regions with cool, moist atmosphere. Propagate by layers, division, or summer cuttings.

Vinca minor L.—Zones 5-10

Periwinkle

One of the best evergreen ground covers. Periwinkle is a trailing plant 6 to 8 inches tall with dark green foliage and purple, blue, or white flowers. It grows well in full sun or partial shade and is especially useful on rocky banks. It is stem rooting, spreading in all directions, and easily propagated. Some recommend inter-planting bulbs to give spring color and others find that a few clumps of *Ajuga* are attractive additions. Periwinkle is one of the first ground covers to consider. There are several flower variants but Bowles Variety with light blue flowers is the best. Propagate by division or root pieces.

Zebrina pendula Schnizl.—Zone 10

Wandering Jew

A succulent, perennial herb native to Mexico used extensively in Florida and in conservatories. The foliage is purple beneath and striped above. The flowers are red-purple. It grows easily in the shade and roots readily so that, while a tender plant, it is not surpassed as a soil cover. It does well on both acid and alkaline soils. A related plant, *Setcreasea purpurea,* Purple Heart, with larger, lance-shaped leaves and vigorous habit is now planted frequently in South Florida in traffic circles and similar divider islands. In full sun the foliage is dark purple. Propagate by division or cuttings.

Literature Cited

Johnson, A. G., D. B. White, and M. H. Smithberg. 1966. Development of ground covers for highway slopes. Interim Report, 1965. Misc. Jour. Sev. Art. 1259. University of Minnesota. 87 p.

Ouellet, C. E. and L. C. Sherk. 1967. Map of plant hardiness zones in Canada. Canada Central Experiment Farm, Ottawa, Ontario.

Skinner, H. T. 1960. Plant hardiness zone map. USDA Misc. Pub. 814. Washington, D. C.

Smithberg, M. K. and A. G. Johnson. 1965. Ground covers—uses and materials. The Minnesota Horticulturist *93* No. 5: 68-69, 80.

Springer, D. K., J. D. Burns, H. A. Fibourg, K. E. Graetz. 1967. Roadside revegetation and beautification in Tennessee. University of Tennessee SP 162, 22 p.

Weston, T. A. and G. Harshbarger. 1962. Plant hardiness zone map. The American Home. The Curtis Publishing Co.

Wyman, D. 1961. Ground cover plants. The Macmillan Company. New York. 175 p.

Wyman, D. and H. L. Flint. 1967. Plant hardiness zone maps. Arnoldia *27* No. 6: 53-56.

Other References on Ground Cover Plants

Butterfield, H. M. 1963. Lawn-grass substitutes in California. University of California (Berkeley). Mimeo. 7 p.

Crevasse, J. M., Jr. 1950. Ground covers for Florida gardens. University of Florida Agricultural Experiment Station Bul. 473. 60 p.

Hoag, D. G. 1964. Ground covers for North Dakota. North Dakota Extension Service Circ. A-448.

Lacy, D. B. 1966. Ground covers. New Jersey Extension Bul. 351.

Lieberman, A. S. and R. G. Mower. 1967. Ground covers for New York State landscape plantings. Cornell Extension Bul. 1178. 13 p.

Link, C. B. 1963. Ground cover plants. University of Maryland Extension Bul. 190. 11 p.

Littlefield, L. 1966. Woody plant for landscape planting in Maine. University of Maine Bul. 506 (reprinted). 58 p.

Stark, N. 1966. Review of highway planting, information appropriate to Nevada. University of Nevada Bul. B-7. 209 p.

Taven, R. 1961. Ornamental ground cover plants for Missouri. University of Missouri Circ. 737.

Williams, T. G., Jr. 1966. Landscape plant materials for Georgia. University of Georgia Extension Bul. 625. 31 p.

Zangger, C. 1966. Iceplants as groundcover. Lasca Leaves *16,* No. 2: 49-53.

27

Specifications for Turfgrass Establishment

Alton E. Rabbitt

National Park Service
Department of the Interior
Washington, D. C.

C. Wallace Miller

Department of the Army
Washington, D. C.

Since World War II there has been a marked increase in contract planting of turfgrass on extensive areas for erosion control, recreation, and beautification.

Additional golf courses, parks, recreational areas, and municipal airports are required as our population grows; and new subdivisions develop into large communities that require thousands of acres of lawns each year. Turfgrasses are planted for erosion control and to improve natural beauty on hundreds of miles of new highway roadsides each year and on extensive acreages of military lands, such as airfields, lawns, earth dams, and training areas. With continuing shortages of labor, high equipment costs, and the need to perform work rapidly and at the proper time, more and more turfgrass is being planted under contract. This trend has increased the need to develop simple, yet detailed specifications to accompany plans (drawings) that will be followed on specific projects.

The "Technical Section of the Specifications" along with "drawings" become a part of the contract and are the major determining factors as to the quality of work performed. The technical writer of specifications should visualize the different conditions that will be encountered during construction and grading operations, so that all plantings and erosion control measures specified in the written documents, and shown on the drawings, will accomplish the desired objective. For example, an initial field inspection prior to writing specifications and reviewing grading plans may show that turf or other vegetation will not be sufficient for erosion control. Thus, additional control measures, such as structures, terraces, and diversion ditches, may be required as an integral part of the overall specifications and plans.

It is imperative that these documents be specific, so that the contractor can bid on work items without misinterpretation. Should a discrepancy occur between the specifications and drawings, the written specification prevails. The technical writer of the specifications is often not present during planting operations except on call or for periodic inspections; consequently, clarity is also essential for interpretation by the supervisor for the Contracting Agency.

Properly developed plans and specifications should clearly outline job requirements and thereby prevent misunderstanding between the contractor and the Contracting Agency by stipulating materials and methods as well as completion dates. Good specifications are essential to assure a stand of grass that will develop into turf suitable for the purpose required, and to eliminate delays, failures, and costly repairs.

The outline specifications presented on the following pages should be used only for guidance. Insertion of special provisions for specific conditions, climate, and locations will be required for each project. The order of work performed should follow the order of the major items discussed under specifications for seeding, sodding, and sprigging.

I. Seeding

1. SCOPE: The work covered by this section consists in furnishing all plant, labor, equipment, and materials, and in performing all operations in connection with seeding, and completion thereof, in strict accordance with the specifications and applicable drawings, and subject to the terms and conditions of the contract.

2. MATERIALS:

a. *Seed* shall be labeled in accordance with U. S. Department of Agriculture Rules and Regulations under the Federal Seed Act and State seed laws. Seed shall be furnished in sealed standard containers unless exception is granted in writing by the Contracting Agency. Each seed container shall bear the date of the last germination, which date shall be within a period of 6 months prior to commencement of planting operations. Seed which has become wet, moldy, or otherwise damaged in transit or in storage will not be acceptable. The kind and minimum percentage by weight of *pure live seed* shall be as follows:

Kind of seed		Hulled or unhulled	Minimum % pure live seed*	Pounds of bulk seed
Common name	Scientific name			
------------	------------	--------	------------	--------
------------	------------	--------	------------	--------

* Germination × Purity = % pure live seed. Total weed seed content shall not exceed 1%. No noxious-weed seed is allowed.

b. *Fertilizer* shall be ________ grade,[1] uniform in composition, free-flowing, pelleted, or ________ and suitable for application with approved equipment. The fertilizer shall be delivered to the site in bags or other convenient containers, each fully labeled, conforming to applicable State fertilizer laws, and bearing the name, trade name or trademark, and warranty of the producer.

c. *Lime* shall be ground limestone containing not less than 85% of total carbonates and shall be ground to such fineness that at least 50% will pass a 100-mesh sieve and at least 90% will pass a 20-mesh sieve.

d. *Soil for repairs:* The soil for fills and topsoiling of areas to be repaired shall be at least of equal quality to soil existing in areas

[1]Grade is expressed in the order N-P_2O_5-K_2O.

adjacent to the area repaired. The soil shall be free from sub-soil, clay lumps, brush, objectionable weeds, and other litter, and shall be free from stones, stumps, and other objects larger than 2 inches in diameter, from roots and toxic substances, and from any other material or substance that might harm plant growth or hinder grading, planting, and maintenance operations.

3. Inspection and Tests:

a. *Seed:* The Contracting Agency shall be furnished with duplicate signed copies of the vendor's statement certifying that each container of seed delivered is fully labeled in accordance with the Federal Seed Act, and is at least equal to the requirement for seed in the Materials paragraph of these specifications. This certification shall appear on or with all copies of invoices for the seed. Each lot of seed shall be subject to sampling and testing at the discretion of the Contracting Agency. Sampling and testing will be in accordance with the latest Rules and Regulations under the Federal Seed Act and State seed laws.

4. Preparation of Seedbed:

a. *General:* The areas to be treated and their respective requirements for seed, fertilizer, lime, and other treatment shall be as indicated on the drawings. Areas in a satisfactory state of tillage and not requiring further tillage and the areas requiring special tillage or applications of materials are so indicated on the drawings. Equipment necessary for the proper preparation of the ground surface and for handling and placing all required materials shall be on hand, in good condition, and shall be approved before the work is started.

b. *Clearing:* Prior to grading and tillage operations, vegetation on the site that might interfere with grading, tillage, or seeding operations shall be mowed, grubbed, raked, and burned or removed from the site, or, when suitable, shall be used for mulch as directed. Prior to or during grading and tillage operations, the ground surface shall be cleared of stumps, stones larger than ____ inches in diameter, roots, cable, wire, grade stakes, and other materials that might hinder proper grading, tillage, seeding, or subsequent maintenance operations.

c. *Grading:* Previously established grades, as shown on drawings of areas to be treated, shall be maintained in a true and even condition. Maintenance shall include necessary repairs to previously graded areas. When grades have not been established, areas shall be graded as shown on the drawings, and surfaces shall be left at the prescribed grades in an even and properly compacted condition so as to prevent the formation of depressions where water will stand.

d. *Tillage:* After areas to be treated have been brought to the grades shown on the drawings, they shall be thoroughly tilled to a depth of at least ____ inches by plowing, disking, harrowing, or other approved methods until the condition of the soil is acceptable. Work shall be performed only during periods when beneficial results are likely to be obtained. When conditions are such, by reason of drought, excessive moisture, or other factors, that satisfactory results are not likely to be obtained, the work may be stopped by the Contracting Agency and shall be resumed only when directed. Undulations or irregularities in the surface that would interfere with further construction operations or maintenance shall be leveled before the next specified operation.

e. *Cleanup:* After completion of the above operations, the surface shall be cleared of stones, stumps, or other objects larger than ____ inches in thickness or diameter, and of roots, brush, wire, grade stakes, and other objects that might be a hindrance to maintenance operations. Paved areas over which hauling operations are conducted shall be kept clean, and soil or debris left on the surface shall be removed promptly. The wheels of vehicles shall be cleaned to avoid leaving soil upon the surface of roads, walks, and other paved areas. Cleaning operations shall be conducted with care to prevent damage to underlying pavements.

5. Application of Fertilizer and Lime:

a. *Application of fertilizer:* Fertilizer shall be distributed uniformly at a rate of ____ pounds per acre over the areas to be seeded as indicated on the drawings, and shall be incorporated into the soil to a depth of at least ____ inches by disking, harrowing, or other acceptable methods within 24 hours after application. (Note: Distribution by means of an approved seed drill equipped to sow seed and distribute fertilizer at the same time will be acceptable, provided fertilizer placement will not retard germination of the seed specified, and where such a drill is authorized.)

b. *Application of lime:* Lime shall be distributed uniformly at a rate of ____ pounds per acre and shall be incorporated into the soil to a depth of at least ____ inches by disking, harrowing, or other acceptable methods within 24 hours following application. Incorporation of lime may form a part of the tillage operation specified above. (Note: When lime is required it will be applied prior to application of fertilizer.)

c. *Leveling:* Undulations or irregularities in the surface resulting from tillage, fertilizing, liming, or other operations shall be leveled before seeding operations are begun.

6. Planting Seed:

a. *General:* All seeding work shall be done between the dates of ______ and ______. A satisfactory method of sowing shall be employed, making use of approved mechanical power-drawn seeders, mechanical handseeders, or other approved methods. When delays in operations carry the work beyond the most favorable planting season for the species designated or when conditions are such, by reason of drought, high winds, excessive moisture, or other factors, that satisfactory results are not likely to be obtained, the work will be stopped by the Contracting Agency and shall be resumed only when directed. If an inspection, either during seeding operations or after seedling emergence, shows that strips have been left unplanted, or other areas skipped, the Contracting Agency may require the sowing of additional seed on these areas.

b. *Broadcast seeding:* Seed shall be broadcast by approved sowing equipment at the rate of____pounds per acre of bulk seed mixture specified in materials. The seed shall be uniformly distributed over the designated areas. On small areas such as lawns, half the seed shall be sown with the sower moving in one direction, and the remainder shall be sown at right angles to the first sowing. The seed shall be covered to an average depth of____ inch by means of a spike-tooth harrow, cultipacker, or other approved device. Broadcast seeding shall not be done during windy weather.

c. *Drill seeding* shall be done with approved equipment with drills not more than____ inches apart. The seed shall be sown uniformly over the designated areas. The seed shall be sown to an average depth of ____ inch and at the rate of____pounds per acre.

d. *Native-grass seeding:* Seeding shall be accomplished with a native-grass-seed drill having the disks equipped with depth control bands. The seed of____ species and____ species shall be mixed in the presence of the Contracting Agency representative and planted through the small seed box. The____ species and____species shall be planted through the chaffy seed box. Depth of planting the seed shall be 1/2 to 3/4 inch. Disks and seed spouts on the drill shall not be spaced more than 10 inches apart.

e. *Hay-mulch seeding:* Mulch containing seed shall be evenly spread at the rate of_____tons per acre over a suitably prepared surface. The material shall be anchored immediately after spreading with a coulter type disk mulch anchoring machine, or by asphalt mulch blower and adhesive, or other approved equipment. On steep slopes and other areas designated on the drawings, the mulch containing seed shall be held in place by methods outlined under Mulching Specifications.

7. COMPACTING: Immediately after seeding, the entire area shall be compacted either with a cultipacker or a roller weighing 60 to 90 pounds per linear foot. If seeding is performed with a cultipacker type seeder, compacting can be eliminated.

8. PROTECTION: Immediately after seeding, the area shall be protected against traffic or other use by erecting barricades, as needed, and by placing approved warning signs at appropriate intervals.

9. ESTABLISHMENT:

a. *General:* The contractor shall be responsible for the proper care of seeded areas. This period shall extend for_____months after the completion of the seeding on the entire project, unless a cover of____% is established in a shorter period. The shorter period of the contractor's responsibility may be authorized by the Contracting Agency. The percent of coverage is defined as the total percent coverage with no one barren spot exceeding 2 feet square.

b. *Mowing:* The seeded areas shall be mowed with approved mowing equipment to a height of____ inches whenever the average height of grass becomes____ inches. When the amount of cut grass is heavy, it shall be removed to prevent destruction of the underlying turf. If weeds or other undesirable vegetation threaten to smother the planted species, such vegetation shall be mowed. If the growth of undesirable species is very rank, plants shall be uprooted, raked, and removed from the area.

c. *Refertilizing:* Areas needing refertilization will be designated by the Contracting Agency at least 15 days prior to the time that the application is required. Refertilizing shall be completed within 25 days of the date of such designation or within such longer period as may be allowed by the Contracting Agency. The fertilizer shall be distributed on the seeded areas between ___ and ___, during a period when the grass is dry. The fertilizer shall be ___ grade and shall be applied uniformly at the rate of ___ pounds per acre. Physical condition, packaging, and marking of the fertilizer shall be as specified (See item 2, Materials—fertilizer).

d. *Reseeding:* Areas that require reseeding will be designated by the Contracting Agency at least 15 days prior to the period specified for reseeding. Reseeding shall be completed within 25 days of date of such designation or within such longer period as may be allowed by the Contracting Agency. Reseeding shall be with the seed specified (See item 2, Materials—seed) and shall be drilled at ___ pounds per acre, in a manner that will cause a minimum of disturbance to the existing stand of grass, and at an angle of not less than 15 degrees from the direction of the rows of prior seedings.

10. Repair: If at any time before completion and acceptance of the entire work covered by this contract, any portion of the surface becomes gullied or otherwise damaged following seeding, or the seedlings have been winter-killed or otherwise destroyed, the affected portion shall be repaired to reestablish the condition and grade of the soil prior to seeding and shall then be reseeded as specified (See item 6, Planting Seed).

11. Methods of Measurement:

a. *Tilling, Seeding, Mowing, Refertilizing, Reseeding, and Repair:* The unit of measurement for tilling, seeding, mowing, refertilizing, reseeding, or repair shall be the acre. The specified area to be paid for shall be the acreage actually seeded, mowed, refertilized, reseeded, or repaired, computed to the nearest 1/10 acre.

b. *Fertilizer and lime:* The unit of measurement for fertilizer or lime shall be the 2,000-pound ton. The tonnage to be paid for shall be the tonnage actually placed as specified, except as provided for lime (See item 2, Materials—lime).

c. *Soil for Repairs:* The unit of measurement for soil needed for repair work shall be the cubic yard. Measurement will be made in the vehicle just prior to dumping on the site.

12. Payment:

a. *Tilling* will be paid for at the contract unit price per acre, which payment shall constitute full compensation for all work covered by this section of the specifications, except as specified below.

b. *Seeding* will be paid for at the contract unit price per acre, which payment shall constitute full compensation for all work covered by this section of the specifications, except as specified below.

c. *Fertilizer and Lime* will be paid for at the respective contract unit prices per ton for fertilizer and lime, which payment shall constitute full compensation for furnishing and delivering these materials to the site, including necessary storage and application.

d. *Mowing, Refertilizing, Reseeding, and Repair* will be paid for at the respective contract unit prices per acre for mowing, refertilizing, reseeding, and repair, which payment shall constitute full compensation for mowing, refertilizing, reseeding, and repair, as specified, except that fertilizer or soil used for such work will be paid for at the respective contract unit price. No payment will be made for materials or operations for refertilizing, reseeding, or repair work resulting from faulty operations or negligence on the part of the contractor.

II. Sodding

1. SCOPE: See I., Seeding Specifications. Substitute sodding for seeding.

2. MATERIALS:

a. *Sod* shall contain a good cover of growing or living grass. Living grass shall be interpreted to include grass that is seasonably dormant during the cold or dry season and capable of renewing growth after the dormant period. At least 70% of the plants in the sod shall be ____ grass. If a mixture of grasses is required, the percent of each species shall be specified. Sod shall be procured from areas having similar growing conditions to the areas where it will be used and from areas with ____ loam or ____ loam topsoil. Cultivated certified sod may be specified when available. Certified sod will insure obtaining specified species grown under State certification regulations. The sod shall be free of weeds or undesirable plants, large stones, roots, and other material that might be detrimental to the development of the sod or to future maintenance. Vegetation more than 5 inches in height shall be mowed to a height of 3 inches or less, and the loose materials on the surface shall be removed at least ____ days before the sod is lifted. When the sod is cut, the height of the grass shall not exceed ____ inches. Sod shall be cut to provide a thickness of ____ inches. (Suitable sod on areas on the site, as designated on the drawings, will be made available for cutting and sodding the specified areas.) All (other) sod shall be furnished by the contractor.

b. *Fertilizer:* See I, Seeding Specification.

c. *Lime:* See I, Seeding Specification.

d. *Soil for Repairs:* See I, Seeding Specification.

e. *Water* shall be free from oil, acid, alkali, salt, and other substances harmful to growth of grass. The water source shall be subject to approval prior to use.

3. Inspection and Tests:

a. *Sod:* Within ____ days prior to commencement of sodding operations, the contractor shall notify the Contracting Agency of the off-site sources from which sod is to be furnished. The sod will be approved prior to lifting and also inspected during laying operations. Sod will be rejected that fails to meet the requirements specified for sod under MATERIALS, or that has been permitted to dry out or become otherwise injured during transportation or storage so that survival is doubtful. Rejected material, if necessary and suitable, may be pulverized and used for filling.

b. *Fertilizer and Lime:* See I, Seeding Specification.

4. Preparation of Sod Bed:

a. *General:* The areas to be treated and their respective requirements for sodding, fertilizer, lime and other treatment shall be as shown. Areas left in a satisfactory state of tillage and not requiring further tillage and the areas requiring special tillage or applications of materials are so shown. Equipment necessary for the proper preparation of the ground surface and for handling and placing all required materials shall be on hand, in good condition, and shall be approved before the work is started. Before starting work the contractor shall demonstrate that the application of the materials required will be made at the specified rates.

b. *Clearing:* See I, Seeding Specification.

c. *Grading:* See I, Seeding Specification.

d. *Tillage:* See I, Seeding Specification.

5. Application of Fertilizer and Lime:

a. *Fertilizing:* See I, Seeding Specification.

b. *Liming:* See I, Seeding Specification.

c. *Leveling:* Undulations or irregularities in the surface resulting from tillage, fertilizing, liming, or other operations shall be leveled before sodding operations are begun.

d. *Cleanup:* See I, Seeding Specification.

6. Procuring and Developing Sod: After inspection and approval of the sod sources, the sod shall be cut into squares or rolled sections with an approved sod cutter. Sod may vary in length but shall be of equal width and of a size that will permit the sections to be lifted and/or rolled without breaking. Care shall be exercised at all times to retain the native soil on the roots of the sod during the process of stripping, transporting, and planting. Dumping from vehicles will not be permitted. The sod shall be placed on a prepared sod bed within 24 hours from the time of stripping, unless stored in a satisfactory manner. Bermudagrass or St. Augustinegrass sod shall be stacked during transit or storage with roots to roots or grass to grass. During delivery and while in stacks, the sod shall be kept moist and shall be protected from exposure to the air and sun and from freezing. Sod that has been damaged by handling or storage will be rejected. Sod shall be cut and

moved only when the soil moisture conditions are such that favorable results can be expected. When the soil is too dry, the sod shall be cut only after the contractor has watered the sod sufficiently to moisten the soil to the depth at which the sod is to be cut.

7. PLANTING SOD:

a. *General:* Sodding shall be performed only during ______ (dates) when satisfactory results can be expected. Only when authorized in writing by the Contracting Agency may sodding be done during unfavorable seasons. With such authorization, the contractor may move the sod during periods of drought, provided the sod at its origin is watered sufficiently to moisten the soil adequately to the depth to which the sod is to be cut, and provided the sod bed is thoroughly watered to a depth of at least 4 inches prior to planting.

b. *Excavation:* When grades are not low enough for sodding, the areas to be solid and strip sodded shall be excavated to a sufficient depth so that the top of the sod when set in place will be from 1/2 to 1 inch below the surrounding soil at the outer edges of the solid sodded area.

c. *Solid Sodding:* The sod shall be laid smoothly, edge to edge, and with staggered joints. The sod shall be pressed immediately into contact with the sod bed by tamping or rolling with approved equipment, so as to eliminate air pockets, provide a true and even surface, and assure knitting without displacement of the sod or deformation of the surfaces of sodded areas. Following compaction, screened soil of good quality shall be used to fill all cracks. Excess soil shall be worked into the grass with rakes or other suitable equipment. The quantity of fill soil shall be such as will cause no smothering of the grass.

d. *Strip Sodding:* Strips of sod shall be laid in continuous parallel rows at right angles to the slope or flow of water so that the centers of adjacent sod strips are ____ inches apart. Each strip of sod shall be ____ inches wide and shall be laid in a trench and firmly rolled or tamped. The surface of the finished sod shall be approximately 1/2 inch below the surface of the adjacent tilled area.

e. *Spot Sodding:* Sod shall be cut into blocks (4" x 4") containing approximately 16 square inches. The individual pieces of sod shall be placed on ____ -inch centers, sod side up, and pressed firmly into the soil by foot pressure or by tamping. The surface of the finished sod shall be approximately 1/2 inch below the surface of the adjacent tilled area.

8. OVERSEEDING: (Note: Overseeding may be required for erosion control on spot-sodded or strip-sodded areas.)

9. FINISHING: After the sodding operation has been completed, the edges of the area shall be smooth and shall conform to the cross sections shown. Suitable excess material from the planting operations shall be spread uniformly over adjacent areas and the remainder disposed of as directed. On slopes steeper than 2 to 1 and elsewhere when

so shown, the sod shall be fastened in place with suitable wooden pins or by other approved methods.

10. Watering: Water shall be applied to the ______ areas__________
____.
Such watering shall be within 12 hours after commencement of____operations on each portion of an area to be planted. If the soil is extremely dry prior to planting, watering of the areas 48 to 72 hours in advance of planting may be required if deemed necessary by the Contracting Agency. Water shall be applied using portable aluminum pipelines, hoses, underground systems or portable containers. When sprinklers are used, they shall be spaced to provide a minimum of 35% overlap of the pattern. Water shall be applied to the planted areas at a rate sufficient to insure thorough wetting of the soil to a depth of 4 inches over the entire planted area which will usually require a minimum of 27,000 gallons per acre. The actual rate will be determined by the Contracting Agency at the time of watering. Watering operations shall be discontinued during and following effective rains and resumed as directed by the Contracting Agency. Watering operations shall be properly supervised to prevent run-off of water. The contractor shall supply all pumps, hoses, pipelines, and sprinkling equipment, unless otherwise specified. The contractor shall have adequate equipment available for watering operations prior to commencement of planting operations. The contractor shall repair areas damaged by watering operations at no cost to the Contracting Agency.

11. Rewatering: On each area specified to be watered, one or two rewaterings may be required after the initial watering, when such rewatering is deemed necessary by the Contracting Agency. Rewatering shall be at the same rate and applied in the same manner as specified for initial watering.

12. Maintenance: Sodded areas shall be maintained until all work on the entire contract or designated portions thereof have been completed and accepted. Maintenance shall consist of providing protection from traffic by erecting the barricades shown and by placing approved warning signs, watering, mowing once all tall grass and weeds that may otherwise smother desired grass species, and repairing areas damaged in these operations.

13. Repair: If at any time before completion and acceptance of all work covered by this contract, any portion of the surface becomes gullied or otherwise damaged after sodding, the affected portion shall be repaired to reestablish the condition and grade of the soil prior to sodding, and shall then be resodded as specified under PLANTING SOD.

14. Methods of Measurement:

a. *Sodding and Repair:* The unit of measurement for sodding or repair shall be the square yard. The solid-sodded or spot-sodded area to be paid for shall be the area actually sodded as specified; the strip-sodded area to be paid for shall be the actual area of the sod placed as specified. The repaired area to be paid for shall be the area actually repaired as specified, measured in the same manner as the type of sodding used.

b. *Fertilizer and Lime:* See I, Seeding Specification.

c. *Soil for Repairs:* See I, Seeding Specification.

d. *Water:* The unit of measurement[2] for water shall be 1,000 gallons. The gallonage to be paid for shall be the number of 1,000-gallon units actually delivered and applied as specified.

15. PAYMENT:

a. *Sodding* will be paid for at the respective contract unit price per square yard for solid sodding, strip sodding, or spot sodding, as specified, which payment shall constitute full compensation for all work covered by this section of the specifications, except as specified below.

b. *Fertilizer and Lime:* See I, Seeding Specification.

c. *Water* will be paid for at the contract unit price per 1,000-gallon unit, which payment shall constitute full compensation for furnishing and applying water as specified.

d. *Repair* work will be paid for at the respective contract unit price per square yard for solid-sodding repair, strip-sodding repair, or spot-sodding repair, which payment shall constitute full compensation for repair work as specified, except that fertilizer or soil used for repair work will be paid for at the respective contract unit price. No payment will be made for materials or operations for repair work resulting from faulty operations or negligence on the part of the contractor.

III. Sprigging

1. SCOPE: See I, Seeding Specifications. Substitute sprigging for seeding.

2. MATERIALS:

a. *Sprigs* shall be the healthy living stems, stolons or rhizomes, and attached roots of ____ grass with or without adhering soil, obtained from approved sources where the sod is heavy and dense. The presence of weeds or other material that might be detrimental to the proposed planting will be cause for rejecting sprigs. Suitable areas on the site from which sprigs may be taken will be designated and made available for harvesting. All other sprigs required to complete the work shall be furnished by the contractor.

b. *Fertilizer:* See I, Seeding Specification.

c. *Lime:* See I, Seeding Specification.

d. *Soil for Repairs:* See I, Seeding Specification.

e. *Water:* See II, Sodding Specification.

---

[2]Where meters for measuring water cannot be installed for sprinkler systems, the unit of measure may be by the acre. This would require calibration of the system to apply the specified number of inches per acre.

3. Inspection and Tests:

a. *Sprigs:* Within ____ days prior to commencement of sprigging operations, the contractor shall notify the Contracting Agency of the off-site sources from which sprigs are to be furnished. The sprigs shall be subject to inspection during the planting period, and will be rejected when they have been permitted to dry out excessively or are not viable.

b. *Fertilizer and Lime:* See I, Seeding Specification.

4. Preparation of Planting Bed:

a. *General:* See II, Sodding Specification.
b. *Clearing:* See I, Seeding Specification.
c. *Grading:* See I, Seeding Specification.
d. *Tillage:* See I, Seeding Specification.

5. Application of Fertilizer and Lime:

a. *Fertilizing:* Fertilizer shall be distributed uniformly at a rate of __ pounds per acre over the areas shown to be sprigged, and shall be incorporated into the soil to a depth of at least ____ inches by disking, harrowing, or other acceptable methods. The incorporation of fertilizer may be a part of the tillage operation specified above. The distribution of fertilizer by means of an approved sprigging machine equipped to sprig and distribute fertilizer at the same time will be acceptable.

b. *Liming:* See I, Seeding Specification.

c. *Leveling:* Undulations or irregularities in the surface resulting from tillage, fertilizing, liming, or other operations shall be leveled before sprigging operations are begun.

d. *Cleanup:* See I, Seeding Specification.

6. Harvesting Sprigs: Sprigs shall be obtained from areas as close as possible to the planting site. Weeds and grasses taller than 3 inches shall be mowed to a height of 2 inches and raked and removed before harvesting begins. Harvesting shall be accomplished in limited areas or blocks so that the maximum amount of sprigs is harvested from each area or block in a continuous operation, and once abandoned, no more sprigs shall be harvested from the area until detached sprigs exposed on the surface are removed. Harvesting may be performed by any acceptable method, including crisscross cultivation, shallow plowing, or disking to thoroughly loosen the sprigs from the soil and to bring them to the surface. Sprigs may be collected or bunched for loading by hand or by raking with a side-delivery rake. Sprigs that heat will be rejected. Harvesting and planting operations shall be synchronized, with every care taken at the harvesting site to prevent exposure of sprigs to the sun for more than 30 minutes before covering and moistening. Not more than 24 hours shall elapse between initial harvesting and sprigging. When adverse weather or other uncontrollable conditions interrupt sprigging operations, an extension of time may be granted by the Contracting Agency provided the sprigs are still viable.

7. PREPARING SPRIGS FOR PLANTING: If required to facilitate planting with hand-fed machines, sprigs may be cut to an average length of from 4 to 6 inches by passing through an ensilage cutter or similar equipment immediately prior to planting. Cut sprigs shall be covered and kept moist until planted. Sprigs will not be cut for planting with automatic sprig planters.

8. PLANTING SPRIGS:

a. *General:* The contractor shall employ a satisfactory method of sprigging, using approved mechanical power-drawn sprigging machines or other approved methods. When sprigging machines are used, provision shall be made by markers or other means to insure that the successive sprigged strips will overlap or be separated by a space no greater than the space between rows planted by the equipment used. Sprigs shall be planted in such quantity as to provide a minimum of 25 viable sprigs or 100 linear inches of viable sprigs per square yard of area. Distribution shall be sufficiently uniform to insure that the maximum spacing of sprigs will not exceed 18 inches. The interval between dropping sprigs and covering with soil shall not exceed 10 minutes. Sprigging shall be done only when satisfactory results can be expected. When conditions are such, by reason of drought, high winds, excessive moisture, or other factors, that satisfactory results are not likely to be obtained, the work will be stopped by the Contracting Agency and shall be resumed only when directed. If inspection, during sprigging operations or after there is a show of green, indicates that strips____ inches or more in width have been skipped, the planting of additional sprigs will be required on such areas.

b. *Broadcast sprigging*[3]: Sprigs shall be broadcast either by hand or by a manure spreader or other suitable device over the prepared surface. The sprigs shall then be forced into the soil to a depth of approximately____ inches with a straight spade or similar hand tool, or with a disk harrow or other approved equipment set to cover the sprigs to the proper depth. On small areas such as golf greens or lawns, the sprigs may be covered with top dressing and kept moist until growth commences.

c. *Row Sprigging:* Sprigs shall be planted in furrows spaced not more than 18 inches apart. Immediately after opening furrows, sprigs shall be placed and covered to a depth of approximately____ inches. The furrows shall be filled in such a manner that the surface is left even at the designated grade. Sprigging machines, when hand-fed, shall not be operated at speeds in excess of 3 miles per hour while planting. Species such as St. Augustine, zoysia, and centipede grasses that cannot be covered with soil will be planted by hand with a portion of the sprig exposed. Steep slopes may be planted in furrows prepared by a turning plow pulled with a team or special tractor. The second pass of the plow will cover the sprigs. (Note: This method may also be utilized for spot sodding steep slopes.)

---

[3]Although broadcast sprigging is acceptable under optimum moisture conditions, row sprigging is usually the most successful method.

d. *Spot Sprigging* shall be performed by planting groups of sprigs at not more than 18-inch intervals to a depth of approximately___ inches. Sprigs shall be covered in such a manner that the surface is left even with the designated grade.

9. Overseeding: (Note: Overseeding is normally not required for sprigged areas. However, under certain conditions it may be specified to obtain a quick cover.)

10. Compacting: Immediately after the above operations have been completed, the planted area shall be compacted with a cultipacker, roller, or other approved equipment weighing 60 to 90 pounds per linear foot. When machine planting is employed, the roller shall operate immediately behind the planter unless otherwise directed. Under certain soil conditions, the Contracting Agency may direct that rolling be delayed for a period of 15 to 30 minutes following planting to avoid balling of soil on the roller or squeezing of water out of furrows. If the soil is of such type that a smooth or corrugated roller cannot be operated satisfactorily, a pneumatic roller, not wobble-wheel, will be required. The pneumatic roller shall have tires of sufficient size to obtain complete coverage of the soil surface. When a cultipacker or similar equipment is used, the final rolling shall be at right angles to existing slopes to prevent water erosion or at right angles to prevailing wind to reduce soil blowing. When soil is such that a roller will not leave a smooth surface, a final leveling operation with a weighted float drag will be specified.

11. Watering: Watering shall be required when the ground is excessively dry, and shall be applied at the time of, or immediately following, sprigging operations. When applied in open furrows, watering shall be at the rate of____ gallons per acre; other sprigged areas shall be watered until the surface soil is wet to the depth of the planted sprigs. Machines for planting large areas should be equipped for application of water in the furrow and supplied by tank truck. Additional applications of water shall be made as directed. See II, Sodding Specification.

12. Protection: See I, Seeding Specification.

13. Establishment:

a. *General:* The contractor shall be responsible for the proper care of the sprigged areas during the period the grass becomes established. This period shall extend for____ months after the completion of sprigging on the entire project, unless the desired cover is established in a shorter period of time. The shorter period of the contractor's responsibility may be authorized by the Contracting Agency.

b. *Mowing:* The sprigged areas shall be mowed with approved mowing equipment to a height of_____inches whenever the average height of grass becomes______inches. If weeds or other undesirable types of vegetation threaten to smother the planted species, such vegetation shall be mowed or, in the case of rank growth, shall be uprooted, raked, and removed from the area.

c. *Refertilizing:* See I, Seeding Specification.

d. *Resprigging:* Areas that require resprigging will be designated by the Contracting Agency at least 15 days prior to the period specified for resprigging. Resprigging shall be completed within 25 days of date of such designation or within such longer period as may be allowed by the Contracting Agency. Resprigging shall be accomplished as specified under Planting.

14. REPAIR: See II, Sodding Specification.

15. METHODS OF MEASUREMENT:

a. *Tilling, Sprigging, Mowing, Refertilizing, Resprigging, and Repair.* The unit of measurement for tilling, sprigging, mowing, refertilizing, resprigging, or repair shall be the acre. The area to be paid for shall be the acreage actually sprigged, mowed, refertilized, resprigged, or repaired, as specified, computed to the nearest 1/10 of an acre.

b. *Fertilizer and Lime:* See I, Seeding Specification.

c. *Soil for Repairs:* See I, Seeding Specification.

d. *Water:* See II, Sodding Specification.

16. PAYMENT:

a. *Tilling* will be paid for at the contract unit price per acre which price shall constitute full compensation for all work covered by this section of the specifications, except as specified below.

b. Sprigging will be paid for at the contract unit price per acre, which payment shall constitute full compensation for all work covered by this section of the specifications, except as specified below.

c. *Fertilizer and Lime:* See II, Sodding Specification.

d. *Water:* See II, Sodding Specification.

e. *Mowing, Refertilizing, Resprigging, and Repair* will be paid for at the respective contract unit price per acre, which payment shall constitute full compensation for mowing, refertilizing, resprigging, or repair, as specified, except that fertilizer or lime used for such work will be paid for at the respective contract unit price for fertilizer or lime. No payment will be made for materials or operations for refertilizing, resprigging, or repair resulting from faulty operations or negligence on the part of the contractor.

IV. Mulching

1. SCOPE: See I, Seeding Specification. Substitute mulching for seeding.

2. MATERIALS:

a. *General:* Acceptable mulch shall be any of the materials named in item 2b or other approved locally available material. Mulch material that includes an excessive quantity of mature weed seed or other species that could be detrimental to the seeding or a menace to adjacent farm land will not be acceptable. Mulches containing mature noxious-weed seeds are not acceptable. Straw or other mulch material that is fresh and excessively brittle or that is in such an advanced stage of decomposition as to smother or retard the growth of grass will not be acceptable. A certified weight certificate for each load of mulch material delivered to the site will be furnished to the Contracting Agency at the time of delivery.

b. *Mulch* shall be the threshed straw of oats, wheat, barley, rye, rice, native hay, sudangrass hay, broomsedge hay, grass clippings, or wood fiber.

c. *Mulch* to be anchored with coulter disk type equipment will have 50% of the material 10 inches or longer.

d. *Wood cellulose fiber mulch*[4] for use with the hydraulic application of grass seed and fertilizer shall consist of specially prepared wood cellulose fiber, processed to contain no growth- or germination-inhibiting factors and dyed an appropriate color to facilitate visual metering of application of the materials. The mulch material shall be supplied in packages having a gross weight not in excess of 100 pounds. The wood cellulose fiber shall contain not in excess of 10% moisture, air dry weight basis. The wood cellulose fiber shall be manufactured so that (1) after addition and agitation in slurry tanks with fertilizers, grass seeds, water, and any other approved additives, the fibers in the material will become uniformly suspended to form a homogeneous slurry; (2) when hydraulically sprayed on the ground, the material will form a blotter-like cover impregnated uniformly with grass seed; and (3) the cover will allow the absorption of moisture and allow rainfall or added water to percolate to the underlying soil. Suppliers shall be prepared to certify that laboratory and field testing of their product has been accomplished and that their product meets all the foregoing requirements based upon such testing.

e. *Asphalt Adhesive* for application with straw or hay mulch shall be liquid asphalt conforming to ASTM Specifications D 2028, designation RC-70, or emulsified asphalt conforming to ASTM Specifications D 977, grade SS-1.

3. Special Seeding and Mulching Equipment:

a. *Seeder:* Equipment to be used for applying a seed-fertilizer mix over prepared slopes shall be a hydraulic seeder designed to pump and discharge a water-borne, homogeneous slurry of seed, fertilizer, and wood cellulose fiber at the desired specified rate. The seeder shall be equipped with a power-driven agitator, and shall be capable of discharging up to 200 gallons per minute at 100 pounds pressure from a nozzle with clearance for ½-inch solids.

[4] Wood cellulose fiber mulches have been successful on level areas or on slopes with slight grades where sufficient moisture is present to obtain a quick germination of grass seed. It should not be specified for steep slopes in areas where drought may prevent germination of the seed or where runoff from heavy rains may cut gullies through the fiber mulch.

b. *Mulch Spreader* to be used for applying straw or hay mulch shall be trailer-mounted, equipped with a blower that is dynamically balanced for at least 2,000 revolutions-per-minute operation and that will discharge hay or straw mulch material through a discharge boom with spout at speeds up to 220 feet per second. The discharge spout shall be capable of 360-degree horizontal rotation and a minimum of 60-degree range of elevation and depression. The mulch spreader shall be equipped with an asphalt-adhesive supply and application system near the discharge end of the boom spout. This system must apply an asphalt adhesive in atomized form to the mulch material at a predetermined rate. The spreader shall be capable of blowing the adhesive-coated mulch, with a high-velocity airstream, over the surface of a graded or otherwise prepared slope at a uniform rate, forming a porous, stable, erosion-resisting cover at a distance of not less than 80 feet.

c. *Wood Cellulose Fiber Mulch Spreader:* Hydraulic equipment used for the application of fertilizer, seed, and slurry of prepared wood pulp shall have a built-in agitation system with an operating capacity sufficient to agitate, suspend, and homogeneously mix a slurry containing up to 40 pounds of fiber plus 70 pounds of fertilizer solids for each 100 gallons of water. The slurry distribution lines shall be large enough to prevent stoppage. The discharge line shall be equipped with a set of hydraulic spray nozzles that will provide even distribution of the slurry on the various slopes to be mulched. The slurry tank shall have a minimum capacity of 1,000 gallons and shall be mounted on a traveling unit, which may be either self-propelled or drawn by a separate unit that will place the slurry tank and spray nozzles near the areas to be mulched so as to provide uniform distribution without waste. (The Contracting Agency may authorize equipment with smaller tank capacity provided that the equipment has the necessary agitation system and sufficient pump capacity to spray the slurry in a uniform coat over the surface of the area to be mulched.)

4. INSPECTION: At least _____ days prior to commencement of mulching operations, the contractor shall notify the Contracting Agency of the sources from which the mulch materials are available and the quantities thereof and furnish representative samples of the proposed materials for approval.

5. PREPARATION OF GROUND SURFACE:

a. *General:* The areas to be treated shall be as shown. Areas left in a satisfactory state of tillage and not requiring further tillage and areas requiring special tillage or application of soil-improvement materials are so shown on the drawings. The equipment necessary for the proper preparation of the ground surface and for handling and placing all required materials shall be on hand, in good condition, and shall be approved before work is started. Before starting work the contractor shall demonstrate that the application of the required materials will be made at the rates specified.

b. *Clearing:* See I, Seeding Specification.

c. *Grading:* See I, Seeding Specification.
d. *Tillage:* See I, Seeding Specification.
e. *Cleanup:* See I, Seeding Specification.

6. Applying and Anchoring Mulch: Mulch shall be spread uniformly in a continuous blanket, using (——tons per acre) (——pounds per 1,000 square feet). Mulch shall be spread by hand or by a manure spreader, a modified grain combine with straw-spreader attachment, a blower-type mulch spreader, or a blower-type mulch spreader so equipped that straw or hay will be ejected simultaneously with asphalt adhesive, or other suitable equipment. Mulching shall be started at the windward side on relatively flat areas, or at the upper part of a steep slope, and continued uniformly until the area is covered. The mulch shall not be bunched. Immediately following spreading, the mulch shall be anchored to the soil by a coulter disk mulch anchor machine designed to force mulch into the soil surface, or other suitable equipment, or by applying an asphalt adhesive. The number of passes needed, not to exceed three, will be determined by the Contracting Agency. When asphalt adhesive is to be applied to a previously placed mulch or on slopes and embankments where farm tractors cannot be operated safely, application shall be by spraying at the rate of 10 to 13 gallons per 1,000 square feet. When applying straw and asphalt simultaneously, using equipment as specified previously, SS-1 emulsion with a penetration index between 150 and 200 shall be used, and shall be applied with the straw at the rate of ——gallons[5] of emulsion per ton of straw. If the emulsion is diluted at a ratio of 60 parts of emulsion to 40 parts of water, the diluted emulsion shall be applied at the rate of —— gallons per ton of straw. The adhesive-coated mulch shall be applied evenly over the surface so that the depth and thickness of the mulch will be approximately uniform throughout the treated area and sunlight will not be completely excluded from the ground surface. The adhesive-coated mulch shall be applied at the rate of 1½ tons per acre. Wood cellulose fiber mulch for use with the hydraulic application of seed and fertilizer shall be as specified.

7. Maintenance: The mulched areas shall be maintained until all work on the entire contract or designated portions thereof have been completed and accepted. Maintenance shall consist of providing protection against traffic by erecting the barricades shown and placing approved warning signs on the various areas immediately after mulching is complete and of repairing any damage. Mulch material that has been removed from the site by wind or from other causes shall be replaced and secured. Repair work that is required because of faulty operations or negligence on the part of the contractor shall be performed without cost to the Contracting Agency.

[5]Specifications may call for 150 gallons, although 75 gallons have been effective in some tests.

8. Method of Measurement: The unit of measurement for mulching shall be the acre. The acreage to be paid for shall be the acreage actually mulched as specified, computed to the nearest 1/10 of an acre.

9. Payment: Mulching will be paid for at the contract unit price per acre which price shall constitute full payment for tillage, furnishing all materials, delivery, and applying the mulch as specified.

V. Tillage

1. Scope: See I, Seeding Specification. Substitute tillage for seeding.

2. Preparations:

a. *General:* The areas to be tilled or requiring any special tillage are indicated on the drawings. The equipment necessary for the proper preparation of the ground surface shall be on hand, in good condition, and shall be approved by the Contracting Agency before work is started.

b. *Clearing:* See I, Seeding Specification.

c. *Grading:* See I, Seeding Specification.

3. Tillage:

a. *General:* See I, Seeding Specification.

b. *Tillage for Vegetative Mulch:* Tillage shall continue until the soil is loose and in a satisfactory condition to allow the mulching materials to be anchored in the surface soil. Where wind erosion is a problem, the tilled areas shall be left in a rough state to aid in the control of dust. Tillage shall be performed within 24 hours prior to mulching, unless otherwise approved by the Contracting Agency.

c. *Tillage for Dust Control:* The areas required to be tilled for dust control shall be loosened to a depth of_____inches by a tiller tool in such manner that clods will be left on the surface of the ground. In areas where the required penetration cannot be accomplished by a chisel point plow in one operation, a heavy scarifier[6] shall be used first. On areas which will not produce clods of sufficient size and quality to provide adequate dust control by the operation specified above, furrows shall be opened to a depth of 5 inches, on approximately 36-inch centers, by using an approved type of lister. Furrows shall be opened in the directions indicated on the drawings, unless otherwise directed. Equipment and operations other than as specified above may be used subject to the approval of the Contracting Agency.

4. Method of Measurement: The unit of measurement for tillage shall be the acre. The acreage to be paid for shall be the acreage actually tilled as specified, computed to the nearest 1/10 of an acre.

[6]Scarifier or ripper teeth attached to heavy industrial equipment.

5. PAYMENT: Tilling will be paid for at the contract unit price per acre which payment shall constitute full compensation for all work covered by this section of the specifications.

VI. Topsoil Planting

1. SCOPE: See I, Seeding Specification.

2. MATERIALS:

a. *Topsoil* with grass to be made available on the site shall be stripped from the areas so shown on the drawings. All other topsoil with grass necessary to complete the work shall be furnished from approved sources off the site. Topsoil with grass shall be natural, friable, ____ soil possessing characteristics of representative soils in the vicinity that produce heavy crops, grass, or other vegetation. The topsoil shall be obtained from naturally well-drained areas, shall be covered with a vigorous growth of grass of species adapted to the area to be planted and to topsoil planting, and shall be subject to approval. The grass shall have a healthy, thick root system that shall be retained in the topsoil when it is stripped and moved. The topsoil with grass shall be reasonably free from sub-soil, clay lumps, brush, objectionable weeds, and other litter and shall be free from stones, stumps, and other objects larger than 2 inches in diameter, tree roots, toxic substances, and any other material or substance that might be harmful to plant growth or a hindrance to grading, planting, and maintenance operations.

b. *Fertilizer:* See I, Seeding Specification.

c. *Lime:* See I, Seeding Specification.

d. *Soil for Repairs:* The soil for fills and topsoiling of areas to be repaired shall be at least of equal quality to that existing in areas adjacent to the area to be repaired and equivalent to that specified in subparagraph 2a above.

e. *Water:* See II, Sodding Specification.

3. INSPECTION AND TESTS:

a. *Topsoil with Grass:* At least ____ days prior to commencement of topsoil planting operations, the contractor shall notify the Contracting Agency of the sources from which topsoil-planting material is to be furnished. The topsoil will be inspected by the Contracting Agency to determine whether the selected soil and grass meet the requirements. At the time of inspection, the contractor may be required to take representative soil samples from several locations on the area under consideration, to be tested for physical properties, pH (or lime requirement), organic matter, and available phosphorus and potash. Samples shall be supplied by the contractor at the contractor's expense, and tests will be made under the supervision of the Contracting Agency without cost to the contractor. Sampling and testing will be in accordance with standard soil testing practices. Topsoil with grass shall be approved prior to use.

b. *Fertilizer and Lime:* See I, Seeding Specification.

4. Preparation of Subgrade:

a. *General:* The areas to be treated and their respective requirements for fertilizer, lime, or other treatment shall be as shown. Areas in a satisfactory state of tillage and not requiring further tillage and the areas requiring special tillage or applications of materials are so shown. Equipment necessary for the proper preparation of the ground surface and for handling and placing all required materials shall be on hand, in good condition, and shall be approved before the work is started. Before starting work the contractor shall demonstrate that the application of the materials required will be made at the specified rates.

b. *Clearing:* See I, Seeding Specification.

c. *Grading:* See I, Seeding Specification.

d. *Tillage:* See I, Seeding Specification.

5. Obtaining topsoil with Grass: After inspection and approval by the Contracting Agency of the source of topsoil with grass, and prior to stripping, excess vegetation, stones, or debris on the surface that might interfere with grading or later tillage operations shall be removed. The topsoil shall be stripped only when the soil is in a moist, friable condition or when it has been satisfactorily watered to the full stripping depth. The topsoil shall then be stripped to a depth of 6 to 8 inches and hauled to the planting site. The stripping operations shall be such that the interval between stripping and final compaction of the soil on the site will not exceed 24 hours. If the material is thoroughly wetted by rain, 24 hours will be allowed after the soil is again in satisfactory condition for handling.

6. Placing Topsoil with Grass: The topsoil with grass shall be uniformly distributed on designated areas and evenly spread to an average depth of____ inches, with a minimum depth of____ inches. Irregularities in the surface resulting from topsoil planting or other operations shall be corrected so as to prevent the formation of depressions where water will stand. Topsoil shall not be placed when the subgrade is frozen, excessively wet, extremely dry, or in a condition otherwise detrimental to planting or proper grading. Should observations immediately after a show of green indicate areas larger than 10 square feet without growing grass, then these areas will receive additional topsoil with grass.

7. Application of Fertilizer and Lime:

a. *General:* See I, Seeding Specification.

b. *Application of Fertilizer:* See I, Seeding Specification.

c. *Application of Lime:* See I, Seeding Specification.

8. Cleanup: See I, Seeding Specification.

9. Overseeding: Overseeding of topsoil planting is sometimes advisable to provide a temporary cover to supplement the planted species. If required, the seed species and rate per acre should be specified.

10. Compacting: Irregularities in the surface resulting from fertilizing, liming, or other operations shall be leveled before compacting. See III, Sprigging Specification.

11. Watering: Watering will be required if topsoil planting is authorized when the ground is excessively dry. Water shall be applied immediately after final compaction. Watering shall be sufficient to thoroughly wet the soil to the full depth of the applied topsoil with grass. Additional applications shall be made as directed for establishment. See II, Sodding Specification.

12. Protection: See I, Seeding Specification.

13. Establishment:

a. *General:* The contractor shall be responsible for the proper care of the topsoil-planted areas during the period when the grass is becoming established. This period shall extend for _____months after the completion of the topsoil planting on the entire project, unless the desired cover is established in a shorter period of time and the shortening of the period of the contractor's responsibility for acceptably established areas is authorized.

b. *Mowing:* The topsoil-planted areas shall be mowed with approved mowing equipment to a height of _____inches whenever the average height of grass becomes _____ inches. If weeds or other undesirable vegetation threatens to smother the planted species, such vegetation shall be mowed or, in the case of rank growth, shall be uprooted and removed from the area.

c. *Refertilizing:* See I, Seeding Specification.

14. Repair: If at any time before completion and acceptance of the entire work covered by this contract, any portion of the surface becomes gullied or otherwise damaged after any part of the area has been topsoil-planted, the affected portion shall be repaired as directed, to reestablish the condition and grade of the soil prior to the damage.

15. Methods of Measurement:

a. *Topsoil with Grass:* The unit of measurement for topsoil with grass shall be the cubic yard. The yardage to be paid for shall be the number of cubic yards placed as specified. (Measurement will be made in the vehicle just prior to dumping on the site. Yardage may be computed on the basis of the specified average depth of topsoil in final position.)

b. *Fertilizer and Lime:* See I, Seeding Specification.

c. *Water:* See II, Sodding Specification.

d. *Mowing, Refertilizing, and Repair:* The unit of measurement for mowing, refertilizing, or repair shall be the acre. The acreage to be paid for shall be the acreage actually mowed, refertilized, or repaired, as specified, computed to the nearest 1/10 acre.

16. Payment:

a. *Topsoil Planting and Repairs* will be paid for at the respective contract unit price per cubic yard for topsoil with grass obtained on the site and placed, furnished and placed, or both, as specified, which payment shall constitute full compensation for all work including tilling and compacting covered by this section of the specifications, except as specified below.

b. *Fertilizer and Lime:* See I, Seeding Specification.

c. *Water:* See II, Sodding Specification.

VII. Topsoiling

1. Scope: See I, Seeding Specification. Substitute topsoil for seeding.

2. Material: The topsoil to be made available on the site, either in stockpiles or in areas from which it is to be stripped, is as designated on the drawings. All other topsoil necessary to complete the work shall be furnished by the contractor from approved sources off the site. Topsoil to be provided by the contractor shall be natural, friable____soil with a minimum organic matter content of____% possessing the characteristics of representative soils in the vicinity that produce heavy crops, grass, or other vegetation and shall be obtained from naturally well-drained areas. The topsoil shall be reasonably free from subsoil, clay lumps, brush, objectionable weeds, and other litter and shall be free from stones, stumps, and other objects larger than 2 inches in diameter, roots, toxic substances, and any other material or substance that might be harmful to plant growth or a hindrance to grading, planting, and maintenance operations.

3. Inspection and Tests: At least_____days prior to commencement of topsoiling operations the contractor shall notify the Contracting Agency of the sources from which topsoil is to be furnished. The topsoil proposed for use will be inspected by the Contracting Agency to determine whether the selected soil or soils meet the requirements. At the time of inspection, the Contracting Agency may require representative soil samples to be taken from several locations on the area(s) under consideration, to be tested for physical properties, pH (or lime requirement), organic matter, and available phosphorus and potash. Samples shall be supplied by the contractor at no additional cost to the Government, and tests will be made under the supervision of the Contracting Agency without cost to the contractor. Sampling and testing will be in accordance with standard practices of soil testing. Topsoil shall be approved prior to use. The depth to which the topsoil is to be stripped shall be as approved and samples drawn from the area shall be taken to the full stripping depth approved.

4. Preparation of Subgrade:

a. *General:* The areas to be topsoiled and areas requiring other treatments are as shown on the drawings. Equipment necessary for the proper preparation of the ground surface and for handling and placing all materials required shall be on hand, in good condition, and shall be approved before the work is started.

b. *Clearing:* See I, Seeding Specification.

c. *Grading:* See I, Seeding Specification.

d. *Tillage:* See I, Seeding Specification. (NOTE: Tillage is required prior to placing topsoil to obtain a more satisfactory bond between the two layers. Tillage shall be across the slope. In certain instances tillage may be omitted on slopes steeper than 1½ to 1 where tillage equipment cannot be operated.)

5. Obtaining Topsoil: After inspection and approval of the source(s) of topsoil, and prior to stripping, rank vegetation, stones, or debris on the surface that might interfere with grading or later tillage operations shall be removed. Sod or other cover that cannot be disked or otherwise incorporated into the topsoil before or after delivery, in such manner that it can be spread properly, shall be removed. Where topsoil is to be made available on areas to be graded, the topsoil shall be removed to ____ depth from the designated areas prior to the beginning of grading operations. The topsoil removed from areas to be stripped or areas to be graded shall be kept separate from other excavated material. Where topsoil is to be made available on areas to be graded, the topsoil shall be removed to the required depth from any designated area and stockpiled[7] as a part of the grading operation.

6. Placing Topsoil: The topsoil shall be uniformly distributed on the designated areas and evenly spread to an average thickness of ____ inches, with a minimum thickness of ____ inches. The spreading shall be performed in such a manner that planting can proceed with little additional soil preparation or tillage. Irregularities in the surface resulting from topsoiling or other operations shall be corrected so as to prevent the formation of depressions where water will stand. Topsoil shall not be placed when the subgrade is frozen, excessively wet, extremely dry, or in a condition otherwise detrimental to the proposed planting or to proper grading.

7. Cleanup: See I, Seeding Specification.

8. Repair: Where any portion of the surface becomes gullied or otherwise damaged, the affected area shall be repaired to establish the condition and grade prior to topsoiling, and topsoil added as specified in paragraph covering Placing Topsoil.

9. Method of Measurement: The unit of measurement for topsoil shall be the cubic yard. The yardage to be paid for shall be the number of cubic yards placed as specified. (Measurement will be made in the

---

[7]Stockpiling may be held to a minimum by synchronizing the topsoiling with the grading operation so that the soil will not have to be moved more than one time. This requires cooperative planning by the agronomist and engineer.

vehicle just prior to dumping on the site or will be computed on the basis of the specified average depth of topsoil in place.)

10. PAYMENT: Topsoiling will be paid for at the respective contract unit price per cubic yard for topsoil obtained on the site and placed, furnished and placed, or both, as specified, which payment shall constitute full compensation for all work covered by this section of the specifications.

VIII. Fertilization of Established Turfgrass Areas

1. SCOPE: For furnishing all labor, equipment, and materials to fertilize the turf areas designated as follows: _____; in accordance with the following specifications and subject to the terms and conditions of the contract.

a. To furnish and apply approximately___tons of commercial mixed granular or pelletized fertilizer on the turf areas of____________

b. To furnish and spread___tons of fertilizer in excess of the amount above and in excess of amounts under increase quantity clause as specified.

2. MATERIALS:

a. *Fertilizer* shall be commercial mixed granules or pelleted fertilizer, analysis_____, of which not less than (25%) of the total nitrogen shall be slowly soluble. It shall be uniform in condition, free flowing and suitable for application as specified in subparagraph "b" below.

b. *Sampling and Testing:* A representative sample will be taken from each truck and mixed for each day's operation, in order to obtain a composite sample. If bulk fertilizer is delivered, sampling will be with a probe device. The fertilizer shall be subject to tests by representatives of state, government, or other approved testing laboratories and at the expense of the Contracting Agency.

3. METHOD OF APPLICATIONS: Fertilizer shall be distributed over the designated areas by an approved tractor-drawn broadcast spreader or other approved equipment and at the rate of___pounds per acre. On large turf areas a truck broadcast spreader may be used depending on soil moisture content. The fertilizer shall not be applied when grass is wet or during windy or adverse weather conditions. The contractor will stop work in inclement weather on request by the Contracting Agency and resume work only when authorized to proceed. All damage caused by the equipment cutting into lawn areas shall be repaired by the contractor to its original condition, and at no cost to the Contracting Agency.

4. TIME FOR COMPLETION: Work shall be scheduled for accomplishment between____to____.

5. INCREASE OR DECREASE IN CONTRACT QUANTITY: The quantity cov-

ered by this contract is approximate only and the Contracting Agency reserves the right to increase or decrease the quantity not exceeding _%.

6. IMPORTANT: Three (3) days' notice prior to commencing work will be required in order to arrange a mutually satisfactory time and to enable the Contracting Agency to arrange for an inspector to be at the job site.

7. INSPECTION OF EQUIPMENT: Inspection of equipment and a program schedule will be made by the Contracting Agency prior to awarding the contract.

8. PENALTY CLAUSE: A penalty as outlined in the uniform state fertilizer bill adopted by the Association of American Fertilizer Control Officers, Inc. will be included in each contract for procurement of fertilizer or for fertilizer furnished by the contractor. (NOTE: The specification writer should obtain the applicable portion of the bill and quote the exact wording in the specification. The penalty would be imposed to insure that fertilizer meets the percentages of plant food specified.)

9. METHOD OF MEASUREMENT: Measurement will be by the ton or portion thereof and certified weight tickets of each load will be delivered to the Contracting Agency's inspector at the job site.

10. PAYMENT: Payment will be by the ton for each ton or portion thereof spread on the turfgrass areas as specified.

An example of a Bid Schedule, to accompany the specifications in the invitation for bids, is as follows:

Item no.	Description	Estimated quantity	Unit	Unit price	Estimated amount
1	Tillage	100	Acre		
2	Liming	200	Ton		
3	Fertilizer	40	Ton		
4	Seeding	100	Acre		
5	Mulching	10	Acre		
6	Solid sodding	200	Sq yd		
7	Strip sodding	100	Sq yd		
8	Soil for repair	100	Cu yd		
9	Water	200	(1,000 gal)		
				Total bid	

Contingencies often occur that are not foreseen during the preparation of specifications. An example of this is an overrun in acreage due to additional grading beyond the limits shown on the grading plan. In order to include this acreage in the turfing contract a change is necessary. If this is discovered prior to opening the bids an addendum to the contract can be issued. If the change is substantial an increase in the advertising period may be necessary to give prospective bidders time to make additional on-site inspections before submitting their bids.

Another type of modification is sometimes used after opening bids and prior to awarding the contract. This procedure requires negotiation with the low bidder.

Change orders are utilized when a change is necessary after awarding the contract. This requires negotiation with the contractor.

When the contract is set up on a unit price basis for each item of work, it may not be necessary to negotiate another price for the specified item to be changed. Unless a unit price has been established in the original bid, negotiation with the contractor may be difficult. Frequently the necessity for change orders results in excessive prices paid for the additional work. All change orders should be closely examined to be sure extension of the contract will not exceed available funds. If funds are lacking it may be necessary to omit part of the work and have an incomplete job.

Every effort should be made during the preparation of specifications to foresee all contingencies so that modification or change orders are not required.

Acknowledgement

The authors wish to express gratitude for the use of material from the Corps of Engineers, Department of the Army, and the National Park Service, Department of the Interior.

References

Anonymous. 1968. Standard specifications for construction of airports, U. S. Department of Commerce, Civil Aeronautics Administration, Washington, D. C.

Anonymous. American Society for Testing Materials.

Anonymous. 1966 and 1967. Changes, Official Methods of Analysis Association of Official Analytical Chemists.

Musser, H. Burton. 1962. Turf management. McGraw-Hill Book Company, Inc., New York, N. Y.

28 Equipment For Turf

Fred V. Grau
Grassyln, Inc.
College Park, Maryland

I. Introduction

Equipment is an essential part of the growing turfgrass industry and has been a significant factor in helping to accelerate its growth and expansion. Hand labor has declined virtually to the vanishing point with the perfection of specialized power equipment. The last two decades have seen greater developments in turf machinery than during all previous years.

Many of the advances in equipment for turf originated with golf course superintendents who sought mechanization to combat rising costs and an uncertain labor market. There was little or no official recognition of the turfgrass industry and its needs prior to 1940. Government and universities considered turf as something that was not entitled to support out of tax funds, primarily because turf and golf were considered as synonymous. During World War II turf work was reduced virtually to zero. Starting in 1945 there was a resurgence of interest in turf and in better machinery. This was the starting point in the grand period of growth. It may be coincidental but we record here that, in 1946, Turf was lifted from obscurity and elevated to its deserved position as a recognized part of agriculture. The catalyst undoubtedly was the organization of a Turf Division within the American Society of Agronomy. With this official recognition by a leading scientific society, land grant colleges logically could justify the allocation of funds and personnel to this expanding industry.

In 1946 the aerifier was built and tested for the rapid cultivation of soil in turfgrass areas. This machine is considered by some to be the greatest single advance in turf maintenance equipment since the power mower. It certainly served to stimulate machinery innovations and to enhance the development of the entire industry.

Good turf begins with well-conceived designs and sound specifications which, when properly implemented, produce desired perfection in initial establishment. Each step in establishment, from ground breaking through seedbed preparation and planting to first mowing, involves equipment which demands thoughtful intelligent operation. With the start of mowing a different set of implements is employed to build and maintain turf as near perfection as possible.

This review of equipment for turf emphasizes wide variety and principles. No claims are made for completeness. It should be obvious that, soon after publication, this chapter will be rendered incomplete by the building of yet another new machine. This is progress.

II. Seedbed Preparation

The *plow* long has been a basic tool for breaking soils to loosen them preparatory to further refinement to reduce clods and produce good tilth (Fig. 1).

Figure 1. Seedbed preparation in one pass is the object of this "train" of implements. Plows are followed in turn by a clod crusher-roller and drill with press wheels. Large turfgrass areas often are prepared in this way; land levelers also are employed, especially for sod farms. Other combinations are possible. (Courtesy: John Deere, Moline, Illinois.)

The *disc* is another standard tool used immediately following the plow to partially smooth the surface, to eliminate air pockets, to firm the soil, and to bring clods, lumps, roots, and debris to the surface for removal or further treatment.

A *harrow* usually follows the disc to ready the seedbed. *Springtooth* harrows dig deeply (adjustable) with heavy spring steel teeth to bring rocks and debris to the surface and to blend and mix. The *spiketooth* harrow is much more gentle and acts more as a smoothing tool. The *meeker* harrow (cut harrow) has circular knives or coulters which are spaced 4 to 6 inches apart on a rigid shaft some 4 to 5 feet long. A series of 4 to 6 shafts, each with cutting blades out of register with one fore or aft, are held in a heavy frame. Thus the knives cut and pulverize clods while the frame drags and smooths.

A *float* may be used as part of the seedbed process. In simple form it is a "raft" of several planks, edge lapped on edge, held together with bolts and strap or angle iron. On slopes, erosion may be accelerated by "floating."

Clods may be crushed with a *cultipacker* which, essentially, is a corrugated roller. Individual sections of the "roller" are 4 to 5 inches wide, 15 to 18 inches high, and they rotate independently on a rigid shaft 6 to 10 feet long. It is best to operate this machine on the contour to reduce rill and gully erosion.

Smooth *rollers* may be used to firm seedbeds, but, in general, they are not recommended for use prior to seeding. The smooth surface which they create may encourage puddling and hasten sheet erosion. They have a place in pushing small rocks into the soil so that they will not interfere with maintenance (Fig. 2).

Figure 2. Finished seedbed is prepared with this grader-seeder. A blade smoothes and levels, clods are crushed, stones are pressed flush, seed is metered, then partially covered by roller with holes. (Courtesy: ADT Mfg. Division, UNITEC Industries, Inc.)

Figure 3. The power rake long has been a valuable tool for windrowing stones and trash, for leveling and finishing seedbeds. (Courtesy: York Modern Corporation)

Stonepickers can save many man-hours of back-breaking work before seeding and can greatly reduce later damage to cultivating machines and to mowers.

The *york rake* is an incomparable finishing tool for grading, for windrowing stones and debris, and for creating a slightly roughened surface ready for seeding (Fig. 3).

Tillers which can develop a reasonable seedbed and can blend soil amendments in one or two passes include the *rototiller,* the *Howard rotavator,* and the *Seaman tiller* (Fig. 4). They virtually eliminate the need for the plow, the disc, and the harrows. Stones must be picked, of course. Tillers sometimes leave the soil so loose that firming with a roller or cultipacker is advisable. When tillers are operated at excessive r.p.m.'s, they tend to float the "fines" to the top which induces severe puddling and crusting.

Figure 4. The rotary tiller combines the effects of plow, disc, harrow, and leveler in one pass. Power lift permits operation in close quarters. Trash tends to be buried. Surface-applied lime, fertilizer, and other soil amendments are thoroughly incorporated. (Courtesy: Howard Rotavator)

Special "once-over" machines have been developed which, by a combination of devices, loosen the soil, push stones aside, smooth, apply lime and nutrients, incorporate them, sow the seed, and firm it into the soil as a final operation. A certain amount of "pre-preparation" renders their operation more effective.

III. Preparation of Soil Mixtures

Certain limited turfgrass areas are designed so that turf is grown on a mixture of materials that affects firmness, porosity, internal drainage, infiltration rates, water-holding capacity, and other characteristics. It is imperative that added materials be thoroughly and uniformly mixed to create an homogeneous blend. Poor mixing may leave "pockets" or "lenses" of materials which greatly affect movement of moisture, nutrients, air, and roots.

On-site mixing, for many years the only practical method, is being discarded as crude, inefficient, only partially effective, and too expensive. In too many cases "pockets" or "lenses" of unmixed materials remain undetected only to cause trouble later. On-site mixing can be accomplished with conventional tillage tools. Tillers are more effective than plows, discs, and harrows and still are used to some extent.

Off-site mixing is popular because it is so very effective; pockets are eliminated and uniformity is assured.

The *rotary screen* is the old time-honored mixing device that is still popular at some places especially for mixing blends of topdressing.

The *power screen* is a vibrator based on the principle of the *scalper,* a seed processing machine (Fig. 5). In essence it lies nearly flat or gently sloping. As the screen is shaken vigorously (power) the finer materials fall through and may be carried to a pile, to a truck, or to a bin by means of a *conveyor.* The rough debris is discarded.

Grinders or *shredders* are used widely for preparing, mixing, and blending (Fig. 6). Some operate with rotating metal bars or hammers which break apart any large clods or lumps. Others employ a rapidly

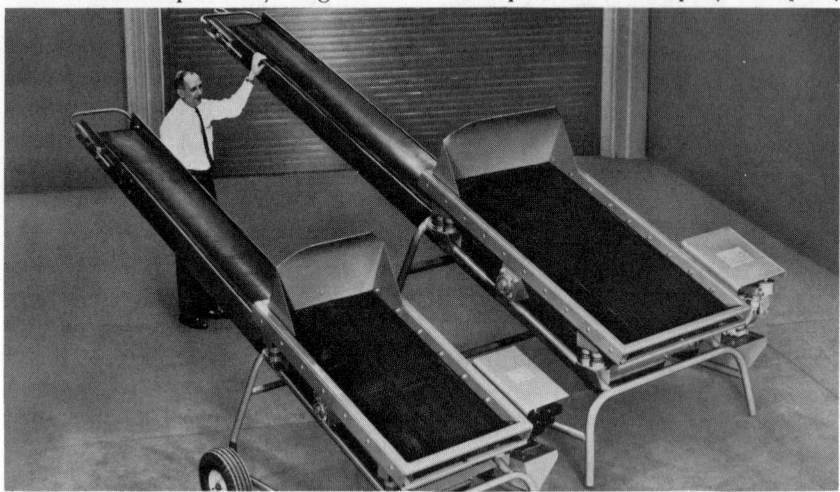

Figure 5. Two sizes of power screens which size material and load it into a convenient truck or bin. Ideally, the shredder is positioned to deliver material directly to the power screen, making it a continuous operation. (Courtesy: Royer Foundry and Machine Co.)

Figure 6. Soil shredders perform valuable services in mixing and blending, screening, and in refining coarse soil and soil amendments. The loading attachment saves handling and provides additional mixing. (Courtesy: Lindig Mfg. Co., Inc.)

moving belt which is studded with hard metal teeth which effectively shred all materials and discards stones and debris. These machines may be fed by hand or with *power scoops* and *front end loaders.* Often they are arranged in series with a power screen and a conveyor, thus automating the process to a high degree.

Clam shells are used to dip proportionate quantities of materials from different piles and to create a new pile of the final mix, still imperfectly blended. The new pile may be homogenized by repiling with the clam shell, by cutting into the edge of the pile with a *motorgrader,* or by employing a power scoop to complete the mixing. Some operators prefer to use the motor grader to create long windrows of the mixture which is homogenized by rolling the windrows over and over.

A series of *bins* has been used wherein each bin contains one ingredient (soil, sand, humus, etc.) each of which flows through chutes at a predetermined rate. All materials meet on a wide conveyor belt which elevates the blend to a pile or into trucks. Conceivably at this point the mixture is homogenous and can be trucked to the ultimate site where it is to be placed. The various bins are recharged by a power scoop or a clam shell.

Cement mixers have been used to good advantage but this is a "batch" affair which is not efficient.

IV. Distribution of Materials

Uniformly beautiful turf depends largely upon an even distribution of added materials such as lime, fertilizer and chemicals, both in the seedbed and for maintenance.

Spreaders come in many shapes and sizes and employ widely varying methods of scattering the materials.

The *hopper-type lime spreader* is well known and, for the most part, dependable. Adjustments tend to be crude and the delivery rate may be affected by speed and by slope. More refined hopper-type spreaders have been developed which can deliver materials in a range from 10 to 1,000 pounds to the acre (Fig. 7).

Figure 7. Accuracy of materials distribution is a cardinal precept in turfgrass management. There are many types of ground- and power-driven spreaders. Each has its champion; each must be understood to be operated properly. (Courtesy: Gandy Company)

Some spreaders employ the *spinning disk* principle (Cyclone, Lely, some commercial rigs) wherein the material falls at or near the center of the rotating disk (with vanes) and is thrown by centrifugal force a certain distance, governed by the speed and shape of the disk and the specific gravity and wind resistance of the particles of material (Fig. 8). Granulated (pelleted) materials are preferred for use in centrifugal spreaders. Powders, obviously, work poorly. A favorable factor is *speed* of application. Width of distribution may be as great as 30 feet compared with the 8- to 10-foot coverage of conventional spreaders. It is claimed also that streaking due to skips or overlaps is minimized. There is controversy on this point.

Figure 8. Spinner seed sowers come in hand- and power-driven models. They have been popular for years on farms and turfgrass areas for distributing seeds, fertilizers, and other materials. Some models are hand-pushed, ground-driven. (Courtesy: The Cyclone Seeder Co., Inc.)

Topdressing spreaders (Fig. 9) have been built that lay down a uniform blanket of a soil mixture through a system of brushes, gates, and a moving belt which forms the bottom of the hopper. Others rely on the central rotor which allows a predetermined quantity of material to fall or to be forced through holes at the bottom.

Airplanes and *helicopters* are used on occasion to spread fertilizer and herbicides on large turfgrass areas. This requires a ground crew of spotters and flag men to guide the pilot. Application cannot be precise, but this method succeeds when soils are too soft to support ground-operated equipment.

V. Vegetative Planters

Many grasses must be planted vegetatively (sprigs, stolons, rhizomes, plugs, sod) in order to maintain genetic integrity since seeds from these grasses result in heterogeneity and loss of quality.

Figure 9. Power-driven topdressing spreaders save time and labor, distribute materials more uniformly than the old-time shovel and rubbing board. (Courtesy: Ryan Equipment Company)

Figure 10. Sprigging machines facilitate vegetative plantings. The development of superior clonal material (no seed available) has created an expanding need for more rapid inexpensive vegetative establishment. (Courtesy: Wichita Equipment Co.)

There are several mechanical planters on the market that insert vegetative material into slits in the soil that have been opened by a coulter and a shoe or knife. A press wheel following firms the soil to insure establishment (Fig. 10). Some planters are homemade.

Hydraulic mulchers and seeders have been modified to handle sprigs and stolons mixed with wood cellulose pulp and water (Fig. 11). The slurry is sprayed to cover the prepared surface. Fertilizer and lime may

Figure 11. This hydraulic seeder is planting vegetatively a water slurry of shredded living grass (roots, rhizomes, stolons, sprigs) combined with wood cellulose pulp and fertilizer. The second view shows a handful of the material as it is applied to the prepared seedbed. (Courtesy: Bowie Machine Works, Inc.)

be added to the slurry. Postplanting care is extremely important. At no time may the planted material be allowed to become dry. Light rolling may be needed to restore contact with the soil.

Plug-setter machines have been developed, but they have not become a major factor in the economy. In general, sod plugs are set by hand. Customer impatience has caused a decline in sod plugs.

VI. Seeding Equipment

One of the earliest seeding tools was the wheelbarrow seeder. A long box with holes in the bottom was mounted on a frame which had a large wheel in front. As the wheel turned, pushed by manpower, a rope in the bottom of the box moved to and fro propelling the seeds through the holes.

The cyclone-type seeder in its simplest form was carried by a man who turned a crank. A canvas hopper held the seeds which dropped through an adjustable opening onto a spinning rotor driven by the crank. Later developments provide the same rotor, now motor driven or ground driven, carried by a tractor (Fig. 8). Drawbacks of spinner distribution include uneven distribution on windy days and lack of positive imbedding or covering of seed.

Another early machine was the *Darmil* seeder. It was not over 18 or 24 inches wide, with a sturdy box mounted over a series of small, sharp, slightly-curved discs at about 3-inch spacings. One man pulled the machine, another man pushed it. Seeds in the box were propelled through openings and dropped into slits cut in the soil or the turf. The Darmil seeder is a museum piece today.

The Darmil principle is embodied in large drills that are tractor pulled and which drop seeds into slits made by sharp-curved discs. They are effective seeders which are capable of planting seeds at precise depths. The *Brillion* seeder carries a precision device to drop seeds between cultipacker-type rollers so that seeds are firmed and covered at the right depth (Fig. 12). The *Gill* seeder is based on a spiking principle wherein seeds are metered precisely so that they fall into shallow pockets punched by spikes. This machine is favored for overseeding established areas.

Figure 12. This precision seeder has fluted rollers that crush clods and firm seeds into shallow depressions for quicker germination and protection from erosion. (Courtesy: Brillion Iron Works, Inc.)

Hydraulic seeders had their prototype in a crude device conceived and designed by C. N. Keyser and F. V. Grau starting in 1938 for use on the original section of the Pennsylvania Turnpike between Carlisle and Irwin[1]. The machine embodied the *Gunite* principle. A mixture of fertilizer, limestone, organic matter, seed, and soil (designated floss) was batch-fed into the Gunite machine[2]. At point of discharge at the end of a hose the dry mixture was engaged with a spray of water so that the highway slope was "plastered" with a thin slurry. It worked!

There are at least five hydraulic seeders (Bowie, Finn, Reinco, Toro, and Spray Baby) that mix the materials in a tank as a water suspension

[1] Records in files of C. N. Keyser, Plymouth Meeting, Pennsylvania (deceased) and Pennsylvania Turnpike Commission.

[2] Grau, Fred V. 1942. "Floss," a suggested term to designate a mixture of materials. J. Amer. Soc. Agron. 34:388.

(slurry) which is pumped through a nozzle and sprayed on the seedbed (see Fig. 3, Chapter 25). The usual practice is to cover the seeded area at once with some type of mulch (see Fig. 4, Chapter 25). Straw mulch is effective but straw is expensive, hard to obtain, and often carries weeds. Wood cellulose pulp has become popular, and it has been recommended as an ingredient in the tank with lime fertilizer and seed for a "one-shot" application. The trend is to apply the wood cellulose pulp as a mulch in a second application immediately following the seeding. In this way the seeds are in close contact with the soil, covered by the protective mulch. In the "one-shot" process many seeds are held away from the soil in the pulp matrix where they may sprout. If the pulp becomes dry and separates from the soil the germinating seeds will die since the roots cannot make contact with soil. Long-chain water-miscible polymers, such as Soil-Seal, can be added to wood cellulose to make the "one-shot" process more reliable.

VII. Mowers

First, there were the sickle and the scythe—and these time-honored implements still are with us, although the skills necessary to their effective use are disappearing.

The sicklebar mower made a natural transition from the hayfield to the playing fields of turf, but, before long, it was superseded by the reel mower with a scissor-like cut. Users of reel mowers, hand-pushed or horse-drawn, continually were plagued by tall seed stalks of weeds (buckhorn, broadleaf plantain, dandelion stems) which would be pushed down flat by the mower, only to spring up again when the machine had passed by. A number of devices were designed to improve the removal of seed stalks with reel mowers, but all have passed out of existence with the advent of effective chemical control.

Reel mowers have become as varied as the turf they are designed to cut. The trend has been toward more blades per reel so as to provide a smooth cut without visible "chatter" marks (Fig. 13). Similarly, reel speeds have been increased so that there are more cuts per unit for each unit of forward travel. Some putting green mowers may have 12 blades per reel (Fig. 14). The trend is toward 3-gang mowers, generally called "triplex greensmowers," adaptable to tees, aprons, and collars.

The rotary mower has been around for little more than 40 years, but it has made tremendous inroads on the reel-mower market. Homeowners, in particular, are attracted to it because it will trim weeds and grass that have grown too tall and thick for a reel mower to handle. It gives the homeowner more leisure time with full knowledge that whenever he got around to his lawn his rotary mower would cut it, even though he might have to rake and remove the hay crop.

The vertical mower is a recent development within the past 20 years. The forerunners were modified cultipackers with wheel units removed and replaced by straight, sharp-rolling coulters or cotton gin saws, evenly spaced about 4 inches apart with the rear unit out of register with the front section. All flat-lying stems of grasses and weeds were severed as the machine was drawn over the area. Essentially the same

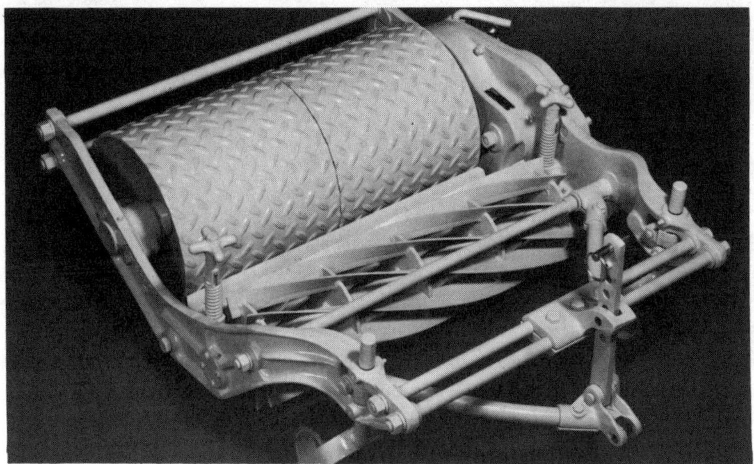

Figure 13. This roller-driven turfgrass mower (30") illustrates several features: (top right)—lever to throw reel out of gear; (center, left and right)—two knobs to adjust bedknife to reel; (front, left and right)—adjustments for caster wheels which regulate height of cut; (front, center)—quick adjustment to raise unit for transport. The multi-blade reel indicates a high frequency of cut suitable for close-cut fairways and estate lawns. (Courtesy: Roseman Mower Corporation)

Figure 14. Putting green mowers set for a 3/16" cut are precision instruments that demand careful intelligent tuning and operation. There is no margin of error if putting surfaces are to be smooth and true. (Courtesy: Jacobsen Manufacturing Co.)

principle was embodied in vertical mowers which have sharp teeth or tines fixed on a horizontal revolving shaft, engine driven. Adjustments permit the teeth to slice into the stems of grasses and weeds at the desired depth. By repeated passes in different directions it is possible to remove most or all of the thatch, or even the turf, and still retain a usable playing surface (Fig. 15).

Figure 15. Aerating and thatch removal may be conducted simultaneously for the good of the turf. (Courtesy: Ryan Equipment Company)

Other mowers which embody the vertical mower principle include the "hammer-knife," and the "flail." Both have free-swinging cutting units which rotate at high speed on a fixed shaft and literally shred the vegetation. Another mower uses free-swinging chains that pulverize almost anything with which they come in contact.

Mowers may be hand-pushed, driven by gasoline engines, by power take-off units, or by electric motors. About 10 years ago there was a flurry of activity in the battery-powered electric mower market, particularly for putting greens using reel mowers. Most of the electric mowers one sees today are rotary mowers on home lawns operated from house current through long power cords.

Mowers may be classed as to the area of their greatest use. Fairway mowers for golf courses have been standardized as 30-inch units (Fig. 16). They may be pulled or pushed by tractors and the number of units may range from 3 to 11. Lift mechanisms are hydraulically operated for the most part (Fig. 17).

Rough mowers (reel type) also are 30-inch units but they do not mow as closely and they have 3 to 5 blades in the reel compared to 7 or 9 in

Figure 16. This 7-gang fairway mower shows how hydraulic controls facilitate exacting work close to bunkers and trees. Two 30-inch units cut grass ahead of the rear tractor drive wheels. In transport position all units are raised to permit passage through openings just wide enough for the tractor. (Courtesy: Toro Manufacturing Corporation)

Figure 17. Mowing in tight quarters among valuable trees with units cutting grass ahead of tractor wheels. (Courtesy: Jacobsen Manufacturing Co.)

Figure 18. Rugged rotary mowers speed the work of maintaining rough areas. Tall seed stalks of weeds and grasses that slip by reel mowers are "consumed" by the horizontal whirling blades. Cutting height can be regulated by adjusting the front caster wheels. (Courtesy: Toro Manufacturing Corporation)

the fairway units. Rotary, flail, or hammerknife mowers are popular for mowing rough areas, parks, and occasional-use areas such as airports (Fig. 18).

VIII. Mower Safety

Any mower is potentially dangerous. Rotary mowers, especially, become engines of destruction unless safeguards are observed. Rapidly rotating blades, unguarded, may pick up stones, debris, or pieces of wire and hurl them with lethal force. Many toes have been amputated unintentionally during careless operation of rotary mowers.

Sharpening. Rotary mower blades cut best when they are razor sharp. A carborundum file, used on the cutting edge after each mowing, will keep the blade in top condition. If the blade is treated in place, be sure to disconnect spark plug or electric power cord. Some blades may be removed easily for sharpening on a bench-grinding wheel.

Reel mowers deserve to be touched up after each use. Only the bedknife should be sharpened and this can be done on home units with a carborundum file. The reel does not need to be sharp; its only function is to bring the grass blades into contact with the sharp-leading edge of the bedknife. Professional units may be "lapped in" on jigs where the reel is run backwards in a bath of carborundum powder in oil or water.

Adjustments. Height of cut is determined by placing the mower on a smooth, flat surface and measuring the distance from the surface to the cutting edge of the blade. Industrial and institutional mowers are adjusted by means of gauges with micrometer adjustments.

Keenness of cut depends upon sharpness and upon the adjustment of the reel in relation to the bedknife. A common device is to use a single thickness of newspaper in a strip placed in the position of a grass blade to be cut. By rotating the reel one can determine proper adjustment, neither too tight nor too loose, just barely tight enough to cut the paper cleanly.

IX. Aerating (cultivation) Tools

Spading (potato) *forks* and dung forks permitted the early turf managers to loosen compacted soils. The solid tines would be inserted deeply, then rocked back and forth to crack the crust and to admit air and water.

Spikers, hand and power driven, became more prominent as turfgrass management advanced. They are in use today more than ever but only as a gentle, remedial tool which does little more than penetrate the surface crust and thatch (Fig. 19). At one time, in the mid-30's, ma-

Figure 19. Spikers have been used in one form or another almost since golf began. Power-driven spikers are useful for overseeding and for gentle aerating in hot weather. Their use enhances water infiltration. Play is not affected. (Courtesy: Power Spiker Manufacturing Co.)

chines were built that employed large solid spikes designed to penetrate several inches deep, forced in by the sheer weight of the machine. These clumsy tools tended to aggravate compaction and never got beyond the prototype stage.

The first effective machine for cultivating turf soils was built by West Point Products Corporation in 1946. It was called the FG Aerifier. The effective principle was a "spoon-type" of tine that penetrated the soil, scooped out a "core" of soil and left a loosened "pocket" to receive water and surface-applied materials and to improve gaseous exchange (Fig. 20).

Figure 20. Large-area turfgrass cultivating units such as this firmly have established the term "aerifying" as a household word everywhere. Soil is loosened with minimum disturbance to playing surfaces. Various models are in regular use on nearly every type of turfgrass area. For athletic fields and golf course fairways soil cultivation is a "must." (Courtesy: West Point Products Corporation)

The success of the aerifier led quickly and surely to competitive machines and to other designs of aerating principles, among them the hollow tine (Fig. 21), the slicer, and other modifications. Probably no other development in turfgrass equipment has had the impact of the first effective soil cultivating tool.

After using an aerating tool the turfgrass surface is littered with soil cores which must be treated before the playing area can be used. It has become almost standard practice to follow with a vertical mower to pulverize the debris, this followed in turn by a steel doormat drag which smoothes the surface and redistributes the soil (Fig. 22). By then mowing the area, using grass catchers, even the finest putting surfaces are ready for immediate play. Experiments proved the value of the treatments in improved water infiltration and penetration of surface-applied nutrients.

X. Renovating Tools

Many turfgrass areas deteriorate with time due to a variety of causes including diseases, insects, low fertility, poor initial choice of grass, and

Figure 21. Coring machines (hollow-tine, straight in-straight out) effectively aerate soils without roughening the playing surface of putting greens. Water penetration greatly is enhanced. Here the soil cores are being windrowed for removal. If soil mixture is favorable, the cores may be allowed to dry, then pulverized with a vertical mower for redistribution as topdressing. (Courtesy: Ryan Equipment Company)

Figure 22. Power-driven steel drag mats have revolutionized the back-breaking job or rubbing in topdressing. (Courtesy: West Point Products Corporation)

thatch buildup. At some point a decision may be made to renovate. This entails thatch removal, soil cultivation, removal of debris, perhaps drainage of some kind, restoration of nutrients, and replanting (seed or vegetative) to an improved grass. It is axiomatic that if the causes for failure are not diagnosed and corrected renovation will be a periodic chore (Fig. 15).

Large tractor-drawn P.T.O. groomers and thatching machines have been perfected which remove surface thatch and till the soil to a shallow depth in one operation (Fig. 23). Some are equipped with revolving brushes which sweep up the debris and throw it into a hopper for disposal (Fig. 24). Some use the vacuum (suction) principle to lift the useless material into a hopper.

Flame-throwers have been used in a limited way to burn excess dead material so as to permit seed to come into contact with the soil. The inconvenience to those who then use the turf (black soot, dirty equipment, delay until fresh turf is playable) most likely will retard acceptance of this approach.

Figure 23. Vigorous, disease-resistant turfgrasses produce more surface stems and blades than are needed for good turf. Here a thatch-removing machine is cross-hatching a turfgrass area to thin the turf and remove excess material. Disposal becomes the next order of business. (Courtesy: Ryan Equipment Company)

Figure 24. This sophisticated power sweeper is combined with a slicer-thatcher to cultivate, to remove excess debris, and to package it in a single pass. (Courtesy: West Point Products Corporation)

Weed control chemicals frequently become a major part of turf renovation; first, to destroy weeds present prior to renovating; second, to prevent germination of soil-borne weed seeds while permitting the planted turfgrasses to develop; and third, to control competing vegetation while the newly planted grasses are becoming established.

XI. Sprayers

Turfgrass managers rely heavily upon dependable spray equipment for uniformly applying various materials to control weeds, insects, diseases, and on occasion to apply grass colorants and fertilizers.

Power may be supplied by hand, by mounted engines, and power-take-off units. Distribution may be effected by a single nozzle (Fig. 25), by a "broom" (several nozzles closely spaced), and by a boom that may cover a swath of 20 feet or more (Fig. 26). Always there is the danger of misapplication—too much in one place, missed strips, clogging, and overlapping.

Figure 25. Hydraulic seeders for highway slopes can be adapted to lawn fertilizing, liming, and insect and grub control. Solid materials are carried in water suspension through non-clog pumps and nozzles. Accuracy and uniformity are responsibilities of the operators. (Courtesy: REINCO, Inc.)

Turbine sprayers employ airplane propeller-type fans which drive an atomized mist with great force for carrying long distances or for penetrating densely canopied areas.

There are roller-type "sprayers" which allow a liquid to drip by gravity onto a roller which, while moving, brings the wetted surface into contact with the turf and the weeds. The absence of "drift" is claimed as one of the great advantages of this system.

Lawn and estate sprayers are made that mount a small (3 to 5 gallon) tank on wheels. As the machine is pushed or pulled by the operator a rotor acts upon a flexible tube, building sufficient pressure to expel the liquid in a fan spray through a single nozzle to a width of 8 or 10 feet.

Figure 26. Spraying chemicals for various purposes (diseases, weeds, insects, nematodes, micronutrients, colorants) is standard operational procedure on turf. This mounted unit can spray putting greens as well as fairways. It is a moderate compromise between hand spraying and huge tractor-drawn boom units usable only on large areas. (Courtesy: Turf-Truckster by Cushman Motors)

Early sprayers used wooden tanks which had to be kept filled with water to prevent cracking. The advent of 2,4-D quickly eliminated the wooden tanks. The chemical permeated the wood and contaminated all subsequent sprays, often with disastrous results. Cleaning tanks of one substance to permit the effective use of a different chemical is not a problem with steel and fiberglass tanks. Caution still is the watch-word but sanitation can be complete.

The proportioner is a type of spray outfit that utilizes the Venturi principle. The water system is attached and turned on. The concentrated spray material in a barrel (constant stirring is recommended) is siphoned out to mix with the stream of water in a known proportion. The diluted spray is directed to cover the turf surface uniformly. "Washing in" with clear water usually follows to reduce the danger of "burn" if a caustic material is involved. Some materials must be left on the surface undisturbed. Several companies make small units for home use. The garden hose supplies the water under pressure and provides the necessary dilution.

Calibration and adjustment of sprayers is essential in order to apply the exact quantity of active ingredient to a unit area. Screens must be kept clean. Nozzles must be checked for clogging and for wear. Speed of travel is extremely important.

Spraying by aircraft or helicopter has assumed gigantic proportions in turf and in farming. Speed and economy are compelling factors. Aircraft can be effective when the soil is too soft to allow ground crews to operate.

XII. Miscellaneous Equipment

A multitude of small tools are essential to the effective management of turfgrass areas. To achieve the perfection demanded in this day and age, it is the attention to the small details that may make the difference between success and mediocrity. To repair an ugly gash in a beautiful piece of turf the manager sends a man out with a $10 plugger and a few plugs of sod, not a huge $10,000 machine.

Pluggers are an integral part of turfgrass management. Repairs can be effected quickly and economically. New grasses can be introduced with ease. Cup-setter pluggers are standard on golf courses.

Whips are in almost universal use to "switch" or "pole" the surface of greens and to reduce dew accumulation, to dispel worm casts and, occasionally, heavy clippings. Whips usually are bamboo, but aluminum and fiberglass are in use.

Dragmats have been mentioned as useful work in topdressing and to smooth surfaces. They may be pulled be manpower or by light power machines (Fig. 22).

Rakes are of several kinds. There are special rakes for bunkers (sand traps); rakes with flexible tines for leaves, sharp-toothed rakes (Cavex) to tear out unwanted grass and thatch, and power-driven rakes for several purposes.

Edgers are essential to maintain neat borders around bunkers, along sidewalks, flowerbeds. They come in hand models and power models with gas engines and electric motors. A few are tractor driven.

Sod cutters are so standard that they could rate a separate section (Fig. 27 and 28). Power-driven sod cutters came into the picture only after World War II. Before that there was the hand-operated goose-neck sod lifter, a back breaker. Then there was the sled which was pulled by men or a horse. Many early golf courses were built with the aid of a horse-drawn sled sod cutter.

Figure 27. Sod cutters now can have sod-rolling attachments. This is a small simple version of hugh sophisticated machines that are especially built for either rolling sod or for prepairing flat-cut sections for fork lift handling on pallets. (Courtesy: Ryan Equipment Company)

Sod cutters today not only cut the sod but roll it and place it on pallets or stack the cut squares and rectangles on pallets for transfer to trucks. The trucks may be refrigerated to insure safe delivery without heating.

Ironically, much turf is damaged or destroyed by the equipment that is designed to maintain and improve it. The damage becomes more severe when the machinery is not kept in optimum condition. Careless operators, and those who do not understand the principles of turfgrass

Figure 28. Sod cutters can be modified to cut a trench into which they pull irrigation tubing. Surface disturbance is minimal with no open trench, no backfill. (Courtesy: Ryan Equipment Company)

maintenance, can create severe problems. Examples include the following.

(1) Dull mowers bruise grass blades and facilitate the entry of disease organisms.

(2) Inadequate grease seals allow lubricants to drip on the grass.

(3) Gas and oil may be spilled when machines are serviced on the turf.

(4) Excessive speed in the operation of machines can damage turf.

(5) Continued operation in one plane or direction is undesirable (each mowing should be made in a different direction).

(6) The movement of heavy equipment on soggy soils can cause severe compaction.

(7) Hose breakage on hydraulic equipment releases fluid that can seriously damage turf.

In the future, cognizance will be given to the effects of equipment operation in evaluating the performance of improved turfgrasses and management practices.

References

Weeds Trees and Turf, December 1967, 1968 Suppliers Guide.
Golfdom, November 1967, 1968 Buyers Guide.

Index

D

E

F

O

P